INTRODUCTION TO

Paralegalism

PERSPECTIVES, PROBLEMS, AND SKILLS

EIGHTH EDITION

INTRODUCTION TO
Paralegalism

PERSPECTIVES, PROBLEMS, AND SKILLS

EIGHTH EDITION

WILLIAM P. STATSKY

❖ Cengage

Australia • Brazil • Canada • Mexico • Singapore • United Kingdom • United States

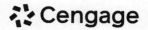

Introduction to Paralegalism: Perspectives, Problems, and Skills, **Eighth Edition**
William P. Statsky

Senior Vice President, General Manager for Skills and Global Product Management: Dawn Gerrain

Product Manager: Katie McGuire

Senior Director, Development/Global Product Management, Skills: Marah Bellegarde

Senior Product Development Manager: Larry Main

Senior Content Developer: Melissa Riveglia

Senior Product Assistant: Diane E. Chrysler

Marketing Manager: Scott Chrysler

Senior Production Director: Wendy Troeger

Production Director: Andrew Crouth

Senior Content Project Manager: Betty L. Dickson

Art Director: Brenda Carmichael, Lumina Datamatics, Inc.

Senior Technology Project Manager: Joe Pliss

Cover image(s): White Marble Ionic Column Scroll Pediment Close-Up Credit: © PeskyMonkey

White Marble Ionic Column Scroll Pediment Close-Up, Credit: © PeskyMonkey

For product information and technology assistance, contact us at **Cengage Customer & Sales Support, 1-800-354-9706** or **support.cengage.com.**

For permission to use material from this text or product, submit all requests online at **www.copyright.com.**

Library of Congress Control Number: 2014957050

ISBN: 978-0-357-67066-8

Cengage
200 Pier 4 Boulevard
Boston, MA 02210
USA

Cengage is a leading provider of customized learning solutions with employees residing in nearly 40 different countries and sales in more than 125 countries around the world. Find your local representative at: **www.cengage.com.**

To learn more about Cengage platforms and services, register or access your online learning solution, or purchase materials for your course, visit **www.cengage.com.**

Notice to the Reader

Printed at CLDPC, USA, 06-22

For Patricia Farrell Statsky,
whose wisdom, light, and love
have sustained more than she knows

BY THE SAME AUTHOR

For all publications by William Statsky, see *statsky.blogspot.com*

The California Paralegal: Essential Rules, Documents, and Resources. Clifton Park, N.Y.: Cengage Learning, 2008 (with S. Sandberg)

Case Analysis and Fundamentals of Legal Writing, 4th ed. St. Paul: West Group, 1995 (with J. Wernet)

Essentials of Paralegalism: Perspectives, Problems, and Skills, 5th ed. Clifton Park, N.Y.: Cengage Learning, 2010

Essentials of Torts, 3d ed. Clifton Park, N.Y.: Cengage Learning, 2012

Family Law: The Essentials, 3d ed. Clifton Park, N.Y.: Cengage learning, 2015

Family Law, 6th ed. Clifton Park, N.Y.: Cengage Learning, 2013

The Florida Paralegal: Essential Rules, Documents, and Resources. Clifton Park, N.Y.: Cengage Learning, 2009 (with B. Diotalevi & P. Linquist)

Inmate Involvement in Prison Legal Services: Roles and Training Options for the Inmate as Paralegal. Chicago: American Bar Association, Commission on Correctional Facilities and Services, 1974

Legal Desk Reference. St. Paul: West Group, 1990 (with B. Hussey, M. Diamond, & R. Nakamura)

The Legal Paraprofessional as Advocate and Assistant: Training Concepts and Materials. New York: Center on Social Welfare Policy and Law, 1971 (with P. Lang)

Legal Research and Writing: Some Starting Points, 5th ed. Clifton Park, N.Y.: Cengage Learning, 1999

Legal Thesaurus/Dictionary: A Resource for the Writer and Computer Researcher. St. Paul: West Group, 1985

Legislative Analysis and Drafting, 2d ed. St. Paul: West Group, 1984

The New York Paralegal: Essential Rules, Documents, and Resources. Clifton Park, N.Y.: Cengage Learning, 2009 (with R. Sarachan)

The Ohio Paralegal: Essential Rules, Documents, and Resources. Clifton Park, N.Y.: Cengage Learning, 2008 (with K. Reed & B. Moore)

Paralegal Employment: Facts and Strategies for the 1990s, 2d ed. St. Paul: West Group, 1993

Paralegal Ethics and Regulation, 2d ed. St. Paul: West Group, 1993

The Pennsylvania Paralegal: Essential Rules, Documents, and Resources. Clifton Park, N.Y.: Cengage Learning, 2009 (with J. DeLeo & J. Geis)

The Texas Paralegal: Essential Rules, Documents, and Resources. Clifton Park, N.Y.: Cengage Learning, 2009 (with L. Crossett)

Torts: Personal Injury Litigation, 5th ed. Clifton Park, N.Y.: Cengage Learning, 2011

Rights of the Imprisoned: Cases, Materials, and Directions. Indianapolis, Ind.: Bobbs-Merrill Company, 1974 (with R. Singer)

What Have Paralegals Done? A Dictionary of Functions. Washington, D.C.: National Paralegal Institute, 1973

CONTENTS IN BRIEF

CONTENTS

PART II

THE SKILLS OF A PARALEGAL   309

PREFACE

Seven editions ago — in 1974 — many were asking the question "What's a paralegal?" That day has long passed, although there is still a great deal of information that people need to have in order to appreciate the outstanding contribution paralegals have made in the delivery of legal services. This book seeks to provide that information and, at the same time, to introduce you to some of the fundamental skills needed to thrive in this still-developing career, a career whose members may one day outnumber attorneys in the traditional and untraditional law office.

It's a fascinating time to study law. So many aspects of our lives revolve around the making, interpretation, and application of laws. As integral members of the attorney's team, paralegals have a unique opportunity to view the legal system in operation as it wrestles with the legal issues of the day.

Back in the 1970s when the first edition of this book came out, Kathy Lowery, a Kansas City paralegal, was asked what impressed her most about the paralegal profession. She said that the two best things about the field were the two constants that were ever present: challenges and opportunities to "learn and grow." Well said about the 1970s and equally true as we continue into the twenty-first century.

CHANGES IN THE EIGHTH EDITION

In addition to the updated material in the book on employment, salaries, roles, ethics, and regulation, a number of particular changes in the eighth edition should be mentioned:

- New categories of assignments have been added, including assignments in critical analysis, the job search, and the core skills of writing, research, ethics, computers, and collaboration. All of the assignments have been placed at the end of each chapter.
- The role of social media is discussed throughout the chapters beginning with the admonition to control one's online reputation.

- Chapter 1 adds a discussion of the important difference between what paralegals need to understand the legal system and what they will need to perform specific tasks on the job.
- Chapter 2 adds extensive material on assertive networking and the use of LinkedIn, Twitter, and Facebook in the job search.
- The extensive coverage of private law firms and state government paralegal jobs has been moved from the end of Chapter 2 to the appendix material at the end of the book.
- Chapter 2 covers the major growth areas of law in the coming years.
- Chapter 2 includes a summary checklist of major job strategies, particularly in markets where competition for jobs is intense.
- Chapter 3 covers the dynamics of working in a multi-generational law office.
- Chapter 3 adds a section on the important and often overlooked skill of listening.
- Chapter 4 adds material on new proposals to end the justice gap, including expanded roles for the paralegal and other nonattorneys.
- Chapter 4 presents the major development of the Limited License Legal Technician in Washington and the favorable climate that exists in many states for recognizing document service providers (DSPs).
- Chapter 5 covers fraudulent "friending" and related ethical misconduct in the use of social media.
- Chapter 5 expands the categories of conflict of interest that paralegals need to understand.
- Chapter 6 adds material on the constitution (e.g., the Bill of Rights) as a foundation of our legal system.
- Chapter 7 has been reorganized to provide more comprehensive treatment of the basic components of legal analysis.
- Chapter 10 introduces predictive coding in the increasingly important arena of e-discovery of big data.

- Chapter 11 has been substantially reorganized in order to focus on the techniques of online legal research, particularly in the free databases.
- Chapter 12 confronts the dangers of copy-and-paste writing in an era when it is deceptively easy to rely on material that is available on the Internet.
- Chapter 12 also adds material on effective email writing.
- Chapter 13 catalogs the variety of social-media sites on the Internet and broadens the scope of security concerns that must be addressed.
- Chapter 13 introduces IoT: the Internet of things.
- Chapter 13 summarizes the major ethical issues covered in the book that result from computer use and misuse in the practice of law.
- The fifty-state survey of ethics in Appendix D expands the coverage of unauthorized practice of law (UPL).
- A new appendix (F) has been added on paralegal blogs.
- Appendix H covers major ways to locate different kinds of law offices as a guide in the job search.

ANCILLARY MATERIALS

Instructor Companion Site

The online Instructor Companion Site provides the following resources:

Instructor's Manual

An Instructor's Manual and Test Bank by the author of the text accompany this edition and have been greatly expanded to incorporate changes in the text and to provide comprehensive teaching support. They include the following:

- Class ideas, such as lecture ideas and suggestions for using selected assignments.
- A test bank of 645 questions, which includes a variety of questions in true/false, multiple-choice, and essay format. An answer key is also provided.

PowerPoint Presentations

- Customizable Microsoft PowerPoint® Presentations focus on key points for each chapter. (Microsoft PowerPoint® is a registered trademark of the Microsoft Corporation.)

Cengage Learning Testing Powered by Cognero is a flexible, online system that allows you to:

- author, edit, and manage test bank content from multiple Cengage Learning solutions.
- create multiple test versions in an instant.
- deliver tests from your LMS, your classroom, or wherever you want.

Start right away!

Cengage Learning Testing Powered by Cognero works on any operating system or browser.

- No special installs or downloads needed
- Create tests from school, home, the coffee shop – anywhere with Internet access

What will you find?

- Simplicity at every step. A desktop-inspired interface features drop-down menus and familiar, intuitive tools that take you through content creation and management with ease.
- Full-featured test generator. Create ideal assessments with your choice of 15 question types (including true/false, multiple choice, opinion scale/Likert, and essay). Multi-language support, an equation editor and unlimited metadata help ensure your tests are complete and compliant.
- Cross-compatible capability. Import and export content into other systems.

To access additional course materials, please go to login.cengage .com, then use your SSO (single sign on) login to access the materials.

MindTap 🌐 MindTap™

MindTap for Statsky/Introduction to Paralegalism is a highly personalized fully online learning platform of authoritative content, assignments, and services offering you a tailored presentation of course curriculum created by your instructor. MindTap for Statsky/Introduction to Paralegalism Law guides you through the course curriculum via an innovative learning path where you will complete reading assignments, annotate your readings, complete homework and engage with quizzes and assessments. MindTap includes a variety of web-apps known as "MindApps" – allowing functionality like having the text read aloud to you as well as MindApps that allow you to synchronize your notes with your personal Evernote account. MindApps are tightly woven into the MindTap platform and enhance your learning experience.

How MindTap helps students succeed

- Use the Progress App to see where you stand at all times—individually and compared to highest performers in your class.
- ReadSpeaker reads the course material to you.
- MyNotes provides the ability to highlight text and take notes – that link back to the MindTap material for easy reference when you are studying for an exam or working on a project.
- Merriam Webster Dictionary and a glossary are only a click away.

- Flashcards are pre-created to help you memorize the key terms.
- Drop boxes are provided for submitting instructor-graded exercises.

Not using MindTap in your course?

- It's an online destination housing ALL your course material and assignments … neatly organized to match your syllabus.
- It's loaded with study tools that help you learn the material more easily.
- To learn more go to www.cengage.com/mindtap or ask your instructor to try it out.

ACKNOWLEDGMENTS

It is difficult to name all the individuals who have provided guidance in the preparation of the eight editions of this book. Looking back over the years, a number of people have played important roles in my initiation and growth as a student of paralegal education. I owe a debt to Jean and Edgar Cahn, founders of the Legal Technician Program at Antioch School of Law, where I worked; Bill Fry, Director of the National Paralegal Institute and a valued colleague since our days together at Columbia Law School, where he was my dean in one of the first paralegal training programs in the country, the Program for Legal Service Assistants; Dan Oran, who helped me plan the first edition; Michael Manna, Ed Schwartz, Bill Mulkeen, Juanita Hill, Willie Nolden, and Linda Saunders.

I wish to thank the following people at Cengage Learning: Paul Lamond, Product Manager; Melissa Riveglia, Senior Content Developer; Diane Chrysler, Senior Product Assistant; Betty Dickson, Senior Content Project Manager; and Scott Chrysler, Marketing Manager.

Finally, a word of thanks to the reviewers who made valuable suggestions for improving the text:

Libby Pace
California State University
Los Angeles, CA

Olga A. Possé
SUNY Buffalo / Millard Fillmore College
Buffalo, NY

Casey D. Thompson
Debbie Vinecour
SUNY Rockland CC
Suffern, NY

[The] expanded use of well-trained…"paralegals," has been an important development. Today there are … double the number of … schools for training paralegals [as the number of schools for training attorneys]… . The advent of the paralegal enables law offices to perform high quality legal services at a lower cost. Possibly we have only scratched the surface of this development.
Warren E. Burger, Chief Justice of the United States Supreme Court, February 3, 1980

Paralegals are an absolutely essential component of quality legal services in the future.
James Fellers, President, American Bar Association, April 4, 1975

The court also commends the firm of Stull, Stull & Brody for the extensive use of paralegals rather than attorneys for various tasks, reducing the cost of litigation.
U.S. District Court Judge Helen Berregan, Feinberg v. Hibernia Corp., 966 F. Supp. 442, 448 (E.D. La., 1997)

Employment of paralegals and legal assistants is projected to grow 17 percent from 2012 to 2022, faster than the average for all occupations. Employers are trying to reduce costs and increase the availability and efficiency of legal services by hiring paralegals to perform tasks once done by lawyers. Paralegals are performing a wider variety of duties, making them more useful.
U.S. Department of Labor, Occupational Outlook Handbook (2010, 2014)
(www.bls.gov/oob/legal/paralegals-and-legal-assistants.htm)

HOW TO STUDY LAW IN THE CLASSROOM AND ON THE JOB

OUTLINE

- Classroom Learning
- On-the-Job Learning: The Art of Being Supervised

OBJECTIVES

After completing this section, you should be able to

- Know why legal education is a lifelong pursuit.
- Distinguish between substantive and procedural law, and rules and skills.
- Understand the importance of a study plan.
- Do a self-assessment of your study habits.
- Do a self-assessment of grammar, spelling, and composition skills.
- Create a self-improvement plan on the basics of writing.
- Know the importance of definitions in the law.
- Increase your note-taking skills.
- Maximize your learning opportunities on the job.
- Use a checklist for major assignments.
- Turn instructions into checklists.
- Know the value of models, background research, new publication lists, feedback, continuing legal education, and evaluations.

CLASSROOM LEARNING

Education does not come naturally to many of us. It is a struggle. This is all the more true for someone entering a totally new realm of training such as legal education. Much of the material may seem foreign and difficult. There is a danger of becoming overwhelmed by the vast quantity of laws and legal material that confront you. How do you study law? How do you learn law? What is the proper perspective that a student of law should have about the educational process? These are our concerns in this introduction to the process of studying law. In short, our theme is training to be trained—the art of effective learning.

The first step is to begin with a proper frame of mind. Too many students have false expectations of what legal education can accomplish. This can interfere with effective studying.

1. Your Legal Education Has Two Phases. Phase I Begins Now and Ends When You Complete This Training Program. Phase II Begins When This Training Program Ends and Is Not Completed Until the Last Day of Your Employment as a Paralegal.

You have entered a career that will require you to be a perpetual student. The learning never ends. This is true not only because the boundary lines of law are vast, but also because the law is changing every day. No one knows all of the law. Phase I of your legal education is designed to provide you with the foundation that will enable you to become a good student in phase II.

2. Your Legal Education Has Two Dimensions: The Content of the Law (the Rules) and the Practical Techniques of Using That Content in a Law Office (the Skills).

Rules

There are two basic kinds of rules or laws:

- *Substantive Law:* The nonprocedural rules that define or govern rights and duties, e.g., the requirements for the sale of land and the elements of battery.

- *Procedural Law:* The rules that govern the mechanics of resolving a dispute in court or in an administrative agency, e.g., a rule on the time by which a party must respond to a complaint.

The law library contains millions of substantive and procedural laws written by courts (in volumes called *reporters*), by legislatures (in volumes called *statutory codes*), and by administrative agencies (in volumes called *administrative codes*). A great deal of the material in these volumes is also available on the Internet, as we will see. A substantial portion of your time in school will involve study of the substantive and procedural law of your state, and often of the federal government as well.

Skills

By far the most important dimension of your legal education will be the skills of using rules. Without the skills, the content of rules is close to worthless. Examples of legal skills include

- How to analyze the facts of a client's case in order to identify legal issues (see Chapter 7)
- How to interview a client (see Chapter 8)
- How to investigate the facts of a case (see Chapter 9)
- How to draft a complaint, the document that initiates a lawsuit (see Chapter 10)
- How to digest or summarize data found in discovery documents (see Chapter 10)
- How to do a cite check or perform other legal research in traditional and online law libraries (see Chapter 11)
- How to write a search query for an online database (see Chapter 13)

The overriding skill that, to one degree or another, is the basis for all others is the skill of legal analysis (Chapter 7). Some make the mistake of concluding that legal analysis is the exclusive domain of the attorney. Without an understanding of at least the fundamentals of legal analysis, however, paralegals cannot understand the legal system and cannot intelligently carry out many of the more demanding tasks they are assigned.

3. You Must Force Yourself to Suspend What You Already Know About the Law in Order to Be Able to Absorb (a) That Which Is New and (b) That Which Conflicts with Your Prior Knowledge and Experience.

Place yourself in the position of training students to drive a car. Your students undoubtedly already know something about driving. They have watched others drive and maybe have even had a lesson or two from friends. It would be ideal, however, if you could begin your instruction from point zero. There is a very real danger that the students have picked up bad habits from others. This may interfere with their capacity to listen to what you are saying. The danger is that they will block out anything you say that does not conform to previously learned habits and knowledge. If the habits or knowledge are defective, your job as a trainer is more difficult.

The same is true in studying law. Everyone knows something about the law from taking government or civics courses as a teenager and from the various treatments of the law in the media. Some of you may have been involved in the law as a party or as a witness in court. Others may have worked, or currently work, in law offices. Will this prior knowledge and experience be a help or a hindrance to you in your future legal education? For some, it will be a help. For many of us, however, there is a danger of interference.

This is particularly so with respect to the portrayal of the law on TV and in the movies. Contrary to what some TV programs may lead you to believe, it is highly unlikely that a judge would say to a witness, "I wouldn't believe you if your tongue came notarized."[1] Furthermore, TV and movies sometimes give the impression that all attorneys are trial attorneys and that most cases are solved by dramatically tricking a hostile witness on the stand into finally telling the truth. Not so.

The practice of law is not an endless series of confessions and concessions that are pried loose from opponents. Every attorney does not spend all day engaged in the kind of case that makes front-page news. Recently a New Jersey paralegal left her job with a sole practitioner to take another paralegal position with a law firm that she thought was going to be like the one on the TV drama she faithfully watched every week. Three months later, she begged her old boss to take her back after discovering the huge gap between reality and the law office on that show.

Another potentially misleading portrayal of the law came in the O.J. Simpson criminal and civil trials, which captivated the nation in the late 1990s. Very few parties to litigation have teams of attorneys, investigators, and experts ready to do battle with each other as they did in the Simpson trials. The vast majority of legal disputes are never litigated in court. Most are either settled or simply dropped by one or both parties. Of the small number that are litigated, most involve no more than two opposing attorneys and several witnesses. In short, it is rare for the legal system to become the spectacle—some would say the circus—that the occasional high-profile case leads us to believe is common in the practice of law. While excitement and drama can be part of the legal system, they are not everyday occurrences. What is dominant is painstaking and meticulous hard work. This reality is almost never portrayed in the media.

Therefore, it is strongly recommended that you place yourself in the position of a stranger to the material you will be covering in your courses, regardless of your background and exposure to the field. Cautiously treat everything as a new experience. Temporarily suspend what you already know. Resist the urge to pat yourself on the back by saying, "I already knew that" or "I already know how to do that." For many students, such statements lead to relaxation. They do not work as hard once they have convinced themselves that there is nothing new to learn. No problem exists, of course, if these students are right. The danger, however, is that they are wrong or that they are only partially right. We are not always the best judges of what we know and of what we can do. Do not become too comfortable. Adopt the following healthy attitude: "I've heard about that before or I've already done that, but maybe I can learn something new about it." Every new instructor, every new supervisor, every new setting is an opportunity to add a dimension to your prior knowledge and experience. Be open to these opportunities. No two people practice law exactly the same way. Your own growth as a student and as a paralegal will depend in large part on your capacity to listen for, explore, and absorb this diversity.

4. Be Sure That You Know the Goals and Context of Every Assignment.

Throughout your education, you will be given a variety of assignments: class exercises, text readings, drafting tasks, field projects, research assignments, etc. You should ask yourself the following questions about each one:

- What are the goals of this assignment? What am I supposed to learn from it?
- How does this assignment fit into what I have already learned? What is the context of the assignment?

For assignments from your textbook, carefully examine the table of contents, chapter objectives, and the variety of headings in a chapter in order to grasp the broader picture into which an assignment fits. Ask questions if the purpose of an assignment and its relationship to paralegalism is not clear. Successfully completing an assignment depends in part on understanding its goals and how these goals relate to the overall context of the course and the career.

5. Design a Study Plan.

Make current lists of everything that you must do in each of your courses. Update the lists regularly. Divide every list into long-term projects (what is due next week or at the end of the semester) and short-term projects (what is due tomorrow). Have a plan for each day. Establish the following norm for yourself:

Every day you will make some progress on everything on your long-term and short-term lists.

Priority, of course, will be given to the short-term tasks. Yet some time, however small, will also be devoted to the long-term tasks. For example, on a day that you will be mainly working on the short-term projects, try to set aside 5 percent of your time for a long-term project by doing some background reading or by preparing a very rough first draft of an outline. Maybe all you can do on an assignment is read a paragraph or review what needs to be done on the assignment. It is critical that you establish momentum toward the accomplishment of all your tasks. This is done by never letting anything sit on the back burner. Set yourself the goal of making at least some progress on everything every day. Without this goal, momentum may be difficult to achieve and sustain.

Once you have decided what tasks you will cover on a given study day, the next question becomes the order in which will you cover them. There are a number of ways in which you can classify the things you must do. For example, you can classify them as

- easy tasks that will require a relatively short time to complete,
- complex tasks requiring more time, and
- tasks with time demands that will be unknown until you start them.

At the beginning of your study time, spend a few moments preparing an outline of the order in which you will cover the tasks that day and the approximate amount of time that you will set aside for each task. You may want to start with some of the easier tasks so that you can feel a sense of accomplishment relatively soon. Alternatively, you may want to devote early study time to the third kind of task listed above so that you can obtain a clearer idea of the scope and difficulty of such assignments. The important point is that you establish a schedule. It does not have to be written in stone. Quite the contrary. It is healthy to have enough flexibility to revise your day's schedule so that you can respond to unfolding realities as you study. Adaptation is not a sign of disorganization, but the total absence of an initial plan often is.

6. Add 50 Percent to the Time You Initially Think You Will Need to Study a Subject.

You are kidding yourself if you have not set aside a substantial amount of time to study law outside the classroom. The conscientious study of law takes time—lots of it. It is true that some students must work or take care of family responsibilities. You cannot devote time that you do not have. Yet the reality is that limited study time can lead to limited education.

Generally, people will find time for what they *want* to do. You may *wish* to do many things for which there will never be enough time. You will find the time, however, to do what you really want to do. Once you have decided that you want something badly enough, you will find the time to do it.

How much of each of your work hours is productive time? For most of us, the answer is about twenty minutes. The rest of the hour is spent worrying, relaxing, repeating ourselves, socializing, checking and posting to social media, etc. One answer to the problem of limited time availability is to increase the amount of productive time that you derive out of each work hour. You may not be able to add new hours to the clock, but you can add to your net productive time. How about moving up to thirty minutes an hour? Forty? You will be amazed at the time that you can "find" simply by making a conscious effort to remove some of the waste. When asked how a masterpiece was created, a great sculptor once responded: "You start with a block of marble and you cut away everything that is not art." In your study habits, start with a small block of time and work to cut away everything that is not productive.

In addition, look for ways to fit study time into your other activities. Always carry something to study in the event that time becomes available. For example, photocopy, scan, or photograph a portion of a chapter in a class textbook and bring it with you whenever you can. It might be perfect for that unexpectedly long wait at the dentist's office. Constantly be on the alert for ways to increase the time you have available or, more accurately, to increase the productive time that you can make available.

There are no absolute rules on how much time you will need to study law. It depends on the complexity of the subject matter you must master. It is probably accurate to say that most of us need to study more than we do—as a rule of thumb, about 50 percent more.

Resolving time management problems as a student will be good practice for you when you are confronted with similar (and more severe) time management problems as a working paralegal. Many law offices operate at a hectic pace. One of the hallmarks of a professional is a pronounced reverence for deadlines and the clock.

Soon you will be gaining a reputation among other students, instructors, supervisors, and employers. You should make a concerted effort to acquire a reputation for hard work, punctuality, and conscientiousness about the time you devote to your work. In large measure, success follows from such a reputation. It is as important, and sometimes more important, than raw ability or intelligence. Phrased another way, your legal skills are unlikely to put bread on the table if you are casual about the clock.

7. Create Your Own Study Area Free from Distractions.

It is essential that you find study areas that are quiet and free from distractions. Otherwise, concentration is obviously impossible. It may be that the worst places to study are at home or at the library unless you can find a corner that is cut off from noise and people who want to talk. If possible, study away from phones, TVs, iPods, and instant computer messaging. Do not make yourself available, except for emergencies. If you study in the corridor, at the first table at the entrance to the library, or at the kitchen table, you are inviting distraction. You need to be able to close yourself off for two to three hours at a time. It is important for you to interact with other people—but not while you are studying material that requires considerable concentration. You will be tempted to digress and to socialize. You are in the best position to know where these temptations are. You are also the most qualified person to know how to avoid the temptations.

Try this idea: never study with your smartphone within reach. Alternatively, shut the phone off when studying. If this is too radical, allow yourself no more than two minutes every hour to turn the phone on in order to find out if a true emergency demands your immediate attention.

8. Conduct a Self-Assessment of Your Prior Study Habits and Establish a Program to Reform the Weaknesses.

If you were to describe the way you study, would you be proud of the description? Here is a partial list of some of the main weaknesses of attitude or practice that students have about studying:

- They have done well in the past with only minimal study effort. Why change now?
- Others in the class do not appear to be studying very much. Why be different?
- They learn best by listening in class. Hence, instead of studying on their own, they wait until someone explains the material in person.
- They simply do not like to study; there are more important things to do in life.
- They can't concentrate.
- They study with lots of distractions, e.g., phones, radios, TVs, computers, iPods. Multitasking is more fun than unitasking.
- They get bored easily. "I can't stay motivated for long."
- They do not understand what they are supposed to study.
- They skim read.
- They do not stop to look up strange words or phrases.
- They study only at exam time—then cram for exams.
- They do not study at a consistent pace. They spend an hour (or less) here and there and have no organized, regular study times.
- They do not like to memorize.
- They do not take notes on what they are reading.

What other interferences with effective studying can you think of? Or, more important, which of the above items apply to you? How do you plead? In law, it is frequently said that you cannot solve a problem until you obtain the facts. What are the facts in the case of your study habits? Make your personal list of attitude problems, study patterns, and environmental interferences. Place these items in some order. Next, establish a plan for yourself. Which item on the list are you going to try to correct tonight? What will the plan be for this week? For next week? For the coming month? What specific steps will you take to try to change some bad habits? If one corrective method does not work, try another. If the fifth does not work, try a sixth. Discuss techniques of improvement with other students and with instructors. Run this search in Google, Bing, or Yahoo: effective study habits. Be a sponge for self-improvement ideas. Prove to yourself that change is possible.

9. Engage in Active Studying.

Even without distractions, the mind often wanders away from what should be the focus of what we are studying. Daydreaming during study time is not uncommon. If this occurs, do some active studying by forcing yourself to do something other than (or in addition to) reading. For example,

- Write out definitions of key terms.
- Create your own chart or graph that contains pieces or components of a topic you are studying.
- Create mnemonics to help you remember important concepts. (On mnemonics, see Section 16 below.)

10. Conduct a Self-Assessment on Grammar, Spelling, and Composition. Then Design a Program to Reform Weaknesses.

The legal profession lives by the written word. Talking is important for some activities, but writing is crucial in almost every area of law. You cannot function in this environment without a grasp of the basics of grammar, spelling, and composition. A major complaint of employers today is that workers consistently violate these basics. The problem is serious. Here are seven steps that will help solve it:

Step One

Take responsibility for your training in grammar, spelling, and composition. Do not wait for someone to teach (or reteach) you the basics. Do not wait until someone points out your weaknesses. Make a personal commitment to train yourself. If English courses are available to you, great. A weekly class, however, may not be enough.

Step Two

Raise your consciousness about the writing around you. When you are reading a newspaper, for example, try to be conscious of semicolons and paragraph structure in what you are reading. At least occasionally ask yourself why a certain punctuation mark was used by a writer. You are surrounded by writing. You read this writing for content. Begin a conscious effort to focus on the structure of the writing as well. This dual level of observation exists in other aspects of our lives. When people come out of the theater, for example, they often comment about how impressive the acting was. In addition to following the story or content of the play or movie, they were aware of its form and structure. These same levels of consciousness (content and form) should be developed for everything you read.

Step Three

Commit yourself to spending ten minutes a day, five or six days a week, on improving your grammar skills. For a total of about an hour a week, drill yourself on the fundamentals of our language. In Google, Bing, or Yahoo, run this search: *English grammar*. Do some surfing to find grammar sites that give basic rules and practice drills that allow you to test yourself on what you know. Avoid sites that charge fees or that are simply selling books. Here are some examples of sites you might find useful:

- www.edufind.com/english/grammar
- andromeda.rutgers.edu/~jlynch/Writing/c.html
- englishplus.com/grammar
- www.tnellen.com/cybereng/32.html

Sites such as these may provide links to comparable sites. Try several. Ask fellow students what sites they have found helpful.

How do you know what areas of grammar you should study? In Google, Bing, or Yahoo, run this search: *grammar self-test*. Find free tests. Take more than one. Make a list of areas where you need improvement. Start eliminating weaknesses one at a time.

One way to test your progress is to try the exercises on different sites. Suppose, for example, you are on a site that discusses the use of commas in *that* clauses and *which* clauses. After you finish the that/which exercises at this site, go to another grammar site and find its section on that/which. Read the examples and do the exercises at this site. Are you reinforcing what you learned at the first site, or are the examples and exercises at the second site making you realize that you need more work understanding this area of grammar? Using more than one site in this way will help you assess how well you are grasping the material.

Step Four

Improve your spelling. Use a dictionary often. Begin making a list of words that you are spelling incorrectly. Work on these words. Ask other students, relatives, or friends to test you on them by reading the words to you one by one. Spell the words aloud or on paper. You can drill yourself into spelling perfection, or close to it, by this method. When you have the slightest doubt about the spelling of a word, check the dictionary. Add difficult words to your list. Again, the more often you take this approach now, the less often you will need to use the dictionary later.

Use the Internet as a resource. In Google, Bing, or Yahoo, run this search: spelling rules. You will be led to sites that will provide guidance.

Many word processors (e.g., Microsoft Word) have spell checkers that not only identify words you may have misspelled but also provide suggested corrections. Does this new technology mean that your spelling problems have been solved forever? Hardly. Spell checkers can catch many spelling blunders, but they can be very misleading. First of all, they cannot tell you how to spell many proper names, such as the surnames of individuals (unless you add these names to the base of words being checked). An even more serious problem is that spell checkers do not alert you to improper word choices. Every word in the following sentence, for example, is incorrect, but a spell checker would tell you that the sentence has no spelling problems:

"Its to later too by diner."

Here is what should have been written:

"It's too late to buy dinner."

Because the first sentence has no misspellings, you are led—that is, misled—to believe that you have written a flawless sentence.

Step Five

Enroll in English and writing courses. Find out if drop-in help labs or remedial centers are available to you. Check offerings at local schools, such as adult education programs in the public schools or at colleges. Call your local public library and ask what resources are available in the community.

Step Six

Find out which law courses in your curriculum require the most writing from students. If possible, take these courses, no matter how painful you find writing to be. In fact, the more painful it is, the more you need to place yourself in an environment where writing is demanded of you on a regular basis.

Step Seven

Simplify your writing. Cut down the length of your sentences. Often a long-winded sentence can be effectively rewritten into two shorter sentences. How can you tell if your sentences are too long? There are, of course, no absolute rules that will answer this question. Yet there is a general consensus that sentences on legal topics tend to be too long.

Several writing scholars have devised readability formulas that allow you to measure the readability of your writing in terms of how difficult it is to read. Among the most popular are the Gunning Fog Index, the Flesch Reading Ease Score, and the Flesch-Kincaid Grade Level Score. You can find them described on many Internet sites such as the following:

- en.wikipedia.org/wiki/Gunning-Fog_Index
- en.wikipedia.org/wiki/Flesch-Kincaid_Readability_Test
- www.nightscribe.com/Education/eschew_obfuscation.htm

Try a readability formula on your own writing. It will take only a few minutes to apply. Find out if the word processor you use (e.g., Word or WordPerfect) has a formula built into the program that is ready to use every time you write something.

Readability formulas are no more than rough guides. Use them to help raise your consciousness about your writing. As you review sentences you have written, you should be asking yourself self-editing questions such as "Would I have been clearer if I had made that sentence shorter?" The conscientious use of readability formulas will help you ask and answer such questions.

For an online manual on writing, including material on readability, see *A Plain English Handbook*, published by the Securities and Exchange Commission (www.sec.gov/pdf/handbook.pdf). Although this manual focuses on financial document filings, it contains many useful guidelines for any kind of writing.

To recap, prepare a self-assessment of weaknesses and set a schedule for improvement. Set aside a small amount of time each day to work on writing weaknesses. Be consistent about this time. Do not wait for the weekend or for next semester when you will have more time. The reality is that you will probably never have substantially more time than you have now. The problem is not so much the absence of time as it is an unwillingness to dig into the task. Progress will be slow and you will be on your own. Hence there is a danger that you will find "good" reasons (excuses) to do something else.

11. Consider Forming a Student Study Group, but Be Cautious.

Students sometimes find it useful to form study groups. A healthy exchange with your colleagues can be very productive. One difficulty is finding students with whom you are compatible. Trial and error may be the only way to identify such students. A more serious concern is trying to define the purpose of the study group. It should not be used as a substitute for your own individual study. Course review, however, is an appropriate group task. Divide a course into parts, with each member of the group having responsibility for reviewing his or her assigned part with the rest of the group.

12. Use Your Legal Research Skills to Help You Understand Components of a Course That Are Giving You Difficulty.

The law library is more than the place to go to find law that governs the facts of a client's case. A great deal of the material in traditional and online law libraries consist of explanations, summaries, and overviews of the same law that you will be covering in your courses. See Exhibit 11-11 in Chapter 11 on doing relatively quick background research on any legal topic. Such research will be invaluable (especially the "dash searches" described in Exhibit 11-11) as outside reading to help resolve conceptual and practical difficulties you are having in class.

13. Organize Your Learning Through Definitions or Definitional Questions.

Among the most sophisticated questions an attorney or paralegal can ask are these:

- What does that word or phrase mean?
- Should it be defined broadly or narrowly?

To a very large extent, the practice of law is a probing for definitions of key words or phrases in the context of facts that have arisen.

- Can a five-year-old be liable for negligence? (What is negligence?)
- Can the government tax a church-run bingo game? (What is the free exercise of religion?)
- Can attorneys in a law firm go on strike and obtain the protection of the National Labor Relations Act? (What is a covered employee under the labor statute?)
- Can one spouse rape another? (What is the definition of rape?)
- Can a citizen slander the president of the United States? (What is a defamatory statement?) Etc.

In every course that you take, you will come across numerous technical words and phrases in class and in your readings. Begin compiling a list of the major words and phrases for each class. When in doubt about whether to include something on your list, resolve the doubt by including it.

Then pursue definitions. Find definitions in class lectures, your textbook, a legal dictionary, or a legal encyclopedia. (For legal dictionaries on the Internet, type "legal dictionary" in Google, Bing, or Yahoo.) See also the online dictionary links in Exhibit 11-11 in Chapter 11.

For some words, you may have difficulty obtaining definitions. Do not give up your pursuit. Keep searching. Keep probing. Keep questioning. For some words, there may be more than one definition. Others may require definitions of the definitions.

Of course, you cannot master a course simply by knowing the definitions of all the key words and phrases covered in the course. Yet these words and phrases are the vocabulary of the course and are the foundation and point of reference for learning the other aspects of the course. Begin with vocabulary.

Consider starting a system of three-by-five or two-by-three cards or sheets of paper to help you learn the definitions. On one side, place a single word or phrase. On the other side, write the definition with a brief page reference or citation to the source of the definition. Using the cards or sheets, test yourself periodically. If you are in a study group, ask other members to test you. Ask a relative to test you. Establish a plan of ongoing review.

14. Studying Ambiguity—Coping with Unanswered Questions.

Legal studies can be frustrating because there is so much uncertainty in the law. Legions of unanswered questions exist. Definitive answers to legal questions are not always easy to find, no matter how good your research techniques are. Every new fact situation presents the potential for a new law. Every law seems to have an exception. Furthermore, advocates frequently argue for exceptions to the exceptions. As indicated, when terms are defined, the definitions often need definitions.

The study of law is in large measure an examination of ambiguity that is identified, dissected, and argued . Search for as much clarity as you can, but do not be surprised if the conclusion of your search brings further questions. A time-honored answer to many legal questions is, "It depends!" Become familiar with the following frequently used equation:

If "fact X" is present, then the conclusion is "A," but if "fact Y is present," then the conclusion is "B," but if "fact Z" is....

The practice of law may sometimes appear to be an endless puzzle. Again, look for precision and clarity, but do not expect the puzzles to disappear.

15. Develop the Skill of Note Taking.

Note taking is an important skill for getting the most out of your formal education. In addition, effective note taking is often a precondition to many law-office tasks.

Take notes on what you are reading for class preparation and for research assignments. Never rely exclusively on your memory. After reading hundreds of pages (or more) in textbooks and online, you will not be able to remember what you have read at the end of the semester, or even at the end of the day. Copy what you think are the essential portions of the materials you are reading. Include definitions of important words and phrases as indicated in Guideline 13 above.

In addition to (and not as a substitute for) taking written notes on your readings, mark up the text if you own it. Use felt pens of different colors. Underline and highlight what appears to be important. Circle key words. Don't read passively. Read with your eyes and hands!

To be sure, note taking will add time to your studying. Yet you will discover that it was time well spent, particularly when you begin reviewing for an exam or writing a memorandum.

In class, you must develop the art of taking notes while simultaneously listening to what is being said. On the job, you will have to do this frequently, such as when

- Receiving instructions from a supervisor
- Talking with someone on the phone
- Doing a follow-up interview of a client
- Interviewing a witness during field investigation

If your supervisor asks you to attend a deposition or a trial, you may need to take detailed notes on the testimony of a particular witness. (A deposition, as you will learn in Chapter 10, is a method of discovery by which parties and their prospective witnesses are questioned outside the courtroom before trial.) A good place to begin learning how to write and listen at the same time is during your classes.

Most students take poor class notes. This is due to a number of reasons:

- They write slowly.
- They don't like to take notes; it's hard work.
- They don't know if what is being said is important enough to be noted until after it is said—when it is too late because the instructor has gone on to something else.
- They don't think it's necessary to take notes on a discussion that the instructor is having with another student.
- They don't think it's necessary to take notes on a topic that's covered in the textbook.
- They take notes only when they see other students taking notes.
- Some instructors ramble.

A student who uses these reasons for not taking comprehensive notes in class will eventually be using similar excuses on the job when precise note taking is required for a case. This is unfortunate. You must overcome whatever resistance you have acquired to the admittedly difficult task of note taking. Otherwise, you will pay the price in your schoolwork and on the job.

Develop your own shorthand system of abbreviations for note taking. Here are some commonly used abbreviations in the law. (Some of the terms have more than one abbreviation; pick the one that works best for you.)

a	action	**d**	danger/dangerous	**jur**	jurisdiction	**rr**	railroad
aa	administrative agency	**dba**	doing business as	**juv**	juvenile	**rsb**	reasonable
a/c	appellate court	**d/e**	direct examination	**K**	contract	**s**	sum
aff	affirmed	**dept**	department	**l**	liable, liability	**S**	statute
aka	also known as	**df**	defendant	**ll**	landlord	**$**	suppose
ans	answer	**dist**	district	**lit**	litigation	**s/b**	should be
app	appeal	**dmg**	damages	**max**	maximum	**sn/b**	should not be
appnt	appellant	**dob**	date of birth	**mfr**	manufacturer	**sc**	supreme court
appee	appellee	**dod**	date of death	**mfg**	manufacturing	**s/f**	statute of frauds
ar	administrative regulation	**dos**	date of separation	**min**	minimum	**s/j**	summary judgment
a/r	assumption of risk	**ee**	employee	**mkt**	market	**sl**	strict liability
assn	association	**eg**	example	**>**	more than; greater than	**s/l**	statute of limitations
atty	attorney	**egs**	examples	**<**	less than; smaller than	**ss**	state statute
b	business	**eq**	equity	**mun**	municipal	**std**	standard
b/c	because	**eqbl**	equitable	**n/a**	not applicable	**sub**	substantial
b/k	breach of contract	**er**	employer	**N**	negligence	**subj**	subject
b/p	burden of proof	**est**	estimate	**natl**	national	**t**	tort
bfp	bona fide purchaser	**ev**	evidence	**negl**	negligence	**t/c**	trial court
©	consideration	**f**	fact	**nj**	injury	**tee**	trustee
¢	complaint	**4cb**	foreseeable	**#**	number	**tp**	third party
ca	court of appeals	**fed**	federal	**O**	owner	**vs**	against; versus
c/a	cause of action	**fs**	federal statute	**op**	opinion	**w**	wife
c/c	counterclaim	**gvt**	government	**p/c**	proximate cause	**w/**	with
cc	child custody	**h**	husband	**p/f**	prima facie	**wd**	wrongful death
c/e	cross-examination	**hdc**	holder in due course	**pg**	page	**w/i**	within
cert	certiorari	**indl**	individual	**pl**	plaintiff	**w/o**	without
c/l	common law	**indp**	independent	**pv**	privilege	**x**	cross
con l	constitutional law	**info**	information	**®**	reasonable	**x/e**	cross-examination
cr	criminal	**ins**	insurance	**re**	real estate	**?**	question
crc	criminal court	**intl**	international	**reg**	regulation	**+**	plus
cs	child support	**IT**	intentional tort	**rep**	representative	****	therefore
ct	court	**j**	judge, justice	**rev**	reverse	**Δ**	defendant
cv	civil	**jj**	judges, justices	**revd**	reversed	**¶**	plaintiff
cz	cause	**jt**	judgment				

If you can't hear the instructor, move closer or ask the instructor to speak up. Ask the instructor to repeat something you missed. Consider taping the class so that you can continue note taking while listening to the tape.

If you are participating in class by talking with the instructor, it will obviously be difficult for you to take notes at the same time. After class, take a few moments to jot down some notes on what occurred during the discussion. Then ask someone else who was in class to review these notes for accuracy and completeness.

Sometimes you will have to begin taking notes at the moment the person starts talking rather than wait until the end of what he or she is saying. Try different approaches to increasing the completeness of your notes.

Don't fill up entire sheets of paper with notes. Keep at least a three-inch right-hand margin that is blank while you take notes. Later, fill in this empty space with notes on things you missed in the lecture or that you better understood as the class progressed. Read the notes of fellow students. When their notes contain material you missed, copy it into the right-margin space.

Sometimes so much is happening and being said during a class that it is difficult to take notes. Things can sometimes get a bit chaotic. When this happens, at least write down what appear to be key nouns or verbs that the instructor uses. Leave additional space around these words so that you can come back later and fill in details and context that you may have missed initially.

Pay particular attention to definitions and lists. Every time the instructor defines something, be sure your notes record the definition exactly. Sometimes instructors will redefine the same term with slight modifications. Take notes on the modifications because they will often help clarify what is being discussed. Also, be conscientious about lists. An instructor might begin a topic by saying that "there are three elements" to a particular rule, or that "we will be examining four major categories of examples of the kinds of cases that can arise." When you hear that a list is coming by such language, have your pen at the ready. Lists of this kind are very important in the law.

16. Studying Rules: The Role of Memory.

Memory plays a significant role in the law. Applicants for the bar, for example, are not allowed to take notes into the exam room. An advocate in court or at an administrative hearing may be able to refer to notes, but the notes are of little value if the advocate does not have a solid grasp of the case. Most of the courses you will be taking have a memory component. This is true even for open-book exams. You will not have time to go through all the course material while responding to the questions.

Students often make two mistakes on the role of memory:

- They think that memorizing is beneath their dignity.
- They think that because they understand something, they know it sufficiently to be able to give it back in an examination.

Of course, you should not be memorizing what you do not understand. Rote memorization is close to worthless. This is not so for important material that you comprehend. Yet simply understanding something does not necessarily mean that you have a sufficient grasp of it for later use.

Many systems for memorizing material can be effective:

- Reading it over and over
- Copying and recopying important parts of it
- Having other students ask you questions about it
- Making summaries or outlines of it
- Tape-recording yourself reading difficult material from a textbook and playing the tape back while driving or doing house chores
- Creating your own mnemonics

Mnemonics are simply aids to memory that you create or adopt. The most common mnemonics consist of a series of letters that represent items on a list. For example, suppose you are studying section § 100, an important larceny statute in criminal law, which requires proof of the following three elements:

- Intent to steal
- Personal property
- Resulting financial harm

To help you remember these elements, you could assign the letter "I" to the first element, "P" to the second, and "R" to the third. You can then scramble these letters to make the word RIP:

Resulting financial harm [R]
Intent to steal [I]
Personal property [P]

The word RIP can now be used to help you remember the elements of § 100. Easy-to-remember words (e.g., RIP) or nonwords (e.g., GGET or ANAR) can be useful mnemonics. You are in control of the letters to be assigned to items on the list. Your goal is to come up with something that will help you recall the list; therefore, only criterion is to come up with something memorable!

If you do not have a photographic mind, you must resort to such techniques. Try different systems. Ask other students for tips on how they memorize material. For more ideas, run this search in Google, Bing, or Yahoo: *student improve memory*.

You will have to find out from your instructor what material you will be expected to know for the course. You can also check with other students who have had this instructor in the past. It may not always be easy to find out how much an instructor expects you to know from memory. Instructors have been known to surprise students on examinations!

17. Studying Skills—the Necessity of Feedback.

Memory is most important when you are studying the basic principles of substantive and procedural law. Memory plays a less significant role in learning the skills of interviewing, investigation, legal analysis, drafting, coordinating, digesting, and advocacy. These skills have their own vocabulary that you must know, but it is your judgmental rather than your memory faculties that are key to becoming competent in such skills.

They are developed primarily by practice drills or exercises. The learning comes from the feedback that you obtain while engaged in the skill exercises. What are the ways to obtain feedback?

- Evaluations on assignments and exams
- Role-playing exercises that are critiqued in class
- Comparisons between your work (particularly writing projects) and models that are provided by the instructor or that you find on your own in the library
- Critiques that you receive from students in study groups

Be constantly looking for feedback. Do not wait to be called on. Do not wait to see what feedback is planned for you at the end of the course. Take the initiative.

- Seek conferences or email contact with your instructors.
- Find out who is available to read your writing or to observe your performance in any of the other skills.
- Set up your own role-playing sessions with your fellow students.
- Seek critiques of your rewrites even if rewriting was not required.
- Look for opportunities to critique other students on the various skills.
- Ask other students to let you read their graded examinations so that you can compare their papers with your own.
- Create your own hypotheticals for analysis in study groups. (A hypothetical is simply a set of facts invented for the purpose of discussion and analysis.)
- Do additional reading on the skills.

In short, become actively involved in your own skill development.

18. The Value of Speed-Reading Courses in the Study of Law.

In the study of law, a great deal of reading is required. Should you, therefore, take a speed-reading course? No, unless the course helps you slow down the speed of your reading! This advice may be quite distasteful to advocates (and salespersons) of speed-reading courses. The reality, however, is that statutes, regulations, and court opinions cannot be speed-read. They must be carefully picked apart and read word for word, almost as if you were translating from one language into another.

If you are troubled by how long it takes you to read, do not despair. Keep reading. Keep rereading. The pace of your reading will pick up as you gain experience. Never strive, however, to be able to fly through the material. Strive for comprehensiveness. Strive for understanding. For most of us, this will come through the slow process of note taking and rereading. It is sometimes argued that comprehension is increased through speed. Be wary of this argument. Reading legal material calls for careful thinking about what you read—and taking notes on these thoughts. There may be no harm in rapidly reading something for the first time. At your second, third, and fourth reading, however, speed is rarely helpful.

ON-THE-JOB LEARNING: THE ART OF BEING SUPERVISED

A great deal of learning will occur when you are on the job. Some of it may come through formal in-house office training and by the study of office procedure manuals. Most of the learning, however, will come in day-to-day interaction with your supervisors as you are given assignments. The learning comes through being supervised. Here are some guidelines to assist you in this important dimension of your legal education.

1. Don't Play "Emperor's Clothes" with the Instructions That You Receive.

Recall the story of the emperor's clothes. He walked around without clothes, but everybody kept saying what a beautiful wardrobe he had. As new people arrived, they saw that he had no clothes, but they heard everyone talking as if he were fully dressed. The new people did not want to appear unintelligent, so they, too, began admiring the emperor's wardrobe. When paralegals are receiving instructions on an assignment, they play "emperor's clothes" when they pretend that they understand all the instructions but in fact do not. They do not want to appear to be uninformed. They do not want to give the impression that they are unsure of themselves. For obvious reasons, this is a serious mistake.

Whenever you are given an assignment in a new area—that is, an assignment on something that you have not done before—there should be a great deal that you do not understand. This is particularly true during your first few months on the job, when just about everything is new! Do not pretend to be something you are not. Constantly ask questions about new things. Do not be reluctant to ask for explanations. Do not assume that the instructions will become clear to you after you start the assignment. Ask for help at the outset. It will not be a sign of weakness. Quite the contrary. People who take steps to make sure that they fully understand all the instructions they receive will soon gain a reputation for responsibility and conscientiousness.

2. Repeat the Instructions to Your Supervisor Before You Leave the Room.

Once your supervisor has told you what he or she wants you to do, do not leave the room in silence or with the general observation "I'll get on that right away." Repeat the instructions back to the supervisor as you understand them. Make sure that you and your supervisor are on the same wavelength by summarizing what you think you were told to do. This will be an excellent opportunity for the supervisor to determine what you did or did not understand and to provide clarifications where needed.

Supervisors will not always be sure of what they want. By trying to obtain clarity on the instructions, you are providing them with the opportunity to think through what they want done. In the middle of the session with you, the supervisor may change his or her mind on what is to be done.

3. Write Down Your Instructions.

Paralegal Jamie Collins has frequently supervised and trained other paralegals and clerical staff. "I cannot tell you," says Jamie, "how many people I have trained that would come back to ask me a question, and never write down a thing, only to return to my office a few moments or hours later or the next day with the exact same question, and no clue how to answer it."[2]

Never go to your supervisor without pen and paper. Preferably, keep an instructions notebook, diary, or journal in which you record the following information:

- Notes on what you are asked to do
- Whether the tasks in the assignment are billable (i.e., whether a particular client will be asked to pay fees for the performance of those tasks)
- The date you received the assignment
- The date by which the supervisor expects you to complete all or part of the assignment; if an exact due date is not provided, an estimate of the amount of time the task should take (sometimes referred to as a *time budget*)
- The date you actually complete the assignment
- Comments made by supervisors or others on what you submit (if no one makes comments, take the initiative and ask for feedback)

The notes will serve as your memory bank. Whenever any questions arise about what you were supposed to do, you have something concrete to refer to.

Exhibit A contains an assignment checklist on which you can record this kind of data for every major assignment you receive.

Exhibit A	Checklist for Major Assignments

- Name of supervisor for the assignment:

- What you have been asked to do:

- Identification of the client or matter for which the task is being done:

- Specific areas or tasks you have been told not to cover, if any:

- Format supervisor expects, e.g., computer text, outline only, rough draft, final copy ready for supervisor's signature:

- Date you are given the assignment:

- Expected due date:

- Time budget (the amount of time the task should take):

(continued)

Exhibit A	Checklist for Major Assignments *(Continued)*

- Is the task billable to a client? If so, to what account? Is there a limit on the number of hours to spend on the assignment?

- Location of samples or models in the office to check as possible guides:

- Possible resource people in the office you may want to contact for help:

- Practice guide, formbook, or manual in the library that might provide background or general guidance:

- Dates you contacted supervisor or others for help before due date:

- Date you completed the assignment:

- Positive, negative, or neutral comments from supervisor or others on the quality of your work on the assignment:

- Things you would do differently the next time you do an assignment of this kind:

4. Ask for a Due Date and a Statement of Priorities.

You need to know when an assignment is due. What's the time budget? Ask for a due date even if the supervisor tells you to "get to it when you can." This phrase may mean "relatively soon" or "before the end of the month" to your supervisor, but not to you. If the supervisor says he or she does not know when it should be done, ask for an approximate due date. Tell the supervisor you want to place the assignment on your calendar so that it can be completed in a timely manner along with all your other assignments. Ask what priority the assignment has. Where does it fit in with your other assignments? If you have more than enough to fill the day, you need to know what takes priority. If you do not ask for a priority listing, the supervisor may assume you are under no time pressures. If you have assignments from different supervisors, gently suggest that the supervisors confer and let you know what the priorities are.

5. If the Instructions Appear to Be Complicated, Ask Your Supervisor to Identify the Sequence of Tasks Involved.

As you receive instructions, you may sometimes feel overwhelmed by all that is being asked of you. Many supervisors do not give instructions in clear, logical patterns. They may talk in a rambling, stream-of-consciousness fashion. When confronted with this situation, simply say:

OK, but can you break that down for me a little more so that I know what you want me to do first? It would help if I approach it one step at a time. Where do you want me to start?

6. As Often as Possible, Write Your Instructions and What You Do in the Form of Checklists.

A methodical mind is one that views a project in "doable" steps and that tackles one step at a time. You need to have a methodical mind in order to function in a busy law office. One of the best ways to develop such a mind is to think in terms of checklists. Attorneys love checklists. A great deal of the practice material published by bar associations, for example, consists of page after page of detailed checklists of things to do and/or to consider when completing a project for a client. Attorneys want to be thorough. An unwritten "rule" of law practice seems to be that you cannot be thorough without a checklist.

A checklist is simply a chronological sequencing of tasks that must be done in order to complete an assignment. Convert the instructions from your supervisor into checklists. In the process of actually carrying out instructions, you go through many steps—all of which could become part of a detailed checklist. The steps you went through to complete the task become a checklist of things to do in order to complete such a task in the future. To be sure, it can be time-consuming to draft checklists. Keep in mind, however, that

- The checklists will be a benefit to you in organizing your own time and in assuring completeness.
- The checklists can be invaluable for other employees who are given similar assignments in the future.
- Your supervisors will probably be very impressed by your initiative and organizational ability.

You will not be able to draft checklists for everything that you do. Perhaps you will not be able to write more than one checklist a week. Perhaps you will have to use some of your own time to write checklists. Whatever time you devote will be profitably spent so long as you are serious about writing and using the checklists. They may have to be rewritten or modified later. This should not deter you from the task. Most things that are worth doing require testing and reassessment.

Here is how one veteran paralegal describes the process:

> When you are doing a multistep task (thinking out each step as you move through it)…create a checklist that will help you do it faster next time. [Also] create a notebook to store it in so that when the job comes around again you can find it! This is trickier to do on a busy day than you may think, but well worth doing. Think of these checklists as expanding your professional options. In time, they may become resources for training you give to newer paralegals.[3]

Many how-to manuals found in law offices were created out of the checklists that workers compiled on tasks they frequently performed.

7. Find Out What Practice Guides and Checklists Already Exist in Your Office.

If practice guides and checklists on the topic of your assignment already exist in your office, you should find and use them. (Also check in computer databases where the office may store frequently used forms and instructions.) Unfortunately, the how-to-do-it information may be buried in the heads of the attorneys, paralegals, and secretaries in the office. No one may have taken the time to write it all down. If this is not so, find out where it is written down and try to adapt what you find to the assignment on which you are working.

8. Ask for a Model.

One of the best ways to make sure you know what a supervisor wants is to ask whether he or she knows of any models that you could use as a guide for what you are being asked to do. Such models may be found in closed-case files, manuals, formbooks, and practice texts. They may also be available on the Internet.

Caution is needed whenever using models. Every new legal problem is potentially unique. What will work in one case may not work in another. A model is a guide, a starting point and nothing more. Changes in the model will often be needed in order to adapt it to the particular facts of your assignment. Whenever you find a possible model your supervisor has not seen, bring it to his or her attention and ask whether it can be adapted and used. (See also Exhibit 10-5 in Chapter 10 on how to avoid abusing standard forms.)

9. Do Some Independent Legal Research on the Instructions You Are Given.

Often you will be told what to do without being given more than a cursory explanation of why it needs to be done that way. Most instructions for legal tasks are based upon the requirements of the law. A complaint, for example, is served on an opposing party in a designated way because the law has imposed rules on how such service is to be made. You may be asked to serve a complaint in a certain way without being told what section of the state code (or of your court rules) requires it to be served in that way. It would be highly impractical to read all the law that is the foundation for an assigned task. It is not necessary to do so and you would not have time to do so.

What you can occasionally do, however, is focus on selected instructions for an assignment and do some background legal research to gain a greater appreciation for why the instructions were necessary. (See the checklist on doing background legal research in Exhibit 11-11 in Chapter 11.) You will probably have to do such legal research on your own time unless the assignment you are given includes doing some legal research. Research can be time-consuming, but you will find it enormously educational. It can place a totally new perspective on the assignment and, indeed, on your entire job.

10. Get on Routing and Mailing Lists for New Legal Material.

A law office frequently buys publications for its law library that are relevant to its practice. The publications can include legal treatises and legal periodicals. Before these publications are shelved in the library, they are often routed to the attorneys in the office so that they can become acquainted with current legal writing that will be available in the library. Each attorney usually keeps the publication for a few hours or a few days for review before passing it on to the next person on the mailing list. If the actual publication is not passed around in this manner, those on the mailing list might receive brief summaries of recent publications or photocopies of their tables of contents. Another option in some offices is the use of email to inform attorneys of new publications.

Ask to be included on these routing or mailing lists. The publications are often excellent self-education opportunities, particularly the articles in legal periodicals.

You can also subscribe to free Internet alerts on your area of practice. Findlaw (www.findlaw.com) allows you to subscribe to free newsletters that give summaries of recent cases in designated areas of law (newsletters.findlaw.com). For example, one of the areas covered by the newsletters is family law. If your office practices in this area, you should consider subscribing.

11. Ask Secretaries and Other Paralegals for Help.

Secretaries and paralegals who have worked in the office for a long time can be very helpful to you if you approach them properly. Everybody wants to feel important. Everybody wants to be respected. When someone asks for something in a way that gives the impression he or she is entitled to what is being sought, difficulties usually result. Think of how you would like to be approached if you were in the position of the secretary or paralegal. What behavior or attitude of another employee would irritate you? What would make you want to go out of your way to cooperate with and assist a new employee who needs your help? Your answers (and sensitivity) to questions such as these will go a long way toward enabling you to draw on the experience of others in the office.

12. Obtain Feedback on an Assignment Before the Date It Is Due.

Unless the assignment you are given is a very simple one, do not wait until the date it is due to communicate with your supervisor. If you are having trouble with the assignment, you will want to check with your supervisor as soon as possible and as often as necessary. It would be a mistake, however, to contact the supervisor only when trouble arises. Of course, you want to avoid wasting anyone's time, including your own. You should limit your contacts with a busy supervisor to essential matters. You could take the following approach with your supervisor:

> Everything seems to be going fine on the project you gave me. I expect to have it in to you on time. I'm wondering, however, if you could give me a few moments of your time. I want to bring you up to date on where I am so that you can let me know if I am on the right track.

Perhaps this contact could take place on the phone or during a brief office visit. Suppose that you have gone astray on the assignment without knowing it? It is obviously better to discover this before the date the assignment is due. The more communication you have with your supervisor, the more likely it is that you will catch such errors before a great deal of time is wasted.

13. Ask to Participate in Office and Community Training Programs.

Sometimes a law office conducts training sessions for its attorneys. Ask if you can be included. Bar associations and paralegal associations often conduct sessions on legal topics relevant to your work. They are part of what is called *continuing legal education* (CLE). Seek permission to attend some of these sessions if they are held during work hours. If they are conducted after hours, invest some of your own time to attend. Also check into what is available on the Internet. Online CLE has become increasingly popular because you can take courses at any time and in any location where you have access to the Internet. To find out what is available, type "continuing legal education" (or "CLE") in the search boxes of national and local paralegal associations and of bar associations in your area (see Appendix B). Your employer may be willing to pay all or a part of the cost of such courses. Even if you must pay the cost, it will be a worthwhile long-term investment.

14. Ask to Be Evaluated Regularly.

When you first interview for a paralegal position, inquire about the policy of the office on evaluations. Are they conducted on a regular basis? Are they done in writing? Will you know in advance the specific criteria that will be used to evaluate your performance? If you are hired in an office that does not have a formal evaluation structure or procedure, take the initiative to let supervisors know that you consider evaluations to be important to your professional development. It may take a while for you to feel confident enough to make this known, but the importance of doing so cannot be overestimated.

For a number of reasons, many offices do not have formal evaluations:

- Evaluations can be time-consuming.
- Evaluators are reluctant to say anything negative, especially in writing.
- Most of us do not like to be evaluated: it's threatening to our ego.

Go out of your way to let your supervisor know that you want to be evaluated and that you can handle criticism. If you are defensive when you are criticized, you will find that the evaluations of your performance will go on behind your back! Such a work environment is obviously unhealthy. Consider this approach that a paralegal might take with a supervisor:

> I want to know what you think of my work. I want to know where you think I need improvement. That's the only way I'm going to learn. I also want to know when I'm doing things correctly, but I'm mainly interested in your suggestions on what I can do to increase my skills.

If you take this approach and mean it, the chances are good that you will receive constructive criticism and gain a reputation for professionalism.

15. Proceed One Step at a Time.

Perhaps the most important advice you can receive in studying law in school and on the job is to concentrate on what is immediately before you. Proceed one step at a time. What are your responsibilities in the next fifteen minutes? Block everything else out. Make the *now* as productive as you can. Your biggest enemy is worry about the future: worry about the exams ahead of you, worry about your family, worry about the state of the world, worry about finding employment, etc. Leave tomorrow alone! Worrying about it will only interfere with your ability to make the most of what you must do now. Your development in the law will come slowly, in stages. Map out these stages in very small time blocks—beginning with the time that is immediately ahead of you. If you must worry, limit your concern to how to make the next fifteen minutes shine.

SUMMARY

Legal education is a lifelong endeavor; a competent paralegal never stops learning about the law and the skills of applying it. A number of important guidelines will help you become a good student in the classroom and on the job. Do not let the media blur your understanding of what the practice of law is actually like. To avoid studying in a vacuum, know the goals of an assignment. Organize your day around a study plan. Assess your study habits, such as how you handle distractions or how you commit things to memory. Then promise yourself that you will do something about your weaknesses.

Increase your proficiency in the basics of writing. How many of the rules about the comma can you identify? Do you know when to use *that* rather than *which* in your sentences? How many of your paragraphs have topic sentences? Are there zero spelling errors on every page of your writing? You have entered a field where the written word is paramount. You must take personal responsibility for the improvement of your grammar, spelling, and composition skills. Use the law library to help you understand difficult areas of the law. But don't expect absolute clarity all the time. Seek out evaluations of your work. Become a skillful note taker. Get into the habit of looking for definitions.

These suggestions also apply once you are on the job. Don't pretend you understand what you don't. Repeat instructions back to your supervisor before you begin an assignment. Ask for due dates. Ask for priorities if you are given several things to do. Write down your instructions in your own notebook or journal. Become an avid user of checklists, including those you create on your own. Find out if an assignment has been done by others in the past. If so, seek their help. Try to find a model and adapt it as needed. Be prepared to do some independent research. Ask if you can be on internal office mailing lists for new publications. Find out what's available on the Internet to keep current in your area of the law. Participate in training programs at the law office and in the legal community. Ask to be evaluated regularly. Seek feedback before an assignment is due.

REVIEW QUESTIONS

1. Why must a student of law be a perpetual student?
2. Distinguish between substantive and procedural law.
3. What are the two dimensions of your legal education?
4. How do you design a study plan?
5. How can you increase your available productive time?
6. What are some of the major interferences with effective studying?
7. What are some of the techniques of active studying?
8. What steps can you take on your own to increase your proficiency in grammar, spelling, and composition?
9. What danger do you need to be aware of when using computer spell checkers?
10. What are readability formulas and how can they assist you?
11. How can study groups help you?
12. How can legal research help you handle difficult aspects of any course?
13. What is meant by expecting ambiguity in the law?
14. Why is note taking important in the study and practice of law?
15. What are some of the steps you can take to increase your powers of retention?
16. Where and how can you obtain feedback on your schoolwork?
17. What is meant by playing "emperor's clothes" with the assignments you receive on the job?
18. What are the major techniques of receiving instructions from your supervisor on assignments?
19. Why is it important to obtain a specific due date and a statement of priorities for assignments?
20. How can you translate instructions into checklists?
21. How can you obtain help on an office assignment from practice guides, manuals, models, independent legal research, secretaries, and other paralegals?
22. How can you obtain feedback on an assignment from a busy supervisor?
23. Why are performance evaluations sometimes ineffective, and what can you do to obtain meaningful ones on the job?

HELPFUL WEBSITES

Study Techniques
- www.how-to-study.com
- www.adprima.com/studyout.htm

Note Taking
- www.sas.calpoly.edu/asc/ssl/notetaking.systems.html
- www.csbsju.edu/academicadvising/help/lec-note.htm
- www.dartmouth.edu/~acskills/success/notes.html
- www.academictips.org/acad/literature/notetaking.html

Online Flashcards for Paralegals
- www.flashcardexchange.com (type "paralegal" in the search box)

Taking Tests
- www.testtakingtips.com/test
- www.studygs.net/tsttak1.htm

Google, Bing, or Yahoo Searches
(On these search engines, run the following searches.)
- grammar help
- study skills
- how to study
- memory skills
- note taking
- test taking
- supervision skills
- "being supervised"
- memory skills
- study groups
- on the job learning

ENDNOTES

[1] Lynda Richardson, *From the Bench, Judgment and Sass*, New York Times, March 27, 2001, at p. A25.

[2] Jamie Collins, *What It Takes to Survive in a Law Office … and Live to Tell the Tale*, KNOW, The Magazine for Paralegals (The Paralegal Society, September 7, 2012) (theparalegalsociety.wordpress.com).

[3] Deborah Bogen, *Paralegal Success* 79 (2000).

The Paralegal in the Legal System

INTRODUCTION TO THE PARALEGAL CAREER

CHAPTER OUTLINE

- Launching Your Career
- Do You Know What Time It Is?
- The Scope of Your Legal Education
- Major Players
- Job Titles
- Definitions of a Paralegal
- Paralegal Fees
- Career Ladders in Large Law Offices
- Paralegal Salaries
- Factors Influencing the Growth of Paralegalism
- "Oh, You're Studying Law?"
- Your Online Reputation
- Conclusion

CHAPTER OBJECTIVES

After completing this chapter, you should be able to:

- Understand the extent of legal disputes in the country.
- Describe the importance of precision in the practice of law.
- List the major organizations in paralegalism and the roles that they play.
- Know the major classifications of paralegal titles.
- Know the definition of a paralegal.
- Outline the major categories of fees.
- Understand the importance of *Missouri v. Jenkins*.
- Identify the major employers that have career ladders for paralegals.
- Identify the factors that determine a paralegal's salary.
- Understand the factors that have contributed to the development and growth of paralegalism.

LAUNCHING YOUR CAREER

Welcome to the field! You probably fall into one or more of the following categories:

- You have never worked in a law office.
- You are or once were employed in a law office and now want to upgrade your skills.
- You want to explore the variety of careers in law for which a paralegal education can be a point of entry.

As you begin your legal education, you may have a large number of questions:

- What is a paralegal?
- Where do paralegals work?
- What are the functions of a paralegal?
- How do I obtain a job?
- How do attorneys and paralegals work together as a team?
- What is the difference between a paralegal and the clerical staff of a law office?
- How do new paralegals adjust to the realities of a law practice?

- How is the paralegal field regulated? Who does the regulating and for what purposes?
- What are the ethical guidelines that govern paralegal conduct?
- What career options are available once a paralegal has obtained experience?

It is an exciting time to be working in the law. So many aspects of our everyday lives have legal dimensions. The law plays a dominant role in a spectrum of issues that range from the status of the unborn to the termination of life-support systems. More than 107 million cases are filed every year in state and federal courts.[1] One study concludes that 52 percent of Americans have a legal problem. One out of three will need the advice of an attorney in the next twelve months.[2] In a large survey of U.S. corporations, 87 percent reported that one or more lawsuits were commenced against them in the past 12 months.[3] The news media are preoccupied with laws that have been broken, laws that no longer make sense, and laws that ought to be passed to create a more just society. Caught up in the whirlwind of these debates is the attorney and the attorney's team, a prominent member of which is the paralegal.

A prominent paralegal was once asked why she became a paralegal. "Deep down," she said, "a good number of us entered the profession because legal proceedings touch everyone on a very personal basis several times during a lifetime, so it is a profession that everyone can relate to. As a paralegal, you . . . also gain the satisfaction of knowing you were able to help solve a problem for a client."[3a]

There are other satisfactions as well. Once you have completed your paralegal education and gained experience on the job, you can explore a variety of career options within traditional paralegal employment settings. In addition:

- An experienced corporate paralegal in a law firm might leave the firm to take a higher-paying position as a securities analyst for a corporation.
- An experienced estates paralegal at a law firm might leave for a more lucrative position as a trust administrator at a bank.

An extensive list of these law-related jobs is given in Exhibit 2-24 at the end of Chapter 2.

Perhaps the most dramatic example of a paralegal position being used as a stepping-stone for other jobs is the large number of former paralegals who have used their legal training and experience to run for political office, particularly at the city and county levels of government. Peggy Marino, for example, used her paralegal background to help her win a seat on the Board of Education in New Jersey. Peggy now serves on the financial and negotiations committees of that Board. She credits her paralegal experience "as having prepared her for those roles."[4] Similarly, when paralegal Deborah Boe was appointed to the Minnesota Board of Medical Practice, she said that she has "read enough legal documents to know how to read between the lines" and "make my way through the issues" that will come before the Board.[5] Representative Mary Squires of the Georgia Legislature feels the same way. She was a paralegal before she ran for office. Because of a paralegal's preparation and organization skills, she felt equipped for the rigorous life of a legislator.[6] After serving in the House, Mary was elected to the state Senate and is currently a candidate for state insurance commissioner. Of course, not all experienced paralegals go into politics, but the experience of these paralegals demonstrates the value and versatility of legal education.

DO YOU KNOW WHAT TIME IT IS?

Perhaps you're wondering what working in the law will be like. One of the hallmarks of legal work is its diversity. In five years, if you meet a fellow classmate and compare notes on what your workdays are like as paralegals, you'll see similarities, but you will probably be startled by the differences.

One way to gauge what working in a law office might be like is to answer a particular question. Stop what you are doing for a moment and answer this question:

Do you know what time it is?

Depending on when you are reading this book, you will probably look at your watch or the clock on the cell phone and answer 9:45 A.M., 1:30 P.M., 3:32 P.M., 11:28 P.M., etc. There could be hundreds of possible answers. But if you answered in this manner, you've made your first mistake in the study and practice of law. Look at the question again. Read it slowly. You were *not* asked, *What time is it*? You were asked, *Do you know* what time it is? There are *only* two possible answers to this question: *yes* or *no*.

Welcome to the law! One of the singular characteristics of the field you are about to enter is its *precision* and *attention to detail*. Vast amounts of time can be wasted by answering the wrong question.[7] In fact, attorneys will tell you that one of the most important skills in the law is the ability to identify and focus on the question—the issue—that must be resolved.

Developing this sensitivity begins with the skill of *listening*—listening very carefully. It also involves *thinking before responding*, noting distinctions, noting what is said and what is not said, being aware of differences in emphasis, and being aware that slight differences in the facts can lead to dramatically different conclusions. Even relatively minor variations in punctuation can sometimes have legal consequences. Compare, for example, the following two statements and note the dramatic difference in meaning that results from the placement of commas:

Johnson said the officer hid the evidence.
Johnson, said the officer, hid the evidence.

In 2008, chief justice of the United States, John Roberts, administered the presidential oath of office by having Barack Obama:

"solemnly swear" that "I will execute the office of President of the United States faithfully."

But the Constitution states that the adverb "faithfully" should go *before* the verb that it modifies:

"solemnly swear" that "I will faithfully execute the office of President of the United States."

After the inauguration ceremony, the chief justice returned and administered the oath again, this time "by the book."

The hallmark of a professional is precision in language and the ability to identify what is different or unique about a particular person or situation. In this sense, highly competent paralegals are true professionals.

Another major characteristic of law is its focus on definitions and intentions. Attorneys are preoccupied with questions such as "What definition did the legislature intend?" and "What does that clause mean?" For example, if a will says, "I give $30,000 to my three children, Bill, Grace, and Sam," does each child receive $30,000 or is this amount to be split among the three children so that each receives $10,000? The answer depends on the intent of the deceased when the will was written. On September 11, 2001, when two airplanes struck the two towers of the World Trade Center sixteen minutes apart, was the landlord of the towers entitled to one insurance payment of $3.5 billion or two payments totaling $7 billion? The answer turned on the definition of the word *occurrence* in the insurance contracts. Was there one attack, one "occurrence," or two? (After extensive litigation, the landlord was not successful in convincing the courts that there were two occurrences under all of the insurance contracts involved in the case.) Another dramatic example of controversy generated by a definition occurred during a famous grand jury hearing that was videotaped and later played on national television. The witness giving testimony under oath was a graduate of the Yale Law School and a former constitutional law professor. In testimony that captivated the nation, he said that his answer to a particular question (involving sexual relations with an intern) would depend on what the "definition of 'is' is" in the question. The attorney giving this testimony was President Bill Clinton.

In a recent discussion on LinkedIn, the social network for professionals, paralegals were asked about the career they have chosen. Here are some of the responses:

- "I'm constantly intellectually stimulated" and have "made amazing friends."
- "I've been with the same firm for 17 years (longer than any of my romantic relationships!) and still have days when my heart beats faster and am excited about something I am doing, usually digging up hard-to-find information, helping a client get much-needed benefits, learning new technology, or writing substantive content. Each day brings something new."
- "If you let it be known that you are looking for a challenge, you will certainly find it in this career field!"

Not every case in a law office makes the headlines, and not every paralegal is satisfied with all aspects of his or her job. Yet the potential is there for a paralegal career to provide substantial fulfillment and a broad range of opportunities. In short, you have a great deal ahead of you in the study of law; it's going to be a fascinating adventure.

THE SCOPE OF YOUR LEGAL EDUCATION

Legal education is a very broad area of study. You will be covering a great deal of material in your courses. Will you use all of this material on the job? Not necessarily. Yet the material must be covered in order to comprehend the legal system and the world of attorneys. For example, you will learning about appellate briefs and sophisticated legal research even though many paralegals never draft such briefs nor perform such research. Yet you need to have a basic understanding of such tasks in order to communicate with attorneys and to perform assignments related to these tasks. In short, understanding the role of a paralegal requires an understanding of and exposure to a wide range of paralegal *and attorney* skills as you begin the journey of comprehending the practice of law and the legal system as a whole.

Areas that are essential to the performance of specific paralegal tasks include:

- the functions of courts, legislatures, and administrative agencies
- the rules of professional responsibility (ethics) governing attorneys and paralegals
- the rules of grammar and clear communication
- the ability to state facts accurately and comprehensively
- the basics of computer hardware and software on your desk and "in the cloud"
- the ability to adapt to the different standards of different attorneys in an environment where time pressures can be intense

Without a grasp of these essentials, a paralegal career can flounder. Hence we will spend a good deal of time on them. Yet we will also cover the big picture, which includes tasks that many attorneys never assign paralegals to perform. This broader perspective is needed to develop into a well-rounded paralegal and to be ready for the great diversity that awaits you within the legal community.

MAJOR PLAYERS

During this course, we will meet many organizations. Here is an overview of some of the major players (not necessarily listed in order of influence):

- National Federation of Paralegal Associations (NFPA)
- National Association of Legal Assistants (NALA)
- NALS, The Association for Legal Professionals (NALS)
- American Bar Association Standing Committee on Paralegals (SCOP)
- Your state bar association (see Appendix B)
- Your local paralegal association (see Appendix B)

These organizations are covered in some detail throughout the remaining chapters of the book, but a brief word about each will be helpful at this point.

All six organizations extensively promote (and most offer) **continuing legal education (CLE)**, which is training in the law (usually short term) that a person receives after completing his or her formal legal training or after becoming employed.

NATIONAL FEDERATION OF PARALEGAL ASSOCIATIONS (NFPA)

(www.paralegals.org)

The NFPA is an association of more than fifty state and local paralegal associations throughout the country. (See Appendix B.) Individual paralegals can also be members, but most are connected to NFPA through their local paralegal association. More than 10,000 paralegals are part of the NFPA network. NFPA offers voluntary **certification** for entry-level paralegals (PCCE: the Paralegal CORE Competency Exam). By entry-level, we mean that the certification credential can be earned without having paralegal job experience. (In the job market, entry-level also refers to a starting position for someone with little or no experience.) NFPA has another voluntary certification program for paralegals with experience (PACE: the Paralegal Advanced Competency Exam). We discuss these credentials in Chapter 4.

continuing legal education (CLE) Training in the law (usually short term) that a person receives after completing his or her formal legal training or after becoming employed.

certification The process by which a nongovernmental organization grants recognition to a person who has met the qualifications set by that organization.

NATIONAL ASSOCIATION OF LEGAL ASSISTANTS (NALA)

(www.nala.org)

NALA is primarily an association of individual paralegals , although eighty-one state and local paralegal associations are affiliated with NALA. (See Appendix B.) More than 18,000 paralegals in the country are represented by NALA. It offers voluntary certification for entry-level paralegals (CLA, Certified Legal Assistant/Certified Paralegal) and for paralegals with experience (APC, Advanced Paralegal Certification). See Chapter 4.

NALS, THE ASSOCIATION FOR LEGAL PROFESSIONALS

(www.nals.org)

The oldest national association in the country is NALS, the Association for Legal Professionals. (See Appendix B.) The association consists of more than 4,000 paralegals and legal secretaries in 100+ chapters throughout the country. NALS offers a voluntary certification examination (PP, Professional Paralegal). See Chapter 4. The National Association of Legal Assistants (NALA) was initially formed as a breakaway association from NALS. Both associations are still headquartered in Tulsa, Oklahoma. (At one time, NALS stood for National Association of Legal Secretaries; the organization kept the abbreviation but changed its meaning.)

See Exhibit 1-1 concerning convention activity of NFPA, NALA, and NALS.

Exhibit 1-1	Annual Conventions: NFPA, NALA, and NALS

Annual convention of the National Federation of Paralegal Associations (NFPA).

Annual convention of the National Association of Legal Assistants (NALA).

Continuing legal education (CLE) session of NALS, the Association for Legal Professionals.

Reprinted with permission of the National Federation of Paralegal Associations; photo courtesy of NALA and Ken Frakes; reprinted by permission of Nancy Harris (PP, PLS) and NALS.

AMERICAN BAR ASSOCIATION STANDING COMMITTEE ON PARALEGALS (SCOP)

(www.americanbar.org/groups/paralegals.html)

The American Bar Association (ABA) is a voluntary association of attorneys; no attorney must be a member. Yet it is a powerful organization because of its resources, its prestige, and the large number of attorneys who have joined. The ABA has a Standing Committee on Paralegals (SCOP) that has had a significant impact on the growth of the field. The role of the ABA has included the publication of research on paralegals, the establishment of a voluntary program of approving paralegal schools, and the creation of an associate membership category for paralegals.

STATE BAR ASSOCIATION OF YOUR STATE
(see Appendix B)

Most state bar associations have been active regarding the role of paralegals in the practice of law. Many of the associations have issued (1) guidelines on the proper use of paralegals by attorneys and (2) ethical opinions that apply the state's ethics code to an attorney's use of paralegals. We examine such guidelines and opinions in Chapter 5 and in Appendix D. Some state bar associations have followed the lead of the ABA and allow paralegals to become associate or affiliate members.

YOUR LOCAL PARALEGAL ASSOCIATION
(see Appendix B)

Paralegal associations fall into at least fourteen categories, some of which overlap:

1. Nationwide (e.g., NFPA, NALA, NALS)
2. Statewide (e.g., Illinois Paralegal Association)
3. Regionwide encompassing more than one state (e.g., Rocky Mountain Paralegal Association)
4. Regionwide within a state (e.g., South Florida Paralegal Association)
5. Countywide (e.g., Santa Clara County Paralegal Association)
6. Citywide (e.g., New York City Paralegal Association)
7. Practice specific (e.g., Houston Corporate Paralegal Association)
8. Division of a bar association (e.g., Paralegal Division of the State Bar of Texas)
9. Association of associations (e.g., Empire State Alliance of Paralegal Associations)
10. Schoolwide (e.g., Fresno City College Paralegal Association)
11. Manager-focused (e.g., International Practice Management Association)
12. Association whose membership is limited to paralegals (e.g., Orange County Paralegal Association)
13. Association whose membership consists of paralegals, legal secretaries, and other nonattorneys (e.g., NALS)
14. Foreign (e.g., Canadian Paralegal Association)

networking Establishing contacts and sharing information with people (a) who might become personal or professional resources for you and (b) for whom you might become a personal or professional resource.

Most paralegals in the country have joined a state, regional, county, city, or bar-affiliated paralegal association. (They are collectively referred to in this book as *local paralegal associations*.) Through CLE and **networking**, a great many paralegals have found major career support and inspiration by active participation in their local paralegal association. If any of them have a student membership rate, you should consider joining now, while you are in this course.

OTHER IMPORTANT ORGANIZATIONS

Although NFPA, NALA, NALS, SCOP, your state bar association, and your local paralegal association will dominate our discussion of paralegalism, we will also be referring to other important groups, such as the following:

- International Practice Management Association (IPMA): an association of paralegal supervisors in large law offices (www.paralegalmanagement.org)
- American Association for Paralegal Education (AAfPE): an association of paralegal schools (www.aafpe.org)
- Association of Legal Administrators (ALA): an association of individuals (mostly nonattorneys) who help administer or manage law offices (www.alanet.org)
- American Alliance of Paralegals, Inc. (AAPI): a national association of paralegals that offers certification without an examination (www.aapipara.org)

JOB TITLES

PARALEGAL AND LEGAL ASSISTANT

For convenience, this book uses the title *paralegal*. At one time, another common title was *legal assistant*. For years most people agreed that these titles were synonymous, just as the titles *attorney* and *lawyer* are synonymous. Yet the titles *paralegal* and *legal assistant* have been the source of confusion and debate. For example, in some state governments, legal-assistant positions are attorney positions. In the federal government, most legal secretaries are called legal assistants. More significantly, many private law offices have changed the title of their legal secretaries to *legal assistants* without changing the requirements for their position or the duties they perform. Those who favor this title change say that it reflects the broader role that many secretaries perform. Cynics, however, argue that the change is due to the fact that courts can give attorneys separate fees for the work of their legal assistants but not for that of their secretaries. We will be examining such fees later in this chapter.

The shift in title from *secretary* to *legal assistant* has not been universal; there are still individuals called legal secretaries in offices throughout the country. Yet the number of legal secretaries now called legal assistants is substantial, and this has led many to conclude that the legal assistant and paralegal titles are no longer synonymous. There is an emerging preference for the *paralegal* title. For example, many local associations have voted to change their name from legal-assistant association to paralegal association. One of the largest paralegal organizations in the country, the Legal Assistant Division of the State Bar of Texas, changed its name to the Paralegal Division of the State Bar of Texas. As indicated, an important committee of the American Bar Association is the Standing Committee on Paralegals. Its former name was the Standing Committee on Legal Assistants.

The National Association of Legal Assistants (NALA), however, is adamant that "the terms legal assistant and paralegal are used interchangeably." This is also the view of the International Practice Management Association (IPMA), yet even IPMA has gone through a name change—it was once known as the Legal Assistant Management Association. NALA itself has acknowledged this trend. As we will see in Chapter 4, if you take and pass NALA's certification exam, you have a choice of being called a certified legal assistant (CLA) or a certified paralegal (CP). The former title has been available since the 1970s; the latter was added as an option in 2004 and is now preferred by those who pass the exam. It is true that some laws (discussed in Chapter 4) treat paralegals and legal assistants as synonyms. Yet the momentum continues on many fronts to separate the positions of legal assistant and paralegal and to prefer the latter.

To summarize:

- At one time, everyone considered paralegal and legal assistant to be interchangeable titles; they were synonymous.
- *Paralegal* became the preferred title after many attorneys allowed their secretaries to be called *legal assistants*.
- Some laws and some organizations, however, still maintain that the titles are interchangeable.

OTHER TITLES

This is not to say that *paralegal* and *legal assistant* are the only titles in the field. Far from it. Many other titles are in use. Several reasons account for this diversity.

First, there are no national standards regulating the paralegal field. Every state is free to regulate or to refuse to regulate a particular occupation. Second, most states have not imposed the kind of regulation on paralegals that would lead to greater consistency on titles within a particular state. For example, most states have not imposed minimum educational requirements or licensing. Hence, few restrictions exist on who can call themselves paralegals, legal assistants, or related titles. Although there are some major exceptions in states such as California, Florida, South Dakota, and Maine that limit who can use specific titles (discussed in Chapter 4), for the most part there are no such restrictions.

To begin sorting through the maze, we examine two broad categories of workers: those who are employees of attorneys (often called **traditional paralegals**) and those who are **independent contractors**. In general, independent contractors are self-employed persons who operate their own business and contract to do work for others. In general, those who hire the services of independent contractors do not control many of the administrative *details* of how the services are performed. The *objectives* or end products of the services, however, are controlled by those who hire them.

We will be examining two kinds of independent contractors in the legal field: those who sell their services to attorneys (a relatively small group) and those who sell their services to the public without attorney supervision (a larger and more controversial group). Within these two categories, you will find considerable diversity (and overlap) in the titles that are used.

traditional paralegals A paralegal who is an employee of an attorney.

independent contractors A self-employed person who operates his or her own business and contracts to perform tasks for others. In general, the latter do not control many of the administrative details of how the work is performed.

Before examining independent contractors, let's first look at traditional paralegals—those who are employees of attorneys.

Employees of Attorneys

The vast majority (over 95 percent) are employees of attorneys. They may be called:

- paralegal (the most common)
- legal assistant
- paralegal/legal assistant
- paralegal assistant
- attorney assistant
- lawyers aide
- lawyers assistant

- legal analyst
- legal paraprofessional
- legal service assistant
- legal technician
- mid-level paralegal
- professional legal assistant

They are all traditional paralegals if they are employees of attorneys. Most are full-time employees. Some, however, are temporary employees who work part-time or who work full-time for a limited period when a law office needs temporary help, usually from paralegals with experience in a particular area of the law.

If a law firm has a relatively large number of paralegals, it might call its entry-level people:

- paralegal I
- legal assistant I
- assistant paralegal
- case clerk
- case handler
- case technician
- clerk/runner
- docketing coordinator
- document clerk

- entry-level paralegal
- intake paralegal
- junior paralegal
- legal assistant clerk
- paralegal case handler
- project case assistant
- paralegal clerk
- project clerk

Large law offices may also have individuals who help recruit, train, and supervise all paralegals in the office. This supervisor might be called:

- paralegal manager
- paralegal administrator
- case manager
- director of legal assistant services
- director of legal assistants
- director of paralegal services
- director of practice support
- legal assistant administrator
- legal assistant coordinator
- legal assistant manager

- legal assistant supervisor
- legal support & professional personnel manager
- manager of paralegal services
- paralegal/case manager paralegal coordinator
- paralegal supervisor
- senior paralegal
- supervising legal assistant

As indicated earlier, these individuals have their own association, the International Practice Management Association (IPMA). For more on entry-level and supervisory paralegals, see the discussion of career ladders later in this chapter.

All of the titles listed thus far are *generic* in that they tell us little or nothing about the person's primary skills or area of the law in which he or she works. Other employee job titles are more specific:

- bankruptcy paralegal
- commercial real estate paralegal
- corporate law analyst
- corporate paralegal
- court researcher/paralegal
- debt recovery paralegal
- demands specialist
- docketing paralegal
- elder care paralegal
- family law paralegal
- foreclosure title paralegal

- government relations paralegal
- health advocate
- health care paralegal
- international trade paralegal
- legal advocate for day laborers
- litigation paralegal
- litigation practice support specialist
- patent prosecution paralegal
- personal injury paralegal
- probate specialist
- public finance paralegal

- real estate paralegal
- senior medical paralegal
- tax paralegal
- water law paralegal
- workers' compensation paralegal

Other special categories include:

- *e-Discovery paralegal:* a person who helps an office identify information stored in digital formats (e.g., emails and spreadsheets) that may have to be exchanged between the parties during the discovery stage of litigation prior to trial.
- *Depo summarizer:* a person who summarizes pretrial testimony, particularly depositions (in which attorneys question potential witnesses outside the courtroom in preparation for trial).
- *Compliance paralegal:* a person who helps assure that clients are following (complying with) regulations that govern insurance, finance, construction, and other regulated industries.
- *Judicial assistant:* a person who works for judges within the federal, state, or local court system.
- *Conflicts specialist* (also called *conflicts analyst* or *conflicts researcher*): a person who helps the office determine whether it should refrain from taking a case because of a conflict of interest with present or prior clients (see Chapter 5).
- *Nurse paralegal:* a nurse who has become a paralegal, using his or her medical training to help personal injury (PI) attorneys locate and decipher medical records and perform other litigation tasks. Nurse paralegals are usually employees of law offices. When they function though their own independent businesses, they are often called *legal nurse consultant* (LNC) or, if certified, *legal nurse consultant certified* (LNCC). See the American Association of Legal Nurse Consultants (www.aalnc.org).

Some law firms divide their paralegals into two broad categories: litigation and transactional. Litigation paralegals work on cases in litigation, particularly in the pretrial stages of litigation. A **transactional paralegal** provides assistance to attorneys with clients engaged in a large variety of transactions, such as entering contracts, incorporating a business, closing a real estate sale, or planning an estate.

A few large law firms have positions called *specialist*, *analyst*, or *consultant*. These are non-attorneys who have a high degree of expertise in a particular area, such as immigration, pensions, medicine, accounting, or environmental regulation. Skilled paralegals are sometimes promoted into these positions.

Occasionally, when an office wants its paralegal to perform more than one job, hybrid titles are used. For example, an office might call an employee:

- paralegal/investigator
- paralegal/librarian
- paralegal/legal secretary
- administrative assistant/paralegal

In general, the smaller the law office, the more likely it is that an employee will be asked to play multiple roles, even if he or she does not have a hybrid title. For example, an employee of an office with one attorney (a **sole practitioner**) could be the paralegal, the bookkeeper, the librarian, the investigator, the secretary, and the receptionist!

Perhaps the strangest—and thankfully the rarest—hybrid title you may see is *attorney/paralegal*. A California law firm placed an ad in a Los Angeles legal newspaper looking for an individual to work under this title. What's going on? The legal job market fluctuates. Depending on the state of the economy, jobs for attorneys might be abundant or scarce. In lean times, parts of the country could be flooded with unemployed attorneys, many of whom are recent law school graduates. Occasionally, these attorneys apply for paralegal jobs. An article in the *American Bar Association Journal*, taking note of the plight of unemployed attorneys, was titled *Post-Law School Job May Be as Paralegal*.[8] Some law firms are willing to hire a desperate attorney at a paralegal's salary because the firm can charge clients a higher billing rate for an attorney's time than for a paralegal's time. Most law firms, however, think it is unwise to hire an attorney for a paralegal's position. The two fields are separate employment categories; firms know that the attorneys are not interested in careers as paralegals. Yet there will continue to be attorneys available for paralegal positions and law firms willing to hire them, particularly when the firms need temporary legal help.

transactional paralegal One who provides paralegal services for an attorney who represents clients in transactions such as entering contracts, incorporating a business, closing a real estate sale, or planning an estate. A paralegal who does not work in litigation.

sole practitioner An attorney who practices alone. There are no partners or associates in the office.

There is a small category of attorneys who *frequently* seek work as paralegals. An attorney who has been disbarred or suspended from the practice of law may try to continue working in a law office by taking a job as a paralegal until he or she can reapply for full admission. Such work is highly controversial because of the temptation to go beyond paralegal work and continue to practice law. Consequently, some states forbid disbarred or suspended attorneys from working as paralegals. In most states, however, it is allowed with restrictions, as we will see in Chapter 5.

Self-Employed Individuals Who Sell Their Services to Attorneys

Independent contractors who sell their services to attorneys perform many different kinds of tasks. For example, they might draft an estate tax return for a probate attorney or digest (i.e., summarize) pretrial documents for a litigation attorney. Most independents work out of a home office. Some do their work in the law offices of the attorneys for whom they work. (See Exhibit 2-2 in Chapter 2 for the Internet site of an independent paralegal and Appendix G on setting up an independent business.) Independents who operate entirely online (as opposed to going to the offices of attorneys who hire them) are called *virtual assistants* or *virtual paralegals*. An independent might work primarily for one law office, although most work for different offices around town. Even though independent contractors are not employees, the attorneys who use their services are still obligated to supervise what they do. (In Chapter 5, we will study the ethical problem of supervising a nonemployee. In addition, we will cover the conflict-of-interest danger that can exist when an independent contractor works for more than one attorney.)

There is no uniform title that these self-employed individuals use. Here are some examples:

- **independent paralegal** (the most common)
- contract paralegal
- freelance legal assistant
- freelance paralegal
- legal technician

Self-Employed Individuals Serving the Public

Finally, we examine those independent contractors who sell their services directly to the public. As a group, they are known as **document service providers (DSPs)**—nonattorneys who work without attorney supervision to provide legal-document assistance to individuals who are representing themselves. DSPs do not work for attorneys. They may have special authorization to provide limited services, as when a statute allows them to assist clients in Social Security cases. To find out what titles they use in your area, check the Yellow Pages under entries such as *paralegal*, *legal*, *divorce*, and *bankruptcy*. Examples of DSP titles include:

- bankruptcy petition preparer (BPP)
- contract paralegal
- independent paralegal
- legal document assistant (LDA)
- legal document preparer (LDP)
- legal technician
- paralegal

In Chapter 4, we will cover an exciting development in the field of independent contractors who sell their services directly to the public without attorney supervision: the creation of the *limited license legal technician (LLLT)* in Washington State. A number of other states are considering similar positions.

Controversy over DSPs has come from three main sources: some of their clients, some bar associations, and some traditional paralegals.

- A few disgruntled clients of DSPs have filed complaints against them that have resulted in state prosecution for the **unauthorized practice of law (UPL)**.
- The organized bar has instigated similar UPL charges on the ground that the public needs protection from DSPs, particularly those who lack formal training. The bar also complains that the public might be confused into thinking that anyone called *paralegal* or who uses the word *legal* in their title works for an attorney. An unstated reason for opposition from the bar is the unwelcome competition that DSPs give to some practicing attorneys.
- A significant number of traditional paralegals resent the use of the paralegal title by some DSPs who work directly for the public. Most traditional paralegals have been through a rigorous training program and are subject to close attorney supervision on the job. These traditional paralegals resent anyone being able to use the paralegal title without similar training and supervision.

---

independent paralegal
(1) An independent contractor who sells his or her paralegal services to, and works under the supervision of, one or more attorneys. (2) An independent contractor who sells his or her paralegal services directly to the public without attorney supervision. Also called *freelance paralegal*, *legal technician*. In some states, however, the paralegal and legal assistant titles are limited to those who work under attorney supervision.

document service provider (DSP) (1) A nonattorney who works without attorney supervision to provide legal-document assistance to individuals who are representing themselves. (2) Someone who helps another prepare or process documents.

unauthorized practice of law (UPL) (1) Using or attempting to use legal skills to help resolve a specific person's legal problem when the assistance is provided by someone who does not have a license to practice law and when the assistance requires such a license or other authorization. (2) A nonattorney's performance of tasks in a law office without adequate attorney supervision when those tasks are part of the practice of law. (3) Delegating tasks to a nonattorney that only an attorney can perform.

In most states, the formidable opposition from these three sources has *not* put DSPs out of business. In fact, their numbers are growing. Although most states allow them to call themselves paralegals, a few states have imposed title restrictions. In California, for example, DSPs cannot call themselves paralegals or legal assistants unless they work under attorney supervision. If a California attorney is not responsible for their work, they must call themselves *legal document assistants (LDAs)*. If they provide landlord-tenant help, they must be called *unlawful detainer assistants (UDAs)*. In Arizona, DSPs who help persons with legal documents are called *certified legal document preparers (CLDPs)*. At the federal level, even greater restrictions have been placed on individuals who provide bankruptcy assistance. In every state, they must be called *bankruptcy petition preparers (BPPs)*. Later, in Chapters 4 and 5, we will more closely examine the controversy generated by DSPs, including proposals in some states to *increase* their role.

DEFINITIONS OF A PARALEGAL

The definition of a **paralegal** we will use in this book is a person who performs substantive legal tasks on behalf of others when those tasks are supervised by an attorney who would be required to perform the tasks if the office did not have a paralegal. Definitions have been written by:

- State legislatures and state courts
- State bar associations
- Local bar associations
- American Bar Association
- American Association for Paralegal Education
- Paralegal associations

To find out if your state has adopted a definition, check Appendix D.

DEFINITIONS WRITTEN BY STATE LEGISLATURES AND STATE COURTS

By far the most important definitions are those written by state legislatures and courts. Not every state has a definition written by its legislature or by its courts, but the number of states that have them is steadily growing. Here is an example of a definition enacted by the state legislature in Illinois. The definition is typical of the definitions used in many states:

> "Paralegal" means a person who is qualified through education, training, or work experience and is employed by a lawyer, law office, governmental agency, or other entity to work under the direction of an attorney in a capacity that involves the performance of substantive legal work that usually requires a sufficient knowledge of legal concepts and would be performed by the attorney in the absence of the paralegal.[9]

Such definitions are often interpreted to include independent contractors who sell their services to attorneys but are not employees of the attorneys.

DEFINITIONS WRITTEN BY ASSOCIATIONS

Many bar associations, paralegal associations, and the main paralegal educators association have adopted definitions that are similar in scope to the Illinois definition. The language of the American Bar Association's definition has been widely adopted (with or without modification) by the other associations. (See Exhibit 1-2.)

CHARACTERISTICS OF THE DEFINITION

Three major characteristics are common to most definitions of a paralegal. A paralegal:

- Has acquired legal skills through education, training, or on-the-job experience
- Works under attorney supervision
- Performs substantive legal work that the attorney would have to perform if the office did not have a paralegal

Under the first characteristic, there are two ways that individuals acquire legal skills: (1) formal education or training programs and (2) on-the-job training (OJT). When the paralegal field

paralegal (1) A person who performs substantive legal tasks on behalf of others when those tasks are supervised by an attorney who would be required to perform the tasks if the office did not have a paralegal. (2) A person with legal skills who works under the supervision of an attorney or who is otherwise authorized to use those skills; this person performs tasks that do not require all the skills of an attorney and that most secretaries are not trained to perform.

Exhibit 1-2	Paralegal Definitions Written by Associations

American Bar Association (ABA)

A legal assistant or paralegal is a person qualified by education, training, or work experience who is employed or retained by a lawyer, law office, corporation, governmental agency, or other entity and who performs specifically delegated substantive legal work for which a lawyer is responsible. (www.americanbar.org/groups/paralegals.html)

American Alliance of Paralegals, Inc. (AAPI)

A paralegal is a person qualified by education, training, or work experience who performs specifically delegated substantive legal work for which a lawyer is ultimately responsible or who is authorized by administrative, statutory, or court authority to perform substantive legal work. (www.aapipara.org/Positionstatements.htm)

American Association for Paralegal Education (AAfPE)

Paralegals [are persons who] perform substantive and procedural legal work as authorized by law, which work, in the absence of a paralegal, would be performed by an attorney. Paralegals have knowledge of the law gained through education, or education and work experience, which qualifies them to perform legal work. (www.aafpe.org)

NALS, the Association for Legal Professionals

NALS has adopted the ABA definition. (www.nala.org)

National Association of Legal Assistants (NALA)

NALA has adopted the ABA definition. (www.nala.org)

National Federation of Paralegal Associations (NFPA)

A paralegal/legal assistant is a person, qualified through education, training, or work experience to perform substantive legal work that requires knowledge of legal concepts and is customarily, but not exclusively, performed by a lawyer. This person may be retained or employed by a lawyer, law office, governmental agency, or other entity or may be authorized by administrative, statutory, or court authority to perform this work. Substantive shall mean work requiring recognition, evaluation, organization, analysis, and communication of relevant facts and legal concepts. (www.paralegals.org)

first came into existence (see discussion of history later in this chapter), most paralegals acquired their skills by OJT. Today, most do so by completing formal programs.

Under the second characteristic, paralegals work under attorney supervision. This covers the vast majority of paralegals in the country, including independent contractors who sell their services to (and are supervised by) attorneys but are not attorney employees. What about independent contractors who sell their services directly to the public without attorney supervision? As we have seen, some states (e.g., California) restrict the paralegal title to persons who work under attorney supervision. The definition of a paralegal in such states would not include independent contractors who sell their services to the public without attorney supervision. This conclusion, however, is not universal. In many states, independent contractors *can* call themselves paralegals even if they do not work under attorney supervision.

Under the third characteristic, the two key themes are (1) the absence test and (2) substantive legal work. We need to take a close look at each of these themes because they will be relevant to the question of whether attorneys can receive *paralegal fees* for the tasks performed by their paralegals.

Absence Test

The third characteristic states the *absence test*. Under this test, a task is a paralegal task if it must be performed by an attorney if the office does not have a paralegal. If a task is a paralegal task, it is not a clerical or secretarial task. Three conditions must be met for a task to be classified as a paralegal task under the absence test:

- Most secretaries do not have the skills to perform the task
- Most paralegals have the skills to perform the task
- An attorney would have to perform the task if the office did not have a paralegal but did have a secretary

To demonstrate, examine the following two tasks:

Task #1: Drafting (writing) a complaint

If the office did not have a paralegal, would an attorney have to perform this task? Yes. A complaint is the plaintiff's first court filing (pleading) that states a legal theory for suing (called a *cause of action*). Legal skills are required to draft even relatively uncomplicated complaints. In general, most experienced paralegals have the skills needed to draft such complaints, but most secretaries do not have such skills. Consequently, if the office did not have a paralegal, the attorney would have to draft the complaint. Therefore, this is a paralegal task.

Task #2: Typing a complaint

If the office did not have a paralegal, would an attorney have to perform this task? No. A secretary could type the complaint. Using a typewriter or word processor does not require legal skills. If the office had a secretary, an attorney would not have to type the complaint. The secretary could type it. Therefore, typing a complaint is a clerical or secretarial task, not a paralegal task.

The absence test requires you to examine who *could* perform a task, not who *actually* performs it in a particular office. Attorneys who type their own complaints are still performing a clerical task. The question is whether the attorney would *have* to perform the task if the office had a secretary, but not a paralegal. Similarly, there are some veteran secretaries who *are* able to draft complaints. This does not mean that such secretaries are performing clerical tasks when they draft complaints. The task is a paralegal task even if there are some secretaries who can perform it. The absence test requires you to focus on the skills of most secretaries and most paralegals.

Substantive Legal Work (SLW)

What is substantive legal work (SLW)? There are two ways of answering this question. First we can simply apply the absence test. If an attorney would have to perform a task because the office has no paralegals, then the task is SLW. In other words, SLW is nonclerical work. Second, we can list specific tasks and say that all tasks like those on the list constitute SLW. In Delaware, for example, a court said that SLW includes "but is not limited to such activities" as:

   (a) Factual investigation, including locating and interviewing witnesses;
   (b) Assistance with depositions, interrogations and document production;
   (c) Compilation of statistical and financial data;
   (d) Checking legal citations;
   (e) Correspondence with clients, opposing counsel, and courts;
   (f) Preparing, reviewing, and answering petitions and other pleadings.[10]

Similarly, note the specificity in the following list from the State Bar of Texas:

Substantive legal work includes, but is not limited to, the following:

   a Conducting client interviews and maintaining general contact with the client;
   b Locating and interviewing witnesses;
   c Conducting investigations and statistical and documentary research;
   d Drafting documents, correspondence, and pleadings;
   e Summarizing depositions, interrogatories, and testimony;
   f Attending executions of wills, real estate closings, depositions, court or administrative hearings, and trials with an attorney.

Substantive legal work does not include clerical or administrative work.[11]

PARALEGAL FEES

INTRODUCTION

The distinction between paralegal and clerical tasks is critical when discussing **fees**, particularly paralegal fees. Paralegals can be a revenue source—a profit center—for a law firm because the firm can collect **paralegal fees** for paralegal work. A *paralegal fee* is a fee that an attorney can collect for the nonclerical tasks of the attorney's paralegal. The fee covers the paralegal's substantive legal work on behalf of the client. Paralegals themselves do not charge or receive these fees; they are paid to the law office that employs the paralegals.

To place paralegal fees in context, four separate financial categories should be distinguished: fees, court costs, special expenses, and operating expenses.

- *Attorney fees and paralegal fees.* Fees are payments for the services provided by attorneys and paralegals, often calculated by the hour unless the client agrees to pay a set amount or percentage of whatever is recovered. The latter is a **contingent fee.** Hourly fees are paid regardless of who wins the case. Contingent fees are paid only if the case is won or satisfactorily settled. (Other categories of fees are discussed in Chapter 14.)
- *Court costs.* **Court costs** are charges or fees (paid to and imposed by the court) that are directly related to litigation in that court. An example is a court filing fee.

fees The amount charged for services rendered.

paralegal fees A fee that an attorney can collect for the nonclerical work of the attorney's paralegal. The fee covers the paralegal's substantive legal work on behalf of the client.

contingent fee A fee that is paid only if the case is successfully resolved by litigation or settlement, regardless of the number of hours spent on the case. (The fee is also referred to as a *contingency*.) A defense contingent fee (also called a *negative contingency*) is a fee for the defendant's attorney that is dependent on the outcome of the case.

court costs Charges or fees (paid to and imposed by the court) that are directly related to litigation in that court. Example: court filing fees.

overhead The operating
expenses of a business
(e.g., office rent, utilities,
insurance, and clerical staff) for
which customers or clients are
not charged a separate fee. It
should be noted, however, that
some attorneys charge clients
for clerical or secretarial time,
which can be ethical if the
client agrees and the amount
charged is reasonable (see
Chapter 5).

engagement letter A letter
that identifies the scope
of services to be provided
by a professional and the
payments to be made for
such services.

American rule Each party
pays his or her own attorney
fees regardless of who wins
the case.

English rule The losing side
in litigation must pay the
winner's attorney fees. Also
called *loser pays*.

fee-shifting Requiring
one party to pay another
party's attorney fees and
paralegal fees because of
prior agreement, bad faith, or
special statute.

bad faith Dishonesty or abuse
in one's purpose or conduct.

frivolous Lacking merit.
Pertaining to a legal position
that cannot be supported by a
good-faith argument based on
existing law or on the need for
a change in existing law.

aggrieved Injured or wronged
and thereby entitled to a
remedy.

statutory-fee cases A case
applying a special statute that
gives a judge authority to
order the losing party to pay
the winning party's attorney
fees (including paralegal fees)
and costs.

remedy (1) The means by
which a right is enforced
or the violation of a right is
prevented, compensated for,
or otherwise redressed. (2) To
correct. The plural is *remedies*.

- *Special expenses.* Special expenses are charges incurred by a law office that are unique to the representation of a particular client. An example is the cost of hotel and travel when an attorney must conduct a trial in another city.
- *Operating expenses.* Operating expenses are charges incurred by the office in order to stay open and provide services to any and all clients. Examples include rent, insurance, and secretaries. Another name for operating expenses is **overhead**. Paralegals are not part of a firm's overhead. They are a source of income for the firm through paralegal fees, which can be substantial.

Most clients pay the first three categories: attorney and paralegal fees, court costs (if any), and special expenses (if any). With limited exceptions, they do not pay for overhead. Clients do not receive a separate bill for their share of the electricity the office used while representing them. The law office is expected to pay for such overhead out of the fees it receives from all its clients. It is possible, however, for a client to agree to pay a separate fee for some secretarial help if the amount charged is reasonable.

When the attorney-client relationship is formed, the attorney and client enter a fee agreement that specifies what fees and other payments will be the responsibility of the client. The agreement is called an attorney-client fee agreement (see an example in Exhibit 8-1 in Chapter 8) or an **engagement letter**.

There are two sources of attorney and paralegal fees. The main source is the attorney's own clients, which is the norm (called the **American rule**) in the United States. Unless the case is taken on contingency, the client pays these fees whether or not the attorney wins the case. Some other countries follow the **English rule** under which an opponent pays the fees of the winning side in litigation. Although we do not follow the English rule, there are three situations in which the losing side *does* pay the attorney and paralegal fees of the winning side. In these limited situations, we follow a version of the English rule. Paying the other side's fees is called **fee-shifting**, which we will now examine.

FEE-SHIFTING

The three situations in which fee-shifting occurs in the United States are triggered by prior agreement, bad faith, and special statutes.

- *Prior agreement.* Parties can always agree to shift payment of fees and related costs. In a separation agreement, for example, the wealthier spouse might agree to pay the fees and costs of the other spouse. (In many states, the divorce court has the power to order such a shift even if the parties have not agreed to do so on their own.) Also, in many consumer contracts, the parties might agree to a clause stating that the buyer of goods or services must pay the fees and costs of the seller if the seller sues the buyer for nonpayment.
- *Bad faith.* **Bad faith** is dishonesty or abuse in one's purpose or conduct. Suppose, for example, that a court is convinced that a party has filed a **frivolous** motion solely to harass the opponent. The court in such a case might require the party making the frivolous motion to pay the fees and costs of the opponent who was forced to respond to the motion.
- *Special statute.* Congress (and some state legislatures) have passed special fee-shifting statutes to encourage **aggrieved** parties to bring litigation in certain areas of law. The purpose of such statutes is to support specific social or policy goals in areas such as civil rights, environmental protection, employment discrimination, antitrust conduct, and securities fraud. Under these statutes, attorney and paralegal fees (and costs) are paid by the defendant *if the plaintiff is successful in the litigation*. The cases in which such fee-shifting can occur are called **statutory-fee cases**. Without fee-shifting, injured parties might not be able to bear the cost of seeking a **remedy** in the courts. Hence, violations of civil rights, environmental laws, and the like would not be remedied. This is not good for society as a whole. Fee-shifting statutes, therefore, have been passed to encourage aggrieved parties to challenge such violations in court.

In the first two categories of fee-shifting cases (prior agreement and bad faith), fees can be awarded regardless of who wins the case. In statutory-fee cases, however, a party can be ordered to pay the fees of its opponent only if the opponent wins the case.

In statutory-fee cases, not all legislatures and courts use the same language in describing the relationship between attorney fees and paralegal fees. Sometimes paralegal fees are referred to as being part of attorney fees. At other times, attorney fees and paralegal fees are treated as separate entities. Regardless of how the relationship is phrased, the result is the same. A court can award two sets of fees: one for attorney work and another for paralegal work.

A major reason paralegalism has blossomed as a new profession is the ability of a law office to collect paralegal fees from its own clients in most cases and from a losing opponent in statutory-fee cases. Paralegal fees in statutory-fee cases can be substantial. In one case, for example, the winning attorney requested $139,238 for more than 1,500 hours of paralegal time.[12]

MARKET RATES IN STATUTORY-FEE CASES

When fees can be shifted in a statutory-fee case, how are fees calculated? For attorney fees, courts use a **lodestar**, under which the number of hours reasonably spent on the case is multiplied by the prevailing hourly rate in the community (called the *market rate*) for similar work by attorneys. Other factors might also be considered above the lodestar in setting the fee, such as the quality of representation, delay in receiving payment, and risk at the outset of the litigation that the attorney will receive no fee.

Before 1989, there was substantial doubt about how paralegal fees would be calculated in statutory-fee cases. Would the market rate for paralegal fees be used, similar to how attorney fees are calculated? Assume that an attorney wins a statutory-fee case. The attorney requests and receives attorney fees based upon the market hourly rate in the area for attorneys working on this kind of case. The attorney also submits a request for paralegal fees for the time the paralegals spent on the winning case. How does the court determine the amount of paralegal fees to award? Two possibilities exist, only one of which uses the market rate:

- Prevailing hourly market rate for paralegals: the market rate is the amount, on average, that law firms in the community charge their own clients for paralegal time (e.g., $110 per hour).
- Actual cost to the law firm: actual cost is the amount that a law firm must pay to keep its paralegal (e.g., $50 per hour to cover the paralegal's salary, fringe benefits, office space, and other overhead costs related to maintaining any employee).

Of course, the winning side in a statutory-fee case will argue that it should receive the market rate for paralegal time, and the losing side will want an actual-cost standard. In 1989, the U.S. Supreme Court, in the landmark case of *Missouri v. Jenkins*, resolved the issue in favor of using market rates. The *Jenkins* holding does not apply to every statutory-fee case, but its influence has been so substantial that the predominant rule today is to use market rates for calculating paralegal fees.

The *Jenkins* case involved a Missouri desegregation suit under § 1988 of the Civil Rights Attorney's Fees Awards Act. (This was a federal statute of Congress that allowed fee-shifting in civil rights cases.) The lower court awarded the winning party $40 an hour for paralegal time, which was the market rate for paralegals in the 1980s in the Kansas City area. On appeal, the losing party argued that it should pay no more than $15 an hour, which at that time was the actual cost to the law firm of having a paralegal in the office. In addition to paralegal fees, the case covered the award of fees for **law clerks**, who are students still in law school or are law-school graduates who have not yet passed the bar. Like paralegals, law clerks are nonattorneys. (For convenience, the Court refers to paralegals and law clerks collectively as paralegals.) As you can see from the opinion, the Supreme Court rejected an actual-cost standard for paralegals under the fee-shifting statute the court was applying.

A footnote in the opinion refers to an **amicus curiae brief** filed by the National Association of Legal Assistants (NALA). This is a "friend of the court" appellate brief submitted by a nonparty that obtains court permission to file the brief with its views on how the case should be resolved.

lodestar A method of calculating an award of attorney fees authorized by statute. The number of reasonable hours spent on the case is multiplied by the prevailing hourly rate in the community for similar work by attorneys. Other factors might also be considered above the lodestar in setting the fee, such as the quality of representation, any delay in receiving payment, and the risk at the outset of the litigation that the prevailing attorney will receive no fee.

law clerks (1) An attorney's employee who is in law school studying to become an attorney or who has graduated from law school and is waiting to pass the bar examination. Also called *clerk*. If law clerks work only in the summer, they are sometimes called *summer associates*. (2) One who provides research and writing assistance to a judge. (3) A nonattorney who is a "trained professional doing independent legal work" in Ontario, Canada.

amicus curiae brief ("friend of the court" brief) An appellate brief submitted by a nonparty who obtains court permission to file the brief setting out its views on how the case should be resolved.

CASE

Missouri v. Jenkins
United States Supreme Court
491 U.S. 274, 109 S. Ct. 2463, 105 L. Ed. 2d 229 (1989)

[To read the opinion online, go to scholar.google.com, select "Case law" and enter "491 U.S. 274" in the search box]

Justice *Brennan* delivered the opinion of the Court.

This is the attorney's fee aftermath of major school desegregation litigation in Kansas City, Missouri. [One of the issues we need to resolve is] should the fee award compensate the work of paralegals and law clerks by applying the market rate for their work.

This litigation began in 1977 as a suit by the Kansas City Missouri School District (KCMSD), the school board, and the children

(continued)

Missouri v. Jenkins
United States Supreme Court (*Continued*)

of two school board members, against the State of Missouri and other defendants. The plaintiffs alleged that the State, surrounding school districts, and various federal agencies had caused and perpetuated a system of racial segregation in the schools of the Kansas City metropolitan area. They sought various desegregation remedies . . . . After lengthy proceedings, including a trial that lasted 7½ months during 1983 and 1984, the District Court found the State of Missouri and KCMSD liable . . . .

The plaintiff class has been represented, since 1979, by Kansas City lawyer Arthur Benson and, since 1982, by the NAACP Legal Defense and Educational Fund, Inc. (LDF). Benson and the LDF requested attorney's fees under the Civil Rights Attorney's Fees Awards Act of 1976, 42 U.S.C. § 1988.* Benson and his associates had devoted 10,875 attorney hours to the litigation, as well as 8,108 hours of paralegal and law clerk time . . . . [T]he District Court awarded Benson a total of approximately $1.7 million and the LDF $2.3 million. [On appeal, the defendant now argues] that the District Court erred in compensating the work of law clerks and paralegals (hereinafter collectively "paralegals") at the market rates for their services, rather than at their cost to the attorney. While Missouri agrees that compensation for the cost of these personnel should be included in the fee award, it suggests that an hourly rate of $15—which it argued below corresponded to their salaries, benefits, and overhead—would be appropriate, rather than the market rates of $35 to $50 . . . .

[T]o bill paralegal work at market rates . . . makes economic sense. By encouraging the use of lower cost paralegals rather than attorneys wherever possible, permitting market-rate billing of paralegal hours "encourages cost-effective delivery of legal services and, by reducing the spiraling cost of civil rights litigation, furthers the policies underlying civil rights statutes." *Cameo Convalescent Center, Inc. v. Senn*, 738 F.2d 836, 846 (CA7 1984).**

Such separate billing appears to be the practice in most communities today.*** In the present case, Missouri concedes that "the local market typically bills separately for paralegal services," Transcript of Oral Argument 14, and the District Court found that the requested hourly rates of $35 for law clerks, $40 for paralegals, and $59 for recent law graduates were the prevailing rates for such services in the Kansas City area . . . . Under these circumstances, the court's decision to award separate compensation at these rates was fully in accord with § 1988 [of the Civil Rights Attorney's Fees Awards Act].

---

*   Section 1988 provides in relevant part: "In any action or proceeding to enforce a provision of . . . the Civil Rights Act of 1964 [42 U.S.C. § 2000d], the court, in its discretion, may allow the prevailing party, other than the United States, a reasonable attorney's fee as part of the costs."

**   It has frequently been recognized in the lower courts that paralegals are capable of carrying out many tasks, under the supervision of an attorney, that might otherwise be performed by a lawyer and billed at a higher rate. Such work might include, for example, factual investigation, including locating and interviewing witnesses; assistance with depositions, interrogatories, and document production; compilation of statistical and financial data; checking legal citations; and drafting correspondence. Much such work lies in a gray area of tasks that might appropriately be performed either by an attorney or a paralegal. To the extent that fee applicants under § 1988 are not permitted to bill for the work of paralegals at market rates, it would not be surprising to see a greater amount of such work performed by attorneys themselves, thus increasing the overall cost of litigation. Of course, purely clerical or secretarial tasks should not be billed at a paralegal rate, regardless of who performs them. What the court in *Johnson v. Georgia Highway Express, Inc.*, 488 F.2d 714, 717 (CA5 1974), said in regard to the work of attorneys is applicable by analogy to paralegals: "It is appropriate to distinguish between legal work, in the strict sense, and investigation, clerical work, compilation of facts and statistics and other work which can often be accomplished by non-lawyers but which a lawyer may do because he has no other help available. Such non-legal work may command a lesser rate. Its dollar value is not enhanced just because a lawyer does it."

*** Amicus National Association of Legal Assistants reports that 77 percent of 1,800 legal assistants responding to a survey of the association's membership stated that their law firms charged clients for paralegal work on an hourly billing basis. Brief for National Association of Legal Assistants as Amicus Curiae 11.

Keep in mind that *Missouri v. Jenkins* is a federal case involving one federal statute: the Civil Rights Attorney's Fees Awards Act. The following categories of cases are *not* required to adopt the conclusion of *Jenkins*:

- Federal cases interpreting other federal statutes
- State cases interpreting state statutes

For example, a *state* court applying a *state* fee-shifting statute could decide to calculate paralegal fees at actual cost rather than at the prevailing market rate. Nevertheless, *Missouri v. Jenkins* has been persuasive. The vast majority of federal and state courts have adopted its reasoning for allowing paralegal fees at market rates in statutory-fee cases. This is why *Missouri v. Jenkins* is a landmark case. The *Jenkins* holding was reinforced in 2008 when the Supreme Court held in *Richlin Security Service Co. v. Chertoff* that paralegal fees were recoverable at market rates under a different federal fee-shifting statute (the Equal Access to Justice Act).[13]

CHALLENGES TO AWARDS OF FEES IN STATUTORY-FEE CASES

Parties who lose statutory-fee cases are often understandably upset when they are faced with losing a judgment *and* paying the attorney fees and paralegal fees of their opponent.

A corporation, for example, might lose an antitrust judgment that requires it to pay its opponent $20 million in damages *plus* millions more to cover the time spent on the case by the attorneys and paralegals of its opponent. Although the losing side will probably lose the argument that seeks an actual-cost calculation of paralegal fees, it may still be able to argue that that there are errors in the winning side's request for fees. Let's look at the steps a party takes to request fees and some of the arguments that challenge the request.

Challenging Fee Requests in a Statutory-Fee Case:

- At the conclusion of the trial, the winning side submits to the trial judge a petition that requests attorney and paralegal fees.
- The petition lists the tasks performed by the attorney and the time taken to perform these tasks. The number of hours is multiplied by the market rate attorneys charge in the area. The result is the total amount requested for attorney fees.
- The petition also lists the tasks performed by a paralegal and the time taken to perform these tasks. The number of hours is divided by the market rate of paralegals in the area. The result is the total amount requested for paralegal fees.
- The losing side can then present challenges to the fee petition. Here are three challenges that will be successful:

  - Some of the tasks performed by the attorney should have been delegated to a paralegal. The attorney should not receive an attorney rate for performing a paralegal task.

  - Some of the tasks performed by the paralegal should have been delegated to a secretary. Paralegal fees in statutory-fee cases are limited to substantive legal work (SLW). Paralegal fees cannot be awarded for clerical tasks performed by a paralegal.

  - Some of the tasks performed by the attorney should have been delegated to a secretary. No fees should be awarded for clerical tasks performed by the attorney.

There is nothing improper or unethical about an attorney performing a paralegal task or a clerical task. Nor is there anything improper or unethical about a paralegal performing a clerical task. In a busy office that is faced with deadlines or that is shorthanded, everyone must pitch in to do what is needed to respond to immediate client needs. In this environment, you will seldom hear someone say, "that's not my job." However, when the times comes for a request for fees in a statutory-fee case, care must be taken to avoid requesting attorney fees for paralegal or clerical tasks and to avoid requesting paralegal fees for clerical tasks.

Suppose, for example, that an attorney performs the following tasks in a statutory-fee case:

- Questions a witness at a deposition (4 hours)
- Reads the transcript of the deposition of this witness and highlights each time the witness mentions any health ailment (2 hours)
- Negotiates a settlement with opposing counsel (10 hours)

The attorney has spent sixteen hours performing these tasks. Assuming the attorney wins the case (a requirement for fee-shifting), can he or she obtain sixteen hours of attorney fees? No. The two hours spent looking for health quotes in the transcript is a paralegal task. The request for attorney fees must be limited to the fourteen hours spent questioning the witness and negotiating the settlement. For an attorney to seek attorney fees for performing paralegal tasks would be the equivalent of Michelangelo charging "Sistine Chapel rates for painting a farmer's barn."[14] See the footnote in the *Missouri v. Jenkins* case in which the court reminded us that the dollar value of a task is not enhanced simply because an attorney performs it.[15] Just as it is improper to seek paralegal fees for clerical tasks, it is also improper to seek attorney fees for paralegal tasks. A Delaware court phrased the concern this way:

> Paralegal fees are not a part of the overall overhead of a law firm. Paralegal services are billed separately by attorneys, and these legal assistants have the potential for greatly decreasing litigation expenses and, for that matter, greatly increasing the efficiency of many attorneys. By permitting paralegal fees, the danger of charging these fees off as the attorney's work is hopefully extinguished. By the same token, the danger of charging off a secretary's services as those of a paralegal is very real and present....[16]

RECORDKEEPING

timekeeping Recording time spent on a client matter for purposes of billing and productivity assessment.

Timekeepers (attorneys and paralegals) must keep careful records of the tasks they perform and the amount of time spent on each task. Accurate **timekeeping** records of this kind will be used to help a court distinguish among attorney, paralegal, and clerical tasks. Again, it is not enough for an attorney to say that task "x" is an attorney task simply because an attorney performed it or that task "y" is a paralegal task simply because a paralegal performed it. The court will want to look at the nature of the task itself in order to determine who should have performed it. Fees will be awarded on the basis of this determination.

It is standard practice in most private law firms for timekeepers to keep detailed time sheets covering the entire workday. A paralegal's supervising attorney may need to enter these time sheets into evidence to justify the award of paralegal fees in statutory-fee cases. Here is an example of what some courts require attorneys to demonstrate in their petition for paralegal fees:

(1) the services performed by the paralegal must be legal in nature;
(2) the performance of these services must be supervised by an attorney;
(3) the qualifications of the paralegal performing the services must be specified in the request for fees in sufficient detail to demonstrate that the person is qualified by virtue of education, training, or work experience to perform substantive legal work (SLW);
(4) the nature of the services performed must be specified in the request for fees in order to allow the reviewing court to determine that the services performed were legal rather than clerical;
(5) as with attorney time, the amount of time expended by the paralegal must be set forth and must be reasonable; and
(6) the amount charged must reflect reasonable community standards—the market rate—for charges by paralegals.[17]

SUMMARY OF RULES ON FEES

To summarize the rules on paralegal fees, let's look at (A) all cases in which attorneys can charge their own clients paralegal fees and (B) special statutory-fee cases in which the losing side can be ordered to pay the paralegal fees of the winning side.

In all cases:

1. Attorneys can charge *their own clients* a separate fee for the work of their paralegals regardless of who wins the case. This is in addition to charging for the attorney's time. If the fee agreement says that the paralegal fee shall be for paralegal tasks, the firm should not charge for clerical tasks performed by the paralegal.
2. Timekeepers must keep detailed records (e.g., time sheets) on the tasks they perform and the time spent performing them. (**Contemporaneous** recordkeeping is preferred over time records that are assembled long after the task is performed.)
3. The amount of time a timekeeper takes to perform a task must be reasonable in light of the nature and complexity of the task.
4. The amount of the fee itself must be reasonable.

contemporaneous Existing or occurring in the same period of time; pertaining to records that are prepared regarding events as the events are occurring or very shortly thereafter.

In statutory-fee cases:

1. The loser can be required to pay the attorney and paralegal fees of the winner.
2. The attorney will be required to demonstrate the paralegal's qualifications (e.g., education and experience) for the fees requested.
3. Attorney fees cannot be awarded when an attorney performs paralegal tasks.
4. Paralegal fees cannot be awarded when a paralegal performs clerical tasks.
5. The amount of the fee is based on the prevailing market rate that attorneys in the legal community charge their clients for paralegal tasks. (This market-rate rule applies if a court adopts the rationale of *Missouri v. Jenkins*, as most courts have.)

CAREER LADDERS IN LARGE LAW OFFICES

There is no career ladder for paralegals working in a small law office that consists of one or several attorneys, a secretary, and a paralegal. In an office with more than three paralegals, career ladders are more likely to exist. When they exist, firms use a wide variety of titles. Exhibit 1-3 presents two examples used in law firms and two used in the law department of a large corporation.

Exhibit 1-3	Examples of Paralegal Career Ladders

Sample Career Ladders in Two Large Law Firms

- Paralegal I (entry level)
- Paralegal II (intermediate)
- Paralegal III (supervisory)

- Case Assistant (0–1 year of experience)
- Entry-Level Paralegal (0–3 years experience)
- Mid-Level Paralegal (3–5 years experience)
- Senior Level Paralegal (5+ years experience)

Sample Career Ladders in the Law Departments of Two Large Corporations

- Entry-level legal assistant (0–1 year of experience)
- Legal assistant (1–3 years experience)
- Senior legal assistant, level one (4–7 years experience)
- Senior legal assistant, level two (8–12 years experience)
- Corporate legal assistant, level one (13+ years experience)
- Corporate legal assistant, level two (20+ years experience)
- Specialist (experience requirement depends on the specialty)

- Legal Research Assistant A
- Legal Research Assistant B
- Legal Administrative Specialist (this is the senior-level paralegal)

At the top of most career ladders, where they exist, is the paralegal coordinator or manager, with duties such as:

- Recruiting and screening candidates for paralegal positions
- Orienting new paralegals to office procedures
- Training paralegals to operate software used in the office
- Training paralegals to perform certain substantive tasks, such as digesting (i.e., summarizing) pretrial testimony
- Coordinating assignments of paralegals among the different attorneys in the office to help ensure that paralegals are given assignments they are able to perform and that they complete them on time

For more details on the role of the paralegal manager, see Exhibit 14-3 in Chapter 14. As indicated earlier, paralegal managers have formed their own association, the International Practice Management Association (www.paralegalmanagement.org).

PARALEGAL SALARIES

How much do paralegals make? Although some data are available to answer this question, there is no definitive answer because of the great variety of employment settings. Here are some relevant statistics:

- According to a 2015 survey by Robert Half Legal, a major legal staffing firm, the salary range for a case clerk/assistant with 0–2 years of experience was:
  - $34,000–44,250 in law firms with 75 or more attorneys
  - $33,250–42,750 in law firms with between 35 and 75 attorneys
  - $31,000–38,500 in law firms with between 10 and 35 attorneys
  - $29,500–34,250 in law firms with between 1 and 10 attorneys
  - $33,750–47,250 in corporate law offices

- The salary range for a midlevel paralegal/legal assistant with 4–6 years of experience was:
  - $59,500–72,750 in law firms with 75 or more attorneys
  - $55,750–73,000 in law firms with between 35 and 75 attorneys
  - $51,250–64,250 in law firms with between 10 and 35 attorneys
  - $43,500–58,500 in law firms with between 1 and 10 attorneys
  - $50,750–74,750 in corporate law offices[18]

- According to the Bureau of Labor Statistics of the U.S. Department of Labor:
  - The median salary of the 277,000 paralegals in the country was $46,990 (2012). (The median wage is the wage at which half the workers in an occupation earned more than the median amount and half earned less.)

- The top 10 percent of paralegals earned more than $75,410.
- The bottom 10 percent of paralegals earned less than $29,420.[19]

- According to a 2013 survey of the National Association of Legal Assistants:
  - The national average salary of paralegals was $54,376 with an average annual bonus of $4,501.
  - $38,867: 1–5 years of experience
  - $51,484: 6–10 years of experience
  - $54,347: 11–15 years of experience
  - $58,952: 16–20 years of experience
  - $60,075: 21–25 years of experience
  - $64,552: more than 25 years of experience[20]

- According to a survey in *Paralegal Today*:
  - The average paralegal salary in 2013 was $54,742.
  - The highest paralegal salary in the survey was $118,500.
  - The lowest paralegal salary in the survey was $24,960.
  - The average paralegal salary in corporations was $63,664.
  - The average paralegal salary in government was $59,840.[21]

Experienced paralegals do very well. If they have good résumés and have developed specialties that are in demand, they usually improve their financial picture significantly. A number of other generalizations can be made about salaries across the country:

- Skilled paralegals and those with considerable responsibility earn high salaries.
- Paralegals who meet or exceed billable-hour expectations tend to be rewarded with higher salary increases and bonuses.
- Paralegals who work in large private law firms tend to make more than those who work in smaller private law firms.
- Paralegals who work in large metropolitan areas (over a million in population) tend to make more than those who work in rural areas.
- Paralegals who work in legal aid or legal service offices that are funded by government grants and charitable contributions to serve the poor tend to make less than most other paralegals.
- Paralegals who work for attorneys who understand the value of paralegals tend to make more than those working for attorneys who have a poor or weak understanding of what paralegals can do.
- Paralegals who work in an office where there is a career ladder for paralegals, plus periodic evaluations and salary reviews, tend to make more than those who work in offices without these options.
- Paralegals who are career oriented tend to make more than those less interested in a long-term commitment to paralegal work.

In addition to the payment of bonuses, other fringe benefits are also relevant to the overall compensation picture (e.g., vacation time, health insurance, and parking facilities).

FACTORS INFLUENCING THE GROWTH OF PARALEGALISM

In the late 1960s, most attorneys would have drawn a blank if you mentioned the words *paralegal* or *legal assistant*. According to Webster's *Ninth New Collegiate Dictionary*, the earliest recorded use of the word *paralegal* in English occurred in 1971. Today, the situation has changed radically. Most law offices either employ paralegals or are seriously considering doing so. (A major exception to this trend is the one- or two-attorney office in which the only staff member is a secretary who often performs paralegal tasks.) Some surveys show that there is one paralegal for every four attorneys in law firms and one paralegal for every two attorneys in the law departments of corporations. It has been estimated that the number of paralegals may eventually exceed the number of attorneys in the practice of law. The U.S. Bureau of Labor Statistics says that there are 277,000 paralegal jobs in the country and that between 2012 and 2022, employment will grow by 17 percent, "faster than the average for all occupations."[22]

What has caused this dramatic change? The following factors have been instrumental in bringing paralegalism to its present state of prominence:

1. The pressure of economics
2. The call for efficiency and delegation
3. The promotion by bar associations
4. The organization of paralegals

I. THE PRESSURE OF ECONOMICS

Perhaps the greatest incentive to employ paralegals has been arithmetic. Law firms simply add up what they earn without paralegals, add up what they could earn with paralegals, compare the two figures, and conclude that the employment of paralegals is profitable. There "can be little doubt that the principal motivation" prompting law firms to hire paralegals is the "economic benefit enjoyed by the firm."[23] The key to increased profits is **leveraging**. Leverage, often expressed as a ratio, is the ability to make a profit from the income-generating work of others. The higher the ratio of paralegals to partners in the firm, the more profit to the partners or owners of the firm (assuming that everyone is generating income from **billable** time). The same is true of associates in the firm. The higher the ratio of associates to partners, the greater the profit to the partners/owners.

In the best of all worlds, some of this increased profit will result in lower fees to the client. For example, Chief Justice Warren Burger felt that some attorneys charge "excessive fees" for tasks such as "**closing** real-estate transactions for the purchase of a home. A greater part of that work can be handled by trained paralegals, and, in fact, many responsible law firms are doing just that to reduce costs for their clients."[24] If the state requires an attorney to do all the work at a closing, the law would have to be changed to allow paralegals to do what Chief Justice Burger suggests. We discuss such changes in Chapter 4.

Exhibit 1-4 provides an example of the economic impact of using a paralegal. In the example, a client comes to a lawyer to form a corporation.[25] We will compare:

(a) the economics of an attorney and secretary performing a task, assuming a fee of $2,500; and
(b) the economics of an attorney, secretary, *and* paralegal working on the same task, assuming a fee of $2,000.

As you can see from the numbers in Exhibit 1-4, with a paralegal added to the team, the firm's profit is increased 6.8 percent in spite of the lower fee to the client, and the attorney has 3.5 hours of billable time to spend elsewhere. Some studies have claimed an even higher profit increase because of the effective use of paralegals.

The average billing rate attorneys charged clients for paralegal time is:

- $92 per hour for paralegals with 1–5 years of experience
- $116 per hour for paralegals with 6–10 years of experience
- $133 per hour for paralegals with 26–30 years of experience[26]

About 28 percent of paralegals with these billing rates are expected to produce a set number of billable hours per week. Most work forty-hour work weeks and are asked to bill at least thirty hours. An expectation of this kind is called a **billable hour quota** or billable hour goal.

Some law firms use the **rule of three** as a general guideline to project the profit they want to generate from paralegal billing. Under this guideline, total or gross revenue generated through paralegal billing should equal three times a paralegal's salary. Of the total revenue brought in through paralegal billing, one-third is allocated to salary, one-third to overhead, and one-third to profit. Phrased another way, when the gross revenue generated through paralegal billing equals three times the paralegal's salary, the firm achieves its minimum profit expectations.

For example, assume that a firm pays a paralegal $40,000 a year and bills the paralegal's time at $100 an hour:

- Paralegal's salary: $40,000
- Paralegal rate: $100 per hour
- Billings the firm hopes this paralegal will generate: $120,000 ($40,000 × 3)

leveraging Making profit from the income-generating work of others.

billable Pertaining to those tasks requiring time that can be charged to (and paid by) a client.

closing The meeting in which a transaction is finalized. An example is the meeting to complete a real estate sale or other transaction. Also called *settlement*.

billable hour quota A minimum number of hours expected from a timekeeper on client matters that can be charged (billed) to clients per week, month, year, or other time period.

rule of three A general guideline used by some law firms to identify budget expectations from hiring paralegals: gross revenue generated through paralegal billing should equal three times a paralegal's salary.

Exhibit 1-4	Profitability of Using Paralegals: An Example

TASK: TO FORM A CORPORATION

a. Attorney and Secretary

Function	Attorney Time	Secretary Time
1. Interviewing	1.0	0.0
2. Advising	1.0	0.0
3. Gathering information	1.0	0.0
4. Preparing papers	2.0	4.0
5. Executing and filing papers	1.0	1.0
	6.0	5.0

Assume that the attorney's hourly rate is $250 per hour and that the overhead cost of maintaining a secretary is $25 per hour.

Attorney (6 × $250)	$1,500
Secretary (5 × $25)	125
Total cost	$1,625

Fee	$2,500
Less cost	1,625
Gross profit	$875

b. Attorney, Secretary, and Paralegal

Function	Attorney Time	Paralegal Time	Secretary Time
1. Interviewing	0.5	0.5	0.0
2. Advising	1.0	0.0	0.0
3. Gathering information	0.0	1.0	0.0
4. Preparing papers	0.5	1.5	4.0
5. Executing and filing papers	0.5	0.5	1.0
	2.5	3.5	5.0

Assume a paralegal hourly rate of $90 per hour.

Attorney (2.5 × $250)	$625
Paralegal (3.5 × $90)	315
Secretary (5 × $25)	125
Total cost	$1,065

Fee	$2,000
Less cost	1,065
Gross profit	$935

COMPARISON

Fee:	a. Attorney and Secretary	$2,500
	b. Attorney, Secretary, and Paralegal	$2,000
Saving to client		$500
Increased profitability to attorney ($935 vs. $875)		$60

By using a paralegal on the case, the attorney's profit increases 6.8% over the profit realized without the paralegal, and the client can be charged a lower fee. Furthermore, the attorney has 3.5 hours that are now available to work on other cases, bringing in additional revenue of $875 (3.5 × the attorney's hourly rate of $250).

Adapted and updated from Jespersen, "Paralegals: Help or Hindrance?," *The Houston Lawyer* 114–116 (March/April 1977). Reprinted with permission of the Houston Bar Association.

Rule-of-three allocation:
- Paralegal salary: $40,000
- Overhead for this paralegal: $40,000
- Profit to the firm: $40,000[27]

Some firms use a rule of 3½, under which gross revenue generated through paralegal billing should equal three and a half times a paralegal's salary.

Of course, the rule of three (or 3½) is not an absolute gauge for determining profit expectations from using paralegals. Other factors affect the profitability of paralegals for an office. A high turnover of paralegals in the office, for example, often means that the office will have substantially increased overhead costs in recruiting and orienting new paralegals. One survey concluded that the annual attrition rate for paralegals is between 11 and 25 percent.[28] Another factor that can offset the rule of three is the extent to which attorneys have more billable time because of a paralegal's performance of *nonbillable* tasks. Some paralegals perform many tasks that cannot be billed to clients. Examples include recruiting new employees, helping to maintain the law library, organizing the office's closed case files, and doing some of the work on certain kinds of cases that an attorney would normally do for free (e.g., probating the estate of the attorney's brother-in-law). The more nonbillable tasks such as these that a paralegal performs, the less time he or she will have available to devote to billable tasks. This, however, does not mean that the paralegal is a drain on profits. A nonbillable task that a paralegal performs is often a task that the attorney, at least in part, does *not* have to perform. This, of course, enables the attorney to direct more of his or her efforts to fee-generating (i.e., billable) matters.

Directly related to a paralegal's profitability is his or her **realization rate**. A law firm does not always collect100 percent of every bill it sends to its clients. Some clients simply refuse to pay, or they bargain down the bills initially sent to them. The realization rate is the percentage of the total amounts billed to clients that a law office actually collects. If, for example, the office fails to collect 10 percent of all the bills sent out during a given period, its realization rate is 90 percent for that period. Attorneys and paralegals have realization rates based on the percentage of the amounts billed from their hours that were actually collected. Of course, a paralegal has no control over whether the office is able to collect every billable hour submitted. Yet many paralegals inquire about their current realization rate for their own information and possible use when discussing their value to the office, perhaps at annual review and bonus time.

2. THE CALL FOR EFFICIENCY AND DELEGATION

Attorneys are overtrained for many of the tasks that they once had to perform in a traditional law firm. It eventually became clear that this was not the way to run an efficient office. The creation of the paralegal role was a major step toward reform. The results have been quite satisfactory, as evidenced by the following comments from attorneys who have hired paralegals:[29]

> A competent paralegal for several years has been effectively doing 25% to 35% of the actual work that I had been doing for many years prior to that time.

> The results of our 3 attorney–3 paralegal system have been excellent. Our office's efficiency has been improved and our clients are receiving better service.

> It has been our experience that clients now ask for the paralegal. Client calls to the attorneys have been reduced an estimated 75%.

In light of such comments, it is surprising that the legal profession took so long to recognize the need to create the position of paralegal. The following historical perspective presents an overview of how attorneys came to this conclusion.[30]

Historical Background

During the American colonial period, the general populace distrusted attorneys because many of them sided with King George III against the emerging independent nation. This is illustrated by the following 1770 census report sent back to the king about a county in New Hampshire:

> Your Royal Majesty: Grafton County consists of 1,212 square miles. It contains 6,489 souls most of whom are engaged in agriculture, but included in that number are 69 wheelwrights, 8 doctors, 29 blacksmiths, 87 preachers, and 90 students at a new college. There is not one lawyer, for which fact we take no personal credit but thank an Almighty and merciful God.[31]

Some colonies tolerated the existence of attorneys but established roadblocks to their practice. In 1641, for example, the Massachusetts Bay Colony prohibited freemen from hiring attorneys for a fee:

> Every man that findeth himself unfit to plead his own cause in any court shall have libertie to employ any man ... to help him, Provided he gave him no fee or reward for his pains.[32]

Furthermore, almost anyone could become an attorney without having to meet rigorous admission requirements. States did not have training requirements to be an attorney until the 1940s.

Up until the nineteenth century, the attorney did not have assistants other than an occasional apprentice studying to be an attorney himself. The attorney basically worked alone. He carried "his office in his hat."[33] A very personal attachment and devotion to detail were considered to be part of the process of becoming an attorney and of operating a practice. In the early nineteenth century, George Wythe said about the education of attorneys:

> It is only by drudgery that the exactness, accuracy and closeness of thought so necessary for a good lawyer are engendered.[34]

realization rate The percentage of total client billings of an attorney or paralegal that the office actually collects. Also called the *collection realization rate*. Because timekeepers often spend time on both billable tasks and nonbillable tasks, a further breakdown is a timekeeper's *billing realization rate*. This is the percentage of the timekeeper's total office time that is billable. For example, paralegals who spend half their time on nonbillable tasks and half on billable tasks have a 50 percent billing realization rate.

The same theme came from Abraham Lincoln in his famous *Notes for a Law Lecture*:

> If anyone ... shall claim an exemption from the drudgery of the law, his case is a failure in advance.[35]

Attorneys would be somewhat reluctant to delegate tasks to someone working for them, according to this theory of legal education.

Attorneys often placed a high premium on the personal relationship between attorney and client. As late as 1875, for example, Clarence Seward and his partners "would have none of the newfangled typewriters" because clients would "resent the lack of personal attention implied in typed letters."[36] The coming of the Industrial Revolution, however, brought about change in the practice of law. Some law offices began to specialize. As attorneys assumed new responsibilities, the concern for organization and efficiency grew. To be sure, large numbers of attorneys continued to carry their law offices "in their hats" and to provide an essentially one-to-one service. Many law offices in the 1850s, however, took a different direction.

Machines created new jobs. The typewriter introduced the typist. Librarians, investigators, bookkeepers, office managers, accountants, tax and fiduciary specialists, and research assistants soon found their way into some large law offices. Although nonattorneys were hired primarily to undertake clerical or administrative responsibilities, they were soon delegated more challenging roles. This can be seen in the following comment from a study of employees in a Midwestern law office:

> In addition, [the workers] were given considerable responsibility in connection with their positions as secretary or head bookkeeper. The head bookkeeper acted as assistant secretary to the partner-secretary of certain charitable corporations the firm represented. In this capacity, she recorded minutes of director's meetings, issued proxy statements, [and] supervised the filing of tax returns for the organization.[37]

In this fashion, attorneys began delegating more and more nonclerical duties to their clerical staff. This was not always done in a planned manner. An employee might suddenly be performing dramatically new duties as emergencies arose on current cases and as new clients arrived in an already busy office. In such an environment, an attorney may not know what the employee is capable of doing until the employee does it. Despite its haphazard nature, the needs of the moment and OJT (on-the-job training) worked wonders for staff development.

By the 1960s, attorneys started to ask whether a new kind of employee should be created. Instead of expanding the duties of a secretary, why not give the expanded duties to a new category of employee—the paralegal? A number of studies were conducted to determine how receptive attorneys would be to this idea on a broad scale. The results were very encouraging. The conclusion soon became inevitable that attorneys can delegate many tasks to paralegals. Today, this theme has become a dominant principle of law office management. Most attorneys no longer ask, "Can I delegate?" Rather they ask, "Why *can't* this be delegated?" or "How can the delegation be effectively managed?" It is a given that substantial delegation is a necessity.

3. THE PROMOTION BY BAR ASSOCIATIONS

The bar associations assumed a large role in the development of paralegals. This has given great visibility to the field. In 1968, the House of Delegates of the American Bar Association established a Special Committee on Lay Assistants for Lawyers (subsequently renamed the Standing Committee on Paralegals) and resolved:

> (1) That the legal profession recognize that there are many tasks in serving client's needs which can be performed by a trained, non-lawyer assistant working under the direction and supervision of a lawyer; [and]
>
> (2) That the profession encourage the training and employment of such assistants.[38]

Most of the state bar associations now have committees that cover the area of paralegal utilization. Many of these committees have established guidelines for the use of paralegals in a law office. (For developments in your state, see Appendix D.)

At present, no paralegals are full members of any bar association. In recent years, however, a number of state and local bar associations have invited paralegals to join their organizations in various capacities. The association might allow the paralegals in as:

- associate or affiliate members of the entire association, including its committees and sections;
- associate or affiliate members of committees or sections only; or
- full members of special paralegal divisions.

Bar associations have different requirements for paralegal membership. For example, an **attorney attestation** may be required, in which an attorney member of the bar confirms (*attests*) that the applicant performs substantive legal work (SLW) under attorney supervision.

An example of an active paralegal unit of a bar association is the Paralegal Division of the State Bar of Texas (www.txpd.org). It has more than 2,300 members. The annual voting membership fee is $70. In some of the bar associations, paralegals are allowed to vote on issues within the section, committee, or division of which they are members, but they cannot vote on general bar association issues.

In 1982, the ABA standing Committee on Paralegals proposed that the ABA create an associate category of membership for paralegals. The National Association of Legal Assistants (NALA) warmly endorsed the proposal, but the National Federation of Paralegal Associations (NFPA) opposed it on the ground that paralegals' organizations should be autonomous and should not become part of a state or national association that regulates them. NFPA and others argued that the organized bar had a conflict of interest in regulating paralegals in light of the profit motive attorneys have in using paralegals. Today, however, this concern is rarely, if ever, raised.

Paralegals take advantage of bar membership for a number of reasons. It looks good on a résumé. It fosters a positive relationship between paralegals and attorneys. Employers often pay all or part of the paralegal's membership fee. Bar association meetings can be an excellent place for networking. Members receive paper or online newsletters and announcements, thus keeping them better informed about developments in the legal community.

> **attorney attestation** A signed statement by an attorney that a paralegal applying for membership in an association meets one or more of the criteria of the association, the most common of which is that the paralegal performs paralegal duties.

4. THE ORGANIZATION OF PARALEGALS

Paralegals have been organizing. There are approximately 200 paralegal organizations throughout the country. (See Appendix B.) This has greatly helped raise everyone's consciousness about the potential of paralegalism. We will be examining the work, impact, and value of these associations in the next several chapters.

"OH, YOU'RE STUDYING LAW?"

"Can the landlord put my furniture out on the curb?" "What happens if I cosign the note and it's not paid?" Once your friends and relatives find out that you are studying law, you will probably start receiving legal questions such as these. Later, in Chapters 4 and 5, we will examine **legal advice** in some detail. You need to be very careful to avoid giving such advice. You do not want to begin your legal career with a charge of engaging in the unauthorized practice of law. Politely refuse to answer all questions that seek to find out how the law applies to particular fact situations. Even if you know the answer, the proper response is "That's something an attorney would have to look into," or simply say, "I don't know."

> **legal advice** A statement or conclusion that applies the law or legal principles to the facts of a specific person's legal problem.

YOUR ONLINE REPUTATION

In today's computer-driven environment, the likelihood is strong that prospective employers will be seeking information about you on the Internet. What will they find? Your online reputation is your *brand*—how you stand out, what makes you distinctive. As a professional, you will need an online presence, and it must be informative, intelligent, engaging, and conservative. In later chapters, we will cover ways to achieve such a presence through LinkedIn, Facebook, Twitter, and other social-media sites. For now, the watchword is caution:

- On Google, Bing, or Yahoo, enter your name as a search term to find out what the Internet currently has or says about you.

- On Google, Bing, or Yahoo, run this search: how to clean up your image on _____ (*in the blank, insert the name of any site you have joined*).
- If something exists about you on the Internet that would not impress a prospective employer, follow the clean-up instructions of the site involved to try to remove it.

Again, we will have more to say about building a positive online presence. In the meantime, find out what that presence is today and start learning how to remove (and avoid) anything negative.

CONCLUSION

As we will learn in subsequent chapters, there have been some dramatic developments in paralegalism in recent years, beginning in 2000, when California inaugurated a major program of paralegal regulation. This has prompted many other states to consider their own versions of regulation. Furthermore, the practice of law, legal education, and the legal profession are going through a period of reexamination. Change is clearly in the air.

In a keynote address, Robert Stein, executive director of the American Bar Association, said that the four most important areas affecting the practice of law in the future were diversity, globalization, electronic contracts, and the growth of paralegalism. "The paralegal profession," he said, "is undergoing a remarkable transformation as the value of a well trained paralegal is recognized by more and more law firms, corporations and governments as a means of providing cost effective services in an era of rising expenses and complex litigation."[39]

Echoing these themes, a recent study of the practice of law came to the following conclusions:

> The combined forces of globalization, technology, and market liberalization are creating new services, new delivery mechanisms, and new forms of competition. Those changes are altering client needs and expanding client expectations. Clients want services to be quicker, cheaper, and smarter. They want more transparency and involvement, and they want to be and stay connected.[40]

These are some of the themes we will be exploring as you now begin the journey of becoming a well-trained paralegal.

CHAPTER SUMMARY

The law has a wide-ranging impact on our society. Large percentages of individuals and companies need legal assistance. Precision and attention to detail are critical attributes of anyone working in the law. Important organizations in paralegalism include the National Federation of Paralegal Associations (NFPA); National Association of Legal Assistants (NALA); NALS, the Association for Legal Professionals; the American Bar Association (ABA); your state bar association; your local paralegal association; and the American Association for Paralegal Education (AAfPE). The national paralegal associations offer certification and, along with the bar associations, promote continuing legal education (CLE). Although some laws and organizations assert that the titles *paralegal* and *legal assistant* are synonymous, the preferred title has become *paralegal* as more and more legal secretaries are called legal assistants. Some states have laws that restrict the use of specific titles, but most states have no such restrictions. Paralegals are either employees of attorneys (traditional paralegals) or independent contractors who sell their services to attorneys or who have authorization to sell limited services directly to the public without attorney supervision. Paralegals who have specialties include

bankruptcy paralegals, corporate paralegals, family law paralegals, real estate paralegals, and e-Discovery paralegals. In small offices, paralegals are likely to perform a variety of paralegal, bookkeeper, librarian, investigator, secretary, and receptionist tasks.

Independent contractors who work without attorney supervision are document service providers (DSPs). They are sometimes charged with the unauthorized practice of law. They must call themselves bankruptcy petition preparers if they work in bankruptcy. In California, they must be called legal document assistants or unlawful detainer assistants. A few other states have similar restrictions and limit the use of the titles *paralegal* and *legal assistant* to those who work under attorney supervision.

A paralegal is a person who performs substantive legal work (tasks) on behalf of others when those tasks are supervised by an attorney who would be required to perform the tasks if the office did not have a paralegal. Definitions of a paralegal have been written by legislatures, courts, the American Bar Association, local bar associations, and paralegal associations. The three most common characteristics of the definitions are that the paralegal has acquired legal skills through education, training, or on-the-job experience; works under attorney supervision; and performs substantive (i.e., nonclerical) legal work that the attorney would have to perform if the office did not have a paralegal.

In most states, attorneys can charge their clients paralegal fees in addition to fees for attorney time. In statutory-fee cases, the losing side in litigation can be forced to pay the attorney fees of the winning side. These fees can include separate fees for paralegal tasks. Under the landmark civil-rights case of *Missouri v. Jenkins* (a statutory-fee case that has been followed by many state courts and by many federal courts in non–civil rights cases), paralegal fees are determined by market rate. Paralegal fees in statutory-fee cases are limited to substantive legal work performed by paralegals. Paralegal fees cannot be awarded in such cases for clerical tasks. Fee challenges in statutory-fee cases can include claims that some of the tasks performed by the attorney for which fees are requested should have been delegated to a paralegal and some of the tasks performed by the paralegal for which fees are requested were clerical. Paralegals must keep detailed (and preferably contemporaneous) records that specify the tasks they performed.

Career ladders for paralegals exist mainly in law offices with more than three paralegals. Paralegal managers in large offices help recruit and train paralegals and coordinate their assignments.

Paralegal salaries are influenced by a number of factors: experience, skills, level of responsibility, kind of employer, geographic area, meeting billable-hour expectations, the employer's understanding of the paralegal's role, and the extent to which the paralegal is committed to the field as a career. One rough measure of paralegal profitability to a firm is the rule of three. Under this guideline, gross revenue generated through paralegal billing should equal three times a paralegal's salary.

Bar associations and paralegal associations have promoted the value of paralegals extensively. The economic impact they have had on the practice of law is the major reason the paralegal field has flourished and grown so rapidly. In a properly leveraged firm, paralegals can be a profit center without any sacrifice in the quality of the service delivered by the firm. Also, a paralegal can help attorneys redirect some of their energies from nonbillable to billable tasks.

KEY TERMS

continuing legal education (CLE) (p. 6)	unauthorized practice of law (UPL) (p. 12)	fee-shifting (p. 16)	leveraging (p. 23)
certification (p. 6)	paralegal (p. 13)	bad faith (p. 16)	billable (p. 23)
networking (p. 8)	fees (p. 15)	frivolous (p. 16)	closing (p. 23)
traditional paralegals (p. 9)	paralegal fees (p. 15)	aggrieved (p. 16)	billable hours quota (p. 23)
independent contractors (p. 9)	contingent fee (p. 15)	statutory-fee cases (p. 16)	rule of three (p. 23)
transactional paralegal (p. 11)	court costs (p. 15)	remedy (p. 16)	realization rate (p. 25)
sole practitioner (p. 11)	overhead (p. 16)	lodestar (p. 17)	attorney attestation (p. 27)
independent paralegal (p. 12)	engagement letter (p. 16)	law clerks (p. 17)	legal advice (p. 27)
document service provider (DSP) (p. 12)	American rule (p. 16)	amicus curiae brief (p. 17)	
	English rule (p. 16)	timekeeping (p. 20)	
		contemporaneous (p. 20)	

ASSIGNMENTS

CRITICAL ANALYSIS

1.1 Assume that you had two employment offers. In one the title of the position is *paralegal*; in the other it is *legal assistant*.

(a) What factors would you consider about the two positions in making a decision about which position to accept?

(b) Assume that the duties of the two positions are substantially the same, but that the salary of the legal-assistant position is 10 percent higher than the paralegal position. How would you go about making a decision?

1.2

(a) Justice William Brennan, in *Missouri v. Jenkins*, said that using a market rate for paralegals will help reduce the "spiraling cost of civil rights litigation." How can forcing a losing party to pay more for paralegals reduce the cost of litigation?

(b) Examine the full text of *Missouri v. Jenkins* to determine why Chief Justice William Rehnquist filed a dissenting opinion

on paralegal fees. Why did he say that allowing paralegal fees would amount to double recovery? If you do not have access to a library to examine the opinion on the shelf, read it online. Follow the Google Scholar instructions beneath the citation of the case in the chapter or use Findlaw (www.findlaw.com/casecode/supreme.html). In Citation Search for Findlaw, type 491 in the first box and 274 in the second box so that it reads 491 US 274.

1.3 The paralegal in the example in Exhibit 1-4 billed at $90 an hour. Under the rule of three:

(a) How many hours a year would this paralegal have to bill if he or she is to earn $40,000 a year?

(b) How many hours a week would this paralegal have to bill if he or she had two weeks of vacation each year?

(c) Assuming that the paralegal bills the number of hours indicated in questions a and b, what could occur that would defeat the firm's profit expectation under the rule of three?

PROJECTS

1.4 Go to the Internet addresses of NFPA, NALA, NALS, SCOP, your state bar association, and your local paralegal association. (If your local association does not have an Internet address, go to the closest paralegal association that has one.) The Internet addresses of these associations are in the chapter (see the section on Major Players). See also Appendix B and E. On each of these sites:

(a) What email address is available to write for additional information about the organization?

(b) Quote any sentence on the site that pertains to paralegal careers. Following the quote, give the citation to the site. In your citation to an Internet page, include the name of the site, the Internet address, and the date you visited the site. Example: National Association of Legal Assistants. Paralegals, *Welcome to NALA*, http://www.nala.org (last visited March 14, 2014).

CORE SKILLS

Among the many skills a paralegal must have, five core skills stand out: writing (both basic English and legal drafting), research, ethics, computer use, and collaboration (working with others). The core-skill assignments introduce and reinforce these skills. Even if you are not asked to do all of the core assignments as part of the course, you should do them on your own. Also, do not wait for the topics in the assignments to be covered in this course or in other courses. Successful paralegals are self-starters. A major characteristic of a self-starter is a thirst for independent study—learning on your own.

CORE SKILL: WRITING

1.5 Run this search in Google, Bing, or Yahoo: commas.

(a) State three comma rules that are new to you or with which you were only vaguely familiar. List the website(s) that you used to answer this question.

(b) Make up three sentences. Each sentence should use all of the following words in any order you choose: *paralegal*, *law*, and *career*. Each sentence should demonstrate the correct use of one of the three comma rules you identified in part a.

CORE SKILL: RESEARCH

1.6

(a) What is the Internet address of the main state judicial system in your state? Run this search in Google, Bing, or Yahoo: aa courts (substituting your state for aa).

(b) What is the Internet address of your state legislature? Run this search in Google, Bing, or Yahoo: aa legislature (substituting your state for aa).

(c) What is the Internet address of every federal court sitting in your state? Run this search in Google, Bing, or Yahoo: aa federal court (substituting your state for aa).

(d) What are the Internet addresses of Congress, the U.S. Senate, and the U.S. House of Representatives? Run three separate searches in Google, Bing, or Yahoo:

Congress

United States Senate

United States House of Representatives

CORE SKILL: ETHICS

1.7

(a) What is the name of the code of ethics that governs attorneys in your state? What is the Internet address where you can find the text of this code? Run this search in Google, Bing, or Yahoo: attorney ethics aa (substituting your state for aa).

(b) Pick any two sentences from different rules in the code. Quote each sentence followed by the citation to the code. The citation should include the name of the code (in italics), the rule of the code you are quoting, the Internet address, and the date you visited the site. Example: *New York Rules of Professional Conduct*, Rule 5.3, https://www.nycourts.gov/rules/jointappellate/NY-Rules-Prof-Conduct-1200.pdf (last visited May 10, 2014).

CORE SKILL: COMPUTERS

1.8 Start a computer notebook (paper or digital). Call it Computer Terminology in the Law (CTL). Throughout the course, make entries in your CTL notebook. There will be two main categories of entries in the CTL: (a) General Computer Terms and (b) Specific Computer Software. General Computer Terms consist of any term connected with computers other than the names of specific products or companies (e.g., database management, cloud computing). Specific Computer Software consists of the names of software products (e.g., Word, Concordance, Summation, TimeSlips). You do not have to wait to have a course or lecture on these concepts before beginning to collect the vocabulary of computers in the law.

To start making entries in the CTL, run one of the following searches on Google, Bing, or Yahoo:

- commonly used software for attorneys
- popular law-firm computer products
- survey computer trends attorney

From these searches, select any two general computer terms and any two software products that are used by law firms. In the CTL, write (or type) a few sentences describing your four terms. The physical act of writing or typing them will enhance the learning process.

Don't worry about alphabetizing the entries in the CTL. Also, don't expect to understand the terms fully at this early stage. The goal now is simply to collect definitions and to write or type them. The world of computers is complex; you will continue learning about computers throughout your career. The starting point is terminology.

CORE SKILL: COLLABORATION

1.9 Pick a task that you know how to perform on a computer. The task must take approximately ten minutes to perform. (Don't select a task that takes seconds or hours to perform.) Write out detailed instructions on how to perform this task. Find someone (e.g., a fellow student) who does *not* know how to perform this task but who has the facilities needed to perform the task (a computer, particular software, Internet access, etc.). Give the written instructions to this person and ask him or her to perform the task solely by following your written instructions. Have the person report back to you on whether he or she could do the task. If possible, let this person show you that he or she can do the task. Do not give oral instructions. The person should try to do the task solely by reading your instructions.

(a) What task did you select?

(b) Describe whether the person was able to perform the task, either by what this person reported back to you or by what you observed.

(c) Did the task take the person approximately ten minutes to perform? If not, select a different task that meets this time requirement.

(d) What lessons did you learn about working with another person whom you are trying to train?

THE JOB SEARCH

(The search for employment cannot wait until the end of a course or of a curriculum. It should begin now. The job-search assignments are designed to introduce you to different aspects of the job search and to build options for you to explore about employment.)

1.10 In Google, Bing, or Yahoo, run the following searches (substituting your state for aa):

law firms aa

"large law firms" aa

(a) Pick any five law firms in your state that mention paralegals on their Internet sites. On the homepage of each site, click words such as *careers, employment, join us, opportunities, people,* or any other words that invite the viewer to learn about personnel at the firm. On the sites that you select, what job titles or job descriptions do you find for individuals who are neither attorneys nor secretaries? Summarize what you find. Include the Internet address of each site you use.

(b) Do any of the sites you selected mention job openings for paralegals? Summarize what you find.

REVIEW QUESTIONS

1. Approximately what percentage of Americans have legal problems and how many will need a lawyer in the next year?
2. Where do most paralegals work?
3. What are the six major organizations in the development of paralegalism?
4. What is certification and which national paralegal associations have certification exams?
5. What is continuing legal education (CLE)?
6. How have state bar associations affected the development of paralegalism?
7. Name fourteen categories of paralegal associations.
8. To what extent are the titles *paralegal* and *legal assistant* synonymous?
9. Why are there many titles in this occupation?
10. What is the distinction between traditional paralegals and paralegals who are independent contractors?
11. What are the two categories of independent contractors?
12. What are some of the major titles that employers use for traditional paralegals?
13. What are some of the major titles that employers use for entry-level paralegals?
14. What are some of the major titles that employers use for supervisory paralegals?
15. Distinguish between a generic and a specific title of a paralegal.
16. What is an e-Discovery paralegal, compliance paralegal, conflicts specialist, nurse paralegal, and legal nurse consultant?
17. What is a transactional paralegal?
18. What is a hybrid title? Give some examples.
19. What are some of the titles used by self-employed paralegals who work for attorneys? What are some of the titles used by self-employed persons who sell their services directly to the public without attorney supervision?

20. What are the three sources of opposition to those who sell their law-related services directly to the public without attorney supervision?
21. What is the unauthorized practice of law?
22. What is the definition of a paralegal?
23. What six entities or organizations have adopted definitions of a paralegal, and which definitions are the most significant?
24. What three characteristics are common to most definitions of a paralegal?
25. What are the two ways that paralegals acquire legal skills?
26. What is the absence test?
27. What are the two ways that substantive legal work can be defined?
28. What is a paralegal fee and to whom is it given?
29. Distinguish fees (attorney and paralegal), court costs, special expenses, and operating expenses.
30. Distinguish between an hourly fee and a contingent fee.
31. What is overhead?
32. What is the document called that specifies the payments a client will make to a law office?
33. Distinguish between the American rule and the English rule.
34. What is fee-shifting?
35. What is a statutory-fee case?
36. What tasks performed by a paralegal can and cannot be the basis of fees in a statutory-fee case?
37. What is a law clerk?
38. What was decided in *Missouri v. Jenkins*? Why is this a landmark case?
39. When a party loses a statutory-fee case, what kinds of challenges does the party sometimes make against the request for fees by the winning side?
40. What are contemporaneous records?

41. What are some of the duties of a paralegal coordinator or manager?
42. What factors determine paralegal salaries?
43. Name four major factors that have been instrumental in the emergence of paralegalism to its present state of prominence.
44. What is meant by leveraging?
45. What is a billable-hours quota?
46. What is the rule of three?
47. What is a realization rate?
48. Give examples of a paralegal's nonbillable tasks.
49. What membership categories have some bar associations created for paralegals?

HELPFUL WEBSITES

Overview of Paralegal Career
- www.mynextmove.org/profile/summary/23-2011.00
- www.mynextmove.org/profile/ext/online/23-2011.00
- www.onetcodeconnector.org/find/result?s=paralegal
- www.nala.org/hrbrochure.htm
- money.usnews.com/careers/best-jobs/paralegal
- en.wikipedia.org/wiki/paralegal

Occupational Outlook Handbook (Paralegals and Legal Assistants)
- www.bls.gov/ooh/Legal/Paralegals-and-legal-assistants.htm
- www.bls.gov/oco

American Bar Association Guidelines on Paralegals
- www.abanet.org/legalservices/paralegals/downloads /modelguidelines.pdf

Paralegal Salaries
- www.roberthalflegal.com/salarycenter
- www.paralegalsalaryinfo.com
- txpd.org/files/file/SalarySurvey /2010ParalegalDivisionCompensationSurveyReport.pdf

Best Jobs (Paralegal Ranking)
- www.careercast.com /jobs-rated/2011-ranking-200-jobs-best-worst
- www.careercast.com /jobs-rated/2011-ranking-200-jobs-best-worst
- www.abajournal.com/news/article /paralegal_is_better_job_than_lawyer_ranking_says
- jobs.aol.com/articles/2009/12/29 /the-8-most-secure-jobs-for-2010

Paralegal Fees
- www.caparalegal.org/index.php/fees

Paralegal Blogs (Blawgs)
- www.abajournal.com/blawgs (click *By Topic* and then *Paralegals*)
- blawgsearch.justia.com/blogs (click *Paralegal*)
- www.criminaljusticedegreeschools.com/top-paralegal-blogs
- See also Appendix F

Social Media Search: LinkedIn, Facebook, and Twitter
- www.hashatit.com (type *paralegal* in the search box)
- www.socialmention.com
- www.hashtagify.me (type *paralegal* in the search box)
- www.tagboard.com (type *paralegal* in the search box)
- www.hashtags.org (type *paralegal* in the search box)

Social Media Search: Other
- www.linkedin.com (type *paralegal* in the search box)
- www.facebook.com (type *paralegal* in the search box)
- www.twitter.com (type *paralegal* in the search box)
- www.reddit.com/r/paralegal

Number of Times "Paralegal" Mentioned by Federal Courts
- legallanguageexplorer.com (type *paralegal* in search box)

Google, Bing, or Yahoo Searches
- (On these search engines, run the following searches, substituting your state for "aa" where indicated)
- paralegal aa
- paralegal jobs aa
- paralegal career aa
- paralegal association aa
- "definition of a paralegal"
- paralegal fees
- "Missouri v. Jenkins" 1989
- Richlin Chertoff
- paralegal billable hour
- paralegal "substantive legal work"
- paralegal "American Bar Association"
- paralegal career ladder
- paralegal salary
- paralegal history
- paralegal profitability
- paralegal economics
- "paralegal profitability v associate"

ENDNOTES

1 U.S. Census Bureau, 2012 *Statistical Abstract of the United States*, Table 335 (2012) (www.census.gov/compendia/statab/2012/tables/12s0335.pdf). See also www.uscourts.gov (enter *filings* in the search box).

2 American Bar Association, *Findings of the Comprehensive Legal Needs Study* (1994).

3 Fulbright & Jaworski, *Fulbright's Litigation Trends Survey* (2011) (www .fulbright.com).

3a Michael Acker, *Three Incumbents Run Unopposed in So. River*, Sentinel (eb.gmnews.com) (June 5, 2007).

4 Joan Centerbury, *President's Column*, 17 On Point 2 (National Capitol Area Paralegal Association, November 1991).

5 Krista Ramsey, *Paralegal Debbie Boe Named to Minnesota Board of Medical Practice*, 27 Paralegal Today 8 (July/August 2010).

6 Cortland Kirkeby, *Paralegal in the House*, 16 Legal Assistant Today 17 (March/April 1999) (www.linkedin.com/in/marysquires).

7 See Jane Cracroft, *Developing Effective Witnesses*, The Legal Investigator, 7 (August 1991).

8 Hope Viner Samborn, *Post-Law School Job May Be as Paralegal*, 81 American Bar Association Journal 14 (March 1995) (www.topattorneys .com/newspdfs/Post-Law_School_Job.pdf).

[9] 5 Illinois Compiled Statutes Annotated § 70/1.35 (2001).

[10] *McMackin v. McMackin*, 651 A.2d 778, 780 (Del. Fam. Ct. 1993). (To read this case online, go to Google Scholar (scholar.google.com), click *case law*, and type the cite (651 A.2d 778) in the search box.)

[11] *Texas Paralegal Standards* (State Bar of Texas 2006) (txpd.org/page.asp?p=Paralegal%20Definition%20and%20Standards). See also *Gill Sav. Ass'n v. Int'l Supply Co., Inc.*, 759 S.W.2d 697, 705 (Tex. App. Dallas 1988). (To read this case online, see the Google Scholar instructions in endnote 10.)

[12] *Rural Water Sys. No. 1 v. City of Sioux Center, Iowa*, 38 F. Supp. 2d 1057, 1061 (N.D. Iowa 1999). (To read this case online, see the Google Scholar instructions in endnote 10.)

[13] *Richlin Sec. Serv. Co. v. Chertoff*, 553 U.S. 571, 128 S. Ct. 2007, 170 L. Ed. 2d 960 (2008). (To read this case online, see the Google Scholar instructions in endnote 10.)

[14] *Ursic v. Bethlehem Mines*, 719 F.2d 670, 677 (3d Cir. 1983). (To read this case online, see the Google Scholar instructions in endnote 10.)

[15] The footnote cites *Johnson v. Georgia Highway Express, Inc.*, 488 F.2d 714, 717 (5th Cir. 1974). (To read this case online, see the Google Scholar instructions in endnote 10.)

[16] *McMackin v. McMackin*, 651 A.2d 778, 780 (Family Court of Delaware 1993). (To read this case online, see the Google Scholar instructions in endnote 10.)

[17] *North Coast Elec. Co. v. Selig*, 151 P.3d 211, 21516 (Wash. Ct. App. Div. 1, 2007). (To read this case online, see the Google Scholar instructions in endnote 10.)

[18] *2015 Salary Guide* (Robert Half Legal, 2015) (www.roberthalf.com/salary-guides).

[19] Bureau of Labor Statistics, *Occupational Outlook Handbook* (2013) (www.bls.gov/ooh/Legal/Paralegals-and-legal-assistants.htm#tab-5). See also www.money.usnews.com/careers/best-jobs/paralegal/salary

[20] NALA, *2013 National Utilization and Compensation Survey Report*, Table 4.7 (2013) (www.nala.org).

[21] Tammy Cravit, *Clearing Skies Ahead:* Paralegal Today's *20th Annual Survey*, 29 Paralegal Today 20 (April/May 2012).

[22] *Occupational Outlook Handbook*, supra note 19.

[23] Subcommittee on Legal Assistants, New York State Bar Association, *The Expanding Role of Legal Assistants in New York State* 7 (1982).

[24] *U.S. News & World Report*, February 22, 1982, at 32.

[25] Adapted and updated from Jespersen, *Paralegals: Help or Hindrance?* The Houston Lawyer 114–16 (March/April 1977).

[26] NALA, *2013 National Utilization and Compensation Survey*, Table 3.6 (2013) (www.nala.org/Upload/file/PDF-Files/13SEC3.pdf).

[27] Adapted from State Bar of Texas, *Attorneys Guide to Practicing with Legal Assistants*, VI(3) (1986).

[28] "How LAMA Data Can Help You Retain Your Paralegals," in *IOMA's Report on Compensation and Benefits for Law Offices* 1 (April 2001).

[29] Legal Assistants Committee, Oregon State Bar, *Legal Assistant Survey* (1977).

[30] The research for this part of the section on the historical background of paralegalism was conducted by the author and subsequently used with his permission in *Expansion of the Lawyering Process through a New Delivery System: The Emergence and State of Paraprofessionalism*, 71 Columbia Law Review 1153, 1169ff (1971).

[31] Thomas Brown, *President's Page*, 19 Virginia Bar Association Journal 2 (Winter 1993).

[32] Body of Liberties, cited in Ralph Warner, *Independent Paralegal's Handbook* 8 (1986).

[33] Lee, *Large Law Offices*, 57 American Law Review 788 (1923).

[34] Lewis, ed., George Wythe, in *Great American Lawyers: A History of the Legal Profession in America* 55 (1907).

[35] John Nicolay & John Hay, eds., Notes for a Law Lecture, in *Complete Works of Abraham Lincoln* 142 (1894). See also Paul Frank, *Lincoln as a Lawyer* 3 (1961).

[36] Robert Swaine, *The Cravath Firm and Its Predecessors: 1819–1947* 365, 449 (1984).

[37] Emily Dodge, *Evolution of a City Law Office*, 1955 Wisconsin Law Review 180, 187.

[38] *Proceedings of the House of Delegates of the American Bar Association*, 54 A.B.A.J. 1017, 1021 (1968)., 54 A.B.A.J. 1017, 1021 (1968).

[39] Robert Stein, Practice of Law in the New Century (American Bar Association 1999).

[40] *CBA Legal Futures Initiative* (Canadian Bar Association 2014).

PARALEGAL EMPLOYMENT

CHAPTER OUTLINE

- The Job Market
- Where Paralegals Work
- Paralegal Specialties: A Dictionary of Functions
- Finding a Job
- Using Social Media in the Job Search
- Résumé
- Cover Letter
- Writing Samples
- Job Interview
- Job-Search Notebook (JSN)
- Volunteering as a Way to Gain Legal Experience
- Summary of Job Strategies
- Your Second Job

CHAPTER OBJECTIVES

After completing this chapter, you should be able to:

- Understand the nature of the job market for paralegals.
- Identify the major employers of paralegals.
- Describe the kinds of tasks paralegals perform in corporations, governments, legal aid offices, special-interest groups, criminal law offices, service companies, and consulting groups.
- Describe the kinds of work performed by independent paralegals.
- Identify tasks performed by many paralegals in corporate law, real estate law, tort law, and other specialties.
- Know the strategies for finding paralegal employment in a competitive market.
- List ways to use social media in a job search.
- Describe the steps for doing background research on a potential employer.
- Write effective résumés, cover letters, and follow-up letters.
- Prepare for job interviews.
- Know the importance of a job-search notebook and what to include in it.
- List ways to use volunteering to gain experience.
- Identify the variety of job opportunities available to experienced paralegals.

THE JOB MARKET

The paralegal job market goes through cycles. (The same is true for attorneys.) There are periods when law offices are desperate for people to hire; at other times, offices are flooded with job applications. Don't be surprised if the job market on the day you begin your paralegal training program is not the same as the market on the day you graduate. Geography also plays an important role. In general, a large metropolitan area will present more employment prospects than rural areas simply because cities have more attorneys seeking paralegal help.

The job market is also affected by the state of the economy. If the country is going through a slump, many businesses cut back on their use of attorneys. A decline in attorney billing usually also means a decline in paralegal employment. It is true that some areas of law practice pick up in a weak economy (e.g., bankruptcy), but usually not enough to make up for losses elsewhere in the marketplace for legal services.

In light of this reality, the safest course is to be prepared for competition when you begin to apply for employment. A central theme of this chapter, therefore, will be job-search strategies that will be needed in a market where there will be more applicants than available jobs. The reason we cover this theme at the beginning of the book is that you need to begin the job search now, not at the end of the course or the curriculum.

It is important to make the distinction between jobs for entry-level paralegals and jobs for experienced paralegals. Almost always, your first job will be the toughest to obtain. A very large number of law offices are seeking paralegals with one, two, three, or more years of law-office experience, often in a particular area of the law. Once you have proven your worth as a practicing paralegal, numerous opportunities open up to you, as we will see later in this chapter (see Exhibit 2-24). Those looking for their first paralegal job may have a tougher time. Don't be discouraged. There are many steps you can take now to increase your chances of finding the job that is right for you.

Competition for paralegal jobs is likely to come from several sources:

- Recent graduates from paralegal training programs
- Secretaries now working in law offices who want to be promoted into paralegal positions
- Paralegals with a year or more of experience who are seeking a job change
- People with no legal training or experience who walk into an office "cold" seeking a job
- People with no legal training or experience but who have connections (a friend of an important client or a relative of a partner)

How long will it take for you to find a paralegal job? Of course, no one can accurately answer this question. Many variables are involved, including the economy, your competence, and the educational record you establish in this program. According to a guideline used by one veteran legal recruiter (a guideline that applies to good nonlegal jobs as well), for every $10,000 in salary you hope to earn, you will need to set aside one month of search time. "So if you want $35,000 per year, your search should take about three and one-half months. But do not be disappointed if it takes longer."[1] Some graduates obtain jobs very quickly. Be prepared, however, for a competitive job market.

In this environment, the two keys to success are information about the employment scene and techniques to market yourself. With these objectives in mind, we turn to the following topics:

- Places where paralegals work
- Paralegal specialties
- Effective job-finding strategies
- Alternative career options

WHERE PARALEGALS WORK

There are nine major settings where paralegals work. They are summarized in Exhibit 2-1, along with the approximate percentage of paralegals working in each location. Later, in Exhibit 2-4, you will find a chart that lists some of the major characteristics of work in these settings. In general, the more attorneys in a law office, the greater the likelihood that significant numbers of paralegals will be working there. (See Appendix H on finding law firms and Appendix I on government paralegals in your state.)

I. PARALEGALS IN PRIVATE LAW FIRMS

The vast majority of paralegals (over 70 percent) work in **private law firms** where revenue is generated mainly from the attorney (and paralegal) fees paid by clients. Although the need for paralegals may be just as great in the other categories, private law firms have been doing most of the hiring. In 1996, there were 24 paralegals for every 100 attorneys in private law firms.[2] Today the ratio is closer to 40 per 100 attorneys. Of course, individual firms can

private law firms A law firm that generates its income mainly from the attorney (and paralegal) fees paid by clients.

Exhibit 2-1	Where Do Paralegals Work and in What Percentages?

1. Private law firms
   A. Small firm: 1–10 attorneys (25%)
   B. Medium firm: 11–50 attorneys (16%)
   C. Large firm: over 50 attorneys (30%)
2. Law departments of businesses (8%)
3. Government
   A. Federal government (6%)
   B. State government (6%)
   C. Local government (3%)
4. Legal aid offices (civil law) (1%)
5. Special-interest groups (0.5%)

6. Criminal law offices
   A. Prosecution (0.5%)
   B. Defense (0.5%)
7. Paralegals as independent contractors (independent paralegals and document service providers) (1%)
8. Legal service providers (0.5%)
9. Other positions (2%)
   A. Law librarian
   B. Paralegal teacher
   C. Paralegal supervisor/office administrator
   D. Elected official, etc.

have dramatically different attorney-paralegal ratios. There are firms that have no paralegals. In some firms the ratio is one paralegal for every two attorneys, and in a few firms paralegals outnumber attorneys.

Many private law firms are engaged in general practice, meaning that they handle a wide variety of legal problems presented by clients. However, firms that specialize (sometimes called **boutique law firms**) are becoming increasingly common, particularly in areas of the law such as employment discrimination, bankruptcy, taxation, and immigration.

Paralegals often wonder about the differences between working for a large private law firm versus a smaller one. Here are some comparisons:

boutique law firms A law firm that specializes in one main area of the law.

- Paralegals in large private law firms:
  - Tend to specialize in one area of the law
  - Are among the highest paid
  - Often have generous employee benefits
  - Are likely to have a variety of supervisors (e.g., a supervising attorney, a paralegal manager, a legal administrator, and a managing partner)
  - Are likely to have the administrative aspects of their job spelled out in a firm-wide employment policy manual
  - Have been politically active in forming paralegal associations and interacting with bar associations
  - Are likely to work in an office that has more than five paralegals
  - Are likely to work in an office that has a career ladder for paralegals
  - Are likely to have in-office training and professional development opportunities
  - Are likely to use sophisticated computer equipment and software
  - Are likely to have access to other support personnel within the office
  - Once experienced, are likely to be able to perform some of the same tasks as newly hired attorneys (occasionally leading to competition between experienced paralegals and newly hired attorneys as both seek to increase their billable hours)
  - Have better opportunities when leaving the office and seeking other paralegal jobs
- Paralegals in smaller private law firms:
  - Have more variety in their tasks (they tend to work in more than one area of the law rather than specialize in one area)
  - Have more client contact
  - Tend to be given more responsibility early in their employment
  - Are more likely to perform clerical/administrative tasks along with their paralegal duties
  - Are more likely to be asked to perform personal errands for a supervisor
  - Are more likely to work for an office with low or no malpractice liability insurance and are more likely to be asked to ignore or participate in unethical conduct by a supervisor (see Chapter 5)
- For more comparisons of paralegals in different work settings, see Exhibit 2-4 later in this chapter.

Of course, these observations do not apply to every large firm and every small firm. Paralegals in some small firms, for example, might experience many of the realities listed for large firms. Each law office tends to have its unique character. In Chapter 3 and in later chapters, we will examine in greater detail some of the realities outlined in these comparisons, and later in this chapter, we will extensively cover techniques for finding employment in *any* law office.

2. PARALEGALS IN LAW DEPARTMENTS OF BUSINESSES

Many large corporations and businesses in the country have their own in-house law department under the direction of an attorney who is often called the **general counsel** or the corporate counsel. The attorneys in this department have only one client: the corporation or business itself. Fees are not involved; the department is funded from the corporate treasury. Attorneys handle the day-to-day legal needs of the organization. If specialized legal help is needed (e.g., when the organization is sued), outside counsel is often hired. The latter work on a fee basis. Unlike attorneys in the law department, outside counsel are not salaried employees of the organization. Examples of businesses and other institutions that often have law departments include manufacturers, retailers, transportation companies, publishers, general insurance companies, real estate and title insurance companies, estate and trust departments of large banks, hospitals, and universities. In increasing numbers, paralegals have been hired in these settings. The average corporate law department employs five paralegals and seventeen staff attorneys. Paralegal salaries are relatively high because the employer (like the large private law office) can often afford to pay good wages.

general counsel
The chief attorney in a corporate law department. Also called *corporate counsel*.

For information about corporate law departments and employment, check:

- Corporate Counsel (lawjobs.com/jobtype/corporate-counsel) (also type *paralegal* in the search box)
- Association of Corporate Counsel (www.acc.com)
- Federation of Defense and Corporate Counsel (www.thefederation.org)
- American Bar Association, Business Law Section (www.americanbar.org/groups /business_law.html)
- Run this search in Google, Bing, or Yahoo: paralegal jobs corporations

Paralegals who work for law departments are often members of national and local paralegal associations, some of which have specialty associations devoted to the interests of in-house paralegals. Examples:

- Metroplex Association of Corporate Paralegals (www.linkedin.com) (type the name of the Metroplex Association in the search box)
- Cincinnati Paralegal Association, Corporate Specialty Section (www.cincinnatiparalegals .org/about/specialty-sections.html)
- San Francisco Paralegal Association, Corporate and Intellectual Property Practice Section (www.sfpa.com/practice_sections)

3. PARALEGALS IN GOVERNMENT

The **civil service** departments of federal, state, and local governments have established standards and classifications for many different kinds of government employees, including paralegals. For every ten government attorneys, there are three paralegals. These paralegals work in four main areas of government:

civil service Nonmilitary government employment, often obtained through merit and competitive exams.

- In the office of the chief government attorney (e.g., attorney general or city attorney) for an entire **jurisdiction** (e.g., state, county, or city)
- In the office of the chief attorney (often called the general counsel) for individual government agencies (e.g., Department of Justice, Transportation Department)
- In the office of the chief attorney (again often called the general counsel) for units within an individual government agency (e.g., civil rights division, enforcement bureau)
- In the office of individual legislators, legislative committees, legislative counsel, or legislative drafting office of the legislature

jurisdiction A geographic area over which a particular court, legislature, or administrative agency has authority. The geographic area can be the entire country, a state, a group of states, a county, a city, etc. (See glossary for an additional meaning.)

paralegal specialist
The major civil service job classification for paralegals who work for the federal government and for some state and local governments.

Federal Government

Thousands of paralegals work for the federal government in the capital (Washington, D.C.) and the main regional cities of the federal government (Atlanta, Boston, Chicago, Dallas, Denver, Kansas City, New York, Philadelphia, San Francisco, and Seattle). The most important job classification for this position is the **paralegal specialist**. The occupational code for this position is GS-0950.[3] (GS means general schedule, the main pay scale in the federal government.) The paralegal specialist performs "legal support functions which require discretion and independent judgment," according to the U.S. Office of Personnel Management (OPM), the federal agency in charge of hiring standards within the federal government. Here is OMP's overview of the duties performed by paralegal specialists in the federal government:

Paralegal Specialist in the Federal Government (GS-0950)

Duties may include the following:

- Interviewing and evaluating potential witnesses; preparing for hearings and court appearances by briefing attorneys on the issues and by assembling and arranging case files, documents, and exhibits
- Examining case files to determine sufficiency of evidence or documentation
- Developing and justifying recommendations for agency action on legal issues
- Searching for legal precedents and preparing digests of points of law involved
- Drafting pleadings and litigation papers for review and approval of attorneys
- Attending court hearings to keep abreast of the status of agency cases in litigation
- Testifying in court concerning exhibits prepared[4]

Paralegal specialists are found throughout the federal government. Some federal agencies are large users of paralegals. For example:

Agency	Number of Attorneys	Number of Paralegals
Department of Justice	9,629	2,073
U.S. Air Force	1,392	960

Other agencies with large numbers of paralegals include the Departments of Health and Human Services, Treasury, Transportation, and Interior. (For a list of federal agencies, see Appendix C.) Paralegals are also employed within the U.S. court system.

Some agencies have their own titles and system of recruiting employees. Here, for example, is an announcement on the website of the Central Intelligence Agency (CIA) for a "paralegal professional":

Paralegal in the CIA

The Central Intelligence Agency is seeking paralegal professionals to provide case management, legal research, case-cite verification, blue book citations and general paralegal support to the Office of General Counsel. Paralegals support legal issues relating to foreign intelligence, counterintelligence activities, and both civil and criminal litigation. All applicants must successfully complete a thorough medical and psychological exam, a polygraph interview and an extensive background investigation. To be considered suitable for CIA employment, applicants must generally not have used illegal drugs within the last twelve months. The issue of illegal drug use prior to twelve months ago is carefully evaluated during the medical and security processing. (Salary: $43,365 to $81,747)

There are many other nonattorney positions in the federal government where legal skills are valued. Examples:

- Civil rights analyst
- Claims examiner
- Clerk of court
- Contract specialist
- Contracts examiner
- Criminal investigator
- Employee benefits specialist
- Environmental protection specialist

- Equal employment opportunity specialist
- Equal opportunity assistant
- Freedom of Information Act/Privacy Act specialist
- Hearings and appeals officer
- Import specialist
- Intelligence analyst
- Internal revenue agent

- Land law examiner
- Legal assistant
- Legal clerk
- Legal instruments examiner
- Legal technician
- Public utilities examiner

- Social services representative
- Tax examiner
- Unemployment insurance specialist
- Wage and hour compliance specialist
- Workers' compensation claims examiner

Here are some Internet sites that can provide extensive information about the federal government and about legal jobs within its various branches, departments, and offices:

Federal Government
- www.usa.gov (click Government Agencies)
- www.whitehouse.gov/our-government
- United States Government Manual (www.gpoaccess.gov/gmanual/index.html) provides descriptions and addresses of all agencies and courts of the federal government.

Employment in the Federal Government
- USAJobs (www.usajobs.gov) is the official job site of the federal government (in the search box, type *paralegal*); upon request, this site can send you email messages (alerts) on all available paralegal job openings (click *Create An Account* to register for this service).
- USA.gov (type *paralegal specialist* in the search box).
- United States Office of Personnel Management (OPM) (www.opm.gov) oversees standards of employment within the federal government.
- In Google, Bing, or Yahoo, type the following search, *how to get a job in the federal government*.

State and Local Government

When looking for work in a state or local government, do not limit your search to paralegal or legal assistant positions. As in the federal government, legal jobs for nonattorneys in state and local government may be listed under a variety of titles, such as research assistant, legal analyst, administrative aide, administrative officer, executive assistant, examiner, assistant, investigator, etc. Here are some steps to find out about such jobs:

- See Appendix I for links to classification standards and examples of paralegal jobs in your state government.
- Go to the National Association of State Personnel Executives (www.naspe.net) (enter *"state government job openings"* in the search box).
- Go to the local government sites for your state in State and Local Government on the Net (www.statelocalgov.net). On the sites of the cities, counties, and towns in your state, look for links to employment or type *employment* in the site's search box.
- Go to the websites of every state court in your state. Such sites often have information on job openings. For courts in your state, see the National Center for State Courts (www.ncsc.org) (type *Court websites* in the search box).
- Go to the website of your representatives in the state legislature; send them an email asking how to find out about employment opportunities in the state legislature. To find your representatives, run this search in Google, Bing, or Yahoo: aa legislature (substituting the name of your state for "aa").
- In Google, Bing, or Yahoo, run this search: aa *state government jobs* (substituting the name of your state for "aa").

4. PARALEGALS IN LEGAL AID OFFICES (CIVIL LAW)

Throughout the country, there are **legal aid offices** that provide legal services for **indigents** (poor or low-income persons without funds to hire a private attorney). A legal aid office might be called community law office, neighborhood legal service office, legal aid foundation, etc. The office obtains most of its funding from the government, often in the form of yearly grants. Here we are referring to **civil** (noncriminal) legal cases. Offices that handle criminal cases are discussed later.

In addition to government funding, legal aid offices are also supported by **IOLTA** (Interest on Lawyers Trust Accounts). Attorneys often have **client trust accounts** containing client funds that earn interest. Under IOLTA programs, this interest is made available to law offices that provide legal services to indigents (www.iolta.org).

legal aid offices An office of attorneys (and often, paralegals) that provides free or low-cost legal services for persons who cannot afford standard legal fees. Also called *legal services office.*

indigent Poor; without means to afford something such as a private attorney or filing fees.

civil Noncriminal. (See glossary for additional meanings.)

IOLTA (Interest on Lawyers Trust Accounts) A program that helps fund legal services for the poor with funds that attorneys are required to turn over from interest earned in client trust accounts containing client funds.

client trust account A bank account controlled by an attorney that contains client funds that may not be used for general operating expenses or for any personal purpose of the attorney.

Legal aid offices make extensive use of paralegals with titles such as:

- Paralegal
- Administrative hearing representative
- Bankruptcy law specialist
- Case advocate
- Community law specialist
- Disability law specialist
- Domestic relations specialist
- Food stamp specialist
- Housing paralegal
- Immigration paralegal

- Information and referral specialist
- Legal assistant
- Legislative advocate
- Paralegal coordinator
- Paralegal supervisor
- Public benefits paralegal
- Social security specialist
- Tenant law specialist
- Tribal court representative
- Veterans law advocate

As we will see in Chapter 4, some administrative agencies permit nonattorneys to represent persons at hearings before those agencies. Legal aid offices take advantage of this authorization. Some of their paralegals undertake extensive agency representation. The distinction between attorneys and paralegals in such offices is less pronounced than in many other settings. Unfortunately, however, these paralegals are among the lowest paid because of the limited resources of the offices where they work.

Here are some examples of the duties of a public benefits paralegal in a legal aid office:

- Interview clients for eligibility for free legal services.
- Interview clients on the facts of the legal matter after the office has accepted the case.
- Assist individuals who are representing themselves in an **uncontested** divorce.
- Represent clients at hearings on the denial of applications for **TANF** (Temporary Assistance for Needy Families) or other public assistance.
- Represent clients at Social Security hearings (see Chapter 15).
- Assist the office to collect data needed for quarterly reports to a funding source.
- Investigate claims of consumer fraud, evictions, discrimination, etc.
- Help prepare (and sometimes distribute) leaflets on poverty law topics, e.g., eligibility for food stamps.

Legal aid offices are not the only way the government helps provide legal services to indigents. Many cities and counties have "volunteer lawyer" organizations that recruit private attorneys to provide **pro bono** (i.e., free or reduced-rate) legal services. These organizations often use paid and volunteer paralegals.

Here are sources of further information about programs that serve indigents and paralegal job opportunities within them:

- Legal service programs in your state:
    - www.lsc.gov (click *Local Programs*) (LSC is the Legal Services Corporation, a federal agency that funds many legal aid programs). For information about paralegals in these programs, type *paralegal* in the search box.
    - www.ptla.org/links/services.htm (click your state).
    - In Google, Bing, or Yahoo, run this search: aa legal services legal aid (substituting your state for "aa").
- Job opportunities for paralegals and attorneys in legal aid offices:
    - In Google, Bing, or Yahoo, run this search: aa jobs paralegal legal aid services (substituting your state for "aa").
    - www.nlada.org/jobs (National Legal Aid and Defender Association (NLADA), covering services in civil and criminal cases) (click your state to look for nonattorney positions).
    - www.abanet.org/legalservices/probono/directory.html (click your state; when you click the site of particular programs in your state, look for links to "Jobs" or "Careers"; most of the pro-bono programs listed are legal aid offices).

5. PARALEGALS IN SPECIAL-INTEREST GROUPS

Many **special-interest groups** exist in our society: unions, business associations, environmental protection groups, taxpayer associations, consumer protection groups, trade

---

uncontested Unchallenged; without opposition or dispute.

TANF (Temporary Assistance for Needy Families) A federal-state welfare program.

pro bono Concerning or involving legal services that are provided for the public good (*pro bono publico,* shortened to *pro bono*) without fee or compensation. Sometimes also applied to services given at a reduced rate.

special-interest group An organization that seeks to influence policy in favor of a particular group or cause, often through lobbying.

associations, citizen action groups, etc. They seek to influence public policy in favor of a particular group or cause. Examples:

- American Bankers Association (www.aba.com)
- National Association of Home Builders (www.nahb.com)
- National Education Association (www.nea.org)
- AFL-CIO (www.aflcio.org)
- National Organization for Women (www.now.org)
- Parents, Families, and Friends of Lesbians and Gays (community.pflag.org)

Large groups may have their own offices, libraries, and legal staff, including paralegals. The legal work often involves monitoring legislation, lobbying, preparing studies, etc. Direct legal services to individual members of the groups are usually not provided. The legal work relates to the needs (or a cause) of the organization as a whole. Occasionally, however, the legal staff will litigate **test cases** of individual members that have a broad impact on the organization's membership.

A different concept in the use of attorneys and paralegals by some special-interest groups is **prepaid legal services**, also referred to as *legal plans* or *group legal services*. Members of unions, for example, might pay a monthly fee to the organization, for which they are entitled to receive designated legal services, such as preparation of a will or representation in an uncontested divorce. The members pay before the legal problems arise. Prepaid legal service systems are a form of legal insurance that operates in a manner similar to health insurance. Specified services are provided if the need for them arises. Here are sources of information about these services:

- American Prepaid Legal Services Institute (www.aplsi.org)
- American Bar Association, Group and Prepaid Legal Services (www.abanet.org/legalservices/prepaid/home.html)
- Legal Shield (www.legalshield.com)

Prepaid legal service plans often employ paralegals, particularly for tasks such as interviewing members and screening cases covered by the plan.

6. PARALEGALS IN CRIMINAL LAW OFFICES

A **crime** is conduct (e.g., theft) the government classifies as a wrong that is serious enough to warrant a criminal proceeding and punishment if convicted. Because a crime is considered an affront against the public peace, criminal cases are brought by the government, not by the victim of the crime. In a criminal case, the victim is the complaining witness, not a party. A *civil* case covers private grievances (called *civil wrongs*) such as a breach of contract or a **tort**. The victim in a civil case brings the action and is a party, not just a witness. Sometimes the same conduct can be both a crime and a civil wrong. For example, a person who steals your car can be punished by the government for the crime of theft and sued by you in a separate civil proceeding for the tort of **conversion**.

Criminal cases are litigated for the government by attorneys called prosecutors, district attorneys, or attorneys general. Defendants are represented by private attorneys if they can afford attorney fees. If they are indigent, they might be represented by **public defenders**, who are attorneys appointed by the court and paid by the government to represent the poor in a criminal case. Public defenders are usually government employees. (To find out if this is so in your state, go to the website of your state or county government and type *public defender* in its search box.) Sometimes a court will appoint a private attorney to represent someone. A court-appointed private attorney in a criminal or civil case is often called **assigned counsel**.

The use of paralegals in the practice of criminal law is increasing, particularly due to the encouragement of organizations such as the National District Attorneys Association and the National Legal Aid & Defender Association. Sources of information on work in criminal justice include:

- National Legal Aid & Defender Association (NLADA) (www.nlada.org)
- National District Attorneys Association (www.ndaa.org) (type *paralegal* in the search box)

test case Litigation that seeks to create a new legal principle or right.

prepaid legal services A legal-insurance plan by which a person pays premiums to cover future legal services that might be needed. Also called *legal plan, group legal services*

crime Conduct the government classifies as a wrong that is serious enough to warrant a criminal proceeding and punishment if convicted.

tort A civil wrong (other than a breach of contract) that causes injury or other loss for which our legal system deems it just to provide a remedy such as damages. Injury or loss can be to the person (a personal tort), to movable property (a personal property tort), or to land and anything attached to the land (a real property tort).

conversion A tort committed by an intentional interference with another's personal property, consisting of an exercise of dominion over the property.

public defender An attorney appointed by a court and paid by the government to represent an indigent defendant in a criminal case.

assigned counsel An attorney (often in private practice) appointed by the court to represent an indigent person in a criminal or civil case. They are paid by the government. Attorneys who are government employees handling criminal cases might be called *public defenders*.

- National Association of Attorneys General (www.naag.org)
- National Association of Criminal Defense Lawyers (www.criminaljustice.org) (type *paralegal* in the search box)
- American Bar Association, Criminal Justice Section (www.abanet.org/crimjust/home.html)
- Office of Defender Services (www.fd.org) (type paralegal in the search box)
- Prosecutor websites (www.prosecutor.info)
- National Criminal Justice Reference Service (www.ncjrs.gov) (type "paralegal" in the search box)

7. PARALEGALS AS INDEPENDENT CONTRACTORS

independent contractor A self-employed person who operates his or her own business and contracts to perform tasks for others. In general, the latter do not control many of the administrative details of how the work is performed.

independent paralegal (1) An independent contractor who sells his or her paralegal services to, and works under the supervision of, one or more attorneys. (2) An independent contractor who sells his or her paralegal services directly to the public without attorney supervision. Also called *freelance paralegal, legal technician.* In some states, however, the paralegal title is limited to those who work under attorney supervision.

As we learned in Chapter 1, some paralegals are **independent contractors** who operate their own business and do contract work for others. An **independent paralegal** is an independent contractor (1) who sells his or her paralegal services to, and works under the supervision of, one or more attorneys; or (2) who sells his or her paralegal services directly to the public without attorney supervision. Here is an overview of both categories of independent paralegals:

Independent Paralegals Supervised by Attorneys

Independent paralegals who are supervised by attorneys perform paralegal services in their own office or in the offices of the attorneys who hire them for special projects. A law firm may be convinced of the value of paralegals but not have enough business to justify hiring a full-time paralegal employee. An independent paralegal is an alternative. This paralegal is almost always someone who was once a traditional paralegal (an employee of an attorney) for a number of years before opening his or her own business. Independent paralegals make their services known in flyers and on the Internet (see Exhibit 2-2).

Exhibit 2-2	Internet Ad for an Independent Paralegal

Improve the quality and
****cost-effectiveness****
of your practice with the help of:
Lawyer's Assistant, Inc.

Here is what the flyer or Internet page of an independent paralegal might say:

Our staff consists of individuals with formal paralegal training and an average of five years of experience in areas such as estates and trusts, litigation, real estate, tax, and corporate law. Whether you require a real estate paralegal for one day or four litigation paralegals for six months, we can provide you with reliable qualified paralegals to meet your specific needs.

Most independent paralegals have websites. To find them in your state, run this search in Google, Bing, or Yahoo: aa *"freelance paralegal"* or aa *"paralegal services"* (substituting your state for "aa").

Independents who operate entirely online (as opposed to going to the offices of attorneys who hire them) are called *virtual assistants* or *virtual paralegals.* The work they do for attorneys is submitted by email attachments or other electronic means. For an example of a virtual office, see Exhibit 2-3. Although many of the services provided by virtual independents are clerical (e.g., typing transcripts of testimony and proofreading), more substantive tasks are also offered (e.g., digesting discovery documents and performing limited legal research). Some virtual assistants have joined the International Virtual Assistants Association (www.ivaa.org).

outsourcing Paying an outside company or service to perform tasks usually performed by one's own employees.

The use of independent paralegals by a law firm is an example of what is called **outsourcing**—paying an outside company or service to perform tasks usually performed by one's own employees. As outsourcing has become increasingly common, ethical and management issues have been raised, particularly when the work is performed in distant countries such as India where low-wage English-speaking workers are available. We will examine these issues in later chapters.

Exhibit 2-3	Example of an Independent Paralegal Service

CONTRACT PARALEGAL SERVICES

We are a full service litigation company. In addition to trial services we provide:

- Contract paralegals for short- or long-term projects. We can provide these services in your office or ours.
- Consulting services for large document cases. Our paralegals are experienced in setting up and implementing procedures for the management of large document cases.
- Document production. Our paralegals have experience in retrieving documents for production. We can provide a team of paralegals to travel to offsite locations to find documents pertinent to subpoenas, disclosure statements, or other production requests.
- Certified training for Summation® litigation support software. We also have experience with CaseSoft®, Sanction®, and Trial Director® products.

Providing low-cost experienced contract paralegal services for:

Corporate legal departments

Government legal departments

Law firms

Trial work & multimedia presentations

Other Paralegal Services Offered

- Preparation of Pleadings/Discovery
- Factual Investigation
- Witness Interviews
- Records Research
- Preparation of Exhibits
- Legal Research

- Deposition Summaries
- Index Discovery Responses
- Attend Document Production
- Create/Manage Document Database
- Trial Preparation/Assistance

Reprinted with the permission of Contract Paralegal Services (www.leedavisandassociates.com/contractparalegals.html)

For an overview on how to start an independent paralegal business, see Appendix G.

Independent Paralegals Not Supervised by Attorneys

As indicated, there are also independent paralegals who sell their services directly to the public without attorney supervision. Because they mostly provide assistance on legal documents, they are collectively referred to as **document service providers** (DSPs). In some states, new titles have been created for these individuals. Examples:

- California: Legal Document Assistants (www.calda.org)
- Arizona: Certified Legal Document Preparers (www.independentparalegals.com)

In some states (e.g., California and Florida), individuals selling law-related services directly to the public without attorney supervision are not allowed to call themselves paralegals or legal assistants. We will examine this and related issues in greater detail in Chapter 4.

8. PARALEGALS WORKING FOR LEGAL SERVICE PROVIDERS (LSPs)

Legal service providers (LSPs), sometimes called consultants and vendors, sell law-related products and services to attorneys and others. Under this definition, the first category of independent paralegal just discussed, is an LSP. Other examples include LSPs that:

- Design graphics for use in litigation
- Select a computer system for a law office
- Design and manage a computer-assisted document control system for a large case
- Manage a large employer's unemployment compensation claims and appeals for its employees
- Establish a marketing strategy
- Design a filing or financial system for the office
- Incorporate a new company in all fifty states
- Conduct a trademark search

document service provider (1) A nonattorney who works without attorney supervision to provide legal-document assistance to individuals who are representing themselves. (2) Someone who helps another prepare or process documents.

- Digest (summarize) discovery documents
- Undertake a UCC (Uniform Commercial Code) search and filing in all fifty states

To accomplish such tasks, LSPs employ highly specialized staffs of management experts, accountants, economists, and former administrators. They also hire experienced paralegals, particularly those with substantial computer skills.

Here are some examples of LSPs:

- Deposums (digesting discovery documents) www.deposums.com/depositionsummaries.html
- Kroll Ontrack (**e-discovery** services) www.krollontrack.com
- LSS (litigation support services) www.litsup.com

A special category of LSP with medical training is the **legal nurse consultant (LNC)**. This person is a nurse who provides a wide range of support services to attorneys in the medical aspects of medical malpractice, products liability, environment, and labor cases. For example, they might be given a large role in obtaining, summarizing, and interpreting medical records. LNCs have formed their own association, the American Association of Legal Nurse Consultants (AALNC) (www.aalnc.org). AALNC considers LNCs to be a specialty practice of the nursing profession rather than a specialty category of paralegals. Nurses who operate their own consulting business as independent contractors are called LNCs. If a former nurse is an employee of a law firm, he or she is often called a **legal nurse**.

9. PARALEGALS IN OTHER POSITIONS

Experienced paralegals may also use their training and experience as:

- Law librarians at law firms
- Teachers or co-teachers of paralegal courses
- Law office administrators
- Appointed or elected politicians
- Judges in lower courts where judges do not have to be attorneys (see, for example, Appendix K for a photo of former paralegal and current probate judge, Arleen Keegan)

It is clear that we have not seen the end of the development of new roles for paralegals within a law office and in other law-related positions. A more extensive list of such roles is provided at the end of this chapter (see Exhibit 2-24).

10. SUMMARY

Exhibit 2-4 presents an overview of some of the major characteristics of the largest employment settings that we began exploring in Exhibit 2-1 at the beginning of this chapter. We will be returning to many of the themes in Exhibit 2-4 in later chapters.

PARALEGAL SPECIALTIES: A DICTIONARY OF FUNCTIONS

Attorneys practice in many different areas of law, with an emphasis on the areas of greatest need. For example, when President Obama's healthcare program was enacted into law in 2010, attorneys anticipated a significant increase in legal issues arising from this major change in the delivery of healthcare in the United States. (See Exhibit 2-5 for projected growth areas of the law).

We turn now to an overview of approximately forty-seven areas of work in a law office. Of course, there is overlap. Even attorneys who specialize in one area often take cases that require client assistance in other areas as well. Note, for example, that there is a separate section on civil litigation (no. 33). This is not meant to suggest that the other areas of specialization do not involve litigation. In fact, between 60 and 70 percent of paralegals work in one form or another of litigation. The section on litigation, therefore, potentially applies to all of the other specialty areas.

For each of the forty-seven specialties outlined in Exhibit 2-6, you will find examples of duties performed by paralegals. For most of the specialties, comments from paralegals or their supervisors about the paralegal's work in the specialty are included. For the six specialties where most paralegals work (corporate law, estate law, family law, litigation, real estate law, and tort law), you will also find excerpts from want ads to give you an idea of what employers are looking for when hiring for those specialties.

---

e-discovery The discovery by a party in litigation of an opponent's data generated by or stored in a computer or other digital device. Examples include data in emails, spreadsheets, memos, Web pages, video, and other digital records. Also called *electronic data discovery (EDD)*.

legal nurse consultant (LNC) A nurse, usually an independent contractor, who examines and evaluates facts involving the delivery of health care on behalf of an attorney, health organization, or other entity.

legal nurse A nurse, usually an employee of an attorney, who examines and evaluates facts involving the delivery of health care on behalf of an attorney.

Exhibit 2-4   General Observations about Paralegal Work in Different Kinds of Law Offices

WHAT IS THE LIKELIHOOD OF A PARALEGAL:

Kind of Office	Being hired without experience	Having very good pay	Having very good benefits	Having variety in assignments	Having clerical tasks to perform	Having a narrowly defined role	Having a career ladder	Having client contact	Having access to support staff	Having formal in-house training	Working with state-of-the-art equipment	Having an hourly billing requirement	Having overtime required by employer	Having work-life balance (diversity)
Large private law firm	Low	High	High	Low	Low	High	High	Low	High	High	High	High	High	High
Medium-size private law firm	Moderate	Moderate	Moderate	Moderate	Low	Moderate	High	Low	High	Moderate	High	High	High	Moderate
Small private law firm	Moderate	Moderate	Moderate	High	High	Low	Low	High	Low	Low	Low	Moderate	Moderate	Moderate
Corporate law department	Moderate	High	High	Moderate	Low	High	High	High	High	High	High	N/A	Low	High
Federal government	Moderate	High	High	Moderate	Low	High	High	High	High	High	High	N/A	Low	High
State government	High	Moderate	High	Moderate	Low	High	High	High	High	High	Moderate	N/A	Low	High
Local government	High	Moderate	Moderate	Moderate	Low	High	High	High	Moderate	Moderate	Moderate	N/A	Low	High
Legal aid office	High	Low	Low	High	High	Moderate	Low	High	Low	Moderate	Low	N/A	Low	Moderate
Special-interest group or organization	Moderate	Moderate	Moderate	High	Moderate	Moderate	Low	Moderate	Moderate	Low	Moderate	N/A	Low	High
Independent paralegal (offering services to attorneys)	Low	Low	Low	Moderate	High	High	N/A	Low	Low	N/A	Low	N/A	N/A	Low

Exhibit 2-5	Growth Areas of Law

Lawyers were asked, "In your opinion, which one of the following areas of Law will experience the most growth in the next three years?"

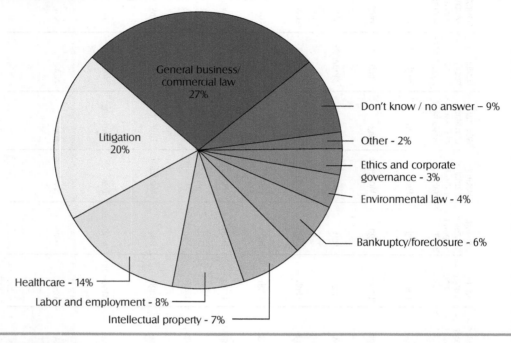

General business/commercial law 27%

Don't know / no answer – 9%

Other – 2%

Ethics and corporate governance – 3%

Environmental law – 4%

Bankruptcy/foreclosure – 6%

Litigation 20%

Healthcare – 14%

Labor and employment – 8%

Intellectual property – 7%

Reprinted with permission of Robert Half Legal (www.roberthalflegal.com/SalaryCenter)

Exhibit 2-6	Paralegal Specialties

1. Administrative law
2. Admiralty law
3. Advertising law
4. Antitrust law
5. Banking law
6. Bankruptcy law
7. Civil rights law
8. Collections law
9. Communications law
10. Construction law
11. Contract law
12. Corporate law
13. Criminal law
14. Elder law
15. Employee benefits law
16. Entertainment law
17. Environmental law

18. Estates, trusts, and probate law
19. Ethics and professional responsibility
20. Family law
21. Gaming law
22. Government contract law
23. Immigration law
24. Insurance law
25. Intellectual property law
26. International law
27. Judicial administration
28. Labor and employment law
29. Landlord and tenant law
30. Law librarianship
31. Law office administration
32. Legislation

33. Litigation (civil)
34. Military law
35. Municipal finance law
36. Native American law
37. Oil and gas law
38. Parajudge (lay judge)
39. Pro bono work
40. Public sector
41. Real estate law
42. Social security law
43. Tax law
44. Tort law
45. Water law
46. Welfare law (public assistance)
47. Workers' compensation law

For all of the forty-seven specialties, you are also given one or more Internet addresses where you will find more information about the kind of law involved in the specialty. Another way to find out what kind of law is practiced in a particular specialty is to go to the Internet site of a major law firm and click the sections called "Areas of Practice," "What We Do," "Services," or "About the Firm." In such sections, specialty areas of the law are listed and described.

For a general overview of paralegal responsibilities in many areas of law, see also:

- www.lectlaw.com/files/pap01.htm
- www.lawcost.com/paras.htm
- www.cobar.org/index.cfm/ID/106/subID/23108/CLAS
- www.caparalegal.org/index.php/duties-skills
- www.paralegals.org (click "Publications," then "Publications Library," then "Paralegal Responsibilities")

1. Administrative Law
- Government Employment

Many paralegals work for specific administrative agencies. (See also Appendix I for links to paralegal functions at state agencies in your state.)

- Process and respond to questions and complaints from the public.
- Perform legal research.
- Provide litigation assistance in agency hearings and court cases brought by or against the agency.
- Represent the government at administrative hearings where authorized.
- Manage the law office within the agency.
- Train and supervise other nonattorney personnel.

- Private Law Firm Compliance Work (see also corporate law and advertising law)

Administrative law is a major focus of law firms with clients who must comply with local, state, and federal government requirements, particularly in regulated industries such as finance, health, environment, and worker safety. For example, the passage of the Sarbanes-Oxley Act (SOX) in 2002 created many new regulations governing banking and finance. This resulted in a great deal of SOX compliance work for attorneys and their paralegals. Paralegals working for the law firms that do compliance work are sometimes called *compliance paralegals.*

- Gather and research information on legal and compliance issues.
- Compile data to demonstrate compliance.
- Maintain records; update log that tracks regulatory compliance filings.
- Draft periodic reports to regulatory agencies documenting compliance.
- Assist in preparing cases before administrative agencies or courts when the client is charged with noncompliance.
- Monitor new government laws affecting compliance obligations of clients.

- Monitor key dates and compliance obligations related to various contracts.
- Provide coordination and follow-through for government contract solicitations.
- Representation of Citizens While Working in Nongovernment Offices

Some administrative agencies authorize nonattorneys to represent citizens at hearings and other agency proceedings. For an example of a paralegal using this authorization while working in a private law office, see the summary of Formal Opinion 1988–103 in Appendix D for California, in which a paralegal represents clients at a workers' compensation hearing. (See also immigration law, pro bono work, public sector, social security law, and welfare law.)

- Interview client.
- Conduct investigation.
- Perform legal research.
- Engage in informal advocacy at the agency.
- Prepare client for the agency hearing and represent him or her at the hearing.
- Draft documents for submission at hearing.
- Monitor activities of the agency (e.g., attend rulemaking hearings to take notes on matters relevant to particular clients).
- Prepare witnesses, reports, and exhibits designed to influence the drafting of regulations at the agency.

- ***Comments on Paralegal Work in This Area* (covering paralegals who are allowed to represent clients at administrative hearings):**

- We "have a great deal of autonomy and an opportunity to develop expertise in particular areas." We have our "own caseloads, interview clients and then represent those clients at administrative hearings." Georgia Ass'n of Paralegals, *Sallye Jenkins Sapp, Atlanta Legal Aid; Sharon Mahaffey Hill, Georgia Legal Services,* 10 Paragraph 5.
- When I got my first case at a hearing before the State Department of Mental Health, I was

"scared to death!" But the attorneys in the office were very supportive. "They advised me to make a good record, noting objections for the transcript, in case of future appeal. Making the right objections was scary." Milano, *New Responsibilities Being Given to Paralegals*, 8 Legal Assistant Today 27, 28.

■ *Job Search in This Area of the Law:*
  ▪ Run the following searches in Google, Bing, or Yahoo: paralegal job "administrative law" paralegal job compliance
  ▪ To narrow these searches, add the name of your state or city to the search query

■ *More on This Area of the Law on the Net:*
  ▪ www.americanbar.org/groups/administrative_law.html
  ▪ www.hg.org/adm.html
  ▪ www.law.cornell.edu/wex/index.php/Administrative_law
  ▪ en.wikipedia.org/wiki/Administrative_law
  ▪ guides.law.csuohio.edu/adminlaw
  ▪ In Google, Bing, or Yahoo, run this search: What do "administrative law" lawyers do

2. Admiralty Law

Admiralty law, also referred to as *maritime law*, covers accidents, injuries, and death connected with vessels on navigable waters. Special legislation exists in this area, such as the Jones Act.

■ Investigation
  ▪ Obtain the facts of the event involved.
  ▪ Arrange to board the vessel to photograph the scene of the accident.
  ▪ Collect facts relevant to the seaworthiness of the vessel.
  ▪ Take statements from witnesses.
■ Legal Research
  ▪ Research liability under the applicable statutes.
  ▪ Research special procedures to obtain compensation.
■ Subrogation (the substitution of one person for another on a debt or insurance claim)
  ▪ Handle small cargo subrogation files.
  ▪ Prepare status reports for clients.
■ Litigation
  ▪ Draft complaints and other pleadings.
  ▪ Respond to discovery requests.
  ▪ Monitor all maritime files needed to keep track of discovery deadlines.
  ▪ Coordinate projects by expert witnesses.
  ▪ Provide general trial assistance.

■ *Comment on Paralegal Work in This Area:*
  ▪ Jimmie Muvern, CLA (Certified Legal Assistant), works for a sole practitioner in Baton Rouge, Louisiana, who specializes in maritime litigation: "If there is a doubt regarding the plaintiff's status as a Jones Act seaman, this issue is generally raised by a motion for summary judgment [which would end the case without a trial] filed well in advance of trial, and it is good practice for the legal assistant who may be gathering facts regarding the client's accident to also gather facts from the client and from other sources, which might assist the attorney in opposing summary judgment on the issue of the client's status as a Jones Act seaman." J. deGravelles & J. Muvern, *Who Is a Jones Act Seaman?*, 12 Facts & Findings 34 (NALA).

■ *Job Search in This Area of the Law:*
  ▪ In Google, Bing, or Yahoo, run this search: paralegal job admiralty
  ▪ To narrow the search, add the name of your state or city to the search query

■ *More on This Area of the Law on the Net:*
  ▪ www.admiraltylawguide.com/index.html
  ▪ corporate.findlaw.com/law-library/maritime-law
  ▪ www.law.cornell.edu/wex/index.php/Admiralty
  ▪ www.washlaw.edu/subject/maritime.html
  ▪ In Google, Bing, or Yahoo, run this search: What do admiralty law lawyers do

3. Advertising Law
■ Compliance Work
  ▪ *Advertising*: Review advertising of company products to identify claims made in the advertising about the product. Collect the data needed to support the accuracy of advertising claims pursuant to regulations of the Federal Trade Commission (FTC), state laws, and company guidelines.
  ▪ *Labels*: Review labels of company products to ensure compliance with federal deception regulations of the FTC and other agencies. Monitor compliance with the Food and Drug Administration (FDA) and company policy on product identity, weight statement, ingredient list, name and address of manufacturer/distributor, and nutrition information.
  ▪ *Product promotions*: Review promotions for company products (coupons, sweepstakes, bonus packs, etc.) to ensure compliance with FTC guidelines, state laws, and company policy.

- Inquiries and Complaints
  - Keep up to date on government regulations on advertising.
  - Help company attorney respond to inquiries and complaints from the public, competitors, the FTC, the FDA, the state's attorney general, etc.

- *Comment on Paralegal Work in This Area:*
  - "On the surface, my job certainly does not fit the 'traditional' paralegal role. [Years ago, if] a fortune teller had ever read my coffee grounds, I might have learned that my paralegal career would include being part of the production of commercials and labels for household products I had grown up with." "My employer, the Procter & Gamble Company, is one of the largest consumer product companies in the United States." Its "Legal Division consists of forty attorneys and nine paralegals. Advertising law is challenging. It requires ingenuity, fast thinking and mastery of tight deadlines." E. Kothman, *Advertising Paralegal Finds Own Label*, National Paralegal Reporter 12 (NFPA).

- *Job Search in This Area of the Law:*
  - In Google, Bing, or Yahoo, run this search: paralegal job "advertising law"
  - To narrow the search, add the name of your state or city to the search query

- *More on This Area of the Law on the Net:*
  - www.hg.org/advert.html
  - www.lawpublish.com
  - www.ftc.gov/bcp/bcpap.shtm
  - In Google, Bing, or Yahoo, run this search: What do "advertising law" lawyers do

4. Antitrust Law

- Investigation/Analysis
  - Collect statistical and other technical data on a company or industry involved in litigation.
  - Check Securities and Exchange Commission (SEC) filings, annual reports, advertising brochures, etc.
  - Obtain data from government bodies.
  - Prepare reports on economic data.
  - Find and interview potential witnesses.

- Administrative Agency
  - Monitor the regulations and decisions of the Federal Trade Commission (FTC) and other agencies.
  - Prepare drafts of answers to requests for information from the FTC and other agencies.

- Litigation
  - Assist in drafting pleadings.
  - Request company witness files and other documents in preparation for depositions.
  - Schedule depositions.
  - Draft interrogatories.
  - Prepare special exhibits.
  - Organize, index, and digest voluminous records.
  - Prepare trial notebook.
  - Attend trial and take notes on testimony of witnesses.
  - Cite-check appellate briefs of attorneys.
  - Provide general trial assistance.

- *Comment on Paralegal Work in This Area:*
  - When Mitchell became a permanent employee at the firm, "he was given three days' worth of files to read in order to familiarize himself with the [antitrust] case. At this point in the case, the firm had already gone through discovery of 27,000 documents. Mitchell analyzed and summarized documents with ten other paralegals hired to work on the case. With a major case such as this one, paralegals did not have a regular nine to five work day. Mitchell frequently worked seventy hours a week (for which he was paid overtime). In January, Mitchell and his team were sent across the country to take depositions for the case ... but this was not a vacation; he worked around the clock." R. Berkey, *New Career Opportunities in the Legal Profession* 47 (Arco).

- *Job Search in This Area of the Law:*
  - In Google, Bing, or Yahoo, run this search: paralegal job antitrust
  - To narrow the search, add the name of your state or city to the search query

- *More on This Area of the Law on the Net:*
  - www.usdoj.gov/atr/index.html
  - www.abanet.org/antitrust
  - www.ftc.gov/bc/antitrust
  - In Google, Bing, or Yahoo, run this search: What do antitrust lawyers do

5. Banking Law

Paralegals employed by banks often work in the bank's trust department or its legal department. They work in the areas of real estate, bankruptcy, consumer affairs, and securities law. In addition to banks, paralegals work for savings and loan institutions and other commercial lenders. Finally, some paralegals are employed in law firms that specialize in banking law. The following overview of duties is limited to the paralegal working for the legal department of a bank.

- Claims: Assist legal staff in assessing bank liability for claims such as negligence and collection abuse.
- Compliance Analysis: Help determine whether the bank is complying with the regulations and statutes that govern the banking industry.
- Monitoring: Keep track of the rulemaking and other activities of the various bank regulatory agencies and the bill-drafting activities of the legislative committees with jurisdiction over banks.
- Litigation: Assist attorneys litigating claims.
- Miscellaneous
  - Draft and/or review loan applications and accompanying credit documents.
  - Perform document analysis on financial statements, mortgages, assignments, and security agreements.
  - Conduct UCC (Uniform Commercial Code) searches.
  - Assemble closing documents.
  - Arrange for and attend loan closings.
  - Notarize documents.
  - Monitor recordation of documents.
  - Act as liaison among the supervising attorney at the bank, the loan officer, and the customer.
  - Perform routine legal research and analysis for the Compliance Department.

- ***Comment on Paralegal Work in This Area:***
  - Ruth Sendecki is the first paralegal at Merchants National Bank, one of the Midwest's largest bank holding companies. Most paralegals employed at banks today work in the trust department. Ruth, however, works with "general banking" at Merchants. Before this job, she worked at a bank, but not in a legal capacity. "You don't have to limit yourself to a law firm. You can combine being a paralegal with other interests." Her "primary responsibility is in the commercial loan department. ... She also serves the mortgage loan, correspondent banking, and the international banking departments." According to her supervisor at the bank, "She is readily accessible for the benefit of the attorney, the loan officer, and the customer to facilitate completion of the arrangements for both sides." Furthermore, she "is expanding her knowledge base, and other departments are drawing on her knowledge." Kane, *A Banker with the Soul of a Legal Assistant*, 5 Legal Assistant Today 65.

- ***Job Search in This Area of the Law:***
  - In Google, Bing, or Yahoo, run this search: paralegal job banking trust department
  - To narrow the search, add the name of your state or city to the search query

- ***More on This Area of the Law on the Net:***
  - www.law.cornell.edu/wex/index.php/Banking
  - www.occ.treas.gov
  - www.fdic.gov
  - In Google, Bing, or Yahoo, run this search: What do banking lawyers do

6. Bankruptcy Law

Paralegals in this area of law may be employed by a law firm that represents the debtor (e.g., an individual, a business); a creditor (e.g., a bank-mortgagee); or the trustee in bankruptcy. (A trustee in bankruptcy does not have to be an attorney. Some paralegals with bankruptcy experience have become trustees.) A few paralegals work directly for a bankruptcy judge as a clerk or deputy in Bankruptcy Court. (Someone who provides bankruptcy assistance as an independent contractor, rather than as an employee of an attorney, is called a *bankruptcy petition preparer* (*BPP*), a position we will examine in Chapter 4.) The following overview assumes that the paralegal works for a firm that represents the debtor.

- Interviewing/Data Collection
  - Help client fill out an extensive bankruptcy questionnaire on assets and liabilities. If needed, visit client's place of business to determine the kinds of records kept there.
  - Help client assemble documents: loan agreements, deeds of trust, security agreements, creditor lists, payables lists, employment contracts, financial statements, leases, etc.
- Investigation
  - Confirm amounts of indebtedness.
  - Identify secured and unsecured claims of creditors.
  - Check UCC (Uniform Commercial Code) filings at the secretary of state's office and at the county clerk's office.
  - Check real property records in the clerk's office in the county where the property is located.
  - Verify taxes owed; identify tax liens.
  - Identify exempt property.
- Asset Control
  - Open bankruptcy file.
  - Prepare inventories of assets and liabilities.
  - Arrange for valuation of assets.
- Creditor Contact
  - Answer inquiries of creditors on the status of the case.
  - Request documentation from creditors on claims.
- Drafting
  - Draft original bankruptcy petition, schedule of liabilities, statement of affairs, status reports, final account, etc.
- Coordination
  - Serve as liaison with trustee in bankruptcy.
  - Coordinate meeting of creditors.
  - Prepare calendar of filing and other deadlines.

- *Comment on Paralegal Work in This Area:*
  - "As a paralegal, you can play a major role in the representation of a Chapter 11 debtor. From pre-filing activities through confirmation of the plan of reorganization, there are numerous duties you can perform to assist in the successful reorganization of the debtor." Morzak, *Organizing Reorganization*, 5 Legal Assistant Today 33.
  - "Bankruptcy work is unusual in a number of ways. e.g., extremely short statutes of limitation ... . The paralegal does everything except sign the papers." Johnson, *The Role of the Paralegal/Legal Assistant in Bankruptcy and Foreclosure*, AALA News 7 (Alaska Association of Paralegals).
- *Job Search in This Area of the Law:*
  - In Google, Bing, or Yahoo, run this search: paralegal job bankruptcy
  - To narrow the search, add the name of your state or city to the search query
- *More on This Area of the Law on the Net:*
  - www.abiworld.org
  - www.hg.org/bankrpt.html
  - www.law.cornell.edu/wex/index.php/Bankruptcy
  - In Google, Bing, or Yahoo, run this search: What do bankruptcy lawyers do

7. Civil Rights Law
- Government Paralegal
  - Help government attorneys litigate discrimination complaints brought by citizens against the government, against other citizens, or against companies.
  - Help identify and resolve discrimination complaints made by government employees against the government. The complaint may be based on sex, race, age, disability, etc.

- Representation of Citizens While Working in Non-government Offices (assist law firms representing citizens in their discrimination complaints filed against the government, other citizens, or companies)
  - In court.
  - In special agencies created to hear discrimination cases, such as the Equal Employment Opportunity Commission (EEOC) or the Human Rights Commission.

- Example: Job Duties of Paralegal at the National Security Project of the American Civil Liberties Union (ACLU)
  - Respond to individuals who contact the National Security Project for legal assistance; utilize and maintain the intake database to respond to requests; and provide support to the Project's attorneys with client and witness interviews, as needed.
  - Conduct Internet and other factual research and collaborate with attorneys in preparing background memoranda on selected policy issues.
  - Cite-check, edit, format, and serve litigation documents, including briefs, memoranda, and correspondence.
  - Draft affidavits, Freedom of Information Act requests, reports, and other legal or public education documents.
  - Review and organize documents related to Freedom of Information Act (FOIA) requests and discovery.
  - Maintain and ensure the accuracy of the Project's litigation docket and calendar.
  - Assist in updating the ACLU website.
  - Oversee the training and work of the Project's Legal Administrative Assistants.

- *Comment on Paralegal Work in This Area:*
  - One aspect that Matthews likes is that each case is a different story, a different set of facts. "There is a lot of interaction with people in the courts and with the public. We do a great deal of civil rights litigation, everything from excessive police force to wrongful termination. Sometimes there are as many as 60 witnesses. The lawyers depend on me to separate the witnesses out and advise them which ones would do best in the courtroom. A lot of time the lawyer does not know the witness and has not seen the witness until the person is in the courtroom testifying." For one case, Matthews reviewed more than 1,000 slides taken in a nightclub, looking for examples of unusual or rowdy behavior. The slides include everything from male strippers to people flashing. Autopsy and horrible injury photographs are also part of the job." *Broadening into the Paralegal Field*, 39 The Docket 7(NALS, the Association for Legal Professionals).

- *Job Search in This Area of the Law:*
  - In Google, Bing, or Yahoo, run this search: paralegal job "civil rights"
  - To narrow the search, add the name of your state or city to the search query

- *More on This Area of the Law on the Net:*
  - www.law.cornell.edu/wex/index.php/Civil_rights
  - www.justice.gov/crt/index.php
  - www.washlaw.edu/subject/civil.rights.html
  - In Google, Bing, or Yahoo, run this search: What do "civil rights" lawyers do

8. Collections Law
- Acceptance of Claims
  - Open file.
  - Prepare index of parties.
  - Prepare inventory of debts of debtor.

- Investigation
  - Conduct asset check.
  - Verify address.
  - Verify filings at secretary of state's office and county clerk's office (e.g., UCC filings).
  - Contact credit bureau.
  - Verify information in probate court, registry of deeds, etc.

- Pursue informal collection efforts (in compliance with the Fair Debt Collection Practices Act)

- **Litigation Assistant (Civil Court, Small Claims Court, etc.)**
  - Draft pleadings.
  - Arrange for witnesses.
  - File documents in court.
  - Assist in settlement/negotiation of claim.
  - Assist in enforcement work, such as wage attachment (prejudgment attachment), supplementary process, execution, and seizure of personal property.[5]

- *Comments on Paralegal Work in This Area:*
  - "O.K. So, [collections work] is not the nicest job in the world, but somebody has to do it, right? If the attorney you work for does not want to do it, there are plenty more in town who will. For a paralegal working in this area, there is always something new to learn. ... It is sometimes difficult to see the results of your labor right away, as very few files are paid in full and closed in a short period of time. It is disheartening to go through many steps and possibly spend a great deal of time just trying to get someone served or to locate someone, and then end up with nothing. I will admit that collections can be very frustrating, but boring they are not!" Wexel, *Collections: Persistence Pay$ Off*, The Paraview (Metrolina Paralegal Association).
  - "I currently have responsibility for some 400 collection cases. My days are spent on the phone talking to debtors, drafting the necessary pleadings, executing forms, and hopefully depositing the money collected. The exciting part of collection is executing on a judgment. We were successful in garnishing an insurance company's account for some $80,000 when they refused to pay a judgment that had been taken against them. We have also gone with the sheriff to a beer distributorship two days before St. Patrick's Day to change the locks on the building that housed gallons and gallons of green beer. The debtor suddenly found a large sum of money to pay us so that we would release the beer in time for St. Patrick's Day." R. Swoagerm, *Collections Paralegal*, The Citator 9 (Paralegal Association of Central Ohio).

- *Job Search in This Area of the Law:*
  - In Google, Bing, or Yahoo, run this search: paralegal job collections
  - To narrow the search, add the name of your state or city to the search query

- *More on This Area of the Law on the Net:*
  - www.consumer.ftc.gov /articles/0149-debt-collection
  - business.ftc.gov/documents /fair-debt-collection-practices-act
  - www.nacm.org
  - www.nclc.org

- In Google, Bing, or Yahoo, run this search: What do collections lawyers do

9. Communications Law

- **Government Paralegal**
  - Assist attorneys at the Federal Communications Commission (FCC) in regulating the communications industry, e.g., help with rulemaking, license applications, and hearings.

- **Representation of Citizens or Companies While Working in Nongovernment Offices**
  - Draft application for license, compliance reports, exemption applications, statistical analyses, etc.
  - Monitor activities of the FCC.
  - Assist in litigation within the FCC and in court.

- *Comment on Paralegal Work in This Area:*
  - The current specialty of Carol Woods is the regulation of television and radio. "I am able to do work that is important and substantive, and am able to work independently. I have an awful lot of contact with clients, with paralegals at the client's office, and with government agencies. One of the liabilities of private practice for both attorneys and paralegals is that there is so much repetition and you can get bored. A lot of times as a paralegal you can't call the shots or know everything that goes into the planning of a project. However, when you can participate in all facets of a project, it's great!" A. Fins, *Opportunities in Paralegal Careers* 84 (Nat'l Textbook Co.).

- *Job Search in This Area of the Law:*
  - In Google, Bing, or Yahoo, run this search: paralegal job "communications law"
  - To narrow the search, add the name of your state or city to the search query

- *More on This Area of the Law on the Net:*
  - www.washlaw.edu/subject/communication.html
  - www.fcc.gov
  - www.law.cornell.edu/wex/index.php /Communications
  - In Google, Bing, or Yahoo, run this search: What do "communications law" lawyers do

10. Construction Law

- **Claims Assistance**
  - Work with engineering consultants in the preparation of claims.

- **Data Collection**
  - Daily manpower hours.
  - Amount of materials used (e.g., concrete poured).
  - Timeline of change orders.
  - PSI (pounds per square inch) testing of concrete.

- **Document Preparation**
  - Prepare graphs, special studies (e.g., compare planned with actual progress on construction project), documents for negotiation/settlement, arbitration claim forms, etc.

- Assist in Litigation
  - See Litigation (Civil)
- *Comment on Paralegal Work in This Area:*
  - "Because of the complex factual issues that arise with construction disputes, paralegals are critical in identifying, organizing, preparing, and analyzing extensive relevant factual information. In many cases, whether a party wins or loses depends on how effectively facts are developed from documents, depositions, interviews, and site inspections. Thus, a successful construction litigation team will generally include a paralegal skilled in organization and management of complex and voluminous facts. ... Construction litigation also provides paralegals with a very distinctive area for expertise and specialization." M. Gowen, *A Guide for Legal Assistants* 229 (Practicing Law Institute).
- *Job Search in This Area of the Law:*
  - In Google, Bing, or Yahoo, run this search: paralegal job "construction law"
  - To narrow the search, add the name of your state or city to the search query
- *More on This Area of the Law on the Net:*
  - www.abajournal.com/blawgs/topic /construction+law
  - www.hg.org/construction-law.html
  - In Google, Bing, or Yahoo, run this search: What do construction lawyers do

11. Contract Law

The law of contracts is involved in a number of different paralegal specialties. See advertising law, antitrust law, banking law, bankruptcy law, collections law, construction law, corporate law, employee benefits law, entertainment law, family law, government contract law, insurance law, intellectual property law, international law, labor and employment law, landlord and tenant law, municipal finance law, oil and gas law, real estate law, and tax law.

- Contract Review
  - Review contracts to determine compliance with terms.
  - Investigate facts involving alleged breach of contract.
  - Do legal research on the law of contracts in a particular specialty.
- Litigation Assistance
  - See Litigation (Civil)
- Preparation of Contract Forms
  - Separation agreements
  - Employment contracts
  - Contracts for sale, etc.
- *Comment on Paralegal Work in This Area:*
  - "The ... paralegal also assists two attorneys in drafting; reviewing; researching; and finalizing a variety of contracts, including entertainment, participant, and operational agreements. Much of the . . .

paralegal's time is spent studying existing contracts, looking for provisions that may answer inquiries or disputes. With hundreds of agreements presently active, researching, reviewing, amending, terminating, revising and executing contracts is an everyday activity for [the] ... Legal Department." Miquel, *Walt Disney World Company's Legal Assistants: Their Role in the Show*, 16 Facts and Findings 29.
  - "Initially, my primary job was to review contracts, and act as Plan Administrator for the 401(k) plan. I was also involved in the negotiation and development of a distributor agreement to market SPSS software to the Soviet Union. Most contract amendments were to software license agreements. The pace picked up when I was promoted to Manager of Human Services, while retaining all of my previous responsibilities." Illinois Paralegal Association, *Spotlight on ... Laurel Bauer*, 20 Outlook 21.
- *Job Search in This Area of the Law:*
  - In Google, Bing, or Yahoo, run this search: paralegal job "contract law"
  - To narrow the search, add the name of your state or city to the search query
- *More on This Area of the Law on the Net:*
  - www.law.cornell.edu/wex/index.php /Commercial_law
  - www.washlaw.edu/subject/contracts.html
  - In Google, Bing, or Yahoo, run this search: What do contracts lawyers do

12. Corporate Law

Paralegals involved in corporate law work in one of two main settings: law firms that represent corporations and law departments of corporations. The following task list covers both settings.

- Incorporation and General Corporate Work
  - *Pre-incorporation.*
    Check availability of proposed corporate name and, if available, reserve it; draft preincorporation subscriptions and consent forms for initial board of directors where required by statute; record articles of incorporation; order corporate supplies for legal law department.
  - *Incorporation.*
    Draft and file articles of incorporation with the state agency for subchapter S corporation, close corporation, and nonprofit corporations; draft minutes of initial meetings of incorporators and directors; draft corporate bylaws; obtain corporate seal, minutes book, and stock certificate book; prepare necessary documents to open a corporate bank account.
  - *Directors Meetings.*
    Prepare and send out waiver and notice of meetings; draft minutes of the meetings; draft the following resolutions to be considered by directors: sale of stock, increase in capitalization, stock split,

stock option, pension plan, dividend distribution, election of officers, etc.

- *Shareholders meetings (annual and special)*
Draft sections of annual report relating to business activity, officers, directors of company, etc.; draft notice of meeting, proxy materials, ballots, etc.; prepare agenda and script of meeting; draft oath, report of judge of elections, and other compliance documents when required; maintain corporate minutes books and resolutions.
- Help prepare other documents: shareholder agreement, employment contract, employee benefit plan, stock option plan, trust agreement, tax return, and closing papers on corporate acquisition.

- **Public Sale of Securities**
  - Compile information on officers and directors for use in registration statement.
  - Assist in research of blue sky requirements.
  - Closing tasks: prepare agenda, obtain certificates from state agencies on good standing of company and certified corporate documents, and prepare index and organize closing binders.

- **Research**
  - Monitor pending legislation that may affect office clients.
  - Obtain requested information from corporate records and documents.
  - Assemble financial data from records on file at SEC (Securities and Exchange Commission) and state securities regulatory agencies.

- **General Assistance**
  - Analyze government regulations to assure that policies and practices of the corporation are in compliance.
  - Maintain tickler system for dates of next corporate meeting, shareholder meeting, upcoming trial, appellate court appearance, etc.
  - Monitor the daily law journal or legal newspaper to identify relevant cases on calendars of courts, current court decisions, articles, etc., and forward such data to appropriate office attorneys.
  - Act as file managers by indexing, digesting, and monitoring documents in the file.
  - Prepare case profiles.
  - Maintain corporate forms file.

- **Miscellaneous**
  - Act as the corporate secretary.
  - Prepare documents for qualification to do business in foreign jurisdictions.
  - Prepare filings with regulatory agencies.
  - Provide assistance in processing patent, copyright, and trademark applications.
  - Coordinate escrow transactions.
  - Work on certificates of occupancy.
  - Prepare documents needed to amend bylaws or Articles of Incorporation.

- Litigation assistance: prepare interrogatories, digest deposition testimony, perform cite checks, etc.

- **Comment on Paralegal Work in This Area:**
  - "At Lyon, Weigand, I manage 230 corporate files. I prepare the corporate and limited liability company documents for the initial filing and file them with the Secretary of State, Department of Licensing, and Internal Revenue Service. I keep the minute books up to date." "I prepare bylaws and limited liability company agreements, leases, corporate renewal documents, and estate planning instruments, and trusts." Carolynn Dodgson, *A Look at Corporate Law*, 22 Legal Assistant Today 88.
  - "When the majority of people describe a legal assistant or a paralegal, they often think of courtroom battles, million dollar lawsuits and mountains of depositions. For those of us in the corporate area, these sights are replaced with boardroom battles, million dollar mergers and mountains of prospectuses. Some of us have NEVER seen the inside of a courtroom or have never touched a pleading. I guess it can be said that 'we don't do windows, we don't type, and we don't do litigation.' A corporate paralegal is never without a multitude of projects that offer excitement or anxiety. This isn't to say, however, that the corporate field is without its fair share of boredom. ... The future is only limited by your imagination. Not every paralegal wants the drama of a landmark case. Some of us are quite content seeing a client's company written up in the *Wall Street Journal* for the first time!" D. Zupanovich, *The Forming of a Corporate Paralegal*, 2 California Paralegal 4.
  - "The company I work for is a major worldwide producer of chemicals ... . I recently had to obtain some technical information about the computer system at a hotel in a foreign country in order to set up documents on a disk that would be compatible with the computer system in that country before one of the attorneys went there for contract negotiations." "One of the most thrilling experiences I have had since working for the company was that of working on the closing of a leveraged buyout of a portion of our business in Delaware. To experience first-hand the intensity of the negotiating table, the numerous last-minute changes to documents, the multitudinous shuffle of papers, and the late, grueling hours was both exhausting and exhilarating." Grove, *Scenes from a Corporate Law Department*, The Paraview 2 (Metrolina Paralegal Association).
  - "Even 'dream jobs' have their moments of chaos. After only two months on the job [at Nestle Foods Corp.] Cheryl had to prepare for a Federal Trade Commission Second Request for Production of Documents relating to an acquisition. She suddenly was thrown into the job of obtaining and organizing over 6,000 documents from around the world, creating a document database and managing up to

10 temporary paralegals at a time. Of course, this preparation included weekends and evenings for a six-week period. Cheryl calls December the 'lost month.'" Scior, *Paralegal Profile: Corporate Paralegal*, Post Script 14 (Manhattan Paralegal Association).

- *Quotes from Want Ads:*
  - Law firm seeks paralegal for corporate work: "Ideal candidate is a self-starter with good communications skills and is willing to work overtime."
  - "Ability to work independently is a must."
  - Paralegal needed to assist corporate secretary: "Analytical, professional attitude essential. Knowledge of state and/or federal regulatory agencies required."
  - "Ability to work under pressure."
  - "All candidates must possess excellent writing and drafting skills."
  - "Ideal candidate is a self-starter with good communication/research skills and is willing to work overtime."
  - "Candidates having less than three years' experience in general corporate legal assistance need not apply."
  - Position requires "word processing experience and ability to manage multiple projects."
  - Position requires "intelligent, highly motivated individual who can work with little supervision."
  - "Great opportunity to learn all aspects of corporate business transactions."
  - Position requires "career-minded paralegal with excellent organizational and communications skills, keen analytical ability and meticulous attention to detail."
  - Position requires "an experienced paralegal with a strong blue-sky background, particularly in public and private real estate syndication."
  - Applicant must have "excellent academic credentials, be analytical, objective, and dedicated to performing quality work and to displaying a professional attitude to do whatever it takes to get the job done and meet deadlines."

- *Job Search in This Area of the Law:*
  - In Google, Bing, or Yahoo, run this search: paralegal job corporate corporation
  - To narrow the search, add the name of your state or city to the search query

- *More on This Area of the Law on the Net:*
  - www.law.cornell.edu/wex/index.php/Corporations
  - www.sec.gov
  - www.acc.com
  - www.washlaw.edu/subject/securities.html
  - In Google, Bing, or Yahoo, run this search: What do corporate lawyers do

13. **Criminal Law**
  - Paralegal Working for a Prosecutor
    - Log incoming cases.

- Help office screen out cases that are inappropriate for arrest, cases that are eligible for diversion, etc.
- Act as liaison with police department and other law enforcement agencies.
- Prepare statistical caseload reports.
- Interview citizens seeking the prosecution of alleged wrongdoers and prepare case files thereon.
- Help the Consumer Fraud Department resolve minor consumer complaints, e.g., contact the business involved to determine whether a settlement of the case is possible without prosecution.
- Conduct field investigations as assigned.
- Help office maintain its case calendar.
- Act as liaison among the prosecutor, the victim, and witnesses while the case is being prepared for trial and during the trial.
- Act as general litigation assistant during the trial and the appeal.
- Prepare documents for UIFSA cases (Uniform Interstate Family Support Act).
- Monitor status of UIFSA cases.

- Paralegal Working for a Criminal Defense Attorney
  - Interview defendants to determine eligibility for free defense counsel (if the paralegal works for a public defender).
  - Conduct comprehensive interview of defendant on matters relevant to the criminal charge(s).
  - Help the defendant gather information relevant to the determination of bail.
  - Help the defendant gather information relevant to eligibility for diversion programs.
  - Conduct field investigations, e.g., interview witnesses.
  - Help obtain discovery, particularly through police reports and search warrants.
  - Act as general litigation assistant during the trial and the appeal.[6]

- *Comment on Paralegal Work in This Area:*
  - Ivy Hart-Daniel "speaks with an obvious love for her current job in the State Attorney's office. In fact, she said she would not want to do anything else! She also said there is no such thing as a typical day in her office, which is one of the many aspects of the job she enjoys. She not only helps interview witnesses and prepare them for trial, but also she often must locate a witness, requiring some detective work! Ivy assisted in a case involving an elderly woman who was victimized after the death of her husband. The woman was especially vulnerable because of her illiteracy. Through the help of the State Attorney's office, the woman was able to recover her money and get assistance with housing and learning to read. Ivy … [says the experience was] very rewarding." Frazier, *Spotlight on Ivy Hart-Daniel*, JLA News 2 (Northeast Florida Paralegal Association).
  - Attorney Kitty Polito "says she and other lawyers at McClure, McClure & Kammen use the firm's

sole paralegal not only to do investigations but also 'to pick cases apart piece by piece.' Polito credits paralegal Juliann Klapp with 'cracking the case' of a client who was accused by a codefendant of hitting the victim on the back of the head. At trial, the pathologist testified that the victim had been hit from left to right. Klapp passed a note to the attorneys pointing out that such a motion would have been a back-handed swing for their right-handed client. Thus it was more likely that the codefendant, who is left-handed, was the one who hit the victim. The defendant won." Brandt, *Paralegals' Acceptance and Utilization Increasing in Indy's Legal Community*, 1 The Indiana Lawyer 1.

- **Job Search in This Area of the Law:**
  - In Google, Bing, or Yahoo, run this search: paralegal job "criminal law"
  - To narrow the search, add the name of your state or city to the search query

- **More on This Area of the Law on the Net:**
  - www.law.cornell.edu/wex/index.php/Criminal_law
  - www.washlaw.edu/subject/criminal.html
  - www.fbi.gov
  - In Google, Bing, or Yahoo, run this search: What do criminal law lawyers do

14. Elder Law

Elder-law attorneys focus on the legal problems of the elderly such as disability, estate planning, probate, Medicare, veterans benefits, and social security. For the roles of paralegals in such areas, see estates, trusts, and probate; family law; public sector; and social security law.

- **Comment on Paralegal Work in This Area:**
  - "Paralegals specializing in elder law need a firm grasp in a wide variety of legal topics." "Elder law paralegals will assist in untangling a web of legal concerns involving employment, disability matters related to the client and possibly the client's children, and estate and retirement planning." Also: elder abuse, patient rights, veteran's benefits, stepchildren, family businesses. "After close to 17 years in the field [Jo Yantz] would say you have to have plenty of patience and understanding with the clients and lots of tissues at the first meeting." "You also need to find a way to leave the emotions and work at the door when you go home or you can burn out really fast." A. McCracken, *The Elder Law Paralegal*, 38 Facts & Findings 17.

- **Job Search in This Area of the Law:**
  - In Google, Bing, or Yahoo, run this search: paralegal job "elder law"
  - To narrow the search, add the name of your state or city to the search query

- **More on This Area of the Law on the Net:**
  - www.washlaw.edu/subject/elder.html
  - www.naela.com
  - www.ssa.gov/disability

  - www.nelf.org
  - In Google, Bing, or Yahoo, run this search: What do "elder law" lawyers do

15. Employee Benefits Law

Employee benefits paralegals work in law firms, banks, large corporations, insurance companies, and accounting firms. The following overview of tasks covers a paralegal working for a law firm.

- Drafting of Employee Plans
  - Assist the attorney, plan sponsor, plan administrator, or trustee in preparing and drafting qualified employee plans, such as stock bonus plans, profit-sharing plans, money purchase pensions, trust agreements, individual retirement account (IRA) plans, annuity plans, HR-10 or Keogh plans, employee stock ownership plans, life and health insurance plans, workers' compensation plans, and Social Security plans.

- Document Preparation and Program Monitoring
  - Gather information.
  - Determine eligibility for participation and benefits.
  - Notify employees of participation.
  - Complete input forms for document assembly.
  - Assemble elections to participate.
  - Determine beneficiary designations.
  - Record elections to contribute.
  - Allocate annual contributions to the individual participant accounts.
  - Prepare annual account statements for participants.
  - Identify potential discrimination problems in the program.

- Government Compliance Work
  - Tax requirements for qualification, amendment, and termination of plan.
  - Department of Labor reporting and disclosure requirements.
  - Insurance requirements.
  - Welfare and Pension Plans Disclosure Act requirements.
  - ERISA (Employee Retirement Income Security Act) requirements.
  - Pension Benefit Guaranty Corporation requirements.[7]

- Miscellaneous
  - Help draft summary plan descriptions for distribution to employees.
  - Help prepare and review annual reports of plans.
  - To assist the office more effectively, become a Certified Employee Benefit Specialist (CEBS).

- **Comment on Paralegal Work in This Area:**
  - "Michael Montchyk was looking to use his undergraduate degree in statistics. ... He now works for attorneys specializing in employee benefits, where understanding numbers and familiarity with the law are key skills." Lehren, *Paralegal Work*

Enhancing Careers of Many, Philadelphia Business Journal 9B.

- "This area is not for everybody. To succeed, you need considerable detail orientation, solid writing skills, self-motivation, the ability to keep up with a legal landscape that is never the same, and a knack for handling crisis situations, which arise when least expected." Germani, *Opportunities in Employee Benefits*, SJPA Reporter 7 (South Jersey Paralegal Association).

- ■ *Job Search in This Area of the Law:*
  - In Google, Bing, or Yahoo, run this search: paralegal job "employee benefits"
  - To narrow the search, add the name of your state or city to the search query

- ■ *More on This Area of the Law on the Net:*
  - www.ifebp.org
  - www.benefitslink.com
  - www.pensionrights.org
  - In Google, Bing, or Yahoo, run this search: What do "employee benefits" lawyers do

16. Entertainment Law

- ■ Types of Client Problem Areas
  - Copyright and trademark law: Apply for government protection for intellectual property, e.g., plays, films, video, music, websites, and novels.
  - Contract law: Help negotiate and draft contracts, and monitor their enforcement.
  - Labor law: Assist clients to comply with the contracts of unions or guilds.
  - Corporate law: Assist in formation of business organizations and mergers; assist on compliance with federal and state reporting laws and regulations.
  - Tax law: Planning and compliance.
  - Report passive royalty income, talent advances, residuals, etc.
  - Allocate expenditures to specific projects.
  - Family law: Assist with related domestic law issues, e.g., prenuptial agreements, divorces, and child custody.

- ■ Miscellaneous Tasks
  - Register copyrights.
  - Help a client affiliate with a guild.
  - Monitor remake and sequel rights to films.
  - Prepare documents to grant a license to use client's music.
  - Check title registrations with the Motion Picture Association of America (MPAA).
  - Read scripts to determine whether clearances are needed for certain kinds of material and references.
  - Apply for permits and licenses.
  - Calculate costs of granting or obtaining property rights.

- ■ *Comment on Paralegal Work in This Area:*
  - "I am a paralegal in the field of entertainment law, one of the fastest growing, and, to me, most

exciting areas of the paralegal profession, and one whose duties are as varied as the practices of the lawyers for whom we work … . I started in a very large Century City firm whose entertainment practice covers everything from songwriters to financing of major motion pictures, and from major recording stars and producers to popular novelists. … My specialty (yes, a specialty within a specialty) is music … . My husband is also an entertainment paralegal who works for 20th Century Fox … . Never, ever a dull moment!" Birkner, *Entertainment Law: A Growing Industry for the Paralegal*, 2 California Paralegal Magazine 7.

- ■ *Job Search in This Area of the Law:*
  - In Google, Bing, or Yahoo, run this search: paralegal job "entertainment law"
  - To narrow the search, add the name of your state or city to the search query

- ■ *More on This Area of the Law on the Net:*
  - www.washlaw.edu/subject/entertainment.html
  - www.hg.org/sport-recreation-law.html
  - www.ascap.com
  - In Google, Bing, or Yahoo, run this search: What do "entertainment law" lawyers do

17. Environmental Law

- ■ Research
  - Research questions pertaining to the environment, land use, water pollution, and the National Environmental Policy Act.
  - Locate and catalog pertinent state and federal statutes, case law, regulations, and law review articles.
  - Obtain nonlegal secondary materials (maps, articles, and books) useful for broadening the information base.
  - Contact, when appropriate, government officials or other informants for information.
  - Obtain and develop personality profiles of members of Congress, members of relevant bureaucracies, and other political figures.
  - Help prepare memoranda of findings, including citations and supporting documents.
  - Develop research notebooks for future reference on new topics in environmental law.
  - Prepare bibliographies on environmental topics.

- ■ Drafting
  - Draft memoranda regarding new federal and state laws, regulations, or findings of research.
  - Draft memoranda discussing pertinent issues, problems, and solutions regarding public policy developments.
  - Draft and edit articles on coastal management programs and problems, conservation, water pollution, and the National Environmental Policy Act.
  - Help edit environmental impact statements.

- Litigation
  - Assist in the preparation of briefs: cite check the brief; develop table of contents, table of authorities, and certificate of service.
  - Locate and schedule witnesses.
  - Gather pertinent research materials (local documents, maps, etc.)[8]

- ***Comment on Paralegal Work in This Area:***
  - (Erin Brockovich was played by Julia Roberts in the movie called *Erin Brockovich*.) Erin Brockovich, "the feisty paralegal helped a California town's residents win $333 million from a utility that had leaked chromium into their water" (www.brockovich.com). "Bill Moyers TV special revealed how the public was kept in the dark about the dangers of toxic chemicals. Every powerful story about fighting for truth and justice has its heroes ... like Erin Brockovich, the paralegal–turned–movie icon who fought against toxic polluters in California" (www.alternet.org/story/10600).
  - Mary Peterson's firm has made a specialty of environmental and land use law. In a major hazardous waste case, "we will try to prove that the paint companies, dry cleaning stores and even the federal government, which used the property to build aircraft during the war," are responsible. "Some of the toxic waste dumped there was cited by federal agencies even back to 1935." Her job is to investigate the types of hazardous wastes and, with the help of the Freedom of Information Act, gather all available evidence. Then she studies it, duplicates, indexes, and writes summaries, which she distributes to the partners and associates. It's a case that has taken eight months so far and may go on for several years "because you don't know what you will uncover tomorrow. The toxins and pollutants could be different. There is no standard, just a constantly changing picture." Edwards, *The General Practice Paralegal*, 8 Legal Assistant Today 49.

- ***Job Search in This Area of the Law:***
  - In Google, Bing, or Yahoo, run this search: paralegal job environmental law
  - To narrow the search, add the name of your state or city to the search query

- ***More on This Area of the Law on the Net:***
  - www.epa.gov
  - www.washlaw.edu/subject/environmental.html
  - www.eli.org
  - In Google, Bing, or Yahoo, run this search: What do environmental law lawyers do

18. Estates, Trusts, And Probate Law

- Estate Planning
  - Collect data (birth dates, fair market value of assets, current assets and liabilities, etc.).
  - Using computer-generated forms, prepare preliminary drafts of wills or trusts.
  - Perform investment analysis in order to provide attorney (who may be the fiduciary of the estate) with information relevant to investment options.

- Office Management
  - Maintain tickler system and the attorney's calendar.
  - Open, index, monitor, and keep current the office file on the client's trust and estate case.
  - Using computer programs, manage the accounting of trusts and estates administered by the office.
  - Act as office law librarian (keeping looseleaf services up to date, etc.).
  - Train secretaries and other paralegals in the system used by the office to handle trusts, estates, and probate cases.
  - Selectively discard certain mail and underline significant parts of other mail.

- Estate of Decedent: Assets phase (physical assets)
  - Collect assets (e.g., bank accounts, custody accounts, insurance proceeds, social security death benefits, safety deposit box contents, and apartment contents).
  - Assist in the valuation of assets.
  - Maintain records (e.g., wills and trusts, vault inventories, powers of attorney, property settlements, fee cards, bill-payment letters).
  - Record and file instruments (e.g., wills and trusts).
  - Notify beneficiaries.
  - Prepare profiles of wills and trusts for attorney review.

- Estate of Decedent: Assets Phase (digital assets)
  - Locate all digital files (documents, photos, etc.).
  - Identify names, addresses, and passwords of digital assets (e.g., email accounts, Facebook, LinkedIn, Twitter, and other social-media accounts, blogs, and other websites).

- Estate of Decedent: Accounting Phase
  - Organize data relevant to taxation of estates.
  - Prepare preliminary drafts of federal and state death tax returns.
  - Apply the income-principal rules to the estate.
  - Prepare accountings: final and accounts current (e.g., set up a petition for a first and final accounting).

- Estate of Decedent: Termination-Distribution Phase
  - Apply for the transfer of securities into the names of the people entitled.
  - Draw checks for the signature of executors.
  - Monitor legacies to charitable clients.
  - File and prepare tax waivers.
  - Assist with closing documents.
  - Calculate distributable net income.
  - Follow up on collection and delivery.

- Litigation
  - Perform legal research.

- Conduct factual research (investigation), e.g., track down the names and addresses of all possible claimants and contact them.
- Prepare pleadings.
- Digest (summarize) depositions; point out inconsistencies in the deposition testimony.
- Prepare drafts of interrogatories.
- Prepare drafts of answers to interrogatories.
- Notarize documents.
- Act as court witness on decedent's signature.

- ■ *Comment on Paralegal Work in This Area:*
  - "What I like best about estate planning is that you work with people on a very individual basis. I don't think that in many other areas of law you get that one-on-one contact with the client. ... You're working with people while they are thinking about the most important things in their lives—their families, their wealth, and how to distribute it, and what they want to happen after they pass on. A lot of the clients contact me directly with their questions for the attorneys. Some of the widows especially are more comfortable calling me with their questions. They seem to think their questions might be 'stupid' and they're embarrassed to ask the attorneys directly. I can take their questions and see that the attorneys respond to them promptly." Bassett, *Top Gun Patricia Adams: Legal Assistant of the Year*, 6 Legal Assistant Today 70.
  - "The position can be very stressful. But it is seldom boring. My typical day involves responding to many telephone inquiries from clients, [writing] memos, or letters requesting additional information concerning life insurance policies, valuation of assets, or simply sending notices of an upcoming hearing 'to all persons entitled,' etc. I draft virtually all documents needed in the administration of an estate, beginning with the initial petition for probate. ... The decedent may have had an interest in a closely-held business, or leave minor or handicapped children, or leave a spouse with no knowledge of the family assets; these all require additional attention. Every case is different. Probate paralegals to some extent must be 'snoopy,' because you do learn a great deal about people, both deceased and living. In most cases your client is facing a difficult time with trepidation and it is your role to provide confidence. The end results are very rewarding." Rose, *Still a Probate Paralegal*, 12 The Journal 5 (Sacramento Valley Paralegal Association).

- ■ *Quotes from Want Ads:*
  - Law firm seeks someone with "experience preparing the 706 estate tax return, asset funding including drafting property deeds and estate planning documents; being a notary public is a plus."
  - Bank has opening for "trust tax administrator, with emphasis on personal and trust planning."

- Paralegal must have "technical understanding of wills and estate plans and terminology; must be self-starter."
- "This is a full-time position with extensive responsibility for both court-supervised and noncourt-supervised estates and trusts."
- Position requires a person who "enjoys writing and proofreading, and who has excellent grammatical skills."
- Job is "for individual who enjoys the complexity and detail of accounting and bookkeeping in a legal environment."
- "Applicants must be prepared to handle tax work."

- ■ *Job Search in This Area of the Law:*
  - In Google, Bing, or Yahoo, run this search: paralegal job estate trust probate
  - To narrow the search, add the name of your state or city to the search query

- ■ *More on This Area of the Law on the Net:*
  - www.actec.org
  - www.washlaw.edu/subject/estate.html
  - www.law.cornell.edu/wex/index.php/Estates_and_Trusts
  - www.hg.org/estate.html
  - In Google, Bing, or Yahoo, run this search: What do estates trusts probate lawyers do

19. Ethics and Professional Responsibility

Paralegals in this area work in two main settings. (1) In large law firms a paralegal can be a conflicts specialist (also called a conflicts analyst or conflicts researcher), helping the firm determine whether a conflict of interest exists between prospective clients and current or former clients. (2) Paralegals also work in state disciplinary agencies or boards that investigate complaints against attorneys for unethical behavior. In addition, paralegals assist attorneys who sue other attorneys for legal malpractice in which the defendant is often charged with negligence and violations of ethics.

- Paralegal Working for a Law Firm
  - Research: Identify all persons or companies with a personal or business relationship with a prospective client; determine whether the firm has ever represented the prospective client and/or any persons or entities related to the prospective client; determine whether the firm has ever represented an opponent of the prospective client and/or any persons or entities related to the opponent of the prospective client.
  - Reports: Notify attorney of data indicating possible conflict of interest.
  - Database work: Update information in client database on current and past clients for purposes of future conflicts checks.

- Paralegal Working for a Disciplinary Agency
  - Screen incoming data on new ethical complaints against attorneys.
  - Help investigate complaints.

- Provide general litigation assistance to disciplinary attorneys during the proceedings at the agency and in court.

- ### Comment on Paralegal Work in This Area:
  - Jane Palmer "does all the research on every prospective client, identifying all the related parties." Her computerized database tells her if the firm has ever represented a party on either side, or been adverse to them. "The most valuable thing has been my experience with the firm, developing somewhat of a corporate memory. The job takes extreme attention to detail. You may not always have all the information you need, so you have to be a detective. Quick response is important; so is making sure to keep things confidential." Sacramento Valley Paralegal Association, *New Responsibilities Given to Paralegals*, The Journal 5.

- ### Job Search in This Area of the Law:
  - In Google, Bing, or Yahoo, run this search: paralegal job conflicts ethics legal malpractice
  - To narrow the search, add the name of your state or city to the search query

- ### More on This Area of the Law on the Net:
  - www.hg.org/practic.html
  - www.legalethics.com
  - www.americanbar.org/groups/professional_responsibility.html
  - www.washlaw.edu/subject/ethics.html
  - In Google, Bing, or Yahoo, run this search: What do ethics legal malpractice lawyers do

20. Family Law

- Problem Areas Covered: Adoption, divorce, contracts (prenuptial agreement, separation agreement, surrogacy agreement, etc.), child support, child custody, annulment, etc.

- Commencement of Action
  - Interview client after attorney has accepted the case.
  - Prepare initial pleadings, including petition, summons and waiver of service, affidavits on child support and child custody, and responses.
  - Draft correspondence to be sent to clients, courts, and other attorneys.
  - Arrange for service of process.

- Temporary Orders
  - Prepare motions for temporary orders, e.g., a temporary injunction, temporary custody and support.
  - Draft notice and request for hearings.
  - Assist in settlement negotiations.
  - Draft stipulations for court orders after negotiations.

- Financial Affidavits
  - Help clients gather and compile financial information.

- Analyze income and expense information provided by the client.
- Coordinate work with accountants, financial advisors, brokers, and other financial experts retained by the client.
- Hire appraisers for real estate, business, and personal property.
- Prepare financial affidavits.

- Discovery
  - Prepare discovery requests.
  - Help clients organize documents and data to respond to discovery requests from the opponent.
  - Organize, index, and summarize materials obtained by discovery.

- Settlement Negotiations
  - Assist attorney in the analysis of proposed settlements.
  - Research legal questions and assist in drafting memoranda and briefs.
  - Assist in drafting separation agreement.

- Hearings
  - Help prepare for hearings on final orders.
  - Assist in the preparation of trial exhibits and trial notebooks.
  - Arrange for expert witnesses; assist in preparing witnesses and the client for trial.
  - Prepare draft of proposed decree.

- Post-Decree
  - Prepare documents for transfers of assets.
  - File and record all transfer documents.
  - Review bills for tax-deductible fees and help prepare opinion letter to client.
  - Draft pleadings for withdrawal from case.

- Special Projects
  - Develop forms for fact gathering from clients.
  - Maintain files on separation-agreement provisions, current case law, resource materials for clients, and experts in various fields (e.g., custody, evaluation, and business appraisals).[9]

- ### Comment on Paralegal Work in This Area:
  - Karen Dunn "draws considerable satisfaction from a divorce case where the client was a woman in her sixties whose husband had left her, a situation that created predictable distress, notably during the discussion of financial issues. She was able to tell me things she couldn't tell the attorney. I found out she had a thyroid condition, so she was able to get more money in the end. I worked with her on the financial affidavit and drafted temporary orders to provide child support and spousal maintenance until the decree was entered." Edwards, *The General Practice Paralegal*, 8 Legal Assistant Today 49.
  - "As the only paralegal in a one-attorney family-law practice, my job responsibilities are numerous. I work for an attorney who believes her paralegal should handle nearly all the legal functions she does,

with the exception of appearing in court on behalf of clients, taking depositions, and giving legal advice. My skills are used to the maximum, as I gather and organize all case information, allowing the attorney to prepare for court and be more cost-effective. I am the liaison person between clients and the attorney. I am able to deal with the human, emotional aspects of our clients, and not just the technical aspects of the law. As each person is different, so is every case, which makes this job a continuing challenge." Lenihan, *Role of the Family Law Paralegal*, 10 Paragram 6 (Oregon Paralegal Association).

- ■ *Quotes from Want Ads:*
  - ▪ Seeking "a highly motivated person with excellent organizational skills and the ability to interface with clients."
  - ▪ "Two swamped attorneys need reliable paralegal to work in fully computerized office. Must have excellent research and writing skills."
  - ▪ Applicant must be "self-motivated, well-organized person who has initiative and can assume responsibility."
  - ▪ Position requires "ability, experience, and attention to detail."
  - ▪ "Looking for very professional applicants."

- ■ *Job Search in This Area of the Law:*
  - ▪ In Google, Bing, or Yahoo, run this search: paralegal job family law
  - ▪ To narrow the search, add the name of your state or city to the search query

- ■ *More on This Area of the Law on the Net:*
  - ▪ www.washlaw.edu/subject/family.html
  - ▪ www.hg.org/family.html
  - ▪ www.divorcecentral.com
  - ▪ www.americanbar.org/groups/family_law.html
  - ▪ In Google, Bing, or Yahoo, run this search: What do family law lawyers do

21. Gaming Law

- ■ Applications
  - ▪ Obtain applications and related documents needed by a business to acquire licenses and permits to operate a gaming business: state gaming business license, local gaming business license, liquor license, state sales/use tax permit, health permit, unemployment insurance registration, and workers' compensation clearance.
  - ▪ Help conduct due diligence and licensing history research.
  - ▪ Coordinate the acquisition of gaming bonds.
  - ▪ Arrange meetings for the execution of licensing applications, affidavits, and declarations.

- ■ Compliance
  - ▪ Research business license and land use regulatory obligations.
  - ▪ Maintain a tickler system for timely filings of compliance reports.

- ▪ File board meeting agendas and related materials.
- ▪ When a regulatory agency investigates the internal operations of a client, assist in providing information on finances, securities, product sales, political contributions, and personal data on senior management.

- ■ Collection and Judgments
  - ▪ Assist on out-of-state (including international) marker collection cases.
  - ▪ Prepare and file judgment renewals.

- ■ *Comment on Paralegal Work in This Area:*
  - ▪ "The commercial casino industry is one of the most heavily regulated industries in the nation." In this position, the "work done for clients translates into a business operation that you can see, watch prosper, and grow. Whether it is assisting a client in the opening of the five-star restaurant … or the newest casino hotel resort, the result of your hard work manifests itself into things that are seen and realized." L. Oehlschlaeger, *The Expanding Role of the Paralegal in the Gaming Industry*, Career Chronicle 42 (NALA).

- ■ *Job Search in This Area of the Law:*
  - ▪ In Google, Bing, or Yahoo, run this search: paralegal job gaming gambling law
  - ▪ To narrow the search, add the name of your state or city to the search query

- ■ *More on This Area of the Law on the Net:*
  - ▪ www.hg.org/gaming.html
  - ▪ www.gaminglawmasters.com
  - ▪ In Google, Bing, or Yahoo, run this search: What do gaming gambling lawyers do

22. Government Contract Law

- ■ Calendar
  - ▪ Maintain calendar for appeal board and court appearances.
  - ▪ On the tickler, record dates when briefs and other filings are due.

- ■ Claims
  - ▪ Gather, review, summarize, and index client files.
  - ▪ Assist in drafting contract claims.
  - ▪ Conduct preliminary research on selected legal issues.

- ■ Appeals
  - ▪ Draft and answer interrogatories and requests for production of documents.
  - ▪ Summarize and index answers to discovery.
  - ▪ Assist in drafting appeals.
  - ▪ Prepare questions for witnesses and summarize their prior testimony.
  - ▪ Maintain documents during hearing.

- ■ Posthearing Briefs
  - ▪ Summarize and index transcripts.
  - ▪ Assist with analysis of government's brief.
  - ▪ Conduct preliminary research on selected issues.
  - ▪ Assist in drafting the posthearing brief.[10]

- **Job Search in This Area of the Law:**
  - In Google, Bing, or Yahoo, run this search: paralegal job government contracts
  - To narrow the search, add the name of your state or city to the search query

- **More on This Area of the Law on the Net:**
  - www.law.cornell.edu/wex/index.php/Government_contracts
  - www.washlaw.edu/doclaw/subject/prop5m.html
  - In Google, Bing, or Yahoo, run this search: What do government contracts lawyers do

23. Immigration Law

- Providing information on: Visas, permanent residency, nonimmigrant status, registration, citizenship, and deportation.

- Deportation: Provide assistance with clients facing deportation proceedings.

- Referral: Refer individuals to foreign consulates, nationality organizations, government officials, etc., for assistance concerning their immigration status.

- Applications/Forms: Assist in filling out visa applications, permanent residency applications, etc.; monitor consular processing procedure.

- **Comment on Paralegal Work in This Area:**
  - "This is not a specialty for the faint-hearted or the misanthrope. The immigration paralegal may deal with much more than the timely filing of paperwork. One distinguishing feature of immigration work is our knowledge of intensely personal aspects of the client's life. We know his criminal record, the success and failure of his personal life, how much money he makes, and his dreams and aspirations … . Some clients have a very laissez-faire attitude towards perjury, and may invite the paralegal to participate without a blush. In America, [said one client] you lie to your attorney. In my country, you cook up the lie with your attorney." Myers & Raman, *Sweet-Talking Clients and Intransigent Bureaucrats*, 15 National Paralegal Reporter 4 (NFPA).
  - Immigration law is "all about seeking available benefits on behalf of those who are eligible for them under the law. This field is personally broadening in that you encounter people from all over the world, and in the process of assisting them, you become a part of their life journey and experience." I. Lefebre, *Immigration Law*, 23 Legal Assistant Today 88.

- **Job Search in This Area of the Law:**
  - In Google, Bing, or Yahoo, run this search: paralegal job immigration
  - To narrow the search, add the name of your state or city to the search query

- **More on This Area of the Law on the Net:**
  - www.uscis.gov
  - www.washlaw.edu/subject/immigration.html
  - www.aila.org
  - In Google, Bing, or Yahoo, run this search: What do immigration lawyers do

24. Insurance Law

Insurance defense work consists of representing insurance companies that challenge claims brought against them (or against their policy holders). A paralegal in this field might work for a law firm hired by an insurance company or may work within an insurance company itself. The most common kind of insurance defense work involves personal injury (PI) claims that arise out of liability policies. The following overview covers paralegals who work for insurance companies.

- Claims
  - Assist in processing disputed claims within the company.
  - Provide trial assistance.

- Outside Counsel
  - Act as liaison between the insurance company and the outside law firm hired by the company to litigate cases brought by or against the company or its policy holders.
  - Help with recordkeeping and oversight of bills submitted by outside counsel.

- Compliance
  - Update government regulations on the insurance industry to assure that insurance policies and other company products are in compliance.
  - Prepare applications for new insurance products to obtain approval from the state departments of insurance.

- Monitoring and Research
  - Monitor regulations of agencies and statutes of the legislatures that affect the insurance industry, particularly the committees of the legislature with jurisdiction over the industry.
  - Provide factual and legal research on inquiries that come into the office from agents and brokers.

- **Comment on Paralegal Work in This Area:**
  - "Compliance is an insurance industry term that refers to keeping the company and its products in compliance with state and federal law, and procuring licenses for the company in states where it is not licensed. Compliance is a good field for paralegals because there is opportunity to work autonomously and also to advance within most companies." I am a "Senior Compliance Analyst" at a life insurance company. "I have met many paralegals who are compliance analysts, compliance specialists, and compliance managers." Maston, *Insurance*, The Citator 8 (Paralegal Association of Central Ohio).

- "Since the attorneys are out of the office frequently, I have a lot of client contact and I also am the first person from the firm to contact the client. I also work with the client in drafting the initial discovery responses." T. Creech, *A Look at Insurance Defense Work*, 22 Legal Assistant Today 88.

- ▪ *Job Search in This Area of the Law:*
  - In Google, Bing, or Yahoo, run this search: paralegal job "insurance law"
  - To narrow the search, add the name of your state or city to the search query

- ▪ *More on This Area of the Law on the Net:*
  - www.law.cornell.edu/topics/insurance.html
  - www.washlaw.edu/subject/insurance.html
  - In Google, Bing, or Yahoo, run this search: What do insurance law lawyers do

25. Intellectual Property Law

Paralegals in this area work on copyrights, patents, and trademarks.

- ▪ Copyrights: Application
  - Help the client apply for copyright registration for a novel, play, or other "original works of authorship" with the U.S. Copyright Office.
  - Help apply for protection in foreign countries.
  - Collect data for the application (e.g., name and nature of the work, date completed, name of creator/author, its owner).
  - Help identify the classification for the copyright.
  - Examine accuracy of certificate-of-copyright registration.

- ▪ Copyrights: Marketing
  - Identify all potential users/licensees of the copyright.
  - Help prepare contracts.

- ▪ Copyrights: Infringement
  - Conduct investigations to determine whether an infringement exists, e.g., compare the copyrighted work with the alleged infringing work.
  - Provide general litigation assistance.

- ▪ Patents: Application
  - Help the inventor apply for a patent with the U.S. Patent and Trademark Office.
  - Help describe the invention by using designs, diagrams, notebooks, etc.
  - Check technical libraries to determine the current state of the art.
  - Conduct a patent search.
  - Determine filing fees.
  - Apply for protection in foreign countries.
  - Monitor the responses from government offices.
  - Examine certificate of patent for accuracy.

- ▪ Patents: Marketing the invention
  - Help identify potential licensees.

- Study the market, solicit bids, conduct financial checks, etc.
- Help prepare contracts.

- ▪ Patents: Infringement
  - Conduct investigation on products that may have violated the patent.
  - Provide general litigation assistance.

- ▪ Trademarks: Registration
  - Research trademark files or order search of trademark (or trade name) preliminary to an application before the U.S. Patent and Trademark Office.
  - Examine indexes and directories.
  - Conduct investigations to determine when the mark was first used, where, on what products, etc.
  - Prepare foreign trademark applications.
  - Respond to actions taken by government offices.
  - Examine the certificate of trademark for accuracy.
  - Maintain files for renewals.

- ▪ Trademarks: Infringement
  - Conduct investigations into who else used the mark, when, where, in what markets, etc.
  - Provide general litigation assistance.

- ▪ *Comment on Paralegal Work in This Area:*
  - "With the right training, trademark paralegals can find richly rewarding experiences waiting for them, whether they remain in paralegal work or go on to build careers in some other facet of trademark law. Trademark work is very dynamic." Wilkinson, *The Case for a Career in Trademark Law*, 7 Legal Professional 29.
  - "Paula Rein was a trademark paralegal before such a job title was even invented. Her career has spanned over 19 years, leading her to some of the biggest corporations and law firms in New York City. Her extensive knowledge of trademark administration has made her one of the most resourceful trademark paralegals in her occupation. In her current 'diversified position,' at a law firm that specializes in intellectual property, she works on the cases of clients in the food and service industries and professional associations. Paula thrives in her current position." Scior, *Paralegal Profile*, Postscript 13 (Manhattan Paralegal Association).

- ▪ *Job Search in This Area of the Law:*
  - In Google, Bing, or Yahoo, run this search: paralegal job intellectual property
  - To narrow the search, add the name of your state or city to the search query

- ▪ *More on This Area of the Law on the Net:*
  - www.copyright.gov
  - www.uspto.gov
  - www.aipla.org
  - www.washlaw.edu/subject/intellectual.html
  - In Google, Bing, or Yahoo, run this search: What do intellectual property lawyers do

26. International law

Paralegals working in international law may be employed by law firms in the United States that represent clients with issues (usually commercial) of international law. Also, the law departments of multinational corporations have attorneys and paralegals on their staff who work on legal problems involving foreign countries. The following example covers a paralegal working on a "dumping" case in international trade. Dumping occurs when a manufacturer tries to control the market for a product in another country by selling the product below its cost or below the price of competing products in the other country.

- Investigation
  - Examine the normal behavior in the industry or market affected by the alleged dumping.
  - Do statistical research (cost and price data).
  - Prepare profiles of domestic competitors.

- Preparation of Documents
  - Help prepare presentation before the U.S. Commerce Department.
  - Help prepare presentation before the U.S. Court of International Trade.

- Accounting Research
  - Coordination of data from members of Congress, foreign embassies, U.S. Department of State, and the U.S. Special Trade Representative.

- *Comment on Paralegal Work in This Area:*
  - Steven Stark works "40–50 hours a week, specializing in international legal assisting, a hot area, while the Japanese are busy buying up American properties. [Steve became the liaison for the firm's Tokyo branch office. He originally expected to stay at the firm only three years but found that] the longer you're here, the more they value you. New things still come up. You work with the constant tension of everyone being expected to perform at a very high level at all times. This is a high-stakes game, with million and billion dollar deals. It's a peaked, emotional atmosphere, with long hours." Milano, *Career Profiles*, 8 Legal Assistant Today 35.
  - "Currently about seven paralegals and 35 Arnold & Porter attorneys work on the international arbitration team. ... Although international commercial arbitration (disputes between or among international parties of different country jurisdictions) has been in existence for a while, my primary focus is international investment arbitration (disputes by foreign investors against the country in which they invested). ... While I work on international arbitration matters exclusively, I also manage and train incoming paralegals in my department." Kelby Ballena, *My Specialty*, 28 Paralegal Today 38.

- *Job Search in This Area of the Law:*
  - In Google, Bing, or Yahoo, run this search: paralegal job international law
  - To narrow the search, add the name of your state or city to the search query

- *More on This Area of the Law on the Net:*
  - www.americanbar.org/groups/international_law .html
  - www.law.cornell.edu/topics/international.html
  - www.washlaw.edu/subject/foreign.html
  - In Google, Bing, or Yahoo, run this search: What do international law lawyers do

27. Judicial Administration

Many courts have law clerks (attorneys who help judges decide cases and write opinions) and administrative clerks (attorneys and nonattorneys who help with the administrative aspects of the court). Recently the U.S. Supreme Court had an opening for an assistant clerk to help screen incoming cases. Some courts have positions that use the paralegal title (e.g., *procedural motions paralegal* in the U.S. Court of Appeals for the Ninth Circuit). A more common title, however, is *judicial assistant*. Examples of tasks performed include determining whether the parties have been properly notified of trial dates, checking filings and proposed orders from attorneys to determine whether anything appears inappropriate or premature, obtaining additional information on a case needed by a judge, etc.

- *Comment on Paralegal Work in This Area:*
  - "The Shreveport City Court has employed me as its paralegal in the civil department for the past six years. The Baton Rouge City Court employs several paralegals." We handle many matters such as determining if the legal delays for pleading have expired "before initialing the pleading and passing it on to the clerk or judge for signature. The most important task is the handling of default judgments. I must certify that proper service has been made. Perhaps I could be called a 'nitpicker' about these cases, but the judge acts on my certificate that everything is in order. It is always challenging to stay informed on our constantly changing procedural laws; I must keep a set of the Civil Procedure [laws] at my desk." Waterman, *The Court's Paralegal*, 3 NWLPA News 5 (Northwest Louisiana Paralegal Association).

- *Job Search in This Area of the Law:*
  - In Google, Bing, or Yahoo, run this search: paralegal job "judicial assistant"
  - To narrow the search, add the name of your state or city to the search query
  - In Google, Bing, or Yahoo, run this search: aa courts (substitute the name of your state for "aa"). Look for links to "employment," "careers," or "jobs" on the site of any court in your state.
  - In Google, Bing, or Yahoo, run this search: aa "federal courts" (substitute the name of your state for "aa"). On the site of any of the federal court in your state, look for links to "employment," "careers," or "jobs."

■ *More on Judicial Administration on the Net:*
- www.fjaa.net/FJAA/FJAA.html (judicial assistants)
- www.law.cornell.edu/wex/index.php/Judicial_ administration
- www.ncsc.org
- In Google, Bing, or Yahoo, run this search: What does a judicial assistant do

28. Labor And Employment Law

■ Investigation
- Sexual harassment.
- Wrongful discharge.
- Violation of occupational safety and health laws.
- Violation of labor laws on collective bargaining, union organizing, arbitration, etc.
- Violation of Civil Rights Act protecting against discrimination on the basis of race, national origin, sex, or physical handicap.
- Violation of Age Discrimination in Employment Act.
- Violation of Americans with Disabilities Act.

■ Compliance
- Assist companies in implementing policies on drug and alcohol testing; AIDS in the workplace; race, sex, disability, and age discrimination, etc.

■ Litigation Assistance
- Help bring labor disputes before the National Labor Relations Board (NLRB), state labor board, civil service commission, human rights board, courts, etc.
- Miscellaneous tasks: Maintain case files, digest and index data in files, arrange for depositions, help draft petition and other pleadings, maintain tickler system of due dates, prepare exhibits, prepare statistical data, help prepare appeals.

■ *Comment on Paralegal Work in This Area:*
- "My experience in the labor and employment area has proven to be both diverse and unique. It is diverse because of the various labor-related issues accessible to me as a paralegal. It is unique because it is an area of specialty that involves very few paralegals in my part of the state." Batke, *Labor and Employment Paralegal*, The Citator 3 (Paralegal Association of Central Ohio).
- "In the labor law area, I was responsible for doing background research, preparing witnesses and drafting arbitration briefs. I also assisted with the drafting of revised language during contract negotiations with unions." Diebold, *A Paralegal of Another Kind*, 16 Facts and Findings 38 (NALA).

■ *Job Search in This Area of the Law:*
- In Google, Bing, or Yahoo, run this search: paralegal job labor employment law
- To narrow the search, add the name of your state or city to the search query

■ *More on This Area of the Law on the Net:*
- www.washlaw.edu/doclaw/subject/emply5m.html
- www.hg.org/employ.html
- www.law.cornell.edu/wex/index.php/Labor
- In Google, Bing, or Yahoo, run this search: What do labor employment lawyers do

29. Landlord And Tenant Law

Paralegals in real estate law firms occasionally become involved in commercial lease cases, such as a dispute over the interpretation of the lease of a supermarket at a large shopping mall. Such landlord-tenant cases, however, are not as common as the cases that arise between landlords and the tenants who live in the apartments they rent. For example, a landlord of a small apartment seeks to evict a tenant for nonpayment of rent. Many of these cases are handled by publicly funded legal aid offices that do not charge fees.

In a few states, nonattorneys are allowed to provide assistance and advice to landlords or tenants in eviction cases. In California, for example, such individuals are called *unlawful detainer assistants* (see Chapter 4). The following overview of duties covers a paralegal who works for a law firm that handles commercial leases.

■ General Duties
- Abstract all leases in files.
- Abstract all amendments to leases in files.
- Enter all alerts and review them for needed action.
- Enter/update lease financials.
- Upload all documents into central lease database.
- Run monthly lease reports.
- Update monthly lease reports.
- Revise financials/clauses/data leases per landlord notices/communications.
- Link lease clauses to PDF pages in actual hard copy of lease.
- Review foreign rents submitted to the office.
- Maintain/organize hard-copy lease files.
- Maintain letter-of-credit reduction schedule.
- Review and obtain insurance binders (subtenants).
- Review insurance binders.
- Act as liaison for audits.
- Submit reconciliation statements.
- Track audit process.
- Draft letters to landlords on financial/ledger information.

■ *Comment on Paralegal Work in This Area:*
- "The Legal Action Center is the largest nongovernmental social service agency in the state. As a paralegal, Virginia Farley handles all eviction calls to the landlord-tenant unit. Three afternoons a week are designated intake times. She screens all eviction cases, determines whether the applicant is eligible for free assistance according to the Center's guidelines, recommends a plan once a case is accepted and assists in carrying out the plan under an attorney's supervision. [After arriving in the city], Farley made a commitment to work directly with the poor and started serving as a volunteer in

five organizations until a job opened up for her at the Legal Action Center." Roche, *Paralegal Profile*, 4 Findings and Conclusions 5 (Washington State Paralegal Association).

- **Job Search in This Area of the Law:**
  - In Google, Bing, or Yahoo, run this search: paralegal job landlord tenant lease law
  - To narrow the search, add the name of your state or city to the search query

- **More on This Area of the Law on the Net:**
  - www.law.cornell.edu/wex/landlord-tenant_law
  - www.hg.org/landlord.html
  - In Google, Bing, or Yahoo, run this search: What do landlord and tenant lawyers do

30. Law Librarianship

There is a separate degree that a law librarian can obtain. This degree, however, is not a requirement to be a law librarian. A number of small or medium-sized law offices are hiring paralegals to perform library chores exclusively or in combination with paralegal duties on cases.

- Administration
  - Order books (traditional and e-books) for law library.
  - File looseleaf services and pocket parts in appropriate volumes.
  - Pay bills of library vendors.
  - Test and recommend computer equipment, software, and services for the law library.
  - Prepare budget for library.
- Cite Checking
  - Check the citations in briefs, speeches, articles, opinion letters, and other legal documents to determine the accuracy of quoted material.
  - Check the citations to determine the accuracy of citation format according to local court rules, the *Uniform System of Citation* (the Bluebook), or other citation guidelines.
- Research
  - Perform factual research.
  - Perform legal research.
- Training
  - Train office staff in traditional legal research techniques.
  - Train office staff in computer research, e.g., Westlaw Next, Lexis Advance, Google Scholar.
  - Train office staff in cite checking.

- **Comment on Paralegal Work in This Area:**
  - "I suppose my entry into the law librarianship profession might be considered unorthodox because I had no formal educational courses in librarianship. My experience was that of working first as a legal secretary and later evolving into a paralegal. My job in a small general practice firm included taking care of the office library such as filing supplements

and pocket parts (because no one else would do it!!); doing the bookkeeping and paying the bills." I did some legal research "as an extension of legal drafting." "In all my working years (and they are many) I had the greatest satisfaction from my work as a law librarian because each day I learned new things." Lewek, *The Legal Assistant as Law Librarian*, 17 Facts & Findings 28 (NALA).

- **Job Search in This Area of the Law:**
  - In Google, Bing, or Yahoo, run this search: paralegal job library
  - To narrow the search, add the name of your state or city to the search query

- **More on This Area of the Law on the Net:**
  - www.aallnet.org
  - www.washlaw.edu/subject/law.libraries.html
  - In Google, Bing, or Yahoo, run this search: What do law librarians do

31. Law Office Administration

At the beginning of Chapter 14, you will find a detailed job description of the legal administrator and of the paralegal manager. (See Exhibits 14-2 and 14-3.) Some experienced paralegals move into management positions at a law office. This might involve helping to administer the entire office, or one component of it, such as the administration of all the paralegals in the office or the administration of the paralegals and other support personnel working on a large case. As we saw in Chapter 1, paralegals who supervise other paralegals in large offices have formed an association, the International Practice Management Association (IPMA). In many smaller offices, paralegals perform office management duties along with paralegal duties.

- **Comment on Paralegal Work in This Area:**
  - "The partners at the firm decided to upgrade their paralegal program and needed a nonlawyer to run it. They offered Linda Katz the new position. The firm is segmented into practice areas, with paralegals dispersed throughout the areas. They report to supervising attorneys for work assignments each day. I serve as administrative supervisor, assuring consistency in how paralegals are treated and utilized, and what opportunities they have for benefits and advancement." Milano, *Career Profiles*, 8 Legal Assistant Today 35.
  - "A good paralegal litigation manager [in a large document case] has both strong paralegal skills and strong management skills. Such a manager must be able to analyze the case's organizational needs, develop methods to cope with them effectively, and often must act as paralegal, office manager and computer expert—all in a day's work." Kaufman, *The Litigation Manager*, 6 Legal Professional 55.

- **Job Search in This Area of the Law:**
  - In Google, Bing, or Yahoo, run this search: paralegal job manager legal administrator

- To narrow the search, add the name of your state or city to the search query

- ***More on This Area of the Law on the Net:***
  - www.paralegalmanagement.org
  - www.alanet.org
  - In Google, Bing, or Yahoo, run this search: What do law legal administrators do (also run this search: What do paralegal managers do)

32. Legislation

- Monitoring
  - Keep track of all events, persons, and organizations involved in the passing of legislation relevant to the clients of the office.

- Legislative History
  - Locate or compile the legislative history of a statute.

- Helping Draft Proposed Legislation

- Lobbying
  - Prepare reports and studies on the subject of proposed legislation.
  - Arrange for and help prepare witnesses to testify at legislative hearings.

- ***Comment on Paralegal Work in This Area:***
  - Margo Horner "is a legislative analyst for the National Federation of Independent Business (NFIB). With paralegal training and a master's degree in history, her job is research, creating legislative strategy, working with [legislators] and their staffs to produce legislation favorable to [NFIB]. Margo likes the frenetic tempo of her life." Smith, *Margo,* 1 Legal Assistant Today 14.

- ***Job Search in This Area of the Law:***
  - In Google, Bing, or Yahoo, run this search: paralegal job lobbying
  - To narrow the search, add the name of your state or city to the search query

- ***More on This Area of the Law on the Net:***
  - www.law.cornell.edu/wex/index.php/Legislation
  - en.wikipedia.org/wiki/Lobbying
  - In Google, Bing, or Yahoo, run this search: What do lobbyists do

33. Litigation (Civil)

Civil litigation involves court disputes in every area of the law other than a case where the government is charging (prosecuting) someone for the commission of a crime. Civil litigation can thus potentially involve every specialty other than criminal law. Also, litigation has many specialties such as medical malpractice and employment discrimination.

- File Monitoring
  - Index all files.
  - Write case profiles based on information in the files.
  - Organize, index, and digest documents obtained through answers to interrogatories, depositions, and other discovery devices.
  - Encode documents into a computer database.

- Investigation
  - Locate records: medical, police, birth, death, marriage, adoption, child custody, incorporation filings, etc.
  - Prepare a profit history report of a company.
  - Identify the corporate structure of a parent company and its subsidiaries.
  - Trace a UCC (Uniform Commercial Code) filing.
  - Find out from court dockets if a particular merchant is being sued, has sued before, etc.
  - Identify the "real owner" of a building.
  - Check housing code agency to find out if a landlord has other building code violations against it on record.

- Discovery (e-discovery and traditional discovery)
  - Access e-discovery data (e.g., emails, blogs, and PDF files).
  - Draft interrogatories.
  - Draft answers to interrogatories.
  - Draft deposition questions.
  - Help prepare witnesses for deposition.
  - Prepare witness books for deposition.
  - Arrange time and place of deposition.
  - Draft requests for admissions.
  - Draft answers to requests for admissions.
  - Draft requests for production of documents.
  - Draft answers to production requests.
  - Ensure that responses to discovery sent out by the office do not contain privileged material.
  - Index and digest discovery data.
  - Work with computer programmer in designing a system to manage discovery documents.

- Filings/Serving
  - File and/or serve documents in court, at agencies, on parties, on attorneys, etc.

- General Assistance
  - Arrange for clients and others to be interviewed.
  - Coordinate ADR (alternative dispute resolution), e.g., help schedule arbitration or mediation.
  - Arrange for expert witnesses to appear in court or at depositions.
  - Reconstruct (from a large collection of disparate records and other evidence) what happened at a particular time and place.
  - Assist clients in completing information questionnaire, especially in class-action cases.
  - Help organize the trial notebook containing items the attorney will need during the trial, such as charts and tables to be used as exhibits.
  - Evaluate prospective jurors from jury book and during voir dire.
  - Sit at counsel's table at trial to take notes and be available to assist trial attorney, e.g., locate documents in digital files the attorney needs for questioning a witness on the stand.
  - Attend (and report on) hearings in related cases.

- Supervise the encoding of documents on a case in litigation.
- Help prepare the notice of appeal.
- Order the trial transcript
- Locate testimony in the transcript needed by the attorney drafting the appellate brief.

- Legal Research
  - Shepardize or KeyCite authority in appellate briefs; perform other cite-check duties.
  - Write preliminary memos and briefs.
  - Prepare bibliographies of source materials related to a case in litigation.

- Pleadings
  - Write preliminary draft of pleadings using standard forms and/or adapting other pleadings written by attorneys on similar cases.

- Experts
  - Assist in obtaining expert opinions for attorneys on taxation, accounting, statistics, economics (e.g., calculation of damages), etc.

- Court Witness.
  - Act as witness if the paralegal did the service of process.
  - Act as witness concerning data uncovered or photographed (e.g., the condition of an apartment building).

- *Comment on Paralegal Work in This Area:*
  - "There are boxes and boxes with an infinite number of documents to be indexed. There are depositions to be summarized. There are cases whose cites need checking. There are trips to the courthouse downtown. There is red-lining of documents to determine changes between two documents. There is Bates-stamping of documents. And there are the exciting trips to visit clients." Lasky, *Impressions of a New Paralegal*, 17 Reporter 5 (Los Angeles Paralegal Association).
  - "Initially, it was overwhelming with the number of files and the names to learn and things to remember, but with help, I learned skills and techniques and polished them day after day as each new case brought with it new quirks and new challenges. I've attended depositions, shaft inspections, and pig farm operations. I've calculated medical expenses, reviewed medical records, and been baffled at how salesmen keep time records! But the ultimate of all experiences, I have to admit, are the trials. You prepare and prepare and hope that you haven't missed any of the details. Then before you know it, the jury has been selected and you're off! The trials keep your adrenaline flowing. They frazzle your patience. They show you your limitations. They elevate you when you win. They shake your confidence when you lose." Riske, *In the Limelight*, 7 Red River Review 4 (Red River Valley Paralegal Association).

- "For almost six years now … , I've experienced the variety (and the drudgery) of preparing civil cases for trial. I've spent countless hours photocopying [and scanning] documents never read by any judge or jury, or worst of all, by anyone else. I've tracked down witnesses and encouraged them to talk, only to find out that they know nothing about the case. In this business of endless paper where no two cases are alike, I've come to understand … that flexibility is essential and a sense of humor is invaluable in dealing with people, be they stressed out attorneys or reluctant witnesses." Vore, *A Litigation Recipe*, 16 On Point 4 (National Capital Area Paralegal Association).
- Rebecca McLaughlin tells of a particularly memorable event during her experience as a paralegal. "It was a few minutes after 12:00 noon on Friday, and presiding Judge Barbour always recesses court at precisely 12:30 on Fridays. The Government's star witness was on the stand and denied he had ever seen a certain letter. One of the trial attorneys motioned me to counsel table and asked if we had any proof that the witness had, in fact, seen this letter." Since there were well over 900 defense exhibits, almost 300 government exhibits, and well over 40 file cabinets filled with supporting documents, Rebecca felt little hope for success [in finding out quickly]. "She hurried across the street to the office, found the witness'[s] original copy of the letter with his handwritten notes in the margin, and returned to the courtroom with a BIG SMILE. The witness was impeached with his own document minutes before recess." "Later, Rebecca received a well-deserved standing ovation from the attorneys, and all the trial team members. It was the highlight of her career." Johnson, *MALA Spotlight: Rebecca McLaughlin*, 8 The Assistant 17 (Mississippi Paralegal Association).

- *Quotes from Want Ads:*
  - "Excellent writing skills and attention to detail are absolute requirements."
  - "Plaintiff's medical malpractice firm seeks non-smoker with word processing, spreadsheet, and database management abilities."
  - Position requires "extensive writing, document summarizing, and medical records research."
  - Must have an ability "to work independently in handling cases from inception through trial preparation; familiarity with drafting motions and pleadings is essential."
  - High-energy candidate "needs to be assertive and should have an excellent academic background."
  - "Wanted: a sharp, take-charge litigation paralegal."
  - "Knowledge of computerized litigation support is essential; good communications and organizational skills are a must."
  - "Candidate must be a multitasker with strong computer skills in Word, Excel, Summation,

Concordance, Access, and document management databases."

- "Applicant must possess a thorough working knowledge of all phases of trial work."
- "Successful candidate will be professional, prompt, pleasant and personable. No egomaniacs or job hoppers, please."
- "Overtime flexibility required."
- "Defense litigation paralegal needed. Must be a self-starter with the ability to accept unstructured responsibility."
- "Applicant must have a thorough knowledge of state and federal court procedures."
- Position requires an ability "to organize and manage documents in large multi-party litigation."
- "Applicants must possess strong supervisory, analytic, writing, and investigative skills, and an ability to perform under pressure."
- "Position requires good analytical and writing skills, and the ability to organize and control several projects simultaneously."
- "Deposition summarizer needed; work in your own home on your own computer."
- "Part-time proofreader for deposition summaries needed."

- **■ *Job Search in This Area of the Law:***
  - In Google, Bing, or Yahoo, run this search: paralegal job litigation
  - To narrow the search, add the name of your state or city to the search query

- **■ *More on This Area of the Law on the Net:***
  - www.americanbar.org/groups/litigation.html
  - www.justice.org
  - www.dri.org
  - www.theolp.org
  - In Google, Bing, or Yahoo, run this search: What do litigation trial lawyers do

34. Military Law

In the U.S. Navy, a nonattorney who assists attorneys in the practice of law is called a *legalman*. Depending upon the assignment, the legalman can work in a large variety of areas of the law, e.g., admiralty law, contracts, and military justice. Similar work is performed by paralegal specialists in the U.S. Army. The following military paralegal job functions are not limited to paralegals in any particular branch of the armed services.

- ■ Military Proceedings
  - Assist in processing the following proceedings: Special court-martial, general court-martial, courts of inquiry, line-of-duty investigations, reclassification board proceedings, etc.
  - Prepare orders designating membership of special and general courts-martial and courts of inquiry.
  - Assure that charges are properly prepared and that specifications are complete and accurate.
  - Make initial determination on jurisdiction of court, status of accused, and subject matter of offenses.

- Examine completed records of investigations and other records requiring legal review to ensure that they are administratively correct.
  - Prepare court-martial sentencing orders.
  - Assure that records of court-martial are correct and complete before disposing of case.
  - Transmit bad-conduct discharge court-martial cases to appropriate officials.

- ■ Claims against the Government
  - Conduct examinations.
  - Help process claims against the United States, e.g., under the Federal Tort Claims Act.
  - Manage claim funds.
  - Undertake research on FLITE (Federal Legal Information through Electronics).
  - Write briefs.

- ■ Administrative Duties
  - Manage records of all court-martial and claim cases within command.
  - Maintain law library.
  - Examine and distribute incoming correspondence, directives, publications, and other communications.
  - Catalog and file books, periodicals, newsletters, etc.
  - Maintain records of discipline within command.
  - Administer office budget.
  - Orient new personnel and monitor their training.

- ■ Court Reporting
  - Use the steno-mask to record legal proceedings.
  - Prepare charges to the jury.
  - Mark exhibits as they are entered into evidence.
  - Transcribe and assemble records of the proceeding.

- **■ *Comment on Paralegal Work in This Area:***
  - "I have been working for the Office of the Staff Judge Advocate (SJA) at Fort Ord, California. The SJA is the Army's lawyer. We serve a military community of just over 90,000 people. Staff within the SJA consists of a combination of military and civilian attorneys, paralegals, legal clerks, and court reporters. I am responsible for claims filed against the federal government under the Federal Tort Claims Act. I am responsible for discovery and investigative efforts, determining legal issues, writing memoranda of law and recommending settlement or denial. Job satisfaction for paralegal professionals is high in the U.S. government. I know that, should I desire to re-enter the civilian work sector, my experience and knowledge of the government legal systems will uniquely qualify me to work for any firm that deals with the government." Richards, *Marching to a Different Drummer: Paralegal Work in the Military*, 2 California Paralegal Magazine 8.

- **■ *Job Search in This Area of the Law:***
  - In Google, Bing, or Yahoo, run this search: paralegal job military
  - Also check the following sites:

- usmilitary.about.com/od/enlistedjob1/a/ln.htm (legalman)
- www.goarmy.com (type "paralegal specialist" in the search box

- *More on This Area of the Law on the Net:*
- www.hg.org/war.html
- www.law.cornell.edu/wex/index.php/Military
- www.washlaw.edu/doclaw/subject/miltary5m.html
- In Google, Bing, or Yahoo, run this search: What do military lawyers do

35. Municipal Finance Law

Attorneys in this area (also called *public finance*) assist governments, nonprofit agencies, and home businesses obtain funding for projects that have a strong public purpose, e.g., libraries, city halls, convention centers.

- Document Preparation
  - Prepare first drafts of basic documents, including bonds, indentures of trust, and financing agreements.
  - Attend drafting sessions and make notes on changes needed on initial drafts.
  - Prepare second and subsequent drafts by incorporating revisions.
  - Prepare first drafts of all closing documents.
  - Prepare second and subsequent drafts by incorporating revisions and red-line changes.
  - Draft official statement/private offering memoranda.
  - Perform due diligence to verify information in the offering document.
  - Prepare second and subsequent drafts by incorporating revisions and red-line changes.

- Coordination
  - Establish timetable and list of participants.
  - Distribute documents to participants.
  - Coordinate the printing of bonds and offering documents.
  - File all documents as required.
  - Coordinate publication of notices of meetings and elections, ordinances, public hearing notices, etc.

- Closing
  - Prepare checklist.
  - Arrange and assist in pre-closings and closings.
  - File special documents prior to closings.
  - Secure requisite documents to be prepared or furnished by other participants.
  - Perform all post-closing procedures.
  - File all documents or security agreements.
  - Supervise preparation of closing binders.

- Formation of Special Districts
  - Prepare documents necessary to organize the district.
  - File documents with city or county and court.
  - Prepare documents for organizational meeting of district.

- Elections (Formation of District or Bond Election)
  - Draft election documents and obtain all necessary election materials.

- Develop and Maintain Research Files
  - IDB procedures for municipalities.
  - Home rule charters.
  - Demographic and economic statistics.
  - Memoranda noting statutory changes.
  - Interoffice research memoranda.
  - Checklists for each type of financing.[11]

- *Comment on Paralegal Work in This Area:*
  - "Because of the wide range of areas of law involved in public finance, paralegals practicing in this area are required to have expertise, or at least a working knowledge, in such diverse areas as real estate, municipal law, corporate law, securities, banking and finance, and tax law. Although demanding, public finance presents paralegals with an opportunity to utilize existing skills in these areas and to acquire expertise in the remainder." For example, "public financing can include every aspect a real estate paralegal would see in the most complicated real estate transactions." Eva M. Merrell, *Career Building Through Public Finance*, 37 Facts & Findings 28.

- *Job Search in This Area of the Law:*
  - In Google, Bing, or Yahoo, run this search: paralegal job municipal public finance
  - To narrow the search, add the name of your state or city to the search query

- *More on This Area of the Law on the Net:*
  - www.hg.org/public-finance.html
  - www.law.cornell.edu/wex/index.php/Local_government_law
  - In Google, Bing, or Yahoo, run this search: What do municipal finance lawyers do

36. Native American Law

Tribal courts on Native American reservations have jurisdiction over many civil and criminal cases in which both parties are Native Americans. Parties are often represented by tribal court advocates who are nonattorney Native Americans. In addition, the judges are often nonattorneys.

- *Comment on Paralegal Work in This Area:*
  - "Lee's career goal is to become an advocate for the Navajo Nation. In March ... she will sit for the Navajo Nation Bar exam, something she is permitted to do as a Native American with an associate degree. If she passes, she will be able to become an advocate for the Navajo Nation, practicing much as an attorney would do on the reservation, although she would not be permitted to practice off the reservation. Her work as an advocate would involve quite a bit of dispute resolution and representing Native Americans in their own tribal courts." J. Roberts, *Unique Specialties (Tribal Law)*, 23 Legal Assistant Today 65.

- As a paralegal, Raylene Frazier "advocates for clients in the Cheyenne River Sioux Tribal Court on a wide range of areas including paternity, custody, and probate cases, often against lawyers representing her opposition." McCullum, *Paralegal Recognized for Work with Native American Community*, 24 Legal Assistant Today 26.

- ***Job Search in This Area of the Law:***
  - In Google, Bing, or Yahoo, run this search: paralegal job tribal native American advocate
  - To narrow the search, add the name of your state or city to the search query

- ***More on This Area of the Law on the Net:***
  - libguides.law.ucla.edu/nativeamerican
  - www.law.cornell.edu/wex/american_indian_law
  - www.hg.org/native.html
  - In Google, Bing, or Yahoo, run this search: What do tribal lawyers do

37. Oil and Gas Law

Some paralegals who work in the area of oil and gas law are referred to as *land technicians* or *landmen*.

- Data
  - Collect and analyze data pertaining to land ownership and activities that may affect the procurement of rights to explore, drill for, and produce oil or gas.

- Leases
  - Help acquire leases and other operating rights from property owners for exploration, drilling, and producing oil, gas, and other natural resources.
  - Monitor the execution of leases and other operating agreements by ensuring that contract obligations are fulfilled (e.g., payment of rent).

- Negotiation
  - Help negotiate agreements with individuals, companies, and government agencies pertaining to the exploration, drilling, and production of oil or gas.

- General Assistance
  - Assist in acquiring oil- and gas-producing properties, royalties, and mineral interests.
  - Process and monitor the termination of leases and other agreements.
  - Examine land titles.

- ***Comment on Paralegal Work in This Area:***
  - "As an oil and gas paralegal, my practice encompasses many different areas of law including real estate, litigation, bankruptcy, and securities, as well as contact with various county, state, and federal government agencies. I frequently spend time searching real estate records in counties … for information on leases to determine such things as who has been assigned an interest in the lease. I have worked in mechanic's lien foreclosures, partition actions, and bankruptcy cases. While researching regulatory information and oil prices, I have obtained information from the Federal Energy Regulatory Commission (FERC) offices in Washington. The variety of work requires a working knowledge of several areas of law, and is always challenging and interesting." Hunt, *Oil and Gas*, The Citator (Paralegal Association of Central Ohio).

- ***Job Search in This Area of the Law:***
  - In Google, Bing, or Yahoo, run this search: paralegal job oil gas
  - To narrow the search, add the name of your state or city to the search query

- ***More on This Area of the Law on the Net:***
  - www.washlaw.edu/subject/oilgaslaw.html
  - www.hg.org/natres.html
  - In Google, Bing, or Yahoo, run this search: What do oil gas lawyers do

38. Parajudge (Lay Judge)

In some states, judges in certain lower courts do not have to be attorneys. Such courts include justice of the peace courts and local magistrate courts.

In New York State, for example, almost 2,000 judges in the state's town and village courts (often called justice courts) are not attorneys. "New York is one of about thirty states that still rely on these kinds of local judges, descendants of the justices who kept the peace in Colonial days, when lawyers were scarce."[12]

As we will see in Chapter 4, some administrative agencies, particularly state and local agencies, allow nonattorneys to conduct administrative hearings within their agencies. The person conducting the hearing (whether an attorney or a nonattorney) is often called an administrative law judge (ALJ), hearing officer, or referee.

- ***More on This Area of the Law on the Net:***
  - In Google, Bing, or Yahoo, run this search: "nonlawyer judges"
  - www.nytimes.com/2006/09/25/nyregion/25courts.html?_r=1&oref=slogin

39. Pro Bono Work

Pro bono work refers to services provided for the public good at no charge (and sometimes at reduced rates). Law firms often give their attorneys time off so they can take pro bono cases, e.g., to defend a poor person charged with a crime. Paralegals are also encouraged to do pro bono work. This is done on their own time or on law-firm time with the permission of their supervisor. Here are examples of the variety of pro bono work performed by paralegals.

- Domestic Violence
  - Draft request for protective orders.
  - Draft divorce pleadings.

- AIDS Patients
  - Interview patient and prepare a memorandum of the interview for the attorney on the case.
  - Assist patient with guardianship proceedings.
  - Draft powers of attorney.

- Homeless
  - Handle a person's Supplemental Security Income (SSI) claims.
  - Make referrals to shelters and drug programs.
- *Comment on Paralegal Work in This Area:*
  - "Asked to share her favorite pro bono experience, Therese Ortega, a litigation paralegal, answered that to choose was too difficult. Any time her efforts result in a benefit to the client, 'I get a warm glow.' One occasion she obviously cherishes was the fight on behalf of some low-income kidney dialysis patients whose eligibility for transportation to and from treatment was threatened. 'Perseverance and appeals paid off,' she says. Rides were re-established through the hearing process, then by information conferences. Finally, the cessation notices stopped." *Spotlight on Therese Ortega*, 13 The Journal 3 (Sacramento Valley Paralegal Association).
- **Finding Pro Bono Opportunities**
  - In Google, Bing, or Yahoo, run this search: paralegal pro bono aa (substituting the name of your state for aa)
  - To narrow the search, add the name of your city to the search query
- *More on This Area of the Law on the Net:*
  - apps.americanbar.org/legalservices/probono/downturn
  - www.probonoinst.org

40. Public Sector

A paralegal in the *private* sector works in an office whose funds come from client fees or from the budget of the corporate treasury. Every other setting is generally considered the *public* sector. More specifically, the latter refers to those law offices that provide civil or criminal legal services to the poor without charge. Often, the services consist of helping clients obtain government benefits such as public housing, welfare, or medical care. Such services are referred to as *public benefits*, and providing such assistance is called public benefits law, or, sometimes, poverty law. Paralegals who are employed by these offices are *public benefits paralegals*. The offices operate with government grants, charitable contributions, and the efforts of volunteers. The offices are called Legal Aid Society, Legal Services Office, Office of the Public Defender, etc. (For examples of the kinds of functions performed by paralegals in these offices, see administrative law, bankruptcy law, civil rights law, criminal law, family law, landlord and tenant law, litigation, pro bono work, social security law, welfare law, and workers' compensation law.)

- *Comment on Paralegal Work in This Area:*
  - "If someone asked me what I disliked most about my job, I would have to answer: the size of my paycheck. That is the only drawback of working for a nonprofit law firm [the Community Legal Aid Society, which represents elderly and handicapped

persons]. Everything else about my job is positive." For example, to "be an integral part of a case where a landlord is forced by the courts to bring a house up to code and prevent a tenant from being wrongfully evicted is a great feeling." The positive aspects of the job "more than compensate for the size of the paycheck." Hartman, *Job Profile*, Delaware Paralegal Reporter 5 (Delaware Paralegal Association).
  - "Mr. Watnick stressed that the organization doesn't have the luxury of using paralegals as 'xeroxers' or errand runners. Staff paralegals have their own caseloads and represent clients before Administrative Law Judges—with a dramatically high rate of success." Shays, *Paralegals in Human Service*, Postscript 16 (Manhattan Paralegal Association).
- *Job Search in This Area of the Law:*
  - In Google, Bing, or Yahoo, run this search: paralegal job public benefits
  - To narrow the search, add the name of your state or city to the search query
- *More on This Area of the Law on the Net:*
  - www.washlaw.edu/subject/poverty.html
  - www.povertylaw.org
  - www.law.cornell.edu/topics/food_stamps.html
  - www.law.cornell.edu/topics/medicaid.html
  - In Google, Bing, or Yahoo, run this search: What do "poverty law" lawyers do

41. Real Estate Law

- General
  - Assist law firms, corporations, and development companies in transactions involving land, houses, condominiums, shopping malls, office buildings, redevelopment projects, civic centers, etc.
  - Research zoning regulations.
  - Prepare drafts of the contract of sale.
- Title Work
  - Order title work from the title company; arrange title insurance.
  - If title work is done by in-house personnel, prepare a map based on a master title plat or the current government survey map; examine title abstracts for completeness; help construct a chain of title that notes liens, easements, or other encumbrances; obtain releases of liens, and payoff statements for existing loans; help draft preliminary title opinions.
- Mortgages
  - Assist in obtaining financing.
  - Review mortgage application.
  - Assist in recording mortgage.
- Closing
  - Arrange a closing time with buyer, seller, brokers, and lender.
  - Collect the data necessary for closing.

- Prepare checklist of expenses covering title company's fee, lender's fee, attorney's fee, prorated taxes and utility bills, tax escrow, discharge of liens, etc.
- Organize documents for closing (deed, settlement statement, note and deed of trust, corporate resolutions, performance bond, waivers, etc.).
- Check compliance with the disclosure requirements of the Real Estate Settlement Procedures Act (RESPA).
- Arrange a rehearsal of the closing.
- Attend and assist at the closing, e.g., take minutes, notarize documents.

- Foreclosure
  - Order foreclosure certificate.
  - Prepare notice of election and demand for sale.
  - Compile a list of parties to be notified.
  - Monitor publication of the notice.
  - Prepare bid letter and other sale documents.

- Eminent Domain
  - Photograph or videotape the property that the state has taken or proposes to take.
  - Prepare inventory of the property taken.
  - Help client prepare business records on the value of the property.
  - Order appraisals of the property.
  - Order soil engineering reports.
  - Review tax appeal records on values claimed by the property owner.
  - Mail notice of condemnation.

- Office Management
  - Maintain office tickler system.
  - Maintain individual attorney's calendar.
  - Manage the client's file: Opening it, keeping it up to date, knowing where parts of it are at all times, etc.
  - Train other staff in the office system of handling real estate cases.

- Tax-Exempt Industrial Development Financing
  - Undertake a preliminary investigation to establish facts relevant to project eligibility, local issuer, and cost estimates of financing.
  - Prepare formal application to the issuer.
  - Prepare timetable of approvals, meetings, and other requirements necessary for closing.
  - Prepare a preliminary draft of portions of the proposal memorandum (relating to the legal structure of the financing) that is submitted to prospective bond purchasers.
  - Obtain confirmation from the Treasury Department that the company is in compliance with the financing covenants of current external debt instruments.
  - Obtain insurance certificates.

- Write the first draft of the resolutions of the board of directors.
- Write the preface and recital of documents for the legal opinion of the company.
- Ask bank to confirm account numbers, amount of money that is to be transferred, and investment instructions.
- Prepare a closing memorandum covering the following documents: Secretary's certificate, including resolutions of the board of directors; certified charter and bylaws of the company, and the incumbency certificate; UCC-1 (Uniform Commercial Code) financing statements, requisition forms; certificate of authorized company representative; deed; legal opinion of the company; transfer instruction letter; officer's certificate, etc.
- Confirm that the money has been transferred to the company's account on the day of closing.
- Order an updated good-standing telegram.
- Send a copy of the IRS election statement.
- Assemble, monitor, and distribute documents to appropriate departments.

- *Comment on Paralegal Work in This Area:*
  - The "paralegal's role in real estate transactions varies widely. [They] may be delegated work on a task-specific basis, such as title examination or closing document preparation. Many times, paralegals handle the transaction entirely, involving the attorney only when legal issues arise. Local statutes or bar ethics opinions, however, may limit the scope of paralegal use." J. Holmgren, *The Road to Closing*, 32 Facts & Findings 22.
  - "Although it may look boring to the untrained eye, and sound boring to the untrained ear, for those of us whose livelihoods depend upon it, real estate law is interesting and exciting. There is always something new to learn or a little flaw to resolve. What can be better than having clients come to you and thank you for your assistance in what would have been a complete disaster without your knowledge and expertise to get them through? I call that total job satisfaction. I am now capable of doing everything in a real estate settlement from opening the file to walking into the settlement room and disbursing the funds. It is not uncommon for me to receive calls from attorneys in the area asking me how certain problems can be solved. That boosts my ego more than any divorce case ever could!" Jaeger, *Real Estate Law Is a Legal Profession Tool*, 14 On Point 9 (National Capital Area Paralegal Association).
  - At a paralegal conference, Virginia Henderson made a seminar presentation on her duties as a paralegal. Her "candor and energetic enthusiasm concerning her profession were encouraging and motivating. She was very explicit about her duties as a commercial real estate paralegal, explaining

that attorney supervision is lessened once the paralegal assumes more responsibility and exhibits initiative as far as his or her duties are concerned. It was refreshing to listen to a veteran of the paralegal profession speak so optimistically about the profession's limitless potential. Here's to having more paralegals as seminar speakers!" Troiano, *Real Estate*, Newsletter 12 (Western New York Paralegal Association).

- "As a foreclosure legal assistant, one of my worst fears is to have a client call and say, 'Remember the Jones property you foreclosed for us last year? Well, we're trying to close on this and it seems there's a problem with the title.' Oh no! What didn't I do! Mortgage foreclosure litigation is fraught with all kinds of pitfalls for the inexperienced and the unwary. An improper or faulty foreclosure could not only be disastrous for the client, it could also be a malpractice nightmare for the law firm." Hubbell, *Mortgage Foreclosure Litigation: Avoiding the Pitfalls*, 16 Facts and Findings 10 (NALA).

- *Quotes from Want Ads:*
  - "Ideal candidate must possess exceptional organization, communication, writing and research skills and be willing to work overtime."
  - "We need a team player with high energy."
  - "Position requires an ability to work independently on a wide variety of matters and to meet deadlines."
  - "Experience in retail real estate or real estate financing a must."
  - "Should be assertive and have excellent analytical skills."
  - Position requires a "self-motivated person."
  - We seek "a TIGER who can accomplish much with a minimum of supervision."
  - "Knowledge of state and federal securities law is essential."
  - "Must be flexible and possess high integrity."
  - Position requires a "self-starter able to deal effectively with executive management, outside counsel, escrow and title companies, brokers, leasing agents, and clients."

- *Job Search in This Area of the Law:*
  - In Google, Bing, or Yahoo, run this search: paralegal job real estate
  - To narrow the search, add the name of your state or city to the search query

- *More on This Area of the Law on the Net:*
  - www.law.cornell.edu/wex/index.php/Real_property
  - www.hg.org/realest.html
  - www.washlaw.edu/subject/property.html
  - In Google, Bing, or Yahoo, run this search: What do real estate lawyers do

42. Social Security Law

As we will see in Chapter 4, paralegals can represent clients (and charge them fees) at social security hearings without attorney supervision. Such representatives are often called social security representatives. In Chapter 15 we will cover techniques for representing clients at such hearings.

Paralegals also work for attorneys who practice elder law, which includes social security cases. Finally, paralegals work for the Social Security Administration itself. The following tasks cover an independent paralegal who represents claimants.

- Problem Identification
  - Applicant is denied benefits, e.g., Medicare, social security retirement or disability benefits.
  - Recipient is terminated from benefits.
  - Recipient is charged with receiving an overpayment.

- Case Preparation
  - Investigate relevant facts.
  - Perform legal research.

- Representation
  - Engage in informal advocacy with social security employees.
  - Represent clients at administrative hearings on denial.
  - Assist attorneys who represent clients at administrative hearings.

- Appeal
  - Help attorney prepare a court appeal of the Social Security Administration's decision.

- *Comment on Paralegal Work in This Area:*
  - "Paralegal representation of a claimant in a Social Security Disability hearing is the closest to a judicial setting that a paralegal may expect to become involved in. For the paralegal, this can be a very complex and challenging field. It can also be extremely rewarding, bringing with it the satisfaction of successfully representing a claimant in a quasi-judicial setting." Obermann, *The Paralegal and Federal Disability Practice in Maine*, MAP Newsletter (Maine Association of Paralegals).

- *Job Search in This Area of the Law:*
  - In Google, Bing, or Yahoo, run this search: paralegal job social security
  - To narrow the search, add the name of your state or city to the search query

- *More on This Area of the Law on the Net:*
  - www.nosscr.org
  - www.ssa.gov
  - www.naela.com
  - www.law.cornell.edu/wex/index.php/Social_Security
  - In Google, Bing, or Yahoo, run this search: What do Social Security attorneys do

43. Tax Law

- Compile all necessary data for the preparation of tax returns: Corporate income tax, employer quarterly tax, franchise tax, partnership tax, sales tax, personal property tax, individual income tax, estate tax, and gift tax.

- Completion of Returns
  - Obtain missing information from client.
  - Compile supporting documents for the returns.
  - Draft extension-of-time requests for late filings.
  - Make corrections in the returns based upon new or amended data.
  - Compute the tax liability or transfer client information to a computer service that will calculate the tax liability.

- Other Tasks
  - Organize and maintain client binder.
  - Compile documentation on the valuation of assets.
  - Maintain tax law library.
  - Read tax looseleaf services and online sources to keep current on tax developments. Let others in office know of such developments.
  - Supervise and train other nonattorney staff.

- *Comment on Paralegal Work in This Area:*
  - "I like the client interaction. Our cases typically involve people who have not filed or paid taxes due to mental illness, physical illness or hard times. I like being able to help them resolve their issues with the tax authorities and help ease their financial burdens. Clients are often very grateful and I enjoy developing personal relationships with them and being a source of information and comfort." Inglesby, *My Specialty: Tax Controversy Law*, 29 Paralegal Today 40 (May/June 2012).
  - A paralegal with the firm "for the past thirteen years, Pat [Coleman] spends a lot of time in her office. She is surrounded by her work, and one gets the idea that Pat knows exactly what is in every file and could put her hand on any information that is needed. Notes are taped next to the light switch; the firm's monthly calendar highlighting important meetings is readily available, and helps her track her many deadlines. Pat is an *Enrolled Agent* (which permits nonattorneys to practice before the Treasury Department), has a lot of tax background, and is competent in that area as well as bookkeeping. One of her least favorite tax forms is the 990 required of not-for-profit organizations. The 990 tax form is second only to private foundation returns when it comes to being pesky and tricky." Howard, *Patricia Coleman of Chicago Creates Her Niche in Taxes, Trusts and ERISA*, 3 Legal Assistant Today 40.

- *Job Search in This Area of the Law:*
  - In Google, Bing, or Yahoo, run this search: paralegal job tax
  - To narrow the search, add the name of your state or city to the search query

- *More on This Area of the Law on the Net:*
  - www.taxsites.com
  - www.irs.ustreas.gov
  - www.naea.org
  - In Google, Bing, or Yahoo, run this search: What do tax lawyers do

44. Tort Law

A *tort* is a civil wrong (other than a breach of contract) that causes injury or other loss for which our legal system deems it just to provide a remedy such as damages. Injury or loss can be to the person (a personal tort), to movable property (a personal-property tort), or to land and anything attached to the land (a real-property tort). Most paralegals working in tort law, particularly on PI (personal injury) cases, are litigation assistants. The major tort areas are negligence, medical malpractice, products liability, defamation, and misrepresentation. Paralegals in this area may also be involved in workers' compensation cases for injuries that occur on the job.

- *Comment on Paralegal Work in This Area:*
  - "Personal injury/products liability cases can be fascinating, challenging, and educational. They also can be stressful, aggravating and very sad. I have been involved in a great many cases in my career, on both sides of the plaintiff/defendant fence. Some of the cases seemed frivolous and somewhat 'ambulance chasing' in nature. Others were significant cases in which the plaintiff had wrongfully suffered injury. There are many talents a good personal injury/products liability paralegal must have. He or she must be creative, tenacious, observant and able to communicate well with people." Lee, *Personal Injury/Products Liability Cases*, 11 Newsletter 7 (Dallas Area Paralegal Association).
  - "Recently, Mary Mann, a paralegal who works on product liability litigation, was asked by her attorney to track down a specific medical article [on a subject relevant to a current case]. The attorney only had a vague description of the article, a possible title, and the name of the organization that might have published it. In her search, Mary spoke by phone to people in New York, Atlanta, Washington, and finally to a doctor in Geneva, Switzerland, who spoke very little English. In her effort to make herself understood by the doctor, Mary continued to speak louder and louder in very simplistic and basic English phrases, as people tend to do when confronted by a language barrier. She is sure her efforts to maintain a professional demeanor were humorous to those passing by her office. However, she did succeed in getting the article

and, in the process, gained a friend in Switzerland!" Fisher, *Spotlight: Mary Mann*, 7 The Assistant 14 (Mississippi Paralegal Association).

- "Asbestos litigation ... opened up in the late 1970s with the lawsuits initiated against the Johns-Mansville Corporation. In 1982 Mansville filed a Chapter 11 bankruptcy to protect its assets from the thousands of claims being filed against it." Huge numbers of paralegals were employed in this litigation. For those paralegals working for Johns-Mansville on the defense team, "the question of morality arose. I get asked about the morality of my job constantly. For me, personal moral judgment does not enter into it. Our legal system is based on the availability of equal representation for both sides. I think I play a small part in making that system work." Welsh, *The Paralegal in Asbestos Litigation*, 10 Ka Leo O'H.A.L.A. 6 (Hawaii Paralegal Association).

- *Quotes from Want Ads:*
  - "Medical malpractice law firm seeks paralegal who is a self-starter, has good communication skills, is organized and detail-oriented."
  - Position in PI firm requires a "take-charge person to handle case details from beginning to end."
  - "Prefer person with experience in claims adjustment, medical records, or nursing." Position requires "dynamic, highly-motivated individual who will enjoy the challenge of working independently and handling a wide variety of responsibilities."
  - "Excellent writing skills a must." "Should be able to perform under pressure."
  - Manufacturer of consumer products "seeks paralegal with engineering background."
  - Must be mature enough to handle "heavy client contact."
  - Position requires "ability to read and summarize medical records."

- *Job Search in This Area of the Law:*
  - In Google, Bing, or Yahoo, run this search: paralegal job personal injury
  - To narrow the search, add the name of your state or city to the search query

- *More on This Area of the Law on the Net:*
  - www.cpsc.gov
  - www.washlaw.edu/subject/torts.html
  - www.toxlaw.com/bookmarks/laws.html
  - www.hg.org/torts.html
  - www.law.cornell.edu/wex/index.php/Tort
  - In Google, Bing, or Yahoo, run this search: What do personal injury lawyers do

45. Water Law
- Water Rights
  - Investigate and analyze specific water rights associated with property

- Do research at Department of Water Resources regarding decrees, tabulations, well permits, reservoirs, diversion records, maps, and miscellaneous statements.
- Do research at other agencies and offices (e.g., Bureau of Land Management, state archives, historical societies, public libraries).
- Communicate in writing and orally with Department of Water Resources personnel regarding status of water rights and wells; with District Water Commissioners regarding status of water rights and wells, historic use, and use on land; and with property owners and managers, ranch managers, and ditch company personnel regarding status of water rights and wells, historic use, and use on land.
- Prepare historic use affidavits.
- Prepare reports, maps, charts, and diagrams on status of water rights and wells, historic use, and use on land.

- Real Estate Transactions
  - Draft documents for the purchase and sale, encumbrance, or lease of water rights and wells.
  - Perform title searches in county clerk and recorder's offices.
  - Perform due diligence investigations.
  - Assist at closings.

- Well Permit Applications
  - Prepare well permit documents for filing: applications, land ownership affidavits, statements of beneficial use, amendments to record, and extensions of time.
  - Coordinate and monitor the well permit and drilling process.
  - Communicate with Department of Water Resources personnel, well drillers, and client.

- Water Court Proceedings
  - Prepare water court documents for filing: Applications, statements of opposition, draft rulings and orders, stipulations, withdrawals of opposition, and affidavits.
  - Maintain diligence filing tickler system; work with client to maintain evidence of diligence.
  - Review, route, and maintain file of term-day notices and orders.
  - Orient attorneys for term day.
  - Monitor water law publications.
  - Read reporter and water court cases, and register for new water law cases and Department of Water Resources regulations.[13]

- *Job Search in This Area of the Law:*
  - In Google, Bing, or Yahoo, run this search: paralegal job water law
  - To narrow the search, add the name of your state or city to the search query

- *More on This Area of the Law on the Net:*
  - www.washlaw.edu/subject/water.html
  - www.hg.org/natres.html
  - In Google, Bing, or Yahoo, run this search: What do "natural resources" lawyers do

46. Welfare Law (Public Assistance)

- Problem Identification
  - Identify nonlegal problems for referral to other agencies.
  - Open a case file or update it.
  - Provide information on benefits such as Temporary Assistance for Needy Families (TANF), Social Security, Medicare, etc.
  - Help client fill out application forms.

- Initial Work
  - Summarize facts for the attorney.
  - Obtain further instructions from attorney.
  - Refer nonlegal problems to other agencies.
  - Do research in law library.

- Investigation
  - Verify information (e.g., call caseworker, visit department office).
  - Search for additional information.
  - Update client file on results of investigation.

- Advocacy
  - Be an informal advocate (to determine if the problem can be resolved without a hearing or court action).
  - Draft letter requesting hearing (if informal advocacy is not successful).
  - In advance of hearing, request that the department send you the documents it will rely on at the hearing.
  - Prepare all witnesses (e.g., explain what hearing will be about; use role-playing to acquaint them with the format and what you will be seeking from the witnesses).
  - Represent client at the hearing: Make opening statement summarizing client's case; state what relief the client is seeking from the hearing; submit documents into the record; conduct direct examination of the client's witnesses, including the client; conduct re-direct examination of witnesses (if allowed); cross-examine their witnesses; re-cross-examine their witnesses (if allowed); make closing statement summarizing the case of the client and repeating the result the client is seeking, etc.

- Follow-up
  - Request a copy of the transcript of the hearing.
  - Consult with attorney to determine whether the hearing result should be appealed in court.
  - Assist attorney in gathering documents needed for appeal.

- Prepare preliminary draft of the legal argument to be made to the trial court handling the appeal.
- Be a general assistant for the attorney in court.

- *Job Search in This Area of the Law:*
  - In Google, Bing, or Yahoo, run this search: paralegal job public benefits
  - To narrow the search, add the name of your state or city to the search query

- *More on This Area of the Law on the Net:*
  - www.law.cornell.edu/wex/index.php/Welfare
  - www.nclej.org
  - In Google, Bing, or Yahoo, run this search: What do "poverty law" lawyers do

47. Workers' Compensation Law

- Initial Work
  - Collect and record details of the workers' compensation claim: date of injury, nature and dates of prior illness, etc.
  - Collect or arrange for the collection of documents, e.g., medical and employment records.
  - Coordinate scheduling of physical examination.

- Drafting
  - Claim for compensation.
  - Request for hearing.
  - Medical authorization.
  - Demand for medical information in the possession of respondent or insurance carrier.
  - Proposed summary of issues involved.

- Advocacy
  - Informal: Contact (call, visit, write a letter to) the employer and/or the insurance carrier to determine whether the matter can be resolved without a formal hearing or court action.
  - Formal: Represent the claimant at the administrative hearing if the state allows nonattorney representation.

- Follow-up
  - Determine whether the payment is in compliance with the award.
  - If not, draft and file statutory demand for proper payment.
  - If such a statutory demand is filed, prepare a tickler system to monitor the claim.

- *Comment on Paralegal Work in This Area:*
  - "I have been working as a paralegal in this area for more than seven years. This is one of the areas of the law in which a paralegal can perform almost all of the functions to properly process a Workers' Compensation claim. A Workers' Compensation practice must be high volume in order to be [profitable]. Thus paralegal assistance in handling a large caseload is an absolute necessity. Extensive paperwork is processed on a daily basis.

Client contact is a major portion of a paralegal's responsibilities. With a large caseload, it is physically impossible for an attorney to communicate with each client on a regular basis. It is not unusual for a paralegal in this field to work on several hundred files each week." Lindberg, *Virtually Limitless Responsibilities of a Workers' Compensation Paralegal*, Update 6 (Cleveland Association of Paralegals).

- "The Company's two workers' compensation paralegals are responsible for reviewing each claimant's file, preparing a summary of medical reports, outlining the issues, and reviewing with the adjusters any questions or circumstances of the case before the claimant's deposition. In addition, they draft any necessary subpoenas, witness lists and settlement stipulations for their respective attorneys, and collect information and draft letters to the Special Disability Trust Fund outlining the

Company's theory of reimbursement for second injury cases." Miquel, *Walt Disney World Company's Legal Assistants: Their Role in the Show*, 16 Facts and Findings 29 (NALA).

- **■ *Job Search in This Area of the Law:***
  - In Google, Bing, or Yahoo, run this search: paralegal job workers compensation
  - To narrow the search, add the name of your state or city to the search query

- **■ *More on This Area of the Law on the Net:***
  - www.law.cornell.edu/wex/index.php/Workers_compensation
  - www.dol.gov/dol/topic/workcomp
  - www.hg.org/workers-compensation-law.html
  - In Google, Bing, or Yahoo, run this search: What do workers compensation lawyers do

Finally, Exhibit 2-7 presents the story of how paralegalism is likely to appear wherever law is involved.

Exhibit 2-7	A Paralegal in the White House

[After working as a paralegal on the Reagan-Bush Campaign Committee], I'm a paralegal in the White House Counsel's office. I believe I'm the first paralegal in this office—in the White House. They've had law clerks in the past, but never have they hired a paralegal. There's one paralegal to nine attorneys at the moment. My responsibilities here are varied. Everybody is still trying to determine what their turf is. But for the first couple of months I've worked on a lot of transition matters, which might be expected. I was the coordinator for our transition audit (congressional transition audit) from the Hill, which just ended a few weeks ago. I have engaged in drafting correspondence concerning the use of the president's name, the use of his image; our policy on gift acceptance by public employees; drafting standards of conduct for public employees in the White House, job freeze litigation, those few controversial things. The last few weeks of my time have been devoted to the Lefever nomination. It's all been fascinating. Anyway, there are a number of areas that we also get involved in, the ethics of government act, for example. It's the first time it has been applied across the board to a new administration. It has been very, very time consuming for all our staff. I've been assisting in that, reviewing each individual file for high level government employees. As I said, I'm in the counsel's office now and intend to stay for a couple of years. But I would like to start my own paralegal firm. I have a close friend who started her own paralegal firm in Florida and we've talked often in the past of expanding it. I think there is a place for more paralegals in the public sector, at least in the White House. I understand the Department of Justice has many, but I'd like to see it expanded and I'd also like to see more people branching out and trying this independent approach. It's risky, but it's worth it."

Source: Meg Shields Duke, *New Roles in the Law Conference*, 93 (1982).

FINDING A JOB

There are many different strategies for finding employment. Those discussed in this section are primarily for individuals who have had very little or no employment experience with attorneys. Many of the strategies, however, are also relevant to people who have worked in law offices as secretaries or who are paralegals seeking other employment opportunities in the field.

BEGIN NOW

You should begin preparing for the job hunt on the first day of your first paralegal class. Do not wait until the program is almost over. Although your school will provide you with guidance and leads, you should assume that obtaining a job will be your responsibility. For most students, the job you get will be the job you find.

In school, your primary focus should be to compile an excellent academic record. In addition, you should start the job search now. It is not too early, for example, to begin compiling the lists called for in the Job-Search Notebook (JSN) that we will examine later in Exhibit 2-21. When school is over, be prepared to spend a substantial amount of additional time looking for employment, particularly if your part of the country is currently a "buyer's market," where there are more applicants than available jobs.

Being a paralegal requires determination, assertiveness, initiative, and creativity. Finding paralegal work may require these same skills. This is not a field for the faint of heart who are easily discouraged.

It may be that you are uncertain about the kinds of employment options that exist. How can you begin looking for a job if you don't yet know what kind of job you would like to have? First of all, many of the suggested steps in this chapter will be helpful regardless of the kind of job you are pursuing. More important, however, the very process of going through these steps will help you clarify your employment objectives. As you begin seeking information and leads, the insights will come to you. At this point, keep an open mind, be conscientious, and begin now.

NETWORKING

Most jobs are obtained by **networking**, which consists of meeting people who might be of help to you (now or in the future) and whom you might be able to help (now or in the future). When you network, you establish contacts and share information with people (a) who might become personal or professional resources for you and (b) for whom you might become a personal or professional resource.

The value of networking is not limited to a job search. It can be used on the job and throughout your career. If you are diligent, creative, and willing to be a giver as well as a receiver of information, there is a very good possibility that networking:

- Will find you your first job, particularly in the "hidden market" where available jobs are not often advertised
- Will lead you to resources that will help you perform the job you obtain
- Will lead you to other jobs when it is time to move on
- Will find you many friends
- Will engage you in the further development of paralegalism as a profession

networking Establishing contacts and sharing information with people (a) who might become personal or professional resources for you and (b) for whom you might become a personal or professional resource.

The Skill of Networking

Networking is something that we all do in our everyday lives. We meet people at school, at work, and at many different kinds of gatherings. If there are mutual interests and a spark of cordiality, we tend to stay in touch and occasionally help each other out. This is fine, but professional networking requires much more. You must become an *assertive* networker—someone who works hard at making new contacts and nurturing them. (See Exhibit 2-8.)

Exhibit 2-8	Assertive Networking

■ **The I-You-What Approach**

When you meet a new person, consider using a three-step approach: I-You-What. "I" stands for introduction, "You" is the other person, "What" is your goal in the contact. Introduce yourself (I), find out something about the new person (you), and only then indicate that you are looking for employment (what). Here are some examples of different comments what you might make at each stage:

- **The "I" Stage** (tell the new person who you are)
  "Hi, my name is Diane Anderson. I'm a student at Iverson Community College. I'm studying to be a paralegal." Etc.

- **The "YOU" Stage** (find out something about the new person and briefly chat about something other than employment)
  "Have you been to these meetings before? This is my first time." … "Do you know what the speaker is going to cover?" … "Are you an attorney?" "Do you work in the law?" "What area of law does your office handle?" "Do you have a card?" Etc.

- **The "WHAT" Stage** (after finding out who this person is and giving him or her an opportunity to share some information about himself or herself or about the event you are both attending, let the person know WHAT you are looking for: work).

"When I graduate next month, I hope to be able to work in an office like yours." "Does your office use paralegals?" "Are there any openings? Do you know of any other offices where I might check?" "I would definitely consider an internship. Would your office be interested in having an intern?" "I'm willing to volunteer in an office in order to gain experience and demonstrate my skills. Does your office accept volunteers? Any suggestions of offices where I might volunteer?" "Could I send you my résumé in case something comes up?" "Can I give you my card?" "I'm a recent graduate of a paralegal program. I'm willing to offer a month of free law office help in order to gain experience. I'm willing to do whatever tasks the office needs. Would you be interested?" Etc. (If the answer is no to the last question, ask if he or she has the name of any other attorneys you could contact about your offer.)

■ Characteristics of Assertive Networkers

- They view *every* adult as a potentially valuable contact.
- They regularly introduce themselves to new people, so long as it is safe to do so. They do not wait for others to make the first move.
- They always look for ways to mingle and interact with people they have never met before.
- They regularly attend gatherings where they will be able to meet people they have not met before.
- They find out where attorneys meet, where paralegals meet, and where legal administrators meet. They then try to go to as many of these places as possible in order to introduce themselves.
- They attend gatherings alone (stag) or, if they go with friends, they do not sit with friends at the gathering; rather, they find new people to sit with.
- They always arrive early at gatherings so that they will have time to mingle with other early arrivals—whom they do not know.
- They join a LinkedIn group (see Exhibit 2-13) and send a message to the group that says (1) they want to network with paralegals in your area, or (2) they are looking for volunteer opportunities in their area, or (3) they are looking for leads on finding a job.
- When they meet someone new, they look them up in LinkedIn and, if there, invite them to be a connection. (See Exhibit 2-13 on LinkedIn.)
- They send tweets on Twitter (see Exhibit 2-13) that can be helpful to others and "follow" people they don't know who might be helpful in their career.
- They search for potential professional contacts on Facebook and try to friend them (see Exhibit 2-13). The contacts are people they know and people they don't know.
- They order their own business cards stating their name, email address, and link to their online profile on LinkedIn (see Exhibit 2-13).
- They join listservs—electronic mailing lists (e.g., one run by their local paralegal association) and send a message to the group asking for leads to employment.
- They look for mentors (knowledgeable, trusted advisors) and make themselves available to mentor others.
- They set networking targets (e.g., while in school, they will contact ten new people a week; after graduation, they will contact twenty new people a week).
- They carry a notebook or small computer device that can be easily used to jot down brief notes about new people they meet (names, email address, line of work, etc.).
- Later, they spend time organizing their notes into categories of contacts (who they met, when, how the contacts might be helpful, how they might be helpful to the contacts, when they last contacted them [or will contact them], etc.).
- They are always open to suggestions for improving their networking techniques (e.g., on Google, Bing, or Yahoo, they run searches such as "how to introduce yourself" and "networking tips").

Strength in Weak Ties

It's possible that the first job you obtain will be a job you saw in an ad. It is much more likely, however, that the job will materialize because a friend of a friend or an acquaintance of an acquaintance found out you were looking and gave you the lead that led to the job, or that led you to another lead that led you to the job.

In what is called "strength in weak ties," you may receive an outstanding lead from a very indirect (weak) contact that you once made. You hope for (and probably expect) help from relatives and good friends, but the help that gets you the job might come from a much wider circle of contacts that you build. Most of networking consists of taking active steps to meet new people. If you limit your contacts to people you already know, you're doing a lot of socializing, but very little networking. Bob Sweat, commenting on a Texas paralegal LinkedIn group, says, "It's tough out there, but people are finding jobs every day." The key is to "network, network, network. Let everyone you have a conversation with know you are looking for work, even the grocery store clerk. Maybe their dad or mom, aunt or uncle, or neighbor is an attorney or works in a firm in a support role."[14]

A great many jobs are part of what is called the *hidden market*. The job opening exists but it may not have been advertised or publicized as yet. How do you find out about such jobs? The answer is networking, indeed, assertive networking.

Many of us like to stay in our comfort zone. When we reach out to strangers, we run the risk of rejection. Yet for a person entering the professional world of law, the risks have to be taken. As one successful paralegal, Eric Bleuel, said about networking and meeting strangers, "I know it's not real fun, kind of humiliating at times, and if you are shy like me it's the last thing you feel like doing. The good news is, all you need is for one" contact to work.[15]

Networking with Attorneys

Begin your networking with a list of attorneys with whom you already have a direct or indirect connection:

- Relatives who are attorneys
- Personal friends who are attorneys
- Friends of friends who are attorneys
- Attorneys you have hired
- Attorneys your relatives have hired
- Attorneys your former employers have hired
- Attorneys your friends have hired
- Attorneys that attend your house of worship
- Attorneys you know who are teachers, politicians, neighbors, etc.

You should consider contacting all of these attorneys. You want to find out:

- Have they hired paralegals in the past?
- If so, are they interested in hiring an additional paralegal?
- If they have never hired paralegals before, would they consider hiring one now?
- Do they know of other attorneys who might be interested in hiring paralegals?
- Would they consider hiring someone part time or on a volunteer basis?

Attorney Directories   Find a directory or list of attorneys. (See Appendix H.) Ask a librarian at any law library or general library in your area. Your Yellow Pages will also list attorneys, often by specialty. Also check with a librarian about national directories of attorneys. Here are some of the major directories:

- *Martindale-Hubbell Law Directory*
  - available in bound volumes
  - available free on the Internet (www.martindale.com) (under Search Tools, click *Law Firms*, then select your state in the pull-down menu, and click Search) (also, click *Jobs* and type *paralegal* in the search box)
  - available for a fee at LexisNexis (www.lexis.com)

- *West's Legal Directory*
  - available free on the Internet (lawyers.findlaw.com) (click *Browse Law Firms*)
  - available for a fee at WestlawNext (www.westlaw.com)

- *Lawyers.com*
  - www.lawyers.com (click your state, then your city, and category of law)

- *National Directory of Legal Employers*
  - www.nalpdirectory.com (select your state in the pull-down menu and click Search)

In addition to these broad-based legal directories, check specialty directories of attorneys. Examples:

- American Immigration Lawyers Association (www.aiia.org)
- National Association of Consumer Bankruptcy Attorneys) (nacba2.memberpath.com)
- American Academy of Matrimonial Attorneys (www.aami.org)
- National Bar Association (African-American Attorneys) (www.nationalbar.org)
- Hispanic National Bar Association (www.hnba.com)
- National Asian Pacific American Bar Association (www.napaba.org)
- Hellenic Bar Association (www.hellenicbarassociation.com)
- American Association of Nurse Attorneys (www.taana.org)

Many of these links will lead you to particular law firms where you can often find biographical data on the attorneys in the firms. If you have something in common with a particular attorney (e.g., you were both born in the same small town or you both went to the same school), mention this fact in a cover letter, email, or phone conversation.

If you find no such connections with any of the attorneys in the directories, consider "cold calling," which we will cover shortly.

Networking with Paralegals

Attend paralegal association meetings. (See Appendix B for links to paralegal associations in your state.) Contact the ones nearest you and ask about joining. Associations often have reduced dues for students. Many associations meet once a month. Attend some of these meetings. Do so even if the meetings do not directly pertain to the areas of law in which you have an interest. If employed paralegals are there, you need to be there. Potentially, they will become your most valuable networking resource.

Other valuable career and employment-searching services that many paralegal associations provide include:

job bank A service that lists available jobs. The list is sometimes available only to members of an organization.

- *Job banks*. Many associations offer a **job bank** service, which lists paralegal job openings. Here is what a paralegal who used this service had to say: "I gained access to an opening to a wonderful job at a law firm exclusively listed in the [Minnesota Paralegal Association] Job Bank … . I would never have heard about the position if I hadn't been a member of [the association]."[16] Not all associations have job bank services and those that have them may not make them available to nonmembers of the association.
- *Mentoring*. Ask if the association has (or would consider creating) a mentoring program in which experienced paralegals volunteer to provide guidance to new entrants to the field.
- *Employment workshops*. Find out if the association has scheduled an employment workshop that you can attend. Such workshops often provide valuable suggestions on how to find work in your area. If none are on the agenda, ask if any were recently held and, if so, whether any handouts or employment manuals from the workshop are still available. Finally, suggest that the association hold an employment workshop in the near future.

continuing legal education (CLE)
Training in the law (usually short term) that a person receives after completing his or her formal legal training or after becoming employed.

- *Continuing legal education*. Almost all associations offer continuing legal education **continuing legal education**, which is training in the law (usually short term) that a person receives after completing his or her formal legal training or after becoming employed. Attend CLE sessions. They may be available at reduced rates to paralegal students. Although most CLE occurs after your formal training program is over, there is no law against your attending while in school. Employed paralegals go to CLE events in large numbers. Hence, they are excellent places to meet and network with experienced paralegals.

Bar associations also sponsor CLE. You will find upcoming CLE events listed on the websites of the bar associations. (See Appendix B.) Many bar associations offer affiliate membership for paralegals. (See Appendix B.) Whether or not other paralegals are present at any particular attorney CLE events that you attend, the events will be excellent opportunities to practice the networking techniques listed in Exhibit 2-8.

Networking with Legal Administrators

On Google, Bing, or Yahoo, run this search: "legal administrator" association aa (substituting your state for "aa"). If there is an legal administrator association meeting near you, consider dropping by. You may or may not be allowed to attend sessions, but you can spend a few minutes trying to meet two or three legal administrators in the corridor before their sessions begin.

ADS

Check classified ads in your daily newspaper and in the legal newspaper (if one exists for your area). (See Exhibit 2-9 for some of the common abbreviations used in ads.) If you are seeking employment in another city, check to see if the online edition of the newspapers in that city (www.50states.com/news) allows you to read want ads without subscribing to the newspaper.

Be alert for "buzzwords" in ads or employment listings. These are key words or phrases that indicate what the employer is looking for (e.g., "computer literacy," "work under pressure," "writing," "immigration," "experience"). Later, when you write your résumé and cover letter in response to an ad or listing, you should try to use (indeed, emphasize) these buzzwords.

blind ad A want ad that does not give the name and address of the prospective employer. The contact is made through a third party, e.g., a newspaper or agency.

An ad may not give the name and address of the employer seeking the paralegal. Instead, it will direct interested parties to an intermediary, such as a newspaper, which forwards all responses to the employer. Such ads are called **blind ads**. Some ads are placed by private employment agencies that specialize in legal placements.

CHAPTER 2   Paralegal Employment

Exhibit 2-9	Common Classified Ad Abbreviations				
Abbreviation	**Translation**	**Abbreviation**	**Translation**	**Abbreviation**	**Translation**
2+	plus means "or more" (years of experience)	DOE	depending on experience	mgmt	management
		EOE	Equal Opportunity	ofc	office
acctg	acounting		Employer	opty	opportunity
advc	advancement	exp nec	experience necessary	ovtm	overtime
agcy	agency	exp pfd	experience preferred	pd vac	paid vacation
appt	appointment	f/pd	fee paid	p/t	part-time
asst	assistant	f/t	full-time	refs	references
begnr	beginner	gd	good	secty	secretary
bkpg	bookkeeping	inq	inquire	sr	senior
bnfts	benefits	k	thousands	w/	with
clk	clerk	LLP	Limited Liability	w/wo	with or without
co	company		Partnership	wpm	words per minute
col grad	college graduate	loc	location or located		
col	college	mfg	manufacturing		

Source: *Finding a Job in the Want Ads* (New Mexico SOICC)

You will find that most want ads seek paralegals with experience in a particular area of practice. Hence, if you are a recent graduate looking for a beginning or entry-level position, you may not meet the qualifications sought in the ads. Entry-level positions are not often advertised. (Later in the chapter we will discuss the Catch-22 dilemma of *no experience/no job* faced by recent graduates seeking their first paralegal job.)

Should you answer ads that specify qualifications such as experience that you do not have? Suppose, for example, that an ad seeks a corporate paralegal with two years of experience. You might consider answering such an ad as follows:

> I am responding to your ad for a corporate paralegal. I do not have the experience indicated in the ad, but I did take an intensive course on corporate law at my paralegal school. I am enclosing my résumé in the hope that you will consider what I have to offer.

When reading want ads, do not limit yourself to the entries for "Paralegal" and "Legal Assistant." Also look for headings for positions that may be law related, such as "Research Assistant," "Legislative Aide," or "Law Library Assistant." (See Exhibit 2-10 for examples.) Of course, some of the jobs with such titles may not be what you are looking for. They may not be directly related to your legal training and experience. Nevertheless, you should read such ads carefully. Some might be worth pursuing.

Exhibit 2-10	Examples of Other Job Titles to Check

RESEARCH ASSISTANT IMMEDIATE POSITION
Social Science Research Institute in downtown looking for coder/editor of legal survey instruments.
Post Box L3040.

LEGISLATIVE ASSISTANT
Good skills essential, dwntwn location, f/t, advc opty, send résumé/sal. requirements to Post Box M 8341.

ADMINISTRATOR—LAW
Medium-size and established estates law firm seeks manager with administrative, financial and personnel experience to supervise all non-legal office activities. Salary and benefits will be commensurate with experience. EOE. Send résumé to Box 9-17-2085.

PROOFREADER
Leading national newspaper for lawyers has an immediate opening for a p/t proofreader of manuscripts and galleys. Attention to detail, some night work. Past exp. preferred. Call Nance, 964-9700, Ext. 603.

SECRETARY AND ATTORNEY POSITIONS

If you see an ad for a legal secretary, docket clerk, word processor, or other clerical position, you might want to respond as follows:

> I saw your ad for a legal secretary. I am a trained paralegal and am wondering whether you have any openings for paralegals. If not, I would greatly appreciate your referring me to attorneys you know who may be looking for competent paralegals.

Should you ever *apply* for a position you are not seeking? A distinction should be made between transitional jobs and career jobs. A transitional job is one taken in the hope that it will eventually turn into the job you really want and for which you have been trained. The latter is a job you would like to keep indefinitely. Should a paralegal take a clerical job as a transitional position? Many paralegals take the view that this would be a mistake. In a tight employment market, however, some believe that a secretarial or clerical position is a way to "get a foot in the door." Their hope is to perform well and eventually graduate into a position in the office that is commensurate with their paralegal training. This "bloom-where-you-are-planted" course of action is obviously a very personal decision that you must make. Clerical staff do sometimes get promoted to paralegal positions in an office, but it is also possible to get stuck in a clerical position. In some offices, success in the clerical position could actually work against you. The office might be reluctant to promote a secretary into a paralegal position because the office does not want to lose a secretary who is doing a good job as a secretary. Finally, it is interesting to keep in mind that some *attorneys* are willing to take a paralegal job in a law office in order to "get a foot in the door" when there is an oversupply of attorneys looking for work in a particular market.

Should you ever respond to want ads for *attorneys*? Of course, a paralegal cannot claim to be an attorney. But any office that is looking for attorneys obviously has a need for legal help. Hence, consider these possible reasons for responding to such ads, particularly when they give the name and address of the office seeking the attorney:

- Perhaps the office is also looking for paralegal help but is simply not advertising for it (or you have not seen the want ad for paralegals).
- Perhaps the office is having difficulty finding the attorney it is seeking and would consider hiring a paralegal for on a temporary basis to perform paralegal tasks while continuing the search for the attorney.
- Perhaps the office has never considered hiring a paralegal instead of an attorney but would be interested in exploring the idea.

Many employers may be totally uninterested in a response by a paralegal to an ad for an attorney. Yet none of the possibilities just described is irrational. The effort might be productive. Even if you receive a flat rejection, you can always use the opportunity to ask the person you contact if he or she knows of any other offices that are hiring paralegals. Here is how you might respond to an attorney ad:

> I saw your ad for an attorney. I am a paralegal and was wondering whether you also have any openings for paralegals. If no full-time positions are open, would you consider hiring a paralegal part-time to perform paralegal tasks while you continue your search for an attorney?

PLACEMENT AGENCIES

Employment agencies advertise their placement services in traditional media and on the Internet. (See Exhibit 2-11 for an example of an ad of a placement agency.) If you are not sure whether an agency covers legal placements, call or email several at random and ask which agencies in the city handle paralegal placement or legal placement in general.

Two main kinds of agencies exist. First there are agencies that place workers who go on the payroll of the offices where they are placed. Second, there are **staffing agencies** that handle the salary, taxes, workers' compensation, and related benefits of the people they place in temporary positions. The office pays the staffing agency, which in turn handles all the financial aspects of the placement.

Some employers hire temporary workers with the goal of hiring them full-time if they fit in and perform well. This arrangement is referred to as *temp-to-hire* or *temp-to-perm*.

For leads to placement agencies on the Internet, see Exhibit 2-12. (See also the employment links for your state in Appendix D.) Paralegal association newsletters (often available on the association's

staffing agency An employment agency that places temporary workers, often directly paying the workers and handling all of the financial aspects of the placement.

| Exhibit 2-11 | Example of an Ad of a Placement Agency |

Help Wanted

| **Paralegal Agency** | | **Fee Paid** |

Paralegal Placement Experts Recognized by Over 200 Law Firms and Corporations

PENSIONS	**LITIGATION**	**MANAGING CLERK**
Outstanding law firm seeks 1+ yrs pension paralegal exper. Major responsibilities, quality clients & liberal benefits. Salary commensurate w/exper.	SEVERAL positions open at LAW FIRMS for litigation paralegals. Major benefits.	Midtown law firm seeks 1+ yrs exper as a managing clerk. Work directly w/top management. Liberal benefits.

These are just a few of the many paralegal positions we have available.
Call us for professional career guidance.

website) and special paralegal magazines such as *Paralegal Today* (www.paralegaltoday.com) may also have this kind of ad. In Google, Bing, or Yahoo, run this search: "legal placement" aa (substituting your city or state for "aa"). Also check your Yellow Pages under "Employment Agencies."

Caution is needed in using placement agencies. Some of them know very little about paralegals, in spite of their ads claiming to place paralegals. You may find that the agency views a legal assistant or paralegal as a secretary with a little extra training. Some agencies will post positions that don't exist in order to generate inquiries and increase their pool of résumés. All agencies charge a placement fee. You must check whether the fee is paid by the employer or by the employee hired through the agency. Read the agency's service contract carefully before signing.

COLD CALLING

Cold calling is contacting someone (usually by telephone) who is not expecting to be contacted by you. You simply call, introduce yourself, and state the purpose of the call: in this instance, to find out if there are any job openings for paralegals. If the person you call knows you or something about you or is expecting your call, it is a "warm" call.

Some job seekers make a list of law firms in their area, obtain basic information about those firms on the Internet (e.g., the kind of law the firm practices), and make cold calls to inquire about employment opportunities. If the office is fairly large, the website might indicate what jobs are open and give the name of the person in charge of hiring. Of course, if you are responding to a published opening, you are making a warm call because such calls are expected.

The approach you take in cold calling must be brief and direct. Example: "My name is Helen Frazer. I recently graduated from the Phoenix Paralegal Institute. I wanted to find out if your office has any openings for paralegals." If the answer is no, ask if you can send a résumé to be kept on file in the event that something opens up in the future. You might also ask about the possibility of volunteering at the office. Finally, ask if the person knows of any other firms in the area where you might check.

Warm calling is certainly preferable to cold calling, but in a tight employment market, you need to consider all options. What about cold résumés (sending a cover letter and résumé to law firms at random even if there is no indication that there are openings at the firm)? Although similar to cold calling, cold résumé sending is less likely to be successful. It's much easier to toss an unsolicited résumé into a trash can than to respond to a cold phone call.

You might consider sending out individually tailored letters inquiring about employment opportunities, but without including your résumé. The letter should include specific information you found out about each law firm on its website, e.g., the kind of law practiced there, a recent court victory. Also check sites that give inside information about law firms (e.g., www.glassdoor.com). After briefly mentioning something about the firm, state your interest in that kind of practice. Include your phone number, email address, and a statement that you would be glad to send in your résumé (and writing samples) if requested. The letter should be addressed to a specific person. (Avoid sending To-Whom-It-May-Concern letters.) If the website does not indicate who is in charge of hiring, send it to a named partner.

INFORMATIONAL INTERVIEWS

informational interview
An interview whose primary purpose is to gain a better understanding of an area of law or kind of employment.

An **informational interview** (sometimes called an *exploratory interview*) is an opportunity to question someone about an area of law or kind of employment. Ideally this is done at the place where the person being interviewed works, although this is not always possible. Unlike a job interview, where you are the one being interviewed, you do the interviewing in an informational interview. You ask questions that will help you learn what working at that kind of office is like.

If, for example, you are a real "people" person who finds antitrust theory fascinating, you should listen to antitrust paralegals discussing their day-to-day work. You may hear that most of them spend years in document warehouses with one lawyer, two other paralegals and a pizza delivery man as their most significant personal contacts. That information may influence your decision about antitrust as a career path.[17]

Do not try to turn an informational interview into a job interview. While on an informational interview, it is inappropriate to ask a person for a job. Toward the end of the interview, you can delicately ask for leads to employment and you can ask how the person obtained his or her job, but these inquiries should be secondary to your primary purpose of obtaining information about the realities of work at that kind of office. Do not use an informational interview as a subterfuge for a job interview that you are having difficulty obtaining.

Although some attorneys and legal administrators may be willing to grant you informational interviews, the best people to talk to are those who were once in your shoes: paralegals. Simply say to a paralegal you have met, "Would it be possible for me to come down to the office where you work for a brief informational interview?" If he or she is not familiar with this kind of interview, explain its limited objective. Many will be too busy to grant you an interview, but you have nothing to lose by asking. If they are willing to accommodate you, they will probably need the permission of their employer before bringing someone into the office. As an added inducement, consider offering to take the paralegal to lunch. In addition to meeting this paralegal, try to have at least a brief tour of the office where he or she works. Observing how different kinds of employees interact with each other and with available technology in the office will be invaluable. If it is not possible to go to an office, try to conduct informational interviews wherever you find working paralegals. For example, go to a paralegal association meeting and ask people at random what kind of work they do. You do not have to use the phrase *informational interview*. If someone you meet mentions an area that interests you, ask the same kinds of questions you would ask if you were interviewing that person in his or her office.

Here are some of the questions you should consider asking:

- What is a typical day for you in your office?
- What kinds of assignments do you receive?
- How much overtime is usually expected? Do you take work home with you?
- How do the attorneys interact with paralegals in this kind of practice? Who does what? How many different attorneys does a paralegal work with? How are assignment priorities set?
- How do the paralegals interact with secretaries and other support staff in the office? What is the hierarchy of the office?
- What kind of education best prepares a paralegal to work in this kind of office? What courses are most effective?
- What is the most challenging aspect of the job? The most frustrating?
- How are paralegals perceived in this office?
- Are you glad you became this kind of paralegal in this kind of office? Would you do it over again?
- What advice would you give to someone who wants to become a paralegal like yourself?

Several of these questions are also appropriate in a job interview, as we will see later. (To learn more, run this search in Google, Bing, or Yahoo: *informational interview*.)

One final word of caution. Any information you learn about clients or legal matters must be kept confidential, even if the person you are interviewing is casual about revealing such information to you. This person may not be aware that he or she is acting unethically by disclosing confidential information. Carelessness in this regard is not uncommon. *Any* information about a client (including the fact that the office represents the client) is confidential, even if some of this information is known by the public.

JOB LEADS ON THE INTERNET

Thus far in this chapter, we have mentioned resources on the Internet a number of times. Exhibit 2-12 presents additional resources available in cyberspace. Keep an open mind about the Internet as a resource. You may have to wade through numerous advertisements and pressures to sign up for services. Yet through the maze, you might come across exactly what you are looking for. Rather than do a blitz of many sites, set aside a certain amount of time each day to devote to checking the various sites listed in Exhibit 2-12.

Exhibit 2-12	Employment Resources on the Internet

For many of the employment sites listed below, find out:
- Whether specific paralegal jobs are posted (if this is not clear, type paralegal or legal assistant or job bank in the search boxes on the sites, even for those sites that appear to be focused primarily on attorneys)
- Whether you can post your résumé on the site for prospective employers to examine
- Whether the service charges a fee
- Whether guidance is available (directly or through links) on résumé writing and job-interview strategies.

Caution
- Use caution when responding to any Internet site. Identity thieves have been known to hack into legitimate employment sites, post bogus job offerings, and collect personal information from unsuspecting job hunters. See additional cautions in Exhibit 2-14.

Paralegal and Other Support Job Sites
- www.linkedin.com/studentjobs (see Exhibit 2-13 on joining LinkedIn)
- www.paralegalmanagement.org (click *Job Bank*)
- www.alanet.org/careers/jobs.asp
- paralegaltoday.com/jobbank
- www.getparalegaljobs.com
- www.mynextmove.org (type *paralegal* in the search box)
- www.paralegals.org (click *NFPA Career Center*)
- www.paralegaljobs.com
- www.litigationsupportcareers.com

Job Alert Sites
(Allows you to sign up to be given email notifications of openings)
- www.careerbuilder.com
- www.legalstaff.com
- www.lawcrossing.com
- www.tweetmyjobs.com

General Legal Employment Search Sites
(For attorneys, paralegals, and other legal staff)
- www.roberthalflegal.com
- www.lawjobs.com

- www.lawcrossing.com
- careers.findlaw.com
- www.hg.org/employment.html
- www.lawyerintl.com
- www.ihirelegal.com
- www.specialcounsel.com/legal-jobs
- www.legalstaff.com
- www.lawtechjobs.com

General Employment Search Sites
(Can be used for paralegal searches; type paralegal in the search boxes on the sites)
- www.refdesk.com/jobsearch.html
- www.indeed.com
- www.careeronestop.org
- www.glassdoor.com
- www.bright.com
- www.careerbuilder.com
- www.careerbliss.com
- www.careerjet.com
- www.careerpath.com
- www.monster.com
- www.simplyhired.com
- www.jobs2careers.com
- www.jobbankinfo.org
- www.vault.com
- www.oodle.com
- www.linkup.com
- www.job-search-engine.com

General Search Engines as Job Resources
In Google, Bing, or Yahoo, run this search: aa paralegal "job search" (substituting your city or state for "aa").

Paralegal Associations and Bar Associations
Paralegal Associations
- Go to the websites of the paralegal associations in your state (see Appendix B). Find out if the associations have a job bank.

Bar Associations.

- Go to the website of the state, city, and county bar associations in your state (see Appendix B). Many associations have job-search services for attorneys, which also cover paralegal employment. On the opening page of the association, type *paralegal employment or paralegal jobs* in the search box. Also look for links on this page for *Career Center, Employment, Jobs, or Job Board.*

Craigslist

- www.craigslist.com (pick your city, then under *Jobs* select *Legal/Paralegal*)

Federal Government Employment

- In Google, Bing, or Yahoo, run this search: paralegal job federal government
- www.usajobs.org
- www.youtube.com (type *usajobs* in the search box)

State Government Employment

- For paralegal job categories in your state government, see your state in Appendix I.
- In Google, Bing, or Yahoo, run this search: aa paralegal job "state government" (substituting the name of your state for aa)
- www.governmentjobs.com

Court Employment

Federal

- www.uscourts.gov (click *Careers*)

State

- www.ncsc.org (type *State Court websites* in the search box) (scroll down to your state; click individual courts and on the sites of these courts, look for links to *Employment* or *Careers*)

Placement Agencies: Temporary Legal Staffing

- In Google, Bing, or Yahoo, run this search: aa "legal staffing" paralegal (substituting the name of your city or state for "aa")
- www.juristaff.com
- www.specialcounsel.com
- www.lumenlegal.com

Salary Information

- www.roberthalflegal.com
- www.salary.com
- www.salaryexpert.com
- www.careeronestop.org

Résumé, Interviewing, and General Job Search Resources

- In Google, Bing, or Yahoo, run this search: paralegal resume help.
- In Google, Bing, or Yahoo, run this search: paralegal job interview help.
- paralegalpost.net/helpfulhints.asp
- www.hg.org/employment.html
- www.careeronestop.org
- www.careerpath.com/resources

Finding Information about Law Offices

The following links will lead you to the sites of many law firms in your state. Those sites will provide information about the firm, e.g., the kind of law it practices.

- See the links in Appendix H
- www.martindale.com
- lawyers.findlaw.com
- www.washlaw.edu (click *Law Firms*)

Volunteer Opportunities to Obtain Experience

(On these sites, type search terms such as *paralegal, legal, lawyer,* or *attorney.*)

- www.volunteermatch.org
- www.idealist.org
- www.casaforchildren.org
- volunteer.gov
- handsonnetwork.org
- www.nationalservice.gov
- www.taprootfoundation.org
- www.serve.gov
- www.allforgood.org

Internships

(Labor laws require that unpaid internships not displace regular employees.) (On the following sites, type search terms such as *legal, paralegal, lawyer,* or *attorney.*)

- internship.com
- www.internjobs.com
- www.youtern.com
- internqueen.com
- www.internmatch.com
- www.vault.com
- On Google, Bing, or Yahoo, run this search: aa finding an internship (substituting your state for "aa")
- On Google, Bing, or Yahoo, run this search: aa unpaid internships legal (substituting your state for "aa")

USING SOCIAL MEDIA IN THE JOB SEARCH

On social-media sites such as LinkedIn, Twitter, and Facebook, you will find a great deal of information. The quality of this information will range from worthless to invaluable. We need to explore ways to obtain the latter. There are five interrelated reasons social-media sites can be an asset in your job search.

- First, they are additional ways for you to become known and, therefore, noticed as a job applicant. Many job seekers use social-media sites to indicate that they are looking for employment.
- Second, they are a way for you to establish your own *brand*, which consists of your strengths, accomplishments, and unique qualities.

- Third, many employers have their own social-media pages that you can use to do background research on them so that you can better target your employment application to their needs. Almost all attorneys, for example, have a LinkedIn page.
- Fourth, job openings are often made known on these sites. Hence, social-media sites can add to and enhance traditional employment-search strategies.
- Fifth, they are the equivalent of forums and discussion groups in which you can ask for specific advice in the job search.

Exhibit 2-13 presents guidelines for using social media in the job search. Cautions you should keep in mind when using social media are listed in Exhibit 2-14.

Exhibit 2-13	Using Social Media in a Job Search

1. General Guidelines

The following general guidelines apply to LinkedIn, Twitter, Facebook, and any other social-media site you are on.

- Joining these social-media sites is free. They all try to sell you extra services, but the free versions are adequate for most job seekers.
- You want to be found on Google and other search engines. One way to be found is to be active on the social-media sites.
- You will be giving out your email address. Be sure that it is professional in tone. If, for example, your email address is ImToughThompson@ hotmail.com, set up a free gmail or yahoo email account with a new name, e.g., hthompson51@gmail.com.
- Use a shoulder and headshot of you in which you appear professional and conservative. No one else should be in the picture.
- You will be asked to select a username on the social-media site. Use your given name with slight modifications if your username is already taken.
- When someone goes to your social-media site, they should not be able to determine your religious views, your political leanings, or your romantic history.
- You need to be active on the social-media sites you join. Simply signing up is not enough. Spend fifteen-to-thirty minutes a day on them, particularly LinkedIn and Twitter. Spend half of this time exploring relevant pages. Spend the other half by creating posts. Post often. For example, at least once a day, post one comment on a LinkedIn discussion, tweet (or retweet) one career-related item on Twitter, and add one career-related item on Facebook.
- Apply the grandma test to everything you post online, particularly on Facebook. If you don't want your grandma to see what you post, you don't want potential employers to see it. Everyone has a brand—the image that the world has of him or her. You want your brand to be professional, skilled, dependable, consistent, and conservative. This brand is not enhanced if there is a picture of you online with a drink in your hand at a bar.
- If you are already on social media and your presence there is more playful than professional (particularly on Facebook and Twitter), you need to clean up your pages and/or create additional accounts on the sites that you will use for career advancement. On Google, Bing, or Yahoo, run these searches:
  - How to clean up your image on _____ (in the blank space, insert the name of any site you may want to try to adjust).
  - How to remove digital dirt.

  Digital dirt (DD) is anything online that is inappropriate or damaging because it casts you in a negative light and interferes with the brand you want to establish for yourself as a competent professional. DD can include party photos, rants about politics, links to off-color humor, etc.

- When communicating with a site (e.g., posting something), don't use your work computer. You may not want your employer to know about your job search or other postings. Using the employer's computer or your work email address may be the equivalent of sending copies of everything to your employer.
- Don't get sidetracked. Once you become familiar with what's available on social media, you could spend all day exploring it all. Limit the time spent and stay focused on whatever will promote your career.
- Be patient. You probably won't see immediate results, but over time social media can help you build a reputation (your personal brand) as someone worth knowing because of your professionalism and your contributions to social media.

2. LinkedIn

LinkedIn is one of the most professional social-media sites on the Internet (www.linkedin.com). It is not a site to share party pictures. It is a site for serious-minded people in the world of business and the professions who want to connect with each other in order to launch, enhance, or restart their careers. Think of LinkedIn as a "live" résumé and business card because of the additions you can make to it and the interaction it can generate with others. Many students looking for their first job have also found the site to be helpful.

- Start by spending a few moments learning the basics of LinkedIn by looking at its overview site (help.linkedin.com) or by typing "LinkedIn" or "LinkedIn tutorial" on www.youtube.com.
- On Google, Bing, or Yahoo, run this search: how to find a job on LinkedIn.
- Sign up to become a registered user. Registration is free. Enter your full name, email address, and a password.

- Before you take the next step (filling out your profile), enter *paralegal student* in the search box. Start by reading through about a dozen or so profiles, noting the ones that have the most professional content and appearance. Keep reading until you have found a fair number of students who have backgrounds and experience similar to yours. Look for phrasing and formats that you can adapt.
- Fill out your own profile in which you tell the LinkedIn community about your professional self, e.g., where you have worked, where you have studied, what skills you have, significant projects you have contributed to, and what hopes you have for the future (such as finding a paralegal job). The more complete and expansive your profile, the more likely you are to reach and be reached by useful contacts.
- Make the profile public so that people can reach you both within LinkedIn and on search engines such as Google. Your profile is the equivalent of an online résumé.
- Start with a concise headline and summary that focuses on your career goal. Be specific as to the type of job you are looking for (e.g., "I am looking for a paralegal job in estates and trusts." As a student, you can be more general if you are not sure what kind of paralegal you want to be.).
- If you have legal experience, list it before education. Otherwise list your education first, followed by job experience. (See the discussion later in this chapter on phrasing experience and education.) Give the complete names of schools and prior employers. You want people to be able to find you if they search for people connected with those schools or employers.
- Include computer programs you have used, substantial volunteer activity, special skills (e.g., speak a foreign language), and any highlights that show you in a positive light (e.g., awards received).
- Include areas of interest outside the law (e.g., photography, fencing, New York Mets). Nonfrivolous hobbies might strike the fancy of someone looking for people with a similar interest.
- Update your profile regularly. When, for example, you finish a course, add the skills learned and the major themes covered on your profile.
- Include links in your profile to your other social sites (e.g., Twitter and Facebook) so long as these sites are professional and conservative.
- Your profile will have a specific Internet address. You will want to link to this address on other social-media sites, on paper résumés, on your email signature, and on business cards. Unfortunately, the LinkedIn profile address is usually long and too unwieldy to place on a paper résumé or business card. Use programs that allow you to shorten such addresses (e.g., www.tinyurl.com, www.snipurl.com).
- Click *Jobs* on the LinkedIn homepage or type jobs in the search box. Then type paralegal in the search box. For corporate paralegal jobs, see: www.linkedin.com/job/corporate-paralegal-jobs-jobs.
- Build a network of connections. On LinkedIn, a connection is simply someone you wish to be associated with, usually because you have something in common. The mutuality can be very broad: e.g., you both work in (or would like to work in) a particular area of law; or very narrow (you both have the same hobby). To find connections, start searching for people you know. Enter names in the general LinkedIn search box. (If, for example, you have fifty people in your email address book, type each name in the LinkedIn search engine to find out if they are already on LinkedIn.) If they are, send each an email on the LinkedIn messaging system in which you invite them to become a connection. On their LinkedIn page, note their connections. Decide which of them you will also send invitations to on the basis of anything you share in common. Slowly you start to build your network of contacts. When you solicit a connection, try to say something personal in the invitation (e.g., make note of something you read on their profile) rather than simply using the generic invitation that is the default invitation provided by LinkedIn.
- When people accept your invitation to be a connection, don't immediately send them a request for a job lead. Let a little time pass and try to interact with them first, such as by commenting on something in their profile or asking them a question about their area of work.
- Join LinkedIn groups that are likely to give you job leads, e.g., paralegal associations. Join as many relevant groups as you can (the maximum allowed is fifty). Do a groups search. Enter "paralegal groups" in the general search box or click Groups and enter "paralegal" in its search box. Start joining groups that are related to your professional goals. Also search for alumni groups for your schools, groups of former employers, groups of houses of worship, social clubs you belong to, etc. They all could provide a rich resource of new connections.
- Read current discussions in the groups you have joined. For example, many of the paralegal groups have discussions on how someone finds a paralegal job with no prior paralegal experience. Scores of answers are often available for you to read, many offering concrete advice.
- Send connection invitations to persons who have made statements in the discussions that are relevant to your career goals.
- Add your own comments to ongoing discussions.
- Discussions often ask a question (e.g., anyone know the name of a good recruiting agency in Atlanta?) or alert the group to something interesting found on the Internet (e.g., a website on legal research, a recent article on a court case).
- Start your own discussion. Add a question or tell the group about something you think will be of interest to it.
- Join the students' LinkedIn section, The Job Portal for Students and Recent Graduates (www.linkedin.com/studentjobs). Use its search box to look for job openings.
- Use LinkedIn for background research on any law firm, company, or association where you may want to apply for work. Type its name in the search box. Use the *Advanced* search feature of LinkedIn to narrow the search for specific firms or companies. The information might include the name of the hiring contact and the profiles of paralegals already employed there.
- LinkedIn has an-easy-to-use format by which members give each other skill endorsements and recommendations on their profile page. An endorsement is given by a single click; a recommendation is praise that is written out. When you scan student LinkedIn profiles, note the endorsements and recommendations that have been received. There are two main ways to obtain endorsements and recommendations:
  - Give them to others. Most people like to receive endorsements and recommendations and are likely to reciprocate with an endorsement or recommendation back about you.
  - Ask for an endorsement or recommendation from your connections. Seek responses from people who are knowledgeable and respected in their field.
  - If people praise your work skills or expertise, ask them to give you an endorsement or recommendation for your LinkedIn profile and show them how easy it is to join LinkedIn and to make endorsements or recommendations.

- Before contacting a prospective employer, find out if any of your LinkedIn connections are connected with anyone at this employer. You may be able to find someone who will be a point of reference for you there.
- Start your own LinkedIn group. Identify something in which you and at least a few others have a mutual interest. An example might be a group consisting of your fellow students. To get ideas, click Groups on the LinkedIn home page. Once the group is formed, start inviting people to join.

3. Twitter

Many attorneys use Twitter (www.twitter.com) regularly, some every day. In addition, legal employment agencies and individual paralegals use Twitter to communicate information about paralegal employment. Tweets are very short messages (up to 140 characters). The messages are powerful because of the links contained within the messages. The link can tell you about a recent job opening, give you background information about a prospective employer, or give you suggestions on how to find a job in today's market.

- Spend a few moments learning the basics of Twitter by looking at its overview site (support.twitter.com) or by typing *Twitter* or *Twitter tutorial* on www.youtube.com. Here, for example, is an excellent short tutorial: www.wikihow.com/Use-Twitter.
- On Google, Bing, or Yahoo, run this search: how to find a job on Twitter.
- Sign up to become a registered user (www.twitter.com/signup). Registration is free. Enter your full name, email address, and a password.
- Select a username. It is called a Twitter handle. Later we will see that the @ sign can be used in front of a username as a search aid. (This @ sign has nothing to do with email addresses.)
- Twitter gives you very little space (140 characters) for your profile (called a Bio). You need to concentrate on the most important aspect of your current situation—what defines you today. For example, you might say: "Paralegal student (will graduate in 20xx) seeking work with a law firm or corporation." If you have a special skill or accomplishment, include it. Examples: "Paralegal student and former nurse (will graduate in 20xx) seeking work in medical malpractice or health law." "Paralegal student (will graduate in 20xx) with excellent computer skills (Excel, Access, etc.) seeking paralegal employment." This statement can be easily modified when your circumstances change, e.g., you finish school.
- Your Twitter Profile/Bio can and should include a link to your more expansive profile/resume on LinkedIn. (See LinkedIn above.)
- Your Twitter page will have a specific Internet address. You will want to link to this address on other social-media sites, on paper résumés, on your email signature, and on business cards.
- Two of the main ways to search Twitter are the search box at the top of the site and the search box when you click the #Discover link. In both of these search boxes, type the following searches:
  - paralegal
  - "paralegal employment"
  - "paralegal student"
  - "employment agency" paralegal
  - "legal recruiters"

You can add the name of your city or state after each search to be more specific.

- From these searches, find people who would probably be helpful in your job search. This could be because they are in the same situation you are in and/or because they may provide job leads or helpful search techniques. For each of these persons, click the "Follow" button. Then go to their home Twitter page. You will be told how many Twitter messages (tweets) they have sent out, how many people they are following, and how many people are following them. Click through the list of people they are following and people who are following them. From these lists, find additional people for you to follow. Build a list of people to follow.
- When you find an interesting or valuable tweet, retweet it. Retweeting is a way of promoting others. You are saying to the original tweeter that his or her tweet is important enough for you to pass it on (retweet it) to your followers. Helping others in this way encourages them to help you.
- Now you are ready to send out your first tweets. You can simply state that you are new on the block. (Examples: "Hello. This is my first tweet." or "I'm in the paralegal field and I hope to learn and contribute to the field through Twitter." Keep within the 140-character limit for each tweet.
- Let the twitterverse (everyone on Twitter) know that you are looking for employment. Example: "In June, I will finish my paralegal education and am looking for job leads in the Los Angeles area."
- Pick a topic that interests you. It could be an area of law or a legal issue. Examples: probate, school vouchers, the First Amendment. Spend ten minutes a day on Google, Bing, or Yahoo searching that topic. Find interesting sites on that topic. For each site you find, write a tweet about it. Simply state the heading of the site and give its web address. Start building a reputation as someone knowledgeable about that topic by your tweets. You do not have to be an expert to tweet. You are on the way to becoming an expert by being a twitterer on a specific topic. Should you wait until you finish school to begin? No.
- Seek followers of your tweets. In the search box, type in names of people you know. If they are on Twitter, follow them and ask them to follow you. Ask your friends, relatives, and colleagues who are not on Twitter to join and to follow you.
- Use hashtag searches to find groups of tweets on the same topic. A hashtag is a group of words with a # before it. For example, type a jobs search hashtag (#"paralegal job") in the Twitter search box. This will lead you to a variety of tweets such as those posted by job recruiters. A broader hashtag (#paralegal) leads you to a larger variety of tweets. As you go through them, select ones to follow that are most relevant to your career goals. Suppose that you come across the name of the law firm of White & Case where you might want to apply for work. Do a hashtag search on this firm (#"white and case").
- In the Help section of Twitter, find out how the "at" sign (@) is used to call out usernames in tweets. Suppose, for example, you find a tweet posted by someone who is hiring. You can connect with that person by sending his or her username an @ message. A username is preceded by the @ sign, which becomes a link to that person's Twitter profile. Again, check Twitter's Help section to learn how to use the @.

- Some sites provide added assistance in the job search via Twitter, e.g., by alerting you to recent tweets on the kind of job you are looking for. Examples:
  - www.tweetmyjobs.com
  - www.twitjobsearch.com

4. Facebook

Facebook (www.facebook.com) is another major social-media site. Most people use it for social interaction as they post pictures and share updates about their lives. Facebook can also be a professional resource in your job search.

- Create an account in Facebook if you don't already have one. Accounts are free. You will be asked to state your name, birthday, gender, and email address.
- Spend a few moments learning the basics of Facebook by looking at its overview site (www.facebook.com/help/basics) or by typing Facebook tutorial or Facebook basics on www.youtube.com.
- On Google, Bing, or Yahoo, run this search: how to find a job on Facebook.
- If you don't want to use Facebook in your job search, change your privacy settings on Facebook to "friends only" so that only persons you have accepted as friends can see your profile, photos, and personal updates. During a job interview, you might be asked for your password so that the prospective employer can learn more about you. In some states, however, it is illegal for the employer to make this request.

The following guidelines assume that you do want to use Facebook in your job search.

- Be sure that your profile does not contain anything frivolous. See the earlier guideline on removing DD (digital dirt). Everything does not have to be excised. Several photos of you camping on a lake with your family help show that you have a well-rounded personality.
- On your Facebook page, link to your profiles on LinkedIn and Twitter.
- Ask former or current coworkers and employers you respect to be your friends. Also tap into the alumni of schools. Friends you make among former classmates could lead to useful job leads.
- Tell people about your career plans. Let your friends know you are looking for a paralegal job.
- Add career-related updates to your page, e.g., completing a course, attending a continuing legal education (CLE) session, or receiving a commendation.
- Find out if the law firm, business, or association where you might like to work has a Facebook page. If it does, "like" it and "follow" it so that you will receive news and updates about it.
- In the Facebook homepage, type the following in the search box:
  - Paralegal jobs
  - Paralegal job aa (substituting your city or state for "aa")
- Use Facebook email to communicate with your friends about your job search. Ask for leads.
- Find career groups on Facebook and join. For example, type *paralegal* in the general search box and click *groups*.

SECURITY AND PRIVACY WHEN USING SOCIAL MEDIA

There are downsides to social-media sites. For example, the sites can use cookies to monitor the Internet activity of users in order to create advertising that is targeted at users. If, for example, you visit a site for boxing matches at the City Arena, don't be surprised if a few days later you see an ad for City Arena boxing when you are reading a story about the mayor while visiting a news site. This bothers some people. Others feel that it is a small price to pay to be able to take advantage of the benefits of the sites. More ominously, social-media sites can facilitate certain kinds of antisocial behavior (e.g., stalking) and crime (identity theft).

Although it is possible to make all or most of your activity on social-media sites private, this would tend to defeat the goal of substantially widening your network of contacts in order to find employment and enhance your career. Hence, a balance must be struck between protection and openness. The guidelines in Exhibit 2-14 should help you strike this balance.

Exhibit 2-14	Caution in Using Social Media

- When on a social-media site (or anywhere on the Internet):
  - Do not use your Social Security number.
  - Do not give your street address or phone number.
  - Do not indicate where you are at any particular moment. Do not state that you are on vacation or away from home (such news is valuable to a burglar).
  - Do not post criticisms of former or current coworkers or employers.
  - Do not post confidential information.

- If you don't feel comfortable sharing something on a site, don't share it.
- Have a strong password (e.g., one with letters and numerals and that is not used on multiple sites).
- Use, know the status of, and regularly update anti-virus software, anti-spyware software, and a firewall (see Chapter 13).
- To remove an account or public profile, check the help section of the site and the following guides:
  - www.accountkiller.com/en
  - Run this search on Google, Bing, or Yahoo: deleting private information
- Educate yourself about security and privacy. On Google, Bing, or Yahoo, run these searches:
  - LinkedIn security privacy
  - Twitter security privacy
  - Facebook security privacy
- There are no guarantees when submitting information (e.g., your employment history) on the Internet. As indicated, identity thieves might find such information useful. Ultimately, you need to become informed about security and privacy so that you can make a judgment of whether you are sending the information into a secure environment.

RÉSUMÉ

Most résumés are **chronological résumés**, which present your education and experience in a chronological sequence, starting with the present and working backward. (Reverse chronological order.) The other major kind of résumé is a **functional résumé**, which covers skills and experience regardless of when they were developed or occurred. The functional résumé also presents reverse chronological data, but in a different overall arrangement. Example of both résumés will be presented in Exhibits 2-15 and 2-16 after we cover résumé guidelines. Although we will focus on these two résumé formats, others exist. To locate different styles of résumés, run this search on Google, Bing, or Yahoo: *kinds of resumes*.

chronological résumé
A résumé that presents biographical data on education, training, and experience in a chronological sequence starting with the present and working backward.

functional résumé A résumé that covers skills and experience regardless of when they were developed or occurred.

GUIDELINES ON DRAFTING AN EFFECTIVE RÉSUMÉ

1. *Advocacy.* A résumé is an advocacy document. You are using it to try to convince someone to give you an interview and, ultimately, to offer you a job. You are not simply communicating information about yourself. A résumé is not a summary of your life or a short autobiography. It is *targeted* advertising—a brief commercial in which you are trying to sell yourself as a person who can make a contribution to a *particular* prospective employer. This means that you will often have to make changes to your résumé every time you send it out. If, for example, you know that an office is looking for a litigation paralegal, you phrase your accomplishments, education, and experience to highlight what you can contribute to a litigation attorney. There is a difference between a general résumé and a targeted résumé. The latter uses language that is responsive to the employment needs of a particular prospective employer. It uses the buzzwords found in the ad for the job you are seeking (e.g., litigation management, office systems, experience with Excel). Background research on the prospective employer (see the following guidelines on doing this research) may suggest other key language (buzzwords) to use in your résumé to help demonstrate that you are the person the office is looking for. A general résumé, in contrast, is a shotgun document that you hope contains data about you that will appeal to any employer. There is nothing wrong with having a general résumé (later we will suggest that you create one). But don't send it out. Use it as the starting point for the creation of targeted résumés that you do send out.

2. *Length.* Generally, the résumé should fit on one page. A second page is justified only if you have unique education or experience that is directly related to the particular law firm or company in which you are interested. Do not submit a résumé that is longer than two pages. Such length is a signal that you don't know how to organize and summarize data. This is not a message that a prospective paralegal wants to convey.

3. *Format: Paper Résumé.* Most résumés will be printed on paper and sent in an envelope. For such résumés:

   - Do not include a photo or business card. You should, however, link to your LinkedIn and Twitter profiles that do contain your photo.

font The design or style of printed letters of the alphabet, punctuation marks, or other characters.

point A measure of the size of printed letters of the alphabet, punctuation marks, or other characters. One point is approximately 1/72 of an inch tall. (See glossary for another meaning.)

PDF Portable Document Format; a file format consisting of an electronic image of a document that preserves the features and styles of the document (e.g., its line spacing, photograph placement, and font size) that existed before it was converted into a digital document.

metadata Data about data. Data about a computer document that are hidden within the document itself, e.g., earlier versions of the document.

- Use at least a one-inch margin throughout. Leave generous white space throughout; do not pack the text into every corner of the page.
- Use headings for the major sections.
- For the body of the résumé, use only one **font** and **point** size (e.g., Times New Roman or Courier New, 11 point). The main headings should be bold and all caps with a slightly higher point size (e.g., 12). Alternatively, you could use a different conservative font for the headings (e.g., Verdana, 11 point).
- Be consistent in fonts and point sizes. For the text, use the same font and point size throughout. Similarly, for the headings, use the same font and point size throughout. If, for example, you use Verdana 11 point, all caps, for the first heading, do the same for all the headings in the résumé.
- Avoid abbreviations except for items such as street, state, and month. Do not, for example, abbreviate the names of educational institutions. Some abbreviations of schools can be confusing to a reader.
- Do not make any handwritten corrections; retype or reprint the résumé after you make corrections.

4. *Format: Digital Résumé.* Some employers will allow (or require) that you submit a résumé as a digital document. There are two main ways this is done. First, you can place the résumé in the body of an email message. Second (and preferably), you can convert the résumé into a **PDF** document and send it as an email attachment. Before you use the first method, send the résumé to yourself in an email message. This will allow you to see it as it would be received by an employer. Bullets, indents, and other format features often become distorted in the body of an email. You may have to make changes (e.g., avoid indents and use asterisks rather than bullets) so that the résumé is presentable upon arrival. A PDF document preserves all the format features and styles you used when you originally prepared the document. Always have a PDF version of your résumés available. It is the cleanest and most professional way to send a digital résumé. (If you used the word-processing program Microsoft Word, run this search on Google, Bing, or Yahoo: how to convert a Word document to a PDF file.)

Some employers might ask you a series of detailed online questions, the answers to which would produce the equivalent of a digital résumé in the format the employer prefers.

Maintain proper formality in whatever you send online. Do not be familiar. Do not address anyone by his or her first name or sign off by using your first name alone.

5. *Metadata.* When you submit any document online, it contains the text of the document *and* **metadata**. The latter is text hidden within the document itself, but recipients of the document may know how to read this metadata. For example, the metadata could consist of an earlier version of the résumé that you sent to another prospective employer. Before sending a digital document, therefore, you need to remove any metadata in it. How this is done may depend on which program you used to create the document. On Google, Bing, or Yahoo, run this search: how to remove metadata.

6. *Honesty.* Studies show that about 30 percent of all résumés contain inaccuracies. Recently, a legal administrator felt the need to make the following comment to other legal administrators about job applicants: "I'm sure we have all had experiences where an applicant has lied on an application about experience, previous salary scales, length of time with previous employers, training, skills, and anything else they can think of that will make them appear more attractive."[18] Although you want to present yourself in the best possible light, don't jeopardize your integrity. All of the data in the résumé should be verifiable. Prospective employers who check the accuracy of résumés usually do so themselves, although some use outside credential-checking services. (For example, see www.myreferences.com.) Finally, be careful in what you say about yourself online on social-media sites such as Facebook. If someone googles your name, you do not want them to find any character traits or facts that are at odds with what you say or imply in your résumé. The picture of you holding a drink with your eyes rolling may have been a big hit among your circle of friends, but it could lead a prospective employer to doubt whether you would be compatible with the culture of the office.

7. *Top of Résumé.* At the top of the résumé, give your name, street address, zip code, email address, and phone (with area code) where you can be reached. (If someone is not always available to take messages while you are away, use an answering machine.) Also give your LinkedIn and Twitter addresses (and Facebook address if the latter is professional in tone and content as outlined in Exhibit 2-13). Do not include information on your health, height, religion, or political party. You do not have to include information that might give a prospective employer a basis to discriminate against you illegally, such as your marital status. Later we will discuss how to handle such matters in a job interview.

8. *Statement of Skills and Accomplishments with Career Objective.* Next should come a short summary of skills and accomplishments (also called a summary of qualifications) that could include a career objective and that is targeted at a particular kind of employer. (The details of the skills and accomplishments will come later in the résumé.) Some studies indicate that recruiters typically spend about six seconds before deciding if the person in the résumé fits what the office is seeking. The opening summary statement on skills and accomplishments at the beginning of the résumé, therefore, must capture the attention of the reader quickly. If it doesn't, the rest of the résumé will probably be ignored.

A flat statement of a career objective alone is usually not sufficient. Example:

Career Objective

A position as a paralegal at an office where there is an opportunity for growth.

There are several problems with this statement. First, it is so general that it gives the unfortunate effect of a mass-mailed résumé. The statement is flat and uninformative. Its generalities could fit any paralegal job. Second, and more seriously, the focus of the statement is on what *you* want. Employers want to know what you can do for *them*—what you can contribute—rather than what you want or need.

A more effective approach is to provide a skills-and-accomplishments statement, which tells the employer what you are seeking in the context of what you can contribute. The statement lets the employer know what you are seeking (a paralegal job) but highlights what you have to offer. Example:

Summary of Major Skills and Accomplishments

Paralegal with ten years of litigation experience with a major law firm (three as senior supervising paralegal) seeks paralegal position in a corporate law department where expertise in accounting, Excel, and database management will make major contributions to the office.

If you are new to the field and do not have legal experience, you can still focus on transferable skills from nonlegal work and volunteer experiences. Later in this chapter when we cover the Job-Search Notebook (JSN), we will cover ways to identify these transferable skills. Example:

Summary of Major Skills and Accomplishments

Recent paralegal honors graduate with seven years of senior sales experience with an online startup and two years in the accounts department of Citibank seeks paralegal position in a law firm where my commercial account experience in sales and finance combined with the investigation, writing, and research skills developed in the paralegal program can be major assets to the office.

The statement should be targeted to a particular employer and therefore must be rewritten just about every time you send out a résumé to a different employer. The first example above is in a résumé sent to the law department of a corporation or of an association. You would not send a résumé with such a statement to a law firm. Similarly, the résumé with the second statement above would go to a law firm, not to a corporation or association.

9. *Education.* Next, state your prior education and training if you have not had any legal work experience. (If you have worked in a law office before, particularly as a paralegal, the next section of the résumé should be work experience, followed by education and training.) List each school or training institution (without abbreviations) and the dates attended. Use a reverse chronological order. Start the list with the most current and work backward. Do not include your high school unless you attended a prestigious high school. When you give your legal education:

- List the major courses.
- State specific skills and tasks covered in your courses that are relevant to the job for which you are applying. (There is no need to use complete sentences so long as you abide by the parallelism rule discussed later.) Also, state major topic areas covered in the courses that demonstrate a knowledge of (or at least significant exposure to) material that is relevant to the job. For example, if you are applying for a corporate paralegal job, relevant courses could be stated as indicated in Exhibit 2-15.

Exhibit 2-15	Phrasing Education

Assume that you are applying for a corporate paralegal job.

Corporate Law:	Formation of a corporation, functions of director and shareholder meetings, corporate mergers, and the dissolution of corporations. Reviewed sample shareholder minutes and prepared proxy statements. Grade received: B+.
Legal Research:	Traditional and online legal research, including title IV of the state corporations code and federal securities law. Grade received: A

- List any special programs in the school, such as unique class assignments, term papers, extensive research, moot court, internship, or semester projects. Give a brief description if the programs are relevant to the job you are seeking.
- State any unusually high grades; give overall grade point average (GPA) only if it is distinctive.
- List any degrees, certificates, or other recognition that you earned at each school or training institution.

10. *Experience.* As indicated, if you have legal experience, list experience before education. For each job you have had, list (in reverse chronological order) your job title, dates of employment, and major duties, preferably phrased as accomplishments. Suppose, for example, that you were once a video store clerk. Here is an ineffective way to state this experience:

Overland Community Video, Assistant Manager, 2005–2008
Responsibilities:

- Kept inventory
- Tracked rentals

Here is a more effective statement focused on *accomplishments* along with duties:[19]
Overland Community Video, Assistant Manager, 2005–2008

- Organizational Experience: Responsible for properly storing, displaying, documenting, and maintaining records for 2,500 leased items without error over a three-year period.

If you cannot specify accomplishments, simply list the major duties. Emphasize duties/accomplishments that are directly relevant to the position you are seeking; e.g., if you are applying for a position in corporate law, state that you drafted corporate minutes or prepared incorporation papers.

Every prior job says something about you as an individual. Phrase your job experience in a manner that will highlight important personality traits. In general, most employers are looking for people with the following characteristics:

- Emotional maturity
- Intelligence
- Willingness to learn
- Ability to get along with others

- Ability to work independently (someone with initiative and self-reliance who is not afraid of assuming responsibility)

- Problem-solving skills
- Ability to handle time pressures and frustration
- Ability to communicate orally, on paper, and online
- Loyalty
- Stability, reliability
- Energy

As you state your job experience, do not use any of the language in this list, but try to state duties/accomplishments in a way that shows how these characteristics apply to you. For example, if you had a job as a camp counselor, state that you:

- Supervised eighteen children for which you received special commendation
- Designed schedules according to predetermined objectives
- Prepared budgets that accurately covered program needs
- Took over camp management in the absence of the camp director, etc.

A listing of such duties/accomplishments will say a lot about you as a person. You are someone who can be trusted, you know how to work with people, you are flexible, etc. These are the kinds of conclusions that you want the reader of your résumé to reach.

11. *Action verbs.* Use action verbs throughout the résumé. Note that the examples we have given used some of the verbs mentioned in the following list of action verbs:

ACTION VERBS TO USE

Creative skills	Financial skills	Management skills	Technical skills
conceptualized	administered	administered	assembled
created	analyzed	analyzed	built
designed	balanced	conducted	calculated
established	budgeted	coordinated	designed
fashioned	forecasted	developed	operated
illustrated	marketed	directed	overhauled
initiated	planned	improved	produced
invented	projected	managed	remodeled
performed		supervised	repaired
prepared		systematized	

Helping skills	Research skills	Communication skills	Administrative skills
assessed	clarified	arranged	arranged
assisted	evaluated	addressed	catalogued
coached	identified	authored	complied
counseled	inspected	briefed	generated
diagnosed	investigated	drafted	negotiated
facilitated	located	formulated	organized
represented	organized	persuaded	processed
	researched	presented	systematized
		summarized	
		wrote	

NONACTION VERBS TO AVOID

was involved in   had a role in

was a part of   was related to

Nonaction verbs are vague. They say very little and give the impression that you are not an assertive person.

12. *Parallelism.* Obey the rule on **parallelism**. The rule requires that you use a consistent (i.e., parallel) grammatical structure when phrasing logically related ideas in a list.

parallelism Using a consistent (i.e., parallel) grammatical structure when phrasing logically related ideas in a list.

Specifically, be consistent in the use of words ending in *-ing*, *-ed*, and *-tion*. Similarly, be consistent in the use of infinitives, clauses, personal pronouns, verb tense, and active voice. See Exhibit 2-16.

Exhibit 2-16	Obeying the Rule on Parallelism

Say: Duties
- Researched securities issues on …
- Drafted medical malpractice complaints in …
- Served papers on opposing parties, including …

Do Not Say: Duties
- Researched securities issues on …
- Drafted medical malpractice complaints in …
- I also serve papers on opposing parties, including …

Note that the first list of duties in Exhibit 2-16 begins with verbs that are all in the past tense and all end in "ed." The verbs are parallel. The verbs in the second list, however, are not parallel. The first two are in the past tense and end in "ed," but the third verb shifts to the present tense ("serve"). To be parallel, all verbs in the list should begin with a verb in the past tense or all should begin with verbs in the present tense. The second list is also not parallel in another way. The first two items begin with a verb ("researched," "drafted"), but the third begins with a personal pronoun ("I"). To be parallel, all three items in the list should begin with a verb or all three items should begin with personal pronouns. (For more on this rule, type *parallelism grammar* in Google, Bing, or Yahoo.)

13. *Reasons for leaving.* Do not state the reason you left each job, although you should be prepared to discuss this if you are granted an interview.
14. *Other experience.* State other experience that does not fall within the categories of education and employment mentioned earlier. Perhaps you have been a homemaker for twenty years, raised five children, worked your way through college, and were the church treasurer, a Cub Scout volunteer, etc. In a separate category on the résumé called "Other Experience," list such activities and state your duties/accomplishments in the same manner described earlier to demonstrate relevant personality traits. Hobbies can be included (without using the word *hobby*) when they are distinctive and illustrate special talents or achievement. We will say more about other experiences and skills later in the chapter when we cover the Job-Search Notebook (JSN).
15. *Special abilities.* State any special abilities (e.g., you can design a database or speak a foreign language), awards, credentials, scholarships, membership associations, leadership positions, community service, publications, etc., that have not been mentioned elsewhere on the résumé. Call this section "Special Abilities" or "Other Abilities."
16. *Weaknesses.* No one has a perfect résumé. There are facts about all of us that we would prefer to downplay or avoid (e.g., sudden change in jobs, school transfer because of personal or family difficulties, and low aptitude test scores). Later, we will see how a functional résumé can be helpful in such cases by steering the reader's attention to your strengths.) Although a résumé does not have to point out weaknesses or potential difficulties in your background, you must be prepared, if granted an interview, to discuss any obvious gaps or problems that might be evident from your résumé.
17. *References.* Prepare a separate sheet on which you give the names, email and business addresses, and phone numbers of persons who know your abilities and who could be contacted by a prospective employer for a reference. Phone or email them and ask (a) if you can list them as references in your job search and (b) whether you can use their street address, email address, and phone number in your list of references. When you submit your résumé, do not include this list of references. Simply be ready to submit it if asked. Résumés sometimes have the following statement at the end of the résumé: "References available upon request." This statement, however, is not needed; all

employers know that the list is available and that they can ask for it. If granted an interview, you can tell the interviewer that you have the list.

18. *Salary.* Do not state salary requirements or your salary history on the résumé. Leave this topic for the interview. If you are responding to an ad that asks for this history, include it in the cover letter.

BACKGROUND RESEARCH ON A PROSPECTIVE EMPLOYER

You should never submit a résumé to a prospective employer if all you know about the employer is that it is a law office. You must do background research on every prospective employer you want to contact. In a law practice and in the business world, background research or investigation is sometimes called performing or doing **due diligence**. Background research on a prospective employer is an example of due diligence.

How do you do background research—due diligence—on a prospective employer? There are two kinds of information that you would like to have: *public* information (facts you can obtain on the Internet or from other generally available sources) and *private* or *inside* information (facts that usually can be obtained only from an insider).

due diligence Reasonable efforts to find and verify factual information needed to carry out an obligation, to avoid harming someone, or to make an important decision, e.g., to determine the true market value of a potential investment, or to decide whether a job prospect is worth pursuing.

Public Information

- What kind of office it is? Law firm? Law department of a corporation? Association? Government office? Other?
- If a law firm, what are its major categories of clients? Any specialties? Any recent major victories?
- If a law department, what are the company's main products or services?
- If an association, what is its mission? How is it funded? Who does it serve?
- If a government office, what kind of office? What is its public purpose? What are the job descriptions of personnel in the office?
- What kinds of personnel does the office have? How many attorneys?
- How long has the office been in existence?
- What does the office say about itself on its website? In its own marketing, how does it project itself?

Inside Information

- Is the office hiring now or in the near future?
- If the office has an opening for a paralegal, why has it decided to hire one now? What needs or problems prompted this decision?
- How many paralegals does the office have? What specific kinds of work do they do? What are the advantages and disadvantages of working there?
- Has the office experienced a high turnover of personnel? If so, why?
- What is the work culture of the office? Conservative? Demanding? Miserly? Collegial?
- How is the office structured or governed? One individual in charge? A management committee?

Here are some of the techniques you can use to try to find these categories of information:

1. Check the main website of the office. Most law offices have websites or are part of a larger organization that has a website. Such sites cover mission statement, kind of law practiced, names (and often photos) of the attorneys at the office, and links to career options or job openings. To find the office on the Internet, type its name in any general search engine.

2. For sites that will help you do background research on companies, see:

   - www.llrx.com/features/co_research.htm
   - www.glassdoor.com
   - finance.yahoo.com

3. Check social media. Find out if the office is on LinkedIn, has a Twitter account, or has a Facebook page.

4. Do a news search. Find out what, if anything, has been said in the news about the office or about any attorney in the office. Check their names in the search boxes of news sites such as:

- news.google.com
- news.yahoo.com

5. Try to obtain an inside perspective from anyone who currently works or who once worked at the office. This includes attorneys, paralegals, administrators, or secretaries. Steps to take to seek inside information:

- Become a student member of your local paralegal association (see Appendix B). Ask paralegals for the names of persons working at the office where you want to apply. The chances are fair to good that you will find someone who works there, who knows someone who works there, or who once worked there
- In LinkedIn, Twitter, and Facebook, check the names of any person you find who works or who once worked in the office. Check their biographical information and any comments they may have posted
- Find out if anyone working in the office is writing a **blog**, which is an Internet journal or diary. As we will see in Chapter 13, many attorneys (and some paralegals) have blogs. (Blogs on legal topics are sometimes called *blawgs*.) Blogs cover different aspects of the law or practice (e.g., recent developments in environmental law, or tax accounting for corporations). To find out if anyone working at the office is writing a blog, type the name of the person or office in standard blog search sites:
  - www.abajournal.com/blawgs
  - www.blawg.com
  - legalblogs.findlaw.com
  - www.google.com/blogsearch
  - In Google, Bing, or Yahoo, type the word *blog* and the name of the office or the person who works at the office

blog An Internet journal or diary on any topic of interest to the blogger (writer) of the blog (sometimes called *blawg* if the topic is mainly legal).

CHRONOLOGICAL AND FUNCTIONAL RÉSUMÉS

Exhibit 2-17 is an example of a *chronological résumé*, which is the traditional format and the one most commonly used by applicants today. As indicated earlier, this résumé presents your education and work history in reverse chronological sequence, beginning with the most recent events and working backward.

A *functional résumé* clusters certain skills, talents, and accomplishments together regardless of the period in which they were developed. See Exhibit 2-18. (Such résumés are sometimes called *skills résumés* or *accomplishments-oriented résumés*.) This style of résumé can be particularly useful:

- when you want to downplay large gaps in education,
- when you are making a radical change of careers, or
- when your skills were not gained in paralegal education, training, or employment.

The functional résumé should not, however, ignore the chronological sequence of the major training and work events of your life; a prospective employer will want to know what this sequence is. Note that the functional résumé in Exhibit 2-18 has a skills cluster early in the résumé, followed by the historical overview in reverse chronological order.[20] Using this format puts the emphasis of the résumé on the skills or abilities and accomplishments highlighted at the beginning. (When a functional résumé includes chronological data on education and employment, it is sometimes called a combination résumé—one that combines the format of a chronological and a functional résumé.)

Exhibit 2-17	Sample Chronological Résumé (targeted at a law firm seeking a trusts and estâtes paralegal)

JOHN J. SMITH
43 Benning Road SE
Salem, Maryland 21455
701-555-0427
jjsmith@gmail.com
linkedin.com/in/johnjsmith
twitter.com/JohnSmith

SUMMARY OF MAJOR SKILLS AND ACCOMPLISHMENTS

Recent high-achieving graduate of intensive paralegal program who completed substantial hands-on trusts and estate taxation projects and who has law office experience (Donaldson & Fry) on e-discovery, drafting, and cite checking. Seeks paralegal position with estates and trusts law firm.

EDUCATION

Maynard Paralegal Institute, Jan. 2014-Jan. 2015
Courses:
Trusts and Estates:

- Overview of probate procedure and the basics of trusts and estates in Maryland
- Client interviews to identify facts needed to prepare the federal 105 long form

Tax I:

- Basics of estate taxation
- Introduction to personal income taxation
- Fundamentals of accounting
- Valuation of personal and real property

Other Courses:

- Introduction to Law, Family Law, Litigation, Legal Research

Internship: Donaldson & Fry, LLP (Sept. 2014-Dec. 2014) Tasks performed under supervision of Alex Fry, Esq.:

- Drafted answer to divorce complaint, including last-minute revisions asked for by the attorney hours before his court appearance
- Successfully maintained the firm's tickler system covering the schedules of ten attorneys handling over 125 active cases
- Coded over forty e-discovery documents pursuant to instructions for newly purchased discovery software
- Cite-checked an appellate brief, bringing several errors to the attention of the drafting attorney

Jefferson Community College, Sept. 2007-June 2009
Courses :

- Business Law; English I, II; Sociology; Creative Writing; French I; Introduction to Psychology

EMPLOYMENT

Salem National Bank, Teller, 2005-2008
Responsibilities:

- Received deposit and withdrawal requests
- Trained new tellers
- Supervised note department in the absence of the assistant manager

ABC Biscuit Company, Driver, 2000-2004

HONORS

2005 Junior Achievement Award for Outstanding Marketing

ASSOCIATIONS

- Financial Secretary, Salem Paralegal Association
- Regional Representative, National Federation of Paralegal Associations
- Member, National Association of Legal Assistants

Exhibit 2-18	Functional Résumé

MARY L. DOE
18 East 7th Ave. Salem,
Maryland 21455
705-555-1943
mldoe@gmail.com
linkedin.com/in/maryldoe
twitter.com/MaryLDoe

SUMMARY OF MAJOR SKILLS AND ACCOMPLISHMENTS

Currently enrolled in paralegal certificate program; will be seeking paralegal position in litigation. Obtained bachelor of arts with major in English and minor in Library Science. Taught creative writing and communications to high school seniors. Worked several years as research and index assistant in records and research department of large international organization. Worked as a part-time volunteer in schools and libraries as librarian and reading tutor.

PROFESSIONAL SKILLS

Communication Skills

- Taught creative writing to high school seniors, several of whom had their work published
- Designed and conducted workshops on library service for newly hired employees
- Co-led workshops on literacy training
- Served as Circulation Representative for *USA Today*, increasing sales by 18 percent over the period worked

Research Skills

- Guided library patrons in use of basic reference materials (twice received patron commendations for services provided)
- Helped write county online resource manual by researching Internet sites (acknowledged in preface for outstanding contribution)
- Recommended subscription purchases for general-circulation library (presented on an Excel spreadsheet with cost comparisons, content
- summaries, and links to vendors)

Organization Skills

- Managed recruitment, staffing, shelving, circulation, and student assistance at school library
- Planned county budget requests for library

EMPLOYMENT HISTORY

9/10-Present: Lincoln Elementary School (Denver): Teacher's Aide (part-time)
6/02-6/10:   International Church Center, Records and Research Section (Philadelphia): Research and Index Assistant
4/10-6/10:   Latin Preparatory School (Dorchester): School Librarian (substitute)
2/09-6/10:   James P. O'Reilly Elementary School (Philadelphia): School Librarian (volunteer)
9/98-6/01   Roosevelt High School (St. Paul): English Teacher Aide

EDUCATION

8/13-Present: LaSalle Community College Paralegal Program (expected date of graduation: 7/15)
Courses :   Introduction to Paralegalism, Litigation, Probate, Contracts, Torts, Legal Research and Writing, Law Office Management, Computers in the Law GPA thus far: 3.9
2003–2004:   University of Massachusetts, Boston Campus Special courses: Library and Urban Children; Design Management
1999–2000:   Harvard Extension, Problems in Urban Education
1989–1993:   University of Minnesota, Minneapolis, B.S., Major: English Minor: Library Science

SCHOOL ACTIVITIES

National Honor Society, Drama Club, Creative Writing Club, YWCA, Minnesota Dance Company

---

cover letter A letter indicating what is being sent in the same envelope or package and that often highlights its contents or purpose. Also called *transmittal letter.*

COVER LETTER

It is often said that you don't get a second chance to make a first impression. That first impression you are likely to make at a law office is when the office opens your **cover letter** and attached résumé. "Research done by recruiting firms has shown that 10 percent of an employer's attention is spent opening an envelope, 80 percent is used reading a cover letter and the other

10 percent focuses on scanning a résumé."[21] Consequently, you need to use considerable care in composing the letter. In one page, it should:

- State the purpose of the letter
- Indicate how you learned about the office
- Summarize why you are qualified for the job, using keywords (buzzwords) related to the specific position, e.g., language used in the want ad
- Include something about the office that you learned from its website or other background research (e.g., that it has a major corporation practice and recently won a federal securities case for a client)
- State that you are enclosing your résumé
- Conclude by saying that you would appreciate the opportunity to discuss the position and how you can be an asset to the office

Much of a résumé is written in sentence fragments found in tightly compacted lists. The cover letter is your one opportunity to use complete sentences in unified paragraphs. Like the résumé itself, the cover letter should give the impression that you are a professional.

It is also important that you communicate a sense of enthusiasm about the position. Try to say something specific in the letter that you learned about the office through your background research. For example, if the office's website says that the firm recently merged with another office, you might say at the end of the letter, "From everything I have learned about your firm, including its recent merger with Davis and Kendle, I feel confident that it would be an exciting place to work and that I would be able to make a contribution."

Note that the cover letter in Exhibit 2-19 is addressed to a specific person. Whenever possible, find out the exact name of the person to whom the résumé should be sent. If you are not sure, call the office and ask. Also check the firm's main Internet site and its social media sites (e.g., LinkedIn) to see if it gives the name of the person at the firm in charge of recruitment or personnel.

Exhibit 2-19	Example of a Cover Letter

43 Benning Road SE
Salem, Maryland 21455
701-555-0427
jjsmith@gmail.com

June 23, 2014
Linda Stenner, Esq.
Stenner, Skidmore & Smith
438 Bankers Trust Bldg
Suite 1200
Salem, Maryland 21458

Dear Ms. Stenner:

I am responding to the ad you placed in the Daily Telegraph of June 14 for a trusts and estates paralegal. My résumé is enclosed for your consideration. I am very interested in working in the field of probate, trusts, and estates. The course work that I did at Maynard Paralegal Institute and my prior work at the Salem National Bank gave me with an appreciation of the complexity of this area of the law. I find the field fascinating.

I am fully aware of the kind of attention to detail that a paralegal in this field must have. If you decide to check my references, I am confident that you will be told of the high level of discipline and responsibility that I bring to the tasks I undertake. I have read several stories in the Salem Bar Register on the Johnson case in which your firm represented the estate petitioners. The description of your firm and its efforts on behalf of the petitioners were eye-opening. It would be an honor to become a member of your team.

I have two writing samples that may be of interest to you: a draft of a will that I prepared in my course on trusts and estates, and a memorandum of law on the valuation of stocks. These writing samples (as well as a list of references) are available on request.

I would appreciate the opportunity to be interviewed for the paralegal position at your firm. I feel confident that my training and experience have prepared me for the kind of challenge that this position would provide.

Sincerely,

Enclosure: Résumé

John J. Smith

When the résumé and cover letter are ready, place them in a large envelope that matches the color (preferably white) of the paper on which you wrote the résumé and letter. Spend the extra money on postage for the envelope so that you do not have to fold the résumé and letter.

About a week after you send the résumé and cover letter, call the office to find out if it was received and when you might have a response. Some offices might consider such calls to be annoying, but if you know that an office will probably have many applicants, your call might help demonstrate your initiative.

PROOFREAD, PROOFREAD, PROOFREAD

Carefully read and reread the résumé and cover letter to be sure that it has no spelling errors, is grammatically perfect, and uses a consistent format. Also ask someone else to proofread it to see if you missed anything. To help you catch errors, print a temporary version of your résumé in substantially different font and point sizes. Read the text in this new format to see if you find problems that were not initially apparent. Then go back to the font and point size that you will use to submit the résumé.[22] Another technique used by careful writers is to read everything backward: word by word, punctuation mark by punctuation mark. Of course, when you do this, you are not reading for meaning. You are isolating everything in the sentence in order to force yourself to ask whether anything might be in need of a dictionary or grammar check.

Reading backward might help reveal glaring spelling or punctuation errors that you have been glossing over. Spell checkers on popular word-processing programs such as Word and WordPerfect can be helpful, but they must be used with caution. They will identify *misspelled* words, not incorrectly chosen words. For example, a spell checker will tell you that there are no misspelled words in the following sentence: "Their is too choices." It is true that this sentence has no spelling errors, but it should have read, "There are two choices."

Do you see any problem with the following sentence from a cover letter?

The description of responsibilities in the want ad fit my experience.

This sentence alone might cause a prospective employer to throw the letter, and its accompanying résumé, in the trash can. The subject and verb do not agree. The sentence should read:

The description of responsibilities in the want ad fits my experience.

The subject of the sentence (description) is singular. A singular subject takes a singular verb (fits). There must be no lapses in your grammar and spelling. Your standard must be perfection. The vast majority of us are unaware of how poor our grammar can sometimes be. We have been lulled into a sense of security because readers of what we have written in the past rarely complained even if we made an egregious error.

Be sure there are no smudge spots from erasures or fingerprints. Avoid submitting a résumé that was obviously reproduced on a poor-quality photocopy machine at a corner drugstore. You want to convey the impression that you know how to write and organize data. Furthermore, it is a sign of respect to the reader when you show that you took the time to make your résumé and cover letter professionally presentable. Law offices are conservative environments. Attorneys like to project an image of propriety, stability, accuracy, and order. Be sure that your cover letter and résumé also project this image.

In the section on studying at the beginning of this book, there are suggestions for improving your writing skills. In the meantime, proofread, proofread, proofread; and then find others to proofread everything that you intend to submit to a prospective employer.

For more guidance, see "Proofreading Your Own Writing" in Exhibit 12-2 in Chapter 12.

WRITING SAMPLES

Later, in connection with the Job-Search Notebook (JSN), we will discuss the importance of having a portfolio that contains many writing samples that you can present to prospective employers. In some parts of the country, it is difficult to obtain a paralegal job without experience. Although writing samples are not the equivalent of experience, they can be part of an effective strategy to try to overcome the experience problem.

JOB INTERVIEW

Once you have overcome the hurdles of finding a prospective employer who will read your cover letter and résumé, the next problem is to arrange for a job interview. In your cover letter, you may want to add the following sentence at the end: "Within the next two weeks, I will give you a call to determine whether an interview would be possible." This strategy does not leave the matter entirely up to the prospective employer as to whether there will be further contact with you. Alternatively, you could make such a call without including in the cover letter a statement of your intention to do so.

Assume that you have been granted an interview and that it's your first legal interview.

Attired in your best interviewing suit, you nervously navigate your way to the reception area of what you hope will be your future employer's office. You are a comfortable ten minutes early. Upon arrival you are directed to the office of the interviewer, whom you greet with a smile and pleasant handshake. She offers you a cup of coffee, which you wisely refuse, since you may spill it. She then looks you in the eye and poses her first question. "Why are you interested in working for this firm?" [Suddenly you go blank!] All thoughts leave your mind as you pray for the ability to speak.[23]

Of course, not all first interviews will be this intense. With proper preparation, you will do fine. If you have done the kind of background research on the office mentioned earlier, you will have a fairly good idea of the structure and mission of the office. Its website or LinkedIn page, for example, might tell you the kind of law it practices, the location of branches, news of recent judgments won by the office, and public service activities of attorneys at the office (such as election to the presidency of the bar association or a pro bono award). These sites often give overviews of areas of the law in which the office specializes. During the interview, you will want to let the interviewer know that you have such information. Interviewers are usually impressed by applicants who have done their homework about the office.

Let's look at some additional interview guidelines.

JOB INTERVIEW GUIDELINES

1. *Location.* Be sure you have the exact address, room number, and time of the interview. Give yourself sufficient time to find the office. If the area is new to you, check the map and directions from standard Internet map services (e.g., www.mapquest.com or maps.google.com). You do not want to start your contact with the office by having to offer excuses for being late. Arrive at least ten minutes early. You will probably be nervous and will need to compose yourself before the interview. It is important that you are as relaxed as possible. Be sure to turn off your cell phone or other mobile devices once you arrive at the office.

2. *Name of interviewer.* Try to find out in advance who will be interviewing you. If you obtain the name of this person, find out if he or she is on LinkedIn, Twitter, or Facebook. Also, type his or her name into a general search engine to find out any available information on him or her. Check to see if he or she is writing (or is mentioned in) a blog. See the discussion earlier on how to find out. If you will be interviewed by an attorney, also check available background information on the attorney in the office's website, on Martindale-Hubbell Law Directory (www.martindale.com), or on the sites mentioned in Appendix H on law firms. Don't be surprised, however, if the person who greets you is a substitute for the person originally scheduled to interview you.

3. *Style of interviewer.* A number of different kinds of people might conduct the interview depending upon the size of the office:

   - The law office manager
   - The managing attorney
   - The supervising attorney for the position
   - The paralegal supervisor
   - A staff paralegal
   - A combination of the above if you are interviewed by different people on the same day or on different days

   The style of the interview may be quite different depending on who conducts it. Someone with management responsibility might stress the interpersonal dimensions of the position, whereas a trial attorney might give you the feeling that you are being cross-examined. Try to determine whether you are being interviewed by the person who has the final authority to hire you. In many large offices, you will be interviewed by someone whose sole task is to screen out unacceptable applicants. If you make it through this person, the next step will usually be an interview with the ultimate decision-maker. You might be lucky enough to talk with someone who has been interviewed by this person before (such as a paralegal now working at the office, another job seeker, or someone at the local paralegal association) so that you can obtain a sense of what to expect. (See also www.glassdoor.com mentioned earlier and below.) Although relatively uncommon, you may have to face a group interview in which several interviewers question you at once, or you might be asked to have the interview online, using the built-in webcam on your laptop and a program such as Skype.

Most interviewers begin with casual conversation about the weather or how long you've lived in the city. Small talk might also include yesterday's game. Before you arrive at the office, it wouldn't hurt for you to check the morning headlines in the sports pages to see who won that game.

4. *Appearance.* Dress conservatively. "A red, wool crepe suit could work well for a professional woman in Los Angeles, Atlanta, Dallas, and Chicago but might seem too flashy in the financial districts of New York or traditional businesses in Boston or Milwaukee. An interview wardrobe is mostly built in solid colors, which offer a more elegant feeling. Both men and women are advised to dress conservatively for the first interview." Suit up for the interview even if the office is having a casual dress day. "The most important thing to remember is that law firms are generally conservative.... . Most firms want to see candidates dressed in traditional, conservative 'Brooks Brothers' looks."[24] You want interviewers to remember what you said, not what you wore.

5. *Propriety and body language.* Be sure that you project yourself positively. Take the initiative in greeting the interviewer. A firm handshake is recommended. (Avoid the fish handshake—lifeless and limp.) Address the interviewer as Mr. or Ms., never by first name, unless expressly invited to do so. (Note: "I'm Bob Sheehan" is *not* an express invitation to call the interviewer "Bob.") Maintain good posture (sitting slightly forward in the chair) and consistent eye contact. While you are talking, do not let your eyes roam around the room. Remember that you are being evaluated. Avoid appearing ill at ease or fidgety. The interviewer will be making mental notes on your body language and forming an opinion of whether you "fit in."

6. *Preparation for the interview.* Many of the principles of résumé writing (discussed earlier) apply to the interview as well. In the résumé and in the interview, you are trying to sell yourself. Know the kinds of questions you will probably be asked (see the next guidelines). Rehearse your responses. Write down a series of questions (tough ones), and ask a friend to role-play an interview with you. Have your friend ask you the questions and critique your responses. Also take the role of the interviewer and question your friend so that you can gauge both perspectives. Many of us have a tendency to say "ah" when pausing as we talk. Avoid doing this. As you rehearse, test yourself. See how many sentences you can speak in a row without saying "ah" or its equivalent. It's appropriate occasionally to pause in order to think about the next thing you want to say. Just don't fill those pauses with sounds that give the impression that you are not sure of yourself.

7. *Discovery.* If you don't already know, you need to find out (discover) what the office is looking for in a paralegal. A major goal of the interview is to relate your education and experience to the needs of the office. To the extent possible, you want to know what these needs are before the interview so that you can quickly and forcefully demonstrate that you are the person the office is looking for. Most offices decide to hire someone because they have a problem: They need someone with a particular skill, they need someone to help them expand, or they need someone who can get along with a particularly demanding supervising attorney. If you are not sure, tactfully ask the interviewer why the office has decided to add a paralegal, what expectations the office has for the person it is seeking, what the primary duties of this person will be, etc. Don't wait until the end of the interview when you are asked if you have any questions. Early on in the interview, you want to try to tailor as many of your answers as possible to the specific needs of the office. The success of the interview is directly related to your ability to identify the problem of the office and to demonstrate how you can solve it for them.

8. *Categories of interview questions. Biographical* questions seek facts about your life, e.g., when did you graduate? *Behavioral* questions gauge your thought process and values, e.g., when was the last time you faced an ethical dilemma in your everyday life and how did you handle it? See Exhibit 2-20 for more categories of possible questions. Keep in mind, however, that no matter how much preparation you do, you may still be surprised by the course the interview takes. Be flexible enough to expect the unexpected. If you are relaxed, confident, and prepared, you will do fine.

Exhibit 2-20	Six Categories of Job Interview Questions

Open-Ended Questions (which are calculated to get you to talk, giving the listener an idea of how you organize your thoughts)
- Tell me about yourself.
- What do you know about our firm?
- Tell me about the kind of position you are seeking.
- What interests you about this job?

Closed-Ended Questions (which can be answered by one or two words)
- When did you receive your paralegal certificate?
- Did you take a course in corporate law?

Softball Questions (which should be fairly easy to answer if you are prepared)
- What are your interests outside of school and work?
- What courses did you enjoy the most? Why? Which were least rewarding? Why?
- Do your grades reflect your full potential? Why or why not?
- Why did you leave your last job?
- How have you grown or developed in your prior jobs? Explain.
- How were you evaluated in your prior jobs?
- What are your strengths as a worker?
- Describe an ideal work environment. What would your "dream job" be?
- What factors make a job frustrating? How would you handle these factors?
- What do you hope to be doing in ten years? What are your long- term goals?
- If you are hired, how long are you prepared to stay?
- Are you interested in a job or a career? What's the difference?
- Why did you become a paralegal?
- What problems do you think a paralegal might face in a busy law office? Which of the problems are the most serious and how would you handle them?
- Can you work under pressure? When have you done so in the past?
- How flexible are you in adapting to changing circumstances?
- Give examples of your flexibility in the last year.
- How do you feel about doing routine work?
- Do you prefer a large or a small law office? Why?
- What accomplishment in your life are you most proud of? Why?
- What was your salary at your last position and what salary expectations do you have?
- What other questions do you think I should ask in order to learn more about you?
- What questions would you like to ask me about this office?
- What was the most recent book you read?

Tension Questions (which are calculated to put you on the spot to see how you handle yourself; your answers will give the interviewer some insight into your thought process and your values)
- No one is perfect. What are your weaknesses as a worker?
- Have you ever been fired from a position? Explain the circumstances.
- What did you like least about your last job?
- Tell me about a time when you experienced failure and the lessons you learned from this experience.
- Why have you held so many jobs?
- Are you a competitive person? If not, why not? If you are, give some examples over the last six months that demonstrate this characteristic.
- Is there something in this job that you hope to accomplish that you were not able to accomplish in your last job?
- Do you type? If not, are you willing to learn? What is your typing speed?
- Where else have you interviewed for a job? Have you been turned down?
- Why wouldn't you want to become an attorney now?
- Everyone makes mistakes. What is the biggest mistake that you made in any of your prior jobs and how did you handle it?[25]
- No job is perfect. What is the least appealing aspect of the job you are seeking here?
- There are over fifty applicants for this position. Why do you think you are the most qualified?

- If you are offered this position, what are the major concerns that you would have about taking it?
- What would make you want to quit a job?
- Give some examples of when you have shown initiative over the last six months in school or at your last job.

Hypothetical (Problem-Solving) Questions (in which you are asked how you would handle a stated fact situation)

- If you were told, "This isn't any good, do it again, and get it right this time," how would you react?
- If you find out late Friday afternoon that you're expected to come in on Saturday, what would you do?[26]
- Assume that you are given the position here and that you work very closely on a day-to-day basis with an attorney. After a six-month period, what positive and negative comments do you think this attorney would make about you as a worker?
- Name some things that would be unethical for someone in a law office to do. What would you do if you found out that the attorney supervising you was doing these things?
- Suppose that your first assignment was to read through and summarize 4,000 documents over an eight-month period. Could you do it? How would you feel about it?
- Assume that two airplanes crash into each other and that your firm represents one of the passengers who was killed. What kind of discovery would you recommend?

Potentially Illegal Questions (because the questions are not relevant to the candidate's fitness and ability to do most jobs)

- Are you married? Do you plan to marry?
- Do you have any children? If so, how old are they? Who takes care of your children?
- If you do not have any children now, do you plan to have any in the future?
- How old are you?
- What is your religion?
- What is your political affiliation?

Finally… (be ready for questions that might throw you; here are two examples designed to gauge how well you can think on your feet; how well you respond to something unexpected[27]):

- Assume that I'm a *third grade student.* Explain to me what a spreadsheet is.
- What's your best clean joke?

9. *STAR method of answering question.* Some questions ask you how you handled certain situations in the past. Other questions ask you how you would handle something in the future. The STAR technique can be a guide to help you answer both kinds of questions.[28] STAR stands for Situation (S) or Task (T), Action (A), and Results (R).

Here are two examples involving past and future situations (S):

Question about the past:

- "What did you like least about your last job?"

The situation (S) is the last job you held and what you least liked about it. Instead of answering solely with a vague generality (e.g., I disliked the travel distance when the firmed moved its office"), refer to this situation and to the action (A) that you took and point out the results (R) of your action. You might say:

- "A year after I was hired, the firm moved across town, which tripled my commute time. I rearranged child care so that I could meet this travel need. It worked for about eight months, but when the firm began planning a further move, which would be even further away for me, I realized that I needed to find a position closer to home."

The action taken (A) was rearranging your schedule and the result (R) of this action was eight months of continued work at the firm. Using STAR, you have demonstrated flexibility, dependability, and resourcefulness.

Question about the future:

- "Name some things that would be unethical for someone in a law office to do. What would you do if you found out that the attorney supervising you was doing these things?"

This question refers to something in the future: being confronted with an ethical problem. Answer such a question about the future, but then try to use STAR to refer to a comparable event in your life. You might say:

- "The first thing I would do is to make sure I understand the facts. What I observed may have appeared unethical solely because I did not understand what the attorney was doing or have the complete picture. I know, for example, that it's unethical to deposit a client award of damages into the general account of the law firm. I would ask the attorney if the check should have gone into the client's separate account. I remember a time at our church when I served on the finance committee. I voted against a motion to censure the church's accountant because I did not think we had enough information to support the motion. The committee agreed to delay the motion until we conducted further investigation."

Using STAR, you briefly described a situation (S: a censure motion at a church meeting), the action taken (A: opposing a motion of censure), and the result of this action (R: further investigation by the committee). Using STAR, you have demonstrated tact, sensitivity, and judgment.

10. *Specialty areas.* If the paralegal job is in a certain specialty, such as probate or corporate law, you may be asked questions designed to assess your familiarity with the area. Prior to the interview, spend some time reviewing your class notes. Type that area of the law in a search engine and read about some of the terminology and major issues of the area (e.g., corporate law legal issues, family law overview). Be sure that you can back up anything you said in your résumé about prior involvement with the area in your school or work experience. Such discussions are always an excellent opportunity for you to present writing samples in that field of the law. As indicated, the websites of many offices discuss their specialties as part of their effort to entice prospective clients to hire the office. If such discussions exist, read them thoroughly before the interview. Look for opportunities to make specific mention of whatever the website says that is relevant to what you have studied and are able to do. You might even ask questions about something said on the site. For example,

- "I read on your website that the firm recently handled the merger of the iBox.net and Granger.com companies. Do paralegals at the firm work on such mergers?"

11. *Illegal questions.* You are not required to answer potentially illegal questions, e.g., "Are you married?" Some employers use the answers to such irrelevant questions to practice illegal sex discrimination. You need to decide in advance how you will handle them if they are asked. You may want to ask why the question is relevant. Or you may simply decide to steer the interview back to the qualifications that you have and the commitment that you have made to a professional career. A good response might be:

- "If you're concerned that my marital status may affect my job performance, I can assure you that it will not."

Follow this up with comments about dedication and job commitment. It may be the perfect time to offer references.[29] Whatever approach you take, be sure to remain courteous. One commentator suggests the following response to an illegal question:

- "Gee, that's interesting. I haven't been asked that question before in a job interview."[30]

Then continue talking about what makes you a dependable worker without allowing the question to control your response.

12. *Criticism of others.* Avoid being critical of anyone even if you are asked a question such as "What did you like least about your last job?" Do not "dump on" your prior employer or school. Criticizing or blaming other organizations, even if justified, is likely to give the interviewer the impression that you will probably end up blaming this organization if you get the job and difficulties arise. If you are asked about dissatisfaction with prior jobs, try to answer in a way that does not criticize others. For example, "The biggest problem I had with the last job was the time I had to be away from my own cases to help train new employees. I was glad to provide the training, but I like to get my own work done well ahead of due dates. I wasn't always able to do that when the office took on new hires."

13. *Self-criticism.* Often you will be invited to criticize yourself when you are asked the seemingly inevitable question, "What are your weaknesses?" Interviewers like such questions because your response gives some indication of how you handle yourself under pressure. You may want to pick a *positive* trait and express it as a negative. For example:

- "I tend to get frustrated when I'm not given enough to do. My goal is not just to collect a paycheck. I want to make a contribution."
- "I think I sometimes have expectations that are too high. There is so much to learn, and I want it all now. I have to pace myself, and realize that the important goal is to complete the immediate task, even if I can't learn every conceivable aspect of that task at the present time."

- "I get irritated by carelessness. When I see someone turn in sloppy work, or work that is not up to the highest standards, it bothers me."

If you use any of these approaches, be sure that you are able to back them up when you are asked to explain what you mean.

14. *Honesty.* Never compromise the truth during an interview. If, for example, you are asked if you know how to prepare trial notebooks, do not say *yes* if you can do little more than define what a trial notebook is. A good answer might be:

- "We studied trial notebooks in our litigation class. I've never prepared one, but I'm a fast learner, and I think that with a good model and clear instructions, I would be able to put together an effective one."

15. *Salary.* Before the interview, find out what you can about paralegal salaries in the area. For example, check recent salary surveys of local and national paralegal associations. (See "Salary Information" in Exhibit 2-12 and the data on salaries in Chapter 1.) During the interview, however, try to avoid the topic of salary until the end of the interview when you have completed the discussion of the job itself. Preferably, let the interviewer raise the issue. Think through how you will handle the topic, but try to avoid discussing it until the appropriate time arises. If asked what salary you are seeking, giving a salary range can be an invitation to limit yourself to the lowest figure stated in the range. Try to get the interviewer to give you information about salaries before you answer. Possible answers:

- "It's difficult to answer that question until I know the complete benefits package and understand all aspects of what the position will require."
- "I will be able to answer that question when I know more about the position and whether there's a mutual fit. It would help me to give a thoughtful answer if I knew the office's salary range for the position. What is the range?"[31]

Of course, the office may not have a range. Often an office has budgeted a specific salary that is not subject to change. Do the best you can to coax the interviewer into telling you what it is. Another way to turn the question back at the interviewer is to say:

- "What do you normally pay someone with my education and experience?"

16. *Law school.* You might be asked if you intend to go to law school. Some offices may limit their hiring to candidates who want to be career paralegals. It is important to let the interviewer know you are excited about the paralegal field. If law school might be a possibility for you in the future, answer the question by leaving your options open. For example,

- "My focus is on being a paralegal. I want to continue learning everything I can about the law. It's difficult to say what might happen way down the road, but right now my main commitment is to be an outstanding paralegal."

17. *Portfolio.* Carry a professional-looking portfolio with you to every interview. It should contain copies of:

- Your résumé
- Writing samples
- Your paralegal certificate
- A list of references
- Letters of recommendation
- Your school transcript (if your grades are impressive)
- Performance reviews at other jobs
- Copies of awards or other recognition of achievement
- Proof of attendance at CLE (continuing legal education) sessions
- Statement of membership in professional associations
- A list of the names of clients and other parties on cases you have worked on in prior employment or volunteer work (see guideline 20 below)
- Anything else that might have a bearing on your employability

At strategic times during the interview, let the interviewer know that you have items in the portfolio that are relevant to what you are discussing. At the end of the interview, summarize anything in the portfolio that has not been mentioned and ask if the interviewer would like you to leave copies.

18. *Your questions.* Be an active participant in the interview even though you let the interviewer conduct it. Avoid one-word answers. Help keep the discussion going by asking your own questions of the interviewer at appropriate times (mainly toward the end of the interview). In effect, you are interviewing the office as much as the other way around. Come with a written list and don't be afraid to let the interviewer see that you have a checklist of questions that you want to ask. It is a sign of an organized person. There is a great deal of information about the job that you could inquire about even if you have done careful due diligence about the office. You want to ask pertinent and intelligent questions that will communicate to the interviewer that you are serious about the paralegal field, that you are prepared, and that you grasp what the interviewer has been telling you about the job and the office.

Here are some topics you could cover in your own questions. Do not, however, ask any of these questions if the answers are already on the firm's website. Such questions would be a signal that you have not done your homework about the firm.

- What type of person is the office seeking to hire? What prompted the need for this kind of person? (Ask this now if you were not able to find out earlier in the interview. See guideline 7.)
- What are some examples of paralegal responsibilities? Will the paralegal specialize in certain tasks or areas of the law? (Ask for a description of a typical workday of a paralegal at the firm.)
- What skills will the paralegal need for the job? Digesting? Investigation? Research? Drafting? Interviewing?
- What kind of writing will the paralegal be doing? Memos? Letters that the paralegal will sign? Letters for attorney to sign?
- How many attorneys are in the firm? Is the number of attorneys growing, declining, or remaining constant?
- How is the firm managed or governed? Managing partner? Management committees? Legal administrator? Is there a policy manual for the firm?
- How many paralegals are in the firm? Is the number growing, declining, remaining constant? Are all the paralegals at the firm full-time? Does the firm use part-time or freelance paralegals? Does the firm have (or has it considered hiring) a paralegal coordinator?
- What kind of supervision does a paralegal receive? Close supervision? From one attorney? Several?
- Will the paralegal work for one attorney? Several? Is there a pool of paralegals available to many attorneys on a rotating basis as needed?
- What kind of client contact will the paralegal have? None? Phone? Email? Meetings? Interviews? Document inspection at client's office?
- Is there a difference between a paralegal and a legal assistant in the office?
- Is there a career ladder for paralegals in the firm?
- How long has the firm used paralegals? What is the average length of time a paralegal stays with the firm? What are the feelings of firm members on the value of paralegals to the firm? Why is this so? How would firm members describe an ideal paralegal employee?
- What opportunities does a paralegal have for further learning? Office training programs? (Do paralegals attend new-attorney training sessions?) Does the firm encourage outside continuing legal education (CLE) for paralegals, e.g., from paralegal associations, bar associations, and area schools?
- How are paralegals evaluated in the office? Written evaluations? Oral? How often?
- Are paralegals required to produce a set number of billable hours? Per day? Per week? Per month? Annually? Is there a **billable hours quota** or billable hour goal? What is the hourly rate at which a paralegal's time is billed to a client? Do different paralegals in the office bill at different rates? If so, what determines the difference?
- How often are paralegals required to record their time? Daily, hourly, in ten-minute segments, etc.?
- What kinds of nonbillable tasks do paralegals perform?
- Does the job require travel?
- What software does the firm use for its major tasks? Word processing? Database management? Litigation support?

billable hours quota A minimum number of hours expected from a timekeeper on client matters that can be charged (billed) to clients per week, month, year, or other time period.

intranet A private network of computers for the sharing of data, software, and services within the organization using features similar to those of the World Wide Web.

- Does the firm use an **intranet**?
- When you make an offer to someone, is there a probationary period he or she goes through before becoming a permanent employee? If there is, what criteria does the office use to decide whether the person will be permanent?

19. *Closing.* After you have thoroughly explored the position during the interview, if you still want the job, ask for it. Be sure that you make a specific request. Some interviewers go out of their way to stress the difficult aspects of the job in order to gauge your reaction. Do not leave the interviewer with the impression that you may be having second thoughts if in fact you still want the job after you have had all your questions answered. Be enthusiastic, but not overly so. You want to let the office know that you want the job, not because you are desperate but because you see it as a challenge offering professional development. You are qualified for the job (don't hesitate to summarize why), and you feel that the office is the kind of place that recognizes valuable contributions from its workers.

   Find out if you can have a brief tour of the office before you leave. Also ask if you can have an opportunity to talk with one or more paralegals currently working at the office. It will be another sign of your seriousness.

   Finally, thank the interviewer by name.

   - "I want to thank you, Mr. Sheehan, for the opportunity to discuss this position with you."

   Try to obtain the business card of everyone you speak to. Accurate names, titles, and addresses will be important for follow-up letters and general networking.

contaminate Cause a conflict of interest to exist in a law office because of prior employment, prior volunteer work, or other factors that could create the conflict.

conflict of interest Divided loyalties that actually or potentially harm (or disadvantage) someone who is owed undivided loyalty.

20. *Contamination.* Don't **contaminate** the office! Later, in Chapter 5, when we study **conflict of interest**, you will learn that a new employee can contaminate an entire office by creating a conflict of interest. Once an office is contaminated, it can be disqualified from representing a client. This could occur if a prospective employee (e.g., a paralegal) once worked or volunteered at another office that represented a client who is an opponent of a current client of the office where the paralegal is seeking employment. Hence, before an office hires an experienced paralegal (or an experienced attorney or secretary), the office needs to know the names of clients at offices where he or she has worked or volunteered. When you are seeking employment as a paralegal, therefore, you must be prepared to provide these names if you have had prior legal experience. This disclosure, however, usually does not have to occur until it is clear that the office is very interested in you and asks for a list of such clients. Never volunteer to show the list to anyone. The names of clients are confidential. But limited disclosure will be required to avoid a disqualification due to a conflict of interest.

21. *Glassdoor.* Some Internet sites give you interview questions that have been asked in the past. Glassdoor (www.glassdoor.com) is such a site. Click *Interviews*. Then type *paralegal* for the job title. Scan through the anonymously posted interview experiences of paralegals who have applied at the various offices in the past. (Also, try this search on Google, Bing, or Yahoo: paralegal job interview questions.)

SEND A FOLLOW-UP LETTER

After the interview (within twenty-four hours, if possible), send a follow-up letter to each person at the office who interviewed you. In a surprising number of cases, the follow-up letter is a significant factor in obtaining the job. In the letter:

- Thank the person for the interview.
- Tell the person that you enjoyed the interview and the opportunity to learn about the office. Personalize this statement by briefly referring to something specific that occurred or was said during the interview, e.g., "I appreciated your detailed description of how employees at the firm are evaluated." "It was very enlightening to hear how your firm handles environmental litigation, particularly in view of the new legislation you mentioned.")
- State that you are still very interested in the position.
- Briefly restate why you are qualified for the position.
- Clarify any matters that arose during the interview.
- Submit references or writing samples that may have been asked for during the interview.

TURNED-DOWN: POST-INTERVIEW FEEDBACK

If you are turned down for a job, try to find out why. Call the office. State that you are disappointed at not getting the job and that you wish the best for the person who was hired. Then politely ask what could have improved your chances. Find out whatever more you can about the criteria the firm used in its decision. Finally, use the occasion to ask for any leads to other prospective employers.

JOB-SEARCH NOTEBOOK (JSN)

Purchase a large three-ring, looseleaf notebook for your Job-Search Notebook (JSN). Include in it the outline of sections presented in Exhibit 2-21. Following the outline, create at least one page for each section.

There are a number of purposes for the JSN:

- To help you identify your strengths based on past legal or nonlegal employment, training, and other life experience
- To help you organize this data for use in your résumés
- To provide you with checklists of contacts that you should start making immediately
- To help you prepare for job interviews
- To provide a place to store copies of résumés, cover letters, writing samples, follow-up letters, notes on job leads and strategies, personal impressions, etc.
- To keep a calendar on all aspects of the job search

The JSN is your own personal document. No one else will see it unless you choose to share its contents with others.

Exhibit 2-21	Outline of Job-Search Notebook (JSN)

Part I. Résumé and Writing Sample Préparation
1. Prior and Current Nonlegal Employment
2. Prior and Current Legal Employment
3. Prior and Current Volunteer Activity
4. Other Life Experiences
5. Nonlegal Education and Training
6. Legal Education and Training
7. Draft of General Résumé
8. Draft of a One-Page Résumé
9. Targeted Résumés
10. Writing Samples
11. Portfolio

Part II. The Search
1. Attorney Contacts
2. Paralegal Contacts
3. Job Interviews

For items in the JSN that you do not want to punch three holes in (e.g., original copies of résumés), use plastic sheet protectors that have three holes on the left and allow you to insert sheets of paper within them.

JSN: PRIOR AND CURRENT NONLEGAL EMPLOYMENT
JSN: PRIOR AND CURRENT LEGAL EMPLOYMENT
JSN: PRIOR AND CURRENT VOLUNTEER ACTIVITY

We begin by analyzing your experience in nonlegal employment, legal employment, and volunteer work. Make three lists:

(1) Every nonlegal job you have held (e.g., cashier, truck driver);
(2) Every legal job you have held (e.g., legal secretary, investigator), and
(3) Every major volunteer activity you have had (e.g., church sale coordinator, political campaign assistant).

Start a separate sheet of paper for each entry on your three lists. For each entry:

- State the name and address of the place of employment or location of the volunteer work. (Include phone numbers, email address, and Internet address.)
- State the dates you were there.

- State the names of your supervisors there. (Circle the names of supervisors who had a favorable impression of you. Place a double circle around the name of each supervisor who would probably write a favorable recommendation for you, if asked.)
- Make a list of every *major* task you performed. Number each task, starting with number 1. (As you write this list, leave a three-inch left-hand margin on the paper. In front of the number for each task, place all of the letters listed in Exhibit 2-22 that apply to that task. When an explanation or description is called for, provide it on attached sheets of paper.)
- Include other characteristics of the task that are not covered in this list.
- See the later discussion on translating this task analysis onto a general résumé and eventually onto targeted résumés.

Exhibit 2-22	Self-Analysis of Your Tasks and Skills in Prior Employment and Volunteer Work
B	The task required you to conform to a BUDGET. (Briefly describe the budget, including its size and who prepared it.)
C	There was some COMPETITION in the office about who was most qualified to perform the task. (Briefly describe why you were the most qualified.)
C/OW	To perform the task, you had to COORDINATE your work with OTHER WORKERS; you did not work alone. (Briefly describe the nature of your interaction with others.)
E	You were EVALUATED on how well you performed the task. (Briefly describe the evaluation of you.)
EI	To perform the task, you occasionally or always had to EXERCISE INITIATIVE; you did not just wait for detailed instructions. (Briefly describe the initiative you took.)
ET	You occasionally or frequently had to devote EXTRA TIME to perform the task. (Briefly describe the circumstances.)
J/C	It was not a mechanical task; you had to exercise some JUDGMENT and/or CREATIVITY to perform it. (Briefly describe the kind of judgment or creativity you exhibited.)
M	MATH skills were involved in performing the task. (Briefly describe what kind of math you had to do.)
OD	OTHERS DEPENDED on your performing the task well. (Briefly describe who had to rely on your performance and why.)
OT	You always or regularly performed the task ON TIME.
P	You had some role in PLANNING how the task would be performed; you were not simply following someone else's plan. (Briefly describe your planning role.)
PI	You did not start out performing the task; you were formally or informally PROMOTED INTO it. (Briefly describe what you did before being asked to perform this task and the circumstances of the promotion.)
PP	You are PERSONALLY PROUD of the way you performed the task. (Briefly describe why.)
R/E	You made RECOMMENDATIONS on EFFICIENCY in which you suggested ways the task could be more efficiently performed or better integrated into the office. (Briefly describe the recommendations you made and what effect they had.)
RR	You RECEIVED RECOGNITION because of how well you performed the task. (Briefly describe the recognition you received and from whom.)
SE	To perform the task, you had to operate SOME EQUIPMENT such as computers or motor vehicles. (Briefly describe the equipment and the skills needed to operate it.)
SO	To perform the task, you had to SUPERVISE OTHERS or help supervise others. (Briefly describe whom you supervised and what the supervision entailed.)
TO	You also TRAINED OTHERS to perform the task. (Briefly describe this training.)
TP	You had to work under TIME PRESSURES when you performed the task; you didn't have forever to perform it. (Briefly describe these pressures.)
W	Performing the task involved some WRITING. (Briefly describe what kind of writing you did.)

JSN: OTHER LIFE EXPERIENCES

Circle *each* of the following experiences that you have had. Do not include experiences that required schooling; schooling will be covered elsewhere in the JSN. Do not include experiences that involved volunteer work unless you have not already included them elsewhere in the JSN. Attach additional sheets as indicated and where more space is needed.

- Raised a family alone
- Helped raise a family
- Traveled extensively
- Read extensively in a particular field on your own
- Learned to operate computer programs on your own
- Learned a foreign language on your own
- Learned a craft on your own (e.g., furniture making or fixing cars)
- Learned an art on your own (e.g., painting or sculpture)
- Developed a distinctive hobby requiring considerable skill
- Other life experiences (list each)

Attach a separate sheet of paper for each of the life experiences or activities that you listed above. Write the activity at the top of the sheet. Answer the following questions for each activity:

- How long did you engage in this activity?
- Have you ever tried to teach this activity to someone else? If so, describe your efforts.
- Do you think you could teach this activity to others? Explain your answer.
- Which of the following characteristics do you think are necessary or very helpful in being able to perform the activity competently? Do not focus at this point on whether you possess these characteristics. Simply compile a list of what would be helpful or necessary.

Ability to work with others	Fortitude	Skill
Ambition	Grace	Sophistication
Cleverness	Imagination	Spirit
Compassion	Independence	Stamina
Competitiveness	Intelligence	Stick-to-itiveness
Congeniality	Judgment	Strength
Conviction	Know-how	Talent
Creativity	Patience	Understanding
Dependability	Perseverance	Willpower
Determination	Poise	Zeal
Dexterity	Punctuality	Others? (list)
Drive	Responsibility	
Efficiency	Self-confidence	
Experience	Self-control	

- Ask *someone else* (whom you trust and who is familiar with you) to look at the list. Ask this person if he or she would add anything to the list. Then ask him or her to identify which of these characteristics apply to you for this activity.
- Now it's your turn. Which of these characteristics do you think apply to you for this activity?
- If there are any major differences in the evaluation of someone else and your self-analysis, how do you explain the discrepancy? Are you too hard on yourself? Do you tend to put yourself down and minimize your strengths?

JSN: NONLEGAL EDUCATION AND TRAINING

On a separate sheet of paper, list every school or training program not involving law that you have attended or are now attending (whether or not you completed it), starting with the most recent. Include four-year colleges, two-year colleges, vocational training schools, weekend seminars, work-related training programs, internships, church training programs, hobby training programs, self-improvement training, etc. Include everything since high school.

Devote a separate sheet of paper to each school or training program, writing its name at the top of the sheet and answering the following questions for it. If more than one course was taught, answer these questions for two or three of the most demanding courses.

1. What were the exact or approximate dates of attendance?
2. Did you complete it? What evidence do you have that you completed it? A grade? A certificate? A degree? A transcript?

3. Were you required to attend? If so, by whom? If not, why did you attend?
4. How did you finance your attendance?
5. What requirements did you meet in order to attend? Was there competition to attend? If so, describe in detail.
6. Describe the subjects taught. Summarize the curriculum.
7. How were you evaluated?
8. What evidence of these evaluations do you have? Could you obtain copies of the evaluations? Do you have a transcript of your record?
9. Describe in detail any writing that you had to do, such as exams or reports.
10. What skills other than writing did you cover, such as organization, research, computer use, speaking, reading, operating equipment, managing or supervising people?
11. What evidence do you have or could you obtain that shows you covered these skills and how well you did in them?
12. Did you receive any special award or distinction? If so, describe it and state what evidence you have or could obtain that you received it.
13. Make a list of every favorable comment you can remember that was made about your work. What evidence of these comments do you have or could you obtain?
14. Was the experience meaningful in your life? If so, explain why. How has it affected you today?
15. What, if anything, did you do that called for extra effort or work on your part beyond what everyone else had to do?
16. Have you ever tried to teach someone else what you learned? If so, describe your efforts. If not, could you? Describe what you could teach.
17. List each teacher or trainer who knew you individually. Circle the name if he or she would probably write you a letter of recommendation if asked.
18. Would an administrator of the training be able to write you a letter of recommendation based on the records of the school or program? If so, who?
19. Does the school or program have a reputation for excellence? If so, describe its reputation.

JSN: LEGAL EDUCATION AND TRAINING

On a separate sheet of paper, list every legal course or training program that you have taken or are now taking, whether formal or informal. Include individual classes, seminars, internships, or workshops at formal schools, on the job, through associations, on the Internet, etc. Devote a separate sheet of paper to each course or program, writing its name at the top of the sheet and answering the following questions for it.

1. What were the exact dates of attendance?
2. Did you complete it? What evidence do you have that you completed it? A grade? A certificate?
3. What requirements did you meet in order to attend? Was there competition to attend? If so, describe in detail.
4. What text(s) did you use? Photocopy the table of contents in the text(s) and circle those items that you covered.
5. Attach a copy of the syllabus and circle those items in the syllabus that you covered.
6. Make two lists: a list of the major themes or subject areas that you were required to know or understand (content, e.g., kinds of corporations) and a list of the things that you were asked to do (skills, e.g., draft a separation agreement).
7. Make a detailed list of everything that you were asked to write for the course or program, such as exams, memos, research papers, or other reports. For every written work product other than exams, give the specific topic of what you wrote. Describe this topic in at least one sentence.
8. Which of these written work products could you now rewrite as a *writing sample*? Whom could you ask to evaluate what you rewrite to ensure that it meets high standards?
9. Describe in detail everything else you were asked to do other than reading assignments. Examples: role-play a hearing, visit a court, orally analyze a problem, interview a client, evaluate a title abstract, search a title, operate a software program, find something in the library, find something on the Internet, or investigate a fact.
10. How were you evaluated? What evidence do you have or could you obtain of these evaluations? Do you have a transcript of your record?

11. Did you receive any special award or distinction? If so, describe it and state what evidence you have or could obtain that you received it.
12. Make a list of every favorable comment you can remember that was made about your work. What evidence of these comments do you have or could you obtain?
13. What, if anything, did you do that called for extra work or effort on your part beyond what everyone else had to do?
14. Describe the most valuable aspect of what you learned.
15. Have you ever tried to teach anyone else what you learned? If so, describe your efforts. If not, could you? Describe what you could teach.
16. Describe every individual who evaluated you. Could you obtain a letter of recommendation from these individuals?

JSN: DRAFT OF GENERAL RÉSUMÉ

Prepare a general résumé and include it here. We are calling it general because it is not directed or targeted at any specific job. It should be comprehensive with no page limitation. Use the guidelines, questions, and checklists in this JSN to help you identify your strengths. The résumés you write for actual job searches will be shorter, specialized, and tailored to the specific jobs you are seeking. Before you write specialized résumés, however, you should write a general one that will be your main point of reference in preparing these other résumés. The general résumé won't be submitted anywhere. Its purpose is to give you the opportunity to take stock of your life to date. Take at least one full day to compile the general résumé. You compiled a lot of data about yourself by going through the preceding exercises on past employment, life experience, education, etc. Identify anything from this data that places you in a positive light from the perspective of a worker and include it in the general resume.

JSN: DRAFT OF A ONE-PAGE RÉSUMÉ

For practice, prepare a one-page resume that includes the essentials and highlights strengths. It will not be targeted to a particular job.

JSN: TARGETED RÉSUMÉS

Every time you write a résumé that is tailored to a specific job, include a copy here. Also include several practice copies of specialized résumés. While taking a course in corporate law, for example, write a résumé in which you pursue an opening at a law office for a corporate paralegal. For each résumé that you write (practice or real), solicit the comments of teachers, administrators, other students, working paralegals, attorneys, etc. Include these comments in this section of the JSN.

JSN: WRITING SAMPLES

Start building writing samples that you will present to prospective employers. Written assignments from your instructors can be turned into writing samples. In addition, take the initiative and create writing samples on your own based on assignments that you give yourself. Examples:

- A brief memorandum of law on the application of a statute to a set of facts (see Chapters 7 and 12)
- A pleading such as a complaint (see Chapter 10)
- A set of interrogatories (see Chapter 10)
- Articles of incorporation and bylaws for a fictitious corporation
- An analysis of a recent court opinion (see Chapters 7 and 11)
- An intake memorandum of law based on an interview that you role-play with another student (see Chapter 8)
- A brief article that you write for a paralegal newsletter or blog on an aspect of your legal education or work experience as a paralegal (see Appendix B and Appendix F)

Don't wait for anyone to tell you that you should turn an assignment into a writing assignment. Do so on your own. Set yourself the goal of completing the program with a *substantial* portfolio of writing samples. The core assignments at the end of every chapter urge you to do assignments on your own that are not required for the course. Many of them can be turned into writing samples.

Characteristics of an Effective Writing Sample

- It is your own work.
- It is clearly and specifically identified. The heading at the top tells the reader what the writing is.
- It is typed (handwritten work should be typed).
- There are no spelling or grammatical errors in it.
- Its appearance is professional.
- Someone whom you respect evaluated it before you put it in final form. You feel that it is a high-quality product.
- It does not violate anyone's right to privacy or confidentiality. (If the sample pertains to real people or events, you have **redacted** it by disguising all names or other identifying features.)

redacted To edit or prepare a document for publication or release, often by deleting, altering, or blocking out text that you do not want disclosed.

Evaluation by others is key. Ask your program director for guidance in selecting samples and in obtaining feedback on them. If possible, try to have a teacher or practicing attorney review each sample. Rewrite it based on their comments. Rewrite it again based on more comments that you solicit. Take the initiative in preparing writing samples and in obtaining feedback from knowledgeable contacts that you make.

The importance of collecting a large pool of writing samples cannot be overemphasized. Even if you eventually use only a few of them, the value of preparing them is enormous. It is sometimes difficult to obtain a paralegal job without experience. Although writing samples are not a substitute for experience, they can be part of an effective strategy to demonstrate your ability to perform practical tasks.

JSN: PORTFOLIO

Have a portfolio that you carry with you to interviews. As mentioned earlier in our discussion of job interviews, the portfolio should contain:

- Your résumé
- Writing samples
- Your paralegal certificate
- A list of references
- Letters of recommendation
- Your school transcript (if your grades are impressive)
- Performance reviews from other jobs
- Copies of awards or other recognition of achievement
- Proof of attendance at CLE (continuing legal education) sessions
- Statement of membership in professional associations
- List of clients and other parties (names of clients and other parties on cases you have worked on in prior employment or volunteer work; this list is never shown to anyone until you are close to having an offer)
- Anything else that might have a bearing on your employability

JSN: ATTORNEY CONTACTS

In the section on assertive networking earlier in this chapter, you were urged to make a list of attorneys with whom you have a direct or indirect connection. For each attorney, include in the JSN the attorney's name, street address, email address, other web address (e.g., LinkedIn), and phone number. Not only do you want to know whether any of these attorneys are interested in hiring paralegals, but equally important, you also want to know if they can give you any leads to other employers who might be interested in hiring.

JSN: PARALEGAL CONTACTS

The section on assertive networking also suggested ways to locate paralegals. You want to talk with as many employed paralegals as possible to obtain leads to possible positions and tips on the job search. Make a list of the names, email and web addresses, and phone numbers of all the paralegals whom you could contact. For those you do contact, include notes on what they told you. If they have nothing useful to say at the present time, ask them if you could check back with them in several months and if you could leave your name and number with them in case they come across anything in the future.

JSN: JOB INTERVIEWS

Here is a checklist for your job interviews:

- Exact location of interview (use an Internet street map)
- Time of arrival
- Professional appearance in dress
- Extra copies of résumé
- Extra copies of writing samples
- Copies of your transcripts
- Name of person(s) who will conduct interview
- Notes from your background research on the firm or company so that you know the kind of law it practices, why it might be considering hiring paralegals, etc.
- Role-playing of job interview in advance with a friend
- Preparation for difficult questions that might be asked, such as why you left your last job so soon after starting it (see Exhibit 2-20)
- List of questions that you will ask the interviewer:
  - Responsibilities of the position
  - Skills needed for the position
  - Methods of supervision
  - Office's prior experience with paralegals
  - Career ladder for paralegals
  - Relationship among paralegals, secretaries, and other clerical staff
  - Whether there will be client contact
  - Opportunities for growth
  - Methods of evaluating paralegals
  - CLE: Continuing legal education opportunities
  - Billable hours expected of paralegals
  - Nonbillable tasks
  - Use of systems in the practice of law
  - Working conditions (typing, photocopying, office arrangement, etc.)
  - Travel
  - Overtime
  - Computers and other equipment use
  - Compensation and fringe benefits

After each job interview that you have, organize your notes around the following themes:

- Date of interview
- Where you interviewed, persons who interviewed you (names, addresses, etc.)
- Kind of position that was open
- Date you sent the follow-up letter
- What you need to do next (send list of references, send writing samples, provide missing information that you did not have with you during the interview, etc.)
- Your impressions of the interview (how you think you did, what surprised you, and what you would do differently the next time you have an interview)
- Notes on why you were not offered the job
- Notes on why you turned down the job offered

VOLUNTEERING AS A WAY TO GAIN LEGAL EXPERIENCE

If you examine job openings for paralegals, you will find that many prospective employers want paralegals with experience. The market for such individuals is excellent. But if you are new to the field and seeking an entry-level position, you are caught in the dilemma of not being able to find a job without experience and not being able to get experience without a job. How do you handle this classic Catch-22 predicament?

- You work even harder to compile an impressive résumé.
- You make sure that you have collected a substantial portfolio of writing samples. Such writing is often the closest equivalent to prior job experience available to you. Each writing sample demonstrates *practical* skills such as clarity of communication and organization.
- When you talk to other paralegals, you seek specific advice on how to present yourself as an applicant for your first job.

- Find out from legal staffing and employment agencies (see Exhibit 2-12) if there are any temporary or part-time positions available that match your qualifications.
- Volunteer.

A major way to gain experience is to volunteer your services. Here are ways to find volunteer options:

Finding Volunteer Opportunities

- Legal aid offices and public interest law firms often encourage volunteer work. On finding such offices, see the steps outlined earlier in this chapter on legal aid offices.
- Here are additional options for finding volunteer opportunities in the public sector:
  - Paralegal associations. At the website of paralegal associations in your state (see Appendix B), look for pro bono links or type "pro bono" in the search box.
  - CASA (Court-Appointed Special Advocate). Find the CASA office in your area (www.casaforchildren.org). In family-law cases, nonattorney volunteers are used as fact finders, interviewers, and investigators. They gather pertinent information relative to the child's case and report on these findings in court.
  - American Bar Association. Check the ABA site for volunteer options in the country (www.probono.net/aba_oppsguide). Many of the programs use attorney and paralegal volunteers. See the Find Opportunities guide at the ABA site.
  - Legal Services Corporation. Go to the site of the Legal Services Corporation, the federal government agency that funds legal service programs (www.lsc.gov). Click your state under Local Programs or type your state in the search box. Links should lead you to legal aid programs in the state, many of which welcome pro bono assistance from attorneys and paralegals.
  - Legal Services Links (www.ptla.org/links/services.htm). Click your state.
  - LawHelp. Find your state at LawHelp, a "gateway to America's nonprofit legal services providers" (www.lawhelp.org). Although this site is primarily for potential clients with specific legal problems, the links to offices providing legal help often use attorney and paralegal volunteers. (Use the Find Help links on the site to get to individual programs.)
  - Volunteer Match. At Volunteer Match (www.volunteermatch.org), type "legal" in the search box. You will be led to organizations seeking volunteer help.
  - See the additional volunteer sites in Exhibit 2-12 under "Volunteer Opportunities to Obtain Experience."
  - As indicated, many offices that use attorney volunteers also use paralegal volunteers. When you find an office that uses attorneys, contact it to find out if paralegals are used as well. Use general search engines to locate offices that use attorney volunteers. In Google, Bing, or Yahoo, run this search "pro bono" volunteer attorney aa (substituting your city, county, or state for "aa").
- Consider volunteering for a recent law-school graduate who is just starting a solo or small-firm law practice. ("The first solo practitioner I approached," commented a person posting on a paralegal listserv, "agreed to allow me to intern with his firm for free. I received a lot of hands-on experience" during the weeks I was there. "That internship was invaluable!")
- Contact a private law firm and offer to perform "runner" services at low or no cost, e.g., delivery of documents, filing, and service of process. Be upfront. For example, say to an attorney, "If I volunteered at your office one afternoon a week, would you have tasks for me that would help me gain practical knowledge and experience in a law office, even if at an introductory level?"

SUMMARY OF JOB STRATEGIES

Exhibit 2-23 presents a summary of the major job-search strategies we have been discussing in this chapter. To a large extent, the strategies will be dictated by the market you will be facing for paralegal employment. In times of plenty when there are many job openings, you can afford to be selective. At other times you need to be more creative in the search.

Exhibit 2-23	Summary: Job Strategies Depending on the Market You Face

Job-Search Strategies Needed in Any Market

1. Know the kinds of law offices in your area and the work that paralegals do in them. Include law firms as well as businesses and associations that employ attorneys.
2. Have a range of high-quality, professional-looking writing samples from your courses.
3. Join and become active now on LinkedIn, Twitter, and Facebook. Do not wait until after graduation. See Exhibit 2-13.
4. Have a business card that states your name, email address, LinkedIn address, and phone number. Refer to yourself as "Paralegal" or, if still in school, "Paralegal Student."
5. Be certain that your résumé(s) and cover letter(s) present your strengths and are perfect in spelling and grammar.
6. Network with all your direct and indirect attorney connections.
7. Network with employed paralegals, e.g., through associations in your area.
8. Do background research on law offices. For each office you contact, check its website or other online information about the office. Locate the career or employment link, if any, on the site. Call the office to obtain the name and title of the person in the office who handles recruitment. Mail (U.S. mail, not email) a cover letter and résumé to that person inquiring about employment there. In your cover letter, refer to something you learned about the firm (e.g., its recent court victory) and retool your résumé (if possible) so that you emphasize a connection between your background and that office. A week after the mailing, call this person to ask if it was received and inquire about paralegal openings.

Job-Search Strategies When the Job Market for Paralegals Is Tight

9. Follow guidelines 1-8 above.
10. Register with recruitment/law employment agencies in your area.
11. Register with staffing agencies in your area.
12. Network with politicians in your area. (They probably know a lot of attorneys and definitely will do what they can to make you a happy voter.)
13. Try to find a temporary paralegal position to get a foot in the door.
14. Do pro bono volunteering, e.g., at a legal aid society, a district attorney's office, a domestic violence center, CASA (Court-Appointed Special Advocate).
15. Ask private attorneys if they would like to have free paralegal work from you (e.g., 5 hours a week).
16. Consider applying for nonparalegal positions at law offices as a way to get a foot in the door, e.g., a job as a file clerk or in the mail room or other clerical position.
17. Create a blog (e.g., use Google Blogspot, www.blogger.com, to start one). Pick an area of law that interests you, e.g., capital punishment. Find recent cases on that area of law by checking Scholar.Google.com regularly. On your blog, enter the cite of each case you find plus one sentence on what the case is about. Include the address of this blog on your résumé.
18. Learn how to set up a simple spreadsheet on Excel or on a free spreadsheet program on the Internet. Example: calculate interest payments on a mortgage based on facts you make up (purchase price, interest rate, etc.). Include the spreadsheet as a writing sample for your portfolio.
19. Cold call law offices.
20. Keep a positive attitude and don't give up!

YOUR SECOND JOB

Once you have had several years of experience and have demonstrated your competence, you will find increased employment options available to you. It will become substantially easier to negotiate salary and articulate your skills in a job interview. You can also consider other kinds of employment where your legal training, skills, expertise, and experience would be valuable. It is not uncommon for a paralegal to be recruited by former or active clients of a first employer. Numerous business contacts are made in the course of a job; these contacts could turn into new careers. In Exhibit 2-24, you will find a list of some of the types of positions that paralegals have taken (often with additional training) after they demonstrated their ability and acquired legal experience.

In short, you face a different market once you have acquired a record of experience and accomplishment. You are in greater demand in law firms and businesses. Furthermore, your legal skills are readily transferable to numerous law-related positions.

Exhibit 2-24	Positions for Experienced Paralegals

- Paralegal supervisor
- Law office administrator (legal administrator)
- Law firm marketing administrator
- Professional development coordinator
- Paralegal consultant
- Freelance/independent paralegal
- Law librarian/assistant
- Paralegal teacher or co-teacher
- Paralegal school administrator
- Placement officer
- Bar association lawyer referral coordinator
- Court administrator
- Court clerk
- Elected official (e.g., legislator, school board member, or mayor)
- Sales representative for legal publisher/vendor
- Investigator
- Customs inspector
- Compliance and enforcement inspector
- Occupational safety and health inspector
- Lobbyist
- Legislative assistant
- Real estate management consultant
- Real estate specialist
- Real estate portfolio manager

- Land acquisitions supervisor
- Title examiner
- Independent title abstractor
- Abstractor
- Systems analyst
- Computer analyst
- Computer sales representative
- Bank research associate
- Trust officer (trust administrator)
- Trust associate
- Assistant loan administrator
- Fiduciary accountant
- Financial analyst/planner
- Investment analyst
- Assistant estate administrator
- Enrolled agent
- Equal employment opportunity specialist
- Employee benefit specialist/consultant
- Pension specialist
- Pension administrator
- Compensation planner
- Corporate trademark specialist
- Corporate manager
- Securities analyst
- Securities compliance officer
- Insurance adjuster
- Actuarial associate

- Claims examiner
- Claims coordinator
- Risk management specialist
- Contracts administrator
- Patient advocate
- Legal journalist
- Legal proofreader
- Environmental specialist
- Editor for a legal or business publisher
- Personnel director
- Recruiter, legal employment agency
- Administrative law judge (ALJ)
- Arbitrator
- Mediator
- Internal security inspector
- Victim witness specialist
- Evidence technician
- Demonstrative evidence specialist
- Fingerprint technician
- Polygraph examiner
- Fraud examiner
- Probation officer
- Parole officer
- Corrections officer
- Bailiff
- Etc.

CHAPTER SUMMARY

Someone once said that finding a job is a job in itself. The first step is to become informed about where paralegals work and what they do at those locations. The first part of this chapter was designed to provide you with this information. The major employers of paralegals are private law firms, corporations and other businesses, the government, and legal aid offices. While other settings also exist, these are the largest. Comparisons were made on working conditions that paralegals are likely to face in each setting.

We then looked at forty-seven specialties such as bankruptcy and criminal law. Our focus was the identification of paralegal functions in these specialties and a brief paralegal perspective of what life might be like in each. For the specialties where most paralegals work (corporate law, estates, family law, litigation, real estate, and tort law), quotations from job ads identified traits and skills employers often seek.

In the second part of the chapter, we turned to strategies for finding employment. The strategies addressed the following questions: When should you begin the search? What are effective networking techniques? How do you locate prospective

attorney employers? How do you locate working paralegals in order to obtain leads to employment? What Internet resources (including social media) are available? How do you arrange an informational interview? How do you do background research (due diligence) on potential employers? What should your résumé contain? What is an effective cover letter? What kinds of writing samples should you prepare, and when should you start preparing them? How should you prepare for a job interview? What kinds of questions should you anticipate? What kinds of questions should you ask? How can you organize all of the contacts, events, and pieces of paper that are involved in a comprehensive job search? What should a Job-Search Notebook (JSN) contain? How do you identify relevant skills that are obtained through nonlegal employment, legal employment, volunteer activity, other life experiences, nonlegal education, and legal education? What strategies can be used to find an entry-level job in a market where employers are looking for experience?

Finally, we examined alternative career opportunities for paralegals, particularly for those who have gained paralegal experience on the job.

KEY TERMS

private law firm (p. 35)	special-interest group (p. 40)	legal nurse consultant (LNC) (p. 44)	PDF (p. 94)
boutique law firm (p. 36)	test case (p. 41)	legal nurse (p. 44)	metadata (p. 94)
general counsel (p. 37)	prepaid legal services (p. 41)	networking (p. 79)	parallelism (p. 97)
civil service (p. 37)	crime (p. 41)	job bank (p. 82)	due diligence (p. 99)
jurisdiction (p. 37)	tort (p. 41)	continuing legal education (CLE) (p. 82)	blog (p. 100)
paralegal specialist (p. 38)	conversion (p. 41)		cover letter (p. 102)
legal aid office (p. 39)	public defender (p. 41)	blind ad (p. 82)	billable hours quota (p. 111)
indigent (p. 39)	assigned counsel (p. 41)	staffing agency (p. 84)	intranet (p. 112)
civil (p. 39)	independent contractor (p. 42)	informational interview (p. 86)	contaminate (p. 112)
IOLTA (p. 39)	independent paralegal (p. 42)	chronological résumé (p. 93)	conflict of interest (p. 112)
client trust account (p. 39)	outsourcing (p. 42)	functional résumé (p. 93)	redact (p. 118)
uncontested (p. 40)	document service provider (DSP) (p. 43)	font (p. 94)	
TANF (p. 40)		point (p. 94)	
pro bono (p. 40)	e-discovery (p. 44)		

ASSIGNMENTS

CRITICAL ANALYSIS

2.1

(a) Why do some attorneys seek paralegal jobs?

(b) How would you characterize the job market for paralegals in your area today? In light of this strategy, write out specific strategies that you will follow for your job search.

PROJECTS

2.2 Exhibit 2-1 lists the major categories of employment for paralegals. Use the links in Exhibit 2-12 and in Appendix H to find the site of one law office in each of the following categories:

(a) private law firm in your state with at least ten attorneys

(b) private law firm in your state with at least thirty attorneys

(c) a legal aid office in your state

(d) a special-interest group located in your state

(e) a state or county prosecution/district attorney office in your state

(f) an independent paralegal (or other nonattorney who is authorized to provide help for persons with legal problems)

2.3 From the list of forty-seven specialties in Exhibit 2-6, pick one that interests you, at least preliminarily.

(a) What specialty did you select? Explain why you might want to work in this area of the law.

(b) Find two Internet sites that provide explanations of any aspect of the substantive or procedural law in this area. (Start by checking the Internet sites presented in the text for that specialty under the heading "More on This Area of the Law on the Net." If needed, check other sites as well.) What sites did you select? Quote at least two sentences from each site on any aspect of the law it covers.

(c) In Appendix H, there are links to finding law offices in every state. Find one law firm in your state that practices this specialty. Quote at least two sentences from this firm's site on what it does in this specialty.

(d) Using the links in Exhibit 2-12, find two paralegal job openings for this area of the law in your state. (Check your local newspaper, available legal newspapers, the Internet, etc.)

2.4 Role-play an interview for an entry-level job in class. The instructor will decide what kind of job the interview will be for and will select students to play the role of interviewer and interviewee. The interviewer should ask a variety of questions such as those presented in the chapter's guidelines for handling a job interview. See also Exhibit 2-20 on categories of interview questions. The interviewee can make up the answers within the guidelines provided by the instructor. The rest of the class will evaluate the interviewee.

(a) What were the strong and weak points in the way the interviewee answered the questions? Were mistakes made? How should the interviewee have dealt with certain questions? Was the interviewee confident? Overconfident? Did the interviewee ask his or her own good questions of the interviewer? Were these questions properly timed? What impressions did the interviewee convey of himself or herself?

(b) Based on this interview, make a list of do's and don'ts for such interviews.

CORE SKILLS

Among the many skills a paralegal must have, five core skills stand out: writing (both basic English and legal drafting), research, ethics, computer use, and collaboration (working with others). The core-skill assignments introduce and reinforce these skills. Even if you are not asked to do all of the assignments as part of the course, you should do them on your own. Also, do not wait for the topics in the assignments to be covered in this course or in other courses. Successful paralegals are self-starters. A major characteristic of a self-starter is a thirst for independent study—learning on your own.

CORE SKILL: WRITING

2.5 Run this search in Google, Bing, or Yahoo: semicolon.

(a) State two semicolon rules that are new to you or with which you were only vaguely familiar. List the website(s) that you used to answer this question.

(b) Make up two sentences. Each sentence should use all of the following words: *corporation, tax*, and *business*. Each sentence should demonstrate the correct use of one of the two semicolon rules you identified in part a.

2.6 Assume that you have just interviewed for a paralegal job at the law firm of Grassley and Sims. You were interviewed by Helen Crowley, an attorney at the firm. She told you that the firm had not yet decided whether the position would be full or part time. Write a follow-up letter to Ms. Crowley. Use the guidelines in the chapter on the purpose of such letters. For the format of the letter, see Exhibit 2-19. Follow this format unless your instructor specifies otherwise. (The letter in Exhibit 2-19 is a cover letter. Adapt it as a follow-up letter.) During the interview, Ms. Crowley asked you for more details on a computer course on word processing that you took at the Adult Learning Center near where you live. Provide these details in the letter. You can make up any details that you need, such as the address of the Center, the address of Grassley and Sims, your address, specifics of the computer course, etc. A major theme of the letter is that you are still very interested in working at Grassley and Sims. Indicate that you are seeking a full-time position but would consider part-time work as well.

CORE SKILL: RESEARCH

2.7 On Google, run this search: Google search techniques tips.

(a) List five Google search techniques that you did not know or with which you were only vaguely familiar. Examples might be how to search for a phrase, how to exclude a term in a search query so that you would be led to sites that did not contain that term, and how to write a search for a three-word phrase when you are not sure of the middle word in the phrase. These are examples; you can use them or others.

(b) Make up any five searches that use the five Google techniques you identified—one search for each of the new techniques. List each of the five searches and give an example of a good site to which each search led you.

CORE SKILL: ETHICS

2.8 In Assignment 1.7 of Chapter 1, you identified the name of the code of ethics that governs attorneys in your state. Dan Walters is an attorney in your state. He posts his résumé on his website. The résumé states that he has trial experience in antitrust cases. This statement is false. Use the index to the code of ethics to find rules and comments in the code that Dan has or may have violated.

CORE SKILL: COMPUTERS

2.9 In Google, Bing, or Yahoo, run each of the following searches:

Microsoft Word tutorial

Microsoft Excel tutorial

Microsoft Outlook tutorial

WestlawNext tutorial

Lexis Advantage tutorial

BloombergLaw tutorial

(a) Give the Internet address of at least two free online tutorials for each of these six programs. (Note: The six software programs listed are not free, but assistance on how to use them (tutorials) often is. You do not have to do the tutorials; simply make note of where the free tutorials are.)

(b) State the main function of Word, Excel, Outlook, WestlawNext, Lexis Advantage, and BloombergLaw.

(c) In the Computer Terminology in the Law (CTL) notebook you started in Assignment 1.8 of Chapter 1, include information you obtain by doing parts a and b.

CORE SKILL: COLLABORATION

2.10

(a) Obtain the email addresses of your classmates in this course. Alternatively, ask your instructor what other options are available for you to communicate with other classmates.

(b) Run this search in Google, Bing, or Yahoo: paralegal blog. See also the list of blogs in Appendix F. Pick any two paralegal blogs that contain useful information. Send an email message to each of your classmates in which you give the addresses to the two blogs you selected. Give specific reasons why you chose these blogs.

(c) You will be receiving the answers on blogs from your classmates. Comment on how helpful you felt their answers were. What did you learn about blogs, paralegals, and collaboration that you did not know before?

THE JOB SEARCH

(The search for employment cannot wait until the end of a course or of a curriculum. It has to begin now. The job-search assignments are designed to introduce you to different aspects of the job search and to build options for you to explore about employment.)

2.11

(a) Start organizing your Job-Search Notebook (JSN). Obtain a notebook. Make headings for each of the fourteen sections of the Notebook as outlined in Exhibit 2-21.

(b) Pick one of the first six sections of the JSN. For the section you select, complete the self-analysis required for that section.

REVIEW QUESTIONS

1. What factors affect the job market for paralegals?
2. What categories of people sometimes compete for paralegal jobs?
3. What are the nine major categories of paralegal employment?
4. What is a private law firm? A boutique law firm?
5. What are some differences between working in large and small private law offices?
6. What is an in-house law department? Who runs it?
7. Name four kinds of offices where government paralegals work.
8. Summarize the major duties of a person in the paralegal specialist series (GS-950) of the federal government.
9. Name some of the ways to find job opportunities in federal, state, and local government.
10. What is a legal aid office?
11. What are IOLTA programs and pro bono legal services?
12. Give examples of special-interest groups that may have legal staffs.
13. What are prepaid legal services?
14. What is the role of public defenders and assigned counsel?
15. What is an independent paralegal?
16. What is meant by outsourcing?
17. Name some of the services offered by legal service providers (LSPs) that use paralegals.
18. What are legal nurses and legal nurse consultants (LNCs)?
19. Pick any three paralegal specialties in which you might want to work upon graduation and list some of the major paralegal duties in each of the three specialties.
20. When should you start looking for paralegal work?
21. What is networking and what benefits can it provide?
22. What is the "I-You-What" approach to networking for employment leads?
23. What are the characteristics of an assertive networker?
24. Name categories of attorneys with whom you may have a direct or indirect connection.
25. How can paralegal associations be used when networking for employment?
26. What is a job bank?
27. What are buzzwords and how should you use them?
28. What is a blind ad?
29. If you need an entry-level position, how might you respond to an ad seeking someone with paralegal experience?
30. What are some job titles you should check in addition to paralegal and legal assistant?
31. Distinguish between a transitional job and a career job.
32. What are some reasons you should consider responding to an ad for an attorney?
33. What is a staffing agency?
34. What is the limited purpose of an informational interview?
35. In what ways can the Internet help you find a paralegal job?
36. What social-media sites should you consider using in your job search?
37. What is a targeted résumé?
38. Summarize guidelines for drafting effective résumés.
39. What is a PDF format and when should you use it?
40. What is metadata in a résumé?
41. What nonaction verbs should you avoid using in a résumé?
42. What is meant by grammatical parallelism?
43. How do you perform due diligence on a prospective employer?
44. Distinguish between the two major kinds of résumés.
45. Name some techniques of an effective cover letter.
46. What are some useful proofreading techniques you should use for your résumé, cover letter, and other writings?
47. Summarize guidelines for effective job interviews.
48. How can you try to phrase "negative" traits in a positive way if you are asked about your weaknesses?
49. What are the six major kinds of questions you should be prepared to answer in a job interview?
50. What is the STAR method of answering interview questions?
51. What should you include in the portfolio that you bring with you to an interview?
52. What are examples of questions you should be prepared to ask the interviewer during a job interview?
53. How can you avoid contaminating a law office where you are seeking employment?
54. What is the function of a follow-up letter after an interview?
55. How should you react if you do not receive a job offer at an office where you have been interviewed?
56. What should you include in a Job-Search Notebook (JSN)?
57. How can you identify relevant skills that you obtained through nonlegal employment, legal employment, volunteer activity, other life experiences, nonlegal education, and legal education?
58. Give examples of writing samples that you could prepare on your own.
59. What are the characteristics of an effective writing sample?
60. What is redaction and when should you redact a writing sample or other writing?
61. How can you try to overcome the Catch-22 predicament that many new paralegals face when looking for entry-level work?
62. Give examples of positions that are often available for experienced paralegals.

HELPFUL WEBSITES

Exhibit 2-12 and Appendix E

For an extensive list of job websites, see Exhibit 2-12 in this chapter. See also the job links for your state in Appendix D.

Finding Employment in Your State

■ www.mynextmove.org (type *paralegal* in the search box)

What Paralegals Do

■ www.lawcost.com/paras.htm
■ www.lectlaw.com/files/pap01.htm

■ www.cobar.org/index.cfm/ID/106/subID/23108/CLAS
■ www.caparalegal.org/index.php/duties-skills
■ www.onetcodeconnector.org/ccreport/23-2011.00
■ www.paralegals.org (click "Publications," then "Publications Library," then "Paralegal Responsibilities")

Social-Media Search: LinkedIn, Facebook, and Twitter

■ www.hashatit.com (type *paralegal job* in the search box)
■ www.socialmention.com

- hashtagify.me (type *paralegal job* in the search box)
- www.tagboard.com (type *paralegal job* in the search box)
- www.hashtags.org (type *paralegal job* in the search box)

Paralegal Résumés
- www.bestsampleresume.com/sample-legal-resume
/paralegal-resume-1.html
- paralegaltoday.com/issue_archive/online_only/paralegal_resumes
.htm
- www.resume-resource.com/exleg6.html
- www.exampleresumes.org/occupational/paralegal.html

25 Things You Should Never Put on a Résumé
- www.hrworld.com/features
/25-things-not-to-put-on-resume-121807

Job-Search Expenses: When Are They Deductible?
- www.irs.gov/uac/Job-Search-Expenses-Can-Be-Tax-Deductible

National Directory of Legal Employers
- www.nalpdirectory.com

Legal Recruiters Directory
- www.law.com/jsp/nlj/legal_recruiters_directory.jsp

Twitter Directory
twitter.com/i/directory (keep clicking through the index until you find paralegal jobs)

Google, Bing, or Yahoo Searches
On these search engines, run the following searches, using quotation marks and substituting your state for "aa" where indicated:

- paralegal aa
- paralegal jobs aa
- paralegal "job alert"
- paralegal career aa
- paralegal roles aa
- paralegal profiles aa
- government paralegal jobs aa
- GS-0950
- corporate paralegal jobs aa
- public sector paralegal jobs aa
- sample paralegal resume
- paralegal resume aa
- functional résumé
- paralegal volunteer aa
- "no experience no job"
- paralegal "job interview" aa
- paralegal "employment interview" aa
- paralegal job market aa
- paralegal specialties aa
- paralegal employment agency aa
- areas of law
- attorney specialties
- illegal job interview questions

ENDNOTES

1. Andrea Wagner, *Tips & Traps for the New Paralegal*, 8 Legal Assistant Today 78 (March/April 1991). (The numbers in the quote were increased, but the guideline remains the same)

2. Knoll Workplace Research, *The Emerging Law Firm Practice* 2 (2009).

3. For more on paralegals in the federal government, run the following search in Google, Bing, or Yahoo: GS-0950.

4. U.S. Office of Personnel Management, *Position Classification Standard for Paralegal Specialist Series*, GS-0950 (1986) (www.opm.gov/fedclass/gs0950.pdf).

5. See Commercial Law League of America, *A Paralegal Approach to the Practice of Commercial Law* (November 14, 1975).

6. J. Stein & B. Hoff, *Paralegals and Administrative Assistants for Prosecutors* (National District Attorneys Association 1974); J. Stein, *Paralegals: A Resource for Defenders and Correctional Services* (1976).

7. Rocky Mountain Paralegal Association, *The Use of the Legal Assistant* (1975).

8. Colorado Bar Association Paralegal Committee, *Guidelines for the Utilization of Paralegals*, "Environmental Law Paralegal" (www.cobar.org/index.cfm/ID/106/subID/23108/CLAS).

9. "Family Law Paralegal," supra note 8.

10. C. Berg, *Annual Survey* (San Francisco Paralegal Association, December 19, 1973).

11. "Municipal Finance," supra note 8.

12. William Glaberson, *In Tiny Courts of New York, Abuses of Law and Power*, New York Times, September 25, 2006, at A1.

13. "Water Law," supra note 8.

14. Paralegal Division of the State Bar of Texas, LinkedIn Group (November 14, 2011) (www.linkedin.com).

15. The Paralegal Society, *Sketches of Our Society—Featured Paralegal: Eric Bleuel* (theparalegalsociety.wordpress.com/2011/12/15/sketches-of-our-society-featured-paralegal-eric-bleuel).

16. *Merrill Advantage* (Spring 1990).

17. Susan Gainen, *Information Interviews: A Strategy*, Paradigm (Baltimore City Paralegal Association, November/December 1989).

18. Jacobi, *Back to Basics in Hiring Techniques*, The Mandate 1 (Association of Legal Administrators, San Diego Chapter, October 1987).

19. Ruth-Ellen Post, *Paralegal Internships*, 39 (Delmar 1999).

20. Rocky Mountain Paralegal Association, *Employment Handbook for legal Assistants* (1979).

21. Judy Waggoner, *Cover Letter as Important as Résumé in Job Search*, Appleton Post-Crescent (August 11, 2005).

22. Gretchen Rubin and Joanna Young, *The Artful Edit* (2007) (see raymondpward.typepad.com/newlegalwriter/2007/07/a-simple-trick-.html).

23. Cunningham, *A Planned Approach to Interviewing*, 5 The LAMA Manager 1 (International Practice Management Association, Fall 1989).

24. Chere Estrin and Stacey Hunt, *The Successful Paralegal Job-Search Guide* 20405 (2001).

25. Moralez, *Sample Interview Questions*, 11 Paragram (Oregon Legal Assistant Association, May 1988).

26. Wendel, *You the Recruiter*, 5 Legal Assistant Today 31 (September/October 1987).

27. Aditi Mukherji, 5 *Intern Interview Questions ... Free Enterprise* (April 24, 2014) (blogs.findlaw.com/free enterprise/2014/04/5-intern-interview-questions-for-smallbusinesses.html?DCMP=NWL-protop).

28. *Sample Interview Questions* (www.wpi.edu/Images/CMS/CDC/Interviews.pdf).

29. Reitz, *Be Steps Ahead of Other Candidates: Understand the Interview Game*, 5 Legal Assistant Today 24, 84 (March/April 1988).

30. Michelle Cottle, *Too Personal at the Interview*, New York Times, April 25, 1999, at BU10.

31. Leslie Hilton, *Interview Scenarios*, San Jose Mercury News, January 26, 2003, at 1PC.

ON-THE-JOB REALITIES: THE ASSERTIVE PARALEGAL

CHAPTER OUTLINE

- The Ideal
- Communication
- The Multigenerational Office
- Expectations
- The Environment of a Law Office
- Office Politics

- Self-Assessment and Employer Evaluations
- Working with Attorneys
- Assertive/Nonassertive/ Aggressive Behavior
- The Skill of Listening
- Keeping a Diary or Journal and a Career Development File

- Paralegal CLE
- Responsibilities of Supervisors
- Relationship with Secretaries
- Sexual Harassment
- Working with Systems

CHAPTER OBJECTIVES

After completing this chapter, you should be able to:

- Identify the major factors that affect paralegal job satisfaction.
- Describe some of the problems a paralegal can encounter on the job.
- Understand the tensions that can exist in a busy law practice.
- List some of the causes of communication problems in a law office.
- Summarize some of the major personality characteristics that can exist in a multigenerational office.
- Know what it means to expect the unexpected in a law office.

- List effective techniques for handling office politics.
- Identify the major components of a paralegal performance review.
- Describe the characteristics of some attorneys that make them good advocates but problematic managers.
- Describe the characteristics of an assertive paralegal.
- List effective techniques of active listening.
- Know the value of a diary or journal and a career development file.

- Understand the importance of continuing legal education (CLE).
- List the techniques of effective supervision.
- Understand reasons why tension may sometimes exist between secretaries and paralegals.
- Distinguish between quid pro quo and hostile-environment sexual harassment.
- Explain why office systems are important but sometimes ineffective.

THE IDEAL

The practice of law is a high-performance arena of challenges, frustrations, and triumphs; it is not for the faint of heart. "Unfortunately, being successful" does not always depend "on being good at what you do but also requires the ability to work with others regardless of how difficult they may be. The good news is that with a little patience and a lot of emotional intelligence, career success is possible."[1] In this chapter, we cover emotional intelligence and related themes by exploring some of the major techniques assertive paralegals use to survive and thrive in the practice of law. Before doing so, we pause to examine the ideal.

What is a "perfect" paralegal job? Perhaps it is impossible to describe perfection in its fullest sense, but if we made the attempt, what would the description contain? Exhibit 3-1 presents such an attempt; it identifies forty factors of an ideal paralegal job environment. The factors are not of equal importance, and some of them overlap. Nor would every paralegal agree that all forty are needed. In general, however, these are the factors (not necessarily listed in order of priority) that must be considered, according to many working paralegals.

Exhibit 3-1	Forty Factors That Can Affect Paralegal Job Satisfaction

1. Your pay and fringe benefits are satisfactory.
2. You are respected and treated as a professional.
3. Attorneys in the office know how to delegate tasks and work with paralegals.
4. Before you are given a new assignment, your supervisor determines how it fits with other assignments still on your agenda. You are never uncertain about what has priority.
5. You are not in competition with new attorneys or other paralegals for billable hours.
6. Secretaries, office clerks, and other support personnel understand and accept your role. The office functions as a team.
7. You share the same values as the people with whom you work.
8. The office has high standards of competence.
9. The office follows high standards of ethical and moral responsibility. The office can be aggressive in the practice of law, but its guiding principle is not to "win at all costs." You are encouraged to raise ethical questions about something the office has done.
10. There are clear lines of authority in the office. You know whom to turn to for help if your immediate supervisor is not available.
11. Your work is adequately supervised.
12. The work you do is challenging.
13. Your paralegal skills are being used by the office; you are delegated meaningful tasks along with your share of mundane work.
14. There is a reasonable variety in the tasks you are asked to perform.
15. Demands on you to perform clerical tasks are reasonable, e.g., you perform them as needed, particularly when deadlines must be met or when the office is short-staffed.
16. Overtime requirements of the job are reasonable. (Overtime does not substantially interfere with maintaining a work-life balance.)
17. There is no undue pressure to meet billable hour goals or quotas.
18. You look forward to coming to work every day.
19. You feel you are making a contribution to the office.
20. Your contribution to the office is acknowledged.
21. Your performance is regularly and constructively evaluated according to clearly articulated standards.
22. In addition to being a business, the office demonstrates a commitment to the community through pro bono work and other volunteer activities that benefit society.
23. There is no sexism, racism, ageism, homophobia, or other inappropriate discrimination in the office.
24. You are given financial support and time off to participate in activities of paralegal associations such as continuing legal education (CLE).
25. Your work area and office equipment are satisfactory.
26. You have adequate access to clerical assistance.
27. Your privacy is respected.
28. When you need help in performing a task, you know what resources are available.
29. You are encouraged to develop new skills.
30. In addition to office training for paralegals, you participate in training for new attorneys, administrative staff, and others when the training is relevant to your job.
31. You have some client contact.
32. You participate in major social events in the office. They are not always attorney-only events.
33. Office politics are manageable.
34. There is a good flow of communication in the office. The grapevine is not the sole source of information.
35. You attend regularly scheduled and well-run staff meetings.
36. People in the office know how to listen.
37. You have good rapport with other paralegals in the office.
38. Office policies and procedures are clearly spelled out.
39. The office has a career ladder for paralegals.
40. You can see (or are told about) the end product of your work even though you may not work on every stage of a case or legal matter.

We move now to the reality of paralegal employment. The forty factors obviously do not exist in every paralegal job. While most paralegals are satisfied with the career they have chosen, problems can arise in any occupation. Our focus in this chapter will be to identify some of these problems and to suggest resolution strategies. Many of the problems we will be discussing are not peculiar to paralegalism. Sexism, for example, and the hassles of worker coexistence are not unique to the law office. Indeed, this chapter is probably as much about human nature as it is about the paralegal career.

Some of the discussion will be directed at attorneys and what they must do to solve a particular employment concern. Yet a major theme of this chapter is what the paralegal can do to overcome difficulties, even those that appear to be beyond the control of the paralegal. According to Beth King, president of the Oregon Paralegal Association:

> Job satisfaction is one of life's most important assets. As such, it is something we should cherish and cultivate. We may blame a lack of job satisfaction on our employer or those with whom we work. In truth, satisfaction with our jobs lies within our control.[2]

COMMUNICATION

A busy law office is often a charged environment, particularly if the office is engaged in litigation or has a large caseload with a relatively high turnover.

> It is difficult to explain to outsiders the pressures of a law firm environment. Client demands [seem] never ending, equipment failures send staff into a frenzy, messengers run throughout the city like maniacs, . . . receptionists cannot find various personnel because they did not check in or out, the accounting [department] is complaining about time and billing, and priorities change every minute.[3]

When large projects or huge sums of money are at stake, careers are on the line. Attorneys, not known for their lack of ego, can at times have unrealistic expectations of those around them. In this atmosphere, communication can occasionally break down. (See, for example, Exhibit 3-2.) According to a survey published by the journal *Legal Management*, "14 percent of each 40-hour workweek is wasted due to poor communication between staff and managers—amounting to a stunning seven weeks a year."[4] The problem may not be as bad as George Bernard Shaw might suggest ("the single biggest problem with communication is the illusion that it has taken place"), but when a breakdown occurs, it can be a trying experience. Here is an example:

> A senior partner thinks he told his paralegal to take care of an important filing. In actuality, all he told the paralegal to do was to draft the necessary documents to make the filing. The paralegal drafts the documents and puts them in the senior partner's in-box for his review. The filing deadline is missed. The senior partner blames his paralegal. The worst part of this scenario is that the paralegal is never told what happened or that she is being blamed. Perhaps the senior partner wishes to avoid a confrontation; perhaps he fears being told that the problem is not only his responsibility, but also his fault. In any event, the paralegal's reputation is smeared among the professional staff.[5]

Attempting to establish the truth in such situations—what actually happened—can sometimes be fruitless. People may simply be in no mood for "explanations."

Exhibit 3-2	Saying and Hearing: Two Separate Skills

Source: Sheila Swanson, 14 *At Issue* 8 (San Francisco Paralegal Association).

The need, of course, is to *prevent* miscommunication. Be aware of the standard factors that contribute to communication problems:

- Distractions
- Time pressures
- Work overload
- Embarrassment over asking for clarification

- Personality conflicts
- Equipment breakdown
- Physical impairment (e.g., hearing difficulty, defective eyeglasses)

You can take specific steps to help avoid miscommunication. Examples:

- Immediately after receiving an assignment, briefly repeat back to the supervisor your understanding of what you have been asked to do.
- Find out what priority each of your tasks should have.
- Ask your supervisor to estimate how many hours he or she thinks the assignment should take to complete.
- For lengthy or complex assignments, send your supervisor a brief note or email message in which you confirm what you have been asked to do and when it is due.
- Keep a personal **work in progress (WIP)** report in which you record your current tasks. (Later in this chapter, we will examine the related topic of job diaries or journals.)

work in progress (WIP) A list of tasks on which one is currently working and the dates they are due.

The danger of miscommunication in a busy law office can be quite high. If, however, you are constantly aware of the danger, you'll be in a better position to help avoid a communication breakdown. It is a little like crossing the street. The busier the intersection, the more caution that is needed to avoid an accident. Many law offices are very busy intersections.

THE MULTIGENERATIONAL OFFICE

There is great diversity in the workforce. "Three-fourths of the world has a personality style that is different than yours. Learning to understand, value and sometimes flex toward the style of others will help you get along and work better with everyone."[6] At one time, tension on the job such as someone's resistance to change was attributed to his or her being old-fashioned or stuck in the past. Today, social scientists have tried to articulate more precise differences among workers that can account for what works and what doesn't on the job.

In many relatively large law offices, four different generations are working side by side: Traditionalists, Baby Boomers, Generation X, and Generation Y. One way to head off miscommunication is to understand this diversity. "Four generations working together in the same work environment present new workforce dynamics and challenges. Moreover, the pending exodus of nearly 80 million retiring Baby Boomers and the entry of Generation Z ... will continue to change workplace dynamics."[7] Exhibit 3-3 describes some of the common characteristics of different workers in a multigenerational office.

Of course, not all law offices are multigenerational. In the office where you work, there may be a substantial unanimity of personality in the workers, even among those who fall into the different generational categories outlined in Exhibit 3-3.[8] Are the characteristics listed in Exhibit 3-3 stereotypes? Yes. Yet it is wise to prepare for the possibility of considerable workforce diversity in order to avoid being surprised by traits that some of the generations might display. If you are not surprised by the diversity, you are more likely to be able to accommodate it without sacrificing your own values. Furthermore, self-awareness of your own personality inclinations is prudent. Ask yourself whether you are inclined to any or all of the common characteristics of your generation or if you have picked up traits often displayed by generations other than your own.

Exhibit 3-3	The Multigenerational Office

Although exceptions exist within any category of worker, there are some characteristics that are common to many individuals within a particular category.

CATEGORY OF WORKER	DATES BORN	CHARACTERISTICS OF MANY IN THIS CATEGORY OF WORKER	
TRADITIONALISTS (also called the Silent Generation, Builders, Greatest Generation, Depression Babies, GI Joe Generation, Matures)	1922–1945	▪ Hardworking, strong work ethic ▪ Loyal (less likely to change jobs) ▪ Sees work as a privilege ▪ Team-player ▪ Civic-minded ▪ Dedicated ▪ Self-disciplined ▪ Prefers a chain-of-command structure ▪ Prefers to work under managers who are decisive, organized, and who are not trendy or touchy-feely ▪ Submissive; unlikely to question authority	▪ Uncomfortable with conflict ▪ Rules-oriented ▪ Favors traditional moral values ▪ Slow to change work habits ▪ Not technologically adept ▪ Inclined to let the job take precedence over family (duty before pleasure) ▪ Prefers formal work clothes ▪ Works only in an office ▪ To communicate, prefers face-to-face communication, memos, letters, and personal notes
BABY BOOMERS (also called Vietnam Generation, Me Generation)	1946–1964	▪ Hardworking ▪ Work-centric ▪ Competitive, but uncomfortable with conflict ▪ Optimistic ▪ Loyal ▪ Team player ▪ Resents newer workers who expect advancement without paying their dues ▪ Prefers to work under managers who treat those under them as equals; dislikes bureaucratic managers	▪ Multitasker ▪ Goal-oriented ▪ Sensitive to feedback ▪ Dislikes absolutes ▪ Has a focus on health ▪ Has a high divorce rate ▪ Prefers business work clothes ▪ May be more concerned with process than results ▪ Works only in an office ▪ To communicate, prefers phone calls and personal interaction
GENERATION X (also called GenX, Baby Busters, Twenty Somethings, Post-Boomers)	1965–1980	▪ Outspoken ▪ Educated ▪ Ambitious ▪ Goal-oriented ▪ Positive ▪ Independent ▪ Prefers to work under managers who encourage independence (dislikes being micro-managed; prefers hands-off management style) ▪ Tends to question and distrust authority ▪ Willing to change jobs ▪ Willing to buck the system ▪ Impatient	▪ Family-centric (disinclined to let the job control everything) ▪ Works with more women colleagues (often part of a two-income family with "latchkey" kids) ▪ Comfortable with new technology ▪ Prefers informal work environment ▪ Has a strong focus on results as opposed to the process of getting to results ▪ Prefers casual work clothes ▪ Flexible about where to work (office, home, etc.) ▪ To communicate, prefers email and voice mail
GENERATION Y (also called Millennials; Gamers, Internet Generation, Nintendo Generation, Digital Generation)	After 1980	▪ Smart ▪ Creative ▪ Self-confident ▪ Were often pampered by doting parents who told them they were special ▪ Feels entitled ▪ Needs constant feedback and praise ▪ Sociable with an emphasis on what is fair ▪ Team-oriented (grew up in team sports)	▪ Multitasker ▪ Techno-savvy (comfortable being online and connected—preferably mobile-throughout the day) ▪ Tends to question authority ▪ Willing to change jobs ▪ Has difficulty accepting criticism ▪ Values work-life balance over career achievements

CATEGORY OF WORKER	DATES BORN	CHARACTERISTICS OF MANY IN THIS CATEGORY OF WORKER	
		■ Comfortable in a diverse workforce ■ Willing to be part of collective action ■ Prefers to work under managers who are motivational and are not threatened by someone's computer skills	■ Prefers comfortable work clothes ■ Flexible about where to work (office, home, etc.) ■ To communicate, prefers text messages, emails, blogs, etc.
GENERATION Z (also called Generation@, Net Generation, Digital Natives)	After the late 1990s	It's unclear what characteristics this generation will bring to the workforce. What is clear is that their lives have been saturated with communication and media diversity	

EXPECTATIONS

To some extent, on-the-job problems are generated by surprise: "I never thought the job would be like this!" Unrealistic expectations, therefore, can be a source of frustration, as Eric Bleuel discovered when he began his first paralegal job:

> Many of the challenges I faced were very unexpected. How do you fix a copy machine when no one is around? How do you serve a subpoena when the guy is running away from you? What do you do when your boss gives you an assignment and you have no idea where to start?[9]

Another example of surprise concerns legal research. Most paralegal programs spend a good deal of time teaching students to do legal research. In many law offices, however, paralegals do not do extensive legal research. As indicated in Chapter 1, research courses are important in your curriculum because of the understanding they give you about the legal system, legal process, and the language of the law. Although you may eventually be given some research assignments, do not enter your first paralegal job expecting to spend a great deal of time in a brick-and-mortar or online law library doing legal research.

One of the objectives of this book is to provide you with information that will help prevent surprise. You need a candid account of what you might find. Chapter 2, for example, outlined steps on doing background investigation (**due diligence**) on a potential employer before you accept a job, such as talking with paralegals who have worked or who still work at the office and finding out what is said about that employer on the Internet, particularly in candid comments available on social media. Following these steps, whenever possible, should give you a more accurate picture of what lies ahead if you take the job.

If you live in a seller's market where there are more applicants than jobs, you may be so anxious to obtain a job that you will overlook its potential negative aspects. This is unfortunate. It is essential that you walk into a job, or any new situation, with open eyes. Not only will accurate information help reduce frustration, but also the information will be the foundation for corrective steps you can begin taking as soon as possible.

You need a lot of information. In the best of all worlds, you would have information relevant to many of the forty factors listed in Exhibit 3-1 that affect potential job satisfaction. Of course, there are limitations on what you can learn in advance of taking a job. Furthermore, even the information you receive can be no more than a guide to your own prediction of how these factors might apply to you as an individual once you are on the job. This should not deter you, however, from going after whatever information is available about the paralegal field in your area and about particular prospective employers. Again, the background research discussed in Chapter 2 should help you obtain such information.

Whether the information you are able to gather is extensive or minimal, the healthiest attitude is to expect the unexpected. Be prepared for surprises about:

- the different kinds of personalities in the office (see Exhibit 3-3),
- what supervisors think you are capable of doing,

due diligence Reasonable efforts to find and verify factual information needed to carry out an obligation, to avoid harming someone, or to make an important decision.

- the level and quantity of assignments you are given,
- how secretaries and other paralegals in the office respond to you,
- who in the office will become the major influences on your growth and success as a paralegal, etc.

This is not to say that everything you encounter will be a surprise, but a healthy perspective might be to proceed as if it will be. In short, be careful of your preconceptions about what is going to happen. Do not let them block the challenges waiting for you.

THE ENVIRONMENT OF A LAW OFFICE

When you walk into a law office, your first impression is likely to be that:

- The office is very formal and organized.
- The people here are set in their ways.

These impressions can be very misleading. A law office is in a state of perpetual becoming. The environment is always changing. New workers are added, established workers leave, new clients come in, old clients are lost, new computer hardware and software are installed, new ways of doing things are developed, personality conflicts arise—numerous factors interact to produce an office that is in constant transition. On the surface, the office may appear to be a model of stability, but underneath all the layers of order and permanence, there is a live office that is in motion.

The consequences of this reality for the paralegal are twofold:

- Do not be deceived by appearances.
- Recognize your own responsibility and ability to help shape the environment in which you are working.

Assume that after being on the job for a while, you become dissatisfied with an office procedure or with billable hour expectations. Avoid becoming defeatist; look for ways to bring about change. To solve the problem, suggest an alternative that others are likely to accept because it is cost effective and nonthreatening to their priorities. If you receive no response, suggest another alternative. Don't give up. As long as you are competent in performing your work, your supervisors will listen to you. Maybe not immediately. Your first suggestion may not be accepted. It may take six months and five more suggestions before you see improvement. Change usually does not occur within the timetable of the person seeking the change. If you are the type of person who wants every possible change made in every area in need of change, and you want all the changes made now, you may not have the temperament needed to survive and thrive in a busy law office. Change is possible, and you can play a role in creating it as long as you are competent, patient, and creative enough to keep looking for ways to try to bring it about.

OFFICE POLITICS

Office politics is the interaction among coworkers who do not always have the same goals, powers, opinions, expectations, abilities, or timetables for performing the work of the office. Because tension can arise out of this interaction, office politics often has a negative reputation. Everyone dislikes it. Most of us want to work where office politics does not exist. If this is not possible, our instinct is to blame others. We do what is right; others play politics.

These attitudes are illusions and interfere with your chances of bringing about change. "There are three things in life you can always count on: death, taxes, and the inevitability of office politics."[10] Whenever two people work together, politics is involved. When fifty people work together, politics is the order of the day. The "people you work with become your second family, complete with squabbles and jealousies. It is not possible to completely avoid confrontations or politics."[11] People often disagree about minor and major matters. As a result, conscious or unconscious negotiation becomes the mechanism by which things get done. Bargaining takes place all the time. More to the point, bargaining in the context of egos takes place

office politics The interaction of coworkers when they do not always have the same goals, powers, opinions, expectations, abilities, or timetables for performing the work of the office.

all the time. There is no alternative to this process. Paralegals who do "not know how to handle office politics will discover the hard way that their career aspirations are limited and may even be derailed from reaching their fullest potential."[12]

If there is harmony in an office, it is because people are engaged in effective office politics. People are trading what others want. The well-known motivational speaker, Zig Ziglar, said that "you can have everything in life you want if you will just help enough other people get what they want."[13] Disharmony usually results from the fact that people are not responding to each other's needs. Here are some examples of disharmony that can exist in law offices, particularly large ones:

- Rivalry among associates to become partners
- Dissatisfaction by partners over associates who do not log enough billable hours
- Dissatisfaction by associates that they are not receiving enough supervision and mentoring from partners
- Conflict among partners over the direction of the office
- Conflict between the office manager and the secretarial pool

Paralegals must be careful not to take sides when such conflict exists. At times, however, the conflict might directly affect them. For example, recently hired young attorneys might be reluctant to delegate tasks to paralegals because the attorneys feel pressured to increase their own billable hours.

Paralegals need a three-part strategy: first, be competent; second, publicize your competence without boasting; and third, look for ways to make others look good. Ultimately, your goal as a practitioner of effective office politics is to demonstrate to others that your competence can help them do their jobs better. To a large extent, the paralegal profession was founded on this principle. Self-promotion by paralegals is not inconsistent with this principle. As you establish your credibility, you need to make sure that others know your worth to them and to the office.

Blow your own horn: let the attorney know how you saved the client thousands of dollars, how you found the hard-to-locate witness, how you organized a huge file in mere hours, how the information you gathered helped win the case, etc. [Attorneys blow their horns in this manner all the time.] Make sure your colleagues know of your special areas of expertise. For example, perhaps you are a good photographer, know everything there is to know about stocks and bonds, or speak several languages. (One paralegal I know dabbles in handwriting analysis; her firm found out and now she is a "handwriting expert.") Show an interest in other matters your firm is handling. Compliment an attorney with whom you are not presently working when you hear he/she won in court, closed a complicated big dollar deal, negotiated brilliantly, etc. . . . Be a real team player.[14]

Ignoring, or worse, denying the ever-present politics of legal environments can be hazardous to your employment. You must be in-tune with the un-spoken; listen to your intuition and the grapevine. Stay out of gossip groups, keeping your ears open and your mouth shut. Watch how the attorneys interact with each other. Monitor power plays and coalitions. Make an effort to understand each of the attorneys you work with on an individual basis, and by that I mean: writing style, organizational preferences, demeanor. You must adapt to each attorney. ... Strategize yourself when possible: work with other attorneys in your firm, or with outside co-counsel; assist baby lawyers without a demeaning attitude. Remember that baby lawyers grow up to be associates and associates grow up to be partners.[15]

What do you think of the following advice from another successful paralegal? "Set your goals and aim for them. Open your mouth and let people know that you're headed up. Search out greater responsibility. Work your tail off—and let everyone know about it."[16] Too extreme? Too risky? People really don't get ahead this way? You don't have to advertise talent because it will eventually be discovered without self-promotion? Maybe. Talk with successful and satisfied paralegals around you. Make inquiries. Take a long look at people you respect in a competitive environment. Try to assess whether their abilities might have gone untapped without a healthy, effective, measured dose of self-assertiveness. You will probably discover that they are comfortable with office politics and are not reluctant to use it to their advantage. (See Exhibit 3-4.)

Exhibit 3-4	Techniques of Effective Office Politics

1. Don't be surprised that office politics exists.
2. Although job competence will not make office politics go away, if you don't perform your job well, you will have difficulty navigating office politics.
3. Be alert to who runs the office through formal power structures (the office's organizational chart or hierarchy) and informal power structures (workers whose voices carry great influence regardless of their titles; those listened to by senior people when important decisions must be made). Find ways (a) to get to know powerful people in the office and (b) to get them to know about your competence and role as a team player who wants the office to flourish.
4. Be alert to (a) workers who constantly complain and (b) workers who always have a positive attitude and are respected for the quality of their work. Spend your time with the second group of workers.
5. Be alert to generational differences between you and others in the office (see Exhibit 3-3); do not expect everyone to do their jobs in the same way or with the same attitude.
6. Immediately defending yourself against criticism can interfere with your ability to hear (listen to) legitimate concerns. When someone attacks you or you feel the urge to attack someone else, pause, stay calm, and breathe. The person criticizing you may have five or six points to make, but you will not hear them all if you immediately point out the first error you think the person has made in his or her comments about you.
7. Stay away from office gossip. Be cordial to everyone and be willing to discuss office matters, but avoid conversations about the personal lives of others.
8. If you happen to hear gossip, don't repeat it.
9. Build relationships by positively interacting with others rather than by joining or aligning yourself with cliques.
10. Get to know coworkers by personal observation and contact rather than by the negative comments others make about them.
11. Make positive comments about others, but avoid empty flattery.
12. Find out what motivates others and what their goals are.
13. When possible, offer to help others with their tasks without seeking credit in return.
14. Be willing to ask others for help, but know when is the best time to ask for this help.
15. When expressing your own objections or criticism of something, do so without whining or self-righteousness and try to present options (more than one) to resolve the concern.
16. Be able to express your feelings while remaining emotionally detached.
17. Brand yourself as someone with integrity, competence, and professionalism, and as someone who is team-oriented.

SELF-ASSESSMENT AND EMPLOYER EVALUATIONS

As emphasized several times, none of the techniques and strategies discussed in this chapter can be a substitute for your own competence as a paralegal. The techniques and strategies are designed to combat unrecognized and unrewarded competence.

Are you competent? To answer this question, you must evaluate yourself and receive the evaluations of others. Here are some suggestions for making both kinds of evaluations more meaningful, now and on the job.

- Carefully read the evaluation form in Exhibit 3-5.[17] (Such evaluations are also called **performance reviews** or performance appraisals.) Note the standards used to earn a "Superior" rating in the nine categories of the evaluation. These standards should be the day-to-day employment goals of every paralegal.

- The ideal evaluation form is one that you and your supervisor design together after you have been employed for a significant period. The goal is to have a form that is specifically geared to the tasks you perform in the office. Even if the office already has an evaluation form, think about ways to adapt it more closely to you as an individual. Make notes on what you would like to see in such a form. Discuss it with your supervisor. Your initiative in this regard will be much appreciated, especially if you make clear that your goal is to use the evaluation to improve communication and to find ways to increase your skills and productivity.

performance reviews An analysis of the extent to which a person or program has met designated objectives. Also called *performance appraisal*.

Exhibit 3-5	Paralegal Evaluation Form

INSTRUCTIONS. Evaluate the paralegal in the nine areas indicated. Check the rating that applies. Use the back of the form to provide explanations as needed.

1. **Work Product.** (Covers the paralegal's ability to understand what is required and to provide a thorough and complete work product. Consider the speed and efficiency with which the work product is returned.)
   - ■ *Superior.* In most cases, needs little instruction. Takes initiative in asking questions if aspects of the task are unclear. Is resourceful in developing more efficient ways to complete projects. Demonstrates ability to consider factors not indicated by the supervising attorney that make the work product more useful. Keeps attorney informed on work progress.
   - ■ *Very good.*
   - ■ *Good.*
   - ■ *Marginal.* Has difficulty understanding the kind of work product that is required. Sometimes does an incomplete job and takes more time than should be needed.
   - ■ *Unacceptable.* Seldom masters what is required and hence cannot do a thorough and complete work product.
   - ■ *No opportunity to form an opinion.*

2. **Efficient Management of Workload.** (Covers the paralegal's efficient use of time to meet deadlines.)
   - ■ *Superior.* Highly efficient. Completes all assignments successfully, on time, and without prompting.
   - ■ *Very good.*
   - ■ *Good.*
   - ■ *Marginal.* Needs to improve efficiency. Assignments sometimes go uncompleted. Often needs substantial attorney supervision.
   - ■ *Unacceptable.* Deadlines are rarely met. Assignments often uncompleted.
   - ■ *No opportunity to form an opinion.*

3. **Ability to Work Well Under Pressure.** (Covers the paralegal's ability to perform quality work under pressure.)
   - ■ *Superior.* Always works well under pressure. Maintains control over assignments. Makes sound decisions consistent with tight schedules. Is never disorganized.
   - ■ *Very good.*
   - ■ *Good.*
   - ■ *Marginal.* Frequently fails to work well under pressure. Tends to become disorganized and to exercise poor judgment.
   - ■ *Unacceptable.* Rarely works well under pressure.
   - ■ *No opportunity to form an opinion.*

4. **Fact Management Skills.** (Covers the paralegal's ability to digest and analyze the facts of a particular case or assignment and the thoroughness of performing factual research.)
   - ■ *Superior.* Is exceptionally thorough in gathering information and mastering facts.
   - ■ *Very good.*
   - ■ *Good.*
   - ■ *Marginal.* Sometimes misses essential information during factual investigation. Knowledge of facts is sometimes incomplete. Often needs substantial attorney direction to analyze facts correctly.
   - ■ *Unacceptable.* Often misses essential information during factual investigation. Knowledge of facts is seriously deficient. Work product needs substantial revision to ensure completeness. Sometimes careless in presentation of facts to attorney.
   - ■ *No opportunity to form an opinion.*

5. **Professionalism.** (Covers the paralegal's initiative and commitment to assigned work, to the law office, and to the paralegal career.)
   - ■ *Superior.* Exhibits exceptionally high level of personal involvement in assignments and is extremely responsible. Takes initiative. Is clearly in alignment with the goals of the office. Is very comfortable with his/her career choice.
   - ■ *Very good.*
   - ■ *Good.*
   - ■ *Marginal.* Frequently appears to lack interest in assignments. Needs substantial follow-up by attorney as to both deadlines and quality of work.
   - ■ *Unacceptable.* Unwilling to assume necessary responsibility.
   - ■ *No opportunity to form an opinion.*

6. **Ability to Work Independently.** (Covers the paralegal's ability to exercise good judgment by making well-reasoned choices while maintaining necessary communication with attorney.)
   - ■ *Superior.* Considers all options and makes good decisions. Always keeps attorney well informed. Knows when to seek assistance.
   - ■ *Very good.*
   - ■ *Good.*
   - ■ *Marginal.* Has difficulty making well-reasoned choices after options are defined. Fails to cover necessary material with attorney and does not readily call upon attorney for assistance or explanation.
   - ■ *Unacceptable.* Is not able to make reasonable choices after options are defined. Rarely keeps attorney informed and lacks understanding as to appropriate area of paralegal work as defined by attorney.
   - ■ *No opportunity to form an opinion.*

7. **Quality of Written Work.** (Covers the paralegal's ability to communicate in writing.)
   - *Superior.* Exceptionally clear, precise, and thorough work that is neat and free from grammatical and spelling errors.
   - *Very good.*
   - *Good.*
   - *Marginal.* Sometimes turns in written material that is weak in significant ways.
   - *Unacceptable.* Work product demonstrates major deficiencies in organization, grammar, and spelling. Lacks initiative to do what is needed to correct the deficiencies.
   - *No opportunity to form an opinion.*

8. **Outside Contact.** (Covers the paralegal's interaction with persons outside the firm, such as co-counsel, clients, state and federal personnel in courts and agencies.)
   - *Superior.* Consistently demonstrates a commendable ability to gain the cooperation and confidence of others as needed for assignments. Establishes excellent working relationships.
   - *Very good.*
   - *Good.*
   - *Marginal.* Unable to handle outside assignments without substantial attorney assistance. Has difficulty developing necessary confidence and cooperation.
   - *Unacceptable.* No understanding of what is required to gain necessary cooperation and confidence. Complaints received with regard to paralegal's behavior.
   - *No opportunity to form an opinion.*

9. **Ethics.** (Covers the paralegal's understanding of and compliance with ethical rules governing attorneys and paralegals.)
   - *Superior.* Has a firm grasp of ethical rules governing the legal profession in this state. Always abides by these rules.
   - *Very good.*
   - *Good.*
   - *Marginal.* Has a weak knowledge of ethical rules.
   - *Unacceptable.* Questions have been raised about the paralegal's ethical conduct.
   - *No opportunity to form an opinion.*

Adapted from Heller, Ehrman, White & McAuliffe.

- Start preparing for an evaluation on the first day of your employment and on the day after your last evaluation. Do not wait until the day of the evaluation itself.[18] Before a regularly scheduled evaluation, write a *pre-evaluation memo* and submit it to your supervisor. The memo should list:
  - the major cases or projects you have worked on since the last evaluation;
  - your functions on each;
  - names of your supervisors and coworkers on each;
  - special accomplishments, events showing initiative (such as weekend work), written or oral quotations from individuals commenting on your work;
  - your **realization rate** (the percentage of total client billings of an attorney or paralegal that the office actually collects; also called the *collection realization rate*. Because timekeepers often spend time on both billable tasks and nonbillable tasks, a further breakdown is a timekeeper's billing realization rate. This is the percentage of the timekeeper's total office time that is billable. For example, paralegals who spend half their time on nonbillable tasks and half on billable tasks have a 50 percent billable realization rate. It is sometimes easier to find out your billing realization rate than your collection realization rate.).

  > **realization rate** The percentage of total client billings of an attorney or paralegal that the office actually collects. Also called the collection *realization rate.*

- When you work on large projects, ask for a "project evaluation" at the conclusion of the project. This evaluation should be in *addition* to any regularly scheduled evaluations you receive.
- Before an evaluation, review your job description. If your duties have been slowly changing, rewrite your job description to reflect these changes. Submit the revision to your supervisor for approval.
- Before an evaluation, review the criteria by which you will be evaluated. If you are unsure, ask your supervisor for the criteria. Knowing in advance the standards by which you will be judged, will be of great assistance in preparing for the evaluation meeting.
- Some law offices ask their paralegals to answer specific self-evaluation questions before meeting with their supervisor for the latter's evaluation. An office in Arizona, for example, asks its paralegals to submit written answers to the following questions before a soon-to-be held performance evaluation conference:
  - How successful overall do you feel you have been in meeting your performance objectives that we set at the last appraisal conference?
  - Do you feel that your performance objectives need to be modified?

- Are there any areas of concern in your job that you would like to discuss?
- What personal assets do you have that enhance your performance on the job?
- What additional training do you feel you need in order to do a better job?
- In what ways can I help as a supervisor?
- Is there anything I can do differently to enable you to reach your potential?
- Is there anything else concerning your job that you would like to discuss?[19]

Even if you work in an office that does not require this level of self-evaluation, you should consider answering such questions on your own before a performance review. You do not have to give your written answers to the supervisor, but you should be prepared to raise some or all of the themes covered by the questions during the meeting with the supervisor.

- If this is your first formal evaluation by a particular supervisor, try to talk with others in the office who have been evaluated by this supervisor before. Find out what you might expect from this person.
- After an evaluation, set measurable improvement goals. Do not simply pledge that you will "work harder." Establish goals that are more concrete. For example:
  - Before January, attend a bar-association seminar or a paralegal-association conference covering an aspect of my job.
  - For the next ten weeks, spend a minimum of ten minutes a day studying topic sentences and paragraph structure in grammar/writing materials that are available online.
  - Once a month for the next six months, go to lunch with a paralegal whose professionalism I respect in order to brainstorm techniques for improvement.
  - Within five weeks, reread the word-processing software manual from cover to cover.

Note that each of these goals can be placed on a calendar. You can determine whether each has been met. Of course, you should also commit yourself to broader goals, like learning how to digest interrogatories or improving your drafting skills. Just be sure to include more objective, short-term, self-measurable goals as well.

- If you receive a negative evaluation, don't react defensively. Although you will want to correct any factual errors made about you in the evaluation, little can be gained by trying to show that the boss is wrong. You might want to thank the supervisor for the comments and then ask for a few days to respond so that you can collect your thoughts. When you do respond, the best approach is to discuss ways in which you can improve your performance.
- Sometimes criticism from a supervisor can be vague. When this occurs, paralegal Elona Jouben recommends that you "ask for specific examples and tell them you want to be sure you understand what they're talking about so you can be sure to address and improve performance in that area. I've learned over the years that it's best to be respectful, but assertive, and insist upon clear examples so that you're not left floundering, not knowing precisely what they're unhappy with or how to improve."[20]
- Before your next regularly scheduled evaluation after a negative evaluation, ask for a follow-up evaluation to determine whether you have made progress on what was considered negative.
- Suppose you work in an office that does not have regularly scheduled performance evaluations. It never uses formal written evaluations. Employees are evaluated, but not on an organized, consistent, written basis. If so, you need to become an advocate for a more structured system of evaluation. You will be successful if you can convince your supervisor of two things: structured evaluations have value and will not take too much of the supervisor's time. Propose the use of evaluation forms such as the one in Exhibit 3-5. Or design your own evaluation form, as suggested earlier.
- If you are unsuccessful in getting a busy supervisor to give you formal evaluations, ask for brief oral comments on your work covering strengths and areas in need of improvement. Take notes on what the supervisor says, type up the notes, and ask the supervisor to read them. All you need say is, "I want to be sure that I have been precise in understanding the comments and concerns you raised."
- A large factor in obtaining and learning from evaluations is your ability to handle criticism. Many of us are defensive when someone tells us something negative about our work or our attitude. Here are some interrelated suggestions on taking criticism:[21]
  - Listen to all comments without trying to influence or criticize the critic.
  - Be sure you understand the complaint.

- Admit when you are wrong; it is a sign of strength.
- Agree with the truth.
- Admit when you do not know something.
- Ask for clarification.
- Ask for instructions or advice on improving your performance; be someone who is teachable.
- Think of ways you can put the advice into action; design measurable goals.

We will have more to say about evaluations later when we discuss ways to support a request for a salary increase.

WORKING WITH ATTORNEYS

Paralegals are sometimes surprised to learn that many (perhaps most) attorneys just out of law school do not have many day-to-day practical skills. Using the **case method** of legal education in which law students spend a vast amount of time studying appellate court opinions, law school teaches students how to think like a lawyer. There is a heavy emphasis on doctrine and theory as opposed to the nuts-and-bolts of representing clients. A bar association president recently commented, "Many new lawyers come out of law school never having drafted a complaint; never having seen a contract; never having interacted with a client, much less an **adverse** witness."[22] Most law-schools try to offset this concern by offering **clinical-education** programs, but such programs are expensive to run and are usually a minor part of the overall three-year law-school curriculum. A complaint frequently heard from veteran attorneys is that graduates of law schools are not "practice-ready." Consequently, the early months of a new attorney's time in a law office is often taken up with basic on-the-job training.

Criticism of law school is not limited to veteran attorneys. In 2013, President Barack Obama suggested that law school should be two years rather than three. At the time, there was widespread concern about:

- the huge debt incurred by law students after three years of school,
- the difficult job market for attorneys, and
- the large number of elective courses (e.g., sports law) taken in the third year that did not have the intellectual rigor of the core courses (e.g., contracts, torts, civil procedure) taken at the beginning of law school.

With a ring of overstatement but a dollop of truth, it is sometimes said that law school scares students to death in the first year, works them to death in the second, and bores them to death in the third.

The turmoil in legal education for attorneys is not due to dwindling demand for legal services. In fact, the need for legal services continues to increase. Unfortunately, the poor and middle class cannot afford attorney fees. Attorneys point out that if fees are too low, they will not be able to operate their offices. Furthermore, many new attorneys carry student-debt loans that take years to repay. We will examine this reality in greater depth in Chapter 4 when we cover reforms in the practice of law. (See Exhibit 4-8 in that chapter.)

The attorney with whom a paralegal usually has the closest association is the paralegal's immediate supervisor (or supervisors if the paralegal works for more than one attorney). The personality of a particular attorney has a great deal to do with the effectiveness of the paralegal-attorney working relationship. Many paralegals speak in glowing terms about their attorney-supervisor. Not only is the attorney easy to work with, but he or she also provides a challenging environment within which the paralegal can grow. Other attorneys, however, fall short of this standard; they do not function well as the leader of a team. This may be due to the rigors of law school (popularized in the movie and TV show, *Paper Chase*) and the unique demands of law practice. According to two experts on the practice of law, a number of characteristics common to many attorneys do not encourage effective team building:[23]

- *Autonomy*: Attorneys are less likely to collaborate than people in other occupations. Often they adhere to their preferred approach even when another is more effective.
- *Critical*: The successful attorney is highly critical. Typically, the focus of the attorney is on what is wrong with an idea. The merits of the idea are often given little consideration or are ignored.
- *Competitive*: The attorney is competitive and adversarial — as is the legal system itself. In policy questions and in personal relationships, progress and truth are achieved through varying degrees of confrontation.

case method Learning law primarily by studying appellate court opinions in which the opinions are *briefed* (broken down into their issue, reasoning, and other essential parts), *synthesized* (read together with other opinions in order to identify rule patterns), and *applied* to new facts presented by the professor.

adverse Opposed to; harmful, unfavorable.

clinical education A training program in which students work on real cases under professional supervision.

A professor of psychology studied twenty professions for optimism and concluded that only one profession, law, was built on pessimism. "Lawyers are trained to look for negative possibilities" and for what is wrong with your logic. Hence, they are not often sensitive listeners.[24]

It may not be easy to work with attorneys who fit these characteristics. The key to survival is assertiveness. According to one expert, many attorneys "prefer to work with assertive paralegals who are competent and knowledgeable. If you are not assertive with attorneys, they will lose confidence in you, and you may find yourself burdened with problems [including] . . . boring work, poor raises, and poor working conditions."[25]

Thus far in this chapter, we have referred to the importance of assertiveness a number of times. We now turn to a closer examination of this theme.

ASSERTIVE/NONASSERTIVE/AGGRESSIVE BEHAVIOR

Assertive persons are positive and self-assured in expressing their views. Nonassertive persons tend to hold back because of a lack of self-confidence. Aggressive persons are in your face; they complain often and rarely worry about how their views affect others. They may be right in many of the things they are saying, but they are so unpleasant that supervisors and coworkers seldom take them seriously.

Successfully assertive people:

- Are competent and display competence.
- Respect the competence of others.
- Are prepared.
- Show initiative; do not always wait to be told what to do.
- Are willing to help others do their job well.
- Know that one of the best ways to help others solve problems is to provide them with options.
- Are self-assured enough to give credit to coworkers and subordinates.
- Are able to give credit to superiors without it being taken as empty flattery or fawning.
- Act like professionals.
- Act like they belong in the office.
- Are always willing to learn.
- Are problem solvers; rarely, if ever, will they state a criticism or problem without offering a menu of realistic solutions.
- Do not shy away from office politics.
- Know the difference between griping and negotiating.
- Understand the necessity of compromise.
- Know the difference between little concerns and major ones; do not treat every problem as a crisis.
- Advocate with resolve, not by carping or fanfare.
- Are secure enough to be able to say no.
- Are not offensive.
- Can express an opinion without putting someone down.
- Appreciate the value of timing; know that "now" is not always the best time to try to resolve a problem.
- Know when and how to lose gracefully.

Assertive paralegals make themselves known. The *backbone* of assertiveness is competence: your work product meets high standards. The *trump card* of assertiveness is timing: you watch for the right moment to come forward. The *foundation* of assertiveness is preparation: you have collected all the facts that support your position.

Suppose, for example, that after being on a job for a while, you feel that you are not earning what you are worth. What do you do? Here are some different approaches:

Nonassertive

You hope that things will get better, but you don't want to rock the boat. After all, your salary isn't that bad; it could be worse. You talk with fellow paralegals about your salary, and you are very frank with your aunt when the two of you talk on the phone about your work. But there's no sense in trying to get the firm to pay you more. The firm probably doesn't earn that much.

And Mr. Smith, the head of the firm, is very pleasant to work with. Money isn't that important. Maybe next year will be better.

Aggressive

Three weeks after you begin your job, you tell your supervisor that your salary is ridiculous. "With inflation, how do you expect me to live on this salary?" When your supervisor is not responsive, you send a memo to all the attorneys in the firm demanding that "something be done about paralegal salaries." When you walk the corridors of the firm, you are always visibly angry.

Assertive

- You make sure that the decision-makers in the firm know who you are and what you have accomplished.
- Months before you ask for a raise, you ask your supervisor to identify those factors that will be taken into consideration in evaluating your overall performance. In the months that follow, you make sure that you organize your efforts and your notes in accordance with the criteria the supervisor initially identified.
- You review written guidelines, if any, on policies of the office regarding compensation. Such guidelines might be in the office procedures manual or employment handbooks for the office.
- You prepare a fact sheet that:
  - Summarizes your contributions to the office, including evaluations of your work.
  - Lists favorable comments that you solicited when you asked supervisors to put in writing favorable oral comments they made to you about your work.
  - Lists cases and projects you have worked on, highlighting special tasks such as helping design part of the forms manual or helping to train a new paralegal or attorney.
  - Lists nonbillable tasks you performed that freed an attorney to devote more of his or her time to billable tasks.
  - Contains data from salary surveys. Examples:
    - *National Utilization and Compensation Survey*, published by the National Association of Legal Assistants (www.nala.org).
    - *Annual Compensation Survey for Legal Assistants/Paralegals and Managers*, published by the International Practice Management Association (www.paralegalmanagement.org).
    - Online salary surveys (on Google, Bing, or Yahoo, run this search: salary paralegal).
- You "know your numbers," consisting of your billing realization rate and, if available, your collection realization rate.
- You attempt to find out as much relevant information about the economics of the firm as possible, e.g., the percentage salary increase that the office generally gives employees, the extent to which the office (or your department in the office) was profitable last year and is profitable this year to date, and unusual expenses in the office, e.g., the purchase of new computer equipment. Such events will inevitably have an impact on salary decisions made by the office.[26]
- You discuss strategies for seeking a raise with other paralegals in the firm, with other paralegals in the area, and perhaps with some attorneys in the firm with whom you have developed considerable rapport.
- You select the right time to meet with your supervisor. (You don't rely on email to state your case for a raise.) You decide to wait until the supervisor is not hassled with a difficult case. You don't wait, however, until the next regularly scheduled performance review. Salary decisions may already have been made by then.
- You may adopt a two-part strategy: you first ask for a meeting with your supervisor to go over your contributions and to discuss ways of increasing your productivity. At a follow-up meeting, you bring up the topic of a salary increase.
- If you are unsuccessful in obtaining the raise you are seeking, you have a fallback position, e.g., you seek a performance bonus in lieu of a raise; additional insurance, educational tuition reimbursement, or other fringe benefits; perhaps a different office setting; or **flextime**.

flextime A system that allows employees some control over aspects of their work schedule, such as the times that they arrive at and leave from work during the day.

If you ask successful paralegals about their secret of success (see Exhibit 3-6), one message will come through loud and clear: Seize the initiative. No one is going to hand you anything simply because you are smart or because you have a certificate. You must prove yourself. You must be assertive.

Exhibit 3-6	Taking the Initiative: Recommendations of Successful Paralegals

Tami Coyne: I have heard this tired refrain many times: "I am a hard worker and just don't get the recognition or the responsibility I deserve." This attitude gets you nowhere. If you believe that it is up to your employer to pick you out of the crowd and reward you just because you do your job, you will be sorely disappointed. In order to advance as a paralegal, you must prove that you are capable of taking on greater responsibility by performing your present duties exceptionally well. Show your initiative by anticipating the next stage of any assignment and completing it before you are asked to do it. Do not wait for recognition or feedback. You must be the one to initiate a feedback discussion after you have completed an assignment.[27]

Shelley Riseden: Be proactive. If you know that your boss is going to ask you to do something, go ahead and do it before he or she has the chance. After you have worked for an attorney for a few months, you can get a feel for what his or her routine is, and what tasks you can do ahead of time. A proactive paralegal can have the work done or the problem solved before his or her boss is even aware it exists.[28]

Renee Sova: Volunteer to draft the next document. Say, "I can do that; will you let me try?" Patience is a virtue. If the lawyer doesn't accommodate your first request, keep asking. Upon receiving and ultimately completing the assignment, there is nothing wrong with asking: "What could I have done differently to make it better?" This shows you truly care about your work product. Always do more than is expected. Few professionals became successful by leaving their careers to fate.[29]

Marian Johnson: The greatest key to success is something no one can give you: a good attitude! Enthusiasm has nothing to do with noise; it has more to do with motivation. It deals with our attitude. An attitude is something you can do something about. I can choose to be enthusiastic or I can choose not to be. Excitement is infectious. It's sort of like a case of the measles. You can't infect someone unless you have the real thing![30]

Ann Pearson: Be the go-to person. Successful paralegals generate billable hours. To do so, you must be available. Be there when they come looking for someone at 5:30 PM to do a last minute project."[31]

Chere Estrin: Be assertive. Take an attorney to lunch![32]

THE SKILL OF LISTENING

attentive listening
Affirmative, ongoing steps taken by an interviewer to let an interviewee know that you have heard what he or she just said and that you consider the meeting with him or her to be important.

Assertive listening is another critical skill we all must learn. Unfortunately, the following two facts are probably true about most of us: (1) we are poor listeners and (2) we think we are excellent listeners. Effective listening is important in many aspects of the practice of law. In Chapter 8 on legal interviewing, for example, we will cover **attentive listening** which consists of affirmative, ongoing steps taken by an interviewer to let an interviewee know that the interviewer has heard what the interviewee has just said and that the interviewer considers the meeting with the interviewee to be important. (See Exhibit 8-12 on Chapter 8 on techniques of attentive learning.)

Most of us tend to shift our listening style, often unconsciously, depending on the circumstances. Examine the following categories of listening, some of which overlap.[33] Ask yourself which categories you use and when you use them. Developing self-awareness in this area can increase your potential as a paralegal. Clearly the category of listening that takes the most work to use, and the category that many of us do not use on a consistent basis, is *active listening*.

■ Passive Listening

Passive listening occurs when we are present in body, but not in mind. We can't wait for the speaker to stop talking so that we can move on to something (or someone) else. We listen passively when we multitask by doing several things at once (only one of which is listening to the person talking) or by thinking about a variety of tasks that need doing once the talker stops. Facial expressions and body language are clues that passive listening is occurring. Eyes wander; the body twitches. The speaker is made to feel that he or she is not important enough to have the other's undivided attention. Listeners may feel justified in what they are doing because of how busy they are, but their approach does not show respect and runs the risk of souring what should be a cooperative relationship. Status can play a role in who receives passive listening from us. We tend to have a short attention span for individuals we deem to be beneath us on the career path or social latter. We're "all ears" for others.

■ Appreciative Listening

The purpose of appreciative listening is to enjoy what is being heard rather than to acquire new facts. We use this kind of listening to enjoy music or to hear a good story teller. We are not irritated if we have heard the music or story before. Appreciative listening is most effective when we are trying to get along with someone. When we meet new people (e.g., a new coworker), appreciative listening helps establish rapport and an inviting atmosphere.

■ Evaluative Listening

The purpose of evaluative listening is to make a decision of some kind. We may be trying to decide whether to buy a certain product or whether someone is believable. We try to separate facts from opinions. We listen for logical arguments that support particular conclusions. We look for holes, inconsistencies, or contradictions. Evaluative listening is critical when interviewing a witness or assessing the merits of a client's case.

■ Judgmental Listening

Judgmental listening is evaluative listening with a sting. The listener is looking for flaws in what others say in order to put them in their place. There is very little effort to understand or empathize. Judgmental listeners are often unaware that their need to control, indeed to win, the conversation indicates insecurity. Some of us are uncomfortable in giving the impression that we don't know something or that what we know less than the other person. Good learners tend to be humble; they rarely if ever listen judgmentally.

■ Empathic Listening

The purpose of empathic listening is to let speakers know that you support them and understand their feelings. You listen for the facts of what the speaker is saying, but just as important, you are sensitive to the overt and underlying emotions that come with the facts. Evaluative listening can get in the way of empathic listening when the listener appears more interested in judging than connecting with the speaker. Empathic listeners may correctly predict what the speaker is going to say and may have solutions that will help the speaker, but the listener holds back in order to allow the speaker to express himself or herself. Only when the speaker feels understood (due to empathic listening) will the speaker be receptive to solutions.

■ Me-Too Listening

A me-too listener is quick to let the speaker know that "The same thing happened to me." You may think that your me-too comment is affirming what the speaker has said, when in fact, the message you are communicating is that what happened to the speaker is nothing special or unusual. Perhaps it isn't, but the speaker may need to feel a moment of importance or symphony. Being too quick with a me-too response may be sending a somewhat insensitive "get-over-it" message.

■ Active Listening

An active listener takes affirmative steps to understand what the speaker is saying. The active listener:
- does not multitask while listening (e.g., the cell phone is off)
- looks at the speaker while he or she is talking
- avoids body language that gives the impression that he or she would prefer to be doing something other than listening to the speaker
- asks clarifying questions
- provides affirming nods or comments (e.g., "I see") to indicate that he or she is following what is said
- occasionally repeats back or paraphrases what the speaker has said to make sure he or she heard correctly
- is never irritated when the speaker is confused or inarticulate
- in appropriate settings, takes notes on what is being said
- has no need to provide a contrary opinion unless specifically invited to provide one
- is in no hurry to respond
- understands that a defensive response (e.g., "what you said about me is not true") should sometimes be postponed (e.g., "let me think about what you said and get back to you") in order to think through the best response

Again, we will have more to say about listening in Chapter 8 on legal interviewing when we cover *attentive listening*, which combines features of appreciative, empathic, and active listening.

KEEPING A DIARY OR JOURNAL AND A CAREER DEVELOPMENT FILE

DIARY OR JOURNAL

Earlier in this chapter, we mentioned keeping a report in which you regularly record your *work in progress* (WIP). In addition, have a job diary or journal that contains the following:

- Notes on the assignments you are given (e.g., what you were asked to do, date you received the assignment, its due date, feedback received before completion, changes in the assignment made by the supervisor, sources consulted, and date completed)
- Names of the parties on both sides of cases on which you performed tasks
- Favorable and unfavorable comments (written or oral) on your work
- Total billable hours per day attributable to billable tasks (i.e., those for which the office can charge the client a fee) and total nonbillable tasks (e.g., helping to orient a new paralegal)
- Your realization rate
- Dates you worked evenings and weekends
- Dates you worked at home
- Dates you were late, were absent, or had to leave early
- Dates you came in early or worked through lunch hour
- Names of clients you referred to the firm
- Time you spent doing your own typing or photocopying
- Time you spend in courses, seminars, or other ventures to improve your skills

You need to have the facts of your employment at your command. The diary or journal is your personal record; you keep it to yourself for use as needed. Not only will the facts be valuable when you are making an argument for a raise, but they might also be essential when misunderstandings arise about what you have or have not done.

Keeping the diary or journal may be burdensome for you at first, and you may not make use of it for a while. It is worth the burden and the wait. You are working in a legal environment that respects someone who has the facts, particularly with dates!

CAREER DEVELOPMENT FILE

In addition, start a *career development file* that contains everything that is relevant to your employment and growth as a paralegal. It should include:

- *Résumés*. A copy of every résumé you have written, including a current one that you should regularly update even if you are not thinking about leaving your current position.
- *Job history*. A record of the dates you were hired in previous and current jobs; who hired you; who supervised you; a copy of your job descriptions; starting salary; amounts and dates of raises, bonuses, and other benefits received; dates and reasons you left.
- *Work accomplishments*. A copy of every written evaluation; letters received from clients commenting on your work; verbal comments made about your work by supervisors that you later wrote down.
- *Professional activities*. Evidence of your involvement with paralegal associations; attendance at conferences, seminars, and classes, including names of teachers, copies of syllabi, etc. (see the discussion of continuing legal education (CLE) in the next section); speaking engagements; articles you have written for paralegal newsletters or blogs.
- *Career client list*. A list of every case on which you worked at any job or volunteer office. Include the exact names of all clients, opposing parties, and opposing attorneys; a brief description of your role in each case; and the dates of your involvement in these cases. Some of this data can come from your diary or journal and work in progress. The difference is that the career client list covers your entire career, not just current cases at your current job. The data may be needed when you seek employment with another law office that wants to avoid being disqualified from a case due to a conflict of interest that arises because of your involvement with a particular party at a prior job. (See the discussion of conflicts checks in Chapter 5 and the Career Client List in Exhibit 5-9 of Chapter 5.)

Now you are ready. You have documented your professional life. You have assembled a catalog of facts that can be very useful weeks and months later when you or someone else in the office asks about a particular case. You have what you need when you sit down with management to discuss the raise for which you have been patiently waiting. If there is a career ladder in the office, you have assembled what will be relevant if the time comes to demonstrate that you deserve the next step up the ladder. Even if you are not looking for another job, you are ready to pursue unexpected opportunities that can't be passed up.[34]

PARALEGAL CLE

Elsewhere in this book we have stressed the reality that your legal education never ends. There is always something to learn. This is true for attorneys, and it is certainly true for paralegals. Education after employment is called continuing legal education (CLE). CLE is offered mainly by bar associations, paralegal associations, and other organizations. (To locate specific CLE programs for paralegals in your state, see Helpful Websites at the end of this chapter.)

There are two main ways in which CLE takes place. The traditional way is to go to a brick-and-mortar building such as a downtown hotel facility. The training might occur on a workday afternoon or on a Saturday. Alternatively, a great deal of CLE is now offered online so that the course can be taken at any time during the week. CLE is usually short term; most courses can be completed in one day or less. You can select CLE that directly and immediately relates to your day-to-day job responsibilities. Here is an example of this reality from Felicia Garant, a paralegal in Maine:

> I had an experience where I attended a half-day title insurance seminar and passed around a memo to attorneys in my section of the firm summarizing what I had learned there. A few minutes after I circulated the memo, an attorney flew out of his office exclaiming, "There's a new law on this subject?" He asked me to help him get a copy of the law since he had a case at that time that would be directly affected. You are the attorney's extra pair of eyes and ears, and you may pick up something at these seminars which will be new to the attorney. Your attendance at seminars, educating yourself, then passing the information on to the attorney not only increases your qualification as a legal assistant, but also makes you a valuable employee.[35]

CLE is not limited to substantive law topics such as insurance, corporations, and taxation. According to one survey, the top CLE subjects were as follows:[36]

- 68% software training
- 59% time management
- 57% getting along with difficult people
- 29% electronic filing (e-filing) of court documents

Often, an employer is willing to pay all or part of your expenses in attending such seminars and to give you time off if they occur during work hours. Even if your employer refuses to pay for them, you should go on your own time and at your own expense. Few things are more important to the professional development of a paralegal than CLE. Furthermore, what you pay out-of-pocket is tax deductible. You cannot deduct the cost of entering a new employment field, but you can deduct the cost of improving your skills in a field you are already in.[37]

In almost every state, attorneys must attend a designated number of CLE hours per year as a condition of maintaining their license to practice law. As we will see in Chapter 4, CLE is required to maintain voluntary certification status with national and some state paralegal associations. In California, failure of a paralegal to comply with the state's mandatory CLE requirement can lead to a fine and imprisonment! Mandatory CLE for paralegals, however, does not exist in most states.

RESPONSIBILITIES OF SUPERVISORS

What is a good attorney supervisor? See Exhibit 3-7 for a checklist of factors that are relevant to this question. Although not all the factors in the checklist are applicable to every law office, they provide a good overview of what many paralegals feel constitute effective supervision. After you have been on the job for a while, you might cautiously consider showing this checklist to your supervisors so that they might evaluate themselves as supervisors. Do not do this, however, until you are well established in your job. Considerable tact is needed when suggesting that a supervisor might be less than perfect.

continuing legal education (CLE) Training in the law (usually short term) that a person receives after completing his or her formal legal training or after becoming employed.

| Exhibit 3-7 | Checklist for Effective Supervision of Paralegals |

1. Gives clear instructions on assignments.
2. Provides adequate training for each assignment given. Takes the time to make sure the paralegal can perform the task.
3. Does not overburden the paralegal with assignments. Before giving a new assignment, determines what the paralegal already has to do.
4. Provides reasonable deadlines on assignments, with adequate time built in for review and redrafting where appropriate.
5. Takes affirmative steps to inquire about the paralegal's progress on assignments to determine if more guidance is needed or if deadline extensions should be given.
6. Delegates a variety of tasks.
7. Occasionally encourages the paralegal to use the law library (via physical books or online) to increase his or her knowledge and to appreciate the broader legal context of a case.
8. Does not unduly pressure the paralegal about producing a quota of billable hours.
9. Whenever possible, allows the paralegal to become involved in a case at the beginning, e.g., at the initial client interview.
10. Permits the paralegal to experience the end product of cases on which he or she is working, e.g., gives the paralegal a copy of the finished product or invites him or her to a court presentation.
11. Keeps the paralegal informed about the status of a case, even with regard to aspects of the case on which the paralegal is not working.
12. When appropriate, includes the paralegal in strategy meetings on cases.
13. Introduces clients to the paralegal, explains the paralegal's role, and expresses confidence in the paralegal.
14. Is supportive when the paralegal makes a mistake; provides constructive, corrective suggestions for the future.
15. Looks for ways the paralegal can increase his or her skills.
16. Encourages paralegals to give their opinions on cases and on office policy.
17. Designs systems with instructions, checklists, forms, etc., to be used by paralegals for the performance of assigned tasks.
18. Encourages experienced paralegals to help write these systems.
19. Evaluates the paralegal, informally and in writing.
20. Gives credit to the paralegal when credit is due.
21. Makes sure others in the firm know about the contribution of the paralegal.
22. Backs the paralegal's reasonable requests on salary and working conditions.
23. Supports the paralegal's need for financial help (and time off) to attend outside training programs (CLE) and to participate in activities of paralegal associations.
24. Considers allowing the paralegal to have reasonable time off to do some **pro bono** work (e.g., time donated to poverty law offices or public interest law firms).

pro bono Concerning or involving legal services that are provided for the public good (*pro bono publico*, shortened to *pro bono*) without fee or compensation. Sometimes also applied to services given at a reduced rate.

RELATIONSHIP WITH SECRETARIES

At one time, many secretaries, particularly those in smaller law offices, resented the hiring of paralegals. This friction arose for a number of reasons, as the following overview points out:

Historically, the legal secretary was "queen" of her territory. The more competent she was, the more control she had over her immediate environment—how the office looked, how the work was done, how the clients were handled, and for that matter, how the lawyer was trained. The longer she worked with one lawyer, the more responsibility she was given, and the better she got at her job. In the office of the sole practitioner, the practice could go smoothly even if the lawyer was in court or out of town. She was just about as indispensable as one person could be. There was a relationship of mutual trust and respect between the legal secretary and the lawyer that was practically impenetrable. Then along came the paralegal, intruding on the legal secretary's territory, doing many of the things that the legal secretary had been doing for years. To add insult to injury, the legal secretary was expected to perform secretarial work for the paralegal![38]

Fortunately, this problem is no longer prevalent. In most law offices, secretaries and paralegals work together smoothly. Yet tension can occasionally surface, particularly over the issue of titles. As we saw in Chapter 1, a large number of secretaries have begun to call themselves legal assistants without obtaining additional legal training. An attorney employer might encourage this title switch in order to increase the likelihood of collecting paralegal fees for their work.

Part of the confusion over titles is due to the fact that there is an overlap of functions in many law offices. There are attorneys who perform paralegal tasks, secretaries who perform paralegal tasks, and paralegals who perform attorney tasks. On paper, the three roles are distinct, but in practice, there can be considerable overlap, particularly in smaller law offices. Furthermore, computers on every desk make it possible for individuals to increase the variety of tasks that they perform. In times of pressure (e.g., during a trial or when a large commercial transaction must be completed before a looming deadline), everyone tends to pull together by doing whatever it takes to accomplish the task at hand. During a crisis, you will rarely, if ever, hear anyone say, "That's not my job."

In light of this reality, it is understandable that some legal secretaries are ambivalent about their title. The paralegal occupation grew out of the legal secretary occupation. Before paralegal training programs became commonplace, a large number of paralegals came from the ranks of legal secretaries. Many secretaries were members of NALS, the National Association of Legal Secretaries. When the paralegal field grew, paralegals started forming their own associations. As pointed out in Chapter 1, the National Association of Legal Assistants (NALA) was initially formed as a breakaway association from NALS. NALS, however, does not consider itself to be a secretaries-only association, as demonstrated by its name change from NALS, the National Association of Legal Secretaries, to NALS, the Association for Legal Professionals (www.nals.org). In addition to its certification program for legal secretaries, NALS also has its own examination for legal assistants and paralegals, leading to certification as a professional paralegal (PP), as we will see in Chapter 4.

In general, the market for legal secretaries has declined as more attorneys (particularly young attorneys) become comfortable with email and word-processing software that enables them to think as they write. Consequently, they do not need the full range of secretarial assistance that they traditionally depended on. According to one expert,

> [T]he old model of the legal secretary as personal assistant is becoming increasingly incompatible with business reality. With some exceptions, today's technology tools often make it more efficient for a lawyer to do something him or herself instead of relying on staff. Email is used for most routine correspondence, and many lawyers are using some combination of speech recognition tools and dictation transcription services. Many of the things that a personal assistant would have done in the 1950s are now more easily done by the lawyer directly on the computer, such as scheduling an appointment with a client while talking to him or her on the phone. After the call, the lawyer can also record the billing entry for the phone call electronically. Even a two-fingered typist can enter a single, simple billing entry.[39]

The job of secretary is not going to disappear, but it is definitely going through a transition that has many secretaries concerned about job security. To make themselves more valuable to the office, some secretaries seek to take on paralegal tasks.

When you begin working in law offices and start your own relationship with secretaries, it is useful to keep this background in mind. Your sensitivity to the ongoing development of the secretary's role will help you to establish good working relationships with legal secretaries.

SEXUAL HARASSMENT

Sexual harassment is unwanted and offensive sexual advances, contact, comments, or other interaction. On the job, two categories of sexual harassment constitute an unlawful employment practice under Title VII of the Civil Rights Act:

- **Quid pro quo sexual harassment:** Submission to or rejection of unwelcome sexual conduct used as a basis for employment decisions on promotion or other job-related benefits.
- **Hostile-environment sexual harassment:** Pervasive unwelcome sexual conduct or sex-based ridicule that unreasonably interferes with an individual's job performance or that creates an intimidating, hostile, or offensive working environment, even if no tangible or economic consequences result.

An example of quid pro quo sexual harassment is a worker who is fired for refusing to become sexually intimate with a supervisor. An example of hostile-environment sexual harassment is an office or other workplace that is pervaded by people telling dirty jokes, displaying obscene pictures, making graphic comments about the bodies of other persons, touching themselves sexually in the presence of others, persistently asking for dates, etc. This can be sexual harassment even if the person offended by such conduct is not being asked to engage in such behavior or is not being denied an employment benefit for refusing to do so.[40]

An employer must actively combat sexual harassment by:

- Establishing a written policy against sexual harassment and publicizing the policy throughout the office

sexual harassment
Unwanted and offensive sexual advances, contact, comments, or other interaction.

quid pro quo sexual harassment Submission to or rejection of unwelcome sexual conduct used as a basis for employment decisions on promotion or other job-related benefits.

hostile-environment sexual harassment Pervasive unwelcome sexual conduct or sex-based ridicule that unreasonably interferes with an individual's job performance or that creates an intimidating, hostile, or offensive working environment, even if no tangible or economic consequences result.

- Investigating all accusations of sexual harassment promptly
- Establishing appropriate sanctions for employees who commit sexual harassment
- Informing employees of their right to bring a charge of sexual harassment under Title VII of the Civil Rights Act of 1964, and telling them how to bring such a charge

It is not a defense for an employer to say he or she did not know that one of the employees engaged in sexual harassment of another employee or that the harassment took place in spite of an office policy forbidding it. If the employer should have known of the harassing conduct, the employer must take immediate and appropriate corrective action beyond merely telling all employees not to engage in sexual harassment.

Studies indicate that the harassment in a law office can come from a superior, a colleague, or a client. Here are some concrete examples:

> The paralegal ... told of one incident in which a partner placed his hand on her knee and asked if she had thought about her future with the firm. "Harassment of women lawyers is only the tip of the iceberg," according to the paralegal. "The support staff has it much, much worse."[41]

> Recently a female paralegal began working with an insecure male lawyer who was a first year associate at the firm. He started "making the moves" on her by constantly asking if she was dating anyone. One day he called her in his office, closed the door, dialed a number on the phone, and handed the receiver to the paralegal. "What I heard was an obscene recording. I laughed, opened the door, and left." She did not believe in pursuing office relationships. Resentment developed when they began working on the same case together. He falsely accused the paralegal of lying and of not completing assignments on time. He made derogatory comments to her co-workers. When she confided in a female lawyer at the firm, she was told that the associate acts that way with all the women at the firm, that the paralegal supervisor and the associate are very good friends, that the partner in charge "sticks to this associate like glue" and does not want to be bothered by "petty personnel problems."[42]

contemporaneous Existing or occurring in the same period of time; pertaining to records that are prepared regarding events as the events are occurring or very shortly thereafter.

When something of this nature happens, make detailed **contemporaneous** notes on who said and did what. Do this immediately after the incident. Should you do anything more? A passive response would be to ignore the problem and hope that it will go away. Another response would be to blame yourself. A conservative female commentator once told the Senate Labor and Human Resources Committee that "men hardly ever ask sexual favors of women from whom the certain response is no."[43] It is highly unlikely, however, that blaming yourself is either correct or productive.

For isolated and less serious problems, all that may be needed is a firm comment to the offender such as:

> Mr. Smith, you know that I respect your ability and authority in the firm. But I want you to know that I do not appreciate the comment you made at that meeting about me as a woman. I did not think it was appropriate or professional.

Unfortunately, this approach may be inadequate when the problem becomes more complicated and persists. All possible internal avenues for resolving the problem should be attempted. The hope is that somebody in a position of responsibility will lend a sympathetic ear. Local paralegal associations should be a source of ideas and support. Speak with officers of the association. Go to general meetings. Ask for advice. It is highly likely that you will find others who have had similar experiences and who can provide concrete suggestions.

Equal Employment Opportunity Commission (EEOC) The federal agency that investigates employment discrimination that might violate federal law (www.eeoc.gov).

If all else fails, you have a powerful weapon at your disposal: the law. Harassment on the basis of sex is a violation of Title VII of the Civil Rights Act of 1964. The federal **Equal Employment Opportunity Commission (EEOC)** as well as state departments of civil rights are available to enforce the law.[44]

Violations can lead to severe penalties. In one case, the legal community was shocked by a jury award of $6.9 million in punitive damages against one of the world's largest law firms, Baker & McKenzie, because of sexual harassment by one of its partners against his legal secretary. With other damages, the award came to $7.1 million. The court later reduced the award to about $3.5 million. The partner's offensive conduct included dumping candy in the front pocket of the secretary's blouse, fondling her breast, and grabbing her hips and asking her repeatedly, "What is the wildest thing you have done?" The jury found that the firm was negligent in the way it responded to her allegations against the partner. It was not enough for the firm to transfer the employee to another attorney when she complained of the behavior. The court was not persuaded by the argument that the partner simply had an "overactive imagination." After the trial, the secretary's attorney said that the case should substantially affect law firms across the country. And the chairman of Baker & McKenzie's executive committee said the firm will handle any future complaints of sexual harassment from its employees very differently.[45]

WORKING WITH SYSTEMS

Some paralegal employment problems are attributed to the fact that the firm has not carefully examined how paralegals can be effectively used in the office. Although paralegals are part of an attorney-paralegal-secretary team, the office may not have done the necessary planning to design the system that the team will execute.

A *system* is simply an organized way of accomplishing a task. All participants are supposed to perform those functions that they are capable of handling and for which they are not overtrained. Here is how many systems are created:

- Select the task that is to be systematized. It will usually be a task that the office performs regularly, such as incorporating a business, probating an estate, filing for divorce, or engaging in discovery. (According to some studies, attorneys perform over 75 percent of their tasks more than once.)
- Carefully study the task to identify its various components. What are the pieces that must always be performed? What facts must always be obtained? What letters must always be sent? What forms must always be drafted?
- Prepare a systems or procedural manual containing a description of the task, instructions or checklists of things to be done, standardized letters, pleadings, forms, and other documents that are customarily used for that task. The manual can be placed in a three-ring notebook and/or on a computer.
- Scan or photocopy statutes, court rules, or other laws frequently used to perform the task and place them in a special section of the manual, often in the appendix.
- Delegate the performance of the components of the task to various members of the team.

It takes considerable sophistication to design a system. Even more sophistication is sometimes needed to implement the system and make it work. The participants must believe in the system and ideally have had a role in its design if it requires changes in their work habits. Many attorneys are notoriously resistant to change, particularly if they believe that the system fails to recognize the role of professional judgment. If you have been doing something the same way for fifteen years, you tend to be suspicious of suggestions that more efficient ways are possible. Furthermore, in the transition from blueprint to operation, the system may have to be modified to work out the "bugs." In short, a precondition for success is a willingness and a determination on the part of the participants to make the new system work.

Unfortunately this willingness and determination do not always exist. When paralegals walk into an office for the first time, they may find a highly structured office with clearly articulated systems being implemented with precision and skill. On the other hand, they may find a different set of circumstances:

- There are few or no systems; most attorneys practice law in their individualistic ways.
- There is talk of systemization, but no one has yet done any serious design work.
- An ineffective system is in place.
- A system is in place, but the participants do not believe in it.
- A system exists on paper, but no one has spent the time and energy to make the system work.

All these environments can make life difficult for the paralegal. A disorganized office can be frustrating.

As you gain experience on the job, don't be reluctant to try to design your own system. Begin modestly with a system for a portion of one of your tasks that you perform multiple times. Start out on a small scale by writing instructions or checklists for functions that you regularly perform. Write the system so that a new paralegal would be able to read it and know what to do. Here is an example of how a project led to the creation of a system:

> Diedre Wilton's organizational skills were really put to the test during a recent assignment which required her to file fictitious business name statements for a client in all counties in California. "Almost every county had a different form!" lamented Diedre. "And I had to arrange for publication in fifty-eight different newspapers." She is creating an extensive file on the project so that ... when the filings come up for renewal, the next person won't have to start from scratch.[46]

Supervisors will be very impressed by such efforts to create systems. A paralegal with this much initiative will soon become a prized member of the office.

CHAPTER SUMMARY

A major theme of this chapter is the critical importance of paralegal initiative. Every occupation has its problems. This chapter covered problems in the paralegal arena and how competence, assertiveness, and initiative are primary vehicles for resolving them. After listing forty factors that influence job satisfaction, we turned to a discussion of the breakdown of communication in the hectic environment of a law practice; the inclinations of workers in different generations (traditionalist, baby boomer, generation X, and generation Y); having realistic expectations of the variety of paralegal jobs and kinds of assignments you can be received; and the dynamics of office politics.

A performance review is an analysis of the extent to which a person or program has met designated objectives. Such reviews are essential to the goal of competence. To prepare for a performance review, write a pre-evaluation memo listing the cases worked on, functions performed on these cases, names of supervisors and coworkers on the cases, special accomplishments, and realization data.

Many recent graduates of law school need on-the-job training at their first job because of the heavy emphasis on doctrine and theory during their three years of law school. A number of characteristics of some attorneys may interfere with them becoming effective team leaders. Some attorneys are less likely to collaborate than people in other occupations; are inclined to adhere to their preferred approach even when another is more effective; tend to focus on what is wrong with an idea as opposed to its merits; and are inclined to seek results through varying degrees of confrontation.

To cultivate active listening, do not multitask while someone is talking, look at the speaker, avoid distracting body language, ask clarifying questions, add reassuring nods or comments, occasionally repeat back or paraphrase what the speaker has said, etc. Keep an ongoing work in progress (WIP) report and a personal job diary or journal in which you record job-related details. Your career development file should contain résumés, job history, work accomplishments, professional activities, and career client list.

Continuing legal education (CLE) is training in the law (usually short term) that a person receives after completing his or her formal legal training or after becoming employed. It is obtained in a brick-and-mortar building or online. Sensitivity is needed in developing a working relationship with some secretaries who may resent the diminishment of the direct relationship they had with attorneys, may be concerned about the loss of their jobs, and may feel that they are able to do some of the tasks that paralegals perform. Employers have an affirmative obligation to take specific steps to prevent sexual harassment, which is unwanted and offensive sexual advances, contact, comments, or other interaction. An office system is an organized way of accomplishing a task in which the participants perform functions that they are capable of handling and for which they are not overtrained. Unfortunately, systems are poorly carried out in some offices.

KEY TERMS

work in progress (WIP) (p. 130)
due diligence (p. 132)
office politics (p. 133)
performance review (p. 135)
realization rate (p. 137)
case method (p. 139)

adverse (p. 139)
clinical education (p. 139)
flextime (p. 141)
attentive listening (p. 142)
continuing legal
    education (CLE) (p. 145)

pro bono (p. 146)
sexual harassment (p. 147)
quid pro quo sexual
    harassment (p. 147)
hostile-environment
    sexual harassment (p. 147)

contemporaneous (p. 148)
Equal Employment
    Opportunity Commission
    (EEOC) (p. 148)

ASSIGNMENTS

CRITICAL ANALYSIS

3.1 According to Douglas McGregor in *The Human Side of Enterprise* (1960), there are two basic views of human behavior at work. "Theory X" says that a person has a natural dislike of work and will avoid it whenever possible. "Theory Y" says that physical and mental work is as natural to a person as any other activity. Under Theory Y, workers do not naturally shy away from responsibility.

(a) Describe a law office using paralegals that is managed under Theory X. How would it function? How would the office handle employee or personnel problems?

(b) Describe a law office using paralegals that subscribes to Theory Y. How would it function? How would the office handle employee or personnel problems?

(c) Which theory do you think is correct?

(d) Which theory describes you?

3.2 Examine the following fact situations. For each situation:

- Identify the problems that you see.
- What strategies do you think would be helpful in resolving the problems? Why?
- What strategies do you think would be counterproductive? Why?
- What do you think could have been done to prevent the problem or problems from occurring in the first place? How could they have been avoided?
- In your responses, specify what you think would be assertive, nonassertive, and aggressive behavior.

(a) Tom has been a paralegal at a firm for three years. His paralegal training in school was in drafting, legal research, investigation, etc. For the entire three years, however, he has been collating and digesting numerous documents in a big antitrust case. It is a very important case, and the firm is reluctant to take him off it due to his familiarity with these documents. The problem, however, is that Tom is becoming bored. He is satisfied with his pay but dreads coming to work each day. He tried to explain this to his supervisor, but he was simply told how important he was to the case. The supervisor said, "If you decide to leave the firm, I hope you will give us six months' lead time so that you can train a replacement." This made Tom all the more depressed because he does not want to leave.

(b) Ellen is a probate paralegal at a firm. She has worked there two years. At a recent paralegal association meeting, she discovered that other probate paralegals in the city with the same experience are making at least $4,000 more per year than she is. She wants to talk with her supervisor (Ed Dooley) about this but is not sure if this is the right time. The last three months have been difficult for her. She has missed work a lot due to illness. She also recently began work on a new complex case. She is struggling to keep up with the new work involved in the case and must constantly ask her supervisor for help. The supervisor appears to be irritated with her progress on the case. Her next scheduled salary review is ten months away.

(c) Fran is a paralegal in a firm where she works for the senior partner—the most powerful person in the firm. Fran receives excellent pay and fringe benefits. She loves her work. Other paralegals in the firm, however, resent her because their benefits are much lower and they receive less desirable assignments.

(d) Same situation as in (c). Fran's supervisor, the senior partner, is currently going through a divorce, and the strain on him has been enormous. One consequence of this is that Fran's workload is increasing. More of his work is being shifted to her. He is extremely sensitive to any criticism about the way he practices law, so Fran is reluctant to talk with him about the extra work—particularly when he is under so much pressure due to the divorce. Yet Fran is worried about her ability to do her job competently in view of the increased work. She hopes that things will get back to normal when the divorce is over.

(e) Tom has been a paralegal at the firm for six years. He works for three attorneys. One day he is told, via a memo from the office administrator, that an outside consultant has been hired to study Tom's job in order to find ways "to increase productivity." The letter instructs Tom to spend the next two days permitting the consultant to follow him around and ask questions about what he does. Tom feels insulted.

(f) Mary has been a paralegal at the firm for two years. She works for one attorney, Mr. Getty. One day a client calls Mary and says, "I'm sending you another copy of the form that Mr. Getty said you lost." This is news to Mary. She works with the client's file every day and knows that she has never lost anything. She pauses, trying to think of what to say to this client over the phone before hanging up.

(g) Veronica works for a law firm where none of the supervisors gives formal evaluations of the paralegals. The supervisors feel that formal evaluations would be too time-consuming and too general to be helpful. They are also afraid that they might be sued for making negative comments about employees. Veronica has received yearly raises, and according to her supervisor, this is the best indication of what the firm thinks of her. Veronica is unhappy, however, with the feedback she has gotten about her work.

(h) George is a paralegal at the office of Kiley & Kiley. His supervisor is Phyllis Kiley, one of the senior partners at the firm. Phyllis knows that George is recently divorced. She often asks him about his dating life. Several times she asked him to accompany her to downtown evening receptions that had nothing to do with the law office or his job. This attention from Phyllis is making George uncomfortable. He is reluctant to say anything because she has a reputation of firing anyone who questions her in any way. Paralegal jobs in the area are scarce and it took George a while to obtain this one. What should George do?

PROJECTS

3.3 Open a LinkedIn account and post basic data about yourself as a new paralegal student. (See Exhibit 2-13 in Chapter 2.) In LinkedIn, do a search for "paralegal student." Read the profiles of current students to obtain ideas for your own profile.

CORE SKILLS

Among the many skills a paralegal must have, five core skills stand out: writing (both basic English and legal drafting), research, ethics, computer use, and collaboration (working with others). The core-skill assignments introduce and reinforce these skills. Even if you are not asked to do all of the assignments as part of the course, you should do them on your own. Also, do not wait for the topics in the assignments to be covered in this course or in other courses. Successful paralegals are self-starters. A major characteristic of a self-starter is a thirst for independent study—learning on your own.

CORE SKILL: WRITING

3.4 Run this search in Google, Bing, or Yahoo: "topic sentence"

(a) Give a definition of a topic sentence and list any three guidelines for writing them. List the website(s) that you used to answer this question.

(b) Write three paragraphs about any aspect of your current job or one of your prior jobs (whether or not the jobs involved the law). Each paragraph must be at least five sentences long and must contain a topic sentence.

CORE SKILL: RESEARCH

3.5 On Bing, run this search: Bing search techniques tips.

(a) List five Bing search techniques that you did not know or with which you were only vaguely familiar. Examples might be how to search for a phrase, how to specifically exclude a term in a search query so that you would be led to sites that did not contain that term, and how to write a search for a three-word phrase when you are not sure of the middle word in the phrase.

(b) Make up any five searches that use the five Bing techniques you identified—one search for each of the new techniques. List each of the five searches and give an example of a good site to which each search led you.

(c) In assignment 2.7 in Chapter 2, you listed five Google search techniques. Do any of the five Google techniques also work in Bing, or does Bing have its own techniques for the same kinds of searches?

CORE SKILL: ETHICS

3.6 Mary works in a law firm that charges clients $225 an hour for attorney time and $100 an hour for paralegal time. She and another paralegal, Fred, are working with an attorney on a large case. She sees all of the time sheets that the three of them submit to the firm's accounting office. She suspects that the attorney is padding his time sheets by overstating the number of hours he works on the case. (As we will see in Chapter 5, *padding* is unethically adding something without justification.) For example, he lists thirty hours for a four-day period when he was in court every day on another case. Furthermore, Fred's time is being billed at the full $100-an-hour paralegal rate even though he spends about 80 percent of his time typing correspondence, filing, and performing other clerical duties.

In assignment 1.7 (Chapter 1), you identified the site that contains the ethics code of your state. (See also Appendix D for links

to your state.) Find ethics code sections that may apply to Mary's concern that the law firm may be falsifying the bills it sends to its clients. Explain why they might apply.

CORE SKILL: COMPUTERS

3.7 Reread assignment 1.8 in Chapter 1. In that assignment you started a Computer Terminology in the Law (CTL) notebook and selected two general computer terms and two software terms. You then entered information about the four terms in your computer notebook.

(a) On the Internet, find additional information about the four terms you selected in assignment 1.8. Enter this additional information in your CTL.

(b) Run the same searches mentioned in assignment 1.8. Select two *new* general computer terms and two new software program terms. Enter the new information in your CTL.

CORE SKILL: COLLABORATION

 3.8

(a) Select what you feel are the ten most important factors in Exhibit 3-1. Write out your list and make a copy. Indicate whether you have ever had any law office work experience as a secretary, a paralegal, etc.

(b) Give the copy of your list to a person in the class whom your instructor will designate as the statistician. The latter will collect all the copies from the students and make the following tabulations: (i) which factors received the most votes on the "top ten" list by the students who have had prior law office experience and (ii) which received the most votes from the other students.

(c) In class, discuss the results of these tabulations. Are there significant differences in the opinions of the two groups? Can you explain the differences or similarities?

 3.9

(a) Open a Twitter account if you do not already have one. (See Exhibit 2-13 in Chapter 2.) Exchange Twitter addresses with other members of your class. Go to these addresses and "follow" your fellow students.

(b) In Google, Bing, or Yahoo, enter this search: "performance reviews" job. Find two different websites on this topic that give recommendations for getting the most out of such reviews.

(c) Post two tweets, one for each of the sites you found.

(d) Jot down the two sites tweeted by each of your fellow students.

(e) Briefly go to each of these tweeted sites. Place the sites in the order in which you think they provide the most useful ideas to prepare for and undergo a performance review.

THE JOB SEARCH

(The search for employment cannot wait until the end of a course or of a curriculum. It has to begin now. The job-search assignments are designed to introduce you to different aspects of the job search and to build options for you to explore about employment.)

3.10

(a) In Google, Bing, or Yahoo, enter this search: paralegal job entry-level. Find two different websites that discuss techniques for finding an entry-level job (one requiring no legal experience).

(b) Tweet your two sites to your classmates.

(c) Go to the sites tweeted by each of your classmates.

(d) Place the sites in the order in which you think they provide the most useful ideas on finding an entry-level job.

REVIEW QUESTIONS

1. What are some of the major factors that paralegals say affect job satisfaction?
2. What are some of the standard factors that can contribute to communication problems in an office?
3. What steps should you take to avoid miscommunication in a busy law office?
4. What is work in progress (WIP)?
5. What is meant by a multigenerational office?
6. Name five generations that can exist (or that will soon exist) in many law offices.
7. Which generation tends to prefer face-to-face communication and a standard chain-of-command structure in the office?
8. Which generation tends to resent newer workers who expect advancement without paying their dues?
9. Which generation were often pampered by doting parents, told they were special, and have a need for constant feedback and praise?
10. What is the major antidote to job frustration resulting from expectations?
11. In what sense can it be said that law office environments are not static?
12. What is meant by office politics and why is it unrealistic to wish that it will go away?
13. What is the three-part strategy for dealing with office politics?
14. What are performance reviews and why are they essential?
15. How should you prepare for a performance review?
16. Give examples of measurable goals before your next evaluation.
17. Why do many recent law-school graduates need on-the-job training at their first job?
18. What characteristics of some attorneys may make them ineffective supervisors and team leaders?
19. What are some differences among assertive, nonassertive, and aggressive persons?
20. What assertive strategies can be used when you are seeking a salary increase?
21. What is a realization rate?
22. What are some of the secrets of successful paralegals?
23. What are some of the techniques of an active listener?
24. What information should be kept in a diary or journal?
25. What should be kept in a career development file?
26. What are the two main ways to obtain CLE?
27. What are some of the major factors of effective paralegal supervision?
28. What are some of the reasons friction once existed between paralegals and some secretaries?
29. What are the definitions of the two kinds of sexual harassment that violate the law?
30. What are the obligations of an employer to prevent sexual harassment?
31. What are law office systems and why are they sometimes difficult to implement?

HELPFUL WEBSITES

Assertiveness

- en.wikipedia.org/wiki/Assertiveness
- www.mindtools.com/pages/article/Assertiveness.htm
- www.mayoclinic.com/health/assertive/SR00042

Job Satisfaction

- www.mindtools.com (enter *job satisfaction* in the search box)
- www.apa.org/monitor/2013/12/job-satisfaction.aspx

Office Politics

- managementhelp.org/interpersonal/office-politics.htm
- www.officepolitics.com

Employment Discrimination and Sexual Harassment

- www.eeoc.gov (enter *harassment* in the search box)
- www.eeoc.gov/laws/types/sexual_harassment.cfm
- www3.uakron.edu/lawrev/robert1.html

Continuing Legal Education (CLE)

Go to the website of your local paralegal association (see Appendix B) to find out what CLE it sponsors or links to.

- www.nala.org/onlineed.aspx

- www.paralegals.org (click *Professional Development*)
- www.nals.org (click *Education*)
- www.cleonline.com
- www.washlaw.edu/subject/continuing.ed.html
- westlegaledcenter.com
- www.findlaw.com/07cle/list.html

Legal Secretaries

- www.bls.gov/oes/current/oes436012.htm
- www.onetonline.org/link/summary/43-6012.00

Listening Skills

- www.mindtools.com/CommSkll/ActiveListening.htm
- www.skillsyouneed.com/ips/listening-skills.html

Paralegal Blogs

See Appendix F

Rate Your Boss

- www.ebosswatch.com

Google, Bing, or Yahoo Searches

On these search engines, run the following searches, using quotation marks and substituting your state for "aa" where indicated.

- paralegal survey
- office politics
- multigenerational workforce
- continuing legal education aa
- "paralegal listserv"
- "employee evaluation"
- salary raise strategies
- assertiveness
- law office environment culture
- effective supervision
- personality types
- sexual harassment aa

ENDNOTES

1. LakishaBealer, *Navigating Law Office Politics*, Paralegal Rainmakers (June 6, 2013) (www.a-paralegal.com).

2. Beth King, *President's Message*, 10 Newsletter 1 (Oregon Paralegal Association, February 1987).

3. Mary Ryan, Human Resources Consultant.

4. *Poor Communication Devours Seven Workweeks Per Year*, Legal Management 14 (November/December 1998).

5. Sgarlat, *The Scape Goat Phenomenon*, 6 The Journal 10 (Sacramento Valley Paralegal Association, June 1986).

6. Rita Milios, *What's Your Personality Style?* 27 Paralegal Today 16 (October/December 2010).

7. Sally Kane, *Ten Trends Reshaping the Legal Industry*, About.com Legal Careers (legalcareers.about.com) (2013).

8. See AARP, *Leading a Multigenerational Workforce*, www.aarp.org (2007).

9. The Paralegal Society, *Sketches of Our Society–Featured Paralegal: Eric Bleuel* (December 15, 2011) (theparalegalsociety.wordpress.com).

10. Chere Estrin, *Political Aspirations*, 16 Legal Assistant Today 94 (May/June 1999).

11. McLaverty, *Office Politics and Communication*, 24 WALS State Journal 50 (January 1990).

12. Lakisha Bealer, *Navigating Law Office Politics*, Paralegal Experts (paralegalexpert.wordpress.com) (June 26, 2013).

13. William Yardley, *Zig Ziglar*, New York Times, November 29, 2012, at B16.

14. Fran Chernowsky, *Toward Greater Visibility*, 15 Reporter (Los Angeles Paralegal Association, August 1986).

15. Michele Boerder, *Four Pointers to Professionalism*, 14 DALA Newsletter 3 (Dallas Area Paralegal Association, December 1990).

16. Oder, *Paralegal Upward Mobility*, 6 National Paralegal Reporter 6 (National Federation of Paralegal Associations, Fall/Winter 1981); Los Angeles Paralegal Association, Reporter (September 1981).

17. Adapted from an evaluation form used at Heller, Ehrman, White & McAuliffe, San Francisco, California.

18. Wojt, *Making the Most of Your Performance Review*, 38 The Docket 22 (April/May 1990).

19. Arthur Greene & Therese Cannon, *Paralegals, Profitability and the Future of Your Law Practice* 133 (ABA Law Practice Management Section 2003).

20. Comment made in Paralegal Today Listserv (paralegaltoday.com/lat-forum).

21. See Barbara Middleton, *Taking Criticism*, 7 Newsletter 25 (Texas Paralegal Division, November 1991).

22. Rachel Zahorsky, *ABA Urges Law Schools to Adopt More Practical Training for Students*, ABA Journal (www.abajournal.com) (August 9, 2011).

23. Stephanie Allen and Andrea Williams, *Team-Building Frenzy Reaches Law Firms*, The National Law Journal, December 17, 1990, at 20.

24. Jean Hollands, *Why Lawyers Are Sometimes Unhappy*, Los Altos Town Crier, May 17, 2000, at 47.

25. Andrea Wagner, *Tips & Traps for the New Paralegal*, 8 Legal Assistant Today 78, 82 (March/April 1991).

26. *Negotiating for More Money in a Tough Market*, Estrin LegalEd Newsletter (June 2007).

27. Tami Coyne, *Strategies for Paralegal Career Development*, National Paralegal Reporter 20 (National Federation of Paralegal Associations, Winter 1990).

28. Shelley Riseden, *How to Impress Your Boss by Being Proactive*, Paralegal Alliance (2013).

29. Renee Sova, *Bridging the Gap from Student to Professional*, 7 Legal Professional 47 (January/February 1990).

30. Marion Johnson, *President's Message*, Newsletter 1 (Arizona Paralegal Association, July 1988).

31. Ann Pearson, *The 6 Minute Paralegal and the Billable Hour* (2013) (www.pearsonresource.com).

32. Chere Estrin, *10 Easy Steps to Leveraging Your Career*, 10 TALA Newsletter 7 (Paralegal Association of Northwest Ohio, October 1989).

33. Adapted from Debra Bruce, "*Are You Tuned In?*" 38 Facts & Findings 14 (National Association of Legal Assistants, 2011); *What Kind of a Listener Are You–It Matters!* (December 1, 2013) (www.impactcommunicationsinc.com).

34. Vicki Kunz, *Personal Management File*, WDALA Summons (Western Dakota Association of Legal Assistants, August 1990).

35. Felicia Garant, *Speech to USM Paralegal Program Graduates*, Newsletter 3 (Maine Association of Paralegals, April 1990).

36. Special Counsel, *Continuing Education Survey*, Legal Management 16 (September/October 2000).

37. Internal Revenue Service, *Tax Benefits for Education* (2012) (www.irs.gov/pub/irs-pdf/p970.pdf).

38. *The Legal Assistant and the Legal Secretary: Friend or Foe*, 8 The Journal 4 (Sacramento Valley Paralegal Association, April 1988). ("Legal assistant" was changed to "paralegal.")

39. Jim Calloway, *Rethinking the Role of Your Law Firm's Support Staff*, LawyersUSA (May 14, 2012).

40. U.S. Equal Employment Opportunity Commission, *Sexual Harassment* (www.eeoc.gov/laws/types/sexual_harassment.cfm).

41. Stephanie Goldberg, Law's "Dirty Little Secret," 76 A.B.A. Journal 34 (October 1990).

42. National Federation of Paralegal Associations, *Harassment: Personnel Problem or Worse?* 9 National Paralegal Reporter 7 (February 1985).

43. Ralph Slovenko, *Psychiatry in Law* 168 (2002) (quoting Phyllis Schlafly).

44. www.eeoc.gov.

45. *Weeks v. Baker & McKenzie*, 63 Cal. App. 4th 1128, 74 Cal. Rptr. 2d 510 (Ct. App. 1998). To read this case online, go to Google Scholar (scholar.google.com), select "Case law," and type *Weeks Baker McKenzie* in the search box.

46. *Paralegal Profile*, 12 Points & Authorities 9 (San Joaquin Ass'n of Legal Assistants, March 1991).

CHAPTER 4

THE REGULATION OF PARALEGALS

CHAPTER OUTLINE

- Kinds of Regulation
- Defining the Practice of Law
- Roles for Paralegals in Court Proceedings
- Roles for Paralegals in Administrative Proceedings
- Licensing
- Reforms in the Practice of Law: Attempts to Close the Justice Gap
- Certification
- Fair Labor Standards Act (FLSA)
- Tort Liability
- Malpractice Insurance

CHAPTER OBJECTIVES

After completing this chapter, you should be able to

- Know the different ways in which paralegals are regulated.
- Understand why it is difficult to define the practice of law.
- List the tests that courts use as a guide to determine what is the practice of law.
- Understand the relationship between professional judgment and legal advice.
- Distinguish between legal information and legal advice.

- Know when document service providers (DSPs) engage in the unauthorized practice of law (UPL).
- Summarize the antitrust argument against some definitions of the practice of law.
- List examples of when nonattorneys are allowed to provide representation in court and in administrative proceedings.
- State the arguments for and against limited licensing.

- Summarize reforms designed to help close the justice gap.
- Distinguish between licensing and certification.
- Identify the major national and state certification programs.
- Explain when paralegals are and are not entitled to overtime compensation.
- Know when attorneys and paralegals are liable for torts and when they are covered by malpractice insurance.

KINDS OF REGULATION

The activities of paralegals could be directly or indirectly regulated in six important ways:

- Laws on the unauthorized practice of law
- Licensing
- Certification
- Fair Labor Standards Act (FLSA)
- Tort law
- Ethical rules

regulation A rule or restriction designed to control the conduct of an organization or individual. The regulation can be issued by a governmental body (e.g., an administrative agency) or by a nongovernmental body (e.g., an association or club).

The first five of these methods of regulation are covered in this chapter. Ethics will be examined in the next chapter. As we explore these methods, you should keep in mind the terminology of **regulation** outlined in Exhibit 4-1.

Exhibit 4-1	Terminology of Regulation

REGULATION

A *regulation* is any rule or restriction designed to control the conduct of an organization or individual. The regulation can be issued by a governmental body (e.g., an administrative agency) or by a nongovernmental body (e.g., an association or club).

KINDS OF REGULATION

Accreditation. A form of acknowledgment (other than certification, registration, or licensing) that a school or training program meets specified standards.

Approval A form of acknowledgment that a school or training program meets specified standards. The acknowledgment may be based on different standards than those used for accreditation.

Certification A formal acknowledgment that a person or organization has met designated qualifications. Most certifications are issued by nongovernmental bodies such as professional associations. Occasionally, however, a government body will issue the certification. Most certification programs are voluntary. Not having certification usually does *not* affect the right of a person to engage in a particular career. Three of the most common qualifications for certification are

- Graduating from a school or training program (see, however, the definition of *certificated* below)
- Passing an examination
- Completing a designated period of work experience

Certified Formally acknowledged as having met the specified qualifications of a certification program. If the certification is issued by a school or training program, say *certificated* rather than *certified.* The word *certified* should be limited to formal recognition by a body *other* than a school or training program. (See next definition.)

Certificated Formally acknowledged as having met specified qualifications of a school or training program.

Code Any set of rules that regulates conduct. Examples include a code of conduct of a professional association or a set of statutes of a legislature. (See the glossary for another definition.)

Ethics Rules or standards of behavior to which members of an occupation, profession, or other organization are expected to conform. In the legal profession, ethics are called *legal ethics, code of professional responsibility,* and most commonly today, *rules of professional conduct.*

Guideline (1) Suggested conduct that will help an applicant obtain accreditation, certification, licensure, registration, or approval. (2) A statement of policy, often with options on carrying it out.

License Government permission to do something that would otherwise be unlawful.

Occupational license Government permission that is required to engage in a specified occupation.

Licensing (also called *licensure*). The granting of a license.

General license Permission by a government body that allows a person who has met designated qualifications to engage in the full range of services that a specified occupation or profession is trained to provide.

Limited license (also called *specialty license*) Permission by a government body that allows a person who has met designated qualifications to engage in specified activities that are customarily (but not always exclusively) performed by another category of license holder. (If, in the future, paralegals are granted a limited license in a particular state, they will be authorized to provide designated services directly to the public without attorney supervision. As we will see later in the chapter, Washington State is the first state to create limited licensing.)

Registration (also called *enrollment*) The process by which the names of individuals or institutions are listed on a roster kept by a governmental or nongovernmental body. There may or may not be qualifications that must be met before a name can go on the list. If qualifications are imposed, registration is often the same as certification.

DEFINING THE PRACTICE OF LAW

The **practice of law** is the use or attempt to use legal skills to help resolve a specific person's legal problem. The **unauthorized practice of law (UPL)** is the use or attempt to use legal skills to help resolve a specific person's legal problem when the assistance is provided by someone who does not have a license to practice law and when the assistance requires such a license or other authorization.

The vast majority of paralegals in the country are employees of attorneys; they are **traditional paralegals**. For the most part, the tasks they perform are authorized due to the attorney supervision they receive on those tasks. Nevertheless, it is possible for traditional paralegals to engage in the unauthorized practice of law (UPL). As we will see in Chapter 5, the two main reasons they can be charged with UPL are (1) they perform tasks that only attorneys are allowed to perform and (2) they receive inadequate attorney supervision on the tasks they are allowed to perform. In this chapter, we will mention traditional paralegals, but our primary concern will be UPL issues involving individuals who do *not* work for or under the supervision of attorneys. These individuals have a variety of titles, but, in general, they fall into the category of what is called **document service providers (DSPs)**.

It's an exciting time to be studying this area of the law because of a current lively debate over whether we need new UPL definitions and new roles for the DSP.

THE CRIME OF UPL

In most states, UPL is a crime. Self-representation is allowed. It is not a crime to represent yourself, but you risk going to jail if you practice law on behalf of someone else. Why such a harsh penalty? Legal problems often involve complicated, serious issues. A great deal can be lost if a person does not receive competent legal assistance. To protect the public, the state requires a license to practice law and will punish anyone who tries to practice without the license. Such individuals are engaged in UPL. As we will see in the Maryland opinion of the attorney general, "The prohibition against unauthorized practice undoubtedly furthers an important goal—to 'protect the public from being preyed upon by…incompetent, unethical, or irresponsible representation.'"

AMBIGUITY IN THE DEFINITION

Unfortunately, the definition of the practice of law is far from clear. The core of the definition is the use of "legal skills" to help another resolve a legal problem, but the phrase "legal skills" is very broad. In essence, it consists of interpreting the law for another. Yet this kind of interpretation takes place throughout society by many different kinds of individuals, including one neighbor who tells another that the city requires overhanging trees to be cut. To try to be more precise, some argue that the practice of law is what attorneys do. But this argument is circular:

- The practice of law is what attorneys do.
- What do attorneys do?
- They practice law.

Efforts by legislatures and courts to define the practice of law in statutes and court opinions have not been successful. The Supreme Court of Texas is quite candid about the weakness of any definition:

"Neither statutory nor judicial definitions offer clear guidelines as to what constitutes the practice of law or the unauthorized practice of law. All too frequently, the definitions are so broad as to be meaningless and amount to little more than the statement that the practice of law is merely whatever lawyers do or are traditionally understood to do."[1]

TESTS TO HELP IDENTIFY THE PRACTICE OF LAW

The difficulty of defining the practice of law, however, has not stopped the effort to try to find a definition. The effort is necessary. How can a state charge someone with the unauthorized practice of law without having a clear definition of the practice of law, or at least having a definition that puts the public on notice of the conduct that could lead to a criminal charge of UPL? Tests have been created to help identify the practice of law. Not all states, however,

practice of law Using or attempting to use legal skills to help resolve a specific person's legal problem.

unauthorized practice of law (UPL) (1) Using or attempting to use legal skills to help resolve a specific person's legal problem when the assistance is provided by someone who does not have a license to practice law and when the assistance requires such a license or other authorization. (2) A nonattorney's performance of tasks in a law office without adequate attorney supervision when those tasks are part of the practice of law. (3) Delegating tasks to a nonattorney that only an attorney can perform.

traditional paralegals A paralegal who is an employee of an attorney.

document service providers (DSP) (1) A nonattorney who works without attorney supervision to provide legal-document assistance to individuals who are representing themselves. (2) Someone who helps another prepare or process documents.

professional judgment Applying the law or legal principles to the facts of a specific person's legal problem. When communicated to this person, the result is called *legal advice.*

legal advice A statement or conclusion that applies the law or legal principles to the facts of a specific person's legal problem.

use the same test. (See Exhibit 4-2; see also Appendix D for the test or definition used in your state.) The test most widely used is **professional judgment**, which is applying the law or legal principles to a specific person's legal problem. When communicated to this person, the conclusion is called **legal advice.**

Exhibit 4-2	General Tests Used by Different States to Define the Practice of Law

States differ on the tests they used to determine whether a service provided by a nonattorney constitutes the practice of law. (See Appendix D for your state.) Here are the main tests, some of which overlap. Note, however, that a state might use more than one test. Also, many activities (e.g., arguing a negligence case in court) would constitute the practice of law under all the tests.

- **Professional-judgment test.** Does the service require an attorney's professional judgment, meaning the special training and skills of an attorney whereby the law or legal principles are applied to a specific person's legal problem? If the answer is yes, the service is the practice of law. Example: questioning a witness at a deposition. (The professional-judgment test is the most widely used test in the country and is closely related to the next test.)

- **General public/personal relationship test.** Is the service offered to the general public rather than to a specific person? If the service is offered to the general public only, it is not the practice of law. Example: an author writes a book on how to draft a will but does not provide personal attention to any individual buyer of the book. If, however, the service connects (applies) the law or legal principles to the facts of a specific person's legal problem, the service is the practice of law.

- **Traditional-areas test.** Is the service one that attorneys have traditionally performed such as representing someone in court or in an agency proceeding, interpreting or drafting legal documents, or giving legal advice? If the answer is yes, the service is the practice of law. Example: drafting a separation agreement in a divorce.

- **Complex/difficult question test.** Does the service seek to resolve a complex or difficult question of law that is beyond the capability of the average layperson? If the answer is yes, the service is the practice of law. Example: giving legal advice on a corporate merger.

- **Important rights/public protection test.** Does the service pertain to important legal rights that can be protected only by someone with special legal skills? If the answer is yes, the service is the practice of law. Example: giving legal advice on a divorce.

- **Commonly understood test.** Is the service commonly understood to be the practice of law? If the answer is yes, the service is the practice of law. Example: making a motion in court. Preparing tax returns, on the other hand, is not commonly understood to be the practice of law.

- **Incidental test.** Is the service an adjunct to (incidental to) the main service provided by the business? If the answer is yes, the incidental service is *not* the practice of law. The service must not be the primary function of the business. Example: the preparation of a sales contract (using standard forms) by a real estate agent for which a separate fee is not charged. Preparing this standard contract is incidental to the primary business of the agent (selling real estate) and, therefore is not the practice of law.

Professional Judgment

In 1969, the American Bar Association said it was hopeless to try to formulate an all-encompassing definition of the practice of law that will cover every case. In effect, there was no bright line that separated the practice of law and the UPL. Instead, the ABA endorsed two of the tests outlined in Exhibit 4-2 (the professional judgment test and the closely related general public/personal relationship test):

It is neither necessary nor desirable to attempt the formulation of a single, specific definition of what constitutes the practice of law. Functionally the practice of law relates to the rendition of services for others that call for the professional judgment of a lawyer. The essence of the professional judgment of the lawyer is his educated ability to relate the general body and philosophy of law to a specific legal problem of a client; and thus, the public interest will be better served if only lawyers are permitted to act in matters involving professional judgment. Where this professional judgment is not involved, non-lawyers, such as court clerks, police officers, abstractors, and many governmental employees may engage in occupations that require a special knowledge of law in certain areas. But the services of a lawyer are essential in the public interest whenever the exercise of professional judgment is required.[2]

The key concept, according to the ABA and most states, is a specific person's legal problem. Anyone can describe the law in general terms without being charged with practicing law. If, however, this description is directed to a specific person's legal problem, the practice of law has taken place. The following factors are irrelevant:

- whether or not the description of the law is correct
- whether or not a charge or fee is paid for the description

Hence, correct, free advice is in the same category as incorrect, expensive advice. Both are the practice of law if they are directed to a specific person's legal problem.

This is the starting point of the analysis to determine whether a service is the practice of law of law. A separate question is whether the service is the *unauthorized* practice of law. We will see that the law allows (authorizes) some individuals to perform tasks that would otherwise be restricted to attorneys only.

Traditional-Areas Test: Representation, Documents, and Advice

We should also briefly look at another popular general test for identifying the practice of law, namely the traditional-areas test listed in Exhibit 4-2. A typical law practice often involves three main (traditional) areas of service: representation, documents, and advice.

- Representing someone in court or in an administrative agency proceeding;
- Interpreting and/or drafting legal documents for someone; and
- Giving someone legal advice.

The third category—giving legal advice—usually takes place while performing the other two activities, although legal advice can also be given independently of them.

LEGAL INFORMATION VS. LEGAL ADVICE

A distinction should be made between providing legal information and providing legal advice.

- **Legal information:** A statement about the law that is not directed at the facts of a specific person's legal problem. General observations or conclusions about the law.

- **Legal advice:** A statement or conclusion that applies the law or legal principles to the facts of a specific person's legal problem.

Examples of legal information include the definition of manslaughter; what court hears divorce cases; how many days a defendant has to answer a complaint. This information does not become legal advice unless it is directed at helping to resolve a specific person's legal problem. According to the American Bar Association,

> Although the line between legal information and legal advice is blurry, there are important differences between the two. Anyone can sell or give you legal information. On the other hand, only a licensed lawyer can give you legal advice. Legal information is supposed to be general and not based on a specific set of facts. Legal advice is provided by a trained lawyer who uses his or her knowledge of the law to tell you how the law applies to your specific circumstances. When you get legal advice from a lawyer, you also enter into an "attorney-client relationship" with the lawyer. This gives you certain legal protections. For example, the lawyer cannot tell someone else what you said without your permission. [The attorney-client privilege prevents this.] Your lawyer can't advise or represent someone whose position or interests will conflict with yours. [This would be a conflict of interest.] You do not have these protections when you get legal information from someone.[3]

The following opinion of the attorney general in Maryland explores the distinction between legal information and legal advice in greater depth. You will note that this opinion allows a paralegal (called a lay advocate) to provide some minimal assistance in filling out court forms ("pointing out where on the form particular information is to be set out"). The reason given is that such assistance does not require much legal skill or knowledge of the law. (The opinion is using the complex/difficult question test outlined earlier in Exhibit 4-2.) Be aware, however, that not all states would agree with this Maryland position. In many states, *any* assistance (other than copying or typing) given to specific individuals in completing legal documents would constitute the practice of law.

legal information Any statement about the law that is not directed at the facts of a specific person's legal problem.

ATTORNEY GENERAL OPINION

Opinion of the Attorney General No. 95–056
State of Maryland
80 Opinions of the Attorney General 138 (December 19, 1995)
www.oag.state.md.us/Opinions/1995/95index.htm (see 80 OAG 138)

You have requested our opinion whether lay advocates who provide certain services to victims of domestic violence engage in the unauthorized practice of law. As you point out, lay advocates often provide important information about medical or social services available outside the court system to victims of domestic violence; activities of this kind raise no significant issue of unauthorized practice of law.

Your concern is with activities that relate to the legal system. Specifically, you ask whether lay advocates may:

(i) provide information to domestic violence victims about legal options and remedies available to them;

(ii) provide information to victims about court proceedings, including the role of witnesses;

(iii) provide assistance to victims in preparing form pleadings, either using their own language or that of the victim;

(iv) provide "non-legal assistance" to victims during judicial proceedings;

(v) sit at trial table with victims; and

(vi) engage in advocacy on behalf of victims' rights before State's Attorneys and other public officials . . . .

I. Scope of the Practice of Law

In general, a person may practice law in Maryland only if admitted to the Bar by the Court of Appeals. §§ 10–206 and 10–601 of the Business Occupations and Professions ("BOP") Article, Maryland Code. The unauthorized practice of law is a misdemeanor and is also subject to injunction. BOP §§ 10–606(a) and 10–406. Moreover, Maryland Rule of Professional Conduct 5.5 (b) prohibits a lawyer from "assist[ing] a person who is not a member of the bar in the performance of activity that constitutes the unauthorized practice of law."

Yet the comment to this rule recognizes a reality of legal practice: "Paragraph (b) does not prohibit a lawyer from employing the services of paraprofessionals and delegating functions to them, so long as the lawyer supervises the delegated work and retains responsibility for their work." In addition, Rule of Professional Conduct 5.3 identifies a lawyer's responsibilities regarding "nonlawyer assistants." Therefore, this opinion's discussion of the potential for unauthorized practice of law by lay advocates does not apply to the activities of lay advocates that are performed on behalf of a lawyer's client and are supervised by the lawyer. Even if some of these activities might constitute the "practice of law," with proper supervision and accountability they are not the "unauthorized practice of law." See In re Opinion 24, 607 A.2d 962 (N.J. 1992).

Our discussion in the balance of this opinion assumes that other lay advocates carry out their activities without a lawyer's supervision. For these lay advocates, the scope of the "practice of law" is crucial.

Exactly what constitutes the practice of law is generally for the courts to decide. Public Service Comm'n v. Hahn Transportation, Inc., 253 Md. 571, 583, 253 A. 2d 845 (1969). In Maryland, as elsewhere, however, the legislative and judicial branches have shared this responsibility, reaching a "comfortable accommodation." Id.

Under the General Assembly's definition of "practice of law," the term encompasses giving legal advice, representing another person before a court or other governmental unit, and preparing or assisting in the preparation of a form or document to be filed in courts. BOP §§ 10–101(h). This is an inevitably imprecise definition, leaving construction on a case-by-case basis to the courts. Hahn, 253 Md. at 583. See also Unauthorized Practice Committee v. Cortez, 692 S.W.2d 47, 51 (Tex. 1985) (courts have inherent power and duty to determine what constitutes the practice of law in any given case).

The Court of Appeals has construed the statute to preclude a layperson from preparing and filing pleadings in a contested case or appearing and engaging in representation at trial on behalf of another. Hahn, 253 Md. at 580–581. Further, the Court of Special Appeals held that even where trial work is not involved, an individual is practicing law if he or she is preparing legal documents, interpreting legal documents, giving legal advice, or "applying legal principles to problems of any complexity." Lukas v. Bar Association of Montgomery County, 35 Md. App. 442, 448, 371 A.2d 669 (1977), cert. denied, 250 Md. 733 (1977) (citations omitted). The test, stated generally, is whether the activity requires "more than the most elementary knowledge of law, or more than that which [a layperson] may be deemed to possess." Id. (citation omitted).

The Court in Lukas made clear, however, that this prohibition does not extend to "mere mechanical" functions, like filling out forms or performing clerical work. Id. Echoing Lukas, an opinion of this office drew the same distinction, finding that "nonlawyers may fill out forms and perform other purely mechanical functions, [but] may not represent [clients] at hearings…, nor may they give legal advice, interpret legal documents, or apply legal principles to any problems of complexity for a client." 65 Opinions of the Attorney General 28 (1980).

We have also concluded that the simple act of providing information about legal rights, as opposed to offering advice about such rights and what to do about them, is not unauthorized.

In deciding that a social worker may inform a birth parent about his or her statutory right to revoke consent to adoption, we stated that the "mere conveying of information about a provision of law" does not constitute the practice of law. 79 Opinions of the Attorney General No. 94–14 (March 7, 1994). Observing that a rule to the contrary would grind commerce and government to a halt, we said that "the line of unauthorized practice is potentially crossed when someone who is not a lawyer purports to give professional advice about another person's legal situation or suggests a course of conduct based on an interpretation of the law, [but] the line is not crossed by the unadorned provision of information." Opinion No. 94–014, at 3.

II. Prohibited and Permissible Services

Under these principles, some of the services [that] lay advocates provide victims of domestic violence constitute the unauthorized practice of law; others do not . . . .

(continued)

Opinion of the Attorney General No. 95–056 (*Continued*)

A. General Information

Lay advocates may provide information to victims about their potential legal rights and remedies. In doing so, however, they must be careful to limit their activity to the unadorned conveyance of information about what rights and remedies exist. They may not help victims decide, based upon the victims' particular circumstances, whether to invoke any of their rights or pursue any of their potential remedies. Providing this latter assistance would be improperly suggesting a "course of conduct." Opinion No. 94–014, at 3. See also *Cortez*, 692 S.W.2d at 50 (advising clients as to whether they qualified to file various petitions and whether they should file various immigration forms required legal skill and was thus unauthorized practice of law).

B. Information about Court Proceedings

Lay advocates may inform victims about purely nonlegal, basic matters such as appropriate attire, where to sit, and so forth. They may also provide a general orientation or overview about the kind of proceeding involved. This kind of information is not legal advice.

Providing any more particular or individualized information about judicial proceedings, such as how to present a case, call witnesses, cross-examine witnesses, introduce documents, and the like, requires a specialized knowledge ordinarily beyond the purview of a layperson. See *Lukas*, 35 Md. App. at 448–49. See also *Matter of Bright*, 171 B.R. 799 (Bankr. E.D. Mich. 1994) (paralegal engaged in unauthorized practice where she advised clients regarding proper testimony and provided them with basic information about local bankruptcy court procedures and requirements). A lay advocate who advised a victim on how her case should be presented or defended would violate BOP § 10–206.

C. Trial Activities

Lay advocates may sit at trial table or stand by the victim in the courtroom, subject to the discretion of the trial judge, provided they do not engage in any activities otherwise prohibited. They may not hold themselves out as representatives of victims or provide victims with any kind of assistance at trial that constitutes unauthorized practice.

D. Preparation of Pleadings

Lay advocates may help a victim fill out a form pleading herself by defining terms in the instructions that might be unclear to the victim or by pointing out where on the form particular information is to be set out. Lay advocates may themselves fill out a form pleading (for a person who is illiterate, for example) only if the assistance is limited to transcribing or recording verbatim the victim's own language. The typing or other transcription of a victim's own words constitutes a "purely mechanical function" permitted by BOP § 10–206. See, e.g., 65 Opinions of the Attorney General at 28. See also *Brammer v. Taylor*, 338 S.E.2d 207, 212 (W. Va. 1985) (merely typing a legal instrument drafted by another person, or merely reducing words of another person to writing, does not constitute the unauthorized preparation of a legal document).

On the other hand, lay advocates may not assist in filling out forms or form pleadings "using their own words," or summarizing information given them by a client. This degree of aid rises impermissibly to the level of applying facts to the law in the "preparation" of a legal document. See *Matter of Bright*, 171 B.R. at 803–04 (deciding where information should be placed on bankruptcy forms and in what format, deciding what property should be listed, and adding language to forms

not dictated by clients constitute unauthorized practice); *Akron Bar Association v. Singleton*, 573 N.E.2d 1249, 1250 (Ohio Bd. Unauth. Prac. 1990) (selling of "dissolution kits" is unauthorized practice of law when layperson prepared dissolution of marriage form pleadings based on information sheet completed by clients); *State v. Hunt*, 880 P.2d 96, 100 (Wash. App. 1994) (preparation of legal forms constitutes unauthorized practice).

E. Government Advocacy

Lay advocates may not urge Assistant State's Attorneys [prosecutors] or other government employees to follow a particular course of action in an individual case, if the advocate purports to do so on behalf of individual victims. This type of advocacy would be "representing" a client before a governmental unit. See BOP § 10–101 (h) (1) (ii). See also *In re Disciplinary Action Against Ray*, 452 N.W.2d 689, 693 (Minn. 1990) (advising clients in legal matter and attempting to negotiate a settlement constitutes unauthorized practice). However, advocates could speak with governmental representatives on behalf of victims' rights generally, without reference to any particular case or individual….

The prohibition against unauthorized practice undoubtedly furthers an important goal—to "protect the public from being preyed upon by…incompetent, unethical, or irresponsible representation." *In re Application of R.G.S.*, 312 Md. 626, 638, 541 A.2d 977 (1988). However, this concern would hardly seem to be paramount in this context. Rather, victims of domestic violence are being "preyed upon" in ways far more threatening than the specter of inadequate representation. Lay advocates could help victims assert legal rights that they would otherwise have no means of pursuing. Battered women need legal assistance desperately and too often cannot find it within the legal community….

[Summary]

1. A lay advocate may:
   (i) provide victims with basic information about the existence of legal rights and remedies;
   (ii) provide victims with basic information about the manner in which judicial proceedings are conducted;
   (iii) assist a victim to prepare a legal pleading or other legal document on her own behalf by defining unfamiliar terms on a form, explaining where on a form the victim is to provide certain information, and if necessary, transcribing or otherwise recording the victim's own words verbatim;
   (iv) sit with a victim at trial table, if permitted by the court; and
   (v) engage in the general advocacy of the rights of battered women as a group.

2. Except under the supervision of an attorney, a lay advocate may not:
   (i) Provide any advice relating to a victim's rights or remedies, including whether a victim's particular circumstances suggest that she should pursue a particular remedy;
   (ii) provide information about the legal aspects of judicial proceedings, such as how to present a case, call witnesses, introduce evidence, and the like;
   (iii) use the advocate's own language in preparing or filling out pleadings or other legal documents; or
   (iv) engage in advocacy before any governmental representative on behalf of an individual victim.

self-help Self-representation. Representing oneself with or without some assistance from an attorney, document service provider (DSP), online legal site, manual, or other materials. (See glossary for an additional meaning.)

pro se (on one's own behalf) Appearing for or representing oneself. Also called *in propria persona* (abbreviated *in pro per*).

litigants A party in a lawsuit.

pleading A formal litigation document filed by a party that states or responds to the claims and defenses the parties have against each other. The major pleadings are the complaint and answer.

independent contractors A self-employed person who operates his or her own business and contracts to perform tasks for others. In general, the latter do not control many of the administrative details of how the work is performed.

SELF-HELP MATERIALS AND DOCUMENT SERVICE PROVIDERS (DSPs)

A great deal of UPL controversy centers on what is called the **self-help** industry, which consists of individuals or companies that provide piecemeal assistance to persons with legal problems who are representing themselves. If the latter are in court, they are called **pro se** parties or pro se **litigants**. (Pro se means appearing for or representing oneself; a litigant is a party in a court case). The type of assistance provided by self-help providers can be varied. Examples:

- selling legal forms, manuals, or books
- typing forms or other documents
- describing legal procedures

Occasionally, a self-represented person will seek assistance from an attorney who will be asked to provide a specific service such as drafting a letter or reviewing a **pleading** that the self-represented person has prepared. (For more on such services by attorneys, see Chapter 5 for a discussion of *limited-scope* services.) More often, the assistance sought by the self-represented person will be from nonattorneys. These nonattorneys and their services are referred to as nonlegal service providers, document production services, or legal document services. Collectively, we call them *document service providers (DSPs)*. They are nonattorneys who work without attorney supervision to provide legal-document assistance to individuals who are representing themselves. Some DSPs have relationships with attorneys, but these are primarily for mutual referrals rather than for ongoing attorney supervision of the DSP. As we saw in Chapter 1, DSPs are **independent contractors**, which are self-employed individuals who perform specific tasks for others.

To gauge the scope of self-help assistance (with or without DSPs), run this search in Google, Bing, or Yahoo: self-help aa yy (for "aa" substitute the name of your state; for "yy" substitute any area of law or legal topic, e.g., self-help texas divorce, self-help maryland probate).

DSPs act within the law if they provide legal information and avoid giving legal advice. In general, they are not allowed to tell their clients which legal forms to use. Nor can they tell them what information should go on the forms. Selecting legal forms to meet the needs of a specific person and guiding someone in filling out those forms is giving legal advice and hence is the practice of law. (Note, however, that the Maryland opinion appears to follow a minority view that "explaining where on a form" a person "is to provide certain information" is *not* legal advice.)

Similar restrictions apply to someone who writes a self-help book or manual. Suppose, for example, you write a book or manual on how to sue your landlord. The book lists all the laws, provides all the forms, and gives precise guidelines on how to use the laws and how to fill out the forms. Are you practicing law? No, because you are not addressing the legal problem of a specific person. It is not the practice of law to sell law books or similar materials to the general public, even if a member of the public uses them for his or her specific legal problem. Suppose, however, that you are a DSP who sells the book and types the forms for customers. Practice of law? No. In most states, this is not the practice of law unless you provide individual help in selecting and filling out the forms. Examples:

- It is proper for nonattorneys to sell divorce forms to their clients and to charge them a fee to type the forms. But in most states, it is UPL to provide personal assistance by telling the clients which divorce forms they need and how to fill them out.
- It is proper for nonattorneys to sell probate forms to their clients and to charge them a fee to type the forms. But in most states, it is UPL to provide personal assistance by telling the clients which probate forms they need and how to fill them out.
- It is proper for nonattorneys to sell bankruptcy forms to their clients and to charge them a fee to type the forms. But in most states, it is UPL to provide personal assistance by telling the clients which bankruptcy forms they need and how to fill them out.

DSPs are controversial because of the allegation that they sometimes select forms for their clients and give them individual assistance in how to fill them out. The charge is that they do not always restrict themselves to typing services and hence are engaged in UPL despite the disclaimers on their websites and on their forms that they are not attorneys, do not work under attorney supervision, and cannot give legal advice. Occasionally, DSPs are prosecuted for engaging in UPL. The prosecution might result from a disgruntled client or an undercover investigation in which a law enforcement officer pretends to hire the DSP and discovers that the services provided include giving legal advice.

Nevertheless, the number of DSPs is steadily growing because of the high costs of hiring an attorney and the explosion in the number of people representing themselves who seek the kind of assistance that DSPs provide. In fact, serious proposals have been considered to expand the role of the DSP through limited licensing, as we will see.

Some DSPs have been given specific titles. Examples:

- Bankruptcy Petition Preparers (BPPs) in all states
- Legal Document Assistants (LDAs) in California
- Unlawful Detainer Assistants (UDAs) in California
- Legal Document Preparers (LDPs) in Arizona
- Limited License Legal Technicians (LLLTs) in Washington State

In many states, DSPs can call themselves paralegals or independent paralegals, although in some states (e.g., California, Florida, South Dakota, and Maine), the title *paralegal* (or legal assistant) can be used only by persons acting with attorney supervision.

Bankruptcy Petition Preparers (BPPs)

The most common type of DSP in the United States is the **Bankruptcy Petition Preparer (BPP)**. A BPP is a nonattorney who (without attorney supervision) is authorized to charge fees for preparing a bankruptcy petition or any other bankruptcy document that a self-represented debtor will file in a federal court. Anyone can be a BPP in any state; there are no education requirements to meet or examinations to pass. A BPP is not allowed to give legal advice or represent people in bankruptcy court. Nor can a BPP tell someone which chapter of bankruptcy to file under, what **exemptions** to claim, what debts can and cannot be **discharged** in bankruptcy, or what the tax consequences are of a bankruptcy decree. In addition:

- A BPP shall not use the word "legal" or any similar term in any advertisements. In a recent case, a court ruled that a BPP's ad offering "paralegal services" is illegal since "the term 'paralegal' fosters consumer confusion."[4]
- A BPP must print his or her name, address, and Social Security number on every document he or she prepares.
- A BPP must give the debtor a copy of each document the debtor signs at the time of signing.
- Within ten days after the filing of a petition, a BPP shall file a declaration disclosing any fee received from the debtor and any unpaid fee charged to the debtor.
- The bankruptcy court will disallow any BPP fee found to be in excess of the value of services rendered for the documents prepared.
- Each violation of the regulations can lead to a fine of $500, and a BPP can be forced to pay the debtor $2,000 or twice the amount the debtor paid for the BPP's services (whichever is greater) plus the debtor's attorney fees.[5]

Legal Document Assistant (LDA) and Unlawful Detainer Assistant (UDA) (California)

California has also imposed substantial restrictions on DSPs. It has created two titles to cover individuals who sell their services directly to the public without attorney supervision: the legal document assistant (LDA) and the unlawful detainer assistant (UDA).

- The **legal document assistant (LDA)** provides self-help assistance to a member of the public who is representing himself or herself in a legal matter.
- The **unlawful detainer assistant (UDA)** provides self-help assistance to landlords or tenants who are bringing or defending actions for the possession of land. (*Detainer* means withholding or keeping something in one's custody.)

Here are some of the important controls imposed on these DSPs to avoid being charged with UPL:

- LDAs and UDAs must meet minimum education requirements.

bankruptcy petition preparer (BPP) A nonattorney who is authorized to charge fees for preparing (without attorney supervision) a bankruptcy petition or any other bankruptcy document that a self-represented debtor will file in a federal court.

exemptions The right of a debtor to keep designated property rather than make it available to creditors to satisfy debts, particularly in bankruptcy. (See glossary for an additional meaning.)

discharged Extinguish; forgive a debt so that it is no longer owed.

legal document assistant (LDA) A nonattorney in California who is authorized to charge fees for providing self-help assistance (without attorney supervision) to anyone representing himself or herself in a legal matter.

unlawful detainer assistant (UDA) A nonattorney in California who is authorized to charge fees for providing self-help assistance (without attorney supervision) to landlords or tenants in actions for the possession of land.

ministerial Involving a duty that is to be performed in a prescribed manner without the exercise of judgment or discretion.

bond An obligation to perform an act (e.g., pay a sum of money) upon the occurrence of a designated condition. Here the condition is a failure to comply with the LDA and UDA regulations.

- LDAs and UDAs are limited to providing self-help services consisting of typing legal documents or otherwise completing them in a **ministerial** manner (meaning that no judgment or discretion is used when helping the client); the documents must be selected by the person being helped, who is representing him- or herself.
- LDAs and UDAs cannot provide any "kind of advice, explanation, opinion, or recommendation to a consumer about possible legal rights, remedies, defenses, options, selection of forms, or strategies."
- LDAs and UDAs must be *registered*. They must obtain a certificate of registration from the county clerk. As we saw in Exhibit 4-1, registration (also called *enrollment*) is the process by which the names of individuals or institutions are listed on a roster kept by a governmental or nongovernmental body. There may or may not be qualifications that must be met before a name can go on the list. For the LDA and UDA, there are government requirements, e.g., minimum education requirements and posting a bond (see below).
- The application for a certificate of registration must be accompanied by a fee of $175 and a $25,000 **bond** to ensure compliance with the regulations.
- The certificate or registration must be renewed every two years. Once an LDA or UDA is properly registered, the county clerk will issue an identification card that lists the title "legal document assistant" or "unlawful detainer assistant," the date the registration expires, a photograph of the registrant, and the following two statements: "This person is not a lawyer" and "The county clerk has not evaluated this person's knowledge, experience, or services." See Exhibit 4-3.
- LDAs and UDAs must give their clients a written contract that states the services to be performed and the cost. The contract must also inform the client where he or she may be able to obtain free or low-cost legal services from an attorney and that the LDA or UDA is not an attorney and cannot give advice, explanations, or recommendations on legal matters.
- An LDA or UDA cannot call him- or herself a paralegal or legal assistant.
- An LDA or UDA cannot retain in his or her possession any original documents of a client.
- If an LDA or UDA violates these regulations, the unpaid fees could be forfeited and the collected fees could be ordered returned to the client. In addition, the LDA or UDA could be fined up to $2,000 and imprisoned for up to a year.
- Suspended or disbarred attorneys cannot register as LDAs or UDAs.[6]

Exhibit 4-3	Example of the Identity Card of a Legal Document Assistant (LDA) in California

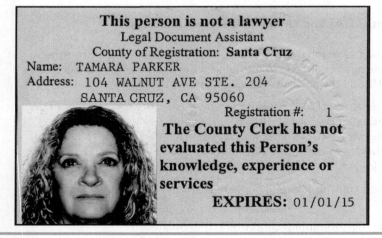

This person is not a lawyer
Legal Document Assistant
County of Registration: **Santa Cruz**
Name: TAMARA PARKER
Address: 104 WALNUT AVE STE. 204
SANTA CRUZ, CA 95060
Registration #:   1
The County Clerk has not evaluated this Person's knowledge, experience or services
EXPIRES: 01/01/15

Reprinted with permission of Tamara Parker (www.legaldocumentassistant.net).

Legal Document Preparer (LDP) (Arizona)

Arizona has also created a DSP position. A **legal document preparer (LDP)** in Arizona is a person who has been certified to "prepare or provide documents" without attorney supervision for citizens engaged in self-representation in any legal matter. More formally, he or she is known as an *Arizona certified legal document preparer (AZCLDP)*. Like the LDA (legal document assistant) in California, Arizona LDPs are subject to significant restrictions on the services they can provide. They can give "general legal information but may not give legal advice."[7]

An LDP must tell their clients that they are not attorneys. To be certified, LDPs must be at least eighteen years old and be of good moral character. In addition, they must meet minimum educational/experience qualifications. Examples of the latter include graduation from paralegal school, law school, or high school plus two years of legal experience under the supervision of an attorney or another certified LDP. Applicants must pass an examination on subjects related to the preparation of legal documents. Once certified, they must complete ten hours of **continuing legal education (CLE)** every year. The program was created by the Arizona Supreme Court and is administered by a Board of Legal Document Preparers, which consists of eleven members, five of whom must have experience as LDPs.

Limited License Legal Technicians (LLLTs) (Washington State)

The newest and most promising DSP in the country is the *limited license legal technician (LLLT)* in Washington State. This DSP is significantly different from the DSPs we have discussed thus far (BPP, LDA, UDA, and LDP). Unlike these other DSPs, the LLLT program in Washington State is designed to *expand* the scope of the services that a nonattorney can provide the public without attorney supervision. A recent law review article called the creation of LLLTs "a single monumental moment for the legal profession and consumers."[7a] We will discuss LLLTs later in the chapter under the topic of the limited license.

Rosemary Furman

One of the first DSPs to gain national recognition was Rosemary Furman, a legal secretary in Florida. Her critics called her a danger to society. Admirers such as the DSPs in the Florida Association of Legal Document Preparers embraced her as our "very own Rosa Parks."[8]

Believing that people should be able to solve uncomplicated legal problems without hiring an attorney, Furman established the Northside Secretarial Service in Jacksonville. She compiled and sold packets of legal forms (for $50) on divorce, name changes, and adoptions. The price included her personal assistance in filling out and filing the forms. The Florida Bar Association challenged her for engaging in UPL. She was convicted and sentenced to thirty days in jail.

Widespread support for Ms. Furman developed. Her case soon became a cause célèbre for those seeking increased access to the legal system for the poor and the middle class.[9] Many were outraged at the legal profession and the judiciary for their treatment of Ms. Furman. The CBS program *60 Minutes* did a story that was favorable to her cause. Other national media, including *Newsweek*, covered the case. Warner Brothers considered doing a docudrama on the story. Rosemary Furman struck a responsive chord when she claimed that for every $50 she earned, an attorney lost $500. An editorial in the *Gainesville Sun* said, "Throw Rosemary Furman in jail? Surely not after the woman forced the Florida bar and the judiciary to confront its responsibility to the poor. Anything less than a 'thank you' note would indeed show genuine vindictiveness on the part of the legal profession." There were, however, other views. An editorial in *USA Today* said that what she was doing was illegal. "If she can give legal advice, so can charlatans, frauds, and rip-off artists." Here is an overview of the main events in the Furman case:

- 1978 & 1979: The Florida Bar Association takes Rosemary Furman to court, alleging that she is practicing law without a license.
- 1979: The Florida Supreme Court rules against her. She is enjoined from continuing the UPL.
- 1982: The Florida Bar Association again brings a complaint against her business, alleging that she was continuing the UPL.
- 1983: A county circuit judge finds her in contempt of court for violating the 1979 order. The judge makes this decision in a nonjury hearing. She is then ordered to serve thirty days in jail.
- 1984: The U.S. Supreme Court refuses to hear the case. This has the effect of allowing the state jail sentence to stand. The Court is not persuaded by her argument that she

legal document preparer (LDP) A nonattorney in Arizona who is authorized to charge fees for providing self-help assistance (without attorney supervision) to anyone representing himself or herself in a legal matter. Also called *Arizona certified legal document preparer (AZCLDP)*.

continuing legal education (CLE) Training in the law (usually short term) that a person receives after completing his or her formal legal training or after becoming employed.

should have been granted a jury trial of her peers rather than having been judged solely by a profession (attorneys and judges) that was biased against her.

- Her attorneys ask the Florida Supreme Court to vacate the jail sentence if she agrees to close her business.
- The Florida Bar Association tells the Florida Supreme Court that the jail term is a fitting punishment and should be served.
- 1984: The Florida Supreme Court orders her to serve the jail sentence for UPL. (To read the opinion, go to scholar.google.com, select *Case law*, and enter *451 So. 2d 808* in the search box.)
- 1984: Rosemary Furman is granted clemency from the thirty-day jail term by the Florida governor and his clemency board. She does not have to go to jail.
- Furman and her attorneys announce that they will work on a constitutional amendment defining the practice of law to make it easier for people obtain help without attorneys in uncomplicated civil cases. Says Ms. Furman, "I have only begun to fight."

The Furman case has had an impact in Florida and elsewhere in the country. Recently, for example, Florida made an important change in the definition of unauthorized practice of law. Under this definition, it

"shall not constitute the unauthorized practice of law for a nonlawyer to engage in limited oral communication to assist a self-represented person in the completion of blanks on a Supreme Court Approved Form. In assisting in the completion of the form, oral communication by non-lawyers is restricted to those communications reasonably necessary to elicit factual information to complete the blanks on the form and inform the self-represented person how to file the form. The nonlawyer may not give legal advice or give advice on remedies or courses of action."[10]

Later in this chapter, we will discuss the even more dramatic concept of limited licensing for paralegals, which is being considered in a number of states. Some have referred to these developments as "the long shadow of Rosemary Furman."

INTERACTIVE COMPUTER PROGRAMS

A good deal of forms assistance is also available through self-help interactive Internet sites or stand-alone computer software programs. They are designed to help individuals complete many legal tasks such as preparing a will, incorporating a business, and drafting divorce pleadings. (In Google, Bing, or Yahoo, run this search: do-it-yourself law assistance.) The question-and-answer format of these programs allows documents to be selected and prepared in response to the specific facts typed in by the users. Some courts have said that this is the equivalent of providing personal assistance on a person's specific legal problem and hence is the practice of law. Most courts, however, have disagreed, on the theory that the website or software is nothing more than the online equivalent of a how-to-do-it book. Yet many traditional attorneys are hostile toward computer-driven self-help services. One attorney argues that they delude and exploit people: "It's like the sick person who calls the doctor and the doctor says 'cough on the phone, I'll tell you what's wrong with you.'"[11]

The online do-it-yourself programs are careful to point out that they do not practice law and cannot give legal advice. They make referrals to attorneys whenever a standard question cannot be answered by standardized answers. If, however, the site has human interaction with the user that consists of making corrections and suggestions based on the answers provided by the user, there is a danger that a court will rule that the program is more than a mere self-help service and that the human interaction turns the transaction into the practice of law.

Such concerns, however, have not stopped the growth of online alternatives to what used to be the exclusive domain of attorneys. Online competition has struck a note of panic in the minds of some bar associations. "A tidal wave is hitting the legal profession," according to the president of the Texas State Bar. Here is the perspective of the new president of the National Conference of Bar Presidents:

"If you think nostalgically about the practice of law and how it used to be, then you are on the train tracks and not on the train…. The development of artificial intelligence along with increased Internet search capabilities is making access to answers for complex legal questions easier and cheaper." Web-based legal information and document sites such as LegalZoom, Cybersettle, CompleteCase.com, and Google Scholar are providing basic legal information that lawyers once provided for a fee. "Why is someone going to pay $700 to have a lawyer prepare a will when they can get it for $49 online?… We have had a monopoly on answering legal questions about the law. But the consumer—our former clients—can now get that information for free on Google…. [T]here are now thousands of small town and small firm lawyers who once depended on those consumers who may not make it."[12]

ANTITRUST ISSUES

To combat the problem of competition from law-related occupations, bar associations have launched two major strategies: (1) adopting statements of principles for law-related industries and (2) creating a model definition of the practice of law. Both of these strategies have failed, largely because of **antitrust law**, which is the law governing unlawful interference with competition such as through price fixing, monopolies, and other restraints of trade.

Some occupations regularly engage in law-related activities. Such occupations include accountants, claims adjusters, real estate agents, life insurance agents, and officers of trust departments of banks. Some of these law-related occupations have gone directly to the legislature to seek enactment of statutes that authorize what would otherwise be the unauthorized practice of law. In many instances, they have been successful. Examples of such authorization:

> Code of Georgia, § 15–19–52. [A] title insurance company may prepare such papers as it thinks proper or necessary in connection with a title which it proposes to insure, in order, in its opinion, for it to be willing to insure the title, where no charge is made by it for the papers.
>
> Utah Code Ann. § 61–2f–306(1). A principal broker may fill out any documents associated with the closing of a real estate transaction.

The effect of such statutes is to allow members of designated occupations to perform certain legal tasks that are intimately related to their work without having to hire attorneys or without forcing their clients to hire them.

Statements of Principles

To try to curtail or eliminate the law-related activities of these occupations, the organized bar negotiated **statements of principles** with them. A statement of principles (sometimes called a treaty) is a set of guidelines negotiated by bar associations and specified law-related occupations that distinguish between those activities of the occupations that do not constitute the unauthorized practice of law and those that do. The guidelines attempt to identify boundary lines and methods of resolving difficulties.

Most of these treaties, however, have been ineffective in defining the kinds of law-related activities that can and cannot be performed by nonattorneys. A tremendous amount of effort and money is needed to negotiate, monitor, and enforce the treaties. The resources are simply not available. Furthermore, there is a concern that such efforts by attorneys to restrain competition might violate the antitrust laws. In light of all these difficulties, the treaties either have been withdrawn or are being ignored.

The speech on the antitrust law and attorney fees in Exhibit 4-4 was delivered by a deputy assistant attorney general in the Antitrust Division of the U.S. Department of Justice (DOJ). He discusses the antitrust implications of the *statements of principles*. The speech mentions two major opinions of the U.S. Supreme Court:

- *Bates v. State Bar of Arizona.* This case held that truthful attorney advertising can no longer be completely banned. Such advertising is commercial speech protected by the First Amendment.[13]
- *Goldfarb v. Virginia State Bar.* This case held that the legal profession could no longer impose **minimum-fee schedules** on attorneys. The schedules required attorneys to charge minimum fees for specified legal services. Charging below that amount was an ethical violation. The Court held that this requirement operated as a fixed, rigid price floor and therefore constituted illegal price fixing.[14]

Bates and *Goldfarb* are landmark decisions because of the dramatic change they brought about in attorney advertising and fee regulation.

antitrust law The law governing unlawful interferences with competition such as through price fixing, monopolies, and other restraints of trade.

statements of principles Guidelines negotiated by bar associations and specified law-related occupations that distinguish between those activities of the occupations that do not constitute the unauthorized practice of law and those that do.

minimum-fee schedules A bar-association list of the lowest fees an attorney can ethically charge for specific kinds of legal services. Such lists (schedules) have been held to violate antitrust laws.

Exhibit 4-4	Antitrust Law and the Legal Profession

The Legal Profession: A Bow to the Past—a Glimpse of the Future
by Joseph Sims

Today, legal services are being advertised on television. [This occurred only after the 1977 decision of the U.S. Supreme Court in *Bates v State Bar of Arizona* that truthful advertising by lawyers is commercial speech protected by the First Amendment and hence cannot be completely banned.] We lawyers as a group have grumbled and argued, fought and yelled, struggled and been confused — but there are now lawyers advertising on television. Even a casual observer cannot fail to appreciate the significance of this change.

Competition, slowly but surely, is coming to the legal profession. This opening of traditional doors, the breaking of traditional barriers is the result of many forces—the number of new lawyers, the awakening of consumerism, [the growth of the Internet], and the growing realization that the complexity of our society requires legal assistance in more and more areas. But one contributing factor has been antitrust litigation and the Department of Justice....

[The Supreme Court fired the shot heard 'round the bar in the 1975 unanimous decision *Goldfarb v. Virginia State Bar.*] The Court held that the minimum-fee schedule challenged by the Goldfarbs violated Section 1 of the Sherman Act. This decision broke the dam and released the flood of change that we see engulfing the profession today. For better or worse, the Goldfarbs had set in motion a series of events that were to change the character of the legal profession forever.

The Court decided several things in *Goldfarb*, but the most important was that the legal profession was subject to the antitrust laws—there was no "professional exemption." The response to *Goldfarb* was fascinating. A large number of private suits were filed challenging various aspects of bar regulation....

[An] area sure to be controversial in the future is unauthorized practice. There is already at least one antitrust challenge, against the Virginia State Bar, seeking to prohibit the bar from promulgating unauthorized practice opinions. This case, which involves title insurance, is a direct challenge to the extraordinary power that the legal profession now has—in most states—to define the limits of its own monopoly. It would be strange indeed for a state to hand over to, say its steel industry, not only the power to regulate entry into the industry and the conduct of those within it, but also the power to define what the industry was. In many states, that is exactly the power the organized bar now has, and that power is being challenged as inconsistent with the antitrust laws.

The heart of this challenge is that lawyers shouldn't be deciding what is the practice of law—defining the scope of the legal monopoly. The papers filed in that case...indicate that the objection is not to such a decision being made; the objection is to the State's delegation of that power to the [legal] profession. [O]f course, the principle behind this lawsuit could be expanded not only to other subject matter areas, but also to arrangements between the organized bar and other professions which have as their basic result the division of commercial responsibilities.

For example, the American Bar Association [once] entered into "statements of principles" with respect to the practice of law with a variety of other professions and occupations ranging from accountants to claim adjusters, publishers, social workers, and even professional engineers. These documents generally set forth the joint views of the professions as to which activities fall within the practice of law and which activities are proper for members of the other profession. They nearly all provide that each profession will advise its clients to seek out members of the other profession in appropriate circumstances.

As a general rule, two competitors may not agree with each other to allocate markets, or bids, or even functions; if they do, they violate the antitrust laws. At the least, this traditional antitrust principle raises some questions about the legal effect of such "statements of principles." [Indeed, because of these questions, such statements are no longer used.]

Model Definition of the Practice of Law

Earlier, we quoted the 1969 view of the American Bar Association that it "it is neither necessary nor desirable to attempt the formulation of a single, specific definition of what constitutes the practice of law." In 2002, the ABA changed its mind and began drafting a model definition of the practice of law. Under the proposal, the practice of law would be defined as the

"application of legal principles and judgment with regard to the circumstances or objectives of a person that require the knowledge and skill of a person trained in the law."[15]

There was nothing dramatically new in this definition. (Indeed, the proposed definition simply restates the professional-judgment test that we examined earlier in Exhibit 4-2.) What was new and highly controversial were some presumptions on what activities would constitute the practice of law under the new definition. The presumptions disturbed the Antitrust Division of the U.S. Department of Justice (DOJ) and a similar division of the Federal Trade Commission (FTC). The DOJ and FTC warned the ABA that the presumptions in the proposal had serious monopoly and antitrust implications.

Under the ABA proposal, a person who engaged in the following activities on behalf of another would be "presumed to be practicing law":

- Selecting, drafting, or completing agreements and other legal documents that affect the legal rights of a person;
- Negotiating legal rights or duties on behalf of a person;

- Representing a person before a body with the authority to resolve a legal dispute (an "adjudicative body"), including, but not limited to, preparing or filing documents or conducting discovery;
- Giving advice or counsel to persons as to their legal rights or responsibilities or to those of others.

The DOJ and FTC said that these provisions, particularly the first two, were overly broad because they would prohibit nonattorneys from offering a number of limited services they currently provide to the benefit of consumers but in competition with attorneys. Here are examples of such services:

- Realtors® selecting, explaining, drafting, and negotiating documents used in the sale of real estate
- Tenants' associations informing renters of landlords' and tenants' legal rights and duties, often in the context of a particular landlord-tenant problem
- Experienced nonattorney employees advising their employer about what their company must do to comply with state labor laws or safety regulations
- Income-tax preparers and accountants interpreting federal and state tax codes, family-law codes, and general-partnership laws, and providing advice to their clients based on this legal information;
- Investment bankers and other business planners providing advice to their clients that includes information about various laws;
- Interactive software allowing consumers to select and draft wills, trusts, and other legal documents.

The DOJ and FTC did not say that a nonattorney should have the same right to practice law as an attorney. They simply said that the ABA failed to provide evidence of the kind of consumer harm that would justify a requirement that only attorneys should be able to provide the services listed in the examples. Indeed, competition between attorneys and nonattorneys for such services is healthy for the consumer:

> Together, the DOJ and the FTC have become increasingly concerned about efforts to prevent nonlawyers from competing with attorneys in the provision of certain services through the adoption of Unauthorized Practice of Law opinions and laws by state bar agencies, courts, and legislatures.... [W]e urge the ABA not to adopt the current proposed Definition, which, in our judgment, is overbroad and could restrain competition between lawyers and nonlawyers to provide similar services to American consumers. If adopted by state governments, the proposed Definition is likely to raise costs for consumers and limit their competitive choices. There is no evidence before the ABA of which we are aware that consumers are hurt by this competition and there is substantial evidence that they benefit from it. Consequently, we recommend that the proposed Model Definition be substantially narrowed or rejected.[16]

Stung by this criticism, the ABA chose to abandon the proposed definition. The ABA did not want to risk an even broader antitrust challenge against the legal profession that the DOJ and FTC appeared to be on the verge of launching.

Unlicensed Practice of Dentistry

Finally, we examine an antitrust case currently in the courts that has implications for the bar association's regulation of nonattorney providers of law and law-related services. The case involved the practice of dentistry:

- The North Carolina State Board of Dental Examiners (BDE) concluded that nondentists who provide teeth-whitening services are engaged in the unlicensed practice of dentistry.
- The Federal Trade Commission (FTC) ruled that the BDE was engaged in unfair competition in violation of the antitrust laws. Furthermore the fact that members of the BDE included dentists who offered teeth-whitening services created a conflict of interest in preventing nondentists from providing these services at a substantially lower cost to the consumer.
- The FTC decision was affirmed by the U.S. Court of Appeals for the Fourth Circuit, which said "It is not difficult to understand that forcing low-cost teeth-whitening providers from the market has a tendency to increase a consumer's price for that service."[16a]

The U.S. Supreme Court has granted certiorari, meaning that it will review the conclusion of the FTC and the Court of Appeals for the Fourth Circuit. If a dental board violates antitrust law by shutting down nondentist providers of a competing dental service, is it a violation of antitrust law for a bar association to take action against nonattorneys who provide competing services? The decisions of the FTC and the Fourth Circuit suggest that the answer is yes. We await a decision of the U.S. Supreme Court to find out whether the BDE violated antitrust law and whether its decision has broader antitrust implications for the legal profession.

ROLES FOR PARALEGALS IN COURT PROCEEDINGS

We turn now to the extent to which nonattorneys can represent clients in courts and in administrative agencies. Court representation by paralegals is nonexistent in most courts and quite limited in a few courts. Yet the extent of nonattorney representation in courts is still worthy of note. Representation at administrative agencies, on the other hand, is more extensive.

COURT APPEARANCES

In the vast majority of courts in this country, only attorneys can represent someone in a judicial proceeding. There are, however, some limited exceptions.

Lower Courts

In some lower courts in the country, particularly in the West, parties can have nonattorneys represent them. Examples include justice of the peace courts, magistrate's courts, and small claims courts. Restrictions might be placed on such representation. The nonattorney might be limited to a one-time representation or to cases involving the nonattorney's family or business associates. Here are two examples of lower-court representation by nonattorneys in Minnesota and the District of Columbia:

- Minnesota

  The conciliation court in Minnesota handles small claims (claims under $7,500) and allows nonattorney representation.

  > Minnesota Statutes Annotated, § 491A.02. A corporation, partnership, limited liability company, sole proprietorship or association may be represented in conciliation court by an officer, manager, or partner…or may appoint a natural person who is an employee…to appear on its behalf to settle a claim in conciliation court…. [This] representation does not constitute the practice of law….

Mary Ford is a paralegal who works for the general counsel of the University of Minnesota. She has represented the university in conciliation court twenty times over the past six years. The university has seven paralegals who have specialties in real estate, health, and international law. The paralegals are given a court document signed by the university that gives them broad authority "to commence, prosecute, defend, satisfy or settle any claim or cause of action brought by or against" the university in conciliation court. Commenting on her role, Mary says, "The more time I have to talk to witnesses, gather evidence and prepare the oral presentation, the more effective I can be in representing the university."[17]

- District of Columbia

  In landlord-tenant actions in the District of Columbia, a corporation can be *defended* in court by one of its nonattorney employees.[18] If, however, the corporation files a **counterclaim**, the corporation must be represented by an attorney. Also, the corporation cannot *bring* or initiate a landlord-tenant action through a nonattorney; the authorization is limited to defending such actions against it.

U.S. Tax Court

The U.S. Tax Court is a **court of record** established by Congress. (See the chart of the federal judicial system in Exhibit 6-4 of Chapter 6.) Representation of clients before the court includes filing petitions, making motions, and acting as a trial advocate.[19] There are two categories of persons who can be admitted to "practice" before the court: attorneys and nonattorneys. Here is the rule on practice by nonattorney applicants:

counterclaim A claim by one side in a case (usually the defendant) that is filed in response to a claim asserted by an opponent (usually the plaintiff).

court of record A court that is required to maintain a record of the proceedings before it, including a word-for-word account of what occurred.

Nonattorney Applicants. An applicant who is not an attorney at law must…, as a condition of being admitted to practice, satisfy the Court, by means of a written examination given by the Court, that the applicant possesses the requisite qualifications to provide competent representation before the Court. Written examinations for applicants who are not attorneys at law will be held no less often than every 2 years….[20]

Native American Courts

Tribal courts on Indian reservations have jurisdiction over designated civil and criminal matters involving Native Americans. In many of these courts, both parties are represented by nonattorney advocates. (See Native American Law in the section on paralegal specialties in Chapter 2.) Examples:

- In Arizona, nonattorneys can be licensed as "tribal advocates" to represent clients before the Salt River Pima-Maricopa Tribal Court.[21]
- In Utah, a party in the tribal court of the Ute Indian Tribe of Utah has the right to be represented by an attorney or by a lay counselor. "Any person appearing as a lay counselor shall be subject to the same ethical obligations of honesty and confidentiality towards his client as would be a professional attorney, and the attorney-client testimonial privilege shall apply."[22]
- In Montana, the Assiniboine and Sioux Tribes Fort Peck Tribal nonattorney lay counselors must pass a bar examination administered by the tribe.[23]
- In Nebraska, a nonattorney who has successfully completed a certified paralegal training program is eligible for admission to practice before the Courts of the Winnebago Tribe.[24]

Nonattorney Government Agency Representatives in Court

Government employees occasionally act in a representative or semirepresentative capacity in court proceedings, even though they are not attorneys. For example, the U.S. Supreme Court has noted that a North Carolina agency (the Department of Social Services) is sometimes represented by nonattorney social workers in cases involving the termination of parental rights.[25]

Nonattorney Court Employees

A number of states have hired nonattorney court employees to act as advisors or facilitators for *pro se* parties (persons who are representing themselves), particularly in divorce and other family-law cases. The employee does not represent the person in court but is available to answer legal questions about which forms or pleadings to file, how to fill them out or draft them, and where to file them—all classic examples of what attorneys do when practicing law.

Calendar Calls

Litigation attorneys often spend unproductive time traveling to court and waiting around simply to give documents to the judge and to set dates for the various stages of pretrial and trial proceedings. Another problem is that an attorney may have to be in two different courtrooms at the same time. For example, an early morning hearing may be unexpectedly extended, preventing the attorney from appearing at a previously scheduled mid-morning proceeding in another courtroom on a different case. In such situations, wouldn't it be helpful if the attorney's paralegal could "appear" in court during **calendar call** for the limited purpose of delivering papers to the judge, asking for a new date that the attorney instructs the paralegal to request, or presenting some other message? In most states, such activity is strictly prohibited. Court appearances are attorney-only functions.

A Kentucky paralegal learned about this prohibition in a dramatic way. Her attorney was involved in a trial at the Jefferson Circuit Court. He asked the paralegal to go to another courtroom during "Motion Hour," where attorneys make motions and schedule future proceedings on a case. He told her to ask for a hearing date on another case that he had pending. She did so. When the case was called during Motion Hour, she rose, identified herself as the attorney's paralegal, and gave the message to the judge, asking for the hearing date. Opposing counsel was outraged. He verbally assaulted the paralegal in the courtroom and filed a motion to hold the paralegal and her attorney in contempt of court for UPL. When a hearing was later

calendar call The time in court when a case on the calendar (docket) is called for a determination by the judge of the next step in the proceeding. Also called *docket call.*

law clerk An attorney's employee who is in law school studying to become an attorney or who has graduated from law school and is waiting to pass the bar examination. If law clerks work only in the summer, they are sometimes called *summer associates*. (See glossary for additional meanings.)

continuance The adjournment or postponement of a proceeding until a later date.

held on this motion, members of a local paralegal association packed the courtroom. Tensions were high. After a hearing on the matter, the judge denied the contempt motion. The audience broke out into loud applause. "Apparently the judge concluded that [the paralegal] had rendered no service involving legal knowledge or advice, but had merely transmitted to the court [the attorney's] message regarding disposition of the motion. She had been performing a function that was administrative, not legal in nature."[26]

A celebrated Illinois opinion, *People v. Alexander*, took a position similar to that of the Kentucky court. In this opinion, the defendant was an unlicensed **law clerk** who appeared before the court to state that his employing attorney could not be present in court at the moment because he was trying a case elsewhere. On behalf of his employer, the law clerk requested a **continuance**. The defendant's actions were challenged. It was argued that *any* appearance by nonattorneys before a court to give information on the availability of counsel or the status of litigation constitutes UPL. The Illinois court in *People v. Alexander* took the unique position that this was not the practice of law.

CASE

People v. Alexander
53 Ill. App. 2d 299, 202 N.E.2d 841
(Appellate Court of Illinois, First District, 1964)

(To read this case online, go to Google Scholar (scholar.google.com), click *Case law*, and type 202 N.E.2d 841 in the search box.)

In the case of *People ex rel. Illinois State Bar Ass'n v. People's Stock Yards State Bank*, 344 Ill. 462 at page 476, 176 N.E. 901 at page 907, wherein a bank was prosecuted for the unauthorized practice of law, the following quotation is relied upon:

According to the generally understood definition of the practice of law in this country, it embraces the preparation of pleadings, and other papers incident to actions and special proceedings, and the management of such actions and proceedings on behalf of clients before judges and courts.

Since this statement relates to the appearance and management of proceedings in court on behalf of a client, we do not believe it can be applied to a situation where a clerk hired by a law firm presents information to the court on behalf of his employer.

We agree with the trial judge that clerks should not be permitted to make motions or participate in other proceedings which can be considered as "managing" the litigation. However, if apprising the court of an employer's engagement or inability to be present constitutes the making of a motion, we must hold that clerks may make such motions for continuances without being guilty of the unauthorized practice of law. Certainly with the large volume of cases appearing on

the trial calls these days, it is imperative that this practice be followed.

In *Toth v. Samuel Phillipson & Co.*, 250 Ill. App. 247 (1928), the court said at page 250,

It is well known in this county where numerous trial courts are sitting at the same time[,] the exigencies of such a situation require that trial attorneys be represented by their clerical force to respond to some of the calls, and that the court acts upon their response the same as if the attorneys of record themselves appeared in person.

After that opinion was handed down, the number of judges was substantially increased in the former circuit and superior courts and the problem of answering court calls has at least doubled. We cannot add to the heavy burden of lawyers who in addition to responding to trial calls must answer pretrial calls and motion calls—all held in the morning—by insisting that a lawyer must personally appear to present to a court a motion for a continuance on grounds of engagement or inability to appear because of illness or other unexpected circumstances. To reduce the backlog, trial lawyers should be kept busy actually trying lawsuits and not answering court calls.

An ethics opinion in North Carolina agrees with the position of the *Alexander* case on calendar calls by nonattorneys:

[A] lawyer may have a non-lawyer employee deliver a message to a court holding calendar call, if the lawyer is unable to attend due to a scheduling conflict with another court or other legitimate reason.[27]

In a few courts, formalized roles for paralegals have been established. In the Allen County Superior Court of Indiana, for example, employees of attorneys are allowed to "set Pre-Trial Conferences and all other hearing dates except trials."[28] A similar program exists in the

Spokane County District Court and Superior Court in Washington State. Once paralegals are registered with the local bar association, they can present **ex parte** and **uncontested** orders to the court. See Exhibit 4-5.

Exhibit 4-5	Paralegals, Rule 10

(Superior Court of Washington State)

Paralegals who are currently registered with the Spokane County Bar Association for the purpose of presentation of such orders may personally present agreed, ex-parte and uncontested orders signed by counsel, based solely upon the documents presented and the record in the file. Said privilege may be revoked or limited by the Court for noncompliance with this rule, or other misconduct, regardless of whether the Paralegal is permitted to present orders before other Courts.

Source: Spokane County Bar Association, Paralegal Registration (www.spokanebar.org/paralegal-reg.html) (www.courts.wa.gov/court_rules).

It must be emphasized that these examples of nonattorney involvement in court tasks such as answering calendar calls in Kentucky, Illinois, North Carolina, Indiana, and Washington State are isolated examples. Such involvement is not allowed in the vast majority of courts in the country. Most states are likely to agree with the Tennessee ethics opinion that concluded that it would be improper for attorneys to allow a paralegal to "make appearances for these attorneys at docket soundings held in open court for the purpose of scheduling cases."[29] Indeed, the opinion said that an attorney who allowed such appearances would be subject to discipline for assisting a nonattorney in UPL. Yet the authorizations do exist in the examples cited and the likelihood is that we will see more such authorizations in the future.

JAILHOUSE LAWYERS

Before turning to nonattorney representation in administrative agencies, we should say a word about incarcerated nonattorneys who provide legal services in our prisons. These nonattorneys cannot represent other inmates in court, but, under certain circumstances, they can give other inmates legal advice and draft their **pleadings**, **memoranda of law**, **appellate briefs**, and other court documents. In fact, if attorney representation is not available, the government has a constitutional duty to provide nonattorney inmate representatives with access to a law library inside prison so that they can provide their legal services to other inmates.

The value of examining inmate legal services is that it tells us something about what sometimes happens when society fails to provide a needed service.

A **jailhouse lawyer** is an inmate, usually a self-taught nonattorney, who has a limited right to provide other inmates with legal services if the institution does not provide adequate alternatives to such services. Jailhouse lawyers clearly practice law, often for fees in the form of cigarettes and cash. Some prisons attempted to prevent jailhouse lawyers from providing this legal assistance even though the prisons provided no meaningful alternatives. This prohibition was struck down, however, by the U.S. Supreme Court in *Johnson v. Avery* in 1969. The basis of the opinion was that without the jailhouse lawyer, prisoners might not have access to the courts. The concurring opinion of Justice William O. Douglas raises significant questions about justice in our society.

Notes on Johnson v. Avery

- "Jailhouse lawyers, or writ writers, as they are sometimes called, have always been part of prison society. But in recent years their numbers as well as the amount of litigation they generate, has increased substantially." One jailhouse lawyer at Soledad Prison "devotes 16 hours a day to his legal work, subscribes to dozens of legal publications (at a cost of $1,800 a year), and files a steady stream of lawsuits." Suing "has become almost a national pastime. Prisoners act no differently from other citizens in a **litigious** society."[30]

---

ex parte With only one side present (usually the plaintiff or petitioner) when court action is requested. An *ex parte order*, for example, is a court order requested by one party and issued before notice is given to the other party.

uncontested Unchallenged; without opposition or dispute.

pleadings A formal litigation document filed by a party that states or responds to the claims and defenses the parties have against each other. The major pleadings are the complaint and answer.

memoranda of law A written explanation of how one or more rules might apply to the facts of a client's case. Also called *memo, memorandum, legal memorandum.*

appellate briefs A document that a party files with an appellate court (and serves on an opponent) in which the party presents arguments on why the appellate court should affirm (approve), reverse, vacate (cancel), or otherwise modify what a lower court has done.

jailhouse lawyer An inmate, usually a self-taught nonattorney, who has a limited right to provide other inmates with legal services if the institution does not provide adequate alternatives to such services. Also called *writ writer.*

litigious (1) Inclined to resolve disputes through litigation. (2) Quarrelsome.

CASE

Johnson v. Avery
United States Supreme Court 393 U.S. 483, 89 S. Ct. 747, 21 L. Ed. 2d 718 (1969)

(To read this case online, go to Google Scholar (scholar.google.com), click *Case law,* and type *393 U.S. 483* in the search box.)

Mr. Justice DOUGLAS, concurring.

While I join the opinion of the Court [in striking down the prohibition on the activities of jailhouse lawyers] I add a few words in emphasis of the important thesis of the case.

The increasing complexities of our governmental apparatus at both the local and the federal levels have made it difficult for a person to process a claim or even to make a complaint. Social security is a virtual maze; the hierarchy that governs urban housing is often so intricate that it takes an expert to know what agency has jurisdiction over a particular complaint; the office to call or official to see for noise abatement, for a broken sewer line, or a fallen tree is a mystery to many in our metropolitan areas.

A person who has a claim assertable in faraway Washington, D.C., is even more helpless, as evidenced by the increasing tendency of constituents to rely on their congressional delegation to identify, press, and process their claims.

We think of claims as grist for the mill of the lawyers. But it is becoming abundantly clear that more and more of the effort in ferreting out the basis of claims and the agencies responsible for them and in preparing the almost endless paperwork for their prosecution is work for laymen. There are not enough lawyers to manage or supervise all of these affairs.... *Yet there is a closed-shop philosophy in the legal profession that [drastically cuts down] active roles for laymen.... That traditional, closed-shop attitude is utterly out of place in the modern world where claims pile high....* [Emphasis added.]

> If poverty lawyers are overwhelmed, some of the work can be delegated.... [to] legal technicians, comparable to nurses and lab assistants in the medical profession. Large law firms employ them, and there seems to be no reason why they cannot be used in legal services programs to relieve attorneys.... Samore, *Legal Services for the Poor,* 32 Albany L. Rev. 509, 515–516 (1968).

The plight of a man in prison may in these respects be even more acute than the plight of a person on the outside.... His imprisonment may give his wife grounds for divorce and be a factor in determining the custody of his children; and he may have pressing social security, workmen's compensation, or veterans' claims.

While the demand for legal counsel in prison is heavy, the supply is light. For private matters of a civil nature, legal counsel for the indigent in prison is almost nonexistent.

- The *Johnson* opinion stressed that the prison provided no alternative to the jailhouse lawyer. If alternatives had been available, the inmate would not be allowed to practice law. The presence of law students in the prison could be an alternative, but only if it were demonstrated that the students were meeting the need for inmate legal services. If the inmates had to wait a considerable period of time, for example, before they could be interviewed by the law students, then no adequate alternative would exist and the jailhouse lawyer could not be prevented from helping other inmates.[31]
- States must either satisfy the legal needs of their prisoners or expand the prison law library to include a more comprehensive collection of law books.[32]

ROLES FOR PARALEGALS IN ADMINISTRATIVE PROCEEDINGS

Some agencies allow representation by nonattorneys. These individuals are usually called agents, practitioners, or representatives. They engage in both *informal advocacy* (e.g., phoning agency officials on behalf of a client) and *formal advocacy* (e.g., representing a client at an **adversarial** administrative hearing within the agency). (A proceeding is adversarial if it involves conflict and an adversary, whether or not the other side is represented.)

In general, attorneys have not been happy with such nonattorney representation. For years, many bar associations argued that administrative agencies should be treated like courts; only attorneys should be allowed to provide representation before the agencies. To a large extent, this argument has not been successful in that many federal and state agencies continue to allow nonattorney representation.

adversarial Involving conflict and an adversary (opponent).

There are four main reasons some agencies allow nonattorney representation:

- Many disputes at administrative agencies do not involve large amounts of money. Hence attorney fees in such cases are relatively low—so low, in fact, that few attorneys are inclined to take the cases. This has encouraged authorities to allow nonattorney representation because nonattorneys are generally satisfied with the fees that these cases generate for them.
- Administrative proceedings often involve factual issues rather than complicated issues of law that require all the skills of an attorney. Although an agency case may raise issues of law, the more common issues before the agency are economic, statistical, or scientific.
- Administrative proceedings are conducted with more flexible procedural rules than court proceedings. Because of the relative informality of agency cases, skilled nonattorneys are deemed to be capable of providing competent representation.
- There is a concern that the combative nature of attorneys would turn every informal agency hearing or conference into a drawn-out battle. Former Chief Justice Rehnquist of the U.S. Supreme Court reflected this concern when he wrote in opposition to a proposal to increase the role of attorneys in administrative hearings. He said that attorneys might cause amicable conferences to become protracted controversies:

> "To be sure, counsel can often perform useful functions…; they may bring out facts ignored by or unknown to the authorities, or help to work out satisfactory compromises. But this is only one side of the coin. Under our **adversary system**, the role of counsel is *not* to make sure the truth is ascertained but to advance his client's cause by any ethical means. Within the limits of professional propriety, *causing delay and sowing confusion not only are his right but may be his duty.* The result [of greater attorney involvement in administrative hearings may] be to turn what might have been a short conference leading to an amicable result into a protracted controversy."[33]

adversary system A method of resolving a legal dispute whereby the parties (alone or through their advocates) argue their conflicting claims before a neutral (impartial) decision maker.

Of course, attorneys counter such concerns by pointing out (1) that resolving factual issues can often be quite complicated, (2) that legal rights can be lost if proper objections are not made even in hearings where the rules are informal, and (3) that attorneys are combative only when needed to prevent injustice.

The most serious objection to nonattorney representation at administrative agencies is that such representation is the unauthorized practice of law (UPL) under any definition of the practice of law. It is clear, for example, that in conducting some adversarial hearings before an agency, the nonattorney is practicing law in a manner that is remarkably similar to an attorney's representation of a client in court. How can an administrative agency allow a nonattorney to engage in activity that is the practice of law? The answer to this question is somewhat different for federal and state agencies.

UPL OBJECTION TO NONATTORNEY REPRESENTATION AT FEDERAL AGENCIES

If the agency permitting nonattorney representation is a federal agency (e.g., the Internal Revenue Service or the Social Security Administration), its authorization takes precedence over any state laws that would prohibit it. This principle was established in the U.S. Supreme Court case of *Sperry v. State of Florida ex rel. the Florida Bar.*[34] The case involved a nonattorney who was authorized to represent clients before the U.S. Patent Office (now the U.S. Patent and Trademark Office). The Florida Bar claimed that the nonattorney was engaged in UPL in violation of the state practice-of-law statute. The Supreme Court ruled that the **Supremacy Clause** of the U.S. Constitution gives federal laws supremacy over conflicting state laws. The Court also said,

Supremacy Clause The clause in the U.S. Constitution (art. VI, cl. 2) that has been interpreted to mean that when valid federal law conflicts with state law, federal law controls.

> Examination of the development of practice before the Patent Office and its governmental regulation reveals that:
>
> (1) nonlawyers have practiced before the Office from its inception, with the express approval of the Patent Office and to the knowledge of Congress;
> (2) during prolonged congressional study of unethical practices before the Patent Office, the right of nonlawyer agents to practice before the Office went unquestioned, and there was no suggestion that abuses might be curbed by state regulation;

(3) despite protests of the bar, Congress in enacting the Administrative Procedure Act refused to limit the right to practice before the administrative agencies to lawyers; and

(4) the Patent Office has defended the value of nonlawyer practitioners while taking steps to protect the interests which a State has in prohibiting unauthorized practice of law.

We find implicit in this history congressional (and administrative) recognition that registration in the Patent Office confers a right to practice before the Office without regard to whether the State within which the practice is conducted would otherwise prohibit such conduct....

Moreover, the extent to which specialized lay practitioners should be allowed to practice before some 40-odd federal administrative agencies, including the Patent Office, received continuing attention both in and out of Congress during the period prior to 1952. The Attorney General's Committee on Administrative Procedure which, in 1941, studied the need for procedural reform in the administrative agencies, reported that "[e]specially among lawyers' organizations there has been manifest a sentiment in recent years that only members of the bar should be admitted to practice before administrative agencies. The Committee doubts that a sweeping interdiction of nonlawyer practitioners would be wise."[35]

Hence, because of the Supremacy Clause, if a federal agency authorizes nonattorney representation, the agency can ignore state UPL rules that would prohibit such representation. Congress could change this result, but has chosen not to do so.

UPL OBJECTION TO NONATTORNEY REPRESENTATION AT STATE AGENCIES

The *Sperry* case involved an unsuccessful attempt by a bar association to prevent nonattorney representation at a federal agency. Suppose, however, that a *state* agency permits nonattorney representation. Can the bar association successfully challenge this authorization? The *Sperry* case would not apply to this question because *Sperry* covered only federal agencies.

Determining whether a state agency can allow nonattorney representation depends on who has the power to regulate the practice of law in a particular state. This is a **separation-of-powers** question. Separation of powers is the constitutional requirement that each of the legislative, executive, and judicial branches of government limit itself to the powers granted to it and not encroach upon the powers granted to the other two branches. Hence we must determine which branch of government the state constitution gives the power to regulate the practice of law.

Assume, for example, that the state legislature passes a statute that authorizes nonattorneys to represent workers' compensation clients before the state workers' compensation agency and that the state bar association challenges this authorization on the ground that such representation by a nonattorney is the UPL. How is this issue resolved? The answer depends, as indicated, on who has the power in the state to regulate the practice of law.

- If the state constitution gives the state judiciary the power to regulate the practice of law, then the legislature interfered with (encroached upon) this power by enacting a statute that granted nonattorneys the right to represent workers' compensation clients at the state agency. Only the courts can decide if nonattorneys can provide this representation. Hence the statute is invalid. The legislature has **usurped** a power of the judiciary. The statute is an unconstitutional violation of separation of powers.
- If the state constitution gives the state legislature the power to regulate the practice of law, then the legislature acted properly when it enacted a statute that granted nonattorneys the right to represent workers' compensation clients at the state agency. The statute is constitutional.

The state's highest court makes the ultimate decision on which branch (its own or the legislative branch) has the power to regulate the practice of law.

In some states, the decision is difficult to make because the state constitution gives *both* the judicial branch and the legislative branch this power. If the workers' compensation statute in our example was enacted in a state where the power to regulate the practice of law is shared by both branches, the highest court must decide if the statute encroaches on the judiciary's share

separation of powers The constitutional requirement that each of the legislative, executive, and judicial branches of government limit itself to the powers granted to it and not encroach upon the powers granted to the other two branches.

usurp To unlawfully exercise a position or power that belongs to another. The noun form is *usurpation*.

of this power. If it does, the statute is unconstitutional as a violation of separation of powers. If it doesn't, the statute is constitutional.

We turn now to an overview of nonattorney representation at agencies, first at federal agencies and then at state and local agencies. Later, in Chapter 15, we will examine specific techniques of paralegal advocacy within administrative agencies. Here our concern is the extent of the authorization that exists to provide this representation.

NONATTORNEY PRACTICE BEFORE FEDERAL ADMINISTRATIVE AGENCIES

Congress has passed a statute, the **Administrative Procedure Act (APA)**, that governs procedures before federal administrative agencies such as the Social Security Administration (SSA) and the Federal Trade Commission (FTC). The act gives each federal agency the power to decide for itself whether only attorneys can represent clients before it:

> **Administrative Procedure Act**, 5 U.S.C. § 555(b) (2001). A person compelled to appear in person before an agency...is entitled to be accompanied, represented, and advised by counsel or, if permitted by the agency, by other qualified representative.[36]

When a federal agency decides to use this power to permit nonattorney representation, it can allow anyone to act as the agent or representative of another before the agency, or it can establish qualifications or standards of admission to practice before it. If the agency takes the latter course, there are a number of qualifications or standards it could impose, such as

- passing a specialized test to demonstrate competency in the subject matter regulated by the agency
- minimum education or experience
- registration or enrollment on the agency's approved roster of representatives
- an agreement to abide by designated ethical rules of practice, a violation of which could result in suspension and "disbarment."

Let's look at some examples of federal agencies that allow nonattorney representation.

U.S. Patent and Trademark Office (USPTO)

The U.S. Patent and Trademark Office (USPTO) has established criteria for individuals to practice before the USPTO as nonattorney **patent agents**. Their services include drafting applications for patents, filing them with the USPTO, and searching legal opinions on patentability. Over 15 percent of USPTO representatives are nonattorneys. To become an agent, an individual must

- Fill out an application for registration.
- Possess good moral character and reputation.
- Pass a registration examination to demonstrate the legal, scientific, and technical qualifications necessary to advise and assist patent applicants.[37]

Internal Revenue Service (IRS)

Perhaps the largest use of nonattorneys in federal agencies is at the Internal Revenue Service within the Treasury Department.[38] Any certified public accountant (CPA) is authorized to practice before the IRS. The American Institute of CPAs (www.aicpa.org) has more than 370,000 members, most of whom are not attorneys.[39] In addition, the IRS has enrolled (i.e., registered) thousands of nonattorneys called **enrolled agents** to represent taxpayers at all administrative proceedings within the IRS. (Once a dispute goes to court, however, an attorney must take over.) To become an enrolled agent, an individual must either pass a written IRS examination or prove that he or she once worked at the IRS for a designated number of years. In most states, there are associations of enrolled agents; the major national organization is the National Association of Enrolled Agents (www.naea.org).

Administrative Procedure Act (APA) The statute that governs procedures before federal administrative agencies. Many states have their own version of the APA for procedures before state administrative agencies.

patent agent A nonattorney licensed to prepare and submit patent applications before the U.S. Patent and Trademark Office. (If an attorney, he or she is more commonly called a *patent attorney*.)

enrolled agent A nonattorney who is licensed to represent taxpayers before the Internal Revenue Service. (Attorneys and certified public accountants can provide such representation without becoming enrolled agents.)

Immigration Court

Immigration courts are administrative tribunals that handle cases on visas, green cards, and asylum. Aliens may be represented in these courts by "accredited representatives" of "recognized" nonprofit organizations. The representatives do not have to be attorneys. There are strict limitations on what the organizations can charge aliens for the services of the representatives.[40]

Social Security Administration (SSA)

Although many federal agencies allow nonattorney representation, relatively few nonattorneys actually use the authority they have. A study by the American Bar Association of thirty-three federal administrative agencies reached the following conclusion: "We found that the overwhelming majority of agencies studied permit nonlawyer representation in both adversarial and nonadversarial proceedings. However, most of them seem to encounter lay practice very infrequently (in less than 5% of adjudications), while only a few encounter lay practice as often as lawyer practice. Thus, although universally permitted, lay practice before federal agencies rarely occurs."[41]

One agency where nonattorney representation is fairly high (about 15 percent) is the Social Security Administration (SSA). Paralegals are frequently appointed by clients to represent them before the agency. According to the results of a study that compared the success of clients at hearings based on who represented them:

- 72.6 percent of clients represented by attorneys were successful.
- 69.8 percent of clients represented by nonattorneys were successful.
- 52.7 percent of clients who represented themselves were successful.[42]

In another study, SSA hearing officers, called **administrative law judges (ALJ)**, were asked to rate the competence of the paralegals and attorneys who represent claimants at the hearings:

- 60 percent rated paralegal representation good or satisfactory.
- 88 percent rated attorney representation good or satisfactory.
- 34 percent rated paralegal competence as better than or about equal to attorney competence.
- 65 percent rated paralegals less or significantly less competent than attorneys.[43]

Social Security representatives have formed the National Organization of Social Security Claimants' Representatives (NOSSCR), consisting of attorneys and "other advocates" (www.nosscr.org) See Chapter 15 on paralegal advocacy on behalf of Social Security claimants.

Attorneys and paralegals can charge fees for their services in representing clients before the SSA, but the agency must specifically approve the fee. This is not to say, however, that attorneys and paralegals are treated alike. If an attorney successfully represents a claimant, the agency will deduct up to 25 percent of the claimant's award, which will be paid directly to the attorney to cover fees. (This is called *direct payment*.) In contrast, if a paralegal successfully represents a claimant, the traditional rule has been that the paralegal must collect the fee from the client; the SSA would not deduct anything from the award in such cases. If, however, the paralegal meets the following conditions, the fee (up to 25 percent) can be paid directly to the paralegal:

- Has a bachelor's degree or "equivalent qualifications derived from training and work experience"
- Passes a written examination administered by SSA on the Social Security Act "and the most recent" agency and court decisions on the Act
- Secures professional liability insurance to protect claimants from malpractice
- Undergoes a criminal background check to ensure fitness to practice, and
- Completes continuing education courses on social security law (including ethics).[44]

Paralegals who do not meet these qualifications must collect their fees from their clients.

Exhibit 4-6 contains the form that claimants must use to appoint representatives.

administrative law judge (ALJ) A government officer who presides over a hearing at an administrative agency. Also called *hearing examiner*. (Most, but not all, ALJs are attorneys.)

Exhibit 4-6	Appointment of Social Security Representative

Social Security Administration
Please read the instructions before completing this form.

Form Approved
OMB No. 0960-0527

Name (Claimant) (Print or Type)	Social Security Number
Wage Earner (If Different)	Social Security Number

Part I   CLAIMANT'S APPOINTMENT OF REPRESENTATIVE

I appoint this individual,_____
                                                     (Name and Address)
to act as my representative in connection with my claim(s) or asserted right(s) under:

☐ Title II (RSDI)   ☐ Title XVI (SSI)   ☐ Title XVIII (Medicare)   ☐ Title VIII (SVB)

This individual may, entirely in my place, make any request or give any notice; give or draw out evidence or information; get information; and receive any notice in connection with my pending claim(s) or asserted right(s).

☐ I authorize the Social Security Administration to release information about my pending claim(s) or asserted right(s) to designated associates who perform administrative duties (e.g. clerks), partners, and/or parties under contractual arrangements (e.g. copying services) for or with my representative.

☐ I appoint, or I now have, more than one representative. My principal representative is:

_____
                            (Name of Principal Representative)

Signature (Claimant)	Address
Telephone Number (with Area Code)	Fax Number (with Area Code)	Date

Part II   REPRESENTATIVE'S ACCEPTANCE OF APPOINTMENT

I, _____ , hereby accept the above appointment. I certify that I have not been suspended or prohibited from practice before the Social Security Administration; that I am not disqualified from representing the claimant as a current or former officer or employee of the United States; and that I will not charge or collect any fee for the representation, even if a third party will pay the fee, unless it has been approved in accordance with the laws and rules referred to on the reverse side of the representative's copy of this form. If I decide not to charge or collect a fee for the representation, I will notify the Social Security Administration. (Completion of Part III satisfies this requirement.)

Check one: ☐ I am an attorney.   ☐ I am a non-attorney eligible for direct payment under SSA law.

☐ I am a non-attorney not eligible for direct payment.

I am now or have previously been disbarred or suspended from a court or bar to which I was previously admitted to practice as an attorney. ☐ YES   ☐ NO

I am now or have previously been disqualified from participating in or appearing before a Federal program or agency.
☐ YES   ☐ NO

I declare under penalty of perjury that I have examined all the information on this form, and on any accompanying statements or forms, and it is true and correct to the best of my knowledge.

Source: Social Security Administration (www.ssa.gov).

NONATTORNEY PRACTICE BEFORE STATE ADMINISTRATIVE AGENCIES

Thus far our focus has been nonattorney practice before federal administrative agencies. At the *state* level, there is often a similar system for authorizing nonattorneys to provide representation at many state administrative agencies. The state agencies most likely to allow nonattorney representation are those with jurisdiction over:

- unemployment insurance
- workers' compensation
- public health benefits
- public assistance benefits
- employment discrimination
- real estate assessments[45]

In New York, 70 percent of New York state agencies and 63 percent of New York City agencies permit some form of nonattorney representation.[46] For example, the New York State Workers' Compensation Board allows nonattorneys to practice before the Board if they pass an exam and demonstrate "competent knowledge of the law and regulations relating to workers' compensation matters" and have "the necessary qualifications to render service to his or her client."[47] The nonattorneys are called *licensed representatives.*

The regulations specify representatives' duties to their clients and the Board. Among other things, representatives are expected to:

- have full knowledge of their client's case,
- prepare diligently for handling all matters relating to the case,
- ascertain and fully disclose to the client the relevant facts and questions of law,
- fairly advise the client as to the merits of the case,
- disclose to the client in writing any potential conflicts of interest,
- transfer or accept transfer of a case only with approval by the Board, and
- withdraw from representing a client only after giving five days" written notice to the client (which must also be filed with the Board).

The regulations also require representatives to:

- conduct themselves as lawyers would in a court;
- maintain a register of their cases for Board inspection;
- display their licenses; and
- appear only in connection with cases in which they have been directly retained.

Representatives may receive fees only if authorized by the Board or by a referee, and are strictly prohibited from receiving any other compensation for their services.[48]

As with all agency representation by nonattorneys, if the case is eventually appealed to a court, an attorney must provide the representation.

LICENSING

A *license* is government permission to do something that would otherwise be unlawful. (See Exhibit 4-1.) *Occupational licensing* is government permission that is required to engage in a specified occupation. Occupational licensing and certification are significantly different. Occupational licensing is a government program that is required for individuals wishing to practice a certain occupation. Certification is a voluntary program run by a nongovernmental organization to recognize individuals meeting the qualifications of the organization. Although exceptions exist to this distinction, it covers most licensing and certification programs.

In 1950, less than five percent of Americans had jobs that required licenses. Today the number is approximately thirty percent.[49] There are two main reasons an occupation may want to be licensed by the government:

- To protect the public
- To enhance the occupation's own image

Licensed occupations such as electricians, brokers, and nurses offer services that require knowledge and skills that most citizens do not have. A license serves as a measure of assurance (although not a guarantee) that license holders are competent to perform their specialized and often technical services. In addition to a desire to protect the public, an occupation may want licensing as a way to enhance its self-image in terms of credibility and professionalism. Toward this end, the occupation often views licensing as a way to prevent less educated and less skilled individuals from working in the field.

No state requires paralegals to be licensed, although there has been considerable discussion (and controversy) over the future of nonattorney licensing. To examine this area, we need to consider traditional paralegals and the document service provider (DSP).

TRADITIONAL PARALEGALS

Traditional paralegals work for and under the supervision of an attorney. For this group, licensing is not a major issue, although many traditional paralegals favor rules that would restrict the use of the paralegal title to persons who work under attorney supervision and meet other designated qualifications. Only a few states (e.g., California, Florida, South Dakota, and Maine) have such title restrictive rules.

The main reason no one is seriously considering the licensing of traditional paralegals is that licensing is not needed to protect the public. Attorneys have an ethical duty to supervise their paralegals (see Chapter 5). The public is adequately protected by this supervision. Why add a vast bureaucratic licensing mechanism that would not increase the protection the public already receives through the attorney's ethical obligation to supervise all law office employees? Many bar associations would agree with the following point of view on paralegal licensing expressed by the North Carolina Bar Association:

> Several states have considered the possibility of adopting a licensing statute for paralegals, but none has done so. Licensing itself is subject to great public and legislative concern at present. So long as the work accomplished by non-lawyers for lawyers is properly supervised and reviewed by a licensed and responsible attorney, there would seem to be no need for a further echelon of licensing for the public's protection. Furthermore, licensing might be more dangerous than helpful to the public. The apparent stamp of approval of a license possibly could give the impression to the public that a person having such a license is qualified to deal directly with and give legal advice to the public.[50]

New Jersey

In 1999, New Jersey almost enacted licensing that would cover traditional paralegals. After five years of study, a Committee on Paralegal Education and Regulation recommended that the Supreme Court of New Jersey adopt a broad-based licensing system run by the judiciary for all paralegals in the state. The system would include minimum educational requirements and an ethics examination. Some paralegal associations endorsed the proposal as enhancing the professionalism of the field and the degree of respect accorded paralegals. Other paralegal associations, however, agreed with the American Bar Association and the New Jersey State Bar Association that the proposal was unnecessary. The New Jersey Supreme Court rejected the plan. The establishment was clearly not in the mood to create the kind of bureaucracy that would be needed to implement and monitor the kind of licensing that would include traditional paralegals.

The New Jersey court acknowledged that "many of the tasks conducted by [traditional] paralegals involve the practice of law." Yet the performance of these tasks was authorized because of the oversight provided by their attorney supervisors. Consequently, "the Court has concluded that direct oversight of paralegals is best accomplished through attorney supervision rather than through a Court-directed licensing system."[51]

California

In 2000, California became the first state to enact extensive regulation of traditional paralegals. The state did not enact licensing, but its new requirements have many features of licensing. From now on, the only individuals who can use the titles *paralegal* and *legal assistant* in California are those who

- Work under the supervision of an attorney;
- Meet stringent education qualifications (e.g., complete an approved paralegal program with a designated number of law-related courses or have a baccalaureate degree and one year of law-related experience under the supervision of a California attorney); and

- Attend mandatory continuing legal education (CLE) (four hours of ethics training every two years and four hours in general law or the law of a specialty every two years).

If you do not work under attorney supervision, you cannot call yourself a paralegal or legal assistant in California. If paralegals sell their services directly to the public, they can no longer call themselves paralegals. This part of the legislation is not new. As we have seen, there are several states (e.g., Maine and Florida) where the titles *paralegal* and *legal assistant* are limited to those who work for attorneys. What was dramatically new about the California legislation was the imposition of education qualifications, mandatory CLE, and a government-backed enforcement mechanism to punish violators. Anyone who violates the requirements of California's new law can be fined $2,500 for the first offense and be imprisoned for subsequent offenses! Violation constitutes a misdemeanor.[52]

It is significant to point out what the California legislation did not do:

- It did not expand the scope of what a paralegal is able to do. The legislation specified what tasks paralegals/legal assistants are able to perform (e.g., case management, interviewing, fact gathering, and drafting legal documents). These tasks, however, are not role expansions. The tasks listed in the legislation are the same tasks that could be performed in California (or in any other state) before the legislation was enacted.
- It did not require paralegals or legal assistants to pass an examination. To be a paralegal or legal assistant in California, you must meet education or experience qualifications, work under attorney supervision, and attend mandatory CLE, but you do not have to take an examination.
- It did not set up a judicial or administrative bureaucracy to administer and enforce the program. There is no central office, agency, or board in the state that administers or enforces any aspect of the regulation governing traditional paralegals. The program does not require registration with anyone. There is no license to obtain. The program is enforced in the following formal and informal ways:
  - The threat of criminal prosecution. The legislation creates a new crime (illegal use of the titles *paralegal* or *legal assistant*) punishable by fine or imprisonment.
  - The threat of a civil suit. "Any consumer injured by a violation of this chapter may file a complaint and seek redress in any municipal or superior court for injunctive relief, restitution, and damages."[53]
  - Self-policing CLE enforcement. Paralegals/legal assistants must keep their own records of CLE attendance. They must demonstrate (i.e., "certify") to their supervising attorneys that CLE obligations have been met. No one else keeps track of CLE hours of attendance. If, however, a criminal charge or civil lawsuit is brought, the paralegal/legal assistant must be prepared to present proof of compliance.
  - Paralegal fees. In **statutory-fee cases**, a judge can order the losing party to pay the attorney fees of the winning party. Attorney fees can include paralegal fees for paralegal tasks performed by a paralegal on the case. This creates an incentive for attorneys to make sure their paralegals comply with California law on the requirements for using the paralegal title.

statutory-fee cases A case applying a special statute that gives a judge authority to order the losing party to pay the winning party's attorney fees (including paralegal fees) and costs.

Although the California legislation did not establish a formal licensing system for traditional paralegals, it did use the force of law to determine who is in and who is out of the paralegal/legal assistant field. That's what licensing does. It is true that most licensing laws prohibit the performance of designated tasks by persons who do not obtain the license. For example, only licensed electricians can wire a house. California did not take this route. A California attorney can ask a secretary or anyone else in the office to perform any paralegal task (e.g., digest a deposition, interview a client, or perform factual research), but such individuals cannot be called paralegals or legal assistants unless they meet the requirements of the law. This, however, does not lessen the dramatic impact of what has occurred in California.

Here are some examples of attorneys and paralegals who have probably violated the California law:

- Charles Kiley, Esq., is a sole practitioner in California. He hires Sally Belmont to be his paralegal. Sally recently graduated from a community college that does not have a paralegal program. Sally has never been formally trained as a paralegal. Kiley wants to train her himself. He does so. Since the day he hired her, Kiley has been very satisfied with the quality of her paralegal work.

- Smith & Smith, a California law firm, promotes one of its veteran secretaries, Mary Adams, to be a paralegal. This secretary has been with the firm for fifteen years and knows more about her specialty than most new attorneys. She does not have a degree and has never attended a paralegal program.
- King, Swenson & Carter, a California law firm, hires Tom Harris to be a paralegal. Tom was a paralegal for ten years in New York before moving to California. The firm where he worked says that he is the finest paralegal the firm has ever had. Tom has a paralegal certificate from a paralegal program in New York, but this program did not have the designated number of law-related courses required for a California paralegal.

Sally Belmont, Mary Adams, and Tom Harris are illegal paralegals. They have not met the requirements of California law no matter how competent their employers think they are. Sally, Mary, and Tom run the risk of going to jail. Their employers must stop calling them paralegals.

Many traditional paralegals in California are thrilled with the new law. Its unexpected enactment was largely due to the determined efforts of individual paralegal associations throughout the state, spearheaded by the California Alliance of Paralegal Associations (www.caPARAlegal.org). The front page of the newsletter of the largest local paralegal association in the state proclaimed, "Hear Ye! Hear Ye! The time has finally come.... After years of struggling to get recognition and affirmation of the role that paralegals play in the legal industry, our time has finally come."[54] No longer can the boss take anyone off the street or from the copy room and call him or her a paralegal or legal assistant. They can have this title and role only if they meet the requirements of the law. The sponsor of the law in the legislature said that her goal was "to elevate the [paralegal] profession with the recognition it so well deserves."[55]

Thus far few states have followed the path taken in California. Most states do not see a need for additional regulation of traditional paralegals. The public is adequately protected because of attorney supervision. Furthermore, these paralegals can achieve increased professional recognition through the certification programs we will discuss later.

DOCUMENT SERVICE PROVIDERS (DSPs)

Document service providers, however, are in a different category. As we have seen, they are self-employed individuals (independent contractors) who offer law-related services to the public without attorney supervision. Because the assistance they provide to self-represented persons is in large measure related to legal documents, they are collectively called *document service providers* (DSPs).

Proponents for expanding the role of DSPs often point to the diversification of personnel in the medical profession. Professor Gilliam Hadfield, for example, makes the following points:

> Does a full-fledged MD have to deliver every service needed to address every medical issue you face in order to receive quality care? No. Medical care is a team sport, provided by a wide variety of medical professionals: nurses, radiologic technologists, pharmacists, nurse practitioners, physical therapists, chiropractors, registered massage therapists, certified nurse midwives, certified registered nurse anesthetists, etc. Many of these providers are licensed and authorized to provide services directly to those with medical problems. They are not limited to working under the direct supervision of MDs. Thank goodness. Because if they were, we'd be paying MD rates for every sore throat and backache.[56]

Professor Hadfield believes that some measure of this diversity is also needed in the delivery of legal services.

Indeed, responsible proposals have been put forward to recognize the valuable services DSPs can provide and to give them the formal recognition of a *limited license*. As we saw in Exhibit 4-1, a limited license (also called a specialty license) is permission by a government body that allows a person who has met designated qualifications to engage in specified activities that are customarily (but not always exclusively) performed by another category of license holder.

As we saw earlier, the rules governing DSPs that currently exist (such as the bankruptcy petition preparer (BPP) in all states and the legal document assistant (LDA) in California) are restrictive in the sense that they do not expand the role of the nonattorney. Limited licensing would be substantially different. It can shift the boundaries lines of what is the practice of law and create new roles for DSPs.

There is, however, a segment of the organized bar that does not relish the prospect of granting limited licenses to nonattorneys. A president of one bar association said of limited licensing, "It's like letting nurses do brain surgery." Here are some other comments from attorneys: "This is the worst thing since the plague!" They think "just about everybody should be able to practice law. I guess they think everybody should be able to slice open a belly and remove an appendix." "I cannot think of anything that would be more injurious to the public." This is an idea "whose time has not yet come." "This is potentially the most fractious and controversial issue ever confronted" by the bar association. Scoffing at the notion that you can carve out tasks that do not require the skills of an attorney, a judge commented, "You never know if you have a simple case until an expert looks at it. It's like a pain in the side. Only an expert can tell whether it should be treated with aspirin or by surgery."[57]

This hostility, however, has not silenced the as-of-now modest movement in the direction of creating limited licenses for nonattorneys. We turn now to an overview of this movement, starting with unexpected support found in position papers of the American Bar Association (ABA).

Position Papers of the American Bar Association (ABA)

The ABA has not formally endorsed limited licensing. Over the years, however, various commissions of the ABA have taken positions in favor of such licensing.

■ *1986: ABA Commission on Professionalism (Page 52)*

A 1986 report of an ABA Commission on Professionalism recommended that attorneys "encourage innovative methods that simplify and make less extensive the rendering of legal services" for middle-class persons. To this end, the commission cautiously suggested—on page 52 of the report—that there be "limited licensing of paralegals" and "paraprofessionals" to perform discrete functions such as handling some real estate closings, drafting simple wills, and performing certain tax work. The report argued that such a proposal could help reduce the cost of legal services:

> No doubt, many wills and real estate closings require the services of a lawyer. However, it can no longer be claimed that lawyers have the exclusive possession of the esoteric knowledge required and are therefore the only ones able to advise clients on any matter concerning the law.[58]

page 52 debate A debate on whether there should be limited licensing for paralegals (based on a recommendation in favor of such licensing on page 52 of a report of an American Bar Association commission).

This remarkable proposal caused quite a stir. Many refer to the controversy it created as the **page 52 debate**. For years, many attorneys were suspicious of paralegalism because of a fear that paralegals might eventually be licensed and compete with attorneys. Then along comes a report of an ABA commission that recommends licensing!

It must be remembered, however, that neither the report nor the commission speaks for the entire ABA. In fact, the 1986 proposal in the report "drew the ire" of other ABA members and was not given serious consideration by the ABA as a whole.

■ *1995: ABA Commission on Nonlawyer Practice*

In 1992, the ABA took another look. It established a Commission on Nonlawyer Practice to conduct hearings throughout the country in order to determine the need for nonattorney assistance, particularly by citizens representing themselves on legal matters. For three years, the commission studied this need and the extent to which it was being met by DSPs. Should DSPs be encouraged? Should they be regulated by a form of limited licensing? The commission heard the testimony of hundreds of witnesses and received thousands of pages of written testimony on these questions. The diversity of points of view presented to the commission was enormous:

> Many suggestions received passionate support and were then opposed with equal vehemence. Experienced lawyers and nonlawyers often testified to diametrically opposed perceptions of consumer needs, risks of harm, nonlawyer capabilities and deficiencies, and the potential economies or effectiveness of any chosen regulatory approach.[59]

Throughout the country, the final report of the commission was eagerly awaited. Supporters of limited licensing were hoping that the report would endorse limited licensing. Some attorneys, however, feared that the commission would move in this direction. At a meeting of bar association leaders, the former president of the New York State Bar Association said, "I will tell you that, unanimously, we reacted in horror to the idea that somehow the ABA might sanction an increase in non-lawyer practice."[60]

When the commission issued its final report in 1995, however, no dramatic recommendations were made. There was nothing comparable to the "page 52 debate" that emerged from the 1986 report. The commission made relatively lukewarm recommendations about expanding the role of the traditional paralegal. What everyone wanted to know was whether the commission was going to conclude that the time was ripe for limited licensing. Its answer to this volatile question was *maybe*. Rather than make a recommendation one way or another, the commission said that each state should decide the question for itself. The main contribution of the commission was to suggest guidelines or criteria that a state should use in deciding whether the state's current regulation of nonattorney activity was sufficient and, if not, what further regulation was needed, including the option of allowing limited licensing of nonattorneys.

First of all, the commission believes a state should ask whether nonattorneys are posing risks to the public. If "there is no serious risk to the consumer even when the nonlawyer's service is poor, then a state may conclude that the activity should be unregulated."[61] The same conclusion might be reached if the state thinks the public is sufficiently able to judge for itself whether a nonattorney is qualified to offer his or her services.

For example, assume that a state reaches the following conclusions about the landlord-tenant legal problems of the public:

- There is a serious shortage of help on these problems.
- It is not economical for attorneys to handle all of these cases.
- Nonattorneys (acting on their own without attorney supervision) can help meet the demand for legal services in this area.
- But serious harm can result if a consumer receives erroneous legal services in a landlord-tenant case.
- Because of the complexity of some landlord-tenant problems, the public may not be able to judge which nonattorneys are qualified to work on them.
- A limited licensing program can be established that meets these concerns. The program would institute standards for training nonattorneys, testing them, requiring them to carry liability insurance, disciplining them for unethical behavior, etc.

The state, however, might also conclude that the benefits of allowing nonattorneys to work in this area are outweighed by the cost of setting up the elaborate licensing scheme that would be needed to make sure the public is protected from the substantial harm that can result from incompetent landlord-tenant legal services. Hence the state would reject a program of limited licensing for these kinds of legal problems. This is the kind of analysis the commission says each state must undertake for all unmet legal needs of the public.

The work of the commission is significant. Its report is the product of the most comprehensive and sophisticated study in the field of paralegalism to date. The first state to come close to implementing the recommendations of the report is Washington State. Before examining what Washington State has done, we need to look at yet another ABA report endorsing limited licensing.

■ 2013: ABA Task Force Report on the Future of Legal Education

In 2013, a draft report of an ABA Task Force on the Future of Legal Education made a number of recommendations to address serious problems in our current system of delivering legal services. A large numbers of people in the country need legal assistance but are unable to afford the fees of attorneys. One recommendation to address this problem was to broaden the pool of providers of legal services through the enactment of limited licensing. At present, the primary person entitled to deliver legal services is the holder of a **Juris Doctor (J.D.)** degree earned after three years of law school and four years of undergraduate college. The time has come, said the report, to broaden the pool:

> *Broader Delivery of Law-Related Services.* The delivery of law-related services today is primarily by lawyers. These services may not be cost-effective for many who are in need of them, and some communities and constituencies lack accessible legal services. State supreme courts, state bar associations, and admitting authorities should devise new or improved frameworks for

Juris Doctor (J.D.) The law degree most American law schools grant its graduates. Also called *Doctor of Jurisprudence.*

licensing providers of legal services. This should include licensing persons other than holders of a J.D. to deliver limited legal services, and authorizing bar admission for people whose preparation may be other than the traditional four years of college plus three years of classroom-based law school education. The current lack of access to legal advice of any kind that exists across the country requires such innovative steps.[62]

The licensing of nonattorney providers of legal services that this report recommends is for DSPs, independent contractors who would be licensed to deliver designated legal services without attorney supervision. To say that this is a breathtaking recommendation would be an understatement.

How likely is it that the recommendation will be implemented? It's difficult to say. Opposition to dramatic change of this kind is likely to be fierce. Each state would have to decide on its own whether to make the change, a decision that could take years of debate, further study, and experimentation. The ABA cannot force any changes on its own. States individually decide what the practice of law is and who is authorized to practice. A commission of the ABA can do no more than make suggestions of what the states should do.

Yet the ABA is a highly influential body and its message may be getting through. There are serious DSP proposals under consideration in several states. For example:

- California. The governing body of the California bar association (the State Bar Board of Trustees) recently "expressed interest in examining a limited-practice licensing program that would create a new class of professionals who could give legal advice.[63]
- New York City. Citing a **justice gap** that leaves more than 2.3 million low-income New Yorkers each year to navigate the civil justice system on their own, the New York City Bar Association recommends that nonlawyers be allowed to practice, with limitations, as "Courtroom Aides" and "Legal Technicians."[64]

justice gap The large numbers of people who do not have access to legal assistance, primarily because of the cost of such assistance.

Other state bars have also expressed interest in exploring this possibility

Thus far, one state has gone beyond the proposal stage and has actually implemented a system of limited licensing: Washington State.

DEVELOPMENTS IN WASHINGTON STATE

Washington State has been a leader in the creation of new roles for nonattorneys in the delivery of legal services. Its Supreme Court is serious about limited licensing.

Limited Practice Officer (LPO)

A number of years ago, the state created a Limited Practice Board that certifies and regulates the **limited practice officer (LPO)**, also called a *certified closing officer*. An LPO is a nonattorney certified by the Washington State Supreme Court to select, prepare, and complete documents that have been approved for use in designated property transactions such as closing a loan, extending credit, or transferring land. The documents include deeds, mortgages, and bills of sale. LPOs are regulated by the Limited Practice Board. Candidates to become LPOs must pass an examination and be "of good moral character" before they can be "admitted" by the Washington State Supreme Court as a LPO.[65] LPOs must follow specific procedures when closing real estate transactions, including identifying themselves as LPOs and making clear they are not attorneys and are not advocates for either party. LPOs are assigned an LPO license number, which they also use when signing documents in their capacity as an LPO.

limited practice officer (LPO) A nonattorney in Washington State who is authorized to select and prepare approved legal documents for designated property transactions.

A number of paralegals in Washington State are licensed LPOs. After meeting LPO requirements, such paralegals typically use the title *paralegal/LPO*. An example is Jeanne J. Dawes, a paralegal with the law firm of Gore & Grewe. She appears on the firm stationery and business cards as "Jeanne J. Dawes, Paralegal/LPO."

Guidelines for Further Limited Licensing

The Washington State Supreme Court also has a Practice of Law Board to investigate complaints of unauthorized practice of law (UPL) and to recommend to the Supreme Court programs in which "nonlawyers may be involved in the delivery of certain types of legal and law-related services" in order to improve access to such services.[66] The guidelines established by the court for making these recommendations are presented in Exhibit 4-7.

Exhibit 4-7	Washington State Guidelines on Proposals for Limited Licensing

- The Practice of Law Board may recommend that nonlawyers be authorized to engage in certain defined activities that otherwise constitute the practice of law.
- The Board shall determine whether regulation under authority of the Supreme Court (including the establishment of minimum and uniform standards of competency, conduct, and continuing education) is necessary to protect the public interest.
- Any recommendation that nonlawyers be authorized to engage in the limited provision of legal or law-related services shall be accompanied by a determination:

  (A) that access to affordable and reliable legal and law-related services consistent with protection of the public will be enhanced by permitting nonlawyers to engage in the defined activities set forth in the recommendation;

  (B) that the defined activities outlined in the recommendation can be reasonably and competently provided by skilled and trained nonlawyers;

  (C) if the public interest requires regulation under authority of the Supreme Court, such regulation is tailored to promote access to affordable legal and law-related services while ensuring that those whose important rights are at stake can reasonably rely on the quality, skill and ability of those nonlawyers who will provide such services;

  (D) that, to the extent that the activities authorized will involve the handling of client trust funds, provision has been made to ensure that such funds are handled in a manner consistent with the ethics rules of the state, including the requirement that such funds be placed in interest bearing accounts, with interest paid to the Legal Foundation of Washington; and

  (E) that the costs of regulation, if any, can be effectively underwritten within the context of the proposed regulatory regime.

- Recommendations to authorize nonlawyers to engage in the limited practice of law shall be forwarded to the Washington State Board of Governors [of the state bar association] for consideration and comment before transmission to the Supreme Court. Upon approval of such recommendations by the Supreme Court, those who meet the requirements and comply with applicable regulatory and licensing provisions shall be deemed to be engaged in the authorized practice of law.

Source: General Rules (GR) 25, Practice of Law Board, Approved by the Washington State Supreme Court (Sept. 1, 2001)

Limited License Legal Technicians (LLLT)

Under these guidelines, the mandate of the Practice of Law Board is not simply to investigate the unauthorized practice of law. The board is charged with determining where the role of paralegals and other nonattorneys might be expanded. Although a number of attorney committees and task forces over the years have recommended expansion of nonattorney roles (e.g., see the earlier discussion of the various ABA reports), the Washington State Supreme Court is the most authoritative *government* entity that has set in motion a process that will actually lead to such expansion.

In 2012, the Washington State Supreme Court created the position of **Limited License Legal Technician (LLLT)**. This person will be trained and authorized to provide "legal assistance or advice in approved practice areas of law." These areas must be approved by the Supreme Court upon recommendations submitted by a newly established Limited License Legal Technician Board. The first area of law to be covered is family law.

LLLTs will be allowed to charge fees for their services and do not have to be supervised by attorneys. The services provided by LLLTs will be for self-represented individuals who are *pro se* clients, meaning that they are representing themselves. Examples of the type of assistance the LLLT will be able to provide include

- Obtaining relevant facts from a client and explaining the relevancy of such facts
- Selecting and completing court forms
- Informing clients of applicable procedures and deadlines that must be met
- Informing clients of the procedures for proper service of process and for filing legal documents

Limited License Legal Technician (LLLT) A nonattorney in Washington State who is authorized to engage in the limited practice of law (without attorney supervision) in approved areas of practice.

- Explaining the meaning of documents the client has received from the other side
- Reviewing and explaining pleadings
- Advising the client of what other documents may be needed in a court proceeding.

The Court referred to such services as "mostly ministerial technical/legal functions."[67] Furthermore, LLLTs will not be able to represent clients in court and will not be able to contact and negotiate with opposing parties on a client's behalf.

The LLLT limited license program will have the following components:

- *Education.* To be an LLLT, an applicant must meet minimum undergraduate and legal education requirements.
- *Experience.* The applicant must have two (or three) years of experience as a paralegal/ legal assistant doing substantive law-related work under the supervision of an attorney (one year of which must be under the supervision of a Washington State attorney). Substantive law-related work means work that requires knowledge of legal concepts and is customarily, but not necessarily, performed by a lawyer.
- *Examination.* The applicant must pass an examination that will cover rules of professional conduct applicable to LLLTs, and rules on privileges, procedural rules, and substantive law issues related to one or more approved practice areas.
- *Continuing legal education (CLE).* There shall be an annual CLE requirement. The Board will establish rules on ways for a LLLT to meet this requirement.
- *Ethics.* The Board will establish rules of professional and ethical conduct for LLLTs.
- *Discipline.* The Board will establish procedures for disciplinary proceedings against LLLTs who violate these rules.
- *Trust accounts.* The Board will establish **client trust account** requirements. When handling client money, LLLTs must use trust accounts that meet these requirements.
- *Pro bono work.* The LLLT must complete at least twenty hours of **pro bono** legal service in Washington State as approved by the Board, no more than two years prior to taking the LLLT examination.
- *Financial responsibility.* The applicant must show proof of ability to respond to claims for damages resulting from his or her acts or omissions in the performance of services. (Example: the Board might require the applicant to post a **surety** bond.)
- *Disclosure.* The LLLT must tell clients that the LLLT is not an attorney and can provide only "limited legal services."
- *Confidentiality.* The LLLT must tell the client that the LLLT has a duty to protect (1) the confidentiality of information provided by the client and (2) the work product associated with the services sought or provided by the LLLT.
- *Privilege.* The **attorney-client privilege** applies to the relationship between an LLLT and his or her client. LLLTs can refuse to disclose communications to and from their clients that pertained to LLLT services.
- *Fiduciary responsibility.* An LLLT has the same **fiduciary** responsibility to his or her client as an attorney has to his or her client.
- *Costs.* The LLLT must pay annual licensing fees.

Notes of Caution: Competence and Competition

The momentum toward limited licensing has its critics as we have seen. The major concerns are as follows:

- *Competence.* Inevitably, the issue of competence arises in any serious discussion of limited licensing for DSPs. Are nonattorneys able to perform the kind of tasks envisioned in Washington State for the LLLT and in the other proposals for limited licensing? Proponents answer this question in the affirmative:

[S]tudy after study has shown that trained lay advocates can effectively represent people in standardized legal proceedings—and even in complex ones when they are specially trained....[68] Professor Deborah Rhode at Stanford Law School [has concluded that] "virtually no experts believe that current prohibitions [on nonlawyer assistance] make sense." Comparative research finds that ... lay specialists can perform as effectively as attorneys. In the one reported survey of consumer satisfaction, nonlawyers rated higher than lawyers."[69] According to Professor

---

client trust account A bank account controlled by an attorney or limited license legal technician (LLLT) that contains client funds that may not be used for general operating expenses or for any personal purpose of the attorney or LLLT.

pro bono Concerning or involving legal services that are provided for the public good (pro bono publico, shortened to *pro bono*) without fee or compensation. Sometimes also applied to services given at a reduced rate.

surety One who is liable for paying another's debt or performing another's duty.

attorney-client privilege (ACP) A client or a client's attorney can refuse to disclose any confidential (private) communication between them if the purpose of the communication was to facilitate the provision of legal services to the client.

fiduciary (1) Pertaining to the high standard of good faith and fair treatment that must be exercised on behalf of another (adjective). (2) A person who owes another good faith and fair treatment in protecting the other's interest (noun).

Rhode, "[a]lmost all of the scholarly experts and commissions that have studied the issue [of expanding nonlawyer assistance] have recommended increased opportunities for such assistance."[70]

Not everyone, however, agrees with Professor Rhode that nonattorneys can perform tasks that now constitute the practice of law. One attorney said that trying to identify legal services that an LLLT or other DSPs can perform is like a plan that would allow nondoctors "to perform minor operations requiring fewer than 15 stitches and incisions of less than 2 inches."

- *Competition.* Not all of the justices on the Washington State Supreme Court agreed that LLLTs should be created. One of the dissenting justices said that it was the equivalent of establishing a "mini bar association" within the state bar association and that attorneys in the state (particularly unemployed and underemployed attorneys) should not be asked to support a program that will compete against them for clients. Another critic made these points:
  - There is no evidence to suggest that the fees LLLTs will charge would be any less than the fees currently charged by solo attorney practitioners, but the service of LLLTs would be much more limited than the service offered by an attorney.
  - Introduction of a new class of limited licensed professionals will continue to erode the economic model of solo and small law firm practice by sucking out from those practices the more routine legal services that are important to sustaining the economic viability of those law firms. It is naive to suggest that solo attorney practitioners should concentrate on doing "more complex legal work" leaving the routine legal work to "limited license professionals. *If the Washington State and the ABA want to deliver a death blow to solo practitioners this is a good way to do it.*[71]

The majority of the judges on the Washington State Supreme Court disagreed. They concluded that clients who will be served by LLLTs have not been able to afford the services of attorneys. Hence, LLLTs will be taking cases that attorneys have traditionally not taken because of cost.

REFORMS IN THE PRACTICE OF LAW: ATTEMPTS TO CLOSE THE JUSTICE GAP

The momentum toward limited licensing has been due to what is called the "justice gap," namely the large unmet need of low- and middle-income people for legal services because of the cost of such services.[72] For many Americans, attorneys have priced themselves out of the market.

Using data from surveys conducted by the ABA and state bar associations, ... at any given time, roughly half of all American households are dealing with about two legal problems each— evictions, divorces, bankruptcies, denials of health care benefits, and so on. Giving these American households just one hour of help from a lawyer to manage a maze of legal documents and court procedures would cost close to $20 billion. This doesn't even consider the cost of what clients want most from lawyers -- advice about how to avoid legal problems. Including this service would add additional tens if not hundreds of billions of dollars.[73]

A 2011 report of the World Justice Project concluded that the United States ranked twentieth out of twenty-three high-income countries in the ability of persons to obtain affordable legal services in civil cases.[74]

Legislatures and the organized bar have tried to respond to this grim picture by creating reforms in the delivery of legal services. Exhibit 4-8 presents an overview of these reforms so that they can be seen in context with proposals for limited licensing. Keep in mind, however, that no single reform in and of itself is sufficient to solve the problem of underrepresentation, which remains a critical deficiency—indeed, an embarrassment—of our legal system. What is needed is a state-wide strategy that establishes multiple reforms. Most of the reforms listed in Exhibit 4-8 have been implemented in varying degrees, but the justice gap is still extraordinarily wide. What is needed is for the reforms to be substantially expanded.

| Exhibit 4-8 | Reforms in the Practice of Law Designed to Increase the Number of People Receiving Legal Services |

- *Pro bono work.* Many law firms and corporations give their attorneys time off to provide pro bono legal services to the poor. Some offices do the same for their paralegals. The ethics codes of all bar associations suggest (and a few require) attorneys to perform a designated number of pro bono hours per year. Pro bono means for free or sometimes at a reduced rate (short for pro bono publico). To find pro bono programs for attorneys and paralegals in your state, run this search in Google, Bing, or Yahoo: pro bono law aa (substituting the name of your state for "aa").

- *Simplified forms.* Many courts and bar associations have helped create legal standardized forms that are relatively easy for the public to use without attorney assistance. To find such forms in your state, run this search in Google, Bing, or Yahoo: forms court aa (substituting the name of your state for "aa").

- *Internet self-help centers of courts.* Many courts have created Internet sites that provide assistance for persons with legal problems who are representing themselves. To find self-help centers in your state, run this search in Google, Bing, or Yahoo: self-help court aa (substituting the name of your state for "aa").

- *Commercial document preparation sites on the Internet.* Many pay sites on the Internet allow users to obtain legal documents after providing data in a question-and-answer format (e.g., www.legalzoom .com). To find such interactive document-assembly services for your state, run this search in Google, Bing, or Yahoo: Internet legal document preparation aa (substituting the name of your state for "aa").

- *Smartphone technology.* The president of the American Bar Association recently called for the creation of programs (apps) written for smartphones to assist the poor. "Consider a young, poor single mother who receives an eviction notice. Imagine if the woman could photograph the eviction notice, email the image to a legal portal, and get some initial advice online.... Given that more than 80 percent of Americans, regardless of income, have access to smart phones, they can be a game changer."[75]

- *Court facilitators.* In some states, volunteer or paid attorneys or paralegals are available at help desks situated in the halls of courtrooms to provide general guidance (but not legal advice or representation) to parties representing themselves in court cases. To find more information, run this search in Google, Bing, or Yahoo: "court facilitator" (add your state to the search to find out if facilitators exist in your state).

- *Prepaid legal services.* Some companies and unions have developed legal-insurance plans that enable participants to pay a set amount each month for designated legal services that might be needed while the participant is in the program. They are called **prepaid legal services**, legal plans, or group legal services. To find such services in your state, run this search in Google, Bing, or Yahoo: prepaid legal services aa (substituting the name of your state for "aa").

- *Attorney advertising.* Media advertising by attorneys (which was once largely prohibited) has arguably made the public more aware of legal services and more inclined to use such services. Advertising can also encourage competition among attorneys, which may allow the public to shop for lower fees among competing attorneys. On attorney advertising, see Chapter 5 and the links to your state in the American Bar Association's site (on www.americanbar.org, type "advertising solicitation" in the search box).

- *Unbundled legal services.* **Unbundled legal services** consist of discrete task representation for which the client is charged per task. As we will see in Chapter 5, an attorney is allowed to provide such services to clients who are representing themselves. This allows clients to obtain some professional assistance at a cost that is substantially less than what an attorney would charge for bundled (all-task) representation.

- *E-filing.* Electronic filing of pleadings and other documents is called **e-filing**. Many courts require e-filers to be attorneys. A pro se litigant would have to make paper filings in such courts. Some courts, however, are changing this rule to allow pro se litigants (who are not attorneys) to e-file.

- *Publicly funded legal services.* Legal aid offices receive substantial funding from the government, donations, and IOLTA. The funds are used to provide free legal services to the poor. (IOLTA—Interest on Lawyers' Trust Accounts—is discussed in Chapter 2.) Most of the legal aid offices employ full-time attorneys and paralegals who work for clients who meet the income guidelines of the programs. For a list of such programs in your state, see the Legal Services Corporation (www.lsc.gov).

- *Social media outreach.* Many organizations that provide legal services to low and moderate income persons are using Facebook, Twitter, YouTube, and other social-media sites to provide information about available legal services, including self-help instructions and guides for persons representing themselves.

- *Modest means panels.* Some states have modest means panels consisting of private attorneys who are willing to provide relatively low-cost (e.g., $60 an hour) legal services in limited areas of law to low-income individuals who are not poor enough to qualify for free legal services at legal aid offices. For more information, run this search in Google, Bing, or Yahoo: "modest means panel" (add your state to the search to find out if the panels exist in your state).

prepaid legal services A legal-insurance plan by which a person pays premiums to cover future legal services that might be needed. Also called *legal plan, group legal services.*

Unbundled legal services Discrete task representation for which the client is charged per task as opposed to a single fee for all tasks to be performed.

e-filing Electronic filing in court of pleadings and other documents.

IOLTA (Interest on Lawyers' Trust Accounts) A program that helps fund legal services for the poor with funds that attorneys are required to turn over from interest earned in client trust accounts containing client funds.

- *Traditional paralegals.* The increased use of traditional paralegals by attorneys can lead to lower client costs because the billing rate for paralegal time is considerably lower than the billing rate for most attorneys. Paralegals can perform many tasks that would otherwise have to be performed by attorneys. (See the discussion of law firm economics and paralegals in Chapters 1 and 14.)

- *Limited licensing?* The big question in the reform movement is whether proposals for limited licensing, like that of Washington State, will come to fruition and have a significant impact in helping to close the justice gap.

CERTIFICATION

Certification is a general term that means formal acknowledgment that a person or organization has met designated qualifications. In paralegalism, the main meaning of certification is formal acknowledgment by a *nongovernmental* organization (e.g., a paralegal association or bar association) that someone has met designated qualifications such as

- Graduating from a school or training program
- Passing an examination
- Completing a designated period of work experience

Paralegal certification is a voluntary process; the failure or refusal of a paralegal to become certified by the programs we will be discussing does not affect his or her ability to work as a paralegal. An occupational license, on the other hand, is a government-granted authorization or permission to engage in a specific occupation. Most license programs are mandatory in that you cannot work in an occupation without the license.

Care is needed to distinguish two related terms:

- *certified*: Formally acknowledged as having met specified qualifications of a certification program of an organization other than a school or training program.
- *certificated*: Formally acknowledged as having met specified qualifications of a school or training program.

Although most certification programs are run by nongovernmental organizations such as paralegal associations, it is possible for a government body to issue certifications. For example, we saw earlier that the Arizona Supreme Court has a certification program for nonattorneys. One of the titles that can be used by persons who meet the requirements of this program is *Arizona Certified Legal Document Preparer*.

The term *registration* is sometimes closely related to, and indeed synonymous with, certification. Registration (also called *enrollment*) is the process by which the names of individuals or institutions are listed on a roster kept by a governmental or nongovernmental body. If qualifications must be met before a name can go on the list, registration is the same as certification. Like certification, most registration programs are voluntary; they are not required for employment.

There has been a steady increase in the number of certification or registration programs in the country. Yet despite this growth, the majority of paralegals in the country do not seek certification or registration. In the few states where the program is run by a bar association, large numbers of paralegals *do* participate, but even in these states, the numbers are usually less than a majority in the state. Perhaps the main reason the programs are not more widely used is that most employers do not require or actively encourage their paralegals to become certified or registered even though the employers are generally pleased when a paralegal employee acquires this credential. In most offices, the credential does not immediately lead to a pay increase. One paralegal commented, "When I passed the exam, my employer at the time chose only to increase my hourly billing rate, but not my salary."[76] Paralegals who most often seek certification or registration are those who are active in local, state, or national paralegal associations. Once certified, these paralegals eloquently promote the value of certification as a way to maintain and enhance the professionalism of the field.

At one time the American Bar Association studied the question of certification. Some suggested that the ABA should certify individual paralegals. It declined the invitation, taking the position that certification should be undertaken by a national body that includes paralegals, attorneys, educators, and members of the general public. Furthermore, the ABA favored specialty certification, not entry-level certification. It felt that the benefits of entry-level certification would not be worth the time, expense, and effort to implement the program.[77] Nevertheless, the momentum toward certification or registration continues, both entry-level and advanced, particularly when the bar association sponsors the certification program.

NATIONAL CERTIFICATION

We begin with the three major national certification programs. They have different requirements, but they all require passing an examination. Here are the credentials offered by the three national associations:

- **National Association of Legal Assistants (NALA)** has two categories of certification: entry level and advanced (www.nala.org) (click *Certification*).
  - Entry-level certification. *Certified Paralegal (CP) or Certified Legal Assistant (CLA)*. Persons who meet the qualifications of this certification can select the CP or CLA credential.
  - Advanced certification. *Advanced Certified Paralegal (ACP)*. The ACP credential is available to a paralegal who has already obtained the CP/CLA credential
- **National Federation of Paralegal Associations (NFPA)** also has two categories of certification: entry level and advanced (www.paralegals.org) (click *Paralegal Certification*).
  - Basic-level certification. Persons who meet the qualifications of this certification become *CORE Registered Paralegals (CRP)*. CORE stands for Competent, Organized, Responsible, and Ethical. The exam is the PCCE, which stands for Paralegal CORE Competency Exam.
  - Advanced certification. *Registered Paralegal (RP) or PACE RP*. Persons who meet the qualifications of this certification can select the RP or the PACE RP credential. PACE stands for Paralegal Advanced Competency Exam (PACE)
- **NALS, the Association for Legal Professionals** has one major paralegal certification called the *Professional Paralegal (PP)*. It has separate certification programs for legal secretaries (www.nals.org) (click *Advance*).

There are some major differences among the certification programs of the three national associations. (See Exhibit 4-9.) Although they all require passing an examination, some are **entry-level certifications**, meaning that they can be achieved without paralegal experience.

There is a fourth national association (American Alliance of Paralegals), which also provides certification. It is much smaller and less well known than the certification programs of NALA, NFPA, and NALS. The certification of the American Alliance is called *AACP* (American Alliance Certified Paralegal). Its requirements include paralegal experience but not an examination (www.aapipara.org).

**entry-level
certifications** Certification acquired by meeting eligibility requirements that do not include work experience.

Exhibit 4-9	National Certification: NALA, NFPA, and NALS

	NALA	NFPA	NALS
Name of Exam	Certified Paralegal Exam	Paralegal CORE Competency Exam (PCCE)	Professional Paralegal Certification Exam
Created and Administered by	National Association of Legal Assistants (NALA)	National Federation of Paralegal Associations (NFPA)	NALS the Association for Legal Professionals
Year Established	1975	2011	2004
Exam Required?	Yes	Yes	Yes
Online Information About the Exam	www.nala.org (click *Certification*)	www.paralegals.org (click *Paralegal Certification*)	www.nals.org (click *Advance*)
Credential Earned by Passing the Exam (For ethical reasons, all signatures using credentials should include the words *paralegal* or *legal assistant* to clarify nonattorney status. See Chapter 5.)	CLA (Certified Legal Assistant) or CP (Certified Paralegal) (the credentials are synonymous) Here is how you would sign your name: ■ Mary Jones, CLA Certified Legal Assistant ■ Mary Jones, CLA Certified Paralegal ■ Mary Jones, CP Certified Legal Assistant ■ Mary Jones, CP Certified Paralegal	CORE Registered Paralegal (CRP) Here is how you would sign your name: ■ Robert Owens, CORE Registered Paralegal ■ Robert Owens, CRP, CORE Registered Paralegal	Professional Paralegal Here is how you would sign your name: ■ Alice Davis, PP, Professional Paralegal ■ Alice Davis, PP, Paralegal

(continued)

Exhibit 4-9 National Certification: NALA, NFPA, and NALS (*Continued*)

	NALA	NFPA	NALS
Required for Employment?	No. Certification is voluntary, although some employers may be impressed by a job applicant who is a CLA or CP.	No. Certification is voluntary, although some employers may be impressed by a job applicant who is a CRP.	No. Certification is voluntary, although some employers may be impressed by a job applicant who is a PP.
Association Membership Required?	No. You can take the exam and become certified without being a member of NALA.	No. You can take the exam and become certified without being a member of NFPA.	No. You can take the exam and become certified without being a member of NALS.
Can the Exam Be Taken Upon Graduating from School—Without Job Experience?	Yes. There are different eligibility categories to sit for the exam. Several do not require paralegal job experience. See Eligibility below.	Yes. There are different eligibility categories to sit for the exam. Several do not require paralegal job experience. See Eligibility below.	Yes. There are different eligibility categories to sit for the exam. Several do not require paralegal job experience. See Eligibility below.
Cost	■ $250 (for members of NALA) ■ $275 (for nonmembers)	$215	■ $200 (for members of NALS) ■ $250 (for nonmembers)
How Exam is Administered	The exam can be taken in January, May, and September at testing centers throughout the country.	The exam can be taken every day except Sundays and holidays at testing centers throughout the country.	The exam can be taken on the first Saturday of March and the last Saturday in September at testing centers throughout the country.
Length of Exam	8 hours	2.5 hours	One day
When Recertification is Required	Recertification is required every two years. It is achieved mainly by attending specified continuing legal education (CLE)	Recertification is required every two years. It is achieved mainly by attending specified continuing legal education (CLE)	Recertification is required every five years. It is achieved mainly by attending specified continuing legal education (CLE)
Subjects Tested	■ Communications ■ Ethics ■ Legal research ■ Judgment and analytical ability ■ Substantive areas of law (American legal system, civil litigation, contracts, business organizations)	■ Paralegal practice (e.g., ethics, the legal system, legal research, civil litigation) ■ Substantive areas of law (e.g., business organizations, contracts, torts)	■ Written communications (e.g., grammar and composition) ■ Legal knowledge and skills (e.g., legal research, interviewing) ■ Ethics and judgment skills ■ Substantive law (e.g., civil procedure, torts, contracts)
Is the Exam State-Specific?	No. The exam is national in scope. It does not test on the law of any particular state.	No. The exam is national in scope. It does not test on the law of any particular state.	No. The exam is national in scope. It does not test on the law of any particular state.
Number Certified	17,000+ (about 44 percent are in Florida and Texas)	183	561
Eligibility: Categories of Criteria to Sit for the Exam	■ Bachelor's degree in paralegal studies ■ Bachelor's degree in any subject plus 1 year of paralegal experience ■ Associate's degree in paralegal studies ■ High school diploma or GED, plus 7 years' experience, and 20 hours of CLE ■ ABA approved paralegal program ■ Other: see website above	■ Bachelor's degree in paralegal studies ■ Bachelor's degree in any subject plus paralegal certificate ■ Associate degree in paralegal studies ■ Associate degree in any subject ■ High school diploma or GED, plus 5 years' experience, and 12 hours of CLE ■ Other: see website above	■ Five years of experience as a paralegal ■ Bachelor's degree in paralegal studies ■ Bachelor's degree in another field plus 1 year of experience as a paralegal ■ Completion of an accredited paralegal program of specified length and content ■ ABA approved paralegal program
Continuing Legal Education (CLE) Requirements	50 hours of CLE every 5 years	8 hours of CLE (including 1 hour of ethics) every two years.	75 hours of CLE (including 5 hours of ethics) every 5 years

(continued)

Exhibit 4-9	National Certification: NALA, NFPA, and NALS (*Continued*)

	NALA	NFPA	NALS
Advanced Certification	NALA also offers advanced certification. It is called *Advanced Paralegal Certification*, which can lead to the Advanced Certified Paralegal (ACP) credential. To earn it, applicants must ■ already have CP/CLA certification, and ■ complete a 20-hour online course in a specific area of law (e.g., family law, contract administration, discovery, trial practice, real estate)	NFPA also offers advanced certification. It is called *PACE RP Certification* (PACE stands for Paralegal Advanced Competency Exam; RP stands for Registered Paralegal.) Applicants must ■ have a bachelor's degree or an associate's degree, and ■ have a designated amount of paralegal experience, and ■ pass an examination	NALS does not offer advanced certification for paralegal. It does offer separate certification for Accredited Legal Secretaries (ALS) and for Professional Legal Secretaries (PLS).
How Those with Advanced Certification Can Identify Themselves	■ John Doe, ACP Contract Administration Paralegal ■ Jane Doe, Advanced Certified Paralegal—Discovery ■ Jane Doe, ACP Advanced Certified Paralegal—Discovery Edward Doe, ACP ACP—Product Liability Paralegal	■ Sam Smith, PACE-Registered Paralegal ■ Sam Smith, RP, Paralegal ■ Sam Smith, RP, Legal Assistant	N/A
Number Who Have Obtained Advanced Certification	3,273	532	N/A

STATE CERTIFICATION

Some states have their own state-specific certification program. Most have exams that test knowledge of the law of a specific state, unlike the national exams of NALA, NFPA, and NALS. State certification exams, like the national ones, are voluntary. They are not required if one wishes to be a paralegal. Some of the state certification programs are run by paralegal associations; others are run by the bar association of the state itself. Exhibit 4-10 presents an overview of the state-specific certification programs of California, Delaware, Florida, Louisiana, Ohio, North Carolina, Pennsylvania, and Texas

FAIR LABOR STANDARDS ACT (FLSA)

Under the federal **Fair Labor Standards Act (FLSA)**, employees are entitled to overtime compensation (one-and-one-half times regular pay) unless they are **exempt**.[78] The FLSA is administered by the U.S. Department of Labor. Before examining whether paralegals are exempt, we need to note two related circumstances that do not involve the FLSA.

■ First, *state* overtime law might be more generous than federal law. Many employees are subject to two wage laws: federal overtime law (the FLSA) and state overtime law. It is possible for an employee to be entitled to overtime under state law but not under federal law. If so, the law that leads to the higher salary controls. In this area of law, federal law does not **preempt** (i.e., displace or take precedence over) state law.
■ Second, unions may negotiate labor contracts that provide better overtime provisions than either federal or state overtime law.

The following discussion is limited to federal overtime law (the FLSA) that covers nonunion employees. (For the link to the state overtime law of your state, see the Helpful Websites at the end of the chapter.)

If employees are not exempt under the FLSA, they must be given overtime compensation. They cannot be pressured by their employers to waive this right. Nor can they be retaliated against if they assert a claim for overtime compensation.

Fair Labor Standards Act (FLSA) The federal statute that regulates conditions of employment such as when overtime compensation must be paid. (29 U.S.C. § 201) (www.dol.gov/whd/flsa).

exempt Not subject to a requirement. The noun form is *exemption*.

preempt Displace or take precedence over. The noun form is *preemption*. Under the Supremacy Clause of the U.S. Constitution, federal laws take precedence over (preempt) any inconsistent state laws when Congress (1) expressly mandates the preemption, (2) regulates an area so pervasively that an intent to preempt the entire field may be inferred, or (3) enacts a law that directly conflicts with state law.

Exhibit 4–10	State Certification Programs:					

STATE	CERTIFICATION CREDENTIAL AWARDED	EXAM ON STATE LAW	PROGRAM RUN BY	DATE BEGAN	REQUIRED FOR EMPLOYMENT?	MORE INFORMATION	COMMENTS
CALIFORNIA	California Advanced Specialist (CAS)	Yes	Commission for Advanced California Paralegal Specialization, Inc.	1995	No. Certification is voluntary.	www.cla-cas.org	Applicants must first have NALA certification before they can become a CAS. See Exhibit 4-9.
DELAWARE	Delaware Certified Paralegal (DCP)	No	Delaware Paralegal Association	2005	No. Certification is voluntary.	www.deparalegals.org /dcp-program.php	
FLORIDA	Florida Registered Paralegal (FRP)	Yes	Florida Bar Association	2007	No. Certification is voluntary.	www.floridabar.org (type *paralegal* in the search box)	There are over 5,000 FRPs in Florida.
FLORIDA	Florida Certified Paralegal (FCP)	Yes	Paralegal Association of Florida	1980	No. Certification is voluntary.	www.pafinc.org (click *Profession* and then *FCP*)	Applicants must first have NALA certification before they can become an FCP. See Exhibit 4-9.
LOUISIANA	Louisiana Certified Paralegal (LCP)	Yes	Louisiana State Paralegal Association	1996	No. Certification is voluntary.	www.la-paralegals.org (click *LCP Certification*)	One qualification to sit for the LCP exam is to have NALA certification. See Exhibit 4-9.
NEW JERSEY	New Jersey Certified Paralegal (NJCP)	No	South Jersey Paralegal Association	2010	No. Certification is voluntary.	www.sjpaparalegals .org	
OHIO	OSBA Certified Paralegal (OSBA stands for Ohio State Bar Association)	Yes	Ohio State Bar Association	2006	No. Certification is voluntary.	www.ohiobar.org (type *paralegal* in the search box)	Over 220 Ohio paralegals are OSBA Certified Paralegals.
NORTH CAROLINA	North Carolina Certified Paralegal (NCCP) North Carolina State Bar Certified Paralegal	Yes	North Carolina State Bar's Board of Paralegal Certification	2005	No. Certification is voluntary.	www. nccertifiedparalegal .org	Over 4,200 North Carolina paralegals are NCCPs.
PENNSYLVANIA	Pennsylvania Certified Paralegal (Pa.CP)	No	Keystone Alliance of Paralegal Associations	2008	No. Certification is voluntary.	www. keystoneparalegals.org	Over 290 Pennsylvania paralegals are PaCPs.
TEXAS	Board Certified Paralegal, Civil Trial Law Board Certified Paralegal, Criminal Law Other areas: estate and probate, personal injury, family, bankruptcy, and real estate	Yes	Texas Board of Legal Specialization of the State Bar of Texas	1994	No. Certification is voluntary.	www.tbls-bcp.org	Over 320 Texas paralegals are board certified.

There are three main categories of exempt employees: executive, professional, and administrative. (They are referred to as the *white-collar exemptions*.) Do paralegals fit within any of them? The answer depends on their primary duties, meaning the main or most important tasks they perform. It does not depend on their title, which, as we saw in chapter 1, can vary from employer to employer. The FSLA uses a duties test, not a titles test to identify who fits within the exemptions. Furthermore, because paralegals perform a wide variety of tasks in many different settings, the question of whether they are exempt must be determined on a case-by-case basis, one paralegal at a time. It is possible for a paralegal in an office to be exempt while another paralegal in the same office is nonexempt.

Here is an overview of the three exemptions and how they might apply to paralegals:

- *Executive exemption*: The employee (1) manages an enterprise such as a department or subdivision that has a permanent status or function in the office; (2) regularly directs the work of two or more employees; and (3) either has the authority to hire, promote, or fire other employees or can recommend such action; if so, the recommendation is given particular weight.

Most paralegal *supervisors* meet all three tests of the executive exemption. They often manage the paralegal unit of the firm, supervise more than two employees, and have great influence on who is hired, promoted, or fired in their department. Paralegals without managerial or supervisory responsibility of this kind do not fit within the executive exemption. If paralegal supervisors meet the requirements of the executive exemption, they do not lose the exemption if they also work on individual client cases in addition to their primary supervisory role.

- *Professional exemption*: The employee performs work that requires advanced knowledge that is customarily acquired by a prolonged course of specialized intellectual instruction. (Advanced knowledge means work that is predominantly intellectual in character and includes work requiring the consistent exercise of discretion and judgment.) There are two categories of exempt professional employees: learned professionals (whose specialized academic training is a standard prerequisite for entrance into the profession) and creative professionals (who work mainly in the creative arts).

Paralegals do not fit within the professional exemption. They are not "learned professionals" because prolonged specialized instruction is not a standard prerequisite to entering the field. A bachelor's degree, for example, is not a prerequisite to becoming a paralegal. (An example of a support occupation that *would* qualify as a learned profession is the registered nurse, because having a specialized advanced degree is a standard prerequisite for becoming a registered nurse.) Also, paralegals are not "creative professionals" because law is not in the same category as music, theater, or one of the other creative arts.

- *Administrative exemption*: The employee (1) performs office work that is directly related to the management or general business operations of the employer or of the employer's customers, and (2) exercises discretion and independent judgment with respect to matters of significance. The question of whether the administrative exemption applies to paralegals is less clear. Historically, the U.S. Department of Labor (DOL) has argued that this exemption does not apply to the vast majority of paralegals.

The first test under the administrative exemption is that the employees perform office work that is directly related to the management or general business operations of the employer or of the employer's customers. This means "assisting with the running or servicing of the business" such as working on budgets, purchasing equipment, or administering the office's computer database. Such tasks, however, are not the primary duties of most paralegals, although they may help out in these areas. In the main, paralegals spend most of their time working on individual cases and hence do not meet the first test.

The second test (which also must be met for the administrative exemption to apply) is that the employees exercise "discretion and independent judgment with respect to matters of significance." The phrase "discretion and independent judgment" involves:

- comparing and evaluating possible courses of conduct and
- acting or making a decision after the various possibilities have been considered.

The phrase implies that the employee has authority to make an independent choice, "free from immediate direction or supervision." An employee does not exercise discretion and independent judgment if he or she merely uses skills in applying well-established techniques, procedures, or standards described in manuals or other sources.

Do paralegals meet the second test of exercising "discretion and independent judgment with respect to matters of significance"? They certainly work on "matters of significance." Yet it is not clear whether they exercise "discretion and independent judgment." Paralegals are often given some leeway in the performance of their work. Yet if they operate "within closely prescribed limits," they are *not* exercising discretion and independent judgment.

The DOL has consistently taken the position that paralegals do not have the kind of independence this exemption requires because of the attorney supervision and approval their work must be given under the rules of ethics. As we will see in Chapter 5, if paralegals make independent choices on client matters, they run the risk of being charged with engaging in unauthorized practice of law (UPL).

For years paralegals debated the desirability of being classified as exempt or nonexempt. The debate was referred to as GOD, the great overtime debate. Those opposed to overtime compensation felt that being classified as exempt gave them increased respect. Attorneys do not receive overtime compensation. Their long hours are rewarded by higher salaries and bonuses. If paralegals were exempt, they would be treated in a similar way. Other paralegals pointed out that there is nothing demeaning about receiving overtime and that many firms offered bonuses to both exempt and nonexempt employees. Today the GOD is relatively quiet. It raged during a time when there was doubt on when the law allowed an exemption. Such doubt no longer exists.

To summarize,

- Paralegals who are not exempt must receive overtime compensation. Paralegals who are exempt are not entitled to overtime compensation.
- Most paralegals who do not supervise others are not exempt under the executive exemption.
- Many paralegal supervisors are exempt under the executive exemption.
- Most paralegals are not exempt under the professional exemption unless they have an advanced degree.
- Most paralegals are probably not exempt under the administrative exemption.

Despite these general principles, disputes continue to arise on whether specific employees should be paid overtime. In 2012, forty-eight lawsuits were pending in which paralegals alleged violations of the overtime law.[79] Not all law offices comply with (or, in some instances, understand) the overtime law.

TORT LIABILITY

Thus far we have discussed a number of ways that paralegal activities are or could be regulated.

- Criminal liability for violating the statutes on unauthorized practice of law (UPL)
- Special authorization rules on practice before administrative agencies and other tribunals
- Licensing
- Certification
- Labor laws

Finally, we come to **tort** liability, which is another method by which society defines what is and is not permissible. A tort action is brought when someone has allegedly caused injury or other damage by committing a civil wrong other than a breach of contract. While a tort is different from a breach of contract and a crime, the same conduct that constitutes a breach of contract or a crime can also constitute a tort.[80]

PERSONAL AND VICARIOUS LIABILITY

Two questions need to be kept in mind. First, when are paralegal employees personally liable for their torts? Second, when are employers vicariously liable for the torts of their paralegal employees? (**Vicarious liability** simply means one person being responsible or liable for what

tort A civil wrong (other than a breach of contract) that causes injury or other loss for which our legal system deems it just to provide a remedy such as damages. Injury or loss can be to the person (a personal tort), to movable property (a personal-property tort), or to land and anything attached to the land (a real-property tort).

vicarious liability Liability imposed on a person for the conduct of another, based solely upon the status of the relationship between the two (e.g., employer and employee). The person liable is not the person whose conduct led to the liability.

another person does because of the relationship that exists between them.) The short answer to the first question is *always*. The short answer to the second question is *when the wrongdoing by the paralegal was within the scope of employment*. After covering both questions, we will then examine the separate question of when malpractice insurance will pay for such liability.

Several different kinds of wrongdoing are possible. The paralegal might commit

- The tort of negligence
- An intentional tort, such as battery
- An act that is both a crime (such as embezzlement) and an intentional tort (such as conversion)

A client who is injured by any of these torts can sue the paralegal in the same manner that a patient in a hospital can sue a nurse. Paralegals are not relieved of liability simply because they work for, and function under the supervision of, an attorney. Individuals have **personal liability** for the torts they commit. If a client suffers harm because of the negligence or other wrongdoing of a paralegal and the client sues the paralegal, it is not a defense that the employee committed the wrongdoing on behalf of someone else (an attorney in a law office).

Next we turn to the employers of paralegals. Are they *also* liable for the wrongdoing committed by their employees? There are four possible theories of employer liability for employee wrongdoing: careless hiring, careless supervision, participation in the wrongdoing, and vicarious liability

- *Careless hiring*: The employer was careless in hiring the employee; the employer should have known that the person was likely to commit wrongdoing. (This theory is called **negligent hiring.**)

- *Careless supervision*: The employer was careless in supervising the employee; the wrongdoing by the employee would not have occurred if the employer exercised proper oversight of the employee's work or provided proper training. (This theory is called **negligent supervision.**)

- *Participation in the wrongdoing*: The employer actually participated in the wrongdoing with the employee; the two of them committed the wrongdoing together.

- *Vicarious liability*: The employer is liable for what the employee did solely because of the special relationship that exists between them—an employer–employee relationship. (As mentioned. this theory is called *vicarious liability*.)[81]

Not all wrongdoing of an employee will result in vicarious liability of the employer. Under the doctrine of **respondeat superior**, an employer will be liable for the wrongdoing of his or her employee if the wrongdoing occurred within the **scope of employment**. This means the wrongdoing was foreseeably done by an employee for the employer's business under the employer's specific or general control. Slandering a client in a law office for failure to pay a law firm bill would be within the scope of employment. It's foreseeable that a paralegal would insult a client for this reason. It's not what the employer would want the paralegal to do, but it is foreseeable and it occurs within the confines and general control of the employer. However, the opposite would probably be true if the paralegal had an argument with a client over a football game and punched the client during their accidental evening meeting at a bar. In the latter example, the client could not sue the paralegal's employer under the theory of respondeat superior for the intentional tort of battery. The battery was not foreseeable by the employer, was not under the employer's control, and was unrelated to the business of the employer. Only the paralegal would be liable for the tort under such circumstances.

When a paralegal's wrongdoing is within the scope of employment (making the paralegal personally liable and the attorney employer vicariously liable under respondeat superior), the client can sue the paralegal or the attorney, or both. This does not mean that the client recovers twice; there can be only one recovery for the tort. Clients are simply given a choice on whom to collect damages from. If, for example, a client is entitled to $75,000 in damages because of the tort committed by the paralegal, the client can recover the entire $75,000 from the attorney, or the entire $75,000 from the paralegal, or part from each until the $75,000 is paid. In most cases, the primary target of the client will be the employer, who is the **deep pocket**—the one who is most likely to have resources from which a judgment can be satisfied.

---

personal liability Liability that can be satisfied out of a wrongdoer's personal as well as business assets.

negligent hiring Carelessly hiring an incompetent person who poses an unreasonable risk of harm to others.

negligent supervision Carelessly monitoring or supervising an incompetent person who poses an unreasonable risk of harm to others.

respondeat superior "Let the master [boss] answer." An employer is responsible (liable) for the wrongs committed by an employee within the scope of employment.

scope of employment That which is foreseeably done by an employee for the employer's business under the employer's specific or general control.

deep pocket (1) An individual, a business, or another organization with resources to pay a potential judgment. (2) Sufficient assets for this purpose. The opposite of *shallow pocket.*

NEGLIGENCE

The most commonly committed tort is **negligence**. This tort occurs when the defendant's failure to use reasonable care causes injury or other loss. When a member of an occupation or profession is charged with negligence, reasonable care is determined by the knowledge and skill commonly possessed by members of that occupation or profession in good standing. Attorney negligence is the failure to exercise the reasonable care expected of an attorney in good standing. An attorney is not an insurer, however. Every mistake will not lead to negligence liability even if it causes harm to the client. The harm must be due to an unreasonable mistake, such as forgetting to file an action in court before the **statute of limitations** runs out. Reasonable attorneys file on time.

CAUSATION

Client victims of negligence must establish that they suffered actual harm. It is not enough to show that a law office failed to use reasonable care. This failure must lead to (i.e., cause) actual harm. Assume that an attorney represents Tom, who wants to sue his employer for $25,000 in back wages. The case is dismissed, however, because his attorney carelessly fails to file the claim before the statute of limitations runs out. Tom now sues the attorney for negligence. What are Tom's damages in this negligence suit? Tom has not lost $25,000 *unless* he can establish that he would have won the case against his employer if it had not been thrown out because of the attorney's filing negligence. If the wage claim was so weak that Tom would have lost it if it had gone to trial, there was no loss of $25,000. Hence, in a negligence action against an attorney, the client must show (a) that the attorney's conduct fell below the standard of reasonable care expected of attorneys, and (b) that the underlying claim would have been successful if the attorney had not been careless.

PARALEGALS

When a *traditional paralegal* (one employed by an attorney) commits negligence for which the attorney becomes liable under respondeat superior, the same standard applies. Because the work product of this paralegal blends into the work product of the supervising attorney, the attorney becomes as fully responsible for what the paralegal did as if the attorney had committed the negligence. Unreasonableness is measured by what a reasonable attorney would have done, not by what a reasonable paralegal would have done.

An *independent contractor* or document service provider (DSP) who does not work under attorney supervision would be treated differently. Because DSPs do not work under attorney supervision, they will be held to the standard of a reasonable DSP. The standard would be the knowledge and skill commonly possessed by a DSP in good standing. If one is charged with negligence, he or she will not be held to the standard of a reasonable attorney—unless the DSP led the client to believe he or she was an attorney or to believe that he or she worked under an attorney's supervision.

There have not been many tort cases in which paralegals have been sued for wrongdoing in a law office. Yet as paralegals become increasingly prominent in the practice of law, more are expected to be named as defendants. The general counsel of the Mississippi Bar Association makes the unsettling point that the prominence of paralegalism means there will be more suits against paralegals. "As paralegals become more and more professional and proficient, they ... will become better targets for disgruntled clients looking for someone to sue."[82] The most common case of paralegal liability has involved false notarization. The paralegal was a notary and improperly notarized signatures under pressure from the supervising attorney. For example, the paralegal may have been asked to notarize the signature of a person the paralegal did not observe signing the document.

MALICIOUS PROSECUTION AND ABUSE OF PROCESS

There are two other torts we need to consider: malicious prosecution and abuse of process. They involve the misuse of legal process. **Process** refers to a summons, writ, or court order by which a court acquires its jurisdiction over a person.

Malicious Prosecution

- *Nature of the tort of malicious prosecution*: Someone maliciously initiates a civil or criminal case for which there is no probable cause and that is won by the party against whom the case was brought.

negligence The failure to use reasonable care that an ordinary prudent person would have used in a similar situation, resulting in injury or other loss.

statute of limitations A law stating that civil or criminal actions are barred if not brought within a specified period of time. The action is time-barred if not brought within that time.

process The means (e.g., a summons, writ, or other court order) used by the court to acquire its power or jurisdiction over a person.

malicious prosecution A tort with the following elements: (1) The initiation (or procuring the initiation) of civil or criminal legal proceedings; (2) without probable cause; (3) with malice or an improper purpose; and (4) the proceedings terminate in favor of the person against whom the proceedings were brought.

> ■ *Example*: A store owner files a criminal complaint for drug dealing against a hated neighbor whom the store owner knows is innocent. The neighbor is eventually found to be innocent. The store owner used the law firm of Adams & Adams for legal advice in bringing the criminal complaint. The store owner initiated legal proceedings without probable cause (the store owner knew the neighbor was innocent), because of hatred (an improper motive), and the neighbor won the case (there was a finding of innocence).

Abuse of Process

abuse of process A tort consisting of the following elements: (1) the use of a civil or criminal proceedings, (2) for a purpose for which the process is not designed, (3) resulting in actual damage.

> ■ *Nature of the tort of abuse of process*: Someone uses process for a purpose for which it was not designed.
> ■ *Example*: A father brings a suit for child custody against the mother (his ex-girlfriend) of his child in order to pressure her to pay a business debt she owes the father. In the suit, the father was represented by the law firm of Smith & Smith. Process was abused because the purpose of custody suits is not to collect unrelated debts.

In these examples, the neighbor can sue the store owner for the tort of malicious prosecution and the mother can sue the father for the tort of abuse of process. They will probably try to join as defendants the attorneys used by the store owner (Adams & Adams) and by the father (Smith & Smith). Such suits against attorneys are seldom successful, however, because attorneys (and their staffs) have a privilege to use the courts on behalf of their clients. It would have to be shown that the attorneys knowingly and maliciously helped their clients misuse process against the neighbor and mother. This is difficult to prove. Yet victims such as the neighbor and mother may be so angry that they will want to join the attorneys as defendants.

MALPRACTICE INSURANCE

malpractice (1) Any professional misconduct such as an ethics violation, breach of fiduciary duty, crime, tort, or other wrongdoing. (2) Negligence committed by a professional.

In the broadest sense, **malpractice** is any professional misconduct such as an ethics violation, breach of fiduciary duty, crime, tort, or other wrongdoing. More narrowly, malpractice refers to negligence committed by a professional. When the professional committing the malpractice is an attorney, the malpractice is called *legal malpractice*. As indicated, attorney negligence (the most common example of legal malpractice) is the failure to exercise the reasonable care expected of an attorney in good standing. Just as doctors purchase malpractice insurance against suits by their patients, so, too, attorneys can buy insurance to cover suits against them by their clients for alleged errors and omissions.

Until the 1940s, not many attorneys bought malpractice insurance because suits by clients were relatively rare. Today, the picture has substantially changed.

- ■ Malpractice claims cost attorneys and their insurers over $4 billion a year.[83]
- ■ Six of the seven insurance companies that insure 80 percent of the 250 largest law firms report a significant increase in claims above $50 million. Two of the insurers said that there was an increase in claims based on the failure of law firms to provide proper training or supervision of new attorneys.[84]
- ■ A study of claims between 2008 and 2011 showed the following percentage of total claims in the practices indicated:
  - 20.3 percent: real estate (residential and commercial)
  - 15.5 percent: personal injury (attorneys representing plaintiffs)
  - 12.1 percent: family law
  - 10.7 percent: estate, trust, and probate
  - 9.2 percent: collection and bankruptcy
  - 3.2 percent: personal injury (attorneys representing defendants)[85]

- ■ The 2008–2011 study showed the following percentage of reasons claims were filed:
  - 13.5 percent: failure to know the law or to apply it properly
  - 9.7 percent: procrastination
  - 7.8 percent: planning error
  - 7.3 percent: inadequate discovery
  - 7.0 percent: lost file, document, or evidence
  - 7.0 percent: failure to obtain client consent
  - 6.9 percent: failure to know a deadline

- 5.7 percent: failure to follow client instructions
- 4.5 percent: fraud by attorney
- 4.3 percent: failure to calendar
- 4.2 percent: conflict of interest
- 3.5 percent: clerical error
- 3.4 percent: abuse of process
- 3.1 percent: failure to file a document
- 3.0 percent: error in record search
- 2.3 percent: failure to react to calendar
- 1.2 percent: violation of civil rights
- 1.3 percent: error in tax law
- 1.8 percent: improper withdrawal from a client's case
- 0.9 percent: libel or slander committed by attorney[86]

- Statistically, a "new attorney will be subjected to three claims before finishing a legal career."[87]
- 16.5 percent of malpractice claims result in payments in excess of $10,000.[88]
- In some cities, the premium for insurance can be between $5,000 and $15,000 per year per attorney.
- An estimated 40 percent of all attorneys do not have malpractice insurance.[89]

It's surprising how many attorneys are willing to **go bare**—that is, practice without liability insurance—in light of the increasing willingness of clients to sue their attorneys for legal malpractice.

> **go bare** To engage in an occupation or profession without malpractice (liability) insurance

The increase in malpractice suits has been due to a number of factors. As the practice of law becomes more complex, the likelihood of error increases. Furthermore, the public is becoming more aware of its right to sue. In spite of disclaimers by attorneys that they are not guaranteeing any results, client expectations tend to be high, and hence clients are more likely to blame their attorney for an unfavorable result. Also, attorneys are increasingly willing to sue each other. In fact, some attorneys have developed a legal malpractice specialty in which they take clients who want to sue other attorneys. (To find attorneys with this specialty, run this search in Google, Bing, or Yahoo: "suing attorneys.") To discourage attorneys from going bare, some states require attorneys with no insurance or with low insurance (e.g., below $100,000) to disclose this fact to their clients or prospective clients.[90]

Typically, legal malpractice claims arise in the context of fee disputes. The sequence is often as follows:

- a client fails to pay agreed-upon attorney fees,
- the attorney sues the client for fees,
- the client responds by suing the attorney for malpractice, and
- the client files an ethics charge with the bar association alleging the same malpractice.

Two kinds of professional liability insurance policies cover attorney malpractice: occurrence policies and claims-made policies. An **occurrence policy** covers all occurrences (such as negligent error or omission) during the period the policy is in effect, even if the claim on such an occurrence is not actually filed until after the policy expires. Insurance companies are reluctant to write such policies because of the length of time it sometimes takes to uncover the existence of the negligent error or omission. Here's an example: An attorney makes a careless mistake in drafting a will. The mistake is not discovered until the person who hired the attorney dies many years later. Under an occurrence policy, the attorney is covered if the mistake occurred while the policy was in effect, even if the actual claim was not filed in court until after the policy terminated. The most common kind of policy sold by insurance companies today is the **claims-made policy** under which coverage is limited to claims actually filed (made) during the period in which the policy is in effect. Covered claims under both occurrence and claims-made policies are subject to limits on the amount the insurance company will pay per claim and over the life of the policy.

> **occurrence policy** Insurance that covers all occurrences (e.g., a negligent error or omission) during the period the policy is in effect, even if the claim is not actually filed until after the policy expires.

> **claims-made policy** Insurance that covers only claims actually filed (i.e., made) during the period in which the policy is in effect.

Malpractice policies usually cover all the attorneys and the nonattorney employees of the law office. One policy, for example, includes within the definition of "the insured"

> Any non-lawyer who was, is now, or hereinafter becomes an employee, leased employee or independent contractor of the Policyholder or Predecessor Firm(s), but solely for acts or omissions while acting within the scope of such person's duties as an employee, leased employee or independent contractor of the Policyholder.[91]

Such inclusion of employees, however, is not always automatic. The policies of some insurance companies do not include paralegals or secretaries unless the law firm specifically requests coverage for them and pays an additional premium for their inclusion. Paralegals should therefore ask their employers if their malpractice policy explicitly covers paralegals.

What about independent paralegals who are not employees of attorneys but who instead sell their services to attorneys and, therefore, work under attorney supervision? Although they may not be considered employees of the firm, they will usually be covered under the firm's policy in the same manner as full-time, in-house (traditional) paralegal employees. So long as the employing attorney supervises and is responsible for the conduct of the paralegal, the malpractice policy usually provides coverage. In the language of one widely used policy, coverage is provided for "any other person for whose acts, errors or omissions the insured is legally responsible,"[92] which would include independent or freelance paralegals. A sophisticated independent paralegal would make sure that this is so before undertaking work for an attorney.

Independent contractors who do not work for attorneys—document service providers (DSPs)—need to purchase their own liability policies if they want protection. As we saw earlier in the chapter, legal document assistants (LDAs) in California are required to purchase a bond in the amount of $25,000. The bond costs approximately $500 a year. In general, liability insurance is expensive and difficult to find. At one time, a company offered "Paralegal Professional Indemnity Insurance" that provided $250,000 in coverage for $1,800 a year. The company offering this policy no longer exists. Most DSPs today "go bare" except in a state like California.

CHAPTER SUMMARY

The major ways in which paralegals could be regulated are laws on unauthorized practice of law (UPL), licensing, certification, labor law (FLSA), tort laws, and ethical rules. Criminal prosecution may result from engaging in UPL. The practice of law is the use or attempt to use legal skills to help resolve a specific person's legal problem. UPL is the use or attempt to use legal skills to help resolve a specific person's legal problem when the assistance is provided by someone who does not have a license to practice law and when the assistance requires such a license or other authorization. The definition of the practice of law is criticized as being too broad. Courts use one or more general tests as a guide to whether a particular service is the practice of law. The most commonly used tests are the professional-judgment test, the general public/personal relationship test, and the traditional-areas test. Legal information is any statement about the law that is not directed at the facts of a specific person's legal problem. Legal advice is a statement or conclusion that applies the law or legal principles to the facts of a specific person's legal problem.

Self-help is self-representation, representing oneself with or without assistance from an attorney, document service provider (DSP), online legal site, manual, or other materials. A DSP is a nonattorney who works without attorney supervision to provide legal-document assistance to individuals who are representing themselves. DSPs are controversial mainly because of the allegation that they sometimes select forms for their clients and give them individual assistance in how to fill them out and hence commit UPL. DSPs can sell forms and other legal materials but cannot give individual help in using them. They can give (and sell) legal information, but they cannot give legal advice. Major types of DSPs include the bankruptcy petition preparer (BPP), legal document assistant (LDA), unlawful detainer assistant (UDA), and legal document preparer (LDP).

Interactive computer programs must point out that they cannot give legal advice and must have no human interaction that makes corrections and suggestions based on the answers provided by the user.

Antitrust law governs unlawful interference with competition such as through price fixing, monopolies, and other restraints of trade. The U.S. Department of Justice has said that efforts by the American Bar Association to enter statements of principles or to write a broad definition of the practice of law could illegally prevent competition with nonattorney service providers without a showing that such competition is harming the public. *Bates v. State Bar of Arizona* held that truthful attorney advertising cannot be completely banned. Such advertising is commercial speech protected by the First Amendment. *Goldfarb v. Virginia State Bar* held that the legal profession cannot impose minimum-fee schedules on attorneys.

For the most part, nonattorneys are not allowed to represent others in court. There are, however, some limited exceptions. Courts that allow nonattorney representation include some small-claims courts, the U.S. Tax Court, and some tribal courts. A few courts will allow a nonattorney to make a limited-purpose calendar-call appearance on behalf of his or her supervising attorney to ask for a continuance or to make some other administrative request.

Johnson v. Avery held that a prison could not bar a nonattorney from giving legal assistance to another inmate if the prison failed to provide alternative legal services that would allow the inmate to exercise his or her constitutional right of access to the courts.

Many administrative agencies allow nonattorney representation because the fees generated from such representation do not attract enough attorneys. The administrative proceedings often involve factual issues rather than complicated issues of law that require all the skills of an attorney. Administrative proceedings are conducted with more flexible procedural rules than court proceedings. Another reason why nonattorney representation is allowed at agencies is the concern that the combative nature of attorneys would turn every informal hearing or conference into a drawn-out battle. The Supremacy Clause gives the federal government the power to authorize nonattorney representation at federal administrative agencies despite state UPL laws. The legality of nonattorney representation at state agencies depends on which branch of state government has the power to define the practice of law. Although nonattorney representation at many federal and state agencies exists, not many nonattorneys provide such representation.

Occupations may seek to be licensed to protect the public and to enhance the occupation's own image. Licensing traditional paralegals is arguably not needed because the public is adequately protected by attorney supervision. There are a few states that have imposed requirements on when the titles *paralegal* and *legal assistant* can be used, but no state has gone so far as to require a license in order to perform paralegal tasks. There are serious proposals, however, for limited licensing in order to help close the justice gap. Washington State has in fact created limited licensing for the Limited License Legal Technician (LLLT).

Reforms designed to help close the justice gap include pro bono work, simplified forms, Internet self-help centers, Internet document preparation sites, court facilitators, prepaid legal services, attorney advertising, unbundled legal services, e-filing, publicly funded legal services, social media outreach, modest means panels, traditional paralegals, and limited licensing.

Certification is a formal acknowledgment that a person or organization has met designated qualifications. Paralegal certification programs are run by nongovernmental organizations and are voluntary in that certification is not required to be a paralegal. The major national certification programs are run by NALA, NFPA, and NALS. The states with state certification programs include California, Delaware, Florida, Louisiana, New Jersey, Ohio, North Carolina, Pennsylvania, and Texas.

The Fair Labor Standards Act (FLSA) requires employers to pay overtime compensation to employees unless the latter are exempt. There are three categories of exemption: executive, professional, and administrative. Most paralegals (other than some paralegal managers) are not exempt and hence are entitled to overtime compensation. State labor laws and union contracts may provide greater overtime rights than those accorded under the federal FLSA.

If a paralegal commits a tort, such as negligence, he or she is personally liable to the defendant. Under the theory of respondeat superior, the supervising attorney is also liable for the wrong committed by a traditional paralegal if it occurred within the scope of employment. Other theories of supervisor (employer) liability include careless hiring, careless supervision, and participation in the wrongdoing. The major attorney errors and misconduct that have led to malpractice insurance claims include failure to know the law and procrastination.

For malpractice insurance, an occurrence policy covers all occurrences (e.g., a negligent error or omission) during the period the policy is in effect, even if the claim is not actually filed until after the policy expires. A claims-made policy covers only claims actually filed (i.e., made) during the period in which the policy is in effect. Most attorneys have an insurance policy that covers their employees, although paralegals should check to be sure that they are covered by such policies.

KEY TERMS

regulation (p. 156)
accreditation (p. 156)
approval (p. 156)
certification (p. 156)
certified (p. 156)
certificated (p. 156)
code (p. 156)
ethics (p. 156)
guideline (p. 156)
license (p. 156)
occupational license (p. 156)
licensing (p. 156)
general licensing (p. 156)
limited licensing (p. 156)
registration (p. 156)
practice of law (p. 157)
unauthorized practice of law
  (UPL) (p. 157)
traditional paralegal (p. 157)
document service provider
  (DSP) (p. 157)
professional judgment (p. 158)
legal advice (p. 158)
legal information (p. 159)
self-help (p. 162)
pro se (p. 162)
litigant (p. 162)
pleading (p. 162)

independent contractor (p. 162)
bankruptcy petition preparer
  (BPP) (p. 163)
exemption (p. 163)
discharge (p. 163)
legal document assistant (LDA)
  (p. 163)
unlawful detainer assistant
  (UDA) (p. 163)
ministerial (p. 164)
bond (p. 164)
continuing legal education
  (CLE) (p. 165)
legal document preparer (LDP)
  (p. 165)
antitrust law (p. 167)
statement of principles (p. 167)
minimum-fee schedule (p. 167)
counterclaim (p. 170)
court of record (p. 170)
calendar call (p. 171)
law clerk (p. 172)
continuance (p. 172)
uncontested (p. 173)
ex parte (p. 173)
pleading (p. 173)
memorandum of law (p. 173)
appellate brief (p. 173)

litigious (p. 173)
jailhouse lawyer (p. 173)
adversarial (p. 174)
adversary system (p. 175)
Supremacy Clause (p. 175)
separation of powers (p. 176)
usurp (p. 176)
Administrative Procedure Act
  (APA) (p. 177)
patent agent (p. 177)
enrolled agent (p. 177)
administrative law judge (ALJ)
  (p. 178)
statutory-fee cases (p. 182)
page 52 debate (p. 184)
Juris Doctor (J.D.) (p. 185)
justice gap (p. 186)
Limited Practice Officer (LPO)
  (p. 186)
Limited License Legal
  Technician (LLLT) (p. 187)
client trust account (p. 188)
pro bono (p. 188)
surety (p. 188)
attorney-client privilege (ACP)
  (p. 188)
fiduciary (p. 188)
prepaid legal services (p. 190)

unbundled legal services
  (p. 190)
e-filing (p. 190)
IOLTA (p. 190)
entry-level certification
  (p. 192)
Fair Labor Standards Act
  (FLSA) (p. 194)
exempt (p. 194)
preempt (p. 194)
tort (p. 197)
vicarious liability (p. 197)
personal liability (p. 198)
negligent hiring (p. 198)
negligent supervision (p. 198)
respondeat superior (p. 198)
scope of employment (p. 198)
deep pocket (p. 198)
negligence (p. 199)
statute of limitations (p. 199)
process (p. 199)
malicious prosecution (p. 199)
abuse of process (p. 200)
malpractice (p. 200)
go bare (p. 201)
occurrence policy (p. 201)
claims-made policy (p. 201)

ASSIGNMENTS

CRITICAL ANALYSIS

4.1 The text discussed the distinction between giving legal information and legal advice. Assume that you are a paralegal talking to Mary Smith, who is thinking about filing for divorce. Give several examples of what you might tell this person that would constitute:

(a) Legal information about her legal rights

(b) Legal advice on her legal rights

4.2

(a) Do you favor broad-based licensing for every paralegal? Limited licensing? Will licensing advance or restrict the development of paralegalism?

(b) If all attorneys in the country drastically cut their fees, would there be a need for paralegal licensing?

4.3 A former paralegal educator made the following observation about paralegal licensing: "The emerging professions and the more established professions have frequently sought greater regulation of their occupational group. They are often motivated, despite the obligatory language on protection of the public interest, to do so in efforts to establish their 'territorial imperative' or to establish barriers to entry into the profession and thereby enhance their economic self-interest." Should paralegals establish such barriers on who can become a paralegal? David Sapadin, *A Comparison of the Growth and Development of the Physician Assistant and the Legal Assistant*, Journal of the American Association for Paralegal Education: Retrospective 1983, 142 (1983).

4.4 Sam Jones is a paralegal at the XYZ law firm. One of his tasks is to file a document in court. He negligently forgets to do so. As a result, the court dismisses the client's case. What options are available to the client?

PROJECTS

4.5 Pick one of the reforms listed in Exhibit 4-8 to help close the justice gap. Prepare a report on that reform. The reform you select must meet the following characteristics: (1) The reform has been tried in your state. (2) You are able to describe the reform in detail. (3) You have found comments about the effectiveness of the reform in closing the justice gap. If the reform you select does not meet these characteristics, select another reform from Exhibit 4-8 that does. To find material on the reform you select, enter relevant terms involving the reform in Google, Bing, or Yahoo. Also run this search: "justice gap" aa (substituting your state for aa).

CORE SKILLS

Among the many skills a paralegal must have, five core skills stand out: writing (both basic English and legal drafting), research, ethics, computer use, and collaboration (working with others). The core-skill assignments introduce and reinforce these skills. Even if you are not asked to do all of the assignments as part of the course, you should do them on your own. Also, do not wait for the topics in the assignments to be covered in this course or in other courses. Successful paralegals are self-starters. A major characteristic of a self-starter is a thirst for independent study—learning on your own.

CORE SKILL: WRITING

4.6

(a) Define the practice of law in your state. Quote from your state code, court rules, or other official authority that is available. See your state in Appendix D.

(b) Apply the practice-of-law rule in your state to the facts of the Rosemary Furman case presented in the chapter in order to determine whether what she did in the 1970s would be the unauthorized practice of law (UPL) in your state today. Explain whether Furman would or would not be prosecuted for UPL in your state today. If you need additional facts about what Furman did, you can make them up so long as they are reasonably consistent with the facts given to you about Furman in the chapter. (If you live in Florida, do this assignment on the basis of *current* UPL law in Florida.) As a guide for your writing, follow the structure of the memorandum of law in Exhibits 7-9 and 7-10 in Chapter 7.

CORE SKILL: RESEARCH

4.7 On Yahoo, run this search: Yahoo search techniques tips.

(a) List five Yahoo search techniques that you did not know or with which you were only vaguely familiar. Examples might be how to search for a phrase, how to specifically exclude a term in a search query so that you would be led to sites that did not contain that term, and how to write a search for a three-word phrase when you are not sure of the middle word in the phrase.

(b) Make up five searches that use the five Yahoo techniques you identified—one search for each of the new techniques. List each of the five searches and give an example of a good site to which each search led you.

(c) In Assignment 2.7 in Chapter 2, you listed five Google search techniques. Do these five Google techniques also work in Yahoo or does Yahoo have its own techniques for the same kinds of searches?

(d) In Assignment 3.5 in Chapter 3, you listed five Bing search techniques. Do these five Bing techniques also work in Yahoo or does Yahoo have its own techniques for the same kinds of searches?

CORE SKILL: ETHICS

4.8 In the section on Roles for Paralegals in Administrative Proceedings, former Chief Justice Rehnquist of the U.S. Supreme Court said that "Under our adversary system, the role of counsel is *not* to make sure the truth is ascertained," and that "sowing confusion" may be an ethical duty of an attorney. What did the Chief Justice mean by these comments?

4.9   Dave Toolan is a nonattorney who sells divorce forms in your state. His business engages in the unauthorized practice of law (UPL) because he also gives his customers legal advice. Dave's good friend is an attorney in the state, Kevin Farrell. Kevin lent Dave money to start his divorce forms business and takes calls from Dave to answer questions that arise in Dave's business. Assume that the state prosecutes Dave for UPL. What ethical rules has Kevin Farrell violated?

In Assignment 1.7 (Chapter 1) you identified the site that contains the ethics code of your state. Use this code to find rules that Kevin Farrell may have violated. (See also Appendix D for ethics links to your state.)

CORE SKILL: COMPUTERS

4.10   In Chapter 13, read the section on word processing. On Google, Bing, or Yahoo, search for terms that will help you answer the following questions:

(a)   What is a word processor?

(b)   What are the main word processors that are sold?

(c)   Which of these word processors is the most widely used?

(d)   What are the main word processors that are free?

(e)   Name one of the free word processors that is considered to be popular.

(f)   Find discussions that compare the word processor you selected in question (c) with the word processor you selected

in question (e). What are some of the differences other than cost?

(g)   In the Computer Terminology in the Law (CTL) notebook you started in Assignment 1.8 of Chapter 1, enter any new terms that you learned by doing parts (a) to (f).

CORE SKILL: COLLABORATION

4.11   In Assignment 3.3 of Chapter 3, you opened a LinkedIn account and wrote your profile. Do a search on LinkedIn for the names of all your classmates. Invite each to be a connection. (Review the discussion of LinkedIn in Exhibit 2-13 in Chapter 2.)

THE JOB SEARCH

(The search for employment cannot wait until the end of a course or of a curriculum. It needs to begin now. The job-search assignments are designed to introduce you to different aspects of the job search and to build options for you to explore about employment.)

4.12   In Google, Bing, or Yahoo, enter this search: "entry level" paralegal job aa (substituting your state for "aa"). Make a list of job openings that meet these criteria. What questions do you have about any of these jobs?

REVIEW QUESTIONS

1.   In what six ways are paralegals regulated?
2.   Define *regulation, accreditation, approval, certification, certified, certificated, code, ethics, guideline, license, occupational license, licensing, general license, limited license,* and *registration.*
3.   What is the practice of law?
4.   What is the UPL?
5.   Under what two circumstances can a traditional paralegal be charged with the unauthorized practice of law (UPL)?
6.   What is a document service provider (DSP)?
7.   Why is UPL a crime?
8.   What is the circular definition of the practice of law?
9.   What is the professional-judgment test?
10.   What is the traditional-areas test?
11.   What is the distinction between legal advice and legal information?
12.   What is self-help?
13.   Why are DSPs controversial?
14.   Describe the roles of the major DSPs: bankruptcy petition preparer (BPP), legal document assistant (LDA), unlawful detainer assistant (UDA), and legal document preparer (LDP) and state how they can avoid engaging in the UPL.
15.   Why was Rosemary Furman prosecuted in Florida?
16.   How do interactive computer programs avoid the charge that they are engaging in UPL?
17.   What is antitrust law and how might it apply to attempts by bar associations to define the practice of law?

18.   What were the holdings of *Bates v. State Bar of Arizona* and *Goldfarb v. Virginia State Bar*?
19.   To what extent can nonattorneys represent others or make appearances in court?
20.   What did *Johnson v. Avery* decide?
21.   What is an adversarial proceeding?
22.   Why do some administrative agencies allow nonattorney representation?
23.   What is the objection to nonattorney representation at federal administrative agencies and how is this objection resolved?
24.   What is the objection to nonattorney representation at state administrative agencies and how is this objection resolved?
25.   What does the federal Administrative Procedure Act (APA) say about nonattorney representation?
26.   What is the extent of nonattorney representation at federal and state administrative agencies?
27.   What is an enrolled agent?
28.   What is the distinction between occupational licensing and certification?
29.   Why do some occupations seek to be licensed?
30.   Why have there been no serious proposals for the licensing of traditional paralegals?
31.   What is limited licensing?
32.   What was the page 52 debate?
33.   What is a Limited License Legal Technician (LLLT)?

34. What is the justice gap?

35. What are the major reforms implemented and proposed to help close the justice gap?

36. What are the most common requirements for many paralegal certification programs?

37. What are the major national certification programs for paralegals?

38. Which states have paralegal certification programs?

39. What are the overtime requirements of the Fair Labor Standards Act (FLSA)?

40. What is the tort liability of paralegals and the attorneys who employ them?

41. What is the most common allegation against paralegals in tort cases?

42. What are the major areas of attorney errors and misconduct that have led to malpractice insurance claims?

43. What is the distinction between an occurrence policy and a claims-made policy, and why are insurance carriers reluctant to issue occurrence policies?

HELPFUL WEBSITES

Regulation Links Collected by the National Federation of Paralegal Associations (NFPA)
- www.paralegals.org (click *Positions and Issues*)

Regulation Links Collected by the National Association of Legal Assistants (NALA)
- www.nala.org (click *About Paralegals*)

Regulation Links Collected by the ABA Standing Committee on Paralegals (SCOP)
- In Google, Bing, or Yahoo, run this search "Directory of Paralegal State Activity"
- www.americanbar.org/groups/paralegals.html (in the search box, *enter Directory of Paralegal State Activity*)

Self-Help Resources
- www.americanbar.org (enter *self-help centers* in the search box)
- public.findlaw.com
- www.nolo.com

Employee Guide to Legal Advice
- courts.mi.gov (enter *"legal advice"* in the search box)

Legal Malpractice and Liability Insurance
- www.americanbar.org (enter "*malpractice insurance*" in the search box)
- www.justia.com/injury/legal-malpractice

Overtime Compensation
- www.dol.gov/dol/topic/wages/overtimepay.htm
- www.dol.gov (enter *paralegal overtime* in the search box)
- www.dol.gov/whd/state/state.htm (state labor laws)

Licensure and Government Regulation of Paralegals
- www.nala.org/licissues.htm

Licensure in Canada
- www.lsuc.on.ca/licensingprocessparalegal

Rosemary Furman Case
- www.law.fsu.edu/library/flsupct/51226/51226.html

Comparison of Certification Programs
- www.nals.org/?page_id=63
- www.paralegals.org/default.asp?page=62 (click the "Comparison" link)

Training for Licensed Limited Legal Technicians (LLLTs)
- papers.ssrn.com/sol3/papers.cfm?abstract_id=2466042 (65 South Carolina Law Review 579)

Legal Document Assistants
- www.calda.org

A Jailhouse Lawyer's Manual
- www3.law.columbia.edu/hrlr/index_jlm.php

Google, Bing, or Yahoo Searches
(on these search engines, run the following searches, using quotation marks and substituting your state for "aa" where indicated)
- paralegal regulation aa
- "unauthorized practice of law" aa
- "The Case for Repealing Unauthorized Practice of Law Statutes"
- overtime paralegal aa
- Fair Labor Standards Act overtime
- paralegal certification aa
- limited licensing
- nonattorney agency representation aa
- legal malpractice aa
- legal malpractice insurance
- professional liability insurance aa
- jailhouse lawyer
- "legal information"
- "legal document assistant" "unlawful detainer assistant"
- "bankruptcy petition preparer" aa
- "limited license legal technician"
- "justice gap"aa

ENDNOTES

1. *Texas Disciplinary Rules of Professional Conduct*, Rule 5.05, Comment 2. (2013) (under *Resources*, click *Rules*).

2. American Bar Association, *Model Code of Professional Responsibility*, Canon 3, EC 3-5 (1969).

3. American Bar Association, *Consumers' Guide to Legal Help* (2012).

4. In *re Moore*, 232 Bankruptcy Reporter 1, 13 (D. Maine 1999).

5. 11 U.S.C. § 110 (2001) (www.law.cornell.edu/uscode/text/11/110).

6. West's Annotated California Business & Professions Code §§ 6400–6450 (2000).

7. Legal Document Preparers (www.azcourts.gov/cld /LegalDocumentPreparers.aspx); (www.azcourts.gov/Portals/26/LDP /Docs/ACJA7208final092106nonleg.pdf).

7a. Stephen Crossland and PaulaLittlewood, *The Washington State Limited License Legal Technician Program*, 65 South Carolina Law Review (2014).

8. Florida Association of Legal Document Preparers (www.faldp.org /rosemary-furman.html) (2013).

9. Peoples and Wertz, *Update: Unauthorized Practice of Law*, 9 Paralegal Reporter 1 (National Federation of Paralegal Associations, February 1985).

10. Rule 10–2.2(a), *Rules Regulating the Florida Bar* (2006). See also *The Florida Bar Re Approval of Forms Pursuant to Rule 10–1.1(B) of the Rules Regulating the Florida Bar*, 591 So. 2d 594 (Fla. 1991); Florida Bar News 12 (August 1, 1989).

11. Dee McAree, *Online Divorce Services Spark Debate*, National Law Journal (July 22, 2003).

12. Mark Curriden, *Future of Law Panel: Change with the Times or Find Another Business*, Law News Now, www.abajournal.com (February 12, 2011).

13. 433 U.S. 350 (1977) (to read this case online, go to scholar.google.com, select *Case law*, and type *433 U.S. 350* in the search box).

14. 421 U.S. 773 (1975) (to read this case online, go to scholar.google.com, select *Care law*, and type *421 U.S. 773* in the search box).

15. American Bar Association, *Task Force on the Model Definition of the Practice of Law*, *Proposed Model Definition of the Practice of Law* (September 18, 2002); www.americanbar.org (type "model definition" in the search box).

16. U.S. Department of Justice and Federal Trade Commission, *Comments on the American Bar Association's Proposed Model Definition of the Practice of Law* (December 20, 2002) (www.justice.gov/atr/public/comments/200604.htm).

16a. *North Carolina State Board of Dental Examiners v. Federal Trade Commission*, 717 F.3d 359, 374 (4th Cir. 2013) (www.ca4.uscourts.gov/opinions/Published/121172.p.pdf).

17. Heidi Lowry, *Paralegal Defends University in a Suit Brought by a Former Student*... Paralegal Today (January/March 2010).

18. District of Columbia Rules of Court, D.C. Court of Appeals Rule 49(11) (2001); www.dcappeals.gov (in the Court of Appeals pull-down menu, click *DCCA Rules*).

19. *About the Court*, www.ustaxcourt.gov/about.htm (2011).

20. U.S. Tax Court, Rule 200 (a) (3)(www.ustaxcourt.gov) (click *Rules*) (2013).

21. Ethics Opinion 99-13 (1999) (Committee on the Rules of Professional Conduct of the Arizona Bar Association) (www.srpmic-nsn.gov/government/court/; (m.azbar.org/RulesofPC/Opinion.aspx?id=507).

22. The Law and Order Code of the Ute Indian Tribe of the Uintah and Ouray Reservation, § 1-5-1 (1988) (www.narf.org/nill/Codes/uteuocode/utebodytt1.htm).

23. Assiniboine & Sioux Comprehensive Code of Justice, § 501(b) (2004) (www.indianlaw.mt.gov/fortpeck/codes/default.mcpx).

24. Winnebago Tribal Code, § 1-403 (2009) (www.winnebagotribe.com/images/tribal_court/2012%20WTN%20TRIBAL%20CODE.pdf).

25. *Lassiter v. Dep't of Social Services*, 452 U.S. 18, 29 (1981). (To read this case online, go to Google Scholar (scholar.google.com), click *Case law*, and type *452 U.S. 18* in the search box.)

26. Winter, *No Contempt in Kentucky*, 7 National Paralegal Reporter 8 (National Federation of Paralegal Associations, Winter 1982).

27. North Carolina State Bar, *Appearance of Non-Lawyer at Calendar Call*, 2000 Formal Ethics Opinion (2001) (www.ncbar.com/ethics).

28. Local Civil Rules of the Allen Superior & Circuit Courts, Rule LR02-AR0021(D) (1), *Authority of Attorneys' Employees* (2000) (www.in.gov/judiciary/files/allen-local-rules.pdf).

29. Tennessee Judicial Ethics Committee, Formal Ethics Opinion 85-F-94 (1985) (tbpr.org/Attorneys/EthicsOpinions/Pdfs/85-F-94.pdf).

30. Michael Kroll, *Counsel Behind Bars: Jailhouse Lawyers*, 7 California Lawyer (June 1987).

31. *Williams v. United States Dep't of Justice*, 433 F.2d 958 (5th Cir. 1970). (To read this case online, go to Google Scholar (scholar.google.com), click *Case law*, and type the *433 F.2d 958* in the search box.)

32. *Gilmore v. Lynch*, 319 F. Supp. 105 (N.D. Cal. 1970), affirmed by the U.S. Supreme Court in *Younger v. Gilmore*, 404 U.S. 15 (1971). (To read these cases online, go to Google Scholar (scholar.google.com), click *Case law*, and type the *319 F. Supp. 105* in the search box and then separately type *404 U.S. 15* in the box).

33. *Walters v. National Ass'n of Radiation Survivors*, 473 U.S. 305, 325, 105 S. Ct. 3180, 3191 (1985) citing Judge Henry Friendly, *Some Kind of Hearing*, 123 U. Pa. L. Rev. 1267, 1288 (1975) (supreme.justia.com/us/473/305/case.html) (emphasis added). (To read this *Walters* case online, go to Google Scholar (scholar.google.com), click *Case law*, and type the *473 U.S. 305* in the search box).

34. 373 U.S. 379, 83 S. Ct. 1322, 10 L. Ed. 2d 428 (1963). (To read this case online, go to Google Scholar (scholar.google.com), click *Case law*, and type the *373 U.S. 379* in the search box).

35. 373 U.S. at 388, 396.

36. www.law.cornell.edu/uscode/text/5/555.

37. U.S. Patent and Trademark Office, *General Requirements Bulletin for Admission to the Examination for Registration to Practice Before the United States Patent and Trademark Office* (www.uspto.gov/ip/boards/oed/GRB_March_2012.pdf).

38. 31 C.F.R. § 10 (2011).

39. www.aicpa.org/About/FAQs/Pages/FAQs.aspx.

40. U.S. Department of Justice, Executive Office of Immigration Review, *Recognition & Accreditation (R&A) Program* (2013) (www.justice.gov/eoir/ra.htm).

41. ABA Standing Committee on Lawyers' Responsibility for Client Protection, *Report of 1984 Survey of Nonlawyer Practice before Federal Administrative Agencies* (October 19, 1984).

42. Office of Hearings and Appeals, Office of Policy Planning and Evaluation, Social Security Administration, *Highlights for Fiscal Year 1993* Tables 1, 2 (November 30, 1993).

43. Elaine Tackett, *Paralegal Representation of Social Security Claimants*, 16 Journal of Paralegal Education and Practice (2000).

44. Direct Payment to Eligible Non-Attorney Representatives (www.ssa.gov/representation/nonattyrep.htm); (www.ssa.gov/OP_Home/ssact/title02/0206.htm).

45. Commission on Nonlawyer Practice, American Bar Association, *Nonlawyer Activities in Law-Related Situations* 146 (1995).

46. Committee on Legal Assistants, New York County Lawyers' Association, *Committee Report* (October 14, 1993).

47. New York State Workers' Compensation Board, *Licensed Representative Regulations* (www.wcb.ny.gov/content/main/wclaws/30213.jsp#sec1b).

48. New York City Bar, *Narrowing the "Justice Gap": Roles for Nonlawyer Practitioners*, 21 (2013) (www2.nycbar.org/pdf/report/uploads/20072450-RolesforNonlawyerPractitioners.pdf).

49. Jacob Goldstein, *So You Think You Can Be a Hair Braider*, N.Y. Times, June 12, 2012.

50. North Carolina State Bar Association, *Report of the Special Committee on Paralegals* 3 (1980).

51. Supreme Court of New Jersey, Press Release (May 18, 1999) (www.judiciary.state.nj.us/pressrel/archives/admpara.htm).

52. West's Annotated California Business & Professions Code §§ 6450 et seq. (2000).

53. *Id.* at § 6455(a).

54. Sharlean Perez, *The New Law of the Paralegal Land*, 20 LAPA Reporter 1 (Los Angeles Paralegal Association, October 2000).

55. *Legislative Report: AB 1761 FAQs*, Recap 7 (California Alliance of Paralegal Associations, Winter 2001).

56. Testimony of Gillian Hadfield, Task Force to Expand Access to Civil Legal Services in New York, *Report to the Chief Judge of the State of New York* 38 (Nov. 2012).

57. Judge William Hogoboom, quoted in Harry Krause, *Family Law* 734 (3rd ed.1990).

58. *In the Spirit of Public Service: A Blueprint for Rekindling of Lawyer Professionalism* 52 (ABA, Commission on Professionalism, 1986). See 112 F.R.D. 243 (1986) (F.R.D. is the Federal Rules Decisions reporter).

59. American Bar Association Commission on Nonlawyer Practice, American Bar Association, *Nonlawyer Activity in Law-Related Situations* 175 (1995).

60. Mike France, *Bar Chiefs Protect the Guild*, The National Law Journal, August 7, 1995, at A1, A28.

61. ABA, *Nonlawyer Activity*, supra note 59 at 177.

62. American Bar Association, Task Force on the Future of Legal Education, *Draft Report and Recommendations* 3 (September 20, 2013) (www.americanbar.org) (in the search box, type "Future of Legal Education").

63. Laura Ernde, *State Bar to look at limited-licensing program*, California Bar Journal (February 2013) (www.calbarjournal.com).

64. New York City Bar, *Narrowing the "Justice Gap": Roles for Nonlawyer Practitioners* (June 2013) (www2.nycbar.org/pdf/report/uploads/20072450-RolesforNonlawyerPractitioners.pdf).

65. Washington State Supreme Court Rule 12; www.courts.wa.gov (in the search box type limited practice officer). See also Washington State Bar Association, www.wsba.org (in the search box type limited practice officer).

66. www.wsba.org (enter *practice of law board* in the search box).

67. *In the Matter of the Adoption of New APR 28—Limited Practice Rule for Limited License Legal Technicians*, Order 25700-A-1005 Washington State Supreme Court, June 14, 2012).

68. Michele Cotton, *Experiment Interrupted: Unauthorized Practice of Law Versus Access to Justice*, 5 DePaul Journal for Social Justice, (2012).

69. Deborah L. Rhode, *In the Interests of Justice: Reforming the Legal Profession* 135-36 (Oxford University Press2000).

70. Deborah L. Rhode, *Symposium: Whatever Happened to Access to Justice?*, 42 Loyola Los Angeles Law Review, 869, 885-86 (2009).

71. Richard Granat, *Limited Licensing of Legal Technicians: A Good Idea?*, eLawyering Blog (September 21, 2013) (www.elawyeringredux.com/2013/09/articles/legal-education-1/limited-licensing-of-legal-technicians-a-good-idea).

72. *Narrowing the "Justice Gap,"* supra note 64.

73. Gillian Hadfield, Lawyers, *Make Room for Nonlawyers*, www.cnn.com.

74. Michele Cotton, *Experiment, Interrupted: Unauthorized Practice of Law versus Access to Justice*, 5 DePaul Journal for Social Science (2012).

75. Jeff Manning, *ABA President Calls for Reform To Meet Legal Needs of the Low-Income*, www.oregonlive.com (October 13, 2014).

76. Barbara Homles, *PACE Testimonial*, 30 National Paralegal Reporter 29 (October/November 2005).

77. ABA Standing Committee on Legal Assistants, *Position Paper on the Question of Legal Assistant Licensure or Certification*, 5 Legal Assistant Today 167 (1986).

78. 29 U.S.C.A. §§ 201 et seq. (1976). See also 29 C.F.R. part 541 and U.S. Department of Labor Wage and Hour Division (www.dol.gov/whd/flsa).

79. Jeanne Johnson. *Paralegals Fight for Overtime Pay*, Paralegal Gateway (February 20, 2012) (www.facebook.com/ParalegalGateway).

80. See William Statsky, *Torts: Personal Injury Litigation* (5th ed. 2011).

81. We are talking here of vicarious *civil* liability or, more specifically, the tort liability of employers because of the torts committed by their employees. In general, employers are not subject to vicarious *criminal* liability. If a paralegal commits a crime on the job, only the paralegal goes to jail (unless the employer actually participated in the crime).

82. Michael Martz, *Ethics, Does a Paralegal Need Insurance?* The Assistant 13 (Mississippi Assn. of Legal Assistants, Fall 1993).

83. Manuel Ramos, *Legal Malpractice*, 70 *Tulane Law Review* 2583 (1996).

84. Debra Weiss, *Lateral Hiring and Law-Firm Mergers Boosted Malpractice Claims, Study Says*, ABA Journal Law News Now (June 20, 2013).

85. James Podgers, *Dubious Honor*, ABA Journal Law News Now (December 1, 2012).

86. Todd Scott, *Recent ABA Study Suggests Emerging New Trends in Legal Malpractice, 28* View (Minnesota Lawyers Mutual, October 2012) (www.mlmins.com).

87. Ronald Mallen & Jeffrey Smith, *Legal Malpractice* 2 (3d ed. 1989).

88. Stephen Gillers, *Regulation of Lawyers* 766 (Aspen, 6th ed. 2001).

89. Kay Ostberg, *If You Want to Sue a Lawyer* (1995).

90. American Bar Association, *Formal Ethics Opinion 93-379* (1993).

91. *Ashby v. Davidson*, 930 N.E.2d 53, 56 (Ind. App. 2010) (To read this case online, go to Google Scholar (scholar.google.com), click *Case law*, and type *930 N.E.2d 53* in the search box.

92. American Home Assurance Company, Lawyers Professional Liability Policy.

CHAPTER 5

ATTORNEY ETHICS AND PARALEGAL ETHICS

CHAPTER OUTLINE

- Ethics in the Real World
- Enforcing Ethics
- Paralegal Codes
- Ethics Rules: Introduction
- Formation of the Attorney-Client Relationship
- Limited-Scope Representation
- Competence
- Diligence/Unwarranted Delay
- Fees
- Misconduct by Attorneys
- Obstructing Access to Evidence
- Crime or Fraud by Clients
- Frivolous Positions and Harassment
- Safekeeping Property
- False Evidence and Statements; Failure to Disclose
- Confidentiality
- Conflict of Interest
- Communication with the Other Side
- Solicitation
- Advertising
- Payment for Referrals or Recommendations
- Reporting Professional Misconduct
- Pro Bono Services
- Withdrawal
- Appearance of Impropriety
- Unauthorized Practice of Law (UPL)
- Paralegals
- Your Ethics or Your Job?

CHAPTER OBJECTIVES

After completing this chapter, you should be able to

- Know the 25 major ethical guidelines for paralegals.
- Distinguish between attorney at law and attorney in fact.
- Explain how attorneys are regulated, including the sanctions that can be imposed for unethical conduct.
- Understand the relationship between attorney codes and paralegal codes.
- State how an attorney-client relationship is formed.
- Give examples of limited-scope representation.
- State the standard of competence and diligence.
- List ways that paralegals can stay competent.
- Identify the major ethical rules that govern attorney and paralegal fees.
- List ways in which wrongdoing by paralegals can lead to sanctions against their supervising attorneys.
- Know the ethical rules governing misconduct by attorneys, paralegals, and clients.
- Know when a position is frivolous.
- Explain an attorney's duty to safeguard client property.
- State when an attorney has a duty to disclose contrary authority.
- Summarize the duty to preserve confidentiality and list the times when an attorney can reveal confidential information.
- List steps paralegals can take to protect client confidentiality.
- Distinguish confidentiality, the attorney-client privilege, and the attorney work-product rule.

- Define conflict of interest and summarize the major conflicts that can exist.
- Explain how a paralegal can contaminate a law office and the ways in which disqualification can be avoided.
- Describe the anticontact rule.
- Know when solicitation and advertising are ethical.

- State the rule on paying for a referral or recommendation.
- State when an attorney must report another attorney's misconduct.
- Explain when an attorney can withdraw from a case.
- Understand what is meant by the appearance of impropriety.
- List the ways in which an attorney illegally assists another in the

- unauthorized practice of law.
- Understand Model Rule 5.3 and other ethical rules governing an attorney's use of paralegals.
- Explain the components of effective supervision of paralegals by attorneys.
- Describe what a paralegal should do when faced with an ethical violation on the job.

ETHICS IN THE REAL WORLD

ethics Rules or standards of behavior to which members of an occupation, profession, or other organization are expected to conform. Ethics governing attorneys are called *legal ethics*.

Ethics are rules or standards of behavior to which members of an occupation, profession, or other organization are expected to conform. Ethics governing attorneys are called legal ethics or codes of professional responsibility.

As you know from the media, a fairly large segment of the general public does not have a favorable opinion of attorneys. Elsewhere in this book, we examine some of the reasons for this hostility. (See, for example, the beginning of Chapter 8.) Here in Chapter 5, we confront one of the main reasons: the perception that attorneys are not very ethical, or, more cynically, the perception that attorneys are ethical only when it doesn't cost them anything.

Courts and legislatures have responded to this problem in different ways. Every law school must offer a required course in legal ethics. Many state bar associations require practicing attorneys to attend annual **continuing legal education (CLE)** courses or seminars on ethical themes. State disciplinary bodies have hired more attorneys (and paralegals) to investigate claims of ethical violations by practicing attorneys.

continuing legal education (CLE) Training in the law (usually short term) that a person receives after completing his or her formal legal training or after becoming employed.

Of course, attorneys are not the only individuals under attack for ethical misconduct. Some commentators claim that the problem is rampant throughout society. Our focus here, however, is the legal profession.

As paralegals, you are about to enter a very special work environment. You will meet many different kinds of attorneys:

- Attorneys whose ethical behavior is beyond reproach,
- Attorneys who engage in blatantly unethical behavior, and
- Attorneys whose who sometimes walk a thin line between ethical and unethical behavior.

Which of these categories of attorneys will one day be your employers and supervisors? The short answer is that you don't know. Hence, you need to prepare yourself for any work environment.

In the abstract, it's easy to be ethical. We all agree that the proper course of conduct is to do the right thing. The problem, however, is that pressures in the real world (particularly financial pressures) can interfere. The niceties of ethics can sometimes give way to the desire to win, the urge to retaliate, or the fear of losing a job or a client. One expert defines ethics as "whether you are willing to do the right thing when it costs more than you are willing to pay."[1] Many attorneys, he argues, feel that they don't "have the luxury of living ethically." Pressures "such as billable hours, overhead costs, and technology cause people to take shortcuts like extending cases too long and lying about billable hours." Attorneys are guilty of a form of rationalization called the Doctrine of Relative Filth, which says that "as long as there's somebody out there worse than you are, you're not that bad."[2]

With these sobering thoughts in mind, you should begin your paralegal career with the resolution of becoming an archconservative on matters of ethics. Our goal in this chapter is to provide you with the tools that will enable you to become this kind of conservative. We begin by presenting an overview of some of the most important ethical guidelines that we will study. Carefully read—indeed, memorize—the twenty-five guidelines in Exhibit 5-1.

In your career, the paramount question must always be "What is the right thing to do?" Answering this question will not always be easy, particularly if you are forced to make a choice between your ethics and your job.

Exhibit 5-1	25 Major Ethical Guidelines for Paralegals

1. *Disclosure of status.* Be sure that everyone with whom you come in contact knows that you are not an attorney. Do not allow people to assume that you are an attorney, which is likely when they learn you work in a law office.

2. *Accepting cases.* Do not "accept" a case on behalf of the office. You can tell someone what kinds of cases the office handles, but you cannot say or imply that the office will take someone's case. Only an attorney can establish an attorney-client relationship.

3. *Setting fees.* Do not "set" a fee. You can tell someone the amount of an attorney's initial consultation fee, but when questioned further about fees, you must say that fees need to be discussed with the attorney.

4. *Sharing fees.* Do not accept a part of the fee of a particular client even if the attorney offers it to you. Attorneys cannot share (split) fees of particular clients with nonattorneys. Your salary will come out of the fees generated by the office, but it is unethical for an attorney to agree in advance to give you a bonus or other compensation on the fee that will be generated by a particular client's case. This is so even if you referred the client to the office, even if you did great work on the case, and even if the client agrees to let you have part of the fee.

5. *Compensation for referring clients.* Do not accept anything of value for recommending an attorney or for referring a case to the attorney. Something of value can include increased salary, a bonus, time off, a promotion, etc.

6. *Confidentiality.* Do not discuss the facts of a case with anyone outside the office (including your spouse or parent) without permission from your supervisor. If you have information related to the case, you must keep the information confidential. This rule is not limited to secrets or personal information about the case. It includes *all* information related to the case, including the fact that a particular person is a client of the office. Although some information about a client may already be public knowledge, abide by the rule that you will not discuss any aspect of the case without permission from your supervisor. KIC: Keep It Confidential.

7. *Confidentiality.* Before sending documents prepared on a computer (or before filing them in court), remove the *metadata* (information hidden within the document itself). Metadata can consist of confidential information.

8. *Confidentiality.* When sending messages or documents over the Internet (e.g., as email attachments), be sure that the client understands that the communication may not be secure. Know how to *encrypt* the communication if your supervisor deems this precaution to be necessary. (Encryption places the text in a code that can be read only by persons with special software.) Extra caution is needed when placing client data on smartphones, tablets, and other small media devices, which are easy to lose and often relatively easy to hack into.

9. *Conflict of interest.* Let your supervisor know immediately if in your prior employment (or volunteer activities) you worked for other law offices with clients who have any connection or relationship with clients of the law office where you now work (or volunteer). Your supervisor must determine if such connections create a conflict of interest.

10. *Conflict of interest.* Avoid romantic or financial relationships with current clients, opposing parties, relatives of opposing parties, or attorneys of opposing parties.

11. *Conflict of interest.* Understand how the office performs its conflicts check on every prospective client so that the office can avoid taking cases that would create a conflict of interest.

12. *Conflict of interest.* Let your supervisor know if a client has offered you a gift. If the gift requires the preparation of a document, the document may have to be prepared by an attorney who does not work in your office.

13. *Competence.* If you do not know how to perform an assigned task, let your supervisor know that you need additional training or a different assignment.

14. *Competence.* Never stop learning the substantive and procedural law that pertains to the tasks you are assigned. Once employed, competence is maintained primarily through self-study and through continuing legal education (CLE).

15. *Communication with other side.* Do not contact an opponent (or anyone connected with an opponent) unless you have the permission of your supervisor and your opponent's attorney. Do not try to become a Facebook friend or establish other kinds of online connections with an opponent or anyone connected with the opponent.

16. *Communication with other side.* If the other side is proceeding *pro se* (without representation) and your supervisor allows you to communicate with him or her, you must not give the impression that you are *disinterested* (impartial or unconnected with the case). He or she must know that you work for the other side.

17. *Solicitation and advertising.* Do not initiate contacts with anyone (in person, by phone, or online (such as by email, on a social media site, in a chat room, etc.) in order to encourage him or her to hire (and pay fees to) your law office unless the person already has a relationship with the law office. (You can, however, recommend your office if someone asks you for a recommendation.) Do not make misrepresentations or false claims in advertising.

18. *Unauthorized practice of law.* Do not give *legal advice* (which is any comment or conclusion that applies the law or legal principles to the facts of a specific person's legal problem.) You can provide *legal information* (any statements about the law that are not directed at

the facts of a specific person's legal problem) but not *legal advice*. When you are asked questions that call for legal advice, refuse to be coaxed into providing it, no matter how innocent the question appears to be, no matter how clear it is that you know the correct answer, and no matter how confident your supervisor is that you can handle such questions on your own. With great caution, you can relay a message from an attorney that contains legal advice, but you cannot explain or elaborate on the message. If the client has any questions about the message, you must tell the client that you will let the attorney know what the questions are. You cannot answer legal questions even if you know the answers.

19. *Unauthorized practice of law*. Avoid performing any task in the office without attorney supervision, even if you have performed the task before and know how to perform it. Attorneys who are confident of the competence of veteran paralegals may not need to provide the kind of supervision that a new paralegal would need. At a minimum, however, the attorney must review the work of both experienced and inexperienced paralegals.

20. *Unauthorized practice of law*. Do not sign a pleading or any document that is filed in court even if the attorney asks you to sign it.

21. *Commingling*. Do not deposit client funds (e.g., proceeds of the sale of a home that is part of a property division in a divorce) into the same account that the law office uses for rent, salaries, or other office expenses. Avoid *commingling*.

22. *Misconduct*. Do not lie or otherwise misrepresent facts (e.g., do not pretend to be a stranger in order to obtain information from someone in an office or on an Internet social media site). Avoid pretexting (online deception to obtain information). Do not notarize a signature unless you were present and saw the signer place his or her signature on the document.

23. *Misconduct*. Do not pad your timesheets by stating that you performed a task you did not perform or spent time on a task that you did not spend. Avoid insider trading (improperly using or passing on to others any nonpublic information you learn about in the office in order to trade in the shares of a company).

24. *Misconduct*. Do not tell anyone how to hide assets so that the assets will not be available to an opponent in litigation and do not tell anyone how to avoid a *subpoena* or other legal *process*.

25. Know the common rationalizations for misrepresentation and other unethical conduct:
   - It's always done.
   - The other side does it.
   - The cause of our client is just.
   - If I don't do it, I will jeopardize my job.

Promise yourself that you will not allow these rationalizations to entice you to participate in unethical conduct even if there are attorneys, paralegals, and others around you who use the rationalizations.

ATTORNEY AT LAW AND ATTORNEY IN FACT

Before we begin examining the themes of ethics in greater detail, we should distinguish between an attorney at law and an attorney in fact. In the broadest sense, an attorney is an **agent**, a representative who is authorized to act for another. The two main categories of attorneys are attorneys at law and attorneys in fact. An attorney at law is someone who engages in the **practice of law**, which consists of using or attempting to use legal skills to help resolve a specific person's legal problem. An **attorney in fact** is someone authorized to act in place of another, often in a business transaction. Examples might include someone given the authority to sign a deed for another or to sell another's business. The document that authorizes another to act as an attorney in fact is called a **power of attorney**. Not all attorneys in fact have business duties. In Shakespeare's *Richard III*, the future king asks the mother of the woman he loves to convince her daughter of his love: "be the attorney of my love to her."

Both attorneys at law and attorneys in fact are agents, but their authority as agents is quite different. An attorney at law practices law on behalf of another. An attorney in fact conducts a transaction on behalf of another. Persons who are attorneys in fact cannot practice law unless they are attorneys at law. Phrased another way, giving a nonattorney a power of attorney does not grant him or her the right to practice law for the person giving the power.[3]

ENFORCING ETHICS

ETHICS AND SANCTIONS

The ethical rules of some organizations are enforced by **sanctions**. A sanction is any penalty or punishment imposed for unacceptable conduct, e.g., the sanction of a fine or expulsion from the organization because of fraud. (A very different meaning of sanction is permission or approval, e.g., the motion could not be filed without the *sanction* of the court.)

agent A person authorized to act for another; a representative. (See glossary for an additional meaning.)

practice of law Using or attempting to use legal skills to help resolve a specific person's legal problem.

attorney in fact One authorized to act in place of another, often in a business transaction.

power of attorney (1) A document that authorizes another to act as one's agent or attorney in fact. (2) The authority itself.

sanctions (1) Penalty or punishment imposed for unacceptable conduct. (2) Permission or approval.

All of the major national paralegal associations have adopted ethical rules, as we will see later in Exhibit 5-4. None, however, are enforced by meaningful sanctions. A paralegal association might occasionally throw someone out of the association because of misconduct, but this is rare, and it is highly unlikely that an expulsion would interfere with his or her ability to work as a paralegal unless the reason for the expulsion would also cause an employer to be upset by what the paralegal did.

Attorneys, on the other hand, *are* subject to enforceable ethical rules that can affect whether they are allowed to continue practicing law. Attorney ethics are backed by sanctions. The rules govern everything an attorney does in setting up, running, and shutting down a law office.

Of course, one of the things an attorney can do in running an office is hire paralegals. Hence the way in which the attorney uses paralegals are subject to ethical rules. Unethical use of paralegals can subject the attorney to sanctions. This can occur in a number of ways. As we will see, an attorney has an ethical obligation to avoid assisting a nonattorney in the **unauthorized practice of law (UPL)**. This can occur by:

- Delegating tasks to a paralegal that only an attorney should perform (e.g., signing a pleading)
- Delegating a task to a paralegal that the latter is allowed to perform, but failing to provide adequate supervision for the task (e.g., not reviewing a pleading written by a paralegal before it was filed in court)
- Helping an independent paralegal set up a business in which the paralegal engages in tasks only attorneys can perform (e.g., helping pay the rent of an independent paralegal who runs a divorce service in which the independent paralegal gives legal advice to his or her clients)

In these three examples, the paralegal is engaging in UPL and the attorney is unethically assisting a nonattorney in UPL.

WHO REGULATES ATTORNEYS?

In most states, the regulation of attorneys is primarily under the control of the highest court in the state (often called the *supreme court*), which determines when an attorney can be granted a license to practice law and under what conditions the license will be taken away or suspended because of unethical conduct. The state legislature may also have some regulatory authority over attorneys, and disputes occasionally arise over which branch of government can control a particular aspect of the practice of law. The judiciary often wins this dispute and becomes the final authority. In practice, however, the judicial branch and the legislative branch usually share regulatory jurisdiction over the practice of law. For example, the state legislature may have the power to impose minimum standards on attorney conduct, but the state supreme court may be able to impose standards that are higher than the minimum.

Neither the courts nor the legislature, however, performs the day-to-day functions of implementing the rules governing attorneys. That role is delegated to an entity such as a state bar association, an office of registration, or a disciplinary board or grievance commission.

Bar associations have a central role in the regulatory process even in states where other regulatory bodies also exist, such as a disciplinary board. There are four kinds of bar associations:

- National (e.g., American Bar Association, Hispanic National Bar Association)
- State (e.g., Illinois State Bar Association, State Bar of Montana)
- Local (e.g., Boston Bar Association, San Diego County Bar Association)
- Specialty (e.g., American Academy of Matrimonial Lawyers, American Association of Justice, National Association of Women Lawyers)

Some bar associations fall into more than one category. The American Academy of Matrimonial Lawyers, for example, is both a national and a specialty association.

All national, local, and specialty bar associations are voluntary; no attorney is required to be a member. At least one *state* bar association in each state, however, is *integrated*, which means that membership is required as a condition of practicing law in the state. (An **integrated bar association** is also referred to as a *mandatory bar association* or a *unified bar association*.)

Under the supervision of the state's highest court, this state bar association can propose revisions in the ethics code, write opinions interpreting sections of the code, and collect dues that are used to help fund the state's system of enforcing ethical rules. Given this dominant role

unauthorized practice of law (UPL) (1) Using or attempting to use legal skills to help resolve a specific person's legal problem when the assistance is provided by someone who does not have a license to practice law and when the assistance requires such a license or other authorization. (2) A nonattorney's performance of tasks in a law office without adequate attorney supervision when those tasks are part of the practice of law. (3) Delegating tasks to a nonattorney that only an attorney can perform.

integrated bar association A state bar association to which an attorney must belong in order to practice law in the state. Also called *mandatory bar association, unified bar association*.

of bar associations, the method of regulating attorneys in America is, in large measure, self-regulation: attorneys regulating attorneys. This is true even in those states that allow nonattorney citizens to serve on some boards or commissions that help regulate the legal profession.

ATTORNEY CODES OF ETHICS

There is no national set of ethical rules that applies to every state. Each state can adopt its own ethics state code to regulate the attorneys in that state. The state code may have different names such as *rules of professional conduct, code of ethics, canons of ethics, code of professional responsibility*, or *model rules*. Although there are some important variations among the state codes, they are substantially similar. The reason for this similarity is the influence of the American Bar Association (ABA).

The ABA is a voluntary national bar association; no attorney must belong to it. Yet approximately 55 percent of the attorneys in America do belong. Paralegals can join as ABA associates (apps.americanbar.org/join). The ABA publishes ethical rules but does not discipline attorneys for unethical conduct. The role of the ABA in this area is to write ethical rules and to propose to the individual states that they be accepted. A state is free to adopt, modify, or reject the ABA rules. The current recommendation of the ABA is found in a document called the ***Model Rules of Professional Conduct (MRPC)***. This document has been very influential throughout the country. Almost every state has adopted it with relatively minor changes. The *Model Rules* (MR) is a revision of the ABA's earlier *Model Code of Professional Responsibility*.

Exhibit 5-2 presents an overview of the major ethical codes governing attorney conduct. Most of these codes include provisions that are directly relevant to paralegals and other nonattorneys who work for attorneys. (See the last column of Exhibit 5-2.) Later in the chapter, we will examine these provisions.

ETHICS OPINIONS

There are two kinds of ethics opinions that interpret and apply specific rules in the ethical codes. First, there are opinions written by courts. These are binding in the state. Second, there are formal and informal ethical opinions written by bodies that regulate attorneys such as bar association committees on ethics or on the unauthorized practice of law (UPL). These opinions are advisory rather than binding. The state's highest court must decide whether to adopt bar association opinions. The court usually does adopt them with minor change. Even those that have not yet been adopted are valuable because of the guidance they provide to practicing attorneys. (See Appendix D for summaries of ethical opinions involving paralegals in your state.)

Attorneys can submit questions to the bar's ethics committee. (To preserve confidentiality, attorneys submit these questions without client names or other identifying information, e.g., "If an attorney represents client A in a case against a local merchant, would it be ethical to…?") The answers to questions are sometimes published as formal or informal opinions so that the entire legal community can benefit from the bar's interpretive advice.

The American Bar Association also writes ethics opinions through its Standing Committee on Ethics and Professional Responsibility. Like the opinions of state and local bar associations, the ethics opinions of the ABA are advisory rather than binding. ABA opinions never become binding because, as a voluntary association, there is no court that oversees what the ABA does. If what the ABA says in an opinion becomes binding, it is because a state has adopted parts or all of the ABA opinion.

ACCUSATION OF UNETHICAL CONDUCT

When an attorney is charged with unethical conduct, the case is investigated by a disciplinary body appointed by the state's highest court. The name for this body differs from state to state, e.g., the Grievance Commission, the Attorney Registration and Disciplinary Commission, the Committee on Professional Conduct, or the Board of Professional Responsibility.

If the investigation shows that **probable cause** exists that a violation has occurred, the next step is usually a disciplinary hearing before a commission, committee, or board. This body decides if a violation occurred and, if it did, what punishment should be imposed. The case then goes before the state's highest court, which is free to accept, reject, or modify the conclusion of the disciplinary body.

Model Rules of Professional Conduct (MRPC) The current set of ethical rules governing attorneys recommended by the American Bar Association. These rules revised the ABA's earlier rules found in the *Model Code of Professional Responsibility (MCPR)*.

probable cause A reasonable belief that good grounds exist to bring charges against someone. (See glossary for additional meanings.)

Exhibit 5-2				Ethical Codes Governing Attorneys			
NAME OF CODE	**DATE**	**WRITTEN BY**	**STATUS**	**STRUCTURE**	**CAN THE CODE BE READ ONLINE?**	**PARALEGALS**
Model Rules of Professional Conduct	1983	American Bar Association	The *Model Rules*: ■ Contain the current recommendations of the ABA. ■ Replace the *Model Code* (see below) ■ Is not binding on attorneys unless a state has adopted it (almost every state has adopted it in whole or with changes)	There are eight rules in the *Model Rules*. All of the rules are followed by interpretative Comments.	Yes. ■ Go to www.americanbar.org (type "Model Rules" in the search box) ■ Run this search in Google, Bing, or Yahoo: "Model Rules of Professional Conduct" ■ Download the Rulebook App. Run this search in Google, Bing, or Yahoo: Rulebook app ABA attorney	■ Rule 5.3 of the *Model Rules* covers the ethical use of paralegals by attorneys. ■ Rule 5.5 covers the unauthorized practice of law. ■ We will cover MR 5.3, MR 5.5, and other relevant rules later in this chapter and in Appendix D.
Model Code of Professional Responsibility	1969	American Bar Association	The *Model Code* is an earlier version of the *Model Rules*	There are nine Canons in the *Model Code*. Within each Canon there are ■ Disciplinary Rules (DR), which are mandatory statements or rules, and ■ Ethical Considerations (EC), which are behavioral guidelines.	Yes. ■ Go to www.americanbar.org (type "Model Code of Professional Responsibility" in the search box) ■ Run this search in Google, Bing, or Yahoo: "Model Code of Professional Responsibility" ■ www.law.cornell.edu/ethics/aba/mcpr/MCPR.HTM	■ DR 3–101 of the *Model Code* covers the unauthorized practice of law. ■ EC 3–6 covers the proper delegation of tasks to paralegals. ■ We will cover DR 3-101 and EC 3–6 later in this chapter.
State Codes	Varies	A state code is adopted by the highest state court in the state, usually after the state bar association proposes the code.	This is the code that is binding on every practicing attorney in the state. Almost all states base their code on the ABA's *Model Rules of Professional Conduct*.	Because most states have adopted the ABA *Model Rules*, the state's ethical code will often be structured like the *Model Rules* (eight main rules followed by interpretative comments)	Yes. ■ See Appendix D for the link to the ethics code of your state. ■ Run this search in Google, Bing, or Yahoo: aa ethics rules attorney (substituting the name of your state for "aa")	■ Because most states have adopted the ABA *Model Rules*, the state code is likely to have Rules 5.3 on paralegals and 5.5 on the unauthorized practice of law. ■ The state may use the same language as the ABA's 5.3 and 5.5 or may substitute its own language. ■ The state may use a numbering system that differs from the ABA's *Model Rules*.
Special Codes	Varies	A separate city, state, regional, or national bar association	These special bar associations may have their own code of ethics.	Varies.	Go to the website of the special bar association. It will link to its ethics code, if any.	Varies

A number of sanctions can be imposed by the court. As you can see from Exhibit 5-3, the sanctions fall into the categories of disbarment, suspension, reprimand, and probation. Some states require attorneys to attend a day of special ethics training (the equivalent of traffic school) as part of the discipline imposed for violating the state's ethical code.

Exhibit 5-3	Sanctions and National Statistics on Attorney Discipline

POSSIBLE SANCTIONS FOR UNETHICAL CONDUCT

- **Disbarment:** The revocation or termination of the right to practice law. Disbarment is often permanent, although some states allow a disbarred attorney to apply for readmission after a designated number of years. If readmitted, conditions may be imposed (see *probation* below).
- **Suspension:** The removal of an attorney from the practice of law for a specified minimum period, after which the attorney can apply for reinstatement. An *interim suspension* is a temporary suspension pending the imposition of final discipline. The attorney may be required to notify clients of a suspension. Sometimes the sanction of suspension is imposed but does not go into effect, i.e., the suspension is *stayed*. The attorney can continue to practice law while operating under a stayed suspension so long as he or she does not commit any further ethical violations. Other conditions might also be imposed (see *probation* below).
- **Reprimand:** An official declaration that an attorney's conduct was unethical. The declaration does not affect the attorney's right to practice law. A *private reprimand* is not disclosed to the public; a *public reprimand* is. Conditions might be imposed along with the reprimand (see *probation* below). In some states, a milder form of private reprimand is called an *admonition, private warning, letter of caution,* or *private reproval.*
- **Probation:** Allowing the attorney to continue to practice but under specified conditions, such as submitting to periodic audits of client funds controlled by the attorney, making restitution to a client whose funds were wrongly taken by the attorney, and obtaining treatment for substance abuse if alcohol or drug use has been a problem. He or she may also be asked to attend additional ethics training and/or to retake the professional responsibility (ethics) portion of the bar exam.

NATIONAL STATISTICS ON ATTORNEY DISCIPLINE

- Number of Attorneys in the United States with Active Licenses to Practice Law: 1,340,602
- Number of Ethical Complaints Filed in One Year against These Attorneys with All Ethics Agencies: 116,384
- Number of Complaints Deemed Worthy of Investigation: 70,238
- Number of Complaints Closed or Dismissed after Investigation: 37,887
- Number of Attorneys Privately Sanctioned: 1,742
- Number Publicly Sanctioned: 4,174
- Number Disbarred: 1,046
- Number Suspended: 2,384
- Number Admonished, Reprimanded, or Censured: 968
- Number Placed on Probation: 895

CLIENT SECURITY FUND

Clients who have been wronged by their attorneys have a number of options:
- Sue the attorney for legal malpractice (see the discussion of such suits in Chapter 4)
- Apply to the state's client security fund for compensation. A number of states have such a fund that is run by a bar association or foundation. The fund provides compensation (e.g., up to $75,000) to clients who have suffered financial losses due to dishonest conduct of attorneys licensed in the state. A portion of annual dues from all attorneys in the state provides the resources for the fund. In New York State, for example, the fund (called the Lawyers' Fund for Client Protection) paid out $163 million to 7,255 clients between 1982 and 2012.

Sources: American Bar Association, *2011 Survey on Lawyer Discipline* (2013). The Lawyer's Fund For Client Protection, Annual Report (2012) (www .nylawfund.org).

Later in the chapter, we will cover one of the most contentious issues in this area: Can a disbarred or suspended attorney continue working in a law office as a paralegal? As we will see, some states say no. The risk is too great that the disciplined attorney will continue to practice law under the guise of being a paralegal. Other states allow it but may do so with restrictions, such as forbidding the attorney/paralegal from having client contact.

APPLICATION OF ATTORNEY CODES TO PARALEGALS

Thus far we have been discussing attorney codes of ethics. Can a paralegal be sanctioned for violating these codes? Not directly. With one exception that we will discuss in a moment, the codes apply to attorneys only. Because paralegals cannot join a bar association as full members, they cannot be sanctioned by a bar association. Serious paralegal wrongdoing, however, can lead to severe consequences:

- The paralegals might be fired by their employer.
- They might be sued for negligence.
- They might face criminal prosecution.
- Their supervising attorney might face ethical charges because of the paralegal's wrongdoing, etc.

Paralegals themselves, however, cannot be punished for unethical conduct by the entity that regulates attorneys. *Attorneys* can be punished for using their paralegals unethically, but paralegals are not directly regulated by, and hence cannot be punished by, the disciplinary system that governs attorneys.

As indicated, there is an exception to the rule that attorney codes apply to attorneys only. Recently, there has been considerable debate over whether the legal profession should allow attorneys and nonlegal professionals to form a **multidisciplinary practice (MDP)**. This is a partnership between attorneys and nonattorneys such as accountants, doctors, therapists, economists, scientists, and environmental consultants. The partnership delivers legal and nonlegal services. In such a partnership, the nonattorney partner would be governed by the ethical code that governs attorneys. At present, only the District of Columbia allows such partnerships, although many states are studying the possibility of allowing them. These entities would be a major departure from the rule that attorneys must not form a partnership with (or share fees with) nonattorneys. Critics warn that MDPs will lead to a loss of attorney control over the practice of law. The big fear is that companies such as Wal-Mart and H&R Block will be able to start offering legal services in direct competition with traditional law firms. Proponents argue that MDPs will open up new markets for law firms, particularly in a global economy where large American law firms often compete in countries that authorize MDPs for their own attorneys.

If MDPs ever become widespread in the United States, they will probably not have a significant effect on paralegals. The goal of an MDP is to allow a law firm to expand its scope of business by partnering with individuals who have nonlegal skills and expertise. There is nothing nonlegal about paralegals! They are an intimate part of the attorney's legal team. While it is possible that a state might one day allow an attorney to form an MDP with a paralegal, the likelihood of this happening is remote.

multidisciplinary practice (MDP) A partnership consisting of attorneys and nonlegal professionals that offers legal and nonlegal services.

PARALEGAL CODES

Now we turn to **paralegal codes**. These are sets of rules and guidelines devoted exclusively to issues of paralegal ethics. There are two kinds of paralegal codes: those written by attorneys, courts, or legislatures and those written by paralegals. See Exhibit 5-4 for an overview of these codes.

paralegal code Rules and guidelines covering ethical issues involving paralegals.

Exhibit 5-4	Paralegal Codes

A. Paralegal Codes Written by Bar Associations
- *ABA Model Guidelines for the Utilization of Paralegal Services* (In Google, Bing, or Yahoo, type the name of this publication in the search box.)
- To find out if your bar association has an ethical code or guidelines for paralegals, go to your state in Appendix D. Also, go to the website of your state bar association (see appendix B) and type *paralegal* in its search box)

B. Paralegal Codes Written by Courts and Legislatures
- To find out if your state court or state legislature has an ethical code or guidelines for paralegals, go to your state in Appendix D.

C. Paralegal Codes Written by National Paralegal Associations
- *Model Code of Ethics and Professional Responsibility and Guidelines for Enforcement* (National Federation of Paralegal Associations 1993) See Appendix E. Also, go to www.paralegal.org, click *Positions and Issues* and then *Ethics*.
- *NALA Code of Ethics and Professional Responsibility* (National Association of Legal Assistants 1995) See Appendix E. Also, go to www.nala.org and type *ethics* in the search box.

■ *NALS Code of Ethics & Professional Responsibility* (NALS, the Association of Legal Professionals). See Appendix E. Also, go to www.nals.org, click *About.*

D. Paralegal Codes Written by State and Local Paralegal Associations

■ To find out if your state and local paralegal association has an ethical code or guidelines for paralegals, go to the links for your state in Appendix B and type *ethics* in the homepage of each of these associations. See also your state in Appendix D.

PARALEGAL CODES WRITTEN BY BAR ASSOCIATIONS, COURTS, AND LEGISLATURES

The ABA has issued *Model Guidelines for the Utilization of Paralegal Services.* Like the ABA's *Model Rules* and *Model Code* (see Exhibit 5-2), the *Model Guidelines* are recommendations to the states. The ABA itself does not discipline anyone for violating the *Model Guidelines.* (Later in this chapter, you will find a discussion of every major guideline or rule contained in the *Model Guidelines.*) To date, about half the states have their own state paralegal codes or guidelines that are similar to the *Model Guidelines.* (For your state, see Appendix D.) Most were adopted by the state bar association or by the committee of the bar association that covers paralegals. Some have been formally approved and adopted by the state's highest court; a few have been written by the state legislature. The *Model Guidelines* and the state paralegal codes/guidelines are primarily directed to attorneys who use paralegals in their practice. Hence, if there are violations by paralegals, it is the supervising attorney who could be subject to sanctions by the state body that enforces attorney ethics.

PARALEGAL CODES WRITTEN BY PARALEGALS

The three major national associations (NFPA, NALA, and NALS) have also written paralegal codes. (See Exhibit 5-4 and Appendix E.) As indicated earlier, these codes are not enforced by meaningful sanctions. The associations might terminate a paralegal's membership in the association for ethical improprieties, but this is rarely done. The associations simply do not have the resources or clout to implement a system of enforcement. This does not mean, however, that the paralegal codes are unimportant. Their main value is to reinforce the critical importance of ethics in the practice of law.

In addition, some state and local paralegal associations have published their own paralegal codes. (For associations in your state, see Appendix E.) These codes closely mirror the themes of the codes written by the national paralegal associations, and most importantly, the themes that govern attorneys as they pertain to paralegals.

ETHICS RULES: INTRODUCTION

We turn now to an overview of specific ethical rules that apply to attorneys. The overview is based on the ABA's *Model Rules of Professional Conduct.* (See Exhibit 5-2.) The rule numbers used in the discussion (e.g., Rule 1.5) refer to the rule numbers of the *Model Rules.* In addition, we will occasionally refer to the ABA's *Model Code of Professional Responsibility*, the earlier version of the *Model Rules.*

Where appropriate, the discussion will include a paralegal perspective based on attorney codes and the other paralegal codes/guidelines mentioned in Exhibit 5-4.

Paralegals are on the front line. One of their primary responsibilities is to help an attorney avoid being charged with unethical conduct. A recent paralegal seminar conducted by the Los Angeles Paralegal Association was entitled "Law Firm Ethics: How to Keep Your Attorneys off '60 Minutes'!" Hence paralegals must be intimately familiar with ethical rules. Our goal in this chapter is to provide you with that familiarity.

One final note before we begin. Most allegations are brought by disgruntled clients who claim to have been harmed by the attorney's alleged unethical behavior. An example would be a client's case that was dismissed because the attorney carelessly forgot to file a pleading in court. We need to emphasize, however, that a person who initiates a charge of unethical conduct does not have to prove he or she suffered actual harm thereby. Suppose, for example, an attorney represents a client with whom the attorney has a clear conflict of interest. The attorney should never have taken the case. Representing the client in the case is unethical even if the attorney wins the case for the client! Proof of harm is not necessary to establish a violation of the ethical rules, although such harm is usually present.

FORMATION OF THE ATTORNEY-CLIENT RELATIONSHIP

An attorney-client relationship arises when
- The attorney and the client expressly agree to form the relationship, or
- The attorney's conduct would lead a reasonable person to believe that he or she has agreed to represent the client even in the absence of a formal agreement to do so.

When an attorney first meets with a prospective client, one of his or her first concerns is whether to accept the case. The attorney may reject a case for a number of reasons, such as

- The attorney's belief that the prospective client does not have a **meritorious** case
- The attorney's current busy caseload does not allow the office to take on the added case
- The attorney's belief that the office does not have the kind of expertise required to represent this prospective client
- The presence of a conflict of interest (see discussion below)
- The likelihood that the office would not be able to collect its fees and costs of representation.

Once the office decides not to take the case, it should send out a **letter of nonengagement** to avoid or refute a later claim by a prospective client that the office was going to provide representation. Initial contacts with the office may have involved a meeting and some phone calls without a clear indication of whether the attorney was going to take the case. As time passes, the situation can become ugly if the **statute of limitations** has run out so that a claim can no longer be asserted. The attorney does not want to be blamed for the fact that the claim is now **time-barred**. Sending a letter of nonengagement helps prove that the attorney never had an ethical or professional duty to act on the case before the claim was barred by the statute of limitations because the attorney never agreed to provide representation.

The main way in which an attorney-client relationship is formed is by the attorney and client expressly agreeing to form such a relationship. The agreement might be called a **retainer** agreement, retainer contract, contract of representation, attorney-client fee agreement, or engagement letter that is signed by the attorney and the client. (See Exhibit 8-1 in Chapter 8 for an example of such an agreement.) The document covers the scope of services to be provided as well as the payments the client will be making for those services. (The verb is *retain*.) *Retainer* also refers to the amount of money (or other property) paid by a client as a deposit or advance against future fees, costs, and expenses of providing services.

Yet a formal agreement is not the only way that an attorney-client relationship can come into existence. It is possible for an attorney to take on a client without intending to do so. The test of whether an attorney-client relationship has been formed is whether a reasonable person would interpret the attorney's conduct as an agreement to provide legal services to a specific person. It does not depend on whether a formal agreement was signed. The test is not whether the attorney wanted or intended to become someone's attorney. The test is how a reasonable person would interpret what the attorney did. In the absence of clear evidence of nonengagement, attorneys can find themselves in an unwanted and unintended attorney-client relationship.

> **Example**: Harry Davis, Esq. meets Mary Patterson for the first time at a party. When Mary finds out that Harry is an attorney, she tells him that she thinks that her boss is trying to fire her because she has rebuffed his romantic overtures to her. Harry tells her that she could write down everything that the boss has said and done since he began acting inappropriately. He also answers her questions about her employment rights. During the conversation, Harry is called away, but before he leaves the party, he gives Mary his card. Nothing else is said.

Is Harry Mary's attorney? Has an attorney-client relationship been formed? The question is critical because if such a relationship exists, Harry has ethical duties pertaining to confidentiality and conflict of interest. He must treat what Mary told him as confidential and he would not be allowed to represent Mary's boss, even if she later hires someone else to represent her in the sexual-harassment case.

Did Harry become Mary's attorney at the party? He gave her legal advice along with his business card after she gave him details about her legal problem. On the other hand, they never signed an agreement or discussed fees. As indicated, however, a formal agreement and fees are

meritorious Having merit; having a reasonable basis to believe that a person's claim or defense will succeed.

letter of nonengagement A letter sent to a prospective client that explicitly states that the law office will not be representing him or her.

statute of limitations A law stating that civil or criminal actions are barred if not brought within a specified period of time. The action is time-barred if not brought within that time.

time-barred (1) Prevented or barred from bringing a civil or criminal action because of the passage of a designated period of time without commencing the action. (2) Being unable to sue because of the statute of limitations.

retainer (1) The act of hiring or engaging the services of someone, usually a professional. (The verb is *retain*.) (2) An amount of money (or other property) paid by a client as a deposit or advance against future fees, court costs, and related expenses of providing services.

not essential to forming an attorney-client relationship. As of the time of the party, if a reasonable person in Mary's position would believe that Harry agreed to provide legal services, then the attorney-client relationship exists. It can always be ended (see the discussion of withdrawal below), but once it is formed, serious consequences can result if the attorney does not act properly before it is ended. The consequences can include the duty to keep confidential what the prospective client said and to refrain from representing the opponent of the prospective client.

The danger of creating an unintended attorney-client relationship is particularly acute on attorney websites. When you go to the website of cautious attorneys, you will often see a statement to visitors that no attorney-client relationship is created simply by reason of the fact that the site is visited or that an email query is sent to the attorney through a link on the site. Before allowing a visitor to send an email question, the attorney may make visitors click "yes" to the question, "Do you understand that the receipt of your email does not in and of itself create an attorney-client relationship between us?" (We will have more to say about the ethical use of websites later in the chapter.) Here is what the American Bar Association says about websites and the attorney-client relationship:

> Websites have become a common means by which lawyers communicate with the public. Lawyers must not include misleading information on websites, must be mindful of the expectations created by the website, and must carefully manage inquiries invited through the website. Websites that invite inquiries may create a prospective client-lawyer relationship.[4] (Model Rule 1.18)

Paralegal Perspective

- Some paralegals work in high-volume law offices that handle a large caseload. Examples might be offices with specialties in workers' compensation or fender-bender negligence cases. Paralegals who are asked to screen the many callers who contact an office about their legal problems must never tell a caller that he or she will be accepted as a client, even if the caller fits the criteria established by the office for the kind of cases it accepts. The most that the paralegal can do is to arrange for the caller to talk with an attorney in the office. Accepting cases is an attorney-only task. An attorney "may not delegate to a paralegal" responsibility for establishing attorney-client relationships."[5]

LIMITED-SCOPE REPRESENTATION

- An attorney can provide limited-scope representation so long as the client clearly understands the limited nature of the services. Model Rule 1.2(c)
- Most states allow attorneys to practice collaborative law so long as the clients clearly understand that the collaborative-law attorneys do not provide litigation services. The attorney's agreement with the client to withdraw from the case if litigation becomes necessary does not compromise the attorney's duty to give vigorous representation to his or her own client.

Most attorney services consist of a mix or bundle of tasks. For example, in a divorce, the bundle might consist of legal advice on the grounds for divorce, investigation of marital assets, document preparation, document review, document filing, legal research, negotiation, and court representation. Collectively, these tasks are called **bundled legal services**.

UNBUNDLED LEGAL SERVICES

Suppose that a client does not want the full range of attorney services. The client might be representing him or herself (**pro se**) but would like the attorney to perform specific tasks, such as reviewing a separation agreement the client has prepared from a sample form found on the Internet. The client is seeking what is called *discrete-task representation* or *limited-scope representation*. Attorneys who agree to such representation are providing **unbundled legal services**. (Charging for such services is called *task-based billing*, *unit billing*, or *project billing*.)

The main ethical danger in providing unbundled legal services is that the client does not have a clear understanding of the limited nature of the representation (Model Rule 1.2). A nightmare example is an attorney who agrees to review a document prepared by a pro se client who believes, wrongly, that the attorney will *also* file a court claim based on that document. The client then loses the claim by default when it is not filed before the statute of limitations expires. Attorneys have an ethical obligation to take all reasonable steps to avoid such misunderstandings in unbundled cases.

---

bundled legal services All tasks needed to represent a client; all-inclusive legal services.

pro se (on one's own behalf) Appearing for or representing oneself. Also called *in propria persona* (shortened *in pro per*).

unbundled legal services Discrete task representation for which the client is charged per task as opposed to paying a single fee for all tasks to be performed. Also called *limited-scope representation*.

In some states, all documents filed in court that were prepared by an attorney must state the attorney's name on the document. In such states, a client who hires an attorney for the limited purpose of drafting a complaint, for example, cannot allow the court to believe that the client drafted it. Ghostwriting is not allowed in such states.

COLLABORATIVE LAW

Collaborative law is an example of limited-scope representation in family-law cases. Attorneys practicing collaborative law refuse to continue representing the parties if they cannot settle their dispute through mediation or other method of **alternative dispute resolution (ADR)**. The representation is limited because the attorneys refuse to litigate.

Each party hires his or her own attorney who practices collaborative law. A four-way agreement is then reached in which the two parties and their attorneys consent to the limited role of the attorneys. To encourage settlement, the agreement provides that the attorneys will refuse to continue representing the parties if litigation becomes necessary because ADR has failed to resolve the disputes. The parties must find other attorneys if the case goes to trial. The collaborative-law attorneys, therefore, do not have a financial incentive to drag the dispute into litigation in order to increase their hourly fees. When collaborative law is successful, the role of the court is limited to reviewing the agreements reached by the parties. Courts often approve such agreements.

Most states say that practicing collaborative law is ethical so long as clients give **informed consent** to the restriction on litigation in a collaborative-law practice. There is a danger that a client who hires a collaborative-law attorney will not understand the litigation restriction and may not realize that he or she can hire other attorneys who are not subject to this restriction.

> Obtaining the client's informed consent requires that the lawyer communicate adequate information and explanation about the material risks of and reasonably available alternatives to the limited representation. The lawyer must provide adequate information about the rules or contractual terms governing the collaborative process, its advantages and disadvantages, and the alternatives. The lawyer also must assure that the client understands that, if the collaborative law procedure does not result in settlement of the dispute and litigation is the only recourse, the collaborative lawyer must withdraw and the parties must retain new lawyers to prepare the matter for trial.[6]

The most troublesome ethical question is whether the four-way agreement not to be litigation attorneys places an attorney under a contractual commitment to an opposing party. This was the concern of one of the few bar associations to take the position that practicing collaborative law is unethical. Most state bars (and the American Bar Association) disagree. It is true that it is unethical for an attorney to represent a party if the representation will be "materially limited" by the attorney's responsibilities to a "third person" (Rule 1.7[b]). In this instance, the third person is the opposing party to whom the attorney has made a contractual commitment to cease providing services to the attorney's own client if ADR collapses and litigation becomes necessary. If, however, a client gives informed consent to the arrangement, the ethical objection is eliminated. The contractual agreement to withdraw from the case places no limits on the attorney's duty to provide competent and vigorous representation before the time litigation becomes necessary. This is the view of most bar associations. They also do not believe that the agreement to withdraw interferes with the attorney's independent judgment regarding whether litigation is needed.

COMPETENCE

- An attorney shall provide competent representation to a client.
- Competence consists of the knowledge, skill, thoroughness, and preparation reasonably necessary to assist a particular client. Model Rule 1.1

A **competent** attorney is one who uses the knowledge, skill, thoroughness, and preparation that are reasonably necessary to represent a particular client. What is reasonably necessary depends on the complexity of the case. A great deal of knowledge, skill, thoroughness, and preparation, for example, will be needed when representing a corporate client accused of complicated antitrust violations. Competence does not mean winning every case. The standard is reasonableness in acquiring and using the knowledge and skill needed to represent a particular client.

collaborative law A method of practicing law in which the attorneys refuse to continue representing the parties if they cannot settle their dispute through mediation or other method of alternative dispute resolution (ADR).

alternative dispute resolution (ADR) A method or procedure for resolving a legal dispute without litigating the dispute in a court or administrative agency.

informed consent Agreement to let something happen after receiving a reasonable explanation of the benefits and risks involved.

competent Using the knowledge, skill, thoroughness, and preparation that are reasonably necessary to represent a particular client. (See glossary for an additional meaning.)

How do attorneys obtain the knowledge and skill needed for particular cases?

- They take the time needed to prepare themselves.
- They use the general principles of legal analysis learned in law school.
- They do legal research in traditional and online law libraries.
- When needed, they formally associate themselves with more experienced attorneys in the area.

Attorneys who fail to take these steps are acting unethically if their failure means that they do not provide the knowledge, skill, thoroughness, and preparation reasonably necessary to represent a particular client.

Some attorneys have so many clients that they could not possibly give proper attention to each. Always looking for more lucrative work, they run the risk of neglecting the clients they already have. As a consequence, they might miss court dates or other filing deadlines, lose documents, fail to determine what law governs a client's case, etc. Such an attorney is practicing law "from the hip"—incompetently and, therefore, unethically.

> **Example**: Mary Henderson, Esq. has a large criminal law practice. She agrees to probate the estate of a client's deceased son. She has never had a probate client before and does not investigate how probate cases should be handled. Five years go by. No progress is made in determining who is entitled to receive the estate. If some minimal legal research had been done, Henderson would have been able to close the case within six months of taking it.

Henderson has acted unethically. The failure to do basic research on a case is a sign of incompetence. The need for such research is clear in view of the fact that she has never handled a probate case. Either she must take the time to find out how to probate the estate, or she must contact another attorney with probate experience and arrange to work with this attorney on the case. Doing neither is unethical.

The vast majority of graduates of law schools need considerable on-the-job study and guidance before they are ready to handle cases of any complexity. Traditional law-school courses give new attorneys a good theoretical understanding of the law. This is different from the practical knowledge and skill needed to work on real cases. Many law schools have **clinical education** programs in which students receive credit for working on actual cases under the supervision of attorneys. For example, the school might operate its own tax clinic for senior citizens or might assign students to work several hours a week on cases of **indigent** clients at a local legal aid office. Although these clinical programs provide practical experience, they are not a major part of the law school curriculum of every law school. Most new attorneys (including those with clinical experience), therefore, are quite nervous when they face their first client on their first paid job. The nervousness is based on the fact that they are acutely aware of how much they don't know. This doesn't necessarily mean they are incompetent to practice law. It simply means they must take the time to prepare themselves and to draw on the assistance of others when needed.

Continuing legal education (CLE) is another vehicle used by attorneys to achieve competence. Most states require attorneys to participate in a designated number of hours of CLE per year as a condition of maintaining their license to practice law. This requirement is called MCLE (mandatory continuing legal education.) CLE sessions are designed to help practicing attorneys stay current in their areas of practice. The sessions are often conducted by a CLE institute affiliated with the bar association. Throughout the year, and particularly during bar conventions, attorneys have the opportunity to attend relatively short CLE sessions, e.g., an afternoon. CLE on the Internet is another option that is becoming increasingly popular.

If an attorney is incompetent, he or she can be sanctioned for being unethical. In addition, the incompetence may have other consequences. The client might try to sue the attorney for the tort of negligence in a legal malpractice case. (Such suits were discussed in Chapter 4.) If the client is a criminal defendant who was convicted, he or she may try to appeal the conviction on the grounds that the attorney's incompetence amounted to a denial of the effective "Assistance of Counsel" guaranteed by the Sixth Amendment of the U.S. Constitution.

Paralegal Perspective:

- One malpractice liability insurance company (Lawyers Mutual) recently made the following observation about malpractice claims that resulted from errors committed by nonattorney staff in the office:

clinical education A training program in which students work on real cases under professional supervision.

indigent Poor; without means to afford something such as a private attorney or filing fees.

Attorney malpractice is on the rise. Each year, Lawyers Mutual processes an increasing amount of claims that can be directly attributed to errors made by support staff. Examples include calendaring incorrect deadlines, title search errors, verified complaints that were not properly filed, and lapsed statute of limitations deadlines that resulted from closing a file prematurely or accidentally removing it from the docket system.[7]

- An attorney has an ethical obligation to recruit paralegals who are competent because of their prior education and whatever additional training and supervision the office will provide to perform the tasks they will be assigned.

- Of course, paralegals have an ethical obligation to take steps to maintain and increase their own competence. Some of these steps are listed below.

- If you are given assignments that are beyond your knowledge and skill, let your supervisor know. Either you must be given training with sufficient supervision, or you must be given other assignments. A "lawyer should explain to the paralegal that the paralegal has a duty to inform the lawyer of any assignment which the assistant regards as beyond his capability."[8]

- Be wary of the attorneys who have so much confidence in your competence that they use your work product with little or no checking for accuracy. This is extremely dangerous, particularly for paralegals who work for busy attorneys. The danger is that you will make a mistake that will not be caught until damage is done to the client. No matter how much experience you develop in an area of the law, unique legal issues often arise. Unless someone is reviewing your work, how will you know whether you have missed one of these issues? Your ego will appreciate the confidence your supervisor expresses in you by delegating so much responsibility, but your competence is not a substitute for supervision. A paralegal is engaged in the unauthorized practice of law (UPL) when performing legal tasks without adequate supervision even if the task is performed correctly and even if the attorney asked the paralegal to perform the task.

- Try to turn assignments into ongoing learning experiences. After a new assignment has been completed, ask your supervisor how it can be improved the next time. You may have to wait until a busy supervisor has time to respond, but don't wait until the year-end evaluation. Every day presents opportunities to increase your competence if you make it part of your agenda to look for and take those opportunities. Your growth as a paralegal will depend on it, and you will be contributing to the ethical mandate of the office to be competent.

- Find out which attorneys, administrators, paralegals, and secretaries in the office have a reputation for explaining things well. Try to spend time with such individuals even if you do not work with them on a daily basis. Take them to lunch. Find time to sit with them on a coffee break. Ask lots of questions. Let them know you respect high-quality work and appreciate anything they can tell you to help you increase your competence.

- Invest in continuing legal education (CLE) *even if you must pay for it yourself*. Find the time to attend CLE sessions. Because the law often changes, you need to use resources like CLE to keep current. Take the initiative in continuing your training after your formal education is over. Do not wait for someone to suggest further training. Attend CLE sessions designed for paralegals. In addition, consider attending CLE sessions for attorneys in the areas of law that are relevant to your work assignments. CLE is often conducted on a weekday afternoon, on a Saturday, or online. Here are ways to find out what CLE opportunities are available in your area:

  - Go to the websites of paralegal associations in your area (see Appendix B). If CLE is not listed on the homepage of an association, type *CLE* or *continuing legal education* in its search box or send an email to the association inquiring about CLE.
  - Go to the website of the bar associations in your area (see Appendix B). If CLE is not listed on the homepage of an association, type *CLE* or *continuing legal education* in its search box.
  - On Google, Bing, or Yahoo, run this search: "continuing legal education" aa (substituting the name of your city or state for "aa").

- In some states, paralegal CLE is not optional. As we saw in Chapter 4, for example, Paralegals and legal document assistants (LDAs) must meet mandatory CLE requirements in California. Also, paralegals who have passed the certification exams of paralegal associations have CLE obligations that must be met in order to maintain their certification status (see Exhibits 4-9 and 4-10 in Chapter 4).

- Review the section in Chapter 4 on malpractice insurance. No matter how competent you are, you could be a defendant in a negligence suit brought against a law firm by a disgruntled client. Find out if the firm has a malpractice policy and whether it covers paralegal employees.

DIGITAL COMPETENCE

At one time, a law office looked with amusement at the older attorneys who refused to join the computer bandwagon in the practice of law. No more. Indeed, all attorneys (young or old) can be disciplined for failing to "keep abreast" of the "benefits and risks associated with relevant technology." (Model Rule 1.3, Comment 6). Attorneys must know how to

- Back up files
- Perform computerized legal research
- Install and update virus and malware protection
- Avoid violating confidentiality when using computer devices in public
- Safeguard confidentiality in the cloud
- Create effective passwords
- Remove ("scrub") *metadata* (discussed later in the chapter)
- Conduct e-discovery
- Avoid *spoliation* of digital evidence (discussed later in the chapter)
- Etc.

Paralegal Perspective:

- There are many steps you can take on your own to increase your own digital competence. See Exhibit 13-1 in Chapter 13, "Developing Your Computer Skills: What You Can Do on Your Own Now." In addition, there is a core computer assignment at the end of every chapter in this book, which you should do whether or not they are required for the course. In particular, start and regularly update the Computer Terminology in the Law (CTL) notebook described in Assignment 1.8 of Chapter 1.

DILIGENCE/UNWARRANTED DELAY

- Attorneys must act with reasonable diligence and promptness (avoiding unwarranted delay) in representing a client. Model Rule 1.3
- Reasonable efforts must be taken to expedite litigation. Model Rule 3.2

"Perhaps no professional shortcoming is more widely resented than procrastination." (Model Rule 1.3, Comment 3) Angry clients often complain that attorneys take forever to complete a case and keep clients in the dark about what is happening. "He never answers my calls." "It took months to file the case in court." "She keeps telling me that everything is fine, but nothing ever gets done." Such complaints do not necessarily indicate unethical behavior by the attorney. Events may be beyond the control of the attorney. For example, the court calendar is crowded or the other side is not responding. Yet this does not excuse a lack of regular communication with clients to keep them reasonably informed about the status of their case.

Other explanations for a lack of diligence and promptness, however, are more serious:

- The attorney is disorganized. The office has not developed adequate systems to process cases. The delays are due to careless mistakes and a lack of skill.
- The attorney is taking many more cases than the office can handle. Additional personnel should be hired to do the needed work, or new cases should not be accepted.
- The office fails to designate backup attorneys to handle ongoing cases of attorneys who are away on vacation or are otherwise unavailable because of pressing work on other cases.

Often the failure to use reasonable diligence and promptness causes harm to the client. For example, the attorney neglects to file a suit before the statute of limitations has run and the client loses the case by default. Unreasonable procrastination, however, can be unethical even if such harm does not result.

Another problem is the attorney who intentionally causes numerous delays in an effort to wear the other side down. It is unethical to engage in such **dilatory** practices. Attorneys must use reasonable efforts to expedite litigation, consistent with protecting the interests of their clients.

dilatory Causing delay, often without merit or justification.

Paralegal Perspective:

- An overloaded attorney probably works with an overloaded paralegal. Successful paralegals often take the initiative by asking for additional work. But reason must prevail. If you have more work than you can handle, you must let your supervisor know. Otherwise, you might find yourself contributing to the ethical problem of undue delay.

- Learn everything you can about office systems, particularly for tasks that the office performs on a regular basis. Find out how systems are created. After you have gained experience in the office, start thinking about designing systems on your own initiative. For example, one component of a system that can be created with relative ease is a folder containing frequently used documents in a divorce or other kind of case the office often handles. The documents in the folder become a source of model documents that can be adapted for future cases. Effective office systems of this kind can reduce the risk of unethical delays in client representation.

- When a busy attorney is in court or cannot be disturbed because of urgent work on another case, someone in the office should be available to communicate with clients who want to know the status of their case. In many offices, the paralegal is in a position to provide this information. The role can be delicate because of two dangers: giving legal advice and creating unreasonable expectations. In addition to asking about the status of their case, clients often ask questions that call for legal advice. Giving such advice may constitute the unauthorized practice of law (UPL). Later we will examine in greater depth the temptations and pressures on a paralegal to give legal advice. Also, clients may want to know if they are going to win their cases. Careless language (e.g., "you have an excellent case") might later give rise to a breach-of-contract suit in which a client argues that the office guaranteed a particular result in the representation. All that can be said to the client is that the office is doing the best it can to achieve the client's objectives.

FEES

- Fees for legal services must be reasonable.
- Factors that determine the reasonableness of a fee include time and labor, complexity, novelty, amount involved, results, experience and reputation, what is customary, and whether other business had to be given up. Model Rule 1.5(a)

WHAT IS A REASONABLE FEE?

A reasonable fee is a fee that is not excessive. There is no absolute standard to determine when a fee is excessive and therefore unreasonable. A number of factors must be considered:

- The time and labor involved
- The complexity of the case
- The novelty of the issues in the case
- The amount of money or other property involved
- The results achieved by the attorney
- The experience and reputation of the attorney
- The customary fee in the locality for the same kind of case
- Whether the attorney had to give up other business in order to take the case, etc.

In one case, a court ruled that $500 an hour was excessive in a simple battery case in which there was no trial (the accused pled guilty) and there were no unusual issues to be resolved. In another case, a court concluded that a fee of $22,500 was excessive in an uncomplicated real-estate case involving very little attorney time. The case was settled through the efforts of someone other than the attorney.

A fee is not necessarily excessive simply because it is large. Cases exist in which courts have approved fees of hundreds of millions of dollars. An example is the tobacco litigation of the 1990s, in which attorneys brought suits that resulted in multibillion-dollar settlements and judgments. Prior to this time, the tobacco industry had remarkable success in winning personal-injury suits brought by sick smokers and by the estates of deceased smokers. In assessing the reasonableness of a fee, a court will consider the initial odds against winning and the uniqueness of the issues raised in the litigation. By these standards, the attorneys who won the cases against the tobacco industry were entitled to very high fees. When the litigation began, few thought the plaintiff attorneys had much chance of winning anything, let alone winning billions. (Later in the chapter, we will discuss the infamous role of a paralegal, Merrill Williams, in the tobacco litigation.)

FEE AGREEMENT

- Most states require contingent fee agreements to be in writing.
- Most states recommend, but do not require, other fee agreements (e.g., hourly-fee agreements) to be in writing. Model Rule 1.5(a)

The basis of the fee should be communicated to the client before or soon after the attorney starts to work on the case. This is often done in the agreement hiring the attorney. (For an example of such an agreement, see Exhibit 8-1 in Chapter 8). Kinds of fees are also discussed in greater detail in Chapter 14.)

In most states, **contingent fee** agreements must be in writing. This is a fee that is paid only if the case is successfully resolved by litigation or settlement regardless of the number of hours spent on the case. States differ on whether non-contingency fee cases must be in writing. In most states, written agreements are recommended but not required. Oral agreements are acceptable as long as the basis of the fee is adequately explained to the client and nothing misleading is said about fees and related expenses. We will have more to say about contingent fees and misleading statements later in the chapter.

EXPENSES

In addition to paying fees for an attorney's time, clients can also be charged for out-of-pocket expenses incurred by the office in the representation. Examples of expenses include **court costs**, witness fees, and long-distance travel. Clients must not be misled about their payment. If an attorney tells clients that they "pay nothing if they don't win," it must make clear whether such statements refer to attorney fees only. If clients must pay an attorney's out-of-pocket expenses even if the case is lost, the clients must be made aware of this at the outset of the attorney-client relationship.

PASSING ON SAVINGS TO CLIENTS

An ethics opinion of the American Bar Association addresses the issue of excessive fees through the following three fact situations:

Case I. John Smith, Esq. (who bills by the hour) has two clients who happen to have separate cases in the same court on May 9, each requiring relatively minor attention from the attorney. If the attorney had gone to court on two separate days, each client could have been billed for three hours. On May 9, however, Smith was able to handle both cases. He spent a total of three hours in court. Can he bill each client three hours for the time spent on May 9, since he would have been able to do so if he went on separate days?

    Answer: No. Smith did not earn six billable hours on May 9. Billing more than one client for the same time is unreasonable. Savings resulting from scheduling must be passed on to clients.

Case II. Mary Jones, Esq. (who bills by the hour) charges a client five hours transportation time to travel by airplane to a meeting with the client in another city. While on the plane, she skips the in-flight movie in order to spend two hours drafting a motion for a different client on another case. Can she bill the first client five hours and the second client two hours to cover the total of five hours on the plane?

    Answer: No. Jones has not earned seven billable hours. Billing more than one client for the same time is unreasonable. Savings resulting from being able to do two things simultaneously (traveling and drafting a motion) for different clients must be passed on to clients.

Case III. George Harris, Esq. (who bills by the hour) bills a client for ten hours to research a problem and draft a memorandum of law covering the issues in the case. Several days later, he uses the same memorandum on a different case for another client who happens to have the same legal problem as the earlier client. Can he bill the second client ten hours for the memorandum?

    Answer: No. Harris has not earned twenty billable hours. Billing more than one client for the same work product (a research memorandum) is unreasonable. Savings resulting from being able to reuse a work product must be passed on to clients. If Harris needed time to adapt the memo to the needs of the second client, he could charge for this time. When billing this client, however, he cannot assume that the prior memo did not exist.[9]

---

contingent fee A fee that is paid only if the case is successfully resolved by litigation or settlement regardless of the number of hours spent on the case. (The fee is also referred to as a *contingency*.) A defense contingent fee (also called a negative contingency) is a fee for the defendant's attorney that is dependent on the outcome of the case.

court costs Charges or fees imposed by and paid to the court that are related to litigation in that court. An example is a court filing fee.

MINIMUM FEES

At one time, bar associations published a list of minimum fees that attorneys should charge for specified legal services. A fee below the minimum was considered unethical. In *Goldfarb v. Virginia State Bar*, the U.S. Supreme Court ruled that such **minimum-fee schedules** are prohibited. The schedules operated as a fixed, rigid price floor and therefore constituted illegal price fixing in violation of **antitrust law**.[10]

MAXIMUM FEES: FEE CAPS

Attorneys cannot be required to charge minimum fees, but they can be subject to maximum fees. Some states have passed statutes that impose **fee caps** on certain kinds of cases. A fee cap is the maximum amount or maximum percentage that can be charged as a fee in a case. For example, a state may say that in a medical malpractice case, fees cannot exceed 20 percent of what is recovered.

CONTINGENT FEES

- Contingent fees are proper in most cases if the client clearly understands when he or she is responsible for paying attorney fees and related expenses of litigation.
- Contingent fees are not allowed in criminal cases.
- Contingent fees are not allowed in family-law cases if the fee is dependent on securing a divorce, on the amount of alimony or support, or the amount of property settlement that is awarded in place of (in lieu) of alimony or support. Model Rule 1.5(c) and (d)

As indicated earlier, most states require contingent-fee agreements (those dependent on the outcome of the case) to be in writing. The benefit of a contingent fee is that it provides an incentive for an attorney to take the case of a client who does not have funds to pay hourly fees while the case is pending.

> **Example**: An attorney agrees to represent a client in an automobile negligence case. If the jury awards the client damages, the attorney will receive 30 percent of the award. If the client loses the case, the attorney receives no fee. Similarly, if the case is settled in the client's favor, the attorney receives 30 percent of the settlement, but no fee if the client obtains nothing through litigation or settlement.

This is a contingent fee because it is dependent on the successful outcome of the negligence case.

In the automobile negligence example, assume that the attorney incurs $5,000 in expenses for filing fees, travel costs, and witness fees. The fee agreement must clearly state who is responsible for these expenses.

- Does the client pay these expenses whether or not the attorney wins the case in court or by settlement?
- If the client must pay these expenses and if the attorney wins the case, are the expenses to be paid in addition to the attorney's fee or must the attorney deduct the expenses from his or her fee?

Contingent fees cannot be used in every kind of case. They are not allowed in criminal cases and in some family-law cases.

> **Example**: Gabe Farrell is a client of Sam Grondon, Esq. in a criminal case. Gabe is charged with murder. Gabe agrees to pay Grondon $100,000 if he is found innocent. Grondon will receive nothing if Gabe is convicted of any crime.

This fee agreement is unethical. Contingent fees are not allowed in criminal cases. Note the pressures on Grondon. He arguably has no incentive to try to negotiate a guilty plea to a lesser charge, e.g., manslaughter, because such a plea would mean a conviction and, hence, no fee. In such a situation, the attorney's own personal interest (obtaining the $100,000) could conflict with the interest of the client (receiving a lesser penalty through a negotiated plea). The fee, therefore, is unethical even if the amount of the contingent fee is otherwise reasonable and is agreed to by the client. Similar inappropriate fee pressures can arise in family-law cases:

> **Example**: Tom Edgers hires an attorney to obtain a divorce from his wife. The fee is $25,000 if the divorce is granted, but no fee if it is not granted.

minimum-fee schedules A bar association list of the lowest fees an attorney can ethically charge for specific kinds of legal services. Such lists (schedules) violate antitrust laws.

antitrust law The law governing unlawful interferences with competition such as through price fixing, monopolies, and other restraints of trade.

fee caps A maximum amount or maximum percentage that can be charged as a fee in a case.

As the case develops, suppose a glimmer of hope arises that the husband and wife might reconcile. Here, again, the attorney's interest (obtaining the $25,000) could conflict with the interest of the client (reconciling). This might lead the attorney to discourage the reconciliation or to set up roadblocks to it. Reconciliation removes the possibility of the contingency—obtaining the divorce—from occurring. In family-law cases, therefore, the following fees would be unethical:

- The attorney will receive a designated fee *if* the divorce is granted.
- The attorney will receive a designated fee *if* the court issues an alimony or support order above a specified dollar amount per month.
- The attorney will receive a designated fee *if* the court issues a property division or settlement order that is in place of (in lieu of) an alimony or support order.

These fees are unethical even if the amount of the contingent fee is otherwise reasonable and is agreed to by the client.

Some states have limited exceptions to the rule on contingent fees in family-law cases. For example, a state might forbid a contingent fee when a client is seeking *future* support but allow it if the client is seeking to collect a support judgment that has already been rendered. If a judgment already exists, the attorney's interest in collecting the contingent fee is less likely to interfere with the continuation or reconciliation of family relationships.

FEE SPLITTING AMONG ATTORNEYS

Attorneys who are not in the same law office can share a fee if
- the client agrees to the arrangement,
- the total fee is reasonable, and
- either
(a) both attorneys do actual work on the case and the fee is split in proportion to the work each does on the case, or
(b) if Attorney #1 does all the work, Attorney #2 agrees to be legally responsible along with Attorney #1 in the event of malpractice or ethical violations by Attorney #1. Model Rule 1.5(e)

fee splitting (1) The division or splitting of a single client's fee between two or more attorneys who are not in the same firm. (2) The division or splitting of a fee between an attorney and a nonattorney. Also called *fee sharing, division of fees.*

forwarding fee A fee received by one attorney from another to whom the first attorney referred a client. Also called *finder's fee, referral fee.*

Attorneys in the same firm share fees all the time. This rarely raises ethical problems. Suppose, however, that attorneys in different firms share a fee. This is an example of **fee splitting**—the division or splitting of a single client's fee between two or more attorneys who are not in the same firm. To explore the ethics of fee splitting, compare the following two situations.

> **Example**: Case A. Attorney #1 finds a client and refers the client to Attorney #2 in a different law firm. Attorney #1 does no work on the case. Attorney #2 pays Attorney #1 a **forwarding fee**.

> **Example**: Case B. Attorney #1 finds a client and asks Attorney #2 in a different law firm to assist Attorney #1 in representing the client. Both attorneys work on the case and the fee that each receives is in proportion to the work they do on the case.

The arrangement in Case A is unethical in most states. Attorneys in different law firms cannot share a fee if one of the attorneys does no work on the case *unless* this attorney agrees to be legally responsible along with the other attorney in the event that the latter commits malpractice or an ethical violation. The splitting of fees in Case B is ethical because both attorneys do actual work on the case. Other requirements for fee splitting are that the total fee paid by the client is reasonable and the client agrees in writing to the fee-splitting arrangement.

Under the Paralegal Perspective below, we will cover the related ethical problem of an attorney splitting a fee with a paralegal or other nonattorney.

NONPAYMENT OF FEES AND THE CLIENT'S FILE

- The failure of a client to pay attorney fees is not a valid reason for the attorney to demand payment as a condition of releasing the file to the client.
- A client's file belongs to the client. Upon request, the attorney must return the file to the client even if fees are outstanding (i.e., unpaid).

When a client has a serious dispute with an attorney over a fee, the client will sometimes dismiss the attorney and ask for a return of the client's file, which may contain many documents such as correspondence, complaints, other pleadings, exhibits, and reports of experts. This file is the property of the client, and in most states the file must be surrendered by the attorney when the client requests it, even if there are unpaid bills for fees and expenses. If the attorney has a claim for payment, the remedy is to sue the client for breach of contract; it is unethical for the attorney to hold the file hostage to ensure payment. The attorney can copy the file before turning it over, but at the attorney's own expense. (For more on an attorney's client-file responsibilities at the close of a case, see Chapter 14.)

Paralegal Perspective:

- *Fee Splitting with Nonattorneys*. Attorneys must not split fees with nonattorneys.

  > **Example**: Frank Martin is a freelance investigator. He refers accident victims to a law firm. For every client he refers to the firm, he receives 25 percent of the fee collected by the firm.

  > **Example**: Helen Gregson is a chiropractor. She refers medical malpractice cases to a law firm, which gives her $500 for each referral who becomes a client.

  These are improper divisions of fees with nonattorneys—even if the amount of the division is reasonable and even if a client brought in by Martin or Gregson gives written consent to their receiving a part of the fee. An attorney cannot share with a nonattorney a portion of a fee paid by a particular client. The rationale behind this prohibition is that the nonattorney might exercise some pressure or control over the attorney in order to protect his or her share of the fee and thereby jeopardize the attorney's independent judgment.

- *Paralegal Salaries*. The salaries of most paralegals are paid out of the fees earned by the office. This does not constitute the unethical sharing of fees with nonattorneys so long as there is no advance agreement to pay a paralegal all or part of *particular* legal fees.
- *Retirement Plan; Bonus*. Suppose that a paralegal is eligible to become part of the firm's retirement plan, which has a profit-sharing component. Or suppose that the firm has a bonus plan for its paralegals. In most states, the same rule applies. Retirement plans and bonuses are ethical so long as there is no sharing or splitting of a *particular* client's fees. There is a major difference between
  - A law firm agreeing to pay a paralegal 10 percent of whatever fees are collected in the *Davis v. Kelly* automobile negligence case on which the paralegal has done good work (unethical in all states) and
  - A law firm giving this paralegal a bonus because the firm appreciates the paralegal's good work on all of the negligence cases (including *Davis v. Kelly*) that resulted in high fees during the year (ethical in most states).
- *Partnerships and Corporations*. An attorney cannot form a partnership with a nonattorney if any of the activities of the partnership consist of the practice of law. If the office practices law as a corporation, a nonattorney cannot own a shareholder interest or be a director or officer. (Professional corporations (PCs) are discussed in Chapter 14.) As we saw earlier, however, if a state allowed the formation of a multidisciplinary practice (MDP), nonattorneys would be allowed to become partners of the firm and thereby share fees.
- *Setting Fees; Accepting or Rejecting a Case*. Paralegals occasionally speak with prospective clients before an attorney does. When this occurs, paralegals must not set fees or say anything that could be interpreted as accepting or rejecting a case. These are attorney-only functions. Is a paralegal allowed to tell a prospective client what the standard fee of the office is? Probably, because this would be considered *communicating* information about fees rather than "*setting*" them. Cautious offices, however, instruct their paralegals to avoid *any* mention of fees except perhaps to state whether there is (or is not) a fee for an initial consultation.
- *Paralegal fees*. Attorneys may charge fees for paralegal work on client cases, referred to as a **paralegal fee**. This is the fee that an attorney can collect for the substantive (nonclerical) legal work of the attorney's paralegal on a client's case. Paralegals record their time on time sheets that eventually become the basis of the bills sent to clients. The amount that an attorney bills for paralegal time must be reasonable as determined by factors such as
  - the experience of the paralegal,
  - the nature of the tasks the paralegal undertakes, and
  - the market rate for paralegals in the area.

paralegal fee A fee that an attorney can collect for the nonclerical work of the attorney's paralegal. The fee covers the paralegal's substantive legal work on behalf of the client.

The attorney-client fee agreements should state the amount a client will be charged for a paralegal's time. (See Exhibit 8-1 in Chapter 8.)

- *Nonclerical tasks.* When a client agrees to pay "paralegal" fees, the fees must be for the performance of paralegal tasks. It is unethical to seek paralegal fees for time the paralegal spent performing clerical duties such as photocopying. A paralegal is allowed to perform such duties, but the office cannot seek paralegal fees from clients for doing so. The costs of secretarial or clerical tasks, rent, utilities, and the like are part of overhead for which clients are not separately charged. In some states, however, a client *can* agree to make separate payments for secretarial or clerical services, but this is not the norm and such services should not be called paralegal services.

- *Statutory-fee cases.* In the vast majority of cases, each side pays its own attorney fees and costs. This is the **American rule**. In special **statutory-fee cases**, however, the losing side can be forced to pay attorney fees (including paralegal fees) of the winning party in litigation. Such fee-shifting cases follow the **English rule**. When attorney (and paralegal) fees are awarded in statutory-fee cases, the fees must be reasonable and cannot cover clerical tasks. As we saw in Chapter 1, some states ask attorneys to submit an affidavit to support the amount claimed for the paralegal's time. The affidavit must give a detailed statement of the time and services rendered by the paralegal, a summary of the paralegal's qualifications, etc.

- *Contemporaneous time records.* The preference (although not a requirement) is that time records should be **contemporaneous**, that is, made at approximately the same time as the events being recorded. Try to avoid entering or recording time long after performing tasks that require time records.

- *Block billing.* Law firms should avoid **block billing** for attorney and paralegal time. Block billing consists of grouping multiple tasks under a single time charge rather than describing each task separately and assigning the actual time associated with each task. Billing records should provide the actual time spent on individually described tasks.

    Example: Block Billing: 19.6 hours: Discovery.

    Itemized Billing: 7.2 hours: Responding to Interrogatories. 3.0 hours: Preparing a Privilege Log. 8.4 hours: Indexing Deposition of Defendant. Total: 19.6 hours.

- *Double billing.* Attorneys and paralegals must avoid **double billing**. It is fraudulent to charge a client twice for the same service.

    Example: Charles is a litigation paralegal in a law firm. One of his tasks is to digest (i.e., summarize) a deposition. The firm bills the client twenty hours for this task at the paralegal's rate ($100 per hour). The firm also bills the client ten hours of Attorney Bedford's time for digesting the same deposition at the attorney's rate ($250 per hour).

The client is being double billed, a grossly unethical practice. It would be proper for an attorney to charge a client for time spent supervising a paralegal's work but not for performing the work the paralegal performed if the paralegal's time is charged separately under the attorney-client fee agreement.

- *Padding.* Do not pad your time sheets. **Padding** is also fraudulent. It occurs when you add hours to your time sheet that were not in fact spent on the client's case (**time padding**) or when you bill for added tasks that were not performed (**task padding**).

    Example: It takes Charles, a litigation paralegal, twelve hours to digest a deposition. His time sheets, however, say he spent twenty hours on the task.

Padding is a serious problem in the practice of law. Here is what one attorney observed about the conduct of some attorneys:

I was routinely told to double and triple bill my time… The lawyers are engaged in pervasive deception of clients, pretending to be doing work that they are not doing, pretending to spend more time than they are spending, pretending that work needs to be done, which in fact does not need to be done. The delivery of legal services is conceptualized principally as a billing opportunity to be manipulated and expanded.[11]

Doing unnecessary work to drive up a client's bill is called *churning*. In 2013, the front page of the New York Times told the story of an attorney's email exhorting another attorney in the firm to "churn that bill, baby!"

---

overhead The operating expenses of a business (e.g., office rent, utilities, insurance, and clerical staff) for which customers or clients are not charged a separate fee. Some states, however, allow attorneys to charge clients for clerical or secretarial time.

American rule Each party pays his or her own attorney fees regardless of who wins the case.

statutory-fee cases A case applying a special statute that gives a judge authority to order the losing party to pay the winning party's attorney fees (including paralegal fees) and costs.

English rule The losing side in litigation must pay the winner's attorney fees. Also called *loser pays.*

contemporaneous Existing or occurring in the same period of time; pertaining to records that are prepared on events as the events are occurring or very shortly thereafter.

block billing Grouping multiple tasks under a single time charge rather than describing each task separately and assigning the actual time associated with each task. The timekeeper enters the total time spent working blocks of tasks without itemizing the time spent on specific tasks for the case.

double billing Fraudulently charging a client twice for the same service.

padding Adding something without justification; adding unnecessary material in order to make something larger.

time padding Inflating a client's bill by charging for time that was not spent.

task padding Inflating a client's bill by charging for tasks that were not performed.

Unfortunately, paralegals can find themselves under a similar pressure, which, of course, must be resisted. In many offices, a paralegal's job security depends on the number of billable hours he or she accumulates. Even if the office does not impose a **billable hours quota**, the number of hours billed is closely watched in order to determine how profitable paralegals are to the office. This should not encourage anyone to engage in double billing and padding.

One of the most common temptations that can corrupt a paralegal's ethics is to inflate billable hours, since there is often immense pressure in law firms to bill high hours for job security and upward mobility. Such "creative billing" is not humorous; it's both morally wrong and illegal. It's also fraudulent and a plain and simple case of theft.[12]

> Paralegals claim that questionable billing is among the most common unethical practice attorneys ask them to perform. [In some offices, paralegals have been] ordered to double bill and bill for time they did not spend working.[13]

When you are employed as a paralegal, you may face such pressure if you work in an office where income is generated through hourly fees. The office wants high billings to increase its income. The paralegal wants high billings to demonstrate to the office that he or she is financially valuable to the office. Fortunately, most paralegals do not submit fraudulent time sheets and billings. But the pressure to do so is real.

- *Summary on Fees*
  - Attorneys must not split fees with nonattorneys.
  - Paralegal salaries, pension benefits, and bonuses can be paid out of the fees generated by the firm so long as these payments are not tied to the fees of particular clients.
  - An attorney cannot form a partnership with a nonattorney or allow a nonattorney to be a shareholder, director, or officer of a corporation engaged in the practice of law.
  - A paralegals cannot set fees, accept cases, or reject cases for an attorney.
  - Attorneys can charge paralegal fees for the substantive (nonclerical) work that paralegal perform on their cases.
  - Preferably, time records should be contemporaneous.
  - Avoid double billing, time padding, and task padding.

MISCONDUCT BY ATTORNEYS

- An attorney must not commit a crime, or engage in dishonesty or misrepresentation, or otherwise violate the rules of ethics.
- An attorney must not knowingly engage in misconduct through the acts of others such as a paralegal or investigator. Model Rule 8.4

As indicated earlier in Exhibit 5-3, over 70,000 allegations of ethical misconduct by attorneys are investigated every year. Some of these allegations involve criminal conduct. Examples include theft of client funds, securities fraud, falsification of official documents, and tax fraud. For such conduct, an attorney can be subject to criminal prosecution and to discipline by the court or agency that enforces ethics in the state.

If an attorney misappropriates a client's funds, the client may be able to receive compensation from a **client security fund** run by a bar association or foundation set up for this purpose. (See Exhibit 5-3.)

Paralegal Perspective:

- *Resisting the pressure.* In the highly charged, competitive environment of a law office, some attorneys may be willing to violate ethics and the law in the interest of winning. Be sensitive to any overt and subtle pressure on you to participate in such violations. If you feel this pressure, resist it, let your supervisors know that you are uncomfortable with the situation, and talk with other paralegals who have encountered comparable pressure. Don't give in and don't sit in silence. In all aspects of your career as a paralegal, adopt the motto "If what you are asked to do doesn't feel right, don't proceed until it does." Value your integrity above all else. A paralegal in Oklahoma offers the following advice: "Insist on the highest standards for yourself and for your employer. One small ethical breach can lead to a series of compromises with enormous" disciplinary and "legal malpractice consequences."[14]

billable hours quota A minimum number of hours expected from a timekeeper on client matters that can be charged (billed) to clients per week, month, year, or other time period.

client security fund A fund (often run by a bar association or foundation) used to compensate victims of designated kinds of attorney misconduct.

pretexting Using online deception as a pretext to obtain information from another person.

■ *Fraudulent "Friending."* Social media sites such as Facebook, Twitter, and MySpace are sources of evidence that attorneys might be able to use in litigation. In a child-custody case, for example, attorneys for the parents routinely check these sites for pictures of partying, drinking, or other behavior that could suggest negative parenting skills. Recently, a judge ordered the parties to exchange each other's passwords for their Facebook and dating websites to allow mutual opportunity for discovery of evidence relevant to their dispute. A paralegal might be asked to comb social-media sites for possible evidence. Care must be used in doing so. It would be unethical to misrepresent your identity in order to gain access to someone's web page through friending or other method of connecting. (Lying—using a pretext—to obtain information is called **pretexting**.) Also, it is unethical to contact an opponent without permission of the opponent's attorney. If the opponent is unrepresented, you must not allow him or her to believe that you are uninvolved (disinterested) in the legal dispute. (See the discussion of the no-contact rule below.)

■ *False notarization.* Paralegals who are also notaries are sometimes asked by their supervisors to notarize documents that should not be notarized. In fact, paralegals "are most often named as defendants for false notarization of a signature."[15] Assume that a law office is sued and the paralegal is named as one of the defendants. If the plaintiff wins, who pays the judgment? As we saw in Chapter 4, the office may have a malpractice insurance liability policy that will pay judgments against it and its employees. The policies, however, often exclude intentional acts of misconduct. (False notarization is usually an intentional act.) Hence, the losing defendants — including the paralegal — must pay the judgments out of their personal pockets. In short, be extremely cautious of what you are asked to sign. The same is true of documents you are asked to witness even if no formal notarization is involved. Don't sign a clause saying you witnessed something being performed or executed (called an **attestation clause**) unless you actually witness it.

attestation clause A clause stating that you saw (witnessed) someone sign a document or perform other tasks related to the validity of the document.

■ *Criminal prosecution.* If your supervisor is charged with criminal conduct, the chances are good that you will be questioned by prosecutors, and you might become a suspect yourself. In 2014, after the prominent law firm of Dewey and LeBoeuf went bankrupt, a paralegal with billing duties was indicted along with senior partners for participating in the falsification of records.[16]

insider trading Improperly using or passing on to others any nonpublic information you learn about in the office in order to trade in the shares of a company.

■ *Insider trading.* Be extremely careful about using any information you learn involving a corporation whose stock is likely to change in value as a result of an event that is not yet known to the public. Assume that Company X is planning to merge with Company Y. The news is not yet public. When it does become public, the value of the stock in Company X is expected to rise dramatically. You work at a law firm that represents Company X, and you find out about the planned merger while at work. If you buy stock in Company X before the announcement of the merger, you would benefit from the increased value of the stock that would result after the announcement. This might be an illegal use of inside information, called **insider trading**. In a dramatic case, a paralegal who worked at a securities law firm in Boston was charged with insider trading by the Securities and Exchange Commission (SEC). While working on a case involving a proposed merger, she learned certain information, which she gave to outside investors who used it to make illegal profits in the stock market. The story made national news. One headline read, "SEC Says Boston Paralegal Gave Tip Worth $823,471." Soon after the incident, she was fired. Criminal prosecution for the crime of insider trading became a very real possibility. All employees of law firms must be extremely careful. Innocently buying stock as a personal investment could turn into a nightmare. One attorney "recommends that any paralegal who would like to buy or sell securities should check first with a corporate attorney in the firm to see if the firm represents the issuer or a company negotiating with the issuer. If it does, an accusation of 'insider trading' might later be made."[17] The same caution applies when a member of the paralegal's immediate family buys or sells such securities.

pirated software Software that has been placed ("loaded") in a computer that is not authorized by the terms of the purchase or lease of the software.

■ *Piracy.* Another problem area is the use of so-called **pirated software**. Some businesses buy or lease one copy of computer software and then copy it so that other employees in the office can use it on other terminals. If the software manufacturer has not authorized such copying as part of the original purchase or lease agreement, the copying is illegal and can subject violators to criminal penalties and civil damages.

OBSTRUCTING ACCESS TO EVIDENCE

- An attorney must not obstruct a party's access to evidence by destroying, altering, or concealing the evidence. Model Rule 3.4

As a matter of basic fairness to an opposing party, an attorney must not obstruct access to evidence by destroying it (e.g., shredding relevant documents), altering it (e.g., backdating financial records), or concealing it (e.g., pretending not to know whether a requested document exists. Nor can the attorney counsel a client to obstruct evidence in these ways. For example, it is unethical for an attorney to tell a client to "clean up" a social networking site by removing photos that were requested in discovery.

A charge of **spoliation** can be brought against attorneys or their clients who intentionally destroy, alter, or conceal evidence. Spoliation is a tort for which an aggrieved party can collect damages from the spoiler. (In Chapter 10 we will discuss the *litigation hold*, which is a notice used by parties to alert opponents not to destroy or alter evidence that might be relevant to contemplated litigation.)

spoliation Intentionally destroying, altering, or concealing evidence.

CRIME OR FRAUD BY CLIENTS

- It is proper for an attorney to discuss the legal consequences of any proposed conduct of the client.
- If, however, the attorney knows that future conduct of a client would be criminal or fraudulent, the attorney must not give the client any advice or other assistance on such conduct. Model Rule 1.2(d)

The client hires the attorney and controls the purpose of the attorney-client relationship. Furthermore, the client is entitled to know the legal consequences of any action he or she is contemplating. This does not mean, however, that the attorney must do whatever the client wants.

> **Example**: The president of a corporation hires Leo Richards, Esq. to advise the company on how to dump toxic waste into a local river.

Note that the president has not asked Richards if the dumping is legal. It would be perfectly ethical for Richards to answer such a question. In the example, the president asks how to dump. If Richards feels that the dumping can legally take place, he can so advise the president. Suppose, however, that it is clear to Richards that the dumping would violate the federal or state criminal code. Under such circumstances, it would be unethical for Richards to advise the president on how to proceed with the dumping. The same would be true if the president wanted help in filing an environmental statement that misrepresented the intentions of the company. Such an application would be fraudulent, and an attorney must not help someone commit what the attorney knows is fraudulent conduct.

When attorneys are later charged with unethical conduct in such cases, their defense is often that they did not know the conduct proposed by the client was criminal or fraudulent. If the law applicable to the client's case is unclear, the attorney can make a good-faith effort to find a legal way for the client to achieve his or her objective. The point at which the attorney crosses the ethical line is when he or she *knows* the client is trying to accomplish something criminal or fraudulent.

In addition to charges of unethical conduct, an attorney could be subjected to civil suits for participating in illegal conduct of a client. For example, as we saw in Chapter 4, an attorney could be sued for the torts of **malicious prosecution** (improperly bringing litigation without probable cause) and **abuse of process** (using civil or criminal process for an improper purpose). Participating in the destruction or alteration of evidence (spoliation) can also have serious consequences.

One final point on the theme of legal services and illegal conduct. Suppose that a senior citizen goes to an attorney for advice on Medicaid. This is a needs-based program; you have to be poor enough to qualify for its health-care benefits (unlike Medicare). Assume that the client has too many assets to qualify. The attorney then describes how the bulk of the assets could be disposed of (e.g., by gifts to children) so that the client would qualify. The strategy was so widespread that Congress (angry that attorneys were "teaching people how to abuse the system") made it a crime to give such advice! The law became known as the "Send Granny's Lawyer to Jail" law. The law certainly made it difficult for attorneys to argue that they did not know that they were participating in something illegal with their clients. The advice itself was illegal! The law created an uproar in the legal community and was immediately challenged in court as a violation of free speech under the First Amendment. The issue eventually became moot when the U.S. Attorney General announced that the Department of Justice would not bring prosecutions under the law because of its dubious legality.

malicious prosecution A tort with the following elements: (1) The initiation (or procuring the initiation) of civil or criminal legal proceedings; (2) without probable cause; (3) with malice or an improper purpose; and (4) the proceedings terminate in favor of the person against whom the proceedings were brought.

abuse of process A tort consisting of the following elements: (1) the use of civil or criminal proceedings, (2) for a purpose for which the process is not designed, (3) resulting in actual damage.

Paralegal Perspective:

■ An attorney will rarely tell paralegals or other staff members that he or she knows the office is helping a client do something criminal or fraudulent. But you might learn that this is so, particularly if there is a close, trusting relationship between you and your supervising attorney. You must let this attorney or some other authority in the office know you do not want to work on such a case.

FRIVOLOUS POSITIONS AND HARASSMENT

An attorney must not bring a claim or assert a defense that
■ is frivolous
■ is intended to harass an opponent or cause unwarranted delay. Model Rules Preamble [5], 3.1

adversary system A method of resolving a legal dispute whereby the parties (alone or through their advocates) argue their conflicting claims before a neutral (impartial) decision maker.

frivolous Lacking merit. Pertaining to a legal position that cannot be supported by a good-faith argument based on existing law or on the need for a change in existing law.

We have an **adversary system** of justice. This means that our method of resolving a legal dispute is to have opposing sides fight it out before an impartial decision maker. (See Chapter 6 for a description of the *inquisitorial system* used in many other countries.) We believe that truth and fairness are more likely to emerge when each side has an equal chance to present its case forcefully. Within this system, clients have the right to hire an attorney to be a vigorous advocate.

But there are limits on how vigorous an advocate can be. It is unethical for an attorney to assert **frivolous** positions as claims or defenses. A position is frivolous if the attorney is unable to make a good-faith argument that existing law supports the position or that existing law should be changed or reversed to support the position. A position is not necessarily frivolous simply because the attorney thinks the client will probably lose. The key is whether there is a good-faith argument to support the position. If the attorney can think of no rational support for the position, it is frivolous. Because the law is often unclear, however, it is difficult to establish that an attorney is acting unethically under the test of good faith.

Closely related to asserting frivolous positions is the unethical practice of asserting positions for the sole purpose of harassing or maliciously injuring someone. "A lawyer should use the law's procedures only for legitimate purposes and not to harass or intimidate others." (Model Rules, Preamble [5])

Federal Rules of Civil Procedure (FRCP) The rules that govern the mechanics of resolving a dispute by a U.S. district court, which is the main federal trial court (www.law.cornell.edu/rules/frcp).

A charge of unethical conduct is not the only consequence for asserting a frivolous position. Under Rule 11 of the **Federal Rules of Civil Procedure (FRCP)**, for example, whenever an attorney in a federal case submits a motion or pleading to the court, he or she must certify that "it is not being presented for any improper purpose, such as to harass or to cause unnecessary delay or needless increase in the cost of litigation" and that "the claims, defenses, and other legal contentions therein are warranted by existing law or by a nonfrivolous argument for the extension, modification, or reversal of existing law or the establishment of new law." Violating Rule 11 can lead to sanctions by the court (e.g., a fine) in addition to a charge of unethical conduct. Many states have their own version of Rule 11 for state-court cases.

Paralegal Perspective:

■ In the heat of controversy, tempers can run high. Attorneys do not always exhibit the detachment expected of professionals. They may so thoroughly identify with the interests of their clients that values can become confused. Paralegals working for such attorneys may get caught up in the same fever, particularly if there is a close attorney-paralegal working relationship on a high-stakes case that has lasted a considerable time. The momentum is to do whatever it takes to win. Although this atmosphere can be exhilarating, it can also create an environment where less and less attention is paid to the niceties of ethics.

SAFEKEEPING PROPERTY

An attorney must
■ hold client property separate from the attorney's own property (no commingling)
■ avoid using client funds improperly
■ safeguard client records
Model Rule 1.15

fiduciaries A person who owes another good faith and fair treatment in protecting the other's interest. (See glossary for an additional meaning.)

Attorneys are **fiduciaries**, individuals who must exercise a high standard of good faith and fair treatment on behalf of their clients. This fiduciary responsibility is particularly important when handling client funds.

COMMINGLING

A law office often receives client funds or funds of others connected with the client's case, e.g., attorneys receive money in settlement of a case or as trustees. Such funds should be held in a **client trust account**. General operating funds of the office should be kept in a separate account. There must be no **commingling** of client funds and office funds. It is unethical to place everything in one account. This is so even if the firm maintains accurate bookkeeping records on what amounts in the single account belong to which clients and what amounts belong to the firm. In a commingled account, the danger is too great that client funds will be used for nonclient purposes.

Law firms are notoriously lax about this requirement "This laxity is borne out by the testimony of … State Bar auditor Bruno DeMolli, who reports that a whopping 60 percent of the law firms he visited during a recent audit sweep were not in compliance with the trust accounting requirements."[19]

RETAINERS

It is also improper for an office to misuse funds on retainer. Clients sometimes deposit funds with an office to cover future fees, court costs, and related expenses. The office should not draw on these fees before they are earned nor withdraw the funds for expenses not yet incurred. This is so even if the funds were never commingled when deposited by the client. For more on the use and abuse of such funds, see Chapter 14.

CLIENT RECORDS

Client records must also be safeguarded. The client's file is the property of the client. When the attorney's representation of the client is over, the firm cannot discard or destroy the file. The client must be given the opportunity to receive it. The firm can keep copies. In fact, many states require that copies of files be kept in storage a minimum period of time (e.g., five years) after the firm has completed its representation of a client on a matter. When a firm is allowed to destroy files, it must do so without breaching confidentiality. It would probably be unethical, for example, to throw unshredded files containing client names and other case information into regular trash bins.

As mentioned earlier, a law office cannot refuse to return a client's file until the client settles his or her final bill.

Paralegal Perspective:

- Use great care when your responsibility involves client funds, such as receiving funds from clients, opening bank accounts, depositing funds in the proper account at a bank, and making entries in law-firm records on such funds. It should be fairly obvious to you whether an attorney is violating the rule on commingling funds. It may be less clear whether the attorney is improperly using client funds for unauthorized purposes. Attorneys have been known to "borrow" money from client accounts and then return the money before anyone discovers what was done. They might even pay the account interest while using the money. Elaborate bookkeeping and accounting gimmicks might be used to disguise what occurred. Such conduct is unethical even if the attorney pays interest and eventually returns all the funds. In addition, the attorney might be charged with theft or criminal fraud. Of course, anyone who knowingly assists the attorney could be subject to the same consequences.

- Be very careful about signatures. An attorney may want to delegate the task of signing for bank deposits, transfers, or withdrawals. It some states, it is unethical for an attorney to allow a nonattorney to sign for transactions involving client property, particularly funds in client trust accounts.

client trust account A bank account controlled by an attorney that contains client funds that may not be used for general operating expenses or for any personal purpose of the attorney. In Washington State, the same obligation applies to accounts controlled by a Limited License Legal Technician (LLLT).

commingling Mixing what should be kept separate, e.g., depositing client funds into an account that also contains funds used for general operating expenses of the office.

FALSE EVIDENCE AND STATEMENTS; FAILURE TO DISCLOSE

An attorney
- must not offer evidence the attorney knows to be false
- must not make a false statement of fact or law to a tribunal,
- must correct any earlier false statements of material fact or law that the attorney made to a tribunal,
- must tell the tribunal about a case, statute, or other authority that the attorney knows will hurt the cause of the attorney's own client if the opposing attorney has failed to tell the tribunal about this authority. Model Rules 3.3, 8.4

FALSE EVIDENCE AND STATEMENTS

material (1) Serious and substantial. (2) Important enough to influence the decision that was made.

Attorneys must not offer false evidence or make false statements. They have an ethical obligation to be truthful to a court. If they later discover that they made a **material** statement in court that they now realize was false, they must correct the statement in court.

Suppose that a client asks his or her attorney to offer into evidence a document that falsely states the earnings of the client's company. If the attorney knows that the document contains false statements, it would be unethical for the attorney to offer it into evidence unless the attorney informs the court of the falsity.

In some states, the obligation of truthfulness applies to statements made to opponents as well as to courts. For example, it would be unethical in such states for an attorney to tell an opposing attorney that that the maximum coverage on a client's liability policy is $100,000 when the attorney knows that the maximum is $300,000. Of course, making such a false statement to a judge would also be unethical.

SOCIAL MEDIA

Attorneys must not make false or misleading statements on Facebook, LinkedIn, or other social media. Attorneys have been disciplined for exaggerating their experience in their online profiles such as by falsely stating that they have handled cases in federal court. In a South Carolina case, an attorney was disciplined for listing practice areas in which he had little or no experience.

DUTY TO DISCLOSE CONTRARY AUTHORITY

An attorney who knows of a law that goes against the claims of his or her own client must tell the tribunal about that law if attorney knows that the opposing attorney has not done so. This requirement is particularly startling.

> **Example**: Karen Singer and Bill Carew are attorneys who are opposing each other in a bitter trial involving a large sum of money. Singer knows about a very damaging but obscure case that goes against her client. But because of sloppy research, Carew does not know about it. Singer never mentions the case, and it never comes up during the trial.

It is certainly understandable why Singer does not want to say anything about the case. Although she does not want to help her opponent, she will pay a price for her silence. She is subject to sanctions for a violation of her ethical obligation to disclose known contrary authority when she knows that her opponent has not cited it.

Paralegal Perspective:

- Chances are high that attorneys who offer false evidence or who lie to a court will pressure their employees to participate in the deception. A paralegal or other employee might be asked to give a false statement to a court clerk, help a client lie (commit perjury), backdate a document, or improperly notarize a deed. Do not compromise your integrity no matter how much you believe in the cause of the client, no matter how much you detest the tactics of the opposing side, no matter how much you like the attorney for whom you work, and no matter how important this job is to you.

CONFIDENTIALITY

GENERAL RULE: An attorney must not disclose information relating to the representation of a client.

EXCEPTIONS TO THE GENERAL RULE

- *Informed Consent:* A client can always agree to allow the disclosure of confidential information.
- *Preventing Death or Substantial Bodily Harm:* Confidential information can be disclosed if the attorney reasonably believes disclosure is necessary to prevent reasonably certain death or substantial bodily harm.
- *Preventing Substantial Injury to Financial Interests or Property:* Confidential information can be disclosed if the attorney reasonably believes disclosure is necessary to prevent the client from committing a crime or fraud that is reasonably certain to cause substantial injury to the financial interests or property of another if the client is using the services of the attorney in committing the crime or fraud that the attorney seeks to prevent by the disclosure.
- *Implied consent:* An attorney has implied consent from the client to disclose confidential information when disclosure is needed to carry out the representation for which the attorney was hired.

■ *Suits between attorney and client.* If the client sues the attorney or vice versa, the attorney can reveal whatever confidential information is necessary for the attorney to defend against the client's suit or to assert the attorney's claims against the client. Model Rule 1.6

Information is **confidential** if others do not have a right to receive it. When access to information is restricted in this way, the information is **privileged**. After we cover ethics and confidentiality, we need to examine the related topics of the attorney-client privilege (ACP) and the attorney work-product rule.

WHAT INFORMATION IS CONFIDENTIAL?

The ethical obligation to maintain confidentiality applies to all or almost all information that relates to the representation of a client, whatever its source. One court has said, "[V]irtually any information relating to a case should be considered confidential … even unprivileged client information."[20] Note also that the obligation is broader than so-called secrets or matters explicitly communicated in confidence. Information can be confidential even if the client does not refer to it as a secret and even if the client does not ask that it not be revealed. Confidentiality has been breached in each of the following examples:

■ At a party, an attorney tells an acquaintance from another town that the law firm is representing Jacob Anderson, who wants to prevent his employer from forcing him to retire. (The identity of a client is confidential. So is the reason the client is seeking legal help.)
■ At a bar association conference, an attorney tells an old law school classmate that a client named Brenda Steck is considering a suit against her brother over the ownership of property left by their deceased mother. (The identity of a client and what lawsuits she is considering are confidential.)
■ A legal secretary carelessly leaves a client's file open on her desk where a stranger (e.g., another client) briefly reads parts of the top sheet. (The contents of a client file are confidential.)

The duty of confidentiality does not apply to information that is already public knowledge. If, in the first example, the media has already reported that Jacob Anderson is represented by the attorney's law firm, the attorney can tell someone that Anderson is a client there. Providing details of the case, however, that have not been reported in the media would be a breach of confidentiality. It should be noted, however, that some law offices recommend nondisclosure of even publically known information. The guideline of such offices is: *no discussion of any information about a case.*

The ethical rule on confidentiality is designed to encourage clients to discuss their case fully and frankly with their attorney, including embarrassing and legally damaging information. Arguably, clients would be reluctant to be open with an attorney if they had to worry about whether the attorney might reveal the information to others. The rule on confidentiality makes it unethical for attorneys to do so.

EXCEPTIONS TO THE RULE ON CONFIDENTIALITY

■ *Informed consent.* Attorneys can disclose confidential information if they receive informed consent to do so from their clients. Well-known trial attorneys who write books about cases of their clients, for example, can include confidential information in the books if they have clear client consent to do so.
■ *Preventing death or substantial bodily harm.* Disclosure can be ethically permissible if the attorney reasonably believes that disclosure is necessary to prevent reasonably certain death or substantial bodily harm.

> **Example**: An attorney represents a husband in a bitter divorce action against his wife. Assume that during a meeting at the law firm, the husband makes one of the following statements to the attorney:
>
> ▪ I am going to use this gun tonight to kill my wife's lover.
> ▪ I killed my wife's lover yesterday with this gun.

The attorney does not have a duty to disclose either of these confidential statements to the police or to anyone else. If, however, the attorney does disclose them, has the attorney breached confidentiality? The answer is *no* for the first statement, but *yes* for the second.

confidential (1) Pertaining to information that others do not have a right to receive. (2) Pertaining to all information related to the representation of a client whatever its source, including the fact that someone is a client.

privileged Protected by a privilege so that disclosure is prohibited or limited.

The first statement is about a future act, the crime of murder that the client says he intends to commit. An attorney can disclose this statement if the attorney reasonably believes that disclosure is necessary to prevent reasonably certain death or substantial bodily harm. The second statement, however, is about a past act. Disclosing it would not prevent death or substantial bodily harm. Hence, disclosure would be unethical.

- *Preventing substantial injury to financial interests or property.* Assume that an attorney learns that the client is about to harm someone financially. The attorney does not have a duty to disclose this confidential information to the person or company that will be harmed. If, however, the attorney does disclose it, the ethical duty of confidentiality is not breached if the attorney reasonably believes that disclosure is necessary to prevent substantial financial harm and if two additional conditions are met: first, the client is going to cause the harm through a criminal or fraudulent act, and second, the client is using the attorney's services to commit the crime or fraud.

    Example: An attorney represents the owner of a company. The attorney advises the owner on a large loan that the owner is seeking from a small bank. The owner tells the attorney that he is going to use false financial data on the loan application and that he intends to file for bankruptcy a few months after the loan is approved once he receives the funds.

In most situations, the attorney does not have a duty to disclose this confidential information to the bank or to anyone else. If, however, the attorney wants to disclose it, the ethical duty of confidentiality is not breached if the attorney reasonably believes disclosure is necessary to prevent the client from committing a crime or fraud that is reasonably certain to cause substantial injury to the financial interests or property of another (the bank) and if the client is using the services of the attorney in committing the crime or fraud that the attorney seeks to prevent. These conditions appear to have been met in the statements the client made to the attorney in the bank example.

- *Implied consent.* The client impliedly consents to those disclosures of confidential information by an attorney that are needed to provide the representation for which the client hired the attorney. In a dispute over alimony, for example, the attorney would obviously have to disclose certain relevant financial information about the client to a court or to opposing counsel during settlement negotiations.
- *Attorney and client suing each other.* Finally, some disclosures can be proper in suits between attorney and client. Suppose, for example, the client sues the attorney for malpractice or the attorney sues the client for nonpayment of a fee. In such proceedings, an attorney can reveal confidential information about the client if disclosure is necessary to defend against the client's claim or to assert the attorney's own claim against the client.

ATTORNEY-CLIENT PRIVILEGE (ACP)

attorney-client privilege (ACP) A client or a client's attorney can refuse to disclose any confidential (private) communication between them if the purpose of the communication was to facilitate the provision of legal services to the client.

The **attorney-client privilege (ACP)** serves a function similar to that of the ethical rule on confidentiality in that both doctrines are designed to encourage open communication between attorney and client. The two doctrines overlap, although the ethical duty of confidentiality is much broader than the ACP:

Ethical duty of confidentiality: Protects all or almost all information (not just client or attorney communications) from any source if the information pertains to a client case and was obtained by a law office while representing the client.

ACP: Protects all communications made in confidence between an attorney and client if the purpose of the communication was to obtain legal services from the attorney. A communication is made in confidence if it was intended to be confidential. If it is made in the presence of strangers (e.g., in front of strangers on an elevator) the ACP is lost.

Everything protected by the ACP is also protected by the ethical duty of confidentiality. The reverse, however, is not always true. All information protected by the ethical duty of confidentiality is not also protected by the ACP.

Example. While investigating the finances of a client's company, an attorney learns from the minutes of a shareholder meeting that the company considered discontinuing a particular product five years ago.

This information is protected from disclosure by the ethical duty of confidentiality. Because, however, the information was not part of a *communication* between attorney and client, the information is not protected by the ACP.

The ACP most often arises in court or administrative proceedings in which the attorney or client is asked a question that pertains to a communication that occurred between them when the client was seeking legal help. The client can refuse to answer on the ground of privilege. If the attorney is the one being asked the question, he or she must refuse to answer on the same ground unless the client gives the attorney consent to answer. Only the client can waive the ACP.

The rule on confidentiality covers sanctions imposed on attorneys when they improperly disclose confidential client information to anyone outside the law office. The ACP tells us when clients and attorneys (or their employees) can refuse to answer questions pertaining to communications involving legal services for a client.

ATTORNEY WORK-PRODUCT RULE

Another rule that is related to (but different from) confidentiality and the ACP is the attorney **work-product rule**. Suppose that, while working on a client's case, an attorney prepares a memorandum that contains research notes but no confidential communications. The memorandum, therefore, is not protected by the ACP. Can the other side force the attorney to provide a copy of the memorandum? Is it **discoverable**, meaning that an opposing party can obtain a copy during discovery at the pretrial stage of a lawsuit? The answer depends on why the memorandum was prepared. If it was prepared in anticipation of litigation, it is protected by the work-product rule and is not discoverable. To the extent that work product is not discoverable, it is privileged.

Work product consists of notes, working papers, memoranda, or similar documents and tangible things prepared by the attorney in anticipation of litigation. An example is an attorney's interoffice memorandum that lays out his or her strategy in litigating a case. Attorneys do not have to disclose their work product to the other side unless the latter convinces a judge that it has a substantial need for the work product. Judges, however, are rarely convinced.

work-product rule Notes, working papers, memoranda, or similar things prepared by or for an attorney in anticipation of litigation are not discoverable by an opponent, absent a showing of substantial need. They are protected by privilege.

discoverable Pertaining to information or materials an opponent can obtain through deposition, interrogatories, or other discovery method.

INADVERTENT DISCLOSURE

A great fear of a law office is that the wrong person will obtain material that should be protected by ethics, by the ACP, by the work-product rule, or by all three. This can have devastating consequences. For example, if a stranger overhears a confidential communication by a client to the attorney or to the attorney's paralegal, a court might rule that the attorney-client privilege has been waived on the theory that it is inconsistent to let a stranger or any third party hear what you claim was confidential. Media celebrity Martha Stewart was confronted with this reality when a court ruled in her criminal trial that she had waived the attorney-client privilege covering the contents of an email with her attorney when Stewart mailed a copy of the email to her daughter.[21] At a recent paralegal conference, a speaker told a stunned audience that a paralegal in her firm accidentally faxed a strategy memorandum on a current case to the opposing attorney! The paralegal punched in the wrong phone number on the fax machine! This could just as easily have occurred by sending an email message or attachment to the wrong address.

Assume that an office receives an email from opposing counsel with an attachment containing a confidential document. The intended recipient was another attorney in a branch office of the sender, but someone typed the wrong email address and the opponent received the document. Many states say that unintended recipients must promptly notify the sender that the document was inadvertently received. If the recipient knows before opening the document that it was received in error, it must not be opened. The recipient must notify the sender and abide by the sender's instructions on what to do with it, e.g., send it back or destroy it.

States use different approaches to decide whether confidentiality and the ACP are always waived (lost) by inadvertent disclosure of confidential information. Some states follow the strict rule (also called the traditional rule) that confidentiality and privilege are lost if a disclosure occurs, whether intentionally or inadvertently. Other states, however, use a case-by-case approach in which the court looks at all of the particular circumstances of each disclosure to decide whether, on balance, justice would be better served by preserving confidentiality and privilege despite the disclosure. The factors the court will look at include whether the office took reasonable precautions to prevent disclosure, the number of disclosures that occurred, and how long it took for the sender to discover what happened and to try to rectify the sending error.

Many law offices routinely include notices at the bottom of every email message they send out, such as the following:

> This message is for the intended individual or entity and may contain information that is privileged. If the reader of this message is not the intended recipient, you are hereby notified that any copying, forwarding, or other dissemination of this message is prohibited. If you have received this communication in error, please notify the sender immediately by email or telephone, and delete the original message immediately.

Paralegal Perspective:

- Rules governing confidentiality and the attorney-client privilege (ACP) apply to paralegals.
  - Confidentiality. In every state, the duty of confidentiality applies to paralegals. Attorneys have an obligation to instruct their paralegals about ethics, particularly the duty not to disclose information relating to a client. Model Rule 5.3 (Comment 2).
  - ACP. In every state, the ACP applies to paralegals. Hence, a paralegal cannot be questioned about what the paralegal and client said to each other on a matter pertaining to the representation of the client by the law office where the paralegal works. Some states have made this result explicit in their statutory code. For example, a Colorado statute provides that

    > "An attorney shall not be examined without the consent of his client as to any communication made by the client to him or his advice given thereon in the course of professional employment; nor shall an attorney's secretary, paralegal, legal assistant, stenographer, or clerk be examined without the consent of his employer concerning any fact, the knowledge of which he has acquired in such capacity."[22]

- As indicated earlier, the major national paralegal associations have their own ethical codes (see Exhibit 5-4 and Appendix E). All of these codes stress the importance of maintaining confidentiality:
  - "A legal assistant must protect the confidences of a client and must not violate any rule or statute now in effect or hereafter enacted controlling the doctrine of privileged communications between a client and an attorney." Canon 7. National Association of Legal Assistants, *NALA Code of Ethics and Professional Responsibility.*
  - "A paralegal shall preserve all confidential information provided by the client or acquired from other sources before, during, and after the course of the professional relationship." "'Confidential information' means information relating to a client, whatever its source, that is not public knowledge nor available to the public." Section 1.5. National Federation of Paralegal Associations, *Model Code of Ethics and Professional Responsibility.*
  - Members of NALS the Association for Legal Professionals must "[o]bserve rules governing privileged communications and confidential information." They must "preserve and protect the confidences and privileged communications of a client." Canon 4. *NALS Code of Ethics & Professional Responsibility.*

- When you are hired, the firm may ask you to sign a formal confidentiality agreement in which you promise not to divulge client information to anyone who is not working on the client's case. (For an example, see Exhibit 5-5.) You, of course, are bound to maintain confidentiality even if your employer does not ask you to sign such an agreement.
- Paralegals face many temptations to violate confidentiality. For example, a paralegal inadvertently reveals confidential information:
  - while networking with other paralegals at a paralegal association meeting;
  - during animated conversation with another paralegal in a common area such as a restaurant or an elevator; or
  - during casual after-work discussions with a relative, spouse, or roommate about interesting cases at the office.

Exhibit 5-5	Example of a Confidentiality Agreement

Confidentiality Agreement

[1] While employed by this firm, you will find yourself exposed to many matters that come within what are known as the "attorney-client" and "work product" privileges. These involve communications between clients and the attorneys in the firm, as well as work conducted, strategies employed, and materials prepared in connection with matters on which we are working for clients. Employees are obliged to keep such information and materials strictly confidential and, except under very limited circumstances, cannot disclose such matters to anyone beyond this office.

[2] As a firm employee, you are also obligated to keep absolutely confidential all communications between our office and our clients (and from clients to our office), the work that we are doing for our clients, and information relating to our cases. Such matters may not be discussed or disclosed outside of our office, even with or to your families and friends. You may not even divulge the *existence* of a case or legal matter that the firm is handling or has handled.

[3] This obligation shall continue in the event that you should, for any reason, leave the firm.

[4] In addition, should you at any time become employed by another law firm, or any legal department, you must refrain from working on or having any contact with any matter in which you or our firm has been involved while working here or that relates to such a matter.

[5] Agreement to these terms and adherence to the "Rules of Professional Conduct" as adopted by the Supreme Court of the State of New Jersey are requirements of your employment by Porzio, Bromberg & Newman, P.C. A copy of the "Rules of Professional Conduct" will be provided at your request.

I agree to the above terms.

_____   _____
Signature   Date

_____
Witness

Source: Reprinted with permission of Porzio, Bromberg & Newman (www.pbnlaw.com).

As indicated, the rule on confidentiality is not limited to damaging or embarrassing information. The rule is much broader. All information relating to the representation of a client must not be revealed to anyone outside the office.

- Some law firms discourage the discussion of even public information with anyone outside the firm. In Philadelphia, paralegals are told that "a client of your office might be offended to learn that a…firm employee has discussed the client's business in public, even if the information mentioned is public knowledge…. [Do] not discuss the business of your office or your firm's clients with any outsider, no matter how close a friend, at any time, unless you are specifically authorized by a lawyer to do so."[23]
- During the Second World War, sailors were told that "loose lips sink ships." The same applies to law firms. Note that the last clause of the following law-firm statement to all paralegals places limits on what can be said to other employees within the same law firm:

  "Throughout your employment, you will have access to information that must at all times be held in strictest confidence. Even the seemingly insignificant fact that the firm is involved in a particular matter falls within the orbit of confidential information. Unless you have attorney permission, do not disclose documents or contents of documents to anyone, *including firm employees who do not need this information to do their work*."[24]

- If you attend a meeting on a case outside the law office, ask your supervisor whether you should take notes or prepare a follow-up memorandum on the meeting. Let the supervisor decide whether your notes or the memo might be discoverable.[25]
- Be very careful when you talk with clients in the presence of third persons. As indicated earlier, overheard conversations might constitute an unintentional waiver of the ACP. Cellular phones can sometimes cause problems. The signal in mobile communications is transmitted by frequency over airwaves. Therefore, outsiders can listen to both ends of a conversation with relative ease. If you are on a cellular phone with a client, warn him or her that confidential information should not be discussed.[26]
- Do not listen to your messages on a phone answering machine when others in the room can hear the messages as well. Clients often leave messages that contain confidential information. When using speakerphones, intercoms, or paging systems, don't broadcast confidential

information. Assume that many people will be hearing you on these public systems and that most of them are not entitled to hear what you are saying.

- Make sure your door is closed when discussing a client's case. If there is no door to the office, find out if there is a private room in the firm you can use for the call. If this is not practical, lower your voice when talking on the phone and be alert at all times to the presence of anyone around you who can hear what you are saying. This is particularly important for paralegals who work in open-cubicle areas.
- When working on your computer, try to position the monitor so that others cannot read the screen, especially when you need to leave your desk. Computers have programs that automatically make the screen go dark or that add a design graphic after a designated period of time when there is no typing. The screen then reappears when you continue typing. Be sure that this screen-saver program is installed on your computer.
- Use a shredding machine when throwing away papers containing confidential information.
- Extra caution is needed when deleting files from a computer. Using the delete key is not enough. A file can be deleted from computer directories but still be readable in the computer's trash bin and elsewhere on your hard drive. In addition to deleting the files in the recycle bin, find out what steps the office takes (or should take) to delete files permanently. Also, most law offices have backup systems that copy data to external drives and/or to the cloud. Deleting a file on an office computer does not simultaneously delete it on external drives or in the cloud. (We will cover these computer terms in Chapter 13.)
- Avoid sending inappropriate **metadata**. When you send someone a document online (e.g., a memo created by Microsoft Word that you send as an attachment to an email message), you are sending more than the data that will be read on the screen when the document is opened or when it is printed. Digital documents also contain metadata, which are data about data. They could consist of hidden information about the document such as earlier drafts of the same document or comments of colleagues on the document. The metadata might contain confidential information. If you do not want a recipient of a document to be able to read the metadata on it, you must delete the metadata before you send the document. To find out how, run this search in Google, Bing, or Yahoo: "removing metadata.")
- Clients often communicate with attorneys and paralegals by email. Most of these communications contain confidential communications that can be read by strangers such as hackers and administrators of network servers. The cautious law office, therefore, will obtain explicit consent from the client to communicate by email after reminding the client that security over the Internet cannot be guaranteed. As an added precaution, email can be **encrypted**, which converts the message into a code that renders the data in the message incomprehensible until they are reconverted to a readable format by a recipient with the right software. Unless requested by a client, however, a law office is not ethically obligated to encrypt all emails it sends.
- Confidential information should never be sent through open formats such as social media, bulletin boards, and listservs. Strangers can often read what is sent over them. We will examine these Internet programs in Chapter 13.
- Find out if anyone other than the client has access to the client's email. If others have such access and read messages to and from the law office, a court might rule that this waives the ACP for those messages.
- Computers and fax machines often store thousands of phone numbers and email addresses to make it easy for you to find an address when you want to send something. The downside of this convenience is that it is very easy to send something to the wrong person. Hence, before you hit the "send" button, follow the three-check rule. Look at the phone number or address you have selected or typed and slowly repeat it to yourself three times.
- When using vendors such as outside printers (e.g., a company that prints appellate briefs) and copying services, make sure that they sign confidentiality agreements stating that they will not disclose the contents of any of the documents on which they will be working.
- Use a stamp marked *privileged* on documents that contain confidential information.
- When transporting file folders or boxes containing case files (e.g., to and from the courthouse), client names should not be visible on the outside of the folder or box.
- When looking for employment, it is often helpful to submit writing samples to prospective employers. If the sample is a document on a real case (e.g., a complaint or research memorandum), seek permission to use it as a writing sample from the employer in the office where you prepared it. Also, be sure to omit or blot out—**redact**—any client names or other confidential information in the samples. During a job interview, never discuss confidential information about prior cases. It would be unprofessional to do so. Later, when we cover

metadata Data about data. Data about an electronic document that are hidden within the document itself, e.g., earlier versions of the document.

encrypt Convert text into a code that renders the text incomprehensible until it is reconverted to a readable format by a recipient with the right software.

redact To edit or prepare a document for publication or release, often by deleting, altering, or blocking out text that you do not want disclosed.

conflict of interest, we will examine the need to provide a prospective employer with a list of names of parties in cases you have worked on in prior jobs. This must be done with great caution, as we will see.

■ One of the most dramatic legal stories of the twentieth century was the tobacco litigation of the 1990s. The cases led to billions of dollars in settlements, judgments, and attorney fees. The litigation is still going on today. A critical event in this drama was a breach of confidentiality by Merrell Williams, a paralegal who once worked at Wyatt, Tarrant & Combs, the largest law firm in Kentucky. The firm represented Brown & Williamson (B&W), maker of Kool and Viceroy. As a $9-an-hour paralegal, Williams was assigned to work on the numerous documents involved in the litigation. The task overwhelmed him. "He was sickened by what he read, as document after document showed the lengths to which the tobacco company executives had gone to cover-up the risks of smoking."[27] He secretly photocopied and distributed confidential internal memos, letters, and other documents exchanged by the law firm and its client. The documents demonstrated that the tobacco manufacturer knew about the danger of smoking but tried to cover it up. The news media made extensive use of this material. No one doubted that Williams had produced the "smoking gun" against the tobacco industry. Here is how a Los Angeles Times article described the impact of the role of Williams in the litigation:

> The ground shifted in 1994, when an obscure paralegal, who had secretly stolen thousands of pages of documents from a [law firm representing] B&W, leaked the purloined papers to Congress and the media.... Now the blood was in the water....[28]

Wyatt, Tarrant & Combs obtained an injunction against Merrell Williams (no longer an "obscure paralegal") to prevent him from continuing to reveal what he knew. The firm said that Williams broke his employment contract that required confidentiality. An ex-smoker himself, Williams has undergone quadruple bypass surgery and has "threatened to seek damages for injuries allegedly caused by smoking and by his exposure during the course of his employment to information that had induced psychological suffering."[29]

This remarkable saga raises critical issues. Clearly, Williams violated client confidentiality. Indeed, it is difficult to think of a violation that has had a greater impact. Yet was his violation justified on moral grounds? Tobacco causes the death of thousands every year in this country and hundreds of thousands around the world. Until Williams committed his act, the tobacco industry was all but invulnerable in the legislatures and in the courts of this country. The disclosure of the documents turned the tide. Was Williams a hero or a common thief? Of course, few paralegals during a job interview will tell an interviewer that Williams is one of their heroes. Such an acknowledgment would probably frighten off any potential employer. Furthermore, the Williams case is complicated by allegations that the attorney to whom Williams gave the documents provided Williams with a home, cars, and cash, either outright or as loans. This raised the further ethical and legal issue of whether stolen evidence was being paid for and received. Nevertheless, the question remains: was Merrell Williams engaged in an act of civil disobedience for which anyone who cares about public health should be grateful?

CONFLICT OF INTEREST

INTRODUCTION

Three words strike dread in the heart of a practicing attorney: **conflict of interest**. Why? Because if it exists, it can lead to the disqualification of the attorney (and his or her entire law firm) from representing the particular client with whom the conflict exists—even if the attorney is in the middle of the representation of this client! In addition, a conflict of interest can subject the attorney to a suit for **legal malpractice**.

A conflict of interest exists because of divided loyalties that actually or potentially harm (or disadvantage) someone who is owed undivided loyalty. A client is entitled to an attorney's zealous representation based on independent professional judgment. It is independent when it is free of compromising influences and loyalties. Furthermore, rules against conflict of interest are needed to safeguard confidentiality.

Independent Professional Judgment

There are two main ways in which an attorney's independent professional judgment might be compromised: when the attorney represents parties who have adverse interests and when the attorney's personal interests interfere with the client's interest.

conflict of interest Divided loyalties that actually or potentially harm (or disadvantage) someone who is owed undivided loyalty.

legal malpractice (1) Malpractice committed by an attorney. (2) Attorney negligence, which is the failure to exercise the reasonable care expected of an attorney in good standing.

adverse (1) Opposed. (2) Hostile. (3) Having an opposing position. (4) Harmful, unfavorable.

adverse interest A goal or claim of one person that is different from or opposed to the goal or claim of another person.

■ Adverse Interests

An attorney's loyalty can be compromised if the attorney represents two persons who have interests that are opposed (**adverse**) to each other. An **adverse interest** is an opposing interest or position.

> **Example**: Smith sues Jones for breach of contract involving the sale of goods. They both want the same attorney to represent them in this case. The parties have adverse interests. They have opposing positions on whether a breach occurred.

■ Personal Interests

An attorney's loyalty can also be compromised by the attorney's own personal interests. An attorney's *professional* interest is to provide (and be paid for) legal services to the client. An attorney's *personal* interest is any other goal or desire that the attorney may have in connection with the client beyond providing (and being paid for) the agreed-to legal services.

> **Example**: Roberts sues Fireside, Inc. for a breach of warranty. Diane Conley, Esq. represents Roberts. Unknown to Roberts, Conley owns substantial stock in Fireside. Conley has a personal interest in something connected to her client. That personal interest is her financial investment in the company she is suing on behalf of her client.

These are just two examples of possible conflicts of interest based on adverse interests and personal interests. As we study these and other examples, we will see that not every conflict of interest will disqualify an attorney.

Confidentiality

The preservation of confidentiality is another major reason that conflict-of-interest rules exist. Attorneys learn many different kinds of facts about their clients. The facts can be financial, emotional, marital, damaging, embarrassing, etc. If these facts are connected or related to the representation, they are confidential. The role of the attorney is to marshal all the facts into the best legal arguments that favor the client's legitimate objectives. Imagine the distress that a former client would feel upon learning that the attorney used some of these facts *against* the client when the attorney represented someone else.

Exhibit 5-6 summarizes the major kinds of conflicts we will be examining. The conflicts can interfere with an attorney's independent professional judgment or can compromise confidentiality. We need to examine when conflicts prevent an attorney from taking a case and when, if the attorney does take the case, he or she must cease the representation because of a court order of disqualification.

Exhibit 5-6	Kinds of Conflicts	
MAJOR CATEGORIES OF CONFLICTS		
Concurrent Representation Conflict	Conflict of interest between two or more current clients	Concurrent representation is an attorney's simultaneous representation of more than one current client who have adverse interests in the same litigated matter, in different litigated matters, in a negotiation, or in a transactional matter.
Successive Representation Conflict	Conflict of interest between a current client and a former client	Successive representation is an attorney's representation of a current client who is opposing a former client of this attorney.
Personal Interest Conflict	Conflict of interest between a client's interest and a personal interest of the attorney.	An attorney's personal interest that could conflict with a client's interest may be the attorney's financial or emotional interest.
Positional Conflict	Conflict of interest due to inconsistent legal positions on behalf of separate clients.	A positional conflict exists (1) if an attorney asserts inconsistent legal positions while representing two current clients in separate, unrelated cases and (2) if success on behalf of a client in one case will harm or disadvantage the current client in the other case.
Third Party Conflict	Conflict of interest between a client and a nonclient	A third party conflict exists if the third party is a nonclient who could interfere with the attorney's duties to his or her client.
Vicarious Conflict	Conflict of interest between a current client and a former client	A vicarious conflict is a conflict that is attributed to every attorney in a law office solely because of an actual conflict caused by one of the attorneys in the office.
Migratory Conflict (another example of a vicarious conflict)	Conflict of interest caused by switching jobs.	A migratory conflict exists when an attorney who has a conflict switches jobs and brings the conflict with him or her to the new job, which may disqualify every attorney at the new job.

CONCURRENT REPRESENTATION

A **concurrent representation** is the simultaneous representation of more than one current client who have adverse interests. The adverse interests can be in the same litigated matter, in different litigated matters, in a negotiation, or in a transactional matter. An *adverse interest* is a goal or claim of one person that is different from or opposed to the goal or claim of another person. Not every concurrent-representation conflict will lead to disqualifications, as we will see.

There are four major categories of concurrent-representation conflicts:

- When two current clients are at odds in the same litigated matter.
- When two current clients are at odds in unrelated litigated matters.
- When two current clients are **coplaintiffs** or **codefendants** in the same litigated matter.
- When two current clients are on the same side in a negotiation or in a **transactional matter** not involving litigation.

Here are examples of these four concurrent-representation conflicts:

Example:

(1) *Two current clients at odds in the same litigated matter.* Tom wants to sue Harry in an automobile negligence case. Both Tom and Harry ask Mary Franklin, Esq. to represent them in this negligence case.

(2) *Two current clients at odds in unrelated litigated matters.* Bill is suing Mary in an automobile negligence case. Mary is suing Bill for sole custody of their daughter. (Bill and Mary are not married.) Alice Sander, Esq. represents Bill in the negligence case and Mary now asks Sander to represent Mary in the custody case against Bill.

(3) *Two current clients who are coplaintiffs or codefendants in the same litigated matter.* Ed is a passenger in a car driven by Kevin. They are both injured when a truck driven by Harry collides with their car. Ed and Kevin, as coplaintiffs, sue Harry for negligence. Walt Francis, Esq. wants to represent both Ed and Kevin.

(4) *Two current clients on the same side in a negotiation or in a transactional matter not involving litigation.* Dan and Charles have lived together for several months. They ask Leon Thomas, Esq. to draft a cohabitation agreement for them so that their property rights and support duties to each other are clarified.

Now let's look at which of these concurrent-representation conflicts will lead to disqualification.

(1) *Two current clients at odds in the same litigated matter*

In most states, an attorney cannot represent two clients who are litigating each other in the same case and who will be making claims against each other. The attorney would be disqualified from such representation. Hence in the first example, Mary Franklin would not be allowed to represent both Harry and Tom in the negligence case. She cannot give her undivided loyalty to both sides. Tom needs to prove that Henry was negligent; Henry needs to prove that he was not negligent, and perhaps that Tom was negligent himself (called contributory negligence). How can Franklin vigorously argue that Henry was negligent and at the same time vigorously argue that Henry was not negligent? How can she give independent professional judgment to two people who have such a conflict? The difficulty is not solved by Franklin's commitment to be fair and objective in giving her advice to both parties. Her role as attorney is to be a *partisan* advocate for the client.

Furthermore, client consent would not change this result. Even if Tom and Henry agree to allow Franklin to represent both of them, it would be unethical for her to do so. In most states, the presence of adverse interests between the parties in the same litigation makes it unethical for an attorney to represent both sides with or without their consent.

Some states, however, make an exception in certain kinds of cases, particularly divorce cases.

Example: Jim and Mary Smith have been married for two months. They are now separated and both want a divorce. There are no children and no marital assets to divide. Neither wants nor is entitled to alimony from the other. George Davidson, Esq. is an attorney that Jim and Mary know and trust. They decide to ask Davidson to represent both of them in the divorce.

In this case of concurrent representation, can Davidson ethically represent both sides? A few states will allow him to do so, on the theory that there is not much of a conflict between the

---

concurrent representation The simultaneous representation of more than one current client who have adverse interests in the same litigated matter, in different litigated matters, in a negotiation, or in a transactional matter.

coplaintiffs Two or more plaintiffs who bring a suit in the same civil case.

codefendants Two or more defendants who are sued in the same civil case or who are prosecuted in the same criminal case.

transactional matter Anything involving a transaction such as entering a contract, incorporating a business, closing a real estate sale, or planning an estate.

parties. The conflict does exist. Jim and Mary will be listed as opposing parties in divorce court, but the conflict appears to be in name only. Jim and Mary want the divorce, there is no custody battle, alimony is not an issue, and there is no property to fight over. All they need is a court to decree that their marriage is legally over. Hence the potential for harm caused by concurrent representation in such a case is almost nonexistent. In these states, if both parties give their informed consent (and are made aware of the risks of concurrent representation), the same attorney would not be disqualified from representing them both.

Other states, however, disagree. They frown on concurrent representation in so-called *friendly* divorces of this kind. The case may have been friendly at the outset, but years later, when everything turns sour, one of the parties inevitably attacks the attorney for having had a conflict of interest. Cautious attorneys always avoid concurrent representation of opposing parties in the same litigation.

(2) *Two current clients at odds in unrelated litigated matters*

Next we look at the second example of concurrent representation where the two current clients would be at odds in unrelated litigated matters. In most states, an attorney would be disqualified from representing two current clients who are litigating each other in unrelated cases. Hence in the second example, Alice Sander, Esq. cannot represent Bill in his negligence case against Mary and simultaneously represent Mary against Bill in the unrelated custody case. Furthermore, in most states, even the consent of both Bill and Mary will not be sufficient to allow Sander to represent them both at the same time (simultaneously) in the two cases.

In the negligence case, Sander must be a loyal advocate for Bill against Mary. Simultaneously she would have to be a loyal advocate for Mary against Bill in the custody case. If Sander says yes to Mary's request that she represent Mary against Bill in the custody case, Bill would have legitimate reason to question Sander's undivided loyalty to him even though the custody case may have nothing to do with his negligence case.

(3) *Two current clients are coplaintiffs or codefendants in the same litigated matter*

Next we look at the third example of concurrent representation where the two current clients would be coplaintiffs or codefendants in the same litigated matter. In most states, an attorney can represent coplaintiffs or codefendants in the same litigated matter *if* the following four conditions are met:

- The attorney reasonably believes he or she can provide competent and diligent representation to both coplaintiffs (if the two current clients are suing in the same case) or to both codefendants (if the two current clients are being sued in the same case).
- The clients will not be asserting claims against each other.
- There is no special law that prohibits the concurrent representation.
- The clients give written informed consent to have the attorney represent both of them. Model Rule 1.7(b)

Written informed consent requires an explanation by the attorney of the risks and as well the benefits of allowing the attorney to both clients.

In the third example, can Walt Francis, Esq. meet all four conditions in order to be able to represent Ed and Kevin as coplaintiffs in their negligence suit against Harry the truck driver? The answer is not clear-cut. Suppose, for example, that the evidence shows that Kevin was negligent in driving his car at the time the truck hit the car. This may give rise to a claim for damages by Ed against Kevin. Also, if Ed is called as a witness, some of his testimony might be unfavorable to Kevin. Hence, Walt may not be reasonable in concluding that he can give competent and diligent representation to both coplaintiffs. If he cannot, the conflict of interest disqualifies him from providing the concurrent representation to the coplaintiffs. The same analysis would apply to two persons being sued as codefendants in the same litigated matter.

(4) *Two current clients on the same side in a negotiation or in a transactional matter not involving litigation*

Finally, we look at the fourth example of concurrent representation where the two current clients would be on the same side in a negotiation or transaction not involving litigation. Leon Thomas, Esq. has been asked by Dan and Charles to draft a cohabitation agreement for them. Both would be his clients in providing the transactional service of writing their contract. Can he do so ethically? The answer depends of the same four conditions mentioned earlier: Leon must reasonably believe he can give competent and diligent representation to Dan and

Charles, these clients must not be asserting claims against each other, there must be no special law against the concurrent representation, and the two clients must give written informed consent to the concurrent representation. The likelihood is that these conditions can be met so that Thomas can draft the agreement. The same conclusion would apply if the attorney were hired to negotiate the agreement between Dan and Charles and someone else drafted it (or they drafted it themselves).

SUCCESSIVE REPRESENTATION

In **successive representation**, an attorney represents a current client who opposes a *former* client of this attorney.

> **Example**: Diane Smithson is a former client of Ron Sullivan, Esq., a sole practitioner. Sullivan once represented Smithson in an antitrust matter against General Motors. Several years after this case was concluded, Smithson has a legal dispute with Wal-Mart. Smithson hires a different attorney (Paul Foley, Esq.) at a different law firm to represent her in the Wal-Mart case. Wal-Mart wants to hire Ron Sullivan to represent it against Smithson in the case of Smithson v. Wal-Mart.

successive representation An attorney's representation of a current client who is opposing a former client of this attorney.

Smithson is a former client of Ron Sullivan. Smithson now has a legal case against Wal-Mart, which wants to hire Sullivan in this case against Smithson. A former client would become an adversary. Can Sullivan represent Wal-Mart against his former client?

The answer depends on the kind of dispute that Smithson has with Wal-Mart. Three possibilities exist:

(1) The matter or case between Smithson and Wal-Mart is the same matter or case that Smithson had in the earlier case with General Motors. The two cases are the same even though the parties are not the same.

(2) The matter or case between Smithson and Wal-Mart is substantially related to the matter or case that Smithson had in the earlier case with General Motors. The two cases are not the same, but they are substantially related even though the parties are not the same.

(3) The matter or case between Smithson and Wal-Mart is totally different from the matter or case that Smithson had in the earlier case with General Motors.

In the third situation, Ron Sullivan is allowed to represent Wal-Mart against his former client, Diane Smithson. In the first two examples, however, Sullivan cannot represent Wal-Mart against Smithson unless Smithson agrees in writing to allow him to do so. The rule is as follows:

Rule on Successive Representation Conflicts

An attorney who once represented a client on a matter cannot later represent another person against the former client in the same matter or in a substantially related matter unless the former client agrees in writing. Model Rule 1.9.

Note the danger that exists in two cases involved in successive representation. In Case #1 when the attorney represented the former client, the attorney learned confidential information about the case. Now this attorney wants to represent a new client against the former client in Case #2. If Case #2 is the same or substantially the same as Case #1, the danger is that the attorney will use the confidential information learned in Case #1 *against* the former client in Case #2. This danger does not exist or is significantly less if Case #1 and Case #2 are totally different.

PERSONAL-INTEREST CONFLICTS

The client's interest is to receive independent professional assistance from an attorney in order to resolve a legal matter. Attorneys may have their own *personal interests* that interfere with this interest of the client. A personal interest is any goal or desire that the attorney may have in connection with a client beyond providing (and being paid for) the agreed-to legal services. Here are four examples of such personal interests. The first three are financial interests and the fourth is an emotional interest:

- Entering a business transaction with the client
- Giving financial assistance to the client such as a loan

> ■ Receiving a substantial gift from the client
> ■ Entering a sexual relationship with the client

overreaching Taking unfair advantage of another's naïveté or other vulnerability, especially by deceptive means.

undue influence Improper persuasion, coercion, force, or deception.

The conflict rules in these areas are designed to prevent **overreaching**, (taking unfair advantage of another's naïveté or other vulnerability) and **undue influence** (improper persuasion) by the attorney. Let's look at how these objectives apply to the four conflicts involving an attorney's personal interest.

Business Transaction with a Client

Clients and attorneys sometimes enter business transactions with each other.

> **Example**: Janet Bruno, Esq. is Len Oliver's attorney. Oliver owns an auto repair business for which Bruno has done legal work. Oliver sells Bruno a 30 percent interest in the repair business. Bruno continues as Oliver's attorney.

Conflict-of-interest problems may exist in this example. Assume that the business runs into difficulties and Oliver considers bankruptcy. He goes to Bruno for legal advice on bankruptcy law. Bruno has dual concerns: to give Oliver competent legal advice and to protect her own 30 percent interest in the business. Bankruptcy may be good for Oliver but disastrous for Bruno's investment. How can an attorney give a client independent professional advice when the advice may go against the attorney's own interest? Bruno's concern for her investment creates the potential that Oliver will be placed at a disadvantage. Divided loyalties exist.

This is not to say, however, that it is always unethical for an attorney to enter a business transaction with a client. If strict conditions are met, the transaction is ethical. The conditions are as follows:

(1) The terms of the transaction are fair and reasonable to the client.
(2) The client is given a written description of the terms of the transaction.
(3) The attorney tells the client (in writing) that the client should seek the advice of another attorney on whether it is wise for the client to enter the transaction.
(4) The client is given sufficient time to seek this additional advice.
(5) The client gives informed consent (in writing) to enter the transaction.

In our example, Oliver must be advised to (and be given sufficient time to) consult with an attorney other than Bruno on letting Bruno buy a 30 percent interest in the business. Bruno would have to give Oliver a clear, written explanation of their business relationship, which must be fair and reasonable to Oliver. Model Rule 1.8(a).

Financial Assistance to a Client

Attorneys, like all service providers, want to be paid. Often, however, a client does not have the resources to pay until after the case is over.

> **Example**: Harry Maxell, Esq. is Bob Smith's attorney in a negligence action in which Smith is seeking damages for serious injuries. While the case is pending, Maxell agrees to lend Smith living expenses and court-filing fees. The loan will be repaid if Maxwell wins the case.

A debtor-creditor relationship now exists between Smith and Maxell in addition to their attorney-client relationship. The loan covered two items: living expenses and court-filing fees. The ethical rule is different for each item.

The financial assistance for living expenses is unethical. Suppose that the defendant in the negligence case makes an offer to settle the case with Smith. Should he accept the offer? There is a danger that Maxell's advice on the offer will be colored by the fact that he has a financial interest in Smith—he wants to have his loan repaid. The amount of the offer to settle may not be enough to cover the loan. Should he advise Smith to accept the offer? Accepting the offer may be in Smith's interest but not in Maxell's interest. Such divided loyalty is an unethical conflict of interest. Furthermore, the rule against providing this kind of financial assistance is designed to discourage attorneys from stirring up litigation by financing it.

The loan covering litigation expenses, such as filing fees and other court costs, is treated differently. Such loans are ethical. In our example, Maxell's loan covering the cost of the filing fees (to be repaid if he wins the case) is proper. Furthermore, if Harry is a poor person (*indigent*), it is ethical for the attorney to pay litigation expenses without asking for repayment. Model Rule 1.8(e).

Gifts from a Client

An attorney must not solicit substantial gifts from clients who are not related to the attorney. Substantial gifts can be accepted, if offered by the client, but they cannot be asked for (solicited).

Suppose, however, that the idea of the gift to the attorney (or to a member of the attorney's family) comes from the client; it is not solicited. Such gifts can be accepted, although this attorney cannot prepare any document that may be needed to complete the gift.

Example: William Stanton, Esq. has been the family attorney of the Tarkinton family for years. At Christmas, Mrs. Tarkinton gives Stanton an expensive computer and tells him to change her will so that Stanton's ten-year-old daughter would receive funds for a college education.

If a document is needed to carry out the gift, it is unethical for the attorney to prepare that document. Its preparation would create a conflict of interest. In our example, the gift of money for college involves a document—Mrs. Tarkinton's will. Note the conflict. It would be in Mrs. Tarkinton's interest to have the will written so that a set or maximum sum is identified for this gift as well as a cutoff date for its use. Stanton, on the other hand, would probably want the will drafted so that there is no maximum amount stated and no cutoff date. His daughter may one day want to go to graduate school. If the language of the will is vague (and if no time limits are inserted), an argument could be made that the gift covers both undergraduate and graduate work. Other questions could arise as well, e.g., does the gift cover room and board at college, and what if the daughter does not go to college until after she marries and raises her own children? It is in Stanton's interest to draft the will to benefit his daughter under all these contingencies. This may not be in Mrs. Tarkinton's interest.

Because of this conflict, an attorney cannot prepare a document such as a will, trust, or contract that results in any substantial gift from a client to the attorney or to the attorney's children, spouse, parents, or siblings. If a client wants to make such a gift, another attorney who is not part of the same law firm must prepare the document. There is, however, one exception. If the client-donor is related to the person receiving the gift, the attorney can prepare the document. In our example, there is no indication that the donor (Mrs. Tarkinton) is related to the attorney or to the attorney's daughter.

There does not appear to be any ethical problem in taking the gift of the computer from Mrs. Tarkinton. No documents are involved. Model Rule 1.8(c)

Paralegal Perspective:

- Can a paralegal accept a substantial gift from a client, e.g., a Christmas present, a trip, or other bonus from a client who just won a big judgment? First of all, never consider accepting gifts from clients unless your supervising attorney approves. Considerations of which you are unaware may make the gift inappropriate. Suppose, however, it is approved, but the gift involves the preparation of a document, which the attorney prepares. Though technically not the same as attorneys preparing the document for a gift to their spouses or children, the similarities certainly create an appearance of impropriety and a court might rule that your supervising attorney should not prepare it.

Sexual Relations with a Client

One of the more dramatic examples of a conflict of interest is the attorney who develops a romantic relationship with a current client, particularly a sexual relationship. Clients often come to an attorney when they are emotionally vulnerable. Under such circumstances, it is unconscionable for the attorney to take advantage of this vulnerability. An attorney with an emotional interest in a client will be looking for ways to increase that interest and to inspire a reciprocal interest from the client. Needless to say, this may not be what the client needs. The attorney's own need could well cloud his or her ability to put the client's welfare first.

The ABA Model Rules prohibit sexual relations between attorney and client, even if consensual, unless the sexual relationship began before the attorney-client relationship began. (Model Rule 1.8(j).) Some states have variations of this rule. In Florida, for example, sexual conduct is prohibited only if it can be shown that the conduct "exploits or adversely affects" the client. (Florida Rules 4-8.4(i).) If the relationship began after the Florida attorney was hired, there is a presumption that the relationship was exploitative. The attorney must overcome the presumption by proving otherwise.

Other Personal Interests

Do you think the attorneys in the following cases have a conflict of interest?

- A homosexual attorney represents a parent seeking to deny custody to the other parent because the latter is gay.
- An attorney who believes abortion is immoral works on a case where the client is Planned Parenthood.
- An attorney whose father was murdered ten years ago represents a client charged with murdering his wife.
- An attorney who is opposed to the death penalty is the prosecutor on a case where the state has asked for the death penalty.

bias (1) An inclination, tendency, or predisposition to think or act in a certain way. (2) Prejudice for or against something or someone. (3) A danger of prejudgment.

The likelihood is that the personal feelings of these attorneys will affect how vigorously (zealously) they will work on behalf of their client. Because of those feelings, it can be argued that they have a **bias**, which is an inclination, a tendency, or a predisposition to think and to act in a certain way.

Clients are entitled to zealous representation even if the character or cause of the client is unpopular. Attorneys are encouraged to provide representation to such individuals. Yet attorneys are not obligated to take every case. Indeed, attorneys should avoid representing someone whose character or cause the attorney regards as so repugnant that the attorney's ability to represent the client zealously is in serious doubt. (Model Rule 6.2.) At one time, attorneys in New York State were explicitly cautioned to decline employment "if the intensity of personal feelings…may impair effective representation of a prospective client."[30] (We will return to the topic of bias in Chapter 8.)

POSITIONAL CONFLICTS

positional conflict A conflict of interest that exists (1) if an attorney asserts inconsistent legal positions while representing two current clients in separate, unrelated cases and (2) if success on behalf of a client in one case will harm or disadvantage the current client in the other case.

A **positional conflict** exists (1) if an attorney asserts inconsistent legal positions while representing two current clients in separate, unrelated cases and (2) if success on behalf of a client in one case will harm or disadvantage a client in the other case. An attorney must avoid positional conflicts unless both clients in writing allow the attorney to assert the inconsistent positions. Model Rule 1.7 (Comment 24).

Example:
Case #1: Diane Bryant, Esq. represents a Mary Thompson who wants § 23(c) declared unconstitutional. In court, Bryant argues that it is unconstitutional.

Case #2: In a separate, unrelated case, Bryant is asked to represent a supplier (Ed Anderson) who would lose substantial business if § 23(c) is declared unconstitutional. In this case, Bryant would have to argue to the court that § 23(c) is constitutional.

In this example, Bryant should not agree to represent Ed Anderson. Winning the case for him is likely to harm or disadvantage Mary Thompson. If both clients agree in writing to allow Bryant to argue these inconsistent positions in the two cases, she can do so. If, however, neither client would be harmed or disadvantaged by the inconsistent legal positions, the attorney would not need their consent to argue the positions in the two cases.

THIRD-PERSON CONFLICTS

Sometimes an attorney's fee is paid by a nonclient.

Example: John Adamson is sued by his landlord for violating the lease on the apartment where he lives. Alice Toomey, Esq. represents John. The company where John works, Towers, Inc., agrees to pay Alice's fees for John

It can be ethical for Alice Toomey to accept payment from Towers, so long as it is clear that her loyalty is to John, not to Towers. Furthermore, (1) John must give written informed consent to allow Towers to pay his fees, (2) Towers must not interfere with the Alice's representation of John, and (3) Alice must not tell Towers anything about the case that would violate John's right of confidentiality. Model Rule 1.8(f).

VICARIOUS CONFLICTS

tainted Having or causing a conflict of interest; contaminated.

When one person causes a conflict of interest in a law office, that person is said to be **tainted**—contaminated. This most often arises in successive-representation conflicts where the attorney seeks to represent a current client against a former client. This conflict taints (contaminates) the attorney and may taint (contaminate) the entire law office so that no attorney in the office can represent the current client against the former client unless the former client agrees to allow the representation.

Example: Two years ago, John Farrell, Esq., of the law firm of Smith & Smith represented the stepfather in a custody dispute with the child's aunt, who represented herself in the case. The stepfather won the case, but the aunt was awarded limited visitation rights. The aunt now wants to sue the stepfather for failure to abide by the visitation order. John Farrell no longer represents the stepfather. The aunt asks John Farrell to represent her. He declines because of a conflict of interest (successive representation) but sends her to his law partner, Diane Williams, Esq., down the corridor at Smith & Smith.

In this example, John Farrell is tainted. He would have a conflict of interest if he tried to represent the aunt against his former client, the stepfather. The two cases involve the same matter, the custody and visitation of the child. When an attorney has a successive-representation conflict such as this one, every other attorney in the firm is also contaminated unless the former client consents to allow the representation. Hence, Diane Williams, Esq. is disqualified from representing the aunt against the stepfather unless the stepfather agrees (consents) to allow Williams to represent the aunt against him.

Diane Williams has a **vicarious conflict**, which is a conflict that exists solely because of someone else's conflict. If a vicarious conflict causes a disqualification, the disqualification is called a **vicarious disqualification**. If the stepfather does not consent to Diane Williams's representation of the aunt, then Williams is vicariously disqualified from representing the aunt because of John Farrell's actual conflict that would prevent him from representing her.

A vicarious disqualification is also called an **imputed** disqualification. *Imputed* simply means attributed to. John Farrell's conflict is imputed (attributed) to Diane Williams. His disqualification is an actual disqualification. If the stepfather does not agree to allow Diane Williams to represent the aunt against him, then Williams's disqualification is an imputed or vicarious disqualification.

MIGRATORY CONFLICTS

Finally, we examine *migratory conflicts*, which exist when an attorney who has a conflict switches jobs and brings the conflict with him or her to the new job, potentially disqualifying every attorney at the new job.

Example:
Law Office I. At Law Office I, Jim Peters, Esq. represents Sue Fisher in the case of Fisher v. Dooley. During the representation, Peters learns confidential information about Fisher.

Law Office II. Peters quits Law Office I and joins Law Office II. One of the clients of Law Office II is Adamson, who is suing Fisher in Adamson v. Fisher, a case that is substantially related to the case of Fisher v. Dooley.

This job switch raises two conflicts questions. First, can Jim Peters at Law Office II represent Adamson against Fisher in the case of Adamson v. Fisher? No. See the earlier discussion of when successive representation is not allowed. Second, can another attorney at Law Office II represent Adamson against Fisher in the case of Adamson v. Fisher?

The second question asks whether every attorney in Law Office II is vicariously disqualified from representing Adamson because of the actual conflict that the tainted attorney, Jim Peters, brought to the office. In many states, there are two possible ways to avoid disqualification: consent and screening.

Avoiding Disqualification through Consent

Consent can avoid vicarious disqualification due to a job switch. In our example, Sue Fisher can be asked if she agrees to allow an attorney in Law Office II to represent Adamson against her in the case of Adamson v. Fisher. Her new attorneys will probably advise her not to give such consent because of the perceived likelihood that Peters will reveal (or has already revealed) confidential information about Fisher to other attorneys at Law Office II.

Avoiding Disqualification through Screening

Another possible method of avoiding vicarious disqualification because of a job switch is by **screening** the attorney from the case in order to eliminate the possibility that the tainted

---

vicarious conflict A conflict attributed to every attorney in a law office solely because of an actual conflict caused by one of the attorneys in the office.

vicarious disqualification The disqualification of every attorney in a law office from representing a client solely because of an actual conflict caused by one of the attorneys in the office. Also called *imputed disqualification*.

imputed Attributed to.

screening Steps taken by a law office to isolate a tainted worker from involvement in a case in order to avoid vicarious or imputed disqualification of the office from representation of a client in that case.

attorney will reveal confidential information to other attorneys in the law office. Screening consists of steps taken by a law office to isolate a tainted worker from involvement in a case. Not all states, however, allow screening of attorneys as a way to avoid disqualification. If a state does not allow attorney screening and if the client at Law Office I does not consent, then every attorney at Law Office II is disqualified from representing that client.

As we will see in the Paralegal Perspective, a job switch by a paralegal can also cause imputed disqualification. To avoid disqualification when a paralegal switches jobs, consent and screening can be used in most states. More states are willing to allow screening to avoid disqualification when a paralegal switches jobs than when an attorney switches jobs.

Paralegal Perspective:

■ *Introduction.* Paralegals and other nonattorney employees can create conflicts that disqualify a law office from representing a particular client. This occurs most often because of the nonattorney's prior employment.

> **Example**: Ted Warren is a paralegal who works for Mary Winter, Esq. Winter represents Apple in the case of Apple v. IBM. Ted has substantial paralegal responsibilities on this case. While the case is still going on, Ted switches jobs. He goes to work for Quinton & Oran, which represents IBM in the litigation with Apple.

Ted is tainted. He brings a conflict of interest to the firm of Quinton & Oran. While Ted worked for Mary Winter, he obviously acquired confidential information about Apple. There are pressures on him to tell the attorneys at Quinton & Oran what he knows about Apple so that they can use the information to the advantage of their client, IBM, in the litigation against Apple. A paralegal's personal interests can also create conflicts. One law firm makes the following statement to all its paralegals: "If you or a temporary paralegal working under your supervision were formerly employed by opposing counsel, this could be the basis for a motion to disqualify" this law firm. "So also could personal relationships such as kinship with the opposing party or attorney or dating an attorney from another firm. Make your attorney aware of such connections."[31]

Similarly, a New Mexico court rule provides the following caution to attorneys:

> A lawyer is responsible to ensure that no personal, social or business interest or relationship of the paralegal impinges upon, or appears to impinge upon, the services rendered to the client…. If a lawyer accepts a matter in which the paralegal may have a conflict of interest, the lawyer will exclude that paralegal from participation in any services performed in connection with that matter. Furthermore, the lawyer must specifically inform the client that a nonlawyer employee has a conflict of interest which, was it the lawyer's conflict, would prevent further representation of the client in connection with the matter. The nature of the conflict should be disclosed. The lawyer will caution the paralegal to inform the lawyer of any interest or association which might constitute or cause such a conflict, or which might give the appearance of constituting or causing such a conflict. In addition, no interest or loyalty of the paralegal may be permitted to interfere with the lawyer's independent exercise of professional judgment.[32]

■ *Avoiding Imputed Disqualification.* As we have seen, there are two ways that contaminated law offices try to avoid imputed disqualification due to tainted attorneys or tainted paralegals whose job switch creates a conflict of interest: client consent and screening. Consent will work to prevent imputed disqualification when the tainted person is an attorney or a paralegal. Screening, however, will work in most states when the tainted person is a paralegal, but in some states will not work if the tainted person is an attorney.

■ *Avoiding Imputed Disqualification by Client Consent:* The cleanest way a contaminated law office can avoid imputed disqualification is to try to obtain the consent of the party who has the most to lose—the party whose confidentiality is in jeopardy. In most cases, the consent of this person will avoid disqualification.

> **Example**. In the Ted Warren example, Apple would have to be asked to consent to the continued representation of IBM by Quinton & Oran, where Warren now works.

■ *Avoiding Imputed Disqualification by Screening:* Screening consists of steps taken by a law office to isolate a tainted worker (attorney, paralegal, or other nonattorney employee) from involvement in a case in order to avoid vicarious or imputed disqualification of the office from representation of a client in that case. The screen is known as a **Chinese wall**

Chinese wall Screening that prevents a tainted worker (attorney, paralegal, or other nonattorney) from having any contact with the case of a particular client in the office because the tainted worker has created a conflict of interest between that client and someone else. Also called *ethical wall, cone of silence.* A tainted worker is also called a *contaminated worker.* Once the Chinese wall is set up around the tainted worker, the latter is referred to as a quarantined worker.

(sometimes called an *ethical wall* or a *cone of silence*). It is built around the tainted worker who brought the conflict of interest into the office. He or she becomes the **quarantined** worker due to a rigid isolation from anything to do with the case that prompted the conflict. To "wall" a person means to screen him or her in an effort to avoid disqualification. The components of screening are outlined in Exhibit 5-7.

quarantined Isolated or kept apart from a case because of a conflict of interest in connection with that case.

Exhibit 5-7	Components of Comprehensive Screening

The following are the most effective guidelines a law office can follow to screen a tainted worker (e.g., attorney, paralegal, investigator, secretary, or other nonattorney) who brings a conflict of interest to the office. The goal is to avoid vicarious (imputed) disqualification by isolating the worker from the case in which he or she has caused the conflict of interest.

1. The screening begins as soon as the tainted worker arrives at the office.
2. At this time, or soon thereafter, the office notifies the opposing party's attorney that the tainted worker has been hired and that comprehensive screening has begun.
3. The office notifies its own client of the screening and the reason for it.
4. The tainted worker signs a statement promising not to discuss what he or she knows about the case with anyone in the office.
5. Those working on the case in the office promise not to discuss it with, or in the presence of, the tainted worker.
6. A written notice is sent to everyone else in the office that identifies the tainted worker and the client's case file in question. Everyone in the office is told not to discuss any aspect of the case with the tainted worker.
7. The tainted worker will not be assigned to work with any untainted attorney, paralegal, secretary, or other staff member who is handling the case in question.
8. Others not working on the case in the office are told that if they learn anything about the case, they must not discuss it with the tainted worker.
9. The receptionist and mail handlers are instructed not to forward anything about the case to the tainted worker.
10. The desk of the tainted worker is in an area that is physically segregated from work on the case in the office. This area is designed to avoid inadvertent access to the case file.
11. The file is removed from the central computer system to which everyone has access or is placed in a separate database to which the tainted worker does not have access. The tainted worker is not given the password that grants access to the restricted file.
12. The paper file of the case is locked in cabinets or other storage facilities to which the tainted worker does not have access.
13. Colored labels or "flags" are placed on each document in the file to indicate it is off limits to the tainted worker. For example, a sticker might say, "ACCESS RESTRICTED: DO NOT DISCUSS THIS CASE WITH [NAME OF TAINTED WORKER]."
14. The tainted worker will not directly earn any profit from, participate in the fees of, or obtain any other financial gain from the case.
15. The firm documents all of the above steps that are taken. This documentation will become evidence, if ever needed, to help rebut an allegation that the tainted worker had any contact with the file.

■ In *Phoenix Founders, Inc. v. Marshall*, a Texas paralegal worked on a case at one firm and then switched jobs to work for opposing counsel on the same case. The court said that if a paralegal does any work on a case, there is a **conclusive presumption** that he or she obtained "confidences and secrets" about that case. There is also a presumption that the paralegal shared this information with her new firm, but this is a **rebuttable presumption**; it is not conclusive. (See Exhibit 5-8.) The presumption can be rebutted by showing that the new firm took "sufficient precautions ... to guard against any disclosure of confidences" through a Chinese wall. At the new firm, "the newly-hired paralegal should be cautioned not to disclose any information relating to the representation of a client of the former employer. The paralegal should also be instructed not to work on any matter on which the paralegal worked during the prior employment, or regarding which the paralegal has information relating to the former employer's representation. Additionally, the new firm should take other reasonable steps to ensure that the paralegal does not work in connection with matters on which the paralegal worked during the prior employment." The *Phoenix Founders* case said

conclusive presumption An assumption or inference of fact that a party will not be allowed to dispute or rebut.

rebuttable presumption An assumption or inference of fact that can be overcome (rebutted) by sufficient contrary evidence but that will be treated as accurate if it is not rebutted.

that disqualification will always be required in three circumstances unless the former client consents to allow the paralegal to continue working at the new firm:

(1) when information relating to the representation of an adverse client is disclosed by the tainted paralegal at the new firm,
(2) when screening at the new firm would be ineffective, or
(3) when the tainted paralegal necessarily would be required to work on the other side of a matter that is the same as or substantially related to a matter on which the paralegal worked at the prior firm.

If any of these three circumstances apply, disqualification is mandatory.[33]

Exhibit 5-8	Presumptions When a Paralegal Switches Jobs

| Paralegal does some work on the case at the first office. | | This creates an irrebuttable (conclusive) presumption that the paralegal obtained confidential information about the case at the first office. | | It also creates a rebuttable presumption that the paralegal shared (revealed) the confidential information at the second office. |

■ In another major case, a contaminated paralegal caused a San Francisco law firm to be disqualified from representing nine clients in asbestos litigation involving millions of dollars. The sole reason for the disqualification was that the firm hired a paralegal who had once worked for a law firm that represented the opponents in the asbestos litigation. Soon after the controversy arose, the disqualified firm laid off the tainted paralegal who brought this conflict to the firm. He was devastated when he found out that he was being let go. "I was flabbergasted, totally flabbergasted." He has not been able to find work since.[34] The case was widely reported throughout the legal community. A front-page story in the *Los Angeles Daily Journal* said that it "could force firms to conduct lengthy investigations of paralegals and other staffers before hiring them."[35]

■ Many paralegals change jobs during their careers. The market for experienced paralegals is outstanding. Bar associations realize that an overly strict disqualification rule could severely hamper the job prospects for such paralegals. According to the American Bar Association, "It is important that nonlawyer employees have as much mobility in employment opportunity as possible consistent with the protection of clients," particularly the protection of client confidentiality.[36]

■ Although such statements from the American Bar Association are comforting, the reality is that tainted paralegals are in a very vulnerable position. Many contaminated offices terminate the tainted paralegal who caused the contamination. Rather than take the risk that a Chinese wall built around this paralegal will be judged too little and too late, the office will probably take the safer course and let the paralegal go.

■ *Career client list.* When you apply for a job, the prospective employer will want to know whether you might bring a conflict of interest to the office if hired. In short, it wants to know if you would contaminate the office. To find out, it must ask you questions about cases you may have worked on in prior jobs or volunteer experiences. (See the discussion of contamination in the section on interviewing for employment in Chapter 2.) You need to compile your own **career client list** as soon as you start working in a law office in any role (e.g., paralegal, secretary, or investigator) as a volunteer, employee, or independent contractor. The list should have five columns consisting of the names of all the parties involved in each case or matter, the name of the office, the names of the attorneys on both sides, the dates of your involvement, and a brief description of your role. (See Exhibit 5-9.) When you apply for a new job, your list will be relevant to whether the law firm will be subject to disqualification if you are hired. If you are unable to produce the list, a conscientious office might refuse to hire you on that basis alone rather than take the risk of finding out later that your prior work created a conflict of interest that could have been identified when you were initially considered for employment. Once you have the list, be very careful. Its contents contain confidential information. Do not attach it to your résumé and randomly send

career client list A confidential list of every client or matter you worked on in any law office (as a paid employee or volunteer) from the beginning of your legal career to the present time. The list is used to help determine whether any of your future work might create a conflict of interest.

Exhibit 5-9	Career Client List

To help determine whether you might create a conflict of interest, keep a confidential list covering the following information for every law office in which you worked or volunteered from the beginning of your career to your current position:

Names of All Parties Involved	Office	Names of Attorneys (both sides)	Dates	Brief Description of Your Role

it around town! Until employment discussions have become serious, do not show it to the prospective employer.

- *Tainted by association.* Assume that an *attorney* in the office is tainted and that the state allows screening to prevent disqualification. Paralegals who work closely with this attorney would probably have to be screened as well. It wouldn't make sense to prevent an attorney from having contact with a particular case but allow his or her paralegal to have such contact. The paralegal, in effect, would become tainted by association.

- Freelance or **independent paralegals** who work for more than one law office on a part-time basis are particularly vulnerable to conflict-of-interest charges. For example, in a large case in litigation involving many parties, two opposing attorneys might unknowingly use the same independent paralegal to work on different aspects of the same case or might use two different employees of this independent paralegal. Another example is the independent paralegal who worked on an earlier case for a client and now works on a different but substantially related case in which that client is the opponent. Attorneys who use freelance or independent paralegals, therefore, must be careful. The attorney cannot simply turn over work and be available to answer questions. At a minimum, the attorney must make inquiries about this paralegal's prior client casework for other attorneys in order to determine whether there are any conflicts.[37]

CONFLICTS CHECKS

How does a law office determine whether any of its attorneys, paralegals, or other employees have a conflict of interest with a prospective client? It does a **conflicts check**. To perform this check, the office needs a comprehensive database containing information such as the following about every former and present client of the office:

- Names of clients (plus any aliases or earlier names before marriage; all names should be checked under varying spellings of the same person or entity)
- Names of spouses of clients
- Names of children of clients
- Names of key employees of clients (including the chief executive officers and directors of corporate clients)
- Names of major shareholders in companies in which the client has an interest
- Names of parent and subsidiary corporations affiliated with the client, plus their chief executive officers and directors
- Names of members of relatively small associations in which the client has a role[38]

Some categories of information can be difficult for the office to obtain. For example:

- Whether an employee in the office holds stock in the company of the adversary of a prospective client
- Whether a spouse, relative, or intimate friend of an employee in the office is employed by or holds stock in the company of the adversary of a prospective client
- Whether an employee in the office is related to or has had a romantic relationship with the adversary of a prospective client or with anyone in the law office that represents the adversary

To discover this kind of information, the office usually must rely on its employees to come forward and reveal such connections.

Some of the data a law firm needs for a conflicts check may be found in the conflicts section of the New File Worksheet that the office fills out when it begins working with a new

independent paralegals (1) An independent contractor who sells his or her paralegal services to, and works under the supervision of, one or more attorneys. (2) An independent contractor who sells his or her paralegal services directly to the public without attorney supervision. Also called *freelance paralegal, paralegal, legal technician.* In some states, however, the paralegal and legal assistant titles are limited to those who work under attorney supervision.

conflicts check Finding out whether a conflict of interest exists that might disqualify a law office from representing a prospective client or from continuing the representation of a current client.

client or with a new matter of a current client. (See the conflicts section on the New File Worksheet in Exhibit 14-4 in Chapter 14.) Large law firms sometimes hire paralegals to go through the office's computer files to try to identify conflict problems that must be addressed by senior attorneys in the office. These paralegals are called *conflicts specialists* (also conflicts analysts and conflicts researchers.)

Detailed conflicts information is also needed when the office is thinking about hiring a new attorney or paralegal from another office (called a **lateral hire**). To determine whether they might contaminate the office, the names of the parties in their prior casework must be checked against the office's current and prospective clients. See Exhibit 5-9, detailing the Career Client List that a paralegal should have available when a prospective employer is considering the paralegal for employment.

When a law office applies for malpractice insurance, the insurance carrier will often inquire about the system the office uses for conflicts checks. Here are examples of questions that might be found on an application for such insurance:

- Do you have a written internal control system for maintaining client lists and identifying actual or potential conflicts of interest?
- Describe in detail the system used by the office to determine whether a conflict of interest exists with respect to prospective, current, and past clients.
- Do firm members disclose to their clients, in writing, all actual conflicts of interest and conflicts they reasonably believe may exist?
- Upon disclosure of actual or potential conflicts to clients, do firm members always obtain written consent from the clients to continue providing legal services?

The insurance carrier will also want to know how conflicts are checked if the law office has merged (or proposes to merge) with another law office. If, for example, the ABC law firm merges with the XYZ law firm, a new group of tainted persons may now exist because of the prior and current caseloads of the two firms. Finding out can be a huge undertaking because of the potentially thousands of cases on which the attorneys and paralegals of the two firms have worked or are working.

Most litigation support and database management software (see Chapter 13) have conflicts-checking functions that enable a law firm to comb through the law firm's database(s) to find possible conflicts. See Exhibit 5-10 for an example.

lateral hire A person hired from another law office.

Exhibit 5-10   **Example of Conflicts Checking by Computer**

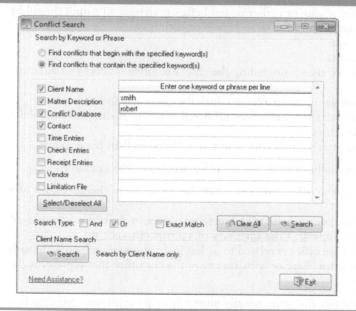

Source: ESILaw (www.esilaw.com).

COMMUNICATION WITH THE OTHER SIDE

- If you know that an opponent is represented by an attorney, you must not contact the opponent about the dispute unless the opponent's attorney consents to the contact. Model Rule 4.2.
- If you have contact with an opponent who does not have an attorney, you must not give the impression that you are uninvolved (disinterested) in the dispute and you must not give legal advice to the unrepresented opponent other than to obtain his or her own attorney. Model Rule 4.3

If an opposing party is represented by an attorney, the permission of the party's attorney is needed to communicate with that party concerning the subject of the case. An unrepresented opposing party must not be misled into thinking that you are **disinterested**, meaning that you are neutral or uninvolved in the case. You are not disinterested if you work for one of the parties in the dispute. The only advice you can give unrepresented opposing parties is to obtain their own attorney.

The **anticontact rule** requires an attorney to avoid communicating with an opposing party unless the latter's attorney consents. The ethical concern here is overreaching—taking unfair advantage of another's naïveté or other vulnerability, especially by deceptive means.

> **Example**: Dan and Theresa Kline have just separated and are thinking about a divorce. Each claims the marital home. Theresa hires Thomas Farlington, Esq. to represent her. Farlington calls Dan to ask him if he would like to settle the case.

It is unethical for Farlington to contact Dan about the case if Farlington knows that Dan has his own attorney. Farlington must talk with Dan's attorney. Only the latter can give Farlington permission to communicate with Dan. If Dan does not have an attorney, Farlington can talk with Dan, but he must not allow Dan to be misled about Farlington's role. Farlington works for the other side; he is *not* disinterested. Dan must be made to understand this fact. The only advice Farlington can give Dan in such a situation is to obtain his own attorney.

A related communication rule is that an attorney should not communicate with the court in the absence of the attorney for the other side. Such **ex parte communications** are forbidden unless specifically authorized by law.

Paralegal Perspective:

- The ethical restrictions on communicating with the other side apply to the employees of an attorney as well as to the attorney. "The lawyer's obligation is to ensure that paralegals do not communicate directly with parties known to be represented by an attorney, without that attorney's consent, on the subject of such representation."[39] If the other side is a business or some other large organization, do not talk with anyone there unless your supervisor tells you that it is ethical to do so. Never call the other side and pretend you are someone else in order to obtain information. (See the earlier discussion on fraudulent "friending," pretexting, and other misuse of social media.) If your office allows you to talk with an opponent who is not represented by an attorney, you cannot give this person any advice other than the advice to secure his or her own attorney.

SOLICITATION

- In-person, live telephone, or real-time electronic solicitation of clients is unethical if a significant reason for the solicitation is to seek fees or other financial benefit unless the contact is with (a) another attorney or (b) someone with whom you have a family, close personal, or prior professional relationship.
- Written, recorded, or standard (not real-time) electronic solicitation of clients is ethical unless (a) the attorney knows that the prospective client does not want to be solicited or (b) the solicitation involves coercion, duress, or harassment.
- Solicitation, when permitted, must not contain untruthful or misleading statements. Rule 7.3

People in distress are sometimes so distraught that they are not in a position to evaluate their need for legal services. They should not be subjected to pressures from an attorney who wants to be hired, particularly if the attorney is not a relative, close friend, or has never represented them in the past. Such in-person (i.e., face-to-face) **solicitation** of clients is unethical, if the attorney has a monetary (**pecuniary**) or other financial goal such as generating fees.

> **Example**: Rebecca Winters, Esq. stands outside the police station and gives a business card to any individual being arrested. The card says that Winters is an attorney specializing in criminal cases.

disinterested (1) Not working for one side or the other in a controversy. (2) Not deriving benefit if one side of a dispute wins or loses; objective.

anticontact rule An advocate must not contact an opposing party without permission of the latter's attorney. Also called *no-contact rule*.

ex parte communications A communication with the court in the absence of the attorney for the other side.

solicitation (1) An appeal or request for clients or business. (2) An attempt to obtain something by persuasion or application.

pecuniary Relating to money. (A pecuniary interest is a financial interest.)

ambulance chasing
Approaching accident victims (or anyone else who might have a legal problem or claim) to encourage them to hire a particular attorney. If the attorney uses someone else to do the soliciting, the latter is called a *runner*. If this other person uses deception or fraud in the solicitation, he or she is sometimes called a *capper* or a *steerer*.

real time Occurring now; happening as you are watching; able to respond or otherwise interact immediately or within seconds.

Winters is obviously looking for prospective clients. Doing so in this manner is referred to as **ambulance chasing**, which is a pejorative term for aggressively tracking down anyone who probably has a legal problem in order to drum up business. (An unkind member of Congress recently told an audience, "If you want to meet a trial lawyer, follow an ambulance."[40]) There is no indication that Winters is related to or is good friends with any of the people going into the police station or that she has any prior professional relationship with them (e.g., they are not former clients). Winters appears to have one goal: finding a source of fees. Hence her conduct is unethical. In-person or live telephone solicitation of clients in this way is not allowed. The same would be true if Winters contacted these individuals through **real-time** electronic communication such as in an Internet chat room. (See Chapter 13 for more on real-time communication.) The concern is that an attorney who contacts potentially vulnerable strangers in these ways may use undue pressure to sign them up as clients.

Undue pressure is less likely to occur if the solicitation is in a writing (e.g., through the mail), a recorded telephone message, or a standard (non–real-time) electronic contact (e.g., an email message). This is true even if the recipients are known to need legal services.

> **Example**: An attorney obtains the names of homeowners facing foreclosure and sends them the following letter: "It has come to my attention that your home is being foreclosed. Federal law may allow you to stop your creditors and give you more time to pay. Call my office for legal help."

Although critics say that such solicitation constitutes "ambulance chasing by mail," the technique is ethical in most states as long as the recipients have not made known to the attorney that they do not want to be solicited; the solicitation does not involve coercion, duress, or harassment; and the solicitation is truthful and not misleading. In-person, live telephone, or real-time electronic solicitation, however, is treated differently because of the added pressure that it imposes. It is "easier to throw out unwanted mail than an uninvited guest."[41]

Some states impose additional regulations on the solicitations that they allow. For example, the state may require the attorney to print the phrase "Advertising Material" on the outside of the envelope or at the top of an electronic message and may prohibit all solicitations to victims and their relatives for a designated number of days after an accident or disaster for which the attorney is offering legal services. Some federal laws impose additional restrictions. For example, the Aviation Disaster Family Assistance Act provides that in the event of an air carrier accident:

> [N]o unsolicited communication concerning a potential action for personal injury or wrongful death may be made by an attorney [...or by an employee of the attorney] to an individual injured in the accident, or to a relative of an individual injured in the accident, before the 45th day following the date of the accident.[42]

In extreme cases, client solicitation can constitute the crime of **barratry**. In 1990, for example, three attorneys and an employee of a law firm were indicted in Texas. They were charged with illegally seeking clients at hospitals and funeral homes soon after twenty-one students were killed and sixty-nine others were injured in a tragic school-bus accident.[43]

barratry The crime of stirring up quarrels or litigation. Persistently instigating lawsuits, often groundless ones. The illegal solicitation of clients.

Paralegal Perspective:

■ An unscrupulous attorney may try to use a paralegal to solicit clients inappropriately. Paralegals are subject to the same prohibitions on solicitation that govern attorneys, e.g., no in-person drumming up of clients in order to earn fees for the office.

> **Example**: Bill Hill is a senior citizen who lives at a home for senior citizens. Andrew Vickers, Esq., hires Bill as his "paralegal." His sole job is to speak with other seniors to find out if they have any legal problems, and if they do, to refer them to Vickers.

Andrew Vickers is engaging in unethical solicitation through Bill Hill. Attorneys cannot hire a paralegal to try to accomplish what they cannot do themselves. Bill Hill is making in-person contact in order to find paying clients for Vickers. This is unethical if none of these other seniors are attorneys, none are family members, and none have a prior professional relationship with the Vickers office.

runner One who solicits business, especially accident cases. (See glossary for an additional meaning.)

■ Attorneys must also avoid using a **runner**—an employee or independent contractor who contacts personal injury victims or other potential clients in order to solicit business for an attorney. If this person uses deception or fraud in the solicitation, he or she is sometimes called a *capper* or a *steerer*. An example would be someone who arranges for an unsuspecting motorist to be involved in a crash with another vehicle, whose driver (by prearrangement with the capper) flees after the collision. The capper then solicits the motorist to hire an attorney for purposes of filing an insurance claim.

■ See also the earlier discussion of fees in which we covered the related topic of unethically splitting fees with a nonattorney and the topic we will discuss shortly on paying someone to recommend the services of an attorney.

ADVERTISING

> ■ Attorneys may advertise in the newspaper, on television, on the Internet, or through other media as long as the advertisements are truthful and do not mislead the public such as by creating unjustified expectations of the results the attorney will be able to obtain. Model Rule 7.2
> ■ The advertisement must include the name and office address of at least one attorney or law firm responsible for its content.

The main goal of advertising and solicitation is to obtain clients. The difference is that solicitation involves direct contact with prospective clients whereas advertising is a broader attempt to draw attention to the legal services being offered.

At one time, almost all forms of advertising by attorneys were prohibited. Traditional attorneys considered advertising to be highly offensive to the dignity of the profession. In 1977, however, the U.S. Supreme Court in *Bates v. State Bar of Arizona* stunned the legal profession by holding that truthful advertising cannot be completely banned.[44] The First Amendment protects such advertising. Furthermore, advertising does not pose the same danger as in-person, live telephone, or real-time electronic solicitation by an attorney. A recipient of advertising is generally under very little pressure to buy the advertised product—the attorney's services. Hence attorneys can ethically use truthful, nonmisleading advertising to the general public in order to generate business.

Attorneys spend millions of dollars every year on television advertising alone, most of it by personal injury (PI) attorneys trying to bring in accident cases that often involve high contingency fees and relatively quick settlements. Former U.S. Chief Justice Warren Burger commented that some attorney ads "would make a used-car dealer blush with shame." Proponents of attorney advertising, however, say that it has made legal services more accessible and has provided the public with a better basis for choosing among available attorneys.

One of the major problems with advertising is that it can be misleading.

Examples of Misleading Ads:

Ad: Flier states, "You pay nothing if we do not win your case."
Problem: The ad may be misleading if the office requires its client to pay court costs and expenses even if it loses the case.

Ad: Man in a wheelchair says, "Fenton and Adams can win $1,000,000. I can vouch for it."
Problem: The ad may raise false expectations. A viewer of the ad may think the law office is saying that it can obtain the same result for the viewer.

Ad: Newspaper box ad says, "Trust your case to a specialist."
Problem: Some states have specialty (specialization) certification programs for attorneys. If a particular state doesn't, calling oneself a specialist may be misleading. If it does, references to the specialty in ads usually must comply with specific regulations, e.g., mentioning the full name of the specialty board that granted the specialty credential.

Many law firms today have Internet sites. Some firms pay search engines to have their sites appear high on the list of results of certain searches. Recently for example, a law firm paid Google $56.24 for each click on a search for "mesothelioma" that led to the firm's website. Google was paid this amount whether or not the searcher hired the firm. A mere click on the link triggered the payment. The firm was willing to pay Google such a high price because someone using this search term is likely to be looking for an attorney who handles cases of workers exposed to asbestos, a field of practice that can led to unusually high attorney fees.

Most law firm websites are designed to provide the public with general information about the firm, particularly the kind of legal services it offers. In addition, some of the firms' Web pages go into detail about an aspect of the law that is relevant to their practice. For example, a family-law attorney might have several pages that list the grounds for divorce in the state or the steps to take to establish paternity. Large law firms may have elaborate Web pages that include pictures of attorneys in the firm and the names and email addresses of its attorneys.

To avoid the charge that a law firm is practicing law on the Internet, a disclaimer will often be printed on the homepage informing readers that the site is not intended to establish an attorney-client relationship or to provide legal advice. The goal is to make clear that the site is simply advertising the firm. As such, it must meet the ethical requirements for advertising, e.g., be truthful and not misleading. The disclaimer should also warn viewers:

- that the laws of different states may differ;
- that the firm makes no representation, warranty, or claim that the information on the site is current or accurate; and
- that viewers should not rely on the information provided on the site without consulting local attorneys.

There will often be an email address on the site that a viewer or prospective client can use to contact the firm. An attorney's response to such email messages should not contain legal advice, particularly to individuals who live in states where the attorneys in the firm are not licensed to practice law. Furthermore, the sender should be told in a disclaimer that

- the firm cannot maintain the confidentiality of any communications sent through the website, and
- until a conflicts check is made, the firm cannot agree to represent anyone.

See also the earlier discussion in the chapter on forming an attorney-client relationship.

Paralegal Perspective:

- In Chapters 1 and 4, we saw that many independent contractors sell law-related services directly to the public without attorney supervision. They are collectively known as **document service providers (DSPs).** A few states place restrictions on what such individuals can call themselves. In California, for example, they cannot call themselves paralegals or legal assistants in their advertising if they do not work under attorney supervision. Similar restrictions exist in a few other states such as Maine and Florida.

- Another example of a DSP is the *bankruptcy petition preparer (BPP)*. A BPP is not allowed to use the word *legal* or any similar term in their advertising. Some courts have concluded that they cannot use the word *paralegal*. (See Chapter 4.)

> **document service providers (DSPs)** (1) A nonattorney who works without attorney supervision to provide legal-document assistance to individuals who are representing themselves. Examples of DSPs include bankruptcy petition preparer (BPP) and legal document assistant (LDA). (2) Someone who helps another prepare or process documents.

PAYMENT FOR REFERRALS OR RECOMMENDATIONS

A lawyer shall not give anything of value to a person for recommending the lawyer's services. Model Rule 7.2(b)

An attorney cannot give compensation, payment, or "anything of value" for referring business to the attorney or for recommending the attorney. An attorney can pay a company for advertising the attorney's services, but not for referring clients to the attorney or for recommending that the attorney be hired. Recommending consists of endorsing or vouching for an attorney's credentials, abilities, competence, character, or other professional qualities. There is nothing wrong with people making recommendations or referrals, but they must not be paid cash or anything else of "value" for doing so.

Paralegal Perspective:

- Paralegals can recommend their law office to others, but the office cannot give paralegals a raise, a bonus, time off, or "anything" else "of value" for making such recommendations.

REPORTING PROFESSIONAL MISCONDUCT

- Attorneys who know that another attorney has violated the ethical rules must report this attorney to the appropriate disciplinary body if the violation is serious enough to cast substantial doubt on the attorney's honesty, trustworthiness, or fitness to practice law. Model Rule 8.3

Attorneys may pay a price for remaining silent when they become aware of unethical conduct by other attorneys. The failure of an attorney to report another attorney may mean that both attorneys can be disciplined for unethical behavior. This is known, pejoratively, as the *rat rule*, the *snitch rule*, or, more euphemistically, the *whistleblower rule*. Not every ethical violation must be reported. The ethical violation must raise a substantial question of the attorney's honesty, trustworthiness, or fitness to practice law, e.g., finding out that another attorney has stolen client funds.

Paralegal Perspective:

■ Suppose that a paralegal observes his or her supervising attorney committing fraud, stealing client funds, or using perjured testimony. Is the paralegal under an ethical obligation to report the offending attorney to the bar association or other disciplinary body? The National Federation of Paralegal Associations (NFPA) thinks so. In its *Model Code of Ethics and Professional Responsibility* (see Exhibit 5-4 and Appendix E) the obligation is stated as follows in EC-1.2(f):

> A paralegal shall advise the proper authority of non-confidential knowledge of any dishonest or fraudulent acts by any person pertaining to the handling of the funds, securities or other assets of a client. The authority to whom the report is made shall depend on the nature and circumstances of the possible misconduct (e.g., ethics committees of law firms, corporations and/or paralegal associations, local or state bar associations, local prosecutors, administrative agencies, etc.). Failure to report such knowledge is in itself misconduct and shall be treated as such under these rules.

■ As pointed out earlier, ethical rules written by paralegals are not binding in the sense that they affect the paralegal's right to work as a paralegal. A paralegal who violates EC-1.2(f) by failing to report his or her attorney to the bar association might be expelled from the paralegal association that has adopted NFPA's Model Code, but it is highly unlikely that this will affect his or her employment prospects so long as the paralegal him- or herself has not participated in the unethical conduct.

■ What should a conscientious paralegal do? Here are some guidelines:

- First and foremost, do not participate directly or indirectly in the unethical conduct.
- Second, consult with fellow paralegals in the office and in your local paralegal association. Without naming names and without breaching client confidentiality, find out how others have handled similar predicaments on the job.
- Third, go to a senior officer at the firm, e.g., a partner, and let him or her know that the conduct you have observed is troubling you.

You may need to confront the offending attorney himself or herself. Whomever you approach, be sure to have your facts straight! What appears to you to be an ethical violation may simply be aggressive or zealous advocacy that is on the edge but still within the bounds of propriety.

■ Should you go to the bar association or to a law enforcement agency? This is obviously a very tough question. The answer may depend on whether you have thoroughly exhausted available routes within the office to resolve the matter to your satisfaction and, more important, whether you think this is the only way to prevent serious harm to a client. (See also "An Ethical Dilemma: Your Ethics or Your Job!" later in the chapter.)

■ The case of *Brown v. Hammond* involves a paralegal and a **whistleblower**, Cynthia Brown, who was fired after she complained about the improper billing practices of her law firm. She then sued the law firm. Her **cause of action** in the suit was **wrongful discharge**. As you read the opinion, keep the following points in mind:

- The case arises on a **motion to dismiss**. The defendant is arguing that even if Brown proves her factual allegations, her facts do not state a cause of action for wrongful discharge and that therefore there is no legal basis for her to recover. If the motion is denied, the case then goes to trial and Brown will be allowed to introduce evidence to support her factual claims. For purposes of ruling on a motion to dismiss, the court will assume that she *will* be able to establish her facts. The issue then becomes whether the state recognizes a cause of action of wrongful discharge on the basis of those facts.
- Like most nonunion employees in the private sector, Brown was an **at-will employee**. The rule governing such employees is that they can be terminated at any time for any reason that does not violate **public policy**.
- Brown's complaint had two counts. Count I is based on the claim that firing her for reporting billing fraud is against public policy. The court's discussion of this count makes a critical distinction between a disclosure that is **gratuitous** (one that is not based on a job duty) and a disclosure someone is obligated to make as part of one's job. Count II is based on the claim that firing her for refusing to participate in fraudulent billing is against public policy.
- The case is in federal court because of **diversity of citizenship**. Plaintiff is a citizen of Texas and defendants are citizens of Pennsylvania. The amount in controversy exceeds $75,000.

whistleblower An employee who reports employer wrongdoing, usually to a government agency.

cause of action A legally acceptable reason for bringing a suit. A rule that constitutes a legal theory for bringing a suit. (See glossary for an additional meaning.)

wrongful discharge Terminating an employee for a reason that is illegal or a violation of public policy.

motion to dismiss. A request, often made before the trial begins, that the judge dismiss the case because the parties have reached a settlement or because of a serious procedural deficiency.

at-will employee An employee who can be terminated for any reason that does not violate public policy. An employee with no union or other contractual protection.

public policy The principles inherent in the customs, morals, and notions of justice that prevail in a state; the foundation of public laws; the principles that are naturally and inherently right and just.

gratuitous Pertaining to what is performed or given without a duty or obligation to do so. (See glossary for another meaning.)

diversity of citizenship The disputing parties are citizens of different states and the amount in controversy exceeds $75,000. This diversity gives subject-matter jurisdiction to a U.S. district court. (When the *Brown* case was decided, the amount had to exceed only $50,000.)

CASE

Brown v. Hammond
United States District Court, Eastern District, Pennsylvania
810 F. Supp. 644 (E.D. Pa. 1993)

(To read this case online, go to Google Scholar (scholar.google.com), click *Case law,* and type 810 F. Supp. 644 in the search box.)

WALDMAN, District Judge.

Plaintiff [Cynthia Brown] is an employee of defendant attorney [Robert Hammond] and his law firm. She is suing for wrongful discharge after having "blown the whistle" on the defendants' allegedly improper billing practices. Jurisdiction is based on diversity of citizenship. Defendants have moved to dismiss the complaint for failure to state a claim upon which relief can be granted, pursuant to Fed.R.Civ.P. [Federal Rule of Civil Procedure] 12(b)(6).

Legal Standard

The purpose of a Rule 12(b)(6) motion is to test the legal sufficiency of a complaint… In deciding a motion to dismiss for failure to state a claim, the court must "accept as true all the allegations in the complaint and all reasonable inferences that can be drawn therefrom, and view them in the light most favorable to the non-moving party." *See Rocks v. Philadelphia,* 868 F.2d 644, 645 (3d Cir. 1989).… A complaint may be dismissed when the facts pled and the reasonable inferences drawn therefrom are legally insufficient to support the relief sought.…

Facts

The pertinent factual allegations in the light most favorable to plaintiff are as follows. From November 4, 1990 to April 4, 1991, plaintiff was employed by defendants at-will as a paralegal and secretary. The time she spent on client matters was billed to clients as "attorney's time" without any notice to such clients that the work was done by a non-lawyer. Her supervisors directed her at times to bill her work directly as attorney's time despite her protests that the practice was improper. She then informed various authorities and affected clients of this practice. Plaintiff does not allege that she had any responsibility for overseeing the firm's billing practices.

Defendants responded by imposing new work rules with respect to hours of employment which applied only to and discriminated against plaintiff. She was subsequently terminated.

In count I, plaintiff asserts that she was terminated in violation of public policy for reporting the wrongful actions of defendants. In count II, she asserts that she was terminated in violation of public policy for refusing to perform wrongful actions.…

Count I

It is well established under Pennsylvania law that "absent a statutory or contractual provision to the contrary…either party [may] terminate an employment relationship for any or no reason." *Geary v. United States Steel Corp.,* 456 Pa. 171, 175–176, 319 A.2d 174 (1974). An employer may determine, without any fair hearing to an at-will employee, that the employer simply wishes to be rid of him. *Darlington v. General Electric,* 350 Pa. Super. 183, 210, 504 A.2d 306 (1986). An employer's right to terminate an at-will employee has been characterized as "virtually absolute." *O'Neill v. ARA Services, Inc.,* 457 F. Supp. 182, 186 (E.D. Pa. 1978).

Pennsylvania law does recognize, however, a… cause of action for wrongful discharge from employment-at-will, but only in the quite narrow and limited circumstance where the discharge violates a significant and recognized public policy. *Borse v. Piece Goods Shop,* 963 F.2d 611, 617 (3d Cir. 1992); *Geary, supra; Darlington, supra.* Such a public policy must be "clearly mandated" and of a type that "strikes at the heart of a citizen's social right, duties and responsibilities." *Novosel v. Nationwide Insurance Co.,* 721 F.2d 894, 899 (3d Cir. 1983). [We must determine whether such a public policy has been violated here.]

Taking [Cynthia Brown's] allegations as true, defendants would appear to have violated the Pennsylvania Rules of Professional Conduct by misrepresenting to clients who had performed work for which they were paying. [See Rule 1.5 (regulating fees), Rule 7.1 (prohibiting false or misleading communications about lawyer's services), and 8.4(c) (defining "professional misconduct" to include dishonesty, fraud, deceit, or misrepresentation)].

Based upon pertinent precedent and persuasive authority, the court must distinguish between gratuitous disclosure of improper employer conduct and disclosures by persons responsible for reporting such conduct or for protecting the public interest in the pertinent area. See *Smith v. Calgon Carbon Corp.,* 917 F.2d 1338, 1345 (3d Cir. 1990)… (discharged chemical company employee not responsible for reporting improper emissions or spills); *Field v. Philadelphia Electric Co.,* 388 Pa. Super. 400, 565 A.2d 1170 (1989) (nuclear safety expert discharged for making statutorily required report to federal agency). See also *Hays v. Beverly Enters.,* 766 F. Supp. 350 (W.D. Pa.), aff'd, 952 F.2d 1392 (3d Cir. 1991) (physician's duty does not extend to plaintiff nurse); *Gaiardo v. Ethyl Corp.,* 697 F. Supp. 1377 (M.D. Pa. 1986). aff'd, 835 F.2d 479 (3d Cir. 1987) (plaintiff not supervisor or responsible for quality control).

The court concludes that plaintiff's termination for gratuitously alerting others about defendants' improper billing practice does not violate the type of significant, clearly mandated public policy required to satisfy the new narrow exception to Pennsylvania's rigid at-will employment doctrine. [As indicated, plaintiff does not allege that she had any responsibility for overseeing the firm's billing practices.]…

Count II

On the other hand, courts are less reluctant to discern important public policy considerations where persons are discharged for refusing to violate the law themselves. See Smith, 917 F.2d at 1344; *Woodson v. AMF Leisureland Centers, Inc.,* 842 F.2d 699 (3d Cir. 1988) (refusal to sell liquor to intoxicated patron); *Shaw v. Russell Trucking Line,* Inc., 542 F. Supp. 776, 779 (W.D. Pa. 1982) (refusal to haul loads over legal weight); *McNulty v. Borden, Inc.,* 474 F. Supp. 1111 (E.D. Pa. 1979) (refusal to engage in anti-trust violations). No employee should be forced to choose between his or her livelihood and engaging in fraud or other criminal conduct. To the extent that plaintiff appears to allege that she was also terminated for refusing herself to engage directly in fraudulent billing, her action may proceed.…

Conclusion

An appropriate order will be entered. [The motion to dismiss Count I is granted; the motion to dismiss count II is denied.]

PRO BONO SERVICES

All attorneys
- have a professional responsibility to provide legal services to persons who are unable to pay, and
- should try to meet the goal of providing a minimum of 50 hours of pro bono services a year at no fee or at a substantially reduced fee.

Model Rule 6.1

Attorneys have an ethical obligation to provide **pro bono** services. Pro bono services are provided free or at a substantially reduced rate. Pro bono is an abbreviated form of the phrase *pro bono publico* (for the public good). The ethics codes of all bar associations suggest (and a few require) attorneys to perform a designated number of pro bono hours per year. The American Bar Association recommends fifty hours.

Paralegal Perspective:

- Many paralegals provide pro bono paralegal services in offices throughout the country such as legal aid offices and domestic-violence clinics. The work is usually done in the evening or on weekends. To find pro bono programs for attorneys and paralegals in your state, run this search in Google, Bing, or Yahoo: pro bono law aa (substituting the name of your state for "aa").
- As we saw in Chapter 4, the Limited License Legal Technician (LLLT) in Washington State is required to complete at least twenty hours of pro bono work. In most states, however, traditional and independent paralegals are not required to do pro bono work as a condition of employment. Yet all paralegal associations strongly urge such work. Here, for example, is what the Kentucky Paralegal Association says to paralegals:

  A paralegal should voluntarily donate paralegal service as a matter of public service. Paralegals are encouraged to donate 25 hours of service a year. Donated service must be performed under the supervision of a lawyer.[45]

pro bono Concerning or involving legal services that are provided for the public good (pro bono publico, shortened to *pro bono*) without fee or compensation. Sometimes also applied to services given at a reduced rate.

WITHDRAWAL

Attorneys are not required to take every case. Furthermore, once they begin a case, they are not obligated to stay with the client until the case is over. If, however, the case has already begun in court after the attorney has filed a **notice of appearance**, withdrawal is usually improper without the permission of the court.

We need to distinguish between mandatory withdrawal (when the attorney must end the attorney-client relationship) and permissive withdrawal (when the attorney is allowed the end the relationship without violating ethical rules).

notice of appearance A formal notification to a court by an attorney that he or she is representing a party in the litigation.

MANDATORY WITHDRAWAL

An attorney *must* end the attorney-client relationship (must withdraw) from a case:
- if the client fires the attorney,
- if continuing on the case violates ethical rules or other laws, or
- if competent representation is jeopardized because of the attorney's physical or mental health.

Withdrawal for these reasons is required unless a court or other tribunal orders the attorney not to withdraw. Model Rule 1.16

In some circumstances, an attorney *must* withdraw from a case that has begun:

- The client fires the attorney. An attorney is an agent of the client. Clients are always free to dismiss their agents.
- Representation of the client would violate ethical rules, e.g., the attorney discovers that he or she has a conflict of interest with the client that cannot be **cured** or remedied even with the consent of the client.
- Representation of the client would violate the law, e.g., the client insists that the attorney provide advice on how to defraud the IRS.
- The attorney's physical or mental health has deteriorated to the point where the attorney's ability to represent the client has been materially impaired. This may be due to alcohol or drug abuse, marital problems, etc.

cured Corrected. Removed a legal defect or error.

PERMISSIVE WITHDRAWAL

- An attorney is allowed to withdraw from a case for any reason if the withdrawal will not harm the client, meaning that withdrawal will not have a material adverse effect on the client.
- If the client would be harmed by the attorney's withdrawal, the attorney can still end the attorney-client relationship (and withdraw from the case) if the attorney has good cause for doing so. Good cause can include the following:
  - The attorney is in fundamental disagreement with the client.
  - The attorney believes the client is acting in a repugnant way.
  - The client has used the attorney's services to commit a crime or fraud.
  - The client has not paid the attorney after being warned that continued nonpayment will result in the attorney's withdrawal. Model Rule 1.16

Attorneys are allowed to change their mind about representing a client even if the representation has begun. They can withdraw so long as a withdrawal would not harm the client. Examples of withdrawal that would harm a client is an attorney who abruptly withdraws on the eve of an important hearing or on the day before the client's cause of action dies because of the expiration of the statute of limitations. It would undoubtedly be burdensome (and probably expensive) for the client to be able to find another attorney on such short notice.

good cause A legally sufficient ground. A justifiable reason. Also called *cause, just cause, sufficient cause.*

If there is a danger that withdrawal would harm a client, the attorney cannot withdraw unless **good cause** is shown. Examples of good cause include fundamental disagreements with the client; repugnant conduct by the client; using the attorney's services for criminal or fraudulent purposes, and financial problems caused by the nonpayment of fees by the client.

LETTER OF DISENGAGEMENT

letter of disengagement A letter sent to a client formally notifying him or her that the law office will no longer be representing the client.

When withdrawal is allowed, the attorney should send the client a **letter of disengagement** (also called, pejoratively, a "kiss-off" letter). It formally notifies the client that the attorney will no longer be representing the client. The letter confirms the termination of the attorney-client relationship. It should state:

- That the attorney-client relationship has ended
- The reason for the attorney is withdrawing
- A summary of the scope of the representation that was attempted
- A statement of the disposition of funds, if any, remaining in the client's account
- A statement of the right of the client to his or her file and how to obtain it
- A recommendation that alternative counsel be obtained as soon as possible

Paralegal Perspective:

- When you have a close working relationship with an attorney, particularly in a small law office, you become aware of his or her professional strengths and personal weaknesses. Bar associations around the country are becoming increasingly concerned about the *impaired* attorney, someone who is not functioning properly due to substance abuse or similar problems. A paralegal with such an attorney for a supervisor is obviously in a predicament. Seemingly small problems have the potential of turning into a crisis. If it is not practical to discuss the situation directly with the attorney involved, you need to seek the advice of others in the office and of other paralegals, particularly members of the local paralegal association.

APPEARANCE OF IMPROPRIETY

How would you feel if you were told that you have not done anything improper, but you are still going to be punished because what you did *appeared* to be improper? That would be the effect of an obligation to avoid even the appearance of professional impropriety. In most states, it was once unethical for attorneys to engage in such appearances. The ABA Model Rules, however, does not list appearance of impropriety as an independent basis for determining unethical conduct. (The ABA Model Code *did* have an appearance rule.) To be disciplined in states that have adopted the Model Rules, an attorney must violate one of the specific ethical rules. Yet even in these states, conservative attorneys are as worried about apparent impropriety as they are about specific, actual impropriety.

Paralegal Perspective

■ In Florida, all Florida Registered Paralegals are told to avoid the appearance of impropriety.

Appearance of Impropriety or Unethical Conduct. A Florida Registered Paralegal should understand the attorney's Rules of Professional Conduct and this code in order to avoid any action that would involve the attorney in a violation of the rules or give the appearance of professional impropriety. It is the obligation of the Florida Registered Paralegal to avoid conduct that would cause the lawyer to be unethical or even appear to be unethical, and loyalty to the lawyer is incumbent upon the Florida Registered Paralegal.[46]

UNAUTHORIZED PRACTICE OF LAW (UPL)

An attorney shall not assist a nonattorney in the unauthorized practice of law (UPL). Rule 5.5

In Chapter 4, we saw that it is a crime in most states for a nonattorney to engage in the *unauthorized practice of law (UPL)*. Our main focus in Chapter 4 was the nonattorney who works for an office other than a traditional law office. An example would be a document service provider (DSP) who owns a do-it-yourself divorce office that sells kits and typing services. Here in Chapter 5, our focus is the paralegal or other nonattorney who works under the supervision of an attorney in a law office. We want to explore the ways in which an attorney might be charged with assisting his or her own paralegal in engaging in UPL because the attorney:

■ Fails to supervise the tasks delegated to a paralegal
■ Fails to prevent a paralegal from giving advice
■ Allows a paralegal to conduct a deposition
■ Allows a paralegal to sign a court document

These and related areas will be discussed below along with an overview of other major ethical issues involving paralegals.

PARALEGALS

Throughout the chapter thus far, we have covered ethical duties involving paralegals in the "Paralegal Perspectives" on the main ethical rules governing attorneys:

■ Maintaining competence
■ Proper fees
■ Misconduct
■ Breaches of confidentiality
■ Conflicts of interest
■ Communication with the other side
■ Solicitation
■ Payment for referrals
■ Reporting misconduct
■ Unauthorized practice of law, etc.

Here we present a more direct treatment of when attorneys can be disciplined for the unethical use of paralegals. We will cover the following topics:

■ Paralegals, the ABA Model Code, and the ABA Model Rules
■ Paralegals and ethics codes in your state
■ Identification of a paralegal's status
■ Doing what only attorneys can do
■ Kinds of supervision
■ Supervision and the independent paralegal

ABA MODEL CODE

The first major statement by the American Bar Association on the ethical use of paralegals by attorneys came in its *Model Code of Professional Responsibility*. (As we saw earlier in Exhibit 5-4, the *Model Code* is an earlier edition of the ABA's *Model Rules of Professional Conduct*.) Here is what the *Model Code* said about nonattorneys in DR (disciplinary rule) 3-101, in EC (ethical consideration) 3-6, and in ABA Formal Opinion 316:

- **DR 3-101(A)**: A lawyer shall not aid a nonlawyer in the unauthorized practice of law.
- **EC 3-6**: A lawyer often delegates tasks to clerks, secretaries, and other laypersons. Such delegation is proper if [three conditions are met]. The lawyer must:
  - maintain a direct relationship with the client,
  - supervise the delegated work, and
  - have complete professional responsibility for the work product.

  This delegation enables a lawyer to render legal services more economically and efficiently.

- **Formal Opinion 316** (American Bar Association, 1967)

  Lawyers can hire paralegals and other nonattorneys to perform any task in a law office except the following three tasks:
  - Counsel clients on legal matters
  - Engage directly in the practice of law
  - Make court appearances

  The attorney must vouch for the paralegal's work to the client and become "responsible for it to the client." The nonattorney must "not do things that lawyers may not do or do the things that lawyers only may do."

ABA MODEL RULES (RULE 5.3)

The Model Rules are more explicit than the Model Code on the ethical duties of attorneys when they use paralegals.

Example: The law firm of Adams & Adams represents Harold Thompson in his breach-of-contract suit against Parker Co. At the firm, Elaine Stanton, Esq. works on the case with Peter Vons, a paralegal she supervises. Peter neglects to file an important pleading in court and carelessly gives confidential information about Thompson to the lawyer representing Parker. All of this causes Thompson great damage.

Under what circumstances can Elaine Stanton be reprimanded, suspended, or disbarred because of what her paralegal did? To answer this question, we turn to **Model Rule 5.3** (see Exhibit 5-11).

> **Model Rule 5.3** The rule in the ABA *Model Rules of Professional Conduct* governing the responsibility of different categories of attorneys for the conduct of paralegals and other nonattorney assistants in a law office.

Exhibit 5-11	Model Rule 5.3

Rule 5.3 in Model Rules of Professional Conduct
Responsibilities Regarding Nonlawyer Assistance

With respect to a nonlawyer employed or retained by or associated with a lawyer:

(a) a partner, and a lawyer who individually or together with other lawyers possesses comparable managerial authority in a law firm shall make *reasonable efforts* to ensure that the firm has in effect measures giving *reasonable assurance* that the person's conduct is compatible with the professional obligations of the lawyer;

(b) a lawyer having direct supervisory authority over the nonlawyer shall make *reasonable efforts* to ensure that the person's conduct is compatible with the professional obligations of the lawyer; and

(c) a lawyer shall be responsible for conduct of such a person that would be a violation of the Rules of Professional Conduct if engaged in by a lawyer if:

(1) the lawyer *orders* or, with the knowledge of the specific conduct, *ratifies* the conduct involved; or

(2) the lawyer is a partner or has comparable managerial authority in the law firm in which the person is employed, or has direct supervisory authority over the person, and *knows* of the conduct at a time when its consequences can be avoided or mitigated but fails to take *reasonable remedial action*.

Comment on Rule 5.3:

Lawyers generally employ assistants in their practice, including secretaries, investigators, law student interns, and paraprofessionals. Such assistants, whether employees or independent contractors, act for the lawyer in rendition of the lawyer's professional services. A lawyer must give such assistants *appropriate instruction and supervision* concerning the ethical aspects of their employment, particularly regarding the obligation not to disclose information relating to representation of the client, and should be responsible for their work product. The measures employed in supervising nonlawyers should take account of the fact that they do not have legal [law school] training and are not subject to professional discipline.... When retaining or directing a nonlawyer outside the firm [e.g., an investigator or independent paralegal], a lawyer should communicate directions appropriate under the circumstances to give *reasonable assurance* that the nonlawyer's conduct is compatible with the professional obligations of the lawyer. [Emphasis added.]

The first line of Rule 5.3 tells us which nonlawyers are covered by the rule:

- nonlawyers "employed" by a lawyer
- nonlawyers "retained" by a lawyer
- nonlawyers "associated" with a lawyer

Employed nonlawyers are **traditional paralegals** who are salaried employees of the firm. A *retained* nonlawyer can be an **independent contractor**, such as an independent paralegal, who works on a contract basis for the firm. An *associated* nonlawyer could be an intern who volunteers at the office. (Note, however, that nonlawyers cannot be called *associates*, as we will see.)

Next, 5.3 lays out the different responsibilities of three different categories of lawyers in the firm. All lawyers are not judged by the same ethical standard. Here are the three categories of lawyers in the rule:

- A lawyer who runs the firm. This can be a partner or a lawyer with managerial authority that is comparable to that of a partner. See 5.3(a) and 5.3(c)(2).
- A lawyer with direct supervisory authority over the paralegal. See 5.3(b) and 5.3(c)(2).
- Any lawyer in the firm. See 5.3(c)(1). Because 5.3(c)(1) does not qualify a category of lawyer, 5.3(c)(1) refers to all lawyers in the office—partners, managing lawyers, supervising lawyers, and every other lawyer in the firm.

Let's analyze 5.3 in detail by applying it to Elaine Stanton, Esq., and Peter Vons in our example of Harold Thomson's suit against Parker Co.. Our analysis will cover the three categories of lawyers in the rule in the order in which they are treated in the rule.

- **Lawyers Who Run the Firm (Partners and Other Managers): Rule 5.3(a)**

  Section (a) of Rule 5.3 gives us the ethical obligation of a partner or other manager. We need to know whether Elaine Stanton is a partner in the firm or is an attorney with managerial responsibilities that are comparable to those of a partner. If so, she has an ethical obligation under Rule 5.3(a) to

  "make reasonable efforts to ensure that the firm has in effect measures giving reasonable assurance" that the paralegal's conduct "is compatible with the professional obligations of the lawyer."

Hence a partner (or comparable manager) who is not supervising a paralegal cannot completely ignore office paralegals in the hope that someone else in the firm is monitoring them. Reasonable steps must be taken by every partner (or comparable manager) to establish a *system of safeguards*. This system is what is meant in 5.3(a) by "measures" that must be taken. The rule does not specify what measures must be taken. Here are some possible examples:

- Make sure that all paralegals in the firm are aware of the ethical rules governing attorneys in the state. Issue a firm-wide requirement that all paralegals must sign a statement that they have read the rules.
- Make sure that all paralegals in the firm are aware of the importance of deadlines in the practice of law and of the necessity of using paper or computer date-reminder (**tickler**) techniques. Ask another lawyer or a legal administrator in the office to let you know when every paralegal in the office has completed a brief in-house course on the tickler systems used by the office.

Because we don't have enough facts in our Elaine Stanton/Peter Vons example to determine who are the partners/managers at Adams & Adams and what reasonable measures they took or failed to take, we cannot at this time determine whether 5.3(a) was violated. We need more facts.

- **Lawyers with Direct Supervisory Authority over the Paralegal: Rule 5.3(b)**

  Next, Rule 5.3(b) gives us the ethical obligation of a lawyer who has direct supervisory responsibility over the paralegal. Such a lawyer must make

  "reasonable efforts to ensure" that the paralegal's conduct is "compatible with the professional obligations of the lawyer."

Peter Vons is supervised by Elaine Stanton, Esq., who, therefore, has "direct supervisory authority" over Peter.

traditional paralegals A paralegal who is an employee of an attorney.

independent contractor, A self-employed person who operates his or her own business and contracts to perform services for others. In general, the latter do not control many of the administrative details of how the work is performed.

tickler A paper or computer system designed to provide reminders of important dates. Also called a *come-up system.*

Assume that Stanton is charged with a violation of 5.3(b) because her paralegal, Peter, failed to file an important pleading in court (relevant to the ethical issue of competence) and disclosed information about a client (relevant to the ethical duty of confidentiality). At Stanton's disciplinary hearing, she would be asked a large number of questions about how she supervised Peter. For example:

- How do you assign tasks to Peter?
- How do you know if he is capable of handling an assignment?
- How often do you meet with him after you give him an assignment?
- How do you know if he is having difficulty completing an assignment?
- Has he made mistakes in the past? If so, how have you handled them?
- Why didn't you prevent the late filing by Peter?
- Why weren't you able to prevent Peter from disclosing confidential information about the Thompson case?

In addition, Peter might be questioned by an investigator from the disciplinary board or called as a witness in Stanton's disciplinary hearing. Peter could be asked questions such as these:

- How long have you worked for Elaine Stanton?
- Why didn't you file the court document on time? Explain what happened.
- Describe the circumstances under which you revealed confidential information to the opponent in the Thompson case.
- How were you trained as a paralegal? What legal courses did you take in school? How was ethics covered?
- What kinds of assignments have you handled in your paralegal career?
- How does Elaine Stanton evaluate your work?
- What do you do if you have a question on an assignment but she is not available in the office?

The purpose of asking these questions of Stanton and of Peter is to find out if 5.3(b) applies. The disciplinary body must determine if Stanton complied with her duty to make "reasonable efforts" to ensure that Peter did not violate ethical standards. Note that lawyer supervisors (as well as partners and managers) do not have to guarantee that a paralegal will act ethically. They simply have to "make reasonable efforts" that this will occur. The preceding questions are relevant to whether Stanton exerted such efforts with respect to Peter. The answers will help determine whether Stanton violated 5.3(b).

Note also that Peter himself is not subject to discipline by the body investigating Stanton. The Model Rules apply to attorneys. Peter is being questioned in order to decide whether Stanton should be disciplined. Peter might be fired by Adams & Adams. If he acted negligently, he might be sued by a client (see Chapter 4). If he engaged in the unauthorized practice of law, he might be prosecuted (see Chapter 4). He cannot, however, be sanctioned by the disciplinary body investigating attorneys at Adams & Adams.

■ Any Lawyer in the Firm Who Orders or Ratifies the Misconduct: Rule 5.3(c)(1)

ratify (1) To adopt or confirm a prior act or transaction, making one bound by it. (2) To give formal approval.

Under Rule 5.3(c)(1), any lawyer in the firm who "orders" the paralegal to commit the wrongdoing in question is ethically responsible for that conduct. The same is true if any attorney "**ratifies**" (that is, approves or endorses) the wrongdoing after the paralegal commits it. There is no indication in the example that Elaine Stanton or any other lawyer at Adams & Adams told (ordered) Peter not to file the important pleading in court or told (ordered) him to give confidential information about Thompson to the other side. Nor is there any indication that any lawyer at Adams & Adams approved of (ratified) Peter's conduct after it occurred. On the facts that we have, therefore, Rule 5.3(c)(1) does not apply.

■ Lawyers Who Run the Firm (Partners or Other Managers) and Lawyers with Direct Supervisory Authority: Rule 5.3(c)(2)

remedial Corrective; intending to correct. (See glossary for an additional meaning.)

Finally Rule 5.3(c)(2) returns to the duty of lawyers who are partners, managers, and supervisors. This section of the rule applies if one of these lawyers "knows" of the paralegal's misconduct at a time when its consequences can be "avoided or mitigated" but fails to take reasonable "**remedial**" (corrective) action to do so. There is no indication in our example that

Elaine Stanton (or any other lawyer in the firm) knew that Peter Vons was going to neglect to file the pleading or that he was going to reveal confidential information. Hence, the lawyers could not take corrective (remedial) steps to avoid what Peter did. Nor do the facts indicate what they could have done to lessen the damage (mitigate) once it occurred. On the facts that we have, therefore, Rule 5.3(c)(2) does not apply.

ETHICS CODE IN YOUR STATE

Every state has a Rule 5.3 (or an equivalent) in its ethics code governing attorneys. (For your state, see Appendix D.) In addition, the paralegal codes and guidelines outlined in Exhibit 5-4 have provisions covering what Peter Vons did in our example. See also Appendix B for links to the paralegal and bar associations that have published these codes and guidelines.

We turn now to other paralegal conduct that can result in ethics trouble for supervising attorneys and their paralegals.

IDENTIFICATION OF PARALEGAL STATUS

A paralegal's status as a nonattorney must be clear to everyone with whom the paralegal comes in contact. To learn how to avoid a misrepresentation of status, intentionally or accidentally, we will examine the following issues:

- Titles
- Disbarred or suspended attorneys as paralegals
- Disclosure of status
- Business cards

- Letterheads
- Websites
- Signature on correspondence
- Name on court documents

- *What Titles Can Be Used?*   Titles must make clear that the individual is a nonattorney. The main titles used in the field are *paralegal* and *legal assistant.* Variations include titles such as paralegal coordinator, senior paralegal, and probate paralegal. These titles are sufficiently clear. There is little danger that someone would think that a person with these titles is an attorney. A few states, however, have restrictions on who can use these titles. In California, for example, the titles can be used only by individuals who work under the supervision of attorneys (and meet specified educational requirements). (See Chapters 1 and 4.) A few other states (e.g., Maine, South Dakota, and Florida) impose similar title restrictions.

  A paralegal should not be called an associate or paralegal associate. The common understanding is that an associate is an attorney.

  As we have seen, special laws have created unique terminology for document service providers (DSPs) who provide services to the public without attorney supervision, e.g., bankruptcy petition preparer (BBP), legal document assistant (LDA), legal document preparer (LDP), and limited license legal technician (LLLT). These titles can be used by persons who meet the requirements for their use.

- *Can a Disbarred or Suspended Attorney Be Called, and Function As, a Paralegal?*   When attorneys have been disbarred or suspended from the practice of law for ethical improprieties, they may try to continue to work in the law as paralegals for attorneys willing to hire them. Some states will not allow this because it shows disrespect for the court that disciplined the attorney and because the individual is highly likely to engage in the practice of law by going beyond paralegal duties. Other states are more lenient but might impose other restrictions, such as not allowing a disbarred or suspended attorney to have any client contact while working as a paralegal. See Appendix D for restrictions, if any, in your state.

- *Should Paralegals Disclose Their Nonattorney Status to Clients, Attorneys, Government Officials, and the General Public?*   Yes, this disclosure is necessary. Compare the following communications by a paralegal:
  - "I work with Ward Brown at Brown & Tams."
  - "I'm from Brown & Tams."
  - "I am a paralegal."
  - "I am a legal assistant."
  - "I am not an attorney."

The fifth statement is the clearest expression of nonattorney status. The first two statements are unacceptable because you have said nothing about your status. For most contacts, the third and fourth statements (paralegal, legal assistant) will be ethically sufficient to avoid any misunderstanding about your nonattorney status. Yet some members of the public may be confused about what a paralegal or legal assistant is. If there is any possibility of doubt, use the magic words "I am not an attorney." Do not assume that a person with whom you come in contact for the first time knows you are not an attorney; the safest course is to assume the opposite.

■ *May a Paralegal Have a Business Card?*   Yes. Every state allows paralegals to have their own business cards if their title is also printed on the card so that their nonattorney status is clear and if the card is not used for unethical solicitation. At one time, some states wanted the word *nonlawyer* or *nonattorney* used along with the paralegal's office title. This is rarely required today.

Because paralegals are not allowed to solicit business for their employer, the card may not be used for this purpose. A paralegal's card can include the name and address of the law office where the paralegal works, but the primary focus of the card must be to identify the paralegal rather than the employer.

■ *May the Letterhead of Law-Office Stationery Print the Name of a Paralegal?*   States differ in their answer to this question, although most now agree that nonattorney names can be printed on law-office letterhead if their title is also printed so that their nonattorney status is clear. (See Exhibit 5-12.) Before 1977, almost no state allowed attorney stationery to print the names of nonattorney employees. The concern was that the letterhead would be used as a form of advertising by packing it with names and titles to make the office look impressive. This concern evaporated in 1977, however, when the Supreme Court held in *Bates v. State Bar of Arizona* that a state could not ban all forms of attorney advertising.[47] After this date, most states withdrew their objection to the printing of paralegal names on attorney letterhead as long as no one would be misled into thinking that the paralegals were attorneys. In Michigan, it was recommended, but not required, that attorney and nonattorney names be printed on different sides of the stationery to "enhance the clarification that the paraprofessional is not licensed to practice law."[48] A few states adhere to the old view that only attorney names can be printed on law office letterhead. Yet, to the extent that this view is still based on a prohibition of attorney advertising, it is subject to challenge.

Though ethically permissible in most states, it should be pointed out that not many law firms in the country print nonattorney names on their law office letterhead.

■ *May the Website of the Law Office List the Names and Qualifications of the Paralegals in the Office?*   Yes. The same reasons that permit paralegal names to be printed on office stationery apply to listing paralegal names and qualifications on law-office websites.

Exhibit 5-12	Example of Law Firm Letterhead with Paralegal Name

HOLLAND & HART LLP
ATTORNEYS AT LAW

DENVER • ASPEN	SUITE 3200	TELEPHONE (303) 295-8000
BOULDER • COLORADO SPRINGS	555 SEVENTEENTH STREET	FACSIMILE (303) 295-8261
DENVER TECH CENTER	DENVER, COLORADO 80202-3979	www.hollandhart.com
BILLINGS • BOISE	MAILING ADDRESS	
CHEYENNE • JACKSON HOLE	P.O. BOX 8749	CAROL J. LEFFLER
SALT LAKE CITY	DENVER, COLORADO 80201-8749	PARALEGAL
WASHINGTON, D.C.		(303) 295-8551
		(303) 713-6223 Fax
		cleffler@hollandhart.com

Courtesy of Holland and Hart LLP.

■ *May a Paralegal Write and Sign Letters on Attorney Stationery?*   There is never an ethical problem with a paralegal writing a letter that will be reviewed and signed by an attorney. Suppose, however, that the attorney wants the paralegal to sign his or her own name to the letter. Most states will permit this if certain conditions are met. For example, a title must be used that indicates the signer's nonattorney status, and the letter must not give legal advice.

We saw in Chapter 4 that paralegals who pass paralegal certification exams are entitled to use the letters that indicate their achievement: CLA, CP, CRP, PP. (See Exhibits 4-9 and 4-10 in Chapter 4.) In most states, however, it would not be appropriate to use these letters alone:

David Johnson, CP   Mary Adams, CRP   Karen Vickers, PP

The general public would not understand what these letters mean, or worse, might think they are attorneys. Hence a title should be used along with the letters:

David Johnson, CP   Mary Adams, CRP   Karen Vickers, PP
Certified Paralegal   CORE Registered Paralegal   Paralegal

In most states, there are no limitations on the persons to whom a paralegal can send letters. Yet, in a few states only an attorney can sign a letter to a client, to an opposing attorney, or to a court. This is an extreme position. So long as the paralegal's nonattorney status is clear, legal advice is not given, and an attorney is supervising the paralegal, restrictions on who can be the recipient of a paralegal-signed letter make little sense. Most states impose no such restrictions.

■ *May an Attorney Print the Name of a Paralegal on a Court Document?*   Occasionally, an attorney may want to print on a document the name of a paralegal who worked on the document *in addition* to the attorney's name and signature. The attorney may simply want to give a measure of recognition to the efforts of this paralegal. Most states permit this as long as there is no misunderstanding as to the paralegal's nonattorney status and no attempt is made to substitute a nonattorney's signature for an attorney's signature.

DOING WHAT ONLY ATTORNEYS CAN DO

There are limitations on what attorneys can ask their paralegals to do. The failure to abide by these limits might subject the attorney to a charge of unethically assisting a nonattorney to engage in the unauthorized practice of law (UPL). The areas we need to examine are as follows:

- Signing court documents
- Legal advice
- Nonlegal advice
- Drafting documents
- Real estate closings
- Depositions

- Executions of wills
- Settlement negotiations
- Court appearances
- Counsel's table
- Administrative hearings
- References to "my client"

■ *May a Paralegal Sign a Court Document?*   We need to separate the question of when paralegals can sign their own name on court documents and when they can sign their attorney's name on them. In most states, the answer to the first question is never. Formal documents that are required in litigation (e.g., **appellate brief, memorandum of law** supporting a motion, or a **pleading** such as a **complaint**) must be signed by an attorney representing a party in the dispute. With rare exceptions, the document cannot be signed by a nonattorney, no matter how minor the formal document may be. In most states, a paralegal can sign a letter on a routine matter to a clerk or other nonjudge, but formal litigation documents require an attorney's signature.

The answer to the second question (can a paralegal sign an attorney's name on a court document) is *almost never*. Of course, a paralegal should never sign someone else's name without authorization. Under limited circumstances, however, a small minority of states authorize nonattorneys to sign an attorney's name on correspondence or pleadings. Missouri,

appellate brief A document that a party files with an appellate court (and serves on an opponent) in which the party presents arguments on why the appellate court should affirm (approve), reverse, vacate (cancel), or otherwise modify what a lower court has done.

memorandum of law A written explanation of how one or more rules might apply to the facts of a client's case. Also called *memo, legal memorandum.* The plural is *memoranda.*

pleading A formal litigation document filed by a party that states or responds to the claims and defenses the parties have against each other. The major pleadings are the complaint and answer.

complaint (1) A plaintiff's first pleading, stating a cause of action against the defendant. Also called *petition.* (2) A formal criminal charge.

for example, allows paralegals to sign an attorney's name on a document if (1) the attorney supervised the production and content of the document, and (2) the paralegal indicates that he or she is signing the attorney's name, such as by placing the paralegal's initials next to the signature.[49]

legal advice A statement or conclusion that applies the law or legal principles to the facts of a specific person's legal problem.

■ *May a Paralegal Give Legal Advice?*   Attorneys use their skills in the practice of law to help clients solve legal problems. Giving them **legal advice** is perhaps the most important of these skills. Legal advice is a statement or conclusion that applies laws or legal principles to the facts of a specific person's legal problem. (See the discussion in Chapter 4 on the distinction between legal advice and legal information.) Attorneys who permit their paralegal to give legal advice (or who fail to take the steps required by Model Rule 5.3 to prevent paralegals from giving such advice) are aiding the paralegal in the unauthorized practice of law (UPL)—and hence are acting unethically.

A number of paralegals have pointed out how easy it is to fall into the trap of giving legal advice:

- Paralegals should be alert to all casual questions (because your answers might be interpreted as legal advice).[50]
- Most of us are aware of the obvious, but we need to keep in mind that sometimes the most innocent comment could be construed as legal advice.[51]
- A...typical scenario, particularly in a small law office where paralegals have a great deal of direct client contact, is that the clients themselves will coax you to answer questions about the procedures involved in their cases, and lead you into areas where you would be giving them legal advice. Sometimes this is done innocently because the attorney is unavailable and they are genuinely unaware of the difference between what you can do for them and what their legal counsel [must] do... They will press you for projections, strategy, applicable precedents—in short, legal advice. Sometimes you are placed in situations where you are not adequately supervised and your own expertise may be such that you know more about the specialized area of law than the attorney.... We have all walked the thin line between assisting in the provision of legal services and actually practicing law.[52]

The consequences of giving legal advice in these situations can be serious. In addition to the sanctions against supervising attorneys described in Exhibit 5-3, insurance problems may exist. Suppose a client sues and alleges that the firm's paralegal gave legal advice. Will the firm's malpractice insurance policy cover this suit? No, according to the General Counsel of the Mississippi Bar Association. "No available insurance policy will cover judgments resulting from a civil suit brought by an angry client based on the theory that a paralegal gave the client legal advice. In fact, if the paralegal gives legal advice, the predominant rule is that coverage is void for such act. Therefore, the paralegal is warned not to give the client advice (even if the paralegal knows the answer) and even though it may be an emergency situation. Why? Giving legal advice constitutes the unauthorized practice of law, and the unauthorized practice of law is not covered."[53]

There are a number of situations, however, in which a paralegal *can* give legal advice. First, a paralegal can tell a client precisely what the attorney tells the paralegal to say, even if the message constitutes legal advice. The paralegal, however, cannot elaborate on, interpret, expand, or explain this kind of message from the attorney.

Example: Helen Vickson is a paralegal in the law office of Sam Kline, Esq. Sam says to Helen, "When the client calls, tell her that she will be in breach of contract if she fails to complete the shipment of the goods." Compare the following three scenarios:

Situation #1: When the client calls, Helen says, "Mr. Kline told me to tell you that you will be in breach of the contract if you fail to complete the shipment of the goods."

Situation #2: When the client calls, Helen says, "Mr. Kline told me to tell you that you will be in breach of the contract if you fail to complete the shipment of the goods." Helen then adds, "The buyer will be able to collect triple damages for failure to deliver."

Situation #3: When the client calls, Helen says, "Mr. Kline told me to tell you that you will be in breach of the contract if you fail to complete the shipment of the goods." The client says, "Does that mean that the buyer will be able to collect extra damages from me?" Helen answers, "Yes."

Only situation #1 is proper; Helen is merely communicating what her attorney told her to say. In situation #2, Helen has elaborated on what the attorney told her to say. The same is true in situation #3.

The second area where paralegals can give legal advice is when they are working in an area of the law where nonattorneys are authorized to represent clients, such as Social Security hearings. (See Chapters 4 and 15.) In such areas, the authorization includes the right to give legal advice.

■ *May a Paralegal Give a Client Nonlegal Advice?* Yes. An attorney may allow a paralegal to render specialized advice on scientific or technical topics. For example, a qualified paralegal can give accounting advice or financial advice. The danger is that the nonlegal advice might also contain legal advice or the client might reasonably interpret the nonlegal advice to include legal advice.

■ *May a Paralegal Draft Legal Documents?* Yes. A paralegal can draft any legal document as long as an attorney supervises and reviews the work of the paralegal. Some ethical opinions emphasize these requirements by insisting that the document must lose its separate identity as the work of a paralegal and must leave the office as the work product of an attorney. The key point is that an attorney must supervise all paralegal work, including document preparation.

■ *May a Paralegal Conduct a Real Estate Closing Alone?* All states allow a paralegal to attend a real estate **closing** with his or her attorney supervisor. States differ on whether paralegals can conduct a closing alone. Most states say they cannot. The sale of real property is finalized at the closing. Many of the events at the closing are formalities, such as signing and exchanging standard documents. Occasionally, however, some of these events turn into more substantive matters where negotiation, legal interpretation, and legal advice are involved. Hence, in only a few states, can paralegals attend *alone* and conduct the closing themselves. Chicago has one of the most liberal rules. There, paralegals can conduct the closing without the attorney-supervisor being present:

- if no legal advice is given,
- if all the documents have been prepared in advance,
- if the attorney-supervisor is available by telephone to provide help, and
- if the other attorney consents.

In some states that allow paralegals to conduct closings, their supervising attorney must be available in the same building where the closing is held.

■ *May a Paralegal Conduct a Deposition?* No. Paralegals can schedule **depositions**, can assist in preparing a witness who will be deposed (called the **deponent**), can take notes at the deposition, and can summarize deposition **transcripts**, but they cannot conduct the deposition. Asking and objecting to questions at a deposition are attorney-only functions.

■ *May a Paralegal Supervise the Execution of an Instrument?* All states allow paralegals to act as a witness to the **execution** of **instruments** such as a will, but states differ on whether paralegals can supervise the execution on their own.

■ *May a Paralegal Negotiate a Settlement?* Most negotiations involve an exchange of opinions on how the law and facts apply to the legal dispute between the parties. Only attorneys can engage in such discussions on behalf of clients. If, however, the opponent is an insurance company, a few states allow a paralegal to negotiate with a nonattorney employee of an insurance company, such as a claims adjuster.

■ *May a Paralegal Make a Court Appearance?* In the vast majority of courts, a paralegal cannot perform even minor functions in a courtroom, such as asking a judge to schedule a hearing date for an attorney. Only attorneys can act in a representative capacity before a judge. As we saw in Chapter 4, however, there are exceptions to this rule. In some specialized courts such as small claims courts, you do not have to be an attorney to represent parties. In a few courts, paralegals can appear at answer calls on behalf of their attorney. These exceptions, however, are rare.

closing The meeting in which a transaction is finalized. An example is the meeting to complete a real estate sale or other transaction. Also called *settlement*.

depositions (1) A method of discovery by which parties and their prospective witnesses are questioned by the opposing party before trial at a location other than the courtroom. (Judges are not present during depositions.) The purpose of discovery is to assist parties in trial preparation by allowing each side to uncover facts from the other side. The person questioned is called the *deponent*. (2) A post trial method of discovery by which the winning party seeks to uncover facts that will help it enforce the judgment it obtained against the losing side.

deponent A person who is questioned in a deposition.

transcripts A word-for-word account of what was said.

execution Signing a document and meeting other requirements needed to finalize the document and make it legal. (See glossary for additional meanings.)

instrument A formal written document that gives expression to or embodies a legal act or agreement, e.g., a contract, deed, will, lease, or mortgage.

■ *May a Paralegal Sit at Counsel's Table during a Trial?*   In many courts, only attorneys can sit at counsel's table during a trial. Yet, in some courts, a paralegal is allowed to sit with the attorneys if permission of the presiding judge is obtained. The paralegal does not take an active role in the trial. He or she provides general assistance for the attorney, e.g., note taking, organizing exhibits, and doing quick database searches for documents and discovery testimony if laptop computers are allowed in the courtroom and if such information is in the database. While at the table, the paralegal is sometimes said to be the **second chair**. This phrase, however, is more accurately used to refer to another attorney assisting the lead attorney, who is the "first chair."

■ *May a Paralegal Represent Clients at Administrative Hearings?*   Yes, when this is authorized at the particular state or federal administrative agency. (See Chapters 4 and 15.)

■ *Can a Paralegal Refer to "My Client?"*   Use care in your choice of pronouns. No matter how long you work on a particular case in a law office, the client is always the attorney's client. It's tempting for a paralegal in casual conversation to refer to "my client." Traditional paralegals, however, do not have clients. Paralegals are assigned to work on the cases of the attorney's clients.

KINDS OF SUPERVISION

It is difficult to overestimate the importance of attorney supervision in the arena of ethics. According to the supreme court of one state, "Without supervision, the work of the paralegal clearly constitutes the unauthorized practice of law [UPL]."[54] Almost every ethical opinion involving paralegals (and almost every attorney malpractice opinion involving paralegals) stresses the need for effective supervision. The justification for the very existence of perhaps 95 percent of paralegal activity is this supervision. Indeed, one of the main reasons many argue that paralegal licensing is not necessary is the protective cover of attorney supervision.

In a recent case, a paralegal made a serious error in failing to give proper notice on **subpoenas** that she issued. Her attorney was disciplined because of this error. "A supervising attorney … has an ethical obligation to establish appropriate procedures to ensure that those duties he or she delegates to subordinates are performed properly." In this case, the attorney "did not assure himself" that the paralegal "had adequate training nor did he adequately supervise her once he assigned her the task of issuing subpoenas."[55] The court was not persuaded by the attorney's argument that sanctions should not be imposed in view of the fact that the error was made by the paralegal and not by the attorney himself. "An attorney may not escape responsibility… by blithely saying that any shortcomings are solely the fault of his employees."[56]

What is meant by supervision? Legal and nonlegal dictionaries provide the same definition: managing, directing, controlling, guiding, and overseeing something or someone. The extremes of supervision are easy to identify. *Absentee supervision* refers to the attorney who is either never around or seldom available. Once tasks are assigned, paralegals are essentially on their own. At the other extreme is *shoulder supervision*, practiced by attorneys who are afraid to delegate. When they do get up enough courage to delegate something, they constantly look over the shoulder of the paralegal. Such attorneys suffer from *delegatitis*, the inordinate fear of letting anyone do anything for them. Both kinds of supervision are misguided.

If you work for an attorney who practices absentee supervision, the potential for disaster is high. Unsupervised or minimally supervised paralegals may not find out about errors they have made until after the errors have caused harm to clients. You may feel flattered by the confidence placed in you; you may enjoy the challenge of independence; you may be highly compensated because of your success. Yet you may be committing UPL.

Shoulder supervision, on the other hand, provides safety at the expense of practicality. Perpetual step-by-step surveillance will ultimately defeat the economy and efficiency motives that originally led the office to hire paralegals. Shoulder supervision may satisfy the ethical duty of supervision, but no ethics code requires such overkill.

Perhaps the most effective kind of supervision is "environmental" supervision, or what might be called holistic supervision. It is far broader in its reach than the immediate task delegated to a paralegal. It addresses this essential question:

What kind of law-office environment is likely to lead to a high-quality paralegal work without sacrificing economy or ethics?

second chair An assistant to the lead attorney at a trial. The assistant, usually another attorney, sits at the counsel's table in the courtroom.

subpoenas (1) To command that someone appear at a certain time and place. (2) A command to appear at a certain time and place.

The components of this kind of supervision are outlined in Exhibit 5-13. "Environmental" supervision requires *hiring* the right people, *training* those people, *assigning* appropriate tasks, *providing* needed resources, *monitoring* progress, *reviewing* the end product, and *rewarding* competence.

Exhibit 5-13	"Environmental" Supervision: The Ethical Ideal

What kind of law office environment is likely to lead to high-quality paralegal work without sacrificing economy or ethics?

1. Before paralegals are hired, the office undertakes a study of its practice in order to identify what tasks paralegals should perform and what level of ability will be required to perform those tasks.
2. As part of the job interview process, the office conducts background checks on applicants for paralegal jobs in order to ensure that competent people are hired who already have the needed skills or who are trainable so that they can acquire these skills on the job.
3. Before the paralegal is hired, the office conducts a *conflicts check* to determine whether he or she might have a conflict of interest with any clients of the office. These conflicts might result from the paralegal's prior legal work as well as from his or her family, romantic, or business connections with anyone who might oppose current clients. Once hired, a similar conflicts check is conducted for every new client or prospective client. (The same conflicts check must be conducted every time the office hires an attorney.)
4. A program of orientation and training is created to introduce paralegals to the office and to prepare them for the tasks ahead.
5. Paralegals are given a copy of the ethical rules governing attorneys in the state, special guidelines (if any) that govern an attorney's use of paralegals, and state ethical opinions (if any) that are relevant to paralegals in the practice of law. In addition to reading these rules and opinions, they are given training on the meaning of this material. (For links to such material in your state, see Appendix D.)
6. Paralegals are told what to do if they feel that an ethical problem exists. Lines of authority are identified if the paralegal needs to discuss the matter with someone other than, or in addition to, his or her immediate supervisor.
7. An attorney reviews all paralegal work. Although paralegals may be given discretion and asked to exercise judgment in the tasks assigned, this discretion and judgment are always subjected to actual attorney review. A paralegal is not reluctant to say to a busy attorney, "would you look this over when you can before it goes out?" even if this attorney is inclined to say, "I'm sure it's fine" and not check it.
8. No task is assigned that is beyond the capacity of the paralegal. Specialized instruction always accompanies tasks the paralegal has not performed before.
9. Once a task is assigned, the paralegal is told where to receive assistance if the immediate supervisor is not available.
10. For tasks that the office performs on a recurring basis, there are manuals, office procedures, checklists, or other written material available to the paralegal to explain how the tasks are performed and where samples or models can be found. If such *systems* material does not currently exist, the office plans to create it.
11. To cut down on misunderstanding, every paralegal assignment includes the following information:
    - *A specific due date.* ("Get to this when you can" is an unwise instruction.)
    - *A priority assessment.* ("Should everything else be dropped while I do this assignment?")
    - *A context.* ("How does this assignment fit into the broader picture of the case?")
    - *A financial perspective.* ("Is the time I work on this assignment billable time?")
    - *A resource perspective.* ("What resources can be used, e.g., fee-based online research?") ("What support services will be available, e.g., the secretary?")
12. At reasonable times before the due date of longer assignments, the supervisor monitors the progress of the paralegal to ensure that the work is being done professionally, accurately, and on schedule.
13. A team atmosphere exists at the office among the attorneys, paralegals, secretaries, and other employees. Everyone knows each other's functions, pressures, and potential as resources. A paralegal never feels isolated.
14. Evaluations of paralegal performance are constructive. Both the supervisor and the paralegal act on the assumption that there will always be a need and opportunity for further learning.
15. The office sends the paralegal to training seminars conducted by paralegal associations and bar associations to maintain and to increase the paralegal's skills.
16. The office conducts periodic surveys and spot checks to monitor compliance with ethical rules.
17. The office knows that an unhappy employee is prone to error. Hence the office makes sure that the work setting of the paralegal encourages personal growth and productivity. This includes matters of compensation, benefits, work space, equipment, and advancement.

Unfortunately, not all law offices practice "environmental" supervision as outlined in Exhibit 5-13. The list represents the ideal. Yet you need to know what the ideal is so that you can advocate for the conditions that will help bring it about.

SUPERVISING INDEPENDENT PARALEGALS

Thus far, our discussion on supervision has focused on the traditional paralegal who works full-time in the office of an attorney. We also need to consider the freelance or independent paralegal who works part-time as an independent contractor for one attorney or for several attorneys in different law firms. Very often this person works in his or her own office at home. (See Appendix G and Exhibit 2-2 in Chapter 2.) How can attorneys fulfill their ethical obligation to supervise such paralegals?

> **Example:** Gail Patterson is an independent paralegal who has her own freelance business. She offers paralegal services to attorneys who hire her for short-term projects, which she performs in her home office.

Attorneys who hire Gail often do not provide the same kind of supervision that they can provide to a full-time paralegal who works in their office. Suppose, for example, that Gail commits an ethical impropriety such as revealing confidential communications. Because she works in her own office, the attorney who hired her may not learn about this impropriety in time to avoid or mitigate its consequences (as required by Model Rule 5.3). Conflict of interest is another potential problem. Gail works for many different attorneys and hence many different clients of those attorneys. It is possible that she could accept work from two attorneys who are engaged in litigation against each other without either attorney knowing that the other has hired Gail on the same case. (See the earlier discussion of this problem when we covered conflict of interest and the tainted paralegal.)

What kind of supervision is needed to prevent such problems? There is no clear answer to this question. It is not enough that the attorney vouches for, and takes responsibility for, the final product submitted by the independent paralegal. Ongoing supervision is also needed under Model Rule 5.3. Furthermore, before an attorney hires an independent paralegal for a task, the attorney must inquire about the paralegal's prior and current work in order to determine whether a conflict of interest exists.

outsourcing Paying an outside company or service to perform tasks usually performed by one's own employees.

Extra ethical care is also needed by offices that are exploring the **outsourcing** of some tasks to a foreign country. Suppose, for example, that a company in India is hired to summarize (digest) a transcript of testimony from a deposition or trial. The transcript can easily be sent to India as an email attachment. Yet how can the attorney be sure that the same company is not doing work for an opponent of the attorney's client? Also, what assurances does the attorney have that the outsource office will maintain client confidentiality? In a recent case that sent shock waves throughout the professional community, a pay dispute led to a threat from a worker in an outsource firm in Pakistan to put confidential records on the Internet if the dispute was not satisfactorily resolved.[57] Extra vigilance, therefore is required in the selection and monitoring (supervision) of an outsource company.

ETHICAL CODES OF PARALEGAL ASSOCIATIONS

As indicated at the beginning of this chapter, there are no binding ethical rules published by paralegal associations. Yet the major national associations have written ethical codes that you should know about. See Exhibit 5-4 for an overview of their structure and functions. For excerpts from these codes, see Appendix E.

YOUR ETHICS OR YOUR JOB?

In this chapter, we have stressed the importance of maintaining your integrity through knowledge of and compliance with ethical rules. There may be times, however, when this is much easier said than done. First of all, you may not be sure whether an ethical violation has been or is being committed. Like so many areas of the law, ethical issues can be complex. Or consider these possibilities:

- No one seems to care about whether an ethical problem exists.
- Your supervisor appears to be the one committing the ethical impropriety.
- the entire office appears to be participating in the impropriety.

Compounding the problem is the fact that people often do not appreciate being told that they are unethical. Rather than acknowledge the fault and mend their ways, they may turn on the accuser, the one raising the fuss about ethics. (See the *Brown* case covered earlier in the discussion on whistleblowing.) Once the issue is raised, it may be very difficult to continue working in the office.

You need someone to talk to. In the best of all worlds, it will be someone in the same office. If this is not practical, consider contacting a teacher whom you trust. Paralegal associations are also an excellent source of information and support. A leader in one paralegal association offers the following advice:

> I would suggest that if the canons, discipline rules, affirmations, and codes of ethics do not supply you with a clear-cut answer to any ethical question you may have, you should draw upon the network that you have in being a member of this association. Getting the personal input of other paralegals who may have been faced with similar situations, or who have a greater knowledge through experience of our professional responsibilities, may greatly assist you in working your way through a difficult ethical situation.[58]

Of course, you must be careful not to violate client confidentiality during discussions with someone outside the office. Never mention actual client names or any specific information pertaining to a case. You can talk in hypothetical terms. For example, "an attorney working on a bankruptcy case asks a paralegal to…." Once you present facts in this sterilized fashion, you can then ask for guidance on the ethical implications of the facts.

If handled delicately, most ethical problems that bother you can be resolved without compromising anyone's integrity or job. Yet the practice of law is not substantially different from other fields of endeavor. There will be times when the clash between principle and the dollar (or egos) cannot be resolved to everyone's satisfaction. You may indeed have to make a choice between your ethics and your job.

CHAPTER SUMMARY

Ethics are the standards of behavior to which members of an occupation, profession, or other organization are expected to conform. Begin your paralegal career by committing yourself to becoming an ethical archconservative. An attorney at law is a person who engages in the practice of law. An attorney in fact is a person authorized to act in place of another, often in a business transaction. Attorneys are regulated primarily by the highest court in the state, often with the extensive involvement of the state bar association. The state legislature may also have some regulatory authority over attorneys. Sanctions for unethical conduct include disbarment, suspension, reprimand, and probation. The American Bar Association is a voluntary association of attorneys; no attorney must be a member. The ABA publishes ethical rules that the states are free to adopt, modify, or reject. The current rules of the ABA are found in its *Model Rules of Professional Conduct*. Because paralegals cannot practice law and cannot become full members of a bar association, they cannot be punished by the bar association (or other attorney regulatory body) for a violation of the ethical rules governing attorneys. Attorneys, however, can be punished if their paralegals engage in unethical conduct.

An attorney-client relationship is formed when the attorney and client expressly agree to form the relationship or when a reasonable person would believe that an agreement to provide representation exists. Limited-scope representation is allowed if the client clearly understands the limited nature of the representation. Collaborative law is an example of limited-scope representation. Attorney competence consists of the knowledge, skill, thoroughness, and preparation reasonably necessary to assist a particular client. Attorneys must act with reasonable diligence and promptness (avoiding unwarranted delay) in representing a client.

Fees must be reasonable as determined by factors such as time, labor, complexity, and what is customary. Most states require contingent fees to be in writing. Such fees are not allowed in criminal cases and in some family-law cases. Under some circumstances, attorneys in different offices can split fees. They must not, however, split the fees of particular clients with nonattorneys. Paralegal salaries, pension benefits, and bonuses can be paid out of the fees generated by the firm as long as these payments are not tied to the fees of particular clients. A paralegal fee is a fee that an attorney can collect for the nonclerical work of the attorney's paralegal. A statutory-fee case is a case applying a special statute that gives a judge authority to order the losing party to pay the winning party's attorney and paralegal fees and costs. Avoid, block billing, double billing, time padding, and task padding.

It is unethical to misrepresent your identity (pretexting) in order to gain access to someone's Web page through friending or other method of connecting. Attorneys can discuss the legal consequences of any proposed conduct of the client, but if the attorney knows that future conduct of a client would be criminal or fraudulent, the attorney must not give the client any advice or other assistance on such conduct. It is unethical to assert a frivolous claim or defense. Attorneys must not commingle general office funds (or an attorney's personal funds) with funds in client trust accounts. Attorneys must not offer false statements to a tribunal nor offer evidence known to be false. The attorney must tell the tribunal about a known case, statute, or other authority that will hurt the cause of the attorney's own client if the attorney knows that the opposing attorney has failed to tell the tribunal about this authority.

Confidential information is information related to the representation of a client whatever its source, including the fact that someone is a client. Attorneys can reveal confidential information under certain circumstances such as when the attorney reasonably believes disclosure is necessary to prevent reasonably certain death or substantial bodily harm. The attorney-client privilege protects all communications made in confidence between an attorney and client if the purpose of the communication was to obtain legal services. The attorney work-product rule provides that notes, working papers, memoranda, or similar things prepared by or for an attorney in anticipation of litigation are not discoverable by an opponent, absent a showing of substantial need. They are protected by privilege.

A conflict of interest is divided loyalties that actually or potentially harm (or disadvantage) someone who is owed undivided loyalty. An attorney's independent professional judgment might be compromised when the attorney represents parties who have adverse interests and when the attorney's personal interests interfere with the client's interest. The major categories of conflict of interest are concurrent representation; successive representation; conflict between a client's interest and a personal interests of the attorney; conflict due to inconsistent legal positions (positional conflict); conflict between a current client and a nonclient; conflict attributed to all attorneys in an office because of the actual conflict of one of the attorneys in the office (vicarious conflict); and conflict when an attorney switches jobs (migratory conflict).

Attorneys or paralegals are tainted when they contaminate an office because of a conflict of interest. Vicarious disqualification due to a job switch might be avoided by client consent or screening. If a paralegal with a conflict of interest because of a case at a former office did any work on the case at the former office, there is a conclusive or irrebuttable presumption that he or she obtained confidences and secrets about that case while there. There is also a presumption that the paralegal shared this information with his or her new firm, but this is a rebuttable presumption.

If an opposing party is represented by an attorney, the permission of the party's attorney is needed to communicate with that party concerning the subject of the case. In-person, live telephone, or real-time electronic solicitation of clients is unethical if a significant reason for the solicitation is to seek fees or other financial benefit unless the contact is with (a) another attorney or (b) someone with whom the attorney has a family, close personal, or prior professional relationship. Written, recorded, or standard (not real-time) electronic solicitation of clients is ethical unless (a) the attorney knows that the prospective client does not want to be solicited, or (b) the solicitation involves coercion, duress, or harassment. Solicitation, when permitted, must not contain untruthful or misleading statements. Attorneys may advertise in the newspaper, on television, on the Internet, or through other media as long as the advertisements are truthful and do not mislead the public such as by creating unjustified expectations of the results the attorney will be able to obtain. An attorney cannot give someone compensation, payment, or anything of value for referring business to the attorney or for recommending the attorney.

Attorneys who know that another attorney has violated the ethical rules must report this attorney to the appropriate disciplinary body if the violation is serious enough to cast substantial doubt on the attorney's honesty, trustworthiness, or fitness to practice law. Attorneys must withdraw from a case if the client fires the attorney, if continuing on the case violates ethical rules or other laws, or if competent representation is jeopardized because of the attorney's physical or mental health. Withdrawing for nonpayment of fees is an example of permissive withdrawal.

Ethical opinions, rules, or guidelines exist in almost every state on the proper use of a paralegal by an attorney. All states have adopted Model Rule 5.3 (or its equivalent), which requires a paralegal's supervising attorney to make reasonable efforts to ensure that the paralegal's conduct is compatible with the professional obligations of the attorney. The titles *paralegal* and *legal assistant* can be used because they do not mislead anyone on the person's nonattorney status.

If there is no misrepresentation of status, paralegals in most states can have their own business cards, can have their names printed on law firm letterhead, can sign most law office correspondence, can give nonlegal advice, can draft legal documents, can assist an attorney at a real estate closing, and can represent clients at agency hearings if authorized by the agency. With few exceptions, paralegals in most states cannot give legal advice, conduct a deposition, sign formal court documents, or make an appearance in court. The key to effective and ethical paralegals in a law office is "environmental" supervision by attorneys, which requires hiring the right people, training those people, assigning appropriate tasks, providing needed resources, monitoring progress, reviewing the end product, and rewarding competence.

KEY TERMS

continuing legal education
(CLE) (p. 210)
agent (p. 212)
practice of law (p. 212)
attorney in fact (p. 212)
power of attorney (p. 212)
ethics (p. 210)
sanction (p. 212)
unauthorized practice of law
(UPL) (p. 213)
integrated bar association
(p. 213)

*Model Rules of Professional
Conduct* (*MRPC*) (p. 214)
probable cause (p. 214)
multidisciplinary practice
(MDP) (p. 217)
paralegal code (p. 217)
meritorious (p. 219)
letter of nonengagement
(p. 219)
statute of limitations (p. 219)
time-barred (p. 219)
retainer (p. 219)

bundled legal services (p. 220)
pro se (p. 220)
unbundled legal services (p. 220)
collaborative law (p. 221)
alternative dispute resolution
(ADR) (p. 221)
informed consent (p. 221)
competent (p. 221)
clinical education (p. 222)
indigent (p. 222)
dilatory (p. 224)
contingent fee (p. 226)

court costs (p. 226)
minimum-fee schedule (p. 227)
antitrust law (p. 227)
fee cap (p. 227)
fee splitting (p. 228)
forwarding fee (p. 228)
fee cap (p. 227)
paralegal fee (p. 229)
overhead (p. 230)
American rule (p. 230)
statutory-fee case (p. 230)
English rule (p. 230)

contemporaneous (p. 230)
block billing (p. 230)
double billing (p. 230)
padding (p. 230)
time padding (p. 230)
task padding (p. 230)
billable hours quota (p. 231)
client security fund (p. 231)
pretexting (p. 232)
attestation clause (p. 232)
insider trading (p. 232)
pirated software (p. 232)
spoliation (p. 233)
malicious prosecution (p. 233)
abuse of process (p. 233)
adversary system (p. 234)
frivolous (p. 234)
Federal Rules of Civil
    Procedure (FRCP) (p. 234)
fiduciary (p. 234)
client trust account (p. 235)
commingling (p. 235)
material (p. 236)
confidential (p. 237)
privileged (p. 237)
attorney-client privilege (ACP)
    (p. 238)

work-product rule (p. 239)
discoverable (p. 239)
metadata (p. 242)
encrypt (p. 242)
redact (p. 242)
conflict of interest (p. 243)
legal malpractice (p. 243)
adverse (p. 244)
adverse interests (p. 244)
concurrent representation
    (p. 245)
coplaintiffs (p. 245)
codefendants (p. 245)
transactional matter (p. 245)
successive representation
    (p. 247)
overreaching (p. 248)
undue influence (p. 248)
bias (p. 250)
positional conflict (p. 250)
tainted (p. 250)
vicarious conflict (p. 251)
vicarious disqualification
    (p. 251)
imputed (p. 251)
screening (p. 251)
Chinese wall (p. 252)

quarantined (p. 253)
conclusive presumption (p. 253)
rebuttable presumption (p. 253)
career client list (p. 254)
independent paralegal (p. 255)
conflicts check (p. 255)
lateral hire (p. 256)
disinterested (p. 257)
anticontact rule (p. 257)
ex parte communication
    (p. 257)
solicitation (p. 257)
pecuniary (p. 257)
ambulance chasing (p. 258)
real time (p. 258)
barratry (p. 258)
runner (p. 258)
document service provider
    (DSP) (p. 260)
whistleblower (p. 261)
cause of action (p. 261)
wrongful discharge (p. 261)
motion to dismiss (p. 261)
at-will employee (p. 261)
public policy (p. 261)
gratuitous (p. 261)
diversity of citizenship (p. 261)

motion to dismiss (p. 261)
pro bono (p. 263)
notice of appearance (p. 263)
cured (p. 263)
good cause (p. 264)
letter of disengagement (p. 264)
Model Rule 5.3 (p. 266)
traditional paralegal (p. 267)
independent contractor (p. 267)
tickler (p. 267)
ratify (p. 268)
remedial (p. 268)
appellate brief (p. 271)
memorandum of law (p. 271)
pleading (p. 271)
complaint (p. 271)
legal advice (p. 272)
closing (p. 273)
deposition (p. 273)
deponent (p. 273)
transcript (p. 273)
execution (p. 273)
instrument (p. 273)
second chair (p. 274)
subpoena (p. 274)
outsourcing (p. 276)

ASSIGNMENTS

CRITICAL ANALYSIS

5.1

(a) Who won the paralegal whistleblower case of *Brown v. Hammond* presented in the chapter? What happens next? In the next proceeding in the case, what does the paralegal have to prove?

(b) Do you think a paralegal has an obligation to report unethical conduct? Should there be a "snitch rule"? If so, to whom should the report be made?

5.2

(a) Paul Emerson is an attorney who works at the firm of Rayburn & Rayburn. One of the firm's clients is Designs Unlimited, Inc. (DU), a clothing manufacturer. Emerson provides corporate advice to DU. Recently, Emerson made a mistake in interpreting a new securities law. As a consequence, DU had to postpone the issuance of a stock option for six months. Has Emerson acted unethically?

(b) Three individuals in Connecticut hire a large New York law firm to represent them in a proxy fight in which they are seeking control of a Connecticut bank. They lose the proxy fight. The firm then sends these individuals a $358,827 bill for 895 hours of work over a one-month period. Is this bill unethical? What further facts would you like to have to help you answer this question?

(c) Victor Adams and Len Patterson are full partners in the law firm of Adams, Patterson & Kelly. A client contacts Len Patterson to represent him on a negligence case. Patterson refers the case to Victor Adams, who does most of the work. (Under an agreement between them, Patterson will receive 40 percent and Adams will receive 60 percent of any fee paid by this client.) Patterson does not tell the client about the involvement of Adams in the case. Any ethical problems?

(d) An attorney establishes a bonus plan for her paralegals. A bonus will be given to those paralegals who bill a specified number of hours in excess of a stated minimum. The amount of the bonus will depend on the amount billed and collected. Any ethical problems?

(e) Mary works in a law firm that charges clients $225 an hour for attorney time and $100 an hour for paralegal time. She and another paralegal, Fred, are working with an attorney on a large case. She sees all of the time sheets that the three of them submit to the firm's accounting office. She suspects that the attorney is padding his time sheets by overstating the number of hours he works on the case. For example, he lists thirty hours for a four-day period when he was in court every day on another case. Furthermore, Fred's time is being billed at the full $100-an-hour rate even though he spends about 80 percent of his time typing correspondence, filing, and performing other clerical duties. Mary also suspects that her attorney is billing out Mary's time at the attorney rate rather than the paralegal rate normally charged clients for her time. Any ethical problems? What should Mary do?

(f) Vince Smith is an attorney who works at the firm of Johnson & Johnson. He represents Ralph Grant, who is seeking a divorce from his wife, Amy Grant. In their first meeting, Smith learns that Ralph is an experienced carpenter but is out of work and has very little money. Smith's fee is $250 an hour. Because Ralph has no money and has been having trouble finding work, Smith tells Ralph that he will not have to pay the fee if the court does not grant him the divorce. One day Smith learns that another of his clients, Helen Oberlin, is looking for a carpenter. Smith recommends Ralph to Helen, and she hires him for a small job. Six months pass. The divorce case is dropped when the Grants reconcile. In the meantime, Helen Oberlin is very dissatisfied with Ralph's carpentry work for her; she claims he didn't do the work he contracted to do. She wants to know what she can do about it. She tries to call Smith at Johnson & Johnson but is told that Smith does not work there anymore. Another attorney at the firm, Georgia Quinton, Esq., helps Helen. Any ethical problems?

(g) Mary Fenton is a paralegal who works for Tom Orson, Esq., a solo practitioner. Mary works extensively on workers' compensation cases. Tom has been tied up for months in a complicated mass tort case. One day a workers' compensation client calls Mary to ask whether his injury qualifies for extended benefits under the state's workers' compensation law. She puts him on hold and calls Tom during a recess of the tort trial. When she asks him the question, he replies, "I don't remember the answer to that, but it's in the code. Just check under injuries or filings and tell the client what you find. Besides, you know more about this area of law than I do." Mary does so. Any ethical problems?

(h) A paralegal quits the firm of Smith & Smith. When she leaves, she takes client documents she prepared while at the firm. The documents contain confidential client information. The paralegal is showing these documents to potential employers as writing samples. What is the ethical liability of attorneys at Smith & Smith under Model Rule 5.3?

(i) Mary is a paralegal at the ABC law firm. She has been working on the case of Jessica Randolph, a client of the office. Mary talks with Ms. Randolph often. Mary receives a subpoena from the attorney of the party that is suing Ms. Randolph. (A subpoena is a command to appear at a certain time and place. Here the subpoena was to give testimony in court.) On the witness stand, Mary is asked by this attorney what Ms. Randolph told her at the ABC law office about a particular business transaction related to the suit. Randolph's attorney (Mary's supervisor) objects to the question. Does Mary have to answer?

(j) George is a religious conservative. He works for a law firm that represents Adult Features, Inc., which runs an X-rated Internet site. The client is fighting an injunction sought by the police against its business. George is asked by his supervisor to do some research on the case. Any ethical problems?

(k) Peter is a paralegal at Smith & Smith. One of the cases he works on is Carter v. Horton. Carter is the client of Smith & Smith. Peter does some investigation and scheduling for the case. Horton is represented by Unger, Oberdorf & Simon. The Unger firm offers Peter a job working in its law library and in its computer department on database management. He takes the job. While at the Unger firm, Peter can see all the documents in the Carter v. Horton case. At lunch, a week after Peter joins the firm, he tells one of the Unger attorneys (Jack Dolan) about an investigation he conducted while working for Smith & Smith on the Carter case. (Jack is not one of the Unger attorneys working on Carter v. Horton.) Two weeks after Peter is hired, the Unger firm decides to set up a Chinese wall around Peter. He is told not to discuss Carter v. Horton with any Unger employee, all Unger employees are told not to discuss the case with Peter, the files are kept away from Peter, etc. The wall is rigidly enforced. Nevertheless, Smith & Smith makes a motion to disqualify Unger, Oberdorf & Simon from continuing to represent Horton in the Carter v. Horton case due to Peter's presence at the Unger firm. Should this motion be granted?

(l) Assume that you owned a successful freelance business in which you provided paralegal services to over 150 attorneys all over the state. How should your files be organized in order to avoid a conflict of interest?

(m) Joan is a paralegal who works for the XYZ law firm, which is representing Goff in a suit against Barnard, who is represented by the ABC law firm. Joan calls Barnard and says, "Is this the first time that you have ever been sued?" Barnard answers, "Yes it is. Is there anything else that you would like to know?" Joan says no and the conversation ends. Any ethical problems?

(n) Mary is a paralegal who is a senior citizen. She works at the XYZ legal service office. One day she goes to a senior citizens center and says the following: "All of you should know about and take advantage of the XYZ legal service office where I work. Let me give you just one example why. Down at the office there is an attorney named Armanda Morris. She is an expert on insurance company cases. Some of you may have had trouble with insurance companies that say one thing and do another. Our office is available to serve you." Any ethical problems?

(o) Sam is a paralegal in the law firm of Orsen and Jacobs. Rachel, a prospective client, calls one day. Sam answers the phone. Any ethical problems based on the following conversation?

Rachel: How much does the firm charge to take a case?

Sam: $200 an hour. What kind of a case is it?

Rachel: I was injured as a passenger in an automobile accident.

Sam: Then the firm will probably take the case on a contingency, meaning that you pay nothing unless we win.

PROJECTS

5.3 Compile a bibliography of sources covering legal ethics applicable to attorneys and paralegals in your state. The bibliography should include paper (book) resources and online resources. Include ethics codes, guidelines, opinions, treatises, articles, and related material. You can also include materials that are national in scope, but the focus of the bibliography should be legal ethics in your state. For leads, see your state in Appendix D and Helpful Websites at the end of this chapter.

CORE SKILLS

Among the many skills a paralegal must have, five core skills stand out: writing (both basic English and legal drafting), research, ethics, computer use, and collaboration (working with others). The core-skill assignments introduce and reinforce these skills. Even if you are not asked to do all of the assignments as part of the course, you should do them on your own. Also, do not wait for the topics in the assignments to be covered in this course or in other courses. Successful paralegals are self-starters. A major characteristic of a self-starter is a thirst for independent study—learning on your own.

CORE SKILL: WRITING

5.4 Run this search in Google, Bing, or Yahoo: grammar self-test. Take several free online self-tests that provide answers to the test questions after you try to answer them. Pick two areas of grammar that the tests indicate need improvement. Devise a plan on how you will work on these two areas in the coming weeks. The plan should state the online resources you will use, the amount of time per week you will spend on those resources, and how you will demonstrate to yourself that the improvement has in fact occurred.

CORE SKILL: RESEARCH

5.5 Run the search *google scholar tutorial* in any search engine. You can also run it in YouTube. Answer the following questions based on what you find:

(a) What is Google Scholar? What is its website?

(b) What kinds of materials are you able to find on Google Scholar?

(c) In Google Scholar, run the search *paralegal "conflict of interest"* to find a court opinion written by a state court in your state in which one of the issues involved paralegals and a conflict of interest. What is the citation of the case? What is the name of the judge who wrote the opinion? In what way did the opinion involve a paralegal conflict of interest?

(c) Run the same search to find two articles on paralegal conflicts of interest. What is the citation of the articles?

CORE SKILL: COMPUTERS

5.6 In Chapter 13, read the short section on spreadsheets. On Google, Bing, or Yahoo, search for key terms in the following questions to help you find the answers.

(a) What is a spreadsheet?

(b) What are the main spreadsheet applications that are sold?

(c) Which of these spreadsheet applications is the most widely used?

(d) What are the main spreadsheets available for free?

(e) Name one of the free spreadsheets that is considered to be popular.

(f) Find discussions that compare the spreadsheet you selected in question (c) with the spreadsheet you selected in question (e). What are some of the differences other than cost?

(g) In your Computer Terminology in the Law (CTL) notebook you started in Assignment 1.8 of Chapter 1, enter all new terms that you learned by doing parts (a) to (f).

CORE SKILL: COLLABORATION

5.7 Draft your own paralegal code as a class project. Use any of the material in Chapter 5 as a resource. First, have a meeting in which you make a list of all the issues that you think should be covered in the code (e.g., what job titles can be used, when a job title must be disclosed, and what tasks a paralegal can and cannot perform). Divide up the issues by the number of students in the class so that every student has roughly the same number of issues. Each student should draft a proposed rule on each of the issues to which he or she is assigned. Accompany each rule with a brief commentary on why you think the rule should be as stated. Draft alternative versions of the proposed rule if different versions are possible and you want to give the class the chance to examine all of them. The class then meets to vote on each of the proposed rules. Students will make presentations on the proposed rules they have drafted. If the class is not happy with the way in which a particular proposed rule was drafted by a student, the latter will redraft the rule for later consideration by the class. One member of the class should be designated the "code reporter," who records the rules accepted by the class by majority vote. After you have completed the code, invite attorneys from the local bar association to your class in order to discuss your proposed code. Do the same with officials of the closest paralegal association in your area.

5.8 Find one site on the Internet that pertains to any legal issue discussed in Chapter 5. It can be a recent news item or case, an ethics website, etc. The site you select should not be a site that is mentioned in Chapter 5. Tweet this site to your classmates. Your tweet should say why you selected it. Don't just tweet the cite of the site. (See Assignment 3.9 in Chapter 3 on opening a Twitter account.)

THE JOB SEARCH

(The search for employment cannot wait until the end of a course or of a curriculum. It needs to begin now. The job-search assignments are designed to introduce you to different aspects of the job search and to build options for you to explore about employment.)

5.9 Use the job links in Exhibit 2-12 in Chapter 2 to find a job opening in your state for a conflicts specialist, i.e., a person who assists a law office determine whether a prospective client would cause a conflict of interest at the office. What does the job entail and what are the qualifications for the position? Give the site address where you found this information. If no openings exist in your state, look for the position in any state. See also "19. Ethics and Professional Responsibility" in the section on paralegal specialties in Chapter 2.

REVIEW QUESTIONS

1. What are ethics?
2. Name twenty-five ethical guidelines for an archconservative paralegal.
3. What is the distinction between an attorney at law and an attorney in fact?
4. How are attorneys regulated?
5. Name three ways that an attorney can be sanctioned for aiding a nonattorney in the unauthorized practice of law (UPL).
6. Name four kinds of bar associations.
7. What is the role of the American Bar Association and its Model Rules of Professional Conduct in the regulation of attorneys?
8. What are the two kinds of ethics opinions?
9. Name four categories of attorney sanctions for unethical conduct.
10. To what extent do attorney codes of ethics apply to paralegals?
11. What is a multidisciplinary practice (MDP)?
12. What are the categories of paralegal codes?
13. When is an attorney-client relationship formed?
14. What is limited-scope representation?
15. How does a collaborative-law practice work?
16. What standard is used to determine attorney competence?
17. What is the function of clinical education and CLE?
18. What is digital competence?
19. In what ways can paralegals achieve and maintain competence?
20. What factors determine the reasonableness of an attorney's fee?
21. Why are minimum-fee schedules illegal?
22. When are contingent fees unethical?
23. When is fee splitting between attorneys allowed?
24. What is the rule on splitting fees with nonattorneys?
25. What is a paralegal fee?
26. What is a statutory-fee case?
27. What is block billing?
28. What are double billing, time padding, and task padding?
29. Give an example of insider trading by a paralegal.
30. When is it unethical for an attorney to advise a client on possible future fraud or crime?
31. Describe our adversary system.
32. What is a frivolous claim or defense?
33. What is a Rule 11 certification under the FRCP?
34. What is a client trust account?
35. Give an example of commingling.
36. When must attorneys make disclosures to a court that attorneys know will hurt their own clients?
37. What is confidential information?
38. When is an attorney allowed to disclose confidential information of clients?
39. Distinguish between the ethical duty of confidentiality and the attorney-client privilege.
40. What is the attorney work-product rule?
41. List steps paralegals can take to avoid breaching client confidentiality.
42. What is a conflict of interest?
43. In what two ways can a conflict of interest interfere with an attorney's independent professional judgment?
44. List seven major categories of conflict of interest.
45. Give four categories of an attorney's personal interests that could become conflicts of interest.
46. When is a worker tainted?
47. What are the two ways that vicarious disqualification due to a job switch might be avoided?
48. What are the components of comprehensive screening?
49. What presumptions arise when a paralegal switches jobs in conflict cases?
50. What is a career client list and how is it used?
51. How can an independent paralegal create a conflict of interest?
52. What is a conflicts check?
53. What is the anticontact rule?
54. When is client solicitation ethical and unethical?
55. When is attorney advertising ethical and unethical?
56. Can someone be paid for recommending an attorney?
57. When must one attorney report unethical conduct by another attorney?
58. What are pro bono services?
59. What is the distinction between mandatory and permissive withdrawal? Give an example of each.
60. What is an appearance of impropriety?
61. What is the unauthorized practice of law (UPL)?
62. Name four ways in which an attorney can be charged with aiding a paralegal in the unauthorized practice of law.
63. What obligation does Model Rule 5.3 place on attorneys who are direct supervisors of paralegals?
64. What obligation does Model Rule 5.3 place on partners or other managers of an office?
65. What are some of the major guidelines on what attorneys can and cannot allow their paralegals to do?
66. What are the major components of comprehensive supervision of paralegals?

HELPFUL WEBSITES

Legal Ethics Links
- www.washlaw.edu/subject/ethics.html
- lawlibguides.seattleu.edu/ethics
- www.hricik.com/StateEthics.html
- www.hg.org/practic.html
- www.law.georgetown.edu/library/research/guides/legal_ethics.cfm
- law.lexisnexis.com/infopro/zimmermans/disp.aspx?z=1623
- www.sunethics.com

State Ethics Rules
- See your state in Appendix D
- www.hricik.com/StateEthics.html
- law.lexisnexis.com/infopro/zimmermans/disp.aspx?z=1623
- www.paralegalethics.net/site/index.htm

State Ethics Opinions
- www.hricik.com/StateEthics.html
- law.lexisnexis.com/infopro/zimmermans/disp.aspx?z=1623

ABA Paralegal Guidelines
- www.americanbar.org (enter *paralegal* in the search box)

Paralegal Ethics
- paralegal-ethics.blogspot.com
- www.paralegalethics.net
- www.paralegalethics.net/site/index.htm

ABA Model Rules of Professional Conduct
- www.americanbar.org (enter *professional conduct* in the search box)

ABA Ethics Opinions
- www.americanbar.org (enter *ethics opinions* in the search box)
- law.lexisnexis.com/infopro/zimmermans/disp.aspx?z=1623

Conflicts of Interest
- www.freivogelonconflicts.com

Attorney Discipline
- www.americanbar.org (enter *Survey on Lawyer Disciplinary Systems* in the search box)
- www.americanbar.org (enter *Directory of Disciplinary Agencies* in the search box)

Attorney Discipline (Finding Out if an Attorney Has Been Disciplined)
- hirealawyer.findlaw.com/choosing-the-right-lawyer /researching-attorney-discipline.html

ABA Center for Professional Responsibility
- www.americanbar.org/groups/professional_responsibility.html

State and Local Bar Associations
- www.americanbar.org (enter *state and local bar associations* in the search box)

Judicial Ethics
- www.ajs.org

Google, Bing, or Yahoo Searches
(on these search engines, run the following searches, using quotation marks and substituting your state for "aa" where indicated)
- attorney ethics aa
- paralegal ethics aa
- "professional responsibility" attorney aa
- code of ethics attorney aa
- competence attorney aa
- attorney fees ethics aa
- "paralegal fees" ethics aa
- "fee splitting" attorney aa
- attorney misconduct attorney
- paralegal misconduct aa
- confidentiality attorney aa
- confidentiality paralegal aa
- "conflict of interest" attorney aa
- "conflict of interest" paralegal aa
- solicitation attorney aa
- "ambulance chasing" aa
- advertising attorney aa
- "unauthorized practice of law" aa
- rule 5.3 paralegal

ENDNOTES

[1] Michael Josephson quoted in *We're All in This Together*, 29 Arizona Attorney 28 (August/September 1992).

[2] R. Bruenderman, *Ethics Expert Josephson Visits Louisville*, 55 Kentucky Bench & Bar 28 (Summer 1991).

[3] In the Minnesota Conciliation Court (a small-claims court), non-attorneys are authorized to represent organizations such as businesses and universities. The document that grants this authorization is called a *power of attorney in fact*. The statute that allows nonattorney representation specifically states that the "representation does not constitute the practice of law." Minnesota Statutes Annotated, § 491A.02. For a copy of the power of attorney in fact, see www.mncourts.gov/ district/4/?page=1824.

[4] American Bar Association, Standing Committee on Ethics and Professional Responsibility, *Formal Opinion 10-457* (August 5, 2010).

[5] *ABA Model Guidelines for the Utilization of Paralegal Services*, Guideline 3 (ABA Standing Committee on Paralegals 2012).

[6] American Bar Association Standing Committee on Ethics and Professional Responsibility, *Formal Opinion 07-447* (August 9, 2007).

[7] Lawyers Mutual Liability Insurance Company of America, *Ethics for Legal Support Staff* 1 (undated) (www.lawyersmutualnc.com).

[8] State Bar of New Mexico, *Rules Governing Paralegal Services*, § 20–110, Commentary (2004).

[9] American Bar Association, *Formal Ethics Opinion 93-379* (1993).

[10] 421 U.S. 773 (1975) (To read this case online, go to scholar.google .com, select *Case law*, and type 421 U.S. 773 in the search box.)

[11] Lisa Lerman, *Scenes from a Law Firm*, 50 Rutgers Law Review 2153, 2159 (1998).

[12] Smith, *AAfPE National Conference Highlights*, 8 Legal Assistant Today 103 (January/February 1991).

[13] Sonia Chan, *ABA Formal Opinion 93-379: Double Billing, Padding and Other Forms of Overbilling*, 9 Georgetown Journal of Legal Ethics 611, 615 (1996).

[14] Tulsa Association of Legal Assistants, *Hints for Helping Your Attorney Avoid Legal Malpractice*, TALA Times (August 1989).

[15] Race, *Malpractice Maladies*, Paradigm 12 (Baltimore Association of Legal Assistants, July/August 1989).

[16] Run this search in Google, Bing, or Yahoo: Dewey LeBoeuf paralegal indictment.

[17] Shays, *Ethics for the Paralegal*, Postscript 15 (Manhattan Paralegal Association, August/September 1989).

[18] 42 U.S.C. § 1320a–7b(a)(6); seniorlaw.com/reno.htm.

[19] Jay Reeves, *How to Avoid Law License "Shrinkage"* (www .lawyersmutualnc.com) (May 1, 2012).

[20] *Phoenix Founders, Inc. v. Marshall*, 887 S.W. 2d 831, 834 (Tex. 1994).

[21] *United States v. Stewart*, 287 F. Supp. 2d 461 (S.D.N.Y. 2003). (To read this case online, go to scholar.google.com, select *Case law*, and type 287 F. Supp. 2d 461 in the search box.)

[22] Colorado Revised Statutes, § 13-90-107(1)(b)(1966).

[23] Professional Responsibility Committee of the Philadelphia Bar Association, *Professional Responsibility for Nonlawyers* (1989) (emphasis added).

[24] *Orientation Handbook for Paralegals* 2 (Lane, Powell, Moses & Miller, 1984) (emphasis added).

[25] Daniels, *Privileged Information for Paralegals*, 17 At Issue 15 (San Francisco Association of Legal Assistants, November 1990).

[26] Betty Reinert, *Cyberspacing around Cowtown*, 13 Cowtown Paralegal Reporter 10 (March/April 1995).

[27] Adam Levy, … *Demise of the Tobacco Settlement*, 2 Journal of Health Care Law and Policy 1, 9 (1998).

[28] Myron Levin, *Years of Immunity and Arrogance Up in Smoke*, Los Angeles Times, May 10, 1998, at D1, D17.

[29] *Brown & Williamson Tobacco Corp. v. Williams*, 62 F. 3d 408, 411 (D.C. Cir. 1995). (To read this case online, go to scholar.google.com, select *Case law*, and type 62 F. 3d 408 in the search box.)

[30] *New York Lawyer's Code of Professional Responsibility*, EC 2-30 (2008).

[31] *Orientation Handbook for Paralegals* 3 (Lane, Powell, Moses & Miller, 1984) (*legal assistant* changed to *paralegal* in the quote).

[32] New Mexico Rules Annotated; State Bar of New Mexico, *Rules Governing Paralegal Services*, § 20–108 (2004).

[33] *Phoenix Founders, Inc. v. Marshall*, 887 S.W.2d 831, 834 (Tex. 1994).

[34] Motamedi, *Landmark Ethics Case Takes Toll on Paralegal's Career; Family*, 7 Legal Assistant Today 39 (May/June 1990); *In re Complex Asbestos Litigation*, 232 Cal. App. 3d 572, 283 Cal. Rptr. 732 (1991). (To read this case online, go to scholar.google.com, select *Case law*, and type 232 Cal. App. 3d 572 in the search box.)

[35] M. Hall, *S.F. Decision on Paralegal Conflict May Plague Firms*, Los Angeles Daily Journal, September 25, 1989, at 1, col. 2.

[36] American Bar Association Committee on Ethics and Professional Responsibility, *Informal Opinion 88-1526* (1988).

[37] See *In re Opinion No. 24*, 128 N.J. 114, 607 A. 2d 962 (1992). (To read this case online, go to scholar.google.com, select *Case law*, and type 607 A. 2d 962 in the search box.)

[38] David Vandagriff, *Computing Your Conflicts*, 10 The Compleat Lawyer 42 (Fall 1993).

[39] New Mexico Rules Annotated; State Bar of New Mexico, *Rules Governing Paralegal Services*, § 20–104 (2004).

[40] *Health Plans Depict Lawyers as Threat*, New York Times, October 8, 1999, at A22.

[41] *Adams v. Attorney Registration...*, 801 F.2d 968, 973 (7th Cir. 1986).

[42] 49 U.S.C. § 1136 (g)(2).

[43] *Four Said to Have Used Bus Crash to Get Business for Law Firm*, New York Times, April 7, 1990, at 8.

[44] 433 U.S. 350 (1977).

[45] Kentucky Paralegal Association, *Paralegal Professional Standards of Conduct* 4 (2d ed. 2010).

[46] *Florida Registered Paralegal Program*, Rule 20-7.1.

[47] 433 U.S. 350.

[48] State Bar of Michigan, Ethics Opinion RI-34 (October 25, 1989).

[49] The Missouri Bar, *Practicing with Paralegals*, 5 (2003).

[50] Beth King, *Ethics and the Legal Assistant*, 10 ParaGram 2 (Oregon Paralegal Association, August 1987).

[51] DALA Newsletter 2 (Dallas Area Paralegal Association, December 1990).

[52] Nancy Spiegel, *How to Avoid the Unauthorized Practice of Law*, 8 The Journal 8–10 (Sacramento Valley Paralegal Association, February 1986).

[53] Michael Martz, *Ethics: Does a Legal Assistant Need Insurance?* The Assistant 13 (Mississippi Paralegal Association, Fall 1993).

[54] *In re Opinion No. 24 of Committee on Unauthorized Practice of Law*, 128 N.J. 114, 121, 607 A. 2d 962, 965 (1992).

[55] *Spencer v. Steinman*, 179 F.R.D. 484 (E.D. Pa., 1998).

[56] *Spencer*, 179 F.R.D. at 489, citing *Attorney Grievance Comm'n v. Goldberg*, 292 Md. 650, 441 A.2d 338, 341 (1982).

[57] David Lazarus, *Special Report, Outsourced UCSF Notes Highlight Privacy Risk*, San Francisco Chronicle (March 28, 2004).

[58] Harper, *Ethical Considerations for Legal Assistants*, Compendium (Orange County Paralegal Association, 1987).

CHAPTER 6

INTRODUCTION TO THE LEGAL SYSTEM

CHAPTER OUTLINE

- Our Legal System
- Introduction to Law
- Judicial Branch
- Executive Branch
- Legislative Branch

CHAPTER OBJECTIVES

After completing this chapter, you should be able to

- List the three levels of government.
- Define federalism.
- List the three branches of government and their functions.
- Explain how checks and balances work.
- Distinguish primary and secondary authority.
- Define the categories of primary authority.
- Summarize the first three articles and the Bill of Rights of the U.S. Constitution.
- Understand the effect of the Supremacy Clause.
- Explain the different meanings of common law and distinguish it from enacted law.
- Explain what is meant by the merger of law and equity.
- Describe the adversary system.
- Distinguish between the power and the geographic or territorial meanings of jurisdiction.
- Know the main categories of subject-matter jurisdiction.
- List the main categories of state and federal courts.
- Explain the different kinds of administrative agencies.
- Outline the legislative process.

OUR LEGAL SYSTEM

What are the components of our legal system and what kind of laws do they produce? These are the concerns of this chapter. We begin by examining the levels of government and the branches of government within each level.

FEDERALISM

Our legal system consists of three levels of government:

- The federal government (also called the national government and the United States government; the phrases "United States" and U.S. often mean *federal*)
- Fifty state governments (plus the District of Columbia, which is often treated like a state)
- Local governments (called counties, cities, townships, etc.)

Our primary focus will be federal and state governments. To a large extent, local governments are dependent on (even though, in many respects, they are separate from) state governments.

A division of powers exists between the federal government and state governments. Some powers are limited to one level. Only the federal government, for example, has the power to declare war, whereas only a state government has the power to issue a marriage license or a divorce decree. Some powers are shared among the levels of government. In the area of public assistance (welfare), for example, both the federal government and the state governments have major roles. The term **federalism** refers to the division of powers between the federal government and state governments. Federalism simply means that we live in a society where some powers are exercised by the federal government, others by the state governments, and still others by both the federal and the state governments.

Two concepts should be kept distinct: federal government and federal system of government. The phrase *federal government* refers to the national government in the nation's capital and in its offices throughout the various states. *Federal system* refers to federalism—the division of powers between the federal government and the state governments.

BRANCHES OF GOVERNMENT

Within the federal, state, and local levels of government, there are three *branches*:

- the branch that makes or enacts laws (**legislative branch**),
- the branch that carries out, executes, or administers laws (**executive branch**), and
- the branch that interprets laws by resolving disputes that arise under them (**judicial branch**).

Here is an overview of the three levels of government and the three branches that exist at each level:

Federal Government

- *Legislative branch*: Congress
- *Executive branch*: President and federal administrative agencies (see the chart in Appendix C)
- *Judicial branch*: U.S. Supreme Court, the U.S. courts of appeals, the U.S. district courts, and other federal courts (see Exhibits 6-4 and 6-5)

State Government

- *Legislative branch*: State legislatures
- *Executive branch*: Governor and state administrative agencies
- *Judicial branch*: State courts (see Exhibit 6-3)

Local Government

- *Legislative branch*: City council, county council, county commission, etc.
- *Executive branch*: Mayor or county commissioner and local administrative agencies
- *Judicial branch*: Local courts (some local courts, however, are considered part of the state judiciary)

CHECKS AND BALANCES

A major component of how the legislative, executive, and judicial branches of government and their laws interact is called **checks and balances**, which are designed to prevent any one branch from becoming too powerful. This occurs by allowing one branch to review, block, or otherwise check another branch so that a balance of powers is maintained among the branches. Let's look some examples.

Checks on Legislative Branch by Executive and Judicial Branches

- The chief executive must give final approval to a proposed law (called a bill) of the legislature before it can become a statute. He or she can veto (i.e., reject) the proposed law.
- The judicial branch has the power of **judicial review** whereby the courts can declare that a statute passed by the legislature is in conflict with the constitution (i.e., is unconstitutional)

federalism The division of powers between the federal government and the state governments.

legislative branch The branch of government with primary responsibility for making or enacting laws.

executive branch The branch of government with primary responsibility for carrying out, executing, or administering laws.

judicial branch The branch of government consisting of courts that have primary responsibility for interpreting laws by resolving disputes that arise under them.

checks and balances An allocation of governmental powers whereby one branch of government can block, check, or review what another branch wants to do (or has done) in order to maintain a balance of power among the legislative, executive, and judicial branches so that no one branch can dominate the other two.

judicial review (1) The power of a court to determine the constitutionality of a statute or other law. (2) The power of a court to determine the correctness of what a lower tribunal has done.

Checks on Executive Branch by Legislative and Judicial Branches

- Although the chief executive can veto a proposed law passed by the legislature, the legislature has the power to override (i.e., nullify) this veto by a two-thirds vote.
- Courts can use their power of judicial review to declare an executive order or administrative regulation to be unconstitutional. Courts can also decide whether an administrative regulation violates a statute.

Checks on the Judicial Branch by Legislative and Executive Branches

- The constitution may give the legislature the power to create new courts and to define the jurisdiction of the courts.
- The legislature must approve the budget of the courts.
- The chief executive may have the power to nominate judges, who must then be approved (confirmed) by the legislature.

The result of all such checks and counterchecks (balances) is an allocation of power among the three branches so that no one branch dominates the government.

INTRODUCTION TO LAW

A **law** is an authoritative rule written and enforced by one or more government bodies. The three branches of government write categories of law that we call primary authority.

PRIMARY AUTHORITY

Primary authority is a law written by one of the three branches of government. The most important primary authorities are constitutions, statutes, opinions, and administrative regulations. These and other categories of primary authority are defined in Exhibit 6-1. **Secondary authority** is any nonlaw that summarizes, describes, or explains the law but is not the law itself. Examples include legal encyclopedias and legal treatises. A special example of secondary authority are **opinions of the attorney general**, which consist of legal advice given by the chief law officer of the government to another government official or agency. These opinions are not primary authority. (The categories of secondary law will be covered in Exhibit 11-6 of Chapter 11.)

law An authoritative rule written and enforced by one or more government bodies.

primary authority A law written by one of the three branches of government.

secondary authority A nonlaw (e.g., a legal periodical article) that summarizes, describes, or explains the law but is not the law itself.

opinion of the attorney general Formal legal advice given by the chief law officer of the government to another government official or agency.

Exhibit 6-1	Categories of Primary Authority

Primary authority is a law written by one of the three branches of government. (Secondary authority is any nonlaw that summarizes, describes, or explains the law but is not the law itself. See Exhibit 11-6 in Chapter 11 for definitions of the major secondary authorities.)

CATEGORY OF PRIMARY AUTHORITY	DEFINITION	WHO WRITES THIS CATEGORY OF LAW?	EXAMPLE	COMMENTS
1. Opinion (also called a *judicial opinion, case,* and *decision*)	A court's written explanation of how it applied the law to the facts to resolve a legal dispute. (See the glossary for additional meanings of *opinion.*)	■ Courts—the judiciary. The vast majority of opinions are written by courts of appeal, also called appellate courts. ■ Occasionally, trial courts also write opinions.	*Miranda v. Arizona,* 384 U.S. 436 (1966). ——— This is an opinion of the U.S. Supreme Court on the rights of persons in custody.	■ Administrative agencies also write opinions, more commonly called *administrative decisions.* (See below) ■ The word *case* has two other meanings: (1) a pending matter on a court calendar and (2) a client matter handled by a law office.
2. Statute (also called *act, statutory law,* and *legislation*)	A law passed by the state or federal legislature that declares, commands, or prohibits something.	■ The legislature. ■ Some states allow the electorate to participate in the enactment of statutes (and constitutional provisions) by popular vote through the *initiative* and *referendum* process (see these terms in the glossary).	18 U.S.C. § 241 (2013). ——— Section 241 of title 18 of the United States Code covers conspiracies to deprive persons of constitutional rights.	■ Local governments also have legislative bodies, e.g., city councils. Their laws are called *ordinances.* (See ordinance below)

3. Constitution	The fundamental law that creates the branches of government, allocates power among them, and defines some basic rights of individuals.	■ Varies. Often a combination of the legislature and a vote of the people. ■ Another option might be a constitutional convention.	U.S. Const. Art. II, § 4. ─── Section 4 of Article II of the U.S. Constitution is on the removal of the president from office.	■ In addition to the federal (U.S.) constitution, each state has its own constitution. ■ At the local level of government, charters have similarities with the constitution at the federal and state levels. (See charter below.)
4. Administrative Regulation (also called *administrative rule*)	A law written by an administrative agency designed to explain or carry out the statutes, executive orders, or other regulations that govern the agency.	Administrative agency	27 C.F.R. § 16.1 (2006). ─── Section 16.1 of title 27 of the Code of Federal Regulations covers health warnings on alcoholic beverages.	■ There are administrative agencies at the federal, state, and local levels of government. All of these agencies write administrative regulations.
5. Administrative Decision (also called *administrative ruling*)	An administrative agency's resolution of a controversy (following a hearing) involving the application of the regulations, statutes, or executive orders that govern the agency.	Administrative agency	*Trojan Transport., Inc.*, 249 N.L.R.B. 642 (1980) ─── This is an administrative decision of the National Labor Relations Board printed on page 642 of volume 249 of N.L.R.B. decisions.	■ Federal agencies frequently write administrative decisions. State and local agencies do so less often.
6. Charter (also called *municipal charter*)	The fundamental law of a municipality or other local unit of government authorizing it to perform designated governmental functions.	Varies. The state legislature often writes charter provisions for cities. The local government itself may be able to create and change the charter.	*N.Y. City Charter* § 394 (1989). ─── Section 394 is in the New York City Charter.	■ At the local level of government, charters can be the equivalent of the constitution at the federal and state levels.
7. Ordinance	A law passed by the local legislature (e.g., city council) that declares, commands, or prohibits something.	The local legislature (e.g., city council, county commission).	Cincinnati, Ohio, Municipal Code § 305-10. ─── Section 305-10 is in the municipal code of Cincinnati.	■ At the local level of government, ordinances are the equivalent of statutes at the federal and state levels.
8. Court Rule (also called *rules of court, rules of procedure,* and *procedural rules*)	A procedural law that governs the mechanics of litigation (practice and procedure) before a particular court.	Courts, often the highest court within the judicial system.	Mo. R. Civ. P. 56.01(b). ─── Rule 56.01(b) is part of the Missouri Supreme Court Rules of Civil Procedure.	■ Administrative agencies that conduct hearings also have rules. They are often called *procedural rules.*
9. Executive order	A law issued by the chief executive pursuant to specific statutory authority or to the executive's inherent authority to direct the operation of governmental agencies.	■ President (for U.S. government) ■ Governor (for state government) ■ Mayor or county executive (for local government)	Executive Order No. 22,796, 3 C.F.R. 359 (1992). ─── This is Executive Order 22,792 of the President on page 359 of volume 3 of the 1992 Code of Federal Regulations (C.F.R.).	
10. Treaty (also called *accord, convention,* and *pact*)	A formal agreement between two or more nations.	The president makes treaties by and with the consent of the U.S. Senate.	Treaty of Friendship, Commerce and Navigation, U.S.-Japan, art. vi, May 24, 1953.	■ If the president has the authority to enter the agreement without Senate approval, it is called an *executive agreement.*

Law offices solve legal problems of clients by applying the different kinds of law outlined in Exhibit 6-1 to the facts presented by client cases. Some cases are straightforward such as a garden-variety automobile accident that might be settled with little or no involvement of the courts. Other cases can be considerably more complex.

Example: Linda Thompson applies for unemployment compensation benefits after being terminated from her job. Her former employer says the termination was due to a slowdown in business at the company. Linda believes she was let go because she is a woman and because she is HIV positive. Here are some possible laws described in Exhibit 6-1 that might be involved in her case:

State Laws:

- Administrative regulations on unemployment compensation of the state unemployment compensation commission and regulations on discrimination of the state fair employment practices agency.
- State statutes on unemployment compensation, civil rights, and sex discrimination.
- State statutes and court rules on evidence and civil procedure if the case is heard in a state court.
- The equal-protection provisions of the state constitution prohibiting sex discrimination.
- State court opinions on unemployment compensation, civil rights, sex discrimination, evidence, and civil procedure.

Federal Laws:

- Administrative regulations on sex discrimination of the U.S. Equal Employment Opportunity Commission (EEOC).
- Federal statutes on civil rights, sex discrimination, and disability discrimination.
- Federal statutes and court rules on evidence and civil procedure if the case is filed in federal court.
- The equal-protection clause of the Fourteenth Amendment of the U.S. Constitution.
- Opinions of federal courts on civil rights, sex discrimination, disability discrimination, evidence, and civil procedure.

These are the kinds of laws that might apply to Linda's case. Note the different levels and branches of government that could be involved. To be able to assist attorneys representing clients such as Linda, paralegals need a keen understanding of how these laws interact in our legal system.

CONSTITUTIONAL LAW

The constitution is the fundamental law that creates the branches of government, allocates power among them, and defines some basic rights of individuals (see Exhibit 6-1). The phrase *constitutional law* refers to the provisions of the constitution itself and to the court opinions that interpret and apply those provisions.

U.S. Constitution

For the federal government, the constitution is the U.S. Constitution. The basic powers of the federal government are contained in articles. Here are the beginnings of the first three articles:

- Article I. Legislative Power. "All legislative Powers herein granted shall be vested in a Congress of the United States, which shall consist of a Senate and House of Representatives."
- Article II. Executive Power. "The executive Power shall be vested in a President of the United States of America."
- Article III. Judicial Power. "The judicial Power of the United States, shall be vested in one supreme Court, and in such inferior Courts as the Congress may from time to time ordain and establish."

The first ten amendments of the U.S. Constitution contain the Bill of Rights. Here are examples of what the amendments cover:

- First Amendment. No government establishment of religion; free exercise of religion; freedom of speech, freedom of the press; right to assemble peaceably, right to petition the government for a redress of grievances.
- Second Amendment. Right of the people to keep and bear arms.
- Third Amendment. Restrictions on when troops can be lodged (quartered) in houses.
- Fourth Amendment. Protection against unreasonable searches and seizures.
- Fifth Amendment. Right to a grand jury and due process of law; prohibitions against double jeopardy, self-incrimination, and the taking of private property for public purposes without just compensation.
- Sixth Amendment. In criminal cases, the right to a speedy and public trial by jury, to subpoena favorable witnesses, to confront opposing witnesses, and to the assistance of defense counsel.

- Seventh Amendment. In civil cases, the right to trial by jury in designated cases.
- Eighth Amendment. Prohibitions against excessive bail, excessive fines, or cruel and unusual punishment.
- Ninth Amendment. An acknowledgment that the rights of the people are not restricted to those specifically mentioned (enumerated) in the constitution.
- Tenth Amendment. State governments are entitled to exercise any power so long as the constitution does not prohibit the states from exercising that power and so long as that power is not delegated to the federal government.

State Constitutions

Every state has its own constitution that sets up the branches of government and defines basic rights. State constitutions tend to be considerably more detailed than the U.S. Constitution. Yet there are basic similarities.

Supremacy Clause

Supremacy Clause The clause in the U.S. Constitution (art. VI, cl. 2) that has been interpreted to mean that when valid federal law conflicts with state law, federal law controls.

What happens if a state law conflicts with a federal law? Suppose, for example, that a state statute allows the use of medical marijuana but federal law prohibits it. In such a conflict, federal law controls. If there is conflict between state law and a valid federal law, the latter is supreme. Under the **Supremacy Clause** in Article VI of the U.S. Constitution, all state laws must be consistent with the U.S. Constitution and with every valid federal statute of Congress and every valid administrative regulation of a federal agency.

indigent Poor; without means to afford something such as a private attorney or filing fees.

The constitutional supremacy of federal law, however, does not mean that states are powerless. The federal constitution sets the minimum standard that must be met in every state. It is possible for a state to go beyond the minimum and to grant greater rights than the federal constitution grants. For example, the U.S. Supreme Court has held that the federal constitution does not require free attorney representation for every **indigent** (poor) person who is charged with civil contempt for failure to pay child support. A state, however, is free to interpret its own state constitution to provide such a right. By so doing, the state constitution would be granting stronger civil rights than those guaranteed by the federal constitution

common law (1) Judge-made law in the absence of controlling statutory law or other higher law. Law derived from court opinions. (2) The court opinions and statutes in England and in the American colonies before the American Revolution. (3) The legal system of England and of those countries such as the United States whose legal system is based on England's.

COMMON LAW, ENACTED LAW, AND EQUITY

Before we examine the structure of our court system, we need to cover common law, enacted law, and equity.

Common Law

The phrase **common law** has three major meanings, the first of which will be our primary concern in this book:

at common law (1) Referring to all the case law and statutory law in England and in the American colonies before the Revolution. (2) Pertaining to judge-made law.

- *Judge-made law in the absence of controlling statutory law or other higher law.* Law derived from court opinions.
- *The court opinions and statutes in England and in the American colonies before the American Revolution.* The phrase **at common law** often refers to this colonial period.
- *The legal system of England and of those countries such as the United States whose legal system is based on England's.* Common law originated in England during the early Middle Ages when judges in the king's courts wrote opinions that created case law based on customs and well-established principles. A unique feature of this law was that it was enforced throughout England—it was *common* throughout the realm. The English **common-law system** was eventually adopted in most of the United States. The counterpart of the common law system is the **civil-law system** of Continental Europe, Latin America, and Louisiana. The origin of civil law includes the Code of Justinian of the Roman Empire. (Also influential in many civil-law countries has been the Code Napoléon of France.) Both the common-law system and the civil-law system rely on statutory codes of legislatures and case law of courts. The difference is primarily one of emphasis. In a common-law system, the role of case law is greater than it is in a civil-law system. On the other hand, in a civil-law system, statutory or code law tends to have a greater prominence than it does in a common-law system. Forty-nine states in the United States have a common-law system. Louisiana is unique in that its law is largely based on civil law due to the historical importance of France in that state. (The word **civil** also has other meanings. It can refer to the state or to the citizens of a state (e.g., the civil right to vote); to a noncriminal matter (e.g., a civil wrong such as a tort); and to a nonmilitary matter (e.g., civil service).

common-law system The legal system of England and most of the United States that places a greater emphasis on case law than do countries that have a civil law system where a greater emphasis is placed on statutory or code law.

civil-law system The legal system of many countries in Continental Europe and Latin America (and Louisiana) that places a greater emphasis on statutory or code law than do countries (such as England and most of the United States) whose common-law system places a greater emphasis on case law.

civil (1) Pertaining to the state or its citizens. (2) Noncriminal. (3) Nonmilitary.

The first definition of common law is the most important: judge-made law in the absence of controlling statutory law or other higher law. Courts are sometimes confronted with disputes for which there is no applicable law. There may be no constitutional provisions or statutes governing the dispute. When this occurs, the court will apply-and if necessary, create—common law to resolve the controversy. This is judge-made law created in the absence of statutory law or of other higher law needed to resolve the case at hand. In creating the common law, the court relies primarily on the unwritten customs and values of the community from time immemorial. Very often these customs and values are described and enforced in older opinions that are heavily cited by modern courts in the continuing process of developing the common law.

The common law grows slowly, case by case. Radical changes are not encouraged and, therefore, are relatively rare. Once a court decides a case, it becomes a potential **precedent** that can be helpful as a standard or guide for the resolution of similar cases that arise in the future. Under the doctrine of **stare decisis**, a court will decide similar cases in the same way (i.e., it will follow available precedents) unless there is good reason for the court to do otherwise. Courts are most comfortable when they can demonstrate that their decisions are rooted in precedent. Knowing this, attorneys and paralegals study precedents in order to try to predict how a court might resolve a current case.

Suppose, for example, that a law office is representing Phil Kelley, who is a defendant in a civil battery case. (Battery is both a crime and a civil wrong. Phil is being sued for the latter where the **cause of action** is battery.) Kelley took a baseball bat and forcefully hit the handlebars of a bicycle on which the plaintiff was riding at the time. The bat did not touch the plaintiff's body. This case raises the question of whether you can batter someone without making contact with his or her body. One of the steps the law office will take in representing Kelley is to do legal research to try to find precedents for this kind of case. Assume that on the shelves of the law library (or in an online legal database), the attorney or paralegal finds the prior case of *Harrison v. Linner*. This case decided that the defendant committed a battery when he knocked over a plate being held by the plaintiff even though the defendant never touched any part of the plaintiff's body. Is *Harrison v. Linner* a precedent for the bicycle case? Is hitting a bicycle handle with a bat sufficiently similar to knocking a plate out of someone's hand? The law office must predict whether a court will apply *Harrison v. Linner* to the bicycle case. Making such a prediction requires legal analysis, which we will be studying in Chapter 7. For our purposes, the example illustrates how precedent is used in our common-law system. When the bicycle case goes before the court, the attorneys for both sides will be spending a good deal of time trying to convince the court that *Harrison v. Linner* is or is not a precedent. The court's resolution of the bicycle issue will become part of the evolving common law.

Note that our main definition of common law says judge-made law in the absence of controlling statutory law or other higher law. There is a hierarchy in the categories of law. Constitutional law, for example, is higher in authority than statutory law. So too, statutory law is higher in authority than common law. Assume that the courts have created common law in an area where no controlling statutes existed. This does not mean that statutes can never play a role in this area. The legislature can now decide to step in and create statutes that change the common law in this area for future cases. Such statutes are said to be *in derogation of the common law*.

One of the best examples of the interplay between common law and statutory law can be found in the area of contracts. A great deal of contract law was created by the courts as common law. Centuries ago, for example, the courts created the principle that a contract was not enforceable unless it was supported by **consideration** (something of value that is exchanged between the parties). Over the years, statutes have been written to change many common-law contract principles. In some kinds of contracts, for example, statutes have changed the common law of consideration. For commercial contracts, the greatest statutory changes were brought about by the Uniform Commercial Code (UCC). Many other contract statutes in derogation of the common law also exist. Today, contract law consists of a mix of statutes and those common-law principles that have not been changed (derogated) by legislatures or indeed by the courts themselves, who are always free to change their own common law. This evolution of the common law has been taking place for centuries and has given us what commentators call the "seamless web" of the common law.

Enacted Law

We need to compare common law with the broader category of law called **enacted law**. As we have seen, a major characteristic of common law is that it is created by the courts, which means that common law is a byproduct of litigation–common law is created *within* litigation.

precedent A prior opinion or decision covering similar facts or issues in a later case that can be used as a standard or guide in the later case.

stare decisis ("stand by things decided") Courts should decide similar cases in the same way unless there is good reason for the court to do otherwise. When resolving an issue, courts should be reluctant to reject precedent—a prior opinion covering similar facts and issues.

cause of action (1) A legally acceptable reason for bringing a suit. A rule that constitutes a legal theory for bringing a suit. (2) The facts that give a person a right to judicial relief. When you *state a cause of action*, you list the facts that give you a right to judicial relief against the alleged wrongdoer.

derogation A partial repeal or abolishment of a law.

consideration Something of value that is exchanged between parties. It can be an act, a forbearance (not performing an act), a promise to perform an act, or a promise to refrain from performing an act.

enacted law (1) Law written by a deliberative body such as a legislature or constitutional convention after it is proposed and often debated and amended. (2) Any law that is not created within litigation.

prospective Governing future events; effective (having an effective date) in the future.

equity Justice administered according to fairness in a particular case, as contrasted with the strictly formalized rules once followed by common-law courts.

remedy The means by which a right is enforced or the violation of a right is prevented, compensated for, or otherwise redressed. (See glossary for an additional meaning.)

damages (1) Money claimed by a person to compensate for the harm caused by an alleged wrongdoer. (2) An award of money paid by the wrongdoer to compensate the person who has been harmed.

equitable (1) Fair; just. (2) Pertaining to any remedy available in an action in equity.

specific performance A remedy for breach of contract that forces the wrongdoing party to complete the contract as promised.

injunction A remedy that orders a person or organization to do or to refrain from doing something.

Enacted law is any law that is *not* created within litigation. Enacted laws include constitutions, statutes, administrative regulations, and ordinances. (See Exhibit 6-1.) The verb *enact* means to pass or adopt a rule after someone has proposed it. The noun is *enactment*, which refers to the result of the process, (e.g., a statute), or to the process of creating the law.

The proposal for an enacted law is often debated by a deliberative body such as a legislature or city council, commented on by the public and by experts, amended, and eventually voted up or down. Most enacted laws are intended to cover broad categories of people or entities (e.g., taxpayers, motorists, or businesses). With few exceptions, the reach of an enacted law is **prospective**—it governs *future* events that will occur after the rule is enacted. A statute, for example, might provide that after a certain date, all motorcycle riders in the state must wear helmets. Most court opinions are significantly different. They result from litigation involving specific parties that, in the main, cover events that have already occurred (e.g., an automobile accident, an allegedly discriminatory firing).

Law and Equity

At one time in our history, most states had two separate state court systems: common-law courts and **equity** courts. A major reason courts of equity were developed was to provide parties with more flexible **remedies** and greater fairness than common-law courts provided. In a common-law court, for example, a victim of a breach of contract would be limited to recovering a money judgment (i.e., **damages**) from the wrongdoer. In some cases, this remedy was inadequate (and, in fact, was referred to as an *inadequate remedy at law*). Suppose, for example, that Tom breaches his contract to sell Mary a painting that Mary's uncle painted before she was born. In a common-law court, she would be limited to winning damages from Tom. In a court of equity, however, she might be able to obtain the **equitable** remedy of **specific performance**, which would direct Tom to perform the contract as promised and turn over the painting to her. If Tom tried to sell the painting overseas, Mary could seek an **injunction** that orders him not to remove the painting. An injunction is another equitable remedy that she could not obtain in a common-law court. She would undoubtedly consider such remedies to be fairer than a mere award of damages.

Most states today no longer have separate common-law and equity courts. Parties can request the application of equitable principles in *any* court. There has been a *merger of law and equity*, meaning that the same court can apply legal and equitable principles. See Exhibit 6-2 that summarizes the various differences between common law and equity courts before they were merged.

Exhibit 6-2	Common Law Courts and Equity Courts (before the Merger of Law and Equity)

CATEGORY OF COURT	OTHER NAMES FOR THIS SEPARATE COURT	WHAT THIS COURT APPLIED	WHEN THIS COURT WAS USED	PROCEDURE	CURRENT STATUS OF COURT
Common Law Court	■ Law court ■ Court of law	■ Legal principles ■ Law (shorthand for legal principles)	When the remedy at law (e.g., damages) was adequate.	The decision of the court was called a *judgment*. Parties could request a jury trial.	Most states have abolished the separate law and equity courts so that the same court can now apply both legal and equitable principles
Equity Court	■ Court of equity ■ Chancery court	■ Equitable principles ■ Equity (shorthand for equitable principles)	When the remedy at law (e.g., damages) was inadequate.	The decision of the court was called a *decree*. There were no jury trials.	See above.

INTERNATIONAL LAW

International law consists of the legal principles and laws that govern relations between nations. A major source of international law is a *treaty*, which is a formal agreement between two or more nations. Treaties require approval by the U.S. Senate. If the president enters an agreement with a nation that does not require Senate approval, the agreement is called an *executive agreement*. (See Exhibit 6-1.)

International law The legal principles and laws governing relations between nations. Also called *law of nations*, *public international law*.

JUDICIAL BRANCH

There are fifty state court systems and one main federal court system. (In addition, the District of Columbia has its own court system.) Within each court system, there are two main kinds of courts: **constitutional courts** (those that derive its jurisdiction from a provision of the constitution) and **legislative courts** (those created by the legislature). In most constitutions, the main constitutional court is the highest court in the judicial system. For the federal government, the highest court is the U.S. Supreme Court.

ADVERSARY SYSTEM

The main function of courts is to **adjudicate** (resolve or decide) legal disputes. (The noun is *adjudication*.) A major characteristic of our courts is that they are **adversarial**. We have an **adversary system** in which legal disputes are resolved by the parties (alone or through their advocates) arguing their conflicting claims before a neutral (impartial) decision maker. This approach is based on the theory that justice and truth have a greater chance of being achieved when the parties to a controversy appear before a neutral judge to present their conflicting positions. We don't expect the judge to control the case by calling witnesses or by extensively questioning them. We leave these functions, by and large, to the parties and their representatives.

Ideally, the parties in an adversary system have an equal opportunity to present their cases.[1] Unfortunately, the system is often criticized for failing to live up to this ideal. In many disputes between a citizen and a corporation, for example, the citizen cannot afford the kind of representation available to the corporation.

Not all countries use an adversary system. Many European countries have an **inquisitorial system** in which the judge has a more active role in questioning the witnesses and in conducting the trial than in countries with an adversary system.

COURTS OF RECORD

Most of our major state and federal trial courts produce a **record** of what occurred during the trial. A record is the official collection of all the trial pleadings, exhibits, orders, and word-for-word testimony given during the trial. If the decision of the court is appealed, the appellate court examines this record to determine if errors were made.

Not all courts, however, are **courts of record**. Some lower-level trial courts (called inferior courts) are not courts of record. The decision or *result* of the proceeding in such courts is recorded, but rarely, if ever, is a complete record made of the proceeding. A party wishing to appeal the decision must start over in the next level of court. A **trial de novo** is required.

JURISDICTION

The lifeblood of any court is its jurisdiction. At the broadest level, **jurisdiction** has two main meanings. First, and most importantly, it refers to the *power* of a court to resolve a legal dispute. When, for example, we say, "The court has jurisdiction over labor strikes," we are referring to a court's power to resolve legal issues involving labor strikes. Second, it refers to the *geographic area* over which a particular court has authority. The latter is called the court's **territorial jurisdiction**. When, for example, a New York state court says, "This is the first time that the question has been raised in this jurisdiction," it is referring to a place or territory —the state of New York. Our primary concern in this section will be the power definition of jurisdiction. As we will see, there are several subdivisions of this power.

The power jurisdiction of a court can be divided into (1) jurisdiction over parties or property and (2) jurisdiction over subject matter.

Jurisdiction over Parties or Property

Personal jurisdiction is a court's power over a person to determine (adjudicate) his or her personal rights. This jurisdiction is also called *in personam jurisdiction*. In addition, a court can exercise *in rem jurisdiction* over property within the geographic boundary or territory of the court even if the claimed owners (or others involved) are not present within the boundaries or territory.

---

constitutional court A court that derives its jurisdiction from a provision of the constitution. (At the federal level, a constitutional court is called an *Article III court* because it derives its jurisdiction from Article III of the U.S. Constitution.)

legislative courts A court created by the legislature. (At the federal level, a legislative court is called an *Article I court* because Article I of the U.S. Constitution gives Congress the authority to create special courts.)

adjudicate To resolve or decide by judicial process; to judge. The noun is adjudication; the adjective is adjudicative.

adversarial Involving conflict and an adversary (opponent)..

adversary system A method of resolving a legal dispute whereby the parties (alone or through their advocates) argue their conflicting claims before a neutral (impartial) decision maker.

inquisitorial system A method of resolving a legal dispute in some countries in which the judge has a more active role in questioning the witnesses and in conducting the trial than in an adversary system.

record The official collection of all the trial pleadings, exhibits, orders, and word-for-word testimony that were part of the trial. (See glossary for additional meanings.)

court of record A court that is required to maintain a record of the proceedings before it, including a word-for-word account of what occurred.

trial de novo A new trial conducted as if a prior one had not occurred.

jurisdiction   (1) The power of a court to resolve a legal dispute. (2) A geographic area over which a particular court, legislature, or administrative agency has authority. The geographic area can be the entire country, a state, a group of states, a county, a city, etc. (3) The power or authority that a person, government, or other entity can exercise.

territorial jurisdiction   The geographic boundaries within which a court has the power to act.

personal jurisdiction   A court's power over a person to determine (adjudicate) his or her personal rights. Also called *in personam jurisdiction*. More limited kinds of jurisdiction include the court's power over a person's interest in specific property (quasi in rem jurisdiction), over the property itself, or over a status such as marriage (in rem jurisdiction).

subject-matter jurisdiction   The court's power to resolve a particular type of legal dispute and to grant a particular type of relief.

limited jurisdiction   The power of a court to hear only certain kinds of cases. Also called *special jurisdiction*.

general jurisdiction   The power of a court to hear any kind of civil or criminal case, with certain exceptions.

exclusive jurisdiction   The power of a court to hear a particular kind of case, to the exclusion of other courts.

concurrent jurisdiction   The power of more than one type of court to hear a particular kind of case.

original jurisdiction   The power of a court to be the first to hear a case before it is reviewed by another type of court. Also called a *court of first instance*.

appellate jurisdiction   The power of a court to review and correct the decisions of a lower tribunal.

Jurisdiction over Subject Matter

The second kind of power jurisdiction that enables a court to adjudicate a dispute is its power over the subject matter of the dispute. By subject matter, we mean the particular kind or category of case involved (e.g., copyright infringement, manslaughter, or divorce). This power is called **subject-matter jurisdiction**. The most common classifications of subject-matter jurisdiction are as follows:

- Limited jurisdiction
- General jurisdiction
- Exclusive jurisdiction
- Concurrent jurisdiction
- Original jurisdiction
- Appellate jurisdiction

Limited Jurisdiction

A court of **limited jurisdiction** can hear only certain kinds of cases. For example, a criminal court is not allowed to take a noncriminal case, and a small claims court is authorized to hear only cases in which the plaintiff seeks damages from the defendant that is at or below the maximum set by statute. If a plaintiff brings a civil case in a criminal court or seeks damages in a small claims court that are above the maximum, the defendant can challenge the court's subject-matter jurisdiction.

General Jurisdiction

A court of **general jurisdiction** can, with some exceptions, hear any kind of civil or criminal case. (Here, the word *civil* means noncriminal.)

- A *state* court of general jurisdiction can hear a wide range of cases that raise state questions (i.e., questions arising from or based on the state constitution, state statutes, state regulations, state common law, or other state laws).
- A *federal* court of general jurisdiction can hear a wide range of cases that raise federal questions (i.e., questions arising from or based on the federal (U.S.) constitution, federal statutes, federal regulations, or other federal laws). In this context, the word *federal* means United States. The main federal court of general jurisdiction is the United States district court.

Exclusive Jurisdiction

A court of **exclusive jurisdiction** is the only court that can handle a certain kind of case. For example, a juvenile court may have exclusive jurisdiction over all cases involving children under a designated age who are charged with acts of delinquency. If this kind of case is brought in another court, there could be a challenge on the ground that the court lacked subject-matter jurisdiction over the case.

Concurrent Jurisdiction

Sometimes two different types of courts have jurisdiction over a case; the case could be brought in either court. Both courts are said to have **concurrent jurisdiction** over the case. For example, a family court and a county court may have jurisdiction to enforce a child-support order.

Original Jurisdiction

A court of **original jurisdiction** is one with the power to be the first to hear a case before it is reviewed by another type of court. The most common kind of court with original jurisdiction is a *trial court* (also called a *court of first instance*).

Appellate Jurisdiction

A court with **appellate jurisdiction** has the power to review and correct the decisions of a lower tribunal (e.g., a lower court or an administrative agency) to determine whether the lower tribunal committed an error of law. For example, at the federal level, the U.S. Supreme Court has appellate jurisdiction to review a decision of a U.S. court of appeals. Similarly, at the state level, the New York Court of Appeals has appellate jurisdiction to review a decision of a lower New York state court. The examination of what the lower tribunal has done is called a **review**. Sometimes, a party who is dissatisfied with a lower court **ruling** can appeal as a matter of right to the appellate court (the court must hear the appeal). In other kinds of cases, the appellate court has discretion on whether it will hear the appeal. Such appeals are called discretionary appeals. If the appellate court uses its discretion to hear the appeal, the court issues a **certiorari** (abbreviated *cert.*). This is a **writ** that orders the lower court to certify the record of the lower court proceeding and send it up to the appellate court for review. If the appellate court uses its discretion to refuse to hear the appeal, the lower court's decision is final. Not all appellate courts use the language of certiorari. In some courts, for example, discretionary reviews are activated by a *writ of review* or *certification for appeal*.

STATE COURTS

With this background overview of court jurisdiction, we first examine state judicial systems—our state courts. The vast majority of litigation in America (over 90 percent) occurs in state courts. States may differ in the names of their courts and in the number of appellate courts that they have, as you can see in Exhibit 6-3.

State Courts of Original Jurisdiction

A court of original jurisdiction is a trial court. Most states will have at least two levels or tiers of trial courts (referred to as tier I and tier II in Exhibit 6-3). Trial courts hear the dispute, determine the facts of the case, and make the initial determination or ruling. In addition, they may sometimes have the power to review cases that were initially decided by an administrative agency.

review The power of a court to examine the correctness of what a lower tribunal has done.

ruling The conclusion or outcome of a decision made by a court or administrative agency.

certiorari (cert.) An order (or writ) by a higher court that a lower court send up the record of a case because the higher court has decided to use its discretion to review that case.

writ A written court order to do or refrain from doing an act.

Exhibit 6-3	State Court Systems

- Most states have at least two levels of trial courts. This chart refers to them as "tiers" (tier I is the highest level; tier II is the inferior level).
- About half the states have two levels of appellate courts: intermediate and final. Other states have only one appellate court level: final.
- The names of state courts differ from state to state. This chart presents an overview of the names that exist. For the specific names of state courts in your state, go to

  ■ www.govengine.com (click your state on the map, then click entries under "Judicial Branch")
  ■ Google, Bing, or Yahoo (type aa "Court System" substituting the name of your state for "aa," e.g., California "Court System")
  ■ www.ncsc.org (type "State Court Web sites" in the search box, then click your state)

Level of Court	Name(s) of Court at this Level in Different States	Function of Court at this Level	Lines of Appeal
Trial courts: tier I	Superior court, circuit court, district court, court of common pleas (in New York, the trial court at this level is called the supreme court)	■ Tier I trial courts are courts of original jurisdiction—trial courts. ■ Tier I trial courts have general jurisdiction.	Cases from tier I trial courts are appealed to the intermediate appellate courts in the state if the state has intermediate appellate courts. If the state does not have such courts, cases are appealed to the court of final resort.
Trial courts: tier II (inferior courts)	Probate court, small claims court, family court, municipal court, county court, district court, justice of the peace court, police court, city court, water court (trial courts at this level are sometimes called *inferior courts*)	■ Tier II trial courts are courts of original jurisdiction—trial courts. A tier II trial court is considered a lower (inferior) level of trial court than a tier I trial court. ■ Tier II trial courts have limited or special jurisdiction. *Examples:* The Probate Court (also called Surrogate Court) hears estate cases of deceased or incompetent persons; the Small Claims Court hears cases involving small amounts of money (damages); the Family Court hears divorce, custody, and other domestic relations matters; the Municipal Court hears traffic cases and those involving petty crimes.	Cases from tier II trial courts (those of limited or special jurisdiction) are often appealed to tier I trial courts of general jurisdiction. Some, however, are appealed to the intermediate appellate courts (if they exist) or to the court of final resort.
Intermediate appellate courts (exist in about half the states)	Court of appeals, court of civil appeals, court of criminal appeals, appellate court, appeals court, district court of appeals, intermediate court of appeals, court of special appeals, appellate division of superior court	■ Intermediate appellate courts are courts of appellate jurisdiction.	An intermediate appellate court hears appeals from trial courts in the state. If the state does not have intermediate appellate courts, appeals go directly from the trial court to the court of final resort.
The court of final resort—the highest court in the state court system	Supreme court, supreme judicial court, supreme court of appeals, court of appeals	■ The court of final resort has appellate jurisdiction.	The court of final resort hears appeals from lower courts in the state. If the state has intermediate appellate courts, appeals are heard from these courts. If intermediate appellate courts do not exist in the state, the court of final resort hears appeals directly from trial courts.

inferior courts (1) A trial court of limited or special jurisdiction. (2) Any court that is subordinate to the court of final resort.

At the lower level are state trial courts are courts of limited or special jurisdiction, the so-called **inferior courts**. (See "Trial courts: tier II" in Exhibit 6-2.) Local courts, such as small claims court, family court, municipal court, and justice of the peace courts, often fall into this category. Some are not courts of record. Inferior courts may have original jurisdiction over relatively minor cases, such as violations of local ordinances and lawsuits involving small sums of money. Also included in this category are special courts that are limited to specific matters, such as surrogate courts or probate courts that hear matters involving the estates of deceased or mentally incompetent persons.

Immediately above the trial courts of limited jurisdiction are the trial courts of general jurisdiction, which usually handle more serious cases, such as lawsuits involving large sums of money. (See "Trial courts: tier I" in Exhibit 6-2.) These trial courts are courts of record. The name given to the trial courts of general jurisdiction varies greatly from state to state. They are known as superior courts, circuit courts, district courts, or courts of common pleas. New York is especially confusing. There, the trial court of general jurisdiction is called the supreme court, a label reserved in most states for the court of final resort, the highest court in the system.

Finally, trial courts may be segmented into divisions. A trial court of general jurisdiction, for example, might be broken up into specialized divisions such as landlord-tenant division, family division, juvenile division, and criminal division.

State Courts of Appellate Jurisdiction

Appellate courts have appellate jurisdiction that allows them to review decisions of a lower tribunal, usually a lower court. The goal of the review is to determine whether the lower court committed any errors of law by incorrectly interpreting or applying the law to the facts of the dispute. In this review process, appellate courts do not make their own findings of fact. No new evidence is taken, and no witnesses are called. The court limits itself to an analysis of the trial-court record to determine if that lower court made any errors of law. Attorneys submit **appellate briefs** containing their arguments on the correctness or incorrectness of what the lower court did.

appellate briefs A document that a party files with an appellate court (and serves on an opponent) in which the party presents arguments on why the appellate court should affirm (approve), reverse, vacate (cancel), or otherwise modify what a lower court has done.

An appellate court often consists of an odd number of judges (sometimes called justices), e.g., 5, 7, 9, 11, or 15. This helps avoid tie votes. Some of the courts hear cases in smaller groups of judges, usually three. These groups are called **panels**. Once a panel renders its decision, the parties have the right to petition for an **en banc** review by the same court. If granted, all (or most) of the judges on the court will review the case.

panels A group of judges, usually three, who decide a case on behalf of a with a larger number of judges. (See glossary for additional meanings.)

Many states have only one level of appellate court to which trial court judgments are appealed. About half the states have two levels of appellate courts. The first level is the *intermediate appellate court*, sometimes called the court of middle appeals. The decisions of this court can in turn be reviewed by the court of final appeals. The latter court, often known as the supreme court, is the **court of final resort**. About half the states do not have intermediate appellate courts. Appeals from trial courts in such states go directly to the court of final resort.

en banc ("on the bench") By the entire court.

court of final resort The highest court within a judicial system.

FEDERAL COURTS

The federal court system, like the state systems, consists of two basic kinds of courts: courts of original jurisdiction (trial courts) and courts of appellate jurisdiction (appellate courts). See Exhibit 6-4. All federal courts listed in this exhibit are courts of record.

Federal Courts of Original Jurisdiction

U.S. district court The main trial court in the federal judicial system with subject-matter jurisdiction over civil and criminal cases.

The main federal court at the trial level is the **U.S. district court**. It hears two main categories of cases: those that raise *federal questions* (e.g., whether an employer has violated the National Labor Relations Act) and those that involve **diversity of citizenship** (e.g., a citizen of Ohio sues a citizen of Idaho claiming $80,000 for a breach of contract). There are federal districts throughout the country, with at least one for every state, the District of Columbia, Guam, the Virgin Islands, and Puerto Rico.

diversity of citizenship The disputing parties are citizens of different states and the amount in controversy exceeds $75,000. This diversity gives subject-matter jurisdiction to a U.S. district court.

District courts exercise general jurisdiction in that they can hear a broad range of civil or criminal cases. In a sense, however, they are courts of limited jurisdiction because they can resolve only those cases that raise federal questions or where the parties have diversity of citizenship.

District courts also serve as courts of review for many cases initially decided by federal administrative agencies. U.S. bankruptcy courts are units of the U.S. district courts. (U.S. bankruptcy judges hear those bankruptcy cases that are referred to them by U.S. district judges.)

In addition to the U.S. district courts, several federal courts exercise limited, original jurisdiction over specialized cases. Such courts include the U.S. Court of Federal Claims (which

Exhibit 6-4	Federal Court System

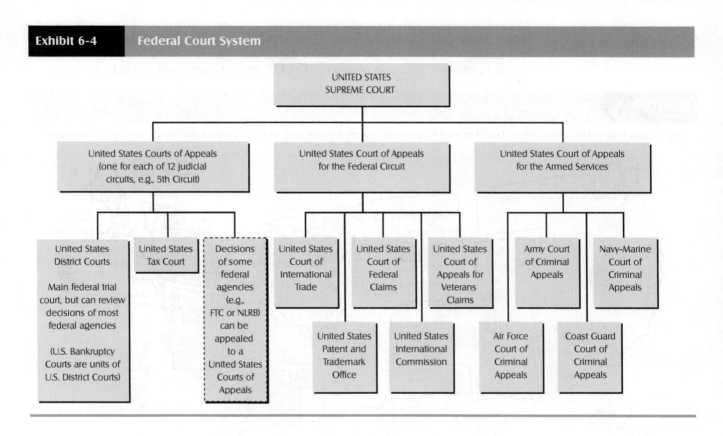

hears contract and other nontort claims against the federal government), the U.S. Court of International Trade, and the U.S. Court of Appeals for Veterans Claims.

Federal Courts of Appellate Jurisdiction

The federal system, like almost half of the fifty state judicial systems, has two levels of appellate courts: intermediate appellate courts and the court of final resort. The primary courts at the intermediate appellate level are the **U.S. courts of appeals** (formerly called circuit courts of appeals). There are twelve of these courts, one for each of the twelve judicial circuits in the country. Eleven of the circuits are made up of groupings of various states and territories. The District of Columbia has its own circuit. The main function of the U.S. courts of appeals is to review the decisions of the federal courts of original jurisdiction, primarily the district courts and the tax court. In addition, decisions of certain federal agencies, e.g., the Federal Trade Commission (FTC) and the National Labor Relations Board (NLRB), are reviewed directly by a court of appeals without first going to a U.S. district court.

There is a specialized court of appeals called the *U.S. Court of Appeals for the Federal Circuit.* This court reviews:

- decisions from the U.S. Court of International Trade, the U.S. Court of Federal Claims, the U.S. Court of Appeals for Veterans Claims, the U.S. Patent and Trademark Office, the U.S. International Commission; and
- some decisions of the district courts where the U.S. government is a defendant.

The U.S. Court of Appeals for the Armed Services reviews decisions of the courts of criminal appeals within the branches of the military. Finally, the United States Foreign Intelligence Court is a special court whose sole function is to review applications for warrants related to national-security investigations. Its decisions are reviewed by the U.S. Foreign Intelligence Surveillance Court of Review.

The federal court of final resort is, of course, the **U.S. Supreme Court,** which provides the final review of the decisions of all federal courts and agencies. The Supreme Court may also review certain decisions of the state courts when these decisions raise questions involving the U.S. Constitution, a federal statute, or other federal law. Although the Supreme

U.S. court of appeals The major intermediate appellate court in the federal court system.

U.S. Supreme Court The court of final resort in the federal court system.

Court has original jurisdiction to conduct trials in certain categories of cases, this jurisdiction is rarely used. The main activity of the Court is based on its appellate jurisdiction.

Exhibit 6-5 illustrates the division of the federal court system into twelve circuits. Each circuit has its own U.S. court of appeals. The U.S. district courts exist within these circuits.

Exhibit 6-5	U.S. Courts of Appeal and U.S. District Courts

(The dotted lines within a state indicate boundary lines for the district courts; if no dotted lines exist in a state, the district covers the entire state.)

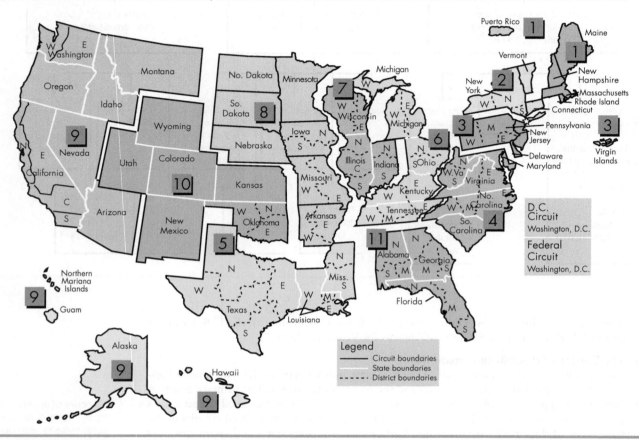

Source: Administrative Office of the United States Courts. January 1983 (www.uscourts.gov/courtlinks).

EXECUTIVE BRANCH

The chief executive of the executive branch of government is the president (at the federal level), the governor (at the state level), and the mayor or county executive (at the local level). Most of the work of the executive branch of government is performed by administrative agencies. An **administrative agency** is a governmental body, other than a court or legislature, that carries out (i.e., administers or executes) the statutes of the legislature, the executive orders of the chief executive, and its own regulations. The most important statute that agencies carry out is the **enabling statute**, which gives the agency specified delegated powers. As we will see, however, many agencies do more than carry out or execute the law; they also have rule-making and dispute-resolution responsibilities.

Administrative agencies can have a wide variety of names. Here are some examples:

- Fire Department
- Board of Licenses and Occupations
- Civil Service Commission
- Agency for International Development
- Department of Defense
- Bureau of Taxation
- Office of Management and Budget
- Legal Services Corporation
- Internal Revenue Service
- Division of Child Support and Enforcement
- Social Security Administration

administrative agency A governmental body, other than a court or legislature, that carries out (i.e., administers or executes) the statutes of the legislature, the executive orders of the chief executive, and its own regulations.

enabling statute The statute that allows (enables) an administrative agency to carry out specified delegated powers.

Certain types of agencies exist at all three levels of government. For example, there is a separate tax collection agency in each of the federal, state, and local governments. Other agencies, however, are unique to one of the levels. For example, only the federal government has a Department of Defense (DOD) and a Central Intelligence Agency (CIA). Nothing comparable exists at the state and local levels of government. The latter have police departments and the highway patrol, but their roles are significantly different from those of the DOD and CIA.

For a list of some of the most important federal agencies, see Appendix C.

There are three main kinds of administrative agencies: executive department agencies, independent regulatory agencies, and quasi-independent regulatory agencies.

- **Executive department agency.** An administrative agency that exists within the executive branch of government, often at the cabinet level. Examples include the Department of Agriculture (DOA) and the Department of Labor (DOL). These agencies are answerable to the chief executive, who usually has the power to dismiss them for any reason. The chief executive does not have to establish **cause** for doing so.
- **Independent regulatory agency.** An administrative agency that regulates an aspect of society such as securities or public utilities. The agency often exists outside the executive branch of government and, therefore, outside the day-to-day control of the chief executive. Examples include the Securities and Exchange Commission (SEC) and the Public Utilities Commission (PUC). To insulate these agencies from politics, those in charge usually cannot be removed at the whim of the chief executive; *cause* must be established.
- **Quasi-independent regulatory agency.** An administrative agency that has characteristics of both an executive department agency and an independent regulatory agency. A quasi-independent regulatory agency has more independence than an executive department agency, yet it might exist within the executive department. An example is the Federal Energy Regulatory Commission (FERC), which exists within the U.S. Department of Energy (DOE).

In a category all its own is the **government corporation**. This is a government-owned entity that has characteristics of a business corporation and a government agency. It is designed to have considerable flexibility and independence in carrying out a predominantly business function in the public interest. Examples include the Tennessee Valley Authority (TVA), the U.S. Postal Service (USPS), and the Corporation for Public Broadcasting (CPB). The government establishes this entity and usually provides its initial funding. Often, however, a substantial portion of its ongoing budget comes from fees and, for some corporations, from private charitable giving. Members of the boards of directors of federal government corporations are usually appointed by the president and confirmed by the Senate.

Many administrative agencies have three functions: execution, rulemaking, and dispute resolution:

- *Execution.* The primary function of the agency is to execute (i.e., carry out or administer) the statutes and executive orders governing the agency as well as the administrative regulations created by the agency itself. This is the agency's executive function.
- *Rulemaking.* The agency often has the authority to write administrative regulations, also called administrative rules (see definition in Exhibit 6-1). In so doing, the agency is "making law" like a legislature. Indeed, such laws are sometimes referred to as **quasi-legislation**. The rulemaking power of the agency is therefore called a *quasi-legislative* power. When considering a new regulation, the agency often publishes the proposed regulation in a register (e.g., the *Federal Register* for federal agencies) in order to give the public an opportunity to comment on the proposed regulation. Once finalized, the regulation is often published in a code (e.g., the *Code of Federal Regulations* for federal agencies).
- *Dispute resolution.* The agency has the authority to interpret the statutes and regulations that govern it. Furthermore, it often has the authority to resolve disputes that arise over the application of such laws. It will hold administrative hearings and issue administrative decisions (see definition in Exhibit 6-1). In so doing, the agency is acting like a court when the latter adjudicates (i.e., resolves) disputes. Indeed, such decisions are sometimes referred to as **quasi-adjudication** and its power to render such decisions is sometimes called a *quasi-judicial power*.

---

executive department agency An administrative agency that exists within the executive branch of government, often at the cabinet level.

cause A legally sufficient reason to do something. Sometimes referred to as *just cause, good cause*.

independent regulatory agency An administrative agency that regulates an aspect of society. The agency often exists outside the executive branch of government.

quasi-independent regulatory agency An administrative agency that has characteristics of both an executive department agency and an independent regulatory agency.

government corporation A government-owned entity that is a mixture of a business corporation and a government agency created to serve a predominantly business function in the public interest. Also called a *quasi-government agency*.

quasi-legislation An administrative regulation enacted by an administrative agency that has some characteristics of the legislation (statutes) enacted by the legislature. The adjective is *quasi-legislative*.

quasi-adjudication An administrative decision written by an administrative agency that has some characteristics of an opinion written by a court.

An agency exercises its quasi-judicial power at several levels.

- At the first level is a hearing, which is similar to a trial in a court of original jurisdiction. The presiding agency official is known variously as the hearing examiner or **administrative-law judge (ALJ)**. This official will, like the judge in a trial court, take testimony of witnesses, examine other evidence, determine the facts of the case, and apply the law to those facts in order to render an administrative decision.
- In many agencies, the findings of fact and the decision of the hearing officer constitute only a recommendation to the director, commissioner, secretary, or other high official who will make the decision at this level.
- Like the courts, many agencies then provide a second, "appellate" level where a body such as a board or commission reviews the decision of the hearing examiner (or other official), corrects errors, and renders the final administrative decision of the agency.

After the parties to the dispute have used all these quasi-judicial avenues of redress within the agency, they have **exhausted administrative remedies** and may then appeal the final administrative decision to a court. For federal and many state administrative agencies, the procedures that must be followed within the agencies are defined in the **Administrative Procedure Act (APA)**.

Here is an example of an agency using all three powers:

Securities and Exchange Commission (SEC)

- *Rulemaking.* The SEC writes regulations that implement statutes of Congress. An example is a statute that require companies to file registration statements with the SEC.
- *Execution.* To carry out the statutes and regulations, the SEC creates a registration office that prepares standard forms to be used by companies to file the registration statements. The office also answers questions of companies on the registration process. When an agency carries out a statute in this way, it is administering or executing that statute.
- *Dispute resolution.* The SEC can hold a hearing to decide whether a company has violated the registration requirements laid out in the statutes and administrative regulations. The end product of the hearing can be an administrative decision.

LEGISLATIVE BRANCH

The legislative process consists of the steps that a **bill** must go through before it becomes a statute. (A bill is a proposed statute.) Exhibit 6-6 outlines these steps for the federal legislature—Congress. The chart in Exhibit 6-6 assumes that the same idea for a bill is introduced simultaneously in both chambers of Congress: the House of Representatives and the Senate. It is, of course, also possible for a bill to be introduced in one chamber, go through all the steps for passage in that chamber, and *then* be introduced in the other chamber. The conference committee step outlined in the chart occurs only when both chambers have enacted their own version of the bill.

Congress is **bicameral**, meaning that it consists of two chambers: the House of Representatives and the Senate. In some state legislatures, the chambers have different names, such as the Assembly and the House of Delegates. Legislatures with one chamber are called **unicameral**. The only state legislature that is unicameral is the Nebraska Legislature. Local legislatures, however, such as city councils, are often unicameral.

The process of enactment can involve six major stages:

- Proposal
- Committee consideration
- Floor debate
- Conference committee
- Floor debate
- Response of the chief executive

The **legislative history** of a statute is what occurs at each of these stages. The history includes hearings, debates, amendments, committee reports, and all other events that occur in the legislature before a bill is enacted into a statute. Also part of the history are later changes, if any, made by the legislature to the statute.

PROPOSAL

A member of the legislature must formally introduce the bill. Where do the ideas for proposed laws originate? Here are the major sources of ideas:

administrative-law judge (ALJ) A government officer who presides over a hearing at an administrative agency. Also called *hearing examiner.*

exhaust administrative remedies To go through all dispute-solving avenues that are available in an administrative agency before asking a court to review what the agency did. Also called *exhaustion of remedies.*

Administrative Procedure Act (APA) The statute that governs procedures before federal administrative agencies. Many states have their own version of the APA for procedures before state administrative agencies.

bill A proposed statute.

bicameral Having two chambers in the legislature. If there is only one chamber, it is *unicameral.*

unicameral Having one chamber in the legislature.

legislative history Hearings, debates, amendments, committee reports, and all other events that occur in the legislature before a bill is enacted into a statute. Also part of the history are later changes, if any, made by the legislature to the statute.

- The chief executive of the government (e.g., the president or governor) may initiate the process by sending the legislature a message stating the reasons for a proposed law.
- Frequently, an administrative agency has made a study of a problem, which is the impetus for the proposal. The agency will usually be the entity with responsibility for administering the proposal if it is enacted into law.
- The bar association might prepare a report to the legislature calling for the new legislation.
- The legislature or chief executive may have established a special commission to study the need for changes in the law and to propose changes where appropriate. The commission might consist of members of the legislature and outside experts.
- Some states have ongoing law revision commissions that frequently make proposals for legislation.
- In many areas, a council of governments made up of neighboring governments studies problems and proposes legislative changes.

| Exhibit 6-6 | The Legislative History of a Federal Statute—How a Bill Becomes a Law |

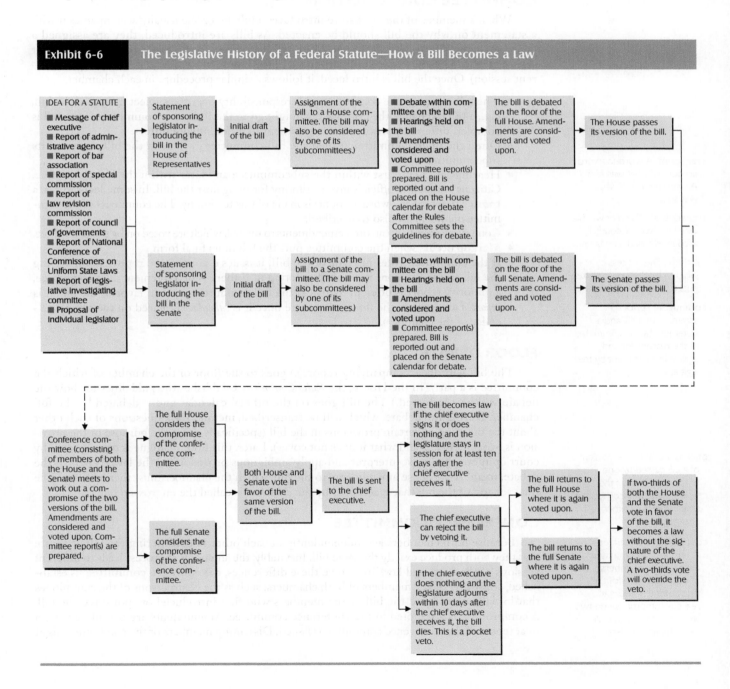

- The National Conference of Commissioners on Uniform State Laws is an organization with members from each state. The conference makes proposals to the state legislatures for the enactment of uniform state laws where it deems uniformity to be desirable.[2]
- Most ideas for legislation come from within the legislature itself. One or both houses may have established an investigating committee to examine a particular problem and propose legislation where needed.
- Individual legislators can also generate ideas for bills, and often do so to fulfill promises made during the campaign that led to their election.

Can private citizens introduce a bill in the legislature? No. They must convince an individual legislator to sponsor their idea for a bill. (As we saw in Exhibit 6-1, however, voters in some states can participate in the enactment of statutes through the initiative and referendum process.)

COMMITTEE CONSIDERATION

When a member of the legislature introduces a bill, he or she usually accompanies it with a statement on why the bill should be enacted. As bills are introduced, they are assigned a consecutive number (e.g., S 250 is the 250th bill introduced in the Senate during the current session; HR 1753 is the 1753rd bill introduced in the House of Representatives during the current session). Once the bill is introduced, it follows a similar procedure in each chamber.

- The bill is sent to the committee with responsibility over the subject matter of the bill, e.g., a bill to change the criminal law might go to the Judiciary Committee. If the bill is complex, different portions of it may be sent to different committees.
- Often the main committee (called the full committee) will send the bill to one of its subcommittees.
- Hearings are held, first within the subcommittee and later within the full committee. Citizens and public officials give testimony for or against the bill. In some legislatures, a **transcript** (word-for-word account) is made of this testimony. The comments of the committee members are also **transcribed**.
- Committee members can offer amendments to the bill, which are voted on by the committee.
- **Markup** occurs when the committee puts the bill in its final form.
- If the committee votes in favor of the bill, it issues a **committee report** summarizing the bill and the reasons in favor of enacting it. If there is disagreement on a committee, a minority report is often prepared. If the full committee votes in favor of the bill, it is *reported out* (sent to the floor) for debate once it is *calendared* (placed on the official calendar of the chamber).

FLOOR DEBATE

The bill with its accompanying report(s) goes to the floor of the chamber of which the committee is a part. (In the House, the *Rules Committee* establishes the guidelines for how the debate will be conducted.) The bill goes on the official calendar and is debated by the full chamber. During the debate, which will be transcribed, members ask questions of each other about the meaning of certain provisions in the bill (specifically, what the purpose of the provision is, what it covers, and what it does not cover). Later, this floor dialogue is often quoted by court opinions that must interpret and apply ambiguous provisions in the law. As part of the debate, members propose amendments to the bill, which the chamber must then vote on. The final version of the bill that is accepted by the chamber is called the **engrossed bill**.

CONFERENCE COMMITTEE

Because both chambers act independently of each other in considering the bill, it is rare that they both produce exactly the same bill. Inevitably, the amendment process leads to different versions of the proposed law. To resolve these differences, a **conference committee** is established, consisting of key members of both chambers, such as the chairpersons of the committees that initially considered the bill or the members who first introduced or sponsored the bill. A compromise is attempted in the conference committee. Amendments are considered and a final report of the conference committee is issued. Dissenting members of the committee might

---

transcript A word-for-word account of what was said. A written copy of what was said.

transcribed Taken down in a word-for-word account. The account is called a *transcript*.

markup The process by which a legislative committee puts a bill in its final form.

committee report A summary of a bill and a statement by the committee of the reasons for and against its enactment by the legislature.

engrossed bill The version of a bill passed by one of the chambers of the legislature after incorporating amendments or other changes.

conference committee A temporary committee consisting of members of both chambers of the legislature that seeks to reach a compromise on two versions of the same bill each chamber passed.

prepare a minority report. The majority report summarizes the major terms of the compromise and explains why it should be enacted by each chamber.

FLOOR DEBATE

The conference committee compromise then goes back to the floor of each chamber where more debate, explanations, and amendments are considered. Again, everything is transcribed. If both chambers pass the same version of the bill, usually by a majority vote, it goes to the chief executive. This version of the bill is called the **enrolled bill**.

RESPONSE OF CHIEF EXECUTIVE

There are three main ways for the bill to become law after it reaches the chief executive.

- He or she can sign it.
- He or she can do nothing. If the legislature stays in session for at least ten days after he or she receives it, the bill automatically becomes law—without requiring a signature.
- If the chief executive rejects or **vetoes** the bill, it can still become law if both chambers of the legislature **override** the veto by a two-thirds vote.

There are two main ways for the chief executive to reject a bill.

- He or she can explicitly veto the bill. It then goes back to the legislature, often with the chief executive's reasons for the rejection.
- He or she can do nothing. If the legislature adjourns within ten days after the chief executive receives it, the bill automatically dies. This is known as a **pocket veto**. Because the legislature is no longer in session, the pocket veto deprives the legislature of the opportunity to override the veto.

enrolled bill A bill that is ready to be sent to the chief executive after both chambers of the legislature have passed it.

veto A rejection by the chief executive of a bill passed by the legislature.

override (1) To supersede or change a result. (2) To approve a bill over the veto of the chief executive.

pocket veto The chief executive's "silent" rejection of a bill by not acting on it within 10 days of receiving it if the legislature adjourns during this period.

CHAPTER SUMMARY

Our legal system consists of three levels of government (federal, state, and local) and three branches of government (executive, legislative, and judicial) within each level. Federalism is the division of powers between the federal or national government and the state governments. To keep any one branch from becoming too powerful, our system imposes checks and balances among the three branches.

There are ten main categories of primary authority: opinions, statutes, constitutions, administrative regulations, administrative decisions, charters, ordinances, court rules, executive orders, and treaties. The first three articles of the U.S. Constitution establish the legislative power in Congress, the executive power in the president, and the judicial power in the U.S. Supreme Court and inferior courts that Congress may establish. The first ten amendments contain the Bill of Rights, such as freedom of speech in the First Amendment. Each state also has a constitution. Under the Supremacy Clause, all state laws must be consistent with the U.S. Constitution and with every valid federal statute and administrative regulation.

The main definition of common law is judge-made law in the absence of controlling statutory law or other higher law. Under the doctrine of stare decisis, a court will decide similar cases in the same way (it will follow available precedents) unless there is good reason for the court to do otherwise. Enacted law is law written by a deliberative body such as a legislature or constitutional convention after it is proposed and often debated and amended. It is any law that is not created within litigation. Common-law courts and courts of equity have been merged in most states so that the same court can provide legal and equitable remedies. Under our adversary system, we resolve a legal dispute by letting the parties (alone or through their advocates) argue their conflicting claims before a neutral (impartial) decision maker.

Jurisdiction refers to the power of a court to resolve a legal dispute and to the geographic area over which a particular court has authority. The latter is the court's territorial jurisdiction. Subject-matter jurisdiction is the court's power to resolve a particular type of legal dispute and to grant a particular type of relief. The six main kinds of this jurisdiction are limited, general, exclusive, concurrent, original, and appellate jurisdiction.

Courts of original jurisdiction are the trial courts. There may be two levels or tiers of trial courts within a judicial system: courts of general jurisdiction and inferior courts of limited jurisdiction. There may also be two levels of courts with appellate jurisdiction: intermediate appellate courts and a court of final resort.

There are three main kinds of administrative agencies: executive department agencies, independent regulatory agencies, and quasi-independent regulatory agencies. (Government corporations are special entities that are a mixture of business corporation and government agency.) Agencies serve three main functions: to carry out (execute) statutes, executive orders, and administrative regulations; to write administrative regulations; and to resolve disputes that arise under laws for which the agency has responsibility.

The federal legislature (Congress) and most state legislatures are bicameral. For a bill to become a statute, it must go through approximately six stages. First, the bill is proposed by being introduced into one of the chambers of the legislature. It may be introduced into the other chamber simultaneously or at a later date. Second, a committee (and its subcommittee) of each chamber gives the bill initial consideration. Third, all of the members of each chamber are given the opportunity to debate and vote on the bill that was approved by the committee. Fourth, if there are differences in the versions of the bill passed by each chamber, a conference committee, made up of members of both chambers, considers the bill. The role of this committee is to try to reconcile differences in the two versions of the bill passed by each chamber. Fifth, the bill goes back to the full membership of each chamber for a vote on what the conference committee produced. Sixth, the chief executive can sign or reject (veto) the bill. If he or she explicitly vetoes the bill, it can still become a statute if two-thirds of each chamber votes to override the chief executive. The legislative history of a statute consists of what happens during these six stages.

KEY TERMS

federalism (p. 286)
legislative branch (p. 286)
executive branch (p. 286)
judicial branch (p. 286)
checks and balances (p. 286)
judicial review (p. 286)
law (p. 287)
primary authority (p. 287)
secondary authority (p. 287)
opinion of the attorney
    general (p. 287)
opinion (p. 287)
statute (p. 287)
constitution (p. 288)
administrative regulation (p. 288)
administrative decision (p. 288)
charter (p. 288)
ordinance (p. 288)
court rule (p. 288)
executive order (p. 288)
treaty (p. 288)
Supremacy Clause (p. 290)
indigent (p. 290)
common law (p. 290)
at common law (p. 290)
common-law system (p. 290)
civil-law system (p. 290)
civil (p. 290)

precedent (p. 291)
stare decisis (p. 291)
cause of action (p. 291)
derogation (p. 291)
consideration (p. 291)
enacted law (p. 291)
prospective (p. 292)
equity (p. 292)
remedy (p. 292)
damages (p. 292)
equitable (p. 292)
specific performance (p. 292)
injunction (p. 292)
international law (p. 292)
constitutional court (p. 293)
legislative court (p. 293)
adjudicate (p. 293)
adversarial (p. 293)
adversary system (p. 293)
inquisitorial system (p. 293)
record (p. 293)
court of record (p. 293)
trial de novo (p. 293)
jurisdiction (p. 294)
territorial jurisdiction (p. 294)
personal jurisdiction (p. 294)
subject-matter jurisdiction
    (p. 294)

limited jurisdiction (p. 294)
general jurisdiction (p. 294)
exclusive jurisdiction (p. 294)
concurrent jurisdiction (p. 294)
original jurisdiction (p. 294)
appellate jurisdiction (p. 294)
review (p. 295)
ruling (p. 295)
certiorari (p. 295)
writ (p. 295)
inferior court (p. 296)
appellate brief (p. 296)
panel (p. 296)
en banc (p. 296)
court of final resort (p. 296)
U.S. district court (p. 296)
diversity of citizenship (p. 296)
U.S. court of appeals (p. 297)
U.S. Supreme Court (p. 297)
administrative agency (p. 298)
enabling statute (p. 298)
executive department
    agency (p. 299)
cause (p. 299)
independent regulatory
    agency (p. 299)
quasi-independent regulatory
    agency (p. 299)

government corporation (p. 299)
quasi-legislation (p. 299)
quasi-adjudication (p. 299)
administrative law judge (ALJ)
    (p. 300)
exhaust administrative
    remedies (p. 300)
Administrative Procedure Act
    (APA) (p. 300)
bill (p. 300)
bicameral (p. 300)
unicameral (p. 300)
legislative history (p. 300)
transcript (p. 302)
transcribed (p. 302)
markup (p. 302)
committee report (p. 302)
engrossed bill (p. 302)
conference committee (p. 302)
enrolled bill (p. 303)
veto (p. 303)
override (p. 303)
pocket veto (p. 303)

ASSIGNMENTS

CRITICAL ANALYSIS

6.1 You will frequently hear complaints about gridlock in government as political parties attack each other. Write an essay in which you discuss whether the system of checks and balances makes gridlock even worse. Your discussion should include pros and cons of our system of checks and balances.

PROJECTS

6.2 Find a recent article in your local general newspaper that meets the following criteria: (1) it refers to more than one kind of law listed in Exhibit 6-1, and (2) it refers to more than one level of government. The article will have no formal citations to laws, so do the best you can to guess what kinds of law and levels of government are involved. Clip out the article or print it if you found it on the Internet. In the margin, next to each reference to a law, place the appropriate abbreviation: FO (if you think the reference is to a federal court opinion); SO (if you think the reference is to a state court opinion); FS (federal statute); SS (state statute); FC (U.S. Constitution); SC (state constitution); FAR (administrative regulation of a federal agency); SAR (administrative regulation of a state agency). Make up your own abbreviation for any other kind of law listed in Exhibit 6-1. If the article refers to the same law more than once, make a margin note only the first time the law is mentioned. (We'll have an informal contest to see which student can find the article with the most different kinds of laws involving more than one level of government.)

6.3

(a) Redo Exhibit 6-3 so that your chart includes all the state courts of your state. Identify each level of state court in your state, using Exhibit 6-3 as a guide. Give the complete name of each court you include and a one-sentence description of its subject matter jurisdiction. Indicate the lines of appeal among these courts. To find out what state courts exist in your state, check the Internet sites presented at the beginning of Exhibit 6-3. See also your state in Appendix J.

(b) Select any state trial court of general jurisdiction in your state. Give its name, address, and phone number. Include the email address and the Internet site if the court has either. Also give the name, phone number, and email address of the chief clerk of this court.

(c) Give the name, address, and phone number of the court to which decisions of the trial court you selected are appealed. Include the email address and the Internet site if the court has either. Also give the name, phone number, and email address of the chief clerk of this appellate court.

6.4

(a) What is the complete name of the federal trial court where you live? Give its address and phone number. Include the email address and the Internet site. Also state the name, phone number, and email address of the chief clerk of this court. Are the decisions of this court available on its Internet site? If so, pick any recent decision, and give the names of the parties and the online address of the decision.

(b) What is the name of the U.S. court of appeals to which decisions of your federal trial court are appealed? Give its address and phone number. Include the email address and the Internet site. Also state the name, phone number, and email address of the chief clerk of this appellate court. Are the decisions of this court available on its Internet site? If so, pick any recent decision, and give the names of the parties and the online address of the decision.

6.5 Give the name, street address, phone number, email address, Internet address, and function (stated briefly) of

(a) Any three federal agencies with offices in your state

(b) Any five state agencies in your state

(c) Any five city or county agencies with offices in your city or county

6.6

(a) What is the Internet address of your state legislature? On this site, can you find current statutes in the code? Current bills in the legislature? Explain what is available.

(b) Give the name, political party, street address, phone number, email address, and fax number of the chief legislator in each chamber of your state legislature, e.g., speaker of the house and president of the senate. (If your state legislature is unicameral [Nebraska], answer these questions for the one chamber that exists.)

(c) What is the full name of the legislative committee in each chamber (e.g., judiciary committee) with primary authority to consider laws that directly affect your state courts, such as procedural laws that govern the conduct of litigation? Give the name, political party, phone number, email address, and fax number of the current chairperson of each of these committees.

6.7 What is the name of the local legislature in your city or county? Give the name, political party, street address, phone number, and email address of the chief legislator of this body. (If you have both a city and a county legislature, answer this question for both.) On these sites, can you find links to current ordinances or other laws in force? Current bills in the legislature? Explain what is available.

CORE SKILLS

Among the many skills a paralegal must have, five core skills stand out: writing (both basic English and legal drafting), research, ethics, computer use, and collaboration (working with others). The core-skill assignments introduce and reinforce these skills. Even if you are not asked to do all of the assignments as part of the course, you should do them on your own. Also, do not wait for the topics in the assignments to be covered in this course or in other courses. Successful paralegals are self-starters. A major characteristic of a self-starter is a thirst for independent study—learning on your own.

CORE SKILL: WRITING

6.8 On Google, Bing, or Yahoo, run this search: readability tests. Find information about tests such as Flesch Kincaid Reading Ease, Flesch Kincaid Grade Level, Gunning Fog Score, Coleman Liau Index, and Automated Readability Index. Others also exist. Many word processors (e.g., Word) have readability tests built into the program.

(a) What is the purpose of readability tests?

(b) Pick any two tests and describe how persons can improve their scores or results on these tests.

(c) Write an essay on your career goals as a paralegal. Cover why you entered the field, what you hope to accomplish, and any obstacles or challenges that you anticipate. The essay should be long enough for you to be able to apply any two readability tests to it.

(d) Apply the two tests to what you wrote. State the results of each test.

(e) Rewrite the essay in order to improve the results you achieved on each test. Apply the two tests to the rewrite. Now what results did you obtain?

CORE SKILL: RESEARCH

6.9 Exhibit 6-1 presents the main categories of law. A great deal of this law is available on the Internet. If, for example, you wanted to find a statute written by the Florida legislature or by Congress, you could start the search by entering "Florida statute" or "federal statute" or "United States statute" in a search engine such as Google. Using this general guide, find one example on any topic of each of the following materials on the Internet. When asked for state material, use the state where you will be working as a paralegal. Give the name or title of what you found and the Internet address where you found it:

(a) a federal court opinion

(b) a state court opinion

(c) a federal statute

(d) a state statute

(e) a clause in the U.S. Constitution

(f) a clause in a state constitution

(g) an administrative regulation of a federal agency

(h) an administrative regulation of a state agency

(i) an administrative decision of a federal agency

(j) a clause in a city or county charter

(k) a city, county, or town ordinance

(l) a court rule of a federal court

(n) a court rule of a state court

(o) an executive order of the president

(p) an executive order of a governor

(q) a treaty signed by the United States

CORE SKILL: ETHICS

6.10 Fred is a paralegal at Harris and Harris. He works on the case of Kevin Crowley, who is being sued by the Securities and Exchange Commission (SEC) for securities fraud. Fred sees an opening at the SEC for a paralegal. He takes the job. What ethical problems do you see? How, if at all, can these problems be resolved?

CORE SKILL: COMPUTERS

6.11 In Chapter 13, read the section on database management. On Google, Bing, or Yahoo, search for key terms in the following questions to help you find the answers.

(a) What is a database management software program?

(b) What are the main database management software programs that are sold?

(c) Which of these programs are the most widely used?

(d) What are the main database software programs that are free?

(e) Name one of the free programs.

(f) Find discussions that compare the program you selected in question c with the program you selected in question e. What are some of the differences other than cost?

(g) In the Computer Terminology in the Law (CTL) notebook you started in Assignment 1.8 of Chapter 1, enter any new terms that you learned by doing parts (a) to (f).

CORE SKILL: COLLABORATION

6.12 For this assignment, you will be teamed up with two other students in the class. The instructor will let you know if the two other students will be assigned to you or whether you can select two on your own. Each of you should redraw Exhibit 6-6 so that your chart and the accompanying narrative explanation include the steps needed for a bill to become a statute in your state legislature. Three weeks before the assignment is due, email your answer to the other two students. The three of you must discuss combining the best or your three work products so that you submit one final answer signed by the three of you. The task of submitting the final product should *not* be performed by one student. An objective of the assignment is for the three of you to work collaboratively. Submit two documents to the instructor: the final product the three of you worked on and your individual answer that you prepared *before* you submitted it to the other two students.

THE JOB SEARCH

(The search for employment cannot wait until the end of a course or of a curriculum. It needs to begin now. The job-search assignments are designed to introduce you to different aspects of the job search and to build options for you to explore about employment.)

6.13 Use the job links in Exhibit 2-12 in Chapter 2 to find a job opening for a paralegal in any state or local government office in your state. What does the job entail and what are the qualifications for the position? Give the address of the site where you found this information. If no openings exist in your state, look for the position in any state. See also Appendix I for your state and the discussion in Chapter 2 of paralegals in government.

REVIEW QUESTIONS

1. What are the three levels of government?
2. What is federalism?
3. What are the three branches of government and their functions?
4. What is meant by checks and balances?
5. What is judicial review?
6. What is the distinction between primary and secondary authority?
7. Define opinion, statute, constitution, administrative regulation, administrative decision, charter, ordinance, court rule, executive order, and treaty.
8. What rights are found in the First Amendment?
9. What is the Supremacy Clause?
10. What are the three major meanings of common law?
11. What is stare decisis?
12. How does enacted law differ from common law?
13. How did law and equity differ before they merged in most states?
14. What is an adversary system?
15. What is a court of record?
16. What are the two main meanings of jurisdiction?
17. What is personal jurisdiction?
18. What is subject-matter jurisdiction? What are the six main kinds of this jurisdiction?
19. What is an inferior court?
20. What are the tiers or levels of courts that can exist in state court systems?
21. Name and distinguish the four main kinds of administrative agencies.
22. What are the three main functions of an administrative agency?
23. What can occur when a party has exhausted administrative remedies?
24. What is the Administrative Procedure Act (APA)?
25. Define bill.
26. Distinguish between unicameral and bicameral legislatures.
27. What steps can a federal bill go through before it becomes a statute?
28. Distinguish between an engrossed bill and an enrolled bill.
29. What is meant by legislative history?

HELPFUL WEBSITES

Government: Federal
- www.usa.gov
- www.whitehouse.gov/our-government

Government: State
- en.wikipedia.org/wiki/State_governments_of_the_United_States
- www.whitehouse.gov/our-government/tate-and-local-government

Government: Local
- www.usa.gov/Agencies/Local.shtml

Legislature: Congress
- congress.gov

Legislature: Fifty States
- thomas.loc.gov/home/state-legislatures.html

Legislature: How Our Laws Are Made (Congress)
- thomas.loc.gov/home/lawsmade.toc.html
- thomas.loc.gov/home/holam.txt
- clerk.house.gov/legislative/legprocess.aspx
- www.thecapitol.net/glossary (definitions of legislative terms)

Legislature: How Our Laws Are Made (Your State)
- In Google, Bing, or Yahoo, try this search: *aa how a bill becomes law is made* (substituting your state for "aa")

Courts: Fifty States
- www.govengine.com (click your state on the map, then click entries under "Judicial Branch")

- Google, Bing, or Yahoo (type aa "Court System" substituting the abbreviation of your state for "aa," e.g., CA "Court System")
- www.ncsc.org (type "State Court Web sites" in the search box, then click your state)

Courts: Federal (Understanding the Federal Courts)
- www.uscourts.gov/FederalCourts.aspx
- www.uscourts.gov/News/JournalistsGuide.aspx
- www.uscourts.gov/uscourts/News/docs/JournalistGuide2011.pdf

Courts: Comparing Federal and State Court Systems
- www.uscourts.gov (enter *compare federal and state courts* in the search box)

National Center for State Courts
- www.ncsc.org

Administrative Agency Links (Federal)
- www.usa.gov (click *Government Agencies and Elected Officials*)

Administrative Procedures Act (APA)
- www.archives.gov/federal-register/laws/administrative-procedure
- en.wikipedia.org/wiki/Administrative_Procedure_Act
- usgovinfo.about.com/library/bills/blapa.htm

Constitutional Law
- www.law.cornell.edu/wex/Constitutional_law
- en.wikipedia.org/wiki/Constitutional_law

Google, Bing, or Yahoo Searches

(On these search engines, run the following searches, using quotation marks and substituting your state for "aa" where indicated.)

- federalism
- "checks and balances"
- "judicial review" aa
- "common law" aa
- stare decisis

- equity law aa
- constitution aa
- Bill of Rights
- Supremacy Clause
- civil law system

- adversary system
- jurisdiction aa
- personal jurisdiction aa
- subject-matter jurisdiction aa
- court system aa
- federal courts
- administrative agency federal
- administrative agency aa

- regulatory agency
- government corporation
- Administrative Procedure Act
- How a law is made Congress
- How a law is made aa
- legislative process aa

ENDNOTES

[1] William Burnham, *Introduction to the Legal System of the United States* 78 (2d ed. 1999).

[2] See uniformlaws.org.

The Skills of a Paralegal

CHAPTER 7

INTRODUCTION TO LEGAL ANALYSIS

CHAPTER OUTLINE

- Legal Analysis Skills: Introduction
- Legal Analysis Skills: Element Identification
- Legal Analysis Skills: Issue Spotting and Phrasing
- Legal Analysis Skills: Definitions
- Legal Analysis Skills: Factor Analysis
- Memorandum of Law
- Introduction to Court Opinions
- Legal Analysis Skills: Briefing an Opinion
- Legal Analysis Skills: Applying an Opinion

CHAPTER OBJECTIVES

After completing this chapter, you should be able to:

- Define legal analysis.
- List some of the major skills involved in legal analysis
- Know how to break a rule into its elements and why this is important.
- Explain the different kinds of issues.
- Know how to spot and phrase issues.
- Distinguish between a comprehensive and a shorthand statement of a legal issue.
- Explain the importance of definitions and know how to phrase them broadly and narrowly.
- Distinguish between element analysis and factor analysis.
- Distinguish between IRAC and IFRAC.
- Explain the components of an opinion.
- Know how to write a comprehensive and a thumbnail brief of an opinion.
- Know how to apply an opinion.
- Write a memorandum of law.

LEGAL ANALYSIS SKILLS: INTRODUCTION

Legal questions are answered by applying rules to facts. The application is called **legal analysis.** The interrelated goals of legal analysis are as follows:

- To avoid a legal dispute (e.g., "Will I get into trouble with the Federal Trade Commission if we merge with our main competitor?")
- To resolve a legal dispute that has already arisen (e.g., "I feel the deduction I took was legitimate, but the IRS has notified me that I now owe interest and penalties because of it.")
- To prevent a legal dispute from becoming worse (e.g., "The police are on the way to question me about the fight I was in. What should I tell them?")

Paralegals need to study legal analysis for two main reasons. First, many paralegals are given assignments that in varying degrees call for legal analysis. Secondly, and perhaps more importantly, attorneys talk the language of legal analysis all the time (issues, rules, exceptions,

legal analysis The application of one or more rules to the facts of a client's case in order to answer a legal question that will help (1) avoid a legal dispute, (2) resolve a legal dispute that has arisen, or (3) prevent a legal dispute from becoming worse.

elements, briefing, reasoning, etc.). A paralegal who knows the basics of legal analysis will be better equipped to understand and communicate with attorneys.

LEGAL ANALYSIS SKILLS

Competent legal analysis may involve a number of basic skills:

- *Legal research*: This skill allows you to find rules that you need to apply to the facts of a client's case. Legal analysis and legal research often occur simultaneously in the sense that preliminary legal analysis helps the researcher decide what laws in the library should be checked.
- *Element identification*: Once you have found a potentially applicable rule, the skill of element identification allows you to break any rule into its essential parts—elements— as a first step in identifying issues.
- *Identifying issues (issue spotting)*: This skill allows you to identify which elements of a rule are in contention. Each element in contention will be the basis of a separate issue.
- *Phrasing issues*: This skill allows you to phrase issues (comprehensively and in shorthand).
- *Defining important language*: This skill allows you to define important language in the element in contention (using available court opinions, if any, that have interpreted and defined the language)
- *Applying definitions*: This skill allows you to apply the definitions to the facts (again using available court opinions, if any)
- *Factor analysis*: This skill allows you to apply a rule when it contains factors.
- *Briefing court opinions*: This skill allows you to understand a court opinion in order to assess whether it might apply.
- *Applying court opinions*: This skill allows you to apply a court opinion to your facts.

The sequence of using the skills that we will examine in this chapter is outlined in Exhibit 7-1.

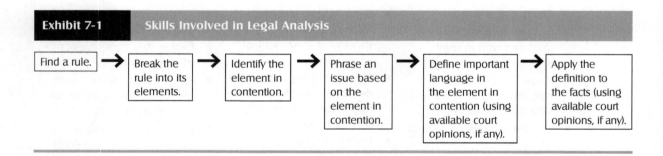

| Exhibit 7-1 | Skills Involved in Legal Analysis |

Find a rule. → Break the rule into its elements. → Identify the element in contention. → Phrase an issue based on the element in contention. → Define important language in the element in contention (using available court opinions, if any). → Apply the definition to the facts (using available court opinions, if any).

FINDING A RULE TO APPLY (LEGAL RESEARCH)

The first task is to find a rule that might apply to the facts of the client's case. The law firm may already be aware of potentially applicable rules because of its prior experience with other clients and the nature of its practice. If not, it must find those rules through the skill of legal research. Because the law is constantly changing, legal research is also needed on an ongoing basis to determine the *current* validity of any rule the law firm is considering. We will cover the skill of legal research in Chapter 11. Here in Chapter 7, we will assume that one or more rules have been identified.

In this chapter, the word *rule* means any **primary authority** that we defined in Exhibit 6-1 in Chapter 6. (**Secondary authority** are nonlaws—nonrules—that we will define in Exhibit 11-6 in Chapter 11.) The most frequently applied primary authorities (rules) in legal analysis are:

- Statutes
- Administrative regulations
- Common-law rules
- Constitutional provisions

In Chapter 6, we also defined **common law** as judge-made law in the absence of controlling statutory law or other higher law. The phrase *common-law rule* refers to any law that was created by the courts—that was judge-made.

primary authority A law written by one of the three branches of government. (For definitions of the primary authorities, see Exhibit 6-1 in Chapter 6.)

secondary authority A nonlaw (e.g., a legal periodical article) that summarizes, describes, or explains the law but is not a law itself. (For definitions of the secondary authorities, see Exhibit 11-6 in Chapter 11.)

common law Judge-made law in the absence of controlling statutory law or other higher law. Law derived from court opinions. (See glossary for additional meanings.)

When someone is sued for a violation of one of these rules, the theory of the suit is called a **cause of action**. The cause of action becomes the rule that the person is alleged to have violated. Although the phrase *cause of action* is most often used in civil cases, it can also be used in criminal cases, as we will see.

LEGAL ANALYSIS SKILL: ELEMENT IDENTIFICATION

Once you have a rule that might apply, the analysis begins by breaking the rule into its basic parts. We call these parts **elements**. An element is simply one of the parts of a rule that must apply in order for the rule to apply. An element is, therefore, a precondition of the applicability of the entire rule.

The element-identification skill requires you to answer two questions: what is the express or implied consequence of the rule, and what must happen before this consequence will be imposed or go into effect? When you answer the second question, you will have identified the elements of the rule.

Every rule has a consequence or an effect if the rule applies. These consequences can vary. For example, there are rules that

- Authorize something
- Prohibit something
- Impose punishments
- Require payments
- Establish a right to sue and receive damages
- Require safety steps to be taken

- Institute procedures
- Make statements of policy
- Declare definitions of important concepts
- Carry out a combination of the above consequences

The consequence might be stated in the rule or it might be implied. After we look at some examples, Exhibit 7-2 will summarize guidelines for the element-identification skill. We begin with some relatively simple rules.

EXAMPLES

Example #1 – Co-op

Rule: § 10. Any business operating within the city must obtain a commercial license.

If § 10 applies, a commercial license must be obtained. This is the consequence of the rule if it applies. To find the elements of § 10, make a numbered list of its essential parts.

Elements of § 10

1. Any business
2. Operating within the city

Note that the list uses the exact language of the rule and that the consequence of the applicability of the rule—obtaining a commercial license—is not listed as one of the elements. To list the consequence of the rule as an element would be circular. It makes no sense to say that one of the preconditions of having a license is to have a license. In some issue statements, you may want to include part of the consequence within an element in order to clarify the context of the element. This, however, should be rare. If you do include the consequence, be sure that you avoid circular reasoning when you apply the element.

Element identification is done in your head or on a scrap piece of paper. It is not handed in to anyone. It is one of the preliminary tasks of legal analysis.

Example #2 - Bike on Road

Rule: § 92(b). The operator of any vehicle riding on a sidewalk shall be fined $100.

If § 92(b) applies, a $100 fine will be imposed. This is the consequence of the rule. Here are the elements of the rule:

Elements of § 92(b)

1. Operator
2. Any vehicle
3. Riding
4. On a sidewalk

cause of action (1) A legally acceptable reason for bringing a suit. A rule that constitutes a legal theory for bringing a suit. (2) The facts that give a person a right to judicial relief. When you *state a cause of action*, you list the facts that give you a right to judicial relief against the alleged wrongdoer.

element A portion of a rule that is a precondition of the applicability of the entire rule.

Example #3 - Pharmacy

Rule: § 25–403. A pharmacist must not sell prescription drugs to a minor.

The effect or consequence of this rule is that something is prohibited—the selling of prescription drugs. For any rule, ask yourself what conditions must exist before the rule applies. Your answer will consist of its elements.

Elements of § 25–403

1. Pharmacist
2. Sell
3. Prescription drugs
4. To a minor

The second element does not say "must not sell." The "must not" language is part of the consequence. If the elements apply, then the "must not" command kicks in.

Example #4 - Additional Punishment

Rule: § 109. A judge may impose additional punishment when a weapon is used by the accused in the commission of a drug offense.

Often there is more than one way to list elements. Here, for example, are two ways to phrase the elements of § 109:

Version A
    Elements of § 109

1. Judge
2. Weapon
3. Is used in the commission of a drug offense
4. By the accused

Version B

1. Judge
2. Weapon
3. Is used
4. In the commission of a drug offense
5. By the accused

The consequence of § 109 is that a judge can impose additional punishment. In version A, note that there are two themes in the fourth element: *use* and *commission*. By combining them in one element, the verb "used" is seen in perspective. The element focuses on the *what* the use involves. Nevertheless, it is possible to separate these concepts into their own elements as seen in version B.

How do you decide which version to use? The facts will usually suggest what is needed. Suppose the accused merely had the weapon (e.g., a loaded gun) in his or her pocket at the time the drug offense was committed. The question would then become whether *possession* could constitute *use* under § 109. The facts would prompt you to discuss "used" separately. Either version, however, would work. If you used the first version, you would simply have to focus on one piece of the third element—used. The main guideline is to be narrow in your list and be willing to break an element into smaller units if the facts call for it.

Example #5 - False Imprisonment

Rule: False imprisonment is confinement of a person within fixed boundaries set by another person who intended to restrain the movement of the person confined.

False imprisonment is a common-law cause of action and, as such, is a common-law rule. False imprisonment is a **tort** cause of action. Other frequently used torts include negligence, medical malpractice, libel, wrongful adoption, strict liability in tort, and false light invasion of privacy. Each of these tort causes of action (like false imprisonment) has its own elements. A major nontort cause of action is breach of contract.

tort A civil wrong (other than a breach of contract) that causes injury or other loss for which our legal system deems it just to provide a remedy such as damages. Injury or loss can be to the person (a personal tort), to movable property (a personal-property tort), or to land and anything attached to the land (a real-property tort).

Elements of False Imprisonment

1. Confinement
2. Of a person
3. Within set boundaries
4. By another person
5. Who intended to restrain the movement of the person confined

If these elements apply, the consequence is that false imprisonment has been committed. Other rules will state other consequences such as the payment of damages.

Example #6 - Place of Trial

Rule: § 971.22. A party may move for a change of the place of trial on the ground that an impartial trial cannot be had in the county. The motion must be made at the time of arraignment.

If § 971.22 applies, parties will know whether they can request a change in the place of the trial and when they must request the change. This is the consequence of the rule.

Elements of § 971.22

1. A party
2. Move for a change of the place of trial
3. On the ground that an impartial trial
4. Cannot be had in the county
5. The motion
6. Must be made at the time of the arraignment

Here is another version:

Elements of § 971.22

1. A party
2. At the time of the arraignment
3. Move for a change of the place of trial
4. On the ground that an impartial trial cannot be had in the county

When you list elements, you are not casting them in stone. Variations are possible. As your analysis proceeds, you may consider a different listing of elements so long as you are rigorously faithful to the language of the rule. You can shift the order of the language if this helps you organize your thoughts about the rule so long as a shift does not change the meaning of any of the elements.

Example #7 - Wrongful Adoption

Rule: An action for wrongful adoption exists for failing to disclose to prospective adoptive parents known facts or conditions that would be relevant to the decision on whether to adopt.

Elements of wrongful adoption

1. Failing to disclose
2. Known facts or conditions
3. To prospective adoptive parents
4. That would be relevant to the decision on whether to adopt

This is another common-law rule on the tort cause of action for wrongful adoption. The consequence of the elements applying is that the tort or wrongful adoption has been committed.

Note the word "or" in the second element. When "or" means two or more alternatives that will satisfy a requirement, place all of the alternatives within the same element. If, however, the rule contains language separated by "and," *additional* requirements are usually indicated. Each additional requirement should be stated in its own element. The same is true if "and" (or "or") is implied rather than explicitly stated in the rule.

Note also that the language in the listing of the four elements of wrongful adoption does not follow the same sequence as the language in the rule itself. The list places "known facts or conditions" immediately after "disclose." So long as the meaning of the rule is not changed, it can be appropriate to alter the sequence of the language in the rule when this is helpful in understanding and analyzing the rule.

Example #8 - Expenses of Litigation

> *Rule*: § 5. While representing a client in connection with contemplated or pending litigation, a lawyer shall not advance or guarantee financial assistance to his client, except that a lawyer may advance or guarantee court costs, expenses of investigation, expenses of medical examination, and costs of obtaining and presenting evidence, provided the client remains ultimately liable for such expenses.

Some rules, particularly statutes and regulations, can be difficult to break into elements when they contain

- Lists
- Alternatives
- Exceptions
- Provisos or conditions

Nevertheless, the same process is used. Take the time to dissect the rule into its component elements. Don't be reluctant to bring subject and verb closer together when the meaning is not changed.

Elements of § 5

1. A lawyer
2. Representing a client in connection with contemplated litigation or in connection with pending litigation
3. Shall not advance financial assistance to his client or guarantee financial assistance to his client, except that the following is proper:
   a. Lawyer advances or guarantees court costs provided the client remains ultimately liable for such expenses, or
   b. Lawyer advances or guarantees expenses of investigation provided the client remains ultimately liable for such expenses, or
   c. Lawyer advances or guarantees expenses of medical examination provided the client remains ultimately liable for such expenses, or
   d. Lawyer advances or guarantees costs of obtaining and presenting evidence provided the client remains ultimately liable for such expenses.

Section 5 tells us what a lawyer "shall not" do. The consequence of the elements applying is that the attorney has violated § 5.

Section 5 contains several alternatives. Note how they are clustered together with the element to which they relate. The same is true of the exception clauses in the rule. Don't be reluctant to repeat parts of the rule within the elements, particularly when the subject and object or the subject and modifying clause are far apart in long rules. Reread § 5 again slowly and then note how the elements repeat clauses in this way.

The most complicated element of § 5 is the third—(3). It contains lists, alternatives, an exception, and a proviso. But they all relate to the same point—the propriety of advancing (providing) or guaranteeing financial assistance to a client. None of the subdivisions of the third element should be stated as a separate element because all the "or" options relate to the element of whether the items listed shall or shall not be advanced or guaranteed.

GUIDELINES FOR IDENTIFYING ELEMENTS

For a summary of the guidelines for identifying elements, see Exhibit 7-2.

Exhibit 7-2	Guidelines for Identifying Elements

- An element is a portion of a rule that is a precondition of the applicability of the entire rule. The skill of element identification requires you to make a list of these elements.
- Element identification is done in your head or on a scrap piece of paper. It is not handed in to anyone. It is one of the preliminary tasks of legal analysis.
- There is often more than one way to list elements. Be prepared to try different combinations in the list. The facts will suggest to you how narrow your list of elements should be. (See Example #4 on the two lists for § 109.)
- The starting point is a rule such as a statute or common-law rule.

■ Know the consequence of the rule if it applies. The consequence may or may not be stated within the rule.

■ The consequence might be to allow something, to forbid something, to define something, etc. The elements of the rule will tell us when this consequence will be effective.

■ In general, don't list the consequence as one of the elements.

■ Read the rule carefully. Make a list of all of the essential parts of the rule. This list comprises the elements of the rule.

■ Use the exact language of the rule in your list of elements. Don't paraphrase with synonyms or use your language. You can, however, make some adjustments in the order of the language so long as you do not change the language or alter the meaning of the rule. One adjustment that may add clarity is to bring verbs and subjects closer together. (See Example #7.) Another is to repeat subjects, clauses, prepositions, or phrases that clearly go together. (See Example #8.)

■ Rules often contain "and" lists. If the items in the list are joined by "and," treat each of the items as a separate element. The "and" will either be explicit or implied. *And* tells you what additional items are required.

■ Rules often contain "or" lists. If the items in the list are joined by "or," you are being told about alternatives. Keep all of the "or" alternatives within the same element. (See Examples ##7 and 8.) The "or" will either be explicit or implied.

■ Rules often contain exception clauses. State them within the relevant element when they are related to the applicability of that element. (See Example #8.) Exception clauses do not contain new requirements. Rather, they tell us when a requirement does not apply.

■ Some rules are very long. A statute, for example, may contain dozens of sentences. The likelihood is that such statutes consist of more than one rule. Look for the possibility that each complete sentence in the statute is a separate rule (or subrule) with its own elements.

ADDITIONAL BENEFITS OF ELEMENT IDENTIFICATION

Element identification has many uses in the law in addition to being an early step in legal analysis. Exhibit 7-3 outlines these other benefits. For example, knowing the elements of rules can help give direction to interviewing and investigation. When you interview and investigate, you are looking for relevant facts. How do you know which facts are relevant? One of the ways is to identify the elements of the potentially applicable rules that both sides will be arguing in the litigation. Facts are relevant if they help show that those elements apply or do not apply. As you can see from Exhibit 7-3, element identification will also help identify issues, draft complaints and answers, conduct depositions, organize memos and exam answers, and charge the jury.

Exhibit 7-3	Uses of Element Identification

■ **Identifying issues.** Once you identify the elements of a rule, the next step is to find the elements that are most likely to be in contention between the parties. These elements become the basis of issues (as we shall see in the next section).

■ **Drafting a complaint.** A *complaint* is the plaintiff's first formal litigation document; it is the plaintiff's first pleading. The complaint states a *cause of action* against the defendant. When drafting a complaint, you often organize your factual allegations around the major elements of the cause of action.

■ **Drafting defenses.** An *answer* is the first pleading of the defendant that responds to the plaintiff's cause of action. The answer will often assert *defenses* such as the statute of limitations. When drafting an answer to a complaint, you often state your defenses by alleging facts that support the elements of each defense.

■ **Organizing an interview of a client.** One of the goals of interviewing a client is to obtain facts that are relevant to every element of the potential causes of action and defenses in the case. Element analysis, therefore, helps you organize the interview and give it direction.

■ **Organizing an investigation.** One of the goals of investigation is to obtain facts relevant to every element of the potential causes of action and defenses in the case. Element analysis, therefore, helps you organize the investigation and give it direction.

■ **Conducting a deposition.** A *deposition* is a method of discovery by which parties and their prospective witnesses are questioned by the opposing party outside the courtroom before trial. During a deposition, many of the attorney's questions are designed to identify facts that are relevant to the elements of the potential causes of action and defenses in the case. Element analysis, therefore, helps the attorney organize the deposition and give it direction.

■ **Organizing a memorandum of law.** A memorandum of law is a written explanation of how one or more rules might apply to the facts of a client's case. The memorandum is organized by issues, which are based on elements of rules that are in contention. Element analysis, therefore, helps identify what is covered and what will be emphasized in the memorandum of law.

■ **Organizing an examination answer.** Some essay examinations in school are designed to find out if the student is able to identify and define the major elements of the rules that should be analyzed.

■ **Charging a jury.** When judges *charge* (instruct) a jury, they will go over each of the elements of the causes of action and defenses in the case. They will tell the jury what standard to use (e.g., beyond a reasonable doubt or preponderance of the evidence) to determine whether facts in support of those elements have been sufficiently proven during the trial. Element analysis, therefore, helps the judge organize the charge and give it direction.

LEGAL ANALYSIS SKILLS: ISSUE SPOTTING AND PHRASING

Identifying elements, as we have seen, is the first step of legal analysis after you have found a rule and want to determine whether it applies to the facts of the client's case. We will turn now to the next skill, which is the identification of issues—issue spotting. This skill will also be dependent on a proper identification of elements.

In the broadest sense, an **issue** is a question that needs to be answered or resolved, usually because of uncertainty or dispute. There are two main categories of issues:

■ Factual issues (also called *issues of fact* or *fact questions*)
■ Legal issues (also called *issues of law* or *legal questions*)

A factual issue is raised when we want to know what happened. A **legal issue** is raised when we want to know what the law is, what the law means or how the law applies to a specific facts. Examples of Factual Issues

■ Was the employee denied a bonus in 2014?
■ How long has Jones been receiving unemployment compensation?
■ What did the parties intend when the buyer agreed in writing to pay the cost of the delivery?
■ Who was present when the vote was taken by the board of directors?
■ Is Paul Davis the biological father of Mary Smith's child?

Examples of Legal Issues

■ Is a bonus includible in the taxable income of an employee?
■ Is Jones eligible for unemployment compensation?
■ Can oral statements be introduced to prove a party's intention when the parties have a written contract?
■ Are the minutes of a meeting of the board of directors conclusive evidence of who was present at the meeting?
■ Is Paul Davis obligated to take and pay for a DNA paternity test?

In a jury trial, the jury answers factual issues in the **verdict** and the judge answers legal issues in the **judgment**. Conclusions on factual issues are called *findings*. Conclusions on legal issues are called *rulings* and *holdings*. In a **bench trial**, there is no jury, so the judge resolves both factual and legal issues.

Most of the issues we will be covering in this chapter will be legal issues. The legal issues presented in the above list are in a shorthand or abbreviated format. We need to learn how to phrase legal issues in their comprehensive format.

With this background, we turn to the interrelated skills of identifying legal issues (issue spotting) and phrasing them properly.

You identify an issue when you identify the **element in contention**. Once you break a rule into its elements, you then determine which element or elements the parties will dispute. An element they will dispute is an element in contention. Such an element then becomes the basis of a *legal issue*. (See Exhibit 7-4.) If a rule has five elements and you anticipate disagreement over all of them, phrase five separate issues. If, however, only one of the five elements will probably be in contention, phrase only one issue. There is no need to waste time over elements that will not be the basis of disagreement.

---

issue (1) A question to be resolved. (2) A question of law. A dispute over what the law is, what the law means, or how the law applies to the facts. Also called *legal issue, issue of law*. (3) A question of fact. A dispute over the existence or nonexistence of the alleged facts. Also called *factual issue, issue of fact, question of fact*. (See glossary for additional meanings.)

legal issue A question of law; a question of what the law is, what the law means, or how the law applies to specific facts. Also called *issue, issue of law*.

verdict The jury's finding or decision on the factual issues placed before it.

judgment The final conclusion of a court that resolves a legal dispute by declaring the rights and obligations of the parties or that specifies what further proceedings are needed to resolve it.

bench trial A trial before a judge without a jury. Also called a *nonjury trial*.

element in contention The portion of a rule about which the parties cannot agree. The disagreement may be over the definition of the element, whether the facts fit within the element, or both.

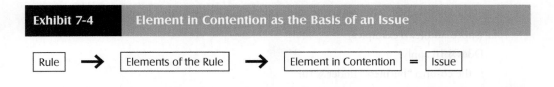

| Exhibit 7-4 | Element in Contention as the Basis of an Issue |

Rule → Elements of the Rule → Element in Contention = Issue

An element is in contention when you can predict that the two sides in the controversy will probably not agree (1) on the definition of the element, (2) on whether the facts fit within the element, or (3) on both the definition and whether the facts fit within it.

- Definition of the element. Example: the plaintiff and defendant have different interpretations of the meaning of "timely" in § 55.
- Whether the facts fit within the element. Example: the parties agree on the meaning of "timely," but disagree on whether the motion was "timely" filed when it was given to the clerk two hours after the deadline and the delay was caused by a snowstorm.
- Both the definition and whether the facts fit within it. Example: the parties disagree on the meaning of "timely" in § 55 and on whether the motion was "timely" filed when it was given to the clerk two hours after the deadline and the delay was caused by a snowstorm.

Let's look again at the eight examples we examined earlier. For each of the rules, you will find a set of facts. By examining these facts, you should be able to anticipate the dispute between the parties, which will lead you to the element in contention.

EXAMPLES

Example #1 – Co-op

Facts: Bill and his neighbors have formed a downtown food co-op (called Neighbors Together) through which members buy their food collectively from a **wholesale** company. All funds received by the co-op go for expenses and the purchase of more food to sell. There is no profit distributed to individual members. The city wants the co-op to obtain a commercial license. The co-op says the license law (§ 10) does not apply to co-ops.

wholesale The purchase of goods in large quantities that will be retailed to consumers by others.

Rule: § 10. Any business operating within the city must obtain a commercial license.

Elements of § 10

1. Any business
2. Operating within the city

The second element is not in contention. The facts say that the co-op is downtown, presumably within the city in question. There is no need, therefore, to base a legal issue on the second element. The element in contention is the first element. The co-op and the city will disagree on whether the co-op is a "business" within the meaning of § 10. Their contention over this element is its definition.

There are two main ways to phrase issues: shorthand and comprehensive. Both consist of only one sentence. Do not phrase a legal issue in more than one sentence.

Shorthand Statement of an Issue

During informal discussions in a law office, you will often find that attorneys and paralegals phrase legal issues in a broad, abbreviated fashion. Examples: Was Tom negligent? Does § 12 apply? Can we use the trespass defense? These are shorthand statements of issues because they state few or no facts and say little or nothing about the element in contention.

Comprehensive Statement of an Issue

Although shorthand issue statements can be useful starting points for discussion, you need to be able to provide a more comprehensive statement of the issue. This is done by including in your issue

- A brief quote from the element in contention, and
- Several of the important facts that are relevant to that contention

In our co-op example, here are shorthand and comprehensive statements of the issue:

Issue (shorthand)(two examples)

Does § 10 apply?

Is the co-op a "business" under § 10?

Issue (comprehensive)

Is a food co-op a "business" under § 10 even though the co-op uses its proceeds for expenses and to buy additional food rather than as profit for individual members of the co-op?

Note the following points about the comprehensive statement of the issue:

- The issue uses an "even though" clause. The use of the phrase "even though" or "when" or "if" is often an effective way to state facts that are relevant to the element in contention.
- The issue does not mention any proper names. The fact that the co-op is called Neighbors Together is not relevant to the element in contention. The issue would be the same if it had some other name. The issue would not be "wrong" if it included proper names; they are simply not needed. What is often important is the *category* in which major facts fit. Neighbors Together is a *food co-op*.
- The issue begins with the element in contention and concludes with the facts relevant to the contention. Facts are stated throughout the issue, but the facts most relevant to the contention are stated after "even though," "when," or "if."

There are other acceptable ways to phrase issues. They are outlined in Exhibit 7-5.

Exhibit 7-5	Different Ways to Phrase the Same Issue

The two critical components of a comprehensive statement of a legal issue are as follows: (1) a brief quote from the element of the rule in contention and (2) several of the important facts that are relevant to that contention. The same legal issue can be phrased in different ways so long as these two essentials are always included. The examples in Exhibit 7-5 use language such as "is," "has," "when," "if," and "whether" to introduce and connect the two essential elements. Be prepared, however, to use other language when it better fits the flow of the issue you are stating. Furthermore, the following ways to phrase an issue are not exhaustive. Other ways are possible so long are the two critical components are present.

Here are a variety of ways to structure a legal issue:

- State the Element in Contention before the Relevant Facts
    Is or *Has* or *Does* or similar verb [include here a short quote from the element in contention] *even though* or *when* [include here a brief statement of facts relevant to that contention].

    Examples:
    Is a food co-op a "business" under § 10 even though the co-op uses its proceeds for expenses and to buy additional food rather than as profit for individual members of the co-op?

    Has there been a "forfeiture" of a tax refund under § 612 when the taxpayer fails to allege misconduct by the investigating auditors?
- State the Relevant Facts before the Element in Contention
    When or similar introductory word [include here brief statement of facts relevant to the element in contention], *is* or *has* [include here a short quote from the element in contention].

    Examples:
    When a food co-op uses its proceeds for expenses and to buy additional food rather than as profit for individual members, is the co-op a "business" under § 10?

    When the taxpayer fails to allege misconduct by the investigating auditors, has there been a "forfeiture" of a tax refund under § 612?
- Begin by Stating the Nature of the Action
    Start with the nature of the suit or action being brought and then present the element in contention before the relevant facts or the relevant facts before the element in contention.

    Examples:
    In an action to require a license, is a food co-op a "business" under § 10 even though the co-op uses its proceeds for expenses and to buy additional food rather than as profit for individual members?

    In an action for a refund, has there been a "forfeiture" of the refund under § 612 when the taxpayer fails to allege misconduct by the investigating auditors?

■ Use a Whether/If or a Whether/When Sentence

Start with the word *whether* and then present the element in contention before the relevant facts or the relevant facts before the element in contention. A question mark is not needed at the end of such issue statements. The first example is in a *whether/if* format. It begins with the word *whether* (quoting from the element in contention) and then uses the word *if* (stating the facts relevant to that contention). The second example is in a *whether/when* format. It begins with the word *whether* (quoting from the element in contention) and then uses the word *when* (stating the facts relevant to that contention).

Examples:

Whether a food co-op is a "business" under § 10 if the co-op uses its proceeds for expenses and to buy additional food rather than as profit for individual members.

Whether there has been a "forfeiture" of the refund under § 612 when the taxpayer fails to allege misconduct by the investigating auditors.

Example #2 - Bike on Road

Facts: Fred pedals his ten-speed bicycle on the sidewalk. He is charged with violating § 92(b).

Rule: § 92(b). The operator of any vehicle riding on a sidewalk shall be fined $100.

Elements of § 92(b)

1. Operator
2. Any vehicle
3. Riding
4. On a sidewalk

The parties will agree that Fred rode his bicycle on a sidewalk and that Fred operated (rode) the bicycle. The first, third, and fourth elements, therefore, should not be made into legal issues. The only disagreement will be over the second element. Hence, it is the element in contention and the basis of the issue.

Issue (shorthand)(two examples)

Did Fred violate § 92(a)?

Is a bike a "vehicle" under § 92(a)?

Issue (comprehensive)

Is a ten-speed bicycle riding on the sidewalk a "vehicle" under § 92(a) when the bicycle runs on pedal power?

Example #3 - Pharmacy

Facts: Harry O'Brien, the pharmacist at the ABC Drugstore, fills a prescription of Vicodin for Helen Jarvis. Helen pays by credit card. She is fifteen years old. With the permission of her parents, she is legally married in the state.

Rule: § 25–403. A pharmacist must not sell prescription drugs to a minor.

Elements of § 25–403

1. Pharmacist
2. Sell
3. Prescription drugs
4. To a minor

The first three elements are not in contention. O'Brien is a pharmacist who sold a drug. We are told that he filled a prescription for the drug; therefore, it is a prescription drug. The element in contention will be the fourth.

Issue (shorthand)(two examples)

Was § 25-403 violated?

Is a married fifteen-year old person a "minor" under § 25–403?

Issue (comprehensive)

Has a pharmacist sold a prescription drug to a "minor" under § 25–403 when the buyer is fifteen years old and legally married?

Note that the name of the specific drug (Vicodin) is not mentioned in the issue. Nor is the fact that payment was by credit card. These facts do not appear to be relevant to the main element in contention—whether the buyer was a minor. The issue would not be wrong if these facts were included in the issue, but they are not needed to understand the nature of the contention. For the same reason the names of the persons involved (Harry O'Brien and Helen Jarvis) are omitted. This particular legal issue is the same regardless of proper name or gender.

Example #4 - Additional Punishment

Facts: On December 12, 2013, John Smith was arrested at 465 East 8th Street, North Boston, at midnight. He was observed selling a substance to another adult, his brother Richard Smith. The substance was later determined to be heroin. When John Smith was arrested on East 8th Street immediately after the sale, Officer Frank Doyle searched him and found a loaded gun in his back pocket. Doyle was not aware of the presence of the gun until this search. At the trial, Smith was convicted of selling heroin. During sentencing, the prosecution asked for additional punishment under § 109 because Smith used a weapon in the commission of a drug crime.

Rule: § 109. A judge may impose additional punishment when a weapon is used by the accused in the commission of a drug offense.

Elements of § 109

1. Judge
2. Weapon
3. Is used
4. In the commission of a drug offense
5. By the accused

The first, second, fourth, and fifth elements won't be in contention. A loaded gun is a weapon; selling heroin is a drug offense, which Smith is charged with committing; and John Smith is the accused. The parties are not going to disagree about these facts. There will be contention, however, over whether the weapon was "used" in the commission of a drug offense. Hence an issue should be based on the third element because it is the element in contention.

Issue (shorthand) (two examples)
> Was the gun "used" for purposes of § 109?
> Can additional punishment be added under § 109?

Issue (comprehensive) (two examples)
> Is a gun "used" in the commission of a drug offense under § 109 when the gun is loaded and is in the back pocket of the accused at the time he is arrested for selling heroin even though the gun played no active role in the drug offense?

> When an accused has a loaded gun in his back pocket at the time he is arrested for selling heroin, has the accused "used" the gun while committing a drug offense under § 109 even though the gun played no active role in the offense?

Example #5 - False Imprisonment

Facts: After George falls asleep in a room, Ted locks the door to the room, knowing that George will not be able to get out. The door is the only way in and out of the room. Before George wakes up, someone else unlocks the door so that when George wakes up and goes out, he never knew that the room had been locked.

Rule: False imprisonment is confinement of a person within fixed boundaries set by another person who intended to restrain the movement of the person confined.

Elements of False Imprisonment

1. Confinement
2. Of a person
3. Within set boundaries
4. By another person
5. Who intended to restrain the movement of the person confined

The second and fourth elements are not in contention because the parties will agree that George and Ted are *persons*. The parties will probably also agree that a room with only one way in and out constitutes "set boundaries" so that the third element is not in contention. There is every indication that Ted wanted (intended) to prevent George from getting out of the room when Ted locked it. Hence the fifth element is unlikely to be in contention. But they probably will disagree with whether the first element applies. The disagreement will be over the definition of "confinement" (or its verb form *confined*). Ted will argue that you can't be confined by a locked door if you were never aware of the door being locked and never had difficulty getting out. The door was locked only while George was asleep. George will argue that his awareness is irrelevant because the room was in fact locked while he was in it.

Issue (shorthand)(two examples)
> Was George falsely imprisoned?
> Can you be confined if you don't know about it?

Issue (comprehensive)
> In an action for false imprisonment, has there been a "confinement" of a person when he is locked in a room while asleep even though the door was no longer locked when he awoke and left?

Example #6 - Place of Trial

Facts: During a hearing on the arraignment of Helen Foley for possession of marijuana in Essex County, the prosecutor asks the judge to move the trial to Fairfax County, a neighboring county, because Helen is a reporter for an Essex County newspaper and has written stories attacking the prosecutor. The prosecutor alleges that these stories have negatively affected the potential pool of jurors for the trial of Foley. Foley objects to the prosecutor's motion.

Rule: § 971.22. A party may move for a change of the place of trial on the ground that an impartial trial cannot be had in the county. The motion must be made at the time of arraignment.

Elements of § 971.22 (we'll use the alternative listing of elements discussed earlier)

1. A party
2. At the time of the arraignment
3. Move for a change of the place of trial
4. On the ground that an impartial trial cannot be had in the county

The first and second elements will not be in contention. The prosecutor is a party and he is making the motion during the arraignment. The third elements will not be in contention because the prosecutor is making a motion for a change in the place of the trial. The element in contention is the fourth element. The parties will disagree over whether Foley's newspaper stories could affect the impartiality of her trial in Essex County.

Issue (shorthand) (two examples)
> Do newspaper attacks on the prosecutor affect impartiality under § 971.22?
> Can the prosecutor get the trial moved under § 971.22?

Issue (comprehensive)
> When a newspaper reporter charged with a drug offense has written stories attacking the prosecutor, can the prosecutor obtain a change in the place of the trial under § 971.22 on the ground that an "impartial trial cannot be had" in the county because of the stories?

Example #7 - Wrongful Adoption

Facts: Jim and Grace Thompson adopted a child through the ABC Adoption Service. ABC told the Thompsons that the child had a heart condition but it failed to tell them that the child had a baby sister who recently died of a heart attack. The agency knew about the death but did not think it was relevant to the adoption by the Thompsons. The Thompsons sue ABC for wrongful adoption.

Rule: An action for wrongful adoption exists for failing to disclose to prospective adoptive parents known facts or conditions that would be relevant to the decision on whether to adopt.

Elements of wrongful adoption

1. Failing to disclose
2. Known facts or conditions
3. To prospective adoptive parents
4. That would be relevant to the decision on whether to adopt

Only the fourth element is in contention. ABC knew about the death of the sister, but failed to disclose it to the prospective patents, the Thompsons. The parties will disagree about whether this failure was "relevant."

Issue (shorthand) (two examples)
Was the failure to disclose the death "relevant" to the adoption?
Was there a wrongful adoption?

Issue (comprehensive)
In an action for wrongful adoption of a child with a known heart condition, is the undisclosed recent death of a young sibling from a heart attack "relevant" to the decision to adopt the child?

Example #8 - Expenses of Litigation

Facts: Karen Jacob, Esq. represents Bob Carey in his negligence action against another driver. Karen wants to hire an expert witness for the case in order to secure some important evidence. The cost of the witness is $4,000. Bob does not have this amount. Karen agrees to pay the fee of the expert. Bob agrees to let Karen deduct this amount from an award of damages from the other driver in his case. Unfortunately, he loses the case and refuses to pay Karen the $4,000. When she tries to collect it from him, he brings an ethics charge against her before the state bar association for violating § 5.

Rule: § 5. While representing a client in connection with contemplated or pending litigation, a lawyer shall not advance or guarantee financial assistance to his client, except that a lawyer may advance or guarantee court costs, expenses of investigation, expenses of medical examination, and costs of obtaining and presenting evidence, provided the client remains ultimately liable for such expenses.

Elements of § 5

1. A lawyer
2. Representing a client in connection with contemplated litigation or in connection with pending litigation
3. Shall not advance financial assistance to his client or guarantee financial assistance to his client, except that the following is proper:
   a. Lawyer advances or guarantees court costs provided the client remains ultimately liable for such expenses, or
   b. Lawyer advances or guarantees expenses of investigation provided the client remains ultimately liable for such expenses, or
   c. Lawyer advances or guarantees expenses of medical examination provided the client remains ultimately liable for such expenses, or
   d. Lawyer advances or guarantees costs of obtaining and presenting evidence provided the client remains ultimately liable for such expenses.

The first element is not in contention because Karen is a "lawyer." The second element is not in contention because what Karen did (paying for the expert) was done "in connection" with "pending litigation." The third element is in contention. She advances "costs of obtaining and presenting evidence," but Bob agrees to let Karen deduct this amount from an award of damages from the other driver in his case. There are two issues in this case: a factual issue and a legal issue.

Factual Issue

First, there is a factual issue on the agreement between Karen and Bob. What was their agreement on payment for the expenses of the expert? We are told that Bob agrees to let Karen deduct this amount from an award of damages from the other driver. Karen will argue that the agreement was not to forgive the debt if the case is lost. The agreement, she would argue, was to allow her to deduct the $4,000 from the winnings, if any, and if Bob lost the case, he impliedly agreed to pay this amount out of his own pocket. Bob, on the other hand, would argue that the agreement was that Karen would pay for the witness and absorb this cost if she did not win the case for Bob. The dispute is factual. What did they intend? What did they agree to do when they discussed the witness fee?

> *Factual Issue*:
>> Did the parties agree that Carey would reimburse Jacob for the $4,000 witness fee whether or not he won the case?

Unlike the legal issues we have been discussing, the statement of factual issues are fairly straightforward. There is no need to make specific reference to the element in contention, although this element will be the focus of the factual dispute. Simply state what the factual issue is. Also, for factual issues, include the actual names of the parties, again, unlike legal issues.

Legal Issue

The legal issue in Example #8 is based the third element—specifically, on the definition of "ultimately liable." Under the third element, the lawyer can advance litigation expenses if ("provided") the client is "ultimately" responsible for paying back the advance. If the factual question is resolved by concluding that Carey must pay the $4,000 whether or not he wins the case, then there is no legal issue. If he must pay it back regardless of the outcome of the case, then he is "ultimately liable" for it. The legal issue arises only if the factual issue is resolved by concluding that the attorney agreed to forget the $4,000 if Carey loses the case. Hence, the legal issue will be phrased *on the assumption* that this is what the attorney agreed to do.

> *Issue* (shorthand)
>> Has Karen Jacob violated § 5?
>
> *Issue* (comprehensive)
>> Does a lawyer violate § 5 when she advances the cost of an expert witness for a client who is "ultimately liable" to repay the lawyer only if the client wins the case?

This relationship between factual issues and legal issues is common. Often a legal issue will arise only if a factual issue is resolved in a certain way.

For a summary of the guidelines for identifying and phrasing legal issues, see Exhibit 7-6.

Exhibit 7-6	Guidelines for Identifying and Phrasing an Issue

These guidelines assume you have found a rule and want to identify and phrase the legal issue based on that rule.

- Identify the rule the parties will be disputing.
- Break the rule into its elements and identify the element that will be in contention. The contention will be over the definition of the element, whether the facts fit within the element, or both the definition and whether the facts fit within the element.
- Identify the specific language in the element in contention that is at the center of the dispute.
- Give a comprehensive statement of the issue. The two critical components of a comprehensive statement of an issue are a brief quote from the element in contention and several of the important facts that are relevant to that contention.
- Put quotation marks around the specific language of the element in contention.
- Phrase the issue in one sentence.
- Do not include complete citations to the rule in the issue, but include the section number (if a statute or regulation) or the name of the cause of action (e.g., negligence).
- Include several facts that are most relevant to the dispute over the specific language in the element in contention.
- In a legal issue, do not include the specific names of any of the parties or major participants. Instead, think of relevant categories into which they fit (e.g., spouse, seller, business, and child.) Gender or race are usually not relevant categories unless the element in contention involves discrimination. A category is relevant if it is related to the element in contention.
- There is no minimum or maximum length for legal issues. A comprehensive statement of an issue should be long enough to comply with the above guidelines, but not be so long that it is unreadable or in violation of grammar.
- See Exhibit 7-5 on variations for the structure of the issue.
- You have more flexibility is phrasing factual issues. State the essence of the dispute. Include the actual names of the parties or major participants in the dispute.

LEGAL ANALYSIS SKILLS: DEFINITIONS

Next we turn to the definitions skill. Important language in the element in contention must be defined. This is so even if the parties are likely to agree over the definition but disagree over whether the facts fit within the definition.

Where do you obtain the definition(s)? You use a two-step approach. First you try to define the terms on your own based on everyday language, the context of the rule, and common sense. Then you check the validity of your definitions by doing legal research of primary authority to find out:

- if a court opinion provides a definition
- if a statute of the legislature provides a definition
- if an administrative regulation or administrative decision provides a definition

In addition,

> **legislative history** Hearings, debates, amendments, committee reports, and all other events that occur in the legislature before a bill is enacted into a statute. Also part of the history are later changes, if any, made by the legislature to the statute.

- if the rule is a statute, check the **legislative history** of the statute for clues to meaning and definition
- and finally, find out if discussions of the rule in respected secondary authority (such as a law review article or legal treatise) provide clues to meaning and definition. As we will see in Chapter 11, courts are not obligated to agree with secondary authority, but a court may find the discussion persuasive. (See the section on persuasive authority in Chapter 11.)

In Chapter 11, we will study legal research techniques of finding cases, statutes, regulations, decisions, legislative history, and secondary authority. In this chapter, we will use the first step of identifying definitions: Coming up with definitions on your own based on the meaning of everyday language, the context of the language in the rule, common sense, and your best guess of the definition each side to the dispute is likely to propose.

In many cases, terms that need a definition can be defined broadly or narrowly. Decide which party would favor the broad definition and provide it. Decide which party would favor the narrow definition and provide it.

Let's look again at the examples we have been following.

Example #1 – Co-op

Facts: Bill and his neighbors have formed a downtown food co-op (Neighbors Together) through which members buy their food collectively from a wholesale company. All funds received by the co-op go for expenses and the purchase of more food to sell. There is no profit distributed to individual members. The city wants the co-op to obtain a commercial license. The co-op says the license law (§ 10) does not apply to co-ops.

Rule: § 10. Any business operating within the city must obtain a commercial license.

Issue: Is a food co-op a "business" under § 10 even though the co-op uses its proceeds for expenses and to buy additional food rather than as profit for individual members of the co-op?

Bill and the co-op would argue for a narrow definition of "business" to avoid being classified as one. The city, on the other hand, would seek a broader definition that would encompass the co-op.

Narrow definition:
A business is a venture in which a person or persons invest funds or other resources in order to earn a profit that can be distributed and used by the individual investors.

Broad definition:
A business is a venture in which a person or persons invest funds or other resources with the objective of earning a return that is greater than its investment.

To help support its definition, each party will do legal research to try to find primary and secondary authority on the meaning of the rule and of the element in contention. While doing the research, the parties may find support for other definitions.

Example #2 - Bike on Road

Facts: Fred pedals his ten-speed bicycle on the sidewalk. He is charged with violating § 92(b).

Rule: § 92(b). The operator of any vehicle riding on a sidewalk shall be fined $100.

Issue: Is a ten-speed bicycle riding on the sidewalk a "vehicle" under § 92(b) when the bicycle runs on pedal power?

Fred would argue for a narrow definition of "vehicle" to avoid being classified as one. The police, on the other hand, would seek a broader definition that would encompass the bicycle.

Narrow definition:
Vehicle means any motorized method of transportation.

Broad definition:
Vehicle means any method of transportation.

To help support its definition, each party will do legal research to try to find primary and secondary authority on the meaning of the rule and of the element in contention. While doing the research, the parties may find support for other definitions.

Example #3 - Pharmacy

Facts: Harry O'Brien, the pharmacist at the ABC Drugstore, fills a prescription of Vicodin for Helen Jarvis. Helen pays by credit card. She is fifteen years old. With the permission of her parents, she is legally married in the state.

Rule: § 25–403. A pharmacist must not sell prescription drugs to a minor.

Issue: Has a pharmacist sold a prescription drug to a "minor" under § 25-403 when the buyer is fifteen years old and legally married?

Harry O'Brien would argue for a narrow definition of "minor" so that Helen would not be classified as one. The state, on the other hand, would seek a broader definition that would include Helen.

Narrow definition:
A minor is any person under the age of eighteen unless that person has obtained legal independence (emancipation) such as by being legally married.

Broad definition:
A minor is any person under the age of eighteen.

To help support its definition, each party will do legal research to try to find primary and secondary authority on the meaning of the rule and of the element in contention. While doing the research, the parties may find support for other definitions.

Example #4 - Additional Punishment

Facts: On December 12, 2013, John Smith was arrested at 465 East 8th Street, North Boston, at midnight. He was observed selling a substance to another adult, his brother Richard Smith. The substance was later determined to be heroin. When John Smith was arrested on East 8th Street immediately after the sale, Officer Frank Doyle searched him and found a loaded gun in his back pocket. Doyle was not aware of the presence of the gun until this search. At the trial, Smith was convicted of selling heroin. During sentencing, the prosecution asked for additional punishment under § 109 because Smith used a weapon in the commission of a drug crime.

Rule: § 109. A judge may impose additional punishment when a weapon is used by the accused in the commission of a drug offense.

Issue: Is a gun "used" in the commission of a drug offense under § 109 when the gun is loaded and is in the back pocket of the accused at the time he is arrested for selling heroin even though the gun played no active role in the drug offense?

John Smith would argue for a narrow definition of "used" to demonstrate that there was no use. The prosecution, on the other hand, would seek a broader definition that would include the gun in Smith's pocket.

Narrow definition:
Used means actively employing or activating a weapon for the purpose of committing the drug offense for which a person is arrested.

Broad definition:
Used means having a weapon in one's possession and readily available as needed while a person is committing a drug crime.

To help support its definition, each party will do legal research to try to find primary and secondary authority on the meaning of the rule and of the element in contention. While doing the research, the parties may find support for other definitions.

Example #5 - False Imprisonment

Facts: After George falls asleep in a room, Ted locks the door to the room, knowing that George would not be able to get out. The door is the only way in and out of the room. Before George wakes up, someone else unlocks the door so that when George wakes up and goes out, he never knew that the room had been locked.

Rule: False imprisonment is confinement of a person within fixed boundaries set by another person who intended to restrain the movement of the person confined.

Issue: In an action for false imprisonment, has there been a "confinement" of a person if he is locked in a room while asleep even though the door was no longer locked when he awoke and left?

Ted would argue for a narrow definition of "confinement" to avoid being charged with false imprisonment. George, on the other hand, would seek a broader definition that would include what Ted did.

Narrow definition:
Confinement is the complete restraint of a person's freedom of movement within fixed boundaries while the person is aware of the restraint.

Broad definition:
Confinement is the complete restraint of a person's freedom of movement within fixed boundaries.

To help support its definition, each party will do legal research to try to find primary and secondary authority on the meaning of the rule and of the element in contention. While doing the research, the parties may find support for other definitions.

Example #6 - Place of Trial

Facts: During a hearing on the arraignment of Helen Foley for possession of marijuana in Essex County, the prosecutor asks the judge to move the trial to Fairfax County, a neighboring county, because Helen is a reporter for an Essex County newspaper and has written stories attacking the prosecutor. The prosecutor alleges that these stories have negatively affected the potential pool of jurors for the trial of Foley. Foley objects to the prosecutor's motion.

Rule: § 971.22. A party may move for a change of the place of trial on the ground that an impartial trial cannot be had in the county. The motion must be made at the time of arraignment.

Issue: When a newspaper reporter charged with a drug offense has written stories attacking the prosecutor, can the prosecutor obtain a change in the place of the trial under § 971.22 on the ground that an "impartial trial cannot be had" in the county because of the stories?

Foley would argue for a narrow definition of "impartial trial" in order to increase the likelihood that the judge will deny the motion to move the trial. The prosecutor will argue for a broad definition in order to increase the likelihood the motion will be granted.

Narrow definition:
Impartial trial means the absence of outside influences that are highly likely to impact the fairness of the trial.

Broad definition:
Impartial trial means the absence of outside influences that could in any way impact the fairness of the trial.

To help support its definition, each party will do legal research to try to find primary and secondary authority on the meaning of the rule and of the element in contention. While doing the research, the parties may find support for other definitions.

Example #7 - Wrongful Adoption

Facts: Jim and Grace Thompson adopted a child through the ABC Adoption Service. ABC told the Thompsons that the child had a heart condition but it failed to tell them that the child had a baby sister who recently died of a heart attack. The agency knew about the death but did not think it was relevant to the adoption by the Thompsons. The Thompsons sue ABC for wrongful adoption.

Rule: An action for wrongful adoption exists for failing to disclose to prospective adoptive parents known facts or conditions that would be relevant to the decision on whether to adopt.

Issue: In an action for wrongful adoption of a child with a known heart condition, is the undisclosed recent death of a young sibling from a heart attack "relevant" to the decision to adopt the child?

ABC will argue for a narrow definition in order to increase the likelihood that the failure to disclose would not be found relevant. The Thompsons will argue for a broad definition of "relevant" in order to increase the likelihood that the failure to disclose was relevant.

Narrow definition:
Relevant means whatever a reasonable prospective adoptive parent would consider critical information about the child.

Broad definition:
Relevant means whatever the prospective adoptive parent would consider important information about the child.

To help support its definition, each party will do legal research to try to find primary and secondary authority on the meaning of the rule and of the element in contention. While doing the research, the parties may find support for other definitions.

Example #8 - Expenses of Litigation

Facts: Karen Jacob, Esq. represents Bob Carey in his negligence action against another driver. Karen wants to hire an expert witness for the case in order to secure some important evidence. The cost of the witness is $4,000. Bob does not have this amount. Karen agrees to pay the fee of the expert. Bob agrees to let Karen deduct this amount from an award of damages from the other driver in his case. Unfortunately, he loses the case and refuses to pay Karen the $4,000. When she tries to collect it from him, he brings an ethics charge against her before the state bar association for violating § 5.

Rule: § 5. While representing a client in connection with contemplated or pending litigation, a lawyer shall not advance or guarantee financial assistance to his client, except that a lawyer may advance or guarantee court costs, expenses of investigation, expenses of medical examination, and costs of obtaining and presenting evidence provided the client remains ultimately liable for such expenses.

Issue: Does a lawyer violate § 5 when she advances the cost of an expert witness for a client who is "ultimately liable" to repay the lawyer only if the client wins the case?

Karen Jacob is being charged with a violation of § 5. She can escape sanctions by showing that her agreement with the client required repayment of the witness fee regardless of who wins the case. Hence she would like a broad definition of "ultimately liable," whereas Bob Carey (hoping to avoid the payment) would argue for a narrow definition.

Narrow definition:
"Ultimately liable" means responsible for payment if the client wins damages from which payment can be made.

Broad definition:
"Ultimately liable" means responsible for payment regardless of who wins the case.

To help support its definition, each party will do legal research to try to find primary and secondary authority on the meaning of the rule and of the element in contention. While doing the research, the parties may find support for other definitions.

For a summary of the guidelines on definitions in legal analysis, see Exhibit 7-7.

Exhibit 7-7	Guidelines on Definitions in Legal Analysis

- Identify the language in the rule that needs a definition. It will be language in the element in contention.
- The language will be in dispute because the parties disagree over the definition of the language, disagree over whether the facts fit within the definition, or disagree over both the definition and whether the facts fit within it.
- First, attempt to define the language on your own based on the meaning of everyday language, the context of the language in the rule, common sense, and your best guess of the definition each side to the dispute is likely to propose.
- Ask yourself whether the language can be defined broadly and narrowly, and if so, which side would argue for the broad definition and which side would argue for the narrow definition. Put yourself in the shoes of each person in the controversy and try to identify what definition of the language each would propose.
- Second, do legal research on the language:
  - Find out if the language has been defined by a court opinion.
  - If the language is in a statute, find out if there is a definitions statute that is part of the same cluster of statutes
  - If the language is in a statute, check to see if the legislative history of the statute will help you define the language
  - Find out of any administrative regulations and administrative decisions have interpreted the language
  - Find out if secondary authority (e.g., a law review article or legal treatise) has interpreted the language
  We will cover these and other legal-research topics in Chapter 11.
- If the language has been defined by a controlling opinion, statute, or other primary authority, the definition is binding regardless of the definition(s) you came up with on your own. Don't be surprised, however, to discover that some language, particularly in statutes, has never been defined by court opinions, statutes, or other primary authority.

LEGAL ANALYSIS SKILLS: FACTOR ANALYSIS

Thus far we have concentrated on the analysis of elements in rules. Elements are preconditions to the applicability of the entire rule. If one element does not apply, the entire rule does not apply. We now turn to a closely related but different kind of analysis: *factor analysis*. A **factor** is one of the circumstances or considerations that will be weighed in making a decision, no one of which is conclusive.

Elements and factors are closely related. Many of the important decisions we make in everyday life involve the equivalent of elements and factors, e.g., buying a home, accepting a job offer, and picking someone to marry. When people look for a house, they consider space, neighborhood, area schools, affordability, etc. If an item is essential, it is an element. Suppose, for example, that you will not buy a house with less than three bedrooms. This is a precondition to the entire purchase in the same manner as any single element of a rule is a precondition to the applicability of the entire rule. A house hunter may also want a large yard and a bus line within walking distance. But if these are not preconditions, they are simply factors to be considered, no one of which is **dispositive** or essential. If the bus line is a factor, the house hunter may decide to buy a particular house even though the bus line is not within walking distance. Why? Because this negative fact was examined in the light of everything else about the house (e.g., the price was fair, the house had a very large yard, it was the right color, it needed few repairs) and, on balance, the decision was to make the purchase. The bus line problem did not outweigh all of the other factors.

In a similar fashion, factors often play an important role in legal analysis. For example:

§ 20. In a hearing to determine whether the penalty for nonpayment of a tax can be waived, the agency shall consider the amount of the nonpayment, the timing of the failure to pay, and the extent to which the nonpayment occurred intentionally or accidentally.

Elements of § 20

1. In a hearing
2. To determine whether the penalty for nonpayment of a tax can be waived

factor (1) One of the circumstances or considerations that will be weighed in making a decision. (2) One of the circumstances or considerations that will be weighed in deciding whether an element applies.

dispositive Pertaining to something that is essential to a decision; pertaining to a deciding factor or consideration.

3. The agency
4. Shall consider

    a. the amount of the nonpayment, and

    b. the timing of the failure to pay, and

    c. the extent to which the nonpayment occurred intentionally or accidentally

The word "and" in factor analysis means that every factor must be considered. Note that "and" is expressly mentioned once in § 20 and implied twice in the list of factors.

The word "waived" is not defined in § 20. Instead of a definition, we are given a list of three items that will be considered by the agency in deciding whether to grant a waiver: (1) the amount of the nonpayment, (2) the timing of the failure to pay, and (3) the extent to which the nonpayment occurred intentionally or accidentally. Nothing in this list is dispositive. Each item on the list is a factor that must be weighed to determine whether a penalty will be waived. These factors are a requirement of the fourth element of § 20.

Once you find factors in a rule, you simply examine the factors one at a time by connecting the facts that you have (or that you must investigate) to each factor. Further investigation is often called for because of the large number of facts that are usually needed to assess each of the factors mentioned in a rule. One of the benefits of this kind of analysis is that it will help the office identify these investigation needs.

There are no magic words that will always signal the need for a factor analysis. You must examine the rule carefully to determine whether you are being told that several items mentioned in the rule must be weighed in order to decide whether the rule applies. The rule may or may not use the word *factor* in the list. Other words that might indicate factors are *consideration*, *consider*, *circumstances*, *assess*, and *evaluate*. The test is whether it is clear from the rule that everything on the list must be weighed or considered. Factor analysis requires a *balancing* act to determine whether an element applies. Each factor is to be considered and balanced against the other factors.

MEMORANDUM OF LAW

We turn now one of the written products of the skills we have been discussing. The word **memorandum** (*memo*) has several meanings. It can refer to a short note, a written record of a transaction, or a **memorandum of law**. A memorandum of law is a written explanation of how one or more rules might apply to the facts of a client's case.

There are two main audiences for a memorandum of law:

- *Internal audience.* If the memo is written solely for individuals in the office where the writer of the memo works, the memo is called *office memorandum of law*, *interoffice memorandum of law*, or simply *office memo*. Such memos must be honest about the strengths *and weaknesses* of the client's case. An internal memorandum is objective in that it points out the weaknesses as well as the strengths. Such honesty will help the attorney devise an appropriate strategy for the client.
- *External audience.* An external memo is addressed to someone outside the office such as opposing counsel, a judge, or an agency hearing officer. Most memoranda for an external audience are advocacy documents that stress the strengths and downplay the weaknesses of the client's case. Here are some of the major categories of external memos:

  - Points and authorities memorandum, trial memorandum, or hearing memorandum. These are examples of memos submitted to a judge or agency hearing officer.

  - Memorandum in support of a motion. If the memo is offered to support a request or a motion (e.g., for a waiver of filing fees), the name of the memorandum will include its purpose, e.g., Memorandum in Support of a Motion for a Waiver of Filing Fees.

Most of the discussion that follows is on the internal memorandum of law.

One of the guidelines that can be helpful in organizing a memorandum is IRAC, or its modified version, IFRAC

IRAC

When your supervisors were in law school, many of their first-year law professors probably taught them **IRAC**. IRAC is an acronym that stands for four components of legal analysis:

- Issue (I)
- Rule (R)

memorandum (1) A short note. (2) A written record of a transaction. (3) A memorandum of law or legal memorandum, which is a written explanation of how one or more rules might apply to the facts of a client's case. The plural of memorandum is *memoranda*.

memorandum of law A written explanation of how one or more rules might apply to the facts of a client's case. Also called *memo*, *legal memorandum*.

IRAC An acronym that stands for the components of legal analysis: issue (I), rule (R), application of the rule to the facts (A), and conclusion (C). IRAC provides a structure for legal analysis.

- Application of the rule to the facts (A). Also called Analysis or Discussion
- Conclusion (C)

(An acronym is simply a memory aid formed by the initial letters in words you want to remember.) IRAC provides a structure for legal analysis and can be helpful when you are ready to organize your memo. Let's take a closer look at IRAC and its variation, IFRAC.

IRAC

- State the issue (I). The issue is based on the element in contention.
- State the rule (R) you are trying to apply to the facts. The rule, of course, will include the element in contention.
- Apply the rule to the facts (A). More specifically, apply the definition of the language of the element that is in contention. Show how both sides would argue their positions.
- State the conclusion (C). Which side do you think has the better argument on whether the rule applies to the facts?

Note that IRAC does not have a separate step for stating the facts, which are critically important in legal analysis. IRAC users certainly include the facts in their legal analysis (usually after stating the issues), but they don't make it part of their acronym. We, however, *will* place the facts (F) into the acronym so that it becomes IFRAC:

- Issue (I)
- Facts (F)
- Rule (R)
- Application of the rule to the facts (A). Also called Analysis or Discussion
- Conclusion (C)

IFRAC An acronym that stands for the components of legal analysis: issue (I), facts (F), rule (R), application of the rule to the facts (A), and conclusion (C). IFRAC provides a structure for legal analysis.

IFRAC

IFRAC is a modification of the IRAC acronym by adding facts (F).

IFRAC

- State the issue (I). The issue is based on the element in contention.
- State the facts (F) that have raised the issue.
- State the rule (R) you are trying to apply to the facts. The rule, of course, will include the element in contention.
- Apply the rule to the facts (A). More specifically, apply the definition of the language of the element that is in contention. Show how both sides would argue their positions.
- State the conclusion (C). Which side do you think has the better argument on whether the rule applies to the facts?

Again, IFRAC is not different from IRAC. Both discuss facts. The difference is that the IFRAC acronym is explicit on including facts. (See Exhibit 7-8.)

Exhibit 7-8	Basic Structure of Legal Analysis: Issue, Facts, Rule, Application, and Conclusion (IFRAC)

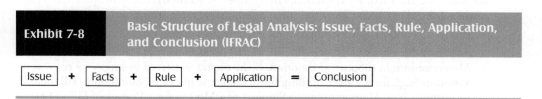

Issue + Facts + Rule + Application = Conclusion

In your academic and paralegal career, you may find that others want you to use a different structure for your written legal analysis. Don't let this concern you. Adapt to what your teachers and supervisors want. Rest assured, however, that the core components—the building blocks—of the analysis will always be the same whether the guideline is IRAC, IFRAC, or some other approach. Learn the basics of IFRAC here, but be flexible and be prepared for variety in how different people write out the basics in documents such as the memorandum of law.

SECTIONS OF A MEMO

A memorandum of law can have the following sections:

- Heading
- Introduction
- Issue(s) and Summary Conclusion(s)
- Facts
- Rule(s)
- Application (also called Analysis or Discussion)
- Conclusion(s)
- Recommendation(s) (if needed)
- Appendix (if needed)

As we examine these sections, you will note that after the preliminary sections (Heading and Introduction), the memo proceeds by following the IFRAC sequence. In the examples, we will be using the skills discussed earlier: breaking rules into elements, identifying and phrasing issues based on the element in contention, defining important language in the elements, and applying those definitions to the facts.

Heading

In the Heading section of the memo, you include basic information about you and the nature of the memo (see the examples in Exhibits 7-9 and 7-10):

- TITLE. A centered title at the top of the page stating the kind of document it is (Office Memorandum of Law)
- TO. The name of the person to whom the memo is addressed (usually your supervisor)
- FROM. Your name (the author of the memo)
- DATE. The date the memo was completed and submitted
- CASE. The name of the case (client's name and opponent, if any)
- OFFICE FILE NUMBER. The internal numbering (and/or lettering) system used by the office to identify files of its clients.
- KIND OF CASE. The general area of law covered in the memo.
- DOCKET NUMBER. The **docket number** is the number assigned to the case by the court clerk (if the suit has already been filed in court).
- RE. The notation **RE** means *regarding*, *concerning*, or *in the matter of*. This notation is followed by a very brief summary of the subject matter of the memo, often in the form of a shorthand statement of the issue.

docket number A consecutive number assigned to a case by the court and used on all documents filed with the court during the litigation of that case.

RE Regarding, concerning; in the matter of.

roadmap paragraph An overview, introductory, or thesis paragraph at the beginning of a memorandum of law that tells the reader what issues will be covered and briefly states the conclusions that will be reached.

Introduction

In the Introduction section of the memo, you write a short **roadmap paragraph** and state any limitations that have been imposed on your assignment. A roadmap paragraph is an overview or thesis paragraph that tells the reader what issues will be covered and briefly states the conclusions that will be reached. Examples:

Introduction

This memorandum examines the question of whether § 34–304(g) of the Civil Code allows substituted service after making only one attempt to serve the defendant at his last known address. Although there are no cases on this new statute, the best reasoning is that it does not allow such service.

Introduction

This memorandum examines the question of whether cyanide sulfate falls within the category of "prohibited substances" under § 154(1)(c) of the environmental code. It does.

Note that the introduction contains a more elaborate presentation of what was briefly summarized in the heading (under Kind of Case and RE).

Often your supervisor will place restrictions or limitations on what the memo should or should not cover. If so, they should be added to the introduction paragraph. Examples:

- You have asked me not to examine the issue of damages.
- You have asked me to spend no more than four hours on the assignment.
- You have asked me not to use fee-based online research services at this time.

If you have any difficulty writing the statement of the assignment, consult with your supervisor immediately. The time to clarify what you are to do—and what you are not to do—is before you spend extensive time researching, analyzing, and writing. The value of clearly articulating the boundary lines of the memo cannot be overemphasized.

Finally, include in the introduction any assumptions that you have been asked to make. Examples:

- You have asked me to assume that only New York law applies. (Or, you have asked me to discuss New York law only.)
- You have asked me to discuss the constitutionality of the client's statement to the police on the assumption that the state will be able to convince a trial judge that the statement was not privileged.

Issue(s) and Summary Conclusion(s)

In the Issue(s) and Summary Conclusion(s) section of the memo, you lay out all of the issues and conclusions. As we have seen, the two critical components of a legal issue are (1) a brief quote from the element of the rule in contention and (2) several of the important facts relevant to that contention. See Exhibits 7-5 and 7-6 on phrasing issues. After you have stated the issues, tell the reader what your answers are in the form of Summary Conclusions. Later in the memo, you will elaborate on the conclusions as needed. Here you provide short answers to the issues raised.

Example of Issues and Summary Conclusions:

Issues

I. Under the statute of frauds, does a purchase option constitute an agreement that can be "performed within a year" if the option cannot be exercised before the completion of construction, which is expected to take eighteen months?

II. Does the "substantial impairment exception" of § 745 of the Corporations Code apply to filing requirements imposed by the government even though the date of incorporation has passed?

Summary Conclusions

I. Yes. The year requirement of the statute of frauds can encompass estimated times.

II. No. The § 745 exception is activated only when the interference results from conduct of the shareholders.

Facts

In the Facts (F) section of the memo, you take great pains to ensure that the statement of facts is concise, accurate, and well organized. The facts should be stated in the memo even if you and your supervisor are familiar with the facts. Later, there may be other readers of the memo who are not as familiar with them.

The statement of facts should include the following:

- *All legally relevant facts.* A fact is legally relevant if it will help prove or disprove one of the elements of a cause of action or of a defense.
- *Unknown facts.* Include facts that are unknown as of the date of the memo if they would be relevant to the dispute. (Example: We do not know if the substance seized by the police is a drug because the lab report has not yet been completed.)
- *Favorable and unfavorable facts.* The reader of an office memo needs an accurate picture of what happened in order to formulate an effective strategy on behalf of the client. This requires an honest and complete presentation of every relevant fact, regardless of which side it favors. (Example: The client insists that he paid for the service with cash. Thus far, however, we have not been able to locate a receipt or other indication that the payment was made.)
- *Procedural facts.* If the client's case is already in litigation, include a summary of what has happened in court to date—the procedural facts. (Example: On March 26, 2015, we filed an action for medical malpractice against Sutter Hospital on behalf of Johnson and are now waiting for service of its answer.) Then proceed to the nonprocedural facts of the dispute.

Do not state legal conclusions in the statement of facts, and do not be argumentative. State the facts as objectively as you can.

If the statement of facts is fairly long, you might begin with a one- or two-sentence summary of the facts. For example:

Facts

> During 12 years of employment at Sinclair Chemicals, Inc., Mary Kiley was subjected to numerous instances of sexual harassment. When she began work there in 1990, she....

Then provide a *chronological* statement of the detailed facts. Occasional variations from strict chronological order can be justified as long as they do not interfere with the flow of the story. Sometimes, it is useful to divide complicated facts into broad categories or topics. Suppose, for example, your office represents three companies suing the same distributor for breach of contract. One way to present the facts would be to begin with the facts that pertain to all three. These facts would be stated chronologically. Then you would list each company individually and provide separate statements of facts—again, in chronological order—that pertain to each company.

An alternative to a chronological statement of facts is a statement that is organized around specific topics or subject matters. For example, there may be separate subheadings for Background Facts, Employment, Termination, Damages, etc. All of the facts related to these topics could be clustered under them.

Rule(s)

In the Rule (R) section of the memo, you list the pertinent parts of each rule that will be discussed. The rule will be the basis of a legal issue. If a rule is long, part of the rule can be given in the body of the memo and the full rule can be given in the appendix at the end of the memo.

As indicated earlier, the most frequent rules involved in legal disputes are statutes, administrative regulations, common-law rules, and constitutional provisions. Each rule can be the basis of a separate issue. Alternatively, an issue might consist of more than one rule such as whether an administrative regulation violates a statute or whether a statute violates the constitution.

For each rule, give its complete citation. If the rule is a common-law rule, the citation will be to the court opinion that applies the rule.

Application (also called Analysis or Discussion)

In the Application (A) section of the memo, you apply the rules to the facts in order to try to answer the legal issue. As indicated, the section might also be called Analysis or Discussion. Assume that the rule being applied is a statute. Here is a summary of the steps that would be taken:

- Break the statute into its elements. List each element separately.
- Briefly tell the reader which elements will be in contention and why. In effect, you are telling him or her why you have phrased the issue(s) the way you did earlier in the memo.
- Go through each element you have identified, one at a time, spending most of your time on the elements that are most in contention.
- For the elements not in contention, simply tell the reader why you think there will not be any dispute about them. For example, you anticipate that both sides will probably agree that the facts clearly support the applicability or nonapplicability of the element.
- For the elements in contention, state the definition each side is likely to ask a court to adopt. Discuss court opinions, if any, that have interpreted the statute; discuss administrative regulations and administrative decisions, if any, that have interpreted the statute; discuss the legislative history of the statute, if any; discuss scholarly interpretation of the statute, if any, in legal periodicals, legal treatises, and other secondary authority.
- Give opposing viewpoints for the elements in contention. Try to anticipate how the other side will interpret these elements. For example, what **counteranalysis** will the other side probably make through court opinions or legislative history?

Counterarguments are particularly important; too often a memo fails to provide them. Avoid presenting only one side in the memo, usually the side you think should win or the side your law office represents. For every sentence you write that contains any analysis or conclusion, use the **STOP** technique:

STOP

- after you write a **S**entence containing any analysis or conclusion
- **T**hink carefully
- about whether the **O**ther side
- would agree with the **P**osition you have just taken in that sentence

If you conclude (once you STOP yourself) that the other side would not agree with what you have written, a counteranalysis to your position will be needed somewhere in the memo. The

counteranalysis Arguments that support a different result or conclusion; counterarguments.

STOP A writing technique alerting you to the need for a counteranalysis: after writing a Sentence that contains facts or analysis, Think carefully about whether the Other side would take a Position that is different from the one you took in the sentence.

counteranalysis does not have to occur immediately after the sentence you wrote. You may decide to present the counteranalysis in a separate paragraph or in a separate section of the memo. STOP is simply a technique to remind you that your analysis will not be complete until you have covered every position the other side will probably raise.

Conclusion(s)

In the Conclusion (C) section of the memo, you give your personal opinion as to which side has the better arguments. Do not state any new arguments in the conclusion. Simply state your own perspective on the strengths and weaknesses of the arguments of both sides.

Recommendation(s) (if needed)

Include recommendations you feel are appropriate in view of the analysis and conclusion you have provided. For example, further facts should be investigated (specify which ones), further research should be undertaken (identify each issue in need of further research), a letter should be written to the government agency involved in the dispute (summarize or submit a draft of the proposed letter), the case should be settled or litigated (summarize why you think so), etc.

If your have already stated your recommendations in the Analysis section of the memo, there may be no need for a separate recommendations section.

Appendix (if needed)

At the end of the memo, include special items, if any, that you referred to in the memo, such as the full text of statutes or other rules, photographs, and statistical tables.

SAMPLE MEMOS

Exhibits 7-9 and 7-10 contain two examples of office memoranda. Both memos apply statutes. Later in the chapter, in Exhibit 7-17, you will find an example of a memo that applies a court opinion.

Note that the memos in Exhibits 7-9 and 7-10 build on the skills we have been covering in this chapter:

- The rule is broken into its elements.
- The element in contention is identified and an issue is based on this element.
- A definition of the element is stated; competing definitions are discussed.
- The structure of the memo follows IFRAC.

The memo in Exhibit 7-9 is based on one of the examples we discussed earlier-Example #4. The memo in Exhibit 7-10 includes the draft of a letter (Exhibit 7-11) that the writer of the memo recommends sending.

Exhibit 7-9	Example 1: Memorandum of Law (Using IFRAC as a Guide)

Office Memorandum of Law

TO: Peter Adams, Esq.
FROM: George Vance, Paralegal
DATE: February 14, 2014
CASE: State v. John Smith
OFFICE FILE NUMBER: 14-391
KIND OF CASE: Criminal Drug Offense
DOCKET NUMBER: E-39571-14

RE: Whether additional punishment can be added under § 109

I. Introduction

You have asked me to examine whether our client, John Smith, can receive additional punishment under § 109 of the Criminal Code because he had a weapon when he was arrested for drug possession. A strong argument can be made that he cannot.

II. Issue and Summary Conclusion

Issue: Is a gun "used" in the commission of a drug offense under § 109 when the gun is loaded and is in the back pocket of the accused at the time he is arrested for selling heroin even though the gun played no active role in the drug offense?

Summary Conclusion: No. Additional punishment requires more than mere possession of the weapon.

III. Facts

On December 12, 2013, John Smith was arrested at 465 East 8th Street, North Boston, at midnight. He was observed selling a substance to another adult, his brother Richard Smith. The substance was later determined to be heroin. When John Smith was arrested on East 8th street immediately after the sale, Officer Frank Doyle searched him and found a loaded gun in his back pocket. Doyle was not aware of the presence of the gun until this search. At the trial, Smith was convicted of selling heroin. During sentencing, the prosecution asked for additional punishment under § 109 because Smith used a weapon in the commission of a drug crime. Smith objected on the ground that he did not use the weapon within the meaning of § 109 because the gun had nothing to do with the heroin. The judge overruled the objection and imposed the additional punishment.

IV. Rule

The governing rule in this case is § 109 of the Criminal Code, which provides as follows:

§ 109. A judge may impose additional punishment when a weapon is used by the accused in the commission of a drug offense. 12 State Criminal Code § 109 (2012)

V. Analysis

There are five elements of § 109:

1. Judge
2. Weapon
3. Is used
4. In the commission of a drug offense
5. By the accused

If these five elements apply, a judge can impose additional punishment on the defendant under § 109. There will not be any dispute between the parties on the first, second, fourth, and fifth elements. Both John Smith and the prosecutor will agree that the request is being made to a judge, that the gun is a weapon, and that it was found on the accused (Smith), who has committed a drug offense. The dispute will be over the third element—whether Smith "used" this weapon in the commission of a crime. The parties will disagree over the definition of "used."

Section 109 was enacted by the legislature last year. No state court has yet ruled on the definition of "used" in the statute.

The prosecution will argue that *used* means having a weapon in one's possession, and readily available as needed, while committing a drug crime. Under this definition, Smith "used" the gun. A person with a gun in his pocket possesses the gun. The gun was loaded. Furthermore, Smith was in possession of the gun while Smith was selling heroin. Hence he used the weapon in the commission of a crime.

Smith, on the other hand, will argue that the prosecution's definition is too broad. When the legislature passed § 109, it intended the word *used* to mean actively employing or activating a weapon for the purpose of committing the drug offense. The legislature could have written the word *possessed* if it merely wanted the weapon to be present during the commission of a drug offense. Instead, however, the legislature wrote the word *used*, which has a more active meaning than *possessed.*

Smith can argue that he did nothing more than possess the weapon. Furthermore it was concealed. He was not going to use it on his own brother. When Smith sold heroin to his brother, he never took out his gun. There is no evidence that his brother knew he was armed. John Smith never actively employed the gun by brandishing it, displaying it, striking anyone with it, or threatening to fire it. Hence he never "used" the gun. Merely possessing it is not enough under § 109. If the weapon played no role in the commission of the drug offense, the legislature did not intend defendants to suffer additional punishment.

VI. Conclusion

Smith has the stronger argument. The word *used* requires activity beyong concealed, passive possession.

VII. Recommendation

The legislative history of § 109 should be checked to see if it sheds any light on what the legislature meant by "used" in the statute.

Exhibit 7-10	Example 2: Memorandum of Law (Using IFRAC as a Guide)

Office Memorandum of Law

TO: Daniel Farrell, Esq.
FROM: Paula Vargas, Paralegal
DATE: March 23, 2015
CASE: *Dept. of Sanitation v. Donaldson*
OFFICE FILE NUMBER: 15-114
KIND OF CASE: Alleged Misuse of Government Property
DOCKET NUMBER: (none at this time; no action has been filed)

RE: Whether Donaldson has violated § 17 of the State Civil Code

I. Introduction

You have asked me to do a preliminary analysis of 23 State Civil Code § 17 to assess whether our client, Jim Davidson, has violated this statute. The argument is strong that he did not. No research has been undertaken thus far, but I will indicate where such research should be pursued.

II. Issue and Summary Conclusion

Issue: When a government employee is asked to rent a car for his agency but makes a personal use of the car before he signs the lease, has this employee violated § 17 which prohibits the use of "property leased to the government" for nonofficial purposes?

Summary Conclusion: No. Until the lease is signed, § 17 does not prohibit personal use.

III. Facts

Jim Donaldson is a government employee who works for the State Department of Sanitation. On February 12, 2015, he is asked by his supervisor, Frederick Jackson, to rent a car for the agency for a two-year period. At the ABC Car Rental Company, Donaldson is shown several cars available for rental. He asks the manager if he could test-drive one of the cars before making a decision. The manager agrees. Donaldson then drives the car to his home in the area, picks up a TV, and takes it to his sister's home. When he returns, he tells the manager that he wants to rent the car for his agency. He signs the lease and takes the car to the agency. The supervisor, however, finds out about the trip that Donaldson made to his sister with the TV. He is charged with violating § 17. Because Donaldson is a new employee at the agency, he is fearful that he might lose his job.

IV. Rule

Section § 17 provides as follows:

§ 17. Use of Government Property

An employee of any state agency shall not directly or indirectly use government property of any kind, including property leased to the government, for other than officially approved activities. 23 State Civil Code Ann. § 17 (2007)

V. Analysis

To establish a violation of § 17, the following elements must be proven:

1. An employee of any state agency
2. (a) Directly uses government property of any kind including property leased to the government or
    (b) Indirectly uses government property of any kind including property leased to the government.
3. For other than officially approved activities

The main dispute in this case will be the second element.

(1) Employee of a state agency

Donaldson works for the State Department of Sanitation, which is clearly a "state agency" under the statute.

(2) Use of property leased to the government

The central issue is whether Donaldson used property leased to the government. There should be no dispute that when Donaldson drove the car to his sister's, he directly used property. (He did not "indirectly" use property such as by causing someone else to drive the car.) The question is whether the car was "property leased to the government" within the meaning of § 17.

Donaldson's best argument is a strong one. When he made the trip to his sister, he had not yet signed the lease. He can argue that "leased" means contractually committed to rent. The general definition of lease is as follows: "A contract by which the rightful possessor of personal property conveys the right to use that property in exchange for consideration." *Black's Law Dictionary,* 970 (9th ed. 2009). I have not yet checked whether courts in our state have adopted language similar to *Black's Law Dictionary.* Under this definition, the car did not become property leased to the government until after he returned from his sister's house. No costs were incurred by the government because of the test drive. Rental payments would not begin until the car was rented through the signing of the lease contract.

The supervisor, on the other hand, will argue for a broader definition of "leased"—that it means the process of obtaining a contractual commitment to rent, including integral steps leading up to that commitment. Under this definition, the car was "leased" to Donaldson when he made the unauthorized trip. The test drive was arguably an integral step in making the decision to sign a long-term leasing contract.

The supervisor will stress that the goal or purpose of the legislature in enacting § 17 should be kept in mind when trying to determine the meaning of any of the language of § 17. The legislature was trying to avoid the misuse of government resources, including the good name of the government. Public employees should not take advantage of their position for private gain. To do so would be a violation of the public trust. Yet this is what Donaldson did. While on the government payroll, he obtained access to a car and used it for a private trip. Common sense would lead to the conclusion that leasing in § 17 is not limited to the formal signing of a leasing contract. Anything that is an integral part of the process of signing that contract should be included. The legislature wanted to prevent the misuse of government resources in all necessary aspects of the leasing of property.

It is not clear from the facts whether the manager of the ABC Rental Company knew that Donaldson was considering the rental on behalf of a government agency when he received permission to take the test drive. The likelihood is that he did know it, although this should be checked. If the manager did know, then Donaldson probably used the fact that he was a government employee to obtain the permission. He held himself out as a reliable individual because of the nature of his employment. This reinforces the misuse argument under the broader definition of "leased" that the supervisor will present.

I have not yet checked whether there are any court opinions or agency regulations interpreting § 17 on this point. Nor have I researched the legislative history of the statute. All this should be done soon.

(3) Officially Approved Activities

Nothing in the facts indicates that Donaldson's supervisor gave him any authorization to make the TV trip. Even if the supervisor had authorized the trip, it would probably not be "officially" approved, since the trip was not for official (i.e., public) business.

VI. Conclusion

Donaldson has the stronger argument based on the language of the statute. The property simply was not "leased" at the time he made the TV trip. I must admit, however, that the agency has some good points in its favor. Unlike Donaldson's technical argument, the agency's position is grounded in common sense. Yet on balance, Donaldson's argument should prevail.

VII. Recommendations

Some further investigation is needed. We should find out whether the ABC Rental Company manager knew that Donaldson was a government employee at the time he asked for the test drive. In addition, legal research should be undertaken to find out if any court opinions and agency regulations exist on the statute. I cited the definition of *lease* from *Black's Law Dictionary*, but I have not yet done any legal research to determine if the legislature intended the same meaning when it passed § 17. The legislative history of the statute should be checked. Finally, I recommend that we send a letter to Donaldson's supervisor, Frederick Jackson, explaining our position. I have attached a draft of such a letter for your signature in the event you deem this action appropriate.

There is one matter that I have not addressed in this memo. Donaldson is concerned that he might lose his job over this incident. Assuming for the moment that he did violate § 17, it is not at all clear that termination would be an appropriate sanction. The statute is silent on this point. Let me know if you want me to research this issue.

Exhibit 7-11	Draft of Proposed Letter for the Donaldson Case

Farrell, Grote & Schweitzer
Attorneys at Law
724 Central Plaza Place
West Union, Ohio 45693
513-363-7519

Daniel Farrell, Esq.
Angela Grote, Esq.
Clara Schweitzer, Esq.

March 25, 2015
Frederick Jackson
Field Supervisor
Department of Sanitation
3416 34th St. NW
West Union, Ohio 45693

RE: James Donaldson
15-114

Dear Mr. Jackson:

Our firm represents Mr. James Donaldson. As you know, a question has arisen concerning Mr. Donaldson's use of a car prior to his renting it for your agency on February 12, 2015. Our understanding is that he was asked to go to the ABC Car Rental Company in order to rent a car that was needed by your agency, and that he did so satisfactorily.

Your agency became responsible for the car at the moment Mr. Donaldson signed the lease for the car rental on behalf of the agency. What happened prior to the time the lease was signed is not relevant to § 17. This statute is quite explicit. It forbids nonofficial use of property "leased" to the government. Such use did not occur in this case. No one has questioned Mr. Donaldson's performance of his duty once he "leased" the car.

If additional clarification is needed, we would be happy to discuss the matter with you further.

Sincerely,

Daniel Farrell, Esq.
DF: ps

opinion A court's written explanation of how it applied the law to the facts to resolve a legal dispute. Also called *case, court opinion, judicial opinion,* and *decision.* (See glossary for additional meanings.)

case (1) A court's written explanation of how it applied the law to the facts to resolve a legal dispute. Also called *opinion, court opinion, judicial opinion, decision.* (2) A pending matter on a court calendar. (3) A client matter handled by a law office.

casebook A law-school textbook containing numerous edited court opinions and related materials assembled for a course.

brief (1) The ten parts of a court opinion: citation, parties, objectives of parties, theories of the litigation, history of the litigation, facts, issues, holdings, reasoning, and disposition. (2) Trial brief. (3) Appellate brief.

trial brief (1) An attorney's written presentation to a trial court of the legal issues and positions of his or her client (also called *trial memorandum*). (2) An attorney's personal notes on how he or she will conduct a particular trial (also called *trial manual, trial book*).

appellate brief A document that a party files with an appellate court (and serves on an opponent) in which the party presents arguments on why the appellate court should affirm (approve), reverse, vacate (cancel), or otherwise modify what a lower court has done.

holding A court's answer to one of the legal issues in the case. Also called *ruling.*

precedent A prior opinion or decision covering similar facts or issues in a later case that can be used as a standard or guide in the later case.

reporter A volume (or set of volumes) of court opinions. Also called case reports. (See glossary for additional meanings.)

INTRODUCTION TO COURT OPINIONS

An **opinion** is a court's written explanation of how it applied the law to the facts to resolve a legal dispute. An opinion is also called case, court opinion, judicial opinion, and decision. The word **case** has several definitions. In addition to meaning court opinion, the word also means a pending matter on a court calendar and a client matter handled by a law office. (In this chapter, the words *case* and *opinion* will be used interchangeably to mean court opinion.) Decisions of administrative agencies are also called opinions, although they are more commonly referred to as *administrative decisions.* (For definitions of these and related terms, see also Exhibit 6-1 in Chapter 6.)

Case analysis is opinion analysis–the study and application of court opinions. In law school, students spend a great deal of time learning to be attorneys by doing case analysis. This approach to studying law is called the *case method* or the *casebook method.* The opinions that they study are in thick textbooks (often over a thousand pages long) called **casebooks.**

Our goal here is to examine two major case-analysis skills: (1) reading cases, called *briefing,* and (2) applying cases, sometimes called *analogizing.*

Before we start learning the skill of briefing, we need to cover the meaning of the word *brief* and examine commonly found features of opinions printed in volumes called *reporters.*

THE MEANINGS OF BRIEF

When someone uses the word **brief,** he or she can be referring to three different documents: case brief, trial brief, or appellate brief.

- *Case brief.* A brief consists of the ten parts of a court opinion: citation, parties, objectives of the parties, theories of the litigation, history of the litigation, facts, issues, holdings, reasoning, and disposition. To brief an opinion is to identify these ten parts. When you do so, you are *briefing* the opinion. A brief (sometimes called a *case brief*) is your own summary of the opinion for later use. You cannot apply an opinion (the main reason for reading opinions) unless you know how to brief it.
- *Trial brief.* A **trial brief** has two main meanings. First, it is an attorney's written presentation to a trial court of the legal issues and positions of his or her client (also called *trial memorandum*). Second, the phrase can mean an attorney's personal notes on how he or she will conduct a particular trial (also called *trial manual* or *trial book*). The notes (often placed in a *trial notebook*) will be on the opening statement, witnesses, exhibits, direct and cross-examination, closing argument, etc. These notes are private; they are not submitted to the court or to opponents.
- *Appellate brief.* An **appellate brief** is a document that a party files with an appellate court (and serves on an opponent) in which the party presents arguments on why the appellate court should affirm (approve), reverse, vacate (cancel), or otherwise modify what a lower court has done. A main focus of the appellate brief is on the claimed errors made below by a lower court.

Here our concern is the first meaning of the word brief—the ten parts of a court opinion. It should be pointed out that paralegals do not spend a lot of time on the job briefing opinions. Yet learning this skill has important benefits. Briefing is an excellent way to increase your understanding of legal analysis as used by judges and attorneys. It will also provide a greater appreciation of how appellate courts and trial courts interrelate within a court system.

DETAILED EXAMINATION OF AN OPINION

All court opinions resolve a legal dispute by applying one or more rules to facts presented by parties in the dispute. The rules that the court applies can be a statute, administrative regulation, common-law rule, constitutional provision, etc. (See the definitions of primary authorities in Exhibit 6-1 of Chapter 6.) As mentioned earlier, a common-law rule is a rule created by the courts in the absence of controlling statutory law or other higher law.

In an opinion, the court resolves the legal dispute by answering the legal issues involved in the dispute. This answer is called a **holding.** Each holding in an opinion becomes a new rule. Consequently, the opinion can be a **precedent** for future court opinions.

We will now examine an opinion as it might appear in a library volume called a **reporter.** (See Exhibit 7-12.) (When we say that a case is *reported,* we simply mean that it is in writing and usually printed in a reporter.) The opinion is *People v. Bruni,* referred to in the discussion as the *Bruni* case or opinion, or simply as *Bruni.* (Names of cases appear in italics.)

The publisher of this reporter is Thomson Reuters, though many of its publications are still known by the name *West*, which was the name of the company before it was acquired by Thomson Reuters. The publisher might also be listed as Thomson West. Most researchers prefer to call them West publications, which we will do here.

Exhibit 7-12	A Court Opinion: *People v. Bruni*

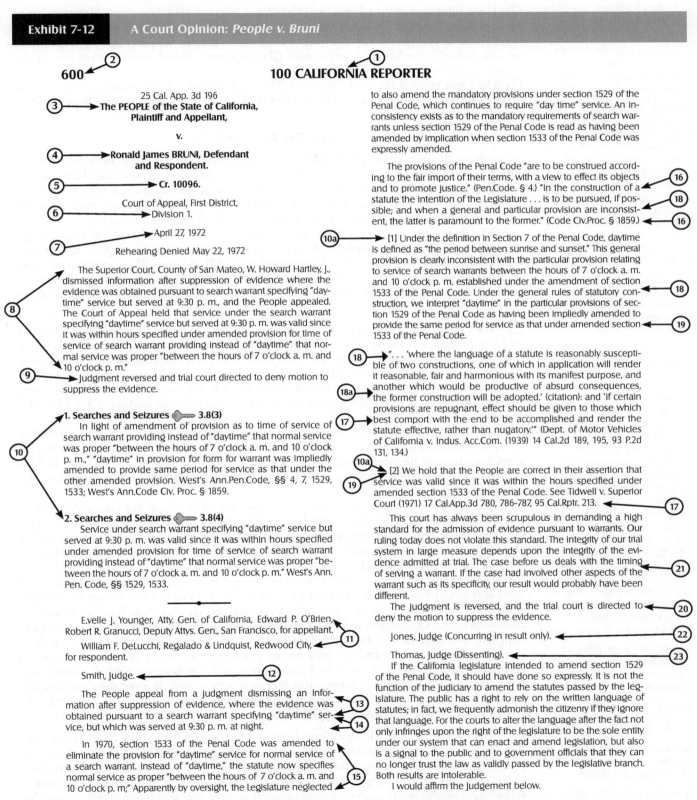

600 ②

① **100 CALIFORNIA REPORTER**

③ 25 Cal. App. 3d 196
The PEOPLE of the State of California,
Plaintiff and Appellant,

v.

④ Ronald James BRUNI, Defendant
and Respondent.

⑤ Cr. 10096.

⑥ Court of Appeal, First District,
Division 1.

⑦ April 27, 1972
Rehearing Denied May 22, 1972

⑧ The Superior Court, County of San Mateo, W. Howard Hartley, J., dismissed information after suppression of evidence where the evidence was obtained pursuant to search warrant specifying "daytime" service but served at 9:30 p. m., and the People appealed. The Court of Appeal held that service under the search warrant specifying "daytime" service but served at 9:30 p. m. was valid since it was within hours specified under amended provision for time of service of search warrant providing instead of "daytime" that normal service was proper "between the hours of 7 o'clock a. m. and 10 o'clock p. m."

⑨ Judgment reversed and trial court directed to deny motion to suppress the evidence.

⑩ **1. Searches and Seizures** 🔑 3.8(3)
In light of amendment of provision as to time of service of search warrant providing instead of "daytime" that normal service was proper "between the hours of 7 o'clock a. m. and 10 o'clock p. m.," "daytime" in provision for form for warrant was impliedly amended to provide same period for service as that under the other amended provision. West's Ann.Pen.Code, §§ 4, 7, 1529, 1533; West's Ann.Code Civ. Proc. § 1859.

2. Searches and Seizures 🔑 3.8(4)
Service under search warrant specifying "daytime" service but served at 9:30 p. m. was valid since it was within hours specified under amended provision for time of service of search warrant providing instead of "daytime" that normal service was proper "between the hours of 7 o'clock a. m. and 10 o'clock p. m." West's Ann. Pen. Code, §§ 1529, 1533.

⑪ E.velle J. Younger, Atty. Gen. of California, Edward P. O'Brien, Robert R. Granucci, Deputy Attys. Gen., San Francisco, for appellant.
William F. DeLucchi, Regalado & Lindquist, Redwood City, for respondent.

⑫ Smith, Judge.

⑬⑭ The People appeal from a judgment dismissing an Information after suppression of evidence, where the evidence was obtained pursuant to a search warrant specifying "daytime" service, but which was served at 9:30 p. m. at night.

⑮ In 1970, section 1533 of the Penal Code was amended to eliminate the provision for "daytime" service for normal service of a search warrant. Instead of "daytime," the statute now specifies normal service as proper "between the hours of 7 o'clock a. m. and 10 o'clock p. m;" Apparently by oversight, the Legislature neglected

to also amend the mandatory provisions under section 1529 of the Penal Code, which continues to require "day time" service. An inconsistency exists as to the mandatory requirements of search warrants unless section 1529 of the Penal Code is read as having been amended by implication when section 1533 of the Penal Code was expressly amended.

⑯⑱⑯ The provisions of the Penal Code "are to be construed according to the fair import of their terms, with a view to effect its objects and to promote justice." (Pen.Code. § 4.) "In the construction of a statute the intention of the Legislature . . . is to be pursued, if possible; and when a general and particular provision are inconsistent, the latter is paramount to the former." (Code Civ.Proc. § 1859.)

⑩a [1] Under the definition in Section 7 of the Penal Code, daytime is defined as "the period between sunrise and sunset." This general provision is clearly inconsistent with the particular provision relating to service of search warrants between the hours of 7 o'clock a. m. and 10 o'clock p. m. established under the amendment of section ⑱ 1533 of the Penal Code. Under the general rules of statutory construction, we interpret "daytime" in the particular provisions of section 1529 of the Penal Code as having been impliedly amended to provide the same period for service as that under amended section ⑲ 1533 of the Penal Code.

⑱ ". . . 'where the language of a statute is reasonably susceptible of two constructions, one of which in application will render it reasonable, fair and harmonious with its manifest purpose, and ⑱a another which would be productive of absurd consequences, the former construction will be adopted.' (citation): and 'if certain provisions are repugnant, effect should be given to those which ⑰ best comport with the end to be accomplished and render the statute effective, rather than nugatory.'" (Dept. of Motor Vehicles of California v. Indus. Acc.Com. (1939) 14 Cal.2d 189, 195, 93 P.2d 131, 134.)

⑩a ⑲ [2] We hold that the People are correct in their assertion that service was valid since it was within the hours specified under amended section 1533 of the Penal Code. See Tidwell v. Superior Court (1971) 17 Cal.App.3d 780, 786-787, 95 Cal.Rptr. 213. ⑰

⑳⑪ This court has always been scrupulous in demanding a high standard for the admission of evidence pursuant to warrants. Our ruling today does not violate this standard. The integrity of our trial system in large measure depends upon the integrity of the evidence admitted at trial. The case before us deals with the timing of serving a warrant. If the case had involved other aspects of the warrant such as its specificity, our result would probably have been different.

⑳ The judgment is reversed, and the trial court is directed to deny the motion to suppress the evidence.

㉒ Jones, Judge (Concurring in result only).

㉓ Thomas, Judge (Dissenting).
If the California legislature intended to amend section 1529 of the Penal Code, it should have done so expressly. It is not the function of the judiciary to amend the statutes passed by the legislature. The public has a right to rely on the written language of statutes; in fact, we frequently admonish the citizenry if they ignore that language. For the courts to alter the language after the fact not only infringes upon the right of the legislature to be the sole entity under our system that can enact and amend legislation, but also is a signal to the public and to government officials that they can no longer trust the law as validly passed by the legislative branch. Both results are intolerable.
I would affirm the Judgement below.

unofficial reporter A volume (or set of volumes) of court opinions printed by a commercial publishing company without special authority from the government.

official reporter. A volume (or set of volumes) of court opinions printed by or under the authority of the government.

citation A reference to any legal authority printed on paper or stored in a computer database that will allow you to locate the authority. As a verb, to cite something means to give its location (e.g., volume number or Web address) where you can read it. The citation is the paper or online "address" where you can read something. (See glossary for additional meanings.)

parallel cite An additional citation where you can find the same written material in the library or online.

public-domain citation (1) A citation that is not dependent on the volume and page number of a reporter. (2) A citation that is both medium neutral (meaning that it can be read in a paper volume or online) and vendor neutral (meaning that it does not contain volume, page, or other identifying information created by particular vendors such as a commercial publisher). In a public-domain citation, each paragraph is consecutively numbered (e.g., ¶1, ¶2) so that you can refer to specific language in the opinion by paragraph number rather than by page number. Also called vendor-neutral citation, generic citation, medium-neutral citation.

appellant The party bringing an appeal because of disagreement with a decision of a lower tribunal. Also called *petitioner.*

plaintiff The party who initiates a civil (and sometimes a criminal) action in court.

defendant The party against whom a civil or criminal action is brought in court.

respondent The party against whom an appeal is brought. Also called the *appellee.*

The circled numbers in the following paragraphs correspond to the circled numbers in the *Bruni* opinion in Exhibit 7-12. When the word *Bruni* is in italics, the reference is to the opinion; when Bruni is not in italics, the reference is to the party in the opinion, Ronald James Bruni. In the discussion, the words *opinion* and *case* are used interchangeably to mean court opinion.

① The *California Reporter* (abbreviated Cal. Rptr.) is an **unofficial reporter** of state opinions in California. The "100" indicates the volume number of the reporter. An unofficial reporter is a collection of cases printed by a private or commercial printer/publisher (here West) without specific authorization from the government. (If the opinion had such authorization, it would be an **official reporter**.

② The *Bruni* opinion begins on page 600. The official **citation** (shortened to *cite*) is given at the top of the first column above the word PEOPLE. The citation that includes both reporters containing this opinion is

People v. Bruni, 25 Cal. App. 3d 196, 100 Cal. Rptr. 600 (1972).

When more than one citation is available, each cite is a **parallel cite**. Citations are highly technical. Note the use of italics, abbreviations, punctuation, and spacing in this cite. We will have a lot to say about the niceties of citation in Chapter 11. An official cite is a reference to the opinion printed in its official reporter. An unofficial cite is a reference to the same opinion printed in an unofficial reporter. The official cite is always listed before the unofficial cite.

The *Bruni* opinion does not have a **public-domain citation**, a citation format that we will examine in Chapter 11. If public-domain citation was used, every paragraph in the opinion would be separately and consecutively numbered, [¶1], [¶2], [¶3], etc. There are ten paragraphs in *Bruni*, so, therefore, the last paragraph would begin with [¶10]. As we will see in Chapter 11, public-domain citation allows you to quote from opinions that are published online where page numbers are not used.

③ When the People or the state brings an action, as here, it is often a criminal-law opinion. *People v. Bruni* is a criminal-law opinion written by an appellate court. Trial court decisions are appealed to the appellate court. The **appellant** is the party bringing the appeal because of disagreement with a decision of a lower tribunal. The state of California brought the case as the **plaintiff** (called prosecutor in criminal cases) in the lower court (Superior Court, County of San Mateo) and is now the appellant in the higher court (Court of Appeal, First District, Division 1).

④ Ronald James Bruni was the **defendant** in the lower court because he was being sued or (in this criminal case) charged with a crime. The appeal is taken against him by the People (appellant) because the people believed that the lower court was in error when it ruled in favor of Bruni. The party against whom a case is brought on appeal is called the **respondent** (also called appellee).

⑤ "Cr. 10096" refers to the *docket number* of the case. "Cr." stands for criminal. A docket number is a consecutive number assigned to a case by the court and used on all documents filed with the court during the litigation of that case. Note that the docket number was not used in the citation of the case presented earlier. Docket numbers are not used in citations unless the opinion has not been reported.

⑥ Make careful note of the name of the court writing the opinion. As soon as possible, you must learn the levels of state courts in your state. (See Exhibit 6-3 in Chapter 6.) In many states, there are three levels of courts: trial level, intermediate-appellate level, and court-of-final-resort level. Opinions in such states are appealed from the trial court to the intermediate-appellate level, and then to the court of final resort. (The court of final resort in most judicial systems is the supreme court.) If a state has only two levels of courts, opinions are appealed from the trial court to the court of final resort. Here, we know from the title of the court that wrote *People v. Bruni* (Court of Appeal) that it is an appellate court. It is not the supreme court because in California the highest court is the California Supreme Court. In California, the Court of Appeal is an intermediate appellate court.

The level of the court is significant because of legal *authority*. If the court is the court of final resort (the supreme court) of the state, then the opinion would govern (and must be followed) in similar future cases throughout the state. It is binding in future cases everywhere in the state. An intermediate-appellate court opinion, however, would govern (and must be followed) in similar future cases only in the geographic area over which that appellate court has jurisdiction. It is not binding in future cases throughout the state.

When you see that the opinion was written by a trial or intermediate-appellate court, you are immediately put on notice that you must check to determine whether the opinion was appealed subsequent to the date of the case. Two of the main systems for checking the subsequent history of an opinion are *Shepard's Citations* and *KeyCite*. As we will see in Chapter 11, these systems are called **citators**.

⑦ When an opinion is cited, only the year (here 1972) is used, not the month or day (April 27). (If the opinion has not yet been reported, then the month, day, and year are used—along with the docket number.) Sometimes the text of the reported opinion will also give you other dates (e.g., the date when a request for a rehearing was denied). The year of the decision is still the critical one for citation purposes.

⑧ Here you are provided with a summary (**syllabus**) of what the opinion says. The summary provides the procedural background of the case, a few of the major facts, and what the court "held." The last item refers to the *holdings* of the opinion. Recently the publisher of these reporters (West) has separated the syllabus into two parts: background (consisting mostly of the procedural steps leading up to the present opinion) and holdings (summarizing the holdings of the opinion). For most courts, the syllabus is written by an editor and not by the court itself.

⑨ Here continues the unofficial summary, providing the reader with what procedurally must happen as a result of the April 27 opinion.

⑩ These are editor's **headnotes** which are short-paragraph summaries of portions of the opinion. Like the syllabus, headnotes are printed before the opinion begins. Each headnote covers a single point of law in the opinion.

The beginnings of the two headnotes in *Bruni* are as follows:

1. **Searches and Seizures** ⚷ 3.8(3)
2. **Searches and Seizures** ⚷ 3.8(4)

Note the sequence of the four parts: a number, a general topic, a key icon, and another number. Let's examine each part:

- The first number

Number 1 corresponds to bracketed [1] in the opinion. Number 2 corresponds to bracketed [2] in the opinion. (See 10a for these bracketed numbers.) When the editors first read the opinion, they decide how many points of law are covered in the opinion. Each of these points of law is summarized in a headnote, all of which are then given consecutive numbers, here 1 and 2. These numbers correspond with the bracketed numbers [1] and [2] in the opinion itself. If, for example, you wanted to read the portion of the opinion that was summarized in the second headnote of the opinion, you would go to the text of the opinion that begins with the bracketed [2].

- A general topic.

Next comes a general topic, here Searches and Seizures. West has over 400 of these general topics such as Divorce, Fraud, Searches and Seizures, and Taxation. (Remember that West is the still-used name of the current publisher, Thomson Reuters.)

- The key icon

The key icon (⚷) tells you that you are using West's system of organizing topics found in court opinions.

- Another number

Following each key icon, there is another number, here 3.8(3) and 3.8(4). This number refers to a subtopic of the general topic. There are hundreds of subtopics of Searches and Seizures. A general topic and the subtopic number that follows it are called a **key number**. A key number, therefore, is a numbered subtopic of a general topic. Key numbers are used by West to organize millions of cases by subject matter.

---

citator A book or online service containing lists of citations that can (a) help you assess the current validity of an opinion, statute, or other item; and (b) give you leads to additional relevant materials.

syllabus A brief summary or outline. For court opinions, it is also called a *case synopsis* and is printed before the opinion begins. It is usually a summary of the entire opinion.)

headnote A short-paragraph summary of a portion of a court opinion (usually covering a single point of law) printed before the opinion begins. These headnotes will also be printed in digest volumes, which serve as an index to all court opinions.,

key number A general topic and a number. The number designates a subtopic of the general topic. For example, key number Divorce 204.5 refers to the subtopic covered in 204.5 of the general topic Divorce. Key numbers are used by West (Thomson Reuters) to organize millions of cases by topic in its multivolume digests.

digest A set of volumes that contain brief summaries of points of law in court opinions. The summaries come from headnotes at the beginning of court opinions. When the summaries are printed in digests, they are sometimes called *abstracts* or *squibs*. (See glossary for another meaning.)

Westlaw A fee-based system of computer-assisted legal research owned by Thomson Reuters. Its current version is WestlawNext.

per curiam opinion An opinion issued "by the [whole] court," usually a short opinion that does not name the judge who wrote it.

memorandum opinion (mem.) The decision of a court rendered with few or no supporting reasons, often because it follows well-known or established principles. Also called *memorandum decision*.

key fact A fact that was very important or essential in reaching a decision.

Headnotes are found in three places: at the beginning of opinions, in the **digest** volumes of West, and on **Westlaw**. Digests are volumes containing headnotes clustered together by topic so that researchers can find similar cases. Westlaw (and its more recent version, WestlawNext) is a fee-based system of computer-assisted legal research owned by Thomson Reuters. We will examine digests and Westlaw in Chapter 11.

Caution is needed in reading the syllabus and headnotes of opinions. They are written by editors, not by the court, and therefore should never be quoted. They are merely preliminary guides to what is in an opinion. To understand the opinion, you must carefully study the language of the opinion itself through the process called *briefing*. Do not follow the example of what is pejoratively called a *headnote lawyer*, someone who overly relies on the summaries of an opinion found in its headnotes without taking the time to brief it in its entirety.

⑪ Here are the attorneys who represented the appellant and respondent on appeal. Note that the attorney general's office represented the People. The attorney general or the district attorney's office represents the state in criminal cases. For recent opinions, many of the attorneys have websites that can be useful if you want more information about them.

⑫ The opinion begins with the name of the judge who wrote the majority opinion, Judge Smith. In this spot you will sometimes find the words Per Curiam, Per Curiam Opinion, or Memorandum Opinion. A **per curiam opinion** is a court opinion that does not mention the individual judge who wrote the opinion. The opinion is issued by the whole court. It is often a short opinion because it covers relatively simple issues. (There are exceptions to this. For example, the famous case of *Bush v. Gore*, 531 U.S. 98 (2000), which led to the election of President George W. Bush, was a per curiam opinion. The name of the justice who wrote the *Bush* opinion was not given, but the issue resolved in the opinion could not be called simple.) **Memorandum opinions**, like per curiam opinions, do not name the judge who wrote the opinion. A memorandum opinion will briefly state the conclusion (holding) of the opinion or the disposition of the case with few or no supporting reasons. Such opinions are issued when the point of law involved is well known or established.

⑬ When briefing an opinion, make note of the *history of the litigation* to date. The lower court rendered a judgment dismissing the information (similar to an indictment) against Bruni after certain evidence was suppressed and declared inadmissible. (This is the *prior proceeding*.) The People have now appealed the judgment. (This appeal is the *present proceeding*.)

If the words *information* and *suppression* are new to you, look them up in a legal dictionary. Do this for every new word. (In this book, also check the definitions of such words in the glossary.)

⑭ It is critical to state the facts of the opinion accurately. Here the facts are straightforward. A search warrant that said "daytime" service was served at 9:30 p.m., and evidence was taken pursuant to this search warrant. Defendant objected to the admission of this evidence at trial. In most opinions, the facts are not this simple. The facts are usually given at the beginning of the opinion. In some opinions, however, the facts are scattered throughout the opinion. If you confront the latter situation, you must carefully read the entire opinion to piece the facts together. Ultimately, your goal is to identify the key facts of the opinion. A **key fact** is a fact that was very important or essential to a decision; here, to the result or holding of the court.

⑮ The next step in reading an opinion is to state the *legal issue* (or issues) that the court was deciding. The issue in *Bruni* is as follows:

When evidence is seized pursuant to a search warrant served at 9:30 p.m., can the evidence be suppressed under § 1529, which requires "daytime" service?

See the discussion of phrasing issues earlier in the chapter in Exhibit 7-5. The issue should include a brief quote from the element of the rule in contention (the word "daytime" in § 1529) and several important facts relevant to that contention (the warrant was served at 9:30 p.m.).

⑯ The court refers to other statutes to support the conclusion it will reach. Note the interrelationship of the statutory sections. One statute is interpreted by interpreting other statutes. Section 4 of the Penal Code ("Pen. Code") says that the sections of the Penal Code are to be interpreted ("construed") according to the meaning and significance of their terms ("according to the fair import of their terms") in order to carry out ("effect") their purpose ("objects") and to promote justice. Section 1859 of the Code of Civil Procedure ("Code Civ. Proc.") says that when a general and a particular section are inconsistent, the latter is preferred ("paramount").

The interrelationship of the statutes in this opinion is as follows:

- Section 1529 of the Penal Code still says "daytime."
- Section 7 of the Penal Code defines daytime as sunrise to sunset.
- Section 1533 of the Penal Code, as amended, says between 7:00 a.m. and 10:00 p.m.
- Section 4 of the Penal Code and § 1859 of the Code of Civil Procedure provide principles for interpreting statutes that are inconsistent.

⑰ In the same manner, a court will refer to other opinions to support its ruling. In this way, the court argues that the other opinions are *precedents* for the issues before the court. The court in *People v. Bruni* is saying that the case of *Dept. of Motor Vehicles of California v. Indus. Acc. Com.* and the case of *Tidwell v. Superior Court* are precedents for its own ruling.

⑮⑯⑱ The **reasoning** of the court is its explanation for resolving the issue the way it did. The reasoning tells us why the court reached the particular *holding* for that issue. The court's reasoning in *Bruni* is that if there is a general statute (such as § 1529) and a specific statute (such as § 1533) that are inconsistent, the specific is paramount and is preferred when this preference would render the statutes "reasonable, fair and harmonious." Hence, the legislature probably intended (but forgot) to amend the more general statute (§ 1529) when it amended the more specific statute (§ 1533).

⑱ₐ Note the use of the single quote mark ('), double quote mark ("), and single and double quote marks together (' "). The double quotation marks are around the main quote. There is a quote within this main quote. The quote within the quote is indicated by single quote marks. Ellipsis dots (…) tell the reader that the court left out some language that was within the original quoted language. Finally, the word *citation* in parentheses (citation) tells us that there was a citation in the quote, but the court decided not to give us this citation.

⑲ The holding of the court ("We hold that…") is that § 1529 was impliedly amended to authorize service up to 10:00 p.m. A holding is also called the court's *ruling*. Courts do not always use the words *hold* or *holding* when stating their holding. Alternative language might be used such as *We conclude* or *Therefore*.

⑳ In *Bruni*, the consequences of the court's resolution of the issue are stated toward the very end of the opinion. The judgment of the lower court is reversed. The lower court cannot continue to suppress (i.e., declare inadmissible) the evidence seized at the 9:30 p.m. search. This is the **disposition** of the court.

An appellate court could take a number of positions with respect to a lower court's decision. It could **affirm** the decision, meaning to accept and confirm the decision. It could reverse, **vacate** or otherwise modify the decision in whole or in part. It could **remand** the case (send it back to the lower court) with instructions on how to proceed, such as how to retry the case.

㉑ In theory, a judge must be very precise in defining the issue before the court and in resolving only that issue. The judge should not say more than must be said to decide the case. The theory, however, is sometimes not observed. This can make your job more difficult; you must wade through the language of the court to identify (1) the precise issues, (2) the key facts for those issues, (3) the holdings for each issue, and (4) the reasoning for each holding. The worst tangent that a judge can stray into is called **dictum**. Dictum is a judge's view of what the law is, or might be, on facts that are not before the court. (The plural of dictum is *dicta*.) Judge Smith indicated that the result of the case might be different if the warrant were not specific, e.g., if it did not name the individual to be searched or what the investigator was looking for. This was not the situation in *Bruni*; therefore, Judge Smith's commentary or speculation is dictum. The statement is dictum because it covers facts that were not before the court.

㉒ On any court there may be several judges. They do not always agree on what should be done. The majority controls. (The majority consists of more than half of the judges who agree on the final result or judgment in the case, including the holdings and reasoning.) In

reasoning An explanation of why the court resolved an issue the way it did. The reasons the court reached its holding on an issue.

disposition A court's final order that is reached as a result of its holding(s). (See glossary for an additional meaning.)

affirm To agree with or uphold the lower court judgment.

vacate To cancel or set aside. (See glossary for an additional meaning.)

remand To send back. For example, to return a case to a lower tribunal with instructions from a higher tribunal (e.g., an appellate court) on how to proceed.

dictum (short for *obiter dictum*, "something said in passing") A statement or observation made by a judge in an opinion that is not essential to resolve the issues before the court; comments that go beyond the facts before the court. (See glossary for an additional meaning.).

majority opinion An opinion whose final conclusion or judgment is agreed to by more than half of the judges hearing the case. The agreement includes the holdings and reasoning for the holdings.

concurring opinion An opinion written by less than a majority of the judges hearing the case. The opinion agrees with the final conclusion or judgment of the majority opinion but wishes to add its own comments or reasoning. If the majority opinion has more than one holding, there can be a concurring opinion on only some of the holdings.

unanimous opinion An opinion in which all of the judges hearing the case agree with the final conclusion or judgment, including all of the holdings and reasoning.

plurality opinion The opinion agreed to by the largest number of judges hearing the case when there is no majority opinion.

dissenting opinion An opinion that disagrees with part or all of the result or judgment reached by the majority or plurality opinion.

Bruni, Judge Smith wrote the **majority opinion**. A **concurring opinion** is one that votes for the result reached by the majority but for different reasons. In *Bruni*, Judge Jones concurred but specified that he accepted only the result of Judge Smith's opinion. Normally, judges in such situations will write an opinion indicating their own point of view. Judge Jones did not choose to write an opinion. He simply let it be known that he did not necessarily agree with everything Judge Smith said; all he agreed with was the conclusion that the warrant was validly served. To reach this result, Judge Jones might have used different reasoning, relied on different opinions as precedent, etc. If all the judges on the bench agree on the result and reasoning, the opinion is called a **unanimous opinion**. If a majority of the judges cannot agree, a **plurality opinion** might be written in which the largest number of judges, short of a majority, agree on the result and reasoning. (Assume, for example, that there are seven judges on the bench, four of whom cannot agree. If any three can agree, their opinion would be the plurality opinion.)

㉓ A **dissenting opinion** disagrees with part or with all of the result and judgment in the opinion of the majority or of the plurality. Dissenting opinions are sometimes heated. Of course, the dissenter's opinion is not controlling. It is often valuable to read, however, in order to determine what the dissenter thinks that the majority or plurality decided.

LEGAL ANALYSIS SKILLS: BRIEFING AN OPINION

Briefing cases requires patience and skill. There is a vast difference between reading a newspaper account of a recent court opinion and reading the opinion itself. In fact, it is more accurate to say that you dissect an opinion than to say that you read it. In short, you *brief* the opinion.

Exhibit 7-13 summarizes the ten parts of a comprehensive brief of a court opinion. Exhibit 7-14 presents a brief of *Bruni* that conforms to the guidelines in Exhibit 7-13. Finally, Exhibit 7-15 is a shortened version of the brief (a thumbnail brief).

Keep in mind as we examine the ten components of a comprehensive brief that not everyone agrees on what the components are, nor on what the components should be called. As with most aspects of the practice of law, you should expect to find diversity among your supervisors on how things are done. Nevertheless, at the core, you will find that the ten components in Exhibit 7-13 are consistent with other briefing formats.

PRE-READ BEFORE BRIEFING

Here are some preliminary steps to follow when briefing:

- Skim the opinion a few times before starting to read it. Start taking short notes.
- Note any headings provided by the court. How a court divides an opinion can help you understand what it does.
- Note who the main parties are; this is usually indicated at the very beginning of the opinion.
- Note the general category into which the opinion fits. Is it a criminal case? An antitrust case? A negligence case?
- Note whether the court states the issue(s) in the case early in the opinion.
- Note who won, usually indicated at the end of the opinion. Occasionally, however, the court will summarize its main conclusion at the beginning of the opinion. If there was no clear winner, note what the court did to resolves the case, e.g., send it back (remand it) to a lower court for further proceedings.
- Now begin your first reading of the entire opinion.
- Start your briefing with the second reading, assembling what you need in order to identify the ten parts of a comprehensive brief outlined in Exhibit 7-13.
- Have access to a paper legal dictionary or an online legal dictionary (e.g., dictionary .law.com) in order to check the meaning of unfamiliar terms. Be cautious, however, in using a dictionary. It can be helpful in understanding common legal terms that the judge assumes the reader already knows (e.g., the definition of *motion*), but a standard legal dictionary will not provide the ultimate answer to the legal issues before the court.

Exhibit 7-13	Ten Parts of a Comprehensive Brief of an Opinion

The ten parts of a comprehensive brief of a court opinion:

I. Citation	VI. Facts
II. Parties	VII. Issue(s)
III. Objectives of the Parties	VIII. Holding(s)
IV. Theories of the Parties	IX. Reasoning
V. History of the Litigation	X. Disposition

I. Citation

Tell the reader where can the opinion be found. Provide a full *citation* to the opinion you are briefing. Include

- Names of the parties
- Volume number of the reporter,
- Abbreviation of the name of the reporter
- Page on which the opinion begins
- Date of decision
- *Parallel cites*, if available. A parallel cite is an additional citation where you can find the same written material in the library or online.
- In Chapter 11, we will cover public-domain citations. If the opinion you are briefing has a public-domain cite, include it as well.

II. Parties

Who are the *parties*? Identify the lead parties, their relationship to each other, and their litigation status.

- Lead parties. If there are numerous parties on both sides of the litigation, include only the first named party on each side. This first party is called the lead party.
- Relationship to each other. Examples: landlord and tenant, buyer and seller, husband and wife, parent and child, government and accused. Think of the categories of the parties in relationship to each other.
- Litigation status. State the litigation status of the parties "below" at the trial when the case began (e.g., plaintiff, defendant), and then state their litigation status "here" in the opinion you are now reading and briefing (e.g., appellee, appellant). If you are briefing a trial court opinion that has not been appealed, the litigation status will be their trial status (e.g., plaintiff, defendant). If there have been several appeals, give the litigation status at each appeal.

III. Objectives of the Parties

When the litigation began, what were the parties seeking? State the ultimate *objectives of the parties* in terms of the end result they want from the litigation. Examples:

- To convict someone of a crime
- To avoid conviction
- To force someone to pay for injuries suffered
- To avoid paying for another's injuries
- To get a job back

The objectives may not be explicitly stated in the opinion. If so, do your best to guess what the objectives were based on what you are told in the opinion. At this point, do not focus on tactical or procedural objectives.

IV. Theories of the Parties

What are the legal *theories* of the parties at each level of the litigation? By theory we mean the rule on which a party is relying as its legal basis in the suit. As we saw earlier, the rule that is the legal theory for bringing a suit is called a *cause of action*. Here are some examples of the plaintiff's legal theory:

- The defendant has violated a statutory rule (e.g., the plaintiff sues the state for violating § 235 of the statutory code on who is entitled to a license).
- The defendant has violated a common-law rule (e.g., the plaintiff sues the defendant for committing negligence in an automobile collision).

The defendant will also have a legal theory in response to the suit of the plaintiff. If the theory (rule) is not explicitly stated, do the best you can to figure out what it is. It may be a simple denial, which is the equivalent of saying that the facts do not support the plaintiff's theory or the plaintiff's theory is defective. Examples:

- A denial that the defendant violated the rule asserted by the plaintiff
- A claim that another rule justified what the defendant did
- An assertion that it was the plaintiff who violated a rule, which the defendant now claims (as the defendant's own cause of action) entitles the defendant to relief from the plaintiff

Briefly state what these theories have been at each stage in the litigation to date.

- If an administrative agency has acted on the case, state the specific legal theories used by the agency (e.g., failure to comply with an administrative regulation), and by other party (e.g., it did comply, or the regulation is invalid because it violates another rule).
- At the trial level of a civil case, name the *cause of action* (e.g., negligence, breach of contract, violation of § 65) and the main *defenses* (e.g., general denial, or failure of plaintiff to prove unreasonable care)
- At the trial level of a criminal case, state what the prosecution was for (e.g., murder) and the response of the defendant (e.g., self-defense). An explicit or implied denial is the equivalent of saying that the facts do not support the plaintiff's legal theory.
- On appeal, briefly state the main legal theory of each party (e.g., the trial judge applied the wrong law).

Note that the rules stated in these legal theories do not include the holding(s) that that will result from the opinion you are briefing. The holdings of the present proceeding will be stated elsewhere in the brief. For this section of the brief (theories of the parties), state the theory asserted at each stage of the prior proceedings and also state the theory of the parties going into the present proceeding.

V. History of the Litigation

What has happened thus far in the litigation? The case may have already been heard by an administrative agency, by one or more trial courts, and by one or more appellate courts before it reached the present proceeding that led to the opinion you are briefing. State the history of the litigation at two main stages.

- For each *prior proceeding*, briefly state the nature of the proceeding, who initiated it, the name of the court or agency involved, and what the court or agency did.
- For the *present proceeding*, briefly state the nature of the proceeding, who initiated it, and the name of the court or agency involved.

The history of the litigation will contain procedural facts, which are the steps the parties took in every proceeding to date to get to the court that wrote the opinion you are briefing. You should also state what each lower court or agency did. You won't state what the present court did until you get to the disposition of the opinion you are briefing.

VI. Facts

What are the *key facts*? The court may give many background facts, but we want the key facts. This is one of the most significant parts of the brief.

- A key fact is a fact that was very important or essential to the result or holding in the court opinion you are briefing. You know you have identified a key fact if you can say that the holding would probably have been different if that fact had not been in the opinion.

For each holding, identify the facts that were most important to the court. Note the facts that the court emphasized by repetition or by the use of adjectives such as "material" or "crucial." A court may provide hundreds of facts to give context to the opinion. Often, however, only a few of those facts are important or significant enough to have persuaded the court to rule in a certain way.

Proper names of parties or witnesses are rarely helpful in the statement of facts, but classifications or categories into which they fit are almost always helpful. If, for example, the opinion is about a purchase that Helen Olson made from Day-Glo Supplies, it will probably be important (key) to say that the opinion is about a purchase made by a buyer from a retail supplier.

Don't confuse the facts of the opinion you are briefing with the facts in other opinions that the court cites. Note, however, that the way the court discusses the facts in these other opinions will often give you clues to what facts were key in the opinion you are briefing.

VII. Issue(s)

What are the issue(s) now before the court? Provide a comprehensive statement of each issue by

- quoting specific language of the rule in controversy (which will be one of the elements of that rule - the element in contention) plus
- several important facts that are relevant to this contention

The court may not use the word *element,* but when it quotes specific language from the rule in dispute, it will be giving you the element(s) in contention. The contention will be over the definition of the element, on whether the facts fit within the element, or on both the definition and whether the facts fit within it.

VIII. Holding(s)

What are this court's answers to the issues? What are the holdings? If you have stated each issue comprehensively, its *holding* will be a simple YES or NO response.

IX. Reasoning

Why did the court answer the issues the way it did? State the *reasons* for each holding. The reasons can be varied. Examples:

- The facts substantially support the conclusion that…
- The legislature intended the statute to have the meaning stated in the holding because…
- The conclusion is supported by precedent, namely the prior opinions of…
- Society would benefit because…
- The statute is unconstitutional because…
- The administrative regulation violates the statute because…
- Etc.

X. Disposition

What order did this court enter as a result of its holding(s)? State the *disposition,* i.e., the consequences of the court's resolution of the issue(s). Examples:

- The defendant must pay damages to the plaintiff.
- The lower court decision is reversed and a new trial is ordered.
- The case is remanded to the trial court in order to …

Exhibit 7-14	Comprehensive Brief of *People v. Bruni*

CITATION:	*People v. Bruni,* 25 Cal. App. 3d 196, 100 Cal. Rptr. 600 (1972).
PARTIES:	People of California/prosecution/plaintiff below/appellant here v. Bruni/accused/defendant below/respondent here
OBJECTIVES OF THE PARTIES:	The people want to convict and punish Bruni for alleged criminal conduct. Bruni wants to avoid conviction and punishment.
THEORIES OF THE PARTIES:	1. TRIAL: The People sought to prosecute Bruni for alleged commission of a crime. (The opinion does not tell us which crime.) Bruni's theory at the trial (also not stated) was probably a denial that he committed the crime or an assertion that the prosecution has not met its burden of proving that he committed one.
	2. APPEAL: Bruni says that the state violated the requirement in § 1529 of "daytime" service when the search warrant was served at 9:30 p.m. The People say § 1529 was impliedly amended by § 1533, which allows service up to 10:00 p.m.
HISTORY OF THE LITIGATION Prior Proceeding:	1. TRIAL: A criminal prosecution was brought by the People (the state) in the Superior Court (San Mateo). RESULT: Judgment for Bruni dismissing the information after the court granted a motion to suppress the evidence obtained from the search warrant.
Present Proceeding:	2. APPEAL: The People now appeal the dismissal of the information to the Court of Appeal (First District, Division 1).
FACTS:	A search warrant that said "daytime" service was served at 9:30 p.m. Evidence was obtained during this search, which the People unsuccessfully attempted to introduce during the trial.
ISSUE:	When evidence is seized pursuant to a search warrant served at 9:30 p.m., can the evidence be suppressed under § 1529, which requires "daytime" service?

HOLDING:	No.
REASONING:	If there is a general statute (such as § 1529) and a specific statute (such as § 1533) that are inconsistent, the specific statute is paramount and is preferred when this preference would render the statutes "reasonable, fair and harmonious." Hence the legislature probably intended to amend the more general statute-§ 1529—when it amended § 1533.
DISPOSITION:	The trial court's judgment dismissing the information is reversed. When the trial resumes, the court must deny the motion to suppress the evidence based on the time of the service.

ADDITIONAL NOTES FOR THE BRIEF

At the end of your brief, you should consider adding some notes that cover the following topics:

- What has happened to the opinion since it was decided? Has it been overruled? Has it been expanded or restricted by later opinions? You can find the later history of an opinion and its treatment by other courts by using citators such as Shepard's Citations or KeyCite. (See Chapter 11.)
- Summary of concurring opinions, if any.
- Summary of dissenting opinions, if any.
- Interesting dicta, if any, in the majority opinion.
- Your own thoughts about the opinion. Was it correctly decided? Why or why not?

THUMBNAIL BRIEF

A *thumbnail brief* is, in effect, a brief of a brief. It is a shorthand version of the ten-part comprehensive brief. A thumbnail brief includes abbreviated versions of six of the components (citation, facts, issues, holdings, reasoning, and disposition) and leaves out four of the components (parties, objectives, theories, and history of the litigation). By definition, you must know how to do a comprehensive brief before you can do a shorthand one. Many students fall into the trap of doing only shorthand briefs. It takes considerable time to do a comprehensive brief. It is highly recommended, however, that early in your career you develop the habit and skill of preparing briefs comprehensively. Shorthand briefs are *valuable* time savers when communicating with colleagues, but they are not substitutes for comprehensive briefs. See Exhibit 7-15.

Exhibit 7-15	Thumbnail Brief of People v. Bruni

CITATION:	*People v. Bruni*, 25 Cal. App. 3d 196, 100 Cal. Rptr. 600 (1972).
FACTS:	A search warrant that said "daytime" service was served at 9:30 p.m. Evidence was obtained during this search, which the People unsuccessfully attempted to introduce during the trial.
ISSUE:	When evidence is seized pursuant to a search warrant served at 9:30 p.m., can the evidence be suppressed under § 1529, which requires "daytime" service?
HOLDING:	No.
REASONING:	A specific statute (§ 1533) is preferred over an inconsistent general statute (1529).
DISPOSITION:	Dismissal of the information is reversed; motion to suppress the evidence obtained at 9:30pm must be denied.

LEGAL ANALYSIS SKILLS: APPLYING AN OPINION

Applying a case (a court opinion) means determining whether the ruling in the opinion (called a *holding*) applies to the facts presented by a client. In a classroom setting, applying a case means determining whether the holding applies to the facts of a **hypothetical** devised by the instructor. In the following discussion, we will refer to the client facts or to the hypothetical facts as the *problem facts* and we will refer to the facts in the opinion as the *case facts* or simply as facts in the opinion.

A court opinion can have two impacts.

- First, it resolves the legal dispute between the specific parties within the opinion. Their controversy is over. Under the doctrine of **res judicata**, they will not be allowed to relitigate any issue that was resolved **on the merits**.
- Second, the opinion might become a precedent for future cases. The rest of the world can read the opinion to assess whether its conclusions (holdings) can be applied to the legal disputes of others.

Under the doctrine of **stare decisis**, similar cases should be decided the same way unless there is a good reason to reach a different decision. Hence, when a client walks into a law office and presents facts that raise legal issues, the office must determine whether any prior cases (opinions) are precedents for the client's case.

The process of finding out is called *applying court opinions, applying cases,* or *analogizing* cases. The word *analogy* means a comparison of similarities and differences. To *analogize* a case is to determine whether it is sufficiently similar to the facts presented by a client (the problem facts) to justify a similar outcome or result. When we say that a case is **analogous**, we are saying that the holding in the case should apply to the client's facts because there is a sufficient similarity between the case and the problem facts to justify a similar outcome or result.

To determine whether an opinion is analogous, we need to use two skills: rule comparison and fact comparison.

RULE COMPARISON

Assume that your client in the problem facts is charged with failing to make "estimated payments" as required by § 23, which is an estate-tax statute.

- Step One is to break the rule (§ 23) into its elements and find the element in contention. The element in contention in this rule is the phrase "estimated payments" in § 23. This becomes the basis of the issue.
- Step Two (after you have phrased the issue) is to do your own analysis based what you think each side would contend is the definition of "estimated payments."
- Step Three is to do some legal research on § 23. Here are some of the research steps you would take, not necessarily listed in the order in which you would take them:

  - Find out if any other statutes help define the phrase.
  - Check the legislative history of § 23 to see if it sheds any light on what the legislature intended by this phrase in § 23.
  - Find out if there are any administrative regulations covering § 23.
  - Find out if any court opinions have interpreted and applied § 23.

Our concern here is the last step. We want to know if there are court opinions that have interpreted and applied § 23. You would not waste time looking for opinions that have interpreted other primary authorities such as housing or pollution rules. You focus on opinions that cover the same rule involved in the client's case—§ 23. This is also true of common-law rules. If, for example, the client has a negligence case involving an attractive nuisance (a rule covering the duty owed to children), you search for negligence opinions interpreting the attractive-nuisance rule.

---

hypothetical (1) A set of facts assumed to exist for purposes of discussion or learning. (2) Not actual or real but presented for purposes of discussion or analysis; based on an assumed set of facts; based on a hypothesis.

res judicata ("a thing adjudicated") A defense raised (a) to prevent the same parties from retrying (relitigating) a claim that has already been resolved on the merits in a prior case or (b) to prevent the litigation of a claim arising out of the same transaction involved in the first case that could have been raised in the first case but was not.

on the merits Pertaining to a court decision that is based on the facts and on the substance of the claim, rather than solely on a procedural ground or other technicality.

stare decisis ("stand by things decided") Courts should decide similar cases in the same way unless there is good reason for the court to do otherwise. When resolving an issue, courts should be reluctant to reject precedent—a prior opinion covering similar facts and issues.

analogous (1) Sufficiently similar to justify a similar outcome or result. (2) Sufficiently similar to lend support. (3) On point; germane. Involving the same or similar issues; involving facts and rules that are similar to those now under consideration.

Suppose, however, that you cannot find opinions interpreting the same rule. Occasionally, you can use opinions applying different rules, but only if they are similar in language and purpose. In the tax example, the problem facts concerned the failure to pay "estimated taxes" under § 23 of the rules governing estate taxes. Assume that you cannot find any opinions interpreting § 23, but that you can find an *income* tax opinion applying § 100, which also uses the phrase "estimated taxes." Can you use such an opinion? Usually not. If, however, you carefully compare the language used in the two rules (§ 23 and § 100) and the reason (purpose or intent) the legislature had in writing them, you may be able to argue that the opinion interpreting § 100 can be helpful in interpreting § 23. To be able to do so, the language and purpose of the two rules must be sufficiently similar.

Assume further that our estate-tax case arose in Maryland and that § 23 was written by the Maryland State Legislature. In our search for court opinions, we will look for opinions written by Maryland state courts, preferably the highest state court in Maryland. Such opinions are **mandatory authority** for all lower state courts in Maryland. If no such opinions exist, can we use opinions from other states that have the same or similar language as § 23 in Maryland? Possibly. There are times when opinions from other states or jurisdictions can be used as **persuasive authority**. For now, however, our focus is on court opinions from the same state.

To summarize, follow these guidelines on rule comparison: Don't try to apply an opinion to problem facts unless the problem facts involve the same rule that was interpreted in the opinion. Also, concentrate on opinions decided by courts in the same jurisdiction where the problem facts will be litigated. Again, there can be exceptions to these guidelines, but use them as starting points.

FACT COMPARISON

Now we come to the critically important skill of fact comparison when trying to apply a court opinion. We are assuming that you have already done a rule comparison and are satisfied that the statute, common-law rule or other primary authority interpreted in the opinion is the same rule you are exploring for the problem facts. For example, your client has been charged with bigamy in the state of Georgia and you are trying to apply an opinion of the Georgia Supreme Court on bigamy. You must now do a fact comparison in order to determine if the opinion applies to the problem facts—to determine if the opinion is analogous.

When comparing facts in an opinion (case facts) with problem facts, follow these three steps:

1. Identify fact similarities, differences, and gaps.
2. Identify the key facts for a holding in the opinion.
3. Compare those key facts with the problem facts.

1. Identify Factual Similarities, Differences, and Gaps
Identify factual similarities, factual differences, and factual gaps between the facts in the opinion (case facts) and the problem facts. The heart of your analysis begins when you start comparing the facts in the opinion with the problem facts. Specifically, you need to identify factual similarities, factual differences, and factual gaps. The comparison should include individual facts and broader categories of individual facts. Don't worry at this point about whether any of these comparisons are significant. Many won't be. For now, however, concentrate on lining up all of the similarities, differences, and gaps. Later, we will weed out what is irrelevant and focus on the comparisons that are significant.

mandatory authority Primary authority that is binding; it must be followed. Examples: the statutes of state "x" are mandatory authority in state "x"; opinions of the highest state court in state "x" are mandatory authority for every lower state court in state "x" so that all lower state courts must rely on the mandatory authority in reaching their decisions.

persuasive authority Any primary or secondary authority that is not binding on a court, but that could be relied on by the court because it finds the authority helpful (persuasive) in reaching its decision.

Example:

Your Facts (problem facts)	The Opinion: *Brey Academy v. Davis*
The client, Barbara Lang, is being sued by Dr. David Orlief for defamation in a Los Angeles Superior Court. Orlief is a Los Angeles dentist. Lang is a former patient of his. On the phone, Lang told Mary Adams, a current patient of Orlief, that the diplomas and awards on the wall of his office are fake. Orlief filed the defamation suit due to his fear that he would lose patients as a result of what Lang said. In the law library, you find the opinion of *Brey Academy v. Davis* and you now need to assess whether it applies to Lang.	In this case, Brey Academy sued Paul Davis for defamation. From Davis's home computer in Sacramento, he wrote on his Facebook page that Brey Academy allowed coaches with known criminal records to teach children at the school. Brey sued Davis for defamation when it began receiving phone calls from people who saw the Facebook post and asked if it had staff members who had criminal records. Brey was concerned about the effect this would have on future enrollment at the school. The court dismissed the suit, holding that Davis has a right to alert the public of the information he provided. The cite of the opinion is *Brey Academy v. Davis*, 54 Cal. 3d 145, 176 P.3d 26 (2011).

The rule comparison for this example is easily stated: Our client is being sued for defamation in California. *Bray Academy v. Davis* is a California opinion that interprets the same rule, defamation.

The next step is a fact comparison. As we list similarities, differences, and gaps, note that the comparisons often categorize individual facts. For example, an individual fact in the client's case is that the Dr. Orlief feared losing patients, and an individual fact in the opinion is that Brey Academy received calls from people who saw the Facebook statement and was concerned about a decline in future enrollment. The list below categorizes these individual facts by saying that both defamation plaintiffs were worried about their *reputation*.

- First, identify all factual similarities:
  - Both Lang in our facts and Davis in the opinion are being sued for damaging or harming the reputation of the plaintiff.
  - There was an economic fear in both controversies. Dr. Orlief feared the loss of patients and Brey Academy feared the loss of future applications. A possible loss of revenue is involved in the dentist suit and in the school case.
  - There is no indication that Orlief has actually lost any patients as a result of Lang's statement. Similarly the opinion does not say that Brey Academy suffered any actual harm as a result to Davis's statement. The opinion does not say that applications have in fact declined as a result of the Facebook post.
  - The allegation of Lang concerns the safety of patients because fake diplomas suggest that Orlief does not have the skills to perform dentistry and, therefore, he might harm his patients. The statement of Davis also concerns the safety of children being coached by persons with criminal records.
- Next, identify all factual differences:
  - Lang is being sued for an oral statement (what she told another patient on the phone) whereas Davis was sued for a written statement (what he wrote on Facebook).
  - The plaintiff (Orlief) in our facts is a person whereas the plaintiff in the opinion is an institution (a school).
  - The defendant in our facts made the statement to one person (Mary Adams), whereas the statement in the opinion was made online, presumably to more than one person.
  - Lang's statement involved a health practitioner (a dentist) whereas Davis's statement involved sports/educational personnel.
- Next, identify all factual gaps, if any:
  - In our facts, the defendant (Lang) had a prior association with the defendant (she is a former patient), whereas in the opinion we do not know if the defendant (Davis) is a

current or former student of Brey Academy or has any other prior or current association with the Academy.

- The recipient of Lang's statement in our facts (Mary Adams) has a current association with the plaintiff (she is his patient), whereas in the opinion we are not told if persons who read the Facebook post were current or former students at Brey Academy or if they had any other association with the academy. We know that Brey received calls about the Facebook statement, but we are not told if any of the callers had any association with Brey.

Again, don't worry about whether any similarities, differences, and gaps are significant. Your job at this stage is to push yourself to think of as many of these comparisons as you can. Let's look at another example.

Example:

Your Facts (problem facts)	**The Opinion: *Smith v. Apex Co.***
The client, Ed Fox, sees an ad in the newspaper announcing a sale at a local store in downtown Boston. He goes to the back of the store and falls into a pit. The only warning in the area was a three-inch sign that said "Danger" near the pit. The client wants to bring a suit in Massachusetts against the store owner, James Jackson, for negligence in failing to use reasonable care in preventing his injury. In the law library, you find the opinion of *Smith v. Apex Co.* and you now need to assess whether it applies to Fox.	In this case, Tom Smith was looking for an address. He was walking down the street. He decided to go into an office building to ask someone for directions. While coming down the corridor, he slipped and fell on a wet floor. There was a small sign in the corridor that said "Wet Floor," which Smith saw. Smith sued the owner of the building (Apex Co.) for negligence. The court held that the owner of a commercial building was negligent for violating the common-law duty to use reasonable care for the safety of users of the premises. The cite of the opinion is *Smith v. Apex Co.*, 223 Mass. 578, 78 N.E.2d 422 (1980).

The rule comparison for this example is easily stated: Our client wants to bring a suit in Massachusetts for negligence, alleging failure to use reasonable care. The same rule was applied in the Massachusetts case of *Smith v. Apex Co.* The next step is a fact comparison. Note the fact categorizations of individual facts in the following comparisons.

- First, identify all factual similarities:
  - The client, Fox, was in a public place (a store). Smith was also in a public place (an office building). Both the store and the office building are commercial entities — businesses.
  - Both situations involved some kind of warning (the danger sign and the wet floor sign).
  - The warning in both situations was not conspicuous (the danger sign was three inches; the wet floor sign was "small").
- Next, identify all factual differences:
  - Fox was in a store, whereas Smith was in an office building.
  - The client's case involved a hole or pit, whereas *Smith v. Apex Co.* involved a slippery surface.
  - Fox was there about a possible purchase, whereas Smith was looking for directions and therefore was not trying to transact any business in the office building.
  - Both the store and the office building were open to the public. There is no indication that anyone was restricted from entering.
- Next, identify factual gaps, if any:
  - Smith saw the wet floor sign, but we do not know whether Fox saw the danger sign.

Ninety percent of your legal analysis is complete if you have been able to make these three categories of fact comparison: factual similarities, factual differences, and factual gaps. Many students either ignore the categories or do a superficial job of laying them out. They do not carefully pick apart the facts in order to identify similarities, differences, and gaps.

2. Identify Key Facts in the Opinion

Identify the key facts for each holding in the opinion you are applying. The next step is to focus on the key facts in the opinion. When you briefed the opinion, you identified the key facts for each holding in the opinion. As we saw earlier, a key fact is one that was very important or essential to the holding or conclusion reached by the court. In a divorce opinion, for example, it probably will not be a key fact that the plaintiff was thirty-three years old. The court would have reached the same result if the plaintiff had been thirty-two or thirty-four. Age may have been irrelevant or of very minor importance to the holding. What may have been key is that the wife postponed her education in order to work so that her husband could complete his education. Without these facts, the court might not have reached the conclusion (holding) that she was entitled to a share in his future earnings in the property settlement. Carefully comb the opinion to read what the judge said about the various facts. Did the judge emphasize certain facts in the opinion? Repeat them? Label them as crucial or important? These are the kinds of questions you must ask yourself to determine which facts in the opinion were key. (See "Facts" in Exhibit 7-13 earlier in the chapter.)

3. Compare Key Facts in the Opinion with the Problem Facts

Compare the key facts in the opinion (for each holding) with the problem facts. Here are your objectives when comparing key facts with the problem facts:

- *If you want a holding to apply to the problem facts, try to show that there is a substantial similarity between ALL the key facts in the opinion for that holding and the problem facts.*
- *If you do not want a holding to apply to the problem facts, try to show that there is a substantial difference between AT LEAST ONE of the key facts for that holding and the problem facts.*

If a holding in an opinion is favorable to your client in the problem facts and you want the holding to apply,

- You emphasize the similarities between the problem facts and all the key facts for that holding in the opinion. They must be substantially similar for the holding to apply.
- If any of your problem facts differ from a fact in the opinion, you try to point out that this is not significant because the latter was not a key fact in the opinion.

If a holding in an opinion is not favorable to your client in the problem facts and you do not want that holding to apply,

- You emphasize the differences between the problem facts and the key facts for that holding in the opinion. You need to show that there is a substantial difference between the problem facts and at least ONE key fact for that holding.

If some of the problem facts are similar to a key fact in the opinion, you try to point out that this is not significant because there is still a dissimilarity with at least one key fact for that holding in the opinion. For a holding to apply, ALL its key facts must be substantially similar to the problem facts.

When you want a holding to apply, the best opinion to find is one that is **on all fours** with the problem facts. The facts in such an opinion are exactly the same as the problem facts, or almost so. Such opinions, however, are relatively rare. Most opinions will have a mixture of similar and dissimilar facts, requiring you to go through the kind of analysis described above.

on all fours Exactly the same, or almost so; a very close precedent.

Handling fact gaps

If you can't fill a factual gap by obtaining more facts, do the best you can to assess its significance. If the factual gap is in the facts of your client's case, you simply go back to the client and ask him or her about the fact. In our negligence example, the paralegal asks the client (Ed Fox) whether he saw the "danger" sign. Suppose, however, that the factual gap is in the opinion itself. Assume that your client was running when he fell into the pit but that the opinion does not tell you whether Tom Smith was running, walking, etc. You obviously cannot go to Smith or to the judge who wrote the opinion and ask. You must make a guess of what the judge would have done in the opinion if Smith was running at the time he slipped on the corridor floor. You may decide that it would have changed the result or that this additional fact would have made no difference to the holding of the court.

Exhibit 7-16 summarizes the fact-comparison steps we have been discussing.

Exhibit 7-16	Fact Comparison When Applying Opinions

1. Identify factual similarities, factual differences, and factual gaps between the facts in the opinion and the problem facts. Compare both individual facts and broader categories of individual facts.
2. In the opinion, identify the holding and the key facts for that holding. (If there is more than one holding in the opinion, do this for each holding that is relevant to the problem facts.)
3. A holding cannot apply to problem facts unless ALL of the key facts for that holding are substantially similar to the problem facts.
4. Compare the key facts in the opinion with the problem facts:
   - If you want a holding to apply to the problem facts, try to show a substantial similarity between *all* the key facts in the opinion for that holding and the problem facts.
   - If you do not want a holding to apply to the problem facts, try to show that there is a substantial difference between *at least one* of the key facts for that holding and the problem facts.
5. If you can't fill a factual gap, do the best you can to assess its significance.

MEMORANDUM OF LAW APPLYING AN OPINION

One of the examples we just examined involved the application of the opinion *Smith v. Apex Co.* to the problem facts of Ed Fox. Let's look at how this application might look in a memorandum of law. (See Exhibit 7-17.) The client's case in the problem facts and the *Smith* opinion involve exactly the same rule, the common-law duty of owners of commercial premises to use reasonable care to assure the safety of users of the premises. Assume that the element in contention in this rule is the requirement of "reasonable care." The contention will be over whether the facts fit within the definition of the element of reasonable care.

Note that the memo in Exhibit 7-17 builds on the skills we have been covering in this chapter:

- The rule is broken into its elements.
- The element in contention is identified and an issue is based on this element.
- A definition of the element is stated (here, the parties agree on the definition but disagree on whether the facts fit within the definition).
- A court opinion is used to help determine how the definition applies.
- The structure of the memo follows IFRAC.

Exhibit 7-17	Example 3: Memorandum of Law (Using IFRAC as a Guide)

Office Memorandum of Law

TO: James O'Toole, Esq.
FROM: Rachel Parker, paralegal
DATE: June 30, 2015
CASE: Ed Fox v. James Jackson
OFFICE FILE NUMBER: 15-3218
KIND OF CASE: Personal Injury/Negligence
DOCKET NUMBER: (the case has not yet been filed)

RE: Whether the store owner, James Jackson, was negligent

I. Introduction
This memorandum addresses the question of whether a store used "reasonable care" for the safety of its occupants such as our client, Ed Fox. My conclusion is that it did not.

II. Issue and Summary Conclusion
Issue: Is a store owner negligent for failure to use "reasonable care" toward someone who is injured by a pit in the store when the only available warning was a small danger sign near the pit?
Summary Conclusion: Yes. Reasonable care requires additional precautions because of the danger.

III. Facts

Ed Fox saw an ad in a newspaper announcing a sale at a local store in downtown Boston. He went to the back of store and fell into a pit. The only warning in the area was a small (three inch) sign that said "Danger" near the pit.

IV. Rule

Under the standard common-law negligence rule in this jurisdiction, "owners of commercial premises must use reasonable care to assure the safety of users of the premises." *Smith v. Apex Co.*, 233 Mass. 578, 588, 78 N.E.2d 422, 430 (1980).

V. Analysis

According to *Smith v. Apex Co.*, there are five elements of the common-law negligence rule on the premises liability of commercial owners:

1. Owners
2. Of commercial premises
3. Must use reasonable care
4. Assure the safety
5. Of users of the premises

The only element that the parties are likely to dispute is the third on reasonable care. The parties will probably agree on the definition of reasonable care (ordinary prudence under the circumstances to avoid injury or other loss) but disagree on whether the facts fit within the definition.

An important opinion on reasonable care that is required of owners of premises is *Smith v. Apex Co.*, 233 Mass. 578, 78 N.E.2d 422 (1980). In this opinion, the holding of the court was that the owner of an office building was liable for negligence when Smith slipped on a wet corridor floor in the building. There was a small "Wet Floor" sign in the corridor. This opinion is substantially similar to our own client's case. Both were in public buildings where owners can expect people to be present. In both situations, the warning was insufficient. The *Wet Floor* sign in the opinion was "small." The *Danger* sign in our situation was "little." Because of these important similarities, it can be argued that the holding in *Smith v. Apex Co.* applies. The court in *Smith* emphasized the "inconsistency of allowing an owner to invite the general public to visit its facilities but do little more than the bare minimum to provide for their safety." Id. at 582, 78 N.E.2d at 428.

Reasonable care should have included additional safety measures such as a sign larger than three inches and a rope or other barrier around the pit.

It is true that in the opinion the judge pointed out that Smith saw the sign. Our facts do not state whether the client saw the *Danger* sign in the store. This, however, should not make any difference. The judge in the *Smith* opinion would probably have reached the same holding if Smith had not seen the *Wet Floor* sign. In fact, the case would probably have been stronger for Smith if he did *not* see the sign. The building was dangerous in spite of the fact that users of the building such as Smith could see the sign. Obviously, the danger would be considered even greater if such users could not see the sign. We should find out from our client whether he saw the *Danger* sign, but I do not think that it will make any difference in the applicability of the holding in *Smith v. Apex Co.*

The store owner will try to argue that the opinion does not apply. His argument might be that a pit is not as dangerous as a wet floor because a pit is more conspicuous than a wet floor and hence not as hazardous. A user is more likely to notice a hole in the floor than to know whether a floor is slippery enough to fall on. Our client could respond by pointing out that the pit was in the back of the store where it may not have been very noticeable. (We need to check this and perhaps photograph the area.) Furthermore, the wet floor in the opinion was apparently conspicuous (Smith saw the *Wet Floor* sign), yet the judge still found the defendant liable for the failure to provide reasonable care.

Finally, Ed Fox is arguably in a better position than Tom Smith. James Jackson was explicitly inviting people like Ed Fox into his store by placing the ad in the paper for the sale to which Fox was responding. Tom Smith, on the other hand, was using the office building for his own purpose — to seek directions. Yet the court still found that the office building failed to provide sufficient protection for Smith's safety. Surely, someone using a building to do business with the owner is entitled to the same, if not greater, protection than someone who is there for no purpose other than his own.

VI. Conclusion

Our client has the stronger argument on whether the store was negligent in failing to use reasonable care. Better warning should have been provided in view of the danger posed by the pit in the store.

CHAPTER SUMMARY

Legal analysis is the application of one or more rules to the facts of a client's case in order to answer a legal question that will help (1) avoid a legal dispute, (2) resolve a legal dispute that has arisen, or (3) prevent a legal dispute from becoming worse. Competent legal analysis requires a number of basic skills: legal research, element identification, identifying issues, phrasing issues, defining important language, applying definitions, factor analysis, briefing court opinions, and applying court opinions. The most frequently applied rules in legal analysis are statutes, administrative regulations, common-law rules, and constitutional provisions.

An element is a portion of a rule that is a precondition to the applicability of the entire rule. Rules can have different consequences such as authorizing or prohibiting something, requiring payments, and declaring definitions. Element identification requires you to list every portion of the rule that must apply in order for the consequence of the rule to apply. The word *and* in a rule usually indicates separate elements of the rule. The word *or* usually indicates alternative options for the same element.

An issue is a question that needs to be answered or resolved. Factual issues pose questions of what happened. Legal issues are raised when we want to know what the law is, what the law means, or how the law applies to specific facts. An element in contention is the portion of a rule about which the parties cannot agree. The disagreement may be over the definition of the element, whether the facts fit within the element, or both. Each element in contention is the basis of an issue. The two components of a comprehensive statement of a legal issue are a brief quote from the element in contention and several of the important facts that are relevant to that contention. The element in contention often contains language that must be defined. The parties may disagree on whether this language should be defined broadly and narrowly. A factor is one of the circumstances or considerations that will be weighted in deciding whether an element applies.

IRAC and IFRAC are acronyms that help you organize your legal analysis. IFRAC stands for issue (I), facts (F), rule (R), application of the rule to the facts (A), and conclusion (C). A memorandum of law can have nine parts: heading, introduction, issue and summary conclusion, facts, rule(s), application (also called analysis and discussion), conclusion, recommendations, and appendix.

An opinion (also called a case) is a court's written explanation of how it applied the law to the facts to resolve a legal dispute. Primary authorities often applied in opinions include statutes, administrative regulations, common-law rules, and constitutional provisions. A holding is the court's answer to an issue. The holding becomes a new rule. The opinion can then become a precedent for future opinions. Terms you need to understand when reading opinions include reporter, citation, appellant, plaintiff, defendant, respondent, syllabus, headnote, key number, reasoning, remand, majority opinion, concurring opinion, etc. The ten parts of a case brief are citation, parties, objectives of parties, theories of the litigation, history of the litigation, facts, issues, holdings, reasoning, and disposition. A thumbnail brief has only six of these parts.

A court opinion resolves the legal dispute between the specific parties within the opinion and might become a precedent for future cases. To be a precedent, the opinion must be analogous. To determine whether an opinion is analogous, we need to make two comparisons: rule comparison and fact comparison. First, you compare the rule (e.g., a statute or common-law rule) that was interpreted in the opinion with the rule you are considering in the client's case. With limited exceptions, the opinion cannot apply unless these two rules are the same. Second, you compare the key facts of a holding in the opinion with the problem facts (the facts of the client's case). If you want a holding to apply to the problem facts, try to show that there is a substantial similarity between all the key facts in the opinion for that holding and the problem facts. If you do not want a holding to apply to the problem facts, try to show that there is a substantial difference between at least one of the key facts for that holding and the problem facts.

KEY TERMS

legal analysis (p. 311)	verdict (p. 318)	memorandum of law (p. 331)	case (p. 340)
primary authority (p. 312)	judgment (p. 318)	IRAC (p. 331)	casebook (p. 340)
secondary authority (p. 312)	bench trial (p. 318)	IFRAC (p. 332)	brief (p. 340)
common law (p. 312)	element in contention (p. 318)	docket number (p. 333)	trial brief (p. 340)
cause of action (p. 313)	wholesale (p. 319)	RE (p. 333)	appellate brief (p. 340)
element (p. 313)	legislative history (p. 326)	roadmap paragraph (p. 333)	primary authority (p. 340)
tort (p. 314)	factor (p. 330)	counteranalysis (p. 335)	holding (p. 340)
issue (p. 318)	dispositive (p. 330)	STOP (p. 335)	precedent (p. 340)
legal issue (p. 318)	memorandum (p. 331)	opinion (p. 340)	reporter (p. 340)

unofficial reporter (p. 342)	syllabus (p. 343)	affirm (p. 345)	res judicata (p. 351)
official reporter (p. 342)	headnote (p. 343)	vacate (p. 345)	on the merits (p. 351)
citation (p. 342)	key number (p. 343)	remand (p. 345)	stare decisis (p. 351)
parallel cite (p. 342)	digest (p. 344)	dictum (p. 345)	analogous (p. 351)
public-domain citation (p. 342)	Westlaw (p. 344)	majority opinion (p. 346)	mandatory authority (p. 352)
appellant (p. 342)	per curiam opinion (p. 344)	concurring opinion (p. 346	persuasive authority (p. 352)
plaintiff (p. 342)	memorandum opinion (p. 344)	unanimous opinion (p. 346)	on all fours (p. 355)
defendant (p. 342)	key fact (p. 344)	plurality opinion (p. 346)	
respondent (p. 342)	reasoning (p. 345)	dissenting opinion (p. 346)	
citator (p. 343)	disposition (p. 345)	hypothetical (p. 351)	

ASSIGNMENTS

CRITICAL ANALYSIS

7.1 Identify the elements of the following rules:

(a) § 200. Parties to a child custody dispute shall attempt mediation before seeking a custody order from the court.

(b) § 75(b). Lawyers shall not enter into a business transaction with a client if they have differing interests therein and if the client expects the lawyer to exercise his or her professional judgment therein for the protection of the client.

(c) § 38. A person or agency suing or being sued in an official public capacity is not required to execute a bond as a condition for relief under this section unless required by the court in its discretion.

(d) § 1.2. A lawyer may not permit his or her paralegal to represent a client in litigation or other adversary proceedings or to perform otherwise prohibited functions unless authorized by statute, court rule or decision, administrative rule or regulation, or customary practice.

(e) § 179(a)(7). If at any time it is determined that application of best available control technology by 1988 will not assure protection of public water supplies, agricultural and industrial uses, and the protection and propagation of fish, shellfish, and wildlife, and allow recreational activities in and on the water, additional effluent limitations must be established to assure attainment or maintenance of water quality. In setting such limitations, the Environmental Protection Agency must consider the relationship of the economic and social costs of their achievement, including any economic or social dislocation in the affected community or communities, the social and economic benefits to be obtained, and determine whether or not such effluent limitations can be implemented with available technology or other alternative control strategies.

7.2 Provide a shorthand and a comprehensive phrasing of the legal issue or issues in each of the following situations:

(a) *Facts*: Tom owns a 2010 Ford. One day it stalls on a hill; the engine stops running. He wants to get the car off the street. He, therefore, pushes the car so that it glides off the street and onto the sidewalk. While Tom is pushing the car on the sidewalk, a police officer stops him.

Statute: § 92(b). The operator of any vehicle riding on a sidewalk shall be fined $100.

(b) *Facts*: Harry Franklin works for the XYZ Agency. In one of the agency's personnel files is a notation that Paul Drake, another agency employee, was once arrested for fraud. Harry obtains this information from this file and tells his wife about it. (She also knows Paul.) Harry is unaware that Paul has told at least three other employees about his fraud arrest.

Regulation: 20(d). It shall be unlawful for any employee of the XYZ Agency to divulge confidential material in any file of the agency.

(c) *Facts*: Jones has a swimming pool in his backyard. The pool is intended for use by the Jones family members and guests who are present when an adult is there to supervise. One hot summer night, a neighbor's child opens an unlocked door of a fence that surrounds the Jones's yard and goes into the pool. (There is no separate fence around the pool.) The child knows that he should not be there without an adult. No one else is at the pool. The child drowns.

Statute: § 77. Property owners are liable for the foreseeable harm that occurs on their property.

(d) *Facts*: Dr. Carla Jones is the family physician of the Richardson family. After an appointment with Mary Richardson, age sixteen, Dr. Jones prescribes birth control pills. Mary tells Dr. Jones that she can't afford the pills and does not want her parents to know she is taking them. Dr. Jones says she will give her a supply of the pills at no cost in exchange for an afternoon of office clerical work at Dr. Jones's office.

Statute: § 12(c). It is illegal to sell prescription drugs to a minor.

(e) *Facts*: Victor and Cathy Moseley own a lingerie store called Victor's Little Secret in a small town in Kentucky. The multinational company, Victoria's Secret, objects to the name of this store on the ground that it can confuse the public and thereby dilute the value of its well-known mark. (A mark is any language or symbols used to identify or distinguish one's product or service.)

Statute: § 43. The owner of a famous mark shall be entitled to an injunction for its dilution.

7.3 In each of the following problems, identify any ambiguous language in elements in contention. Give broad and narrow definitions of this language, and state which side would argue which definition.

Do not do any legal research.

(a) *Facts*: Alice Anderson is nine months pregnant. A police officer gives her a ticket for driving in a carpool lane in violation of § 101. The officer said he gave her the ticket because she was alone in the car at the time.

Regulation: § 101. Carpool lanes can be used only by cars and only when there is at least one passenger with the driver.

(b) *Facts*: Mary is arrested for violating § 55. She is charged as a felon. She forced open the lock on the driver's side of a van at 5 p.m. Mary didn't know that the door on the passenger side was unlocked. She went into the back of the van and fell asleep on the floor. The police arrested her after waking her up at 9 p.m. The owner of the van claims that a $20 bill is missing. Mary had a $20 bill on her, but she said it was her own.

Statute: § 55. A person who breaks and enters a dwelling at night for the purpose of stealing property therein shall be charged as a felon.

7.4 Section 100 provides as follows: "Motorists shall be liable for the foreseeable harm or damage caused by their driving. To determine foreseeability, the court must consider road conditions, speed, weather, visibility, and any other circumstance that would affect the likelihood of the harm or damage occurring." Charles Wilson ran his truck into the side of a parked car when he came to an abrupt stop at an intersection. There was some oil on the road. Wilson's truck skidded on the oil when he tried to stop at the intersection. The incident occurred at 7 p.m., just after rush hour. Was the damage caused by Wilson foreseeable? Do a factor analysis on the applicability of § 100. In your analysis, identify further facts that you would need to investigate. State how such facts might be relevant to your factor analysis. If there are unknown facts that you need, state what they are and the factors to which they are (or might be) relevant.

7.5 Prepare a comprehensive and a thumbnail brief of each of the following opinions:

(a) Your instructor will give you the citation of the opinion. (To read the opinion online, go to scholar.google.com, select *Case law*, and type the citation in the opinion your instructor will give you.)

(b) In Google Scholar, select "Case law" and run the following search aa bb (substituting your state for "aa" and a legal topic that interests you for "bb" (example: Florida capital punishment). Find a court opinion written by a state court in your state on your topic. Pick an opinion that is under 10 pages.

(c) *Brown v. Hammond*, printed in Chapter 5.

7.6 Read the following facts taken from an opinion. Then read a quote by the judge who wrote this opinion. What is dictum in this quote and why?

Facts in the opinion: Plaintiff sues a cable company for an injury to his foot allegedly caused by a hole the company left in the sidewalk. He claims that it was dark out at the time and that he was unconscious after he fell. When he woke up, he saw the hole. His leg was twisted, and he saw that his sneaker had come off. The company asked the court to dismiss the complaint because the plaintiff had failed to produce enough evidence of where he fell and what caused the fall.

Quote of judge writing this opinion: "The cable company's position lacks merit. It is true that negligence claims will be dismissed if causation is based on pure speculation. In this case, however, plaintiff did in fact identify the cause and location

of his accident. While he could not recall the exact manner in which his foot became entrapped in the alleged defect, and could not describe the way it looked on the night of the accident prior to his fall, he repeatedly identified the hole between the sidewalk and the depressed cable vault cover as the condition that trapped his foot and caused him to fall. Plaintiff also specifically identified, by circling and initialing on a photographic exhibit, the exact location and condition that caused his fall. The company's position would have merit if the accident had been caused by a transitory condition such as ice or a slippery liquid of nebulous nature. Here, however, plaintiff woke up with his leg twisted, then saw the hole, and even saw his sneaker off."

7.7 In the following situations, point out all factual similarities, differences, and gaps between the client facts and the facts of the opinion. Do not analyze the law of negligence in (a) or the law of neglect in (b). Focus solely on factual similarities, differences, and gaps.

(a) *Client facts*: Jim is driving his car 30 m.p.h. on a dirt road at night. He suddenly sneezes and jerks the steering wheel slightly, causing the car to move to the right and run into Bill's fence. Bill sues Jim for the negligence.

Opinion: A pedestrian brings a negligence action against Mary. Mary is driving her motorcycle on a clear day. A page of a newspaper unexpectedly flies into Mary's face. Because she cannot see where she is going, she runs into a pedestrian crossing the street. The court finds for Mary, ruling that she did not act unreasonably in causing the accident.

(b) *Client facts*: Helen is the mother of David, age four. The state is trying to take David away from Helen on the ground that Helen has neglected David. Helen lives alone with David. She works part-time and leaves David with a neighbor. Helen's job occasionally requires her to travel. Once she was away for a month. During this period, David was sometimes left alone because the neighbor had to spend several days at the hospital. When David was discovered alone, the state began proceedings to remove David from Helen on the ground of neglect.

Opinion: The state charged Bob Thompson with the neglect of his twins, aged ten. The state wishes to place the twins in a foster home. Bob is partially blind. One day he accidentally tripped and fell on one of the twins, causing severe injuries to the child. Bob lives alone with the twins but refuses to hire anyone to help him run the home. The court ruled that Bob did not neglect his children.

PROJECTS

7.8 A federal depository library is a public or private law library that must give you free access to the federal laws (e.g., federal statutes and regulations) that the library receives from the federal government. See Exhibit 11-4 in Chapter 11 on depository libraries in your state.

(a) What federal depository libraries are within an hour's driving distance of where you live?

(b) Use Exhibit 11-4 to find out what state depository libraries, if any, are within an hour's driving distance.

CORE SKILLS

Among the many skills a paralegal must have, five core skills stand out: writing (both basic English and legal drafting), research, ethics, computer use, and collaboration (working with others). The core-skill assignments introduce and reinforce these skills. Even if you are not asked to do all of the assignments as part of the course, you should do them on your own. Also, do not wait for the topics in the assignments to be covered in this course or in other courses. Successful paralegals are self-starters. A major characteristic of a self-starter is a thirst for independent study—learning on your own.

CORE SKILL: WRITING

7.9 The Pepsi Cola Bottling Company is authorized to do business in Florida. It wishes to prevent another Florida company from calling itself the Pepsi Catsup Company because this name violates § 225.25. The Pepsi Catsup Company denies that its name is in violation of this statute. The secretary of state has the responsibility of enforcing this statute.

> 48 State Code Ann. § 225.25 (1999). The name of a company or corporation shall be such as will distinguish it from any other company or corporation doing business in Florida.

Your supervisor asks you to prepare a memorandum of law on the applicability of this statute. The office represents the Pepsi Catsup Company. Analyze the language of the statute (§ 225.25) in a manner similar to the analysis of the statute (§ 17) in the sample office memorandum of law in Exhibit 7-10. Do no legal research at this time, although you should point out what research might be helpful. After you complete the memo, draft a letter to the secretary of state giving the position of your office on the applicability of the statute. You can make up the names and addresses of the people involved as well as any dates that you need. For guidance in composing the letter, see Exhibit 7-11.

7.10 Anthony Bay is a paralegal who works for Iverson, Kelley, and Winters in Philadelphia. He is an at will employee. His supervising attorney is Grace Swenson. One day, Bay notices that Swenson deposited a client settlement check in the general law firm account. Bay calls the bar association disciplinary committee and charges Swenson with commingling funds unethically.

(Attorneys have an ethical obligation to keep client funds and general law firm funds in separate accounts. Commingling or mixing these funds in one account is unethical, as we saw in Chapter 5.) Bay is fired for disloyalty. In the meantime, the bar investigates the charge of commingling and finds that the charge is accurate. Swenson is eventually disciplined. Can Bay sue Swenson and Iverson, Kelley, and Winters for wrongful dismissal? Write a memorandum of law that applies *Brown v. Hammond* to answer this question. Do not do any additional legal research. Use the memo in Exhibit 7-17 as a guide. The text of the *Brown* opinion is in Chapter 5.

CORE SKILL: RESEARCH

7.11 In Google, Bing, or Yahoo, run this search: *court opinions aa* (substituting your state for "aa"). Make a list of every paper or online site that prints the opinions of any of the state courts in your state. For additional leads, see section called Finding Case Law in Chapter 11.

CORE SKILL: ETHICS

7.12 Frank Adams is a paralegal in the one-attorney office of Jolene Richards, Esq. Adams has paralegal, secretarial, accounting, and receptionist duties. Richards has one account in a local bank, Heritage Savings. She has authorized Frank to make deposits and withdrawals from the account. Frank's paycheck is a check drawn on this account at the bank. Richards has several personal-injury cases. When a case settles, the insurance company sends Richards a check. She endorses it and instructs Frank to deposit it in the Heritage account. After deducting her fee, she will write a Heritage check for the balance payable to the client. Discuss ethical problems, if any, with this arrangement.

CORE SKILL: COMPUTERS

7.13 In Google, Bing, or Yahoo, run this search: *kinds of operating systems*. Write a report in which you discuss and compare the different kinds of operating systems used for various devices. In the Computer Terminology in the Law (CTL) notebook you started in Assignment 1.8 of Chapter 1, enter any new terms that you learned by doing this assignment.

CORE SKILL: COLLABORATION

7.14 In this chapter on legal analysis, we covered legal issues, court opinions, briefing, the memorandum of law, etc. In Google, Bing, or Yahoo, search for two sites that pertain to any topic covered in the chapter (e.g., how to brief an opinion). In Assignment 3.9 of Chapter 2, you obtained the Twitter addresses of students in your class. Send two tweets to these students (and to the teacher) that contain links to the two sites that you found. Prepare a report in which you list the sites that were tweeted to you, state whether you found them helpful, and explain why. Your two tweets should be different from any of the sites listed in the Helpful Websites section at the end of the chapter.

THE JOB SEARCH

(The search for employment cannot wait until the end of a course or of a curriculum. It needs to begin now. The job-search assignments are designed to introduce you to different aspects of the job search and to build options for you to explore about employment.)

7.15 Use the job links in Exhibit 2-12 in Chapter 2 to find a job opening for an entry-level paralegal in a corporation in your state. What does the job entail and what are the qualifications for the position? Give the site address where you found this information. If no openings exist in your state, look for the position in any state. For additional leads, see the section in Chapter 2 called Where Paralegals Work. In this section, see Paralegals in Law Departments of Businesses.

REVIEW QUESTIONS

1. What is legal analysis?
2. What are two reasons paralegals should study legal analysis?
3. What basic skills are required for competent legal analysis?
4. What are the most frequently applied rules in legal analysis?
5. What is an element?
6. Name some consequences of when a rule applies.
7. What is the relationship between the elements of a rule and the consequences of the rule?
8. How are "and" items treated in element identification? How are "or" items treated?
9. Name some of the benefits or uses of element identification.
10. What is an issue and how does a factual issue differ from a legal issue?
11. What is an element in contention and what is its relationship to issues?
12. What are the two components of a comprehensive statement of a legal issue?
13. What kind of disagreement do parties often have over the definition of language in the element in contention?
14. What is a factor?
15. What is IFRAC and how can it be helpful?
16. Name nine parts that a memorandum of law can have.
17. What is a roadmap paragraph?
18. What is an opinion?
19. What categories of primary authority are often applied in opinions?
20. What is a holding and how does it relate to precedents in future opinions?
21. What is a reporter and how does an official reporter differ from an unofficial one?
22. How does the syllabus differ from a headnote?
23. What is a key number?
24. How does a majority opinion differ from a concurring opinion?
25. What is meant by the reasoning of the opinion?
26. What is the disposition of an opinion?
27. What are the ten parts of the brief of a court opinion?
28. What are the six parts of a thumbnail brief?
29. What are the two impacts of an opinion?
30. What is res judicata?
31. What is stare decisis?
32. What is meant by analogous?
33. What is the distinction between mandatory and persuasive authority?
34. To apply an opinion, what two comparisons must be made?
35. What are the three components of fact comparison?
36. What fact arguments does an advocate make if he or she wants a holding to apply? What fact arguments does an advocate make if he or she does not want a holding to apply?

HELPFUL WEBSITES

Legal Analysis
- user www.sfsu.edu/dlegates/URBS513/howtodoa.htm
- www.law.uky.edu/files/docs/clinic/legal_analysis.pdf

IRAC
- www.lawnerds.com/guide/irac.html
- en.wikipedia.org/wiki/IRAC

How to Brief a Case
- www.csun.edu/~kkd61657/brief.pdf
- www.cjed.com/brief.htm
- www.lawnerds.com/guide/reading.html
- www.lib.jjay.cuny.edu/research/brief.html
- people.virginia.edu/~rjb3v/briefhow.html
- law2.umkc.edu/faculty/profiles/glesnerfines/bateman.htm

Phrasing Issues
- legalwritingtips.blogspot.com (click *Issue Statement*)
- disputedissues.blogspot.com (type *issues in the* search box)

Outline of a Judicial Opinion
- www.supremecourt.ohio.gov/ROD/manual.pdf (pages 123, 132, 135)

Legal Research Basics
- lib.law.washington.edu/ref/basic.html
- www.lawschool.cornell.edu/library (enter *legal research* in the search box)
- libraryguides.missouri.edu (enter *legal research* in the search box)

Google, Bing, or Yahoo Searches
(on these search engines, run the following searches, using quotation marks where indicated)

- "legal analysis"
- "legal reasoning"
- IRAC school
- "how to brief a case"
- "memorandum of law" write
- "applying court opinions"
- "issue spotting"
- "legal issues" school write
- "defining legal terms"
- "legal writing"
- analogizing cases
- "applying precedent"

LEGAL INTERVIEWING

CHAPTER OUTLINE

- Introduction
- Client Relations in an Era of Lawyer Bashing
- Hiring the Firm
- Context of Interviewing in Litigation

- Format of an Intake Memo
- What Facts Do You Seek? Guides to the Formulation of Questions
- What Does the Client Want?

- Assessing Your Own Bias
- Communication Skills: Analysis of an Interview
- Improving Your Interviewing Skills
- The "Difficult" Client

CHAPTER OBJECTIVES

After completing this chapter, you should be able to

- Interview a client.
- Understand the importance of the skill of legal interviewing.
- Describe the image of the legal profession in the media and what the paralegal can do to bolster that image.
- Know the meaning of *retainer*.
- Summarize a typical attorney-client fee agreement.
- Distinguish between an engagement and a nonengagement letter.

- Explain the role of interviewing in litigation.
- Outline what is included in an intake memo.
- List guides for the formulation of interview questions.
- Explain the value of fact particularization (FP).
- Understand the difficulty some clients have in describing what they want.
- Recognize the danger of your own bias.
- Know how to prepare for an interview.
- Enumerate ways to begin an interview.

- Define and give examples of the different kinds of interview questions.
- Explain the techniques of attentive listening.
- Know how to achieve factual comprehensiveness in an interview.
- List the dangers of ethical violations in interviews and how to avoid them.
- Know how to end an interview.
- Give examples of "difficult" clients and how to deal with them.

INTRODUCTION

Most paralegals do not do a lot of client legal interviewing. Exceptions include:

- High-volume law offices where the office handles many of the same kind of case, e.g., automobile negligence, bankruptcy, or DWI (driving while intoxicated)
- An office bringing a class action in which there may be numerous clients or potential clients
- Legal aid offices that provide free legal services to low-income persons
- Government agencies that have extensive interaction with the public

An example of a high-volume office is Harris, Mitchell & Hancox, which represents many clients charged with DWI. "When a new client arrives … a receptionist obtains client information, including address, telephone numbers, court location, appearance date, and other data concerning the charge…. Next a paralegal takes a client through a 15-page preliminary interview form covering all aspects of the arrest…. Only after these preparatory stages does the client meet an attorney."[1]

In most other offices, however, paralegals are more likely to do occasional follow-up interviews after the attorney has conducted the main interview. Nevertheless, all paralegals should know the dynamics of the interview process in order to increase their understanding of the overall practice of law and to be ready for the time when they are called on to conduct a legal interview. Paralegal Chris Baker was glad she was ready when her supervisor surprised her with an unusual assignment: interview all the players on a women's high school basketball team about whether their coach had inappropriate contact with them.

CLIENT RELATIONS IN AN ERA OF LAWYER BASHING

Before we begin, we need to examine some preliminary matters that often influence client relationships today.

Some clients you will be working with may be hiring an attorney for the first time. Their image of the legal profession is often heavily influenced by the portrayal of attorneys in the media. The media can be quite negative about attorneys. In a steady stream of commercials, cartoons, and jokes, attorneys are sometimes held up to public ridicule. Indeed, there is so much unfavorable publicity that some bar associations have accused the media of lawyer bashing and have urged their members to take affirmative steps to improve the image of the profession. Improvement is clearly needed. Almost two-thirds of Americans think lawyers are necessary but are overpaid; about half think they do more harm than good; and four in ten think they are dishonest, according to a nationwide survey commissioned by Columbia Law School.[2]

This may be the environment in which a paralegal comes into contact with clients. How they perceive you matters a great deal. The way you dress, how you communicate, and how you perform your job can reinforce the negativism or help reverse it. Whether you are interviewing the client, relaying a message to or from a client, or have roles that require no client contact, it is extremely important that you project yourself as a professional. There is no better way to combat negative stereotypes of attorneys than for everyone in the office to maintain a high level of integrity and competence.

You should act on the assumption that every large or small task you perform on a client's case is of critical importance. Even if you have only a small role in a particular client's case, you should assume that how you perform your role will help determine whether the client is satisfied with the services rendered by the entire office and whether he or she will readily recommend the office to relatives, friends, and business associates. This is particularly important because about 40 percent of a law office's new business comes from referrals and recommendations of satisfied clients.[3]

Admittedly, you cannot single-handedly correct the public's perception of attorneys. It is due to forces beyond your control. To a significant extent, the public does not have a clear understanding of the role of attorneys in society. A federal judge recently made the following comment about the legal profession and how attorneys are trained to think: "From the first day of law school, would-be lawyers learn not how to seek the truth, but how to advocate effectively for a client's version of the truth, expressed as a legal position."[4] Some citizens find this reality difficult to accept, as reflected in the question attorneys are often asked, "Would you represent a guilty person?" Under our constitution, everyone is entitled to his or her day in court. The legal system would collapse if attorneys refused to represent anyone who was not clearly innocent.

Attorneys sometimes take unpopular cases such as defending people charged with committing heinous crimes. When interviewed on TV or radio, these attorneys seldom generate much sympathy when they suggest that the accused is the victim. A well-known trial attorney once commented on his technique for dealing with the public. "Always tell reporters things are going great," he said, "even if 14 nuns have just taken the stand to identify your client as the man who pulled the trigger."[5]

Attorneys are frequently injected into the middle of bitter disputes where they become lightning rods for underlying and overt hostility. Opponents often accuse the other attorney of causing the hostility or of setting up roadblocks to resolution in order to increase fees. Although you cannot eliminate these perceptions, you can perform your job in such a way that the client feels that his or her case is the most important case you are working on and that you are doing everything possible to help the office keep costs to a minimum. This kind of professionalism will be a significant step in the direction of correcting public misconceptions about the practice of law.

HIRING THE FIRM

As we saw in Chapter 5, there are several ways in which an attorney-client relationship is created and formalized. The main way is by signing an *attorney-client fee contract*. See Exhibit 8-1 for an example. (It might also be called a **retainer** agreement, retainer contract, contract of representation, or fee agreement.) The document covers the scope of services to be provided as well as the payments the client will be making for those services. The payments will be for attorney fees, paralegal fees, court costs (e.g., filing fees), and any other expenses (e.g., witness fees and travel costs) that may be involved in the representation. The noun *retainer* has several meanings. It is the act of hiring or engaging the services of someone, usually a professional. (The verb is *retain*.) Retainer also refers to the amount of money (or other property) paid by a client as a deposit or advance against future fees, costs, and expenses of providing services.

retainer (1) The act of hiring or engaging the services of someone, usually a professional. (The verb is *retain*.) (2) An amount of money (or other property) paid by a client as a deposit or advance against future fees, costs, and related expenses of providing services.

Exhibit 8-1	Example of an Attorney-Client Fee Contract

Attorney-Client Fee Contract

This ATTORNEY-CLIENT FEE CONTRACT ("Contract") is entered into by _____ (Client) and _____ (Attorney)

1. **CONDITIONS.** This Contract will not take effect, and Attorney will have no obligation to provide legal services, until Client returns a signed copy of this Contract and pays the deposit called for under paragraph 3.

2. **SCOPE AND DUTIES.** Client hires Attorney to provide legal services in connection with _____. Attorney shall provide the legal services reasonably required to represent Client, and shall take reasonable steps to keep Client informed of progress and to respond to Client's inquiries. Client shall be truthful with Attorney, cooperate with Attorney, keep Attorney informed of developments, abide by this Contract, pay Attorney's bills on time, and keep Attorney advised of Client's street address, telephone number, email address, social media addresses and passwords, and whereabouts.

3. **DEPOSIT.** Client shall deposit $ _____ by _____. This sum will be deposited in a client trust account, to be used to pay costs, expenses, and fees for legal services. Client hereby authorizes Attorney to withdraw sums from the trust account for such payments. Any unused deposit at the conclusion of Attorney's services will be refunded.

Note that paragraph 2 is careful to say that the attorney will take "reasonable" steps to represent the client. This is to make clear that the attorney is not guaranteeing results. This disclaimer is made more explicit in paragraph 10. An attorney's duty is to act as a reasonable attorney.

Paragraph 3 refers to a client trust account. Funds in this account must not be mixed (i.e., commingled) with general office funds. Such commingling is unethical, as we saw in Chapter 5. Client trust funds are also discussed in Chapter 14.

(Continues)

4. **LEGAL FEES.** Client agrees to pay for legal services at the following rates: Partners: $ _____ an hour. Associates: $ _____ an hour. Paralegals: $ _____ an hour. Law clerks: $ _____ an hour. Note: Attorneys and paralegals charge in minimum units of 0.2 hours.

5. **COSTS AND EXPENSES.** In addition to paying legal fees, Client shall reimburse Attorney for all costs and expenses incurred by Attorney, including, but not limited to, process servers' fees, fees fixed by law or assessed by courts or other agencies, court reporter fees, long-distance telephone calls, messenger and other delivery fees, postage, in-office photocopying at $ _____ a page, parking, mileage at $ _____ a mile, investigation expenses, consultant fees, expert witness fees, and other similar items. Word processing in excess of 15 pages will be charged at $ _____ a page. Client authorizes Attorney to incur all reasonable costs and to hire any investigators, consultants, or expert witnesses reasonably necessary in Attorney's judgment, unless one or both of the following clauses are initialed by Client and Attorney.
_____ _____ Attorney shall obtain Client's consent before incurring any cost in
excess of $ _____.
_____ _____ Attorney shall obtain Client's consent before retaining outside investigators, consultants, or expert witnesses.

6. **STATEMENTS.** Attorney shall send Client periodic statements for fees and costs incurred. Client shall pay Attorney's statements within _____ days after each statement's date. Client may request a statement at intervals of no less than 30 days. Upon Client's request, Attorney will provide a statement within 10 days.

7. **LIEN.** Client hereby grants Attorney a lien on any and all claims or causes of action that are the subject of Attorney's representation under this Contract. Attorney's lien will be for any sums due and owing to Attorney at the conclusion of Attorney's services. The lien will attach to any recovery Client may obtain, whether by arbitration award, judgment, settlement, or other means.

8. **DISCHARGE AND WITHDRAWAL.** Client may discharge Attorney at any time. Attorney may withdraw with Client's consent or for good cause. Good cause includes Client's breach of this Contract; Client's refusal to cooperate with Attorney or to follow Attorney's advice on a material matter; or any other fact or circumstance that would render Attorney's continuing representation unlawful or unethical.

9. **CONCLUSION OF SERVICES.** When Attorney's services conclude, all unpaid charges shall become immediately due and payable. After Attorney's services conclude, Attorney will, upon Client's request, deliver Client's file to Client. Subject to paragraph 7 on liens, Client funds or property, if any, in Attorney's possession will be returned to the Client.

10. **DISCLAIMER OF GUARANTEE.** Nothing in this Contract and nothing in Attorney's statements to Client will be construed as a promise or guarantee about the outcome of Client's matter. Attorney makes no such promises or guarantees. Attorney's comments about the outcome of Client's matter are expressions of opinion only.

11. **EFFECTIVE DATE.** This Contract will take effect when Client has performed the conditions stated in paragraph 1, but its effective date will be retroactive to the date Attorney first provided services. The date at the beginning of this Contract is for reference only. Even if this Contract does not take effect, Client will be obligated to pay Attorney the reasonable value of any services Attorney may have performed for Client.

Attorney Signature _____
Date Signed _____, 20 ___

Client Signature _____
Date Signed _____, 20 ___

Paragraph 4 makes clear that separate fees are paid for paralegal services. The minimum charge for attorney and paralegal time is 12 minutes (0.2 hour). If, for example, a phone call with a client takes 8 minutes, the office will charge the client for 12 minutes. (See Chapter 14 on billing.) Law clerks are still in law school or are graduates waiting to pass the bar examination.

For an example of a client bill, see Exhibit 14-10 in Chapter 14.

An attorney lien is the right of an attorney to hold a client's funds or property (*retaining lien*) or to keep a part of funds coming to the client (a *charging lien*) until the attorney's fees and costs have been paid. The lien, however, does not cover the client's file. See paragraph 9.

In most states, the client's file must be returned upon request even if attorney fees are still due.

If the case has already been filed in court, the attorney will need the permission of the court to withdraw.

Courtesy of Everett Nollkamper, Fundamentals of Law Office Management: Systems, Procedures, and Ethics. © 1994 Cengage Learning.

The attorney-client relationship might also be formalized by an **engagement letter** that specifies the scope of the professional services to be rendered. At the end of the letter there is space for the prospective client to sign, indicating agreement with the terms stated in the letter.

Suppose, however, the attorney decides not to accept the case. This may happen for a number of reasons. There may be a conflict of interest because the law office once represented the opponent of the prospective client (see Chapter 5). The attorney may feel that the case lacks merit because there is no legal justification for what the client wants to accomplish. More commonly, the attorney will refuse to take the case for economic reasons. The client may not be able to afford the anticipated legal fees, and the party the client wants to sue may not have enough cash or other resources to pay a winning judgment. (Such an opponent is said to lack a **deep pocket**.)

Whatever the reason, it is important for the office to document its rejection of prospective clients by sending them a letter explicitly stating that the office will not be representing them. The document is called a **letter of nonengagement** or a **declination** letter. Its purpose is to avoid any misunderstandings if the person later claims to have been confused about whether the office had agreed to take the case. This person may try to assert that he or she took no further action on the case because of the belief that the office was going to provide representation. The ultimate nightmare occurs when this person loses the case by **default** because no one showed up in court at a scheduled hearing and the **statute of limitations** ran out before any action was taken to bring the claim. The attorney may now face a legal-malpractice lawsuit based on the person's reasonable assumption that the attorney was going to pursue the case. One way to avoid this predicament is by sending prospective clients an emphatic letter of non-engagement (sometimes humorously referred to in the office as the "Dear Not Client Letter"). The letter will often conclude with a statement such as the following: "Although our office cannot represent you, we urge you to protect your rights by seeking other counsel."

CONTEXT OF INTERVIEWING IN LITIGATION

There are three main kinds of legal interviews:

- Initial client interview
- Follow-up client interview
- Field interview of someone other than the client

In the initial client interview the attorney-client relationship is formally established and legal problems are identified as the fact-collection process begins. Follow-up interviews occur after the initial interview. The client is asked about additional facts and is consulted on a variety of matters that require attention, consent, or other participation. The field interview is conducted during investigation. The interviewer, as investigator, will contact individuals outside the office in order to try to verify facts already known and to uncover new relevant facts. Investigation will be examined in the next chapter. Here our focus will be the initial and follow-up client interviews.

Interviewing is among the most important skills in a law office. Many assume that the skill is relatively easy to perform (all you need is a person to interview, the **interviewee**, a pleasing personality, and some time). Yet interviewing is much more than good conversation. To avoid incomplete and sloppy interviewing, the interviewer must establish a relationship with the client that is warm, trusting, professional, and goal-oriented as the office goes about its mission of identifying and solving legal problems. The materials in this chapter, particularly the charts and checklists, are designed to help you achieve this relationship.

The *initial client interview* is critical because it sets the foundation for the entire litigation process. (See Exhibit 8-2.) The facts obtained from this interview are further pursued through *field investigation*. Subsequent or *follow-up interviews* are often needed to clarify new facts and pursue leads uncovered during investigation. The laws governing the facts are *researched* in a traditional law library, online, or both. The facts and the governing law are informally argued between counsel for the parties in an effort to *settle* the case through *negotiation*. If there is no settlement, a *trial* is held in which the facts are formally established. Finally, the process may end with one or more *appeals*. Everything begins with the facts obtained through the initial client interview. A poor job done at this stage can have major negative consequences throughout the remaining steps of the litigation.

---

engagement letter A letter that identifies the scope of services to be provided by a professional and the payments to be made for such services.

deep pocket (1) An individual, a business, or another organization with resources to pay a potential judgment. (2) Sufficient assets for this purpose. (The opposite of *shallow pocket*.)

letter of nonengagement A letter sent to prospective clients that explicitly states that the law office will not be representing them.

declination A formal rejection.

default (1) The failure to take action. (2) The failure to exercise a legal duty.

statute of limitations A law stating that civil or criminal actions are barred if not brought within a specified period of time. The action is time-barred if not brought within that time.

interviewee The person being interviewed.

| Exhibit 8-2 | Interviewing in the Context of Litigation |

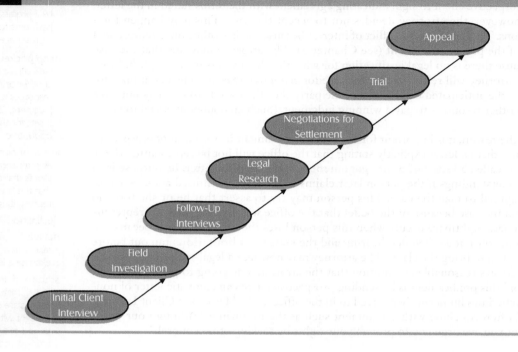

FORMAT OF AN INTAKE MEMO

intake memo A memorandum that contains the facts given by a client during the initial client interview and comments by the interviewer about the client and the case.

Before analyzing the interviewing process, we should look briefly at one of the end products of the interview—a document that is sometimes called the **intake memo**. It contains the facts given by a client during the initial client interview and comments by the interviewer about the client and the case. The intake memo becomes part of a newly opened case file on the client. The memo often has five parts:

1. *Heading.* The heading provides the following information at the top of the first page:
   - The title of the document (here, Intake Memo) centered at the top of the page
   - The supervisor in charge of the case to whom the memo is addressed
   - The name of the person who wrote the memo
   - The date the memo was completed and submitted
   - The date the interview was conducted
   - The name of the case (client's name and opponent, if any)
   - The office file number of the case (the internal numbering (and/or lettering) system used by the office to identify files of its clients)
   - The kind of case (general area of the law covered in the interview, e.g., mortgage foreclosure, child custody)
   - The notation **RE**, which means concerning, in the matter of, or in reference to. After RE, provide a brief overview of what is covered in the memo.

RE Regarding, concerning; in the matter of.

2. *Personal data*:
   - Name of the client
   - Home address (mailing address, if different from residence)
   - Phone numbers where the client can be reached; email address(es)
   - Age of client
   - Marital status
   - Address of employment
   - Etc.

3. *Statement of assignment.* The first paragraph of the memo should state the precise objective the paralegal was given in conducting the interview. It is a more detailed statement of what was listed under RE in the heading.

4. *Body of memo.* Here the facts are presented in a coherent, readable manner according to a number of possible organizational principles:

- A chronological listing of the facts so that the events are unfolded as a story with a beginning, middle, and end
- A categorizing of the facts according to the major topics or issues of the case (e.g., Background, Accident, Causation, and Medical Expenses), each with its own subject heading under which the relevant facts are placed
- Any other format called for by the supervisor

5. *Conclusion.* Here different kinds of information could be included. Examples:

- The paralegal's impressions of the client's personality and the facts presented during the interview, such as:
  - How knowledgeable the client appeared to be
  - How believable the client appeared to be
- A list of the next steps, such as:
  - What further facts should be sought through investigation
  - What legal research should be undertaken
  - Other recommendations on what should be done on the case based on what was learned during the interview
- A list of anything the paralegal told the client to do, such as:
  - Bring in specified documents relevant to the case.
  - Check on further facts and call back.
  - Return for another interview.

Exhibit 8-3 shows a sample of the introductory parts of an intake memo.

Exhibit 8-3	Beginning of an Intake Memo

Intake Memo

TO: Ann Fuller, Esq.	**CASE:** John Myers vs. Betsy Myers
FROM: Jim Smith, Paralegal	**OFFICE FILE NUMBER:** 15-102
DATE of MEMO: March 13, 2015	**KIND OF CASE:** Child Custody
DATE of Interview: March 12, 2015	**RE:** Intake Interview of John Myers

Personal Data
Name of Client: John Myers
Address: 34 Main Street, Salem, Massachusetts 01970
Phone: 966-3954 (H) 297-9700 (x301) (W)
E-mail: jmyers@aol.com
Age: 37
Marital Status: Married but separated from his wife, Betsy Meyers
Employment: ABC Construction Co, 2064 South Street, Salem, Massachusetts 02127

You asked me to conduct a comprehensive intake interview of John Myers, our client, in order to obtain a listing of his assets and the facts surrounding his relationship with his children.

A. ASSETS

John Myers owns...

WHAT FACTS DO YOU SEEK? GUIDES TO THE FORMULATION OF QUESTIONS

grounds Reasons that are legally sufficient to obtain a particular remedy or result.

relevant Logically tending to establish or disprove a fact. Pertinent. Relevant evidence is evidence having any tendency to make the existence of a fact more probable or less probable than it would be without the evidence. (See glossary for an additional meaning.)

Unless you know what to accomplish in an interview, valuable time will be wasted. For example, suppose you are interviewing a client on the **grounds** for divorce. You do not simply write down all the facts about the marriage and the client's problems in it. The facts must be clustered or arranged in categories that are **relevant** to each element of the grounds for divorce. Unless you have this objective in mind before and during the interview, you can end up with a confusing collection of facts and may have to conduct a second interview to go over matters that should have been covered initially. (As all-star Yankee catcher Yogi Berra once said, "If you don't know where you are going, you might wind up someplace else.") This does not mean that the interview must avoid any topic that is not directly related to the objective, but it does mean that each interview must have a definite focus.

There are six major ways to achieve focus in the formulation of questions to be asked of a client:

- Instructions of the supervisor for the interview
- Evidence, Procedural Law, and Substantive Law
- Checklists
- Fact particularization (FP)
- Common sense
- Flexibility

These methods overlap; at various times during an interview, you may be using all six. The goal of the methods is to help you avoid all the following examples of an ineffective interview:

- You fail to seek the information that the supervisor wanted you to obtain.
- You miss major relevant facts.
- You fail to probe for greater details about unpleasant or unflattering facts that the client glossed over or avoided.
- You fail to ask questions about the extent to which the client was sure or unsure about the major facts the client gives you.
- You fail to pursue leads the client provides about other relevant topics that may not have been part of the supervisor's explicit instructions or may not have been within the scope of your initial questions.

evidence Anything offered to establish the existence or nonexistence of a fact in dispute. Separate determinations must be made on whether a particular item of evidence is relevant or irrelevant, admissible or inadmissible.

substantive law Nonprocedural laws that define or govern rights and duties, e.g., the duty to use reasonable care to avoid injuring someone. *Procedural law* consists of the rules that govern the mechanics of resolving a dispute in a court or administrative agency, e.g., a rule on the time by which a party must respond to a complaint.

cause of action (1) A legally acceptable reason for bringing a suit. A rule that constitutes a legal theory for bringing a suit. (2) The facts that give a person a right to judicial relief. When you *state a cause of action*, you list the facts that give you a right to judicial relief against the alleged wrongdoer.

INSTRUCTIONS OF THE SUPERVISOR FOR THE INTERVIEW

The instructions of the supervisor control what you do in the interview. You may be asked to do a limited interview or a comprehensive one. Be sure to write down what the supervisor wants from the interview and include those instructions at the beginning of your intake memo. If possible, try to sit in on an interview conducted by your supervisor to observe his or her method of questioning and the amount of detail sought. Also, examine some closed or open case files that contain intake memos. Ask the supervisor if any of these memos is exemplary, and if so, why. A factually detailed memo can be useful as a guide. Later in Exhibit 8-8 we will cover more of these preparatory steps.

EVIDENCE, PROCEDURAL LAW, AND SUBSTANTIVE LAW

Paralegal Sally Kane points out that fact gathering in interviewing and investigation "should always be guided by the legal theories of the case and the facts and **evidence** you will need to support them."[6] You do not have to be experts in every area of the law or in any particular area of the law in order to conduct an interview. At the very least, however, you should have a general understanding of evidence and civil procedure, or, if the case is a criminal case, evidence and criminal procedure. You should understand the basic procedural steps in litigation in order to see how facts can be used in different ways at different steps in the litigation process. Also, you should have a general understanding of the **substantive law** that will be involved. In this regard, it would be sufficient to know what the basic **cause of action** and defenses are likely to be.

We will cover evidence in Chapter 9 and provide an overview of civil and criminal litigation in Exhibits 10-3 and 10-4 in Chapter 10. Regarding the substantive law involved in the interview, you can obtain a quick overview of any area of the law on the Internet. Suppose, for example, you wanted to find the basic terminology, causes of action, and defenses for an automobile negligence case. You could run this search in Google, Bing, or Yahoo: automobile negligence law aa (substituting the name of your state for "aa"). Many of the sites from this search will be attorney ads, but even the ad sites may provide useful overviews. As we will see in Chapter 11, an office would *not* rely on such overviews in a memorandum of law or appellate brief. Overviews of the law found on the Internet are no more than starting points. (On assessing the reliability of law on the Internet, see Chapter 11.)

CHECKLISTS

The office where you work may have checklists that are used in conducting interviews. For some kinds of cases, such as probate or bankruptcy, the checklists may be extensive. If such checklists are not available, you should consider writing your own for the kinds of cases in which you acquire experience. Caution is needed, however, in using checklists:

- You should find out why individual questions were inserted in the checklist.
- You should be flexible enough to ask relevant questions that may not be on the checklist.

By definition, a checklist is nothing more than a standard form. Use it as a guide that must be adapted to the case and client in front of you, rather than as a rigid formula from which there can be no deviation. There is a danger of being so tied to a checklist that you fail to hear and respond to what the client is saying.

FACT PARTICULARIZATION

How much detail should you try to obtain in an interview? Attorneys like facts. During three years of law school, they were constantly asked by their law professors, "What are the facts?" The likelihood is that the attorney for whom you work will want considerable detail from the interview. Even if you are told to limit yourself to obtaining the basic facts from the client, you may find that the supervisor wants a lot of detail about those basic facts. When in doubt, the safest course is to be detailed in your questioning.

Fact particularization (FP) is a skill that will help you obtain factual details. To particularize a fact means to ask an extensive series of questions about that fact in order to explore its uniqueness. Fact assessment is critical to the practice of law; fact particularization (FP) is critical to the identification of the facts that must be assessed. FP is a fact-collection technique. It is the process of viewing every person, thing, or event as unique—different from every other person, thing, or event. Each important fact a client tells you in an interview should be particularized. You do this by asking a large number of initial and follow-up questions (who, what, where, how, when, and why) once you have targeted the fact you want to explore. (See Exhibit 8-4.)

FP can be a guide in formulating factual questions that need to be asked in different settings:

- In a client interview (our focus in this chapter)
- In investigations (see Chapter 9)
- In **interrogatories ("rogs")** during **discovery** (see Chapter 10)
- In a **deposition** during discovery (see Chapter 10)
- In an administrative or court hearing (in which witnesses are formally questioned; see Chapters 10 and 15)

fact particularization (FP)
A fact-gathering technique to generate a large list of factual questions (who, what, where, how, when, and why) that will help you obtain a specific and comprehensive picture of all available facts relevant to a legal issue.

interrogatories ("rogs")
A method of discovery by which one party sends written questions to another party.

discovery Methods used by parties to force information from each other before trial to aid in trial preparation. Examples of such devices include interrogatories and depositions. The methods can also be used to aid in the enforcement of a judgment.

deposition (1) A method of discovery by which parties and their prospective witnesses are questioned by the opposing party before trial at a location other than a courtroom. (Judges are not present during depositions.) The person questioned is called the *deponent.* (2) A posttrial method of discovery by which the winning party seeks to uncover facts that will help it enforce the judgment it obtained against the losing side.

Exhibit 8-4	Fact Particularization (FP)

To *particularize* a fact you already have,

- Assume that what you know about this fact is woefully inadequate.
- Assume that there is more than one version of this fact.
- Ask a large number of who, what, where, how, when, and why questions about the fact, which, if answered, will provide as specific and as comprehensive a picture of that fact as is possible at this time.
- The questions do not have to be asked in any set order so long as the multiple questions are asked for each fact connected to the case.

Example of FP:

You are working on an automobile negligence case. Two cars collide on a two-lane street. They were driven by Mary Smith and Ed Jones. Jones is a client of your law office. One of the facts alleged by Jones is that Smith's car veered into Jones's lane moments before the collision. Your job is to particularize this fact by trying to obtain a much more detailed picture of the alleged veering. This is done by seeking a comprehensive elaboration of this fact. Using FP, here are examples of commonsense who-what-where-how-when-why questions you could ask to particularize the fact of veering:

- What does Jones mean by "veered into" the lane?
- How much veering was done? An inch? A foot? Did the entire car come into the other lane? How much of an angle was there?
- Who saw this happen? According to Jones, Smith's car veered. Did Jones see this happen himself? Who else saw it, if anyone? Any passengers in Jones's car? Any passengers in Smith's car? Were there any bystanders? Has the neighborhood been checked for witnesses, e.g., people who live or work in the area or people who frequently sit on public benches in the area?
- Were the police called after the accident? If so, who was the officer? Was a report made? If so, what does it say, if anything, about the car veering into the other lane? Where is this report? How can you obtain a copy?
- What time of day did the accident occur?
- Why did Smith's car veer, according to Jones or anyone else who alleges that this occurred?
- How fast was Jones's car going at the time of the veering? Why was Jones going at this speed? Who would be able to substantiate the speed? Who might have different views of how fast Jones was going?
- How fast was Smith's car going at the time of the veering? Why was Smith going at this speed? Who would be able to substantiate the speed? Who might have different views of how fast Smith was going?
- Have there been other accidents in the area? If so, how similar have they been to this one?
- What was the condition of the road at the time Smith started to veer? At the time of the collision?
- What was the weather at the time?
- How was visibility?
- What kind of a road is it? Straight? Curved at the area of the collision? Any inclines? Any hills that could affect speed and visibility?
- What kind of area is it? Residential? Commercial?
- Is there anything in the area that would distract drivers, e.g., potholes?
- Where is the nearest traffic light, stop sign, or other traffic signal? Prepare a diagram or obtain an online street map (e.g., through *maps.google.com* or *www.mapquest.com*) on which you note their location. How, if at all, did they affect traffic at the time of the accident?
- What is the speed limit in the area?
- What kind of car was Smith driving? Were there any mechanical problems with the car? Would these problems have helped cause the veering?
- What prior accidents has Smith had, if any?
- What kind of car was Jones driving? Were there any mechanical problems with the car? What prior accidents has Jones had, if any?
- Etc.

Of course, the interviewee may not have the answer to all of such questions. The job of the interviewer, however, is to probe. You can't know in advance what questions will or will not be productive.

In legal interviewing, the starting point for the FP process is an important fact that the client has told you during the interview. Here are additional examples: "I tried to find work";

"the car hit me from the rear"; "the pain was unbearable"; "the company was falling apart"; "he told me I would get the ranch when he died"; "he fired me because I am a woman." With these starting points, you then ask the client the basic who-what-where-how-when-why questions that we used in the Smith and Jones driving example. As a guide to help you organize these questions, Exhibit 8-5 presents eight categories of questions and aids that can be asked in order to achieve competent FP.

Exhibit 8-5	Categories of Questions for Fact Particularization (FP)

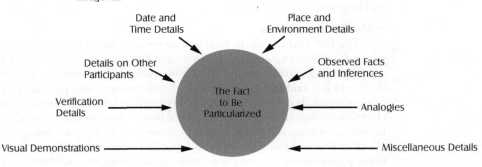

FACT PARTICULARIZATION

Steps: Begin by obtaining a general picture of what happened. Next, particularize every important fact you obtain by seeking comprehensive details on that fact through who-what-where-how-when-why questions that are relevant to the following interrelated categories:

Date and Time Details

Place and Environment Details

Details on Other Participants

Observed Facts and Inferences

Verification Details

The Fact to Be Particularized

Analogies

Visual Demonstrations

Miscellaneous Details

The seven categories are not mutually exclusive, and all eight categories are not necessarily applicable to every fact that you particularize. Again, the questions need not be asked in any prescribed order as long as you are comprehensive in your search for factual detail. The point of FP is to get the wheels of your mind rolling so that you will think of a large number of questions and thereby avoid conducting a superficial interview.

▪ Date and Time Details

When did the fact occur or happen? Find out the precise date and time. The interviewer should be scrupulous about all dates and times. If more than one event is involved, ask questions about the dates and times of each. If the client is not sure, ask questions to help jog the memory and ask the client to check his or her records or to contact other individuals who might know. Do not be satisfied with an answer such as "It happened about two months ago." If this is what the client says, record it in your notes, but then probe further. Show the client a calendar and ask about other events going on at the same time in an effort to help him or her be more precise.

▪ Place and Environment Details

Be equally scrupulous about geography. Where did the event occur? Where was the thing or object in question? Where was the client at the time? Ask the client to describe the surroundings. Ask questions with such care that you obtain a verbal photograph of the scene. If relevant, ask the client to approximate distances between important objects or persons. You might want to have the client draw a diagram, or you can draw a diagram on the basis of what you have been told and ask the client if the drawing is accurate. (Also consider printing one of the online maps mentioned earlier.) Ask questions about the weather or about lighting conditions. You want to know as much as you can about the environment, or whatever the client could observe about the environment, through the senses of sight, hearing, smell, and touch.

■ Details on Other Participants

Who else was involved? Ask questions about who they were, their roles, their ages, appearance, etc., if relevant. Where were they at the time? When did they act? Why did they act? Why did they fail to act? Could you have anticipated what they did or failed to do? Why or why not? Have they ever acted or failed to act in this way before? Ask questions designed to obtain a detailed picture of who these other participants were and their precise relationship to the fact being particularized.

■ Observed Facts and Inferences

inference A deduction or conclusion reached from facts.

Interviewers must also carefully distinguish between observed facts and **inferences** of fact.[7] *Observed* facts are what the client directly experienced through the senses (e.g., "I saw the car weaving back and forth over the center line"; "I smelled alcohol on his breath"). An inference is a deduction or conclusion from facts (e.g., "He was driving carelessly"; "He was drunk"). Part of being comprehensive in an interview is to uncover all the observed facts that led to the inferences made by a client. This is not always easy to do. Opinionated clients sometimes confuse facts and opinions. They may state an opinion but think it is a fact because they "swear" it is true. But opinions are mere inferences. Let a client express them during an interview and record them in your notes, but follow up with probing questions that identify underlying observed data. All of the categories of fact particularization will help you achieve this goal.

■ Verification Details

The fact that the client tells you something happened is *some* evidence that it happened. Verification details are *additional* evidence that supports what the client has said. Always pursue verification details. Ask yourself how you would establish the truth of what the client has said if the client suddenly disappeared and you had to rely exclusively on other sources. Inquire about documents (such as letters or check stubs) that support the client's statements. Inquire about other people who might be available to provide confirmation. Asking the client for verification details does not mean that you distrust the client or that you think the client is lying. It is simply a good practice to view a fact from many perspectives. You are always seeking the strongest case possible. This calls for probing questions about verification details.

■ Analogies

analogy A comparison of similarities and differences.

Some facts you are particularizing are difficult to pin down, e.g., "The pain was unbearable." "I was careful." "It looked awful." "I was scared." In the interview, you should ask the client to explain such statements. Sometimes it is helpful to ask the client to use **analogies** to describe what is meant. When you ask clients to use an analogy, you are asking them to explain something by comparing it to something else. For example:

- What would you compare it to?
- Was it similar to anything you have ever seen before?
- Have you observed anyone else doing the same thing?
- Have you ever been in a similar situation?
- Did it feel like a dentist's drill?
- On a scale of 1 to 10 (with 10 being the worst pain you have ever experienced), what number would you use to describe the pain?

First, you ask the client to compare the fact to something else. Then you ask about the similarities and differences. Through a series of directed questions, you are encouraging the client to analogize the fact to some other fact. This is done in a further attempt to obtain as comprehensive a factual picture as possible.

■ Visual Demonstrations

Under place and environment details we mentioned the use of diagrams and maps as aids. Other visuals should also be considered. Creative interviewers realize that a brief demonstration, drawing, or exhibit can sometimes be effective in eliciting greater factual detail. One interviewer who works on many automobile negligence cases has a set of toy cars at her desk. She will occasionally line them up on the desk and ask the client to explain what happened by using the toy cars. "People love visual demonstrations. As powerful as words can be, charts, maps, graphs, re-enactments, diagrams, timelines, and other visual aids" can be very effective in communicating information.[8]

Drawing a **timeline** can be helpful when a story involves some complexity. The simplest format of a timeline is a straight line that lists significant events chronologically along the line. Each event might be drawn within a separate box that includes the date when the event occurred (see Exhibit 8-6). During the interview, draw a rough sketch of a timeline based on the facts given to you and show it to the client. A diagram such as this gives the client a visual overview of what occurred and may prompt further questions and clarifications.

timeline A chronological presentation of significant events, often using text and diagrams.

Exhibit 8-6	Example of a Timeline

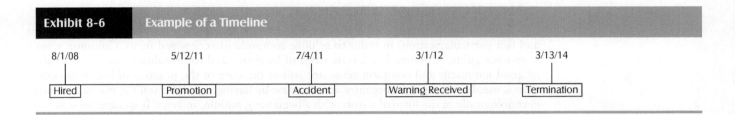

(For a more elaborate timeline that a paralegal helped design in a medical-malpractice case, see Exhibit 10-11 in Chapter 10.)

■ **Miscellaneous Details**

Here, you ask about any details that were not covered in the previous categories of questions. Include questions on anything else that might help in particularizing the fact under examination.

EXTENT OF CERTAINTY AND UNCERTAINTY

Everything the client tells you can be placed somewhere on the *spectrum of certainty*. (See Exhibit 8-7.) It would be a mistake, for example, to record that the client said a letter was received two weeks ago when in fact the client said, "I think it came two weeks ago." Do not turn uncertainty into certainty by sloppy listening and sloppy recording in your notes and intake memo of what the client said. Of course, it may be possible for a client to be uncertain about a fact initially but then become more certain of it with the help of your questioning. If so, record this transition by saying, "The client at first did not remember who else was present, but then said she thought Fred was 'probably' there."

Exhibit 8-7	Spectrum of Certainty

As a client answers questions, make note of how certain the client is of each answer. Where on the spectrum does the answer fit?

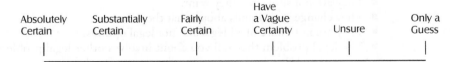

At the outset, explain to the client how critical it is for you to obtain accurate information. Encourage the client to say, "I'm not sure" when that is the case. A client may not want to be hesitant about facts that are favorable to what they are trying to accomplish. Clients must be relaxed and unthreatened before they will be honest and frank about what they know and, equally important, about what they do not know. A lot depends on the attitude of the interviewer in asking questions and in reacting to answers. Let the clients know that when you ask a question, you are looking for no more than the best of their recollection.

Never be irritated or disappointed when a client cannot answer a question with absolute certainty. Do not keep saying, "Are you sure?" after every client answer. Probing will often be necessary in order to find out where on the spectrum of certainty a fact falls. Yet probing must be undertaken with sensitivity. Repeating what the client has said in the form of a question can be a tactful way to reinforce the importance of obtaining precise dates and times (e.g., "You said the delivery was made at 1:30 in the afternoon. Do I have that right?"). We will cover similar interviewing techniques later in the chapter in Exhibit 8-12 on attentive listening.

COMMON SENSE AND FLEXIBILITY

Thus far we have examined a number of guides for formulating questions (e.g., checklists and fact particularization) in order to achieve comprehensiveness and focus. Common sense is another guide. Although law has its share of legalisms and technicalities, the related traits of good judgment and common sense are still at the core of the practice of law. It is common sense, for example, to organize an interview by having the client tell the relevant events chronologically in the form of a story with a beginning, middle, and end. It is common sense to ask further questions that follow up on a potentially important topic the client mentions even though you had not anticipated the topic. If the client says something you do not understand, common sense dictates that you ask what the client means before continuing with the interview. At times, it may be common sense to stop the interview for a moment to obtain further guidance from your supervisor.

The best frame of mind an interviewer can have is to be prepared but to be flexible enough to expect the unexpected. Although you lead the interview and give it direction, you must be ready to go where the interview takes you. It could be a serious mistake to block out topics that arise solely because they were not part of your game plan in conducting the interview or are not on your checklist. As with so many areas of the law, you may not know what you are looking for until you find it. In interviewing a client about incorporating a business, for example, you may stumble across a lead from something the client says that could involve fraud or criminal prosecution on a matter unrelated to the incorporation. Don't block this out. Make note of it for further questions later and for further instructions from your supervisor.

WHAT DOES THE CLIENT WANT?

Recently, a veteran paralegal reflected on her years of experience working with clients. She said,

"The greatest challenges are in dealing with the people. We see the best in people, the worst, and everything in between. Different clients need different levels and types of support from their legal team. Sometimes it takes several interactions with a client and some wrong turns to figure out their needs and expectations."[9]

CLIENTS IN DISTRESS

A number of points can be made about many clients, particularly new ones:

- They are not sure what they want.
- They change their minds about what they want.
- They are not aware of all legal and nonlegal options.
- The legal problem they tell you about involves other legal problems that they are not aware of and that even you may not be aware of at the outset.

Suppose a client, Tom Kelly, walks into the office and says, "I want to declare bankruptcy." The following observations might be possible about Kelly:

- He has an incorrect understanding of what a bankruptcy is.
- He says he wants to declare bankruptcy because he thinks this is the only remedy available to solve his problem.
- If he knew that other options exist (e.g., credit counseling and free mentoring advice from the Small Business Administration), he would consider them.
- What really troubles Kelly is that he is under pressure from organized crime in the neighborhood; bankruptcy is the only way he thinks he can escape the pressure.

If any of these observations is correct, think of how damaging it would be for someone in the office to take out the standard bankruptcy forms and start filling them out immediately after the client says, "I want to declare bankruptcy." Kelly needs a consultation with an attorney in order to find out (1) what bankruptcy entails and (2) what alternatives to bankruptcy should be considered.

One technique used by an experienced paralegal is to ask clients what they think would happen if the office were able to accomplish *xyz* for them. When they answer, the paralegal then asks, "Is that what you want to happen?" The question can sometimes help the client put the matter in perspective. "Maybe they don't really want a divorce, but they don't know of other options. Maybe they don't really need a will; perhaps other forms of estate planning will meet their need."[10]

This is not to say that a law office must psychoanalyze every client or that it should distrust everything clients say when they first seek legal help. Rather, it is a recognition of the fact that most people are confused about the law and make requests based on misinformation about what courses of action are available to solve problems. Common sense tells us to avoid taking all statements at face value. People under emotional distress need to be treated with sensitivity. We should not expect them to articulate their intentions with clarity all the time in view of the emotions involved and the sometimes complicated nature of the law.

ASSESSING YOUR OWN BIAS

You need to be aware of how your personal feelings might affect your work on a case. Such feelings are the foundation of **bias**, which is an inclination, tendency, or predisposition to think or to act in a certain way. How would you answer the following question: "Am I objective enough that I can assist a person even though I have a personal distaste for what that person wants to do or what that person has done?" Many of us would quickly answer "yes" to this question. We all like to feel that we are levelheaded and not susceptible to letting our prejudices interfere with the job we are asked to accomplish. Most of us, however, have difficulty ignoring our personal likes and dislikes.

Examine the following fact situations. In each situation, to what extent might an individual be hampered in delivering legal services because of personal reactions toward the client? Identify potential bias.

bias (1) An inclination, tendency, or predisposition to think or act in a certain way. (2) Prejudice for or against something or someone. (3) A danger of prejudgment.

1. Mr. Smith, the client of your office, is being sued by his estranged wife for custody of their two small children. Mr. and Mrs. Smith live separately, but Mr. Smith has had custody of the children during most of their lives. Mrs. Smith has charged that Mr. Smith often yells at the children, leaves them with neighbors and day care centers for most of the day, and is an alcoholic. Your investigation reveals that Mrs. Smith will probably be able to prove all these allegations (and more) in court.

2. Mrs. Jones is being sued by Mr. Jones for divorce on the ground of adultery. Mrs. Jones is the client of your office. Thus far your investigation has revealed that there is considerable doubt over whether Mrs. Jones did in fact commit adultery. During a recent conversation with Mrs. Jones, however, she tells you that she has worked as a prostitute.

3. Jane Anderson is seeking an abortion. She is not married. The father of the child wants to prevent her from having the abortion. Jane comes to your office for legal help. She wants to know what her rights are. You belong to a church that believes abortion is murder. You are assigned to work on the case.

4. Paul and Victor are a gay couple who want to adopt Sammy, a six-month-old baby whose parents recently died in an automobile accident. Sammy's maternal grandmother is not able to adopt him because of her age and health. She opposes the adoption by Paul and Victor because of their lifestyle. Paul and Victor are clients of your office in their petition for adoption. You agree with the grandmother's position, but have been assigned to work on the case.

5. Tom Donaldson is a client of your office. His former business associate is suing Tom for breach of contract. Your job is to help Tom collect a large volume of records concerning the business. You are the only person in the office who is available to do this record gathering. It is clear, however, that Tom does not like you. On a number of occasions, he has indirectly questioned your ability.

Keep in mind that in each of these situations, the person paying the bills is the person against whom you may have a bias. In the vast majority of law offices, the last thing an attorney wants to do is antagonize a paying client.

When confronted with unpleasant feelings, we rarely can wish them away or successfully pretend that they do not exist. Furthermore, the following admonitions are rarely helpful: "Be **objective**," "be dispassionate," "don't get personally involved," "control your feelings." Such admonitions are too general, and when viewed in the abstract, they may appear not to be needed because we want to believe that at work we are objective, detached, and in control.

We must recognize, however, that there are facts and circumstances that arouse our emotions and tempt us to impose our own value judgments. Perhaps if we know where we are vulnerable, we will be in a better position to prevent our reactions from interfering with our work. It is not desirable for you to be totally dispassionate and removed. A paralegal who is cold, unfeeling, and incapable of empathy is not much better than a paralegal who self-righteously scolds a client. It is clearly not improper for a paralegal to express sympathy, surprise, and perhaps even shock at what unfolds from the client's life story. If these feelings are genuine and if they would be normal reactions to the situation at a given moment, they can be expressed. The problem is knowing where to draw the line between expressing these feelings and reacting so judgmentally that you interfere with your ability to communicate with the client now and in the future. The starting point is to recognize how easy it is to go over the line.

Some paralegals apply what is called the "stomach test." If your gut tells you that your personal feelings about the case are so intense that you may not be able to do a quality job for the client, you need to take action.[11] Talk with your supervisor. You may have some misunderstandings about the case that your supervisor can clear up. You may be able to limit your role in the case or be reassigned to other cases. Without breaching client confidentiality (see Chapter 5), contact your local paralegal association to try to talk with other paralegals who have handled similar situations. They may be able to give you some guidance.

As mentioned earlier, attorneys often take unpopular cases involving clients who have said or done things that run the gamut from being politically incorrect to being socially reprehensible. As professionals, attorneys are committed to the principle that *everyone* is entitled to representation. Paralegals should have this same commitment. But attorneys and paralegals are human beings. No one can treat every case identically. In the final analysis, you need to ask yourself whether your bias is so strong that it might interfere with your ability to give the needs of the client 100 percent of your energy and skill. If so, you have an obligation not to work on the case.

Ethical concerns also dictate this result. As we saw in Chapter 5, attorneys have an ethical obligation to avoid a conflict of interest. Such a conflict exists when an attorney has divided loyalties. An obvious example is an attorney who represents opposing parties in a legal dispute. A less obvious example is an attorney whose personal feelings could interfere with his or her obligation to give a client vigorous representation. The attorney's personal feelings should not be in conflict with a client's legitimate need for undiluted advocacy. Is the attorney going to be loyal to his or her personal feelings and values, or to the client's cause? Clients should not be subjected to such conflicts of loyalties. When a conflict of this kind exists, the attorney has an ethical obligation not to take the case. The same obligation applies to paralegals. There should be no interference with a client's right to receive total commitment from everyone in the law office.

COMMUNICATION SKILLS: ANALYSIS OF AN INTERVIEW

INTRODUCTION

We will now examine portions of a **hypothetical** interview involving Sam Donnelly, who walks into the law office of Day & Day seeking legal assistance. Last month he was a passenger in a car that collided with a truck.

Our goal in this analysis is to identify guidelines that can help you conduct competent interviews. In particular, we want to increase your sensitivity to the large variety of factors that affect the quality of communication between client and interviewer.

Assume that Mr. Donnelly is in the office of William Fenton, Esq., one of the partners of Day & Day. During their meeting, the law firm agrees to represent Mr. Donnelly. The arrangement is confirmed in the attorney-client fee contract that Mr. Donnelly signs. (See Exhibit 8-1

objective Dispassionate; not having a bias.

hypothetical Not actual or real but presented for purposes of discussion or analysis; based on an assumed set of facts. (See the glossary for an additional meaning.)

for a sample contract.) At the conclusion of the meeting, Mr. Fenton calls his paralegal, Jane Collins. He asks her to come to his office so that he can introduce her to Mr. Donnelly.

Attorney: [*As the paralegal walks into Mr. Fenton's office, he says*] Mr. Donnelly, I want to introduce you to Jane Collins who will be working with me throughout the case. I have asked her to schedule an appointment with you to do a comprehensive interview that will cover the facts you and I began to discuss today. Jane will be an additional contact for you throughout the case. If at any time you can't reach me because I am in a meeting or in court, let Jane know what concerns, questions, or needs you have. I will be reviewing all of Jane's work and will be meeting with her regularly. Jane is a trained paralegal. She is not an attorney and therefore can't give legal advice, but she can do many things to help me represent you.

Client: Nice to meet you.

Paralegal: [*Jane walks over to where Mr. Donnelly is sitting and, with a smile, extends her hand to offer a firm handshake.*] I'm very pleased to meet you, Mr. Donnelly. I look forward to working with you on the case. Let me give you one of my cards so that you'll know how to reach me.

Client: Thank you.

Attorney: I've already explained to Mr. Donnelly that you will be doing an in-depth interview with him on the case. He can't stay today for the interview so it will have to be scheduled.

Paralegal: Yes…. Before you leave today, Mr. Donnelly, let's discuss when it would be convenient for you to have the interview. Or if you need to check your calendar, I can call you.

It is important to note that the supervising attorney, Mr. Fenton, has taken the initiative to introduce the client to the paralegal. This sets the tone for the client-paralegal relationship. Many clients have little more than a general understanding of what a paralegal is. Here, the introduction by the supervising attorney is very specific in identifying Jane as a nonattorney who cannot give legal advice but has been trained to help attorneys represent clients. She will also act as a liaison between the attorney and the client.

Note also the manner in which the paralegal treats the client. She walks toward the client to greet him with a firm handshake and a smile. She tells the client that she looks forward to working with him. She gives him her business card. (This is often appreciated because the client is probably meeting several new faces during the first few visits to the law office.) She is very deferential to the client on when it would be convenient for him to schedule an interview with her. These are signs of a paralegal who is willing to go out of her way to make the client feel important and at ease.

PREPARING FOR THE INTERVIEW

How do you get ready for an interview? Exhibit 8-8 lists some of the major steps you should take to prepare. The list assumes that this is one of the first legal interviews you have conducted.

Exhibit 8-8	Preparing for an Interview

- Schedule the interview during a time when you will not be rushed or constantly interrupted.
- Schedule the interview at a location that will be private and convenient for the client.
- Find out from your supervisor if the client has any special needs such as wheelchair accessibility.
- Call or write the client in advance to confirm the date and place of the interview. Give an estimate of how long the interview will take. If the directions are complex, offer to send a map (hand-drawn if necessary). Remind the client of anything you want him or her to bring to the interview, e.g., insurance policies or copies of tax returns.
- Anticipate and prepare for the client's comfort, e.g., a comfortable chair, a pad and pencil in case the client wants to take notes, and a supply of tissues. Know where you can quickly obtain fresh water or coffee after offering them to the client early in the interview.

- Before the interview, read everything in the office file on the client. Bring (or copy) any documents in the file that you may want to question the client about or have the client review during the interview.
- Have a final brief meeting (or phone conversation) with your supervisor to make sure you understand the goals of the interview.
- Find out if the office has any checklists you should use in asking questions. If none exist, prepare an outline of about a dozen major questions you will ask the client. You will have many more questions in the interview, but you can use this outline as a guide.
- If possible, spend some time in the law library (or online) doing general background research in the area of the law involved in the client's case to obtain an overview of some of the major terminology and legal issues. This overview may suggest additional questions you will want to ask during the interview.
- Prepare any forms you will ask the client to sign during the interview, e.g., consent to release medical information, or authorization to obtain employment history records.
- Have your own supplies ready for note taking. Some interviewers recommend using different colored pens so that you can switch colors when the client is telling you something you want to give particular emphasis in your notes.[12]
- Walk into the interview with the attitude that the client will be telling you a story that you have never heard before. Do not assume you know what the client is going to say even if you have handled many cases of this kind.

In addition to the suggestions in Exhibit 8-8, try to observe someone interviewing a client. Find out if anyone else in the office will be conducting an interview soon. If so, ask permission to sit in. Watching others interview can be very instructive. Another way to prepare is to read some intake memos or other reports written after interviews in other cases. They can be found in the open or closed files of office clients. Pay particular attention to the amount and kind of information obtained in these cases.

Your mental attitude in preparing for the interview is very important. You need to approach each interview as if it is going to be a totally new experience for you. It is dangerous to think that you know what the client is going to say, no matter how many times you have worked on a particular kind of case in the past. The danger is that you will not be listening carefully to what the client is saying. An interviewer who has an I've-heard-it-all-before attitude may block out what is unique about the facts of *this* client's case.

The hallmark of the *professional* is to view every client, every problem, and every incident as different and potentially unique ("There's never been one like this before"). A professional interviewer, therefore, keeps probing for more facts to try to show that this case is not like all the rest. The goal of the professional is to find out what makes this case stand out. The inclination of the *bureaucrat*, on the other hand, is to see the similarities in clients, problems, and incidents. (You've seen one, you've just about seen them all.) The bureaucrat clusters things together into coherent groupings and patterns so that time can be saved and efficiency achieved. The bureaucrat feels that chaos could result if we viewed everything as potentially unique. An interviewer who has a bureaucratic attitude usually does not spend much time probing for facts; his or her goal is to fit this case into a category of similar cases handled in the past.

We all have within us professional and bureaucratic tendencies that are sometimes in conflict with each other.[13] Our bureaucratic self is very practical; our professional self can be a bit extreme in its search for uniqueness. When conducting legal interviews, however, or engaging in any task in the representation of a client, our goal is to try within reason to let our professional selves dominate.

ENVIRONMENT

You need to consider the impact of the physical setting or environment in which you conduct the interview. It will usually take place in the office of the interviewer. If this office is not private enough, however, try to reserve the conference room or borrow an available office from someone else if it would be more private than your own. In our example, let us assume that Jane Collins's office is suitable for her interview with Sam Donnelly.

[*There is a knock at Jane Collins's door. She gets up from her chair, goes over to the door, opens it, and says, as she extends her hand*],

Paralegal: Hello, Mr. Donnelly. I'm Jane Collins, Mr. Fenton's paralegal. It's good to see you again. Won't you come in?... Did you have any trouble finding the office?

Client: No, I had to use the bus, but it worked out fine.

Paralegal: Let me take your coat for you. Please have a seat. [*The paralegal points the client toward a chair on the opposite side of the desk from where she sits. They face each other.*]

In Exhibit 8-9, note the seating arrangement the paralegal selects as illustrated in diagram A. ("I" is the interviewer and "C" is the client.) A number of seating arrangements are possible. The chairs can be arranged so that the interviewer and the client sit on opposite sides of a desk (diagram A), diagonally across a desk (diagram B), on the same side of a desk (diagram C), or in another part of the room away from the desk altogether (diagram D). Seating arrangements are usually made at the convenience of the "owner" of the office. Rarely, however, is enough thought given to how a particular arrangement may help or hurt the flow of communication. Sometimes the seating arrangement will create an austere and official atmosphere; other settings may be close and warm.

Exhibit 8-9	Possible Seating Arrangements During Interviews

Diagram A

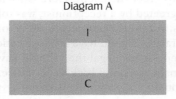

A number of other seating arrangements could have been used.

Diagram B   Diagram C   Diagram D

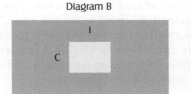 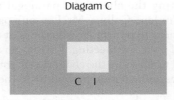 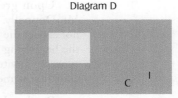

Of the four seating arrangements diagrammed in Exhibit 8-9, which do you think would be most effective? Which would you feel most comfortable with? Which do you think the client would be most comfortable with? There is probably no single seating arrangement that will be perfect for all situations. The interviewer must be flexible enough to experiment with different arrangements. For most legal interviews, you will be taking extensive notes as the client answers your questions. If you are going to make any notes about the client that you may not want him or her to see (e.g., "appears reluctant to answer"), you will want to select a seating arrangement that does not allow the client to read what you are writing.

To some extent, seating arrangements can be a reflection of your personality. How do you want to project yourself? As an authority figure? If so, you might be inclined toward the seating arrangement in diagram A. Do you, on the other hand, want the client to feel closer to you and not to have the impression that you are hiding behind a desk? When clients look up, do you want them to be looking straight at you (diagram A) or do you think that it might be more comfortable for them to be able to face in other directions (diagram B) without appearing to scatter their attention?[14]

Of course, an office is much more than an arrangement of desks and chairs. Describe the potential benefits or disadvantages of the following:

- Numerous posters on the wall display political slogans, e.g., "Down with the Wasteful Spenders in Congress!" or "Pro Choice IS Pro Family."
- A copy of the latest issue of a Rush Limbaugh newsletter is on the desk.
- A sign on the wall says, "Don't even think of smoking here."
- The desk is cluttered with papers, books, and half-eaten food.

Be careful about explicit messages around the room. Your political views may clash with those of the client. Do not broadcast your politics by having partisan literature on the walls or desk. The no-smoking sign is too abrupt. Courtesy would suggest a more friendly way of letting clients know that they should not smoke in your room (e.g., "Thank you for not smoking"). You want the office to project a professional image of you. Slogans and a messy desk usually suggest the opposite.

GETTING STARTED

Note that the paralegal, Jane Collins, went to the door to greet the client. Suppose that, instead, she had remained in her chair and called, "Come in," in a loud voice. Do you think it makes any difference whether the interviewer walks over to the client? When you walk into a room with someone, you are communicating the message, "Come share my room with me." If, however, you are seated at your desk and call the visitor in, the message to the visitor is likely to be, "This is my room; I control it; you have my permission to enter." Although this is not necessarily an inappropriate message, it is not as friendly and warm as going to the door to escort the client in.

Note also, however, that the paralegal apparently did not go out to the front entrance of the law firm to greet the client. Here is what may have happened: the client came to the front door, was greeted by a receptionist, was told to wait in the reception area, and was then given directions to find the paralegal's office on his own. If this is what happened, it was a mistake. The paralegal should have left instructions with the receptionist to call her when the client arrived, and the paralegal then should have gone out to the reception area to greet the client and personally walk him back to her office. This would be the most courteous approach. Furthermore, you do not want clients roaming around offices—even if they know the way. A wandering client may overhear confidential conversations between other members of the firm or see open files of other clients on the desks of secretaries. This danger is minimized if the paralegal escorts the client from the front door to her office.

Upon greeting the client, the paralegal reintroduced herself to the client: "Hello, Mr. Donnelly. I'm Jane Collins, Mr. Fenton's paralegal. It's good to see you again." She does not expect the client to remember who she is. It is a sign of courtesy to reintroduce yourself at the beginning of a second meeting. Finally, never call a client by his or her first name unless expressly invited to do so by the client. Furthermore, do not interpret a client's calling you by your first name as an invitation for you to do the same with the client's name.

Paralegal:	Thank you for coming in today, Mr. Donnelly. Are you ready for today's session?
Client:	Ready as I can be.
Paralegal:	Good…. How have you been?
Client:	Not bad considering all this mess. I can't believe all this is happening.
Paralegal:	Being involved in an accident can be very upsetting. It must be very hard for you…. Our office has handled cases like this before. While no one can predict how a case will turn out, you can rest assured that we will be doing everything possible to lessen the burden on you and to resolve the matter.
Client:	Thank you.
Paralegal:	Let me ask you, Mr. Donnelly, is there anything that you want to cover now before we begin?
Client:	This letter came in the mail this morning. It looks like the truck company has its lawyers on the case.
Paralegal:	[*She takes the letter from Mr. Donnelly and spends a few moments reading it.*] This is a letter from the attorney representing the truck company seeking information from you. They obviously don't know yet that we represent you. Once they know you are represented, it is improper for them to contact you directly. They need to go through your attorney. I'll let Mr. Fenton know about this letter right away. I'll scan it before you leave so that you can keep the original for your records. After Mr. Fenton sees this, we'll let you know if there is anything you need to do about the letter. For now, let us take care of it.

Early on, the paralegal thanked the client: "Thank you for coming in today." Throughout the case, the office may ask the client to do many things such as come to meetings, sign documents, and collect information. Each time, you should express appreciation for doing what was asked. Never expect the client to thank you, although this may occur. You do not want the client to have the impression that you are doing the client a favor. The reverse is always true. Hence, constantly be appreciative.

Soon after inviting the client in, the paralegal asked, "Did you have any trouble finding the office?" And a little later, "How have you been?" It is a good idea to begin the interview at a personal level with some small talk about the weather, how the client is doing, or a recent sports event the client might know something about. (Within reason, of course, since clients are being charged by the hour unless they have a **contingency case** with the office.) Small talk helps put the client at ease. The client may still be a bit nervous about the accident or whatever led to the conflict and the involvement of attorneys. Being a little lighthearted and personal for a few moments at the beginning of the interview may help break the ice.

When clients are particularly stressed or overwhelmed, you need to provide reassurance that the office will be actively working on the case and that the situation is manageable. The paralegal did that here when she told the client the office has handled similar cases in the past and would be doing everything possible to lessen the burden on him and to resolve the matter. Comments such as these should help reassure the client. Of course, many clients want to be told they are going to win their cases. Avoid making any statement that could be interpreted as a promise or guarantee of success. Otherwise, the office could be sued for **breach of contract** if the case is not successful. Instead of telling a client, "You've got a great case," say something like the following: "There is no way of telling how a case will turn out. You've got a lot of good points in your favor, and we're going to work as hard as we can for you."

The paralegal also told the client, "Being involved in an accident can be very upsetting. It must be very hard for you." Here, the paralegal is expressing understanding and empathy for the client's predicament. This is important. The comment tells the client that the paralegal is listening to what the client is saying. Mr. Donnelly refers to the "mess" he is in and says, "I can't believe all this is happening." Rather than ignoring this comment, the paralegal lets the client know that she has heard what he said. This is comforting. On the other hand, you don't want to be patronizing or condescending. A comment such as "You poor fellow" would obviously fall into this category.

Interviewers often learn a large number of highly personal facts about the client's life. Think of how you would feel if you were revealing such facts about yourself to a stranger. Think of how you would want this person to react to what you are revealing. At such a vulnerable time, clients need understanding and compassion. This does not mean that you should lose your objectivity. As indicated earlier, if it would be natural for you to express an emotion in response to what a client tells you, express the emotion. For example, "I'm very sorry to hear that" or "I can understand why you'd be angry." At the same time, you need to have an appropriate professional distance from the emotions and drama of the client's story.

Some clients will be understandably reluctant to talk about certain topics. Indeed, as an interviewer, you may feel uncomfortable delving into them. Examples might be prior bankruptcies a client has gone through, violence engaged in by the client in the past, or the client's marital history with a spouse. If, however, these topics are relevant to the legal services sought by the client, they must be covered. The client will be looking for signs that you are not embarrassed by such topics and that you can talk about them with appropriate sensitivity.

Of course, never be judgmental of the client. Do not ask the client, "Why did you do that?" if your tone is one of suspicion or disbelief. Clients should not feel that they are required to justify their actions or inactions to you. This obviously would not encourage open communication between interviewer and client.

Also important was the paralegal's question, "is there anything that you want to cover now before we begin?" Early in the interview, find out if the client has any immediate concerns or questions on his mind. This should be done not only as a matter of courtesy but also as a technique to make sure the client has your undivided attention. On the way into the law office, the client may have been thinking of several things he wants to ask about. He may be worried that he will forget them. Or he may be a little embarrassed about asking his questions. Give the client a chance to express anything on his mind at the outset before you begin your barrage of questions. In our example, this technique worked. Mr. Donnelly did have something on his mind—the letter he received from opposing counsel.

contingency case A case in which clients pay attorney fees only if they win through litigation or settlement.

breach of contract A cause of action seeking a court remedy (usually damages) for the alleged failure of a party to perform the term(s) of an enforceable contract.

Paralegal: Our goal today is to obtain a comprehensive statement of the facts of the accident. It will take at least an hour, maybe a little more. As Mr. Fenton told you, I am a paralegal, not an attorney. I'll be able to help on the case in many ways, but I won't be able to give you legal advice. That will have to come from Mr. Fenton. If anything comes up today that calls for legal advice, I'll bring it to Mr. Fenton's attention so that we can get you the response you need. Since I work for an attorney, you should know that everything you tell me is protected by the attorney-client privilege.

Client: Fine.

Paralegal: Before we begin, Mr. Donnelly, you mentioned that you had to take the bus in. Is there a problem with your car? Was it involved in the accident with the truck?

Client: No, no…. I let my brother borrow my car today.

Paralegal: All right…. I want to start by getting an overview of what happened on the day of the accident. Then we'll go back and fill in the details. I'll be taking detailed notes to make sure that I remember everything you say…. OK, what happened that day?

This is the second meeting between the paralegal and Mr. Donnelly. Although the supervising attorney, Mr. Fenton, told Mr. Donnelly that Jane Collins was not an attorney, it is a good idea for the paralegal to reinforce this point herself. Paralegals who have contact with clients are sometimes pressured to give legal advice. Making it clear at the outset that this is inappropriate can cut down on this pressure, although, unfortunately, it will not eliminate it.

The paralegal also told the client that what he tells her "is protected by the attorney-client privilege." The client needs to know this, but not in this way. The phrase *attorney-client privilege* is legal **jargon**. It is specialized or technical language that may not be understood by the general public. Avoid jargon unless the client needs to know it and you explain it in language the client can understand. When you use jargon or confusing terms, do not interpret the client's lack of questions to mean that the client understands the jargon. Do not wait for the client to ask you to explain unfamiliar terms. Take the initiative to provide explanations. In our example, it probably would have been sufficient to tell Mr. Donnelly that what he tells her will be confidential rather than using the more technical phrase *attorney-client privilege*.

Another useful technique for beginning an interview is to briefly state the major goal of the interview—here, to obtain a comprehensive statement of the facts of the accident. Give the client an overview of what you hope to accomplish and how long it may take. Do this even if you gave the client this information when you set up the appointment.

Let the client know you will be taking notes in order to have an accurate record of what he says during the interview. As indicated earlier, the document that contains the detailed report of the interviewer is sometimes called the intake memo (see Exhibit 8-3). This will be prepared after the interview based on the interviewer's notes.

Some interviewers recommend against taking detailed notes, particularly at the beginning of the interview when you want to maintain eye contact and establish rapport. If you follow this advice, at least some notes should be taken at the outset as reminders of the topics you need to come back to later for detained questioning and note taking.

Occasionally, your supervisor will want you to tape-record the interview. Be sure the client consents to the recording. At the beginning of the interview, say, "This is Jane Collins, a paralegal in the law office of Day & Day. Today's date is March 12, 2015. I am in our law office with Mr. Samuel Donnelly. Mr. Donnelly, have you agreed to have this interview tape-recorded?" The latter question will help disprove any allegations that you secretly recorded the interview. On the tape, also state the names of other persons, if any, who are in the room during the taping.

A good interviewer is always listening for clues to other legal or relevant nonlegal problems. There is always a danger that an interviewer will block out anything that does not fit within the topics scheduled for discussion. In our example, the paralegal said to Mr. Donnelly, "You mentioned that you had to take the bus in. Is there a problem with your car?" Although the car apparently has nothing to do with the case, it was worth inquiring into. Suppose, for example, the client is not driving because of injury to his eyes caused by an eye doctor. Or perhaps the client had a contract dispute with an auto mechanic. It is a good idea to listen for suggestions or clues to other problems provided by a client. If you do not want to cover

jargon Specialized or technical language used by a particular group or profession that may not be understood by the general public.

the matter immediately, make a note to raise it later in the interview at a more appropriate or convenient time.

The major techniques and guidelines for beginning an interview are summarized in Exhibit 8-10.

Exhibit 8-10	Beginning the Interview

- Introduce yourself by name and title. If this is your second meeting with the client, reintroduce yourself.
- Do not call a client by his or her first name unless invited to do so by the client. Do not ask the client for permission to use his or her first name. Wait to be asked to do so.
- Express appreciation each time the client does something the office asks, e.g., comes in for an interview, or reads and signs a document.
- Make sure the client understands that you are not an attorney and cannot give legal advice.
- Start at a personal level (e.g., with some small talk) rather than launching right into the main task at hand.
- Review the goals of the interview with the client (based on the assignment from your supervisor), and provide an estimate of how long the interview will take.
- Make the client feel that his or her case is special. Avoid giving the impression that you are engaged in anything boring or routine.
- Never tell a client how busy you are. It suggests to the client that he or she is bothering you and might give the impression that the office is disorganized.
- Express understanding and empathy for the client's predicament without being condescending.
- Never be judgmental.
- Make sure the client understands that what he or she tells you is confidential.
- Find out if there are immediate concerns that the client wants to raise.
- Avoid legal jargon unless the client needs to become familiar with the jargon and you provide clear definitions and explanations.
- Let the client know you will be taking notes, and why.
- Listen for clues to other legal and relevant nonlegal problems that the office may need to explore.
- Begin new topics with open-ended questions. (See Exhibit 8-11 on the kinds of questions an interviewer might ask.)
- Spend the first few minutes obtaining an overview/outline of the entire event or transaction. Then go back to obtain the details.
- Encourage the client to give you the facts chronologically as a story with a beginning, middle, and end. If more than one event is involved in the case, cover them separately in the same chronological way. Then go into how the events are interconnected.
- If the client appears overwhelmed or unusually distressed, try to provide reassurance by letting him or her know that the office is actively working on the case and is doing everything it can. Do not, however, promise results or say anything that a client could interpret as a promise or even as a prediction of what the outcome of the case will be.

KINDS OF QUESTIONS

One of the early questions the paralegal asked Mr. Donnelly was "what happened that day?" This is known as an **open-ended question**. It is a broad, relatively unstructured question that rarely can be answered in one or two words. An open-ended question gives the client more control over the kind and amount of information to be provided in response. It also gives the interviewer an opportunity to size up the ability of the client to organize his or her thoughts in order to present a coherent response. Here are additional examples of open-ended questions: "What brings you in today?" "What led to the crisis at the bank?" One of the most frequently used categories of open-ended questions is the **overview question**, which asks for a summary of something such as an important event. For example, "What happened during your first year in college?" or Jane Collins's question, "What happened that day?" An open-ended *request* (e.g., "Tell me about the problem") invites the same kind of broad response but is phrased as a request rather than as a question.

Open-ended questions (or requests) invite the person questioned to give a long and potentially rambling answer. Hence they should not be overused. These questions are often most effective when beginning a new topic in the interview.

At the opposite extreme is the **closed-ended question**, which is a narrowly structured question that usually can be answered in one or two words. Examples: "How old are you?" "What time did the accident occur?" "Did you receive the letter?" Closed-ended questions give the interviewer more control over the interview because they let the client know precisely what information is sought.

If the facts of a case are relatively complex, you should consider spending the first few minutes asking overview questions in order to obtain an outline of the entire event or transaction, and then going back to obtain the details, using closed-ended questions as

open-ended question A broad, relatively unstructured question that rarely can be answered in one or two words.

overview question An open-ended question that asks for a summary of an event or condition.

closed-ended question A narrowly structured question that usually can be answered in one or two words, often yes or no. Also called a *directed question*.

needed. Once you have the big picture, you will be better able to see connections among the individual facts. The paralegal in our example took this approach when she said, "I want to start by getting an overview of what happened on the day of the accident. Then we'll go back and fill in the details." She followed this up with the open-ended overview question, "What happened that day?"

Both the request for an overview and the detailed questioning should be designed to encourage the client to tell the events of the case chronologically. The case may have many confusing aspects. The client may be inclined to talk about four or five things simultaneously—the accident, the hospitalization, the events leading up to the accident, the deceitfulness of the other side, etc. The best way to conduct an orderly interview is to help the client structure the case as a story with a beginning, middle, and end. Hence you should regularly ask **chronological questions** such as "What happened next?" or "What did you do then?" If the client says something substantially out of chronological sequence, politely say, "Could we get to that in a moment? First I want you to finish telling me what happened after...." Although you want to see the interconnections among the various events of the case, the discussion may become tangled and confusing unless you cover one topic at a time in the same methodical manner. In most instances, the most methodical way is chronologically.

In general, avoid asking **leading questions** in which an answer is suggested in the question. For example, "You didn't return the call, did you?" "Did he tell you about the defect in the engine after you already said you would buy it?" The danger of a leading question is that a nervous client or witness will simply give you the answer you appear to want. Leading questions might sometimes be useful when trying to challenge something that a **hostile** witness is saying, but this approach should obviously not be needed with the office's own client. If a client is having difficulty remembering something (e.g., the weather on a particular day), a leading question might help jog the memory (e.g., "Was it raining that day?"). If a client needs constant prodding through leading questions, however, you may have reason to doubt the client's entire story.

Another category is the **corroborative question**, which seeks to verify (or corroborate) by seeking additional or supportive facts. For example, "Were there any passengers in the car who will back that up?"

Avoid **combination questions**—those with more than one part. They can confuse the person being interviewed. There are two kinds of combination questions: multiple-choice and add-on. A **multiple-choice question** asks the client or witness to choose among options presented by the interviewer. It is an "or" question. For example, "Did you personally review the balance sheet, or did you rely exclusively on what the accountant told the committee?" The interviewee may not remember both options and respond only to the last part of the question. An **add-on question** consists of several questions phrased as one. It is an "and" question. For example, "When did you arrive in Dallas, and how long did you stay there?" Two questions asked at once are sometimes referred to as *double-barreled questions*. Of course, add-on questions could have more than two parts: for example, "What was your salary when you began work at the company, at the time of the accident, and on the date you were terminated?" Avoid add-on questions for the same reason you should avoid most multiple-choice questions: they can be confusing.

There are some combination questions that are relatively simple. For example, "Was he driving a car or a truck?" and "What is your husband's name, and where was he born?" Yet the danger of confusion still exists, and the better practice is to break all combination questions into individual questions that are asked separately.

The final question that should always be asked at the end of the interview (or at the end of a separate topic during the interview) is the **wrap-up question**. It asks whether the interviewee thinks everything has been covered. "OK, before we conclude, have we gone over everything you wanted to say about...?" This gives clients the opportunity to raise or reinforce anything of particular importance to them.

See Exhibit 8-11 for an overview of the major kinds of questions an interviewer can ask.

---

chronological questions A question designed to encourage the interviewee to describe what happened in the order in which events occurred—by date and time, step by step.

leading questions A question that suggests an answer within the question.

hostile Unfriendly or antagonistic.

corroborative question A question designed to verify (corroborate) facts by seeking additional or supportive facts.

combination questions A question that has more than one part.

multiple-choice question A question that asks the interviewee to choose among two or more options stated in the question.

add-on question A question that is added to the end of another related question, both stated in one sentence. Also called *double-barreled question*.

wrap-up question A question asked at the end of the interview (or at the end of a separate topic within the interview) in which the interviewee is asked if there is anything he or she thinks has been left out or inadequately covered.

Exhibit 8-11	Kinds of Interview Questions

Here are some of the major categories of questions, some of which overlap:

- *Open-ended question.* A broad, relatively unstructured question that rarely can be answered in one or two words. The question encourages interviewees to express what is on their mind in as much detail as they choose. Examples: "What can we do for you today?" "Tell me what happened on the day of the accident?" "What kind of a marriage did you have?"
- *Overview question.* An open-ended question that asks for a summary of an event or condition. Examples: "Would you first give me a general picture of what happened?" "What are the major incidents that led to the dismissal?" "Could you start me off by giving a brief description of what happened at the party before the shooting?"
- *Closed-ended question.* A narrowly structured question that usually can be answered in one or two words, often yes or no. Examples: "Are you seeking a divorce?" "Were you wearing your glasses when you saw the accident?" "Did your husband ever hit you?" "What time did it occur?"
- *Chronological question.* A question designed to encourage the interviewee to describe what happened in the order in which events occurred—by date and time, step by step. Examples: "Then what happened?" "What did he say after he saw the accident?" "What happened next?"
- *Leading question.* A question that suggests an answer within the question. Examples: "Where was the fender dented?" "The car wasn't damaged when you received it, was it?" "You were traveling 75 mph?"
- *Corroborative question.* A question designed to verify (corroborate) facts by seeking additional or supportive facts. Examples: "Who else saw the accident?" "Were you the only one who complained?" "Do you have receipts?"
- *Combination question.* A question that has more than one part. Examples: "Did you accept the offer, reject it, or ask for more time to respond?" (multiple choice) "What school does your child attend, and are you satisfied with how well he is doing there?" (add-on).
- *Wrap-up question.* A question asked at the end of the interview (or at the end of a separate topic within the interview) in which the interviewee is asked if there is anything he or she thinks has been left out or inadequately covered. Examples: "Have we covered everything?" and "Anything more on the phone calls you received?"

ATTENTIVE LISTENING

Some studies have shown that clients rate "evidence of concern" as more significant than the results they obtain from a law office.[15] This is a remarkable conclusion. Of course, clients want to win their cases. Yet they are also desperate for a sympathetic ear. Being involved in a legal dispute is often traumatic. In addition to wanting to be treated competently as a plaintiff or defendant, clients want a law office that is genuinely concerned about them as persons.

One of the best ways to demonstrate concern is through **attentive listening**. This requires taking affirmative steps to let clients know that you have heard what they just said and that you consider every client meeting to be important. Unfortunately, listening is not a skill that comes naturally to us. "Too many times in today's society, what passes for listening is merely waiting quietly for your turn to talk."[16] According to the International Listening Association (www .listen.org), when we are going through the motions of listening to someone, we are in fact preoccupied with something else about 75 percent of the time. To help combat this problem, Exhibit 8-12 summarizes some of the major techniques of attentive listening.

Some experienced paralegals handle the same kind of case over and over. Clients, however, want to feel that their case deserves and will receive individual attention; they do not want their cases handled in an assembly-line or mass-production manner. They appreciate having experienced attorneys and paralegals working for them, but they are particularly pleased when they feel that the office is treating their case as special. (See the earlier discussion on the tension between the professional self and the bureaucratic self.)

For more on the skill of listening, see the categories discussed in Chapter 3: passive listening, appreciative listening, evaluative listening, judgmental listening, empathic listening, me-too listening, and active listening.

attentive listening
Affirmative, ongoing steps taken by an interviewer to let an interviewee know that you have heard what he or she just said and that you consider the meeting with him or her to be important.

Exhibit 8-12	Techniques of Attentive Listening

- Make it obvious to the client that he or she has your full attention. If a receptionist answers incoming calls to the office, let the client hear you tell the receptionist that you are in an interview and do not wish to be disturbed. If you know that there might be an interruption during the interview, alert the client and apologize in advance.
- Occasionally lean forward toward the client as he or she speaks.
- Avoid being fidgety or appearing nervous.
- Take notes. This is an obvious sign that you think what the client is saying is important. (As indicated earlier, however, some interviewers avoid extensive note-taking at the beginning of an interview in order to help establish rapport through concentrated attention.)
- Maintain eye contact whenever you are not taking notes.
- As the client speaks, give frequent *yes* nods. Also say, "Ah hum," "OK," or "I see" when the client momentarily pauses while answering your questions. Connecting or reinforcing words such as these let the clients know you are following what they are saying.
- Several times during the interview, use the client's name, e.g., "Mr. Jones, was that the first time you spoke to your accountant last year?" and "Did I hear you say, Mrs. Phillips, that you lease the car rather than own it outright?"
- Periodically let the client know he or she is providing useful information. Make comments such as "That could be very important" or "I'm glad you recall the event in such detail."
- In addition to listening to the words of the client, "listen" to the feelings the client is expressing through body language. Words are not the only way a client lets you know he or she is anxious, suspicious, worried, or in pain. Frowns, hand gestures, eye contact, and a lack of eye contact are examples of body language (nonverbal communication).
- At appropriate times, restate a feeling the client is trying to describe, e.g., "The stress you were under must have been overwhelming." You may want to do this in the form of a question, e.g., "You were really angry when you found out, weren't you?"
- Occasionally read something from your notes out loud to the client and ask if you have correctly recorded what he or she has said. This reinforces the value of precision in the practice of law as well as letting the client know how important this interview is.
- Recap regularly. Often during the interview, paraphrase and summarize what the client has said and ask if your paraphrase or summary is correct. ("Let me see if I understood what you have said….")
- Occasionally (or often if needed), ask the client to clarify or elaborate on something he or she has said.
- Ask spontaneous questions that occur to you while listening to an answer of the client. This helps demonstrate that you are not trying to fit the client's answers into your preconceived notions about the case. Rather, you are following the client's train of thought.
- Refer back to what the client said earlier, e.g., "When we were discussing the purchase, you said that your father wanted his brother to manage the property. Could you tell me what you meant?"
- Never express impatience, no matter how frustrated you are at the client's failure to answer what you feel should be an easy question.
- While a client is answering a question, try to avoid interrupting unless he or she is rambling and you need clarification before the client moves to another point.
- Do not finish the sentences of clients no matter how certain you are of what they are trying to say. Finishing someone's sentences demonstrates your impatience and is condescending.

COMPREHENSIVENESS

A major goal of most legal interviews is to achieve factual comprehensiveness; you want to obtain as many relevant facts as the client is able to give. The most important technique in accomplishing this goal is *fact particularization (FP)*, discussed earlier in the chapter. (See Exhibits 8-4 and 8-5.) Also important are *corroborative questions* that ask about documents or other individuals who can support the version of the facts the client is relating. (See Exhibit 8-11.)

Most clients want to give you facts that support their case. Yet you need to encourage them to tell you negative as well as positive facts. Let them know how important it is for the attorney to know all the facts. One of the preoccupations of the other side is to find the facts that will hurt the client's case. The client's attorney must know all the facts in advance so that he or she can prepare a response when these facts come out, as they inevitably do.

Earlier we said that checklists of questions can be helpful in preparing for an interview. Be careful, however, when using checklists. Although they can provide guidance on what to cover in the interview, you must be flexible enough to deviate from the checklist when relevant topics come up that are not on the checklist. Use the checklist (whether written by others or prepared on your own) as no more than a starting point. Suppose, for example, you are interviewing a client about her financial assets. You are working from a checklist of questions on wages, real estate holdings, stocks, bonds, etc. During the interview, the client happens to mention an ailing grandparent who is very fond of the client. This suggests the possibility of another possible asset: inheritance from this grandparent. Suppose, however, the checklist contains no questions about future inheritances. Common sense (one of the guides to formulating questions discussed earlier in the chapter) should tell you to ask whether the client thinks she might be a beneficiary in someone's will. Hence, if you have a checklist of questions, use it, but don't be so tied to the checklist that you fail to hear or respond to something the client says that does not fit into the checklist.

Take accurate notes on the facts the client gives you, including the extent of the certainty or uncertainty a client expresses about a fact. (See Exhibit 8-7 on the spectrum of certainty.) Suppose the client tells you, "I'm not sure" how fast an approaching car was going, but then says it was "about 50 mph." Your final report based on your notes should say, "When I asked the client how fast the other car was going, he said he was 'not sure.' Then he estimated, 'About 50 mph.'" This lets the supervising attorney know that the client may be vulnerable as a witness in court if questioned about the matter of speed. An interviewer does not achieve the desired factual comprehensiveness unless he or she asks about and records the extent to which the client is certain or uncertain about the facts conveyed.

The techniques for obtaining factual comprehensiveness are summarized in Exhibit 8-13.

Exhibit 8-13	Achieving Factual Comprehensiveness

- Apply the technique of fact particularization to all the major facts the client tells you about the case. (See Exhibits 8-4 and 8-5.)
- Ask corroborative questions. (See Exhibit 8-11.)
- Encourage the client to tell you negative facts by explaining why you need to know them, namely to allow the attorney to prepare a response to them if they come up during negotiations or litigation.
- Probe beneath client opinions to obtain the underlying facts, particularly observed facts.
- Distinguish between facts the client has directly experienced through the senses (observed facts) and conclusions he or she has made about the facts (inferences).
- Follow available checklists of questions, but be prepared to ask questions not on the checklist if they are related to topics on your prepared agenda of questions.
- Ask questions to determine the extent to which the client is certain or uncertain about an important fact. (See Exhibit 8-7.)
- Where appropriate, use demonstrations and exhibits to elicit further information. For an example, see the timeline in Exhibit 8-6.
- After each separate topic is covered during the interview (and at the end of the entire interview), ask wrap-up questions to determine if the client thinks anything has been left out or has not been covered adequately. (See Exhibit 8-11.)

ETHICS AND INTERVIEWING

Paralegal: [*Telephone rings.*] Excuse me, Mr. Donnelly. "Yes, hello. How are you?... No, the Jackson case has been resolved. Mr. Jackson decided not to go through with his suit after McDonald made its offer.... You're welcome." Sorry, Mr. Donnelly, let's get back to the....

A legal interview must be conducted competently and *ethically*. Unfortunately, there are more than a few opportunities for an interviewer to run afoul of ethical rules.

Mr. Donnelly has just heard the paralegal discuss the Jackson case on the phone. This is a violation of the paralegal's ethical obligation to preserve client confidentiality. Even though Mr. Donnelly may not have understood anything about the Jackson and McDonald case, he was not entitled to hear what he heard. He should not even know that Jackson or McDonald is a client of Day & Day. Revealing information about a client is a breach of confidentiality, whether it is done intentionally or carelessly. Mr. Donnelly may now have the impression that the paralegal will be as careless about discussing his case in front of strangers.

Client: A friend of mine told me that if another car rams into you and commits a clear traffic violation, their negligence is automatic. Is that true?

Paralegal: That's a good question. I'll take it up with Mr. Fenton and get back to you. All legal questions like that need to be dealt with by an attorney.

Another major ethical danger that can arise during an interview is giving **legal advice**. As we saw in Chapters 4 and 5, legal advice a statement or conclusion that applies the law or legal principles to the facts of a specific person's legal problem. The more contact a paralegal has

legal advice A statement or conclusion that applies the law or legal principles to the facts of a specific person's legal problem.

with clients, the greater the likelihood the paralegal will be asked to give legal advice. This is especially true during legal interviews. Clients are often hungry for answers. Mr. Donnelly is no exception. He asked the paralegal whether a traffic violation makes one's negligence "automatic." Even general questions about the law could be interpreted as questions that call for legal advice. Mr. Donnelly is probably trying to understand how the courts will handle his case.

Suppose the paralegal knows the correct answer. Think of how tempting it would be for her to answer the question. It takes a lot of willpower for her to refrain from answering. She wants to appear intelligent. We all want to show off what we know. Be conservative, however, about ethics. (See Exhibit 5-1 in Chapter 5 for a summary of twenty-five major ethical guidelines a paralegal must follow.) To be safe, avoid giving an answer. The paralegal told Mr. Donnelly that she would "get back" to him after consulting with Mr. Fenton. This is better than coldly saying, "I'm not allowed to answer that question." When she said, "All legal questions like that need to be dealt with by an attorney," she is also helping to train the client about the limitations inherent in the paralegal's role. This may cut down on future pressures from Mr. Donnelly to seek legal advice from her.

Some of the main areas of ethical concern are summarized in Exhibit 8-14.

Exhibit 8-14	Avoiding Ethical Problems During Interviews

- Do not "accept" a case on behalf of the office and do not set fees. You can tell someone what kinds of cases the office handles, but you cannot tell someone that the office will take his or her case. Only an attorney can establish an attorney-client relationship or set fees. Do not discuss fees with a client except to state the amount of an initial consultation fee, if any.
- If you cannot avoid phone interruptions or visits by others to your office during the interview, be sure that you do not discuss the facts of other clients' cases. Never mention the names of clients (or their opponents) in front of another client even if you are certain that the latter will not recognize these names. Excuse yourself and leave the room if you must discuss anything about other cases.
- While talking to the client, do not have open files of other clients on the desk.
- Do not let the client wander in the corridors of the office, e.g., to go to the coffeepot. You do not want the client to overhear conversations about other cases among attorneys, paralegals, secretaries, or other employees.
- Make sure the client understands you are not an attorney.
- Resist pressures from the client to give legal advice. When in doubt about whether a question you are asked calls for legal advice, do not answer. Refer the matter to your supervising attorney.
- Avoid saying anything that could be interpreted as a prediction of how the case will be resolved.
- If the client says anything during the interview that suggests the possibility of a conflict of interest (e.g., the client tells you that the opposing side's spouse was once represented by your law firm), stop the interview and check with your supervisor about whether you should continue.

ENDING THE INTERVIEW

The interview is over when you have accomplished the objectives of the interview or when the client is not able to provide you with additional information. The client may need to check some of his records at home or contact a family member or business associate in order to answer some of your questions. The missing data can probably be communicated on the phone.

Use wrap-up questions to give the client the opportunity to raise anything he thinks should have been covered. For example, you could say, "Before we end today's session, let me ask you if there is anything you think we haven't covered or haven't covered enough." If the client raises anything, you may want to take some additional time now to go over the client's areas of concern, or you may have to tell the client that you'll get back to him on when you will be able to go over those concerns. The important point is to find out how the client feels about what was discussed during the interview and to respond to any of his concerns.

Often the client needs to sign documents that authorize the office to obtain confidential information about the client, e.g., a consent to release medical information. Be sure to explain the document clearly to the client and give him time to read through what he is being asked to sign. Do not brusquely hand the client a document and say, "I'll need your signature on this form that will allow us to get your medical records." Here is a more appropriate approach:

Paralegal: [*Handing the document to him.*] Mr. Donnelly, I want you to take a look at this document. It's a consent to release medical information. We'll use it

> to ask doctors, hospitals, or other medical providers to give us information about your medical condition. Your signature tells them that you agree to let them release the information to us. Would you please take a moment to read through it and let me know if you have any questions about it. If not, there's a space at the end of the document for your signature.

Client: OK.

Paralegal: Once you sign it, I'll keep the original and get you a copy for your records.

The client will want to know what is going to happen next—after the interview. Remind the client of any scheduled appointments, e.g., doctor visits or depositions. If there are none, tell the client that you will be preparing a report for the attorney on the interview and that the office will be getting back to the client. Also, summarize anything you asked the client to do during the interview, e.g., call you to provide the exact address of a former employer.

Begin preparing a draft of your intake memo soon after the interview is over, while the data and your notes are fresh in your mind. (See Exhibit 8-3.) Do this even if you need to obtain additional facts to include in your memorandum by follow-up interviewing or investigation. Word processing makes it relatively easy to make additions to memos or other documents. (See chapter 13.) Do not wait until you have all the facts before you start writing.

Also, make a notation in the client's file that you conducted the interview. If the file does not have a summary sheet on which client events can be recorded, place a brief note in the file stating the date and place of the interview. Someone else in the office working on the case (e.g., supervising attorney, law clerk, or secretary) should be able to look at the file and know what has been done to date.

For a summary of these and similar steps to take at the end of an interview, see Exhibit 8-15.

Exhibit 8-15	Ending the Interview

- Ask the client to sign any standard forms needed by the office, e.g., consent to release medical information, or authorization to obtain employment history records. Before doing so, clearly explain what the document is designed to do and give the client the opportunity to ask any questions about the document before he or she signs it.
- Use wrap-up questions to ask the client if there is anything else on his or her mind that he or she would like to raise before the interview is concluded. Ask if the client thinks any of the topics covered need more discussion.
- Let the client know precisely what the next step will be in the office's representation of the client, e.g., the attorney will call the client, or the paralegal will schedule a medical examination of the client.
- Remind the client of how to reach you. Have additional copies of your business card on the desk.
- Thank the client for the interview.
- Start preparing a draft of your intake memo soon after the client leaves. In the client's file, make a brief note of the fact that you conducted the interview. Include the date and place of the interview.

PERSONALITY OBSERVATIONS

After conducting an interview, you should formulate some preliminary observations about the client's personality, particularly as they pertain to his or her sincerity, credibility, and persuasiveness. Here is how one attorney described this aspect of the interview:

> "Assess the client's personality" and whether you think the office "can work with this person.... Watch for red flags or danger signals, including the client who is emotionally distraught or vengeful; is inconsistent with the story or avoids answering questions; has unrealistic objectives; suggests use of improper influence or other unethical or illegal conduct; rambles, wanders off the subject, or constantly interrupts you ... tells the office how to run the case; has already discharged or filed disciplinary complaints against other lawyers; has a personality disorder; or is flirtatious."[17]

In your intake memo to your supervisor, include your observations and assessments relevant to concerns such as these.

IMPROVING YOUR INTERVIEWING SKILLS

There are many ways to improve your interviewing skills. They are summarized in Exhibit 8-16. Be a perpetual student; always be inquisitive. Never be totally comfortable with any of your skills. One of the fascinating aspects of working in a law office is the availability of infinite opportunities to grow and improve.

Exhibit 8-16	Improving Your Interviewing Skills

- There is a good deal of literature on legal interviewing. On Google, Bing, or Yahoo, run searches such as "interview skills" or "the art of interviewing." Even though some of the results of such searches will lead you to sites on job interviewing, you may find techniques covered that apply to many interview settings.
- On YouTube, enter the search terms "how to interview clients" and "techniques of client interviews" in order to find relevant tutorials on interviewing.
- Try to attend seminars that include the topic of legal interviewing, e.g. CLE (Continuing Legal Education) seminars for attorneys conducted by bar associations or CLE seminars conducted by paralegal associations.
- Ask someone you respect in the office to observe you interviewing a client and then give you a critique. (You will need the advance permission of the client for this person to sit in.)
- In addition to whatever feedback your supervisor gives you about the intake memo that you submit on the case, ask him or her for suggestions on how the memo and the interview could have been improved.
- Ask others you respect in the office to read your intake memo and critique it. An experienced interviewer will be able to see if there appear to be any gaps in what you covered in your memo.
- Try to sit in when others in the office are interviewing clients. Read their memos on the interview and ask them questions about their interviewing techniques. (To observe someone else's interview, you will need the consent of the interviewer and of the client interviewee.)
- Ask attorneys and other paralegals about their interviewing experiences even if you are not able to watch them conduct an interview.

THE "DIFFICULT" CLIENT

Once someone is accepted as a client, the relationship between the office and the client is likely to be smooth and mutually beneficial. Occasionally, however, you will encounter clients who can be troublesome. Here are some examples.

- ### *The Client Who Knows All the Law*
    Some clients are quick to tell the office that they know the law. They may have been in litigation before, have taken courses on law, have a close relative who is an attorney, or have read a good deal about the law on the Internet. The difficulty arises if such clients are always second-guessing the way the office is handling their case or are unduly critical of anyone trying to help them. Ultimately, the attorney in charge of the case must decide if the office can continue to work with such clients. All clients, of course, are entitled to their opinions about the legal system and about anyone trying to help them. (Indeed, clients have the right to fire their attorneys at any time.) The central question is whether a client is prepared to listen to the advice provided by the attorney. The client is not obligated to follow every recommendation, but there may be no point in continuing with the attorney-client relationship if the client does not trust the attorney's professional judgment. Paralegals working with such clients must be careful to avoid arguing with them or giving them legal advice. If a client starts lecturing a paralegal about the law, the best response is to listen respectfully and then respond by saying, "I'll be sure to let the attorney know what you have said."

As with all client contacts, make a brief note in the file on this exchange, indicating the date of the contact, what the client wanted, and what you said or did in response.

- ### *The Angry Client*

    Some clients can be very angry. They may feel outrage at the injustice someone has allegedly committed against them. It is important that such clients be given a chance to express themselves. At the very least, they need to know that the office they have hired understands what they have been through and how they feel. They need an opportunity to vent. If, however, they continue to be angry after they have had this opportunity, the office may have difficulty providing them with effective representation. As indicated earlier, it is important to show empathy for a client by making comments such as "This must be a very difficult time for you" or "I can understand why that would be upsetting." These comments can have a settling effect on clients without engulfing the office in an emotional thicket. You do not want to lose your professionalism by adopting the same pessimistic or hostile frame of mind as the client.

- ### *The Demanding or Suspicious Client*

    Some clients have difficulty believing that everyone in the office is not preoccupied with their case. They demand instant attention and results ("Why is it taking so long? I want this thing over!"). They may interpret delays as a tactic by the office to run up fees. An obvious response is to explain that the courts and the legal system often work at a slow pace unless an extreme emergency exists.

    During the initial interview, the office needs to head off or offset any unrealistic client expectations about how much time the case will take by providing a time range to complete such cases. The client also needs to be told that complications (e.g., new counter-demands by the opponent) almost always create additional delays.

    Generally, it is not helpful to point out that there are other clients who also need the attention of the attorneys and paralegals in the office. One possibly effective approach is to keep demanding clients constantly informed of the status of their case. The office could send them copies of documents as these are prepared for them and also send periodic reports on the status of their case.

- ### *The Client Who Lies*

    There is a difference between clients who give facts a favorable interpretation and clients who lie. Assume, for example, that an office represents a husband who is seeking sole custody of his children in a bitter divorce case. It is understandable that he will attempt to portray himself as a loving father. He may glowingly describe the positive effect he has had on his children by attending sports events with them and by helping them with their homework. Careful questioning and further investigation will help determine whether he has exaggerated his role. If he has, an experienced legal team will know how to present his case in a favorable light without compromising the truth.

    Suppose, however, that the father goes beyond exaggeration. For example, he may falsely claim that he does not use corporal punishment on the children, or he may deny that he takes illegal drugs in front of them in spite of evidence to the contrary. Of course, if negative facts can reasonably be interpreted in the father's favor, the office has an obligation to present this interpretation to the court. Yet it may eventually become clear to the office that the client has a tendency to lie. Serious ethical problems can arise in such cases. As we saw in Chapter 5, an attorney has an ethical obligation to avoid telling the court something that is known to be false and to avoid actively helping a client lie to the court. Withdrawal from a case by an attorney is justified when continued representation of the client would cause the attorney to violate an ethical obligation.

    Furthermore, it may be impossible for the attorney to provide competent representation without knowing all available facts. The client must be told that the attorney cannot rebut negative facts without knowing what those facts are before someone else reveals them. The client cannot make those facts go away by lying about them or concealing them. If the office cannot convince the client of this reality, the likelihood of representing the client effectively and ethically is low.

CHAPTER SUMMARY

To a large extent, public disfavor of the legal profession is based on misunderstanding of the role of the attorney in our system of justice. Attorneys often take unpopular cases and can find themselves in the middle of bitter disputes. The attorney-client fee agreement (retainer) creates and formalizes the attorney-client relationship. An attorney may decide not to take a case because of conflict of interest, lack of merit, or the client's inability to pay fees. If the office decides not to represent the prospective clients, it should send them a letter of nonengagement. The three main kinds of legal interviews are initial client interview, follow-up client interview, and field interview of someone other than the client.

Legal interviewing is designed to obtain facts that are relevant to the identification and eventual resolution of a legal problem. These facts are often reported in a document called an intake memo. Guides to the questions to ask include instructions of the supervisor; a general understanding of evidence, procedural law, and substantive law (causes of action and defenses) involved in the interview; checklists; fact particularization (FP); common sense; and flexibility. Determining what the client wants often takes probing and a presentation of options by an attorney. Otherwise, the office might fail to identify client objectives. Most of us are not fully aware of how our own bias affects our performance.

The supervising attorney can help set the tone for an effective interview by introducing the client to the paralegal and explaining the latter's role. The professional interviewer strives to uncover facts that make the case of each client unique. There are many ways to prepare for an interview such as scheduling the interview at a convenient time, reading everything in the file, having supplies available, and preparing initial questions. The seating arrangement should facilitate communication. The walls, desk, and overall appearance of the office should project a professional image. The interviewer should go out to greet clients when they arrive at the reception desk. Always be appreciative of what the client does. Some small talk at the beginning of the interview can help decrease client tension. Avoid making any promises of what the office can accomplish. Express empathy without being condescending or losing objectivity. Find out if there are any immediate concerns on the client's mind. Avoid legal jargon unless the client needs to know it and clear explanations are given. Briefly restate the purpose of the interview for the client. Let the client know why you are taking notes. Listen for clues to other problems the office should know about.

The following are the major kinds of questions an interviewer can ask (some of which overlap): open-ended, overview, closed-ended, chronological, leading, corroborative, combination, and wrap-up. One of the most important ways of building a relationship with the client is through attentive listening techniques such as maintaining eye contact and occasionally repeating back what the client tells you. Ask questions that will ferret out whatever observed facts helped lead to the inferences drawn by the client so that facts and opinions can be clearly identified and differentiated. Factual comprehensiveness is achieved through fact particularization (FP), corroborative questions, probing, etc. The paralegal interviewer must be alert to potential ethical problems such as breaching confidentiality and giving legal advice.

At the conclusion of the interview, ask the client to read and sign needed forms, find out if the client has any concerns not addressed during the interview, tell the client what next steps are planned, and make sure the client knows how to reach you. As soon as possible, make a note to the file that you conducted the interview. Begin writing the report (intake memo) soon after the interview, making note of any personality characteristics relevant to working with the client. To improve your interviewing technique, read literature and attend CLE seminars on interviewing, seek the critique of others, try to observe others interview, etc.

Special sensitivity is needed when working with potentially difficult clients such as those who claim to know all the law, who are angry, who are demanding, or who lie. Every effort should be made to accommodate such clients while maintaining professionalism, but ultimately the office may have to decide whether continued representation is feasible or ethically appropriate.

KEY TERMS

retainer (p. 365)
engagement letter (p. 367)
deep pocket (p. 367)
letter of nonengagement (p. 367)
declination (p. 367)
default (p. 367)
statute of limitations (p. 367)
interviewee (p. 367)
intake memo (p. 368)
RE (p. 368)
grounds (p. 370)

relevant (p. 370)
evidence (p. 370)
substantive law (p. 370)
cause of action (p. 370)
fact particularization (FP) (p. 371)
interrogatories ("rogs") (p. 371)
discovery (p. 371)
deposition (p. 371)
inference (p. 374)
analogies (p. 374)
timeline (p. 375)

bias (p. 377)
objective (p. 378)
hypothetical (p. 378)
contingency case (p. 383)
breach of contract (p. 383)
jargon (p. 384)
open-ended question (p. 385)
overview question (p. 385)
closed-ended question (p. 385)
chronological question (p. 386)
leading questions (p. 386)

hostile (p. 386)
corroborative question (p. 386)
combination question (p. 386)
multiple-choice question
   (p. 386)
add-on question (p. 386)
wrap-up question (p. 386)
attentive listening (p. 387)
legal advice (p. 389)

ASSIGNMENTS

CRITICAL ANALYSIS

8.1

(a) List some of the times in your life when you have interviewed someone on any subject in any setting. List some of the times when you have been interviewed by someone.

(b) Describe what you feel are the central ingredients of a good interview.

(c) Describe a bad interview. From your experience, what are some of the worst mistakes an interviewer can make?

(d) Describe what you think are some of your strong and weak points as an interviewer. What can you do to improve?

8.2 Think about your past and present contacts with people who have irritated you the most. Make a specific list of what bothered you about these people. Include examples that involve a serious clash of values between you and that person. Suppose that you are working in a law office where a client did one of the things on your list. Could you handle such a case? Explain why or why not. Assume that there is no one else in the office available to work with this client.

8.3

(a) The instructor asks the class if anyone was involved, in any way, in a recent automobile accident. If someone says yes, this student is asked if he or she would be willing to be interviewed by another class member whose job is to obtain as complete a picture as possible of what happened. At the outset, the interviewer knows nothing other than that some kind of an automobile accident occurred. The interviewee can make up any sensitive facts if he or she wishes to keep some of the actual events confidential.

(b) The instructor asks the class if anyone has recently had trouble with any government agency (e.g., the post office or the department of motor vehicles). If someone says yes, this student is asked if he or she would be willing to be interviewed by another class member whose job is to obtain as complete a picture as possible of what happened. The interviewer at the outset knows nothing other than the fact that the person being interviewed has had some difficulty with a government agency. The interviewee can make up any sensitive facts if he or she wishes to keep some of the actual events confidential.

PROJECT

8.4 In Google, Bing, and Yahoo, run this search: client legal interviewing -jobs -employment. (This search tells the search engines you want sites on legal interviewing but not the kind of interviewing that occurs when looking for employment. Note, however, that the search may still turn up some job sites).

Which of the three search engines was the most productive in leading you to material on the themes covered in Chapter 8? Run the same search in the Articles database of Google Scholar (scholar.google.com). How would you compare the results in Google Scholar to the results achieved by the general search engines (Google, Bing, and Yahoo)? Limit yourself to examining the articles you found through Google Scholar that you can read in full for free. Make a list of any ten sites found through steps a and b. The list should begin with the most useful site, then the next most useful site, etc. For each site, state its www address; what Chapter 8 themes it covered; and whether you found the site in Google, Bing, or Yahoo or in Google Scholar.

CORE SKILLS

Among the many skills a paralegal must have, five core skills stand out: writing (both basic English and legal drafting), research, ethics, computer use, and collaboration (working with others). The core-skill assignments introduce and reinforce these skills. Even if you are not asked to do all of the assignments as part of the course, you should do them on your own. Also, do not wait for the topics in the assignments to be covered in this course or in other courses. Successful paralegals are self-starters. A major characteristic of a self-starter is a thirst for independent study—learning on your own.

CORE SKILL: WRITING

8.5 When an office represents a debtor, one of the paralegal's major responsibilities may be to interview the client in order to write a comprehensive report on the client's assets and liabilities. Assume that your supervising attorney has instructed you to conduct a comprehensive interview of the client in order to write such a report. Assets are everything the client owns or in which the client has an interest. Liabilities are everything owed; they are debts. These are the only definitions you need; you do not need any technical knowledge of law to conduct this interview. All you need is common sense in the formulation of questions

Your instructor will role-play the client in front of the room. It will be a collective interview. Everyone will ask questions. Take detailed notes on the questions asked by every student (not just your own) and the answers provided in response. You will have to write your individual report based on your own notes.

Raise your hand to be recognized. Be sure to ask follow-up questions when needed for factual clarity and comprehensiveness. You can repeat the questions of other students if you think you might elicit a more detailed response. Any question is fair game as long as it is directly or indirectly calculated to uncover assets or liabilities. There may be information the client does not have at this time, such as bank account numbers. Help the client determine how such information can be obtained later. In your notes, state that you (or another interviewer) asked for information that the client did not have and state what the client said he or she would do to obtain the information. To achieve comprehensiveness, you must obtain factual detail. This means that you go after names, addresses, phone numbers, dates, relevant surrounding circumstances, verification data, etc. In short, you want fact particularization (FP). (See Exhibits 8-4 and 8-5.)

The heading of your report will be as follows:

Office Memorandum

To: [name of your instructor]

From: [your name]

Date: [date you prepared the report]

RE: Comprehensive Interview of _____

Case File Number: _____

(Make up the case file number.) The first paragraph of your memo should state what your supervisor has asked you to do in the memo. Simply state what the assignment is. Organization of the data from your notes is up to you. Use whatever format you think will most clearly communicate what you learned from the client in the interview. Use clear headings to help the reader grasp the volume and variety of facts covered in the memo.

CORE SKILL: RESEARCH

8.6 It is often said that client recommendations are a large source of future clients for a law office. Write a report on this theme. (In Google, Bing, or Yahoo, run this search: marketing attorney client recommendations.) Your report must cite at least five different sources that you found on the Internet.

CORE SKILL: ETHICS

8.7 Mrs. Jones is being sued by Mr. Jones for divorce on the ground of adultery, which she has denied. Mrs. Jones is the client of your office. Thus far your investigation has revealed that there is considerable doubt over whether Mrs. Jones did in fact commit adultery. During a follow-up interview with Mrs. Jones she tells you that she is a prostitute. She asks you not to say anything about this to anyone because she has just started therapy for drug addiction. What should the paralegal do? Identify ethical problems that are likely to result from the various responses the paralegal could make to this request by the client.

CORE SKILL: COMPUTERS

8.8 In Google, Bing, or Yahoo, run this search: e-discovery. Write a report in which you describe what e-discovery is. Select any two software products on e-discovery that is available to attorneys. Explain what these two products do. Do not use any term in your report that you do not understand. If, for example, the program you select says that it covers interrogatory answers, find a definition of interrogatory if you do not know what it is. At the end of your report, include a glossary of every word you had to check the meaning of and include the definition. Also enter these words in the Computer Terminology in the Law (CTL) notebook you started in Assignment 1.8 of Chapter 1.

CORE SKILL: COLLABORATION

8.9 In this exercise, fact particularization (FP) will be role-played in class. (See Exhibits 8-4 and 8-5.) One student will be selected to play the role of the client and another, the role of the paralegal interviewer. The rest of the class will observe and fill out the FP Score Card on the interview. The FP Score Card is on page 398.

Instructions to interviewer. You will not be conducting a complete interview from beginning to end. Instead, you will be trying to particularize a certain fact that is given to you. Go through all the categories of FP outlined in Exhibit 8.5. Use any order of questioning you want. Probe for comprehensiveness (see also Exhibit 8-13 on comprehensiveness). Your instructor will select one of the following facts to be used as the basis of the interview:

(a) "I was hit in the jaw by Mary."

(b) "He neglects his children."

(c) "I have not been promoted because I am a woman."

(d) "The computer system the store sold me is useless."

(e) "I'm buried in debt."

After the client makes one of these five statements to you, your opening statement to the client will be, "Tell me what happened." Then use the process of FP to particularize the statement.

Instructions to client. The interviewer will ask you what happened. Make one of the five statements above as selected by the instructor. Then the interviewer will ask you a large number of questions about the statement. Make up the answers—ad lib your responses. Do not, however, volunteer any information. Answer only the questions asked.

Instructions to class. Observe the interview. Use the FP Score Card to assess how well you think the interviewer particularized the fact. Do not, however, focus on the score card while the interview is underway. Peruse the score card briefly before the interview begins and close your book until the interview is over. Concentrate on the interview itself.

The FP Score Card for Assignment 8.9 is on page 398.

8.10 The following exercise involves an interview role-played in class. After watching this interview, you will be asked to deduce some principles of communication for interviewing.

Legal Interviewing Communications Score (LICS)

In this exercise, two students will role-play a legal interview in front of the class. The rest of the class will observe the interview and comment on it, using the LICS on page 398.

Instructions to client. You will role-play the part of a client. A month ago you sprained your back while lifting a computer and carrying it from one room to another. You are an accountant. When you came to work that day, you found the computer on your desk. It did not belong there, and you did not know how it got there. You decided to move it to another desk. That was when you sprained your back.

You have come to the law office for legal advice. You have already seen an attorney in this office who has agreed to take your case. An interviewer has been assigned to conduct an interview with you to obtain a complete picture of what happened. This interview will now be role-played in front of the class.

The basic facts involve the accountant and the computer. You can make up all other facts to answer the interviewer's questions. Make up the name of the company for which you work, the details surrounding the accident, etc. You can create any set of facts as long as your answers are reasonably consistent with the basic facts given to you above.

Instructions to interviewer. You will play the role of the interviewer in the case involving the sprained back. You are a paralegal in the office. All you know about the case thus far is that the client's back was injured in a work-related accident. You have been assigned to interview the client for detailed information about the client and about the accident. Start off by introducing yourself and your role. State the purpose of the interview. Then proceed to the questions. Take notes on the client's answers.

You do not need to know any law in order to conduct the interview. Let common sense be your guide. Your goal is to compile as comprehensive a picture of the facts as you can prompt this client to convey. Consult the material in Exhibits 8-4 and 8-5 on fact particularization (FP) as you prepare and formulate questions. Be sure to listen carefully to the answers so that you can ask appropriate follow-up questions that seek more details on the facts contained in the answers.

The class will observe you in order to assess the manner and content of the interview. A good deal of constructive criticism may develop from the class discussion. As you listen to the criticism, try to be as objective as you can. It is difficult to conduct a comprehensive interview and probably impossible to conduct one flawlessly. For every question that you ask, there may be ten observations on how you could have asked it differently. Hence, try not to take the comments personally.

Instructions to class. You will be watching the interview involving the sprained back. You have two tasks:

(1) Read through the Legal Interviewing Communications Score (LICS) form on page 398. Then close your book so that you will give your complete attention to the interview. After the interview, fill out the LICS form. The teacher will ask you to state the total score you gave the interview or to submit this score to someone who will calculate the average score from all students' scores.

(2) Identify as many dos and don'ts of interviewing as you can. If you were writing a law office manual on how to interview, what would you include? What guidance would you give an interviewer on taking notes during the interview, asking follow-up questions, maintaining eye contact with the client, etc.? After you observe the interview, discuss specific suggestions on what an interviewer should or should not do. Ideas will also come to mind while you are filling out the LICS form.

The LICS form for Assignment 8.10 is on page 398.

8.11 Form a circle of chairs with a single chair in the middle. The student sitting in the middle will play the role of the client. The students in the circle (numbering about 10)

will be the interviewers, in rotation. The instructor will ask one of the students to begin the interview. As this student runs into difficulty during the interview, the student to his or her right picks up the interview, tries to resolve the difficulty in his or her own way, and then proceeds with the interview. If this student cannot resolve the difficulty, the student to his or her right tries, and so on. The objective is to identify as many diverse ways of handling difficulties as possible in a relatively short period. No interviewer should have the floor for more than a minute or two at any one time. The student playing the role of the client is given specific instructions about how to play the role. For example, sometimes he or she is asked to be evasive; other times, demanding. The client should not overdo the role, however. He or she should respond naturally within the role assigned. Here are four sets of instructions for this "interview in rotation."

(a) The interviewer greets the client and says, "I am a paralegal." The client is confused about what a paralegal is. The interviewer explains. The client is insistent upon a comprehensive definition that he or she can understand.

(b) The client is being sued by a local store for $750.00 in grocery bills. The client has a poor memory and is having difficulty remembering what was or was not purchased at this store (where the client has shopped for over a year). The interviewer must think of ways to help him or her remember. The client wants to cooperate but is having trouble remembering.

(c) The client wants to sue an auto mechanic. The client gives many opinions, conclusions, and judgments (such as "The mechanic is a crook," "I was their best customer," or "The work done was awful"). The interviewer is having difficulty encouraging the client to state the facts (observed data) underlying the opinions. The client insists on stating conclusions.

After each exercise, the class should discuss principles, guidelines, and techniques of interviewing.

THE JOB SEARCH

(The search for employment cannot wait until the end of a course or of a curriculum. It needs to begin now. The job-search assignments are designed to introduce you to different aspects of the job search and to build options for you to explore about employment.)

8.12 In Assignment 8.5 you prepared a memo based on an interview of a client concerning assets and liabilities. Rewrite this memo so that it can be a writing sample for your portfolio when you are looking for employment. The memo must have no spelling or grammar errors. The paragraphs must be skillfully organized. Find two individuals who are willing to evaluate the memo. They do not have to be paralegals or attorneys. You want an evaluation that covers spelling, grammar, paragraph structure, and overall organization and clarity. Rewrite the memo based on their critiques.

FP Score Card (to be used with Assignment 8.9)

Effective in obtaining date and time details	5 4 3 2 1	Weak in obtaining date and time details
Effective in obtaining place and environment details	5 4 3 2 1	Weak in obtaining place and environment details
Effective in obtaining details on other participants	5 4 3 2 1	Weak in obtaining details on other participants
Effective in finding out where the client's statements fall on the spectrum of certainty	5 4 3 2 1	Weak in finding out where the client's statements fall on the spectrum of certainty
Effective in seeking verification details	5 4 3 2 1	Weak in seeking verification details
Effective in using analogies to obtain greater detail	5 4 3 2 1	Weak in using analogies to obtain greater detail
Effective in obtaining miscellaneous details	5 4 3 2 1	Weak in obtaining miscellaneous details

Following the interview, put a check on the appropriate number for each of the preceding categories of assessment. A *5* score means you thought the interview was very precise or effective in fulfilling the goal of the particular FP category being assessed; a *1* score means the opposite. Also, make notes of questions you think the Interviewer *should have asked*. These questions, and your scores, will be discussed in class after the interview.

Legal Interviewing Communications Score (LICS) (to be used with Assignment 8.10)

How to Score:

You will be observing the role-playing of a legal interview and evaluating the Interviewer on a 100-point scale. These 100 points will be earned in the four categories listed below. The score is not based on scientific data. It is a rough approximation of someone's oral communication skills in a legal interview. A score can be interpreted as follows:

> 90–100 Points: Outstanding Interviewer
> 80–89 Points: Good Interviewer
> 60–79 Points: Fair Interviewer
> 0–59 Points: A Lot More Work Needs to Be Done

(Of course, the LICS does not assess the Interviewer's ability to *write* an intake memo for the file. See Exhibit 8-3 and the discussion of the intake memo earlier in this chapter.)

Category I: Role Identification

On a scale of 0–5, how well did the interviewer explain his or her role and the purpose of the interview?
(A 5 score means the interviewer took time to explain clearly what his or her job was in the office and what he or she hoped to accomplish in the interview. A low score means the interviewer gave little or no explanation or mumbled an explanation without being sensitive to whether the client understood.)

Category I Score: ☐

Category II: Factual Detail

On a scale of 0–80, how would you score the interviewer's performance in asking enough questions to obtain factual comprehensiveness? How well was FP performed?
(An 80 score means the interviewer was extremely sensitive to detail in his or her questions. A low score means that the interviewer stayed with the surface facts, with little or no probing for the who-what-where-how-when-why details. The more facts you think the interviewer did not obtain, the lower the score should be.)

Category II Score: ☐

Category III: Control

On a scale of 0–10, how would you score the interviewer's performance in controlling the Interview and in giving It direction?
(A 10 score means the interviewer demonstrated excellent control and direction. A low score means the interviewer rambled from question to question or let the client ramble from topic to topic.)

Category III Score: ☐

Category IV: Earning the Confidence of the Client

On a scale of 0–5 how would you score the interviewer's performance in gaining the trust of the client and in setting him or her at ease?
(A 5 score means the interviewer appeared to do an excellent job of gaining the trust and confidence of the client. A low score means the client seemed to be suspicious of the interviewer and probably doubted his or her professional competence. The more the interviewer made the client feel that he or she was genuinely concerned about the client, the higher the score. The more the client obtained the impression that the interviewer was "just doing a job," the lower the score.)

Category IV Score: ☐

Total Score: ☐

REVIEW QUESTIONS

1. In what kinds of law offices are paralegals likely to conduct legal interviews?
2. Why should a paralegal understand the dynamics of legal interviewing?
3. What are some of the reasons the public perception of attorneys is often negative?
4. What can paralegals do to help combat the negative perception of attorneys?
5. What is a retainer?
6. Why might an attorney decide not to take a case?
7. What is a deep pocket?
8. What is the function of a letter of nonengagement?
9. What are the three kinds of legal interviews?
10. What is an intake memo? Name its five parts.
11. What guides can be used to know what questions to ask in an interview?
12. State five reasons why an interview can be ineffective.
13. What law should a legal interviewer know?
14. What is fact particularization (FP)?
15. What are the categories of questions for fact particularization (FP)?
16. What is a timeline?
17. Why do some clients have difficulty stating what they want?
18. What is bias, and how can an interviewer's bias against a client interfere with effective interviewing?
19. What steps are needed to prepare for an interview?
20. Distinguish between a professional and a bureaucratic perspective or attitude.
21. What is jargon and how should it be handled in an interview?
22. What could a paralegal tell a client that might result in a breach-of-contract suit against the law office, and how can this be avoided?
23. What are some of the techniques and guidelines for beginning an interview?
24. What is the definition of the following kinds of questions: open-ended, overview, closed-ended, chronological, leading, corroborative, combination, and wrap-up?
25. What are some of the techniques and guidelines for attentive listening?
26. What are some of the techniques and guidelines for achieving factual comprehensiveness during an interview?
27. How can an interviewer avoid ethical violations in an interview?
28. What are some of the techniques and guidelines for ending an interview?
29. List ways to improve your legal interviewing skills.
30. What are examples of some so-called "difficult" clients and how should the office respond to them?

HELPFUL WEBSITES

Interviewing Basics
- www.americanbar.org/newsletter/publications/youraba/201312article02.html
- courses.washington.edu/civpro03/resources (click *interviewing.doc*)

Client Intake/Interview Forms
- www.gabar.org/committeesprogramssections/programs/lpm/forms.cfm

Interviewing: Selected Articles
- www.rongolini.com/Interviewing.html

What Clients Want
- lawprofessors.typepad.com/legal_skills/2012/05/what-clients-want.html

Reasons Not to Take a Case
- www.americanbar.org/publications/gp_solo/2011/march/the_wayward_client.html

Attentive Listening
- www.businesslistening.com/listening_skills-3.php
- www.skillsyouneed.com/ips/active-listening.html
- www.taft.cc.ca.us/lrc/class/assignments/actlisten.html
- www.abelsonlegalsearch.com/pdf/HarnessthePowerofActiveListening.pdf

Difficult Clients

- blogs.hbr.org/2013/04/how-to-deal-with-a-toxic-clien
- www.lawyersmutualnc.com/7-scary-law-office-scenarios

Attorney Stereotypes

- solopracticeuniversity.com/2011/12/01
  /why-people-hate-lawyers-getting-beyond-the-stereotypes

Paralegal Role in Improving Reputation of Legal Profession

- www.sddt.com/news/article.cfm?SourceCode=20070214crb#
  .UucWZxDTlhE

Nonengagement Letters

- www.lawyersmutualnc.com/blog
  /making-the-case-for-non-engagement-letters

International Listening Association

- www.listen.org

Google, Bing, or Yahoo Searches

(On these search engines, run the following searches, using quotation marks and substituting your state for "aa" where indicated.)

- client interviewing
- law office client interview
- kinds of interview questions
- attorney stereotypes
- lawyer bashing
- engagement letter
- retainer aa
- nonengagement letter
- fee agreements attorney
- attentive listening
- intake memo
- "difficult clients"

ENDNOTES

[1] David Vandagriff, *Take My Breath Away*, 80 American Bar Association Journal 95 (May 1994).

[2] *Americans Find Lawyers Necessary, but Overpaid and Dishonest* (2002) (www2.law.columbia.edu/news/surveys/survey_opinion_index.shtml).

[3] Brent Roper, *Practical Law Office Management* 121 (1995).

[4] Jeremy Fogel, "*Justice Denied" Is a National Problem*, San Jose Mercury-News, February 12, 2006, at 3P.

[5] Robert McFadden, *Thomas Puccio, 67, Lawyer with Infamous Clients, Dies*, N.Y. Times, November 19, 2008, at B16.

[6] Sally Kane, *Tap Into Your Inner Sleuth*, Legal Assistant Today 25 (May/June 2009).

[7] Kenney F. Hegland, *Introduction to the Study and Practice of Law*, 161 4th ed. 2003).

[8] Claire Summerhill, *Imagine This*, Paralegal Today 78 (July/ August 2004).

[9] *My Specialty: Divorce Law*, 27 Paralegal Today 27 (April/June 2010).

[10] Anita McCracken, *How to Keep Your Client's Sanity Without Losing Yours*, The Paralegal Society Blog (September 5, 2012).

[11] Shari Caudron, *Crisis of Conscience*, 12 Paralegal Today 73, 75 (September/ October 1994).

[12] Denise Clemens, *Client Interviewing*, 11 California Paralegal Magazine 12, 13 (October/December 1991).

[13] William P. Statsky & Philip C. Lang, *The Legal Paraprofessional as Advocate and Assistant: Roles, Training Concepts, and Materials* (Center on Social Welfare Policy & Law, 1971).

[14] Arthur White, *Architectural Suggestions for a Law Office Building*, 2 Practical Lawyer 66 (December 1956).

[15] Harrop Freeman & Henry Weihofen, *Clinical Law Training, Interviewing and Counseling* 13 (1972).

[16] Jim Calloway, *The Initial Client Interview*, 73 Oklahoma Bar Journal (2002).

[17] *The Initial Interview*, 12 Family Advocate 6 (Winter 1990).

INVESTIGATION IN A LAW OFFICE

CHAPTER OUTLINE

- Paralegal Roles in Investigation
- Nature and Context of Investigation
- Fact Analysis: Organizing the Options
- Distortions in Investigation

- Sources of Evidence/ Sources of Leads
- Gaining Access to Records
- Evaluating Evidence
- Interviewing Witnesses
- Special Investigative Problems

- License to Investigate?
- Basics of Evidence Law
- Evidence Log
- Taking a Witness Statement
- Settlement Work-Up
- Ethics and Investigation

CHAPTER OBJECTIVES

After completing this chapter, you should be able to

- Identify paralegal roles in investigation.
- List the major guides to fact gathering in investigation.
- Describe the nature of investigation.
- Know the standard methods of discovery.
- Understand the importance and limitations of fact versions.
- Explain the major distortions that can occur in investigation.
- List the standard sources of evidence and leads.
- Know how to gain access to records.

- Explain ways to evaluate the reliability of evidence.
- Outline the techniques of interviewing a witness.
- Summarize steps in collecting a judgment, finding missing persons, doing a background investigation, and investigating an automobile accident.
- Know whether a license is needed to investigate a case.
- List the four ways that a party can establish its version of the facts at a trial.

- Explain the evidence law of admissibility, relevance, competence, opinions, hearsay, privilege, authentication, and parol evidence.
- Understand the purpose of an evidence log.
- Know how to take a witness statement.
- Explain the purpose and format of a settlement work-up.
- List the major ethical requirements of an investigation.

PARALEGAL ROLES IN INVESTIGATION

For relatively large and important cases, law offices often hire private investigators or specialists who investigate certain kinds of cases. Examples of specialty areas include criminal fraud and **forensic** accounting (involving tasks such as examining paper and digital corporate records for evidence of fraud or embezzlement). In law practices such as criminal law, insurance law, or **mass torts**, the office may have its own investigators on staff. In the vast majority of cases, however, investigative work is performed by attorneys and paralegals as part of their regular duties. Here are some comments by paralegals doing such work:

> In "personal injury litigation, particularly representing the injured party, paralegals routinely perform a variety of investigative tasks,... sometimes without leaving the office."[1]

> "What I love most of what paralegals do is the investigation; digging and researching for information or **skiptracing** to find witnesses."[2]

> "I really enjoy doing the nitty-gritty investigative work, whether it be medical record analysis, researching plaintiffs' criminal backgrounds, or Facebook research."[3]

It is now standard practice for many paralegals to seek background information about parties by Googling their names and checking their pages on Facebook, Twitter, LinkedIn, and other social networking sites. In addition, there are the inevitable unexpected assignments:

> "Many of us have been approached by our attorneys at the last minute to interview a witness and 'Find out what he knows.'"[4]

There are many different kinds of investigation assignments that a paralegal might be given. Here are some more specific examples:

- Contact all witnesses to an accident and obtain a witness statement from each.
- Verify information given by a witness.
- Go to the scene of an accident and photograph the area.
- Search for and order aerial photographs.
- Determine a company's registered agent so that the agent can receive **service of process** for that company.
- Find out if a company is publicly traded or privately held.
- Obtain the names of the board of directors and shareholders of a company.
- Find out if a national corporation headquartered in another state has any assets in your state.
- Obtain a "D&B" on a prospective client (D&B is the abbreviation for Dun & Bradstreet, a company that provides financial information on businesses) (www.dnb.com).
- Help conduct **due diligence** on a company (e.g., ascertain the fair market value of its assets, trace its income and profit history, determine its actual and potential exposure to liability from customers, competitors, or staff).
- Determine whether prior judgments have been filed against a potential client.
- Find out if there is pending litigation against a particular individual or company.
- Determine whether someone has a criminal record.
- Locate an expert witness.
- Research the background of an opposing witness.
- Find an automobile engine of the same make and year as one destroyed in a collision that a client had with the defendant.
- Trace the ownership and repair history of a motor vehicle through its VIN (vehicle identification number).

In the movie *Erin Brockovich*, based on a true story, Julia Roberts won an Academy Award for her role as a nonattorney employee who was given a major investigation assignment in the law office where she worked. She investigated the link between a highly toxic antirust chemical agent (chromium-6) used by a major public utility and the life-threatening diseases suffered by residents in the area where the utility had dumped the agent. Their water supply had become contaminated. Brockovich's work helped the office obtain a $333 million settlement for the victims. Brockovich was given a $1 million bonus by her grateful supervising attorney. Of course, most paralegal investigation assignments will not be this dramatic. Yet the movie

forensic (1) Pertaining to the use of scientific techniques to discover and examine evidence. (2) Belonging to or suitable in courts of law. (3) Concerning argumentation. (4) Forensics (ballistics or firearms evidence).

mass tort A general term for various causes of action asserted by a large number of persons who have been harmed by the same or similar conduct or product of a relatively small number of defendants. The causes of action include negligence, strict liability in tort, breach of warranty, misrepresentation, and violations of deceptive trade acts.

skiptracing Efforts to locate persons (e.g., debtors) or assets.

service of process A formal delivery of notice to a defendant that a suit has been initiated to which he or she must respond. *Process* is the means used by the court to acquire or exercise its power or jurisdiction over a person.

due diligence Reasonable efforts to find and verify factual information needed to carry out an obligation, to avoid harming someone, or to make an important decision, e.g., to determine the true market value of a potential investment or to decide whether a job prospect is worth pursuing.

certainly highlighted the importance of investigation and the critical role that nonattorneys can have in this arena of fact gathering.

Many paralegals look forward to their investigation assignments, particularly in an era when so much can be accomplished on the Internet. "One of the things I enjoy most in the profession is the investigative part of cases. I take it as a personal challenge to [find out how much the other side has] inadvertently or deliberately left out of their answers to discovery. It becomes an even bigger challenge when that person is out of state."[5] Whether you are "diving deep for information on a multinational corporation" or "just checking the background of a witness," good investigative skills can be a major asset in a paralegal's professional development.[6]

NATURE AND CONTEXT OF INVESTIGATION

Legal investigation is the process of gathering additional facts and verifying presently known facts in order to advise a client on how to avoid or solve a legal problem. A **fact** is an actual event or real occurrence. It is anything that can be shown to exist. It can be an incident (such as a fire), a state of mind (such as an intention to enter a contract), or an emotion (such as anger or remorse).

Our study of investigation will focus on three main topics:

- The nature of investigation
- Techniques of investigation
- Evidence law and investigation

In Chapter 8, on legal interviewing, we examined six major guides to fact gathering:

- Instructions of the supervisor
- Evidence, procedural law, and substantive law
- Checklists
- Fact particularization (FP)
- Common sense
- Flexibility

You should review these guides because they are equally applicable to investigation. **Fact particularization (FP)** is especially important.

We begin our study of legal investigation with some general observations about its nature and context:

1. *Investigative techniques are individualistic.* Styles, mannerisms, and approaches to investigation are highly personal. Through a sometimes-arduous process of trial and error, the investigator develops effective techniques. Some of these techniques come from the suggestions of attorneys and fellow paralegals. Most, however, are acquired from on-the-job experience.

2. *It is impossible to overemphasize the importance of hustle, imagination, and flexibility.* If there is one characteristic that singles out the effective investigator, it is a willingness to dig. Many investigation assignments are relatively straightforward. For example:

- Check court records to find out if a doctor has other malpractice cases pending against him or her.
- Find out if someone has filed a workers' compensation claim.
- Obtain a copy of an ambulance report.
- Photograph the ceiling of a bathroom that a tenant claims is falling down.

Other assignments are more involved because they are open ended. For example:

- Find out what property or other assets of the defendant might be available to pay a judgment.
- Investigate the cause of an automobile accident.

An extensive range of options and conclusions is possible in such assignments. The answer is not always there for the asking. In open-ended assignments, investigators must be prepared to identify and pursue leads, be unorthodox, and let their feelings, hunches, and intuition lead

fact An actual event; a real occurrence. Anything that can be shown to exist, e.g., an incident, a relationship, an intention, an opinion, or an emotion. (When we say that an opinion is a fact we are referring to whether or not a person has or holds a particular opinion, not to the opinion itself.)

fact particularization (FP) A fact-gathering technique to generate a large list of factual questions (who, what, where, how, when, and why) that will help you obtain a specific and comprehensive picture of all available facts relevant to a legal issue.

where they will. In short, formal guidelines of investigation must give way to hustle, imagination, and flexibility.

Here are two examples of paralegals who demonstrate these qualities:

- Edna Wallace, an Indianapolis paralegal, recently needed to find out the name of the bank of a company that was avoiding payment of a judgment that her firm had obtained against it. Her ingenious strategy was to have dinner at one of the company's restaurants and to pay by check. Once it was cashed and returned to her, she was able to determine where the company banked and what its account number was. Her firm immediately sought a court order to freeze the company's bank account.[7]
- Traci Brown, a Michigan paralegal, recently made herself "look like a rockstar using Facebook." A private investigator was not able to locate a party who needed to be served. The party was not at any of the addresses the office had for him. Without using deception, Traci went to the party's Facebook page and found out the name of the party's girlfriend. Traci then went to the girlfriend's page, where publicly available information listed the girlfriend's city. Using another site, Traci found the address of the girlfriend. A process server was sent to this address and "sure enough," the party was at this address. The boss was "pretty impressed," with Traci, especially in view of the inability of the private investigator to accomplish what Traci did.[8]

Good investigators are always in pursuit. They are on the offensive and do not wait for the facts to come to them. They know that legwork is required. They know that 75 percent of their leads will turn out to be dead ends. They are not frightened by roadblocks and therefore do not freeze at the first hurdle. They know that there are no perfect ways of obtaining information. They know that they must take a stab at possibilities and that it takes persistent thinking and imagination to come up with leads. At the same time, good investigators are not fools. They do not stay on blind alleys. After being on the job for a while, they have developed "a feel" for whether a possibility or lead is worth pursuing. They have been able to develop this feel because, when they first started investigating, they had open minds and were not afraid to try things out.

3. *Investigation and interviewing are closely related.* The investigator builds on the report or intake memo (see Exhibit 8-3 in Chapter 8) prepared by the interviewer on what the client said. The investigation needs may be clear from this report, or they may become clear only after the investigator and his or her supervisor have defined them more precisely.

    The investigator should approach the interview report with a healthy skepticism. Thus far, all the office may know is what the client has said. The perspective of the office is therefore narrow. Without necessarily distrusting the client's word, the investigator's job is to verify the facts obtained in the interview and to determine whether new facts exist that were unknown or improperly identified during the interview. The interview report should not be taken at face value. New facts may be revealed or old facts may for the first time be seen in a context that gives them an unexpected meaning. The investigator must approach a case almost as if the office knows nothing about it or as if what the office knows is invalid. By adopting this attitude, the investigator may be able to give the case an entirely different direction when this is warranted.

4. *The investigator must be guided by goals and priorities.* The starting point in an investigation assignment is a set of instructions from the supervisor. These instructions determine the investigator's goals and priorities.

5. *Investigation, negotiation, discovery, and trial are closely related.* There are two questions that should guide the investigator's inquiry into every fact being investigated:

- How will this fact assist or hurt the office in attempting to settle or negotiate the case without a trial?
- How will this fact assist or hurt the office in presenting the client's case at trial?

settlement An agreement resolving a dispute without full litigation. (See glossary for additional meanings.)

A large percentage of legal claims never go to trial. Opposing counsel hold a number of bargaining sessions in which they attempt to hammer out a **settlement** acceptable to their clients. Very often they discuss the law that they think will be applicable if the case goes to trial. Even more often, they present each other with the facts that they think they will be able to establish at trial. Here, the investigator's report becomes invaluable. As a result of this report, the attorney may be able to suggest a wide range of facts that could be used at trial ("we have reason to believe…" or "we are now pursuing leads that would tend to establish that…" etc.). The attorney's bargaining leverage is immeasurably increased by a thorough investigation report.

If negotiations do not produce a settlement, the investigator's report can help the attorney:

- Determine whether to go to trial.
- Help the attorney plan **discovery.**
- Decide what witnesses to call.
- Choose questions to ask of witnesses.
- Decide how to **impeach** (challenge) opposing witnesses.
- Anticipate how the other side might try to impeach your client and witnesses.
- Determine what tangible (physical) evidence to introduce.
- Decide how to attack the tangible evidence the other side will introduce.

For an overview of the discovery methods, see Exhibit 9-1.

discovery Methods used by parties to force information from each other before trial to aid in trial preparation. Examples of such devices include interrogatories and depositions. The methods can also be used to aid in the enforcement of a judgment.

impeach To challenge; to attack the credibility of.

Exhibit 9-1	Standard Discovery Methods
Deposition	1. A method of discovery by which parties and their prospective witnesses are questioned by the opposing party before trial at a location other than the courtroom. (Judges are not present during depositions.) The purpose of depositions and other discovery methods is to assist parties in trial preparation by allowing each side to uncover facts from the other side. The person questioned is called the *deponent.* 2. A posttrial method of discovery by which the winning party seeks to uncover facts that will help it enforce the judgment it obtained against the losing side.
Interrogatories ("rogs")	A method of discovery by which one party sends written questions to another party. An interrogatory is simply a question submitted by one party to another.
Request for Admission (RFA)	A method of discovery by which one party sends a request to another party that the latter agree that a certain fact or legal conclusion is true or valid so that there will be no need to present proof or arguments about that matter during the trial.
Request for Production (RFP)	A method of discovery by which one party requests that another party provide access to electronically stored data, paper documents, or other tangible things for copying or inspection. The method can also include a request to enter the party's land for inspection.
Independent Medical Examination (IME)	A method of discovery by which a party obtains a court order for a professional examination of a person whose physical or mental condition is in controversy, e.g., the extent of the plaintiff's alleged injuries.

After the discovery methods have been used, the investigator may be asked to study all the facts that the methods disclose in order to

- Cross-check or verify these facts, and
- Look for new leads (names, addresses, incidents) that could be the subject of further discovery and investigation.

evidence Anything offered to establish the existence or nonexistence of a fact in dispute. Separate determinations must be made on whether a particular item of evidence is relevant or irrelevant, admissible or inadmissible.

proof Enough evidence to establish the existence or nonexistence of an alleged fact.

standard of proof A statement of how convincing a version of a fact must be before the trier of facts (usually the jury) can accept it as true.

beyond a reasonable doubt The standard of proof that is met when there are no doubts about the evidence that would cause prudent persons to hesitate before acting in matters of importance to themselves.

preponderance of the evidence The standard of proof that is met when the evidence establishes that it is more likely than not that the facts are as alleged. Also called *fair preponderance of evidence*.

clear and convincing evidence A standard of proof that is met when the evidence demonstrates that the existence of a disputed fact is much more probable than its nonexistence. This standard is stronger than preponderance of the evidence but not as strong as beyond a reasonable doubt.

substantive law Nonprocedural laws that define or govern rights and duties, e.g., the duty to use reasonable care to avoid injuring someone.

networking Establishing contacts and sharing information with people (a) who might become personal or professional resources for you and (b) for whom you might become a personal or professional resource.

inferences A deduction or conclusion reached from facts.

6. *It is important to distinguish between proof of a fact and evidence of a fact.* **Evidence** is anything that is offered to establish the existence or nonexistence of a fact in dispute. Examples of evidence include testimony, documents, and fingerprints. **Proof** is enough evidence to establish the existence or nonexistence of an alleged fact. Investigators are looking for evidence. They should not stop looking simply because they have not found proof. It is the role of the judge and jury to resolve questions of proof by applying the **standards of proof** used in criminal and civil cases (**beyond a reasonable doubt** in criminal cases and **preponderance of the evidence** or **clear and convincing evidence** in civil cases). The function of investigators is to identify reasonable options or fact possibilities. To be sure, they can speculate on whether a judge or jury would believe an alleged fact to be true. But the presence or absence of proof is not the test that should guide them in their investigations. The test that an investigator should apply in determining whether to investigate a fact possibility is "Am I reasonable in assuming that a particular fact will help establish the case of the client and/or of the opponent?" It is important to be able to approach the case from the perspective of the opponent, even to the point of assuming that you work for the other side! What facts will the opponent go after to establish its case? What is the likelihood that such facts will be accepted?

7. *The investigator must know some law.* As pointed out in Chapter 8, interviewers and investigators do not have to be experts in any particular area of the law in order to perform their job. For their fieldwork to have a focus, however, they should have at least a general understanding of evidence, procedural law (civil procedure), and the **substantive law** governing the facts of the client's case. They should know the meaning of *hearsay* and *relevance* (see the discussion on evidence later in the chapter) and understand the basic procedural steps in litigation in order to see how facts can be used in different ways at different steps in the litigation process. (For an overview of civil and criminal litigation, see Exhibits 10-3 and 10-4 in Chapter 10.) The investigator does not need to know substantive law in any great depth. In a negligence case, for example, it would be sufficient to know the basic elements of a negligence cause of action and the standard defenses raised against it.

8. *The investigator must network regularly.* There is a good deal of practical information that investigators need to have about the area in which they work. At the court clerk's office, for example, which employee is most helpful? If you want something done at city hall, whom do you see? What government agencies provide good service? **Networking** with numerous individuals, particularly other paralegals, is an excellent way to answer such questions.

FACT ANALYSIS: ORGANIZING THE OPTIONS

One of the hallmarks of a good investigator, and indeed of all paralegals, is the ability to organize facts, or more accurately, to organize *versions* of facts. Carolyn Saenz, a veteran Ohio paralegal, says, "I've become quite good at reading body language and listening to people. It's amazing how many different versions of one story can be told."[9]

A number of fundamental characteristics of facts should be kept in mind:

- Events take place.
- Events mean different things to different people.
- Different people, therefore, can have different versions of events.
- Inconsistent versions of the same event do not necessarily indicate fraud or lying.
- Although someone's version may claim to be the total picture, it probably will contain only a piece of the picture.
- In giving a version of an event, people may mix statements of why the event occurred (e.g., he wanted to retaliate for being fired) with statements of what occurred (he was terminated on May 1st). Or worse, they may tailor their description of what happened to fit the version that they wish occurred.
- In giving a version of an event, people may mix *observed facts* (what they directly experienced through the senses, e.g., I saw him get in the car) and **inferences** (conclusions reached about the facts, e.g., he lost control of the car because of his speed).
- Whenever it is claimed that an event occurred in a certain way, one can logically expect that certain signs, indications, or traces (evidence) of the event can be found.

Given these truisms, you should plan an investigation along the lines indicated in Exhibit 9-2.

It is possible for a single client's case to have numerous individual facts that are in dispute. Furthermore, facts can change, or people's versions of facts can change in the middle of a case. Each new or modified fact requires the same comprehensive process of fact analysis outlined in Exhibit 9-2.

Exhibit 9-2	Planning an Investigation: Fact Versions

Starting Point

All the facts you currently have on the case:
- Arrange the facts chronologically.
- Place a number before each fact that may have to be established in a legal proceeding.

State the Following Versions of Each Fact

Version I: The client's
Version II: The opponent's (as revealed to you or as assumed)
Version III: A witness's
Version IV: Another witness's
Version V: Any other reasonable version (e.g., from your own deductions)

As to Each Version
- State precisely (using quotes if available) what the version is.
- State the evidence or indications that tend to support the version according to persons presenting the version.
- State the evidence or indications that tend to contradict this version.
- Determine how you will verify or corroborate the evidence or indications.

Of course, not every fact will necessarily have multiple versions. It is recommended, however, that you assume there will be more than one version until you have demonstrated otherwise to yourself.

Obtaining different versions of a fact is sometimes difficult because the differences may not be clear on the surface. People will not always be willing to share their accounts or versions of facts with you. If you are not successful in convincing them to tell their story, you may have to make assumptions of what their story is likely to be and then check out these assumptions. In short, you will have to do some probing to uncover the versions that exist. Better to do so now than for the office to be confronted with a surprise at trial or at an agency hearing.

DISTORTIONS IN INVESTIGATION

Investigators are not mere newspaper reporters or photographers who simply report what they see, hear, or otherwise experience. You have a much more dynamic role. In a very significant sense, you sometimes have the power to influence what someone else says about the facts. This can have both positive and negative consequences.

1. *Leading questions.* Be alert to the danger of asking questions in such a manner that you are putting words into someone's mouth. The primary technique that can bring about this result is the **leading question**, which suggests an answer in the statement of the question. For example, "You were in Baltimore at the time, isn't that correct?" "You earn over $200 a week?" "Would it be fair to say that when you drove up to the curb, you didn't see the light?" (For more on the different kinds of questions that can be asked, see Exhibit 8-11 in Chapter 8.)

Questions can intentionally or unintentionally manipulate someone's answer by including a premise that has yet to be established. It sometimes takes an alert person to say to such questions, "I can't answer your question (or it is invalid) because it assumes another fact that

leading question A question that suggests an answer within the question.

I haven't agreed to." In the following examples of questions and answers, the person responding to the question refuses to be trapped by the form of the question:

Q: How much did it cost you to have your car repaired after the accident?
A: It's not my car and it wasn't an accident; your client deliberately ran into the car that I rented.

Q: Can you tell me what you saw?
A: I didn't see anything; my brother was there and he told me what happened.

Suppose that a different answer had been given to the last question:

Q: Can you tell me what you saw?
A: The car was going about 70 mph.

In fact, the person answering the question did not see this himself; his brother told him that a
car was traveling at this speed. This person may have failed to tell the investigator that he did
not see anything first hand for a number of reasons:

- Perhaps he did not hear the word "saw" in the investigator's question.
- He may have wanted the investigator to think that he saw something himself; he may
  want to feel important by conveying the impression that he is special because he has
  special information.
- He may have felt that correcting the investigator's false assumption was not important
  because the investigator was more interested in what happened than in who saw what
  happened.

Whatever the reason, the investigator has carelessly put him or herself in the position of miss-
ing a potentially critical fact, namely, that the person is talking from second-hand knowledge.
Before asking what the person "saw," the investigator should ask, "Were you there?" and if so,
"Did you see anything?"

2. *The use of definite articles in the question.* Be careful about the use of the definite article
   ("the") and the indefinite articles ("a" or "an") in the way you phrase a question. "Research
   indicates the wording of questions to witnesses significantly affects their recall. For example, more uncertain or 'don't know' responses are given if a witness is asked about an
   indefinite item (e.g., 'Did you see *a* knife?') than occurs when the question contains a
   definite article ('Did you see *the* knife?')."[10]
3. *Questions not asked.* Communication is often blurred when the questioner concentrates
   on some themes to the exclusion of others. If you do not ask questions about certain
   matters, intentionally or otherwise, you are likely to end up with a distorted picture
   of a person's version of the facts. For example, assume that Smith and Jones have an
   automobile collision. The investigator, working for the attorney who represents Jones,
   finds a witness who says that she saw the accident. The investigator asks her to describe what she saw, but fails to ask her where she was at the time she saw the collision.
   In fact, she was sitting in a park more than two blocks away and could see the collision
   only through some shrubbery. The investigator did not ask questions to uncover this
   information and it was not volunteered. The investigator, therefore, walked away with
   a potentially distorted idea of how much light this individual could shed on what took
   place. This is similar to the distortion that can result from the use of questions that
   contain an unestablished premise.
4. *Jarring the memory and uncooperative witnesses.* In some instances, however, questions
   that would otherwise distort can have beneficial results. For example, a leading question might help jar someone's memory, making a shy or inarticulate person better
   able to recall the facts. If, however, this person constantly needs leading questions in
   order to remember, you have strong reason to suspect that the person knows little or
   nothing.

Suppose a witness is uncooperative or has a version of the facts that is damaging to the
client of the investigator's office. It may be that the techniques described in this section can
be used to challenge a version of the facts. A leading question with an unestablished premise,

for example, may catch an individual off guard and give the investigator reasonable cause to believe that the person is not telling the truth.

If you doubt someone's willingness to tell you what he or she knows, a leading statement or question might be helpful in ferreting out additional facts. "A technique I've found very successful is to ask a question I feel will evoke a factual answer. For example, I would ask Mr. John Doe, 'Mr. Doe, you claim that you are a witness to the accident when, in fact, I understand you were not in a position to see everything that happened.' Often, the person will respond with a defensive answer similar to, 'I was in a position to see everything,' and then continue to tell me their location and what they saw."[11]

SOURCES OF EVIDENCE/SOURCES OF LEADS

As we have seen, evidence is anything offered to establish the existence or nonexistence of a fact in dispute. Exhibit 9-3 presents a partial checklist of some of the standard sources of evidence—or leads to such evidence. Of course, once evidence is identified, it often becomes its own lead to further evidence.

Exhibit 9-3	Checklist of Standard Sources of Evidence and Leads

(Some of the records in this list are online. For Web addresses, see Helpful Websites at the end of the chapter.)

- Statements of the client
- Documents the client brings or can obtain
- Information that may be voluntarily provided by the opposing attorney
- Information involuntarily provided by the other side through discovery (see Exhibit 9-1)
- Information from the attorneys involved with the case in the past
- Accounts of eyewitnesses
- Postings on Facebook, LinkedIn, Twitter, and other social media sites
- Hearsay accounts (see discussion of hearsay later in the chapter)
- Letters requesting information
- Pleadings (e.g., complaints) filed thus far in the case
- Other court records (e.g., abstracts of judgments, liens, unlawful detainers)
- Newspaper accounts (available online)
- Public records of municipal, state, and federal administrative agencies (see Helpful Websites at the end of the chapter for public-records sites)
- Business records (e.g., canceled receipts)
- Fictitious business name records (often filed with the secretary of state or the state corporations office)
- Death, marriage, and divorce records (on Google, Bing, or Yahoo, run this search: "vital records" aa, substituting the name of your state for "aa")
- Bureau of vital statistics and missing persons
- Autopsy reports
- Employment records, including job applications
- Photographs
- Hospital records
- Informers
- Surveillance of the scene
- Reports from the police and other law enforcement agencies (see Exhibit 9-4)
- Fingerprints
- School records
- Military records (www.archives.gov/veterans/military-service-records)
- Use of aliases
- Weather reports
- Professional license records (see Helpful Websites at the end of the chapter for public-records sites)
- Hunting and fishing permit records
- Weapons permit records
- Voter registration records
- County election records (e.g., for information on political contributions)
- Workers' compensation records
- Office of politicians
- Records of Better Business Bureaus and consumer groups
- Telephone books
- *Polk City Directory* (www.citydirectory.com/polk)
- Reverse phone directory
- Boat registry
- Automobile records (DMV; VIN number searches)
- County assessor (for real property)
- Tax assessor's office
- Post office (record of forwarding addresses)
- Object to be traced (such as an auto)
- Credit bureaus
- Reports of investigative agencies
- Associations (trade, professional, etc.)
- *Who's Who* directories
- Insurance Company Clearing House
- Standard and Poor's *Register of Directors and Executives*
- Telling your problem to a more experienced investigator and asking for other leads
- Shots in the dark

Exhibit 9-4	Request for a Copy of Police Accident Report

(On the value of this report in the investigation of an accident, see the beginning of Exhibit 9-11 on auto accident analysis later in the chapter.)

Form CR-91
(Rev. 08/14)
Page 1 of 1

REQUEST FOR COPY OF
PEACE OFFICER'S CRASH REPORT

Mail To: Crash Data and Analysis, Texas Department of Transportation, P.O. Box 12879, Austin, Texas 78711

Make check or M.O. payable to: Texas Department of Transportation   **Questions? Call:** 512/486-5780

CHECK TYPE OF SERVICE DESIRED:

☐ Copy of Peace Officer's Crash Report - $6.00 each   ☐ Certified Copy of Peace Officer's Crash Report - $8.00 each

DATE OF REQUEST   **CLAIM OR POLICY NO.**

Transportation Code, Sec.550.065. **RELEASE OF CRASH REPORTS.** (b) Except as provided by Subsection (c), a crash report held by the department is privileged and for the confidential use of: the department; and an agency of the United States, this state, or a local government of this state having use for the report for crash prevention purposes. (c) allows release of a crash report on written request and payment of required fee: (4) a person who provides the department or law enforcement agency with two or more of the following: date of the crash; the name of any person involved; the specific location of the crash.

Please provide as accurate and complete information as possible.

CRASH DATE

MONTH/DAY/YEAR

CRASH LOCATION

COUNTY   CITY   STREET OR HIGHWAY

WAS ANYONE KILLED IN THE CRASH?   IF SO, NAME OF ONE DECEASED

INVESTIGATING AGENCY AND/OR OFFICER'S NAME (if known)

DRIVER'S FULL NAME	DRIVER INFORMATION (if available)		ADDRESS (if available)
	DATE OF BIRTH	TEXAS DL NUMBER	

PASSENGER'S FULL NAME	PEDESTRIAN or PEDALCYCLIST (if available)	ADDRESS (if available)

* Texas Statute allows the investigating officer 10 days in which to submit his/her report.
* Requests should not be submitted until at least 10 days after the crash date to allow time for receipt of the report.
* The Law also provides that if an officer's report is not on file when a request for a copy of such report is received, a certification to that effect will be provided in lieu of the copy and the fee will be retained for the certification.

Source: Texas Department of Transportation (www.txdot.gov/driver/laws/crash-reports.html). To obtain a copy of an accident report in your state, run this search in Google, Bing, or Yahoo: accident crash police report aa (substituting your state for "aa").

GAINING ACCESS TO RECORDS

Gaining access to records can sometimes be difficult. There are four categories of records you may need to examine on behalf of a client:

- Those already in the possession of a client or an individual willing to turn them over to you on request
- Those in the possession of a governmental agency (see Exhibits 9-5 and 9-6) or of a private organization and available to anyone in the public
- Those in the possession of a governmental agency or of a private organization and available only to the client or to the individual who is the subject of the records
- Those in the possession of a governmental agency or of a private organization and claimed to be confidential except for in-house staff

Obviously, there should be no difficulty in gaining access to the first category of records unless they have been misplaced or lost, in which event the person who once had possession would ask the source of the records to provide another copy. As to records in the latter three categories, the checklist in Exhibit 9-5 should provide some guidelines on gaining access, including use of the **Freedom of Information Act (FOIA)** or other **sunshine laws** for government records.

Freedom of Information Act (FOIA) A statute that gives public access to certain information in the possession of the government. There is a FOIA for the federal government (www.foia .gov) (5 U.S.C. § 552) and equivalent FOIAs for state and local governments (www.nfoic.org).

sunshine laws A statute that requires some government agencies to have open meetings and to provide public access to designated public records.

Exhibit 9-5	Guidelines for Gaining Access to Records

1. Write, phone, or visit the organization and ask for the record.
2. Have the client write, phone, or visit and ask for the record. If needed, draft a letter for the client to sign that asks for it.
3. Have the client sign a form stating that he or she gives you authority to see any records that pertain to him or her and that he or she specifically waives any right to confidentiality with respect to such records. (For special HIPAA rules and forms pertaining to the privacy of medical records, see www.hhs.gov/ocr/hipaa.)
4. Find out if one of the opposing parties has the record, and if so, ask his or her attorney to send you a copy. (Caution: Do not directly ask a represented opposing party for a copy. As we saw in Chapter 5, it is unethical to contact an opponent without permission of the latter's attorney.) Once a lawsuit has begun, it is often possible to obtain copies of records through discovery methods such as a request for production (RFP).
5. Find out if someone else has it (e.g., a relative of the client or a co-defendant in this or a prior court case) and ask that person if he or she will provide you with a copy. (If the co-defendant has separate counsel, the request must be made to his or her attorney.)
6. For records available to the public, find out where these records are and go use them. For government records, check the Internet site of the government agency that has the records. Find out if they are available online at this site. (See the public-records sites in the section on Helpful Websites at the end of the chapter.)
7. If you meet resistance, make a basic fairness pitch to the organization as to why you need the records.
8. Find out (by legal research) if there are statutes, administrative regulations, or cases that arguably provide the client with the right of access to records kept by government agencies. Access may be available through the federal or state Freedom of Information Act (FOIA) (see Exhibit 9-6). Go to the Internet site of the federal or state agency that has the records you need. Find out if the site provides instructions on filing a FOIA request at that agency. Try typing "freedom of information" in the search box of the agency. See also the sites on the Freedom of Information in Helpful Websites at the end of the chapter.
9. If the first person at the agency turns down the request for access, appeal the decision formally or informally to his or her supervisor, and up the chain of command to the person with final authority. The websites of agencies usually indicate the names of department or bureau heads to whom you can address your appeal.
10. Solicit the intervention of a politician or some other respected and independent person in trying to gain access.
11. Let the organization know that your office is considering (or is preparing) a suit to establish a right to the record (when this is so).

Exhibit 9-6	Sample Freedom of Information Act (FOIA) Letter

Agency Head or FOIA Officer
Title
Name of Government Agency
Address of Agency
City, State, Zip

Re: Freedom of Information Act (FOIA) Request

Dear FOIA officer:

Please send me copies of [describe the documents or information you seek in as much detail as possible. Include any file names or numbers, if applicable.]
I agree to pay all necessary costs associated with this request.

[or]

I agree to pay all necessary costs up to the amount of $xx.00. Please contact me if you expect the costs will exceed that amount.

If you deny all or any part of this request, please cite each specific exemption you think justifies your refusal to release the information and notify me of appeal procedures available under the law.

Sincerely,

Your name, address, and phone

Source: Adapted from Office of the Missouri Attorney General (www.ago.mo.gov/sunshinelaw/requestform.htm). For FOIA resources in your state, see www.nfoic.org.

EVALUATING EVIDENCE

parol evidence Evidence of an oral statement.

tangible evidence Physical evidence; evidence that has a physical form. Evidence that can be seen and inspected. *Intangible evidence* (e.g., a right or belief) is evidence without physical form. Intangible evidence is sometimes embodied or evidenced by something physical, e.g., a written contract.

At all times, you must make value judgments on the usefulness of **parol evidence** (oral) and **tangible evidence** (physical) that you come across. A number of specific criteria can be used to assist you in assessing the worth of what you have. The checklists in Exhibits 9-7 and 9-8 can help in determining this worth.

Most people overrate the value of eyewitness evidence. In one experiment, over 2,000 persons were shown a thirteen-second video of a mugging. They were then shown a lineup of six persons and asked to identify the perpetrator. Only 13 percent were able to do so correctly. In another experiment, 150 college students were shown videos of a shooting followed by a five-person lineup. Every student identified a suspect even though the perpetrator was not in the lineup.[12] Commenting on the frailty of our attention span and memory, a judge pointed out how often one dinner partner will turn to another halfway through a meal and ask, "Is that our waiter?"[13]

Exhibit 9-7	Checklist on Evaluating Parol (Oral) Evidence

CHECKLIST ON EVALUATING THE BELIEVABILITY OF A STATEMENT MADE BY A PERSON WHO IS SPEAKING FROM FIRST-HAND (EYEWITNESS) OBSERVATION

Example: Ed tells you about a fight he saw on a bus.

- How long ago did the event (the fight) occur?
- How good is the memory of this person (Ed)?
- How far from the event was Ed at the time?
- How good is Ed's eyesight? (Does he wear glasses?)
- What time of day was it and would this affect vision?
- What was the weather at the time and would this affect vision?
- Was there a lot of commotion at the time and would this or similar distractions affect vision or ability to remember?
- What was Ed doing immediately before the incident?

CHECKLIST ON EVALUATING THE BELIEVABILITY OF A STATEMENT MADE BY A PERSON WHO IS RELAYING WHAT SOMEONE ELSE (THE DECLARANT) HAS SAID

Example: At a restaurant, Mary tells you that John told her he was sick with the flu last May. John is the declarant (the person who has made a statement we are evaluating).

- How well does the person (Mary) remember what the declarant (John) told her?
- How sure is Mary of what John said?
- Is John now available to confirm or deny what Mary says he told her? If not, why not?
- Under what conditions did John allegedly make the statement (e.g., was John healthy at the time)?

- How old is Ed?
- What was the last grade of school he completed?
- What is Ed's employment background?
- What is the Ed's reputation for truthfulness?
- Was Ed ever convicted of a crime? Are any criminal charges now pending against him?
- Does Ed have technical expertise or other qualifications relevant to what he is saying?
- Is Ed related to, an employee of, or friendly with either side in the litigation? Would it be to Ed's benefit, in any way, to see either side win?
- Does any direct evidence exist to corroborate (confirm) what Ed is saying?
- Does any hearsay evidence exist to corroborate it?
- Is Ed defensive when asked about what he knows?
- Are there any inconsistencies in what he is saying?
- How does he react when confronted with the inconsistencies? Defensively?
- Are there any gaps in what Ed is saying?
- Does Ed appear to exaggerate?
- Does he appear to be hiding or holding anything back?
- Is he willing to sign a statement covering what he tells the investigator? Is he willing to say it in court?

- Does any direct or indirect evidence exist to corroborate that John had the flu in May?
- How old is Mary? How old is John?
- What are the educational and employment backgrounds of both?
- What is their reputation for truthfulness?
- Was either ever convicted of a crime? Are any criminal charges pending against either?
- Does Mary or John have technical expertise or other qualifications relevant to what was said?
- Is Mary or John related to, an employee of, or friendly with either side in the litigation? Would it be to the benefit of Mary or John to see either side win?
- Is Mary defensive when asked about what John told her?
- Are there any inconsistencies in what Mary is saying?
- How does Mary react when confronted with the inconsistencies? Defensively?
- Are there any gaps in what Mary is saying?
- Does she appear to exaggerate?
- Does she appear to be hiding or holding anything back?
- Is Mary willing to sign a statement covering what she says John told her? Is she willing to say it in court?

Exhibit 9-8	Checklist on Evaluating Tangible (Physical) Evidence

CHECKLIST ON EVALUATING SOMETHING THAT IS WRITTEN

- Who wrote it?
- Under what circumstances was it written?
- Is the original available? If not, why not?
- Is a copy available?
- Who is available to testify that the copy is in fact an accurate copy of the original?
- Is the alleged author available to testify about what he or she wrote? If not, why not?
- Is there any other available evidence to corroborate (confirm) the authenticity of the writing, namely that it was written by that person?
- What doubts exist, if any, about the accuracy of statements made in the writing?
- What evidence is available to corroborate or contradict what is said in the writing?
- Can you obtain sample handwriting specimens of the alleged author?
- Who found it and under what circumstances?

CHECKLIST ON EVALUATING NONWRITTEN MATERIAL

- What is it (e.g., jewelry, cash, weapon, clothing, vehicle, drugs)?
- Where was it found?
- Why would it be where it was found? Was it unusual to find it there?
- Who is available to identify it?
- What identifying characteristics does it have?
- Who owns it? Who used it?
- Who owned it in the past? Who used it in the past? Who has had possession?
- Who made it?
- What is its purpose?
- Does it require laboratory analysis?
- Is it stolen?
- Is there any public record available to trace its history?
- What facts does it tend to establish?
- Was it planted where it was found as a decoy?

INTERVIEWING WITNESSES

Francis Ritter, a seasoned investigator, tells us that there are six parts to every conversation: three for the speaker and three for the listener.

For the speaker:

- What the speaker wants to say,
- What the speaker actually says, and
- What the speaker thinks he or she said.

For the listener:

- What the listener wants to hear,
- What the listener actually heard, and
- What the listener thinks he or she heard.[14]

Keep these sobering observations in mind as we examine the following guidelines that apply to all witness interviews:

1. *Whenever possible, interview a witness with no other potential witnesses present.* If other people are in the room when you interview a witness, they are likely to be influenced by what the witness says. If two people have different versions of an event, you are more likely to find this out if you talk to each one separately than if they are together. Of course, this may not always be possible. A witness may be uncomfortable talking with you alone and, indeed, you may feel safer if others are present. Do the best you can under such circumstances. Later you may be able to telephone them individually to ask that they clarify something they said earlier. This might increase the chance you will obtain an account that is uninfluenced by what others have said.

2. *Know what image you are projecting of yourself.* In the minds of some people, an investigator is often involved in serious and dangerous undertakings. How would you react if a stranger introduced himself or herself to you as an investigator? This might cause some people to be guarded and suspicious, so you may not want to call yourself an investigator. You may want to say, "My name is ___, I work for (name of law office), and we are trying to get information on ___ ."

   Can you think of different people who would respond more readily to certain images of investigators? The following is a partial list of some of the images that an investigator could be projecting by dress, mannerisms, approach, and language:

   - A professional
   - Someone who is just doing a job
   - Someone who is emotionally involved in what he or she is doing
   - A neutral bystander
   - A friend
   - A manipulator or opportunist
   - A salesperson
   - A wise person
   - An innocent and shy person

   You must be aware of (a) your own need to project yourself in a certain way, (b) the way in which you think you are projecting yourself, (c) the way in which the person to whom you are talking perceives you, and (d) the effect that all this is having on what you are trying to accomplish.

   Here is how one paralegal, Janet Jackson, describes her approach:

   [The] basic techniques are to approach the person as a friend, make him or her feel comfortable talking, and gain his or her trust. One simple way of doing this is using the principle that people respond to their names. I address the contact by name several times throughout the interview. I also use a friendly, soft, nonthreatening, inquisitive tone of voice. The first few moments … are always the most difficult and the most important. Usually in these few moments the contact makes the decision whether to talk. So, a strong opening is needed. I plan, write out, and practice my opening so I can deliver it smoothly and quickly in a friendly, confident voice…. I say, "Hello, Mr. Jones, my name is Janet Jackson and I work for the law firm of X, Y & Z. We have been retained by the T. Company to represent them in a lawsuit brought against them by Mr. John Smith. I would like to ask you a few questions about the lawsuit…." I then identify myself as a legal assistant and explain that I am collecting information. Often I have found that saying "I am a legal assistant, not an attorney," causes people to relax and let down their guard.[15]

3. *There are five main kinds of witnesses: hostile, skeptical, friendly, disinterested or neutral, and a combination of the above.* Hostile witnesses want your client to lose; they may try to set up roadblocks in your way. Skeptical witnesses are not sure who you are or what you want in spite of your explanation of your role. They are guarded and unsure whether they want to become involved. Friendly witnesses want your client to win and will cooperate fully. **Disinterested** or neutral witnesses do not care who wins. They have information that they are usually willing to tell anyone who asks. Hostile and friendly witnesses have probably prejudged the case. They may be incapable of examining all the facts dispassionately; they are already inclined to think or act in a certain way. They have a **bias**. Friendly witnesses may have a bias—in your favor.

disinterested (1) Not working for one side or the other in a controversy. (2) Not deriving benefit if one side of a dispute wins or loses; objective.

bias (1) An inclination, tendency, or predisposition to think or act in a certain way. (2) Prejudice for or against something or someone. (3) A danger of prejudgment.

If the hostile witness is the opposing party who has retained counsel, it is unethical for the investigator to talk directly with this person without going through his or her attorney (see Chapter 5 for a discussion of the **anticontact rule**). If the opposing party is not represented by an attorney, check with your supervisor on how, if at all, to approach this party. Never do anything to give an unrepresented party the impression that you are disinterested.

To complicate matters, it must be acknowledged that witnesses are seldom totally hostile, skeptical, friendly, or neutral. At different times during the investigation interview, and at different times throughout the various stages of the case, they may shift from one attitude to another. Although it may be helpful to determine the general category that witnesses fit into, it would be more realistic to view witnesses as individuals in a state of flux in terms of what they are capable of saying and what they want to say. In view of this reality, it is usually recommended that a witness statement be taken soon after the incident in question whenever possible. (Witness statements are discussed later in the chapter.) This helps offset the danger of a witness changing his or her story at a later date.

4. *The investigator must have the trust of the witness.* You have the sometimes-difficult threshold problem of sizing up the witness from whom you are trying to obtain information. Here are some of the states of mind that witnesses could have:

   ■ They want to feel important.
   ■ They want to be "congratulated" for knowing anything, however insignificant, about the case.
   ■ They want absolute assurance from you that they will not get into trouble by talking to you. They shy away from talk of courts, lawyers, and law.
   ■ They are willing to talk only after you have given full assurance that you will not reveal the source of the information they give you.
   ■ They are willing to talk to you only in the presence of their friends.
   ■ If they know your client, they want to be told that you are trying to keep the client out of trouble.
   ■ They want the chance to meet you first and then have you go away so that they can decide whether they want to talk to you again.
   ■ They are not willing to talk to you until you fulfill some of their needs, e.g., listen to their troubles or act in a fatherly or motherly manner.

   In short, the investigator must gain the trust of individuals by assessing their needs and by knowing when they are ready to tell you what they know. To establish communication, sensitivity to such undercurrents is often required. The most effective approach may not be to take out your notebook immediately upon introducing yourself. What are often needed are persistence, the right tone, and the right language. This is amply demonstrated by Minnesota paralegal Deborah Rohan, who describes how she handles someone who is initially reluctant to talk with her: "I tell him I'm not going to try to sway him to either side of the issues. I say … I just want to get the facts. If that doesn't work, I say 'Okay, I won't formally interview you, but could I ask you a few questions?' Often the person will consent to that."[16] Similarly, Deborah Andrews, a New Jersey paralegal, says she obtains better results when she avoids using the word *witness*. "Do not ask if the person was a witness— simply ask what they know of the incident."[17]

5. *The investigator should assess how well the witness would do under direct examination and cross- examination.* As witnesses talk, ask yourself a number of questions and be prepared to let your supervisor know your answers to these questions:

   ■ Would they be effective on the witness stand if they agreed to testify or if they were **subpoenaed**?
   ■ Do they know what they are talking about?
   ■ Do they have a reputation for integrity and truthfulness?
   ■ Are they defensive?
   ■ Would they know how to say "I'm not sure" or "I don't understand the question," as opposed to giving an answer for the sake of giving an answer or to avoid being embarrassed?
   ■ When they talk, are they internally consistent?
   ■ Do they know how to listen as well as talk?
   ■ Do they understand the distinction between right and wrong, truth and lying?

anticontact rule
An advocate must not contact an opposing party without permission of the latter's attorney. Also called *no-contact rule*.

subpoena (1) To command that someone appear at a certain time and place. (2) A command to appear at a certain time and place.

SPECIAL INVESTIGATIVE PROBLEMS

JUDGMENT COLLECTION; LOCATING ASSETS

judgment creditor The
person who wins and
therefore has a right to
collect a money judgment.

judgment debtor The
person who loses and
therefore must pay a money
judgment.

The person who wins a money judgment in court is called the **judgment creditor**. Unfortunately, collecting that judgment can be a difficult undertaking. An investigator may be asked to assist the law firm in ascertaining the financial assets of a particular individual or corporation against whom the judgment was obtained, called the **judgment debtor**.

One of the best starting points for such an investigation is government records. The following is a partial list of records available from the county clerk or court office:

- Real property records (check grantee and grantor indexes)
- Real and personal property tax assessments
- Filings made under the Uniform Commercial Code (UCC)
- Federal tax liens
- Court dockets to determine whether the judgment debtor has been a plaintiff or defendant in prior litigation (check the abstract-of-judgment index)
- Inheritance records to determine whether the judgment debtor has inherited money or other property (determined by checking records of the surrogate's court or probate court, which handles inheritance and trust cases)

Any of these records could reveal a good deal of information on the financial status of people you are investigating. You might find out whether they own or have an interest in valuable personal or business property. Even though tax records often undervalue the property being taxed, they are some indication of a person's wealth. Another indication is the existence of past suits against the party. If a party has been sued in the past, someone made a determination that he or she probably had a **deep pocket** at that time, meaning sufficient assets to satisfy a judgment.

deep pocket (1) An
individual, a business, or
another organization with
resources to pay a potential
judgment. (2) Sufficient
assets for this purpose. The
opposite of *shallow pocket*.

For corporations that are judgment debtors, check the records of state and federal government agencies (such as the state Secretary of State and the federal Securities and Exchange Commission [SEC]) with whom the corporation must file periodic reports or disclosures on its activities and finances. You should also check with people who have done business with the corporation (customers or other creditors) as well as with its competitors in the field. These records and contacts could provide leads.

A great deal of this information is now online so that it can be searched through computers. For resources available on the Internet (paid and free), see Helpful Websites at the end of the chapter. In Exhibit 9-9 you will find examples of some of the major databases and libraries available on Westlaw (WestlawNext) and LexisNexis (Lexis Advance), the two largest fee-based online commercial research services. Even if you do not have access to these services (they are expensive to use), reading the following overview will give you a good idea of the kinds of data that law firms try to obtain. The data are valuable when conducting *due diligence* investigations, such as when you need to verify the information given by a prospective business associate.

Exhibit 9-9	**Examples of Financial Data on Fee-Based Databases (Westlaw and Lexis-Nexis)**

DUE DILIGENCE SEARCHES ON WESTLAW (WESTLAWNEXT)

Asset Locator (ASSET). Identifies real property tax assessor records, real property transaction records, pre-foreclosure records, unclaimed property records, aircraft records, watercraft records, and corporation stock records.

Executive Affiliation Records (EA–ALL). Provides name, title, business address, and phone number of millions of executives nationwide.

Uniform Commercial Code (UCC) Provides information on UCC filings, which can include debtor names and addresses, filing numbers, dates of filing, secured parties and assignees, status, filing locations, collateral, filing histories, and tax liens.

Dun & Bradstreet Business Records Plus (DUNBR). Provides information on a company's history, operations, and financial performance as well as intracompany relationships for millions of companies worldwide.

Combined Corporate and Business Registration Records (CORP–ALL). Provides abstracts of business addresses; officers, directors, and partners; and location of registered agents.

Bankruptcy Filings (BKR–ALL). Provides summaries (abstracts) of filings in U.S. bankruptcy courts. Includes business filings in all 50 states and personal filings in selected states.

Lawsuits (LS). Provides abstracts of civil lawsuits filed in selected state and local courts.

Dow Jones–All Plus Wires (ALLNEWSPLUS). Provides business news reports from newspapers, magazines, journals, newsletters, government press releases, transcripts of television shows, radio shows, congressional testimony, and newswires.

DUE DILIGENCE SEARCHES ON LEXIS-NEXIS (LEXIS ADVANCE)

ASSETS (DEEDS) (ALLOWN). Provides leads to the location and assessed value of corporate and individual real estate, hidden assets, parties and witnesses, and current tax mailing addresses for service of process. Also assesses the collectability of judgments, and locates property for judgment lien attachment.

Bankruptcy (INSOLV) (ALLBKT). Provides business and consumer bankruptcy filings; background data on parties, witnesses, and judgment debtors; tracks business and consumer bankruptcies; and helps assess the collectability of potential judgments.

Business Filings (INCORP). Provides access to state and local business filings, including corporate registrations, limited partnership registrations, limited liability company registrations, county d/b/a (doing business as) filings, and professional licenses.

Business Reports (BUSRPT). Provides business reports from Dun & Bradstreet and Experian that will help establish a company's existence, assess financial performance, ascertain client solvency, and confirm company ownership for determining potential conflicts of interest.

Courts (DOCKET). Provides information from civil and criminal court indexes and dockets from local and federal courts.

Liens (ALLUCC) (ALLIEN). Provides information on Uniform Commercial Code (UCC) liens, state and federal tax liens, and judgments from state courts. The data contain debtor names, addresses, secured parties, assignees, and types of pledged collateral.

License (LICNSE). Provides information on professional licenses, liquor licenses, driver licenses, pilots, tax practitioners, etc. This information helps locate self-employed individuals, verify their license status, and locate their business assets.

Personal Property (P–PROP). Provides information from registrations of boats, motor vehicles, and aircraft.

Verdicts and Settlements (ALLVER). Provides information on civil verdicts and settlements from the databases of National Jury Verdict Review & Analysis (NTLREV); Verdicts, Settlement & Tactics (VERST); and Medical Litigation Alert (MDALRT).

MISSING PERSONS

An investigator may be asked to locate a missing heir, a relative of a client, a person who must be served with process in connection with current litigation, etc. A missing person is generally not difficult to locate—unless this person does not want to be found.

A number of effective locator or skiptracing services are available online. For Internet resources (free and fee-based), see the section on "Finding People" in Helpful Websites at the end of the chapter. The major fee-based databases also have powerful finding tools:

- Westlaw (WestlawNext): People Finder (PEOPLE-FIND); PeopleMap
- LexisNexis (Lexis Advance): FINDER (EZFIND, P-TRAK, P-FIND, B-FIND, P-SEEK, DCEASE)

The Social Security Administration will not disclose personal information on recipients. Knowing the person's social security number, however, might provide a clue. Before 2011, the first three digits of a social security number (called the area number) indicated the state in which the card was issued. For example:

545–573	California	010–034	Massachusetts	540–544	Oregon
602–626	California	362–386	Michigan	159–211	Pennsylvania
261–267	Florida	468–477	Minnesota	449–467	Texas
589–595	Florida	135–158	New Jersey	627–645	Texas
318–361	Illinois	050–134	New York	387–399	Wisconsin
212–220	Maryland	268–302	Ohio		

For more, see "Social Security Numbers and States" in Helpful Websites at the end of the chapter. People who "disappear" sometimes return to the state where they grew up, which often is the state where they obtained their social security card.

Local libraries sometimes make old telephone directories available online or in print. John Lehe, a legal investigator, suggests that you begin with the easily available resources: telephone books and directory assistance operators. "In contacting directory assistance operators, ask for telephone numbers for anyone with the same last name on the street of the last known address. It is possible for relatives to live on the same street and they may be able to provide the [missing person's] current address or place of employment."[18]

Check online for criss-cross or cross-reference directories, sometimes known as *reverse look up*. They may allow you to obtain an address if you have a phone number or vice versa. If all you have is the address of a person, they may also allow you to find out who lives at that address, plus his or her surrounding neighbors.

Try sending a registered letter to the person's last known address, "return receipt requested," which asks the post office to send you back a notice with the signature of the person who signed to receive the letter.

BACKGROUND INVESTIGATIONS

Exhibit 9-10 presents a form used by a large investigative firm for its general background investigations on individuals.

Exhibit 9-10	Background Investigations

Identification of Subject

1. Complete Name_____ Age_____ SS#_____ Marital Status _____
   Spouse's Name; Pertinent Info _____

   Children's Names and Ages _____

2. Current Residence Address and Type of Neighborhood _____

   Prior Residence Info _____

3. Business Affiliation and Address, Position, Type of Bus. _____

Antecedent History

1. Place & Date of Birth_____
   Parents' Names & Occupations _____

   Where Did They Spend Their Youth? _____

2. Education—Where, Which Schools, Dates of Attendance _____

   Degree? What Kind?_____ Any Other Info Pertaining to Scholastic Achievement, Extracurric.
   Activities _____

3. First Employer, to Present—F/T or P/T, Position or Title, Job Description, Exact Dates of Employment, Type
   of Company _____

4. Relationship with Peers, Supervisors, Subordinates—Where Do Subj.'s Abilities Lie? Any Outside Activities? Reputation
   for Honesty, Trustworthiness, Integrity? Does Subj. Work Well under Pressure? Anything Derogatory? Reasons for
   Leaving? Would They Rehire? Salaries? Health? Reliability? Job Understanding? Willingness to Accept Responsibility?

If Self-Employed—What Was the Nature of the Business? With Whom Did Subj. Deal? Corp. Name?

_____

Date & Place of Incorporation _____

Who Were Partners, If Any? _____

What % of Stock Did Subj. Own? _____ Was Business Successful? _____ What Happened to it? _____

If Sold, to Whom? _____

Any Subsid. or Affiliates? _____

_____

_____

5. What is Subj.'s Character or Personality Like? Did Informer Know Subj. Personally?

_____

Hobbies? _____

Family Life? _____

Even-Tempered? _____ Loner or Joiner? _____

Introverted, Extroverted? _____ Written or Oral Abilities? _____

Does Informer Know Anyone Else Who Knows Subj.? _____

6. Credit Information _____

_____

_____

7. Subj.'s Involvement in Litigation _____ Civil _____ Criminal _____ Bankruptcy _____

State _____ Federal _____ Local _____

_____

8. Banking—Financial: Bank _____

Types of Accounts—Average Bal. _____

How Long Did Subj. Have Accounts? _____ Any Company Accounts? _____

_____

Is Subj. Personally Known to Officers of the Bank? _____ Any Borrowing? _____

Secured or Unsecured? _____ If Secured, by What? _____

Do They Have Financial Statement on the Subj.? _____

What Is Net Worth of Subj.? _____ Other Assets? Real Estate _____

Stocks _____

Equity in Subj.'s Co., etc. _____

AUTOMOBILE ACCIDENT INVESTIGATIONS

A great deal of precision is required when investigating an automobile accident, as demonstrated in Exhibit 9-11.

Exhibit 9-11	Auto Accident Analysis

Accidents don't just happen.[19] Except in instances of mechanical failure or acts of God, vehicle collisions occur because of driver negligence. If a collision is properly investigated and analyzed, the person(s) at fault can usually be determined. If, for example, the analysis reveals that the defendant was negligent, demonstrative evidence can be used to show jurors how the defendant's negligence caused the collision.

Law offices need to know the fundamentals of automobile accident investigations even in the era of smart car designs in which computers embedded in a car can record operating data at the time of the accident including vehicle speed, steering angle, brake status, force of impact, seatbelt status, and airbag deployment. The device is called an *event data recorder (EDR)*. It functions like the "black box" in airplanes. EDRs are controversial. They are not yet required in all new vehicles, but many predict that it's only a matter of time when they become standard. Plaintiffs' attorneys eagerly await the day. Yet an EDR is not a substitute for the basic kind of data that can be obtained with more traditional investigation techniques, which we will explore here.

Many vehicle-accident cases could be settled without a trial if insurance adjusters were shown definitive or scientific facts demonstrating where fault lies. Insurance adjusters, like jurors, are receptive to scientific analysis of liability.

It is important to investigate as quickly as possible. Accident scenes change and witnesses move. Of course, you often do not get a case until months after the accident occurred. Even then, the investigation should be started immediately. Bits of evidence and many helpful facts may still be available.

Reports

Begin the investigation by getting a complete statement of facts from the client. Then, get a police report of the collision. (See Exhibit 9-4.) This report may include the officer's estimate of the damage to each vehicle as well as the location of the damage. Often the report will list names, addresses, and telephone numbers of the witnesses, as well as the statements that each party gave to the officer at the scene. The report will show who was ticketed and why. Reports often include a sketch of the accident scene as well as the officer's analysis of the factors contributing to the collision.

Sometimes, however, these drawings may be inaccurate. The officer's analysis of contributing factors may not make sense. In most instances where an insurance company denies liability, it is because an investigating officer indicated that the plaintiff was in some way at fault. Here the plaintiff's law office must prove that the police officer's analysis was not correct.

In serious collisions, investigating police officers will often keep notes, take photographs, and make a scale drawing of the scene. You can obtain these by subpoena.

After obtaining a police report, take witness statements, being careful that each statement (written or taken with a voice recorder) includes all facts the witness knows. (See Exhibit 9-14 later in the chapter for more on witness statements.) A full investigation also includes taking appropriate measurements and determining the point of impact based on data obtained from physical evidence at the scene, the police report, and witness statements.

Photographs

The vehicles involved and the accident scene should be photographed as soon as possible because vehicles may be repaired quickly and accident scenes may change due to construction, resurfacing or installation of traffic control devices. Law offices should own and know how to use a good quality digital camera, even if they hire full-time investigators or photographers. Many times, if you wait for someone else to take photographs, it will be too late.

Know what photographs you need and make sure that the proper ones are taken. The only way to be sure to get the right photograph is to take many of them. Using a slow pre-digital camera, the late Axel Hanson, one of the greatest investigators who ever lived, once said that he took 211 photographs of a vehicle involved in a fatality, and just one proved to be the key to liability.

Photographers should

- Move around the vehicle in a circle, taking photographs every five minutes on the hands of a clock.
- Take close-ups of damaged areas and use a flash to ensure that shadows do not obscure these areas.
- Take shots from beneath the damaged part of the vehicle, an area that will often reveal the severity of the impact.
- Take shots while focusing straight down on the damaged area; these pictures will reveal the angle of impact.

To obtain the straight-down shots, you need to stand on a ladder, or, if allowed, stand on the vehicle itself. Downward shots of the vehicle involved in a collision can be matched to illustrate the angle at which the vehicles collided.

Also take pictures of any internal damage to the vehicle, including the speedometer and seats. In a rear-end collision the seats will often be bent backward or broken off at the frames. Jurors can readily understand that an impact strong enough to break seats would be severe enough to injure a human being.

A 50-mm lens best approximates the view as seen by the human eye. To illustrate what each driver saw, work from as far back as 1,000 feet from the point of collision. (If drivers did not travel 1,000 feet on the road in question before impact, photos should be taken starting from the point where each driver entered the roadway.) Take photographs every 100 feet until 300 feet from the collision site; then every 50 feet until 100 feet from the point of impact; then every 25 feet to the point of impact. Only in this way can photographs show what the driver of each vehicle could see when approaching the collision site. Video, of course, can also be used to obtain these scenes, but not as a substitute for still photos arranged in a collage that can be held in the hand and studied.

In photographing a severe crash scene, you should try to obtain the same types of vehicles that were in the actual accident from a used-car lot or car dealership. Measurements should be made to determine driver's-eye height. Set tripods at this height to take approach shots. If a bus or truck is involved, measure driver's-eye height in the same type of vehicle. In these instances, you must use ladders to get eye-height shots of what the drivers could see as they approached the collision site. A foot or two can make a world of difference in what a driver can see. These photographs should show any obstructions to a driver's view.

Photographs should also be taken of all road signs, not only to show their wording but also to show their location. At the point of impact, photos should be taken of gouge marks, scrapes, and any other damage the vehicles caused to the road surface or surrounding area. Both distance and close-up shots should be taken to pinpoint the damage. For close-up shots, it is often advisable to include a ruler or a pencil in order to indicate the scale.

Light Bulbs

Examining the light bulbs near a vehicle's damaged area will reveal whether they were operating at the time of the crash. During a collision, a heated light filament will stretch or break, while an inoperative cool filament will not. A bulb with a stretched or broken filament can easily be compared with a new bulb to show whether the bulb in question was functioning at the time of the collision. This principle applies to taillights; brake lights; turn indicators (front, back, or side); and headlights. In all rear-end collisions at night, taillights are a factor. Brake lights and turn signals may be factors day or night. If bulbs figured in the crash, they should be removed by an investigator and retained. It may be many months before the plaintiff's lawyer learns that the defendant is claiming that the plaintiff did not have the appropriate lights on or failed to give a turn signal.

Be sure to document the removal of bulbs, which should be placed in a padded, labeled box. It is important to indicate the vehicle the bulbs came from, their location on the vehicle, the person who removed them, and the date and time of removal. (See Exhibit 9-13 later in the chapter on the *evidence log* where notations such as these need to be entered.) In *Golleher v. Herrera*, the court ruled that to introduce expert testimony concerning whether a vehicle's light bulb was functioning at the time of a collision, not only must the bulb be put into evidence but there must also be testimony that the bulb was the one that came from a particular location on a vehicle in the collision. 651 S.W.2d 329, 333–34 (Tex. Ct. App. 1983).

Skid Marks

Careful measurements of all skid marks at the scene are essential. Before measuring them, the investigator should ensure that the skid marks were laid down in the collision in question. To avoid measuring the wrong marks, it is best to have someone who can definitively identify the marks. This could be the client, a witness, or an ambulance driver at the scene for the investigation. Of course, this also applies to measuring gouges, scrapes, and other physical damage at the accident site.

Here are the major formulas that can be used to determine the minimum speed of the vehicle before the driver applied the brakes:

- *Straight-skid speed formula.* Often a vehicle traveling at a high rate of speed leaves only a few feet of skid marks because the brakes were not applied until the instant before impact. In those instances, determining the speed from skid marks may not be possible. But where skid marks were laid down over a long distance, the straight-skid speed formula may reveal that the colliding vehicle was traveling at excessive speed.
- *Yaw-mark formula.* A yaw mark is left on a road surface by the sideward motion of a tire when the driver turned the wheel sharply, usually to avoid a collision or to take a curve at excessive speed. A yaw mark will reveal the speed at the time the vehicle made the mark. A yaw mark should not be confused with a skid mark. A yaw mark is a scuff mark made while the tire is rotating. It is easily identified by striations left on the roadway by the tire sidewall.
- *Flip-vault formula.* If an object was thrown from either vehicle because of the impact, the investigator can calculate the minimum speed of the colliding vehicle if the exact point of impact of the vehicles and the exact point where the item first

contacted the ground are known. The calculation is done using the flip-vault formula. Therefore, when examining the scene, the investigator should look for anything that may have been thrown from either vehicle. For example, if a toolbox was thrown from the back of a truck and it can be determined exactly where it hit the ground, applying the flip-vault formula can determine the speed of the colliding vehicle at impact. In one case, a screwdriver with the driver's name taped to the handle was thrown from the colliding vehicle, and the screwdriver stuck blade-first into the ground many feet away from where the vehicles collided. The investigator applied the flip-vault formula to determine speed.

- *Fall formula.* Investigators can use the fall formula to determine the speed of a vehicle that ran off an embankment. The investigator must measure the horizontal distance that the vehicle traveled before hitting the ground and then measure the vertical distance that the vehicle dropped. This formula can be helpful in proving whether a vehicle that went off an embankment was speeding.

Drag Factor

Investigators cannot determine speed from skid marks or yaw marks unless they know the drag factor of the roadway. The drag factor is the coefficient-of-friction, plus or minus grade. It is that percentage of the weight of an object that is required to push or pull it along a surface. The grade takes into account whether or not the object was going uphill or downhill.

To determine speed from skid marks, investigators must measure the drag factor accurately. Many books and other publications give drag-factor ranges for dry concrete, wet concrete, dry asphalt, wet asphalt, gravel and ice. These ranges are best used only to get a general idea of what might be expected for each surface. The drag factor can vary greatly, even on the same roadway. To determine speed from skid marks or a yaw mark, you must conduct a drag-factor test at the specific point where the marks were made. Just as important, the test must be conducted in the same direction that the vehicle was traveling to take into account the plus or minus grade.

Measurements and Scale Drawings

In examining a collision scene, the investigator should take all measurements relative to a fixed reference point located close to the point of impact like a telephone pole or a corner of a building. The best method is to use a north-south, east-west grid and locate each distance measured north, south, east, or west of the reference point. Using this method, investigators can make an infinite number of measurements and plot each point on a scale drawing of the scene.

Besides the obvious distances that must be measured, such as the width of each roadway and the location of all traffic signs, the exact locations of any buildings or obstructions to clear view between the vehicles should be precisely determined.

A 1:20 scale is one scale to use for drawings in most cases. The drawing helps in performing a time-and-distance analysis, as well as in seeing the entire collision process on paper. Along with minimum speed calculations, a scale drawing of the accident scene can be persuasive when presented to an insurance adjuster. If the case does not settle, a scale drawing can be used to prove a plaintiff's case at trial.

Time-and-Distance Analysis to Help Determine Fault

Once the investigation is complete and a scale drawing made, the collision can be analyzed to help determine fault (negligence).

Time and distance must be taken into account in every collision or vehicle-pedestrian accident. Every moving mass is traveling at a certain speed that converts to either miles per hour or feet per second. To determine the feet per second a vehicle was traveling, multiply miles per hour times 1.47.

- One mile = 5,280 feet
- One hour = 3,600 seconds
- To determine feet per second, divide 5,200 by 3,600
- The answer is 1.47 feet per second

If you convert miles per hour to feet per second, you can work backward from the point of impact and place the vehicles at the various points on the scale drawing for each second (or even one-tenth of a second) before the collision occurred. With the scale drawing and the locations of each vehicle at different intervals before impact, you can see the view each driver had of the scene and of each other, determine to what extent speed of each driver was a factor, and determine what action or actions could have been taken by either driver to avoid a collision.

Of course, the miles-per-hour figure may come from the testimony of the driver. In many instances, a defendant driver will say in deposition that the vehicle was going at a slower rate of speed than it actually was. The statement may hurt the defense because at the lower speed the defendant would have had more time to see plaintiff's vehicle and come to a stop or turn in order to avoid a collision.

Time and distance can also be used to refute contributory negligence on the part of the plaintiff. For example where the defendant pulled out in front of the plaintiff or made a left turn into the plaintiff's path, time-and-distance calculations can be used to show that the legal speed at which the plaintiff was traveling did not allow stopping before colliding with the defendant. It takes three-quarters of a second to realize that you need to brake. It takes another three-quarters of a second to move your foot to the brake pedal. In many instances, taking into account the judicially accepted three-quarters-of-a-second reaction time will show that the plaintiff did not even have time to apply the brakes.

A time-and-distance analysis is especially helpful in pedestrian cases. Pedestrians have a normal walking speed of about three miles per hour. At this speed it takes several seconds to walk just a few steps. It can usually be shown that in those several seconds the driver had more than ample time to avoid striking the pedestrian.

The *flip-vault formula* can also be applied in pedestrian cases. If the point of impact and the point where a pedestrian hit the ground after impact are known, the speed of the striking vehicle can be determined. Often, doing a time-and-distance analysis and applying the flip-vault formula will clearly demonstrate a driver's fault.

Determining Negligence

To assess fault, let's look at six examples on page 422. Examples 1-3

In Example 1, the driver (S) was traveling at a speed (25 mph) that was safe for the circumstances (an uncontrolled intersection ahead with a view obstruction on the right). The driver looked to the right and as soon as an approaching vehicle (T) was observed, applied the brakes and yielded the right-of-way.

In Example 2, the driver (S) was traveling at a speed too great for existing conditions. At 35 miles per hour, even though the driver maintained a proper lookout and saw the approaching vehicle (T), the driver could not stop in time to avoid colliding with it.

In Example 3, the driver (S) was traveling at a safe speed (25 mph) but was not looking to see if a vehicle was approaching from the right. By the time the driver saw the approaching vehicle (T), it was too late. Failure to keep a proper lookout was the cause of the collision.

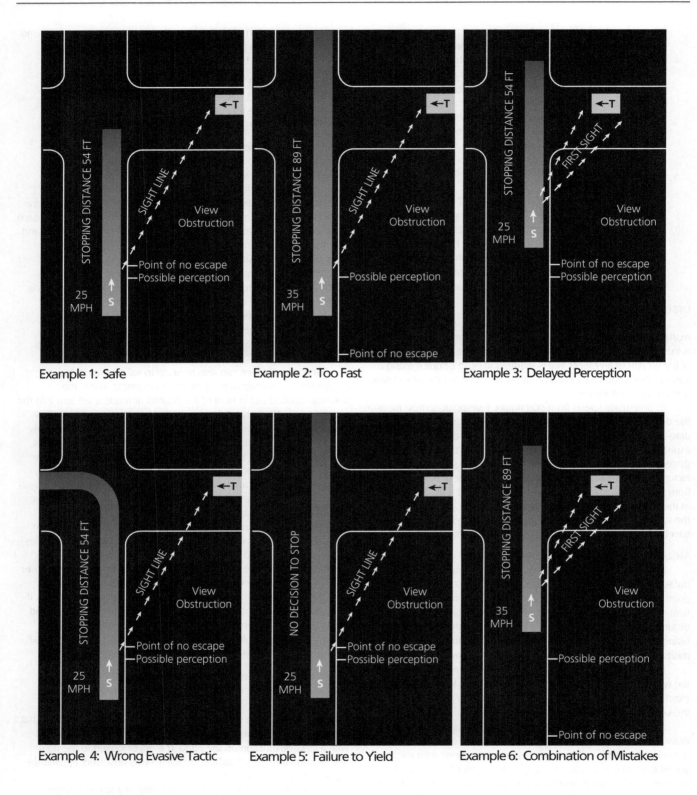

Example 1: Safe

Example 2: Too Fast

Example 3: Delayed Perception

Example 4: Wrong Evasive Tactic

Example 5: Failure to Yield

Example 6: Combination of Mistakes

Examples 4-6

In Example 4, the driver (S) was traveling at a speed (25 mph) that was safe for conditions and kept a proper lookout. However, the driver chose the wrong evasive tactic. The driver tried to turn left in front of the approaching vehicle (T) rather than apply the brakes and yield the right-of-way to the vehicle.

In Example 5, the driver (S) was traveling at a safe speed (25 mph), kept a proper lookout, but did nothing to avoid the collision. The driver (S) simply failed to apply the brakes.

Example 6 shows a combination of errors. The driver (S) was traveling at a greater speed (35 mph) than existing conditions permitted and failed to keep a proper lookout.

An analysis similar to Examples 1-6 on your scale drawing will clearly illustrate to an insurance adjuster, a defense lawyer, and (if those two are hardheaded) a jury precisely what the defendant did wrong. After seeing and understanding this type of accident analysis, jurors are less likely to fall for the defendant who testifies, "I don't know where he came from. He just came out of nowhere."

Rear-End Collisions

Where the rear-ended vehicle is stopped, the colliding driver may have been negligent in speed, lookout, or brake application. But what about a rear-end collision that occurs as two cars are traveling down a roadway at about the same speed and the first car has to stop for some unexpected reason? Alleging that speed caused the collision is faulty, because the first driver was traveling at the same rate of speed as the second. If the second driver testifies that the instant he saw the first driver's brake lights come on, he slammed on his brakes, he is probably telling the truth. Usually this type of rear-end collision is not the result of negligent speed, lookout, or brakes application. It is the result of following too closely.

Analysis Works

Accident analysis works, but it will not work unless law offices put their best efforts into it. If they ensure that a proper investigation is done and perform an accident analysis in each case, the results will be rewarding.

Reprinted and updated with permission of TRIAL (February 1991) Copyright the Association of Trial Lawyers of America.

LICENSE TO INVESTIGATE?

In some states, persons who conduct investigations must be licensed. In Montana, for example, a statute provides that you need a license if you investigate the cause of accidents or injuries or if you gather "evidence to be used before any court."[20] The statute is administered by an administrative agency called the Board of Private Security Patrolmen and Investigators. Private investigators in the state took the position that *anyone* who investigates must be licensed, including paralegals. The Montana Paralegal Association asked the legislature to clarify the law by amending the statute to specifically exclude paralegals from this requirement. Testimony in support of this exclusion was submitted by the major national paralegal associations: NALA and NFPA. The exclusion was adopted by the Montana legislature and signed by the governor. Under § 37-60-105(4)(b) of the M.C.A. (Montana Code Annotated), the license requirement

"does not apply to ... a paralegal, or legal assistant employed by a licensed attorney."

This did not, however, end the controversy. Private investigators argued that the language of the exemption only covers paralegals who work for *one* attorney or *one* law firm. (The statute says "a" licensed attorney.) If a paralegal does investigative work for more than one law firm, the private investigators took the position that he or she would still have to be licensed. In effect, freelance or independent paralegals who perform investigation assignments for several attorneys or firms would need to be licensed under this interpretation.

The Board of Private Security Patrolmen and Investigators agreed with this interpretation! It adopted an administrative regulation that said, "the word 'paralegal' will be interpreted to mean a paralegal employed by only one law firm. Paralegals employed by more than one firm at the same time will be required to be licensed."

The Montana Paralegal Association again expressed organized opposition to this interpretation. Its effective lobbying led to another change in the statute to clarify the law. The license exemption statute, § 37-60-105(f), now reads as follows:

[This chapter does not apply to a] paralegal, or legal assistant employed by one *or more* lawyers, law offices, governmental agencies, or other entities [emphasis added]

This finally settled the controversy to the satisfaction of traditional and freelance paralegals.

These events demonstrate the need of paralegals to be vigilant in the protection of their interests and the effectiveness of paralegal organizations in providing that protection.

BASICS OF EVIDENCE LAW

INTRODUCTION

We turn now to a closer look at the relationship between investigation and the law of evidence. One of the goals of investigation is to uncover and verify facts that will be **admissible** in court as determined by the law of evidence. Admissible means allowed into court to determine its truth or believability.

admissible Allowed into court to determine truth or believability.

During a trial, each party attempts to establish its version of the facts. There are four main ways that this can be done:

- Admission
- Judicial notice
- Presumption
- Evidence without aid of the above three

Admission

admission An assertion of the truth of a fact. (See glossary for an additional meaning.)

Paula sues Dan for negligence following an automobile accident. Paula claims that Dan has prescription eyeglasses and that he was not wearing them at the time of the accident. Before the trial, Dan concedes that he wears glasses but denies that he was not wearing them at the time of the accident. Dan's statement that he needs glasses is an **admission**, which is an assertion of the truth of a fact. It is one of the facts that Dan's opponent needs to prove. He has not admitted that he was not wearing glasses at the time of the accident, but he has admitted that he needs glasses.

One of the ways in which such acknowledgments (admissions) are made during discovery is through a *request for admissions* (RFA). As we saw in Exhibit 9-1, this is a discovery method by which one party sends a request to another party that the latter agrees that a certain fact or legal conclusion is true or valid.

stipulation ("stip") An agreement between opposing parties about a particular matter. The verb is stipulate. (See glossary for an additional meaning.)

Facts that are admitted as true do not have to be proven in the trial. Another way to accomplish the same result is by **stipulation**, which is an agreement between the parties about a particular matter. For example, the parties can stipulate that there were no passengers in Dan's car at the time of the accident. (We will return to the topic of admission later when we discuss admission by a party opponent as an exception to the hearsay rule.)

Judicial Notice

judicial notice A court's acceptance of a well-known fact without requiring proof of that fact.

Some facts are so well accepted that the court can acknowledge them without requiring either party to prove those facts. This is known as **judicial notice**. An example is that water freezes at 32 degrees Fahrenheit or that there are 31 days in July.

Presumption

presumption An assumption or inference that a certain fact is true once another fact is established.

rebuttable presumption An assumption or inference of fact that can be overcome (rebutted) by sufficient contrary evidence but that will be treated as accurate if it is not rebutted.

irrebuttable presumption An assumption or inference of fact that cannot be overcome (rebutted) because evidence to the contrary will not be considered. The presumption is conclusive.

A **presumption** is an assumption or inference that a certain fact is true once another fact is established. If a party proves that fact #1 exists, then fact #2 is established. An example in many states is that proof a person has disappeared for seven years raises the presumption that he or she is dead. Also, proof that a letter was properly addressed and mailed raises the presumption that the addressee received it. There are two kinds of presumptions. First, a **rebuttable presumption** is an inference of fact that can be overcome (rebutted) by sufficient contrary evidence but that will be treated as accurate if it is not rebutted. Evidence to the contrary can be introduced. For example, the presumption of death after a disappearance of seven years is rebuttable in most states. Therefore, evidence that the missing person may still be alive could be introduced. An example of such evidence might be that someone recently used the Social Security number of a person who has been missing for eight years. Second, an **irrebuttable presumption** is an inference of fact that cannot be overcome (rebutted) because evidence to the contrary will not be considered. The presumption is conclusive. An example is the presumption that a child under seven years of age is incapable of forming the intent necessary to commit a crime. This is a conclusive presumption. Evidence that a six-year-old child has the intelligence of a teenager, therefore, would not be admitted.

Evidence

bench trial A trial before a judge without a jury. Also called a *nonjury trial*.

Most facts are established by the introduction of evidence without the aid of admissions, judicial notice, or presumptions. Evidence, as we have seen, is anything that could be offered to establish the existence or nonexistence of a fact in dispute. Admissible evidence is evidence that the judge will permit the court (usually the jury) to consider. The jury is free to conclude that it does not believe the evidence that the judge ruled admissible. In a **bench trial** where there is no jury, the judge can conclude that specific evidence he or she ruled was admissible is not believable.

Two important categories of evidence can be admissible: *direct* and *circumstantial* evidence. See Exhibit 9-12.

| Exhibit 9-12 | Direct and Circumstantial Evidence | |

CATEGORY	DEFINITION	EXAMPLES
Direct Evidence	Evidence (based on personal knowledge or observation) that tends to establish a fact (or to disprove a fact) without the need for an inference. Also called *positive evidence*.	▪ Ellen Foley says that she saw it raining on Tuesday at noon. This statement is direct evidence that it was raining on Tuesday at noon.
Circumstantial Evidence	Evidence of one fact from which another fact (not personally observed or known) can be inferred. Also called *indirect evidence*.	▪ Tom Richards says that on Tuesday at noon he saw a person run into the building with drops of water falling from his raincoat. This is circumstantial evidence that it was raining on Tuesday at noon. The conclusion about rain at this time is the inference.

Investigation Guideline:

Direct evidence is preferred over circumstantial, although both kinds of evidence may be admissible. Identify the inference in the circumstantial evidence. Then try to find direct evidence of whatever was inferred.

RELEVANCE

Relevant evidence is evidence that logically tends to establish or disprove a fact. Phrased another way, evidence is relevant when it tends to make the existence of a fact more probable or less probable than it would be without that evidence. Relevancy is a very broad concept. It means that the evidence may be helpful in determining the truth or falsity of a fact involved in a legal dispute. The test of relevancy is common sense and logic. If, for example, you want to know whether a walkway is dangerous, it is relevant that people have slipped on this walkway in the immediate past. Prior accidents under the same conditions make it more reasonable for someone to conclude that the walkway is dangerous.

All relevant evidence, however, is not admissible evidence. Some highly relevant evidence is considered so potentially inflammatory or prejudicial that a judge will rule it to be inadmissible. An example might be evidence of a defendant's prior convictions for the same kind of crime for which the defendant is currently being tried. Similarly, it would be very relevant to know that the defendant told his attorney he was driving 80 mph at the time of the accident, yet the **attorney-client privilege** would make such a statement inadmissible. Also, relevant evidence is not necessarily conclusive evidence even if it is admissible. The jury will usually be free to discount relevant evidence it does not believe. Relevancy is simply a tendency of evidence to establish or disestablish (disprove) a fact. It may be a very weak tendency. Prior accidents may be relevant to show danger, but the jury may still conclude, in the light of all the evidence, that there was no danger.

Investigation Guideline:

Let common sense and logic be your main guide in pursuing relevant evidence. So long as there is some logical connection between the fact you are pursuing and a fact that must be established at trial, what you are pursuing is relevant.

COMPETENCE OF WITNESSES

Witnesses are **competent** to testify if they

▪ understand the obligation to tell the truth,
▪ have the ability to communicate, and
▪ have knowledge of the topic of their testimony.

Children or mentally ill persons are not automatically disqualified. They are competent to testify if the judge is satisfied that the above criteria are met. This, however, does not mean that a competent person will always be allowed to testify nor that the fact-finder will believe

relevant (1) Logically tending to establish or disprove a fact. Pertinent. Relevant evidence is evidence having a tendency to make the existence of a fact more probable or less probable than it would be without the evidence. (2) Contributing to the resolution of a problem or issue. The noun is *relevancy*.

attorney-client privilege (ACP) A client or a client's attorney can refuse to disclose any confidential (private) communication between them if the purpose of the communication was to facilitate the provision of legal services to the client.

competent Having the legal capacity to give testimony because the person understands the obligation to tell the truth, has the ability to communicate, and has knowledge of the topic of his or her testimony. The noun is *competency*. (See glossary for an additional meaning.)

the testimony if the competent person is allowed to testify. Keep in mind the following distinctions:

- *Competence*: Having the legal capacity to give testimony because the person understands the obligation to tell the truth, has the ability to communicate, and has knowledge of the topic of his or her testimony.
- *Admissible*: Allowed into court to determine its truth or believability.
- *Relevant*: Logically tending to establish or disprove a fact. Pertinent.
- *Credibility*: The extent to which something is believable or worthy of belief.

credibility The extent to which something is believable or worthy of belief.

Recall the example given earlier of the statement a defendant gave his attorney that the defendant was driving 80 mph at the time of the accident. The statement is certainly *relevant* to whether the defendant caused an accident. The defendant probably understands the obligation to tell the truth, is able to communicate, and knows something about the speed of his own car. Therefore, he is *competent* to testify. If allowed to testify, the fact-finder (the jury in a jury trial and the judge in a bench trial) would probably find his statement to be highly believable (*credible*). But the statement is not *admissible*. The attorney-client privilege allows persons to refuse to testify about what they told their attorneys when seeking legal assistance. Competent, relevant, credible evidence is not always admissible.

Investigation Guideline:

Although the ultimate goal of investigation is to uncover admissible, competent, credible evidence, the major guideline of the investigator is to go after whatever is relevant to the issues in the case. If what you find is relevant, bring it to the attention of your supervisor who will decide how, if at all, the evidence is usable on behalf of the client.

OPINIONS

In Chapter 8, we covered the distinction between observed facts and inferences. Observed facts are what someone directly experiences through the senses (e.g., "I saw the car weaving back and forth over the center line" or "I smelled alcohol on his breath"). An inference is a deduction or conclusion from facts (e.g., "He was driving carelessly" or "He was drunk"). An inference is an example of an **opinion**, which is a judgment, belief, or appraisal of something that may or may not be based on fact or proof. For example, after you watch George stagger down the street and smell alcohol on his breath, you come to the conclusion that he is drunk. The conclusion is your opinion. This opinion is based on the alleged facts of seeing George stagger and smelling alcohol on George's breath.

opinion A judgment, belief, or appraisal of something that may or may not be based on fact or proof. (See glossary for additional meanings.)

Investigation Guideline:

Know when a person is stating an inference or opinion. Pursue all the underlying facts (particularly observed facts) that support the conclusion in the opinion.

HEARSAY

Hearsay is an out-of-court statement quoted or reported by someone who did not make the statement when offered into evidence to prove the truth of the matter asserted in the statement.[21] There are four conditions to the existence of hearsay: (1) a witness in court gives testimony, (2) about a statement made out of court by another person (called the *declarant*), (3) in order to establish the truth of the matter in the statement, (4) so that the value of the statement depends on the credibility of the declarant.[22] If evidence is hearsay, it is inadmissible *unless* one of the exceptions to the hearsay rule applies.

hearsay An out-of-court statement quoted or reported by someone who did not make the statement when offered into evidence to prove the truth of the matter asserted in the statement.

Example: Sam, a witness in court, says, "Fred told me when I met him on Elm Street that he was speeding."

Note that Sam is telling us what he learned from someone else—Fred. Fred is the declarant, the person who has made a declaration or statement. The problem of hearsay arises when someone tries to give testimony about what a declarant has said or communicated. Is Sam's testimony hearsay? It depends on whether the four conditions for hearsay can be met:

Testimony in court	The witness, Sam, is on the stand.
Statement made out of court	The statement made by Fred (the declarant) was made on Elm Street, not in court.
Offered to assert the truth of The matter in the statement	Assume that the purpose of the attorney questioning Sam is to show that Fred was speeding—that the statement is true.
The value of the statement depends on the credibility of the out-of-court declarant	Fred is the out-of-court declarant. The value of the statement depends on how believable or credible Fred is.

If the statement is not offered to prove the truth of the matter asserted in the statement, it is not hearsay. Suppose, for example, that the attorney wants to prove that Fred was alive immediately after the accident—that death was not instantaneous. The above statement ("Fred told me when I met him on Elm Street that he was speeding") would be admitted to prove that Fred actually said something, i.e., that Fred was alive long enough to make a statement. If the testimony of the witness (Sam) is offered to prove that the words were spoken by Fred rather than to prove that Fred was speeding, then the statement is not hearsay. The testimony on what Fred told Sam would therefore be admissible. The jury would have to be cautioned to examine the testimony for the limited purpose for which it is offered and not to consider it as evidence that Fred was speeding.

Conduct intended as a substitute for words (called *assertive conduct*) can also be hearsay. For example, the witness is asked "What did Fred say when you asked him if he was speeding?" The witness answers, "He nodded his head yes." This testimony is hearsay if it is offered to prove that Fred was speeding. Conduct—nodding the head—was intended as a substitute for words.

Investigation Guideline:
Know when hearsay exists so that you can try to find alternative, nonhearsay evidence to prove the truth of the assertions made in the hearsay. See also the second column of Exhibit 9-7 for a checklist on assessing the believability of secondhand statements.

There are a number of exceptions to the hearsay rule that have the effect of making evidence admissible even though it fulfills all the conditions of hearsay. In the following examples of exceptions to the hearsay rule, assume that the person making the statement (the declarant) is not available to testify:

- *Statement against self-interest.* A statement against self-interest is an out-of-court statement that was against the financial interest of the declarant at the time it was made. Example: John tells a friend at a ball game, "I still owe the bank the money."
- *Dying Declaration.* A dying declaration is an out-of-court statement concerning the causes or circumstances of death, made by a person who is conscious of his or her imminent death. Example: Tom dies two minutes after he was hit over the head. Seconds before he dies, he says, "Linda did it." Many states limit the dying-declaration exception to criminal cases. Some states, however, would also allow this statement to be used in a civil case, such as in a civil battery or wrongful death case against Linda.
- *Excited Utterance.* An excited utterance is an out-of-court statement relating to a startling event or condition made while the declarant was under the stress of excitement caused by the event or condition. Example: Fred says, "I heard John say, 'Oh my God, the truck just hit a child.'"
- *Statement of Present Sense Impression.* A statement of present sense impression is an out-of-court statement describing or explaining an event or condition, made while the declarant was perceiving the event or condition or immediately thereafter. Example: Janice says, "As the car turned the corner, a bystander turned to me and said, 'That car will never make it.'"
- *Statement of Existing Mental, Emotional, or Physical Condition.* An out-of-court statement of an existing state of mind (such as motive, intent, or plan) or of an emotional, sensory, or physical condition (such as a mental feeling, pain, or bodily health). Example: Bob says, "A second before Sheila fell, she said to me, 'I feel dizzy.'"

A statement in some written records can also qualify as an exception to the hearsay rule. Example:

- *Business Record.* A business record is a record kept in the course of a regularly conducted business activity. The exception also applies to nonprofit organizations such as universities. Example: A hospital record containing a description of a patient's condition upon entering the emergency room.

PRIVILEGE

privilege A special legal benefit, right, exemption, or protection. (See glossary for an additional meaning.)

A **privilege** is a special legal benefit, right, exemption, or protection. In the law of evidence, a privilege is the right to refuse to testify or the right to prevent someone else from testifying on a matter.[23]

1. *Privilege against self-incrimination.* Under the privilege against self-incrimination, an accused person cannot be compelled to testify in a criminal proceeding or to answer incriminating questions, which are questions that directly or indirectly connect the accused to the commission of a crime.
2. *Attorney-client privilege.* A client or a client's attorney can refuse to disclose any confidential (private) communication between them if the purpose of the communication was to facilitate the provision of legal services to the client. The attorney cannot disclose the communication without the consent of the client. Closely related to the attorney-client privilege is the **work-product rule**. Under this rule, an attorney's notes, working papers, memoranda and the like prepared by or for an attorney in anticipation of litigation is privileged. With rare exceptions, the other side's request to be shown this work-product will be denied.

work-product rule Notes, working papers, memoranda, or similar things prepared by or for an attorney in anticipation of litigation are not discoverable by an opponent, absent a showing of substantial need. They are protected by privilege.

3. *Doctor-patient privilege.* A patient or a patient's doctor can refuse to disclose any confidential (private) communications between them that relate to the patient's medical care. The doctor cannot disclose the communication without the permission (consent) of the patient.
4. *Clergy-penitent privilege.* A penitent and a member of the clergy can refuse to disclose any confidential (private) communications between them that relate to spiritual counseling or consultation. The minister, priest, rabbi, or cleric cannot disclose the communication without the consent of the penitent.
5. *Marital-communications privilege* A person can refuse to testify and can prevent his or her spouse or ex-spouse from testifying about any confidential communications made between them during the marriage. Also called *marital privilege, husband-wife privilege.*
6. *Government Information.* Some information collected by the government about citizens is confidential and privileged. Examples include most adoption and tax records. The privilege would not prevent use of the information to prosecute the citizen in connection with the citizen's duty to provide accurate information. It could, however, prevent third parties from gaining access to the confidential information.

Investigation Guideline:

When a privilege applies, try to find alternative, nonprivileged sources of obtaining the information protected by the privilege. (See also Exhibits 9-4, 9-5, and 9-6.)

privilege log A list of information or documents claimed to be covered by privilege and, therefore, protected from disclosure in discovery or during trial.

A task that litigation paralegals are sometimes asked to perform is to prepare a **privilege log** that lists all of the information or documents that the office will refuse to disclose because of a claim of privilege.

Great care must be taken to preserve a legitimate privilege. Suppose, for example, that a third party is told (or accidentally overhears) a conversation protected by the attorney-client privilege. In some cases, this could destroy the privilege. See the example in Chapter 5 in which Martha Stewart lost her privilege when she told her daughter about a conversation she had with her attorney.

AUTHENTICATION

authentication The use of evidence that a writing or other physical item is genuine and that it is what it purports to be. (See glossary for an additional meaning.)

Authentication is the use of evidence that a writing (or other physical item) is genuine and that it is what it purports to be. An example of such evidence would be the testimony of witnesses who saw a **testator** sign a document and, while doing so, stated that it was his or her last will and testament.

PAROL-EVIDENCE RULE (PER)

Under the **parol-evidence rule (PER)**, prior or **contemporaneous** oral statements cannot be introduced to alter or contradict the terms of a written document if the parties intended the written document to be a complete statement of the agreement.

EVIDENCE LOG

In representing a client, a law firm often collects documents (e.g., drafts of a contract) and other tangible things (e.g., a defective consumer product) that might become evidence in a client's litigation. It is important to be able to account for the **chain of custody** of the evidence, which is a list that covers the movement of evidence (and the persons who had it in their possession) from the time the evidence was obtained to the time it is offered in court. To keep track of evidence, a paralegal might be asked to help prepare and monitor an **evidence log**. The log is an ongoing, in-office record that provides identification and related data about documents and other tangible objects that might eventually be introduced into evidence. The office needs to keep careful records on what the evidence is, how the office came into possession of it, and to whom it was released either before trial (e.g., to an expert for examination) or at the conclusion of the litigation. The evidence log is one way to manage this important information (see Exhibit 9-13).

Exhibit 9-13	Evidence Log

EVIDENCE LOG

CASE	FILE NAME	EVIDENCE COLLECTED	DESCRIPTION/ IDENTIFYING MARKS	PERSON WHO COLLECTED THE EVIDENCE	DATE COLLECTED	CIRCUMSTANCES LEADING TO COLLECTION	RELEASED TO/ DATE	REASON RELEASED	CURRENT CUSTODIAN/ LOCATION

TAKING A WITNESS STATEMENT

There are four major kinds of witness statements:

- Handwritten statement taken from a witness in your presence
- Recorded statement in question-and-answer format (on a voice recorder or video camera)
- Responses to a questionnaire that is mailed to the witness to answer
- Statement taken in question-and-answer format with court reporters

The most common kind of statement is the first, which we shall consider here.

In a handwritten statement, the investigator writes down what the witness says, or the witness writes out the statement himself or herself. There is no formal structure to which the written statement must conform. The major requirements for the statement are clarity and accuracy. Here is how one paralegal explains the process to the witness: "What I'd like to do today is take a written statement from you. After we talk about what you recall about the accident, I'd like to write it down, then have you review it, verifying with your signature that this statement is indeed what you have said about the matter."[24]

Sidebar definitions:

testator One who has died leaving a valid will.

parol-evidence rule (PER) Prior or contemporaneous oral statements cannot be introduced to alter or contradict the terms of a written document if the parties intended the written document to be a complete statement of the agreement.

contemporaneous Existing or occurring in the same period of time; pertaining to records that are prepared on events as the events are occurring or very shortly thereafter.

chain of custody A list that covers the movement of evidence (and the persons who had it in their possession) from the time the evidence was obtained to the time it is offered in court.

evidence log An ongoing record that provides identification and related data about documents and other tangible objects that might eventually be introduced into evidence.

From whom should you take a witness statement? "Many people feel that a witness can only be someone who has actually viewed the event or occurrence. Obviously, this is not true. Quite often the so-called **occurrence witness** cannot offer as significant a contribution in testimony as the **pre-occurrence witness** or **post-occurrence witness.** An alert, intelligent post-occurrence witness can shed a great deal of light upon the matter in dispute by testifying as to physical facts such as positions of cars or skid marks. He or she could also testify as to statements made immediately after the occurrence by a party to the lawsuit. The pre-occurrence witness can testify as to the condition of premises or machinery immediately before the accident. Therefore, the paralegal should be interested in interviewing witnesses who can set the stage for the scene of the accident, in addition to those who actually witnessed the occurrence."[25]

Suppose that a person says he or she knows nothing. Should a "witness" statement be taken of this person? Some recommend that you should take a "negative statement" to discourage this person from coming back later to claim "remembered information." Here's an example of such a statement:

> "I was not at the abc address on xyz date and did not see a traffic accident at the time. I did not see anything happen at the abc location. I did not hear anything. I talked to no one about this accident, nor did I hear anyone say anything about it."[26]

The witness statement should begin by identifying (1) the witness (name, street and email address, place of work, names of relatives, and other identifying data that may be helpful in locating the witness later); (2) the date and place the statement was taken; and (3) the name of the person to whom the statement is being made. See the example of the beginning of a witness statement in Exhibit 9-14.

occurrence witness Someone who actually observed an event.

pre-occurrence witness Someone who did not observe an event but who can give an account of what happened before the event.

post-occurrence witness Someone who did not observe an event but who can give an account of what happened after the event.

Exhibit 9-14	Witness Statement

Statement of Patricia Wood

I am Patricia Wood. I am 42 years old and live at 3416 34th Street, N.W., Nashua, New Hampshire 03060. I work at the Deming Chemical Plant at Region Circle, Nashua. My home phone is 966–3954. My work phone is 297–9700 x301. My e-mail address is pwood@pacbell.com. I am married to John Wood. We have two children, Jessica (14 years old) and Gabriel (11 years old). I am making this statement to Rose Thompson, a paralegal at Fields, Smith and Farrell. This statement is being given on March 13, 2014 at my home, 3416 34th Street, NW.

On February 15, 2014, I was standing on the corner of…

In the body of the statement, the witness provides information about the event or occurrence in question such as an accident that was observed, what the witness did and saw just before a fire, where the witness was on a certain date, etc. Be sure that the statement includes facts relevant to the ability of the witness to observe, e.g., amount of light available, weather conditions, and obstructions. This lends credibility to the statement. It is often useful to have the witness give the facts in chronological order, particularly when many facts are involved in the statement.

At the end of the statement, the witness should say that he or she is making the statement of his or her own free will, without any pressure or coercion from anyone, (e.g., "I have carefully read all 3 pages of this statement. To the best of my knowledge, everything in it is accurate. I have made this statement of my own free will without coercion or pressure from anyone.") The witness then signs the statement and writes the date next to his or her signature. The signature goes on the last page. Each of the other pages is also signed or initialed. If others have watched the witness make and sign the statement, they should also sign an **attestation clause,** which states that they observed the witness sign the statement.

Before the witness signs, he or she should read the entire statement and make any corrections that need to be made. Each correction should be initialed by the witness. Every page should be numbered with the total number of pages indicated each time. For example, if there are four pages, the page numbers would be 1 of 4, 2 of 4, 3 of 4, and 4 of 4. Each of these page numbers should be initialed and dated by the witness. The investigator should not try to correct any spelling or grammatical mistakes made by the witness. The statement should exist exactly as the witness spoke or wrote it.

attestation clause A clause stating that you saw (witnessed) someone sign a document or perform other tasks related to the validity of the document.

Investigators sometimes use tricks of the trade to achieve a desired effect. For example, if the investigator is writing out the statement as the witness speaks, the investigator may intentionally make an error of fact, e.g., write "2014" when the witness said "2015." When the witness reads over the statement, the investigator makes sure that the witness catches the error and initials the correction. This becomes added evidence that the witness carefully read the statement. The witness might later try to claim that he or she did not read the statement. The initialed correction helps **rebut** this position.

rebut To refute or oppose.

If possible, every page of the witness statement (other than the last) should end in the middle of a sentence or somewhere before the period. This will help rebut a later allegation that someone improperly added pages to the witness statement after it was signed. The allegation is difficult to support if the bottom line of one page contains a sentence that is continued at the top of the next page.

Witness statements are generally not admitted into evidence at the trial. If, however, a witness gives testimony in court that is inconsistent with what he or she said in a witness statement, the statement might be allowed into evidence to demonstrate the inconsistency. The main value of witness statements is thoroughness and accuracy in case preparation. Trials can occur years after the events that led to litigation. Witnesses may disappear or forget. Witness statements taken soon after the event can be helpful in tracking down witnesses, helping them recall the details of the event, and, discouraging them from changing their story.

SETTLEMENT WORK-UP

One of the end products of investigation is the **settlement work-up**, which is a summary of the major facts obtained through investigation, client interviewing, answers to interrogatories, deposition testimony, etc. It is also called a *demand package* or *settlement brochure*. The work-up is used in negotiation with the other side or with the other side's liability insurance company in an effort to obtain a favorable settlement in lieu of trial. In addition to the presentation of the facts of a case, the settlement work-up might also summarize the law that will govern those facts.

Exhibit 9-15 shows a memo containing data for a proposed settlement work-up.[27] Note its precision and attention to detail. Excellent FP (fact particularization; see Exhibit 8-5 in Chapter 8) had to occur in order to obtain the kind of detail presented in this report.

settlement work-up A summary of the major facts in the case presented in a manner designed to encourage the other side (or its liability insurance company) to settle the case. Also called *demand package*, *settlement brochure*.

Exhibit 9-15	Draft of a Memorandum on a Proposed Settlement Work-Up

Office Memorandum

To: Mary Jones, Esq.
From: Katherine Webb, Paralegal
Date: October 12, 2015
Re: Joseph Smith vs. Dan Lamb
    Case Summary—Settlement Work-Up

I. Facts of Accident

The accident occurred on September 6, 2013, in Orange, California. Joseph Smith was driving westbound on Chapman Avenue, stopped to make a left turn into a parking lot, and was rear-ended by the one-half-ton panel truck driven by Dan Lamb. The defendant driver, Mr. Lamb, was cited for violation of Vehicle Code Sections 21703 and 22350, following too close, and at an unsafe speed for conditions.

II. Injuries

Injuries included severe cervical and lumbar sprain, superimposed over pre-existing, albeit asymptomatic, spondylolisthesis of pars interarticularis at L5–S1, with possible herniated nucleus pulposus either at or about the level of the spondylolisthesis; and contusion of right knee. Please see attached medical reports for further details.

III. Medical Treatment

Mr. Smith felt an almost immediate onset of pain in his head, neck, back, and right knee after the accident and believes that he may have lost consciousness momentarily. He was assisted from his car and taken by ambulance to the St. Joseph Hospital emergency room, where he was initially seen by his regular internist, Raymond Ross, M.D.

Dr. Ross obtained orthopedic consultation with Brian A. Ewald, M.D., who reviewed the multiple X-rays taken in the emergency room and found them negative for fracture. Lumbar spine X-rays did reveal evidence of a spondylolisthesis defect at the pars interarticularis of L5, but this was not felt to represent acute injury. Dr. Ewald had Mr. Smith admitted to St. Joseph Hospital on the same day for further evaluation and observation.

On admission to the hospital, Mr. Smith was placed on complete bed rest, with a cervical collar and medication for pain. On September 10, neurological consultation was obtained with Michael H. Braniff, M.D., who, although he did not find any significant objective neurological abnormality, felt that there might be a herniated disc at L4–L5, with possible contusion of the nerve roots.

Drs. Ewald and Braniff followed Mr. Smith's progress throughout the remainder of his hospitalization. He was continued on bed rest, physiotherapy, and medication, and fitted with a lumbosacral support. He was ultimately ambulated with crutches and was discharged from the hospital on September 25, 2013, with instructions to continue to rest and wear his cervical collar and back brace.

On discharge from the hospital, Mr. Smith was taken by ambulance to the Sky Palm Motel in Orange, where his wife and children had been staying during his hospitalization. Arrangements were made for home physiotherapy and rental of a hospital bed. Mr. Smith was taken by ambulance on the following day to his residence in Pacific Palisades.

After returning home, Mr. Smith continued to suffer from headaches, neck pain, and severe pain in his lower back, with some radiation into both legs, especially the right. He was totally confined to bed for at least two months following the accident, where he was cared for by his wife. Daily physical therapy was administered by Beatrice Tasker, R.P.T.

Mr. Smith continued to receive periodic outpatient care with Dr. Ewald. By the end of December 2013, Mr. Smith was able to discontinue the use of his cervical collar and was able to walk, with difficulty, without crutches. At the time of his office visit with Dr. Ewald on December 21, he was noted to be having moderate neck discomfort, with increasingly severe low back pain. At the time, Dr. Ewald placed Mr. Smith on a gradually increasing set of Williams exercises and advised him to begin swimming as much as possible.

Mr. Smith continued to be followed periodically by Dr. Ewald through March 2014, with gradual improvement noted. However, Mr. Smith continued to spend the majority of his time confined to his home and often to bed, using a cane whenever he went out. In addition, he suffered periodic severe flare-ups of low back pain, which would render him totally disabled and would necessitate total bed rest for several days at a time.

During this period of time, Mr. Smith also experienced headaches and blurred vision, for which Dr. Ewald referred him to Robert N. Dunphy, M.D. Dr. Dunphy advised that the symptoms were probably secondary to his other injuries and would most likely subside with time.

On April 1, 2014, Mr. Smith consulted Dr. Ewald with complaints of increased back pain following an automobile ride to San Diego. Dr. Ewald's examination at that time revealed bilateral lumbar muscle spasm, with markedly decreased range of motion. Due to his concern about the extremely prolonged lumbar symptoms, and suspecting a possible central herniated nucleus pulposus, Dr. Ewald recommended that Mr. Smith undergo lumbar myelography. This was performed on an inpatient basis at St. Joseph Hospital on April 4, 2014, and reported to be within normal limits.

Mr. Smith continued conservative treatment with Dr. Ewald, following the prescribed program of rest, medication, exercise, and daily physiotherapy administered by his wife. He was able to graduate out of his lumbosacral support by approximately October 2014, resuming use of the garment when he experienced severe flare-ups of low back pain.

In his medical report dated January 2, 2015, Dr. Ewald stated that he expected a gradual resolution of lumbar symptomatology with time. However, in his subsequent report, dated January 10, 2015, Dr. Ewald noted that since his original report, Mr. Smith had suffered multiple repetitive episodes of low back pain, secondary to almost any increase of activity. At an office visit on February 25, Mr. Smith was reported to have localized his discomfort extremity well to the L5–S1 level, and range of motion was found to have decreased to approximately 75%.

Since his examination in February, Dr. Ewald has discussed at length with both Mr. Smith and his wife the possibility of surgical intervention, consisting of lumbar stabilization (fusion) at the L5–S1 level, secondary to the spondylolisthesis present at that level. Dr. Ewald has advised them of the risks, complications, and alternatives with regard to consideration of surgical stabilization, noting that surgery would be followed by a 6-to-9-month period of rehabilitation, and further warning that even if the surgical procedure is carried out, there is no guarantee that Mr. Smith will be alleviated of all of his symptomatology.

As stated in Dr. Ewald's medical report dated March 10, 2015, Mr. Smith is himself beginning to lean toward definite consideration with regard to surgery, although he is presently continuing with conservative management.

Dr. Ewald recommends that in the event Mr. Smith does choose to undergo surgery, a repeat myelogram should be performed in order to rule out, as much as possible, the presence of a herniated nucleus pulposus either above or at the level of the spondylolisthesis.

IV. Residual Complaints

Mr. Smith states that his neck injury has now largely resolved, although he does experience occasional neck pain and headaches. However, he continues to suffer from constant severe pain in his low back, with some radiation of pain and numbness in the right leg.

Mr. Smith notes that his low back pain is worse with cold weather and aggravated by prolonged sitting, walking, driving, or nearly any form of activity. He finds that he must rest frequently and continues to follow a daily regimen of swimming, Williams exercises, pain medication, and physiotherapy administered by his wife. He has also resumed the use of his lumbosacral brace.

Mr. Smith was an extremely active person prior to the accident, accustomed to working 10 to 12 hours per day and engaging in active sports such as tennis. Since the accident, he has had to sell his business and restrict all activities to a minimum, because he has found that any increase in activity will trigger a flare-up of low back pain so severe that he is totally incapacitated for several days at a time.

As stated by Dr. Ewald, Mr. Smith is now seriously considering the possibility of surgical stabilization, despite the risks and complications involved. He has always viewed surgery as a last resort but is now beginning to realize that it may be his only alternative in view of his prolonged pain and disability. However, he currently intends to delay any definite decision until after the summer, during which time he intends to increase his swimming activity and see if he can gain any relief from his symptomatology.

V. Specials

(Copies of supporting documentation are attached hereto.)

A. Medical

Southland Ambulance Service (9/6/13).	$ 2,937.12
St. Joseph Hospital (9/6/13-9/25/13)	$ 122,046.22
Raymond R Ross, M.D. (Emergency Room 9/6/13)	$ 12,025.68
Brian A. Ewald, M.D. (9/6/13-4/28/15)	$ 5,604.94
Michael H. Braniff, M.D. (9/10/15-9/22/15)	$ 4,140.12
Wind Ambulance Service (9/25/15)	$ 1,939.22
Wind Ambulance Service (9/26/15)	$ 1,989.71
Beatrice Tasker, R.P.T. (9/21/13-10/22/13)	$ 4,825.10
Abbey Rents (Rental of hospital bed and trapeze bar, 9/25/13-11/25/13)	$ 822.00
Allied Medical & Surgical Co. (Purchase of cane, 1/10/13)	$ 50.45
Rice Clinical Laboratories (2/1/14)	$ 314.00
Robert N. Dunphy, M.D. (2/1/14-4/15/14)	$ 2,895.00
St Joseph Hospital (X-rays and lab tests, 2/9/14)	$ 1,756.00
St Joseph Hospital (Inpatient myelography, 4/23/14-4/24/14)	$ 3,851.60
Medication	$ 6,357.70
Total Medical Expenses	$ 171,554.86

B. Miscellaneous Family Expenses

(During plaintiffs hospitalization, 9/6/13-9/25/15)

1. Sky Palm Motel (Lodging for wife and children).	$ 6,050.50
2. Taxicab (9/6/13).	$ 62.45
Total Miscellaneous Expenses.	$ 6,112.95

C. Business and Wage Loss

At the time of the accident, Mr. Smith was employed as president and co-owner, with Mr. George Frost, of the Inter Science Institute, Inc., a medical laboratory in Los Angeles. As stated in the attached verification from a CPA, John Mamikunian, Mr. Smith was earning an annual salary of $48,000, plus automobile, expenses, and fringe benefits.

In a telephone conversation with Mr. Smith on May 6, 1995, he advised that Inter Science Institute had grossed $512,000 in 2013 and $700,000 in 2014. He further confirmed that prior to the accident of September 6, 2013, both he and Mr. Frost had been approached on at least two to three different occasions by companies, including Revlon and a Canadian firm, offering substantial sums of money for purchase of the business. On the basis of the foregoing, both Mr. Smith and Mr. Frost place a conservative estimate of the value of the business at $2,000,000.

Due to injuries sustained in the subject accident, Mr. Smith was unable to return to work or perform the necessary executive and managerial functions required in his position as president and part owner of the business. As a result, on or about October 26, 2013, while still totally incapacitated by his injuries, Mr. Smith was forced to sell his 50% stock interest in the Inter Science Institute for a total sum of $300,000.

On the basis of the prior estimated value of the business at $2,000,000, Mr. Smith sustained a loss of $700,000 in the sale of his one-half interest in Inter Science Institute, Inc., in addition to the loss of an annual salary of $48,000, plus automobile, expenses, and fringe benefits. His salary loss is $84,000 based on an annual salary of $48,000 up to October 12, 2015.

D. Totals

Medical Expenses.	$ 171,554.86
Miscellaneous Expenses.	$ 6,112.95
Business Loss.	$ 700,000.00
Salary Loss.	$ 84,000.00
Totals.	$ 961,667.81

Adapted from Katherine Webb, Legal Assistant at Cartwright, Sucherman, Slobodin & Fowler, San Francisco, California.

ETHICS AND INVESTIGATION

When carrying out an investigation assignment, great care must be used to comply with all of the ethical obligations discussed in Chapter 5 that govern law offices. For example:

pretexting Using online deception as a pretext to obtain information from another person.

- Do not violate the *anticontact rule*. Do not communicate with an opponent or an employee of an opponent unless the opponent's attorney allows you to do so. If you are not sure whether someone has attorney representation, ask him or her.
- If the opponent is unrepresented, do not allow him or her to think that you are *disinterested*. Because you work for one side in the matter, it is deceptive to allow someone to think you are neutral.
- Do not lie about your identity, the purpose of your contact with someone, or the advocacy connection you have with one side in a legal dispute. Attorneys and their paralegals have an ethical duty not to deceive. For example, do not use deception (**pretexting**) to obtain information that is not publicly available on social media such as Facebook. (It is "impermissible deception to seek to friend a witness without disclosing the purpose of the friend request, even if the witness is not a represented party."[28] For more on deception in this area, see Chapter 5.
- Do not allow anyone to think you are an attorney even if you have made no affirmative misrepresentations about your status.
- Do not give any other false statements of fact while communicating with a potential witness.
- Do not expressly or implicitly promise someone something of value (e.g., money) if he or she agrees to bring or drop a lawsuit.
- Do not expressly or implicitly encourage someone to alter or destroy evidence. This can lead to a charge of **spoliation**.

spoliation Intentionally destroying, altering, or concealing evidence.

- Do not expressly or implicitly encourage someone to leave the area so that a court would not be able to reach him or her with process (e.g., service of process).
- Do not secretly record a conversation with someone.
- Do not reveal personal information about other people.
- Be careful when monitoring the activities of someone so that you are not accused of stalking.

Finally, avoid careless waiver of the attorney-client privilege. While working on a client's case, you undoubtedly will learn a great deal of information that is protected by the attorney-client privilege. Be very careful about mentioning any of this information while talking with a witness. As we saw in Chapter 5, the disclosure of such confidential information may result in a waiver of the privilege, even if the witness is friendly to your side.[29]

CHAPTER SUMMARY

In large relatively complex cases, law firms hire professional investigators. For less involved investigation needs, attorneys and paralegals perform needed investigation tasks. Legal investigation is the process of gathering additional facts and verifying presently known facts in order to advise a client on how to avoid or solve a legal problem. The major guides to fact gathering are instructions of the supervisor; evidence, procedural law, and substantive law; checklists; fact particularization (FP); common sense; and flexibility. Investigation is a highly individualistic skill where determination, imagination, resourcefulness, hustle, and openness are critical. A good investigator has a healthy suspicion of preconceived notions of what the facts are because such notions might interfere with uncovering the unexpected. A good investigation report can help an attorney plan discovery strategy.

The main discovery methods are deposition, interrogatories, requests for admissions (RFA), requests for production (RFP), and independent medical examinations (IME). In the search for the facts, the standard that guides the search is not truth or proof; the guideline of the investigator is to pursue any evidence that might help either side in the dispute.

People often have different perspectives on what did or did not happen, particularly in regard to emotionally charged events. When different versions of facts exist, the investigator must seek them out and distinguish between observed facts and conclusions (inferences and opinions) that people reach about the facts they observe.

Competent investigation requires an understanding of the kinds of distortions that can occur in an investigation, a knowledge of the standard sources of information, an ability to use the techniques of gaining access to records, and an ability to evaluate the trustworthiness of both oral and physical evidence.

Investigators must be aware of the image they project of themselves, be prepared for witnesses with differing levels of factual knowledge, be ready for witnesses who are unwilling to cooperate, and be able to gain the trust of witnesses.

Investigators should understand the four ways a version of the facts can be established at trial, admissibility, the distinction between direct evidence and circumstantial evidence, the nature of relevance, when a witness is competent to give testimony, the nature of hearsay, and the major exceptions that allow hearsay to be admitted. Investigators also need to understand the effect of the privilege against self-incrimination, the attorney-client privilege, the doctor-patient privilege, the clergy-penitent privilege, the privilege for marital communications, confidentiality of some government information, authentication of evidence, the parol-evidence rule (PER), and the function of an evidence log.

Two important documents that are the products of competent investigation are a witness statement, which is taken to preserve the testimony of an important witness, and a settlement work-up, which is an advocacy document that compiles and organizes facts in an effort to encourage a favorable settlement.

Ethical investigators do not improperly contact an opposing party who has attorney representation, lie about their identity, allow anyone to think they are attorneys, make false statements of fact, make promises in exchange for an agreement to bring or drop a lawsuit, encourage anyone to alter evidence or avoid process, secretly record an interview, reveal personal information about others, or engage in stalking. They are also careful to avoid waiving the attorney-client privilege.

KEY TERMS

forensic (p. 402)
mass tort (p. 402)
skiptracing (p. 402)
service of process (p. 402)
due diligence (p. 402)
fact (p. 403)
fact particularization (FP) (p. 403)
settlement (p. 404)
discovery (p. 405)
impeach (p. 405)
deposition (p. 405)
interrogatories ("rogs") (p. 405)
request for admission (RFA) (p. 405)
request for production (RFP) (p. 405)
independent medical examination (IME) (p. 405)
evidence (p. 406)

proof (p. 406)
standard of proof (p. 406)
beyond a reasonable doubt (p. 406)
preponderance of the evidence (p. 406)
clear and convincing evidence (p. 406)
substantive law (p. 406)
networking (p. 406)
inference (p. 406)
leading question (p. 407)
Freedom of Information Act (FOIA) (p. 411)
sunshine law (p. 411)
parol evidence (p. 412)
tangible evidence (p. 412)
disinterested (p. 414)
bias (p. 414)
anticontact rule (p. 415)

subpoena (p. 415)
judgment creditor (p. 416)
judgment debtor (p. 416)
deep pocket (p. 416)
admissible (p. 423)
admission (p. 424)
stipulation (p. 424)
judicial notice (p. 424)
presumption (p. 424)
rebuttable presumption (p. 424)
irrebuttable presumption (p. 424)
bench trial (p. 424)
direct evidence (p. 425)
circumstantial evidence (p. 425)
relevant (p. 425)
attorney-client privilege (p. 425)
competent (p. 425)
credibility (p. 426)

opinion (p. 426)
hearsay (p. 426)
privilege (p. 428)
work-product rule (p. 428)
privilege log (p. 428)
authentication (p. 428)
testator (p. 429)
parol-evidence rule (PER) (p. 429)
contemporaneous (p. 429)
chain of custody (p. 429)
evidence log (p. 429)
occurrence witness (p. 430)
pre-occurrence witness (p. 430)
post-occurrence witness (p. 430)
attestation clause (p. 430)
rebut (p. 431)
settlement work-up (p. 431)
pretexting (p. 434)
spoliation (p. 434)

ASSIGNMENTS

CRITICAL ANALYSIS

9.1 Which of the following statements do you agree or disagree with? Why? How would you modify the statements you disagree with to reflect your own view?

(a) There is a great difference between investigation conducted by the police and that conducted by a paralegal working for a law office.

(b) An investigator is an advocate.

(c) It is impossible for the investigator to keep from showing his or her personal biases while in the field investigating.

(d) There is often a need for a second investigation to verify the results of an earlier investigation.

(e) A good investigator will probably be unable to describe why he or she is effective. There are too many intangibles involved.

(f) If someone is willing to talk to and cooperate with an investigator, there is reason to suspect that this person has a bias.

9.2 Design a detailed investigation strategy for the following situations:

(a) Sam owes Tom $50,000. When Tom asks for his money, Sam tells him that he is broke. Tom suspects differently.

(b) Tom's uncle once lived in Boston. After spending two years in the army, he started traveling across the country; he has not been heard from for five years. Tom wants to locate his uncle.

(c) A welfare department has told a client that it is going to terminate public assistance because the client's boyfriend is supporting her and her family. The client denies this. Tom is assigned to the case.

(d) A client has been to the office seeking help in obtaining custody of his children from their mother (to whom he is not married). He claims that she is not taking proper care of the children.

9.3 Examine the following four situations. Discuss the relevance of the evidence indicated and what the evidence proves and does not prove.

(a) Mrs. Phillips is being sued by a department store for the cost of a gas refrigerator. Mrs. Phillips claims that she never ordered and never received a refrigerator from the store. The attorney for Mrs. Phillips wants to introduce two letters: (1) a letter from Mrs. Phillips's landlord stating that her kitchen is not equipped to handle gas appliances and (2) a letter from another merchant stating that Mrs. Phillips bought an electric refrigerator from him a year ago.

(b) Phil Smith has been charged with burglary in Detroit on December 16, 2013. His attorney tries to introduce testimony into evidence that on December 7, 8, 11, 15, and 22, 2013, the defendant was in Florida.

(c) Al Neuman is suing Sam Snow for negligence in operating his motor vehicle. Al's attorney tries to introduce into evidence the fact that Snow currently has pending against him four other automobile negligence cases in other courts.

(d) Jim is on trial for the rape of Sandra. Jim's attorney wants to introduce into evidence (1) the fact that Sandra is the mother of Jim's child, who was born three years ago when they were dating (they separated in bitterness five months after the birth and never married); (2) the fact that Sandra has a Facebook page on which she has posted provocative pictures of herself boasting of having multiple boyfriends; and (3) the fact that Sandra is a member of Alcoholics Anonymous.

9.4 Make a list of the questions that you would ask in order to uncover the underlying facts that formed the basis of the following opinions:

(a) He was insane.

(b) She couldn't see.

(c) It was cold out.

(d) He was traveling very fast.

9.5 Is hearsay evidence involved in the following situations? Examine the four conditions of hearsay in each.

(a) Tom is suing Jim for negligence. On the witness stand, Tom says, "Jim was speeding at the time he hit me."

(b) Tom is suing Jim for negligence. While Tom is on the stand, his attorney introduces into evidence a mechanic's bill showing that the repair of the car cost $578.

(c) Mary and George were passengers in Tom's car at the time of its collision with Jim. George testifies that just before the collision, Mary shouted, "Look out for that car going through the red light!"

(d) He told me he was God.

9.6 Smith is being sued for assaulting Jones, who later died. Smith is on the stand when the following exchange occurs.

Counsel for Smith: Did you strike the decedent, Jones?

Smith: Yes.

Counsel for Smith: Did Jones say anything to you before you struck him?

Counsel for Jones's estate: Objection, your honor, on the grounds of hearsay. Smith cannot give testimony on what the decedent said, since the decedent is obviously not subject to cross-examination.

(a) If Smith is allowed to answer the last question, he will say, "Yes, Jones told me that he was going to kill me." Would this statement be hearsay?

(b) If so, under what circumstances, if any, can it be admissible?

9.7 Assume that the settlement work-up in Exhibit 9-15 is not successful. The case is not settled and must now go to trial. Prepare a report for the attorney litigating the case of all the evidence that should be collected and considered for use at the trial.

(a) List all possible witnesses your side (representing Joseph Smith) might call and give a summary of what their testimony is likely to be.

(b) List all possible witnesses the other side (representing Dan Lamb) might call and give a summary of what their testimony is likely to be.

(c) List all possible physical evidence your side should consider using and give a summary of what each item might establish.

(d) List all possible physical evidence the other side is likely to consider using and give a summary of what each item might establish.

(e) What further facts do you think need to be investigated?

PROJECTS

9.8 Select any member of the class and take a witness statement from this person. (Alternatively, select someone at your home or work for the statement.) The statement should concern an accident of any kind (e.g., a serious mishap at work, a highway collision) in which the witness was a participant or an observer. (The witness, however, should not be a party to any litigation growing out of the accident.) You write out the statement from what the witness says in response to your questions. Do not submit a statement handwritten by the witness; the only handwritten matter should be his or her signature, initials, or corrections, if any. Use complete paragraphs in your report. Do not simply write out the question-and-answer exchanges between you and the person you interviewed. To help you obtain factual specificity, review the categories of fact particularization in Exhibits 8-4 and 8-5 in Chapter 8. As a guide for the reader, use descriptive headings for different parts of the statement. Assume that you (the investigator-paralegal) work for the law firm of Davis and Davis, which represents someone else involved in the accident.

CORE SKILLS

Among the many skills a paralegal must have, five core skills stand out: writing (both basic English and legal drafting), research, ethics, computer use, and collaboration (working with others). The core-skill assignments introduce and reinforce these skills. Even if you are not asked to do all of the assignments as part of the course, you should do them on your own. Also, do not wait for the topics in the assignments to be covered in this course or in other courses. Successful paralegals are self-starters. A major characteristic of a self-starter is a thirst for independent study—learning on your own.

CORE SKILL: WRITING

9.9 Select one of the hearsay problems in Assignment 9.5 and write a memo. For the format of the memo, use Exhibit 7-17 in Chapter 7. Apply the law of your state. Use the following steps to locate this law:

(a) In Google Scholar (scholar.google.com), select the "Case law" database and type this search query: aa hearsay law (substituting the name of your state for "aa").

(b) In the general search engine of Google, Bing, or Yahoo, type this search query: aa hearsay law (substituting the name of your state for "aa").

The memo must apply at least one opinion written by a state court in your state that defines hearsay. Pick an opinion whose facts are as close as possible to the fact situation you selected from Assignment 9.5. You can make up any additional facts that you need (e.g., the name of your supervisor, the city were the incident arose.) so long as these facts are reasonably consistent with the facts that you are given.

CORE SKILL: RESEARCH

9.10 In Google, Bing, or Yahoo, run this search: companies headquartered in aa (substituting the name of your state for aa). Select any corporation that has its home office or headquarters in your state, has a Web address, has a large number of employees, and is publicly traded (i.e., has shareholders who are members of the general public). Answer the following questions about this company using the suggestions in the chapter as well as the Internet resources listed in Helpful Websites at the end of the chapter.

(a) What is the name of the company? What are its street and Internet addresses?

(b) What kind of corporation is it?

(c) What are the names of five major officers of the corporation?

(d) Give a biographical summary of the president.

(e) What are the names of the members of the board of directors of the corporation?

(f) What is the earnings history of the corporation over the last five years?

(g) What major litigation has been brought by or against the corporation over the last 10 years?

9.11 Using the suggestions covered in the chapter and the Internet resources listed in Helpful Websites at the end of the chapter, answer the following questions:

(a) The average life span of a lobster.

(b) The maiden name of the wife of the first married governor of your state.

(c) The assessed property tax value of the tallest commercial building in your city in 1980.

(d) The weather in your state capital at noon on January 1 of last year.

(e) The estimated number of vehicles using diesel fuel that drove in or through the state last month.

(f) At the largest airport in the state, the salary of the air traffic controller with the most seniority on duty on the day last year when the airport experienced the largest rainfall of the year.

CORE SKILL: ETHICS

9.12 Make up a fact situation in which a paralegal on an investigation assignment violates at least five different ethical rules in the ethics code of your state. As pointed out in Chapter 5, the ethics code applies to attorneys. For purposes of this assignment, assume that the attorney knows about and gives advance approval for what the paralegal does in the investigation. This would make the attorney directly responsible for the ethical violations. To find the ethics code, enter this search in Google, Bing, or Yahoo: attorney ethics aa (substituting your state for aa). See also Assignment 1.7 in Chapter 1 and Appendix D for your state. For each violation, quote language from the code and explain how the facts violate this language.

CORE SKILL: COMPUTERS

9.13 In Google, Bing, or Yahoo, run this search: Apple attorney legal software hardware. Prepare a report in which you list Apple products that are used in any aspect of the practice of law. For each product, give a brief description of what it does and how it is used in a law office. Give the citation of each Internet site that you use.

CORE SKILL: COLLABORATION

9.14 In Google, Bing, or Yahoo, run this search: top twitterers legal.

(a) Select 10 twitterers who cover an aspect of law in which you have an interest. State why you selected each.

(b) Give two examples of tweets from each of the ten twitterers you selected.

(c) In Assignment 3.9 in Chapter 3, you opened a Twitter account, obtained Twitter addresses of as many fellow students as you could, and began following them. Select three of your ten twitterers and send a tweet to all your classmates in which you tell them about the three. Send your classmates three tweets, one each for the twitterers you selected. Include in the tweet why you selected the twitterer.

(d) Make a list of all of the twitterers your classmates tweeted you about. Go to the home pages of the twitterers. For each, state whether you think the twitterer is worth following for your own career.

THE JOB SEARCH

(The search for employment cannot wait until the end of a course or of a curriculum. It needs to begin now. The job-search assignments are designed to introduce you to different aspects of the job search and to build options for you to explore about employment.)

9.15   In Assignment 9.8 you did a witness statement. Rewrite this memo so that it can be a writing sample for your job portfolio when you are looking for employment. The memo must have no spelling or grammar errors. The statement must be at least two pages long. (Redo Assignment 9.8 if you do not have enough facts for a memo of this length.) The statement must have at least five paragraphs, and each paragraph must have at least five sentences. The paragraphs must be skillfully organized and have headings that facilitate ease of reading. Find two individuals who are willing to evaluate the memo. They do not have to be paralegals or attorneys. You want an evaluation that covers spelling, grammar, paragraph structure, and overall organization and clarity. Rewrite the statement based on their comments.

REVIEW QUESTIONS

1. What are some examples of investigation tasks performed by paralegals?
2. What kinds of tasks are performed in a forensic accounting?
3. What is legal investigation?
4. What is a fact?
5. What are the six major guides to fact gathering?
6. What are some characteristics of an effective investigator?
7. What is the relationship between the initial client interview and investigation?
8. How can the investigator assist the attorney who is trying to negotiate a settlement?
9. What is the goal of impeaching someone?
10. Name and define five discovery methods.
11. What is the distinction between evidence and proof?
12. What are the three standards of proof?
13. What test should an investigator use in determining whether to pursue a fact possibility?
14. What law should an investigator know?
15. What are some of the fundamental characteristics of facts and of peoples' perceptions of facts?
16. What is the distinction between observed facts and inferences?
17. How should an investigator plan an investigation via fact versions?
18. What is a leading question, and what are the dangers and advantages of using them?
19. List four categories of records to which you may want to obtain access.
20. What is a FOIA request?
21. What are some of the major techniques of gaining access to records?
22. Give examples of major questions you would ask yourself to determine the validity of eyewitness evidence.
23. Give examples of questions you would ask yourself to determine the validity of what someone else (the declarant) has said.
24. Give examples of questions you would ask yourself to determine the validity of something that is written.
25. Why should you try to interview someone with no other potential witnesses present during the interview?
26. What are the different images you might project of yourself when you investigate?
27. What are the five kinds of witnesses?
28. What is a disinterested witness?
29. What is the anticontact rule?
30. Name some of the states of mind witnesses can have.
31. What are some of the questions investigators must ask themselves when evaluating how well a witness might do on direct examination and on cross-examination?
32. What is the distinction between a judgment creditor and a judgment debtor?
33. What do we mean when we say that a witness has a deep pocket?
34. Name some of the kinds of information that a judgment creditor might try to seek online (from free and paid services) about the financial condition of a judgment debtor.
35. Name formulas to determine the minimum speed of a vehicle before the driver applied the brakes.
36. Name four ways a party can establish its version of the facts at a trial.
37. What is the difference between a rebuttable and irrebuttable presumption?
38. What is the consequence of evidence being declared admissible?
39. What is the difference between direct evidence and circumstantial evidence?
40. What is the difference between relevant evidence and admissible evidence?
41. What three conditions determine the competency of a witness?
42. What is the difference between the competency of a witness and the credibility of a witness?
43. What are the four conditions for the existence of hearsay?
44. What are the major exceptions to the hearsay rule?
45. What are the major evidentiary privileges?
46. What is the work-product rule?
47. What is the function of authentication?
48. What is the parol-evidence rule (PER)?
49. What is an evidence log?
50. What is the chain of custody?
51. Define a pre-occurrence witness, an occurrence witness, and a post-occurrence witness.
52. What are the four main kinds of witness statements?
53. What is a settlement work-up?
54. Name the major dos and don'ts of ethical investigators.

HELPFUL WEBSITES

Factual Information on the Internet (General)
- www.ipl.org
- indorgs.virginia.edu/portico
- vlib.org
- infomine.ucr.edu
- www.about.com
- dir.yahoo.com

General Investigation Resources
- www.refdesk.com
- www.llrx.com/features/ciguide.htm
- www.melissadata.com/lookups
- journalistsresource.org
- www.journaliststoolbox.com (click Investigative)
- www.reporter.org/desktop
- www.blackbookonline.info
- www.gao.gov/assets/200/198282.pdf
- www.gao.gov/products/osi-97-2
- www.docusearch.com
- jolt.richmond.edu/v12i4/article17.pdf
- law.lexisnexis.com/infopro/zimmermans/disp.aspx?z=2178
- www.reporter.org/desktop/tips/johndoe.htm

Public Records on the Internet
- publicrecords.searchsystems.net
- usgenweb.com
- rootsweb.com
- indorgs.virginia.edu/portico
- www.brbpub.com/free-public-records
- www.zabasearch.com
- blackbookonline.info
- www.zoominfo.com
- pipl.com
- www.spokeo.com
- www.publicdata.com
- locateplus.com

Finding People
- www.zabasearch.com
- www.snitch.name
- www.spokeo.com
- www.whitepages.com
- www.peoplesmart.com
- www.intelius.com
- www.pipl.com
- www.knowx.com
- www.switchboard.com
- www.accurint.com
- virtualprivatelibrary.blogspot.com/Finding%20People.pdf
- www.llrx.com/features/companyresearch.htm
- publicrecords.searchsystems.net/United-States/Missing

Locating Deceased Persons
- www.ehow.com/how_5864933_deceased-people.html
- www.rootsweb.com
- www.tributes.com
- familysearch.org

Birth, Death, Marriage, Divorce Records
- www.cdc.gov/nchs/howto/w2w/w2welcom.htm
- www.vitalrec.com
- www.vitalchek.com
- search.ancestry.com/search/db.aspx?dbid=3693

Social Security Numbers and States
- socialsecuritynumerology.com/prefixes.php
- www.mrfa.org/ssn.htm

Finding Information about Businesses
- www.sec.gov/edgar.shtml
  (SEC filings; EDGAR)
- www.annualreports.com
- www.bloomberg.com
- www.hoovers.com
- www.dnb.com
- www.corporateinformation.com

Business Directories and Search Engines
- www.yellowpages.com
- www.dexonline.com

Due Diligence Searches
- www.wysk.com

Finding Assets
- www.knowx.com
- www.ussearch.com
- www.tracerservices.com
- www.members.tripod.com/proagency/ask8.html
- www.accurint.com
- locateplus.com
- www.abajournal.com/news/article/podcast_monthly_episode_23
- www.assetsearchblog.com

Background Checks
- www.backgroundchecks.com
- www.employeescreen.com
- www.ussearch.com

Freedom of Information
- www.foia.gov
- www.usdoj.gov/oip/foi-upd.htm
- www.tncrimlaw.com/foia_indx.html
- www.sba.gov (type "freedom of information" in the search box)
- www.nfoic.org

Open Records and Sunshine Laws
- www.rcfp.org/open-government-guide
- www.kcnn.org/open_government

Political Contributors
- fec.gov
- www.melissadata.com/lookups
- www.opensecrets.org

Motor Vehicle History Search
- www.vehiclehistory.gov

Party Search in Court Records
- State courts: online index
- Federal courts: www.pacer.gov

Deep Web Research
- www.llrx.com/features/deepweb2013.htm

Big Data Online
- www.llrx.com/features/statisticsdataresources.htm

Statistics
- www.census.gov
- www.census.gov/compendia/statab
- factfinder2.census.gov
- fedstats.sites.usa.gov
- www.cdc.gov/nchs/products/vsus.htm
- www.archives.gov/research/genealogy/index.html

The Ethical Investigator
- www.ethicalinvestigator.com

Accident Investigation
- www.actar.org/links.html

Settlement Brochure/Demand Package
- www.thecalifornialitigator.com (type *settlement* in the search box)

Witness Statement
- a4m.co/topics/jZg6w5RXXPqK8vaN.html
- thecalifornialitigator.com (type *witness* in the search box)

Historical Weather Sites
- www.ncdc.noaa.gov/cdo-web
- www.ncdc.noaa.gov/data-access/quick-links
- www.weather.gov
- www.wunderground.com

Climate Reports
- www.noaa.gov
- www.ncdc.noaa.gov

Medical Information and Research
- www.nlm.nih.gov
- www.med.yale.edu/departments/index.aspx#page1
- med.stanford.edu/research
- library.umassmed.edu/index

Military Searches
- www.military.com/buddy-finder
- pibuzz.com/find-people-in-the-us-military

Expert Witness Directory
- www.tasanet.com
- www.expertlaw.com
- www.expertpages.com

News Searches
- news.google.com
- www.bing.com/news
- news.yahoo.com
- www.onlinenewspapers.com

Erin Brockovich
- www.brockovich.com

Your Local Public Library
Check to find out what online databases are available free to anyone with a library card. Examples of what might be available:
- Gale's Business Directory
- RefUSA
- Academic Search (full-text access to scholarly articles)
- Legal Information Reference center

Google, Bing, or Yahoo Searches
(On these search engines, run the following searches, using quotation marks and substituting your state for "aa" where indicated.)
- "people search"
- "public records"
- "accident reconstruction"
- "Erin Brockovich"
- expert witnesses
- witness interviews
- "witness statement"
- finding assets
- locating missing persons
- background investigation
- evidence rules aa
- legal investigation aa
- hearsay evidence
- evidence privilege
- "settlement brochure"
- freedom of information
- "legal investigation"
- due diligence

ENDNOTES

1 Tracey Young, *Paralegal as Investigator*, National Paralegal Reporter, 22 (October/November 2010).

2 Christine Drapac-Taylor, *Why I Became a Paralegal* (June 16, 2011).

3 Theresa Carrico, IV *The Paralegal Mentor*, Issue 47 (December 15, 2011).

4 Lana Clark, *Developing a Strategy for Witness Interviews*, 10 Legal Assistant Today 65 (January/February 1993).

5 Tracy Girrens, *Paralegal Profession the Best*, KLAS ACTION 9 (Kansas Paralegal Association, May 1998).

6 Neal Bevans, *Diving Deep*, 22 Legal Assistant Today 70 (September/October 2004).

7 See Edna M. Wallace, *Regulation: The Good, the Bad and the Ugly* (linkedin.com/pub/edna-wallace/6/970/2aa) (2006).

8 Paralegal Today Forum (March 15, 2012) (www.paralegaltoday.com/lat-forum/default.htm).

9 Carolyn Saenz, Paralegal, *P.I.*, 16 Legal Assistant Today 56 (May/June 1999).

10 A. Daniel Yarmey, *The Psychology of Eyewitness Testimony* 9 (Free Press, 1979); E. Loftus et al., *Powerful Eyewitness Testimony*, Trial Magazine 64–66 (April 1988).

11 Byron Keith, *Dealing Smartly with Different Witnesses*, The Legal Investigator 38 (November 1991).

12 *When Witnesses Are Mistaken*, The Week, November 11, 2011, at 13. See also Melissa Dittmann, *Accuracy and the Accused*, American Psychological Association (2004).

13 Adam Liptak, *Justices Weigh Judges' Duties to Assess Reliability of Eyewitness Testimony*, N.Y. Times, November 13, 2011, at A20.

14 Francis Ritter, *The Art of Hearing Between the Lines*, The Legal Investigator 9 (February 1992).

15 Janet Jackson, *Interviewing Witnesses*, At Issue 1 (San Francisco Association of Legal Assistants April 1994). Reprinted with permission of the San Francisco Paralegal Association.

16 Julie Bassett, *Hot Tips for Interviewing Witnesses*, 9 Legal Assistant Today 23, 27 September/October 1991).

17 Deborah Andrews, *Ask the Experts*, SJPA Reporter (South Jersey Paralegal Association, July 1991).

18 John Lehe, *Techniques for Locating Missing Parties*, 11 Legal Assistant Today 80, 81 (January/February 1994).

19 Adapted from Dale W. Felton, 27 Trial Magazine 60 (February 1991). Reprinted with the permission of *Trial* (February 1991) © Copyright The Association of Trial Lawyers of America.

20 *Montana Code Annotated*, § 37-60-101 (2013) (codes.lp.findlaw.com/mtcode/37/60/1/37-60-101).

21 Roger Haydock and John Sonsteng, *Trial* 209 (1991).

22 E. Cleary, ed., *McCormick's Handbook of the Law of Evidence* 584 (1972).

23 For an overview of privilege in federal court, see Rule 803, Federal Rules of Evidence (2014) (www.law.cornell.edu/rules/fre/rule_803).

24 K. Wilkoff, *Writing Witness Statements That Win Cases*, 12 Legal Assistant Today 51, 52 (September/October 1994).

25 Yetta Blair, *Interviewing Witnesses and Securing Their Signed Written Statements*, 14 Points and Authorities 10 (Fresno Paralegal Association, May 1992).

26 Kathryn Andrews, *Interviews and Statements* 10 (Oregon Paralegal Association, October 1988).

27 Adapted from Katherine Webb, Legal Assistant at Cartwright, Sucherman, Slobodin & Fowler, San Francisco, California.

28 San Diego County Bar Association, *SDCBA Legal Ethics Opinion* 2011-2 (May 24, 2011) (www.sdcba.org/index.cfm?pg=LEC2011-2).

29 Beth L. King, *The Successful Witness Interview*, 29 National Paralegal Reporter 6 (National Federation of Paralegal Associations October/November 2004).

CHAPTER 10

LITIGATION ASSISTANTSHIP

CHAPTER OUTLINE

- Introduction
- Overview of Civil and Criminal Litigation
- Alternative Dispute Resolution (ADR)
- Litigation Assistant: Pretrial Stage
- Litigation Assistant: Trial Stage
- Litigation Assistant: Appeal Stage
- Litigation Assistant: Enforcement Stage

CHAPTER OBJECTIVES

- Describe the extent of litigation in the United States.
- Distinguish between civil and criminal litigation.
- Outline the major steps in bringing and defending a civil case.
- Outline the major steps in bringing and defending a criminal case.
- Outline the major steps in bringing and defending a case before an administrative agency.
- Explain the different categories of alternative dispute resolution (ADR).
- List the major roles of paralegals in the pretrial stage of litigation.
- List the major roles of paralegals in the trial stage of litigation.
- List the major roles of paralegals in the appellate stage of litigation.
- List the major roles of paralegals in the enforcement stage of litigation.

INTRODUCTION

litigious (1) Inclined to resolve disputes through litigation. (2) Quarrelsome.

litigation (1) The formal process of resolving a legal dispute through the courts. (2) A lawsuit.

America is a **litigious** society, meaning we are prone to engage in disputes and **litigation**. Every year over 100 million new cases are filed in state courts and over 330,000 in federal courts (not including 1.2 million bankruptcy filings in federal bankruptcy courts).[1] Litigation is the formal process of resolving legal controversies through the courts. Administrative agencies can also resolve some legal disputes, as we saw in Chapter 6. In fact, a good deal of litigation begins in administrative agencies, whose decisions can be appealed in court.

OVERVIEW OF CIVIL AND CRIMINAL LITIGATION

Paralegals can perform many functions in assisting attorneys who are litigating cases. Before studying what these functions are, read the following overview of litigation, which will provide a context for understanding the roles of the attorney and paralegal. The overview is presented in the form of a story—the litigation woes of Michael Brown, who finds himself embroiled in a civil trial, a criminal trial, and an administrative dispute. At the end of the story, you will find most of this overview in outline form in Exhibits 10-3 and 10-4.

There are two broad categories of litigated disputes: civil and criminal. A **civil dispute** consists of

civil dispute A legal controversy in which (a) one private person or entity (e.g., a business) sues another; (b) a private person or entity sues the government; or (c) the government sues a private person or entity for a matter other than the commission of a crime.

- One private person or entity (e.g., a business) sues another private person or entity. Examples: Jones sues Smith for negligence after an automobile collision; Ajax, Inc. sues Tomas Vine Co. for breach of contract), or
- One private person or entity sues the government. Examples: a senior citizen sues the Social Security Administration for denial of disability benefits; an inmate sues a state prison for violation of civil rights), or
- The government sues a private person or entity for a matter other than the commission of a crime. Example: the state department of revenue sues the Dayglow Restaurant for the failure to deduct state taxes from the wages of servers.

criminal dispute A legal controversy in which the government alleges the commission of a crime.

A **criminal dispute** is a legal controversy in which the government alleges the commission of a crime.

THE LEGAL ODYSSEY OF MICHAEL BROWN: AN ANATOMY OF THE LITIGATION PROCESS

Michael Brown is a salesman for the Best Bread Company. Several years ago, as Brown was walking home from work, Harold Clay, an old friend from the past, stopped and offered him a ride. They had not seen each other since Clay had moved cross-country a number of years ago. They carried on an excited conversation as Clay drove. After a few blocks, a car driven by George Miller, a resident of a neighboring state, ran through a red light and struck Clay's car. All three individuals were seriously injured and were taken to a local hospital. Clay died two weeks later from injuries received in the crash.

Several days after the accident, Brown's boss, Frank Best, wrote Brown a letter. In it, Best said he had learned that the police had found about half an ounce of heroin under the front passenger seat of Clay's car and were planning to charge Brown with possession of narcotics with intent to distribute. Best also stated that several thefts had occurred at the company warehouse recently and that he now suspected Brown of having been involved in them. For these reasons, he decided to fire Brown, effective immediately.

At least three different legal disputes involving Brown could arise out of this fact situation:

1. A dispute among Brown, Miller, and Clay's estate regarding civil liability for the accident
2. A dispute between Brown and the government regarding the criminal drug charge
3. A dispute among Brown, the Best Bread Company, and the State Unemployment Compensation Board concerning Brown's entitlement to unemployment compensation benefits. This, also, is a civil dispute

Each of these disputes could lead to a number of court decisions. The third dispute might involve an administrative decision, possibly followed by one or more court decisions, all concerning Brown's claim for unemployment compensation.

I. CIVIL LIABILITY

Brown suffered substantial injury as a result of the crash. This raised important questions. From whom could he collect *damages*? Who was *liable* for the accident? Was Miller at fault? Clay? Was each of them *jointly and severally liable*?

Damages: An award of money paid by the wrongdoer to compensate the person who has been harmed.

Liable: Legally responsible.

Joint and several liability: Legally responsible together and individually. Each wrongdoer is individually responsible for the entire debt or judgment. The injured party can choose to collect the full debt or judgment from one wrongdoer or from all of them until the debt or judgment is satisfied.

Brown *retained* Brenda Davis, Esq. to represent him. Once Brown signed the attorney-client fee contract (in which Brown agreed to pay Davis a *contingent fee* of one-third of whatever Brown wins in a judgment or settlement), Davis entered an *appearance* and become the *attorney of record*.

Retain: To hire; to place or keep in one's service. The noun is **retainer**.

Retainer: The act of hiring or engaging the services of someone, usually a professional. The verb is *retain*. (See glossary for an additional meaning.)

Contingent fee: A fee that is paid only if the case is successfully resolved by litigation or settlement, regardless of the number of hours spent on the case. (The fee is also referred to as a *contingency*.)

Appearance: Formally coming before a tribunal as a party or as a representative of a party. The attorney usually appears by filing a *notice of appearance* in court, which in some courts is accomplished through a *praecipe*. A praecipe is a formal request to the court (usually directed to the court clerk) that something be done. Here, the request is that the attorney become the attorney of record.

Attorney of record: The attorney noted in the court files as the attorney representing a particular party. Once litigation has begun, attorneys of record may need court permission to withdraw from the case before it is concluded.

The attorney explained that a number of factors had to be considered before deciding on the *forum* in which to sue Miller and Clay's *estate*. Brown might be able to bring the suit in a number of courts: (1) in a state trial court where Brown lives, (2) in a state trial court where Miller lives, (3) in a state trial court where Clay lived and where his estate is now located, (4) in a federal trial court sitting in Brown's state, (5) in a federal trial court sitting in Miller's state, or (6) in the federal trial court sitting in the state where Clay lived. All of these courts would have *subject-matter jurisdiction* over the dispute. The reason Brown could sue in a federal court is the existence of *diversity of citizenship*. Davis advised Brown to sue in federal court. The suit would be brought in the *U.S. district court* sitting in Brown's own state because this would be the most convenient *venue* for Brown.

Forum: (1) A court. (2) The place where the parties are presently litigating their dispute. (3) A court or other tribunal hearing a case.

Estate: All of the assets and liabilities of a decedent (one who has died) at the time of his or her death. When we say that an estate is sued (or brings a suit), we are referring to the decedent's representative who is authorized to resolve claims involving the decedent's assets and debts. (For other meanings of estate, see the glossary.)

Subject-matter jurisdiction: The court's power to resolve a particular type of legal dispute and to grant a particular type of relief.

Diversity of citizenship: The disputing parties are citizens of different states and the amount in controversy exceeds $75,000. This diversity gives subject-matter jurisdiction to a U.S. district court.

U.S. district court: The main trial court in the federal judicial system with subject-matter jurisdiction over civil and criminal cases. (See Exhibits 6-4 and 6-5 in Chapter 6.)

Venue: The proper county or geographical area in which a court with jurisdiction may hear a case. In most judicial systems, there is more than one trial court. For example, there may be one for each county or district. The selection of a particular trial court within a judicial system is referred to as a *choice of venue*.

Having decided on a court, Davis was ready to begin the lawsuit. She instructed her paralegal, Ted Alexander, to prepare the first draft of the *complaint*, naming Brown as the *plaintiff* and *stating a cause of action* for *negligence* against Miller and Clay's estate as *codefendants*. The complaint was the first *pleading* of the case. In the complaint, Davis stated the facts she felt constituted a cause of action for negligence. Some of the factual *allegations* were based on Brown's personal knowledge, while others were based on *information and belief*. The *prayer for relief* in the complaint contained an *ad damnum clause* that asked for $100,000. When Davis finished drafting the complaint, she signed it. The signature (called a *subscription*) of the attorney is sufficient for this pleading. The signature (subscription) of a party (Brown) is not needed. If it was needed, it would be called a *verification*. Because this was not to be a *bench trial*, Davis included a written demand for a *jury trial* and instructed her paralegal to *file* the complaint and a *civil cover sheet* with the clerk of the court. When this was done, the clerk *docketed* the case.

Complaint: (1) A plaintiff's first pleading, stating a cause of action against the defendant. Also called *petition*. (2) A formal criminal charge.

Plaintiff: The person who initiates a civil (and sometimes a criminal) action in court.

Cause of action: (1) A legally acceptable reason for suing. A rule that constitutes a legal theory for bringing a suit. (2) The facts that give a person a right to judicial relief.

Negligence: The failure to use reasonable care that an ordinary prudent person would have used in a similar situation, resulting in injury or other loss.

Stating a cause of action: Including facts in a pleading (e.g., a complaint) that, if proved at trial, would entitle the party to the judicial relief sought (assuming the other party does not plead and prove a defense that would defeat the effort).

Codefendant: Two or more defendants who are sued in the same civil case or who are prosecuted in the same criminal case.

Pleading: A formal litigation document filed by a party that states or responds to the claims and defenses the parties have against each other. The major pleadings are the complaint and answer.

Allegation: A claimed fact. A fact that a party will try to prove at trial.

Information and belief: Good-faith belief as to the truth of an allegation, not based on firsthand knowledge. A standard legal term used to indicate that the allegation is not based on the firsthand knowledge of the person making the allegation, but that the person, nevertheless, believes in good faith that the allegation is true.

Prayer for relief: The request in a pleading for damages or other forms of judicial relief.

Ad damnum clause: A clause stating the damages claimed. (See "prayer for relief" in Exhibit 10-6 later in the chapter.)

Subscription: (1) A signature. (2) The act of signing one's name.

Verification: A formal declaration that a person has read a document (e.g., a complaint) and swears that it is true to the best of his or her knowledge.

Bench trial: A trial before a judge without a jury. Also called *nonjury trial*.

Jury trial: A trial in which a group of persons resolves the issues or questions of fact. The judge decides the issues or questions of law. In a bench trial, the judge decides both the questions of law and the questions of fact.

File: (1) To deliver a document to a court officer so that it can become part of the official collection of documents in a case. (2) To deliver a document to a government agency.

Civil cover sheet: A form filed in court in a civil case that indicates the names and addresses of the parties and their attorneys, the kind of action being filed, etc. The form is filed with the complaint. Also called *civil action cover sheet*.

Docket: A court's list of its pending cases. Also called *calendar*. Once all the necessary papers have been filed, the case is "docketed" by the clerk, i.e., placed on the court's official calendar. (See glossary for an additional meaning.)

Service of process came next. It was accomplished when a copy of the complaint, along with the *summons*, was served on both Miller and the legal representative of Clay's estate. Miller and the estate had to respond to the summons in order to avoid a *default judgment*. Neither Davis nor her paralegal served Miller and the estate. Davis used a *process server*, who then had to file with the court a *proof of service* indicating the circumstances under which service was achieved. Service was made before the *statute of limitations* on the negligence cause of action had run out. Once the defendants were properly served, the court acquired *personal jurisdiction* over them. All the parties then sent *litigation holds* to each other.

Service of process: A formal delivery of notice to a defendant that a suit has been initiated to which he or she must respond. The most common method of service of process is to place the complaint and summons in the hands of the defendant. This is called *personal service*. If another form of service is allowed (e.g., service by mail), it is called *substituted service* or *constructive service*.

Process: The means (e.g., a summons, writ, or other court order) used by the court to acquire or exercise its power or jurisdiction over a person.

Summons: A notice directing the defendant to appear in court and answer the plaintiff's complaint or face a **default judgment**. The summons is served on the defendant.

Default judgment: A judgment against a party for failure to file a required pleading or otherwise respond to an opponent's claim.

Process server: Someone who serves or delivers process.

Proof of service: A sworn statement (or other evidence) that a summons or other process has been served on a party in an action. Also called *certificate of service*, *return of service*.

Statute of limitations: A law stating that civil or criminal actions are barred if not brought within a specified time. The action is time-barred if not brought within that time.

Personal jurisdiction: A court's power over a person to determine (**adjudicate**) his or her personal rights. Also called *in personam jurisdiction*. More limited kinds of jurisdiction include the court's power over a person's interest in specific property (quasi in rem jurisdiction), over the property itself (in rem jurisdiction), or over a status such as marriage (also in rem jurisdiction).

adjudicate: To resolve or decide by judicial process; to judge. The noun is *adjudication*; the adjective is *adjudicative*.

Litigation hold: A notice that a legal dispute has occurred and that information pertinent to the dispute must be preserved by the person or organization in possession or custody of such information. The failure to do may result in sanctions for **spoliation**.

Spoliation: Intentionally destroying, altering, or concealing evidence.

Both Miller and Clay's estate filed *motions to dismiss* for *failure to state a cause of action*. The court issued a *ruling* that denied both motions.

Motion: An application or request made to a court or other decision-making body seeking to obtain a favorable action or ruling, e.g., a motion to dismiss. The party making the motion is called the **movant**. The verb is *move*, as in "I move that the court permit the demonstration" or "I move that the case be dismissed."

Movant: A party masking a motion or request.

Motion to dismiss: A request, often made before the trial begins, that the judge dismiss the case because the parties have reached a settlement or because of a serious procedural deficiency.

Failure to state a cause of action: Failure of a party to allege enough facts that, if proved, would entitle the party to judicial relief. Even if the party proved every fact he or she alleged, the facts would not establish a cause of action entitling the party to recover against the opponent. The motion to dismiss for failure to state a cause of action is sometimes referred to as (a) a *demurrer* or (b) a *failure to state a claim upon which relief can be granted*.

Ruling: The conclusion or outcome of a decision made by a court or administrative agency.

Because the case had been filed in a federal court, the *procedural law* governing the case would be found in the *Federal Rules of Civil Procedure*. (The *substantive law* of the case would be the state law of negligence.) According to the Federal Rules of Civil Procedure, Miller and Clay's estate were each required to file an *answer* to Brown's complaint within 20 days. Miller filed his answer almost immediately. Because Clay was dead and unable to tell his attorney what happened at the accident, the attorney for the estate had some difficulty preparing an answer and was unable to file it within the 20 days. To avoid a default judgment against the estate, the attorney filed a motion asking for an extension of 30 days within which to file the answer. The motion was granted by the court, and the answer was filed within the new deadline.

Procedural law: The rules that govern the mechanics of resolving a dispute in court or in an administrative agency, e.g., a rule on the time by which a party must respond to a complaint.

Federal Rules of Civil Procedure (Fed. R. Civ. P.)(FRCP): The rules that govern the mechanics of resolving a dispute by a U.S. district court, which is the main federal trial court (www.law.cornell.edu/rules/frcp).

Substantive law: Nonprocedural laws that define or govern rights and duties, e.g., the duty to use reasonable care to avoid injuring someone.

Answer: The first pleading of the defendant in response to the plaintiff's claims. (See glossary for an additional meaning.)

The answers contained the parties' *defenses*. The answer filed on behalf of Clay's estate denied all allegations of negligence and raised an *affirmative defense* of *contributory negligence* against Brown on the theory that if Clay had been partially responsible for the collision, it was because Brown had carelessly distracted him through his conversation in the car. Finally, the answer of Clay's estate raised a *cross-claim* against the codefendant Miller, alleging that the accident had been caused by Miller's negligence. The estate asked $1,000,000 in damages.

Defense: An allegation of fact or a legal theory offered to offset or defeat a claim or demand. The word *defense* also means the defendant and his or her attorney.

Affirmative defense: A defense raising facts or arguments that will defeat the opponent's claim even if the opponent's allegations in the claim are proven.

Contributory negligence: The failure of plaintiffs to use such reasonable care for their own protection as an ordinary prudent person would have used in a similar situation, thereby helping to cause their own injury or other loss.

Cross-claim: A claim brought by one defendant against another defendant or by one plaintiff against another plaintiff in the same action. Also called a *cross action*.

Miller's answer also raised the defense of contributory negligence against Brown and stated a cross-claim against Clay's estate, alleging that the accident had been caused solely by the negligence of Clay, or of Clay and Brown together. On this same theory (that Brown together with Clay had negligently caused the accident), Miller's answer also stated a *counterclaim* against Brown, to which Brown immediately filed a *reply*. Miller sought $50,000 from Brown and $50,000 against Clay's estate as damages.

Counterclaim: A claim by one side in a case (usually the defendant) that is filed in response to a claim asserted by an opponent (usually the plaintiff).

Reply: A plaintiff's response to the defendant's counterclaim, plea, or answer.

For a time, Miller and his attorney considered filing a *third-party complaint* against his own automobile insurance company, because the company would be liable for any judgment against him. They decided against this strategy because they did not want to let the jury know that Miller was insured. If the jury knew this fact, it might be more inclined to reach a verdict in favor of the plaintiff and for a high amount of damages. The strategy was also unnecessary because there was no indication that Miller's insurer would *contest* its obligation to compensate Miller (within the policy limits of his insurance) for any damages that he might have to pay Brown or Clay's estate in the event that the trial resulted in an *adverse judgment* against him.

Third-party complaint: A defendant's complaint against someone who is not now a party on the basis that the latter may be liable for all or part of what the plaintiff might recover from the defendant.

Contest: (1) To challenge. (2) To raise a defense against a claim.

Adverse judgment: A judgment or decision against you.

At this point, five claims had been filed by the parties. A sixth, Miller's third-party claim against his insurer, had been considered but ultimately had not been filed. These claims and their relationship to each other are illustrated in Exhibit 10-1.

1. Plaintiff Brown's complaint (seeking $100,000) for negligence against Miller
2. Plaintiff Brown's complaint (seeking $100,000) for negligence against Clay's estate (Miller and the estate are codefendants)
3. Defendant Miller's counterclaim (seeking $50,000) for negligence against plaintiff Brown
4. Defendant Miller's cross-claim (seeking $50,000) for negligence against his codefendant, Clay's estate

Exhibit 10-1	Claims in the Brown/Miller/Clay's Estate Litigation

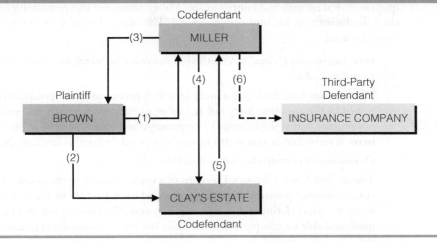

5. Defendant estate's cross-claim (seeking $1,000,000) for negligence against its codefendant, Miller
6. Third-party complaint that defendant Miller considered but ultimately decided not to file against his insurance company

Once the pleadings were filed, the first *pretrial conference* was held before a *magistrate*. The main purpose of the conference was to go over any anticipated concerns about *discovery*, the next stage in the proceedings. The magistrate also obtained an overview of the case from the parties and made inquiries about the possibility of settling the dispute without a trial. Neither side, however, was interested in *settlement*, so discovery began after the magistrate issued a *scheduling order*.

Pretrial conference: A meeting of the attorneys and the judge (or magistrate) before the trial to attempt to narrow the issues, to secure **stipulations**, and to make efforts to settle the case without a trial. Also called a *trial management conference*.

Stipulation ("stip"): An agreement between opposing parties about a particular matter. The verb is *stipulate*. Once the parties have reached a stipulation about a fact, neither side is required to offer evidence as to the existence or nonexistence of that fact at trial. (See glossary for another meaning.)

Magistrate: A judicial officer having some but not all of the powers of a judge. In federal trial courts (U.S. district courts), the magistrate may conduct many of the preliminary or pretrial proceedings in both civil and criminal cases. (See glossary for an additional meaning.)

Discovery: Methods used by parties to force information from each other before trial to aid in trial preparation. Examples of such methods include interrogatories and depositions. The methods can also be used to aid in the enforcement of a judgment.

Settlement: An agreement resolving a dispute without full litigation. (See glossary for additional meanings.)

Scheduling order: A pretrial order of a magistrate or judge that sets time limits for discovery, filings, further pretrial conferences, and other related pretrial matters.

Each attorney first served *interrogatories ("rogs")* on the opposing parties. These were followed by *depositions* and *requests for admissions (RFAs)*. Miller was also served with a *subpoena duces tecum*, which ordered him to bring his driver's license and car registration to his attorney's office, where his deposition took place. He complied with this *order*. (An alternative way in which Miller could have obtained copies of these records would have been to file a *request for production (RFP)*.) During the deposition, Miller refused to answer several questions. As a result, Brown's attorney had to file a discovery motion in court, seeking an order compelling Miller to answer. A court *hearing* was subsequently held on the motion. After listening to arguments by all of the attorneys, the judge granted the motion in full, ordering Miller to answer the questions. Faced with the court's order, Miller answered the remaining questions. Each party then filed a motion for *summary judgment*. The judge denied these motions, and the case was ready for trial.

Interrogatories ("rogs"): A method of discovery by which one party sends written questions to another party.

Deposition: A method of discovery by which parties and their prospective witnesses are questioned by the opposing party before trial at a location other than the courtroom. (Judges are not present during depositions.) The person who is questioned (*deposed)* is called the **deponent.** A recording or **transcript** (a word-for-word account) is made of the deposition.

Deponent: A person who is questioned in a deposition.

Transcript: A word-for-word account of what was said. A written copy of what was said. The **court reporter** prepares this transcription, which is paid for by the parties requesting it. In many courts, **real-time** transcription is also available whereby a draft of the typed testimony is made available on computer screens while the witness is testifying in court.

Court reporter: The person who takes down and transcribes proceedings.

Real time: Occurring now; happening as you are watching; able to respond or otherwise interact immediately or within seconds.

Request for admission (RFA): A method of discovery by which one party sends a request to another party that the latter agree that a certain fact or legal conclusion is true or valid so that there will be no need to present proof or arguments about that matter during the trial.

Subpoena duces tecum: A command to appear at a certain time and place and bring specified things such as documents. (If ordered to give testimony, the subpoena would be a *subpoena ad testificandum*.)

Order: An official command by a court requiring, allowing, or forbidding something.

Request for production (RFP): A method of discovery by which one party requests that another party provide access to electronically stored data, paper documents, or other tangible things for copying or inspection. The method can also include a request to enter the party's land for inspection.

Hearing: A proceeding designed to resolve issues of fact or law. An impartial officer presides at the hearing, the parties present evidence, etc. The hearing is **ex parte** if only one party is present; it is **adversarial** if both parties are allowed to be present even if only one side is before the hearing officer. Hearings occur in court as well as in administrative agencies.

Ex parte: With only one side present (usually the plaintiff or petitioner) when court action is requested.

Adversarial: Involving conflict and an adversary (opponent).

Summary judgment: A judgment of the court that is rendered without a full trial because of the absence of conflict on any of the material facts. A motion for a **summary** judgment is a request by a party that a decision be reached on the basis of the submitted documents and already agreed-to facts without going through a full trial. A summary judgment is normally allowed only when there is no dispute between the parties as to any of the material or significant facts. Summary judgment can be granted on the entire case or on individual claims or defenses within the case.

Summary: Quick, expedited, without going through a full adversary hearing.

As the trial date neared, each of the attorneys received a notice asking them to appear before the magistrate for another pretrial conference. During the conference, the magistrate, with input from the attorneys, prepared a pretrial statement for the trial judge on the case. It contained a statement of the facts that had been stipulated by the attorneys and the facts that were still at *issue*. It also listed the *tangible evidence* and witnesses that each attorney intended to *introduce* at the trial.

Issue: (1) A question to be resolved. (2) A question of law. A question of what the law is, what the law means, or how the law applies to the facts. Also called *legal issue, issue of law*. The judge resolves such issues. (3) A question of fact. A dispute over the existence or nonexistence of the alleged facts. Also called *factual issue, issue of fact, question of fact*. The jury resolves factual issues in a jury trial, but in a bench trial, the judge resolves them. (See glossary for additional meanings.)

Tangible evidence: Physical evidence; evidence that has a physical form. Evidence that can be seen and inspected. *Intangible evidence* (e.g., a right or a belief) is evidence without physical form. Intangible evidence is sometimes embodied or evidenced by something physical, e.g., a written contract.

Introduce evidence: To place evidence formally before a court or other tribunal so that it will become part of the record for consideration by the judge, jury, or other decision-maker.

After some delay, the case was finally *set for trial*. All of the parties and their attorneys assembled in the courtroom. The judge entered, took the bench, and ordered the *bailiff* to summon a *jury panel* for the trial. Once the potential (prospective) jurors were seated in the courtroom, *voir dire* began. Several jurors were *challenged for cause* and dismissed—one because she has worked for the insurance company that had issued the policy on Miller's car. The position as to this prospective juror was that she has or might have a *bias*. Several other jurors were dismissed as a result of *peremptory challenges*. Twelve jurors plus two *alternates* were eventually *empaneled* and seated in the jury box.

Set for trial: To schedule a date when the trial is to begin.

Bailiff: A court employee who keeps order in the courtroom and renders general administrative assistance to the judge.

Jury panel: A group of citizens who have been called to jury duty. From this group, juries for particular trials are selected. Also called *venire, jury pool*.

Voir dire: ("to speak the truth") A preliminary examination of (a) prospective jurors for the purpose of selecting persons qualified to sit on a jury or (b) prospective witnesses to determine their competence to testify (see definition of *competent* below).

Challenge for cause: A request from a party to a judge that a prospective juror not be allowed to become a member of this jury because of specified causes or reasons.

Bias: (1) An inclination, tendency, or predisposition to think or act in a certain way. (2) Prejudice for or against something or someone. (3) A danger of prejudgment.

Peremptory challenge: A request from a party to a judge asking that a prospective juror not be allowed to become a member of this jury without stating a reason for this request. Each side is allowed a limited number of such challenges. The request will be granted unless it is used to discriminate on the basis of race, sex, or ethnicity.

Alternate: An extra juror who will take the place of a regular juror if one is removed or becomes incapacitated during the trial.

Empanel: Select and swear in (referring to a jury). Also spelled *impaneled*.

Before the jury was brought into the courtroom, Brown's attorney made a *motion in limine*. She wanted to prevent the other attorneys from introducing into evidence any reference to a case five years ago when Brown was sued for negligently causing a brush fire in his neighborhood. The judge granted the motion.

When the jury was seated, Brown's attorney told the judge that she wanted to invoke the *rule on witnesses*. The judge agreed to *sequester* them. The bailiff led all of the witnesses (except for the parties themselves) out of the courtroom. Brown's attorney then began the trial with her *opening statement* to the jury. When she finished, Miller's attorney also delivered an opening statement. The attorney for Clay's estate, however, decided to reserve his opening statement until it was time for him to present the estate's case.

Motion in limine: A request raised preliminarily such as asking the court for a ruling on the admissibility of evidence prior to or during trial but before the evidence has been offered.

Rule on witnesses: A rule that requires certain witnesses to be removed from the courtroom until it is time for their individual testimony so that they will not be able to hear each other's testimony.

Sequester: (1) To separate or isolate a jury or witness. (2) To seize and hold funds or other property. Sometimes called *sequestrate*.

Opening statement: An attorney's statement to the jury (or to the judge alone in a bench trial where there is no jury) made before presenting evidence. The statement summarizes or previews the case the attorney intends to try to establish during the trial. Unrepresented parties make the statement themselves. Also called *opening argument*.

Brown's attorney, whose client had the *burden of proof*, called her first witness, a 10-year-old boy who had seen the accident. Miller's attorney immediately rose and requested a *sidebar conference*. When all the attorneys had gathered around the bench, he stated that he had an *objection* to the witness on the basis that the witness was not *competent* to testify. The judge then *excused the jury* temporarily while he conducted a brief *examination* of the witness. The judge *overruled* the objection upon being satisfied that the boy was mature enough to understand the obligation to tell the truth, had the ability to communicate, and had knowledge of the topic about which the attorney wanted to question him.

Burden of proof: The responsibility of proving a fact at the trial. Generally, the party making the factual allegation has the burden of proof as to that allegation.

Sidebar conference: A discussion between the judge and the attorneys held at the judge's bench so that the jury cannot hear what is being said. Also called a *bench conference*.

Objection: A formal challenge, usually directed at the evidence that the other side is trying to pursue or introduce.

Competent: Having the legal capacity to give testimony because the person understands the obligation to tell the truth, has the ability to communicate, and has knowledge of the topic of his or her testimony. The noun is *competency*. (See glossary for an additional meaning.)

Excuse the jury: Ask the jury to leave the courtroom.

Examination: Questioning of someone, who usually must answer under oath.

Overrule: To decide against or deny. (Overrule also means to reject or cancel a holding in an earlier opinion by rendering an opposite decision on the same question of law in a different litigation.)

The jury was brought back into the courtroom, and Brown's attorney began her *direct examination*. After a few questions, Miller's attorney again objected, this time on the *ground* that if the child was allowed to answer the question ("What did your father tell you about the accident?), the answer would be *hearsay*. The judge *sustained* the objection. Brown's attorney continued her examination of the witness for a few minutes before announcing that she had no further questions. The attorney for the estate then rose to conduct a brief *cross-examination* of the boy. He was followed by Miller's attorney, whose cross-examination was also brief. There was no *redirect examination* and, therefore, no *recross-examination*.

Direct examination: The first questioning of a witness at a hearing by the party who called the witness. Also called *examination in chief*.

Grounds: Reasons that are legally sufficient to obtain a particular remedy or result.

Hearsay: An out-of-court statement quoted or reported by someone who did not make the statement when offered into evidence to prove the truth of the matter asserted in the statement.

Sustain: To uphold or agree with. (See the glossary for additional meanings.)

Cross-examination: Questioning of a witness at a hearing by an opponent after the other side has conducted a direct examination of that witness. Generally, the person conducting the cross-examination must limit himself or herself to the topics or subject matters raised during the direct examination of this witness by the other side.

Redirect examination: Another direct examination of a witness after he or she was cross-examined. The attorney who conducted the direct examination conducts the redirect examination.

Recross-examination: Another cross-examination of a witness after the witness has been through a redirect examination. The attorney who conducted the cross-examination conducts the recross-examination.

Brown's attorney, Davis, called several other witnesses who had seen the accident. Each witness was examined and cross-examined in much the same fashion as the boy had been. Davis was about to call her fourth witness, Dr. Hadley, when the judge announced a recess for lunch. The judge admonished the jury not to discuss the case with anyone, even among themselves, and ordered everyone to be back in the courtroom by 2:00 p.m.

Dr. Hadley was called to the stand immediately after the lunch recess. Brown's attorney began her direct examination with a series of questions about the doctor's medical training and experience in order to *qualify* him as an *expert witness*. (See Exhibit 10-2.) She then moved that Dr. Hadley be recognized as an expert witness. The *court*, with no objections by either defense counsel, granted the motion.

Qualify: To present evidence of a person's education and experience sufficient to convince the court that the witness has expertise in a particular area.

Expert witness: A person qualified by scientific, technical, or other specialized knowledge or experience to give an expert opinion on a fact in dispute.

Court: (1) The judge. (2) A government tribunal for the resolution of legal disputes.

Exhibit 10-2	Examination of a Witness

Attorney Davis conducts a direct examination of Dr. Hadley, the doctor who treated plaintiff Michael Brown.

Photo courtesy of James L. Shaffer.

Brown's attorney then asked the doctor to testify as to the nature and extent of the injuries that the plaintiff, Brown, had suffered as a result of the accident. In addition to multiple cuts and bruises, the doctor stated that Brown had suffered a broken knee. The knee, in the doctor's opinion, had been permanently injured, and Brown would continue to suffer periodic pain and stiffness due to the injury. To show the expense of these injuries, the attorney produced the original copies of the bills that the doctor sent to Brown. She handed the bills to the *clerk*, who marked them as plaintiff's *exhibit* number one. After allowing defense counsel to inspect the bills, Brown's attorney handed them to the doctor, who promptly identified them. The attorney then *moved the bills into evidence* and turned the witness over to defense counsel for cross-examination.

Clerk: The court employee who assists judges with recordkeeping and other administrative duties.

Exhibit: A document, chart, or other object offered or introduced into evidence.

Move into evidence: To request that an item be formally declared admissible. This is not the same as declaring it to be true. *Admissible* means that the item will be admitted simply for consideration as to its truth or believability.

It was late in the afternoon when Brown's attorney finished with her final witness, Brown himself. The judge did not want to recess for the day, however, until the attorneys for the defendants completed their cross-examination of Brown. After about an hour, all the defense attorneys completed their questioning of Brown, and Brown's attorney *rested* her case. She had concluded her *case-in-chief*. The judge *adjourned* the trial until the following morning.

Rest: To announce formally that you have concluded the presentation of evidence (through the introduction of tangible evidence, through direct examination of your own witnesses, etc.). While the other side presents its case, however, you will be entitled to cross-examine its witnesses.

Case-in-chief: The main presentation of evidence by a party, not including any rebuttal evidence this party may want to present later.

Adjourn: To halt the proceedings temporarily.

On the following morning, the attorney for Clay's estate advised the judge that he had a preliminary matter to bring up before the jury was brought into the courtroom. He then proceeded to make a motion for a *judgment as a matter of law* in favor of the estate on Brown's claim of negligence. The judge listened to arguments by the attorneys on the motion. He decided that he would neither deny nor grant the motion but would take it under *advisement*. Miller's attorney also moved for a judgment as a matter of law on the negligence claim of Clay's estate against Miller. After hearing the arguments on this motion, the judge denied it because Clay's estate had introduced sufficient evidence to make out a *prima facie case* of Miller's negligence. Hence he would allow this claim of negligence to go to the jury.

Judgment as a matter of law: A judgment on an issue in a jury trial that is ordered by the judge against a party because there is no legally sufficient evidentiary basis for a reasonable jury to find for that party on that issue. A judgment as a matter of law may be rendered before or after the verdict. In federal courts and in some state courts, this judgment is called a **directed verdict** if it is rendered before the jury reaches a verdict and is called a **judgment notwithstanding the verdict (JNOV)** if it is rendered after the jury reaches a verdict.

Directed verdict: A judge's decision not to allow the jury to deliberate because only one verdict is reasonable.

Judgment notwithstanding the verdict (JNOV or judgment n.o.v.): A judgment by the trial judge that is contrary to the verdict reached by the jury because the verdict was not reasonable, in effect, overruling the jury.

Advisement: Careful consideration. If a decision is taken under advisement, it is delayed until the judge has time to consider it later.

Prima facie case: A party's presentation of evidence that will prevail unless the other side presents more convincing counterevidence.

The jury was summoned into the courtroom and seated in the jury box for the second day of the trial. The attorney for the estate began his case by making an opening statement to the jury, reserved from the previous day. He then proceeded to call his witnesses. He had only two witnesses and was able to conclude his case just before noon, at which time he introduced Clay's death certificate into evidence. The judge then declared a recess for lunch.

Miller's attorney began to present his case in the afternoon, and by late afternoon, he, too, had rested his case. The judge dismissed the jury until the following morning and told the attorneys to be prepared for *closing arguments* at that time. He also asked them to submit any *jury instructions* they would like to request so that he could review them. Brown's attorney requested an instruction that the codefendants had to overcome a *presumption* of negligence against them. The judge denied this request. Finally, he announced that he had decided to deny the estate's earlier motion for a judgment as a matter of law.

Closing argument: The final statement by an attorney to the jury (or to the judge alone in a bench trial where there is no jury). The statement summarizes the evidence that was presented during the trial and requests a favorable decision. Unrepresented parties make the argument themselves. Also called *closing statement*, *final argument*, *summation*, and *summing up*.

Jury instructions: A statement of the law given to the jury by the judge for use in deciding the issues of fact in its verdict. The instructions to the jury are also referred to as the *charge* to the jury. The attorneys are allowed to submit proposed instructions for consideration by the judge.

Presumption: An assumption or inference that a certain fact is true once another fact is established. The presumption is *irrebuttable* (conclusive) if a party is not allowed to introduce evidence to show that the assumption is false. The presumption is *rebuttable* if a party is allowed to introduce evidence to show that the assumption is false.

In the closing arguments, each attorney carefully reviewed the evidence for the jury and argued for a *verdict* in favor of his or her client. Following a brief recess for lunch, the judge began to instruct the jurors on the law they were to follow in finding the facts and in reaching a verdict. He said that they, as jurors, were the finders of fact and were to base their decision solely upon the testimony and exhibits introduced during the trial. He explained the concept of burden of proof and stated which party had to carry this burden as to each of the various *elements* of negligence. Each element had to be proved by a *preponderance of the evidence*. This was the *standard of proof* for this kind of case. Finally, he described the manner in which they should compute the amount of damages, if any, suffered by the parties. The jury was then led out of the courtroom to deliberate on its verdict. The judge retired to his chambers, and the attorneys settled back with their clients to wait.

Verdict: The jury's finding or decision on the factual issues placed before it.

Element: A portion of a rule that is a precondition of the applicability of the entire rule. Here, the rule is a cause of action for negligence.

Preponderance of the evidence: The standard of proof that is met when the evidence establishes that it is more likely than not that the facts are as alleged. Also called *fair preponderance of evidence*.

Standard of proof: A statement of how convincing a version of a fact must be before the trier of fact (usually the jury) can accept it as true. The main standards of proof are proof *beyond a reasonable doubt* (in criminal cases), proof by *preponderance of evidence* (in most civil cases), and proof by *clear and convincing evidence* (in some civil cases).

After about an hour, the judge received a note from the foreman of the jury, asking that the jury be allowed to view several of the exhibits. The items requested were the medical bills allegedly incurred by Brown and Clay. The attorneys for Brown and for the estate took this as a good sign. The jury had probably decided the case against Miller and was now trying to compute damages.

A second note arrived in another hour, announcing that the jury had reached a verdict. The bailiff summoned everyone back to the courtroom, and the jury came in a few minutes later. At the clerk's request, the foreman rose to read the verdict.

1. On Brown's complaint (seeking $100,000) for negligence against Miller, the jury found for Brown, awarding Brown $30,000 in damages.
2. On Brown's complaint (seeking $100,000) for negligence against Clay's estate, the jury found for the estate.
3. On Miller's counterclaim (seeking $50,000) for negligence against Brown, the jury found for Brown.
4. On Miller's cross-claim (seeking $50,000) for negligence against the estate, the jury found for the estate.
5. On the estate's cross-claim (seeking $1,000,000) for negligence against Miller, the jury found for the estate, awarding the estate $750,000 in damages.

The judge entered a *judgment* against Miller in the amounts awarded by the jury. After denying a motion by Miller for a judgment as a matter of law, he thanked the jurors and dismissed them.

Judgment: The final conclusion of a court that resolves a legal dispute by declaring the rights and obligations of the parties or that specifies what further proceedings are needed to resolve it. Many judgments order the losing party to do something (such as pay damages) or to refrain from doing something. A **declaratory judgment** establishes the rights and obligations of the parties, but it does not order the parties to do or refrain from doing anything.

Declaratory judgment: A binding judgment that declares rights and obligations without ordering anything to be done.

Miller's attorney immediately made a *motion for a new trial*, arguing several possible grounds. When this motion was denied by the trial judge, he moved for a reduction of the verdict on the grounds that the amounts awarded were excessive. This motion was also denied, and the attorney announced his intention to seek an *appeal*. The judge granted Miller a *stay* of the judgment, conditioned upon his filing a *timely notice of appeal* and arranging for the appropriate *bond*.

Motion for a new trial: A request that the judge set aside the judgment and order a new trial because the evidence is insufficient to support the judgment, newly discovered evidence, or errors committed during the trial.

Appeal: A proceeding in which a higher tribunal reviews or reconsiders the decision of an inferior tribunal.

Stay: The suspension or postponement of a judgment or proceeding.

Timely: Within the time set by contract or law.

Notice of appeal: A party's notice given to a court (through filing) and to the opposing party (through service) of an intention to appeal.

Bond: An obligation to perform an act (e.g., pay a sum of money) upon the occurrence of a designated condition. Here the bond secures the payment of the judgment.

Miller asked his attorney what the $30,000 verdict against him meant. Brown had originally sued for $100,000. Could Brown later sue Miller again for the rest of the amount he claimed? The attorney explained that, because of the stay granted by the judge, Miller would not have to pay anything until a decision on appeal had been reached. Furthermore, Brown could not sue Miller again on the same cause of action because Brown had received a *judgment on the merits* that would be *res judicata* and would *bar* any later suit based on the same facts. This would also be true of a later action by Clay's estate against Miller.

Judgment on the merits: A judgment (rendered after evidentiary inquiry and argument) that determines which party is in the right, as opposed to a judgment that is based solely on a technical point or procedural error.

Res judicata: ("a thing adjudicated") A defense raised (a) to prevent the same parties from retrying (relitigating) a claim that has already been resolved on the merits in a prior case or (b) to prevent the litigation of a claim arising out of the same transaction involved in the first case that could have been raised in the first case but was not.

Bar: Prevent or stop.

Miller's attorney filed his notice of appeal with *the U.S. court of appeals* and posted bond the following week. As representative for this *appellant*, the attorney had to see to it that the *record*, including transcripts and copies of exhibits, was transmitted to the court of appeals and that the case was *docketed* by the clerk of that court. Miller's attorney then had 40 days in which to draft and file his *appellate brief* with the court of appeals. He served copies of the brief on the attorneys for the *appellees* (Brown and Clay's estate) who in turn filed their appellate briefs concerning the *issues on appeal*.

U.S. court of appeals: The main intermediate appellate court in the federal court system. (See Exhibits 6-4 and 6-5 in Chapter 6.)

Appellant: The party bringing an appeal because of disagreement with a decision of a lower tribunal. Also called *petitioner*.

Record: The official collection of all the trial pleadings, exhibits, orders, and word-for-word testimony that were part of the trial. (See glossary for additional meanings.)

Docketed: Placed on a court's list of pending cases.

Appellate brief: A document that a party files with an appellate court (and serves on an opponent) in which the party presents arguments on why the appellate court should affirm (approve), reverse, vacate (cancel), or otherwise modify what a lower court has done. Both the appellant and the appellee prepare appellate briefs. If the appellant responds to the appellate brief of the appellee, it is often called a *reply brief*.

Reply brief: An appellate brief of the appellant that responds to the appellate brief of the appellee. (A reply brief can also refer to any appellate brief that responds to an opponent's appellate brief.)

Appellee: The party against whom the appeal is brought (also called the *respondent*). Often, the appellee is satisfied with what the lower court did and wishes the appellate court to affirm (approve) the lower court's rulings.

Issue on appeal: A claimed error of law committed by a lower court. The appellate court does not retry the case. No witnesses are called, and no testimony is taken by the appellate court. The court examines the record and determines whether errors of law were committed by the lower court.

Several months passed before the attorneys finally received a notice from the clerk of the court of appeals that the appeal had been scheduled for *oral argument* before a three-judge *panel* of the appellate court. The arguments were heard a few weeks later. Six months after oral argument, the attorneys received the decision of the court in its written *opinion*. By a vote of two to one (one judge dissenting), the court *affirmed* the judgments against Miller. The only error that the majority found was the admission of certain testimony offered through Brown's expert witness. However, because Miller's attorney had not objected to this testimony at trial, the opinion stated, he had *waived* this defect.

Oral argument: A spoken presentation to the court on a legal issue, e.g., telling an appellate court why the rulings of a lower tribunal were valid or were in error.

Panel: The group of judges, usually three, who decide a case on behalf of a court with a larger number of judges. (See glossary for additional meanings.)

Opinion: A court's written explanation of how it applied the law to the facts to resolve a legal dispute. Also called *judicial opinion*, *case*, *decision*. (See glossary for additional meanings.) One case can contain several opinions: a **majority opinion**, a **concurring opinion**, a **plurality opinion**, and a **dissenting opinion**. Opinions are often collected in official and unofficial **reporters**.

Majority opinion: An opinion whose final conclusion or judgment is agreed to by more than half of the judges hearing the case. The agreement includes the holdings and reasoning for the holdings.

Concurring opinion: An opinion written by less than a majority of the judges hearing the case. The opinion agrees with the final conclusion or judgment of the majority opinion but wishes to add its own comments or reasoning. If the majority opinion has more than one holding, there can be a concurring opinion on only some of the holdings.

Plurality opinion: The opinion agreed to by the largest number of judges hearing the case when there is no majority opinion.

Dissenting opinion: An opinion that disagrees with part or all of the result or judgment reached by the majority or plurality opinion.

Reporter: A volume (or set of volumes) of court opinions. Also called *case reports*. (See glossary for additional meanings.)

Affirm: To agree with or uphold the lower court judgment. If the appellate court **remands** the case, the court sends it back to the lower tribunal with instructions on how to proceed, e.g., instructions on correcting the errors made by the lower tribunal. If the appellate court reverses the court below, it changes the result reached below.

Remand: To send back. For example, to return a case to a lower tribunal with instructions from a higher tribunal on how to proceed.

Waive: To lose a right or privilege because of an explicit rejection of it or because of a failure to claim it at the appropriate time. The noun is *waiver*. Here, the court is referring to the rule that failure to object during trial is an implied waiver of the right to complain about the alleged error on appeal.

Miller, undaunted, *petitioned* for a *rehearing* by the court *en banc*. The petition was denied. Miller then discussed the possibility of further appeal with his attorney. The attorney explained that Miller could, if he desired, try to appeal to the U.S. Supreme Court. He cautioned Miller, however, that he could not *appeal by right* in this case but would be limited to a petition for a *writ* of *certiorari*. He advised Miller that it was extremely unlikely that the Supreme Court would grant the petition and that it probably would not be worth the expense. Miller agreed, and no further appeal was attempted. The court of appeals issued its *mandate* affirming the trial court's judgment. Shortly thereafter, Miller, through his insurance company, *satisfied* the judgment. There was no need to ask the sheriff to force compliance of the judgment through *execution*.

Petition: (1) A formal request or motion. (2) A complaint.

Rehearing: A second (or later) hearing by a court to reconsider the decision it made after an earlier hearing.

En banc: ("on the bench") By the entire court. The panel of judges that heard the first appeal may have consisted of three judges, yet the number of judges on the full court may be much larger. En banc refers to this larger number.

Appeal by right: The appeal of a case that an appellate court must hear; it has no discretion on whether to take the appeal.

Writ: A written court order to do or refrain from doing an act.

Certiorari (cert.): An order (or writ) by a higher court that a lower court send up the record of a case because the higher court has decided to use its discretion to review that case. (Also referred to as *writ of certiorari*.) The writ is used in a case in which the appellate court has discretion to accept or reject the appeal. If the writ is denied, the court refuses to hear the appeal, and, in effect, the judgment below stands unchanged. If the writ is granted, the lower court "sends up" the record and the appeal proceeds.

Mandate: An order of a court. Here, the mandate of the appellate court is to affirm the trial court's judgment.

Satisfy: To comply with a legal obligation (here, to pay the judgment award). The noun is *satisfaction*.

Execution: A command or writ to a court officer (e.g., sheriff) to seize and sell the property of the losing litigant in order to satisfy the judgment debt. Also called *general execution, writ of execution*. (See glossary for additional meanings.)

2. CRIMINAL LIABILITY

As Brown was leaving the hospital, having recovered from his injury, he was met at the door by two police officers. The officers produced a *warrant* and advised Brown that he was under arrest. After he was read his rights, he was taken to the police station. Hence, in addition to suing Clay's estate and Miller, Brown was now defending himself in a criminal *prosecution*. The criminal charge was drug possession. After the collision of the Clay and Miller vehicles, the police found drugs under the passenger seat where Brown was sitting.

Warrant: An order from a judicial officer authorizing an act, e.g., the arrest of an individual or the search of property.

Prosecution: (1) Bringing and processing criminal proceedings against someone. The words *prosecution* and *prosecute* can also refer to bringing and processing civil proceedings against someone, although the words are more commonly used in criminal proceedings. (2) The attorney representing the government in a criminal case. Also called the *prosecutor*.

The following morning Brown was taken before a judge for his *initial appearance*. The judge advised Brown that he had been charged with a *felony*, possession of narcotics with intent to distribute. He then advised Brown of his rights, including his right to be represented by an attorney. Because Brown was unemployed and without adequate funds to pay an attorney (he had not yet won the judgment against Miller), the judge asked him if he would like the court to appoint an attorney to handle the case. Brown said yes and was given *assigned counsel* to represent him. The judge, at the attorney's request, then agreed to give Brown a chance to confer with his new attorney before continuing the hearing.

> **Initial appearance:** The first criminal court appearance by persons accused of a crime during which the court (a) informs them of the charges and of their rights, (b) makes a decision on bail, and (c) determines the date of the next court proceeding.

> **Felony:** (1) Any crime punishable by death or by imprisonment for a term exceeding a year. (2) A crime more serious than a misdemeanor.

> **Misdemeanor:** (1) Any crime punishable by fine or by detention (often for a year or less) in an institution other than a prison. (2) A crime less serious than a felony.

> **Assigned counsel:** An attorney (often in private practice) appointed by the court and paid by the government to represent an **indigent** person in a criminal or civil case. Attorneys who are government employees handling criminal cases might be called *public defenders*.

> **Indigent:** Poor; without means to afford something such as a private attorney or filing fees.

When the case was recalled, Brown and his court-appointed attorney again approached the bench and stood before the judge. The attorney formally entering his name as attorney of record for Brown and advised the judge that he was prepared to discuss the matter of *bail*. He proceeded to describe for the judge the details of Brown's background—his education, employment record, length of residence in the city, etc. He concluded by asking that he be released on *personal recognizance*. The prosecutor was then given an opportunity to speak. He recommended a high bond, pointing out that the defendant was unemployed and had no close relatives in the area. These facts, he argued, coupled with the serious nature of a felony charge, indicated a substantial risk that the defendant might try to flee. The judge nevertheless agreed to release Brown on his personal recognizance and set a date for a *preliminary hearing* the following week.

> **Bail:** (1) Money or other property deposited with the court as security to ensure that the defendant will reappear at designated times. Failure to appear forfeits the security. (2) Release of the defendant upon posting this security.

> **Personal recognizance:** Release of a defendant in a criminal case without posting a bond, based solely on a promise of the defendant to appear at all scheduled times. Also called *release on recognizance (ROR)*.

> **Preliminary hearing:** A pretrial criminal proceeding to determine if **probable cause** exists that the accused has committed a crime. Also called *probable-cause hearing*, *bindover hearing*.

> **Probable cause:** A reasonable belief that a specific crime has been committed and that the accused committed the crime. (See glossary for additional meanings.)

Before the preliminary hearing was held, the parties engaged in discovery. The prosecution is required to disclose to Brown any evidence it has collected thus far that indicates guilt or innocence. In a criminal case, defendants do not have to disclose as much evidence as they do during discovery in civil cases. The main reason for this is the Fifth Amendment right of defendants not to incriminate themselves by being forced to answer questions about the alleged crime.

At the preliminary hearing, the only witness was the police officer who investigated the accident. The officer testified that when he helped pull Brown out of the car, he noticed a small paper sack sticking out from under the passenger's side of the front seat. Several glassine envelopes containing a white powdery substance, the officer said, had spilled out of the sack. The substance, totaling about one-half ounce, was tested and proved to be 80 percent pure heroin. Brown's attorney cross-examined the officer briefly, but little additional information came out. The judge found that there was probable cause to hold the defendant and ordered the case *bound over* for *grand jury* action. He continued Brown's release on personal recognizance.

Bound over: Held or transferred for further court proceedings.

Grand jury: A jury of inquiry (not a trial jury) that that sits for a designated period of time (often a month), receives accusations in criminal cases, hears the evidence of the prosecutor (but not the evidence of the suspects), and issues **indictments** when satisfied that a trial should be held.

Indictment: A formal document issued by a grand jury accusing the defendant of a crime. (If the state has no grand jury, the accusation is often contained in a document called an **information.**)

information: A document accusing the defendant of a crime. The document is issued by a prosecutor when a grand jury is not used or does not exist. Also called *bill of information.*

Shortly after the preliminary hearing, Brown's attorney went to the prosecutor to see if he could work out an informal disposition of the charge. He tried to convince the prosecutor to enter a *nolle prosequi* on the charge, explaining that Brown had simply been offered a ride home and was not aware that the heroin was in the car. The prosecutor was unwilling to drop the charge. However, he was willing to "nolle" the felony charge of possession with intent to distribute if Brown would agree to *plead* guilty to the lesser offense of simple possession of a dangerous drug, a misdemeanor. The attorney said he would speak to his client about it.

Nolle prosequi ("not to wish to prosecute"): A statement by the prosecutor that he or she is unwilling to prosecute the case. The charges, in effect, are dropped. (Abbreviated nol-pro or nolle.)

Plead: To file a pleading, enter or make a plea, or argue a case in court. In a criminal case, to plead means to enter a specific plea to the charges. Usual plea options are guilty, not guilty, or **no contest.** (A no-contest plea does not admit guilt but does not dispute the charge.)

No contest: A plea that does not admit guilt but that does not dispute the charge so that its effect is a conviction. Also called *nolo contendere* ("I will not contest.")

He spoke to Brown that same afternoon about the prosecutor's offer of a *plea bargain.* Brown was not interested. He felt he was innocent and was unwilling to plead guilty, even to a misdemeanor.

Plea bargain: An agreement whereby an accused pleads guilty to a lesser included offense or to one of multiple charges in exchange for the prosecution's agreement to support a dismissal of some charges or a lighter sentence. Also called *negotiated plea.*

Several weeks went by before Brown's attorney was notified that the grand jury had returned an indictment against his client. The next step would be the *arraignment* on the following Monday. On this date, Brown and his attorney appeared before the judge, and Brown was formally notified of the indictment. He entered a plea of not guilty to the charge. The judge set a trial date ten weeks from that day and again agreed to continue Brown's release on personal recognizance.

Arraignment: A pretrial criminal proceeding in which the defendant is formally charged with a crime and enters a plea. Arrangements are then made for the next proceeding.

The day for the trial arrived. Brown's attorney and the prosecutor announced that they were ready. Voir dire was held, and a jury was empaneled. The trial itself was relatively uneventful, lasting less than a day. The prosecutor, following a brief opening statement, presented only two witnesses: the police officer who had been at the scene and an expert from the police lab who identified the substance as heroin. He then rested his case. Brown's attorney made his opening statement and presented his only witness, Brown himself. The jury listened attentively as Brown, on direct examination, explained the events leading up to the accident and his subsequent arrest. Not only had he been unaware of the heroin, he testified, but he had never even seen it because he had been knocked unconscious by the accident and had not revived until he was in the ambulance.

Brown had a previous conviction for shoplifting. The prosecutor on cross-examination was about to use this conviction to *impeach* Brown's testimony when Brown's attorney objected. She asked for a sidebar conference so that the jury could not hear her objection to any questions about the shoplifting conviction. She argued that the conviction, which had occurred eight years previously, was too remote to be *relevant* and would constitute *undue prejudice.*

The judge agreed and prohibited any mention of the prior conviction. After a few more questions, the prosecutor concluded his cross-examination, and the defense rested its case.

Impeach: To challenge; to attack the credibility of.

Relevant: Logically tending to establish or disprove a fact. Pertinent. Relevant evidence is evidence having any tendency to make the existence of a fact more probable or less probable than it would be without the evidence. (See glossary for an additional meaning.) The noun is *relevancy*.

Undue prejudice: The persuasiveness of the evidence is outweighed by the harm it could cause a party because of the emotions the evidence could stir up in the minds of the jury.

Both sides presented their closing arguments following the lunch recess. The judge then instructed the jury. He described the elements of the offense and explained that the burden of proof in a criminal case is on the *government*. That burden, he continued, is to prove each element of the offense *beyond a reasonable doubt*. The jury took less than 45 minutes to reach its verdict. All parties quickly reassembled in the courtroom to hear the presiding juror (foreman) announce the verdict *acquitting* Brown of the offense. A *poll* of the jury, requested by the prosecutor, confirmed the result, and the judge advised Brown that he was free to go.

Government: In a criminal case, the prosecutor.

Beyond a reasonable doubt: The standard of proof that is met when there are no doubts about the evidence that would cause prudent persons to hesitate before acting in matters of importance to themselves.

Acquit: To declare that the accused is innocent of the crime.

Poll: To ask each member of a body (e.g., a jury) that has just voted to state how he or she individually voted. (See glossary for an additional meaning.)

Generally, criminal cases in which the defendant is acquitted may not be appealed by the prosecutor. A second prosecution would be *double jeopardy*. Hence, in this case, there was no appeal of the trial judgment. If a defendant is convicted, he or she is sentenced. A convicted defendant *does* have the right to appeal.

Double jeopardy: (1) A second prosecution for the same or substantially same offense after acquittal or conviction. (2) Multiple punishments for the same or substantially same offense.

3. ADMINISTRATIVE DISPUTE

The day after his indictment on the felony charge, Brown went down to the state employment office to apply for *unemployment compensation*. After being interviewed by a clerk, he filled out an application form. The clerk told Brown that he would receive a letter in about a week notifying him of the agency's initial determination of his eligibility. If he were eligible, his benefits would start in ten days.

Brown received the letter a few days later. It advised him that, although he was otherwise eligible for benefits, a routine check with his former employer had disclosed that he had been fired for misconduct. For this reason, the letter stated, he would be deemed disqualified for a nine-week period. Moreover, the benefits due for those nine weeks would be deducted from the total amount he would otherwise have been entitled to receive. If he wished to appeal this decision, the letter went on, he needed to request an *administrative hearing* within ten days.

Unemployment compensation: Temporary income from the government to persons who have lost their jobs (often after being laid off) and are looking for work. Also called *unemployment insurance*.

Administrative hearing: A proceeding at an administrative agency presided over by a hearing officer (e.g., an administrative law judge) to resolve a controversy involving the application of the regulations, statutes, or executive orders that govern the agency. The hearing is usually conducted less formally than a court hearing or trial.

Brown felt that he needed some legal advice, but he was still out of work and broke. (The lawsuit in the civil action had not been filed yet; it would be well over a year before the case would be tried, the appeal completed, and the judgment award actually paid.) Brown, therefore, decided to obtain help from the local *legal aid office*. He explained his problem to a receptionist and was introduced to the paralegal who would be handling his case. The paralegal, an expert in unemployment-compensation law, interviewed Brown and helped him fill out a form requesting a hearing. He said he would let Brown know as soon as the date was set. Brown left and the paralegal, after consulting with his supervisor, began to research and draft a *memorandum* to submit to the *hearing examiner* on Brown's behalf.

> **Legal aid office:** An office of attorneys (and paralegals) that provides free or low-cost legal services to persons who cannot afford standard legal fees. Also called *legal services office*.
>
> **Memorandum:** A memorandum of law or legal memorandum, which is a written presentation of how one or more rules might apply to the facts of a client's case. (See glossary for additional meanings.)
>
> **Hearing examiner:** One who presides over an administrative hearing and makes findings of fact and rulings of law, or who recommends such findings and rulings to someone else in the agency who will make the final decision. Also called *administrative law judge (ALJ)*, *referee*, *hearing officer*.

In Brown's state, a *claimant* can have nonattorney representation at unemployment-compensation hearings. Therefore, the paralegal at the legal aid office was allowed to represent Brown at his hearing. The only witnesses at the hearing were Brown and his former boss, Frank Best. Best told the examiner about Brown's arrest and about the thefts from the warehouse. Taken together, he argued, these events make it impossible for him to trust Brown on the job any longer. Brown, in turn, denied any participation in the thefts and maintained his innocence on the drug charge. (Brown had not yet been acquitted of the felony.) The hearing examiner, at the close of the proceedings, thanked the parties and promised a decision within a few days.

The hearing examiner's decision was mailed shortly thereafter in a document labeled *Proposed Findings and Rulings*. The last paragraph contained the examiner's recommended decision. The hearing examiner agreed with Brown that his boss's mere suspicion that Brown was involved in the thefts was not enough to justify a finding of misconduct. However, the decision went on, the pending criminal charges for a drug-related offense did provide the employer with *good cause* to fire Brown because drug involvement could affect his ability to operate a company vehicle safely. The paragraph concluded by recommending a finding of misconduct and the imposition of a nine-week penalty period.

> **Claimant:** A person asserting or making a claim.
>
> **Proposed findings and rulings:** Recommended conclusions presented to someone else in the administrative agency who will make the final decision.
>
> **Good cause:** A legally sufficient ground. A justifiable reason. Also called *cause, just cause, sufficient cause*.

A second mailing arrived ten days later containing the *administrative decision* of the agency. The letter, signed by the director of the local agency, adopted the recommended decision of the hearing examiner. This decision, the letter concluded, could be appealed within fifteen days to the State Unemployment Compensation *Board of Appeals*. Brown immediately appealed.

> **Administrative decision:** An administrative agency's resolution of a controversy (following a hearing) involving the application of the regulations, statutes, or executive orders that govern the agency. Sometimes called *ruling, administrative ruling*. (See also Exhibit 6-1 in Chapter 6.)
>
> **Board of appeals:** The unit within an administrative agency to which a party can appeal a decision of the agency.

Copies of the hearing transcript along with memoranda from both sides were filed with the Board of Appeals. The Board, exercising its *discretion*, refused to allow oral arguments before it and reversed the decision. It issued a short administrative decision stating that Best may have had cause to be suspicious of Brown, but there was not sufficient evidence of actual misconduct on Brown's part. The Board, in this final administrative decision, ordered the local office to begin paying benefits immediately, including *retroactive* benefits to cover the period since Brown had first applied.

Discretion: The power to choose among various courses of conduct based on one's reasoned judgment or preference.

Retroactive: Applying to facts that arise before as well as after the effective date.

Best decided to appeal this administrative decision in a state court. He was allowed to do so, because he had *exhausted his administrative remedies*. He filed a complaint in the county court seeking review of the Board's decision. He submitted the entire record from the proceedings below and asked the court for a *trial de novo*. Brown, now represented by an attorney from the legal aid office, filed his answer and immediately made a motion for summary judgment. The court, upon a review of the record and the pleadings, granted the motion and affirmed the judgment of the Board of Appeals. Best, after discussing the case at length with his attorney, decided against a further appeal of the case to the state court of appeals.

Exhaust administrative remedies: To go through all dispute-solving avenues that are available in an administrative agency before asking a court to review what the agency did. A court generally will not allow a party to appeal an administrative decision until administrative remedies are exhausted. Also called *exhaustion of remedies*.

Trial de novo: A new trial conducted as if a prior one had not taken place.

Many of the steps described in the litigation woes of Michael Brown, which you have just read, are outlined in Exhibit 10-3 (overview of civil litigation) and in Exhibit 10-4 (overview of criminal litigation).

Exhibit 10-3	Overview of Civil Litigation

Possible proceedings where administrative decisions, court rulings, and opinions could be written. The events presented here and their sequence are examples only. The examples assume that the litigation begins in an administrative agency. If no agency is involved, the litigation begins in court at the pretrial stage.

EVENT	DECISIONS, RULINGS, AND OPINIONS AT THIS STAGE	DEFINITIONS	POSSIBLE PARALEGAL ROLES AT THIS STAGE
I. AGENCY STAGE	**I. AGENCY STAGE**	**I. AGENCY STAGE**	**I. AGENCY STAGE**
1. Someone protests an action taken (or not taken) by the *administrative agency* 2. *Administrative hearing* 3. Appeal *within the agency* to a commission, board of appeals, director, or secretary. (If no agency is involved, the litigation begins in court at the pretrial stage.)	■ A mid-level agency official (e.g., hearing examiner or administrative law judge) writes a recommended decision (*proposed findings and rulings*). ■ The commission, board of appeals, director, or secretary writes an *administrative decision*, which becomes the final decision of the agency.	■ *Administrative agency:* A governmental body, other than a court or legislature, that carries out (i.e., administers or executes) the statutes of the legislature, the executive orders of the chief executive, and its own regulations. ■ *Proposed findings and rulings:* Recommended conclusions presented to someone else in the administrative agency who will make the final decision. ■ *Administrative decision:* An administrative agency's resolution of a controversy (following a hearing) involving the application of the regulations, statutes, or executive orders that govern the agency. Also called *ruling, administrative ruling.*	a. Open a case file. b. Interview client or do follow-up interview of client. c. Interview witnesses. d. Conduct investigation. e. Draft documents pertaining to the case f. Organize and help manage the case file. g. Represent client at agency hearing (if agency allows nonattorney representation).
II. PRETRIAL STAGE	**II. PRETRIAL STAGE**	**II. PRETRIAL STAGE**	**II. PRETRIAL STAGE**
4. Plaintiff files a *complaint*	■ The trial court often makes *rulings* on the pretrial events listed in the first column but rarely writes an *opinion* on any of the rulings.	■ *Complaint:* A plaintiff's first pleading, stating a cause of action against the defendant (also called *petition*).	a.–f. Same as above if the case begins in court rather than in an administrative agency.

(continued)

Exhibit 10-3	Overview of Civil Litigation *(Continued)*

EVENT	DECISIONS, RULINGS, AND OPINIONS AT THIS STAGE	DEFINITIONS	POSSIBLE PARALEGAL ROLES AT THIS STAGE
5. Court clerk issues a *summons* 6. *Service of process* on defendant 7. Defendant files an *answer* 8. *Compulsory mediation* ordered by court (in some kinds of cases) 9. *Pretrial conference* (including *settlement* efforts) 10. *Discovery* by *interrogatories* (*"rogs"*) 11. *Discovery* by *deposition* 12. Other discovery 13. Final pretrial conference 14. Pretrial *motions* 15. *Voir dire*	■ Occasionally, a party may be allowed to appeal a pretrial ruling to an appellate court, which may write an opinion affirming, modifying, or reversing the ruling. Such an appeal is called an *interlocutory appeal*. It takes place before the trial court reaches its final judgment.	■ *Summons:* A notice directing the defendant to appear in court and answer the plaintiff's complaint or face a *default judgment*. ■ *Default judgment:* A judgment against a party for failure to file a required pleading or otherwise respond to an opponent's claim. ■ *Service of process:* A formal delivery of notice to a defendant that a suit has been initiated to which he or she must respond. ■ *Answer:* The first pleading of the defendant in response to the plaintiff's claims. ■ *Compulsory mediation:* In some kinds of cases (e.g., medical malpractice), the parties are required to try to resolve their dispute by mediation before proceeding with their case in court. ■ *Mediation:* A method of alternative dispute resolution (ADR) in which the parties avoid litigation by submitting their dispute to a neutral third person (the mediator) who helps the parties resolve their dispute, but does not render a decision that resolves it for them. ■ *Pretrial conference:* A meeting of the attorneys and the judge (or magistrate) before the trial to attempt to narrow the issues, to secure stipulations, and to make efforts to settle the case without a trial. Also called a *trial management conference*. ■ *Settlement:* An agreement resolving a dispute without full litigation. ■ *Discovery:* Methods used by parties to force information from each other before trial to aid in trial preparation. (Also used to aid in the enforcement of a judgment.) ■ *Interrogatories ("rogs"):* A method of discovery by which one party sends written questions to another party. ■ *Deposition:* A method of discovery by which parties and their prospective witnesses are questioned by the opposing party before trial at a location other than a courtroom. ■ *Motion:* An application or request made to a court or other decision-making body seeking to obtain a favorable action or ruling (e.g., motion to dismiss). ■ *Voir dire:* A preliminary examination of (a) prospective jurors for the purpose of selecting persons qualified to sit on a jury or (b) prospective witnesses to determine their competence to testify. ■ *Ruling:* The conclusion or outcome of a decision made by a court or administrative agency. ■ *Opinion:* A court's written explanation of how it applied the law to the facts to resolve a dispute. ■ *Interlocutory appeal:* An appeal of a trial court ruling before the trial court reaches its final judgment.	g. Perform preliminary legal research. h. Help draft complaint and other pleadings. i. Schedule discovery. j. Draft discovery requests and motions. k. Draft responses to discovery requests and motions. l. Summarize (digest) facts obtained through discovery. (For other discovery tasks, see Exhibit 10-7 later in the chapter.) m. Assemble trial notebook. (A trial notebook, discussed later in the chapter, is a collection of documents, arguments, and strategies that an attorney plans to use during a trial.) n. Help prepare and coordinate trial exhibits. o. Draft voir dire questions for attorney to consider for prospective jurors. p. Help attorney evaluate prospective witnesses during voir dire.
III. TRIAL STAGE	**III. TRIAL STAGE**	**III. TRIAL STAGE**	**III. TRIAL STAGE**

16. *Opening statement* of plaintiff
17. *Opening statement* of defendant
18. Plaintiff presents its case:
  a. *evidence* introduced
  b. *direct examination*
  c. *cross-examination*
  d. re-direct and recross-examinations
19. Motions to dismiss
20. Defendant presents its case:
	■ The trial court often makes rulings on trial events listed in the first column, but rarely writes an *opinion* on any of the rulings.
	■ Occasionally, a party may be allowed to appeal a trial-court ruling to an appeals court before the trial is over. The appeals court may then write an *opinion* affirming, modifying, or reversing the ruling. Such an appeal is called an *interlocutory appeal*. It takes place before the trial court reaches its final judgment.
		■ *Opening statement:* An attorney's statement to the jury (or to the judge alone in a bench trial where there is no jury) made before presenting evidence. The statement summarizes or previews the case the attorney intends to try to establish during the trial. Unrepresented parties make the statement themselves. Also called *opening argument*.
		■ *Evidence:* Anything offered to establish the existence or nonexistence of a fact in dispute.
		■ *Direct examination:* The first questioning of a witness at a hearing by the party who called the witness. Also called *examination in chief*. (Redirect examination of this witness can occur after cross-examination.)
		■ *Cross examination:* Questioning a witness at a hearing by an opponent after the other side has conducted a direct examination of that witness. (Recross-examination of this witness can occur after redirect examination.)
		■ *Closing argument:* The final statement by an attorney to the jury (or to the judge alone in a bench trial where there is no jury). The statement summarizes the evidence that was presented during the trial and requests a favorable decision. Unrepresented parties make the argument themselves. Also called *closing statement, final argument, summation, summing up*.
			a. Coordinate scheduling of witnesses.
			b. Take notes during trial.
			c. Assist attorney with documents and exhibits.
			d. Perform last-minute legal research.
			e. Compare a witness's trial testimony with what he or she said during discovery (e.g., in a deposition) and inform the attorney of any inconsistencies.
			f. Perform other tasks needed by the attorney conducting the trial.

(continued)

Exhibit 10-3	Overview of Civil Litigation *(Continued)*

EVENT	DECISIONS, RULINGS, AND OPINIONS AT THIS STAGE	DEFINITIONS	POSSIBLE PARALEGAL ROLES AT THIS STAGE
a. *evidence* introduced **b.** *direct examination* **c.** *cross-examination* **d.** *re-direct and recross-examinations* **21.** *Closing arguments* to jury by attorneys **22.** Requests by attorneys for specific *jury instructions* by judge (the charge) **23.** Jury instructions given by judge (the charge to the jury) **24.** *Verdict* of jury **25.** *Judgment* of trial court	■ After the trial, the trial court delivers its judgment. Rarely will the trial court write an opinion explaining its judgment. (Most opinions are written by appellate courts rather than by trial courts.) ■ Several trial courts, however, do sometimes write trial-court opinions. Examples of such trial courts are federal trial courts (U.S. district courts) and New York State trial courts.	■ *Jury instructions:* A statement of the law given to the jury by the judge for use in deciding the issues of fact in its verdict. Also called the *charge.* Parties are allowed to request specific instructions. ■ *Verdict:* The jury's finding or decision on the factual issues placed before it. ■ *Judgment:* The final conclusion of a court that resolves a legal dispute by declaring the rights and obligations of the parties or that specifies what further proceedings are needed to resolve it.	
IV. APPEAL STAGE	**IV. APPEAL STAGE**	**IV. APPEAL STAGE**	**IV. APPEAL STAGE**
26. Filing of *notice of appeal* **27.** Filing of *appellate brief* of *appellant* **28.** Filing of *appellate brief* of *appellee* **29.** Filing of appellant's *reply brief* **30.** *Oral argument* by attorneys **31.** Judgment of court	■ An opinion of the intermediate appellate court might be written. ■ The decision of the intermediate appellate court might be appealed to the highest court, which might write its own opinion. (Note, however, that in some states there is no intermediate appeals court. An appeal in such states goes directly from the trial court to the highest state court. See Exhibit 6-3 in Chapter 6.) (In the federal judicial system, there are intermediate appellate courts. See Exhibit 6-4 in Chapter 6.)	■ *Notice of appeal:* A party's notice given to a court (through filing) and to the opposing party (through service) of an intention to appeal. ■ *Appellate brief:* a document that a party files with an appellate court (and serves on an opponent) in which the party presents arguments on why the appellate court should affirm (approve), reverse, vacate (cancel), or otherwise modify what a lower court has done. ■ *Appellant:* The party bringing an appeal because of disagreement with a decision of a lower tribunal. Also called *petitioner.* ■ *Appellee,* The party against whom the appeal is brought. Also called *respondent.* ■ *Reply brief:* An appellate brief of the appellant that responds to the appellate brief of the appellee. A reply brief also refers to any appellate brief that responds to an opponent's appellate brief. ■ *Oral argument* A spoken presentation to the court on a legal issue, e.g., telling an appellate court why the rulings of a lower tribunal were valid or were in error.	**a.** Draft and file the notice of appeal. **b.** Order the trial transcript. **c.** Summarize (digest) trial testimony relevant to issues to be raised on appeal. **d.** *Cite check* the appellate brief. (Cite checking consists of examining citations in a document to determine their accuracy such as whether the format of the citation is correct, whether a *parallel cite* is needed, whether quoted material is accurately quoted, and whether the law cited is still valid. A *parallel cite* is an additional citation where you can find the same written material in the library or online. See Chapter 11 for a discussion of these tasks.)
V. ENFORCEMENT STAGE	**V. ENFORCEMENT STAGE**	**V. ENFORCEMENT STAGE**	**V. ENFORCEMENT STAGE**
32. *Posttrial discovery* **33.** *Execution* by the sheriff if the judgment debtor refuses to pay the judgment.	■ Court opinions or rulings are not common at the enforcement stage unless the parties disagree about something that requires a decision from a judge.	■ *Posttrial discovery:* Methods used by parties to force information from each other to aid in the enforcement of a trial judgment. An example would be a deposition conducted by a *judgment creditor* (who won the litigation) of a *judgment debtor* (who lost the litigation) in order to help identify the judgment debtor's assets. ■ *Execution:* A command or writ to a court officer (e.g., sheriff) to seize and sell the property of the losing litigant (the judgment debtor) in order to satisfy the judgment debt.	**a.** Investigate judgment debtor's assets. **b.** Schedule posttrial discovery of the judgment debtor. **c.** Arrange for the sheriff to begin execution of the judgment if the judgment debtor refuses to pay the judgment.

Exhibit 10-4	Overview of Criminal Litigation

Possible proceedings where court rulings and opinions could be written. The events and their sequence presented here are examples only.

EVENT	DECISIONS, RULINGS, AND OPINIONS AT THIS STAGE	DEFINITIONS	POSSIBLE PARALEGAL ROLES AT THIS STAGE
I. PRETRIAL STAGE	**I. PRETRIAL STAGE**	**I. PRETRIAL STAGE**	**I. PRETRIAL STAGE**
1. *Arrest* 2. *Booking* 3. *Initial appearance* before a judge or magistrate 4. *Discovery* 5. *Preliminary hearing* 6. *Indictment* by grand jury 7. *Arraignment* 8. *Plea bargaining* 9. Pretrial motions 10. *Voir dire*	■ The trial court often makes *rulings* concerning the pretrial events listed in the first column but rarely writes an *opinion* on any of the rulings. ■ Occasionally, a party may be allowed to appeal a pretrial ruling to an appellate court, which may write an opinion affirming, modifying, or reversing the ruling. Such an appeal is called an *interlocutory appeal.* It takes place before the trial court reaches its final judgment.	■ *Arrest:* Taking someone into custody to bring him or her before the proper authorities, here to answer a criminal charge. ■ *Book:* To enter charges against someone in a police register. The process is called *booking.* ■ *Initial appearance:* The first criminal court appearance by persons accused of a crime, during which the court (1) informs them of the charges and of their rights, (b) makes a decision on bail, and (c) determines the date of the next court proceeding. ■ *Preliminary hearing:* A pretrial criminal proceeding to determine if *probable cause* exists that the accused has committed a crime. Also called *probable-cause hearing, bindover hearing.* ■ *Probable cause:* A reasonable belief that a specific crime has been committed and that the accused committed the crime. ■ *Indictment:* A formal document issued by a grand jury accusing the defendant of a crime. (If the state has no grand jury, the accusation is contained in a document called an *information.)* ■ *Arraignment:* A pretrial criminal proceeding in which the defendant is formally charged with a crime and enters a plea. Arrangements are then made for the next proceeding. ■ *Plea bargain:* An agreement whereby an accused pleads guilty to a lesser included offense or to one of multiple charges in exchange for the prosecution's agreement to support a dismissal of some charges or a lighter sentence. Also called a *negotiated plea.* ■ *Voir dire:* A preliminary examination of (a) prospective jurors for the purpose of selecting persons qualified to sit on a jury or (b) prospective witnesses to determine their competence to testify. ■ *Ruling:* The conclusion or outcome of a decision made by a court of administrative agency. ■ *Opinion:* A court's written explanation of how it applied the law to the facts to resolve a dispute. ■ *Interlocutory appeal:* An appeal of a trial court ruling before the trial court reaches its final judgment.	**a.** Help conduct investigation of the charges. **b.** Prepare facts needed to argue for a low bail or *release on personal recognizance (ROR).* **c.** Help draft motions, e.g., motion to suppress. **d.** Draft discovery requests and motions. **e.** Summarize (digest) facts obtained through discovery. (For other paralegal discovery tasks, see Exhibit 10-7 later in the chapter.) **f.** Assemble *trial notebook.* (A trial notebook, discussed later in the chapter, is a collection of documents, arguments, and strategies that an attorney plans to use during a trial.) **g.** Help prepare and coordinate trial exhibits. **h.** Draft voir dire questions for attorney to consider for prospective jurors. **i.** Help attorney evaluate prospective witnesses during voir dire.
II. TRIAL STAGE	**II. TRIAL STAGE**	**II. TRIAL STAGE**	**II. TRIAL STAGE**

11. *Opening statements* of attorneys
 12. Government presents its case against the defendant:
   a. *evidence* introduced
   b. *direct examination*
   c. *cross-examination*
   d. re-direct and recross-examinations
 13. Motions to dismiss
 14. Defendant presents its case:
   a. *evidence* introduced
   b. *direct examination*
   c. *cross-examination*
   d. re-direct and recross-examinations
 15. Closing arguments to jury by attorneys
	■ The trial court often makes rulings on trial events listed in the first column, but rarely writes an *opinion* on any of the rulings.
	
	 ■ Occasionally, a party may be allowed to appeal a trial-court ruling to an appellate court before the trial is over. The appeals court may then write an opinion affirming, modifying, or reversing the ruling. Such an appeal is called an *interlocutory appeal.* It takes place before the trial court reaches its final judgment.
		■ *Opening statement:* An attorney's statement to the jury (or to the judge alone in a bench trial where there is no jury) made before presenting evidence. The statement summarizes or previews the case the attorney intends to try to establish during the trial. Unrepresented parties make the statement themselves. Also called *opening argument.*
		 ■ *Evidence:* Anything offered to establish the existence or nonexistence of a fact in dispute.
		 ■ *Direct examination:* The first questioning of a witness at a hearing by the party who called the witness. Also called *examination in chief.* (Redirect examination of this witness can occur after cross-examination.)
		 ■ *Cross-examination:* Questioning a witness at a hearing by an opponent after the other side has conducted a direct examination of this witness. (Recross-examination of this witness can occur after redirect examination.)
		 ■ *Closing argument:* The final statement by an attorney to the jury (or to the judge alone in a bench trial where there is no jury). The statement summarizes the evidence that was presented during the trial and requests a favorable decision. Unrepresented parties make the argument themselves. Also called *closing statement, final argument, summation,* and *summing up.*
			a. Coordinate scheduling of witnesses.
			 b. Take notes during trial.
			 c. Assist attorney with documents and exhibits.
			 d. Perform last-minute legal research.
			 e. Compare a trial witness's trial testimony with what he or she said in discovery and inform the attorney of any inconsistencies.
			 f. Perform other tasks needed by the attorney conducting the trial.

(continued)

| Exhibit 10-4 | Overview of Criminal Litigation *(Continued)* | | |

EVENT	DECISIONS, RULINGS, AND OPINIONS AT THIS STAGE	DEFINITIONS	POSSIBLE PARALEGAL ROLES AT THIS STAGE
16. Requests by attorneys for specific *Jury instructions* by judge (the charge) 17. Jury instructions given by judge (the charge to the jury) 18. *Verdict of* jury 19. *Judgment* of court, including the sentence if defendant is convicted	■ After the trial, the trial court delivers its judgment. Rarely will the trial court write an opinion explaining its judgment. (Most opinions are written by appellate courts rather than by trial courts.) ■ Several trial courts, however, do sometimes write trial-court opinions. Examples of such trial courts are federal trial courts (U.S. district courts) and New York State trial courts.	■ *Jury instructions:* A statement of the law given to the jury by the judge for use in deciding the issues of fact in its verdict. Also called the *charge.* Parties are allowed to request specific instructions. ■ *Verdict:* The jury's finding or decision on the factual issues placed before it. ■ *Judgment:* The final conclusion of a court that resolves a legal dispute by declaring the rights and obligations of the parties or that specifies what further proceedings are needed to resolve it.	
III. APPEAL STAGE	**III. APPEAL STAGE**	**III. APPEAL STAGE**	**III. APPEAL STAGE**
20. Filing of *notice of appeal* 21. Filing of *appellate brief of appellant* 22. Filing of *appellate brief* of appellee 23. Filing of *reply brief* of appellant 24. Oral argument by attorneys 25. Judgment of court	■ An opinion of the intermediate appellate court might be written. ■ This decision of the intermediate appellate court might be appealed to the highest court, which might write its own opinion. ■ (Note that in some states, there is no intermediate appeals court; the appeal goes directly from the trial court to the highest state court. See Exhibit 6-3 in Chapter 6.) (In the federal judicial system, there are intermediate appellate courts. See Exhibit 6-4 in Chapter 6.)	■ *Notice of appeal:* A party's notice given to a court (through filing) and to the opposing party (through service) of an intention to appeal. ■ *Appellate brief:* a document that a party files with an appellate (and serves on an opponent) in which the party presents arguments on why the appellate court should affirm (approve), reverse, vacate (cancel), or otherwise modify what a lower court has done. ■ *Appellant:* The party bringing an appeal because of disagreement with a decision of a lower tribunal. Also called *petitioner.* ■ *Appellee:* The party against whom the appeal is brought. Also called *respondent.* ■ *Reply brief:* An appellate brief of the appellant that responds to the appellate brief of the appellee. A reply brief also refers to any appellate brief that responds to an opponent's appellate brief. ■ *Oral argument:* A spoken presentation to the court on a legal issue, e.g., telling an appellate court why the rulings of a lower tribunal were valid or were in error.	a. Draft and file the notice of appeal. b. Order the trial transcript. c. Summarize (digest) trial testimony relevant to issues to be raised on appeal. d. *Cite check* the appellate brief. (Cite checking consists of examining citations in a document to determine their accuracy such as whether the format of the citation is correct, whether a *parallel cite* is needed, whether quoted material is accurately quoted, and whether the law cited is still valid. A *parallel cite* is an additional citation where you can find the same written material in the library or online. See chapter 11 for a discussion of these tasks.)

ALTERNATIVE DISPUTE RESOLUTION (ADR)

As you can see, litigation can be an involved and costly process. Consequently, disputing parties usually spend considerable time and effort trying to avoid full litigation by negotiating a mutually acceptable resolution, called a *settlement*. Negotiations usually begin when the attorney for the aggrieved party sends a demand letter to the other party or the latter's attorney. More letters are often exchanged along with memos and supporting reports. If there is some progress in these initial exchanges, the attorneys will have a number of face-to-face negotiation sessions.

A more formal method of seeking a settlement and avoiding litigation is called **alternative dispute resolution (ADR)**. Most ADR methods involve a neutral third person in the process. In some kinds of cases, e.g., medical malpractice, parties are required to try ADR before being allowed to have a court trial.

Here are the major categories of ADR:

ARBITRATION

Arbitration is a method of alternative dispute resolution in which the parties avoid litigation by submitting their dispute to a neutral third person (the arbitrator) who renders a decision resolving the dispute. **Judicial arbitration** occurs when a court refers or orders the parties to arbitration. If the parties have decided on their own to arbitrate the dispute, the arbitration is

alternative dispute resolution (ADR) A method or procedure for resolving a legal dispute without litigating the dispute in a court or administrative agency.

arbitration A method of alternative dispute resolution (ADR) in which the parties avoid litigation by submitting their dispute to a neutral third person (the arbitrator) who renders a decision resolving the dispute.

judicial arbitration Court-referred or court-ordered arbitration.

contractual arbitration
Arbitration that the parties have agreed (contracted) to use. Also called *private arbitration.*

called **contractual arbitration** or *private arbitration.* Many consumer purchase contracts and service agreements have a clause in which both sides agree to use arbitration if a dispute arises.

Contractual arbitration is used extensively. One paralegal points out that we "live in an age when everything from your bank account to the forms you fill out in a doctor's office contain a clause requiring any dispute that arises to be resolved by arbitration. [Hence when disputes arise in these situations], the modern paralegal is far more likely to help prepare for arbitration than for trial. Only a small minority of cases go to trial, and that is partly because more and more disputes are governed by arbitration."[2]

award The decision of an arbitrator. (See glossary for another meaning.)

In both judicial and contractual arbitration, the arbitrator listens to the evidence and makes a decision (often called an **award**). Arbitrators are not judges or government employees and they do not have to be attorneys. They are often hired through organizations such as the American Arbitration Association (www.adr.org). An arbitration proceeding is not as formal as a court trial. Elaborate objections to evidence, for example, may occur in court cases, but they are relatively rare in arbitration proceedings. Parties appear before the arbitrator on their own or through their attorneys.

Both judicial and contractual arbitration can be binding or nonbinding. The parties decide. If they choose binding arbitration, the arbitrator's decision is not appealable to a court or is subject to limited court appeal. In nonbinding arbitration, a party who is unhappy with an arbitrator's decision can appeal the decision in court. If, however, the end result of the court appeal is the same as the arbitration decision (or is more favorable to the other party), some states will punish the party who appealed by making him or her pay the attorney fees and costs incurred by the other party in litigating the case in court.

MEDIATION

mediation A method of alternative dispute resolution (ADR) in which the parties avoid litigation by submitting their dispute to a neutral third person (the mediator) who helps the parties resolve their dispute, but does not render a decision that resolves it for them.

Mediation is a method of alternative dispute resolution (ADR) in which the parties avoid litigation by submitting their dispute to a neutral third person (the mediator) who helps the parties resolve their dispute, but does not render a decision that resolves it for them. The mediator, however, may make suggestions or recommendations for a resolution. Parties appear before the mediator on their own or through their attorneys. Mediators do not have to be attorneys.

A variation on this ADR is called *binding mediation* in which the mediator *does* render a decision that resolves the dispute but only after the parties have attempted mediation and failed. This is similar to med-arb, discussed next.

MED-ARB

med-arb A method of alternative dispute resolution (ADR) in which the parties first try mediation, and if it does not work, they try arbitration.

Med-arb is a method of ADR in which the parties first try mediation, and if it does not work, they try arbitration. Once it is clear that mediation will not be successful, the mediator can switch roles and make a decision as an arbitrator.

PRIVATE JUDGING

private judging A method of alternative dispute resolution (ADR) consisting of arbitration or mediation in which the arbitrator or mediator is a retired judge. Sometimes misleadingly called *rent-a-judge.*

Private judging is a method of ADR consisting of arbitration or mediation in which the arbitrator or mediator is a retired judge. It is sometimes misleadingly referred to as *rent-a-judge.* The name is misleading because the retired judge has no more authority or power than any other arbitrator or mediator. Private judging is not a government proceeding.

NEUTRAL EVALUATION

neutral evaluation A method of alternative dispute resolution (ADR) in which both sides hire an experienced attorney or an expert in the area involved in the dispute who will listen to an abbreviated version of the evidence and the arguments of each side and offer an evaluation in the hope that this will stimulate more serious settlement discussions. Also called *case evaluation.*

Neutral evaluation is method of ADR in which both sides hire an experienced attorney or an expert in the area involved in the dispute (e.g., a chemist in a patent dispute) who will listen to an abbreviated version of the evidence and the arguments of each side and offer an evaluation in the hope that this will stimulate more serious settlement discussions. The process is sometimes called *case evaluation.*

SUMMARY JURY TRIAL; SUMMARY BENCH TRIAL

In a *summary jury trial* or *summary bench trial*, the attorneys present their cases in summary form without calling witnesses. A jury listens to the attorneys if a summary jury is used; a judge listens to the attorneys if a summary bench trial is used. The jury or judge will then reach a nonbinding conclusion on the dispute. The hope is that this conclusion will encourage the parties to settle. If the settlement efforts fail, the case goes to trial. The parties begin anew as if the summary jury or bench trial had not occurred.

COLLABORATIVE LAW

Collaborative law is a method of practicing law in which the attorneys refuse to continue representing the parties if they cannot settle their dispute through mediation or other method of ADR. The goal is to encourage settlement. If ADR fails and the parties want to start litigation, the collaborative-law attorneys withdraw from the case so that the parties must now find litigation attorneys. The cost of paying for a new set of attorneys is a strong incentive to settle.

collaborative law A method of practicing law in which the attorneys refuse to continue representing the parties if they cannot settle their dispute through mediation or other method of alternative dispute resolution (ADR).

ONLINE ADR

Parties can engage in alternative dispute resolution (ADR) online. One settlement site for medical claims (www.cybersettle.com) asserts that it has settled over $1.9 billion in disputes since it became available online.

LITIGATION ASSISTANT ROLES IN ADR

Paralegals have many roles in assisting attorneys who have cases in ADR. For example, a paralegal can organize files, schedule discovery and ADR sessions, conduct investigations, summarize or digest data from discovery, help prepare the client for ADR, and assist the attorney during the ADR proceeding in much the same fashion as paralegals assist attorneys during regular trials. Paralegals often prepare *mediation summaries* (particularly in personal-injury cases) that:

- outline the issues of the case,
- present the facts (including a description of the incident),
- list the medical expenses and lost wages incurred by the client,
- summarize medical records, and
- state the costs incurred by the law firm to date.

"Some firms use a [standard] form for this where you simply 'plug in' the information." One paralegal helps her attorney prepare for mediation by scanning all documents and supportive evidence into the attorney's laptop computer and making a PowerPoint presentation of this data that the attorney can use during the mediation session.[3] If ADR leads to a resolution of the case, paralegals can be involved in finalizing the settlement such as by preparing a draft of the document that lays out the terms of the agreement that the parties reached.

In addition, some paralegals have become arbitrators and mediators themselves. In most states, as indicated, you do not have to be an attorney to conduct arbitration or mediation. (For more information, run this search in Google, Bing, or Yahoo: paralegal mediator.) Service companies are available that offer arbitration and mediation services to parties involved in disputes. A few of these companies hire people with paralegal training and experience to be arbitrators or mediators.

LITIGATION ASSISTANT: PRETRIAL STAGE

For a list of paralegal functions in litigation, see Exhibit 2-6 in Chapter 2 ("Paralegal Specialties: A Dictionary of Functions"). Note the separate entry on litigation as well as the trial and other litigation tasks listed under most of the forty-seven specialty entries presented in this exhibit of Chapter 2.

Trial work can be challenging because of the high stakes and high energy involved. Litigation paralegal Jennifer Swails "assists lawyers with everything from submitting the first draft of discovery to following through to the end of a trial." Recalling her first trial, she remembers experiencing "every possible emotion." "I was scared to death, nervous, and tired."[4] Not all paralegals, however, have the same responsibility during litigation. Some, like Jennifer, perform a broad range of tasks. Others are given more narrow litigation tasks. Let's take a closer look at this variety of paralegal roles during litigation, beginning with the pretrial stage.

At the *pretrial stage*, many paralegal tasks fall into the following categories:

1. Pleadings
2. Service of process and court filings
3. Calendar control and scheduling
4. Discovery
5. Trial notebooks
6. Settlement
7. Expert witnesses
8. Interviewing
9. Investigation
10. Legal research

The remainder of the chapter will cover most of these tasks, particularly those at the beginning of the list. Some are also discussed in Chapter 8 on interviewing, Chapter 9 on investigation, Chapter 11 on legal research, Chapter 13 on computers in the law, and Chapter 14 on law office administration.

1. PLEADINGS

The major pleadings in litigation are the complaint and the answer. Very often a law office will use standard forms as the starting point in drafting pleadings or **instruments** such as a will, contract, or mortgage. The standard forms come from old case files or from **templates** in document-assembly programs, which we will examine in Chapter 13. (See also Exhibit 10-5 on finding these forms.) With word processors such as Microsoft Word and Corel's WordPerfect (alone or with their office suites) you can create your own template. For example, once you have typed the basic format of a complaint, you can save the format for reuse in other cases. The format typically includes the heading of the complaint, the spacing between lines, the consecutive numbering of each line (if this is required by court rules), etc.

instruments A formal written document that gives expression to or embodies a legal act or agreement, e.g., a will, contract, or mortgage.

templates A file containing text and a format that can be used as the starting point for creating frequently used documents.

Standard Forms

Before we look at an example of a standard form for a complaint, we need to cover some basic guidelines on the need to adapt such forms to the needs of current clients. The guidelines are outlined in Exhibit 10-5.

Exhibit 10-5	How to Avoid Abusing a Standard Form

- A standard form is an example of the document that you need to draft. It could be a pleading (e.g., a complaint) or an instrument (e.g., a contract).
- Standard forms are found in a number of places: formbooks, manuals, practice texts, statutory codes, and court rules. Computer templates in document-assembly programs are also used as starting points for creating standard forms. On the Internet, for example, see www .USCourtForms.com and the sites listed in Helpful Websites at the end of the chapter. Searches such as "negligence form" or "contract form" on Google, Bing, or Yahoo will often lead to standard forms that can be purchased or used for free.
- Most standard forms are written by private attorneys. Occasionally, however, a standard form will be written by the legislature or by the court as the suggested *or required* form to use.
- Considerable care must be exercised in the use of a standard form. A form can be deceptive in that it appears to require you to do little more than fill in the blanks. The intelligent use of these forms usually requires much more.
- The cardinal rule is that you must always *adapt* the form to the particular law and facts of the client's case. You fit the form to the client's case, not the client's case to the form. If there are facts already in the form, be sure that those facts are consistent with the facts of your client's case. Clauses may have been included in the form to cover specific legal requirements. You must decide if these clauses are needed by the client and if other clauses must be added to cover the client's situation.
- Do not be reluctant to change the preprinted language in the form if you have a good reason. Whenever you make such a change, be sure to alert your supervisor so that it can be approved.
- You should never use a standard form unless and until you have satisfied yourself that you know the meaning of every word and phrase on the form. This includes *boilerplate*, which is standard language commonly used in the same kind of document. Too often, form users ignore what they do not understand. Find out what everything on the form means by
  - Using a legal dictionary (often a good starting point)
  - Asking your supervisor
  - Asking other knowledgeable people
  - Doing other legal research
- Once you have found a form that appears useful, look around for another form that attempts to serve the same purpose. Analyze the different or alternative forms available. Which one is preferable? Why? Keep questioning the validity and effectiveness of any form.
- If you leave any blank spaces on the form, be sure that your supervisor approves leaving them blank.
- If the form was written for another state, be aware that the form may be unadaptable to your state because of differences in the laws of the two states.
- Often, you will go to an old case file to find a document that can be used as a model for a similar document that you need to draft on a current case. All the above cautions apply to the adaptation of documents from other case files.

Complaints

Exhibit 10-6 illustrates the basic structure of many complaints. Note that the complaint includes the following components:

- Caption
- Designation of the pleading
- Statement of jurisdiction
- Facts relevant to venue
- Body of complaint

- Prayer for relief
- Jury demand
- Subscription
- Verification
- Notarization

Not all complaints will contain these components. You need to check the requirements in the statutes and court rules that govern the structure for complaints in the court where your office is filing the action. Detailed requirements may exist on matters such as size, weight, and type of paper that can be used; permissible margins; font and type size; line spacing and numbering; and the use of a colored backing to which the complaint may have to be fastened.

Electronic filing (e-filing) of complaints and other pleadings is discussed in the next section.

Exhibit 10-6	Structure of a Complaint

Caption

STATE of _____
COUNTY of _____
SUPERIOR COURT
Mary Smith, Plaintiff
v.   Civil Action No. _____
Fred Jones, Defendant

Designation of Pleading →

COMPLAINT FOR NEGLIGENCE

The plaintiff, through her attorney, alleges:

Statement of Jurisdiction → (1) The jurisdiction of this court is based upon section _____, title _____ of the State Code (2013).

Facts Relevant to Venue

(2) The plaintiff is an accountant who resides at 12 Arch St. in the City of _____, County of _____. She has resided here for five years immediately preceding the filing of this complaint.

(3) Upon information and belief, defendant is a truck driver who has resided at 465 Hamilton St., City of _____, County of _____ for an indefinite period.

Body of Complaint

(4) On March 13, 2012, the truck of defendant collided with the car of plaintiff. This occurred on the corner of First Street and Via Dios in the City of _____, County of _____

(5) The collision occurred as a result of the negligent operation of the defendant's truck as to speed and control of his truck.

(6) As a result of the negligence of the defendant asserted in paragraph 5, the plaintiff has been subjected to great pain and suffering and has incurred medical expenses, loss of income, and automobile repair expenses.

Prayer for Relief → (7) Therefore, plaintiff demands judgment in the amount of $350,000 plus the costs and disbursements of this action.

Jury Demand → (8) The plaintiff demands a trial by jury on all issues so triable.

Subscription →

_____
Linda Stout
Attorney for Plaintiff
234 Main St.
_____, ____ 07237
STATE of _____
COUNTY of _____

_____

Verification

Mary Smith, being first duly sworn on oath according to law, deposes and says that she has read the foregoing complaint and that the matters stated therein are true to the best of her knowledge, information, and belief.

Notarization

Subscribed and sworn to before me on this _____ day of _____, 20 ____

_____

Notary Public
My commission expires _____

caption The heading or introductory part of a pleading, court opinion, memo, or other document that provides identifying information such as the kind of document it is, the names of the parties, and the court involved, if any.

docket number A consecutive number assigned to a case by the court and used on all documents filed with the court during the litigation of that case.

Caption of Complaint

A **caption** of a complaint is the heading that provides identifying information, such as the kind of document it is, the name of the court, the name of the parties, and, if available, the **docket number** assigned to the case by the court.

Designation of the Pleading

The title of the pleading is stated at the top of the pleading as part of the caption. The pleading for our example in Exhibit 10-6 is a Complaint for Negligence.

Statement of Jurisdiction

If the court requires a statement of the court's *subject matter jurisdiction*, the citation to the statute or other law conferring this jurisdiction must be included. (Subject-matter jurisdiction is the court's power to resolve a particular type of legal dispute and to grant a particular type of relief.) The main federal trial courts—U.S. district courts—require a statement of subject-matter jurisdiction in complaints. Rule 8 of the *Federal Rules of Civil Procedure (FRCP)* provides that a claim for relief shall contain "a short and plain statement of the grounds for the court's jurisdiction." Not all states have the same requirement. Some state courts require a statement of subject matter jurisdiction; others do not.

Venue

For purposes of determining *venue*, the complaint may also have to allege the residence of the parties, where the accident or wrong allegedly occurred, etc. Venue is the proper county or geographical area in which a court with jurisdiction may hear a case. In most judicial systems, there is more than one trial court. For example, there may be one for each county or district. The selection of a particular trial court within a judicial system is referred to as a *choice of venue*.

Body of Complaint

The claims or causes of action of the plaintiff are stated in the *body* of the complaint. A cause of action is a legally acceptable reason for suing, a set of facts that gives a party the right to judicial relief. Every separate cause of action used by the plaintiff should be stated in a separate "count," e.g., Count I, Count II, or simply as First Cause of Action, Second Cause of Action, etc. (This is not done in Exhibit 10-6 because only one cause of action is alleged in this complaint–negligence.) Throughout the complaint, the paragraphs should be consecutively numbered. Each paragraph in the body should contain a single fact or a closely related grouping of facts.

In federal courts and in many state courts, the complaint does not have to state every detail of every fact that the plaintiff will try to prove in the trial. These courts require only **notice pleading**, which is a short and plain statement of the claim showing that the pleader is entitled to relief. There are times, however, when specificity in the pleading is required. For example, allegations of fraud must be stated with specificity or particularity. Also, when **special damages** are sought in defamation cases, the facts must be pleaded with specificity.

When the plaintiff lacks personal knowledge of a fact being alleged, the fact should be stated upon *information and belief*, as in the third paragraph of Exhibit 10-6.

notice pleading A short and plain statement of the claim showing that the pleader is entitled to relief.

special damages Economic losses (e.g., medical expenses and lost wages) that must be alleged and proven. They are not presumed to exist. Also referred to as *specials*. Special damages is a category of *compensatory damages*, which is money paid to restore an injured party to his or her position prior to the injury or other loss.

Prayer for Relief

In the *prayer for relief*, the complaint asks for a specific amount of damages or for some other form of relief such as an injunction against a nuisance. (If the prayer asks for damages, the clause requesting it is called the *ad damnum clause*.) In the event that the defendant fails to appear and answer the complaint, a *default judgment* is entered against the defendant. The relief given the plaintiff in a default judgment cannot exceed what the plaintiff asked for in the prayer for relief. (A default judgment is a judgment against a party for failure to file a required pleading or otherwise respond to an opponent's claim.)

Demand for a Jury Trial

Not all cases can be tried by jury, although negligence cases between private parties usually can. If a plaintiff in a civil negligence case wants a jury, most states require a request (demand) for a jury to be made in the complaint.

Subscription

A *subscription* is someone's signature. If an attorney wrote the complaint, his or her subscription is required. If the plaintiff wrote the complaint and is acting as his or her own attorney in the case, the plaintiff signs.

Verification

A *verification* is a formal declaration stating that a person has read a document (e.g., a complaint) and swears that it is true to the best of his or her knowledge. Not all courts require a verification. When required, it is signed by a party on whose behalf the pleading is prepared.

Notarization

If court rules require notarization, the notary's seal is usually placed at the end of the complaint.

Civil Cover Sheet

Along with the complaint, the plaintiff must file a *civil cover sheet*, which is a form filed in court in a civil case that indicates the names and addresses of the parties and their attorneys, the kind of action being filed, etc.

OTHER PLEADINGS

The response of the defendant is the *answer*, which is the first pleading filed by the defendant that responds to the plaintiff's claims. The answer may simply deny the assertions in the complaint. The answer can also assert an *affirmative defense*, which raises facts or arguments that will defeat an opponent's claim even if the opponent's allegations in the claim are proven. If the defendant wants to assert a claim against the plaintiff, it is done in a *counterclaim*.

SERVICE OF PROCESS AND COURT FILINGS

The lawsuit begins with *service of process*, which is a formal delivery of notice to a defendant that a suit has been initiated to which he or she must respond. The defendant receives a copy of the complaint and *summons*. The latter is a notice directing the defendant to appear in court and answer the plaintiff's complaint or face a *default judgment*, which is a judgment against a party for failure to file a required pleading or otherwise respond to an opponent's claim. Delivery of the complaint and summons to the defendant is usually accomplished in person. An adult (someone other than the plaintiff) hands the documents to the defendant. Under some circumstances, the law allows **substituted service** such as by registered mail. Before substituted service is allowed, the plaintiff may be required to file an **affidavit** on the efforts taken to find the defendant in the state.

Another service task involves witnesses who are called to appear for a deposition, for a court hearing, or for the trial itself. To compel witnesses to appear, they are often served with a **subpoena**, which is a command to appear at a certain time and place. (If the command is to bring documents or things, it is a *subpoena duces tecum.)* A paralegal may be asked to serve process or to serve a subpoena. Alternatively, the law firm may hire a service company that is a professional process server. If so, a paralegal may have the responsibility of hiring and monitoring the company.

Completing a service yourself takes preparation and care. You must know the local rules on how to serve someone properly. In addition, you need to anticipate the kinds of difficulty you might encounter "on the street." Here is how paralegal David Busch describes his first service assignment.

> "I was given a subpoena to serve on a lady for a hearing the next day. I rushed to the courthouse to pick up the subpoena and immediately proceeded to the address given to me by the attorney. I spent over an hour looking for the address when I realized that it was a bad address. I frantically [tried to call] the lawyer." He was in court. His secretary "gave me a work address. I rushed to the work address to find out that she was on vacation for two weeks beginning yesterday.... Frustrating! This was my first service and I could not even find the lady." I realized that process serving is not as easy as handing someone a copy of a lawsuit.[5]

substituted service An approved method of completing service of process other than by handing the process documents in person to the defendant or to the defendant's authorized representative (e.g., service by mail or by publication in a newspaper). Also called *constructive service.*

affidavit A written or printed statement of facts made under oath by a person (called the *affiant*) before someone with authority to administer the oath.

subpoena (1) To command that someone appear at a certain time and place. (2) A command to appear at a certain time and place.

Filing documents in court also requires careful preparation and compliance with court rules. Court clerks usually have little sympathy for filers who fail to comply with such requirements.

> There are few things more frustrating to the paralegal than getting something to the courthouse for filing, often on the very last day it is due, and having it returned, not filed, because of a technical error or oversight. Since the paralegal is the "last checkpoint" for pleadings and other documents being sent to the courthouse, it falls on him or her to ensure those documents are complete and acceptable.[6]

Litigation paralegal, Erin Schlemme, recommends the following basic steps for successful filings:

- Know the correct address of the court where the filing must be made.
- Phone in advance or check the court's website to determine the exact hours when the clerk's office will be open to accept filings.
- Use the correct format, including the proper size of paper, content of the cover sheet, etc.
- Have the correct fees, and know whether the clerk can accept a personal check or a law-firm check, or will insist on cash.

The traditional method of initiating a lawsuit is to go to the court clerk and hand over the original complaint, a copy to leave with the court, and copies for each of the parties. The clerk assigns a docket number (or special computer coding number) to the case and stamps this number on the original and on each of the copies. The date is also stamped on the front of the original and each copy. Most courts require the *summons* to be attached to the complaint.

e-filing Electronic filing in court of pleadings and other documents.

Many courts now allow electronic filing, referred to as **e-filing**, which can occur at any hour of the day on any day of the week. Of course, as with traditional filing, deadlines must be met. A cause of action can be lost if not filed (by hand or electronically) before the statute of limitations expires.

PACER (Public Access to Court Electronic Records) An electronic public access service that allows subscribers to obtain case and docket information from federal courts via the Internet (www.pacer.gov).

In federal courts (trial, bankruptcy, and appellate), the e-filing system is called Case Management/Electronic Case Filing (CM/ECF). The system for gaining access to the 500+ million case file documents is called Public Access to Court Electronic Records (**PACER**). Most state courts have their own systems for e-filing and access. In one county in Arizona, for example, the online system for state courts is called Electronic Court Record (ECR). Great care is needed in order to use these systems correctly. Special rules apply. Here, for example, is the rule in one state:

> "Any document that is electronically filed with the court after the close of business on any day shall be deemed to have been filed on the next court day. 'Close of business,' as used in this paragraph, shall mean 5 p.m. or the time at which the court would not accept filing at the court's filing counter, whichever is earlier."[7]

Online assistance is often available to learn the e-filing system, including its special rules and the mechanics of navigating the system.

PDF (portable document format) A file format consisting of an electronic image of a document that preserves the features and styles of the document (e.g., its line spacing, photograph placement, and font size) that existed before it was converted into a digital document.

E-filed documents are often presented in an image or digital format, the most popular being **PDF** (portable document format). A document as a PDF file is a digital document that preserves all the features and styles of the document before it was converted into a digital document. When you read a PDF file, you are reading an exact duplicate of the original document. A special code in the program allows a user to insert a digital signature that verifies the authenticity of the document you are sending. To read PDF files, many law firms use free or paid versions of Adobe products. The PDF standard is not the only format used in e-filing systems. Another is the XML (extensible markup language) standard.

3. CALENDAR CONTROL AND SCHEDULING

Recently a paralegal commented that her "greatest challenge is staying on top of schedules. The attorney I work for ... is incredibly overloaded and the amount of juggling I have to do sometimes makes me feel like I should be in Ringling Brothers and Barnum & Bailey instead of a law office."[8]

Here are five words that a paralegal (and anyone else in a law office) should never be heard saying: "Oh, was that due today?" [9]. The clock is a dominant presence in every well-run law office. Calendar control is so critical that some legal-malpractice insurance companies will not insure attorneys that do not have approved reminder systems built into their case-management program. One of the most common grounds for legal-malpractice claims against attorneys is allowing the statute of limitations to run on a cause of action. The failure to file a lawsuit within the time allowed by law can result in the permanent loss of a client's right to assert a cause of action, no matter how good a case the client would have had in court.

The task of controlling dates and schedules can become all the more hectic when unanticipated events force an office to recalculate large numbers of due dates. One paralegal recalls the time when a judge unexpectedly postponed a trial that was about to begin. "Here we are, three days before trial," and everything comes to an abrupt halt. The parties had subpoenaed over twenty witnesses, rooms had been reserved, equipment had been rented, expert witnesses had been prepared, and numerous exhibits were ready to be used. Suddenly the judge's clerk called to announce a two-month postponement.[10]

In this environment, a major method of achieving calendar control is the tracking system called the **tickler** (also called a *come-up system*). This is a paper or computer system used to record important dates and to remind everyone to take appropriate action on these dates. A key responsibility of many paralegals is to operate and monitor these tracking or calendar systems. Attorneys need constant reminders of due dates, particularly when they are working on more than one case and when more than one attorney is working on a single case.

Ticklers operate in different ways. Most offices use computer programs that have reminder or tickler systems built into them. Case management and calendar software programs can automatically send out email reminders as the date of a calendared event approaches. Once you insert future events in the online calendar, you can receive pop-up reminders (and beep sounds) prior to and on the due dates indicated on the calendar. The software can be keyed to the deadlines found in court rules of particular courts. When you tell the software what kind of case you have and the date on which you filed your complaint, you will be given alerts on when litigation events must occur such as the date when the answer must be filed, the earliest date when discovery can begin, etc. Online calendaring services of this kind are also available.

Some offices still use a manual or paper tickler as a backup to the computer tickler. Suppose, for example, that an attorney must conduct a deposition on May 23. Weeks before this date, the attorney's paralegal will enter this date on a specially designed, multipart form. One of the parts of the form is torn off and sent to the attorney as a reminder of the deposition. Another part will be torn off and sent to the attorney as a further reminder a few days before May 23. In addition, secretaries, paralegals, and attorneys would enter the same due dates in their individual diaries.

An important part of calendar control is *redundancy*, meaning more than one system to accomplish the same task. For example, there could be a central computer tickler for all cases in the office, a separate tickler built into the case management software used on a particular case, a manual tickler, and individual diaries. With these tools, the likelihood of missing a date is substantially decreased.

tickler A paper or computer system designed to provide reminders of important dates. Also called a *come-up system*.

4. DISCOVERY

Methods of Discovery

To help a party prepare for trial, the following discovery methods are available:

- deposition
- interrogatories ("rogs")
- request for admission (RFA)

privilege log A list of data or documents claimed to be covered by privilege and, therefore, protected from disclosure in discovery or during trial.

attorney-client privilege (ACP) A client or a client's attorney can refuse to disclose any confidential (private) communication between them if the purpose of the communication was to facilitate the provision of legal services to the client.

redact To edit or prepare a document for publication or release, often by deleting, altering, or blocking out text that you do not want disclosed.

discoverable Pertaining to information or materials an opponent can obtain through deposition, interrogatories, or other discovery method.

- request for production (RFP) of documents and things; request for entry on land for inspection and other purposes
- independent medical examination (IME)

Discovery is used by parties to force information from each other to aid in trial preparation. There are many tasks paralegals can perform during the discovery stage of litigation. For example, when responding to discovery requests, they can help prepare the **privilege log** that lists all of the information or documents that the office will refuse to disclose because of a claim of privilege such as the **attorney-client privilege (ACP)**, which protects communications between attorney and client that are part of the legal services the attorney is providing the client. If only part of a document is protected by privilege, the paralegal can be assigned the task of **redacting** (blocking out or shielding) the part that is not **discoverable** so that the rest can be disclosed. For an overview of discovery and paralegal tasks, see Exhibit 10-7.

E-Discovery

The information obtained in discovery can consist of written answers to questions (e.g., what doctors treated you in the last five years?); documents (e.g., provide bank records for the last three years); and the large quantities of **e-evidence** that are now part of many lawsuits. E-evidence is known as electronically stored information (ESI). When e-evidence is sought in discovery, the process is called **e-discovery** or electronic data discovery (EDD).

Exhibit 10-7	**Overview of Discovery and Paralegal Roles**

DEPOSITION:

DEFINITION	WHO MUST COMPLY?	POSSIBLE PARALEGAL ROLES
■ A method of discovery by which parties and their prospective witnesses are questioned by the opposing party before trial at a location other than the courtroom. The person questioned is called the *deponent*. ■ If the deponent has not seen the questions before they are asked, the deposition is called a *deposition by oral examination*. (Such questions are always asked by an attorney.) ■ If the deponent is given the questions in writing, the deposition is called a *deposition by written questions*. (Such questions are often asked by a stenographer or court reporter rather than by an attorney.) ■ On depositions in federal trial courts, see Rules 30 and 31 of the Federal Rules of Civil Procedure)(www.law.cornell.edu/rules/frcp/#chapter_)	■ A deposition can be taken of a party to the suit. ■ A deposition can also be taken of a nonparty witness.	**a.** Schedule time and place for the deposition, usually in the conference room of one of the law offices. In an electronic deposition (e-deposition) conducted on the Internet, the attorney asking the questions and the deponent may be in different locations. **b.** Make entries in office tickler on due dates for scheduled depositions and related court motions. **c.** Prepare the *subpoena*, which orders a nonparty to come to the deposition to be deposed. **d.** Prepare *subpoena duces tecum*, which requires the deponent (the witness being deposed) to bring specified things (e.g., documents) with him or her. **e.** When a client is being asked to bring things to the deposition under a subpoena duces tecum, prepare the *privilege log* in order to have a list of what is not *discoverable* by the other side in discovery. **f.** Prepare a list of suggested questions for the attorney to ask the deponent. (This is done after reading everything in the file to date, e.g., complaint, answer, interview reports, investigation reports, and answers to interrogatories.) **g.** Prepare exhibits the attorney will use when questioning the deponent. **h.** Arrange for scheduling and payment of stenographer or reporter. **i.** Order transcript of deposition. **j.** Take notes at the deposition. **k.** Prepare motion to force compliance by other side. **l.** Prepare motion to have matters not answered deemed admitted. **m.** Prepare an index of the deposition testimony. The index should include an alphabetical list of all major topics covered in the deposition. **n.** Digest (summarize) the deposition testimony. See Exhibit 10-8 for different ways to prepare digests. **o.** Compare the deposition testimony with the answers to the interrogatories. Identify patterns, look for inconsistencies, etc.

(continued)

Exhibit 10-7	Overview of Discovery and Paralegal Roles *(Continued)*

INTERROGATORIES ("ROGS"):

DEFINITION	WHO MUST COMPLY?	POSSIBLE PARALEGAL ROLES
▪ A method of discovery by which one party sends written questions to another party. The answers are submitted in writing. ▪ On interrogatories in federal trial courts, see Rule 33 of the Federal Rules of Civil Procedure) (www.law.cornell.edu/rules/frcp/#chapter_)	▪ Limited to parties only. Nonparty witnesses do not have to answer and cannot send interrogatories.	a. Prepare a list of the interrogatories to be sent. (This is done after reading everything in the file to date, e.g., complaint, answer, interview reports, investigation reports, and deposition transcript, if available.) b. Prepare a draft of answers to interrogatories received from the other side. c. Enter due dates in office tickler to serve as reminders of the dates interrogatories must be sent and must be answered. d. Arrange conference with client to go over questions and answers. e. Prepare the privilege log in order to have a list of what is not *discoverable* by the other side through interrogatories. f. Draft a motion to compel a response to interrogatories. g. Draft a motion to have matters not answered be deemed admitted. h. Prepare an index of the answers to the interrogatories. The index should include an alphabetical list of all major topics covered in the rogs. i. Digest (summarize) the interrogatory answers. See Exhibit 10-8 for different ways to prepare digests. j. Compare the interrogatory answers with deposition testimony. Identify patterns, look for inconsistencies, etc.

REQUESTS FOR ADMISSION (RFA):

DEFINITION	WHO MUST COMPLY?	POSSIBLE PARALEGAL ROLES
▪ A method of discovery by which one party sends a request to another party that the latter agree that a certain fact or legal conclusion is true or valid so that there will be no need to present proof or arguments about that matter during the trial. ▪ On RFAs in federal trial courts, see Rule 36 of the Federal Rules of Civil Procedure) (www.law.cornell.edu/rules/frcp/#chapter_)	▪ Limited to parties only. Nonparty witnesses do not have to respond to and cannot send RFAs.	a. Read everything in the file to date, (e.g., complaint, answer, interview reports, investigation reports, interrogatory answers, deposition transcript) in order to prepare a list of facts or legal conclusions the other side will be requested to admit or accept. b. Index and digest the responses from the other side. c. Enter due dates in office tickler. d. Prepare the privilege log in order to have a list of what is not discoverable by the other side by using an RFA.

REQUESTS FOR PRODUCTION (RFP)

DEFINITION	WHO MUST COMPLY?	POSSIBLE PARALEGAL ROLES
▪ A method of discovery by which one party requests that another party provide access to electronically stored data, paper documents, or other tangible things for copying or inspection. ▪ The method can also include a request to enter the party's land for inspection. ▪ On RFAs in federal trial courts, see Rule 34 of the Federal Rules of Civil Procedure) (www.law.cornell.edu/rules/frcp/#chapter_)	▪ Limited to parties only. Nonparty witnesses do not have to respond to and cannot send RFPs. ▪ The party must be in possession or control of the data, document, thing or land in question. ▪ If you want a nonparty to turn over documents and other materials you can seek a deposition of this nonparty and use a *subpoena duces tecum* to specify what should be brought to the deposition.	a. Prepare a draft of a request for production of electronic data, paper documents, or other things, specifying what you want to copy, inspect, or test, and when you want to do so. b. Arrange who will do the inspecting, copying, etc., payment of costs involved, etc. c. Draft a motion to compel the inspection, copying, etc. d. Index and digest the report(s) based on the inspection, copying, etc. e. Enter scheduled dates for inspection, copying, etc. in the officer tickler. f. Prepare the privilege log in order to have a list of what is not discoverable by the other side in a RFP.

INDEPENDENT MEDICAL EXAMINATION (IME):

DEFINITION	WHO MUST COMPLY?	POSSIBLE PARALEGAL ROLES
▪ A method of discovery by which a party obtains a court order for a professional examination of a person whose physical or mental condition is in controversy. ▪ On IMEs in federal trial courts, see Rule 35 of the Federal Rules of Civil Procedure) (www.law.cornell.edu/rules/frcp/#chapter_)	▪ Limited to parties only and to persons under the control of parties, e.g., the child of a party. (In a few courts, the employees of a party can also be forced to undergo a physical or mental examination.)	a. Prepare court motion to order the examination. b. Schedule appointment and payment of doctor or other professional who will conduct the examination. c. Enter dates pertaining to the examination in office tickler. d. Prepare court motion to have matters relevant to the examination be deemed admitted for failure to submit to the examination.

E-evidence consists of e-mail, instant messages (IMs,) text messages, voice mail, social-media posts, spreadsheets, Web pages, digital video, and other digital data. Because storage of digital data is relatively inexpensive, many companies keep tremendous quantities of data in their offices. In addition, a recent trend is to store digital data in the *cloud*, meaning in secure sites on the Internet.

e-evidence Evidence generated by or stored in a computer or other digital device. Examples include email, Web pages, digital spreadsheets, computer-generated memos, and other digital data.

e-discovery The discovery by a party in litigation of an opponent's data generated by or stored in a computer or other digital device. Also called *electronic data discovery (EDD)*. The discovery of electronically stored information (ESI).

E-discovery seeks two broad categories of relevant digital data: current data and legacy data. Current data is information that is in current or recent use, e.g., a list of customers or an exchange of emails from merger negotiations. Legacy data is largely inactive data that is part of the history of the company and that may have been collected on now-outdated technology.

Digesting Discovery Transcripts and Documents

A discovery task that some paralegals frequently perform is digesting or summarizing transcripts and documents, particularly depositions. Here is how Dana Nikolewski describes a recent experience with this seemingly never-ending task:

> It's Thursday and I'm on page 20 of a 300-page deposition, which I really should have finished summarizing last week. The phone rings and I relish the thought of this brief interruption, until I recognize the voice on the other end as none other than our local courier announcing the arrival of 200 more depositions which I know need to be summarized ASAP.[11]

Similarly, Aaron Paker says that within fifteen minutes of arriving at a new position, "I was handed over 2,000 pages of discovery for a Murder 1 case and asked to summarize and index it."[11a] Litigation paralegals can indeed spend a good deal of time digesting. Occasionally, you will see a want ad for paralegals to digest depositions full-time. Such individuals are sometimes called **depo summarizers**. While all litigation paralegals do not perform the task full-time, the experience of Dana Nikolewski and Aaron Paker is not unusual.

Before digesting can occur, every page of a discovery document may have to be sequentially numbered. Your **digest** will refer to specific page numbers in these documents. You will be inserting the page numbers. A variety of numbering formats are possible (e.g., 1, 2, 3, 4; 0001, 0002, 0003, 0004; or ABC-1, ABC-2, ABC-3, ABC-4). You can combine names with numbers. The pages of the Jackson deposition, for example, might be numbered Jackson01, Jackson02, Jackson03, Jackson04, etc. Page numbering is often performed with a desk tool called a **Bates stamp**. Each time a page number is stamped using this tool, the number on the tool automatically advances so that the next page will be stamped with the next number. Whoever is inserting or stamping the page numbers does not have to advance the number on the Bates stamp manually. Numbering pages with this tool is referred to as *Bates numbering*. If the document being digested is an electronic or digital document (e.g., a PDF file), it can be sequentially numbered by using special Bates stamping software. An Adobe product such as Acrobat is an example of software that can insert page numbers on PDF documents.

At depositions and in court proceedings, a reporter is present to record everything that is said and to certify that the recording is accurate. The attorneys then purchase a *transcript* (a word-for-word account of the deposition questions and answers) from the reporter. To qualify as a reporter, an individual may be required to "write" at a speed of up to 225 words per minute with over 95 percent accuracy. The reporter works with a computer and a stenotype machine that uses its own form of shorthand. Software in the computer translates the data into English. Reporters are able to make the transcript available on a disk so that the law office can immediately load the deposition directly into their litigation software. Other formats for court reporting include digital audio and digital video recording. Real-time transcription, whereby a draft of the transcript is made available to the attorneys on computer screens while the witness is being questioned, is also possible.

Once the law office receives the transcript of the deposition from the reporter (on paper or in a digital format), paralegals are often asked to digest (summarize) it. Three major kinds of digests can be prepared: page/line, chronological, and topical. A **page/line digest** is a summary of a deposition transcript that presents the questions and the deponent's answers in the order in which the questions were asked along with the page and line numbers where the questions and answers appear. (The lines on every page of the transcript are numbered sequentially with the first line of each page being number "1.") A **chronological digest** is a summary of a deposition transcript that presents the events described in the deponent's answers in their chronological order. Finally, a **topical digest** is a summary of a deposition transcript organized by specific topics covered in the answers of the deponent. For examples of these different styles of digests, see Exhibit 10-8.

As a rule of thumb, every ten pages of a deposition can be digested into one page. The ten-to-one ratio, of course is not absolute. The length of the digest depends on what the supervisor wants summarized and on the complexity of the testimony being summarized.[12]

depo summarizers An employee whose main job is digesting (summarizing) discovery documents, particularly depositions.

digest An organized summary or abridgment. (See glossary for an additional meaning covering volumes that summarize court opinions.)

Bates stamp A tool with which to manually or digitally insert a number (usually sequential) on a page. After using the tool on a page, it automatically advances to the next number, ready to stamp the next page.

page/line digest A summary of a deposition transcript that presents the questions and the deponent's answers in the order in which the questions were asked along with the page and line numbers where the questions and answers appear.

chronological digest A summary of a deposition transcript that presents the events described in the deponent's answers in their chronological order.

topical digest A summary of a deposition transcript organized by specific topics covered in the answers of the deponent.

Exhibit 10-8	Examples of Different Styles of Deposition Digests

PAGE/LINE DIGEST

Page/Lines	Summary	Topic
1:1–35	John Smith, 12 Main St. Buffalo NY 14202. 716–456–9103	Personal Data
1:36–40	Mechanic, Acme Factory. Began work 9/23/90. Became supervisor 5/1/10.	Employment
2:1–28	Met Adams (coworker) 7/29/14. Supervised Adams on odd jobs; trained him to operate equipment	Relationship to plf (Adams)
2:29–47	Was working at Combine #7 on date of the injury; Adams saw plank fall on Smith	Accident
Etc.		

CHRONOLOGICAL DIGEST

Date	Page	Topic
3/13/43	12	Mary Smith's date of birth
1950	15	Father died; mother returned to work
1950–1964	12	Attended Buffalo parochial schools
1964–1966	12, 14	Attended Bayling Community College
May 1965	13	First job–Elway Mall
6/23/68	13	Married John Smith
Etc.		

TOPICAL DIGEST

Topic	Page	Summary
Education	1, 3	John Smith grew up/was educated in Buffalo pub schools (1940s); took evening auto body courses (approx 1951)
Prior Employment	3, 5	First job: assistant on milk delivery truck (1954); day laborer (1957–1960); used car salesman (1960–63)
Prior Medical History	2, 5, 6	Rheumatic heart trouble as teenager–brief hosp in Syracuse; minor cuts and bruises in HS football–treated by school nurse; began seeing MD about kidney stones in 1982–last incident was 1990.
Accident	6–10	Foreman asks Smith to work early shift; arrives two hours earlier than normal. Floor was wet from a recent mopping. Plank needed to be moved because of malfunction of one at regular location. Smith asks foreman for help. Vague response. Smith attempts to move it himself. Falls on his foot.
Etc.		

Many software programs are available (sold separately or as part of litigation management packages such as Summation iBlaze) to facilitate the creation of deposition digests. When transcripts are on disk, searching for specific topics is relatively easy with this software. You simply run a "find" search for whatever you need, e.g., every mention of "Giles MD" in the entire transcript. For more on the use of computers in the law office for such tasks, see Chapter 13.

Of course, depositions are not the only discovery documents a paralegal may be asked to summarize. Answers to interrogatories, medical reports, on-site inspection reports, and responses to requests for admission can also be summarized. A paralegal may be asked to examine all of these documents to summarize specific topics, to look for inconsistencies, or to identify gaps in information that could require further discovery or investigation. Exhibit 10-9 provides general guidelines for all these digesting tasks.

Exhibit 10-9	Guidelines for Digesting Discovery Documents

- Obtain clear instructions from your supervisor. What precisely have you been asked to do? What kind of digest is required? What have you, expressly or by implication, been told not to do? How much time do you have to complete the digest? To what case will your time be billed? Write down the supervisor's instructions. If you have never worked with a particular supervisor before, show him or her your work soon after you begin the assignment to make sure you have understood the instructions.

- Find out if the law firm has an office manual that gives instructions on digesting. If not, check closed-case files for samples of the kind of digesting that the firm has done in the past. Ask your supervisor if you should use such samples as models.

- Keep a list (or know where to find a list) of every document in a file. Some digesting assignments will require you to examine everything in the file.

- Know the difference between paraphrasing testimony and quoting testimony. To *paraphrase* is to phrase the testimony partly or entirely in your own words. To *quote* is to use the exact words of the witness even though you may leave out part of what the witness said. For many digesting assignments, you will be asked to quote, not paraphrase. Use ellipsis dots (…) to indicate that you left something out of a quote. Assume, for example, that the full sentence says, "Jones is 24 years old and works at Telco." A summary with ellipsis dots indicating that you left something out of the quote might read: "Jones … works at Telco."

- Do not "editorialize," i.e., inject your personal comments, unless your supervisor asks you for such comments. For example, do not say that the response of a witness whose testimony you are digesting is "unbelievable."

- Know the case inside and out so that you can grasp the context of what you are digesting. You cannot digest something you do not understand. Read the client file, including interview and investigation reports, pleadings, interrogatory answers, other discovery documents, etc.

- Each summary should include the specific document you used (e.g., the 3/13/15 deposition of Ann Davis, MD) and the page numbers that you summarized. The page/line digest should also include line numbers.

- The answers given in a deposition often ramble. (The same may be true of some interrogatory answers.) Therefore, act on the assumption that the same topic is covered in more than one place in the discovery document. Look for this diversity and record it in your summary by pointing out each time the same topic is mentioned.

- Do not expect the answers to be consistent, even from the same witness. Do not consciously or unconsciously help the witness by blocking out potential inconsistencies. If on page 45 the witness said she saw a "car" but on page 104 said she saw a "van," do not block out the distinction by saying she saw a "motor vehicle," or by failing to mention both. The danger of doing this is more serious than you may think, particularly when you are reading hundreds of pages and are getting a little red in the eyes.

- When doing topical digests, think of the categories of facts that would be most useful for the attorney. The categories may be as broad as the name of a given witness. More precise examples of categories include

  - Background information
  - Education
  - Past employment
  - Present employment
  - Medical history
  - Insurance
  - Prior claims
  - Pre-accident facts
  - Accident facts
  - Post-accident facts
  - Medical injuries from this accident
  - Damage to property
  - Prior statements made

- Update the summaries. After you finish your digest, more facts may become known through further investigation and discovery. Ask your supervisor if you should add these facts to your earlier summary reports.

Outsourcing

outsource Pay an outside company or service to perform tasks usually performed by one's own employees.

In large cases, some law firms will **outsource** digesting tasks to countries such as India where the cost of attorneys can be considerably less than that of attorneys and experienced paralegals in the United States. See Chapter 5 for a discussion of ethical problems that can arise when work is outsourced.

Big Data and Predictive Coding

predictive coding A method of training software to find data that meets defined parameters.

We live in an era of *big data*, which are vast quantities of information collected by commercial and government computers. When law firms are engaged in litigation that involves big data, they often hire IT (information technology) consulting firms to capture, transfer, store, visualize, and analyze the data. The trend in such large cases is to use **predictive coding** to find relevant documents in vast databases. Predictive coding (also referred to as *technology-assisted review*) consists of computer programs that search for documents that are relevant to a case. "After documents are loaded into the program, a lawyer manually reviews a batch [of the documents] to train the program how to recognize what is relevant to a case. The manual review is repeated until the program has developed a model that can accurately predict relevance in the rest of the documents."[13] A 2012 study that compared document review by humans and by predictive coding concluded that humans found an average of about 60 percent of relevant documents, while predictive coding found an average of 77 percent.[14]

5. TRIAL NOTEBOOKS

A **trial notebook** is a collection of documents, arguments, and strategies that an attorney plans to use during a trial. It is often organized in a looseleaf binder with tabbed sections for easy use by the attorney (see Exhibit 10-10). The notebook becomes the attorney's checklist for conducting the trial. The contents of the notebook are not submitted to anyone outside the law office.

trial notebook A collection of documents, arguments, and strategies that an attorney plans to use during a trial. Also called *trial binder.*

Exhibit 10-10	Example of a Trial Notebook

Source: Bindertek, Amherst MA, www.bindertek.com.

Not all trial notebooks are organized the same way. Litigation assistant Pam Robtoy cautions us that "[j]ust as each attorney has different preferences on how they want you to perform different tasks, each notebook you organize will be different, depending on which attorney will be utilizing the notebook and the particular requirements of the case. For example, a trial notebook for a medical malpractice case would likely contain a section for medical research regarding the surgical procedure, medication, etc. that is the focus of the case." A trial notebook for a breach-of-contract case would not.[15]

A comprehensive trial notebook might contain the following sections:[16]

- Table of contents of the trial notebook
- To-do list
- Trial schedule/deadlines
- Trial team (street addresses, phone numbers, email addresses)
- Case outline
- Statement of facts
- Pleadings
- Trial briefs/trial memoranda outlining the facts and law of the case
- Law relied on for causes of action, defenses, and admissibility of evidence
- Outline of liability
- PDF copy of email posts
- Our exhibits
- Opposition's exhibits

- Our witnesses
- Opposition's witnesses
- Witness statements
- Requests for production (RFP)
- Responses to RFPs
- Requests for admission (RFA)
- Responses to RFAs
- Direct examination outline of questions
- Anticipated cross-examination questions
- Outline of damages
- Evidence to offer as foundation for admissibility
- Motions
- Deposition summaries
- Voir dire questions

- Juror information
- Jury chart
- Records
- Opening statements
- Plaintiff testimony
- Requests for jury instructions

- Defendant testimony
- Closing arguments
- Settlement proposals
- Evidence log (see Chapter 9)
- Privilege log

It's often the paralegal's job to collect the material that will go into the notebook, organize it, keep it current, and help make it useful to the attorney as a vehicle for trial preparation and management. Specifically, the paralegal might do the following:

- Prepare summaries of deposition testimony.
- Prepare a list of all parties and witnesses plus people who are expected to be mentioned during testimony; index this list to the rest of the trial notebook.
- Prepare sample questions to ask witnesses, particularly when needed to lay the foundation for evidence to be introduced.
- Prepare a summary description or log of all the exhibits to be used.
- Prepare an abstract (brief summary) of the contents of every document.
- State the location of relevant documents and exhibits that will not be contained in the trial notebook itself.
- Cross-index material on particular witnesses or on legal theories.
- Summarize all information known about each juror from voir dire.
- Prepare end tabs for each section of the notebook.
- Color-code different kinds of documents and information (Examples: blue sheets for citations to authorities that support claims, yellow sheets for deposition testimony and other statements of the opposing party, etc.).

Again, you need to adapt these tasks to the particular needs of your supervisor. One paralegal recently color-coded all the tabs (green for exhibits, orange for discovery data, etc.) before she discovered that the attorney using the trial notebook was color blind!

6. SETTLEMENT

Throughout the pretrial stage of litigation, the opposing attorneys often engage in efforts to negotiate a settlement of the case in order to avoid a trial. One of the formal documents the parties sometimes use during negotiations is the **settlement work-up**, also called a *settlement brochure*. It contains a summary of the major facts in the case presented in a manner designed to encourage the other side (or its liability insurance company) to settle the case. Paralegals often have a large role in helping draft this document. For a memorandum on a settlement work-up, see Exhibit 9-15 in Chapter 9.

7. EXPERT WITNESSES

Paralegals may have different tasks in working with expert witnesses that the trial attorney may want to use. The first task is to locate potential experts for consideration. Many can be located online. A paralegal can use free and paid Internet sites to locate specific kinds of experts. If, for example, the office has a products-liability case involving an allegedly defective steering wheel on a 1997 Buick, it is often relatively easy to use online resources to find experts who have testified in the past on this defect or on a closely related defect. Once you find such an expert, the next step is to use online resources to check that expert's credentials and to obtain recommendations by contacting law offices that have used the expert on their cases. See the sites on expert witnesses in the Helpful Websites section at the end of this chapter and Chapter 9.

Once an expert is selected, your office sends him or her a formal engagement letter. Patricia Gustin, a paralegal who has helped draft such letters, recommends that the letter include[17]

- Confirmation of all past discussions (by phone, email, letter, or in-person meetings) about hiring the expert
- A summary of the case, including the case name and docket number, if the case has already been filed in court

settlement work-up A summary of the major facts in the case presented in a manner designed to encourage the other side (or its liability insurance company) to settle the case. Also called a *settlement brochure*.

- Anticipated dates for the expert's testimony at deposition, at trial, or both
- The scope of the expert testimony to be provided
- A list of articles or documents enclosed with the letter that the expert should review
- Names of the primary contacts in the office that the expert should use
- A list of support people and available resources in the law office for the witness
- A summary of the financial terms for hiring the expert

After experts are hired, the paralegal may be asked to monitor the ongoing relationship with them. This often includes keeping a detailed log on everything sent to the expert for review. The log will note what was sent (e.g., memos, scientific studies, exhibits, and fee payment checks); the format used for the communication (e.g., disk, email, and paper); and the dates these items were sent.

LITIGATION ASSISTANT: TRIAL STAGE

The role of paralegals at trial depends, in part, on the involvement they have had with the case up to trial. If the involvement has been minimal, they will probably have no role during the trial. Once the attorney is in court conducting the trial, most paralegals are working on other cases. If, on the other hand, a paralegal has been working closely with the attorney on the case all along, the paralegal might be given tasks during the trial. In addition to the tasks listed in Exhibit 10-3, paralegal trial tasks might include

- Visiting the courtroom in advance of the trial to determine the location of the following items within the courthouse itself and within walking distance of the courthouse building: points from which Internet access can be obtained, telephones, photocopy machines, fax machines, food take-out facilities, vending machines, stationery supply stores, public restrooms, etc. If the trial will be out of town, the paralegal might be asked to set up a secure hotel conference room (sometimes called a "war room") where the litigation team can regularly meet between trial sessions.
- Monitoring all the files, documents, and evidence needed by the attorney to plan and replan strategy as outlined in the trial notebook.
- Obtaining copies of laws needed by the attorney or doing spot legal research (online or in available volumes) on issues that come up during the trial that require a quick answer.
- Preparing preliminary drafts of certain motions and other documents that are required during the course of the trial.
- Assuring the presence of witnesses; assisting the attorney in preparing them for direct examination and in anticipating questions that might be asked of them on cross-examination.
- Using a laptop or tablet, taking notes on the testimony of witnesses. The attorney may be able to use these notes in preparing for other segments of the trial (e.g., closing argument). A transcript (typed or digital) of the testimony from the court reporter may not be available until after the trial.
- Monitoring the reactions of the jury as the trial unfolds. For example, if juror #7 lights up when the attorney makes a certain point or if juror #10 does not appear to be paying attention, the paralegal will let the attorney know about these reactions during a recess or at the end of the day so that the attorney can decide if anything should be emphasized or if a different strategy is needed when the trial resumes.[18]
- Making suggestions to the attorney on what questions to ask a witness based on what has happened thus far in the trial and based on the paralegal's involvement with the documents and files prepared during the pretrial stage.
- Assisting with trial exhibits.

In some courtrooms, a judge will allow a paralegal to sit with the attorney at counsel's table during the trial. This can provide invaluable assistance to the attorney. For example, if the paralegal knows how to search online documents such as the deposition testimony of a witness now on the stand, the paralegal may be able to help the attorney quickly find earlier deposition testimony of this witness on the same topic.

Here is how one attorney describes the benefits of having paralegals close at hand during a trial:

> At trial, the paralegal sitting with counsel can be extremely helpful. Paralegals should be trained to take notes while counsel is examining witnesses and to monitor the admission of exhibits. Thereafter, they can prepare a binder of all exhibits for subsequent trial days and can digest the transcripts. At the end of a day of trial, the file may be out of order, and paralegals can reorganize it for the next day. Finally, paralegals can assist the attorney by calling witnesses to arrange testimony, meeting witnesses in the hall, and talking with the client and his family. Generally, the attorney has so much to concentrate on during a trial that paralegals can give the client the needed attention while providing a "buffer" between lawyer and client.[19]

EXHIBITS

timeline A chronological presentation of significant events, often using text and diagrams.

Trial exhibits can include photographs, X-rays, medical illustrations, video presentations, anatomical models, surgical appliances, computer reenactments, etc. Some paralegals are able to design exhibits. See, for example, the graphic designed by Kathleen Evans, a litigation paralegal, in Exhibit 10-11. Notice that the graphic contains a **timeline** that shows when significant events occurred in a birth case where the graphic was used. The head was delivered at 1:47 and the baby at 1:53, indicating a total of six minutes when the baby was deprived of oxygen. Timelines can help the jury visualize the impact of crucial facts. For a less elaborate example of a timeline, see Exhibit 8-6 in Chapter 8.

Exhibit 10-11	Timeline Trial Graphic Designed by a Paralegal

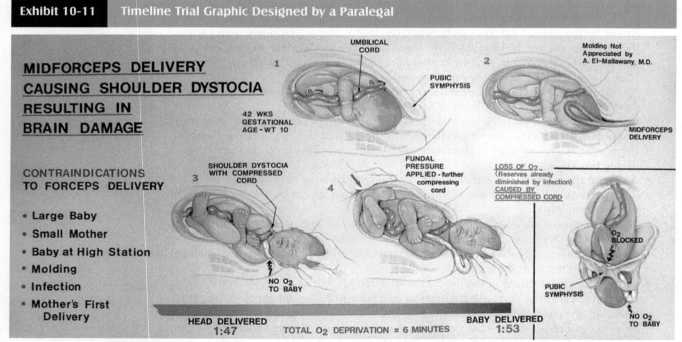

Timeline illustration created by paralegal Kathleen Evans of Litigation Visuals, Inc., that helped win a $3.9 million verdict.

Here are some additional examples of paralegal work creating trial exhibits:

- In a case brought against Wal-Mart, paralegal Susan Sharp designed "a 5-foot long by 3.5-foot tall poster board filled with one-sixteenth of an inch squares, each representing $1 million, to graphically illustrate Wal-Mart's wealth."[20] Her poster board was used by the trial attorney during the damages stage of the trial.

- Paralegal Catherine Astl created a medical treatment calendar chart. "We painstakingly … thumbed through literally stacks of records, making a list of all therapy visits, doctor visits, pain injection procedures and hospitalizations. We then color coded these events, such as all therapy visits color blocked in blue, all hospitalizations in green, etc. We then gave this information to our exhibit vendor where they shaded in each appropriate box, each of which represented a day on the calendar, for the particular event. For example, if March 4–8 was a hospitalization event, those days were shaded in green. When completed, the jury could visually see the amounts of 'greens' or hospitalizations over several years, the number of 'blues' spent in therapy, the amount of time spent in doctor offices, and the total number of days this poor soul spent in agony after a treatment."[21]

Different versions of the chart created by Catherine Astl are often used as exhibits in personal-injury cases. One of the most popular is the *life activity calendar* that presents a day-in-the-life video or chart on the plaintiff. The exhibit carefully catalogs the minute-by-minute activities of the plaintiff in order to help demonstrate the impact of the injury.

If the office hires a litigation consultant to create such graphics, the role of the paralegal might be to help monitor the work of the consultant. Computer graphics presentation programs such as Microsoft's PowerPoint are available to help create graphics. They can generate slides that contain text, pictures, drawings, and maps. PowerPoint also allows videos or movies to be integrated into the presentation. (For more on these computer programs, see Chapter 13.)

Displaying trial exhibits often requires the use of computers, overhead projectors, video players, magnetic boards, blackboards, chart holders, and the like. The judge's permission is needed to bring such devices into the courtroom if they are not already present. Permission is usually sought through the judge's clerk, secretary, or other court personnel.

MOCK TRIALS AND SHADOW JURORS

If the office is about to begin an important and potentially complex trial, it may decide to conduct a mock trial to give the participants stand-up practice and feedback. A mock trial is a pretend trial staged by one side to operate as close as possible to the upcoming real trial. The office can hire strangers to play the role of jurors. Attorneys in the office will play the role of opposing counsel. Paralegals and secretaries might be asked to play the role of witnesses. After each "side" presents its case, the jury renders its "verdict" and makes itself available to critique the strength of the evidence and the performance of the attorneys. This can be very helpful to the attorney who will be trying the case. The exercise is the equivalent of assembling a focus group to obtain reactions to a product or presentation.

Another option is to use **shadow jurors**. These are persons hired by one side to observe a trial as members of the general audience. Typically a law firm will use a jury consultant to select citizens as close demographically (e.g., race, occupation, and income level) to the actual jury as possible. During recess and at the end of the day, these "jurors" will tell the consultant what they thought of the physical evidence, the witnesses, and the performance of the trial attorneys. The consultant will give this information to the attorney who hired the consultant and shadow jurors. Based on this feedback, the attorney will decide whether any shift in trial strategy is warranted for the remainder of the trial. Paralegals might be used to help coordinate the work of the jury consultant as the trial progresses.

shadow jurors Persons hired by one side to observe a trial as members of the general audience (gallery) and, as the trial progresses, to give feedback to the trial attorney who will use the feedback to assess strategy for the remainder of the trial.

LITIGATION ASSISTANT: APPEAL STAGE

Once the trial is over, the central question becomes whether to appeal. (The party bringing the appeal is the *appellant*; the party against whom the appeal is brought is the *appellee*.) In some cases, both sides might decide to appeal if neither party obtained everything it wanted at the trial. Attorneys must review all of the documents and transcripts from the trial in order to identify grounds for an appeal. A paralegal may be asked to go back over the record and do the following:

■ Find the page number in the record that supports a statement of fact that the attorney mentions in his or her appellate brief.

table of authorities (TOA) A list of primary authority (e.g., cases and statutes) and secondary authority (e.g., legal periodical articles and legal treatises) that a writer has cited in an appellate brief or other document. The list includes page numbers where each authority is cited in the document.

cite checking Examining citations in a document to determine their accuracy, such as whether the format of the citation is correct, whether a parallel cite is needed, whether quoted material is accurately quoted, and whether the cited law is still valid.

parallel cite An additional citation where you can find the same written material in the library or online.

citators A book or online service containing lists of citations that can (a) help you assess the current validity of an opinion, statute, or other item; and (b) give you leads to additional relevant materials.

public defender An attorney appointed by a court and paid by the government to represent an indigent defendant in a criminal case.

brief bank A collection of appellate briefs and related documents drafted in prior cases that might be adapted for current cases and used as models.

judgment debtor The person who loses and therefore must pay a money judgment.

judgment creditor The person who wins and therefore has a right to collect a money judgment.

contempt Conduct that defies or disrespects the authority of a court or legislative body. When the court is defied or disrespected, it is called *contempt of court*.

■ Make a list of every time the trial attorney objected to something during the trial. Include the page number where the objection is found, a brief summary of what the objection was, and the ruling of the judge on the objection.
■ Make a list of every time opposing counsel made reference to a particular topic, such as the plaintiff's prior involvement in other litigation.
■ Make a list of every time the judge asked questions of witnesses.

This information can be critical when the attorney prepares the appellate brief. Arguments made in the brief must refer the judge to specific parts of the trial record and transcript that are relevant to the arguments being made. (These references to specific pages in the trial record are called *record cites*.) The office must be scrupulous in ensuring that references to the record are accurate, particularly quotations from trial transcripts.

Other important paralegal roles on the appellate brief are preparing the table of authorities and cite checking. The **table of authorities (TOA)** is a list of every primary authority (e.g., cases and statutes) and secondary authority (e.g., legal periodical articles and legal treatises) that a writer has cited in a document such as an appellate brief and indicates where they are mentioned in the document. (For an excerpt from a table of authorities, see Exhibit 12-6 in Chapter 12. In Chapter 13, we will also examine software used to help create these tables.) The task of **cite checking** the appellate brief is performed by examining citations in a document to determine their accuracy such as whether the format of the citation is correct, whether a **parallel cite** is needed, whether quoted material is accurately quoted, and whether the law cited is still valid. Has it been overruled, repealed, or otherwise modified? We will cover the skill of cite checking (including the use of major **citators** such as Shepard's and KeyCite) in Chapter 11.

Once the appellate brief is complete, paralegals can be asked to help monitor its printing (in-house or through an outside printing vendor), filing in court, and service on the opposing side.

When an opponent's appellate brief is received by the office (e.g., the *reply brief*), the paralegal might be asked to check the accuracy of all quotes to the record and to use the standard citators to determine whether any of the laws cited in the opponent's brief have been overruled, repealed, or otherwise modified.

Some highly skilled paralegals are also given responsibility for drafting part of an appellate brief itself, particularly if the appeal involves an issue the office has often litigated in the past. For example, the appellate office of a **public defender** might often appeal search-and-seizure issues in criminal cases. A paralegal who works for such an office might be asked to locate earlier briefs on this issue in the office's **brief bank** and to adapt one to the facts of the particular case currently on appeal.

LITIGATION ASSISTANT: ENFORCEMENT STAGE

If a money judgment was awarded to the client, considerable work may be required in collecting it from the **judgment debtor**, the party obligated by the court to pay the judgment. (The person who won the judgment and must be paid is the **judgment creditor**.) See Chapter 9 on investigations to uncover assets. If the judgment debtor refuses to pay the judgment, the paralegal for the judgment creditor can help arrange for the sheriff to begin *execution*, which is the process of carrying out or enforcing a judgment. The judgment debtor may be ordered by the court to submit to an examination about his or her assets. This examination is an example of a posttrial deposition designed to help enforce a judgment. In some cases, the attorney may be able to petition the court for a finding of **contempt** against the judgment debtor for noncompliance with court orders. The paralegal can help by assembling the factual basis to support this charge and drafting some of the court papers involved.

CHAPTER SUMMARY

Litigation is the formal process of resolving a legal dispute through the courts. Civil litigation begins with the filing of a complaint, the service of process on the defendant, and the filing of a response (answer) by the defendant. In the complaint and answer (pleadings), the parties state their causes of action and defenses. The next major event is discovery, which can include interrogatories, depositions, requests for admission (RFAs), requests for production (RFP), and independent medical examinations (IMEs). If motions for summary judgment are denied, the trial proceeds. After voir dire and opening statements to the jury, the party with the burden of proof puts on its case through the introduction of evidence and the direct examination of witnesses. The latter can be cross-examined by the other party. When the first party rests, the other goes through the same steps. A motion for a judgment as a matter of law (known as a motion for a directed verdict in some courts) will be granted if there is no legally sufficient evidentiary basis for a reasonable jury to find for the party against whom the motion is made. After closing statements to the jury and the instructions of the judge, the case goes to the jury. Its verdict (if accepted by the court) becomes the basis of the court's judgment.

If dissatisfied with the judgment, the appellant files a notice of appeal and an appellate brief. The appellee also files an appellate brief. After oral argument, the appellate court affirms, reverses, vacates, or otherwise modifies what the lower court has done. A further appeal to a higher appellate court might also be possible.

Criminal litigation often begins with an arrest warrant, followed by an initial appearance. Once the decision on bail is made, the prosecution proceeds to the preliminary hearing to determine whether probable cause exists. If so, the grand jury will then determine whether to issue an indictment. The arraignment is next. If plea bargaining is unsuccessful, the case goes to trial, where guilt must be established beyond a reasonable doubt. The criminal trial then proceeds in a manner similar to a civil trial: voir dire, opening statements, etc. The appeal process is also similar: notice of appeal, appellate briefs, etc.

In an administrative hearing, a hearing examiner makes a decision on the dispute within the agency. His or her decision will usually be in the form of a recommendation to a higher official or body within the agency. When a party has exhausted administrative remedies, he or she can appeal the agency's decision to a court.

Alternatives to litigation (alternative dispute resolution) can include arbitration, mediation, med-arb, private judging, neutral evaluation, summary jury trial, summary bench trial, and collaborative law.

Among the roles fulfilled by paralegals during litigation are the following: drafting complaints and other pleadings, serving and filing documents, maintaining the calendar, digesting discovery transcripts and documents, helping prepare the trial notebook, assisting with settlement efforts, coordinating trial exhibits, working with expert witnesses, providing assistance as needed during the trial, retrieving and digesting facts in preparation for appeal, and providing general assistance with collecting a judgment.

KEY TERMS

litigious (p. 441)
litigation (p. 441)
civil dispute (p. 442)
criminal dispute (p. 442)
damages (p. 442)
liable (p. 442)
joint and several liability (p. 442)
retain (p. 443)
retainer (p. 443)
contingent fee (p. 443)
appearance (p. 443)
attorney of record (p. 443)
forum (p. 443)
estate (p. 443)
subject-matter jurisdiction (p. 443)
diversity of citizenship (p. 443)
U.S. district court (p. 443)
venue (p. 443)
complaint (p. 444)
plaintiff (p. 444)
cause of action (p. 444)
negligence (p. 444)
stating a cause of action (p. 444)

codefendant (p. 444)
pleading (p. 444)
allegation (p. 444)
information and belief (p. 444)
prayer for relief (p. 444)
ad damnum clause (p. 444)
subscription (p. 444)
verification (p. 444)
bench trial (p. 444)
jury trial (p. 444)
file (p. 444)
docket (p. 444)
service of process (p. 444)
process (p. 445)
summons (p. 445)
default judgment (p. 445)
process server (p. 445)
proof of service (p. 445)
statute of limitations (p. 445)
personal jurisdiction (p. 445)
adjudicate (p. 445)
litigation hold (p. 445)
spoliation (p. 445)
motion (p. 445)
ruling (p. 445)

movant (p. 445)
motion to dismiss (p. 445)
failure to state a cause of action (p. 445)
procedural law (p. 445)
Federal Rules of Civil Procedure (FRCP) (p. 445)
substantive law (p. 446)
answer (p. 446)
defense (p. 446)
affirmative defense (p. 446)
contributory negligence (p. 446)
cross-claim (p. 446)
counterclaim (p. 446)
reply (p. 446)
third-party complaint (p. 446)
contest (p. 446)
adverse judgment (p. 446)
pretrial conference (p. 447)
stipulation ("stip") (p. 447)
magistrate (p. 447)
discovery (p. 447)
settlement (p. 447)
scheduling order (p. 447)
interrogatories ("rogs") (p. 448)

deposition (p. 448)
deponent (p. 448)
transcript (p. 448)
court reporter (p. 448)
real-time (p. 448)
request for admission (RFA) (p. 448)
subpoena duces tecum (p. 448)
order (p. 448)
request for production (RFP) (p. 448)
hearing (p. 448)
ex parte (p. 448)
adversarial (p. 448)
summary judgment (p. 448)
summary (p. 448)
issue (p. 448)
tangible evidence (p. 449)
introduce evidence (p. 449)
set for trial (p. 449)
bailiff (p. 449)
jury panel (p. 449)
voir dire (p. 449)
challenge for cause (p. 449)
bias (p. 449)

peremptory challenge (p. 449)
alternate (p. 449)
empanel (p. 449)
motion in limine (p. 449)
rule on witnesses (p. 49)
sequester (p. 450)
opening statement (p. 450)
burden of proof (p. 450)
sidebar conference (p. 450)
objection (p. 450)
competent (p. 450)
excuse the jury (p. 450)
examination (p. 450)
overrule (p. 450)
direct examination (p. 450)
grounds (p. 450)
hearsay (p. 450)
sustain (p. 450)
cross-examination (p. 450)
redirect examination (p. 450)
recross-examination (p. 450)
qualify (p. 451)
expert witness (p. 451)
court (p. 451)
clerk (p. 451)
exhibit (p. 452)
move into evidence (p. 452)
rest (p. 452)
case-in-chief (p. 452)
adjourn (p. 452)
judgment as a matter of law
   (p. 452)
directed verdict (p. 452)
judgment notwithstanding the
   verdict (p. 452)
advisement (p. 452)
prima facie case (p. 452)
closing argument (p. 453)
jury instructions (p. 453)
presumption (p. 453)
verdict (p. 453)
element (p. 453)
preponderance of the evidence
   (p. 453)
standard of proof (p. 453)
judgment (p. 454)

declaratory judgment (p. 454)
motion for a new trial (p. 454)
appeal (p. 454)
stay (p. 454)
timely (p. 454)
notice of appeal (p. 454)
bond (p. 454)
judgment on the merits (p. 454)
res judicata (p. 454)
bar (p. 454)
U.S. court of appeals (p. 454)
appellant (p. 454)
record (p. 454)
docketed (p. 455)
appellate brief (p. 455)
reply brief (p. 455)
appellee (p. 455)
issue on appeal (p. 455)
oral argument (p. 455)
panel (p. 455)
opinion (p. 455)
majority opinion (p. 455)
concurring opinion (p. 455)
plurality opinion (p. 455)
dissenting opinion (p. 455)
reporter (p. 455)
affirm (p. 455)
remand (p. 455)
waive (p. 456)
petition (p. 456)
rehearing (p. 456)
en banc (p. 456)
appeal by right (p. 456)
writ (p. 456)
certiorari (p. 456)
mandate (p. 456)
satisfy (p. 456)
execution (p. 456)
warrant (p. 456)
prosecution (p. 456)
initial appearance (p. 457)
felony (p. 457)
misdemeanor (p. 457)
assigned counsel (p. 457)
indigent (p. 457)
bail (p. 457)

personal recognizance (p. 457)
preliminary hearing (p. 457)
probable cause (p. 457)
bound over (p. 458)
grand jury (p. 458)
indictment (p. 458)
information (p. 458)
nolle prosequi (p. 458)
plead (p. 458)
no contest (p. 458)
plea bargain (p. 458)
arraignment (p. 458)
impeach (p. 459)
relevant (p. 459)
undue prejudice (p. 459)
government (p. 459)
beyond a reasonable doubt
   (p. 459)
acquit (p. 459)
poll (p. 459)
double jeopardy (p. 459)
unemployment compensation
   (p. 459)
administrative hearing (p. 459)
legal aid office (p. 460)
memorandum (p. 460)
hearing examiner (p. 460)
claimant (p. 460)
proposed findings and rulings
   (p. 460)
good cause (p. 460)
administrative decision (p. 460)
board of appeals (p. 460)
discretion (p. 461)
retroactive (p. 461)
exhaust administrative remedies
   (p. 461)
trial de novo (p. 461)
alternative dispute resolution
   (ADR) (p. 465)
arbitration (p. 465)
judicial arbitration (p. 465)
contractual arbitration (p. 466)
award (p. 466)
mediation (p. 466)
med-arb (p. 466)

private judging (p. 466)
neutral evaluation (p. 466)
collaborative law (p. 467)
instrument (p. 468)
template (p. 468)
caption (p. 470)
docket number (p. 470)
notice pleading (p. 470)
special damages (p. 470)
substituted service (p. 471)
affidavit (p. 471)
subpoena (p. 471)
e-filing (p. 472)
PACER (p. 472)
PDF (p. 472)
tickler (p. 473)
privilege log (p. 474)
attorney-client privilege (ACP)
   (p. 474)
redact (p. 474)
discoverable (p. 474)
e-evidence (p. 474)
e-discovery (p. 474)
depo summarizer (p. 476)
digest (p. 476)
Bates stamp (p. 476)
page/line digest (p. 476)
chronological digest (p. 476)
topical digest (p. 476)
outsource (p. 478)
predictive coding (p. 478)
trial notebook (p. 479)
settlement work-up (p. 480)
timeline (p. 482)
shadow jurors (p. 483)
table of authorities (TOA)
   (p. 484)
cite checking (p. 484)
parallel cite (p. 484)
citator (p. 484)
public defender (p. 484)
brief bank (p. 484)
judgment debtor (p. 484)
judgment creditor (p. 484)
contempt (p. 484)

ASSIGNMENTS

CRITICAL ANALYSIS

10.1 In large cases there is often a great deal of digital data involved in discovery. In Google, Bing, or Yahoo run this search: "predictive coding" attorney. Write an essay in which you cover the following topics:

(a) What is predictive coding and how is it used?

(b) To what extent does predictive coding mean a loss of jobs for attorneys and paralegals?

   Give citations to the authorities on which you rely in your answers.

PROJECTS

10.2 The attorney for whom you work has just won a $1,000,000 judgment against a defendant who is independently wealthy and is the sole owner of a company that makes cosmetics in your state. The defendant, however, claims to have no assets. On Google, Bing, or Yahoo, run the following search: collecting a judgment in aa (substituting the name of your state for aa). Prepare a memo to your supervisor on the specific steps that can be tried to find assets and collect the judgment. Give citations that support the use of all of the steps you propose.

CORE SKILLS

Among the many skills a paralegal must have, five core skills stand out: writing (both basic English and legal drafting), research, ethics, computer use, and collaboration (working with others). The core-skill assignments introduce and reinforce these skills. Even if you are not asked to do all of the assignments as part of the course, you should do them on your own. Also, do not wait for the topics in the assignments to be covered in this course or in other courses. Successful paralegals are self-starters. A major characteristic of a self-starter is a thirst for independent study—learning on your own.

CORE SKILL: WRITING

10.3 You are a paralegal working for the office of Linda Stout, Esq., who represents Mary Smith. Re-write Mary's complaint in Exhibit 10-6 for your state. If the complaint could be filed in more than one state court in your state, select one of the courts. Check all relevant court rules and statutes available online for requirements on the format and content of complaints. (Your complaint should not include the labels or arrows to the left of the complaint in Exhibit 10-6.) In your complaint, use the names provided (Mary Smith, Fred Jones, and Linda Stout). You can make up any facts additional to those currently in Exhibit 10-6 so long as the added facts are reasonably consistent with the facts currently given in Exhibit 10-6. Attach a brief memo that lists the sources you used to prepare your complaint.

CORE SKILL: RESEARCH

10.4 Ted Smith says that he injured his arm at work. He files a workers' compensation claim in your state. The claim is denied on the ground that the injury did not occur at work. Ted appeals this decision in the agency and, after a hearing, loses. He then appeals the agency's decision in a state court. Rewrite the first column of Exhibit 10-3 so that it covers Ted's case for your state at the four states (I to IV) listed in the first column: Agency Stage, Pretrial Stage, Trial Stage, and Appeal Stage. Use the actual names of the agency and court(s) in your state that would hear Ted's case. If your state would include steps that are not in the first column of Exhibit 10-3, include them in your answer. Provide citations to court rules, statutes, and forms that support what you include in your answer.

Your answer does not have to be presented in a boxed chart like Exhibit 10-3. You can present your answer in full sentences with descriptive headings. If needed, you can add facts to Ted's story in order to cover more fully the litigation steps that could be involved at the workers' compensation agency and court levels in your state.

CORE SKILL: ETHICS

10.5

(a) On Google, Bing, or Yahoo, run this search: attorney ethics opinions aa (substituting the name of your state for aa). See also the ethics links for your state in Appendix D. What is the Internet address of the site that contains these opinions?

(b) Find any ethics opinion in which an attorney was disciplined for a matter involving fees. What is the name and Internet address of this opinion? What was the ethics rule the attorney was charged with violating and what conclusion did the opinion reach on whether the rule was violated?

CORE SKILL: COMPUTERS

10.6 In Google, Bing, or Yahoo, run the search "litigation software" and select any three software programs that meet the following characteristics. Each program is produced by a different company. The website of the company describes the program in some detail. The programs can cover the same or different aspects of litigation. Write a report in which you explain the three products. Do not use any term in your report that you do not understand. If, for example, the program you select says that it covers docket control, find a definition of *docket* if you do not know what it is. At the end of your report, include a glossary of every word you had to check the meaning of and include the definition. Also place these words in the Computer Terminology in the Law (CTL) notebook (see Assignment 1.8 of Chapter 1 on the notebook) along with the meaning of those words.

CORE SKILL: COLLABORATION

10.7 In Assignment 3.3 (Chapter 3), you opened a LinkedIn account and posted basic data about yourself as a new paralegal student. In Assignment 4.11 (Chapter 4), you invited your fellow students to be connections. Start adding more connections—at least 10. See the suggestions in Exhibit 2-13 in Chapter 2 on who to invite and ways to build your network of connections.

THE JOB SEARCH

(The search for employment cannot wait until the end of a course or of a curriculum. It needs to begin now. The job-search assignments are designed to introduce you to different aspects of the job search and to build options for you to explore about employment.)

10.8 Use the job links in Exhibit 2-12 in Chapter 2 to find two job openings in your state for a litigation assistant (a paralegal who will assist attorneys in litigation). One of the openings should be for a paralegal with experience and the other for an entry-level paralegal (someone with no experience). For each opening, list the duties and qualifications for the position. Give the site addresses where you found this information.

REVIEW QUESTIONS

1. What is litigation?
2. What is a litigious society?
3. What are the three categories of civil disputes?
4. What is a criminal dispute?
5. What are damages?
6. What are the consequences of joint and several liability?
7. What are the forum choices when citizens of two different states have a legal dispute involving negligence?
8. How does a lawsuit begin?
9. How does a party state a cause of action?
10. What is service of process?
11. What is the distinction between subject-matter jurisdiction and personal jurisdiction?
12. What procedural and substantive laws apply in diversity-of-citizenship cases in federal court?
13. Distinguish complaint, answer, counterclaim, cross-claim, and third-party complaint.
14. What is a pretrial conference?
15. Name and define the major methods of discovery.
16. When is a subpoena duces tecum used in a deposition?
17. When will a court grant a motion for summary judgment?
18. What is the distinction between a question of law and a question of fact and how are they resolved?
19. What are the two kinds of challenges can be made against prospective jurors during voir dire?
20. What are the functions of the opening statement and closing argument?
21. How does the court resolve a competency challenge to a prospective witness?
22. Who conducts direct, cross, re-direct, and re-cross examination and in what sequence?
23. What is a judgment as a matter of law and when is it made?
24. What is a standard of proof? What are the standards in civil and criminal cases?
25. What is res judicata?
26. What is an appellate brief?
27. What are the different kinds of opinions that an appellate court can write?
28. What is a writ of certiorari (cert.)?
29. In a criminal case, what happens at the initial appearance, preliminary hearing, and arraignment?
30. What happens if a prosecutor issues a nolle prosequi?
31. What is the function of an administrative hearing?
32. How does an administrative agency reach a final conclusion when it has a legal dispute with a citizen?
33. What are some paralegal tasks at the agency stage of civil litigation?
34. What are some paralegal tasks at the pretrial stage of civil litigation?
35. What are some paralegal tasks at the trial stage of civil litigation?
36. What are some paralegal tasks at the appeals stage of civil litigation?
37. What are some paralegal tasks at the enforcement stage of civil litigation?
38. What are some paralegal tasks at the pretrial stage of criminal litigation?
39. What are some paralegal tasks at the trial stage of criminal litigation?
40. What are some paralegal tasks at the appeals stage of criminal litigation?
41. How do the major kinds of alternative dispute resolution (ADR) function?
42. What are some paralegal tasks in alternative dispute resolution (ADR)?
43. Define the two major pleadings.
44. What are the major components of a complaint?
45. What is a civil cover sheet?
46. What is substituted service?
47. What is e-filing?
48. What is a tickler?
49. What is redundancy, and how is it used in calendar control?
50. What is a privilege log?
51. What is redacting?
52. Who must comply with the various discovery methods an opponent wants to use?
53. What is e-discovery?
54. What kinds of e-evidence are often sought in e-discovery?
55. Describe three styles of deposition digests.
56. What is predictive coding?
57. What is a trial notebook and what roles can paralegals play in its preparation?
58. What is the function of a settlement work-up?
59. How can paralegals assist attorneys with expert witnesses?
60. What is the function of shadow jurors?
61. What is an appellate brief?

HELPFUL WEBSITES

Courts: Fifty States
- www.ncsc.org (enter *court charts* in the search box)

Courts: Federal (Understanding the Federal Courts)
- www.uscourts.gov
- www.uscourts.gov/FederalCourts.aspx
- www.fjc.gov/federal/courts.nsf (click *Search* and type *How Cases Move*)

Courts: Comparing Federal and State Court Systems
- www.uscourts.gov (enter *compare federal and state courts* in the search box)

National Center for State Courts
- www.ncsc.org

The Litigation Process
- www.stoel.com/how-does-a-lawsuit-work-basic-steps-in
- www.hg.org/article.asp?id=20845
- sautersullivan.com/process-of-litigation
- www.youtube.com/watch?v=oRPvm7z4BYA

Trial Overviews (jury handbooks)
- www.mnd.uscourts.gov/JuryInfo/jury-handbooks.shtml
- www.state.ak.us/courts/forms/j-180.pdf
- www.wicourts.gov/services/juror/docs/handbook.pdf

Alternative Dispute Resolution
- www.adr.org
- www.cpradr.org
- www.mediate.com
- en.wikipedia.org/wiki/Alternative_dispute_resolution

Rules of Procedure and Evidence in Federal Courts
- www.law.cornell.edu/rules/frcp
- www.uscourts.gov/uscourts/rulesandpolicies/rules/ap2009.pdf
- www.law.cornell.edu/rules/fre
- www.law.cornell.edu/rules/frap

Court Forms
- forms.lp.findlaw.com
- www.USCourtForms.com
- www.lectlaw.com/forma.htm
- www.blumberg.com/forms/index.html

E-Filing
- www.pacer.gov
- www.legaldockets.com

E-Discovery
- www.discoveryresources.org
- en.wikipedia.org/wiki/Electronic_discovery
- www.aceds.org (Association of Certified E-Discovery Specialists)

Managing Discovery of Electronic Information (in Court)
- www.fjc.gov/public/pdf.nsf/lookup/eldscpkt.pdf/$file/eldscpkt.pdf

Internet Depositions
- www.youtube.com/watch?v=aDxQLhYAELo
- www.gramannreporting.com

Deposition Summaries
- deposummary.com
- www.deposums.com/depositionsummaries.html

Expert Witnesses
- www.jurispro.com
- www.tasanet.com
- www.witness.net

Famous Trials
- www.law.umkc.edu/faculty/projects/ftrials/ftrials.htm
- law2.umkc.edu/faculty/projects/ftrials/ftrials.htm

Manual for Complex Litigation
- www.fjc.gov/public/pdf.nsf/lookup/mcl4.pdf/$file/mcl4.pdf

National Association of Professional Process Servers
- www.napps.org

Google, Bing, or Yahoo Searches
(On these search engines, run the following searches, using quotation marks and substituting your state for "aa" where indicated)
- "steps in a trial" aa
- courts aa
- paralegal trial roles
- litigation process aa
- civil litigation overview aa
- trial discovery process aa
- pretrial procedure aa
- federal court procedure
- court jurisdiction aa
- pleadings aa
- alternative dispute
- resolution aa
- service of process aa
- e-evidence aa
- e-discovery aa
- criminal procedure aa
- criminal litigation aa
- administrative agency hearing aa
- PACER
- trial notebook
- privilege log

ENDNOTES

1 State Court Caseload Statistics (www.courtstatistics.org); United States Courts (www.uscourts.gov) (type *statistics* in search box) (2014).

2 Jane Heath, *Alternative to Trial* 20 Legal Assistant Today 81 (July/August 2003).

3 Catherine Astl, *Inside the Bar*, 78 (iUniverse 2003).

4 Rachel Campbell, *Above and Beyond*, 21 Legal Assistant Today 60 (November/December 2003).

5 David Busch, *A Job and an Adventure*, 12 AAPLA Advocate 3 (Alamo Area Professional Legal Assistants, October/November 1993). (*Legal assistant* was changed to *paralegal* in the quote.)

6 Erin Schlemme, *Courthouse Etiquette*, 11 The TALA Times 4 (Tulsa Area Paralegal Ass'n, February 1993).

7 California Civil Procedure Code § 1010. 6(3)(3).

8 Alan Gelb & Karen Levine, *A Survival Guide for Paralegals* 6 (2003).

9 Christofer French, *The Professional Paralegal Job Search* 18 (1995).

10 Email post on a paralegal listserv (Paralegals@yahoogroups.com) from "Lil Mermaid" (September 29, 2003).

11 Dana Nikolewski, *Just Call Me Dorothy*, 13 Newsletter 5 (Dallas Area Paralegal Association, April 1989).

11a *Your First Legal Job: What Was It and What Do You Remember Most?* Paralegal Network (www.linkedin.com)(tinyurl.com/k9zr772) (2014).

12 Oliver Gierke, *Deposition Digests*, 24 Legal Assistant Today 86 (September/October 2006).

13 Joe Palazzolo, *Why Hire a Lawyer? Computers Are Cheaper*, Wall Street Journal, June 18, 2012.

14 Ibid.

15 Pam Robtoy, *Preparing Trial Notebooks*, 14 Legal Paraphernalia 5 (St. Louis Paralegal Association, July/August 1994).

16 Hollins, *Assignment: Trial Prep*, 2 California Paralegal 30 (April/June 1990); Feder, *Translating Professional Competence into Performance Competence*, 15 Legal Economics 44 (April 1989).

17 Patricia Gustin, *Making the Expert Witness Part of the Legal Team*, 27 Facts & Findings 14 (November 2000).

18 Debra Martinelli, *A Winning Team*, 19 Legal Assistant Today 54 (July/August 2002).

19 Lynne Z. Gold-Bikin et al. *Use of Paralegals in a Matrimonial Practice*, 16 FAIR$hare 9 (September 1996).

20 Lee Scheier, *A Very Sharp Legal Team*, 19 Legal Assistant Today 68.

21 Catherine Astl, *Behind the Bar* 84 (iUniverse 2003).

CHAPTER 11

LEGAL RESEARCH

CHAPTER OUTLINE

- Introduction
- What Is a Legal-Research Expert?
- Perseverance and Legal Research
- Terminology of Legal Research
- Legal Research on the Internet
- Finding Traditional Law Libraries

- Ask an Online Librarian
- CARTWHEEL
- Kinds of Authority
- Citation
- Cite Checking
- The First Level of Legal Research
- Finding Case Law
- Finding Statutes
- Finding Constitutional Law

- Finding Administrative Law
- Finding Court Rules (Rules of Court)
- Finding Local Law
- Finding International Law
- Finding Secondary Authority (Subject-Matter Research)
- Westlaw and LexisNexis
- Research Self-Audit

CHAPTER OBJECTIVES

After completing this chapter, you should be able to

- Distinguish between fact research and legal research.
- Know why legal research cannot answer every legal question.
- Explain why you may need to forget the law you learned in school.
- State the four categories of legal sites on the Internet and their reliability.
- Know where to find traditional law libraries.
- Describe the value of Ask-an-Online-Librarian services.

- Explain how to CARTWHEEL a legal-research problem.
- Distinguish the different kinds of authority.
- State the hierarchy among primary authorities.
- Know the major categories of secondary authority.
- Know how to cite cases, constitutions, statutes, administrative regulations, and other sources.
- Know how to cite check a document.

- Outline techniques for obtaining the "big picture" at the outset of a legal-research assignment.
- List major sources for finding and updating case law and statutory law.
- Know how to find other major categories of primary and secondary authority.
- Describe the features of Westlaw and LexisNexis.
- Know how to do a research self-audit.

INTRODUCTION

Many paralegals do *fact* research in which they perform tasks such as finding the names of a company's board of directors or locating a report on weather conditions on the day a client had an accident. Fact research is covered in Chapter 9 on investigation. Here in Chapter 11 our focus is *legal* research, which consists of finding law in a traditional or online library to help resolve a legal issue.

If asked whether they do legal research, a few experienced paralegals will answer, "All the time." For most paralegals, however, the answer will be either *no* or *occasionally*. An attorney might ask a paralegal to:

- Bring me § 120 from the state code.
- Find the statute that allows us to request an extension of time to file an answer.
- Check the online site of the secretary of state for the forms to file when a business wants to incorporate.
- At the library (or online), get me a copy of every case cited in the motion of an opponent. (This is sometimes called "pulling cases.")
- Cite check an appellate brief. (Cite checking involves making sure all the citations are in proper citation form, all quotations are accurate, etc.)
- Go on PACER and find me the Foley complaint. (PACER is the online system of obtaining case and docket information on cases filed in federal courts.)
- Recently a paralegal (Tina R.) described an incident involving a tax question that she and her supervising attorney were discussing. The attorney did not know the answer, so he called a CPA friend. The CPA did not know the answer either, but while the attorney and CPA were on the phone discussing the question, Tina did a Google search of the IRS website and found the answer! "Wow, she's really good," the CPA said to the attorney when he told her what Tina just found.

In most law offices, however, broader research questions are performed by attorneys. Examples: Has the employer committed age discrimination? Is the city liable for injuries to patrons injured in a public park?

Nevertheless, paralegals should have a comprehensive understanding of legal research. First of all, like most legal skills, you won't know if you'll use them until you find out what your particular supervisor will ask you to do. More importantly, the study of legal research exposes you to numerous dimensions of our legal system. Library research gives you hands-on interaction with primary sources such as court opinions, statutes, regulations, and constitutions. Directly or indirectly, each of these sources is often a product of delicate and hard-fought policy deliberations in our major government institutions. Furthermore, legal research is closely interconnected with the skills of legal analysis and writing. An excellent way to understand the heart of the practice of law is to listen and watch attorneys talk and write about cases, statutes, and other primary authorities, all of which begin in the aisles of law libraries and on the websites of legal databases.

So, will you be doing extensive legal research on the job? Perhaps, but probably not. Should you nevertheless become skilled in the techniques of legal research? Definitely *yes*.

WHAT IS A LEGAL RESEARCH EXPERT?

This chapter does not cover every aspect of legal research, nor does it treat every conceivable legal resource that could be used in a law library. Rather, the chapter examines the major components of legal research with the objective of identifying effective starting points.

When you walk into a law library, your first impression is likely to be one of awe. You are confronted with row upon row of books, most of which seem unapproachable; they do not invite browsing. The same is true of **online** legal materials on the Internet. The amount of law that is available online is overwhelming. To cope with this quantity of material so that you are able to use brick-and-mortar and online law libraries, you need to learn the techniques of legal research and understand the limitations of the law library.

A major misunderstanding about the law library is that it contains the answer to every legal question. Often, legal questions have no definitive answers because the courts have not

online (1) Connected to another computer or computer network, often through the Internet. (2) Residing on a computer and available for use; activated and ready for use on a computer.

addressed the question or because they have given us inconsistent answers. You may have heard the story of a client who walked into a law office and asked to see a one-armed attorney. When asked why he required an attorney meeting such specifications, he replied that he was tired of presenting problems to attorneys and having them constantly tell him that "on the one hand" he should do this but "on the other hand" he should do that. He hungered for an attorney who would give him an answer. This concern is well taken. A client is entitled to an answer, to clear guidance. At the same time (or, on the other hand), part of the attorney's job is to identify alternatives or options and to weigh the benefits and disadvantages of each option. Good attorneys are so inclined because they understand that our legal system teems with unknowns and ambiguities. Good paralegals also have this understanding. They are not frightened by ambiguities; they thrive on them

Not all legal-research problems fall into this category. Indeed, many problems can be answered by basic (easy) legal research. Suppose, for example, you want to know the name of the state government agency in charge of incorporating a business or the maximum number of weeks one can receive unemployment compensation. Finding the answer is not difficult if you know what books or other resources to go to and how to use their indexes or other points of access.

In school, you will learn a good deal of law. Eventually, you will probably forget most of it. If you don't, you should! No one can know all of the law, even in a specialty. Furthermore, the law is always changing. In just one year (2013), more than 100,000 statutes, 160,000 administrative regulations, and 285,000 court opinions were written by the three branches of government.[1] Consequently, a law office cannot practice on the basis of rules learned in school. Those rules may no longer be valid by the time you try to use them in actual cases. Thousands of courts, legislatures, and administrative agencies spend considerable time writing new laws and changing, interpreting, or adapting old ones. In light of this reality, you need to focus on the *techniques* of doing legal research covered in this chapter. These techniques will remind you to distrust the law you think you know and will equip you to find out what the law is *today*.

The law library and the techniques of legal research are the indispensable tickets of admission to current law. School teaches you to think. You teach yourself the law through the skill of legal research. Every time you walk into a law library or click on a legal database, you are your own professor. You must accept nothing less than to become an expert on the topic of your research, no matter how narrow or broad the topic. The purpose of the law library is to enable you to become an expert on the current law of your topic. Do not fall into the trap of thinking that you must be an expert in an area of the law to research it properly. The reverse is true. A major way for you to become an expert in an area is by discovering on your own what the law library can teach you about that area.

Never be reluctant to undertake legal research on a topic simply because you know very little about the topic. Knowing very little is often a beneficial starting point for the researcher. Preconceptions about the law can sometimes lead you away from avenues in the library that you should be traveling.

Becoming an expert through comprehensive legal research does not necessarily mean that you will know everything about a particular topic or issue. An expert has answers and knows how to formulate the questions that remain unanswered even after comprehensive legal research. An expert is someone who can say:

This is what the current law says, and these are the questions that are still unresolved.

Of course, you cannot know what is unresolved until you know what is resolved. The law library will tell you both.

PERSEVERANCE AND LEGAL RESEARCH

You are in the position of the king who sadly discovered that there is no royal road to geometry. If he wanted to learn geometry, he had to struggle through it like everyone else. Legal research is a struggle and will remain so for the rest of your career. The struggle will eventually become manageable and even enjoyable and exciting, but there is no way to avoid the struggle no matter how many shortcuts you learn. The amount of material in a law library is simply too massive for legal research to be otherwise, and, as indicated, the material is growing every day with new laws, new formats for law books, new technology for accessing the law, and new publishers offering new services that must be mastered.

Unfortunately, some cannot handle the pressure that the law library sometimes seems to donate in abundance. Too many attorneys, for example, stay away from the library and consequently practice law "from the hip." They act on the basis of instinct and bravado rather than on the basis of the most current law uncovered through comprehensive legal research. Such attorneys need to be sure that they have adequate malpractice insurance!

Legal research will be difficult for you at the beginning, but with experience and the right attitude, you will overcome the difficulties. The most important advice is *stick with it*. Spend a lot of time in the library (physical and online). Be inquisitive. Ask questions of fellow students, teachers, librarians, attorneys, paralegals, legal secretaries, etc. Be constantly on the alert for tips and techniques. Take strange books from the shelf and try to figure out what they contain, what they try to do, how they are used, and how they duplicate or complement other law books with which you are more familiar. Do not wait to be taught how to use sets of books that are new to you. Strike out on your own. Do the same online. Visit research sites often. Take advantage of links to click your way around sites you are on and sites to which you are led.

We will be saying a good deal about computers in this chapter and in Chapter 13. Computers can be very helpful, but they do not eliminate the need to learn book basics. Keep this caution in mind:

> The computer will become your best friend only when you have acquired the techniques of traditional book (i.e., paper) legal research that will allow you to find what you need without a computer.

Intelligent use of computers requires an understanding of the fundamental techniques of legal research. Furthermore, computer legal research can be expensive. A good deal of free legal information is now available on the Internet, but as we will see, it is not always as current, accurate, or user friendly as information available in traditional library volumes and in commercial (fee-based) computer research services.

At this stage of your career, most of the frustration will center on the question of how to *begin* your legal research of a topic. Once you overcome this frustration, the concern will then become how to *end* your legal research. After locating relevant material, you will worry about when to stop. In this chapter, our major focus will be the techniques of beginning. Techniques of stopping are more troublesome for the conscientious researcher. It is not always easy to determine whether you have found everything that you should find. Although guidelines do exist and will be examined in the chapter, a great deal of experience with legal research is required before you can make the judgment that you have found everything available on a given topic. The techniques you need will come with time and practice. Don't be too hard on yourself. You will not learn everything now; you can only begin the learning that must continue throughout your career. There is no royal road, but there are pathways that, once learned, can make the journey fascinating.

TERMINOLOGY OF LEGAL RESEARCH

Exhibit 11-1 contains a list of research terms that you should know. They are defined in this chapter, in other chapters (see, for example, Exhibit 6-1 in Chapter 6), and in the glossary. (Also use the "Define:" search technique described in Exhibit 11-1.) The terms in Exhibit 11-1 are the foundation for all of legal research. Assignment 11.2 at the end of the chapter covers these terms. It is recommended that you begin this assignment now.

Exhibit 11-2 contains a short list of some of the major abbreviations that you should know.

Exhibit 11-1	The Terminology of Legal Research: Basic Terms

Definitions
- Some of the terms are defined in this chapter. Others are defined in Chapter 6 and in the Glossary at the end of the book.
- For online definitions, type *Define:* (include the colon), the word or phrase you want to define plus the word *law*. For example, if you wanted an online definition of mandatory authority, enter this search in Google, Bing, or Yahoo, *Define: "mandatory authority" law*. (Use quotation marks for phrases.)

(continued)

Exhibit 11-1   The Terminology of Legal Research: Basic Terms (*Continued*)

- act
- administrative decision
- administrative regulation
- advance sheet
- *ALR Index*
- American Digest System
- *American Jurisprudence, 2d*
- *American Law Reports (ALR)*
- analogous
- annotated
- annotation
- appellant
- appellee
- attorney general opinion
- authority
- bill
- black letter law
- Bloomberg Law
- caption
- CARTWHEEL
- case in point
- charter
- citation (cite)
- citator
- cite checking
- code
- common law
- constitution
- *Corpus Juris Secundum*
- court rules (rules of court)
- *Descriptive Word Index (DWI)*

- deskbook
- dictum
- digest
- enacted law
- equity
- executive order
- federal depository library
- Google Scholar
- headnote
- historical note
- holding
- hornbook
- id.
- infra
- key number
- KeyCite
- law review (law journal)
- legal encyclopedia
- legal periodical
- legal treatise
- legislation
- legislative history
- Lexis Advance
- LexisNexis
- mandatory authority
- looseleaf service
- National Reporter System
- on all fours
- opinion (case)
- ordinance
- parallel cite

- per curiam
- persuasive authority
- pocket part
- practice guide
- precedent
- primary authority
- public domain citation
- regional reporter
- register
- reported
- reports
- Restatement
- search engine
- secondary authority
- series
- session law
- shepardize
- slip law
- slip opinion
- stare decisis
- star paging
- statute
- statutes at large
- supra
- table of authorities (TOA)
- terms and connectors
- treaty
- uniform laws
- unpublished opinion
- Westlaw
- WestlawNext

Exhibit 11-2   Legal Abbreviations You Should Know

- For more on abbreviations, run this search in Google, Bing, or Yahoo: legal abbreviations United States
- To obtain definitions of the materials abbreviated in this list, run a Define colon (:) search in Google, Bing, or Yahoo. Type "Define:", the term you want to define and the word "law."

- A. or Ann. (annotated)
- A.3d (Atlantic Reporter, Third Series)
- A.L.R. (American Law Reports)
- A.L.R.6th (American Law Reports, Sixth Series)
- Am. Jur. 2d (American Jurisprudence 2d)
- art. (article)
- B.R. (Bankruptcy Reporter)
- c. (Chapter)
- Cal. Rptr. 3d (California Reporter, Third Series)
- cert. (certiorari)
- C.F.R. (Code of Federal Regulations)
- C.J.S. (Corpus Juris Secundum)
- ch. (chapter)

- Ct. App. (Court of Appeals)
- F.3d (Federal Reporter, Third Series)
- Fed. R. Civ. Proc. or FRCP (Federal Rules of Civil Procedure)
- Fed. Reg. (Federal Register)
- Fed. R. Evid. or FRE (Federal Rules of Evidence)
- F. Supp. 2d (Federal Supplement Second Series)
- L. Ed. 2d (United States Reports, lawyers Edition, Second Series)
- L. Rev. (law review)
- N.E.2d (North Eastern Reporter, Second Series)

- N.W.2d (North Western Reporter, Second Series)
- op. (opinion)
- P.3d (Pacific Reporter, Third series)
- s. or § (section)
- S. Ct. (Supreme Court Reporter)
- S.E.2d (South Eastern Reporter, Second Series)
- So. 2d (Southern Reporter, Second Series)
- S.W.2d (South Western Reporter, Second Series)
- T.C. (U.S. Tax Court)
- U.S. (United States Reports)
- U.S.C. (United States Code)
- U.S.C.A. (United States Code Annotated)

LEGAL RESEARCH ON THE INTERNET

As indicated, there is a tremendous amount of law on the Internet. Indeed, some law offices cancelled many of their subscriptions to paper publications once they realized what they could obtain from fee-based and free law sites on the Internet.

There are three kinds of legal materials in a brick-and-mortar library and in online legal databases:

- **Primary authority.** Any law: constitutions, statutes, opinions, court rules, administrative regulations, administrative decisions, executive orders, ordinances, charters, and treaties (see the definitions of these laws in Exhibit 6-1 of Chapter 6).
- **Secondary authority.** Any nonlaw that summarizes, describes, or explains the law. Examples: legal periodicals, legal treatises, and legal encyclopedias. (For definitions, see Exhibit 11-6 later in the chapter.)
- Finding and updating resources. These are tools that allow you to locate (find) primary and secondary authority. The tools also allow you to update primary authority by telling you if the primary authority you have found is current or has been changed in any way. Examples of finding and updating resources include digests, Shepard's Citations, and KeyCite. (These examples will be defined later in the chapter.) Secondary authority can also help you find primary authority, as we will see.

Our main concern here is *primary* authority that you find on the Internet. How reliable is it?

RELIABILITY OF LAW ON THE INTERNET

There are three main categories of legal sites on the Internet: fee-based private sites, free government-run sites, and free private sites.

- Fee-Based Private Sites

There are two groups of fee-based sites based on cost:

- Very expensive. The three giants and most expensive online legal-research sites are Westlaw (WestlawNext), LexisNexis (Lexis Advance), and Bloomberg Law. (See their websites in Exhibit 11-3.)
- Moderately expensive. (See examples in Exhibit 11-3.)

These fee-based private sites are highly reliable for obtaining the full-text of primary authority. They employ an army of attorneys and other staff to ensure that the material on them is current and that special finding features are added to enhance the user-friendly experience of their paying customers. The sites also contain secondary authority as well as finding and updating resources.

- Free Government-Run Sites

Almost every federal, state, and local government body has a website that contains the full text of all or most of the primary authority it writes. The sites are maintained by legislatures, courts, the chief executive, and administrative agencies. The sites are also very reliable — and they are quite popular. A high percentage of attorneys rely on the law they find on them. The sites, however, are generally not as user friendly and comprehensive as the fee-based sites.

Occasionally a government site will caution the user that the law on the site may not be current. One state (Kentucky) has a more ominous warning:

The files making up this Internet version of the *Kentucky Revised Statutes* do not constitute official text of the statutes and are intended for informational purposes only. No representation is made as to the accuracy or completeness of these sections.[2]

Hence caution is needed when relying on the law found on government sites. Updating steps must be taken, as we will see.

In order to improve public confidence in the government sites, some states have passed the **Uniform Electronic Legal Material Act (UELMA)** to provide a method of letting users know that the law contained on the government site is authentic. The method can consist of placing the law on a secure website or using a special electronic symbol (a digital thumbprint of some kind) to indicate authenticity. "If electronic legal material is authenticated, it is presumed to be an accurate copy of the legal material."[3] It should be noted, however, that law offices

primary authority A law written by one of the three branches of government.

secondary authority A nonlaw (e.g., a legal periodical article) that summarizes, describes, or explains the law but is not a law itself.

Uniform Electronic Legal Material Act (UELMA) A statute that provides a method of letting users of government sites know that the law contained on the sites is authentic.

continue to flock to government sites to obtain the text of primary authority, even in states that have not enacted the UELMA.

Many of the free-government sites also give summaries and interpretations of primary authority. These summaries and interpretations are modern examples of secondary authority.

- Free Private Sites

Finally, there is a great variety of free private sites on the Internet:

- Sites that have their own databases containing the full text of primary authority. A major example is Google Scholar (scholar.google.com) for court opinions.
- Sites containing numerous links to government sites that provide the full text of primary authority. A major example is Public Library of Law (www.plol.org) for many categories of primary authority. (Other examples will be presented in Exhibit 11-3.)
- Sites of law offices, associations, foundations, businesses, and individuals that contain summaries and interpretations of those primary authorities that pertain to their areas of interest or expertise.

With one exception, there are no absolute guidelines to determine the reliability of what you find on free private sites. Although sites such as Google Scholar and the links to the government sites have good reputations, caution is the order of the day.

The exception concerns the summaries and interpretations of primary authority that appear to saturate the Internet. Never rely on them as substitutes for the primary authorities themselves. The summaries and interpretations may be valuable if they contain references or links to primary authority. Follow the references and links, but never take the risk that the summaries or interpretations of primary authority are accurate or current. You must rely on the text of the primary authority and not solely on what a law firm, association, foundation, business, or individual says about the primary authority.

WIKIPEDIA

Perhaps the largest free private Internet site that summarizes and interprets legal and nonlegal topics is Wikipedia (www.wikipedia.com). You need to be cautious about the content of legal materials on Wikipedia, not simply because the site allows users to make corrections and additions to its millions of entries, but mainly because the site does not contain the full text of reliable and current primary authority. Attorneys or paralegals would look foolish if, for example, they cited Wikipedia as their only source for the law of collective bargaining. Researchers need to rely on and cite collective-bargaining statutes, cases, and regulations — the primary authorities. Yet free private sites such as Wikipedia can be quite valuable to a legal researcher. They will often provide references and links to primary authority. Furthermore, when you need to do background research on a topic, they can be quite useful as we will see when we cover the techniques of background research in Exhibit 11-11.

BEGIN WITH GOOGLE?

Of course, you should have no hesitation in using general search engines to find legal materials. In a 2013 study, 587 attorneys were asked where they begin a research assignment. One third said that they frequently or very frequently start with a Google search. Just under another third said they occasionally do so.[4] The major search-engine competitors to Google (Bing and Yahoo) are also excellent starting points.

Suppose, for example, you are working in a law office where the client is Jane Richards, a five-year old passenger in a Ford Taurus, who was injured when the airbag in the car activated on its own without a collision or other impact. Here are some possible searches to try in Google, Bing, or Yahoo:

- airbag injury
- injury defective airbag
- airbag self-activation
- Ford Taurus airbag defect
- child injury airbag activation

Add the name of your state to each of these search queries to narrow the search further. The goal of such searches is to lead you to relevant primary authority and, for background research, to summaries and interpretations of such primary authority.

GOOGLE SCHOLAR

It's not too early to become familiar with the valuable resource called Google Scholar (scholar.google.com). On its home page, you can select

- *Case law* to obtain access to the full text of court opinions
- *Articles* to obtain articles on a large variety of legal and nonlegal topics. To read some of the articles, you must pay a fee, although there are links to numerous free articles as well.

To learn more about Google Scholar, run this search in Google, Bing, or Yahoo: how to use google scholar.

FINDING LAW ON THE INTERNET

Exhibit 11-3 contains links to the various categories of law sites we have been discussing.

Exhibit 11-3	Finding Law on the Internet

- The following sites (a) will lead you to the full text of opinions, statutes, administrative regulations, and other primary authority; (b) will act as gateways or portals that provide links to full-text sites; or (c) will summarize and interpret primary authority.
- Later in the chapter, additional links will be provided to specific categories of primary authority.

Law of Your State
- See the sites for your state in Appendix D.
- Run the following search in Google, Bing, or Yahoo: aa "free legal research" (substitute your state for aa).
- To find the state law library in your state, run the following search in Google, Bing, or Yahoo: aa state law library (substitute your state for aa). The sites of state law libraries often provide numerous links to the primary law of the state.

All 50 States: Cases, Statutes, and Other Primary Authorities
- www.washlaw.edu
- www.statelocalgov.net
- www.lawsource.com
- govengine.com
- www.romingerlegal.com

Federal Law: Cases, Statutes, and Other Primary Authorities
- www.uscourts.gov
- congress.gov
- www.gpo.gov/fdsys
- www.usa.gov
- law.duke.edu/lib/researchguides/fedadminlaw
- govengine.com/fedgov/index.html
- www.washlaw.edu/reflaw/reflawfed.html

Court Rules (Rules of Court) State and Federal
- Go to the home page of any court and click the link to *rules,* or enter *rules* in its search box.
- To find links to the courts in your state, go to www.ncsc.org (type *court charts* in the search box)
- www.llrx.com/courtrules
- law.duke.edu/lib/researchguides/courtr
- www.plol.org

Comprehensive General Legal Sites
- www.findlaw.com
- www.plol.org
- www.hg.org
- www.law.cornell.edu
- www.ilrg.com

Legal Research Guides
- www.loc.gov/law/help/guide.php
- www.law.gmu.edu/library/guides
- www.washlaw.edu/reflaw/researchguides.html
- library.law.yale.edu/research-guides
- lib.law.washington.edu/ref/guides.html
- law.duke.edu/lib/research_guide
- guides.library.harvard.edu/law
- libguides.law.virginia.edu/researchguide
- www.law.georgetown.edu/library/research/guides/index.cfm

Legal Research by Subject Matter (e.g., bankruptcy, women's rights)
- lib.law.washington.edu/ref/guides.html
- www.washlaw.edu/subject/index.html
- guides.library.harvard.edu/law
- law.lexisnexis.com/infopro/zimmermans
- www.hg.org
- law.okcu.libguides.com/browse.php
- www.law.georgetown.edu/library/research/guides/index.cfm

International Law
- lib.law.washington.edu/ref/intlegal.shtml
- www.law.cornell.edu/wex/international_law
- www.un.org/law
- www.law.cornell.edu/wex/International_law

(continued)

| Exhibit 11-3 | Finding Law on the Internet (*Continued*) |

Blawgs Relevant to a Law Practice
- blawgsearch.justia.com
- www.abajournal.com/blawgs

Legal Forms
- www.washlaw.edu/legalforms/index.html
- law.duke.edu/lib/researchguides/formbks
- forms.lp.findlaw.com
- www.romingerlegal.com/practice/forms.html
- www.lectlaw.com//form.html
- www.formsguru.com

Legal News
- www.abajournal.com/news
- legalnews.findlaw.com
- www.washlaw.edu/reflaw/reflegalnews.html
- www.law.com
- www.cnn.com/JUSTICE
- abovethelaw.com

Tweets Relevant to a Law Practice
- twitter.com/search-home (type your practice area in the search box, e.g., patent law)
- twitter.com (type your practice area in the search box (e.g., Florida negligence law))

Full-Text Access to Primary Authority: Free
- Google Scholar (cases)(scholar.google.com)
- Cornell Legal Information Institute (www.law.cornell.edu)
- Findlaw (www.findlaw.com)

- Justia (www.justia.com)
- Public Library of Law (PLoL) (www.plol.org)

Full-Text Access to Primary Authority: Fee-Based, Expensive
- Westlaw (WestlawNext) (www.westlaw.com)
- LexisNexis (Lexis Advance)(www.lexis.com)
- Bloomberg Law (www.bloomberglaw.com)

Full-Text Access to Primary Authority: Fee-Based, Moderately Expensive
- Most state bar associations (and some local bars) give their members free access (as a membership benefit) to legal-research databases. Paralegals may be able to sign in under authorization of their supervisors who are members of the bar.
- www.fastcase.com (Fastcase)
- www.casemaker.us (Casemaker)
- estore.loislaw.com (Loislaw)
- www.versuslaw.com (VersusLaw)

New and Experimental Legal Search Engines
- www.ravellaw.com
- casetext.com
- wellsettled.com
- www.courtlistener.com

Public Records and Other Factual Research
(Background and due-diligence investigations, finding people, locating assets, business directories, government statistics, maps, etc.)
- See Helpful Websites at the end of Chapter 9

FINDING TRADITIONAL LAW LIBRARIES

TRADITIONAL LAW LIBRARIES

Assume that you want to use a traditional law library—a brick-and-mortar facility where you can hold books in your hand. What are your options? There may be such a library in the office where you work, although, as mentioned, a number of offices have cancelled their subscriptions to some paper publications, relying instead on free and fee-based material online.

The availability of traditional law libraries outside your office depends to a large degree on the area where you live, study, or work. Rural areas, for example, have fewer possibilities than larger cities or capitals. Begin your search by running the following search in Google, Bing, or Yahoo: aa "law library" (substituting the name of your state for "aa"). Examples:

- Dallas Texas "law library"
- Boston Massachusetts "law library"
- Albany "New York" "law library"

federal depository library
A public or private library that receives free federal government publications (e.g., the statutes of Congress) to which it must allow access by the general public without cost. (In some states there is a comparable program for *state* government publications.)

Look for libraries that are run or funded by the government. Check their websites to determine whether the public can use them. In general, court law libraries will not allow public access, whereas the state law library and county law libraries, if any, will allow such access. If unsure, call the library and ask. College and university libraries are restricted to their own students unless they are depository libraries. See the next section.

DEPOSITORY LIBRARIES

A **federal depository library** is a public or private library that receives free federal government publications to which it must allow access by the general public. The publications include federal statutes, federal regulations, and federal court opinions. If the library is private, e.g., a private university library, the public right of free access may be limited to those publications the library receives from the federal government under the federal depository program. The private library has the right to prevent the public from using the rest of its collection.

The federal depository library program (FDLP) gives you access to federal laws. Some states have comparable *state* depository library programs for state laws. To find both kinds of depository libraries, see Exhibit 11-4. Some libraries are both federal and state depository libraries.

Exhibit 11-4	Depository Libraries

Federal Depository Libraries

- Go to www.gpo.gov/libraries.
- Alternatively, enter this search in Google, Bing, or Yahoo: federal depository library.
- On the site, find the links on locating a federal depository library.
- Click your state.
- Click the link to the library closest to you or do a search in Google, Bing, or Yahoo for the name of that library.
- On the site, look for information on gaining access to the print collections that are part of the federal depository library.
- Some libraries discourage use of their facilities by directing you to the *online* sites of federal laws. If, however, you want to use the paper volumes, the library must give you access to them.

State Depository Libraries

- To find out if there is a *state* depository library in your state that contains state laws, run this search in Google, Bing, or Yahoo: aa depository law library (substituting the name of your state for aa).
- Every state has a central state law library. Go to the site of this library by running this search: aa state law library (substitute the name of your state for aa)
- If your state has a state depository library for state laws, the above searches should lead you to information about how it works and how to find state depository libraries nearest you.

YOUR NEIGHBORHOOD PUBLIC LIBRARY

Surprisingly, nonlaw libraries often have legal materials on their shelves, e.g., the current state statutory code. In the card or online catalog of your neighborhood or central public library, find out (1) what legal materials it has on its shelves and (2) how current (up-to-date) any particular legal material is. Some of these libraries have very little legal material and what they have may not be up-to-date. Nevertheless, it is worth checking what is available.

ASK AN ONLINE LIBRARIAN

Before we leave the topic of law libraries, you should know about a frequently overlooked resource that is available to you. "Ask a Librarian" programs exist throughout the country. The Library of Congress, for example, has an Ask program that provides "legal and legislative research assistance" for federal and state law (www.loc.gov/rr/askalib). Most Ask programs are available by email to help answer questions about where to find legal information (e.g., statutes on divorce) and factual information (reports on airline crashes). The programs cannot give legal advice, but they can provide useful leads. You can ask general questions (e.g., where can I find the regulations of the Environmental Protection Administration?) and specific questions (e.g., how can I find out how to appeal a Missouri workers' compensation decision?).

The Ask programs are sometimes limited to designated populations such as the students of a particular university. The website of the program will list any restrictions that exist. Don't be reluctant to contact Ask programs located outside your state. Many are eager to help no matter where the inquirer is located. Furthermore, the Ask program does not have to be located within a law library. Good leads can come from any skilled reference librarian to whom your question will be directed.

Finding Ask-a-Librarian Programs
Run any of the following searches in Google, Bing, or Yahoo:
"ask a librarian"
"ask a librarian" law
"ask a librarian" aa (substitute the name of your state for aa)
"ask a librarian" law aa (substitute the name of your state for aa)

CARTWHEEL

CARTWHEEL A technique designed to help you think of a large variety of words and phrases to check in online search engines and in book indexes.

What search terms should you try in a search engine or in the index to a book? This is not always an easy question to answer once you find out that your first few attempts with the search engine or index have not been successful in leading you to what you need. When this occurs, try the **CARTWHEEL**, which is a technique designed to help you think of a large variety of words and phrases to check in search engines and indexes. Here is what a veteran teacher of legal research, Professor Roy Steele, says about using this technique:

I think it is important for students to understand that they cannot just walk into a library and start pulling books off the shelf. That is the quickest way to become frustrated. Legal research requires thoughtful planning. A student must determine which resources will be checked. It is not enough that a student knows [that] a certain resource has an index or table of contents. The student must know what he/she is looking for. This requires the student to develop a list of search terms. Some people would call the development of this list *brainstorming*. However, brainstorming is somewhat hit or miss; it lacks structure and organization. The CARTWHEEL is one of the most effective ways of systematically developing a list of search terms. [It is] a method of analyzing a legal problem and developing a list of descriptive words, which can be used to search indexes.

Professor Steel's comment applies to search engines as well. The objective of the CARTWHEEL can be simply stated: to help you develop the habit of phrasing every word involved in the client's problem *in multiple ways*. When you go to a search engine or book index, you naturally begin looking up the words and phrases that you think should lead you to relevant material. If you do not find anything on point, two conclusions are possible:

- There is nothing on point in the book or on the Internet.
- You checked the wrong words in the index or search box.

Too often we make the mistake of thinking that the first conclusion is accurate. Nine times out of ten, the second conclusion is more accurate. The solution is to be able to phrase a word in as many different ways and in as many different contexts as possible—hence the CARTWHEEL. See Exhibit 11-5.

Exhibit 11-5	The CARTWHEEL: Generating Search Terms for Indexes and Search Engines

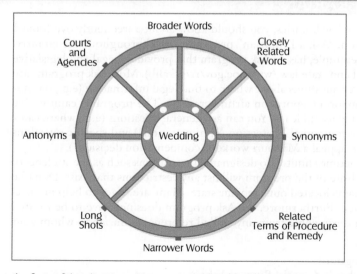

1. Identify all the *major words* from the facts of the client's problem or the assignment (e.g., wedding). One at a time, place each word or small set of related words in the center of the CARTWHEEL.
2. Look up all of these words in the index of law books or type them into a search engine.
3. Identify the *broader categories* of the major words.
4. Look up all of these broader words in the index of law books or type them into a search engine.

(continued)

| Exhibit 11-5 | The CARTWHEEL: Generating Search Terms for Indexes and Search Engines (*Continued*) |

5. Identify the *narrower* categories of the major words.
6. Look up all of these narrower words in the index of law books or type them into a search engine.
7. Identify all *synonyms* of the major words.
8. Look up all of these synonyms in the index of law books or type them into a search engine.
9. Identify all of the *antonyms* (words that mean the opposite) of the major words.
10. Look up all of these antonyms in the index of law books or type them into a search engine.
11. Identify all words that are *closely related* to the major words.
12. Look up all of these closely related words in the index of law books or type them into a search engine.
13. Identify all terms of *procedure and remedy* related to the major words.
14. Look up all of these procedure and remedy terms in the index of law books or type them into a search engine.
15. Identify all *courts* and *agencies,* if any, that might have some connection to the major words.
16. Look up all of these courts and agencies in the index of law books or type them into a search engine.
17. Identify all *long shots.*
18. Look up all of these long shots in the index of law books or type them into a search engine.

Note: The above categories are not mutually exclusive.

Let's look at an example. A bride and a caterer have a dispute involving food that was ordered. Assume that one of the major words in the dispute is the word *wedding.* Place this word in the center of the CARTWHEEL. It will be the first word that will be CARTWHEEL-ed. Look up the word *wedding* in the index of every law book you are checking. Type the word in the search box of Google or whatever search engine you are using. If you are not successful with this word, it may be because (1) the word is not in the index, (2) the page or section references after the word in the index do not lead you to relevant material in the body of the book, or (3) the sites the search engine led you to are equally unproductive.

The next step is to think of as many different phrasings and contexts of the word *wedding* as possible. This is where the steps of the CARTWHEEL can be useful. If you applied the steps of the CARTWHEEL to the word *wedding,* here are some of the words and phrases that should come to mind:

1. *Broader words:* celebration, ceremony, custom, festivity, formality, matrimony, observance, rite, ritual, sacrament, service, etc.
2. *Narrower words:* church wedding, civil wedding, double wedding, formal wedding, golden wedding, group wedding, informal wedding, military wedding, proxy wedding, religious wedding, same-sex wedding, sham wedding, shotgun marriage, Vegas wedding, etc.
3. *Synonyms:* espouse, join in wedlock, jump the broom, marriage ceremony, nuptial, tie the knot, etc.
4. *Antonyms:* alienation, annulment, break-up, divorce, legal separation, separation, split-up, etc.
5. *Closely related words:* anniversary, betrothal, blood test, bride, children, cohabitation, community property, conjugal, connubial, consummation, contract, domestic, domicile, family, home, husband, license, marital, marital relations, matrimony, minister, monogamy, name change, premarital, relationship, residence, sexual relations, spousal, spouse, vows, wedlock, wife, etc.
6. *Procedure and remedy terms:* action, breach of contract, complaint, court case, defense, discovery, jurisdiction, lawsuit, legal proceedings, legal process, petition, process, statute of limitations, suit, trial, etc.
7. *Courts and agencies:* bureau of vital statistics, county clerk, county court, court, department of social services, enforcement, family court, justice of the peace, juvenile court, license bureau, office of child support, superior court, supreme court, etc.
8. *Long shots:* alimony, antenuptial, bigamy, chastity, common law, consent, custody, dowry, fraud, gifts, illegitimate, impotence, incest, paternity, pregnancy, property division, relationship, religion, remarriage, separate maintenance, single, blood, support, virginity, etc.

If the CARTWHEEL can generate this many words and phrases from a starting point of just one word (wedding), potentially hundreds more can be generated when you subject all of the important words from the client's case or assignment to the CARTWHEEL. Do you check all of these words in the index volume of every law book or type them all in search engines? No. You cannot spend your entire legal career working on one case or one assignment! Common sense will tell you when you are on the right track and when you are needlessly duplicating your efforts. You may get lucky and find what you are after in a few minutes. For important tasks in any line of work (or play), however, being comprehensive is often time-consuming.

The categories in the CARTWHEEL will overlap; they are not mutually exclusive. Also, it is not significant whether you place a word in one category or another as long as the word comes to your mind. The CARTWHEEL is, in effect, a word-association game that should become second nature to you with practice. Perhaps some of the word selections in the wedding example seem a bit far-fetched. You will not know for sure, however, whether a word will be fruitful until you try it. Be imaginative, and take some risks.

You do not need a thesaurus to generate words for the CARTWHEEL, but you may find one to be helpful. Most word processors such as Word and WordPerfect have a built-in thesaurus that is easy to use. In addition, you can use a standard thesaurus such as West's *Legal Thesaurus/Dictionary*, Ballentine's *Legal Dictionary and Thesaurus*, or *Roget's International Thesaurus*.

Example of a legal thesaurus

OTHER INDEX SEARCH SYSTEMS

The CARTWHEEL is not the only technique for using indexes and search boxes effectively. Others include Descriptive Words and TAPP.

Descriptive Words

The publisher Thomson Reuters suggests a five-part descriptive-word framework for generating search terms:

Parties	Defenses
Places or Things	Relief Sought
Basis of Action or Issue	

By trying to identify terms that fall into these categories, you will be generating numerous words to check in indexes and search engines.

Parties Identify persons of a particular class, occupation, or relation involved in the problem you are researching (e.g., commercial landlords, children born out of wedlock, physicians, sheriffs, aliens, or collectors). Include any person who is directly or indirectly necessary to a proper resolution of the legal problem.

Places or Things Identify all significant objects, namely the places and things perceptible to the senses that are involved in the research problem (e.g., automobiles, sidewalks, derricks, garages, or office buildings). An object is significant if it is relevant to the cause of action or dispute that has arisen.

Basis of Action or Issue Identify the alleged wrong or infraction (e.g., negligence, loss of goods, assault, failure to pay overtime, or sex discrimination).

Defenses Identify reasons in law or fact why there arguably should be *no* recovery (e.g., assumption of the risk, failure of consideration, act of God, or infancy).

Relief Sought Identify the legal remedy being sought (e.g., damages, injunction, or annulment).

Example At a professional wrestling match, the referee was thrown from the ring in such a way that he struck and injured the plaintiff, who was a front-row spectator. The following descriptive words for this problem should be checked:

- *Parties.* Spectator, patron, arena owner, wrestler, referee, promoter, pugilist, ticket holder, etc.
- *Places and things.* Wrestling match, amusement place, theater, show, playhouse, hall, arena, etc.
- *Basis of action or issue.* Negligence, injury, personal injury to spectator, liability, carelessness, recklessness, due care (lack of), etc.
- *Defense.* Assumption of risk, contributory negligence, comparative negligence, etc.
- *Relief sought.* Damages, compensation, recompense, etc.

TAPP

Another system of generating search terms is to think of TAPP categories: Things, Acts, Persons, or Places involved in the problem you are searching.

- *Things.* Automobile, pool, knife, blood, etc.
- *Acts.* Swimming, driving, rescue, accounting, etc.
- *Persons.* Mother, pedestrian, driver, etc.
- *Places.* State freeway, residence, etc.

A variation is TARPP, in which an R category is added to prompt you to think of relief or remedy words to check.

- *Relief/Remedy.* Suit, damages, litigation, injunction, specific performance, etc.

A further variation is TARP: Things (e.g., circus, dog bite), Actions (e.g., breach of contract), Relief (e.g., damages, injunction), and Persons or Parties (e.g., spouse, employer).

KINDS OF AUTHORITY

Legal research is a search for authority, which is anything written that could be relied upon in making a decision. Our overview of authority will cover these themes:

- The two major categories of authority: primary authority (any law) and secondary authority (any nonlaw)
- Primary authority, which can be either mandatory authority or persuasive authority
- The hierarchy among primary authorities
- Secondary authority, which can be persuasive authority

PRIMARY AUTHORITY

As we have seen, primary authority is any law written by one of the three branches of government. For example, the judicial branch writes opinions, the legislative branch writes statutes, and the executive branch writes administrative regulations. There are two kinds of primary authority: mandatory and persuasive.

Mandatory Authority

Mandatory authority is primary authority that is binding; it must be followed. The court must rely on and apply mandatory authority in reaching its decision. To understand this principle, we need to examine three questions: When is state law mandatory, when is federal law mandatory, and what law is mandatory when state law conflicts with federal law?

- State constitution. The provisions of the state constitution are mandatory authority in that state. For example, the provision in the Idaho Constitution on the right to a jury trial is mandatory authority in Idaho.
- State statutes. The statutes of the state legislature are mandatory authority in that state. For example, an Illinois statute on divorce is mandatory authority in Illinois.
- State court opinions. The **holdings** of the opinions of the highest state court in the state are mandatory authority in that state. All lower state courts in the state must follow those holdings. For example, the holding of an opinion of the California Supreme Court on eminent domain is mandatory authority in every lower state court in California such as in one of California's superior (trial) courts.
- State administrative regulations. The administrative regulations of state administrative agencies are mandatory authority in the state. For example, a regulation of the Arkansas Workers' Compensation Commission on filing a claim is mandatory authority in Arkansas.
- Federal constitution. The provisions of the U.S. Constitution are mandatory authority throughout the country for any power that this constitution gives to the federal government. For example, the provision in the U.S. Constitution giving the U.S. (federal) government the power to print money is mandatory authority everywhere. New Jersey could not create its own currency.
- Federal statutes. The statutes of Congress are mandatory authority throughout the country if the statutes are carrying out a power granted to Congress by the U.S.

mandatory authority
Primary authority that is binding; it must be followed. Examples: The statutes of state x are mandatory authority in state x; opinions of the highest state court in state x are mandatory authority for every lower state court in state x, so that all lower state courts must rely on the mandatory authority in reaching their decisions.

holdings A court's answer to one of the legal issues in the case. Also called a *ruling*.

Constitution. For example, a statute of Congress that regulates interstate commerce is mandatory authority because the U.S. Constitution gives Congress the power to regulate interstate commerce.

■ Federal administrative regulations. The administrative regulations of federal agencies are mandatory authority throughout the country if the regulations are carrying out a power properly delegated to the agency by Congress. For example, a regulation of the Social Security Administration on eligibility for social security is mandatory authority throughout the country because the regulation is carrying out the Social Security Act, a statute of Congress.

■ Federal court opinions. The holdings of the opinions of the highest federal court (the U.S. Supreme Court) are mandatory authority for all lower federal courts in the country. They are also mandatory authority for all state courts in the country, but only if the holdings are interpreting the U.S. Constitution or some other federal law based on this constitution. For example, a holding of the U.S. Supreme Court that the Equal Protection Clause of the U.S. Constitution prohibits race discrimination in voting is mandatory authority in every federal court and in every state court. On the other hand, if a holding of an opinion of the U.S. Supreme Court is interpreting the *meaning* of a clause in the Iowa Constitution (a state law), the holding would not be mandatory authority on any state court in Iowa. Iowa courts have the final say on the meaning of Iowa law and on whether anyone has violated Iowa law.

■ Conflict between federal and state law. Federal courts are the final authority on the meaning of federal law. A state court is the final authority on the meaning of its state law. If, however, state law conflicts with valid federal law, the controlling (mandatory) authority is federal law. The result is based on the **Supremacy Clause** of the U.S. Constitution.

■ Example of conflict. A New York statute (§ 102) says that alimony can be granted to divorcing "spouses in need." An opinion of the highest state court in New York holds that § 102 applies to needy ex-wives but not to needy ex-husbands. This holding is mandatory authority in all lower state courts in New York. New York courts have the final say on the meaning of New York state law. A federal court, however, can rule that a state statute that grants alimony to needy ex-wives, but not to needy ex-husbands, violates the Equal Protection Clause of the U.S. Constitution. Under the Supremacy Clause, federal courts have the final say on whether a state law violates federal law. This is quite different from the question of what a state law *means*. State courts decide this question. Federal courts, however, can decide the question of whether a state law violates federal law.

Persuasive Authority

Persuasive authority is any primary authority or secondary authority that is not binding, but that could be relied on by a court because it finds the authority helpful (persuasive) in reaching its decision. When we covered mandatory authority earlier, one of the examples presented was the holding in the opinion of the California Supreme Court on eminent domain, which we said is mandatory authority in every lower state court in California such as one of its superior courts. This holding would not be mandatory authority in the state courts of any other state. Suppose, however, that a Florida state court likes the reasoning used by the California Supreme Court when it reached its eminent-domain holding. If the Florida court decides to use (follow) the California opinion, the latter will become persuasive authority for the Florida court. For an example of secondary authority that can be persuasive authority, see the paragraph after Exhibit 11-6.

HIERARCHY AMONG PRIMARY AUTHORITIES

Before leaving the topic of primary authority, we should say a word about the hierarchy of laws among primary authorities. The following principles apply:

■ The highest authority is the constitution, which is the fundamental law that creates the branches of government, allocates power among them, and defines some basic rights of individuals.

■ Statutes, court opinions, rules of court, administrative regulations, and all other primary authorities must be consistent with the constitution. The constitution is higher in authority than these other primary authorities.

■ Administrative regulations must be consistent with statutes. Statutes are higher in authority than regulations.

Supremacy Clause The clause in the U.S. Constitution (art. VI, cl. 2) that has been interpreted to mean that when valid federal law conflicts with state law, federal law controls.

persuasive authority Any primary or secondary authority that is not binding, but that could be relied on by a court because it finds the authority helpful (persuasive) in reaching its decision.

- **Common law** is judge-made law in the absence of controlling statutory law or other higher law. Statutes are higher in authority than common law. The legislature can pass a statute that changes the common law. Such statutes are said to be *in derogation of the common law*. (See the example of such a statute in Chapter 6 involving a statute that changed the common law of consideration in contracts.)

common law Judge-made law in the absence of controlling statutory law or other higher law. (See glossary for additional meanings.)

derogation A partial repeal or abolishment of a law.

SECONDARY AUTHORITY

Secondary authority is any nonlaw that summarizes, describes, or explains the law but is not a law itself. The major examples of secondary authorities, as summarized in Exhibit 11-6, are legal encyclopedias, legal periodicals, legal treatises, practice guides, looseleaf services, and legal dictionaries. Opinions of the attorney general are a special category of secondary authority.

Exhibit 11-6   Major Categories of Secondary Authority

KIND OF SECONDARY AUTHORITY	DEFINITION	EXAMPLES	FINDING SECONDARY AUTHORITY
Legal Encyclopedia	A multivolume set of books that summarizes almost every important legal topic.	▪ *Corpus Juris Secundum (C.J.S.)* ▪ *American Jurisprudence, 2d (Am. Jur. 2d)*	▪ The paper versions of C.J.S. and Am. Jur. 2d are usually found only in large law libraries. ▪ C.J.S is also available on Westlaw. ▪ Am. Jur. 2d is also available on Westlaw and on LexisNexis.
Legal Periodical (published by law schools, bar associations, and commercial publishing companies)	A pamphlet issued at regular intervals (e.g., quarterly) containing articles and notes on legal topics. Later the pamphlets are often bound.	▪ *Harvard Law Review* ▪ *Yale Journal of Law and Feminism* ▪ *American Bar Association Journal* ▪ *Boston Bar Journal*	▪ The paper versions of legal periodicals are usually found only in large law libraries. ▪ They are also found on Westlaw and LexisNexis. ▪ The major indexes to them are *Index to Legal Periodicals and Books* (paper and online) and *LegalTrac* (online). ▪ You may also find links to the articles on Google Scholar (scholar.google.com). ▪ See more links in Helpful Websites at the end of the chapter.
Legal Treatise	A book written by a private individual (or by a public individual writing as a private citizen) that provides an overview, summary, or commentary on a legal topic.	▪ *McCormick on Evidence* ▪ Johnstone and Hopson, *Lawyers and Their Work*	▪ Print versions of legal treatises are found mainly in large law libraries. A few are also on Westlaw and LexisNexis.
Practice Guide (also called formbook, practice manual)	A legal treatise that provides practical advice on an aspect of the practice of law, often including standard forms and checklists.	▪ Dellheim, *Massachusetts Practice* ▪ Moore's *Federal Practice*	▪ Print versions of practice guides are found in large law libraries. A few are also on Westlaw and LexisNexis.
Looseleaf Service	A law book with a binding (often three ringed) that allows easy insertion and removal of individual pages for updating.	▪ *Corporate Practice Series* (BNA) ▪ *Medicare-Medicaid Guide* (CCH)	▪ Print versions of looseleaf services are found in large law libraries. A few are also on Westlaw and LexisNexis.
Legal Dictionary	An alphabetical list of legal words and phrases that are defined.	▪ *Black's Law Dictionary* (single volume) ▪ *Words and Phrases* (multi-volume)	▪ Almost all law libraries have the paper version of *Black's Law Dictionary*. It also exists on Westlaw. ▪ See Helpful Websites at the end of the chapter for links to online legal dictionaries. ▪ *Words and Phrases* is found only in large law libraries.
Opinion of the Attorney General (also called Opinion of Legal Counsel)	Formal legal advice given by the chief law officer of the government to another government official or agency.	▪ U.S. Department of Justice, Opinions of the Attorney General (now, Opinions of the Office of legal Counsel) ▪ Legal Opinions of the Attorney General (California)	▪ Opinions of the attorney general are a special category of secondary authority. Although often quoted and relied upon, the opinions are not primary authority.

An example of the use of secondary authority as persuasive authority is a judge who cites the analysis of an article in a scholarly legal periodical on an issue before the court. The court is under no obligation to agree with the article (secondary authority cannot be mandatory authority), but cites the article with approval because the judge finds the article to be persuasive.

A major value of secondary authority is the background research that it can provide when you are researching areas of law that are new to you. For an overview of secondary authorities that can provide such background, see Exhibit 11-11.

CITATION

citation A reference to any authority printed on paper or stored in a computer database that will allow you to locate the authority. As a verb, *to cite* something means to give the location (e.g., volume number or Web address) where you can read it. The citation is the paper or online "address" where you can read something. (See glossary for additional meanings.)

In this section, we cover the **citation** of the most important primary and secondary authorities. A citation is a reference to any authority printed on paper or stored in a computer database that will allow you to locate the authority. Citation is shortened to *cite* (to be distinguished from *site*, which is a place such as a playground or a page on the Internet). A citation gives you the "address" where you can go in the library or online to find whatever is cited. Citation rules and manuals tell you what to abbreviate in the citation, where spaces and commas must be inserted, in what order the information in the citation must be provided, when to include a parallel cite, etc.

CITATION RULES

If you pick up different law books and examine the citations of similar material within them, you will notice great variety in citation form. You will find that people abbreviate things differently, do not include information in the same order in the cite, use parentheses differently, use punctuation within the cite differently, include different amounts of information in the same kind of cite, etc. There does not appear to be any consistency. Yet, in spite of this diversity and confusion, you may be admonished for failing to use "proper citation form." What, you may well ask, is proper?

Start by checking the court rules or statutes governing the court that will have jurisdiction over the problem you are researching. They may or may not contain *official* citation rules, which tell you how you must cite authorities within documents submitted to courts. If official citation rules exist, they must be followed no matter what any other citation guide may say. The rules are, in effect, citation laws.

Official citation rules might also be found in official style manuals. Examples:

- *Writing Manual* (Supreme Court of Ohio) (www.sconet.state.oh.us/ROD/manual.pdf)
- *New York Style Manual* (www.nycourts.gov/reporter/New_Styman.htm)
- *California Style Manual* (www.sdap.org/downloads/Style-Manual.pdf)

To find out if your state has citation rules (and perhaps a style manual covering such rules), run this search in Google, Bing, or Yahoo: citation rules law aa (substitute the name of your state for "aa"). See also the research references for your state in Appendix D.

BLUEBOOK AND ALWD GUIDE

Suppose, however, that there are no official citation rules in your state. In such circumstances, ask your supervisor what citation format you should use. You may be told to use one of the two major citation guidebooks:

- *The Bluebook: A Uniform System of Citation* (Harvard Law Review Association) (www.legalbluebook.com) (www.law.cornell.edu/citation)
- *ALWD Guide to Legal Citation* (Association of Legal Writing Directors) (www.alwd.org) (Click Publications)

The Bluebook (BB) is the older of the two guidelines. A job ad recently posted on a paralegal manager's site (www.paralegalmanagement.org) called for an individual with "exceptional bluebooking skills." At one time there were minor differences between the citation rules in the BB and in the *ALWD Guide*. Beginning in 2014, this is no longer true. The two guides are now substantially alike in their requirements for proper citation format.

Excellent overviews of these citation guides are available online:

- Introduction to Basic Legal Citation (www.law.cornell.edu/citation) (www.access-to-law.com/citation/basic_legal_citation.pdf)

- Video Tutorials on Citation
  (www.access-to-law.com/citation)
- A Bluebook Guide
  (www.suffolk.edu/law/library/19543.php)
- On Google, Bing, or Yahoo, run this search: legal citation guide

The beginning pages of *The Bluebook* are called *Bluepages*. These pages cover the citation formats used in everyday practice. After the Bluepages you will find the citation formats used by law reviews and journals of law schools. For example, law reviews often use large and small caps in their abbreviations (e.g., Ga. Code Ann.), whereas everyday memorandum and brief writing in a law office uses a standard cap format (Ga. Code Ann.). If you go to the pages covering your state in the back of *The Bluebook*, you will find a list of citation formats for every major category of law.

The *ALWD Guide to Legal Citation* is arguably more user-friendly and does not have as much material for the specialized needs of law reviews. The *Guide* also covers the citation formats for the major categories of law in your state.

GENERAL CITATION GUIDELINES

Before examining specific citation rules, review the general citation guidelines in Exhibit 11-7.

Exhibit 11-7	Citations: General Guidelines

1. Find out if there are official citation rules in the court rules or statutes that govern what you are trying to cite. The following sites will let you know if such laws exist in your state:

   - www.law.cornell.edu/citation
     (Click "Cross Reference Tables," then "Table: State-Specific Practices")
   - www.access-to-law.com/citation/basic_legal_citation.pdf
     (Scroll down to section 7-500 before the Topical Index)

2. Ask your supervisor if he or she has any special instructions on citation form. What guidelines should you follow? *The Bluebook* or *ALWD*?
3. Consult the specific citation guidelines presented below. Most of these rules are based on the *Bluebook* and *ALWD*.
4. Remember that the *functional* purpose of a citation is to enable readers to locate your citation in a library or online. You must give enough information in the cite to fulfill this purpose. Courtesy to the reader in providing this help is as important as compliance with the niceties of citation form—so long as you are not violating any explicit citation law or instruction of your supervisor on citation form.
5. At the beginning of some books, you will be told how to cite the book. ("Cite this book as....") Ignore this instruction! Instead, follow guidelines 1–4 above.
6. When in doubt about whether to include something in a citation after carefully following guidelines 1–4 above, resolve the doubt by including it in the cite.

CITING COURT OPINIONS (CASES)

Court opinions (cases) are printed in volumes called **reporters**. **Official reporters** are printed by or under the authority of the government. The cite to an official reporter is called an official cite. **Unofficial reporters** are printed by commercial publishing companies without special authority from the government. The cite to an unofficial reporter is called an unofficial cite. Here, for example, is a citation of the landmark abortion case of *Roe v. Wade* in the official reporter (U.S.) and in two unofficial reporters (S. Ct. and L. Ed. 2d):

> *Roe v. Wade*, 410 U.S. 113, 93 S. Ct. 705, 35 L. Ed. 2d 147 (1973).

In this cite, U.S. is the abbreviation for *United States Reports*, the official reporter for cases of the U.S. Supreme Court. S. Ct. is the abbreviation for *Supreme Court Reporter*, which is an unofficial reporter. L. Ed. 2d is the abbreviation for *United States Supreme Court Reports, Lawyers Edition, Second Series*, which is another unofficial reporter.

In a cite to a case, the number to the left of the abbreviation of the reporter is the volume number of the reporter. The first number to the right of the abbreviation of the reporter is the page number of the reporter where the case begins. Hence in the *Roe* cite,

reporters A volume (or set of volumes) of court opinions. Also called *case reports*.

official reporters A volume (or set of volumes) of court opinions printed by or under the authority of the government.

unofficial reporters A volume (or set of volumes) of court opinions printed by a commercial publishing company without special authority from the government.

- 410 is the volume number of U.S. Reports (U.S.) containing the *Roe* case
- 113 is the page number of U.S. Reports (U.S.) where the *Roe* case begins
- 93 is the volume number of Supreme Court Reporter (S. Ct.) containing the *Roe* case
- 705 is the page number of Supreme Court Reporter (S. Ct.) where the *Roe* case begins
- 35 is the volume number of Lawyers Edition 2d Series (L. Ed. 2d.) containing the *Roe* case
- 147 is the page number of Lawyers Edition 2d Series (L. Ed. 2d.) where the *Roe* case begins

Parallel Cites

parallel cite An additional citation where you can find the same written material in the library or online.

A **parallel cite** is an additional citation where you can find the same written material in the library or online. Hence for the *Roe v. Wade* case,

- 93 S. Ct 705 is a parallel cite of 410 U.S. 113.
- 35 L. Ed. 2d 147 is another parallel cite of 410 U.S. 113.

If the opinion is also available on the Internet, the Internet cite would be an additional parallel cite to the cites in paper volumes.

Exhibit 11-8 contains another example of a citation to an opinion with parallel cites:

Cashen v. Spann, 66 N.J. 541, 334 A.2d 8 (1975).

The 1975 case of *Cashen v. Spann* is printed in two reporters: New Jersey Reports (abbreviated N.J.), the official reporter, and Atlantic Reporter 2d Series (abbreviated A.2d), the unofficial reporter.

Exhibit 11-8	Components of a Typical Case Citation

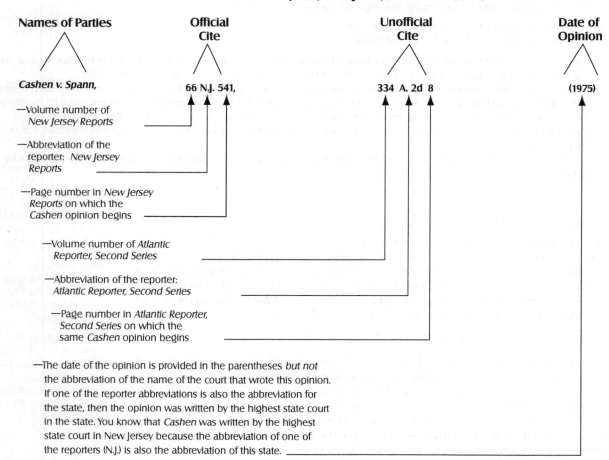

Names of Parties

Official Cite

Unofficial Cite

Date of Opinion

***Cashen v. Spann,* 66 N.J. 541, 334 A. 2d 8 (1975)**

Cashen v. Spann,   66 N.J. 541,   334 A. 2d 8   (1975)

—Volume number of *New Jersey Reports*

—Abbreviation of the reporter: *New Jersey Reports*

—Page number in *New Jersey Reports* on which the *Cashen* opinion begins

—Volume number of *Atlantic Reporter, Second Series*

—Abbreviation of the reporter: *Atlantic Reporter, Second Series*

—Page number in *Atlantic Reporter, Second Series* on which the same *Cashen* opinion begins

—The date of the opinion is provided in the parentheses *but not* the abbreviation of the name of the court that wrote this opinion. If one of the reporter abbreviations is also the abbreviation for the state, then the opinion was written by the highest state court in the state. You know that *Cashen* was written by the highest state court in New Jersey because the abbreviation of one of the reporters (N.J.) is also the abbreviation of this state.

When to Include the Name of the Court in a Case Citation

The citations to *Roe v. Wade* and to *Cashen v. Spahn* include a date in parentheses at the end of the citation: (1973) and (1975). In other citations, the parentheses will also include an abbreviation of the court that wrote the case. This is not needed, however, for the *Roe* and *Cashen* cases. Here is why:

- If one of the reporters is abbreviated by the name of the state (e.g., N.J, Cal. 2d), you know that the case was written by the highest state court in the state. Hence you know the *Cashen* was written by the highest state court in New Jersey (Supreme Court of New Jersey) because the reporter abbreviation in 66 N.J. 541 is the abbreviation of New Jersey.
- If "U.S." is the abbreviation of one of the reporters in the cite, you know that the case was written by the U.S. Supreme Court. You know that *Roe* was written by the U.S. Supreme Court because U.S. is in the abbreviation of one of the reporters (410 U.S. 113).

Sometimes you will find an abbreviation of a court in the parentheses before the date. Let's look at three examples:

Snuszki v. Wright, 751 N.Y.S.2d 344 (Sup. Ct. Niagara Co. 2002).

- The abbreviation of the reporter (N.Y.S.2d) is not the abbreviation of New York state (N.Y.). Hence you know that *Snuszki* was not written by the highest state court in New York (which is the New York Court of Appeals). The reader, therefore, needs to be told in the parentheses what court wrote it. The *Snuszki* case was written by the Supreme Court of Niagara County. The abbreviation for this court is Sup. Ct. Niagara Co. (The reporter in this cite is N.Y.S.2d—New York Supplement, 2d series.) (In New York, the supreme court is *not* the highest state court.)

In re Estate of Hewitt, 721 A.2d 1082 (Pa. 1998).

- The abbreviation of the reporter (A.2d) is not the abbreviation of any state. The reader, therefore, needs to be told in the parentheses what court wrote the *Hewitt* case. It was written by the Supreme Court of Pennsylvania. You can abbreviate the highest state court by using the abbreviation of the state. The abbreviation of Pennsylvania is "Pa.". This abbreviation, therefore, is used in the parentheses for the highest state court in Pennsylvania. The highest state court in a state is always the abbreviation of that state, here Pa. (The reporter in this cite is A.2d—Atlantic Reporter, 2d series.)

McHenry v. Fla. Bar, 21 F.3d 1038 (11th Cir. 1994).

- The abbreviation of the reporter (F.3d) is not the abbreviation of any state or court. The reader, therefore, needs to be told in the parentheses what court wrote the *McHenry* case. It was written by the U.S. Court of Appeals for the 11th Circuit (abbreviated 11th Cir). (The reporter in this cite is F.3d—Federal Reporter, 3d series.)

Most of the abbreviations in these examples are covered in the list of major abbreviations in Exhibit 11-2.

When to Include a Parallel Cite

In the examples we have seen thus far, you will note that some have parallel cites and some do not. For most citations, you do *not* need a parallel cite. We will cover when they are required in the section below called "More Examples of Case Citations."

Citation to a Portion of a Case

Sometimes you will want to refer the reader to a particular part of a case, perhaps a quotation of the judge. Here again is our citation of *Cashen*:

Cashen v. Spann, 66 N.J. 541, 334 A.2d 8 (1975).

Assume that the quote is on page 554 of New Jersey Reports (N.J.) and on page 14 of Atlantic 2d Series (A.2d). In the citation, you would pinpoint these page numbers by including them *after* the page numbers on which the opinion begins. Here is how the citation would look:

Cashen v. Spann, 66 N.J. 541, 554, 334 A.2d 8, 14 (1975).

The reference to specific material within a document (in addition to the citation of the entire document) is called a **pinpoint cite.**

pinpoint cite A reference to specific material within a document (e.g., a quote) in addition to the citation of the entire document. Also called a *jump cite.*

Public Domain Cites

The case citations we have examined thus far contain a volume and page number. A volume-and-page citation is referred to as a *traditional* citation. In the following traditional Illinois citation of *Wirtz v. Quinn*, decided in 2011, the reporter is North Eastern Reporter, 2d Series (abbreviated N.E.2d). The case is found on page 899 of volume 953 of N.E.2d. As in all traditional citations, the year the case was decided is given in parentheses at the end of the citation.

> *Wirtz v. Quinn*, 953 N.E.2d 899 (Ill. 2011).

In some courts, there is an additional citation format that is *not* dependent on volume and page numbers of reporters. It is called a **public-domain citation**. Illinois uses such citations. Here again is a citation to the same case of *Wirtz v* Quinn, this time using a public-domain citation:

> *Wirtz v. Quinn*, 2011 IL 111903.

Note the differences between the traditional citation (TC) and public-domain citation (PDC) of this case:

- There is no volume number in the PDC. Instead, it uses the year the case was decided (2011).
- There is no abbreviation of a reporter in the PDC. Instead, the state is abbreviated as IL.
- There is no page number in the PDC. Instead, there is a number assigned by the court to the entire case (111903).
- The special abbreviation for the state in the PDC is IL. Its abbreviation in the TC is Ill. (Both are abbreviations of the state; hence we know that the case was written by the highest state court in Illinois, the Illinois Supreme Court.)

The number assigned to the case by the court (111903) is a consecutive number so that the next case issued by the court in 2011 will be assigned number 11904 (2011 IL 111904). The one after that will be 111905, etc.

Not all courts have PDCs and those that have them do not have the same format, although they will be similar to the format in Illinois.

When a court starts using PDCs, it will number each paragraph: ¶1, ¶1, ¶2, ¶3, etc. (Before this time, paragraph numbers were not numbered in this way.) If you wanted to quote or refer to something in ¶64 of the opinion, you would pinpoint this number. The pinpoint cite of a case with a PDC, therefore, would look like the following:

> *Wirtz v. Quinn*, 2011 IL 111903, ¶64.

Most opinions that have a PDC also have a TC. They are parallel cites to each other. If both exist for a case, provide both. The *Wirtz* case has a PDC and a TC. Hence, here is its citation:

> *Wirtz v. Quinn*, 2011 IL 111903, 953 N.E.2d 899.

There is no need to include the parentheses (Ill. 2011) in a cite that includes both a PDC and a TC. The year is already included as part of the PDC. There is also no need to include the name of the court that wrote the opinion. You know that the highest court in the state wrote the opinion because one of the abbreviations of the reporters is also the abbreviation of the state (IL).

Finally, let's look at this cite with pinpoint references. Assume that you wanted to quote a sentence that is in ¶57 of the PDC and on page 910 of the TC. Here is the pinpoint cite you would use:

> *Wirtz v. Quinn*, 2011 IL 111903, ¶57, 953 N.E.2d 899, 910

More Examples of Case Citations

Let's look at some additional case citation examples. In the examples (A–G), note when parallel cites are included and when they are not. Here are the guidelines on when they must be included:

- Citations to federal court cases do not need a parallel cite. See Examples A, B, and C.
- Citations to state court cases do not need a parallel cite unless the rules of the court (where you are submitting the document containing the citation) require parallel cites.
- If the court uses public-domain citations, include the parallel cite.

Example A: Format of a citation to an opinion of the highest federal court (the U.S. Supreme Court) in United States Reports (U.S.).

> *Taglianetti v. United States,* 394 U.S. 316 (1969)
> (Earlier we included parallel cites for the U.S. case of *Roe v. Wade.* This was done to show you what parallel cites are, but such cites are not required.)

Example B: Format of a citation to an opinion of a federal intermediate appellate court (the U.S. Court of Appeals for the Second Circuit) in Federal Reporter 3d Series (F.3d).

> *Podell v. Citicorp Diners Club, Inc.,* 112 F.3d 98 (2d Cir. 1997)

Example C: Format of a citation to an opinion of a federal trial court (the U.S. District Court for the District of Pennsylvania, Eastern District) in Federal Supplement 2d Series (F. Supp. 2d).

> *Stratton v. Marsh,* 71 F. Supp. 2d 476 (E.D. Pa. 1999)

Example D: Format of a citation to an opinion of the highest state court (California Supreme Court) that is printed in three reporters: California Reports, 4th Series (Cal. 4th), California Reporter 2d (Cal. Rptr. 2d), and Pacific Reporter 2d Series (P.2d). Assume that a parallel cite is required.

> *People v. Sargent,* 19 Cal. 4th 1206, 81 Cal. Rptr. 2d 835, 970 P.2d 409 (1999)

Example E: Format of a citation to an opinion of a lower state court (Connecticut Superior Court, Appellate Session) printed in Connecticut Supplement (Conn. Supp.). Assume that a parallel cite is required.

> *Huckabee v. Stevens,* 32 Conn. Supp. 511, 338 A.2d 612 (Super. Ct. 1975)

Example F: Format of a citation to an opinion of a lower state court (Connecticut Superior Court) that includes a pinpoint cite. The pinpoint cites in Example F are 520 (for the Conn. Supp. reporter) and 632 (for the A.2d reporter).

> *Huckabee v. Stevens,* 32 Conn. Supp. 511, 520, 338 A.2d 612, 632 (Super. Ct. 1975)

Example G: Format of citation that includes a public-domain citation to an opinion of the Supreme Court of Maine in Atlantic Reporter 2d Series (A.2d) and a pinpoint citation to the third paragraph, which is also on page 599 of A.2d.

> *Pine Ridge Realty, Inc. v. Mass Bay Ins. Co.,* 2000 ME 106, ¶ 3, 752 A.2d 595, 599

Examples of Case Citations for Your state

To see online examples of citations of state cases for your state, go to
www.law.cornell.edu/citation
(Click "Cross Reference Tables," then "Table: State-Specific Practices.")

CITING CONSTITUTIONAL LAW

Constitutions are cited to the abbreviated name of the constitution, the article (art.) number, and the section (§) number.

U.S. Const. art. I, § 9
N.M. Const. art. IV, § 7

When citing constitutions currently in force, do not give the date of enactment. Give the date only if you are citing a provision that is no longer in effect.

CITING STATUTES

Citing Federal Statutes

The federal statutes of Congress are published in three main sets of codes:

- United States Code (U.S.C.), published by the government;
- United States Code Annotated (U.S.C.A.), published by West (Thomson Reuters); and
- United States Code Service (U.S.C.S.), published by LexisNexis.

Citations begin with a title number, followed by the abbreviation of the code, then the section (§) number of the statute being cited, and ending with the date in parentheses. Mention the name of the publisher only for U.S.C.A and U.S.C.S. Here are examples of the citation of the same statute in each of the three codes:

42 U.S.C. § 3402 (2006)
42 U.S.C.A. § 3402 (West 2012)
42 U.S.C.S. § 3402 (LexisNexis 2013)

The year to use is the year the volume you are using was published, not the year the statute was enacted.

Citing State Statutes

Citations to state codes vary from state to state. Here are some examples:

Fla. Stat. Ann. § 23.8911 (West 2010)
Cal. Fam. Code § 100(b) (West 2008)

For the citation format you should use for your state, check state rules for citation in your state (if any), the charts for your state in the *Bluebook* and in the *ALWD*. Also go to
www.law.cornell.edu/citation
(Click "Cross Reference Tables," then "Table: State-Specific Practices.")

CITING ADMINISTRATIVE REGULATIONS

Citing Federal Administrative Regulations

Federal administrative regulations are published in the *Federal Register* (Fed. Reg.). Cites to the Fed. Reg. are to the volume number of the register, the abbreviation of the register, the page number in that volume that contains the regulation, and the full date of the register. Example:

77 Fed. Reg. 2092 (March 13, 2013)

codify To arrange laws or rules in a systematic order, usually by subject matter, regardless of when the laws or rules were enacted. (The noun is *codification*.)

Many federal regulations are later **codified** in the *Code of Federal Regulations* (C.F.R.). When any group of laws is codified, the laws are arranged in a systematic order, usually by subject matter, regardless of when they were enacted. (The noun is codification.) Cites to the C.F.R. are to the title number of the code, the abbreviation of the code, the section number of the regulation, and the year of the code you are using. Example:

29 C.F.R. § 102.60(a) (2007)

Citing State Administrative Regulations

The format for citing *state* administrative regulations is similar to the format used for federal administrative regulations. Both the *Bluebook* and the *AWLD* have a table that gives the name of the administrative code and register of every state. To see online examples of citations of state administrative regulations for your state, go to
www.law.cornell.edu/citation
(Click "Cross Reference Tables," then "Table: State-Specific Practices.")

Here is an example of a state regulation published in a register (Massachusetts) and one published in an administrative code (Virginia):

1136 Mass. Register 26 (Aug. 7 2009)

4 Va. Admin. Code § 15-40-140 (2009)

CITING OTHER AUTHORITIES

- Administrative Decision (National Labor Relations Board). Example:
  Standard Dry Wall Products, Inc., 91 N.L.R.B. 544 (1950)
- Court Rules (Federal Rules of Civil Procedure). Example:
  Fed. R. Civ. P. 15
- Executive Orders. Example:
  Exec. Order No. 12,893, 3 C.F.R. 359 (1992)
- Opinion of the Attorney General. Example:
  40 Op. Att'y Gen. 423 (1945)
- Annotations in American Law Reports (A.L.R.). (Annotations are explained later in the chapter.) Example:
  James J. Watson, Annotation, *Attorney's Fees: Cost of Services Provided by Paralegals*, 73 A.L.R.4th 938 (1989)
- Legal Treatise. Example:
  Alice W. Rand, *International Tribunals* 370 (2d ed. 1970).
- Legal Periodicals. Example:
  William P. Statsky, *The Education of Legal Paraprofessionals: Myths, Realities, and Opportunities*, 24 Vand. L. Rev. 1083 (1971)
- Legal Encyclopedias. Examples:
  83 C.J.S. *Subscriptions* § 3 (2006)
  77 Am. Jur. 2d *Vendor and Purchaser* § 73 (2007)
- Restatement (A **Restatement** is a special category of legal treatise of the American Law Institute that states the law and indicates changes in the law that the Institute would like to see implemented. Examples:
    > Restatement (Second) of Torts § 37 (1965)
    > Restatement (Third) of the Law Governing Lawyers § 159(c) (2000)

CITING INTERNET SOURCES

When you do want to cite something that exists *only* on the Internet, provide (1) the name of the author, if given; (2) the title or top-level heading of the material you are citing; (3) the Uniform Resource Locator (URL), which is its Internet address; (4) the date of the site, if available; and the date you last visited the site. Example:

National Association of Legal Assistants/Paralegals, *Welcome to NALA*, http://www.nala .org (last visited November 5, 2014)

For more, run this search in Google, Bing, or Yahoo: bluebook citation internet sources.

CITE CHECKING

Documents such as a **memorandum of law**, **appellate brief**, and **motion** often contain many citations. **Cite checking** such documents requires an examination of each citation in the document to determine its accuracy. For example, you want to make sure that

- The format of the citation is correct
- Parallel cites (where required) are provided
- Quoted material is accurately quoted
- Cases cited have not been reversed or overruled
- Statutes cited have not been amended, repealed, or declared unconstitutional
- Administrative regulations cited have not been amended, repealed, or declared unconstitutional

In a cite-checking assignment, you are given a document written by someone else and asked to check the citations provided by the author of the document.

Restatement A special legal treatise of the American Law Institute that states the law and indicates changes in the law that the Institute would like to see implemented.

memorandum of law A written explanation of how one or more rules might apply to the facts of a client's case. Also called *memo, memorandum, legal memorandum.* The plural of memorandum is *memoranda.*

appellate brief A document that a party files with an appellate court (and serves on an opponent) in which the party presents arguments on why the appellate court should affirm (approve), reverse, vacate (cancel), or otherwise modify what a lower court has done.

motion An application or request made to a court or other decision-making body seeking to obtain a favorable action or ruling. The person making the motion is the *movant.* The verb is *move.*

cite checking Examining citations in a document to determine their accuracy such as whether the format of the citation is correct, whether a parallel cite is needed, whether quoted material is accurately quoted, and whether the cited law is still valid.

Although our focus in this section will be cite checking documents written by others, the guidelines discussed here are in large measure equally applicable to your own writing. (Subjecting what you have written to your own criticism and review is called *self-editing*.)

See Exhibit 11-9 for guidelines to follow in cite-checking assignments.

Exhibit 11-9	Guidelines for Cite Checking

1. The first step is to obtain clear instructions from your supervisor on the scope of the assignment. Should you do a "light check" that merely makes sure that the format of the citations is correct? Or should you do a comprehensive check that includes checking citation format, finding and inserting needed parallel cites, checking quotation accuracy, and determining the current validity of the laws cited? (The remaining guidelines assume that you have been asked to do a comprehensive check.)
2. Make sure that you have a *copy* of the document on which you can make comments. Avoid using the original.
3. If the pages of the document already have pencil or pen markings made by others (or by the author who made last-minute insertions), use a pencil or pen that is a different color from all other markings on the pages. In this way, it will be clear to a reader which corrections, notations, or other comments are yours. If you find that you do not have enough room to write in the margins of the pages, use separate sheets of paper. You can increase the size of the margins by photocopying the document on a copier that will reduce the size of what is copied.
4. It is also possible to do a cite check entirely on a computer without any markings on a paper document. Start by making a digital copy of the document. On the copy, use red print (or some other bright color) to indicate every addition you have made to the document. Use the strike-out key (~~key~~) for whatever you want to remove from the document. These format notations make it easy for the writer of the document to scroll through it and find your additions and omissions. The "Track Changes" feature of word-processing programs such as Word will automatically insert the format notations for you. The programs also allow you to include margin comments in which you explain why you made a particular change. In the remainder of these guidelines, we will assume that you are doing the cite check in the traditional way—on paper—rather than entirely on the computer.
5. If the document will be submitted to a court, be sure that you are using the court's official citation rules, if any, that must be followed for all citations in documents submitted to that court. If official citation rules do not exist, find out what rules or guidelines on citation format the supervisor wants you to use: *Bluebook?* Another format?
6. Before you begin, try to find a model. By going through old case files in the office, you may be able to locate a prior document, such as an old appellate brief, that you can use as a general guide if it still has the markings and notations on it made by the person who cite-checked it. Ask your supervisor to direct you to such a document. Although it may not cover all the citation variations you will encounter in your own document, you will at least have a general guide approved by your supervisor.
7. Check the citation format of every cite in the document. This includes any cites in the body of the text, the footnotes (or endnotes), the appendix material, and the introductory pages of the document, such as the **table of authorities (TOA)** at the beginning of a brief. (A table of authorities is a list of the primary and secondary authority the writer is using in an appellate brief or other document. The table will indicate on what page(s) in the document each authority is discussed or mentioned. Be sure that these page references are accurate. (For more on TOAs, see Chapter 12.)
8. For long documents, you will need to develop your own system for ensuring the completeness of your checking. For example, you might want to circle every cite that you have checked and found to be accurate, and place a small box around (or a question mark next to) every cite that is giving you difficulties. You will want to spend more time with the latter, seeking help from colleagues and your supervisor as needed.
9. When you find errors in the form of the citation, make the corrections in the margin of the pages where they are found.
10. For some errors, you will not be able to make the corrections without obtaining additional information, such as a missing date or a missing parallel cite. If you can obtain such data by going to the relevant library books (or available online resources), do so. Otherwise, make a notation in the margin of what is missing or what still needs correction.
11. Consistency in citation format is extremely important. On page 2 of the document, for example, the author may use one citation format, but on page 10, he or she may use a slightly different format for the same kind of legal material. You need to point out this inconsistency and make the consistency corrections that are called for.
12. Often your document will quote from cases, statutes, or other legal materials. For example, the document may quote a sentence from a case and give this pinpoint cite to the case:

    Miranda v. Arizona, 384 U.S. 436, 451 (1966)

    The quoted sentence should be on page 451 of the *Miranda* case. Check the accuracy of these quotations. Go to the material being quoted and find the quote. Confirm that it is on page 451. Now check the quote itself line by line, word by word, and punctuation mark by punctuation mark to be sure that the document is quoting the case accurately. Be scrupulous about the accuracy of quotations.
13. If available to you, use standard citators (e.g., *Shepard's Citations*, KeyCite, or GlobalCite) to check the cites. We will discuss citators later in the chapter.
14. Check the accuracy of every *supra* reference. Supra means "above" or "earlier." It refers to something already mentioned (and cited) in the document you are cite checking. For example, assume that footnote 8 on page 23 of the document contains the following cite:

    [8]Robert G. Danna, *Family Law* 119 (1992).

The particular reference is to page 119 of Danna's book. Now assume that 10 pages later—in footnote 17—the document again refers to Danna's book, this time to page 35. A full citation to this page would be as follows:

[17]Robert G. Danna, *Family Law* 35 (1992).

But a full citation is not needed. You can use a **short-form citation**. This is an abbreviated citation of an authority that you use after you have already given a full citation of that authority earlier in the document. For the short-form citation of a legal treatise such as the Danna book on family law, use the author's last name followed by the supra reference:

[17]Danna, supra note 8, at 35.

This means that the full cite of Danna's book was already given earlier (supra) in the document in footnote 8. There is no need to repeat the full cite. The cite checker must simply go to footnote 8 and make sure that the full cite of the book is provided there.

15. Check the accuracy of every *infra* reference. Infra means "below" or "later" and refers to something that will come later in the document. In the same manner as you checked the supra references, you must determine whether the infra references are accurate.

16. Check the accuracy of all of short-form *case* citations. Assume that in the body of the document the following reference is given:

Sierra Club v. Sigler, 695 F.2d 957, 980 (5th Cir. 1983).

The pinpoint cite is to page 980 of the *Sierra Club* opinion, which begins on page 957 of the Federal Reporter, Second Series, volume 695. Now assume that the author wants to refer to page 962 of the same case later in the document. As with the Danna book example, there is no need to repeat the entire citation. The following short form may be used:

Sierra Club, 695 F.2d at 962.

To check the accuracy of this cite, you must go back in the document to make sure that the *Sierra Club* opinion has already been cited in full.

17. Do not use *supra* when you are citing cases. Supra can be used for many items, such as legal treatises and legal periodicals. With rare exceptions, however, do not use it in citations to court opinions. When you wish to avoid repeating the full citation of an opinion, follow the example above of the *Sierra Club* short-form citation.

18. Check the accuracy of every *id.* reference. Id. means the same as something previously mentioned. Use id. when you are citing an authority that is also the immediately preceding authority cited in a footnote. (Id. is more specific than supra. Supra means above or earlier. Id., however, means *immediately* above.) Assume, for example, that footnote 21 in an appellate brief says

[21]*Kohler v. Tugwell*, 292 F. Supp. 978 (E.D. La. 1968).

And footnote 22 says

[22]Id. at 985.

The Id. reference means that here in footnote 22 you are referring to the immediately preceding authority—the *Kohler* opinion in footnote 21.

19. For more information about cite checking and citation in general, see

- lib.law.washington.edu/ref/citecheck.html
- library.law.emory.edu (type "cite checking" in the search box).
- libguides.law.ucla.edu/citechecking
- proparalegal.com/cite-checking-checklist

THE FIRST LEVEL OF LEGAL RESEARCH

There are three interrelated levels of researching a problem:

- *Background Research*. Provides you with a general understanding of the area of law involved in your research problem. Background research uses secondary sources to give you the "big picture" to help guide you into the specific needs of your research assignment.
- *Specific Research*. Provides you with primary and secondary authority that covers the specific facts of your research problem.
- *Validation Research*. Provides you with information on the current validity of all the primary authority you intend to use in your research memorandum on the problem.

At times, all three levels of research go on simultaneously. If you are new to legal research, however, it is recommended that you approach your research problem in three separate stages or levels. Our concern in this section is the first level: background research. The other two levels are covered throughout the remainder of the chapter.

Exhibit 11-10 presents a catalog of the kinds of information you should try to obtain from background research. Exhibit 11-12 lists some of the major resources you can use to try to obtain the kind of information called for in Exhibit 11-11.

table of authorities (TOA) A list of primary authority (e.g., cases and statutes) and secondary authority (e.g., legal periodical articles and legal treatises) that a writer has cited in an appellate brief or other document. The list includes page numbers where each authority is cited in the document.

short-form citation An abbreviated citation format of an authority for which you have already provided a complete citation earlier in the document.

Exhibit 11-10	Checklist of Information to Try to Obtain through Background Research

Major Areas of Law That May Be Involved in the Research Problem
(circle those that preliminarily seem applicable)

antitrust	corporations	immigration	sales
bankruptcy	criminal law	insurance	sea
children	employment	international	securities
civil procedure	environment	labor relations	sports
civil rights	estates and probate	landlord–tenant	taxation
commercial	ethics	military	torts
communications	evidence	municipalities	trademarks
constitutional law	family	partnership	transportation
consumer	fraud	patents	women
contracts	gifts	public benefits	other
copyright	health	real estate	

Jurisdictions That May Need to Be Checked
(circle those that preliminarily seem applicable)

Federal	State	Local	International

Primary Authority That May Need to Be Checked
(circle those that preliminarily seem applicable; see Exhibit 6.1 in chapter 6 for definitions)

opinions	administrative regulations	ordinances	treaties
statutes	administrative decisions	court rules	
constitutions	charters	executive orders	

Major Causes of action And Defenses That Need to Be Explored

Major Terms of Art That Appear to Be Critical and That Need to Be Defined

Citations to Major Statutes That Might Be Applicable

Citations to Major Administrative Regulations That Might Be Applicable

Citations to Major Court Opinions That Might Be Applicable

Exhibit 11-11	Resources for Doing Background Research on a Topic: Obtaining the Big Picture

Goal
Use the following resources to obtain the background research called for in Exhibit 11-10.

1. Legal Dictionaries
Have a legal dictionary close by as you begin your research. The definitions in dictionaries are not as authoritative as the definitions you may eventually find in statutes, regulations, and cases, but the legal dictionary is a good place to start.

Online Legal Dictionaries
- dictionary.law.com
- legal-dictionary.thefreedictionary.com
- dictionary.lp.findlaw.com
- www.nolo.com/dictionary
- For online definitions: in Google, Bing, or Yahoo, type *Define:* (include the colon), the word or phrase you want to define plus the word *law*. Use quotation marks for phrases.

Examples:
define: consideration law
define: "res ipsa loquitur" law

Paper Legal Dictionaries
- *Black's Law Dictionary*
- *Oran's Law Dictionary*
- *Statsky's Legal Thesaurus/Dictionary*

(continued)

| Exhibit 11-11 | Resources for Doing Background Research on a Topic: Obtaining the Big Picture (*Continued*) |

2. Dash Searches In Google, Bing, or Yahoo

In Google, Bing, or Yahoo, type the word "law" followed by a dash and the subject matter of your search. Add the name of your state. Some of the sites you will find in these searches will be those of law firms looking to be hired. Such sites sometimes provide summaries or links that can be of use.

Examples:

- law-abortion California
- law-manslaughter Pennsylvania
- law-civil rights Florida
- law-guardianship Illinois
- law-attractive nuisance Texas

3. Legal Encyclopedias

- *American Jurisprudence, 2d* (national)
- *Corpus Juris Secundum* (national)
- State legal encyclopedia. Some states, e.g., California, Florida, and Michigan, have a legal encyclopedia covering only that state. To find out if your state has one, run the following search in Google, Bing, or Yahoo: aa legal encyclopedia (substituting your state for aa).
- Wikipedia (www.wikipedia.com). Although not a legal encyclopedia, this site covers may legal topics and can provide useful links to primary authority.

4. Legal Periodicals

Here are the main indexes to legal periodical literature found in law libraries:

- *Index to Legal Periodicals and Books* (ILP)
- *Current Law Index* (CLI)
- *LegalTrac* (the online version of CLI)
- Google Scholar (scholar.google.com). Click "Articles" and enter your search term(s). Some of the articles will require a fee to read, but you will probably find free ones as well.

5. Reports/Studies of Special Interest Groups

There are *special interest* groups for almost every area of the law, e.g., unions, bar associations, environmental associations, tax associations, insurance, and other business associations. They often have position papers and studies. Although one-sided, such literature should not be ignored. The best place to find this literature is on the websites of the organizations. A wealth of links and information is often available in these papers and studies, waiting to be sifted through.

Examples:

- Seeking an overview of adoption law? Check the many reports and policy statements of the National Council for Adoption (www.adoptioncouncil.org).
- Seeking an overview of tobacco litigation? Check the website of a tobacco manufacturer (e.g., www.altria.com) and an antismoking organization (e.g., www.tobacco.neu.edu).

6. Reports/Studies of Administrative Agencies

Many legal problems involve an administrative agency of the federal, state, or local government. If you go to the website of the agency, you will often find summaries of the law that governs the agency. There may also be links to reports or studies that directly pertain to the subject of your research.

7. Reports of Legislative Committees

If you already have the cite to a statute that you think will be relevant to your research, find out if one or more committees of the legislature wrote committee reports on the statute before it was enacted into law. The reports often provide invaluable overviews of why the statute was passed and what it does.

- If you know the popular name of the statute (e.g., Civil Rights Act of 1964), enter it in Google, Bing, or Yahoo along with the phrase "committee report" or "legislative history."
- See the ideas listed later in the chapter on the techniques for compiling a legislative history.

Let us assume you are researching a topic that is new to you. Where do you begin? What law books do you take off the shelves, or what online sites do you start checking? More specifically:

- Should you start looking for federal law or state law?
- Should you begin looking for statutes or for court opinions?
- Should you start by checking constitutional law?
- Should you start by checking procedural law?
- Should you start by checking administrative law?
- Should you start by checking ordinances or other local laws?

term of art A word or phrase that has a special or technical meaning.

on point (1) Raising or covering the same issue as the one before you. (2) Relevant to the issues of a research problem.

analogous (1) Sufficiently similar to justify a similar outcome or result. (2) Sufficiently similar to lend support. (3) On point; germane. Involving the same or similar issues; involving facts and rules that are similar to those now under consideration.

digest A set of volumes that contain brief summaries of points of law in court opinions. The summaries come from headnotes at the beginning of court opinions. When the summaries are printed in digests, they are sometimes called *abstracts* or *squibs*. (See glossary for another meaning.)

headnote A short-paragraph summary of a portion of a court opinion (usually covering a single point of law) printed before the opinion begins. See Exhibit 7-12 in Chapter 7 for an example. The headnotes will also be printed in digest volumes, which serve as an index to all court opinions.

key number A general topic and a number. The number designates a subtopic of the general topic. For example, key number Divorce 204.5 refers to the subtopic covered in 204.5 of the general topic Divorce. Key numbers are used by West (Thomson Reuters) to organize millions of cases by topic in its multivolume digests. See Exhibit 7-12 in Chapter 7 for an example of a key number.

By definition, you don't know the answers to such questions—we are assuming that you have never researched a problem like the one now before you. Of course, you will want to ask your supervisor for direction on where to begin. Also, you should try to seek out a colleague who may be able to give you some initial guidance. Suppose, however, that such assistance is fairly minimal or is simply not available. Where do you begin?

As a general rule, it is a good idea to start with the statutory code. CARTWHEEL the major facts in your research problem (see Exhibit 11-5) and try the results in the index of the statutory-code volumes and in the search box for the online version of the code. If relevant statutes exist, you need to find them as soon as possible because they are likely to be central to the problem.

Try some of the resources for doing background research outlined in Exhibit 11-11. Spend an hour or two (depending on the complexity of the problem) with these resources. This will give you an overview or "big picture" of the area(s) of law involved in your research problem. With this general understanding (including the relevant **terms of art**), you will be in a better position to be able to identify the major questions or issues you need to address and where to begin or where the next step should be. Of course, while doing this background research, you will probably also come up with leads that will be helpful in the second and third levels of research.

Next we turn to the second level of research: finding specific primary authority that applies you your facts. Our overview will cover finding cases, statutes, constitutional law, administrative law, court rules, local law, and international law.

FINDING CASE LAW

The goal in the search for case law is to find cases **on point** or **analogous**. Your starting point is a set of facts in a client matter or in a class assignment. You want to find case law (opinions) that covers similar facts and issues. (The words *case* and *opinion* are interchangeable.)

For a list of state and federal courts that write opinions, see Exhibits 6-3 and 6-4 in Chapter 6. See also the material in Chapter 7 on the structure and kinds of court opinions. Exhibit 7-12 dissects an opinion (*People v. Bruni*) and Exhibit 7-14 briefs it.

DIGESTS AND ANNOTATIONS

The two major traditional case finders are digests and annotations.

- A **digest** is a set of volumes that contain brief summaries of points of law in court opinions. The summaries come from **headnotes** at the beginning of court opinions. In Chapter 7, we saw examples of headnotes in Exhibit 7-12 and explained how the digests can be used to find case law through the **key number** system. You should review that material. Most states have individual digests that allow you to search for case law from courts in their state, e.g., *California Digest*, *New York Digest*. In addition, there are national digests that are part of the *American Digest System*, which covers every federal and state court in the country. The index to these digests is called the **Descriptive Word Index (DWI)**. This index will allow you to find key numbers for the issues you are researching. The key numbers are then used in the main volumes of the digest to the find the case summaries. The publisher of the digests is West (Thomson Reuters), which also makes them available on Westlaw.

- Another major traditional case finder are the **annotations** in the volumes of *American Law Reports (A.L.R.)*. An annotation is a research paper. In the volumes of A.L.R., there are thousands of annotations on a wide variety of legal issues. In each annotation you will find one case printed in full plus an extensive research paper that summarizes hundreds of cases from all courts on the main issue covered in the annotation. To find an annotation on the issues you are researching, the main index to use is called *ALR Index*. The publisher of A.L.R. annotations is West (Thomson Reuters), which also makes them available on Westlaw and on LexisNexis.

Cases can be read in print volumes (called reporters) and online. Here are the reporters and online sites for the most recent cases of the major federal and state courts. For the online sites, use their search boxes to locate opinions on the areas of your research.

WHERE CAN YOU FIND AND READ FEDERAL CASES?

(An asterisk (*) indicates an online site that is fee-based.)

U.S. Supreme Court Opinions

- *United States Reports* (U.S.) (an official reporter)
- *Supreme Court Reporter* (S. Ct) (an unofficial reporter)
- *United States Reports, Lawyers' Edition, Second Series* (L. Ed. 2d) (an unofficial reporter)
- www.supremecourt.gov/opinions/opinions.aspx
- www.findlaw.com/casecode/supreme.html
- www.law.cornell.edu/supct
- scholar.google.com (select "Case law")
- www.justia.com/courts
- www.plol.org
- www.westlaw.com(*)
- www.lexisnexis.com(*)
- www.bna.com/bloomberglaw (*)
- estore.loislaw.com(*)
- www.fastcase.com (*)
- See also the links in Exhibit 11-3

U.S. Courts of Appeals Opinions

- *Federal Reporter, 3d Series* (F.3d) (an unofficial reporter)
- www.uscourts.gov/Court_Locator/CourtWebsites.aspx
- www.uscourts.gov/court_locator.aspx (click an area of the map for the court of appeals covering your state, click the link to that court to go to its website, find the link to the cases of that court on its website)
- caselaw.findlaw.com/court/us-federal-circuit
- www.law.cornell.edu/federal/opinions
- scholar.google.com (select "Case law")
- www.justia.com/courts
- www.plol.org
- www.westlaw.com(*)
- www.lexisnexis.com(*)
- www.bna.com/bloomberglaw (*)
- estore.loislaw.com(*)
- www.fastcase.com (*)
- See also the links in Exhibit 11-3

U.S. District Courts Opinions

- *Federal Supplement, Second Series* (F. Supp. 2d) (an unofficial reporter)
- www.uscourts.gov/Court_Locator/CourtWebsites.aspx
- www.uscourts.gov/court_locator.aspx (click an area of the map for your state, click the link to a district court to go to its website, find the link to the cases of that court on its website)
- In Google, Bing, or Yahoo run this search: aa United States district court (substituting your state for aa). On the site of a district court, click the link to the opinions of that court)
- www.law.cornell.edu/federal/districts#circuit
- www.findlaw.com/casecode/district-courts.html
- law.justia.com/cases/federal/district-courts
- scholar.google.com (select "Case law")
- www.plol.org
- www.westlaw.com(*)
- www.lexisnexis.com(*)
- www.bna.com/bloomberglaw(*)
- estore.loislaw.com(*)
- www.fastcase.com (*)
- See also the links in Exhibit 11-3

Descriptive Word Index (DWI) The main index to the digests of West (Thomson Reuters). The index will lead you to key numbers, which is the heart of the organization system used by the digests to find case law.

annotations (1) A research paper in sets of volumes called *American Law Reports (A.L.R.).* (2) A note or commentary that summarizes or explains something.

ALR Index The main index to annotations within the volumes of *American Law Reports.*

reversed To reject or cancel a holding on appeal in the same litigation.

overruled To reject or cancel a holding in an earlier opinion by rendering an opposite decision on the same question of law in a different litigation. (See glossary for an additional meaning.)

precedent A prior opinion or decision covering similar facts or issues in a later case that can be used as a standard or guide in the later case.

cited Mentioned or discussed.

citator A book or online service containing lists of citations that can (a) help you assess the current validity of an opinion, statute, or other item; and (b) give you leads to additional relevant materials.

shepardize To use Shepard's Citations (in book form or online) to obtain validation and other data on a case, statute, or other document you are shepardizing.

slip law A single act passed by the legislature and printed in a single pamphlet.

session law A statute passed by the legislature and printed in volumes that are organized by date (chronologically) rather than by subject matter. Sometimes called *statutes at large.*

statutory code A collection of statutes organized by subject matter rather than by date. An *official* statutory code is one published by the government or by a private company with special permission or authority from the government. An *unofficial* statutory code is one published by a private company without special permission or authority from the government.

WHERE CAN YOU FIND AND READ STATE CASES?

(An asterisk (*) indicates an online site that is fee-based.)

- Go to the regional reporter that includes your state. In Google, Bing, or Yahoo, run this search: national reporter system map. When you find the map, you will be able to see which regional reporter publishes the cases of the state courts in your state.
- In Google, Bing, or Yahoo, run the search: aa courts (substituting your state for aa). On the site of any of the state courts in your state, click the link to the opinions of that court.
- www.findlaw.com/casecode/state.html
- law.justia.com
- www.plol.org
- www.westlaw.com(*)
- www.lexisnexis.com(*)
- www.bna.com/bloomberglaw(*)
- estore.loislaw.com(*)
- www.fastcase.com (*)
- See also the links in Exhibit 11-3

HOW DO YOU FIND OUT IF A CASE IS STILL GOOD LAW?

Assume that you have a case that you want to rely on in your memorandum or other writing. Before you do so, you must find out:

- whether the case has been appealed
- whether the case has been **reversed** (rejected or canceled by a higher court in the same litigation)
- whether the case has been **overruled** (rejected or canceled in a different litigation)
- whether the case has been found to be persuasive (has been followed) by later courts

If you are reading a recent case by a lower court, you must determine whether the parties in the case appealed it to a higher court. If the case was affirmed on appeal, then it is still good law. The opposite is true, however, if the case was reversed on appeal. Some time later, in a different litigation, the same court or a higher court may have overruled the case so that it no longer has value as **precedent**. Also, you need to know whether the case was mentioned (**cited**) by the courts. If many courts have cited the case and followed (adopted) its holding, then the value of the case as precedent is increased. The case can be said to be persuasive because other courts have agreed with it.

How do you find out if a case has been appealed, reversed, overruled, or cited? You use a **citator**. A citator is a book or online service containing lists of citations that can (a) help you assess the current validity of an opinion, statute, or other item; and (b) give you leads to additional relevant materials.

The Major Citators

- *Shepard's Citations* (available in paper volumes and online on LexisNexis). When you use *Shepard's Citations* to check the validity of a cite, you are shepardizing the cite (the verb is **shepardize**).
- *KeyCite* (available online on Westlaw)
- *BCiting* (available online on Bloomberg Law)
- *GlobalCite* (available online on Loislaw)

FINDING STATUTES

Statutes are first published as *slip laws*, then in *session law* volumes, and finally, if they are of general public interest, in a *statutory code.*

A **slip law** is a single act passed by the legislature and printed in a single pamphlet. A **session law** (sometimes called a *statutes at large*) is a statute passed by the legislature and printed in volumes that are organized by date (chronologically) rather than by subject matter. A **statutory code** is a collection of statutes organized by subject matter rather than by date. The most important session laws are eventually printed in a statutory code.

STATUTORY CODES

There are official and unofficial statutory codes. An *official statutory code* is one published by the government or by a private company with special permission or authority from the government. An *unofficial statutory code* is one published by a private company without special permission or authority from the government. Most session laws are published by the government and, therefore, are official.

Except for recently enacted statutes, researchers rarely consult session laws. Once a session law has been placed in a statutory code, it is much easier to find and read. The references below, therefore, are to the code versions of statutes.

WHERE CAN YOU FIND AND READ FEDERAL STATUTES?

Library Statutory Code Volumes

- *United States Code* (U.S.C.) (official)
- *United States Code Annotated* (U.S.C.A.) (unofficial)
- *United States Code Service* (U.S.C.S.) (unofficial)

Online Statutory Codes
(An asterisk (*) indicates an online site that is fee-based.)

- www.gpo.gov/fdsys (click *United States Code*)
- uscode.house.gov
- www.law.cornell.edu/uscode/text
- congress.gov
- www.plol.org
- law.justia.com
- codes.lp.findlaw.com/uscode
- www.westlaw.com(*)
- www.lexisnexis.com(*)
- www.bna.com/bloomberglaw(*)
- estore.loislaw.com(*)
- www.fastcase.com (*)
- See also the links in Exhibit 11-3

WHERE CAN YOU FIND AND READ STATE STATUTES?

Library Statutory Code Volumes

- Most law libraries will have a copy of the state code on their shelves. In addition, the main public nonlaw library in your city will probably have a copy. You need to determine if a library's subscription to the code is kept current.
- Most libraries are less likely to have print volumes of a state's session laws. Researchers often rely on online sites (particularly the site of the legislature) for access to session laws.

State Legislature Websites

- www.ncsl.org (enter *state legislature directory* in the search box)
- tdlp.wikispaces.com/Primary+Legal+Research+Sources+by+State

Online Statutory Codes
(An asterisk (*) indicates an online site that is fee-based.)

- In Google, Bing, or Yahoo, run the following search: aa statutes (substituting your state for aa). Click the site that contains the current state code.
- www.findlaw.com/casecode/state.html
- www.llsdc.org/state-legislation
- law.justia.com
- www.plol.org
- www.westlaw.com(*)
- www.lexisnexis.com(*)

- www.bna.com/bloomberglaw(*)
- estore.loislaw.com(*)
- www.fastcase.com (*)
- See also the links in Exhibit 11-3

HOW DO YOU FIND OUT IF A STATUTE IS STILL GOOD LAW?

Once you have a relevant statute, you need to find out if it has been repealed or amended by the legislature. You also need to find out whether the statute has been interpreted by the courts.

Repeals or Amendments of Statutes

pocket part A pamphlet inserted into a small pocket built into the inside back (and occasionally front) cover of a hardcover volume. The pamphlet contains text that supplements or updates the material in the hardcover volume.

- Many of the print volumes of statutory codes have **pocket parts**. Otherwise, they are often updated by separate supplement volumes. Suppose, for example, you are reading § 107(b) in the main volume of the code. To find out if there have been changes in § 107(b) such as repeals or amendments, you would go to

  - the pocket part of that volume (if any), and
  - a supplement volume of the code (if any)

In the pocket part and supplement volume, you would look up § 107(b). If you do not find this section, no changes have occurred since the date the pocket part or supplement was published. If § 107(b) does appear, you will be told about changes and perhaps cases that have interpreted the section.

annotate To provide notes or commentary. A text is *annotated* if such notes and commentary are provided along with the text.

- Most current *online* versions of statutory codes do not need special update features. Repeals, amendments, or any other changes to the code are automatically included in the results of any search that you enter.

Court Interpretations of Statutes

annotated statutory code A collection of statutes organized by subject matter rather than by date, along with research references such as historical notes and summaries of court opinions (notes of decision) that have interpreted the statutes.

Courts often interpret statutes. They might, for example, declare that a statute is invalid because it violates the constitution. More commonly, a court will apply the statute to specific fact situations in dispute and thereby help to define the meaning of the statute. It is, therefore, important to be able to find cases, if any, that have interpreted a statute. The two major ways of doing so are notes of decisions and citators.

notes of decisions Summaries of opinions that have interpreted a statute, usually printed beneath the text of the statute in annotated statutory codes.

- *Notes of Decisions.* Most statutory codes are **annotated**. An **annotated statutory code** is a collection of statutes organized by subject matter rather than by date, along with research references such as historical notes and summaries of court opinions that have interpreted the statutes. The summaries of court opinions are often called **notes of decisions**. These notes are printed under the text of the statute in the code. If, for example, you want to find out whether § 105(b) has been interpreted by the courts, you would go to the text of § 105(b) in the main volume of the code (and in the pocket parts and supplemental volumes of the code, if any). Beneath the statute, you will find the notes of decisions, if any exist.

legislative history Hearings, debates, amendments, committee reports, and all other events that occur in the legislature before a bill is enacted into a statute. Also part of the history are later changes, if any, made by the legislature to the statute.

- *Citators.* We saw earlier that citators such as *Shepard's Citations* and KeyCite can be used to find out if a case has been reversed, overruled, or followed by other cases. The citator can serve a comparable function for statutes. The citator will tell you if a statute has been repealed, amended, or otherwise changed. The citator will also tell you if the statute has been declared unconstitutional or otherwise interpreted by court opinions.

HOW DO YOU FIND AND READ THE LEGISLATIVE HISTORY OF A STATUTE?

committee report A summary of a bill and a statement by the committee of the reasons for and against its enactment by the legislature.

The **legislative history** of a statute is often used to help interpret the statute. (For more on legislative history, see Exhibit 6-6 in Chapter 6.) For example, when a committee of the legislature recommends the passage or defeat of a bill, it often writes a **committee report** that explains the purpose of the statute. Although this report and other documents of legislative history are not binding on a court interpreting the statute, they are often cited by the court to help it interpret and apply the meaning of the statute.

The first place to look for legislative history is in the **historical note** that is printed after the statute in an annotated statutory code. Many statutes have a **popular name**, e.g., Civil Rights Act of 1964, in addition to their citation in codes (e.g., 42 U.S.C. § 1981). If you know the popular name of a statute, it can sometimes be helpful in the search for its legislative history. In Google, Bing, or Yahoo, type the phrase "legislative history" along with the popular name (e.g., "legislative history" Civil Rights Act of 1964).

Other Resources

- Government Law Library Website. Go to the main law library of the government that wrote the statute. At this site, look for links to legislative history of statutes. Call or email the library to ask for assistance in compiling the legislative history of your statute. (Use the service, Ask an Online Librarian, mentioned earlier in the chapter.)
- For federal statutes (Library of Congress): www.loc.gov/law.
- For state statutes:
  - See the link to the state law library of your state in Appendix J
  - Run this search in Google, Bing, or Yahoo: state law library aa (substituting the name of your state for "aa").
- Legislature. Try to contact the committee in the legislature that considered the statute. It might provide leads to the legislative history of that statute. The office of your representative or senator might be able to assist you.
- Depository library. Contact a depository library in your state to ask for leads. See the discussion of such libraries earlier in the chapter.
- Guides to legislative history
  - law.indiana.libguides.com (click *Legislative History*)
  - www.llsdc.org (enter *legislative history* in the search box)
  - www.llsdc.org/sourcebook
- Fee-based Services. Sites such as Westlaw and LexisNexis also provide extensive access to legislative histories.

historical note Information on the legislative history of a statute printed after the text of the statute.

popular name A phrase or short title identifying a particular statute.

FINDING CONSTITUTIONAL LAW

Constitutions are published in the *annotated statutory code* along with the statutes of the jurisdiction. In addition, you will find the text of the constitution online. (An asterisk (*) indicates an online site that is fee-based.)

- www.law.cornell.edu/constitution/overview
- In Google, Bing, or Yahoo, run this search: United States Constitution
- In Google, Bing, or Yahoo, run this search: aa state constitution (substituting your state for aa)
- constitution.org/c5
- www.findlaw.com/casecode/state.html
- www.law.depaul.edu/library/pdf/constitutional_law.pdf
- www.plol.org
- www.westlaw.com(*)
- www.lexisnexis.com(*)
- www.bna.com/bloomberglaw(*)
- estore.loislaw.com(*)
- www.fastcase.com (*)
- See also the links in Exhibit 11-3

FINDING ADMINISTRATIVE LAW

As indicated when we covered citation, administrative regulations are usually published in a *register* and then, if adopted, they are codified in an *administrative code*. (An asterisk (*) indicates an online site that is fee-based.)

Federal Register (Fed. Reg.)
- www.ofr.gov
- www.gpo.gov/fdsys (click Federal Register)
- www.gpo.gov/fdsys/browse/collection.action?collectionCode=FR
- law.justia.com
- www.plol.org
- www.westlaw.com(*)
- www.lexisnexis.com(*)
- www.bna.com/bloomberglaw(*)
- estore.loislaw.com(*)
- www.fastcase.com (*)
- See also the links in Exhibit 11-3

Code of Federal Regulations (CFR)
- www.ecfr.gov
- www.ofr.gov
- www.gpo.gov/fdsys (Code of Federal Regulations)
- www.gpo.gov/fdsys/browse/collectionCfr.action?collectionCode=CFR
- www.law.cornell.edu/cfr/text
- law.justia.com
- www.plol.org
- www.westlaw.com(*)
- www.lexisnexis.com(*)
- www.bna.com/bloomberglaw(*)
- estore.loislaw.com(*)
- www.fastcase.com (*)
- See also the links in Exhibit 11-3

State Registers
- The name of the register for your state is listed in the back of the two main citation guides: *Bluebook* and *ALWD Guide to Legal Citation.*
- www.administrativerules.org
- www.administrativerules.org/administrative-rules
- www.llsdc.org/state-legislation
- www.plol.org
- www.westlaw.com(*)
- www.lexisnexis.com(*)
- www.bna.com/bloomberglaw(*)
- estore.loislaw.com(*)
- www.fastcase.com (*)
- See also the links in Exhibit 11-3

State Codes of Administrative Regulations
- The name of the administrative code for your state is listed in the back of the two citation guides: *Bluebook* and *ALWD Guide to Legal Citation.*
- www.findlaw.com/casecode/state.html
- tdlp.wikispaces.com/Primary+Legal+Research+Sources+by+State
- law.lexisnexis.com/infopro/zimmermans/disp.aspx?z=1966
- www.administrativerules.org
- www.administrativerules.org/administrative-rules
- www.plol.org
- www.westlaw.com(*)
- www.lexisnexis.com(*)
- www.bna.com/bloomberglaw(*)
- estore.loislaw.com(*)
- www.fastcase.com (*)
- See also the links in Exhibit 11-3

Federal and State Administrative Decisions
- Go to the website of the agency involved and look for links to its administrative decisions.
- Use the Ask-an-Online-Librarian resource discussed earlier.

Executive Orders
- Federal. On the site of the President (www.whitehouse.gov), enter *executive orders* in the search box.
- Federal. www.archives.gov/federal-register/executive-orders/disposition.html
- State. On the site of the governor of your state, enter *executive orders* in the search box.

Opinions of the Attorney General
- Federal: Opinions of the Attorney General of the United States
  - www.justice.gov/olc/opinions.htm
  - law.lexisnexis.com/infopro/zimmermans/disp.aspx?z=1198

- State: On the site of the attorney general of your state, enter *executive orders* in the search box

FINDING COURT RULES (RULES OF COURT)

(An asterisk (*) indicates an online site that is fee-based.)

Federal and State Court Rules
- www.llrx.com/courtrules
- Go to the website of the federal or state court and look for links to its court rules.
- law.duke.edu/lib/researchguides/courtr
- www.plol.org
- www.westlaw.com(*)
- www.lexisnexis.com(*)
- www.bna.com/bloomberglaw(*)
- estore.loislaw.com(*)
- www.fastcase.com (*)
- See also the links in Exhibit 11-3

Federal Court Rules
- In Google, Bing, or Yahoo, run this search: federal court rules
- law.lexisnexis.com/infopro/zimmermans/disp.aspx?z=1458

State Court Rules
- in Google, Bing, or Yahoo, run this search: aa court rules (substituting your state for aa).
- law.lexisnexis.com/infopro/zimmermans/disp.aspx?z=1958

FINDING LOCAL LAW

(An asterisk (*) indicates an online site that is fee-based.)

General
- Go to the website of the city, county, or town and look for links to its laws and regulations
- www.westlaw.com(*)
- www.lexisnexis.com(*)

Municipal Codes
- www.municode.com/library
- www.findlaw.com/11stategov/municipal.html
- www.sterlingcodifiers.com/codes-online

FINDING INTERNATIONAL LAW

(An asterisk (*) indicates an online site that is fee-based.)

U.S. Treaties in Force
- www.state.gov/s/l/treaty/tif/index.htm

Laws of the United Nations
- www.un.org/en/law

Guides to International Law
- www.worldlii.org
- www.findlaw.com/12international/index.html
- www.nyulawglobal.org/Globalex
- library.law.yale.edu/research/guides/country-guide
- www.asil.org/resources/electronic-resource-guide-erg
- www.law.cornell.edu/world
- www.law.cornell.edu/wex/international_law
- www.law.northwestern.edu/depts/library (click *International Law* and *Foreign and Comparative Law*)
- www.westlaw.com(*)
- www.lexisnexis.com(*)
- www.bna.com/bloomberglaw(*)

FINDING SECONDARY AUTHORITY (SUBJECT-MATTER RESEARCH)

There are collections of online links to many specific subject matters, e.g., abortion, capital punishment, consumer law, family law, real estate law, social security, and war.

- See the links in Chapter 2 in the section on Paralegal Roles: A Dictionary of Functions. After each category of law, there are one or more links to the law on the area of law involved.
- In Google, Bing, or Yahoo, enter aa, the subject matter of your research, and the word *law*, substituting your state for aa. Example: Hawaii abortion law
- In Google, Bing, or Yahoo, run the law dash searches (e.g., law-abortion California) explained in Exhibit 11-11.

Here are some major research guides covering many subject matters:

- guides.library.harvard.edu/law
- www.llrx.com/category/1048
- lib.law.washington.edu/ref/guides.html
- law.lexisnexis.com/infopro/zimmermans

WESTLAW AND LEXISNEXIS

As we have seen in Chapter 9 and here in Chapter 11, a great deal of legal and factual information is available on the Internet for free. Much of this information is also available for a substantial fee from the major commercial online services, Westlaw and LexisNexis (affectionately referred to together as Wexis, a nonlegal term) and the most recent large service, Bloomberg Law. These giants, however, are unlikely to go out of business because of competition from the free resources on the Internet. Westlaw, LexisNexis, and Bloomberg Law spend a great deal of editorial time and money ensuring the accuracy and currentness of the information they make available. No comparable control mechanisms exist for much of the free information found on the Internet. The reliability of free information is increasing (particularly at government-run sites that provide access to the government's own statutes, cases, court rules, and administrative regulations), but these free sites are not yet able on their own to satisfy the legal community's need for accurate and current online legal information. Westlaw, LexisNexis, and Bloomberg Law (and some smaller fee-based services such as Loislaw, Fastcase, and VersusLaw) will continue to play major roles in online research.

Because of the cost of fee-based legal-research services, most paralegals, when given research assignments, will be directed to the free sources outlined in this chapter. Nevertheless, paralegals should be aware of the fee-based alternatives. Let's take a closer look at the two giants in the field of fee-based legal research: Westlaw and LexisNexis.

Westlaw (and its recent version, WestlawNext) are products of Thomson Reuters (www.westlaw.com). LexisNexis and its recent version (Lexis Advance) are products of Reed Elsevier (www.lexisnexis.com).

SCOPE OF WESTLAW AND LEXISNEXIS

Westlaw and LexisNexis allow you to search the full text of primary authority such as constitutions, statutes, administrative regulations, administrative decisions, court rules, treaties, and local law. You can also conduct full-text searches of secondary authority such as legal periodicals, encyclopedias, treatises, and newsletters. In addition, Westlaw and LexisNexis give you access to a large variety of factual information such as the following:

- The status of pending lawsuits in federal, state, and local courts
- Records of judgments in bankruptcy courts, other federal courts, state courts, county courts, and other local courts
- Statistics on jury awards for specific kinds of injuries
- Mechanic's lien filings
- Uniform Commercial Code (UCC) filings
- Business and personal addresses
- Names of key personnel in particular companies (e.g., officers, members of the board of directors)
- Major properties (e.g., land, stock, commercial equipment) owned by particular individuals and businesses
- Financial status of companies based on sales data, stock market prices, and property holdings
- Financial details and status of proposed mergers and acquisitions
- Chain-of-title records on specific property
- Medical research (e.g., side effects of particular drugs)
- News stories on particular topics, companies, or individuals in newspapers and other media throughout the world
- Birth and death records
- Social science studies

See also Exhibit 9-9 in Chapter 9 on financial data available on Westlaw and LexisNexis.

This overview is not meant to suggest that the contents of Westlaw and LexisNexis are identical. Each claims to outdo the other in special features, ease of use, comprehensiveness, and diversity of coverage. Yet as demonstrated by the above overview, the coverage in both systems is substantially similar.

SEARCHES ON WESTLAW AND LEXISNEXIS

There are two main methods of phrasing search questions (queries) on Westlaw and LexisNexis: (1) natural language and (2) terms and connectors. These two methods also exist on many of the free research sites on the Internet. Keep in mind, however, that each research site can establish its own way of phrasing queries. You will note similarities, but watch for differences among the various sites.

Natural-Language Searching

Natural-language searching uses everyday speech to phrase questions. LexisNexis calls its natural-language method *Freestyle;* Westlaw calls its natural-language method *Natural Language.* Here are some examples of natural-language questions that can be posed in both services:

- What is the statute of limitations for embezzlement in Virginia?
- When can a minor enter a contract in California?
- Can strict liability be imposed for harm caused by smoking in Illinois?

Type the query in the same way that you would ask a question in plain English to a friend or colleague. (Such natural-language queries or questions can also be used in general search engines such as Google, Bing, and Yahoo.)

natural language Plain English as spoken or written every day, as opposed to language that is specially designed for computer communication.

Terms-and-Connectors Searching

A more precise method of phrasing queries on Westlaw and LexisNexis uses **terms and connectors**. (This method is based on rules of search logic referred to as Boolean logic.) In a terms-and-connectors search, you specify relationships between terms in a search query in order to identify the documents you want included in or excluded from the search. The relationships are indicated by powerful connectors such as *and*, *&*, *or*, and *not*.

Here is an example of a terms-and-connectors search in Westlaw:

marijuana & arrest

Let us assume you want to use this query to search for opinions of your state courts. The query tells the computer to find every opinion in the database that contains the term *marijuana* anywhere in the opinion and that also contains the term *arrest* anywhere in the opinion. The terms being searched are marijuana and arrest. The AND connector (phrased in Westlaw by using the word AND or by using an ampersand, &) tells the computer that you want to be given every opinion in the database that contains both terms.

Of course, if your search query consists of a single term, you do not need connectors. You are simply telling the computer to find every document that contains that term. Single-term searches, however, are usually unproductive because they produce too many documents. (This is also true of general search engines such as Google, Bing, or Yahoo.) Suppose, for example, you entered the following search query in Westlaw:

law

This query would probably identify hundreds of thousands of documents because of the large number of documents that contain this term. In fact, Westlaw will quickly flash a message on the screen telling you to change your query because the one you are using is likely to generate too many documents. Hence, unless your single term is a unique legal term (e.g., asportation) or an unusual surname (e.g., Wyzinski), your query should include more than one term. When it does, connectors are needed to state the relationship between the terms. Although in the following discussion we will use some single-term queries for purposes of highlighting a particular search technique, keep in mind that multiple-term searches are usually more effective than single-term searches.

Universal Character (*) in Westlaw and LexisNexis Both Westlaw and LexisNexis use the asterisk (*) as a **universal character** that stands for any single character, such as a letter of the alphabet. A universal character is useful when you are not sure of the spelling of a term you want to search. For example, in the drug arrest example we just examined, suppose you were not sure whether the drug was spelled marijuana or marihuana. You could enter the search this way:

mari*uana & arrest

This query will find any document that spells the term as marijuana, marihuana, mariiuana, marizuana, etc. Because the asterisk stands for *any* single letter or character, it is called the universal character. You are not limited to one universal character per term. The following query:

int**state

will find every document that contains the term *interstate* anywhere in the document and every document that contains the term *intrastate* anywhere in the document.

Similarly, the query

s****holder

will find

- Every document that contains the term *shareholder* anywhere in the document, and
- Every document that contains the term *stockholder* anywhere in the document, and
- Every document that contains the term *stakeholder* anywhere in the document.

The query

w**nst**n

will find any document that contains words with the following spellings (or misspellings) anywhere in the document: *Weinstein, Weinstien, Weinsteen, Wienstein, Wienstien,* and *Wiensteen.*

Root Expander (!) in Westlaw and LexisNexis   Both Westlaw and LexisNexis use the exclamation point (!) as a **root expander**. When added to the root of any term, the ! acts as a substitute for one or more characters. (The root expander and the universal character are examples of **wildcards**, which are special characters that can be used to represent one or more characters in a search query.) The root expander in Westlaw and LexisNexis is inserted at the end of a term (or at the end of a fragment of a term) in order to broaden the scope of the search. If your query is

> litig!

you will find every document that contains any of the following terms anywhere in the document: *litigable, litigate, litigated, litigating, litigation, litigator, litigious,* and *litigiousness.* The root expander is quite powerful and can be overused. The query:

> tax!

will find every document that contains any of the following terms anywhere in the document: *tax, taxability, taxable, taxation, taxational, taxer, Taxco, taxeme, taxes, tax-deductible, tax-exempt, tax-free, taxi, taxicab, taxidermy, taxidermist, taxied, taximeter, taximetrics, taxing, taxis, taxiway, taxman, taxol, taxon, taxonomist, taxonomy, taxpayer, tax-shelter, taxy,* and *taxying.* Hence, if you use *tax!* as a search query in a large database, you are likely to find many documents that are irrelevant to your research problem.

Plurals in Westlaw and LexisNexis   In Westlaw and LexisNexis searches, it is not necessary to use the universal character or the root expander to search for the plural of a term. The query

> prosecutor

will give you every document that contains the term *prosecutor* or the term *prosecutors* anywhere in the document. The same is true of irregular plurals:

- The query *child* will give you every document that contains the term *child* or the term *children* anywhere in the document.
- The query *memorandum* will give you every document that contains the term *memoranda* or the term *memorandums* anywhere in the document.

Entering the singular form of a term will automatically result in a search for the plural form of that term also.

Thus far we have examined the universal character (*) and root expander (!). Again, keep in mind that this discussion applies only to Westlaw and LexisNexis. When you are searching in other search resources (e.g., on general search engines), you may find that these notations (* and !) serve related but different functions.

Tutorials   To understand how specific queries are phrased in Westlaw and LexisNexis, check available tutorials on the Internet:

- In Google, Bing, or Yahoo, run this search: Westlaw tutorial
- In Google, Bing, or Yahoo, run this search: WestlawNext tutorial
- In Google, Bing, or Yahoo, run this search: LexisNexis tutorial
- In Google, Bing, or Yahoo, run this search: Lexis Advance tutorial

CITATORS IN WESTLAW AND LEXISNEXIS

As we have seen, a citator helps you assess the current validity of a law (e.g., opinion, statute) and gives you leads to other relevant materials. The online citator in Westlaw is called *KeyCite.* The online citator in LexisNexis is called *Shepards.* (The latter is the electronic version of the paper volumes called *Shepard's Citations.*)

Suppose, for example, you want to know whether a particular court opinion is still good law. Has the opinion been reversed on appeal? Have any other courts followed it or criticized it? Has the opinion been overruled? One of the ways to answer such questions is by using the online citators of Westlaw and LexisNexis. Both systems use colored alert signals to tell users about changes in the court opinion, statute, or other authority they are checking in the citator.

root expander An exclamation mark (!) that stands for one or more characters added to the root of a term you are searching in Westlaw or LexisNexis.

wildcard A special character (e.g., *, !, ?) that can be used to represent one or more characters in a search query.

ALTERNATIVE FEE-BASED SERVICES

As indicated, the giant services (Westlaw, LexisNexis, and Bloomberg Law) are expensive. Less expensive alternatives include:

- www.casemaker.us (Casemaker)
- www.fastcase.com (Fastcase)
- estore.loislaw.com (Loislaw)
- www.versuslaw.com (VersusLaw)

RESEARCH SELF-AUDIT

The checklist in Exhibit 11-12 is designed to help you achieve the comprehensiveness that is essential to all aspects of legal research. Fill out a separate research self-audit for each issue you research. Start by summarizing the issue in the box at the top of the checklist. The checklist serves as a reminder to make sure that you have covered all bases. Note that part IV tells you to keep a research log. You not only want to be comprehensive but also you want to be able to tell others (and remind yourself) what steps you took along the way.

Exhibit 11-12	Research Self-Audit

ISSUE #___ (briefly state issue researched)

I. What I Have Checked: Legal Materials

A. *Primary Authority*

■ federal court opinions	■ state court opinions	■ ordinances
■ federal statutes	■ state statutes	■ charter
■ federal constitution	■ state constitution	■ local court rules
■ federal court rules	■ state court rules	■ local administrative regulations
■ federal administrative regulations	■ state administrative regulations	■ local administrative decisions
■ federal administrative decisions	■ state administrative decisions	■ international law

B. *Secondary Authority and Finding Aids*

■ legal periodicals	■ legal treatises	■ looseleaf services
■ ALR annotations	■ legal encyclopedias	■ legal newsletters
■ *Words and Phrases* (legal dictionary)	■ digests	

II. What I Have Checked: Nonlegal Materials

When relevant to the research problem, I have checked nonlegal literature in the areas of:

■ medicine	■ psychology	■ psychiatry
■ statistics	■ accounting	■ sociology
■ biology	■ chemistry	■ business management

III. What I Intend to Rely On in My Research Memo

For every primary authority I intend to use, I have:

- Used paper citators to determine whether it is still valid (e.g., Shephard's Citations)
- Used online citators to determine whether it is still valid (e.g., Shephard's, KeyCite)
- Checked other standard updating features (e.g., pocket parts, supplement pamphlets, history tables)

IV. Research Log

For each paper volume or online resource (free or fee-based Internet) that I checked, I have made the following brief notations in my research notebook or log:

- The name or address of the resource
- The major words/phrases I have checked in the resource
- Which library I used for this resource (if more than one)

V. People Consulted for Guidance/Leads before Completeion

People with whom I have shared my research strategy to determine whether they think I have omitted something:

■ supervisor	■ law clerk	■ ask a librarian
■ other attorney(s) in office	■ experienced paralegal	■ other
■ law librarian	■ experts	

CHAPTER SUMMARY

The law is changing every day. The only dependable way to find out about all of these changes is through legal research. The ticket to current law is legal research. Research skills will take time and determination to develop. You do not have to be an expert in an area of the law in order to research that area. The major categories of law sites on the Internet are fee-based private sites, free government sites, and free private sites. The first two categories are the most reliable for providing the full text of primary authority. All sites, however, are potentially useful for providing links to primary authority and may help with background research.

Law libraries are available in traditional brick-and-mortar buildings and online. A federal depository library is a public or private library that receives free federal government publications (e.g., the statutes of Congress) to which it must allow access by the general public without cost. In some states there is a comparable program for *state* government publications. The CARTWHEEL is a technique designed to help you think of a large variety of words and phrases to check in search engines and indexes.

The two major categories of authority are primary authority and secondary authority. Primary authority is any law written by one of the three branches of government. Primary authority can be mandatory or persuasive. The constitution is the highest authority. Statutes are higher in authority than regulations and the common law. The major categories of secondary authority are legal encyclopedias, legal periodicals, legal treatises, practice guides, looseleaf services, and legal dictionaries.

A citation is a reference to any authority printed on paper or stored in a computer database that will allow you to locate the authority. Some courts require specific citation formats in documents submitted to that court. Citation rules and manuals tell you what to abbreviate in the citation, where spaces and commas must be inserted, in what order the information in the citation must be provided, when to include a parallel cite, etc. A parallel cite is an additional citation where you can find the same written material in the library or online. A public-domain citation is a citation that is not dependent on the volume and page number of a reporter; it is both medium neutral (meaning that it can be read in a paper volume or online) and vendor neutral (meaning that it does not contain volume, page, or other identifying information created by a particular vendor, such as a commercial publisher). Cite checking is examining citations in a document to determine their accuracy such as whether the format of the citation is correct, whether a parallel cite is needed, whether quoted material is accurately quoted, and whether the cited law is still valid.

The three levels of research are background research, specific research, and validation research. Some of the main sources of background research include legal dictionaries; general search engines; legal encyclopedias; legal periodicals; and the reports/studies of special-interest groups, administrative agencies, and legislative committees.

A citator is a book or online service containing lists of citations that can (a) help you assess the current validity of an opinion, statute, or other item; and (b) give you leads to additional relevant materials. Major citators include *Shepard's Citations* and *KeyCite*. The largest fee-based research services are Westlaw and LexisNexis. A research self-audit is a final assessment consisting of a checklist of research tasks to help insure that you have covered everything that needs to be covered for your research problem.

KEY TERMS

online (p. 491)
primary authority (p. 495)
secondary authority (p. 495)
Uniform Electronic Legal
   Material Act (UELMA) (p. 495)
federal depository library (p. 498)
CARTWHEEL (p. 500)
mandatory authority (p. 503)
holding (p. 503)
Supremacy Clause (p. 504)
persuasive authority (p. 504)
common law (p. 505)
derogation (p. 505)
legal encyclopedia (p. 505)
legal periodical (p. 505)
legal treatise (p. 505)
practice guide (p. 505)

looseleaf service (p. 505)
legal dictionary (p. 505)
opinion of the attorney general
   (p. 505)
citation (p. 506)
reporter (p. 507)
official reporter (p. 507)
unofficial reporter (p. 507)
parallel cite (p. 508)
pinpoint cite (p. 509)
public-domain citation (p. 510)
codify (p. 512)
Restatement (p. 513)
memorandum of law (p. 513)
appellate brief (p. 513)
motion (p. 513)
cite checking (p. 513)

table of authorities (TOA) (p. 515)
short-form citation (p. 515)
term of art (p. 518)
on point (p. 518)
analogous (p. 518)
digest (p. 518)
headnote (p. 518)
key number (p. 518)
Descriptive Word Index (DWI)
   (p. 519)
annotation (p. 519)
ALR Index (p. 519)
reverse (p. 520)
overrule (p. 520)
precedent (p. 520)
cited (p. 520)
citator (p. 520)

shepardize (p. 520)
slip law (p. 520)
session law (p. 520)
statutory code (p. 520)
pocket part (p. 522)
annotate (p. 522)
annotated statutory code (p. 522)
notes of decisions (p. 522)
legislative history (p. 522)
committee report (p. 522)
historical note (p. 523)
popular name (p. 523)
natural language (p. 527)
terms and connectors (p. 528)
universal character (p. 528)
root expander (p. 529)
wildcard (p. 529)

ASSIGNMENTS

CRITICAL ANALYSIS

11.1

(a) Computers can perform functions much faster than humans can. Discuss whether it is therefore true that traditional legal research should not be used when computer research is available.

(b) A famous cartoon in the New Yorker shows a dog sitting in front of a desktop telling another dog, "On the Internet, nobody knows you're a dog." To what extent is this comment relevant to laws found or described on free or fee-based Internet sites?

PROJECTS

11.2 Define all of the research terms in Exhibit 11-1. Use the definitions in Chapters 6 and 11, the glossary, the "define colon" technique listed at the top of Exhibit 11-1, and the online legal dictionaries listed in the section on Helpful Websites.

11.3 Go to the website of your local public library. Make a list of available free databases that might be of assistance to a paralegal doing factual or legal research. Describe each database and state how it might be helpful to the paralegal.

CORE SKILLS

Among the many skills a paralegal must have, five core skills stand out: writing (both basic English and legal drafting), research, ethics, computer use, and collaboration (working with others). The core-skill assignments introduce and reinforce these skills. Even if you are not asked to do all of the assignments as part of the course, you should do them on your own. Also, do not wait for the topics in the assignments to be covered in this course or in other courses. Successful paralegals are self-starters. A major characteristic of a self-starter is a thirst for independent study—learning on your own.

CORE SKILL: RESEARCH

11.4 Using the guidelines of Exhibit 11-5, CART-WHEEL the following words or phrases:

(a) paralegal

(b) woman

(c) cruelty

(d) support

(e) paternity

11.5 In your state and in any two others, what is the minimum age to enter a valid marriage without the consent of his or her parents or guardians? Cite and quote from the primary authority you used to answer this question.

11.6 Cite and quote from primary authority of your state that answers the following questions:

(a) Can a woman agree (for a fee) to bear the child of another woman using in vitro fertilization?

(b) Can a doctor assist a patient to commit suicide?

(c) Can a church be forced to pay taxes on profits from its bingo games?

(d) Can a local government use its zoning laws to try to close a bar that features topless dancers?

(e) Can a minor daughter challenge the validity of a deceased parent's will that leaves everything to the parent's pet cat?

(f) Can a burglar bring a civil suit against a homeowner for injuries received when the burglar fell because of a defective floor in the house being burglarized?

(g) Can a husband be prosecuted for raping his wife?

(h) Can a man prevent an abortion from being performed on the woman he impregnated when the woman is a mentally retarded, unmarried adult living with her parents, who are arranging the abortion?

(i) Can a parent invalidate the marriage of his 13-year-old daughter who married her first cousin, also 13 years old?

(j) Can a patient prevent his doctor from telling the patient's health insurance company about the patient's AIDS status?

11.7 Here are five separate queries. If they were run in either Westlaw or LexisNexis, what terms in documents would they find?

1. para!

2. assign!

3. crim!

4. legis!

5. e****e

CORE SKILL: WRITING

11.8 Write a memorandum of law based on the facts of one of the problems in Assignment 11.6. For the format of the memorandum, see Exhibits 7-9, 7-10, and 7-17 in Chapter 7. You can make up additional facts (e.g., the names of the parties and your supervisor and more details about the question asked).

CORE SKILL: ETHICS

11.9 The attorney for whom you work has a case before a court in your state. The attorney asks the court to award the client triple damages for the kind of injury caused by the opposing party. There is, however, a recent court opinion in the state that held that parties are not eligible for triple damages in this kind of case. The attorney does not tell the judge about this opinion and the opposing attorney is unaware of it because of sloppy legal research. What ethical rule has the attorney violated by failing to tell the judge about the opinion? Cite and quote from the specific ethics rule that applies in your state. See the discussion in Chapter 5 on the duty to disclose contrary authority. To find the ethics code in your state, see Appendix D and the Helpful Websites at the end of Chapter 5.

CORE SKILL: COMPUTERS

11.10 In Google, Bing, or Yahoo, run this search: compare fee legal databases research sites that cover both federal and state law. Write an essay in which you compare any three fee-based legal-research services. The comparisons should cover strengths, weaknesses, and costs of the three. For each of the three, you must cite at least two websites. In the Computer Terminology in the Law (CTL) notebook you started in Assignment 1.8 of Chapter 1, enter any new terms that you learned by doing this assignment.

CORE SKILL: COLLABORATION

11.11 This Chapter mentions several free and fee-based sites on which you can find the full text of primary authority, not just links to the laws. Your instructor will assign you one free and one fee-based full-text site. Answer the following questions about your two sites:

(a) What is the Web address of the site?
(b) What are its major features?
(c) Does the site have a citator? If so, how does it work?

Email your answers to each member of your class. Incorporate their answers into a report that covers your two sites and the sites assigned to other students.

THE JOB SEARCH

(The search for employment cannot wait until the end of a course or of a curriculum. It needs to begin now. The job-search assignments are designed to introduce you to different aspects of the job search and to build options for you to explore about employment.)

11.12 Create a blog on Google Blogspot that can be included on your resume. Call it YY's Legal Research Links for AA Law. For AA, substitute the name of your state. For YY, substitute your name or a made-up name. Use any of the sites from this chapter (and in Appendix J) as leads to law in your state. The entries on your blog should include both paper and online resources. For every entry, include a one-sentence description of what you are including. Your blog must cite a minimum of ten paper volumes and ten Internet sites. Try, however, to include more than the minimum. Your entries should include the constitution, statutes, court opinions, administrative regulations, administrative decisions, and local laws of your state. (See Exhibit 6-1 for the definitions of these primary authorities.) You can also include links to secondary authorities on the law of your state. (See the definitions of secondary authorities in Exhibit 11-6.) Here are resources on setting up a blog:

- Instructions for creating a blog (bloginstructions.blogspot.com)
- Tutorial on creating a blog (On YouTube, type this search: *blogspot tutorial*)

REVIEW QUESTIONS

1. Why should paralegals have a comprehensive knowledge of legal research?
2. Why can't legal research always provide definitive answers to legal problems?
3. What is the difference between the law you learn in school and the law you learn through legal research?
4. Is it a good idea to limit your research to areas in which you already have expertise?
5. When experts have done legal research, what conclusion should they always reach about the law they have researched?
6. What are the main categories of legal sites on the Internet?
7. What is the reliability of these categories?
8. What is a federal depository library?
9. What is the CARTWHEEL and what are its eight categories?
10. What are the two major categories of authority?
11. What is the distinction between mandatory and persuasive authority?
12. What is the Supremacy Clause?
13. When is state and federal law mandatory authority?
14. What is the hierarchy of authority among primary authorities?
15. What are the main categories of secondary authority?
16. What is a citation?
17. What are citation rules or laws that must be followed?
18. What are the two major citation guides?
19. What is the distinction between official and unofficial reporters?
20. What is a parallel cite?
21. What can you tell about the court that wrote an opinion if the abbreviation of one of the reporters is the abbreviation of a state?
22. When do you abbreviate the name of the court in the parentheses at the end of a cite to a case?
23. What is a pinpoint cite?
24. What is a public-domain cite?
25. Name three reporters for opinions of the U.S. Supreme Court and state whether each is official or unofficial.
26. Name three codes that contain the statutes of Congress and state whether each is official or unofficial.
27. What are a memorandum of law, appellate brief, and motion?
28. What is cite checking?
29. What is a table of authorities?
30. What is a short-form citation?
31. What are the functions of the three levels of legal research?
32. What are the major sources of background research?
33. When is meant by analogous and on point?
34. How do digests and A.L.R. annotations serve as case finders?
35. What information about a case do you seek when you want to know if it is still good law?
36. What is the function of a citator?
37. Name four citators.
38. What is meant by shepardizing?
39. What are slip laws, session laws, and statutory codes?
40. What is a pocket part?
41. What is an annotated statutory code?
42. What are notes of decisions?
43. What is legislative history?
44. What is a committee report?
45. What is an historical note?
46. What is a popular name?
47. What are some of the main fee-based legal-research services?
48. What is the distinction between natural-language and terms-and-connectors searching?
49. What is a universal character?
50. What is a root expander?
51. What is a research self-audit?

HELPFUL WEBSITES

Research Tutorials
- www.law.harvard.edu/library/research/tutorials
- library.uchastings.edu/research/tutorials/index.php
- www.law.uc.edu/library/circlulation/Legal-Research-Webinars
- www.law.georgetown.edu/library/research/tutorials
- library.law.yale.edu/introduction-legal-research-video-tutorials
- www.law.du.edu/index.php/library/research/tutorials /basic-legal-research-tutorial

Free Online Resources: General
- www.law.gmu.edu/library/research
- www.nyls.edu/library/library_services/dragnet1/dragnet
- blog.library.si.edu/2013/03/finding-current-research-online /#.UyuKVfldV8F

Links to Academic Law Library Resources (Links to the research resources of numerous law libraries)
- www.aallnet.org/sections/all/resources/Academic-Law-Libraries .html

American Law Reports (A.L.R.)
- en.wikipedia.org/wiki/American_Law_Reports
- law.lexisnexis.com/infopro/zimmermans/disp.aspx?z=1168

Citators
- www.law.depaul.edu/library/pdf/citators.pdf
- en.wikipedia.org/wiki/Citator
- lawlibguides.byu.edu/content.php?pid=225319&sid=1961819

Digests
- www.law.georgetown.edu/library/research/guides/digests.cfm
- libguides.law.ucla.edu

Looseleaf Services
- joneslawlibrary.org/jsllibrary/looseleafs.pdf
- www.law.depaul.edu/library/pdf/book_research.pdf

Legal Forms
- www.llrx.com/courtrules
- forms.findlaw.com
- forms.lp.findlaw.com
- www.legalforms.com

Legal Research Basics
- papers.ssrn.com/sol3/papers.cfm?abstract_id=2159932
- www.lawschool.cornell.edu/library/index2.cfm (type *resaerch basics* in the search box)

U.S. Supreme Court Oral Arguments (audio)
- www.supremecourt.gov/oral_arguments/argument_audio.aspx
- lawlibraryblog.seattleu.edu/tag/audio-recordings

Legal Periodicals
- scholar.google.com (select *Articles*)
- www.lawreview.org
- www.americanbar.org/aba.html (enter *online law review* in the search box)
- lawreviewcommons.com
- www.ssrn.com/en

Legal News
- www.abajournal.com
- legalnews.findlaw.com
- www.jurist.org

Legal Blawgs
- www.abajournal.com/blawgs
- blawgsearch.justia.com

Online Legal Dictionaries
- dictionary.findlaw.com
- dictionary.law.com
- www.nolo.com/dictionary
- www.law.cornell.edu/wex
- justice.law.stetson.edu/lawlib/Dictionaries.htm

Legal Research Competencies
- www.aallnet.org (type *competencies* in the search box)

Bluebook and ALWD Citation Resources
- citeuslegalus.com
- lawlibraryguides.bu.edu (click *Citation*)
- lib.law.washington.edu/ref/writing3.html
- lib.law.washington.edu/content/guides/bluebook-101
- www.law.georgetown.edu (enter *citation* in the search box)
- www.citestack.com/bluebook.htm

Crowdsourcing Legal Research
(sites that seek input from users)
- www.mootus.com
- www.casetext.com
- www.jurify.com

Public Records Search; Data and Statistics Sources
- See Helpful Websites at the end of Chapter 9

Useful Twitter Tags
- @LawLibCongress
- @LibraryStuff
- @legalresearchpl
- @Westlaw
- @LexisNexis
- #legalresearch
- #lawlibrary
- www.tagboard.com (type *legal research* in the search box)
- www.hashatit.com (type *legal research* in the search box)

Google, Bing, or Yahoo Searches
(On these search engines, run the following searches, using quotation marks and substituting your state for "aa" where indicated.)

- "legal research" aa
- legal citation aa
- finding court opinions cases aa
- finding statutes aa
- finding constitution aa
- finding court rules aa
- finding ordinances aa
- finding federal law
- finding international law
- "how to shepardize"
- using digests in legal research
- using ALR annotations in legal research
- legal research tutorial aa

ENDNOTES

[1] Technology Seen as a Major Driver of US Legislation, Regulations, PRWEB (February 19, 2014)

[2] Kentucky Revised Statutes, General Information (www.lrc.ky.gov /Statrev/general%20info.htm) (2014)

[3] American Association of Law Libraries, *Uniform Electronic Legal materials Act* (March 2014) (www.aallnet.org/Documents /Government-Relations/UELMA/UELMAFAQs.pdf)

[4] A Study of Attorneys' Legal Research Practices, 12 (American Association of Law Libraries, June 2013) (www.aallnet.org/sections/all /storage/committees/practicetf/final-report-07102013.pdf)

LEGAL WRITING

C H A P T E R   O U T L I N E

- Introduction
- Dangers of Copy and Paste
- Letter Writing

- Email Writing
- Instruments
- Pleadings
- Memorandum of Law

- Appellate Brief
- General Writing Guidelines

C H A P T E R   O B J E C T I V E S

After completing this chapter, you should be able to:

- Understand the importance of legal writing in the practice of law.
- Explain the different meanings of the phrase legal writing.
- Know the preliminary steps for all legal-writing assignments.
- Know the techniques of proofreading your own writing.

- Explain the dangers of copy-and-paste writing.
- List the different kinds of letters in a law office and their standard components.
- Write appropriate email posts.
- Explain the role of software and formbooks in the drafting of instruments and pleadings.

- List the major components of an appellate brief.
- Apply general guidelines for achieving clarity and precision in all categories of writing.

INTRODUCTION

Legal writing is an important skill in the practice of law. To a large extent, the legal profession lives by the written word. Any important task of an attorney, judge, or legislator is almost always heavily documented in writing. Everyone is reluctant to rely on oral communication alone. Consequently, a busy law office generates a vast quantity of paper—even in the age of digital communication. Once documents are prepared on a computer, they are often printed as **hard copy**, i.e., on paper.

Competent attorneys tend to be very particular about how something should be written. You need to learn the style of your supervising attorney, such as by reading documents he or she has written in prior client matters. A paralegal who works for more than one attorney should not expect that they would all have the same style. This can sometimes be disconcerting. What pleases one attorney may upset another.

d copy A paper copy of
nat has been prepared
n a computer. Also called
printout. A soft form of
xt is what exists on disk
· on a computer screen.

Before examining ways to cope in this environment, it is important to understand that the phrase *legal writing* can be used to describe different tasks:

- Preparing documents that require *legal analysis*
- Preparing documents that require *legal research*
- Making sure that legal documents conform to *special formats*
- Using clear and precise language to *communicate* effectively in any legal document

Although these four tasks are often interrelated, our primary focus in this chapter will be the latter two tasks: an introduction to the formats used in some of the documents commonly prepared in a law office and an overview of important general communication techniques that can improve writing in any legal document. Legal analysis is covered in Chapter 7. Legal research is covered in Chapter 11.

We begin with suggestions that can be helpful for all writing assignments in a law office. See Exhibit 12-1.

---

format (1) The way in which something is arranged, designed, or styled on a page. (2) In word processing, the layout of the page when printed, e.g., the font and margin settings.

font The design or style of printed letters of the alphabet, punctuation marks, or other characters.

point A measure of the size of printed letters of the alphabet, punctuation marks, or other characters. (One point is approximately 1/72 of an inch tall.) (See glossary for another meaning.)

draft (1) A document in one of its preliminary stages. (I was asked to proofread a draft of a contract before it was printed.) (2) To write. (She drafted a memorandum.)

Exhibit 12-1	Initial Steps when Receiving a Writing Assignment

1. Obtain basic instructions on the assignment you are given:
   - What are you asked to write? (Letter, memo, etc.?)
   - Who will be reading it? Who is the audience?
   - When is it due? Does it have priority over other assignments? (If you have assignments from different supervisors, ask the supervisors to establish the priorities; don't guess.)
   - Is your time working on this assignment billable? If so, to what clients or accounts?
   - What **format** should you use in the document you will be preparing? For example, what **font** and **point** size should you use?
   - What resources can you use? For example, if your assignment requires legal research, can you use fee-based electronic research, e.g., Westlaw (WestlawNext), LexisNexis (Lexis Advance), or Loislaw (see Chapters 11 and 13)?
   - Will the supervisor (or anyone else in the office) be available to provide feedback on a complete or partial **draft** of the assignment before the final product is due?
2. Find out if the office has its own style manual. Someone in the office may have collected general format instructions for different kinds of writing the office often prepares. Everyone may be expected to follow these instructions. The style manual may also include sample documents that conform to these instructions. If such a manual exists, it may be in a notebook or in a computer database.
3. Find out if the office uses any published texts as guides for commonly prepared documents. Is there a bar practice manual that is considered the bible for the procedural and substantive area of law involved in the assignment? Have courts in the state written a style manual (e.g. *Oregon Appellate Courts Style Manual*)? Are other guides favored by your supervisors (e.g., Bryan Garner's *The Redbook: A Manual of Style*)?
4. Ask your supervisor (or others) where in the office you can find copies of documents on other cases that you may be able to use as a model or guide for the document you are asked to prepare.
5. Once you have a model, adapt it to the specific facts and instructions of the writing assignment you are given. See "How to Avoid Abusing a Standard Form" in Exhibit 10-5 in Chapter 10.
6. For complex assignments or writing tasks that you have not performed before, seek early feedback before submitting the final draft. For example, prepare an outline of the document and ask for feedback on the outline to make sure you are on the right track. (This will not be needed for relatively simple documents or ones that you have prepared often in prior assignments.)
7. Carefully and regularly proofread to make sure there are no grammar or spelling errors in your final draft. See Exhibit 12-2 for self-proofreading techniques.

Exhibit 12-2	Proofreading Your Own Writing

Proofreading your own writing is an example of *self-editing.* The task is critical because it is very easy to overlook our own typos, spelling errors, grammar errors, and format inconsistencies. For many of us, the more familiar we are with the writing, the more likely we are to overlook problems in the writing.

Proofreading Techniques
- Do not do the proofreading immediately after you finish drafting the document. A short (or long) break, if possible, will help you look at the document with fresh eyes.

- If you wrote the document on the computer, print a draft of the document and do the proofreading on the hard copy of the draft. Do this in addition to proofing it on the screen.
- If possible, email the document to yourself so that you can proofread it as an email post.
- Quietly read your text aloud to yourself. This may turn up errors that were overlooked by silent reading and rereading.
- Make a copy and read the document to another person who will follow the text as you read.
- Reverse the steps. Have the other person read the document as you follow the text being read from the copy.
- On the computer, temporarily change the font and point size of the document. Also change the margins. If the document is single spaced, temporarily double-space it when you proofread it. Reading the document with these changes may help you identify errors.
- On a hard copy, reread it with a ruler or a blank sheet of paper beneath each line.
- Read your text backward. This might help reveal glaring errors in spelling or punctuation even though you are not reading for content.
- As you read, tap every word and punctuation with your finger or the eraser end of a pencil. For the same effect, use a felt pen to place a red dot over every word and punctuation mark as you read. Slowing down your reading this way can be beneficial.
- Spell checkers in **word processors** (see Chapter 13) are sometimes helpful. Be careful, however, in using a spell checker. It will tell you if you misspelled the word *there*, but it will not tell you if you should have used the word *their*. (For a list of such words that a spell checker won't catch, run this search in Google, Bing, or Yahoo: **homophone**.) If you asked your spell checker to check the sentence, "Due eye cents that you are a frayed?" you would be told that there are no spelling errors, although it should have read, "Do I sense that you are afraid?" Spell checkers are useful, but they cannot check the meaning or proper use of correctly spelled words.
- If you have grammar-checking software, use it even though it may be able to catch only basic grammatical errors. (Popular word-processing programs such as Word have built-in spell-check and grammar-check programs.)
- Proofread the document more than once.

DANGERS OF COPY AND PASTE

Today it is relatively rare for people to write with pen and paper. It does happen, but writing with computers is far more common. The major word processors (Word, Pages, WordPerfect) that we will discuss in Chapter 13 substantially increase the efficiency and speed of drafting, editing, and finalizing what we write. There are, however, dangers that must be avoided.

The first danger is **plagiarism**, which is passing off someone's original ideas or expressions as our own. It is very easy to go on the Internet and find text that is relevant to what we are writing. The text can be reports, **blogs**, essays, studies, etc. With little effort, we can highlight the text, copy (cut) it, and drop (paste) it in our own writing so that it appears as if that text is our own. It isn't.

To avoid plagiarism, cite the sources of the text you want to use. (See Chapter 11 on citation.) In some instances, however, citation is not enough. **Copyright** law may require permission to use the text. We are entitled to the **fair use** of portions of someone else's work, particularly if we are not writing for a commercial purpose. Furthermore, some written works are in the **public domain**, meaning that permission to use is not needed. (See the links on fair use and public domain in Helpful Websites at the end of the chapter.) Yet even if permission is not required, the failure to cite the source constitutes plagiarism.

Many colleges and other schools are so concerned about plagiarism that they use sophisticated software to detect it. They scan student writing into the software and quickly obtain a report on whether the writer may have plagiarized.

As we saw in Chapter 5, there are ethical rules against falsifying documents. One way to falsify a document is to allow readers to think that someone's else's idea or expression is our own when in fact it isn't. In short, don't misrepresent anything that you write.

The second danger of copy-and-paste writing is style. Assume that George Smith finds a few sentences or paragraphs on a website that are highly relevant to the theme of the paper he is writing. Assume further that George wants to use this text *without citing its source*. He wants the reader to think that all of the ideas in his paper are his own. He highlights it, copies it, and drops it in his paper. He then makes a few word changes and tries to conform the format of the Internet text to the format of what he is writing. For example, if the font of the text in the website is New Roman, 10 point and George's paper is using Courier New, 11 point, he

word processor Software that allows you to enter and edit data in order to create and revise documents. It processes words, allowing you to write sentences, paragraphs, and pages on the computer.

homophone Words that sound alike but have different meanings (e.g., aid/aide, prey/pray).

plagiarism Taking another's original ideas or expressions and using them as if they are one's own. One school defines plagiarism as "copying and representing as one's own the works of another in whole or in part regardless of whether such work is copyrighted; using the ideas of another without proper attribution; or any other effort to pass off the works of another, in whole or in part, as the work of the student." Cleveland-Marshall College of Law, Student Handbook 76 (2010–2011).

blogs An Internet journal or diary on any topic of interest to the blogger (writer) of the blog. Sometimes called *blawg* if the topic is mainly legal.

copyright (©) The exclusive right for a fixed number of years to print, copy, sell, or perform original works (17 U.S.C. § 101).

fair use The privilege of limited use of copyrighted material without permission of the copyright holder.

public domain Work product or other property that is not protected by copyright or patent. A status that allows use by anyone without fee.

changes the web language to Courier New, 11 point. Such changes, however, are usually not enough. Experienced readers say that it is relatively easy to detect the presence of text from other sources. To a trained eye, the style of someone else's writing is noticeably different from our own style despite efforts synchronize the styles.

Consequently, the ethical and safest course to follow is to cite what you want to use in your writing and to avoid using copyrighted material without permission.

Most of the legal writing in a law office falls into the following categories:

- Traditional Letters
- Emails
- Instruments

- Pleadings
- Memoranda of law
- Appellate briefs

LETTER WRITING

First we examine traditional letters—those that are sent on paper. A law office sends out different kinds of letters:

- Cover letter (transmittal letter)
- Demand letter
- Informational letter
- Status letter
- Confirmatory letter
- Opinion letter

There is overlap in these categories because a single letter may seek to accomplish more than one purpose. Exhibit 12-3 presents the standard components of many business letters. The sample letter in Exhibit 12-4 contains these components.

Exhibit 12-3	Standard Components of Many Business Letters

- *Heading.* The heading at the top of the letter contains the law office's letterhead, usually preprinted and centered. The letterhead identifies the office by full name, street address, phone number, fax number, Internet home page address, and email address. Attorney names are also preprinted on the letterhead.
- *Date.* Give the full date (month, day, and year) the letter will be sent. It is often placed flush left at the left margin under the heading. (*Flush left* means aligned along the left margin.)
- *Method of Delivery.* There is no need to indicate how the letter was delivered if the sender uses standard mail via the U.S. Postal Service. The sample letter in Exhibit 12-4 uses standard mail. If, however, another method is used, it should be indicated under the date (flush left). Options include in-person delivery (VIA HAND DELIVERY), special handling (VIA CERTIFIED MAIL), facsimile (VIA FACSIMILE), overnight carrier (VIA FEDEX), etc.
- *Recipient.* Give the full name, title, and address of the person who will be receiving the letter (the addressee). It is often placed at the left margin (flush left).
- *RE.* A reference line (RE) is a brief statement that indicates the case or matter to which the letter pertains, and occasionally the major theme of the letter. Example:

RE: Henderson v. Jones, Civ. 03.179.
Request for Extension of Time to
File Responsive Declaration

RE means *concerning* or *in the matter of* (RE is short for *in re*) The reference line is placed either (1) at the left margin (flush left) after the address of the recipient and just before the salutation or (2) at the right margin opposite the address of the recipient. (The example in Exhibit 12-4 uses the first option.)

- *Salutation.* Here, you address the recipient: Dear _____: A colon (:) follows the name of this person. If he or she is a doctor, professor, or important public official, use his or her title. The salutation starts at the left margin (flush left) on the line under the address.
- *Body.* The body of the letter often includes
  - *Identification line.* In the first line of the letter, let the reader know who is sending the letter, unless this is already obvious to the recipient because of prior contact.

- *Purpose line.* Shortly after the identification line, briefly tell the reader the main purpose of the letter.
- *Request line.* If you are asking the recipient to do something, include a specific request line that makes this clear.
- *Elaboration.* As needed, explain why you are writing the letter.
- *Courtesy conclusion.* As the end of the body, include a final courtesy paragraph. It might say something like "If you have any questions about this matter, please do not hesitate to contact me," or "Thank you for your consideration in this matter."

■ *Closing.* Close the letter with a complimentary close such as *Sincerely* or *Very Truly Yours.* Next comes space for a signature followed by the name and title of the signer. As we saw in Chapter 5 on ethics, when nonattorneys sign letters, their title should clearly indicate their nonattorney status. The titles *paralegal* and *legal assistant* comply with this ethical obligation. Titles such as *CLA, CP, RP, PACE,* and *PP,* when used alone, do not because they give no clear indication that the signer is not an attorney. (On the meaning of these abbreviations, see Exhibit 4-9 in Chapter 4.)

■ *Copies Sent.* If you are sending a copy of the letter to someone, indicate this by saying "cc:" followed by the name of the person(s) receiving the copy ("cc" stands for carbon copies; this abbreviation is still used even though carbon is seldom the method used today to make copies). Suppose you do not want the recipient to know that you are sending copies to others. On the recipient's letter, you say nothing about copies. On the office copy of the letter, say "bcc:" (blind carbon or courtesy copy) followed by the name of the person(s) receiving the copies. In this way, only your copy of the letter indicates who received bcc copies. The letter sent to the primary recipient is silent ("blind") on this point. (This also works with email messages. Beneath the cc box in your email program, you will find (or you can add) a bcc box. The main recipients of the message will not know the names of anyone entered in the bcc box.)

■ *Enclosures.* If you are enclosing something with the letter, say "Encl." If enclosing more than one item, say "Encls."

■ *Initials.* If someone else typed the letter for you, place your initials in capital letters, followed by a colon (:) and the initials (in lowercase) of the person who did the typing.

A **cover letter** (also called a *transmittal letter*) tells the recipient what physical items (e.g., pleadings, photographs) are being sent in the envelope or package and often the reason for sending them. The list of what is being sent should be detailed. If a response is expected, it should be clearly stated. For example:

Enclosed for your records are the following:

- A copy of the defendant's answer (4 pages; dated May 3, 2015) filed with the court on May 5, 2015
- A copy of our response to the answer (5 pages; dated May 18, 2015)

Also enclosed:

- A letter of authorization that allows us to obtain your confidential employment records from the personnel department.

Please read the letter of authorization, sign and date it, and return it to us. We will need it before May 30. If you have any questions, don't hesitate to call us.

A **demand letter** is an advocacy letter that asks the recipient to take specific action (e.g., pay a debt owed to the client) or to refrain from taking specific action (e.g., not to terminate the client). The letter will often

- Tell the recipient that the office represents the client.
- Specify what the recipient is being asked to do or to refrain from doing.
- Present essential facts and legal principles that support the demand.

If the recipient is a nonattorney, citations to authority are relatively rare except when a single statute or regulation is central to the demand. A demand letter seeking the collection of money must conform to the Fair Debt Collection Practices Act. For example, the letter must not use any "false, deceptive, or misleading representation or means in connection with the collection of any debt."[1]

An **informational letter** provides information to the recipient, seeks information from the recipient, or both. See Exhibit 12-4 for a sample informational letter. One category of informational letter is a **status letter** written to a client to inform him or her of what has happened in the case thus far and to indicate what next steps are expected.

cover letter A letter indicating what is being sent in the same envelope or package and often highlights its contents or purpose. Also called *transmittal letter.*

demand letter An advocacy letter that asks the recipient to take or refrain from specific action affecting the client, e.g., to compensate the client for harm allegedly caused by the recipient.

informational letter A letter that provides or seeks information.

status letter A letter that updates someone on a matter. Example: telling a client what has happened in the case thus far and what next steps are expected.

Exhibit 12-4	Example of an Informational Letter

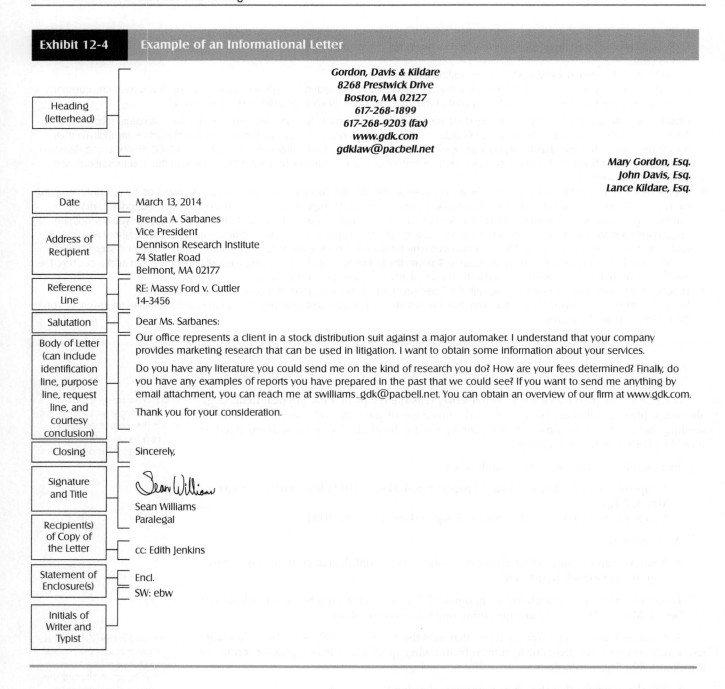

Heading (letterhead)

Gordon, Davis & Kildare
8268 Prestwick Drive
Boston, MA 02127
617-268-1899
617-268-9203 (fax)
www.gdk.com
gdklaw@pacbell.net

Mary Gordon, Esq.
John Davis, Esq.
Lance Kildare, Esq.

Date

March 13, 2014

Address of Recipient

Brenda A. Sarbanes
Vice President
Dennison Research Institute
74 Statler Road
Belmont, MA 02177

Reference Line

RE: Massy Ford v. Cuttler
14-3456

Salutation

Dear Ms. Sarbanes:

Body of Letter (can include identification line, purpose line, request line, and courtesy conclusion)

Our office represents a client in a stock distribution suit against a major automaker. I understand that your company provides marketing research that can be used in litigation. I want to obtain some information about your services.

Do you have any literature you could send me on the kind of research you do? How are your fees determined? Finally, do you have any examples of reports you have prepared in the past that we could see? If you want to send me anything by email attachment, you can reach me at swilliams_gdk@pacbell.net. You can obtain an overview of our firm at www.gdk.com.

Thank you for your consideration.

Closing

Sincerely,

Signature and Title

Sean Williams
Paralegal

Recipient(s) of Copy of the Letter

cc: Edith Jenkins

Statement of Enclosure(s)

Encl.
SW: ebw

Initials of Writer and Typist

---

confirmatory letter A letter that verifies or confirms that something important has been done or said.

In a **confirmatory letter**, you confirm that something important has been done or said.

Examples:

> This is to confirm that you have agreed to accept $5,000 in full settlement of the contract dispute between…

> Thank you for coming to the office on Tuesday to discuss the extension of insurance coverage for the employees in the Southeast region of your company's operations. I want to state my understanding of what took place at the meeting. Please let me know if the following summary is consistent with your understanding…

This kind of letter is important because it provides written confirmation of matters that might be subject to misunderstanding with the passage of time. It is also a good way to provide a record for the file and to prompt the recipient to voice any disagreements he or she may have with the contents of the letter.

In an **opinion letter**, the office writes to its client to explain the application of the law and to advise the client what to do. Giving such advice constitutes the practice of law. Opinion letters try to clarify technical material. Unlike an appellate brief or legal memorandum, the opinion letter does not make extensive reference to court opinions or statutes. The client's need is for clear, concise, practical advice.

opinion letter A letter to a client explaining the application of the law and providing legal advice based on that explanation.

EMAIL WRITING

Here are some important guidelines when writing emails:

- Find out what policy the office follows on email communications going out of the office. What can and cannot be done in emails? Are you allowed to send and receive personal emails on the email system of the office? When sending emails, what format should you use? For example, is there a standard signature line that prints the name of the office?
- If the email contains information about a case, it is probably confidential information. Have explicit permission from your supervisor on whether you can include such information in an email. Find out if the office requires emails to be **encrypted** so that they go out in a code and can be read only by persons with special software.
- Be aware that emails are not private, even those you are allowed to send on personal matters. Whatever is sent on company email systems is company property.
- Write a clear subject line to indicate what the email is about.
- Introduce yourself and state the purpose of the post (e.g., to request something) at the beginning of the message. If the message is long, the last paragraph should repeat the request.
- In general, avoid informality. For example, do not use breezy abbreviations such as BTY (by the way) or IMHO (in my humble opinion). Of course, avoid emoticons such as the smiley :-). Treat emails with the same seriousness as a business letter to a stranger.
- Avoid using special formatting features such as underlining. The recipient may not be able to read them on their email system.
- Address the recipient professionally with a formal salutation followed by a colon (e.g., Dear Mr. Foley:) unless the email is to someone you know well and is comfortable with first-name use.
- Use correct spelling and grammar. If the email program has built-in spell and grammar checkers, use them, but recognize their limitations. See Exhibit 12-2 on self-proofreading.
- Close the post by typing your full name and title. The title should indicate nonattorney status (e.g., paralegal).
- Because tone can't be heard in an email, there is a danger that anything strongly felt will be misinterpreted. When we speak, we rely on voice inflection and pace to communicate nuance. Doing the same in writing is very difficult. Caution, therefore, is needed.
- Do not write in all capitals for emphasis. (All caps reads as if you are shouting.)
- Avoid long sentences and long paragraphs. They are difficult to read on the screen.
- Use gender-neutral language (e.g., police officer rather than policeman).
- When you reply to an email, do not leave out the message thread. Your response should appear above the message that was sent to you.
- Most email programs have an auto-address feature that suggests names once you start typing any letter. Although convenient, there is a substantial possibility of the email going to unintended recipients. (See Chapter 5 on the ethical issues that result from the wrong people seeing or hearing what is said. Such mistakes can be a breach of confidentiality and result in the loss of the attorney-client privilege.) The problem is most serious when the email is going to more than one person. You can get distracted as the auto-address feature selects people it thinks you mean. Hence, before you hit the send button, say the name of each addressee aloud at least twice.
- Read the entire email twice before you hit the send button.
- If you have time, send the email to yourself before you send it to the addressee. Reading the email that comes back can be an excellent proofreading technique and a way to rethink the way you phrased and organized the post.

encrypt Convert text into a code that renders the text incomprehensible until it is reconverted to a readable format by a recipient with the right software.

instrument A formal written document that gives expression to or embodies a legal act or agreement, e.g., a contract, deed, will, lease, or mortgage.

transactional paralegal One who provides paralegal services for an attorney who represents clients in transactions such as entering contracts, incorporating a business, closing a real estate sale, or planning an estate. A paralegal who does not work in litigation.

templates A file containing text and a format that can be used as the starting point for creating frequently used documents.

pleading A formal litigation document filed by a party that states or responds to the claims and defenses the parties have against each other. The main pleadings are the complaint and answer.

memorandum (1) A short note. (2) A written record of a transaction. (3) A memorandum of law or legal memorandum, which is a written explanation of how one or more rules might apply to the facts of a client's case.

memorandum of law A written explanation of how one or more rules might apply to the facts of a client's case. Also called *memo* and *legal memorandum*.

brief A summary of a court opinion that consists of ten parts: citation, parties, objectives of the parties, theories of the litigation, history of the litigation, facts, issues, holdings, reasoning, and disposition. Also called *case brief, brief of a case*.

trial brief (1) An attorney's written presentation to a trial court of the legal issues and positions of his or her client (also called *trial memorandum*). (2) An attorney's personal notes on how he or she will conduct a particular trial (also called *trial manual, trial book*).

- Don't infect the office. Be suspicious of attachments sent to you. This includes attachments that appear to come from someone you know. An attachment might contain a virus. The sender may have captured someone's address book and sent the infected attachment to everyone on the list so that it appears to have come from a person on the list. Find out what virus protection the office uses for attachments.
- Include a copy of the message to yourself as a bcc.

INSTRUMENTS

An **instrument** is a formal written document that gives expression to or embodies a legal act or agreement. Examples of instruments include contracts, deeds, wills, leases, and mortgages. Paralegals who work with instruments are often called **transactional paralegals**.

Instruments are seldom drafted from scratch, particularly in law offices that have many clients with the same kind of case. An example is a real-estate practice where deeds, mortgages, leases, and related documents are often prepared. Most attorneys prefer to start with an already-prepared document or form that can be adapted to a current client than to start with a blank sheet of paper (or blank computer screen).

Formbooks and document-assembly software programs provide useful **templates** and forms. A template is a file containing text and a format that can be used as the starting point for creating frequently used documents such as instruments and pleadings. This output is then adapted to the facts of particular clients. Alternatively, the office can adapt documents already in its own computer files from prior client cases. Word processors can make needed adaptations with relative ease.

On adapting standard forms, see Exhibit 10-5 in Chapter 10.

PLEADINGS

A **pleading** is a formal litigation document filed by parties that state or respond to the claims and defenses they have against each other. The major pleadings are the complaint and the answer to the complaint. As indicated, pleadings, like instruments, are seldom drafted from scratch. Numerous sample pleadings can be found in formbooks and software programs. Law offices make extensive use of such samples for adaptation to the facts of current clients. See the discussion of pleadings, particularly the sample negligence complaint in Exhibit 10-6 in Chapter 10.

MEMORANDUM OF LAW

The word **memorandum** (*memo*) can mean a short note or a written record of a transaction. It can also mean **memorandum of law** or legal memorandum, which is a written explanation of how one or more rules might apply to the facts of a client's case. (The plural of memorandum is memoranda.)

See Chapter 7 where you will find an overview of the different kinds of memos along with sample memos (Exhibits 7-9, 7-10, and 7-17). Also covered in Chapter 7 are the phrasing of legal issues and the application of court opinions in memos.

APPELLATE BRIEF

As we saw in Chapter 7, the word *brief* has several meanings:

- *Case brief.* A **brief** is a summary of a court opinion that consists of ten parts: citation, parties, objectives of the parties, theories of the litigation, history of the litigation, facts, issues, holdings, reasoning, and disposition. To brief an opinion is to identify these ten parts. A brief is your own summary of the opinion for later use. You cannot apply an opinion unless you know how to brief it. We covered briefing cases in Chapter 7 (see Exhibits 7-13, 7-14, and 7-15 in Chapter 7).
- *Trial brief.* A **trial brief** has two main meanings. First, it is an attorney's written presentation to a trial court of the legal issues and positions of his or her client (also called *trial memorandum*). Second, the phrase can mean an attorney's personal notes on how he or

she will conduct a particular trial. The notes (often placed in a **trial notebook**) will relate to the opening statement, witnesses, exhibits, direct and cross-examination, closing argument, etc.

■ *Appellate brief.* An **appellate brief** is a document that a party files with an appellate court (and serves on an opponent). In the brief, the party presents arguments on why the appellate court should affirm (approve), reverse, vacate (cancel), or otherwise modify what a lower court has done. A main focus of the appellate brief is on the claimed errors made **below** by the lower court.

The appellate brief is one of the most sophisticated kinds of legal writing. If the office prepares many appellate briefs, extra copies might be stored in its **brief bank**, where they can be easily accessed to determine whether they can be adapted for future similar cases.

The first appellate brief that is submitted is the *appellant's* brief. The **appellant** (also called the *petitioner*) is the party initiating the appeal because of disagreement with a decision of a lower tribunal. Then the *appellee's* brief is filed in response. The appeal is taken against the **appellee** (also called the *respondent*). Finally, the appellant is often allowed to submit a **reply brief** to counter the position taken in the appellee's brief.

Occasionally, a court will permit a nonparty to the litigation to submit an appellate brief. This is referred to as an **amicus curiae** (friend of the court) **brief**. The *amicus* brief presents the nonparty's view on whether the appellate court should affirm, reverse, or otherwise modify what the lower court has done.

Not all appellate briefs have the same look. Court rules often specify:

■ the structure or format the brief should take
■ the print (point) size of the text
■ the maximum number of pages or words that can be used
■ the number of the copies to be submitted
■ the color of the paper that must be used for the title page
■ whether the brief can be submitted online as a **PDF** file, etc.

THE STRUCTURE OF AN APPELLATE BRIEF

■ Caption
■ Statement of Jurisdiction
■ Table of Contents (with point headings)
■ Table of Authorities (TOA)
■ Questions Presented

■ Statement of the Case
■ Summary of Argument
■ Argument
■ Conclusion
■ Appendixes (if needed)

■ *Caption:* The caption of an appellate brief states the names of the parties, the name of the court, the court file number or docket number of the case, and the kind of appellate brief it is. The caption goes on the title page (i.e., front cover) of the brief.

■ *Statement of Jurisdiction:* In this section of the brief, there is a short paragraph stating the **subject-matter jurisdiction** of the appellate court. For example:

> This Court has jurisdiction under 28 U.S.C. § 1291 (1997).

The jurisdiction statement may also give some of the essential facts that relate to the jurisdiction of the appellate court, such as how the case came up on appeal. For example:

> On January 2, 1998, a judgment was entered by the U.S. Court of Appeals for the Second Circuit. The U.S. Supreme Court granted certiorari on February 6, 1998. 400 U.S. 302.

Later in the brief there is a Statement of the Case, which often includes more detailed jurisdictional information.

■ *Table of Contents:* The table of contents is an outline of the major components of the brief, including **point headings**, and the page number in the brief on which each component begins. (A point heading is the party's conclusion it wants the court to adopt for a particular issue. Every word in a point heading is in capital letters. Point headings are printed in the table of contents and later in the body of the appellate brief itself.) The function of the table of contents is to provide the reader with quick

---

trial notebook A collection of documents, arguments, and strategies that an attorney plans to use during a trial. Also called *trial binder*.

appellate brief A document that a party files with an appellate court (and serves on an opponent) in which the party presents arguments on why the appellate court should affirm (approve), reverse, vacate (cancel), or otherwise modify what a lower court has done.

below Pertaining to a lower level of court in the hierarchy of a court system. (See glossary for another meaning.)

brief bank A collection of appellate briefs and related documents drafted in prior cases that might be adapted for current cases and used as models.

appellant The party bringing an appeal because of disagreement with a decision of a lower tribunal. Also called *petitioner*.

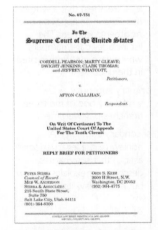

Front cover (title page) of an appellate brief submitted to the U.S. Supreme Court

Source: U.S. Supreme Court

appellee The party against whom an appeal is brought. Also called the *respondent*.

reply brief (1) An appellate brief of the appellant that responds to the appellate brief of the appellee. (2) Any appellate brief that responds to an opponent's appellate brief.

amicus curiae brief ("friend of the court" brief) An appellate brief submitted by a nonparty who obtains court permission to file a brief presenting its views on how the case should be resolved.

PDF (portable document format) A file format consisting of an electronic image of a document that preserves the features and styles of the document (e.g., its line spacing, photograph placement, and font size) that existed before it was converted into a digital document.

subject-matter jurisdiction The court's power to resolve a particular type of legal dispute and to grant a particular type of relief.

point heading A conclusion that a party wants a court to accept on one of the issues in the case.

table of authorities (TOA) A list of primary authority (e.g., cases and statutes) and secondary authority (e.g., legal periodical articles and legal treatises) that a writer has cited in an appellate brief or other document. The list includes page numbers where each authority is cited in the document.

primary authority A law written by one of the three branches of government.

secondary authority A nonlaw (e.g., a legal periodical article) that summarizes, describes, or explains the law but is not a law itself.

and easy access to each portion of the brief. Because the page numbers will not be known until the brief is completed, the table of contents is the last section of the brief to be written. Exhibit 12-5 is an excerpt from the brief of the respondent (appellee). It illustrates the structure of a table of contents that includes the point headings as part of the "argument."

Exhibit 12-5	Table of Contents (with Point Headings) in an Appellate Brief

TABLE OF CONTENTS

- *Table of Authorities:* The **table of authorities (TOA)** lists all the **primary authority** (e.g., cases, statutes, administrative regulations, administrative decisions, constitutional provisions, charter provisions, ordinances, and court rules), and **secondary authority** (e.g., legal periodical articles and legal treatises) cited in the brief. All the cases are listed in alphabetical order, all the statutes are listed in alphabetical and numerical order, etc. The page numbers on which each of these authorities is discussed in the brief are presented so that the table acts as an index to these authorities, as shown in Exhibit 12-6. The major word processing programs (e.g., Word and WordPerfect) include built-in assistance for creating tables of authorities. See the sites mentioned in "Helpful Websites" at the end of the chapter.)

Exhibit 12-6	Table of Authorities in an Appellate Brief

TABLE OF AUTHORITIES

- *Questions Presented:* The label used for the **questions presented** section of the brief varies. Other names for it include "Points Relied On for Reversal," "Points in Error," "Assignments of Error," and "Issues Presented." Regardless of the label, its substance is essentially the same. It is a statement of the legal issues that the party wishes the appellate court to consider and decide.

- *Statement of the Case:* The **statement of the case** has two main components. The first is a summary of the procedural history of the dispute—what has happened in the lower courts and in the current court up to the time the brief is filed. The second is a presentation of the essential facts of the case. The statement of the case may also include the basis of the appellate court's subject-matter jurisdiction to hear the appeal. Exhibit 12-7 presents an example of a statement of the case. Note that the statement provides specific page references to the trial **transcript** (often abbreviated "Tr."). A transcript is a word-for-word account of something. Throughout the appellate brief, references to what occurred during the trial (e.g., the testimony of a particular witness, or a motion made by counsel) should be accompanied by cites to pages of the transcript on which those occurrences are recorded.

questions presented A statement of the legal issues in an appellate brief that a party wants the appellate court to resolve.

statement of the case The portion of an appellate brief that summarizes the procedural history of the case to date and presents the essential facts of the dispute. It may also state the appellate court's subject-matter jurisdiction.

transcript A word-for-word account of what was said. A written copy of what was said.

Exhibit 12-7	Statement of the Case in an Appellate Brief

STATEMENT OF THE CASE

This action is based on the Federal Tort Claims Act, 28 U.S.C. § 1346(b), initiated by the appellants, Garrett Freight Lines, Inc., and Charles R. Thomas in the United States District Court for the District of Idaho. The appellant alleged that appellee's employee, Randall W. Reynolds, while acting within the scope of his employment, negligently caused injury to appellants. The United States denied that the employee was acting within the scope of his employment.

On March 27, 2008, appellant Garrett made a motion for limited summary judgment on whether Reynolds was acting within the scope of his employment when the collision occurred. The actions of Garrett and Thomas were consolidated by order of the court, and appellee later moved for summary judgment (Tr. p. 204).

The District Court held, under the authority of *Berrettoni v. United States*, 436 F.2d 1372 (9th Cir. 1970), that Reynolds was not within the scope of his employment when the accident occurred and granted appellee's motion for summary judgment. It is from that order and judgment that the injured now appeals.

Staff Sergeant Reynolds was a career soldier in the United States Military and, until November 9, 2005, stationed at Fort Rucker, Alabama. On or about July 30, 2005, official orders directed that Reynolds be reassigned to Japan, which occurred on....

- *Summary of Argument:* The major points to be made in the brief are summarized in this section.

- *Argument:* In the Argument, the attorney explains the legal positions of the client. The positions are presented in the order of the point headings listed in the table of contents. The point headings are printed in the body of the argument exactly as they are printed in the table of contents. All the primary and secondary authority relied on are analyzed.

- *Conclusion:* The conclusion states what action the attorney is asking the appellate court to take.
- *Appendixes:* If needed, the appendixes contain excerpts from statutes or other primary authority, excerpts from the trial transcript, charts, descriptions of exhibits entered into evidence at the trial, etc.

GENERAL WRITING GUIDELINES

A law professor once famously said: "There are two things wrong with almost all legal writing. One is its style. The other is its content."[2] Too often legal writing is "intentionally verbose and obscure, to distinguish lawyers from [the general public]. Only another lawyer could understand the lengthy documents filled with Latin and legalese, thereby ensuring that all parties would seek legal counsel."[3]

Equally serious is the complaint that legal writing is often deficient in writing basics. In 2011, the U.S. Court of Appeals for the Seventh Circuit chastised an attorney for submitting a complaint that had "rampant" grammatical errors. Noting the lack of punctuation, the court said that "[a]t least 23 sentences contained 100 or more words." An isolated case? Not so. The court said, "We acknowledge the unfortunate reality that poor writing occurs too often in our profession."[4] In the same year, the U.S. Court of Appeals for the Fifth Circuit said,

> Usually we do not comment on technical and grammatical errors, because anyone can make such an occasional mistake, but here the miscues are so egregious and obvious that an average fourth grader would have avoided most of them. For example, the word "principals" should have been "principles." The word "vacatur" is misspelled. The subject and verb are not in agreement in one of the sentences, which has a singular subject ("incompetence") and a plural verb ("are").[5]

Recently a large group of future attorneys in law school was given a straightforward grammar and spelling test. The results were discouraging:

- 68% thought that "between you and I" was grammatically correct.
- 84% thought "principle" meant main or primary.
- 85% did not know that the pronoun reference in the following sentence was incorrect: "A student came into the facility without realizing that they needed a pass."
- 94% thought that teachers "illicit" responses from their students.
- 62% thought that the letterhead of a law firm was "stationary."
- 97% could not identify and correct the misuse of the passive voice.[6]

Would you make the same errors?

———————————————

SELF-IMPROVEMENT

Review the self-improvement suggestions on grammar, spelling, and composition presented before Chapter 1 in "How to Study Law in the Classroom and on the Job."

Also, the writing assignments after each chapter cover core writing topics, particularly grammar basics on commas, semicolons, and topic sentences. You should do the assignments whether or not they are required for your course.

GUIDELINES

Everything you write, including email messages, should meet the high standards of communication that will be expected of you as a law-office professional. Here are some guidelines to help you with this objective. Most of the guidelines involve style such as word choice. These are important, but not as important as the grammar and composition guidelines that are the basis of the core writing assignments at the end of every chapter in the book.

1. *Do not use circumlocutions.*

A **circumlocution** is the use of more words than needed to express something. An example is the use of a pair of words that have the same effect. Here is a list of circumlocutions commonly found in the law. Avoid using them. Pick one of the words and discard the other.

circumlocution The use of more words than are needed to express something.

Do not say:	Say:	Or say:
alter and change	alter	change
any and all	any	all
by and with	by	with
each and every	each	every
final and conclusive	final	conclusive
full and complete	full	complete
made and entered into	made	entered
order and direct	order	direct
over and above	over	above
sole and exclusive	sole	exclusive
type and kind	type	kind
unless and until	unless	until

If language adds nothing to the sentence, don't use it. There is an easy test to find out if a phrase, clause, or sentence uses language that adds nothing. Remove it and ask yourself whether you have altered the meaning or emphasis desired. If not, keep it out.

Compare the sentences in these two columns:

Your maximum recovery is $100 under the provisions of the Warsaw Convention.	Your maximum recovery is $100 under the Warsaw Convention.

When we remove "the provisions of" from the first sentence, we lose neither meaning nor emphasis. Hence we don't need it.

Use the language in the second column unless you have a valid reason to use the language in the first column:

Do not say:	Say:
(1) all of the	(1) all the
(2) by means of	(2) by *or* with
(3) does not operate to	(3) does not
(4) despite the fact that	(4) because
(5) due to the fact that	(5) because
(6) during the course of	(6) during
(7) in light of	(7) because
(8) in the time of	(8) during
(9) in order to	(9) to
(10) or in the alternative	(10) or
(11) owing to the fact that	(11) because
(12) period of time	(12) period *or* time
(13) prior to	(13) before
(14) provision of law	(14) law
(15) State of New Jersey	(15) New Jersey
(16) subsequent to	(16) after
(17) until such time as	(17) until

2. *Use shorter words when longer ways of expressing the same idea add nothing.*

Use the language in the second column unless you have a valid reason to use the language in the first column:

Do not say:	*Say:*
(1) adequate number of	(1) enough
(2) at such time as	(2) when
(3) at the present time	(3) now
(4) because of the fact that	(4) because
(5) call your attention to the fact that	(5) remind you
(6) during such time as	(6) while
(7) enter into a contact	(7) contract (verb)
(8) for a period of	(8) for
(9) for the duration of	(9) during
(10) for the purpose	(10) for
(11) for the purpose of entering	(11) to enter
(12) for the reason that	(12) because
(13) give consideration to	(13) consider
(14) give recognition to	(14) recognize
(15) have need of	(15) need
(16) in case	(16) if
(17) in a number of	(17) in some
(18) in cases in which	(18) when
(19) in connection with	(19) in *or* on
(20) in many cases	(20) often *or* sometimes
(21) in many instances	(21) often *or* sometimes
(22) in my considered opinion	(22) I think
(23) in regard to	(23) about
(24) in relation to	(24) about *or* toward
(25) in the case of	(25) if *or* in
(26) in the event of *or* that	(26) if
(27) in the matter of	(27) in *or* on
(28) in the nature of	(28) like
(29) in the majority of instances	(29) usually *or* most often
(30) in view of	(30) because
(31) is able to	(31) can
(32) is applicable	(32) applies
(33) is binding on	(33) binds
(34) is dependent on	(34) depends on
(35) is entitled to	(35) may
(36) is permitted to	(36) may
(37) is required to	(37) shall
(38) is unable to	(38) cannot
(39) is directed to	(39) shall
(40) it is your duty to	(40) you shall
(41) make an appointment of	(41) appoint
(42) make a determination of	(42) determine
(43) make application	(43) apply

Do not say:	*Say:*
(44) make payment	(44) pay
(45) make provision for	(45) provide for
(46) on a few occasions	(46) occasionally
(47) on behalf of	(47) for
(48) on the part of	(48) by *or* among
(49) prohibited from	(49) shall not
(50) provided that	(50) if
(51) the question as to whether	(51) whether
(52) with reference to	(52) on
(53) with the exception that	(53) except

3. *Use a less complicated or less fancy way of expressing the same idea when meaning or emphasis is not lost.*

Use the language in the second column unless you have a valid reason to use the language in the first column:

Do not say:	*Say:*
(1) accorded	(1) given
(2) afforded	(2) given
(3) afford an opportunity	(3) allow, *or* let
(4) approximately	(4) about
(5) attempt (verb)	(5) try
(6) at the time	(6) when
(7) cause it to be done	(7) have it done *or* do it
(8) commence	(8) begin
(9) contiguous to	(9) touching
(10) deem	(10) consider
(11) endeavor (as a verb)	(11) try
(12) evince	(12) show
(13) expiration	(13) end
(14) expires	(14) ends
(15) forthwith	(15) immediately
(16) have knowledge of	(16) know
(17) in accordance with	(17) under
(18) in the interest of	(18) for
(19) is authorized to	(19) may
(20) is directed to	(20) shall
(21) is empowered to	(21) may
(22) is entitled (for a name)	(22) is called
(23) is hereby authorized	(23) may
(24) is not prohibited	(24) may
(25) of service to	(25) serves
(26) per annum	(26) per year
(27) render service	(27) give service

4. Words to Avoid (Without a Good Reason to Use Them)

- abeyance
- above [as an adjective]
- above-mentioned
- afore-granted
- aforementioned
- aforesaid
- before-mentioned
- henceforward
- hereby
- herein
- hereinafter

- hereinbefore
- hereunto
- pursuant
- said (as a substitute for the, that, or those)
- same (as a substitute for it, he, him, she, or her)
- thenceforth
- thereunto
- therewith
- to wit

- under-mentioned
- unto
- whatsoever
- whensoever
- wheresoever
- whereas
- whereof
- whosoever
- within-named
- witnesseth

5. *Use action verbs and adjectives.*

Avoid **nominalizations**, which are nouns formed from verbs or adjectives. Examples:

nominalizations A noun formed from a verb or adjective.

- the noun *consideration* from the verb *consider.*
- the noun *effectiveness* from the adjective *effective.*

term of art A word or phrase that has a special or technical meaning.

Nominalizations are not grammatically incorrect. In most cases, however, they weaken a sentence. Unfortunately, the legal profession is addicted to nominalizations. Avoid this addiction yourself.

Note, however, that if a word or phrase is a **term of art**, you need to use it even if it is a nominalization or is awkward or verbose. The word *consideration*, for example, is a contract term that means something of value exchanged between the parties. In the following sentence, the word is used correctly:

- The agreement failed because of inadequate consideration.

When *consideration* is used as a substitute for the word *consider*, the word is a nominalization that generally should be avoided.

Weak: After consideration of the proposals by the parties, the meeting ended.
Better: After the parties considered the proposals, the meeting ended.

Compare the sentences in these two columns:

A	B
He came to the realization that the effort is futile	He realized the effort is futile.
She made the decision to retire.	She decided to retire.
A determination of who should pay was made by the court.	The court determined who should pay.

The nominalizations in column A are *realization*, *decision*, and *determination*. The sentences in column B use verbs (*realized*, *decided*, and *determined*) and are more forceful and direct. The sentences in column A that use the nominalizations are more stilted and verbose. Using nominalizations often leads to longer words and longer sentences. It also encourages the use of the passive voice (in the third example), as we will see. Hence avoid nominalizations unless they are terms of art.

Do not say:	*Say:*
(1) give consideration to	(1) consider
(2) give recognition to	(2) recognize
(3) have knowledge of	(3) know
(4) have need of	(4) need
(5) in the determination of	(5) determine
(6) is applicable	(6) applies

(7) is dependent on	(7) depends on
(8) is in attendance at	(8) attends
(9) make an appointment of	(9) appoint
(10) make application	(10) apply
(11) make payment	(11) pay
(12) make provision for	(12) provide for
(13) make an analysis	(13) analyze

6. *Use active voice.*

Use **active voice** rather than **passive voice** by making the doer of the action the main focus of the sentence. Compare the sentences in the following two columns:

A (passive voice)	*B (active voice)*
The decision was announced by the judge.	The judge announced the decision.
The report will be prepared.	I will prepare the report.
The court was cleared.	The clerk cleared the court.
The strike was ended by the injunction.	The injunction ended the strike.
By Friday, the bridge will have been blown up by the workers.	By Friday, the workers will have blown up the bridge.

active voice The grammatical verb form in which the subject or thing performing or causing the action is the main focus.

passive voice The grammatical verb form in which the object of the action is the main focus. The emphasis is on what is being done rather than on who or what is performing or causing the action.

The verbs in the sentences in the A column are in the passive voice. The verbs in the sentences in the B column are in the active voice. Sentences with verbs in the *passive voice* have the following characteristics:

- The doer of the action is either unknown or given less emphasis than what was done.
- The doer of the action, if referred to at all, is mentioned after the action itself.
- The subject of the sentence receives the action. The subject is acted upon.

If you do not mention the doer of the action in the sentence, the verb form is a **truncated passive**. In the following sentence, for example, you don't know who fired Jim:

- The report will be prepared.
- The court was cleared.
- Jim was fired at noon.

truncated passive A form of passive voice in which the doer or subject of the action is not mentioned.

Sentences with verbs in the *active voice* have the following characteristics:

- The doer of the action is the important focus.
- The doer of the action is mentioned before the action itself.
- The subject of the sentence performs the action. The subject is the doer of the action.

The passive voice is often less effective because it is less direct and often less clear. It can dilute the forcefulness of a statement.

Weak: It is no longer allowed to take law library books overnight.
Better: The law library no longer allows you to take books overnight.
Or: The law library no longer allows students to take books overnight.

The action in these sentences is the prohibition on taking books overnight. In the rewrites, we know who has performed this action—the law library. In the first sentence, we are not sure. The subject (and center of attention) in the rewrites is the law library; the subject (and center of attention) in the first sentence is the prohibition—the action.

Of course, there are times when a speaker or writer wants to hide behind the haziness of the passive voice. A glaring example is when politicians are charged with improprieties and respond with vague generalities:

"Mistakes have been made."

7. *Use positive statements.*

Phrase something positively rather than negatively whenever possible.

Do not say:	*Say:*
It is not difficult to imagine.	It is easy to imagine.
The paper is not without flaws.	The paper has flaws.

Whenever possible, replace a negative phrase with a single word that has the same meaning.

Do not say:	*Say:*
(1) not able	(1) unable
(2) not accept	(2) reject
(3) not certain	(3) uncertain
(4) not unlike	(4) similar *or* alike
(5) does not have	(5) lacks
(6) does not include	(6) excludes *or* omits
(7) not many	(7) few
(8) not often	(8) rarely
(9) not the same	(9) different
(10) not...unless	(10) only if
(11) not...until	(11) only when

When asked about the questionable fundraising activities of a supporter, President Bill Clinton said,

"I had no reason to believe that he didn't know what the law was and wouldn't follow it."[7]

Alternatively, the president could have said,

"I expected him to follow the law."

8. *Use shorter sentences.*

There is no rule on how long a sentence must be. In general, however, the longer a sentence is, the more difficult it is to follow. Although readers are able to understand most long sentences, such sentences tend to tax the patience of readers unduly. As a general guideline, try to avoid sentences longer than twenty-five words. Some authorities are even stricter. Judge Arthur Gilbert, for example, says, "If a sentence has more than twenty words, it usually needs to be redrafted."[8] Unfortunately, sentences are almost always too long in legal writing. Here is an example from a legal memorandum. In the rewrite, we have broken a fifty-seven–word sentence into four smaller, more readable sentences.

Weak: Claims for child support were not fully and finally adjudicated pursuant to a North Carolina divorce judgment where the North Carolina court did not have personal jurisdiction over the husband and could not adjudicate any child support claims without this kind of jurisdiction and therefore Florida is not precluded from collecting monies from the husband toward arrearages.

Better: The North Carolina divorce judgment did not fully and finally adjudicate the claims for child support. The reason is that the North Carolina court did not have personal jurisdiction over the husband. It could not adjudicate child support claims without this jurisdiction. Florida is therefore allowed to collect monies from the husband toward arrearages.

Other examples:

Weak: In May of 2013, a district personnel administrator informed Mary Miller that the district had decided to transfer her to a different school, which was a decision that was based on information Miller provided, however the administrator had never talked to Miller in person prior to the decision.

Better: In May of 2013, a district personnel administrator informed Mary Miller that the district will transfer her to a different school. The district based its decision on information Miller provided. The administrator, however, never talked to Miller in person prior to the decision.

Weak: Her new job at the firm as the legal administrator in charge of personnel and finances was enjoyable, lucrative, educational, and challenging, but confusing and frightening at times.

Better: Her new job at the firm as legal administrator in charge of personnel and finances was enjoyable, lucrative, educational, and challenging. At times, however, it was also confusing and frightening.

Weak: The final issue for discussion concerns the status of the national and international parties that has been the main stumbling block in the contract negotiations thus far.

Better: The final issue for discussion is the status of the national and international parties. This issue has been the main stumbling block in contract negotiations thus far.

9. *Be careful with pronoun references.*

Avoid pronouns (e.g., *he, she, it, they*) unless the nouns to which the pronouns refer are clear. Using pronouns with ambiguous referents can confuse the meaning of a sentence. If the pronoun could refer to more than one person or object in a sentence, repeat the name of the person or object to avoid ambiguity.

> **Do Not Say:** After the administrator appoints a deputy assistant, he shall supervise the team. [Who does the supervising? The administrator or the deputy? If the latter is intended, then]
>
> **Say:** After the administrator appoints a deputy assistant, the deputy assistant shall supervise the team.

When a writer uses pronouns, their *antecedents* (what the pronouns stand for) must be clear.

10. *Avoid sexism in language.*

Avoid gender-specific language when the intent is to refer to both sexes. If neutral language is not available, rewrite the sentence to avoid the problem.

Gender-Specific Language	*Gender-Neutral Alternatives*
(1) actress	(1) actor
(2) businessman	(2) executive, member of the business community
(3) chairman	(3) chairperson, chair, moderator, head, presiding officer
(4) clergyman	(4) minister, priest, rabbi, member of the clergy
(5) crewman	(5) crew member
(6) draftsman	(6) drafter, writer
(7) fireman	(7) firefighter
(8) foreman	(8) supervisor, manager
(9) man	(9) person, human, humankind
(10) man-hours	(10) worker hours
(11) mankind	(11) humanity, human race, people
(12) manpower	(12) workforce, personnel
(13) policeman	(13) officer, police officer
(14) mailman	(14) letter carrier, postal worker
(15) salesman	(15) seller, sales representative
(16) reasonable man	(16) reasonable person
(17) waitress, waiter	(17) server

parallelism Using a consistent (i.e., parallel) grammatical structure when phrasing logically related ideas in a list.

11. *Follow the rule of parallelism.*

   Parallelism means using a consistent (i.e., parallel) grammatical structure when phrasing logically related ideas in a list.

■ The following sentence is not parallel because the list uses two *ing* words (driving, skiing) and one infinitive (to read).

   The defendant enjoys driving, skiing, and to read.

Corrections that make the sentence parallel:

   The doctor enjoys driving, skiing, and reading.

   The doctor likes to drive, ski, and read.

■ The following sentence is not parallel because the list contains two clauses in the active voice and one in the passive voice:

   The attorney expected to present the case to the jury, make closing arguments, and have questions asked of him.

Corrections that make the sentence parallel:

   The attorney expected to present the case to the jury, make closing arguments, and answer questions.

■ Not parallel:

   The nationalities of reporters in the room consisted of the French, the Russians, Spanish, and there were Greeks.

Corrections that make the sentence parallel:

   The nationalities of reporters in the room consisted of the French, the Russians, the Spanish, and the Greeks.

   The nationalities of reporters in the room were French, Russian, Spanish, and Greek.

12. *Use plain English*

   In the 1970s, the plain-English or plain-language movement began, with the goal of adding greater clarity to our written communication, particularly commercial and government communication. The federal government and more than half the states passed laws requiring certain documents (e.g., insurance contracts and securities disclosure statements) to be written in plain English. In general, the components of plain English are those that we have been discussing in this chapter:

   ■ Avoid long sentences.
   ■ Use the active voice rather than the passive voice.
   ■ Use strong verbs rather than nominalizations.
   ■ Avoid superfluous words.
   ■ Phrase things positively.
   ■ Avoid multiple negatives.

Some of the laws impose a *readability* level based in part on the number of words used in sentences or the average number of syllables per word. The lower the number of words a document uses in its sentences, on average, the better the overall readability score the document will have. (Readability refers to the ease with which someone can read a passage.) One way to force writers to use shorter sentences is to mandate that the document have a specified readability score.

   The Plain Language Consumer Contract Act contains guidelines a court must consider when determining whether a contract is written in plain language. Here, for example, are the guidelines for contracts in Pennsylvania:

   1. The contract should use short words, sentences, and paragraphs.
   2. The contract should use active verbs.
   3. The contract should not use technical legal terms, other than commonly understood legal terms, such as mortgage, warranty, and security interest.

4. The contract should not use Latin or foreign words or any other word whenever its use requires reliance upon an obsolete meaning.
5. If the contract defines words, the words should be defined by using commonly understood meanings.
6. The contract should not use sentences that contain more than one condition.
7. The contract should not use cross-references, except cross-references that briefly and clearly describe the substance of the item to which reference is made.
8. The contract should not use sentences with double negatives or exceptions to exceptions.[9]

Plain-English laws do not apply to most of the kinds of writing prepared in a law office, such as a memorandum of law or appellate brief. The laws are designed to help citizens understand written materials prepared by governments and by businesses. Yet the writing principles proposed by the plain-English movement can be applied to *any* writing. It would be a high compliment to say of any document prepared by an attorney or paralegal (particularly a document that covers complex legal material) that it was written in plain English.

13. *100+ Commonly Misspelled Words*

Avoid spelling errors. The best way to overcome commonly misspelled words is to memorize the correct spelling. In the following list, the correct spelling of a word is followed by frequent misspellings of that word.

- absence (absense)
- acceptable (acceptible)
- accidentally (accidentaly)
- accommodate (accomodate)
- accumulate (acumulate)
- achievement (acheivement)
- acquaintance (acquaintence)
- acquitted (acquited)
- advice (as a noun) (advise)
- advise (as a verb) (advice)
- amateur (amater)
- analyze (analyse)
- apparatus (apparatis)
- attendance (attendence)
- balance (balence)
- beginning (begining)
- believe (beleive)
- beneficial (benificial)
- calendar (calander)
- cemetery (cemitery)
- changeable (changable)
- chose (past tense) (choose)
- choose (present tense) (chose)
- commission (commision)
- compelled (compeled)
- conceivable (conceivible)
- conceivable (concievable)
- conferred (confered)

- conscience (consience)
- conscientious (conscientous)
- conscious (conscous)
- controversial (controversal)
- criticize (criticise)
- deferred (defered)
- definitely (definitly)
- desperate (despirate)
- discipline (disipline)
- dissatisfied (disatisfied)
- eligible (eligable)
- embarrass (embarass)
- eminent (eminint)
- encouragement (encouragment)
- environment (enviroment)
- equipped (equiped)
- especially (especialy)
- exaggerate (exagerate)
- exceed (excede)
- fascinate (fasinate)
- February (Febuary)
- forty (fourty)
- government (goverment)
- grammar (grammer)
- grandeur (grandor)
- guarantee (guarante)
- harassment (harasment)
- heroes (heros)
- hindrance (hindrence)
- humorous (humerous)
- hypocrisy (hypocricy)
- incidentally (incidentaly)
- incredible (incredable)

- independence (independance)
- inevitable (inevitible)
- laboratory (labratory)
- leisure (liesure)
- liaison (laision)
- license (licence)
- lightning (weather condition) (lightening)
- lightening (make brighter) (lightning)
- maintenance (maintenence)
- maneuver (manuver)
- mischievous (mischivous)
- misspelled (mispelled)
- necessary (necesary)
- neighbor (nieghbor)
- ninety (ninty)
- noticeable (noticable)
- occasionally (occasionaly)
- occurred (occured)
- occurrence (occurence)
- omitted (omited)
- pastime (pasttime)
- performance (performence)
- permissible (permissable)
- perseverance (perseverence)
- possession (possesion)
- practically (practicaly)
- precedence (precedance)
- preference (preferance)
- preferred (prefered)
- prevalent (prevalant)
- profession (profesion)

- quizzes (quizes)
- recommend (recomend)
- reference (referance)
- referring (refering)
- salary (salery)
- separate (seperate)
- separation (seperation)
- sergeant (sergent)

- shining (shinning)
- sophomore (sophemore)
- specifically (specificaly)
- succession (succesion)
- supersede (supercede)
- temperamental (tempramental)
- tendency (tendancy)

- transferring (transfering)
- truly (truely)
- unnecessary (unnecesary)
- until (untill)
- usually (usualy)
- weird (wierd)

14. *Grammar Saves Lives*

Finally, examine how punctuation in the following sentences dramatically changes the meaning of the sentence. The last example proves that good grammar can save lives.

The defendant said the witness lied.

Woman without her man is nothing.

Let's eat grandma.

The defendant, said the witness, lied.

Woman, without her, man is nothing.

Let's eat, grandma.

CHAPTER SUMMARY

Legal writing is critical in the practice of law. The phrase *legal writing* can refer to preparing documents that require legal analysis or legal research. It can also refer to special formats for legal documents and general communication techniques for any kind of writing. When given a writing assignment, determine basics such as the audience, due date, models to use, and availability of resources and feedback before the due date. Proofreading should allow you to spot typos, spelling errors, grammar errors, and format inconsistencies. Some of the major techniques of self-proofreading include reading a hard copy of the draft, reading it aloud to yourself and to another person, reading it in a different font and point size, and reading it backward.

The two main dangers of copy-and-paste writing are plagiarism (the failure to cite sources) and style inconsistency (the text pasted in does not adequately conform to the style of the writing into which it is pasted—copied).

Law offices often write traditional letters, emails, pleadings, instruments, memoranda of law, and appellate briefs. The standard components of most letters are heading, date, method of delivery, recipient, RE, salutation, body, and closing. Letters can also include notations for enclosures and the initials of the typist. A cover letter states what is being sent in the same envelope or package and often the reason for sending it. A demand letter is an advocacy letter that asks the recipient to take or refrain from specific action affecting the client. An informational letter provides or seeks information. A status letter updates someone on a matter. A confirmatory letter verifies or confirms that something important has been done or said. An opinion letter is a letter to a client explaining the application of the law and providing legal advice based on that explanation.

Email writing requires conformity to office policy on email communication (e.g., the use of encryption), the formality of a business letter, the absence of special formatting, correct spelling and grammar, indication of nonattorney status (if the writer is not an attorney), caution in tone, care to avoid sending the email to the wrong person, care to avoid virus contamination, and careful proofreading.

Instruments are written documents that give expression to or embody a legal act or agreement, e.g., a contract, deed, will, lease, or mortgage. Pleadings are formal litigation documents filed by a party that state or respond to the claims and defenses the parties have against each other. The main pleadings are the complaint and the answer. The starting point in drafting instruments and pleadings is often a standard form or template that is available on software, in formbooks, or in old case files. A memorandum of law or legal memorandum is a written explanation of how one or more rules might apply to the facts of a client's case.

An appellate brief is a document that a party files with an appellate court (and serves on an opponent) in which the party presents arguments on why the appellate court should affirm (approve), reverse, vacate (cancel), or otherwise modify what a lower court has done. The major components of many appellate briefs are caption, statement of jurisdiction, table of contents (with point headings), table of authorities, questions presented, statement of the case, summary of argument, argument, conclusion, and, if needed, appendixes.

Writers that follow a number of important guidelines will increase the clarity and effectiveness of any kind of writing. Avoid circumlocutions and nominalizations, use shorter and simpler words when possible, use action verbs and the active voice, express something positively whenever possible, avoid long sentences, make pronoun references (their antecedents) clear, avoid sexist language, follow the rule on parallelism, use plain English, spell correctly, and obey all grammar rules.

KEY TERMS

ASSIGNMENTS

CRITICAL ANALYSIS

12.1 How do you react to the student who says, "I'm here to learn the law, not grammar"?

PROJECTS

12.2 Find a recent general circulation newspaper published near where you live. In any of the columns of the paper, find three examples of the passive voice. Rewrite each of the three sentences containing the passive voice so that the passive voice is turned into the active voice. Don't just remove the passive voice. Turn it into the active voice.

CORE SKILLS

Among the many skills a paralegal must have, five core skills stand out: writing (both basic English and legal drafting), research, ethics, computer use, and collaboration (working with others). The core-skill assignments introduce and reinforce these skills. Even if you are not asked to do all of the assignments as part of the course, you should do them on your own. Also, do not wait for the topics in the assignments to be covered in this course or in other courses. Successful paralegals are self-starters. A major characteristic of a self-starter is a thirst for independent study—learning on your own.

CORE SKILL: WRITING

12.3 Prepare a letter for each of the following situations. You will need more facts to complete the letters (e.g., the address of the recipient, your address, and more details on the purpose of the letter). You can make up any of these facts as long as they are reasonably consistent with the facts provided. In each case, your supervisor is an attorney who wants you to draft the letter for his or her signature.

(a) The office represents Richard Clemens, who is a plaintiff in an automobile accident case against George Kiley. The latter's insurance company has offered to settle for $10,000. Draft a letter to Richard Clemens in which you tell him about the offer and ask him to call the office to schedule an appointment with your supervisor to discuss the offer. Point out that the supervisor is not pleased with the low amount of the offer but that the decision on whether to accept it will be entirely up to the client.

(b) Draft a letter to a client who failed to appear at two meetings last month with her attorney (your supervisor) at the office to discuss her case. The client is Diane Rolark. She is very wealthy. The office hopes to keep her as a client in the future on other cases. Hence the office does not want to antagonize her. The letter should remind her of the next appointment with her attorney (three weeks from today).

(c) Write an opinion letter to a client, James Duband, in which you explain any legal concept that you have learned in another course. Assume that this concept is relevant to the case of this client and that the client has written the office asking your supervisor to explain the concept as it pertains to his case. The client is a construction worker who never finished high school.

12.4 Rewrite any of the following sentences that contain language that can be simplified without interfering with the meaning or effectiveness of the sentence.

(a) You are required to pay the fine.

(b) The period of time you have to render assistance is three months.

(c) For the duration of construction, it shall be unlawful for a person to enter or to attempt entry.

(d) If you are unable to enter into a contract with him for the materials, the oral commitment is still binding on you.

(e) She consulted with a lawyer with respect to possible litigation.

(f) She accepted the appointment due to the fact that she was qualified.

(g) It is green in color.

(h) Ask the witness questions about the bills.

(i) Judge Jones is currently on the bench.

12.5 Rewrite any of the following sentences that use the passive voice. If you need to add any facts to the sentences to identify the doer of the action, you may make them up.

(a) Examinations are not enjoyed.

(b) No drugs were prescribed after the operation.

(c) It has been determined that your license should be revoked.

(d) Consideration is being given this matter by the attorney.

(e) It is believed by district officials that the expense is legal.

(f) The fracture was discovered by the plaintiffs in 1998.

(g) As the semester came to a close, the students prepared for their exams.

12.6 Rewrite any of the following sentences that are too long.

(a) A short time later, as George approached the intersection of Woodruff and Fuller, someone in the middle of the street started shooting, but George kept driving when he heard about fifteen shots that sounded like different guns firing, one of which hit his Pontiac, damaging the front windshield and dashboard.

(b) By way of illustration, presidential candidate Ross Perot and basketball player Michael Jordan arguably may have achieved such pervasive fame as to have become public figures for all purposes, while Dr. Jack Kevorkian may have voluntarily placed himself into the public controversy over euthanasia and physician-assisted suicide so as to have become a public figure for a limited range of issues.

(c) The board can, within sixty days of the receipt of a certification from the secretary, take action to return ownership of property to persons or corporations certified as owners from whom the property was acquired by expropriation or by purchase under threat of expropriation.

CORE SKILL: RESEARCH

12.7 Run this search in Google, Bing, or Yahoo: aa plain English language (substituting your state for "aa"). Write a report in which you describe what is meant by plain English or plain language and the efforts to promote or require plain English in your state.

CORE SKILL: ETHICS

12.8 For a client in 2013, James Donovan prepared a memorandum in support of a motion to dismiss. The fee for preparing the memorandum was $1,000, based on three hours of work. In 2015, Donovan has a different client who needs a memorandum in support of a motion to dismiss in the same kind of case as the 2013 case. To use the 2013 memorandum for the 2015 client, Donovan changes the names and dates on the 2013 memorandum. This takes ten

minutes. Donovan charges the 2015 client $1,000 for preparing the memorandum. Is this ethical? What sections of your state's ethics code apply to this question? See Assignment 1.7 in Chapter 1 on the ethics code of your state, Chapter 5 on ethics and fees, and Appendix D on ethics in your state.

CORE SKILL: COMPUTERS

12.9 On Google, Bing, or Yahoo, rule this search: attorney tablet computer.

(a) What is a tablet computer?

(b) Write a report in which you describe the different ways in which law offices use tablet computers. The report must cite at least three separate Internet sites.

(c) In the Computer Terminology in the Law (CTL) notebook you started in Assignment 1.8 of Chapter 1, enter any new terms that you learned by doing parts (a) and (b).

CORE SKILL: COLLABORATION

12.10 Write one paragraph on any topic. The paragraph must have at least seven sentences. The writing must be your own. Do not copy any text from the Internet or other source. Send your paragraph to another student in the class and ask that student to send his or her paragraph to you. (If that student has already received someone's paragraph, try another student.)

(a) Subject the other student's paragraph to the Fog Index. See the links on readability in Helpful Websites at the end of the chapter. (Also enter this search in Google, Bing, or Yahoo: fog index readability.) Send your Fog index result to the writer. The result will assess the difficulty of reading your passage as measured by the grade level a reader would need. A score of 11, for example, means that a reader would need at least an eleventh grade education to understand your passage with relative ease.

(b) When you receive the score for your paragraph, rewrite it in order to obtain a score that would improve readability. Run the Fog Index test on your revised paragraph.

(c) Send your revised paragraph and new score to the other student who scored your original paragraph. Ask him or her if he or she has any suggestions on how you could improve the readability of the paragraph even more.

Summary. You will (1) exchange paragraphs with another student, (2) use the Fog Index to score the readability of the other student's paragraph, (3) send the score to the other student, (4) rewrite your paragraph when you receive your score, (5) score your rewritten paragraph, (6) send your revision and score to the other student, and (7) provide the other student with suggestions on how he or she could improve his or her score even more.

THE JOB SEARCH

(The search for employment cannot wait until the end of a course or of a curriculum. It needs to begin now. The job-search assignments are designed to introduce you to different aspects of the job search and to build options for you to explore about employment.)

12.11   Use the job links in Exhibit 2-12 in Chapter 2 to search for paralegal jobs or job descriptions that mention any kind of writing that is part of the job. Find a variety of such jobs and descriptions. Write a report in which you summarize what you find. Mention kinds of writing and writing skills that are used or required. In addition to the job sites in Exhibit 2-12, run this search in Google, Bing, or Yahoo: large law firm aa (substituting your state for aa). Check the websites of several large law firms to see if they mention any of the paralegals on staff and if there is any mention of writing that the paralegals do. On the home page of a law firm's site, click words such as *careers, employment, join us, opportunities, people,* or any other words that invite the viewer to learn about personnel at the firm.

REVIEW QUESTIONS

1. What are the different meanings of the phrase *legal writing*?
2. What general guidelines should be followed when receiving any writing assignment in a law office?
3. What are the goals of proofreading?
4. What are some of the major techniques of self-proofreading?
5. What is copy-and-paste writing?
6. What is plagiarism?
7. What are the two dangers of copy-and-paste writing?
8. Name six categories of writing that law offices often prepare.
9. What are the standard components of most letters?
10. What is a cover letter?
11. What is a demand letter?
12. What is an informational letter?
13. What is a status letter?
14. What is a confirmatory letter?
15. What is an opinion letter?
16. What happens when something is encrypted?
17. What are some of the major guidelines for email communications?
18. What is an instrument?
19. What is a transactional paralegal?
20. What is a pleading?
21. How are instruments and pleadings often drafted?
22. What are a memorandum and a memorandum of law?
23. What are the different meanings of brief?
24. What is a brief bank?
25. What is the distinction between an appellant and an appellee?
26. What is a reply brief?
27. What is an amicus curiae brief?
28. What are the major components of an appellate brief?
29. What is subject-matter jurisdiction?
30. What does PDF mean?
31. What is a point heading?
32. What is a table of authorities (TOA)?
33. What is the distinction between primary and secondary authority?
34. What is the question presented?
35. What is contained in the statement of the case?
36. What is a transcript?
37. What are some major guidelines for all writing?
38. What is circumlocution?
39. What is nominalization?
40. What is the distinction between active and passive voice?
41. What is a truncated passive?
42. What is parallelism?

HELPFUL WEBSITES

Writing Resources
- owl.english.purdue.edu/exercises
- lib.law.washington.edu/ref/writing.html
- sfruehwald.com/ex.htm
- www.kentlaw.edu/academics/lrw/grinker
- law.lclark.edu/programs/legal_analysis_and_writing/resources.php

Grammar Basics
- writing-program.uchicago.edu/resources/grammar.htm
- libraryspot.com/grammarstyle.htm
- owl.english.purdue.edu/owl/section/1/5
- www.grammarbook.com

Plain English/Writing
- www.sec.gov/news/extra/handbook.htm
- www.sec.gov/pdf/handbook.pdf
- plain-writing-association.org
- www.plainlanguage.gov
- plainlanguagenetwork.org
- www.plainenglishcampaign.com

Legal Writing Blogs
- www.lawprose.org/blog
- www.wordrake.com/writing_tips_writetothepoint
- raymondpward.typepad.com/newlegalwriter
- blogs.utexas.edu/legalwriting
- lawprofessors.typepad.com/legalwriting
- lawyerist.com/tag/legal-writing
- www.adamsdrafting.com/blog
- mariebuckley.com
- ladylegalwriter.blogspot.com

Letter Writing
- www.4hb.com/letters
- esl.about.com/cs/onthejobenglish/a/a_basbletter.htm
- www.writinghelp-central.com/letter-writing.html

Demand Letters
- www.nolo.com/legal-encyclopedia/demand-letter-settle-dispute-30105.html

Writing to Clients
- www.michbar.org/journal
  /article.cfm?articleID=449&volumeID=33

Avoiding Ambiguity in Legal Writing
- www.archives.gov/federal-register/write/legal-docs/ambiguity
  .html

Principles of Clear Writing
- www.archives.gov/federal-register/write/legal-docs
  /clear-writing.html
- owl.english.purdue.edu
- www.bartleby.com/usage
- grammar.ccc.commnet.edu/grammar

Legal Style Manuals
- www.nycourts.gov/reporter/New_Styman.htm
- www.sconet.state.oh.us/ROD/manual.pdf
- www.sdap.org/downloads/Style-Manual.pdf
- www.sec.gov/pdf/handbook.pdf
- www.nlrb.gov/reports-guidance/manuals

Online Appellate Brief Manuals
- www.courts.ca.gov/4941.htm
- www.ca7.uscourts.gov/Rules/handbook.pdf
- www.supreme.courts.state.tx.us/ebriefs/ebriefs.asp

Style Manual (U.S. Government)
- www.gpo.gov/fdsys/search/pagedetails.
  action?granuleId=&packageId=GPO-STYLEMANUAL-
  2008&fromBrowse=true

Elements of Style
- www.bartleby.com/141

Fonts and Point Requirements
- typographyforlawyers.com/court-rules-about-typography.html
- www.ca7.uscourts.gov/Rules/type.pdf

Writer's Diet (have a sample of your writing tested)
- www.writersdiet.com/WT.php

Appellate Briefs Online
- www.americanbar.org/publications/preview_home/alphabetical.html
- www.legaline.com/freebriefslinks.html
- supreme.findlaw.com/supreme_court/briefs.html
- www.txcourts.gov/supreme (click *Electronic Briefs*)
- briefmine.com

Table of Authorities
- office.microsoft.com/en-us (type *table of authorities* in the search box).
- www.wordperfect.com/us/product/perfect-authority
- guides.law.csuohio.edu/content.php?pid=358376&sid=2931015

Memorandum of Law
- See Helpful Websites at the end of Chapter 7

Proofreading
- www.paperrater.com
- www.lrcom.com/tips/proofreading_editing.htm

Readability of Writing

Fog Index
- en.wikipedia.org/wiki/Fog_Index
- www.readabilityformulas.com/gunning-fog-readability-formula
  .php

Flesch-Kincaid
- en.wikipedia.org/wiki/Flesch%E2%80%93Kincaid_readability_tests

General
- www.readabilityformulas.com
- www.writing-information-and-tips.com/fog-index.html
- www.dailywritingtips.com/
  whats-the-reading-level-of-your-writing

Plagiarism
- www.plagium.com
- www.plagiarismtoday.com
- www.lwionline.org/publications/plagiarism/policy.pdf

Public Domain
- www.teachingcopyright.org/ (click *Resources* and then *Public Domain*)
- en.wikipedia.org/wiki/Public_domain

Useful Twitter Hashtags: (tagboard.com)

#PlainEnglish

#legalwriting

#legalenglish

Twitters on Legal Writing

@BryanGarner

@MadamGrammar

@ChicagoManual

@APStylebook

Google, Bing, or Yahoo Searches
(On these search engines, run the following searches, using quotation marks and substituting your state for "aa" where indicated.)
- legal writing drafting
- business letter writing
- plain english writing
- readability writing
- grammar tutorials
- "appellate brief" aa
- "appellate brief writing"
- legal style manual
- "table of authorities"
- drafting legal instruments aa
- email writing guidelines
- drafting pleadings aa

ENDNOTES

1 15 U.S.C. § 1692e (www.law.cornell.edu/uscode/text/15/1692e).

2 Fred Rodell, *Goodbye to Law Reviews*, 23 Virginia Law Review 38 (1936).

3 Wendy Davis, *Consequences of Ineffective Writing*, 8 Perspectives: Teaching Legal Research and Writing 97 (Winter 2000).

4 *Stanard v. Nygren*, 658 F.3d 792, 798 (7th Cir. 2011).

5 *Sanches v. Carrollton-Farmers Branch Independent School Dist.*, 647 F.3d 156, 172 (5th Cir. 2011).

6 Ann Nowak, *Tough Love: The Law School That Required Its Students to Learn Good Grammar*, 28 Touro L. Rev. 1369 (2012).

7 William C. Rempel et al., *Indictment Likely Speeded Trie's Return From Abroad*, Los Angeles Times, February 5, 1998.

8 Bryan A. Garner, *Judges on Briefing: A National Survey*, 8 The Scribes Journal of Legal Writing 1, 9 (2001–2002).

9 73 Pennsylvania Statutes § 2205 (2007) (www.pacode.com/secure /data/037/chapter307/chap307toc.html).

CHAPTER 13

COMPUTERS IN A LAW OFFICE

CHAPTER OUTLINE

- Introduction
- What to Do on Your Own…Now
- Review of the Basics
- Introduction to the Internet
- Internet Searching
- Security on the Internet
- Ethical Issues

CHAPTER OBJECTIVES

After completing this chapter, you should be able to

- Know the kind of computer questions a paralegal might be asked in a job interview.
- List the steps that you can start taking now to develop computer skills on your own.
- Understand the basic hardware components of computers.
- Know the difference between operating software (OS) and application software.
- Distinguish between ROM and RAM.
- List the major storage devices.
- List the major input devices.
- List the major output devices.

- List the major communication devices.
- Distinguish between LANs and WANs.
- Distinguish between an intranet and extranet.
- List the major categories of software used in a law office.
- Understand the basic formatting options in word processing.
- Explain what a macro is.
- Give examples of the use of software for spreadsheets, database management, presentation graphics, litigation support, case management, and knowledge management.
- Understand the origins and basic components of the Internet.

- List the major kinds of social media.
- Know the techniques of effective search-engine searching.
- Know how to assess the reliability of a website.
- Understand the kinds of malware that exist and how to protect against malware.
- List the major ethical issues that can arise in the use of computers in a law office.

INTRODUCTION

Computers dominate many aspects of the practice of law. "Technology has irrevocably changed and continues to alter the practice of law in fundamental ways."[1] Yet some attorneys are conservative by nature and are usually not first in line to try the latest hardware or software, as noted by the following comment made as recently as 2012:

> Paralegals often find that attorneys are afraid to adopt new technology, whether it is purchasing the newest hardware device like an iPad or netbook, to purchasing the newest software to assist in processing discovery documents, or even buying the newest smartphone. Many feel that they are too old or too busy to learn to use the newest "gadget" or they do not understand the benefits available with using such technology in their law practice. They are afraid of embracing this technology for fear of it becoming a "monster" and consuming their time and their money.[2]

To counter this instinct, bar associations and management consultants bombard law offices with messages on what computers have to offer. As we saw in Chapter 5, ethical codes are now mandating change. Attorneys can be disciplined for failing to "keep abreast" of the "benefits and risks associated with relevant technology."[3] Sometimes external events force offices to learn new technology, such as when a court allows (or requires) the **e-filing** of pleadings **online**. Although most attorneys have responded by moving their practices into the twenty-first century, some remain hesitant. As one veteran paralegal commented, "It is amazing how many attorneys do not want to learn the new ways, so they depend on their paralegals to know how to handle electronic formats and filings." Paralegals with these skills, therefore, are in "high demand."[4]

In some large law offices (those with 50+ attorneys), the use of computers has been at the expense of attorney jobs. A law-school dean recently commented that attorney jobs at some of these firms have been "wiped away by innovations such as software that takes seconds to do the document discovery that once" created numerous billable hours for junior attorneys.[5]

In short, the practice of law continues to be in a state of change because of technology. The best approach of paralegals about to enter the legal employment world for the first time is to become as knowledgeable as possible about computers. In your first job interview, don't be surprised if you are asked questions such as the following:

- What are your computer skills?
- How skilled are you in Word?
- What apps are you comfortable with?
- Which operating systems have you used?
- What litigation support software have you used?[6]

e-filing Electronic filing in court of pleadings and other documents.

online Connected to another computer or computer network, often through the Internet. (See glossary for another meaning.)

WHAT TO DO ON YOUR OWN...NOW

You can learn a great deal about computers on your own. Don't wait for someone to explain it all to you. Take the initiative by pursuing an aggressive program of self-education. Exhibit 13-1 presents an overview of steps you can start now and continue after you graduate. Indeed, you will probably need to be a student of computers for the remainder of your career. Because computer products are constantly changing, the steps outlined in Exhibit 13-1 are all the more important because they are designed to keep you current.

Exhibit 13-1	Developing Computer Skills: What to Do on Your Own Now

- **Build A Notebook: Computer Terminology in The Law (CTL)**
  - In Assignment 1.8 at the end of Chapter 1, you are asked to start a computer notebook (paper or digital) called Computer Terminology in the Law (CTL). Each chapter in this book has a core computer assignment, which requires you to learn or review computer basics and to build the CTL with the terminology that you come across in the process of doing the assignments. It is recommended that you do the assignments whether or not they are required for the course. See the instructions for Assignment 1.8 on setting up the CTL.

- The goal of the CTL is to build an extensive terminology databank. Do not use the CTL to take extensive explanatory and how-to-do it notes on computer topics. Such notes will quickly overwhelm the notebook. Limit this CTL to definitions of computer software and hardware terminology. Use another notebook for class notes, chapter outlining, etc. Limit the terminology notebook—the CTL—to terminology.
- The core computer assignments after each chapter are not the only way to build the CTL. The steps outlined below duplicate some of these assignments and provide more opportunities. Fill the notebook with definitions of terms you come across in every aspect of the paralegal curriculum.
- There are computer dictionaries and glossaries in book form and on the Internet. (See the links to online legal dictionaries in Helpful Websites at the end of Chapter 11.) Make use of them, but *do not use them as a substitute for writing out your own definitions.*
- Another technique for finding definitions is *define* (:). In Google, Bing, or Yahoo, type the word *define*, followed by a colon, followed by the word or phrase you want defined. Example: define: cloud computing.

Setting Aside Time

- The suggestions below will take time beyond the time required by your coursework. How much time? That depends on you. Ideally, you would devote a minimum of twenty minutes a day, seven days a week. Too much? Then lessen the time to what is more realistic for you. It is critical, however, that you establish a momentum. Don't wait for the weekend, a vacation, or the end of the school year. The amount of material you need to learn is vast. A daily commitment is needed.

Tutorials

- In Google, Bing, or Yahoo, include the word *tutorial* at the end of each of the following search terms (Example: computer basics tutorial):

computer basics	eDiscovery	Microsoft Windows
Android platform	Google Chrome	Microsoft Word
apps for lawyers	Google Scholar	online security
Bing search techniques	Google search techniques	operating systems
Bloomberg law	Internet basics	Pacer federal courts
Boolean search	iPad	smart phones
cloud computing	iPod	spreadsheets
computer servers	Lexis Advance	Summation software
computer tablets	LexisNexis	Westlaw
computer virus	Litigation support	WestlawNext

- Run the same searches on YouTube.
- Of course, you won't be able to watch and read tutorials on all of these topics. You should consider the list a career-long project. Self-learning in the world of computers should occur while you are in school, while you are looking for employment, and while you are employed. As indicated, computer learning is a life-long endeavor.
- Once you start finding tutorial sites through the searches, which ones should you select? Begin with the search for *computer basics tutorial.* You want sites that are effective and free. The quality of the sites will vary a great deal. Try out different sites. Ask your fellow students what sites they like. Ask your teachers. You will eventually find what you need. Don't be reluctant to spend time with tutorials that are trying to sell products but that give previews. They can be effective learning resources.

Courses, Meetings, and Groups

- *Courses.* Take computer courses. Find out what is available at your school. Also check if free or low-cost computer courses exist in your community, e.g., adult education courses. Some may last no more than an afternoon. Call your local public library for leads. Once you know what is available, ask your instructor what courses would be most relevant to someone working in a law office. Anything on the basics of operating systems (e.g., Windows), word processing (e.g., Word), or the Internet will probably be valuable.

- *Computer events at paralegal associations.* Contact your local paralegal association to find out what upcoming events will cover computer use. Check their websites (see Appendix B) for what is on the schedule. There may, for example, be a continuing legal education (CLE) session covering the Internet. Ask if you can attend as a paralegal student. If there is a fee, ask if a reduced rate is available for students. Some of the meetings and sessions may be geared to experienced paralegals. Nevertheless, you should consider attending because the more exposure you have to computer topics, the more you will eventually absorb. Take detailed notes, even if you will not fully understand all of them until later. Furthermore, any contact you have with a paralegal association can be an excellent networking opportunity.

- *Computer events at bar associations.* Your state and local bar association may also have CLE sessions that cover computer basics for attorneys. Find out if you can attend at a reduced rate. Go to the Internet sites of these associations (see Appendix B) to find out what programs are scheduled.

REVIEW OF THE BASICS

Before examining specific computer programs, we will briefly review computer essentials that will be helpful in understanding these programs.

HARDWARE AND SOFTWARE

hardware The physical equipment of a computer system.

software A computer program that tells or instructs the hardware what to do.

central processing unit (CPU) The hardware of the computer that contains the processor chip that controls all computer parts.

Hardware is the physical equipment (i.e., devices) of a computer system. Hardware is what you take out of the box and plug together when you buy a computer system. Examples include the keyboard, central processing unit (CPU), monitor, cables, mouse, speakers, and printer. **Software** is a computer program (also called an *application* or *app*) that tells the hardware what to do.

The **central processing unit (CPU)** is the computer hardware that contains the *processor chip* that controls all computer parts. The CPU is the computer's "brain." The processor chip performs the calculations that are needed for processing tasks. CPUs perform operations and carry out software commands. In most computer systems, the CPU is the unit that contains the on/off button or switch and the ports that are used to connect the computer to other devices.

Software can come on a disk, but today is more often available only through an online download. Updates to software are almost always made through downloads, whether the software was purchased on a disk or thorough an initial download. Most software is subject to a license, which is an agreement that places limitations on the use of the software. For example, the license may specify that the software cannot be used on more than one computer.

There are two main categories of software: (1) operating software (OS) and (2) applications (apps).

operating software (OS) Software that tells the computer how to perform its major functions such as starting (executing) programs, managing its memory, and controlling printers and other attached devices (peripherals). Also called *operating system*.

The **operating software (OS)**, also called the *operating system*, is software that tells the computer how to perform its major functions, such as starting (executing) programs, managing its memory, and controlling printers and other attached devices (peripherals). The OS is the master or central software program that the hardware and all other software depend on to function. When you buy a computer, an OS is already installed. Once you turn on or restart a computer (called *booting up*), the OS system is the first program that is run or executed.

The major operating system in use today is Windows, developed by Microsoft. Others include Android, iOS, Mac OS, Chrome OS, BlackBerry, UNIX, and a special version of UNIX called Linux. Software is written in programming language called *source code*. Most software manufacturers keep their source code secret. If, however, the software's source code is freely available to the public for use and modification, the software is called *open-source software*. Linux is a prominent example of open-source software.

application (app) Software that performs tasks for an end user other than the major tasks of running the computer itself. The most commonly used apps today are downloaded on mobile devices.

An **application (app)** is software that performs tasks commonly needed by the consumer or end user. Examples of applications include word processing, spreadsheets, and database management.

At one time the major hardware option for a computer was the stationary desktop. The options have increased dramatically, particularly in the area of mobile devices with wireless communication capability. Major examples include the following:

Wi-Fi Technology that uses radio waves to allow wireless communication between computers (including the Internet) within a designated area.

- *Laptops*. A laptop is a portable version of a desktop computer. Laptops can be carried to wherever the user can gain access to the Internet, such as at home or where outdoor **Wi-Fi** connections can be made. Laptops run the same or similar software as desktops and also have similar hardware. Lighter and thinner categories of laptops are called *ultrabooks*, *netbooks*, and *subnotebooks*.
- *Tablet computers*. A tablet is a computer that operates mainly by touchscreen rather than by physical keyboard or mouse. The keyboard is on the screen. The tablet may come with a *stylus*, which is a small pen-shaped tool with which you can tap icons that execute programs, type numbers and letters of the alphabet on a touchscreen keyboard, and make handwritten notes that can be turned into digital text. Windows is the operating system (OS) of some tablets. For most tablets, however, the OS is Apple's iOS or Google's Android. Examples of tablets include Apple's iPad, Microsoft's Surface, Google's Nexus, and Samsung's Galaxy. (If the primary function of the tablet is to read documents, it is an *e-book reader* such as Amazon's Kindle.)

- *Smartphones.* A smartphone is a mobile phone that performs many of the functions of a computer. The device operates by touchscreen. It offers Web searching, email, text messaging, video, and photo taking in addition to voice telephoning. Examples of smartphones include Apple's iPhone, phones that run the Google Android OS, and phones that run the Windows OS.

These devices can be taken anywhere and connected to the Internet or to the office's network. Technology has allowed attorneys and paralegals to, in effect, bring their office with them so that they can work from home, the courthouse, the airport, or anywhere they can obtain an Internet connection. A 2013 study of the future of law firms said that 78 percent of attorneys telecommute to some extent and 88 percent use their smartphone for law-related tasks while away from their primary offices. "With smartphones, tablet computers, wireless networks and cloud computing [discussed below], **telecommuting** is on the rise. The physical footprint of today's law firm is shrinking. Some offices are even going completely **virtual**. Technology has leveled the playing field to a great extent, enabling solo practitioners and small law firms to establish a large-firm-like presence online and serve clients in locations that fall outside their historical/traditional geographic reach."[7]

MEMORY

Computers can hold a great deal of data. The internal storage capacity of a computer is called its *memory*. There are two main kinds of memory: read-only and random access. **Read-only memory (ROM)** is memory that stores data that cannot be altered, removed, or added to; the data can only be read by the computer. When you shut the computer off, the data in ROM are not erased. ROM contains critical data such as the code needed to boot the computer. **Random access memory (RAM)** is memory that stores temporary data. You write data (e.g., a letter) to RAM. When you shut the computer off, such data vanish unless you have properly saved the data. Newer applications require increasing amounts of RAM. As long as your device has enough RAM, you can run more than one application at the same time (called multitasking). For example, you can simultaneously run a word processor, a spreadsheet, your Internet connection, and a game of solitaire. (Inadequate RAM was once such a common problem that RAM was humorously referred to as Rarely Adequate Memory.)

The amount or quantity of memory is measured by units called **bytes**. A byte is the storage equivalent of one space or one character of the alphabet typed into a computer. Bytes are expressed in the quantities indicated in Exhibit 13-2.[8]

Exhibit 13-2	Storage Capacities in Bytes		
NAME	ABBREVIATION	NUMBER OF BYTES (approximate)	EXAMPLE OF WHAT THIS MANY BYTES CAN HOLD (approximate)
kilobyte	K	One thousand	A one- or two-line email
megabyte	MB	One million	4 books (200 pages each)
gigabyte	GB	One billion	4.4 thousand books (200 pages each)
terabyte	TB	One trillion	4.5 million books (200 pages each)
petabyte	PB	One quadrillion	4.5 billion books (200 pages each)
exabyte	EB	One quintillion	4.8 trillion books (200 pages each)

STORAGE SYSTEMS

Here is a list of the major storage devices:

- *Hard drive.* A **hard drive** is a computer storage device for data that uses rapidly rotating platters inside a sealed casing. If the drive is located inside the CPU, it is called an internal hard drive. If it sits outside the CPU as a freestanding unit, it is called an external hard drive. (In many computer systems, the internal hard disk is the C drive. If the system also has an external drive, the latter might be the D drive.) Hard drives have

telecommuting Working from home or other remote settings through the Internet, email, telephone and other means of communication that do not require presence at a traditional office.

virtual Carried out by computer. Existing in a computer-generated environment.

read-only memory (ROM) Memory that stores data that cannot be altered, removed, or added to. The data can be only read by the computer.

random access memory (RAM) Memory that stores temporary data that are erased (unless properly saved) whenever the computer's power is turned off.

byte The storage equivalent of one space or one character of the alphabet typed into a computer.

hard drive A computer storage device for data that uses rapidly rotating platters inside a sealed casing. Also called *hard disk drive*.

read/write capability, meaning that you can read the data on them and write new data to them. (If you can read data but not add additional data, the drive has read/only capability.) External drives are frequently used to back up data on other drives.

- *Removable Drive.* A removable drive is a portable device used to store data. A major example is the *flash drive* (also called a *thumb drive*). You can insert the flash drive into one computer, copy data onto it, remove the drive, insert it into another computer, and transfer the data to the second computer. A common point of entry for removable drives is a USB port on the CPU. USB means *universal serial bus*, which allows fast connections between a computer and external devices such as flash drives and cameras. A port is a slot into which you can plug a connection.
- *Magnetic tape system.* A magnetic tape system stores data on tape reels or tape cartridges. Because they store data sequentially, these systems are often slower than disk systems. Sequential storage means that the data is stored in sequence so that the data on it is accessed or retrieved in the order in which it was recorded, unless the user fast-forwards or rewinds the tape. RAM data, on the other hand, can be accessed in any order.
- *Optical Storage device.* An **optical storage device** is a device that uses laser light or beams to write data onto plastic disks. Examples include CDs, DVDs, and Blu-ray disks. Because of the large capacity of these devices, they are often used for movies and other multimedia material.
- *Cloud.* The **cloud** is the part of the Internet where users can (a) obtain and update programs (apps) and (b) read, store, and manage data. Cloud computing means using the Internet to obtain, process, and store data. Large companies such as Google, Microsoft, and Dropbox make it possible for users to store vast amounts of data in Internet data centers or "warehouses" where the data can be accessed from any computer, or indeed, from a cell phone. A major example of data stored "in the cloud" is emails created on Gmail and other web-based email programs.

INPUT DEVICES

To place information into a computer, you need an input device. The most commonly used input device is the keyboard. When you type something on the keyboard, text is entered at the cursor on the screen of the monitor. Other input devices include the mouse, speech recognition programs, and scanners, all of which can be used along with the keyboard. Speech recognition programs allow you to enter information by speaking rather than by typing on the keyboard. As you speak words and commands into a small microphone, the computer enters the words on the screen or executes the commands. A **scanner** is an input device that converts text and images into an electronic or digital format that a computer can recognize. The process by which a scanner digitizes text or images is called **imaging** (or *document imaging*). When a document is scanned into the computer, an exact image of the document appears on the screen, most commonly as a **PDF** (portable document format) file. The file can then be read on a free Adobe reader. PDF is an example of a fixed-layout format. (An alternative to Adobe PDF is Microsoft XPS.) If *optical character recognition (OCR)* software is used, you can perform searches of the text in the scanned document and use a word processor to make changes in the text.

Scanners have other uses as well. For example, a **bar code** can be placed on every document in a large project and then read by a *bar code scanner* in much the same way that supermarkets use scanners for purchases at checkout. A bar code is a sequence of numbers and vertical lines of different shapes that can be read by an optical scanner. The bar code scanner can be effective in helping law offices keep track of multiple documents used by different people in the office.

Two other important input devices are the digital camera and the digital camcorder. Images taken by these devices can be easily transferred to the computer and then used in variety of ways, such as preparing a day-in-the-life trial exhibit in a personal-injury case.

OUTPUT DEVICES

Once data is in a computer, you need an *output device* to receive the data and display it as text, images, sound, or other media. The major output devices are *monitors* and *printers*. Another output device is a *sound card*, which can activate the computer's speakers and enhance sound from the computer.

---

optical storage device
A device that uses laser light or beams to write data onto plastic disks. Examples include CDs, DVDs, and Blu-ray disks.

cloud The part of the Internet where users can (a) obtain and update programs (apps) and (b) read, store, and manage data.

scanner An input device that converts text and images into an electronic or digital format that a computer can recognize.

imaging The process by which a scanner digitizes text or images. Also called *document imaging*.

PDF (portable document format) A file format consisting of an electronic image of a document that preserves the features and styles of the document (e.g., its line spacing, photograph placement, and font size) that existed before it was converted into a digital document.

bar code A sequence of numbers and vertical lines of different shapes that can be read by an optical scanner.

The newest output device that has caught everyone's imagination is the 3-D printer, which can print a three-dimensional solid object from a digital model. The printer can print model buildings, parts for machinery, toys, and even body parts! "Sometime in the not-too-distant future, a doctor will tell a patient that his liver is failing and offer comfort by saying, 'We're going to print you a new one'"[9]

COMMUNICATION DEVICES

Computers at different locations can exchange data by using communications devices. A **modem** is a communications device that allows computers to send and receive data to and from each other. The exchange can be through telephone or cable lines. A wireless modem connects through the air and is most often used by smartphones, iPads, and other handheld computers. Wi-Fi, as indicated earlier, uses radio waves to allow wireless communication between computers (including the Internet) within a designated area.

Other communication devices include digital phone lines such as T1, ISDN (integrated services digital networks), and DSL (digital subscriber lines). They can transmit text, voice, and *real-time* video (e.g., **videoconferencing**) at high speeds.

Real time means occurring now, as you are watching. Suppose, for example, you are on the Internet watching a witness answer questions in a deposition in another city. You would be watching in real time if the witness were talking in the room where the deposition was taking place at the same time you were watching this witness on your computer screen in another room or building. If, however, you were watching a deposition that was recorded earlier, you would not be experiencing the deposition in real time. Similarly, you are communicating in real time if what you type on your screen appears on the screens of others as you type. Videoconferencing is a meeting that occurs in more than one location among individuals who can hear and see each other on computer screens in real time.

LOCAL AREA NETWORKS (LANs); WIDE AREA NETWORKS (WANs)

Computers in a busy law office need to be connected with each other for many reasons. They may need to share the same data (e.g., a client file, calendars, time and billing records) or the same equipment (e.g., a printer). If the computers are relatively close to each other, such as within the same building, they can be connected by a **local area network (LAN)**. Once their computers are connected (i.e., networked), computer users can share calendars, have meetings, exchange email, and work on files together. If the computers are not geographically close, they can still be networked on what is called a **wide area network (WAN)**. Large law offices with branches in different cities, for example, can be linked on a WAN. (Computers that are not connected to a network are called **stand-alone computers**.)

INTRANET AND EXTRANET

The networks in law offices might include the equivalent of a mini-Internet for private, internal use. It is called an **intranet**. The general public would not have access to it. The intranet could give employees access to vacation schedules, court dates of current cases, client databases, current litigation documents, brief banks and legal forms, staff directories (with pictures), personnel manuals, training manuals, and **continuing legal education (CLE)** programs available at the office. The employees can be in the same office or (similar to a WAN) in branch offices around the world. It is possible for the office to allow selected outsiders to have online access to its intranet. (Such access converts the intranet to an **extranet**.) For example, the office could permit a client to read all documents prepared for the client that are on the office's intranet.

SOFTWARE IN A LAW OFFICE

Exhibit 13-3 lists major software programs used in a law office.[10] Some programs are suites or **integrated packages** that allow the user to perform multiple tasks such as word processing, spreadsheet calculations, and database management. All of the major software vendors have websites that provide detailed information about their programs, including the ability to download new features and corrections to errors or "bugs" in previous versions of the software.

---

modem A communications device that allows computers at different locations to exchange data using telephone lines, cables, or wireless connections.

videoconferencing Meeting between individuals in more than one location who can hear and see each other on computer screens in real time.

real time Occurring now; happening as you are watching; able to respond or otherwise interact immediately or within seconds.

local area network (LAN) A multiuser system linking computers that are in close proximity to each other so that they can share data and resources.

wide area network (WAN) A multiuser system linking computers over a large geographical area so that they can share data and resources.

stand-alone computer A computer that is not connected to a network.

intranet A private network of computers for the sharing of data, software, and services within the organization using features similar to those of the World Wide Web.

continuing legal education (CLE) Training in the law (usually short term) that a person receives after completing his or her formal legal training or after becoming employed.

extranet The part of an intranet to which selected outsiders have been given access.

integrated package Software that combines more than one application (e.g., word processing, spreadsheet calculations, and database management) in a single program.

Exhibit 13-3	Software Used in Many Law Offices

Note: Software manufacturers do not all use the same terminology to describe their applications. The functions in some of the following applications overlap. Also, a software package or suite can combine more than one of these applications into a single suite or integrated package that is sold or leased.

SOFTWARE	FUNCTION
Accounting	Tracks financial information needed for the operation of a law office.
Case management	Combines multiple tasks in the control or management of a case. The tasks often include calendaring, document control, document assembly, document tracking, and billing.
Computer-assisted legal research (CALR)	Performs legal research in computer databases, e.g., Westlaw, LexisNexis, Loislaw, and free Internet sites.
Conversion utility	Converts a document created by a word processor into a PDF (portable document format) file so that all the features and styles of the document remain intact. (Such conversion is often needed for e-filing). Alternatives to PDF exist, e.g., the XPS format of Microsoft.
Custom-made software	Meets specialized needs. It is software that is written (programmed) for the needs of a particular office. If the software is usable by a wide variety of offices, it is sometimes called *off-the-shelf software*. As indicated, however, most software today is sold by download rather than on a disk or in a package.
Database management	Organizes, searches, retrieves, and sorts data, e.g., conflict-of-interest records, client lists, and research materials.
Document assembly	Creates standard documents through templates and forms. A *template* is a file containing text and a format that can be used as the starting point for creating frequently used documents.
Document control	Helps maintain control over schedules, e.g., appointments and case deadlines.
Document management	Manages documents and allows them to be searched by all users of a network in the office.
Electronic mail (email)	Sends and receives mail electronically, including complete documents that can be sent as email attachments.
Groupware	Allows computer users on a network to work together, e.g., to share documents and work on the same information.
Knowledge management (KM)	Captures and reuses the knowledge and work product of a law office.
Litigation support	Stores, retrieves, and tracks facts, documents, testimony, and other litigation materials.
Operating software (OS) (operating system)	Tells the computer how to perform its major (operating system) functions, such as starting (executing) programs, managing its memory, and controlling printers and other attached devices (peripherals).
Presentation graphics	Combines text with charts, graphs, pictures, video, clip art, and sound in order to communicate data more effectively.
Project management	Helps manage large projects by tracking the sequence and timing of the events and tasks of the project.
Spreadsheet	Performs calculations on numbers and values entered by the user. The program organizes, compiles, tracks, and calculates numerical data.
Timekeeping and billing	Tracks time and expenses; prepares client invoices.
Web browser	Allows users to read pages on the World Wide Web.
Word processing	Allows you to enter and edit data in order to create and revise documents, e.g., letters, briefs, and memos.

Here is a closer look at of seven of the programs outlined in Exhibit 13-3.

- Word processing
- Spreadsheets
- Database management
- Presentation graphics
- Litigation support
- Case management
- Knowledge management

Legal research sites are covered in Chapter 11.

Word Processing

A **word processor** is a software program that allows you to enter and edit data in order to create and revise documents. Word processors are enormous improvements over standard typewriters. When you make an error on a word processor, for example, you do not reach for

word processor Software that allows you to enter and edit data in order to create and revise documents. It processes words, allowing you to write sentences, paragraphs, and pages on the computer.

Exhibit 13-4	Word Processing Terms and Functions

Note: Many of the terms below are also used in other programs such as spreadsheets.

TERM	FUNCTION
Backspace	The key that allows you to delete the character to the left of the cursor.
Block move	To copy, delete, or change the position of text you highlight. The text you identify is called a *block*. You highlight it by giving it a contrasting background.
Bold	Heavy or dark type. **This sentence is printed in bold.**
Bullet	A special character (e.g., • or ▪) used at the beginning of every line in a list.
Character	A letter, number, or symbol.
Character enhancement	Altering the appearance of words or characters, such as by underlining, **bolding**, or *italicizing* them.
Clipboard	The part of memory that holds the last text you deleted or that holds other temporary text.
Cursor	A blinking character on the screen that shows where the next character will appear.
Default setting	The value used by the word processor when it is not instructed to use any other value. For example, the default for spacing may be single space unless you change the default to double spacing or some other value.
Editing	Adding to, subtracting from, or otherwise changing text.
Endnote	A numbered citation or explanatory text printed at the end of a document or chapter. If printed at the bottom of each page, the citation or text is called a *footnote*.
Global	Pertaining to the entire document. For example, a global spelling change of *principle* to *principal* means that every time the word *principle* appears in the document, it is to be changed to *principal*. The change can be made once (globally) with one click rather than each time the word *principle* appears in the text.
Format	The layout of a page when printed, e.g., the font and margin settings.
Grammar checker	Identifies possible grammatical errors in a document, and suggests corrections.
Hard copy	A paper copy of what has been prepared on a computer. Also called *printout*. A *soft* copy of text is what exists on disk or on a computer screen.
Header	The same text printed at the top of each page of a document, usually identifying the name of the document and, sometimes, its author.
Insert mode	When new text is typed in a line that already has text, the line opens to receive the new text. Nothing is erased or overtyped. (The opposite of insert mode is typeover mode. See below.)
Justification	Every line is even (i.e., aligned) at the left margin (called left justified), at the right margin (called right justified), or at both margins (called full justification).
Landscape	Printing that occurs along the long edge of the page so that when you look at the page, it is shorter than it is wide. The alternative is *portrait* printing. See below.
Macro	The use of one or a few keystrokes to insert frequently used text or to perform other repetitive functions. A keyboard shortcut to perform repetitive tasks.
Paginate	To insert consecutive page numbers at the top or bottom of each page of a document.
Paste	To insert (drop) text or an image into a document that you have copied or cut from somewhere.
Print preview	A screen that presents text (and graphics, if any) as it will appear once sent to the printer and becomes a hard copy.
Portrait	Printing on a page in which the height of the page is greater than the width. When you look at the page, it is taller than it is wide. The alternative is *landscape* printing. See above.
Scroll	To move the cursor and lines of text (or images) either up or down or left or right without altering the content of the text or images.
Spell checker	The identification of possible spelling errors in a document, with suggested corrections.
Status line	A message line (usually at the bottom of the screen) that can state the current position of the cursor (e.g., line 3, column 15) and provide other formatting information.
Subscript	A character that prints below the usual text baseline. For example, the number 7 in the following text is in subscript: Court$_7$.
Superscript	A character that prints above the usual text baseline. For example, the number 7 in the following text is in superscript: Court^7.
Table	A feature that allows the creation of a table of information using rows and columns.
Text file	A file containing text that you create. (A file containing a program is called a systems or application file.)
Thesaurus	Identifies word alternatives that a user can substitute for words initially used or considered.
Tool bar	A list of shortcuts (often represented by icons) that can quickly execute commonly used functions such as saving a document or sending it to the printer.
Typeover mode	When new text is typed in a line that already has text, the old text is erased (i.e., overtyped) with each keystroke.
Word wrap	When a word would extend beyond the right margin, the word is automatically sent to the beginning of the next line.
WYSIWYG	What You See (on the screen) Is What You (will) Get (when the screen is printed).

a bottle of correction fluid (White Out) to take out the error. Instead, you simply press the backspace or delete key over the error and type your new text. If you left something out of a paragraph, you point the cursor to where the additional text should go and insert what you want to add. When you are in *insert mode*, the line can open up to make room for the new text. See Exhibit 13-4 for the definition of insert mode and other standard features of word processors.[11] With relative ease, you can copy, save, and paginate (insert page numbers on) your text; insert footnotes or endnotes; underline or italicize text; and create tables or charts. Most word processors also allow you to spell check and grammar check your writing. Be careful, however, when using spell checkers. They do not check for correct word usage. For example, if you write *its*, the spell checker will not tell you that you should have written *it's*. Similar cautions are needed when using grammar check programs. They can help point out difficulties you should address, but they are not comprehensive.

Justification and Indents   If you want to justify your margins, the word processor will allow you to do so quickly. In the language of printers and typesetting, justification means every line is even (i.e., aligned) at the left margin, at the right margin, or at both margins. Lines are aligned if they come out even (as opposed to being ragged) at the margin. **Left justified** means that every line on the left margin is aligned (except for the first line of a paragraph if the first line is indented). **Right justified** means that every line on the right margin is aligned, except for the last line if it ends before the margin. Full justification means that every line of the paragraph is aligned on both margins, with the possible exception of the first and last lines. (See Exhibit 13-5 for examples of justification and various indentation formats.)

left justified Every line of a paragraph on the left margin is aligned except for the first line if the first line is indented.

right justified Every line of a paragraph on the right margin is aligned except for the last line if it ends before the margin.

Exhibit 13-5	Justification and Indents Using a Word Processor

The text you are now reading is an example of text created on a word processor that is *left justified* only. Note that the text is straight or even along the left margin but ragged along the right margin.   — Left justification

The text you now are reading is an example of text created on a word processor that is *right justified* only. Note that the text is ragged along the left margin, but straight (even) along the right margin.   — Right justification

The text you are now reading is an example of text created on a word processor that has *full justification*. Note that the text is straight, not ragged, along both the left margin and the right margin (except for the last line).   — Full justification

The text you are now reading is an example of text created on a word processor that uses *first line indent*. Note that only the first line is indented in traditional paragraph format. The text is left justified only.   — First line indent

The text you are now reading is an example of text created on a word processor that uses the *double indent* feature. Note that the entire text is indented the same amount from both the left margin and the right margin. Such indentation is often used when presenting a long quote. (This text is left justified only.)   — Double indent

The text you are now reading is an example of text created on a word processor that uses the *hanging indent* feature. Note that the first line hangs or "sticks out" to the left.   — Hanging indent

Macros   One of the special features of word processors (and of other programs) is the ability to create **macros** that allow you to perform repetitive tasks without extensive retyping. Suppose, for example, that when you prepare a letter, you always type a heading at the top of the sheet containing your name, street address, city, state, zip code, phone number, and email address. As you type the heading, you carefully center each line. Assume that this task consists of 100 keystrokes and takes about two minutes to complete. An alternative is to create a macro to perform the task. Within the word processor's macro feature, you go through the steps of creating a macro. First, you name the macro. Let's call our example *heading*. Next, you type the repetitive text (all 100 strokes). You have now created a macro called *heading*. From now on,

macro The use of one or a few keystrokes to insert frequently used text or to perform other repetitive functions. A keyboard shortcut to perform repetitive tasks.

every time you are preparing a new letter, you simply tell the word processor to run the *heading* macro. This is done by typing (or clicking) the word *heading* within the macro feature of the word processor. In less than a second, all 100 keystrokes appear on the screen in the format you want. In addition to being a time saver, this macro insures that all of your letters will have a perfectly consistent heading.

Here is another example. Suppose you are typing a memorandum of law that frequently uses the phrase *federal subject-matter jurisdiction*. To avoid constantly retyping this phrase, you could create a macro called *fsmj* (or you could call it *f*). Now every time you run the *fsmj* macro (or the *f* macro if you used the shorter name), the full phrase automatically goes into your memorandum wherever you want it to appear. Macros can be quite versatile. Within a macro, for example, you can also insert commands such as to save the document or insert a number from another software application.

Word, WordPerfect, and Free Alternatives   The two main word processors that can be purchased are Word by Microsoft and WordPerfect by Corel. Word is the most popular. Both Word and WordPerfect have features or editions that are geared to specific needs of attorneys in the practice of law. For example, they assist you in creating a **table of authorities (TOA)**. (This is a list of primary and secondary authority referred to in a document with the page number where each authority is cited in the document. See Exhibit 12-6 in Chapter 12 for an example.) As an extra service to attorneys, Microsoft has prepared an online guide to how law offices can effectively use Word in the practice of law. To find the latest version of this guide, type "Legal User's Guide" in Google, Bing, or Yahoo. To find comparable help for law offices that use WordPerfect, run a search for "wordperfect law office."

Free word processors are also available. Run this search in Google, Bing, or Yahoo: free alternative Microsoft Word.

PDF Files and E-Filing   Word processors such as Microsoft Word allow you to convert their files into PDF (portable document format) files. As we saw earlier, a PDF file is an electronic image of a document that preserves the features and styles of the document (e.g., its line spacing, photograph placement, **font**, and **point** size) that existed before it was converted into a digital document. Another method of converting word-processed documents into PDF files is by using software such as Acrobat, made by Adobe.

The conversion to PDF is essential for courts that allow (or require) e-filing in PDF format. As we saw in Chapter 10, e-filing in federal courts is called Case Management/Electronic Case Filing (CM/ECF). Documents filed in federal court are PDF files.

Spreadsheets

A **spreadsheet** application is a software program that performs calculations on numbers and values that you enter. Spreadsheets can perform many kinds of number-crunching tasks such as calculating future damages, tax liability, alimony, child support, lost wages, and mortgage payments. The spreadsheet lets you create many groups of interrelated numbers within a series of rows and columns. Once this is done, you can play "what if" by changing one of the numbers to see what happens to the result. The spreadsheet will quickly recalculate all numbers that are dependent on the one that was changed. Suppose, for example, you are considering a loan to purchase a building and want to know what the monthly payments will be. Among the factors that will determine the amount of these payments are the interest rate, length of the mortgage, and amount of the loan. Entering these three numbers into a spreadsheet will give you the amount of the monthly payments. You can then change one or more of the numbers (e.g., enter a lower interest rate) to see what happens to the monthly payments.

What-if calculations can also be used in settlement negotiations. In a **structured settlement**, for example, the payment of damages will be spread over a period of time rather than paid in a lump sum. To calculate what these payments will be, the attorneys must make certain assumptions about the rate of inflation over this period. A spreadsheet will allow the attorneys to try different assumptions in order to see what impact they would have on the amounts to be paid over the period.

Spreadsheet programs such as Microsoft Excel and Apple's Numbers can create charts (e.g., a pie chart) that graphically illustrate the results of these calculations. To locate free alternatives, run this search in Google, Bing, or Yahoo: free alternative spreadsheet Excel.

---

table of authorities (TOA) A list of primary authority (e.g., cases and statutes) and secondary authority (e.g., legal periodical articles and legal treatises) that a writer has cited in an appellate brief or other document. The list includes page numbers where each authority is cited in the document.

font The design or style of printed letters of the alphabet, punctuation marks, or other characters.

point A measure of the size of printed letters of the alphabet, punctuation marks, or other characters. (One point is approximately $\frac{1}{72}$ of an inch tall.) (See glossary for another meaning.)

spreadsheet Software that performs calculations on numbers and values that you enter.

structured settlement An agreement in which a party fulfills a financial obligation (e.g., the payment of damages) by making periodic payments over a designated period. The payments are sometimes funded through an annuity.

Database Management

database management
Software that allows you to organize, search, retrieve, and sort data.

Database management is software that allows you to organize, search, retrieve, and sort data. Such programs are sometimes called *database management systems (DBMS)*. For example, a law office can create a database containing a list of all of its past and present clients. Within this database, the categories of data for each client could include the following:

- Client's name
- Street address
- Phone
- Email address
- Facebook site
- Internet site
- Type of case
- Case number

- Name of opponent
- Names of other parties
- Dates representation was provided
- Attorney who brought the case to the firm
- Fees and expenses billed
- Dates bills were sent out
- Dates payments were received (realization rate)

This database will allow the firm to accomplish a number of useful tasks. For example, it can check for possible conflicts of interest. When the firm is considering a new client, it must find out if the firm has ever represented the opponent of the prospective client. One way to find out is to search that opponent's name in the firm's client database. (For an example of conflicts checking by computer, see Exhibit 5-10 in Chapter 5.) In addition, the database in our example can quickly:

- Generate a list of all probate and estate clients in order to send them a mailing on a new tax law.
- Generate a list of every case that the firm closed in 2015.
- Generate a list of every client who has bills that have not been paid for more than sixty days since they were sent.
- Name the attorney who brought in clients with the largest billing totals in 2016.

Major database software used by law firms includes Microsoft's Access and MySQL. To locate free alternatives, run this search in Google, Bing, or Yahoo: free alternative database management Microsoft Access.

Presentation Graphics

In many settings, a law office must communicate a client's version of the facts. For example, during negotiations with opposing counsel or in a closing argument before a jury, an attorney may want to demonstrate:

- An injured plaintiff's loss of income for the months immediately after the accident
- The expenses of a parent seeking sole custody of a child in a divorce case
- The share of the market controlled by a company accused of antitrust violations
- The chemical components of a lake into which a manufacturing plant allegedly dumped pollutants over a ten-year period

presentation graphics
Software used to combine text with charts, graphs, pictures, video, clip art, and sound in order to communicate data more effectively.

The attorney can use **presentation graphics** (also called *business graphics*) to help communicate such facts forcefully by combining text with charts, graphs, video, clip art, and sound. In a courtroom, a trial judge will probably allow an attorney to use a laptop computer to project charts or graphs as a slide show on a large screen in front of the jury. To demonstrate the costs of caring for a particular child, for example, the attorney could prepare a pie chart that uses different colors and fonts to illustrate the percentage of the budget that each expense consumes. Visually appealing graphics of this kind can be very effective, particularly in cases where the facts are numerous and relatively complicated.

The use of presentation graphics programs is not limited to litigation. A law-office manager might use the software to report on expenses, billable hours, fee collection, cash flow, and other budget matters to a committee of senior partners. The software can also be effectively used by speakers at seminars or by instructors in office training programs. For examples of computer-generated charts and graphs, see Exhibits 14-7 and 14-8 in Chapter 14. See also the baby delivery graphic in Exhibit 10-11 in Chapter 10 and the the Wal-Mart and color-coded medical treatment graphics described after Exhibit 10-11.

Major presentation graphics software used in law offices includes Microsoft's Power-Point and Corel's Presentations. To locate free alternatives, run this search in Google, Bing, or Yahoo: free alternatives PowerPoint.

Litigation Support

Lawsuits often involve numerous documents. Examples:

- correspondence
- memoranda
- transcripts of depositions
- interrogatories
- answers to interrogatories (rogs)
- requests for admission (RFA)
- responses to RFAs
- requests for production (RFP)

- responses to RFPs
- medical reports
- investigation reports
- complaints
- answers
- motions
- briefs
- business records

In complex litigation on issues of product liability, consumer fraud, and environmental law, the quantity of documents can be enormous. In a tobacco case, for example, the attorney representing Lorillard Tobacco Company told the court:

> Lorillard has produced approximately 1.8 million pages of documents in this lawsuit. If you were to take those documents and stack them…one on top of the other, they would be 666 feet high. That's the equivalent of a 66-story office building.[12]

Whether a case is small or large, **litigation support** software can be of great assistance. The software stores, retrieves, and tracks facts, documents, testimony, and other litigation materials.

A major advantage of the software is the time it can save when you are searching for information in documents, particularly when you need to search the full text (i.e., every word) of those documents. In a medical-malpractice case, for example, suppose you wanted to locate every document in the litigation that mentions Dr. Daniel Summers, one of the primary witnesses in the case. If the full text of every document is in the computer database, you would conduct a **full-text search** of these documents. The software would search every word in every document to find those that mention Dr. Daniel Summers.

Of course, to be able to conduct such searches, the complete text of every document must be in the database. (The primary method of entering complete documents is *scanning*.) If entering the full text of every document is not practical because of the time needed to scan the documents, the office can create summaries or **abstracts** of every document and then conduct a search of these abstracts. The search would find every document whose abstract mentioned Dr. Daniel Summers. (Paralegals are sometimes assigned the task of creating and entering these abstracts. Alternatively, the office might hire *document coders* to create and enter abstracts.)

If computers were not available, the searches would have to be done manually (reading line by line). One study by a bar association found that a manual search of 10,000 documents took sixty-seven paralegal hours and produced fifteen relevant documents, while the same search conducted with litigation support software took a few seconds and produced twenty relevant documents.[13]

Numerous litigation support programs exist. Examples include Concordance, CaseMap, Summation, and Zylab.

In large cases, special software is available to sort through vast quantities of information (referred to as *big data*) to find relevant documents. For example, an office might use **predictive coding**, which is a method of training software to find data that meets defined parameters. As we saw in Chapter 10, predictive coding begins with a manual review by a person who looks for specified data. Soon the program picks up patterns of what data is sought and is able to continue the search on its own based on what it learned from the manual searches.

Case Management

Case management software combines multiple tasks in the control and management of a case. The tasks often include calendaring, document control, document assembly, document tracking, and billing. Time is at the center of most of these tasks. A law office cannot practice law without managing the clock with precision. Representing clients often involves numerous appointments and deadlines. The calendar is filled with

litigation support Software that stores, retrieves, and tracks facts, documents, testimony, and other litigation materials.

full-text search A search of every word in every document in a database.

abstract A summary or abridgment.

predictive coding A method of training software to find data that meet defined parameters.

case management Software that combines multiple tasks in the control and management of a case. The tasks often include calendaring, document control, document assembly, document tracking, and billing.

scheduled interviews, strategy meetings, negotiating sessions, hearing dates, and filing deadlines. For example:

- The date of a client meeting
- The date of a meeting with opposing counsel to discuss settlement options
- The date a lease must be renewed
- The date a stock option must be exercised
- The date a complaint must be filed
- The number of days within which the answer to the complaint must be filed
- The number of days within which answers to interrogatories must be served
- The date of a deposition
- The date of a trial
- The number of days within which an appeal of a judgment must be filed
- The date client bills are due

tickler A paper or computer system designed to provide reminders of important dates. Also called a *come-up system.*

Case management software is designed to help a law office meet these and related commitments. Any system that reminds the office of important dates is called a **tickler**—it prods or tickles the memory about what must be done by certain dates.

statute of limitations A law stating that civil or criminal actions are barred if not brought within a specified time. The action is time-barred if not brought within that time.

default judgment A judgment against a party for failure to file a required pleading or otherwise respond to an opponent's claim.

The consequences of missed deadlines can be devastating. A nightmare of every plaintiff's attorney, for example, is the dismissal of an action because the failure to file a complaint before the **statute of limitations** bars the action; a nightmare of every defendant's attorney is the entry of a **default judgment** because of a failure to file an answer to the complaint within the time allotted by law. Surprisingly, such devastating lapses are not uncommon. When an insurance company is considering an application for malpractice insurance by a law firm, one of the primary concerns of the company is whether the firm has effective case-management systems in place for calendar control.

In addition to calendar control, the software can also store related information such as email and street addresses, organize to-do lists, perform billing functions, and manage email.

Commonly used case-management software includes Abacus Law, Amicus Attorney, Tabs, PracticeMaster, and Outlook.

Knowledge Management

As you can see, law offices generate a large quantity of documents. All of these documents contain what attorneys sell: knowledge. The intellectual property of a law firm is its vast collection of briefs, memoranda, pleadings, deposition and trial transcripts, contracts, corporation and banking instruments, wills, trusts, estate plans, government applications, checklists, form files, manuals, emails, reports, etc. Too often, however, once these documents are generated and used, they become an untapped resource. When the office completes work on a client's case, the file gets stored away and everyone moves on to the next client. There may be no systematic way to tap into and reuse prior work product in current cases. For example, a document created for a real estate case in 2008 might be relevant to the case of a corporate client in 2015. Yet the attorneys and paralegals working on the 2015 case may never find out about the 2008 document. This is all the more true if they are working in a branch office that is hundreds of miles away from the office that generated the 2008 document. Consequently, wasteful reinvention of the wheel can occur on a regular basis.

brief bank A collection of appellate briefs and related documents drafted in prior cases that might be adapted for current cases and used as models.

Brief banks are helpful. They contain copies of old appellate briefs and related documents that can be used as models and adapted for current cases. But not all law-office documents are in brief banks, and the banks are not smoothly integrated into the everyday operation of the office. More effective systems are needed to tap into the vast knowledge pool generated in hundreds of thousands of documents over the years. Such systems are being created as computers become more sophisticated. The systems are called **knowledge management (KM)**. KM is a system for linking into the knowledge base of a law office that is embodied in the documents generated by all of the cases handled by the office. The goal is to be able to use this knowledge so that the office can better meet the needs of current and prospective clients. KM is a way to avoid starting every case from scratch. The companies that produce Westlaw and LexisNexis are both designing KM software that can be used in conjunction with their legal-research systems. Other vendors are also creating products. KM is a relatively new concept in the law. Many are excited by its potential to increase efficiency.

knowledge management (KM) A productivity program for capturing and reusing the knowledge and work product of a law office. KM is a system of linking into the knowledge base of a law office embodied in the documents generated by all of the cases it has handled so that it can better meet the needs of current and prospective clients.

INTRODUCTION TO THE INTERNET

Hundreds of millions of people around the world use the **Internet**, a mostly self-governing network of networks, popularly known as the information superhighway, on which users can share information. A **network** is two or more computers (or other devices) that are connected by telephone lines, fiber-optic cables, satellites, or other systems in order to share hardware, software, messages, media, and other data. These different networks can communicate with each other because they all follow a set of specifications called *protocols* that make the communication possible.

Activity on the Internet is vast. Every 60 seconds,

- 7,610 searches are made on LinkedIn.
- 48,000 apps are downloaded by Apple users.
- 277,000 tweets are sent on Twitter.
- 2,000,000 videos are watched on YouTube.
- 2,400,000 items are shared on Facebook.
- 4,000,000 searches are made on Google.
- 20,000,000 photos are viewed on Flickr.
- 204,000,000 emails are sent.[14]

ORIGINS OF THE INTERNET

The Internet was developed in the 1960s by the U.S. Department of Defense to link a handful of computers in the event of a nuclear attack.[15] The idea was to design a system that would allow communication over a number of routes between linked computers. Thus, a message sent from a computer in Boston to a computer in Seattle might first be sent to a computer in Philadelphia, and then be forwarded to a computer in Pittsburgh, and then to Chicago, Denver, and Salt Lake City, before finally reaching Seattle. If the message could not travel along that path (because of military attack, technical malfunction, or other reason), the message would automatically be rerouted, perhaps from Boston to Richmond, and then to Atlanta, New Orleans, Dallas, Albuquerque, and Los Angeles, and finally to Seattle. This type of transmission and rerouting could occur in a matter of seconds without human intervention or knowledge.

When the government no longer needed this link, it turned the system over to the public. Hence no single governmental, corporate, or academic entity owns or administers the Internet. It exists and functions because hundreds of thousands of separate operators of computers and computer networks independently decided to use common data transfer protocols to exchange communications and information with other computers (which in turn exchange communications and information with still other computers). There is no centralized storage location, control point, or communications channel for the Internet. Indeed, it would not be technically feasible for a single entity to control everything that is conveyed on the Internet. An individual country may be able to create a "kill switch" that blocks access to the Internet in that country, but the resulting uproar would probably make the attempt short-lived.

CONNECTING TO THE INTERNET

To connect to the Internet, you need a company or organization that provides access, called an **Internet service provider (ISP)**, e.g., AT&T, Comcast, or EarthLink. Once connected, most of your online time will be spent on the **World Wide Web (WWW)**. The Web is a system of sites using **hypertext** to enable you to display and link information in different locations on the same site or on different sites. When you are on a Web page, you will see words, pictures, or buttons that are highlighted in some way, often with the use of color or underlining. If the words, pictures, or buttons on a site are highlighted (i.e., hypertexted), you can click on them and you will be taken to another section of the site or to a different site. The program that allows you to read pages on the Web is called a **web browser**. (The most popular browsers are Chrome, Explorer, Safari, and Firefox.)

Internet A worldwide electronic network of networks on which millions of computer users can share information.

network (1) A group of computers that are linked or connected together by telephone lines, fiber-optic cables, satellites, or other systems. (2) Interconnected persons or things.

Internet service provider (ISP) A company that provides access to the Internet, usually for a monthly fee.

World Wide Web (WWW) A system of sites on the Internet that can be accessed through hypertext links.

hypertext A method of displaying and linking information found in different locations on the same site or on different sites of the World Wide Web.

web browser A program that allows you to read pages on the World Wide Web.

INTERNET ADDRESSES

uniform resource locator (URL) The address of a resource (or any page) on the Internet.

The address of a resource (or any page) on the World Wide Web (e.g., a document or an image) is called the **uniform resource locator (URL)**. Here is an example of a URL:

http://www.loc.gov

Http means hypertext transfer protocol. As we saw earlier, the protocol is the set of specifications or standards that allow computers to communicate with each other. Because most web browsers assume you are using the http protocol, you do not need to type http://.

server (1) A computer program that provides resources or services to other computers. (2) A system that manages resources on a network. (3) A computer that processes requests.

After the protocol in our URL example comes the address of the **server** (www.loc.gov) on which the resource is located. A server is a computer program that provides resources or services (e.g., access to data) to other computers. Typing the address of the server will usually lead you to its opening page (the home page, also called the *start page*). The last three digits of the server address (.gov) are the domain name or identifier, which indicates the category or type of server. Our example (www.loc.gov) will lead you to a government agency, the Library of Congress (loc). Here are the original categories of domain names:

.com (commercial entity)
.gov (government office)
.org (organization, often nonprofit)
.edu (educational institution)
.mil (military institution)
.net (network provider)

Many more specific categories are being added (e.g., .church, .hotel, .nyc).

After the URL's server name, you may find additional characters. For example:

www.loc.gov/law/index.php

The additional characters (/law/index.php) bypass the home page and take you directly to specific documents, images, or links available on the site.

When you type in a long address, you will occasionally find that no results (or "hits") are produced. You may get a message telling you that "your search did not match any documents." You may be trying to access a site that no longer exists or that no longer exists at the address you are using. Before giving up, check the exact spelling of the address you typed. Make sure that the slashes were correctly typed (/ should not be typed as \) and that you have not added any spaces to the address. If your address is still unproductive, remove everything from the address except the beginning of the address up to the domain name. Hence, www.loc.gov/law/index.php, becomes www.loc.gov. This will bring you get back to the home page. On this page, you may find links that will lead you to what you are looking for. Or you may find a search option on the home page in which you can try some new search terms.

email Electronic mail. A message sent electronically.

EMAIL

e-discovery The discovery by a party in litigation of an opponent's data generated by or stored in a computer or other digital device. The discovery of electronically stored information (ESI). Examples include email, instant messages (IMs), text messages, voice mail, social-media posts, spreadsheets, web pages, digital video, and other digital data. Also called *electronic data discovery (EDD)*.

Email (electronic mail) is a message sent electronically. When you obtain an Internet account, you are given an email address that will allow you to communicate with millions of persons in the world who also have an email address. Many law offices purchase Outlook, a Microsoft software application that is part of its Office suite. Outlook manages the flow of email and provides storage folders, address directories, and ways to divert unwanted email (spam). The general public is more inclined to use Gmail, the free email program of Google, or the email programs of other giant companies such as Yahoo.

A major advantage of email is that you can include attachments that can contain text, sound, images, or video. There are limits, however, on the size of an email or attachment that can be sent. A message with many high-resolution photos attached, for example, or even a short video attachment may be too large.

Email programs allow you to create multiple folders in which you can store messages that have been read (or that will be read later). Such folders, however, can quickly become clogged with a large volume of messages. Hence, many offices transfer their client-related email messages into the records department or another unit of the office where they can be safely stored and searched as needed.

litigation hold A notice that a legal dispute has occurred and that information pertinent to the dispute must be preserved by the person or organization in possession or custody of such information. The failure to do may result in sanctions for *spoliation*.

In Chapters 5 and 14 we examined the ethical requirement of a law office to preserve client records, usually for a designated time after the case is closed. This rule applies to emails that pertain to client cases. As we saw in Chapter 10, **e-discovery** requires parties to turn over email messages that are potentially relevant to litigation. A **litigation hold** is designed to prevent the destruction of such data.

INSTANT MESSAGING

Email messages can take several seconds, minutes, or longer to reach the intended recipient (s). **Instant messaging (IM)**, on the other hand, is electronic communication in real time, usually on smartphones and other hand-held mobile devices. IMs, like emails, can contain text, images, short videos, and various hyperlinks.

instant messaging (IM) Electronic communication in real time.

ELECTRONIC MAILING LIST

An **electronic mailing list** (often referred to as a *listserv*) is a program that manages computer mailing lists automatically. These lists consist of individuals interested in receiving and sending email to each other on a topic of mutual interest. To become a member of a list, you send an email to its administrator asking to join. Thousands of topics are covered on the lists, e.g., travel, higher education, hobbies, and yoga. Numerous *legal* lists cover a large variety of law and law-related topics, e.g., bankruptcy, law office management, job hunting, paralegals, and the law of a particular state. (On Google, Bing, or Yahoo run this search: "legal listserv" or "paralegal listserv".) Once you have subscribed to a list, you can read the comments, questions, and replies sent by everyone else on the list. By reading these messages, you can keep abreast of developments in the subject matter of the group.

Here are examples of the kinds of questions that might be posted on different electronic mailing lists. On a paralegal list, a paralegal asks:

electronic mailing list A program that manages computer mailing lists so that members of the list can receive and send messages and read what other members send to each other. Also called *elist*, *maillist*, *email list*, *listserv*.

I'm thinking about taking NALA's certification exam (CLA/CP), NFPA's certification exam (PACE), or NALS's certification exam (PP). Can any of you help me with a comparison of these paralegal tests?

A paralegal member of a California real-estate list asks:

We have a client who bought and sold land in Georgia in 1985. I'm trying to find a copy of the standard purchase agreement used by the Georgia Association of Real Estate Agents in the 1970s before they substantially changed the format of the contract. Georgia people: Can you help me? I'd appreciate it. Help!

At the beginning of the week, a New York attorney, in immediate need of locating Mississippi regulations on nursing homes, sends out the following urgent email to the members of his list:

I'm looking for the Mississippi Department of Health regulations on nursing homes. I didn't find them on Westlaw, LexisNexis or on the free sites. The Department tells me it can't supply them until Friday. Anyone willing to send me a copy as an email attachment?

Someone who uses Microsoft Word sends this email to members of a Word users list:

I just got the upgrade and I can't get it to hook up with my HP 6620 printer. Are any of you using the upgrade with this printer after downloading the latest driver from the HP site? Were you able to get the two to work together?

Depending on the number of members in the listserv, you could receive scores of replies. Many members who have had their questions answered send "thanks-for-saving-my-life" messages to the group. Even if you do not send any questions yourself, you will probably find it instructive—and fun—to read the questions and answers others are sending to each other on topics that are relevant to your work. (Reading online messages of others without sending any of your own is called *lurking*, an activity engaged in by most of the members of the list.)

SOCIAL MEDIA

Social media refers to websites that allow users to engage in different kinds of interaction or networking with each other, such as by posting information about themselves and their interests and commenting on what others post. The exchange among the users creates a kind of virtual community centered on shared likes and dislikes. In the early days, the main function of the Internet was to provide users with information. In the next stage of Internet development (so-called Web 2.0), users can interact with the site and each other in building the information that is shared. To a large extent, Web 2.0 consists of popular add-your-own-content sites.

social media Websites that allow users to engage in different kinds of interaction or networking with each other such as by posting information about themselves and their interests and commenting on what others post.

See Exhibit 13-6 later in the chapter on ways to check the reliability of social-media and other sites.

Kinds of Social Media

- *Social Networking.* Interact with people of similar backgrounds and interests by making friends or business connections. Examples: Facebook (www.facebook.com), LinkedIn (www.linkedin.com).
- *Collaborative Sites.* Interact by helping to build a body of knowledge on topics of interest. Examples: Wikipedia (www.wikipedia.com), Wikia (www.wikia.com).
- *Blogs.* Interact by commenting on the specific topic of the blog. A **blog** is an Internet journal or diary on any topic of interest to the blogger (writer) of the blog. (Sometimes called **blawg** if the topic of the blog is mainly legal.) Directories of blogs include ABA (www.abajournal.com/blawgs) and Justia (blawgsearch.justia.com/blogs).
- *Microblogs.* Interact by participating in blogs that allow short posts. The main example is Twitter (twitter.com).
- *Social Photo and Video Sharing.* Interact by posting (uploading) pictures and video clips, labeling (tagging) the posts, and commenting on the posts of others. Examples: Flickr (www.flickr.com), Instagram (instagram.com), Pinterest (pinterest.com), YouTube (www.youtube.com), Vimeo (www.vimeo.com), DailyMotion (www.dailymotion.com).
- *News Networking* (Social News). Interact by sharing, voting on, and commenting on articles or stories of interest. Examples: Reddit (www.reddit.com), Digg (www.digg.com).
- *Social Bookmarking.* Interact by sharing websites and labeling (tagging) them so that others can find them by subject or topic. Examples: Delicious (delicious.com), StumbleUpon (www.stumbleupon.com), Blinklist (blinklist.com).
- *Ratings and Reviews.* Interact by recommending services and products and commenting on the recommendations of others. Examples: Yelp (www.yelp.com), Citysearch (www.citysearch.com), Angie's List (www.angieslist.com).
- *Virtual Worlds.* Interact by creating a simulated world or environment. Examples: Second Life (secondlife.com), World of Warcraft (us.battle.net/wow/en).

LinkedIn, Facebook, and Twitter

Three of the major social media sites (LinkedIn, Facebook, and Twitter) are discussed in Chapter 2. See Exhibit 2-13 (Using Social Media in a Job Search) and Exhibit 2-14 (Caution in Using Social Media).

ALERTS

Some sites let you sign up for email alerts that notify you of new content. An example is Google Alert (www.google.com/alerts). Suppose, for example, that you are interested in the topic of "surrogate motherhood" or "acid rain." You could set up an alert so that every time a website mentions your term(s), you will receive an email telling (alerting) you about it. If your name has a unique spelling, you could set up an alert for your name. Broad topics (e.g., law) or common names (e.g., Robert Smith) are unlikely to be productive as alerts because of the large number of responses you will receive. Alerts can be useful in a job search. Suppose, for example, you are interested in working for Garvey, Foley, and Adams. In addition to checking the website of this law firm and doing a news search for stories about the firm, you could also create an alert for its name so that you will receive an email every time the firm is mentioned on the Internet. As we saw in Chapter 2, potential employers are often impressed by job applicants who are knowledgeable about their organization.

RSS

A different notification system is **really simple syndication (RSS)**. Assume that you have twenty must-visit sites that contain important material (e.g., new cases on a court site, and job openings for paralegals on a job placement site). If these twenty sites offer RSS feeds, you can subscribe to them and receive notification whenever anything new exists on any of the sites. (When a site allows RSS feeds, it is called *syndicating its content.*) The notification is not through email but instead through an RSS list that can be placed on your browser. You go to this list to find out which of your sites, if any, are mentioned. If, for example, only two of your favorite sites are on the list, you simply click on them to find out what is new. You can ignore

---

blog An Internet journal or diary on any topic of interest to the blogger (writer) of the blog. Sometimes called *blawg* if the topic of the blog is mainly legal.

blawg An Internet journal or diary on a mainly legal topic.

really simple syndication (RSS) A method of notifying subscribers of new content on an Internet site by syndicating (feeding) notice of the new content to subscribers.

the other eighteen. Their absence from the RSS list means there is nothing new for you to check on them. To give you an idea of RSS feeds on law-related topics, enter this search in Google, Bing, or Yahoo: RSS law. For sites about paralegals that have RSS feeds, try this search: RSS paralegal.

PODCASTS

A **podcast** (sometimes called an *audioblog*) is an Internet radio-type audio file that the public can download and listen to through a browser or on audio devices such as iPods and MP3 players. Many legal podcasts are available (e.g., Legal Talk Network). To find podcasts on the law, run this search on Google, Bing, or Yahoo: podcast law.

podcast An Internet audio file that the public can download and listen to through a browser or on audio devices such as iPods and MP3 players. Also called an *audioblog*.

THE INTERNET OF THINGS (IoT)

What if everything around you—people, animals, and objects—could be given a unique identifier and thereby become connected on the Internet through smart sensors, data centers, and cameras? Chips would be embedded everywhere. Your refrigerator, for example, would signal your smartphone that you are running low on milk, your toothbrush would let another smart device know what areas you tend to miss when brushing your teeth, and your bathroom scale would alert your computer how much you are behind this week on your weight-loss program.[16] "What if the wearable device you used in the workplace could tell you when and where you were most active and productive and shared that information with other devices that you used while working?"[17] Welcome to the *Internet of Things* (IoT), sometimes called the Internet of Everything.

The scope of the IoT is vast when you think of the billions of things that might be connected through the Internet. Government proponents see great public health benefits as volumes of pollution data provide up-to-the minute data on dangers. Businesses see expanded opportunities to sell us what we need close to the moment when the need arises—and, indeed, before we know we have the need! Yet IoT scares a lot of people. Where is all of this mega-big data going to be kept and who will have access to it? The potential security and privacy issues are mindboggling. "Will someone be able to hack into your toaster and thereby get access to your entire network?"[18]

INTERNET SEARCHING

Most of us use Google—a lot. Indeed, we probable feel that we are very good at using this search engine. Unfortunately, many of us are mistaken in this belief. According to one recent study,

> The prevalence of Google in student research is well-documented, but the Illinois researchers found something they did not expect: students were not very good at using Google. They were basically clueless about the logic underlying how the search engine organizes and displays its results. Consequently, the students did not know how to build a search that would return good sources.[19]

This concern does not apply to Google alone. There are widespread deficiencies in the use of other search engines as well. To overcome this concern, see the guidelines in Exhibits 13-6 and 13-7.

Exhibit 13-6	Search Engine (SE) Techniques and Assessing the Reliability of What You Find

Search Techniques

- Be prepared to try your search on more than one search engine (SE). (See the choices in Exhibit 13-7.) The most widely used SEs today are Google, Bing, and Yahoo.
- Every SE has its own help section that gives instructions and suggestions on how to use it to search effectively. On the home page of the SE, look for links called More, Help, How to Search, Advanced Search, etc. (If you don't find these links, enter *search help* in each SE, e.g., Google search help, Bing search help, Yahoo search help.) Read this help section carefully for every SE you try. The section will have suggestions on how to rephrase an unproductive query by narrowing it (e.g., use more specific search terms in the query) or by broadening it (e.g., add synonyms to the query). Unfortunately, many researchers do not check this help section. They type in their search terms and quickly abandon the search site if the first page of results is not productive. Unproductive results, however, may be due to a failure of the researcher to take the time to learn how to use the SE. Someone once said that the best SE is the one that you take the time to learn to use.

(continued)

Exhibit 13-6	Search Engine (SE) Techniques and Assessing the Reliability of What You Find *(Continued)*

- Run this search in any SE: tutorial aa search (substituting the word Google, Bing, Yahoo, or any other SE for aa). (Example: tutorial Bing search). Such tutorials are an additional way for you to become proficient in online search.
- Here are some important questions you want answered about every SE you use. Try to answer these questions by checking the SE's help section:
  - How do you search for phrases? Do you need to add quotation marks around the phrase, e.g., "capital punishment"?
  - How do you search for plurals (e.g., vehicles or children)? Does the SE automatically search for plurals when you enter the singular form of a search term?
  - Does the SE have an AND connector? (A connector is a character, word, or symbol used to show the relationship between words and phrases in a database query.) When your search query has more than one term (e.g., battery woman), how do you indicate that you want sites that contain all of your terms? Do you add AND between the terms (*battery AND woman*)? Do you place a plus sign (+) immediately in front of each term (*+battery +woman*) that must appear in the site? Do you use another method?
  - Does the SE have an OR connector? How do you express alternative terms in your search query? Do you add OR between the terms (e.g., *zoning OR easement*) or does the SE automatically treat every space between search terms as an OR so that OR does not have to be typed?
  - How do you search for synonyms? Is the OR connector used (e.g., *divorce* OR *dissolution*)?
  - Does the SE have a BUT NOT or an AND NOT connector? How do you tell the SE to avoid specific categories of sites? For example, how do you tell it that you want sites on penicillin for adults only? Do you use the BUT NOT connector (*penicillin BUT NOT child*) or the AND NOT connector (e.g., *penicillin AND NOT child*), or do you place a minus sign (–) immediately in front of any term that must not appear (*+penicillin +adult –child*)?
  - If you are not sure how to spell a term (e.g., Gieco? Geico?), can you use a wildcard such as * (G**co) or ! (G!!co)? A wildcard, also called a *universal character*, is a special character (e.g., *, ! or ?) that can be used to represent one or more characters in a search query.
  - How does the SE treat common words, e.g., *a, an, the*, and *that* (sometimes called *stop words*)? If you type them as part of your query, does the search engine ignore them? If you want them included (and searched for) along with the other words in your query, how is this done? Some SEs require the use of quotation marks around the language that includes the common words if you want them included.
  - Are searches *case sensitive* or *case insensitive*? Will the SE give you the same results if all your search words are in capital letters (GUN AND THEFT), in all lowercase letters (gun and theft), or in a combination of capital and lowercase letters (Gun AND Theft)? A search is case insensitive if the use of capital letters has no effect on the search results. The search is case sensitive if the results would differ when capital letters were used. In general, passwords and usernames (but not search terms) are case sensitive, although this should be checked in the help section of the SE.
- Be specific in your use of search terms. For example, if you are looking for attorney fee cases in litigation involving the Ojibwa tribe in Maine, type +attorney +fee +Ojibwa +Maine (or *attorney AND fee AND Ojibwa AND Maine*); do not simply type +attorney +fee (or *attorney AND fee*).
- Refine your search terms as you continue to search. Some of the early sites you come across may not be what you need, but these sites may suggest new search terms to try. Also, watch for hyperlinks within every site you visit. A less-than-productive site may allow you to "jump" to a productive one.
- If you have more than one search term, type the most important term first. For example, if you are looking for sites on the incompatibility grounds of divorce, your query might be +divorce +incompatibility +grounds (or *divorce AND incompatibility AND grounds*).
- Search the *invisible web* to try to find materials that are not picked up by regular SEs. For sites that help you search the invisible Web, see Exhibit 13-7.
- Once you enter a site, you can often use the *find* command (e.g., ctrl-F or Cmd F) to try to find your search terms within the pages of the site.
- When you need the definition of a legal term, use the powerful definition search feature (define:) available on many SEs. For example, run the following search on Google, Bing, or Yahoo: define: habeas corpus.

Assessing Reliability

- Once you have found something on the Internet through these techniques, you need to assess its reliability. The saying "You can't believe everything you read in the newspaper" applies with greater force to what you read on the Internet. Because the Internet is essentially unregulated, everyone can post whatever they want on the information superhighway. The expensive fee-based sites (Westlaw, LexisNexis and Bloomberg Law) are substantially reliable because of the large editorial staffs they employ. For other sites, here are some general guidelines to keep in mind:
  - Be sensitive to when a site states facts as opposed to opinions. If you find a fact on a site (e.g., a statistic) that you want to use in a memo or other writing, look for whatever support the site gives for the fact. Sites that give sources for their facts may be more reliable that those that do not. Also be alert to whether the site is relying on any links to other sites as its source. Go to these linked sites to see if they verify their facts. It is possible for false information to be posted on a site and then republished by dozens of other sites, none of which have independently checked its accuracy.
  - In general, the most reliable free sites are those with government domains (.gov). On the reliability such sites, see Reliability of Law on the Internet toward the beginning of Chapter 11.
  - The reliability of sites with educational institution domains (.edu) or association domains (.org) depends on the quality and reputation of the institution or association.
  - At the bottom of a page on a site, particularly its home page, look for an "Updated On" or "Last Updated" date, which will give you an indication of how current the material is. Be extra cautious of sites that do not provide such dates. The data on some sites may be months or even years old without any indication that this is so.

(continued)

Exhibit 13-6 Search Engine (SE) Techniques and Assessing the Reliability of What You Find *(Continued)*

- Try to find out who owns the site (*e.g.,* enter the address of the site at www.whois.net). The most reliable sites have "About Me" or "About Us" links that will provide background information about the authors of the site. This can help you assess reliability.
- Type the Web address of the site *in the search box* of Google, Bing, or Yahoo rather than in the address box at the top of your browser. This may lead to sites that provide additional information about the site you are checking.
- If you are on a site with a long address, go to the home page of the site by deleting everything in the address after the site's domain name. You may be given more information about the site on this page.
- Approach Wiki sites with added care. These are sites that allow anyone to add content; they have a collaborative authorship. The most widely used Wiki site is the online encyclopedia Wikipedia (wikipedia.org). Hundreds of thousands of people with varying degrees of expertise have written the sections of this encyclopedia. Be hesitant about relying on something found on a wiki site, although the site may be helpful in giving you background information as you start your research on a topic that is new to you. The site may also give you links to other sites that are more appropriate for your needs. (See Exhibit 11-11 in Chapter 11 on doing background research to get the big picture.)
- For more information on determining the reliability of Internet sites, run this search in Google, Bing, or Yahoo: web reliability. Also check:
  - www.lib.unca.edu/library/lr/evalweb.html
  - www.hopetillman.com/findqual.php

Exhibit 13-7 Search Engines

- **LISTS OF AVAILABLE SEARCH ENGINES (SEs)**
  - www.thesearchenginelist.com
  - www.searchengineguide.com/searchengines.html
  - en.wikipedia.org/wiki/List_of_search_engines
  - www.beaucoup.com
  - www.searchenginecolossus.com

- **MAJOR SEARCH ENGINES**
  - www.google.com
  - www.bing.com
  - www.yahoo.com
  - www.duckduckgo.com
  - www.gigablast.com
  - www.aol.com

- **SEARCH ENGINE COMPARISON CHARTS**
  - infopeople.org/content/best-search-tools-chart
  - en.wikipedia.org/wiki/Comparison_of_web_search_engines
  - www.lib.berkeley.edu/TeachingLib/Guides/Internet/SearchEngines.html

- **GLOSSARIES OF SEARCH ENGINE TERMS**
  - searchenginewatch.com/article/2066763/Search-Engine-Glossary
  - www.searchenginedictionary.com
  - www.cadenza.org/search_engine_terms

- **METASEARCH ENGINES**
  (These search multiple search engines simultaneously.)
  - www.dogpile.com
  - www.ixquick.com
  - mamma.com

- **DIRECTORIES: BROWSING BY SUBJECTS, TOPICS, OR TAGS**
  - www.ipl.org
  - dir.yahoo.com
  - www.dmoz.org

- www.galaxy.com
- en.wikipedia.org/wiki/List_of_web_directories

- **BLOG SEARCH**
  - www.google.com/blogsearch
  - www.blogsearchengine.org
  - www.icerocket.com

- **TWITTER SEARCH**
  - twitter.com/search-home
  - twitter.com/twittersearch

- **QUESTION AND ANSWER ENGINES**
  - answers.yahoo.com
  - www.quora.com
  - www.ask.com

- **NATURAL LANGUAGE SEARCHING**
  - www.bing.com
  - www.ask.com
  - www.lexxe.com

- **ACADEMIC SEARCH ENGINES**
  - scholar.google.com (click *Articles*)
  - infomine.ucr.edu
  - www.refseek.com
  - www.teachthought.com (type *academic research* in the search box)

- **SEARCHING THE INVISIBLE WEB**
  (Searching on sites that are often not reachable by standard search engines and directories)
  - www.lib.berkeley.edu/TeachingLib/Guides/Internet/InvisibleWeb.html
  - websearch.about.com/od/invisibleweb/a/invisible_web.htm
  - en.wikipedia.org/wiki/Deep_Web

LEGAL RESEARCH ON THE INTERNET

On free and fee-based legal research on the Internet, see

- Exhibit 11-3 Finding Law on the Internet (Chapter 11).
- Exhibit 11-11 Resources for Doing Background Research on a Topic: Obtaining the Big Picture (Chapter 11).
- Helpful Websites at the end of Chapter 11.

FACTUAL RESEARCH ON THE INTERNET

On free and fee-based factual research on the Internet, see

- Exhibit 9-9 Examples of Financial Data on Fee-Based Databases (Westlaw and LexisNexis) (Chapter 9).
- Helpful Websites at the end of Chapter 9.

SECURITY ON THE INTERNET

CONFIDENTIALITY

In a law office, many clients often communicate with attorneys, paralegals, and secretaries by email. Almost all of these client communications contain confidential communications that might be read by strangers such as **hackers** and administrators of network servers. The cautious law office, therefore, will obtain explicit consent from the client to communicate by email after reminding the client that security over the Internet cannot be guaranteed. As an added precaution email messages can be **encrypted**, which converts the messages into a code that renders the message data incomprehensible until the messages are reconverted to a readable format by the client or other authorized recipient. For more on the ethical use of email, see Chapter 5.

SPAM

Spam consists of unsolicited email messages, often containing commercial advertising (junk mail). Most computers have spam filters that that try to identify spam so that it can be diverted to a junk folder and eventually deleted with relative ease.

MALWARE

Malware, short for malicious software, is software that seeks to disable, disrupt, or otherwise damage computers. In addition, malware can be a major way to commit **identity theft**, which is the acquisition and use (or attempted acquisition and use) of another person's private identifying information with the intent to commit any unlawful activity. Of course, identity theft can be committed without malware, such as by stealing and using someone's credit cards.

Examples of Malware

- *adware*: sends advertising (e.g., pop-ups); may contain spyware (see the definition on the next page)
- *bot* (short for robot): allows someone to take over your computer; large numbers of infected computers (called zombies) can then be activated for malicious purposes such as sending spam, phishing (see below), and making denial-of-service attacks against a website, which must shut down because of the overwhelming traffic generated by the zombies; a denial-of-service attack floods a site with bogus traffic
- *chargeware*: charges a fee to the user's account without the user's knowledge or consent
- *keylogging*: tracks and stores keystrokes you press on your keyboard when typing passwords, credit-card numbers, etc.; a form of spyware (see the definition on the next page)
- *phishing*: fraudulently attempts to obtain personal information by tricking the recipient of an email message into believing that the sender seeking the information is legitimate
- *ransomware*: freezes a computer system and demands a payment (ransom) to restore the system
- *ratware*: automates email spam for mass mailings
- *rootkit*: installs itself remotely on a computer to gain access to the programs and data on the computer

hacker One who gains (or seeks to gain) unauthorized access to computer data.

encrypt Convert text into a code that renders the text incomprehensible until it is reconverted to a readable format by a recipient with the right software.

spam Unsolicited email messages, often consisting of commercial advertising; unsolicited junk mail.

malware Software that seeks to disable, disrupt, or otherwise damage computers. Examples: virus, Trojan horse.

identity theft Acquiring and using (or attempting to acquire and use) another person's private identifying information with the intent to commit any unlawful activity.

- *spyware*: monitors (spies on) the user's movement on the Internet, usually for purposes of advertising
- *trojans*: masquerades as legitimate programs and, when activated, can destroy data, send spam, etc.
- *virus*: inserts itself into and becomes a part of a computer; it can spread to and thereby infect other computers; the virus can look for passwords or other personal information, send spam, delete data, cause denial-of-service attacks, etc.
- *worm*: sends a copy of itself (self-replicates) to everyone in your address book so that it appears that the message comes from you; the virus can then find passwords or other personal information, send spam, delete data, etc.

Preventing Malware

- Install anti-malware software.
- Install **firewalls**. A firewall is a security program for computers on a network that analyzes incoming data to determine whether the data should be allowed into the network based on predetermined rules or criteria on what can be trusted.
- Keep anti-malware software and firewalls up to date in order to protect against newly created malware.
- Regularly download updates of the operating software (OS) (e.g., Windows) and applications (e.g., Microsoft Word). The updates (often called *patches*) may fix security bugs or flaws.
- Encrypt email that is sent from the office.
- Use great care when opening email attachments. They can contain malware. The email may appear to come from someone you know because that person's address list has been captured by a hacker. If you are not expecting an attachment, do not open it without running it through a malware detection program or contacting the sender to confirm that this person has sent you an email with an attachment. Hence, the safest guideline to follow on attachments is as follows: don't click them open unless (1) you know the sender *and* (2) you are expecting the attachment.

firewall A security program for computers on a network that analyzes incoming data to determine whether the data should be allowed into the network based on predetermined rules or criteria on what can be trusted.

Cookies

A **cookie** is a small text file that a website inserts on your computer when you visit the site with your browser, giving the site information about your browsing visit. For example, if you entered your email address on a visit, the next time you visit the site, the address will be remembered (via the cookie) so that you do not have to retype it. For many sites, the cookie will follow you even if you do not enter anything in the site. Suppose, for example, that you click on the site of a Hilton hotel in Boston but leave before doing anything other than reading the site's general information on the hotel. Don't be surprised to find an ad for the Boston Hilton on a news site or a sports site that you visit days later when you have long forgotten about a hotel in Boston.

In general, cookies do not spread viruses or other malware. Yet the cookies make some people uncomfortable because of the information they contain about sites they visit. To erase cookies or to stop them from being inserted on your computer, go to the help or settings page of your browser and read about your options on cookies. You could also enter this search in Google, Bing, or Yahoo: understanding cookies in aa (substituting the name of your browser for aa).

cookie A small text file that a website inserts on your computer when you visit the site with your browser, giving the site information about your browsing visit.

ETHICAL ISSUES

See Chapter 5 for a discussion of the following ethical issues involved in the use of computers in a law office:

- Incompetence. It is unethical to fail to keep current on computer technology to the extent needed to provide competent client representation.
- Deception. It is unethical to misrepresent your identity in order to obtain information online that pertains to a client's case. Avoid **pretexting**.
- Breach of confidentiality. It can be unethical to send documents without removing **metadata** that can contain confidential information.

pretexting Using online deception as a pretext to obtain information from another person.

metadata Data about data. Data about an electronic document that are hidden within the document itself, e.g., earlier versions of the document.

Other ethical concerns:

- Inadvertent establishment of an attorney-client relationship. This can occur when a person contacts a website that does not have adequate disclaimers that the contact does not create an attorney-client relationship.
- Failure to provide adequate supervision of persons performing **outsourced** work online.

outsource Paying an outside company or service to perform tasks usually performed by one's own employees.

CHAPTER SUMMARY

The computer plays a major role in the practice of law. You need to take every opportunity to learn as much as you can about computers. Start compiling a notebook of computer terminology, take online tutorials, take short-term computer courses available in the community, attend computer events at paralegal and bar associations, etc.

Hardware is the physical equipment of a computer system. Software is a computer program that tells the hardware what to do. The two main categories of software are operating software (OS) and application software (apps). The OS is a program that tells the computer how to perform its major functions, such as starting (executing) programs, managing its memory, and controlling printers and other attached devices. An app is software that performs tasks commonly needed by the consumer or end user, such as word processing. The central processing unit (CPU) is the hardware that contains the processor chip, which in turn controls all of the computer's parts. Mobile devices with wireless communication features, such as smartphones and tablet computers, allow users to work from remote locations.

The two main kinds of memory are read-only memory (ROM) and random access memory (RAM). Data in memory are measured in bytes. Storage devices with read/write capability allow users to read the data on the device and write additional data on the device. You cannot write data on a read-only device. Major storage devices include hard drives, removable drives, magnetic tape systems, optical storage devices, and the cloud. Input devices that place information in a computer include the keyboard, the mouse, speech recognition programs, and scanners. The main output devices are monitors, printers (including 3-D printers), and sound cards. A modem is a communications device that allows computers at different locations to exchange data using telephone lines, cables, or wireless connections. Computers can be connected by a local area network (LAN) if they are relatively close to each other, or by a wide area network (WAN) if they are not close. An intranet is a private network of computers for the sharing of data, software, and services within the organization using features similar to those of the World Wide Web. An extranet is the part of an intranet to which selected outsiders (e.g., clients) have been given access.

A word processor is a software program that allows you to enter and edit data in order to create and revise documents. Special formatting features and shortcuts using macros make the creation of documents relatively easy. A spreadsheet is a software program that performs calculations on numbers and values that you enter. Database management software allows you to organize, search, retrieve, and sort data. Presentation graphics software can combine text with charts, graphs, pictures, video, clip art, and sound in order to communicate data effectively. Litigation support software can store, retrieve, and track facts, documents, testimony, and other litigation documents. Case management software combines multiple tasks in the control and management of a case. The tasks include calendaring, document control, document assembly, document tracking, and billing. Knowledge management (KM) software helps a law office capture and reuse its knowledge and work product generated from prior cases.

The Internet is a worldwide network of networks on which millions of computer users share information. The hypertext features of the World Wide Web allow relatively easy access to a vast quantity of data. Personal communication among users often occurs through email and instant messaging (IM). Electronic mailing lists manage computer mailing lists so that members of the list can receive and send messages and read what other members send to each other. The lists can be a useful way to keep current on specialty topics. Social media allow interaction with and among users through comments, votes, uploads, and the like. Categories of social media include social networking, collaborative sites, blogs and blawgs, microblogs, social photo and video sharing, news networking, social bookmarking, ratings and reviews, and virtual worlds. Alerts notify you of new content on topics of interest that you identify. Really simple syndication (RSS) is a method of notifying subscribers of new content on an Internet site by syndicating (feeding) notice of the new content to subscribers. A podcast is an Internet audio file that the public can download and listen to through a browser or on audio devices such as iPods and MP3 players. The Internet of Things (IoT) envisons that every person, animal, and object is given a unique identifier and is connected through the Internet.

The major Internet search tool is the search engine. Check its help feature to identify its unique search techniques. Learn how a search engine handles phrases, plurals, connectors, synonyms, wildcards, stop words, case sensitivity, find commands, and definitions. Once you have found something on the Internet, you must assess its reliability. Malware is software that seeks to disable, disrupt, or otherwise damage computers. Examples of malware include adware, chargeware, keylogging, phishing, ransomware, ratware, rootkits, spyware, trojans, viruses, and worms. To prevent malware, install (and keep current) anti-malware software and firewalls, update operating software and application software, encrypt email, and exert great care in opening attachments.

Ethical problems in the use of computers include incompetence, deception, improper sharing of metadata, inadvertent establishment of an attorney-client relationship, and failure to provide adequate supervision of persons performing outsourced work.

KEY TERMS

e-filing (p. 562)
online (p. 562)
hardware (p. 564)
software (p. 564)
central processing unit (CPU) (p. 564)
operating software (OS) (p. 564)
application (app) (p. 564)
Wi-Fi (p. 564)
telecommuting (p. 565)
virtual (p. 565)
read-only memory (ROM) (p. 565)
random access memory (RAM) (p. 565)
byte (p. 565)
hard drive (p. 565)
optical storage device (p. 566)
cloud (p. 566)
scanner (p. 566)
imaging (p. 566)
PDF (p. 566)
bar code (p. 566)
modem (p. 567)

videoconferencing (p. 567)
real time (p. 567)
local area network (LAN) (p. 567)
wide area network (WAN) (p. 567)
stand-alone computer (p. 567)
intranet (p. 567)
continuing legal education (CLE) (p. 567)
extranet (p. 567)
integrated package (p. 567)
word processor (p. 568)
left justified (p. 570)
right justified (p. 570)
macro (p. 570)
table of authorities (TOA) (p. 571)
font (p. 571)
point (p. 571)
spreadsheet (p. 571)

structured settlement (p. 571)
database management (p. 572)
presentation graphics (p. 572)
litigation support (p. 573)
full-text search (p. 573)
abstract (p. 573)
predictive coding (p. 573)
case management (p. 573)
tickler (p. 574)
statute of limitations (p. 574)
default judgment (p. 574)
brief bank (p. 574)
knowledge management (KM) (p. 574)
Internet (p. 575)
network (p. 575)
Internet service provider (ISP) (p. 575)
World Wide Web (WWW) (p. 575)
hypertext (p. 575)
Web browser (p. 575)
uniform resource locator (URL) (p. 576)

server (p. 576)
email (p. 576)
e-discovery (p. 576)
litigation hold (p. 576)
instant messaging (IM) (p. 577)
electronic mailing list (p. 577)
social media (p. 577)
blog (p. 578)
blawg (p. 578)
really simple syndication (RSS) (p. 578)
podcast (p. 579)
hacker (p. 582)
encrypt (p. 582)
spam (p. 582)
malware (p. 582)
identity theft (p. 582)
firewall (p. 583)
cookie (p. 583)
pretexting (p. 583)
metadata (p. 583)
outsource (p. 584)

ASSIGNMENTS

CRITICAL ANALYSIS

13.1 In Google, Bing, or Yahoo, run this search: lawyers in the cloud.

(a) What is meant by the phrase "practicing law in the cloud"? Give specific examples.

(b) Why are some attorneys reluctant to practice in the cloud? Is this reluctance justified?

In the Computer Terminology in the Law (CTL) notebook you started in Assignment 1.8 of Chapter 1, include information you obtain by doing parts a and b.

Projects

13.2 Run this search in Google, Bing, or Yahoo: legal technology trends aaaa (substitute the current year for aaaa). Write a report in which you discuss trends for this year. You must cite at least five different websites, only one of which can be the site of a law firm. Be specific on how the trend may affect the practice of law. In the Computer Terminology in the Law (CTL) notebook you started in Assignment 1.8 of Chapter 1, include information you obtain by doing this assignment.

13.3 Run this search in Google, Bing, or Yahoo: how do attorneys use Google+? Write a report in which you describe

the different uses law firms have made of Google+. Your report must cite at least five different sources on the Web. In the Computer Terminology in the Law (CTL) notebook you started in Assignment 1.8 of Chapter 1, include information you obtain by doing this assignment.

13.4 Go to HowStuffWorks (www.howstuffworks.com) and select the Tech category. Pick any five topics about computer hardware or software about which you are unfamiliar. Write a summary of what you learned about each topic. In the Computer Terminology in the Law (CTL) notebook you started in Assignment 1.8 of Chapter 1, include information you obtain by doing this assignment.

13.5 Make a list of computer topics that you feel you need to learn more about. Be specific in the list. Some of the topics will probably involve doing something at the computer (e.g., writing a macro). All of the topics will involve learning terminology associated with the topic (e.g., macro, word processor, Excel). Assume that you want to learn all of the terminology in the next six months. Write a plan for doing so. By what dates will you complete the learning of the terminology of what topics? Write a target calendar. You do not have to write out all the terms that you will learn. Just write the topics for your plan.

CORE SKILLS

Among the many skills a paralegal must have, five core skills stand out: writing (both basic English and legal drafting), research, ethics, computer use, and collaboration (working with others). The core-skill assignments introduce and reinforce these skills. Even if you are not asked to do all of the assignments as part of the course, you should do them on your own. Also, do not wait for the topics in the assignments to be covered in this course or in other courses. Successful paralegals are self-starters. A major characteristic of a self-starter is a thirst for independent study—learning on your own.

CORE SKILL: WRITING

13.6 Select a word processor to which you have access. If you don't already have one on your computer, use one of the free word processors on the Internet. (Run this search in Google, Bing, or Yahoo: free alternative Microsoft Word.) Write two paragraphs on this word processor. Use five features of this word processor that you have not used before and that you did not know about. What are the five features? Explain how you used them to write your two paragraphs. In the Computer Terminology in the Law (CTL) notebook you started in Assignment 1.8 of Chapter 1, include information you obtain by doing this assignment.

CORE SKILL: RESEARCH

13.7 In Google, Bing, or Yahoo, run this search: mobile attorney. Write a report in which you describe the different ways in which technology allows attorneys to be mobile. Indicate the major difficulties of such mobility. Your report must cite at least three different websites, one of which you obtained from the articles database of Google Scholar (scholar. google.com). In the Computer Terminology in the Law (CTL) notebook you started in Assignment 1.8 of Chapter 1, include information you obtain by doing this assignment.

CORE SKILL: ETHICS

13.8 An office wants you to read ten court opinions for the case of a current client. The choices are (1) traveling to a large law office in the city that has all of the bound volumes, (2) using case databases on Westlaw or on LexisNexis or (3) using the case databases on Google Scholar. What is the most ethical decision the office can make when faced with these choices? Cite and apply relevant ethical rules. (See Chapter 5 and the ethics code of your state in Appendix D.)

CORE SKILL: COMPUTERS

13.9 In Google, Bing, or Yahoo, run any two of the following searches on software programs:

Concordance software attorney
Summation software attorney
Amicus attorney

Write a report in which you describe how law offices use the first of the two programs you selected. Your report must cite at least three websites. Do the same for the second program you selected. In the Computer Terminology in the Law (CTL) notebook you started in Assignment 1.8 of Chapter 1, include information you obtain by doing this assignment.

CORE SKILL: COLLABORATION

13.10 On Google, Bing, or Yahoo run these searches:
Google docs
Google drive

Also run these searches in the search box of YouTube. Explain how Google Docs and Google Drive can be used to collaborate with others. Assume that five people have been working on a contract. How would they work together on this contract using Google Docs or Google Drive? In the Computer Terminology in the Law (CTL) notebook you started in Assignment 1.8 of Chapter 1, include information you obtain by doing this assignment.

THE JOB SEARCH

(The search for employment cannot wait until the end of a course or of a curriculum. It needs to begin now. The job-search assignments are designed to introduce you to different aspects of the job search and to build options for you to explore about employment.)

13.11 Assume that you wanted to add a computer certification to your resume.

(a) What are the programs in Microsoft Office?
(b) What are the steps in becoming certified in Microsoft Office?

In the Computer Terminology in the Law (CTL) notebook you started in Assignment 1.8 of Chapter 1, include information you obtain by doing this assignment.

REVIEW QUESTIONS

1. What are some of the computer questions you may be asked about during an employment interview?
2. What self-help steps can you take to further your training about computers?
3. Distinguish between hardware and software.
4. What is the function of the CPU?
5. Distinguish between operating software (or systems) (OS) and applications software.
6. What is open-source software?
7. What are the major operating systems in use today?
8. What are the major mobile devices with wireless communication capability?
9. What is the distinction between the two major kinds of memory, ROM and RAM?
10. What are the main storage devices?
11. What are the main input devices?
12. What is the cloud?
13. What is PDF and what is Microsoft's version of PDF?
14. What are the main output devices?
15. What is the function of a modem?
16. What is videoconferencing?
17. What does real time mean?
18. Distinguish between a LAN and a WAN.
19. Distinguish between an intranet and an extranet.
20. What is an integrated software package?
21. List some of the major kinds of software used in a law office.
22. Distinguish between custom-made and off-the-shelf software.
23. What is a word processor?
24. What is justification in word processing?
25. What is a macro?
26. What is a table of authorities (TOA)?
27. Distinguish between fonts and points.
28. What is a spreadsheet?
29. How can a what-if spreadsheet calculation be used in a structured settlement?
30. What is the function of database management software?
31. What is the function of presentation graphics software?
32. What is the function of litigation-support software?
33. Distinguish between searching databases by full text and searching by summaries or abstracts.
34. What is predictive coding?
35. What is the function of case management software?
36. What is a tickler?
37. What is a brief bank?
38. What is the function of knowledge management (KM)?
39. What is the Internet, and how was it created?
40. What is the World Wide Web (WWW)?
41. What is hypertext?
42. What are the components of a URL address?
43. What is an electronic mailing list?
44. What is social media?
45. What are some of the categories of social media?
46. What is an alert site?
47. What is RSS?
48. What is a podcast?
49. What is the Internet of Things (IoT)?
50. What are some of the major techniques for searching the Internet?
51. How can you assess the reliability of data found on the Internet?
52. What is the invisible Web?
53. What is a hacker?
54. What does it mean to encrypt something?
55. What is malware?
56. What is identity theft?
57. What are some examples of malware?
58. What steps should be taken to protect against malware?
59. What is a cookie?
60. What are some major examples of ethics violations that can arise when using computers in a law office?

HELPFUL WEBSITES

Online Dictionary of Computer Terms
- foldoc.org
- www.csgnetwork.com/glossary.html
- www.computeruser.com/resources/dictionary
- www.learnthenet.com/english/glossary/glossary.htm

Law Office Technology Resources
- www.americanbar.org (type *legal technology* in the search box)
- www.lawtechnologytoday.org
- marketcenter.findlaw.com/software.html
- www.llrx.com

Tutorials on the Internet
- www.sc.edu/beaufort/library/pages/bones/bones.shtml
- www.lib.berkeley.edu/TeachingLib/Guides/Internet/FindInfo.html
- www.livinginternet.com
- www.gcflearnfree.org/topics
- searchenginewatch.com/page/resources

- www.anniston.lib.al.us/computerinternettutorial.htm
- www.comptechdoc.org/basic/basictut

Metadata
- en.wikipedia.org/wiki/Metadata
- www.niso.org/publications/press/UnderstandingMetadata.pdf

Intranets
- en.wikipedia.org/wiki/Intranet

Listservs
- www.washlaw.edu/listserv
- www.lsoft.com/lists/listref.html
- tile.net/lists
- groups.yahoo.com
- groups.google.com

Paralegal Electronic Mailing Lists (Listservs)
- paralegaltoday.com/lat-forum

Legal Blogs

- blawgsearch.justia.com
- blawgsearch.justia.com/blogs/categories/podcasts
- legalblogwatch.typepad.com
- 3lepiphany.typepad.com/3l_epiphany/2006/03/a_taxonomy_of_l.html

Paralegal Blogs

- See Appendix F

Computer Security

- www.microsoft.com/security
- en.wikipedia.org/wiki/Computer_security
- computersecuritynews.us

Privacy

- www.llrx.com/features/privacyresources2015.htm

Google, Bing, or Yahoo Searches

(On these search engines, run the following searches, substituting your state for "aa" where indicated.)

- introduction to computers
- computer basics
- computer tutorial
- Internet tutorial
- search engine tutorial
- attorney software
- law office software
- mobile computing

- Internet security
- malware protection
- blawgs aa
- paralegal blogs
- intranet extranet
- litigation technology
- predictive coding

ENDNOTES

[1] James Podgers, *Come the Evolution: Ethics 20/20 Proposals Seek to Adapt Existing Professional Conduct Rules*, ABA Journal (www.abajournal.com/mobile/article/come_the_evolution_ethics_20_20_proposals_seek_to_adapt_existing_profession).

[2] Carl Morrison and Gavin Manes, *Does Your Attorney Suffer From Technophobia?* 61 @Law 8,9 (NALS Summer 2012).

[3] *Model Rules of Professional Conduct*, Rule 1.1, Comment 8 (ABA 1983).

[4] Vicki Voisin, *Interview of Dana Martinez-Jones*, IV The Paralegal Mentor (May 3, 2012) (email newsletter).

[5] Vincent Rougeaujun, *Fix Law Schools*, The Atlantic (June 19, 2012).

[6] Chere Estrin and Stacy Hunt, *The Successful Paralegal Job Search Guide* 71, 236 (2001).

[7] Robert Half, *Future Law Office: Technology's Transformation of the Legal Field*, 1 (www.roberthalf.com/legal/future-law-office) (2013).

[8] Computer Hope (www.computerhope.com/issues/chspace.htm) (2014).

[9] *3D Printing Turns Dreams into Reality*, Time Inc. News Group (www.timeincnewsgroupcustompub.com/sections/130902_3DPrinting.pdf). See also Brian Greene, *3-D Printing*, Fortune, September 2, 1013 at 34.

[10] See Matthew Cornick, *Using Computers in the Law: Basic* (2013) and Steven Mandell, *Introduction to Computers* (3d ed. 1991).

[11] See Steven Mandell, *Introduction to Computers* (3d ed. 1991) and Matthew S. Cornick, *Using Computers in the Law* (6th ed. 2012).

[12] *State of Minnesota and Blue Cross and Blue Shield of Minnesota v. Philip Morris, Inc.*, Trial Transcript, Closing Argument, 1998 WL 242426 (D. Minn. May 7, 1998).

[13] Brent Roper, *Using Computers in the Law* 333 (4th ed. 2004).

[14] *Internet Users Send 204 Million Emails Per Minute*, Mashable (mashable.com/2014/04/23/data-online-every-minute) (2014).

[15] See the historical overview in *American Civil Liberties Union v. Reno*, 929 F. Supp. 824, 832–34 (E.D. Pa. 1996).

[16] John Naughton, *The Internet Of Things: It's a Really Big Deal*, The Observer (June 14, 2014).

[17] Jacob Morgan, *A Simple Explanation of "The Internet Of Things"* Forbes (May 13, 2014).

[18] Ibid.

[19] Steve Kolowich, *What Students Don't Know*, Inside Higher Ed (August 22, 2012).

INTRODUCTION TO LAW OFFICE ADMINISTRATION

CHAPTER OUTLINE

- Practice of Law in the Private Sector
- Legal Administrator
- Paralegal Manager
- Outsourcing

- Virtual Law Practice
- Costs of Running a Law Office
- Timekeeping
- Categories of Fees

- Billing
- Client Trust Accounts
- Administrative Reports
- Client File Management

CHAPTER OBJECTIVES

After completing this chapter, you should be able to

- Provide statistics on attorneys in the United States.
- List the main settings where attorneys practice law.
- Explain the legal consequences of practicing as a sole proprietorship.
- Distinguish between personal and limited liability.
- Understand ethical issues that can arise in an office-sharing arrangement.
- Explain the legal consequences of practicing as a partnership.
- Describe the major categories of attorneys

that can exist in a partnership.
- Explain the legal consequences of practicing as a professional corporation.
- Describe the major responsibilities of a legal administrator.
- Describe the major responsibilities of a paralegal manager.
- Describe kinds of outsourcing and understand ethical issues that can arise when tasks are outsourced.
- List the major costs of operating a law office.
- Know how timekeepers record their time.

- Explain the purpose of a new file worksheet.
- Distinguish between billable and nonbillable time.
- Describe the different kinds of attorney fees.
- Know why some clients dislike hourly fees.
- Explain the billing process.
- Understand ethical issues that can arise in client trust accounts.
- List some of the major administrative reports.
- Explain how law offices manage client files.

PRACTICE OF LAW IN THE PRIVATE SECTOR

Our study of law-office management begins with some statistics about attorneys:

- In 1983, there were 612,000 attorneys in the United States. In 2012, the number was 1,225,452. (Of this number, 759,800 were employed as attorneys.) Approximately 30 percent of attorneys are women, 5 percent are African American, and 8 percent are Asian, Hispanic, or Latino.[1]
- In 2012, there were 146,288 students enrolled in over 195 law schools in the country; just under half were women and almost 25% were minorities. In this year, 46,364 graduates were awarded juris doctor (J.D.) or bachelor of laws (LL.B.) degrees.[2] (The J.D. and LL.B. degrees are equivalent.)
- In 2012,there were 82,920 persons who took a bar examination; 55,253 passed (a pass rate of approximately 67 percent).[3] For the pass rate in your state, run this search in Google, Bing, or Yahoo: aa bar admission statistics (substituting your state for aa).
- In 2012, the median wage of attorneys was

  - $113,530 for all attorneys
  - $ 54,130 or less for 10 percent of attorneys[4]

(The median wage is the wage at which half the workers in an occupation earned more than that amount and half earned less.)

- Upon graduation from law school in 2013,

  - 11 percent of the graduates did not have a job.
  - 67 percent were employed in positions that required or preferred a law degree.
  - 22 percent were employed in positions that did not require or prefer a law degree.[5]

About 70 percent of attorneys practice in **private law firms**, which are offices that generate their income from the attorney (and paralegal) fees paid by clients and, as we will see, by opposing parties in **fee-shifting** cases. Another 10 percent work in the legal departments of corporations. The remainder practice in the public sector for government, for **legal aid offices**, or for organizations such as unions, trade associations, and public interest groups, or they do not practice law.

In the private sector, law is practiced in a variety of settings:

- Sole proprietorship
- Office-sharing arrangement
- Partnership
- Professional corporation
- Limited liability entity
- Corporate law department

SOLE PROPRIETORSHIP

Any business can operate as a **sole proprietorship**, which means that one person, the sole proprietor, owns all the assets of the business (including all profits) and assumes all of its debts or liabilities. (The business does not have a separate legal identity.) Because this person has **personal liability**, creditors can reach his or her personal assets (e.g., a family checking account, a vacation home) *in addition to* his or her business assets (e.g., a business bank account, office furniture). If sole proprietors had **limited liability**, a creditor would be limited to pursuing their business assets when collecting business debts. The liability of sole proprietors, however, is not limited; it is personal.

Sole proprietorship does not mean that the attorney practices alone. He or she can hire other attorneys as employees. The latter receive a salary; they do not share in the profits or become responsible for the debts or liabilities of the office. Attorneys who do practice alone are **sole practitioners**, also called *solo practitioners*. They are said to be "going solo."

An attorney can practice as a generalist or a specialist. A generalist is the equivalent of a doctor in general practice. An attorney who is a **general practitioner (GP)** often handles many different kinds of cases. If, however, a case is unusually complex or if the attorney is very busy with other cases, he or she might consult with an attorney in another firm or refer the case to another attorney. Some attorneys specialize in one main area of the law. Their practice might be limited, for example, to tax cases, criminal cases, or, more commonly, to **PI cases** (personal injury). Specialty offices are sometimes called **boutique law firms** no matter how many attorneys work in them.

---

private law firm A law firm that generates its income mainly from the attorney (and paralegal) fees paid by clients.

fee-shifting Requiring one party to pay another party's attorney fees and paralegal fees because of prior agreement, bad faith, or special statute.

legal aid office An office of attorneys (and paralegals) that provides free or low-cost legal services to persons who cannot afford standard legal fees. Also called *legal services office*.

sole proprietorship A form of business that does not have a separate legal identity apart from the one person who owns all assets and assumes all debts and liabilities.

personal liability Liability that can be satisfied out of personal as well as business assets of a debtor or wrongdoer.

limited liability Restricted liability; liability that can be satisfied only out of business assets, not out of personal assets of a debtor or wrongdoer. Protection from personal liability for business debts and claims.

sole practitioner An attorney who practices alone. His or her office has no partners, associates, or employees who are attorneys.

general practitioner (GP) A professional who handles many different kinds of cases.

PI cases Personal injury (tort) cases.

boutique law firm A law firm that specializes in one main area of the law.

Many attorneys, particularly those in small to moderately sized offices, become known as plaintiff law offices (because their clients are mostly or exclusively plaintiffs who initiate lawsuits) or as defendant or defense law offices (because their clients are mostly or exclusively defendants who are sued). Several reasons account for this concentration. First, once the office becomes successful, it tends to attract new clients who are similar to current clients. Second, many offices *brand* themselves as offices that handle certain kinds of cases. Third, rules on conflict of interest (see Chapter 5) may limit the kinds of clients an office can take. For example, if an office defends hospitals in medical-malpractice cases, it may have to turn away a potential client who wants to sue one of the hospitals the office once defended in an earlier litigation.

Most sole proprietorships have few employees. There might be a secretary, who often performs many paralegal functions along with the traditional clerical responsibilities of typing, filing, and reception work. He or she may also perform bookkeeping chores. The most common job title of this individual is *legal secretary*, although he or she might be called a *legal assistant* or a *paralegal/secretary*. You will sometimes find job ads for small offices seeking paralegals with clerical skills. These skills are often phrased as administrative or word processing skills, but they are, in essence, clerical. In recent years, however, more small offices have begun to hire one or more paralegals who are given minimal or no clerical duties.

The office may also have a **law clerk**. This is a full-time or part-time law-office employee who is studying to be an attorney or who has graduated from law school and is waiting to pass the bar examination. (*Law clerk* is also the title of someone who provides research and writing assistance to a judge.) Another name for a worker in the office who is still a student in law school is **legal intern**. The primary goal of interns, who are often unpaid, is to obtain practical experience in the law.

OFFICE-SHARING ARRANGEMENT

It can be expensive to start a practice, particularly in high-rent areas of the country. One cost-saving alternative is **office sharing**, in which two or more attorneys with independent practices share the use and **overhead** costs of an office. For example, each pays a portion of the monthly office rent and also shares the cost of buying or leasing computers or other equipment. If the office has a secretary/receptionist or a paralegal, each attorney pays a part of this person's salary. The attorneys do not practice together as a partnership or corporation; in most office-sharing arrangements, each attorney practices alone in a sole proprietorship.

In office sharing arrangements, special care must be used to prevent the ethical problems we discussed in Chapter 5. Clients must not be confused into thinking that the attorneys are partners or associated together in a single practice. To preserve confidentiality, the files of the attorneys must be kept separate and be inaccessible to each other. For example, when an attorney is not in the office, his or her files should be locked. If the attorneys are casual about discussing their cases and in covering for each other, a court might conclude that each attorney is not an independent office. This could mean that there would be a conflict of interest if the attorneys have clients with **adverse interests**. Such conflicts would not exist in an office-sharing arrangement if each attorney rigidly maintained the separateness and independence of his or her practice.

PARTNERSHIP

A **partnership** is a business or other venture jointly owned by two or more persons who share its profits and losses. Here are the major characteristics of a partnership:

- Each partner has personal liability for the debts of the partnership. (In this respect, a partnership is similar to a sole proprietorship.)
- Each partner is liable for the **torts** or other wrongdoing committed by every other partner if the wrong arises out of the business.
- A partnership is a **pass-through entity**, meaning that the income tax of the partnership is not paid by the partnership; it is paid on the personal tax returns of the partners. There is no double taxation, which would occur if the partnership paid income taxes on its earnings and the partners then paid income tax on the same earnings when they were distributed to them. Instead, the income of the partnership flows through the partnership to the individual partners.

We live in an era when law offices are increasingly subjected to suits for fraud and legal malpractice. As indicated, this can lead to personal liability for wrongs committed by the any of the partners. Consequently, traditional partnerships often explore restructuring themselves

---

law clerk (1) A law firm employee who is in law school studying to become an attorney or who has graduated from law school and is waiting to pass the bar examination. Also called *clerk*. If law clerks work only in the summer, they are sometimes called *summer associates*. (2) One who provides research and writing assistance to a judge. (See glossary for another meaning.)

legal intern A student in a law office seeking practical experience.

office sharing Attorneys who are sole practitioners but share the use and overhead costs of an office.

overhead The operating expenses of a business (e.g., office rent, utilities, insurance, and clerical staff) for which customers or clients are not charged a separate fee. Some states, however, allow attorneys to charge clients for clerical or secretarial time.

adverse interest A goal or claim of one person that is different from or opposed to the goal or claim of another person.

partnership A business or other venture jointly owned by two or more persons who share its profits and losses.

tort A civil wrong (other than a breach of contract) that causes injury or other loss for which our legal system deems it just to provide a remedy such as damages. Injury or loss can be to the person (a personal tort), to movable property (a personal-property tort), or to land and anything attached to the land (a real-property tort).

pass-through entity A partnership, limited-liability entity, or other business whose income tax is paid by the individual partners or owners of the entity rather than by the entity itself.

into entities that would provide limited liability, as we will see when we examine the professional corporation (P.C.) and the limited liability partnership.

If a partnership is relatively large, it will probably be organized into a series of departments (such as an antitrust department and a litigation department) based on the kinds of clients represented by the office. Large offices are usually managed through a series of committees, such as a partners' committee of the whole, an executive committee, a recruitment committee, a paralegal committee, a library and records committee, etc. (See Exhibit 14-1 for an example of the organization structure of a large law firm.)

Exhibit 14-1	Large Law Firm Organization Chart: An Example

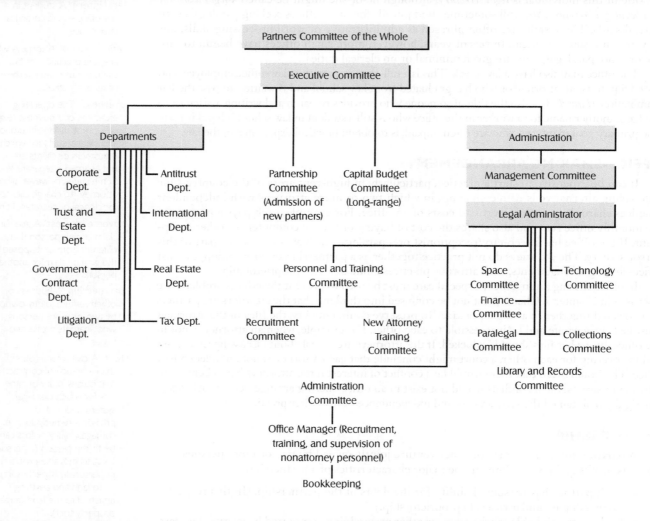

A partnership can include a number of different categories of attorneys, the most common of which are:

- Partner
- Associate
- Staff attorney
- Of counsel
- Contract attorney

Partner

Partners own the firm; they share its profits and losses pursuant to an elaborate partnership agreement. In a system referred to as "eat what you kill," the amount paid to partners often depends in large part on how much business they generate for the firm. (Any attorney who attracts business due to contacts and/or reputation as a skilled attorney is called a **rainmaker**.) Partners decide how the firm should be managed; when to take on new partners; whether to merge with another firm; what attorneys, paralegals, and other employees to hire; etc. Most of this is done through the various committees outlined in Exhibit 14-1.

A firm may have different categories of partners (senior partner, junior partner, etc.) depending on such factors as the amount of capital the attorney contributed to the firm, his or her rainmaking prowess, and how involved he or she is in the firm's management. Large firms may also distinguish between a **nonequity partner** (also called an *income partner*) and an **equity partner** (also called a *capital partner*). An equity partner is a full partner in the sense of owning the firm and sharing in its profits and losses. At the other end of the partner spectrum is the nonequity or income partner who has not been promoted from associate to full partner or who does not aspire to become one. Generally, nonequity partners receive a salary rather than a share of the profits. Equity partners might receive a salary, a **draw**, or both. A draw is an advance against profits (or net income).

Associates

Associates are attorney employees of the firm who are hoping for eventual promotion to partnership. Often they are hired right out of law school while studying for the bar examination. As students, they may have worked for the firm as a law clerk. Other associates, however, are hired from other law firms. They are known as **lateral hires**. (When partners and paralegals switch law firms, they also are referred to as lateral hires.) After a certain number of years at the firm (e.g., seven), associates are usually considered for partnership. If they are *passed over* for partner, they often leave the firm to practice elsewhere, although a few may be invited to stay as **senior associates** or *senior attorneys*. Such lawyers, in effect, become permanent associates.

Staff Attorney

Staff attorneys (sometimes called *second-tier attorneys*) are employees hired with the understanding that they will never be considered for full partnership. This is what distinguishes them from associates.

Of Counsel

There is no fixed definition of an attorney who is **of counsel**. He or she is not a full partner or associate but has a special relationship at the firm. An attorney who is *of counsel* may be a semiretired partner or may work on a mixture of firm cases and his or her own cases. Not all firms use the title "of counsel." Some prefer "special counsel" or simply "counsel."

Contract Attorney

Contract attorneys (sometimes called *project attorneys*) are hired when the firm has a temporary shortage of attorneys or needs expertise in a certain area for a limited period. Often paid on an hourly basis, the contract attorney is not a full-time employee.

PROFESSIONAL CORPORATION

In most states, it is possible for persons with professional licenses (e.g., attorneys and doctors) to incorporate their venture (business) as a **professional corporation (P.C.)** through which they can provide professional services. A law firm that incorporates its practice uses the P.C. designation after its name, e.g., Jamison & Jamison, P.C. The partners of the firm become its shareholders, but are still called partners. A major advantage of incorporation is that the owners of a corporation have limited liability, unlike owners of a sole proprietorship or traditional partnership. As we saw earlier, if the owner of a business has limited liability, his or her business debts are satisfied out of business assets, not out of personal assets. If the owner has personal liability, his or her personal as well as business assets can be reached to satisfy business debts.

A disadvantage of many corporations is *double taxation:* the same income is taxed twice. First, the corporation pays corporate taxes on its taxable income. Second, shareholders pay individual taxes on the salaries, bonuses, and fringe benefits they receive from the corporation. This means that the same corporate earnings could be taxed twice—at the corporate level and at the shareholder level. There are ways, however, for a professional corporation to pay a lower

partner One who shares in the profits and losses of a jointly owned business or other venture. Partners make the ultimate decisions on how the business (e.g., law firm) should be managed.

rainmaker An attorney who brings fee-generating cases into the office due to his or her contacts and/or reputation as a skilled attorney.

nonequity partner A special category of partner who does not own the firm in the sense of an equity or capital partner. Also called *income partner*.

equity partner A full owner-partner of a law firm. Also called *capital partner*.

draw A partner's advance against profits or net income.

associate An attorney employee of a partnership who hopes eventually to be promoted to partnership.

lateral hire A person hired from another law office.

senior associate An attorney who has been passed over for partner status but who remains at the firm.

staff attorney A full-time attorney employee who has no expectation of becoming a full partner. Also called *second-tier attorney*.

of counsel An attorney who is semiretired or has some other special status in the law firm.

contract attorney An attorney hired to work for a relatively short period, usually on specific cases or projects. Also called *project attorney*.

professional corporation (P.C.) A corporation consisting of persons performing services that require a professional license, e.g., attorneys.

limited liability entity A company or partnership whose owners are taxed like a partnership and have the limited liability of a corporation.

corporate law department A law office within a corporation containing salaried attorneys (in-house attorneys) who advise and represent the corporation. Also called *legal department*.

general counsel The chief attorney in a corporate law department. Also called *corporate counsel*.

managing partner A partner of a law firm who has day-to-day responsibility for the overall management of the firm.

legal administrator An individual, usually a nonattorney, who has responsibility for the day-to-day administration of a law office.

tax rate than other kinds of corporations and, perhaps, to avoid the corporate tax altogether. For example, the professional corporation may be able to pay all of its earnings to shareholders in the form of salary, bonus, and benefits, thus leaving no corporate taxable income to declare.

Like any corporation, the owners of a professional corporation are its shareholders. They elect the board of directors, who in turn appoint officers. In most states, shareholders, directors, and officers of a professional corporation must be attorneys in order to avoid ethical violations such as nonattorney control or interference with the professional judgment of an attorney (see Chapter 5).

The day-to-day operation of a professional corporation is practically identical to the operation of a traditional partnership. A client would hardly notice the difference.

LIMITED LIABILITY ENTITY

In many states, a law firm can be organized as a **limited liability entity**. It can be a limited liability company (LLC) or a limited liability partnership (LLP). These entities are hybrid structures in that they combine features of a corporation and a partnership. In general, the owners are taxed like a partnership and have the limited liability of a corporation.

CORPORATE LAW DEPARTMENT

Many large business corporations have a **corporate law department** (sometimes called *legal department*) headed by a **general counsel** (sometimes called *corporate counsel*), who may also be a vice president of the company. Other attorneys in this office can include deputy or associate general counsels, senior attorneys, staff attorneys, etc. They are in-house attorneys who handle the day-to-day tasks of advising the company on legal matters. They have one client—the corporation that hires them and that pays them a salary. Frequently, paralegals work with these attorneys along with other support staff such as secretaries and bookkeepers. There are, of course, no client fees. Funds to operate the department come directly from the corporate treasury. When trial or other expertise is not available "in-house," the general counsel will hire "outside" attorneys from law firms.

LEGAL ADMINISTRATOR

The practice of law is a profession, but it is also a business. The larger the practice (law firm or corporate law department), the more likely its business component will be managed by individuals whose main or sole responsibility is administration rather than helping clients. The owners of a law firm, for example, may delegate management duties to a **managing partner**, often an attorney with a small case load or none at all. More and more offices are hiring new categories of management personnel who are not attorneys. One such individual is the **legal administrator** who works under the supervision of the managing partner or of an executive or management committee of the office.

JOB DESCRIPTION

One way to obtain an overview of law-office management is to examine the job description of the legal administrator. Exhibit 14-2 sets out the range of his or her responsibilities, and indeed of the business component of the practice of law. See also the Association of Legal Administrators (www.alanet.org).

Exhibit 14-2	Legal Administrator: Job Description

Summary of Responsibilities

The legal administrator manages the planning, marketing, and business functions, as well as the overall operations, of a law office. He or she reports to the managing partner or the executive committee and participates in management meetings. In addition to having general responsibility for financial planning and controls, personnel administration (including compensation), systems, and physical facilities, the legal administrator identifies and plans for the changing needs of the organization; shares responsibility with the appropriate partners for strategic planning, practice management, and marketing; and contributes to cost-effective management throughout the organization.

(continued)

| Exhibit 14-2 | Legal Administrator: Job Description (*Continued*) |

DIRECTLY OR THROUGH A MANAGEMENT TEAM, THE LEGAL ADMINISTRATOR IS RESPONSIBLE FOR MOST OR ALL OF THE FOLLOWING:

Financial Management:
- Planning
- Forecasting
- Budgeting
- Variance analysis
- Profitability analysis
- Financial reporting
- Operations analysis
- General ledger accounting
- Rate analysis
- Billing and collections
- Cash flow control
- Banking relationships
- Investment
- Tax planning and reporting
- Trust accounting
- Payroll and pension plans
- Other related functions

Systems Management:
- Systems analysis
- Operational audits

- Procedures manual
- Cost-benefit analysis
- Computer systems design
- Programming and systems development
- Information services
- Records and library management
- Office automation
- Document construction systems
- Information storage and retrieval
- Telecommunications
- Litigation support
- Conflict-of-interest docket systems
- Legal practice systems
- Other related services

Facilities Management:
- Lease negotiations
- Space planning and design
- Office renovation
- Purchasing and inventory control
- Reprographics
- Reception/switchboard services

- Telecommunications
- Mail messenger services
- Other related functions

Human Resource Management:
- Recruitment, selection, and placement
- Orientation, training, and development
- Performance evaluation
- Salary and benefits administration
- Employee relations
- Motivation and counseling
- Discipline
- Termination
- Workers' compensation
- Personnel data systems
- Organization analysis
- Job design, development of job descriptions
- Resource allocation
- Other human resource management functions for the legal and support staff

AS A MEMBER OF THE LEGAL ORGANIZATION'S MANAGEMENT TEAM, THE LEGAL ADMINISTRATOR MANAGES AND/OR CONTRIBUTES SIGNIFICANTLY TO THE FOLLOWING:

General Management:
- Policymaking
- Strategic and tactical planning
- Business development
- Risk management
- Quality control
- Organizational development
- Other general management functions

Practice Management:
- Attorney recruiting
- Attorney training and development
- Paralegal supervision
- Work-product quality control
- Professional standards
- Substantive practice systems
- Other related functions

Marketing:
- Management of client-profitability analysis
- Forecasting of business opportunities
- Planning client development
- Marketing legal services: enhancement of the firm's visibility and image in the desired markets

Job Requirements

- **Knowledge:** Familiarity with legal or other professional service organizations and experience in managing business operations, including planning, marketing, financial and personnel administration, and management of professionals.

- **Skills and Abilities:** Ability to identify and analyze complex issues and problems in management, finance, and human relations, and to recommend and implement solutions. Ability to manage office functions economically and efficiently, and to organize work, establish priorities, and maintain good interpersonal relations and communications with attorneys and support staff. Excellent supervisory and leadership skills, as well as skills in written and oral communication. Demonstrated willingness and ability to delegate.

- **Education:** Graduation from a recognized college or university with major coursework in business administration, finance, data processing, or personnel management, or comparable work experience.

OTHER PERSONNEL IN A LARGE LAW OFFICE

The job description of the legal administrator in Exhibit 14-2 covers an individual who works for a large law office—one with seventy-five or more attorneys. The support staff for such an office can also be quite extensive. Here are some examples:[6]

- Legal administrator
- Paralegal manager
- Accounts payable clerk
- Accounts receivable clerk
- Analyst
- Billing clerk
- Bookkeeper

- Chief financial officer
- Collections clerk
- Comptroller
- Computer specialist
- Conflicts specialist
- Copy room clerk
- Credit/collections manager

- Data processing operator
- Director of marketing
- Docket clerk
- E-discovery specialist
- Employee benefits manager
- Equipment manager

- Facilities manager
- File room clerk
- Financial manager
- Investigator
- IT specialist (information technology)
- Librarian
- Library aide
- Litigation support professional
- Mail clerk

- Marketing director
- Messenger/page
- Office manager
- Payroll specialist
- Personnel manager
- Pricing analyst
- Proofreader
- Purchasing clerk
- Receptionist
- Records information manager

- Recruiter
- Reservation clerk
- Risk manager
- Secretary
- Telephone operator
- Time and billing assistant
- Word processing supervisor
- Word processor

PARALEGAL MANAGER

paralegal manager A paralegal who helps recruit, train, and supervise paralegals in a law office.

As paralegals grow in importance in the practice of law, large offices often rely on **paralegal managers** to help the office handle the administrative concerns that are unique to the paralegal profession. Almost all paralegal managers are individuals who once had considerable experience as paralegals working on individual cases. For a sample job description of a paralegal manager, see Exhibit 14-3. See also the International Practice Management Association (www.paralegalmanagement.org).

Exhibit 14-3	Paralegal Manager: Job Description

POSITION DESCRIPTION
POSITION TITLE: Paralegal Manager
DEPARTMENT: Paralegal Administration

- **Summary**
Responsible for supervision of the paralegal staff, including recruiting, coordinating work assignments, and administering all firm policies regarding the paralegal staff.

- **Primary Duties and Responsibilities**
  - Recruits, hires, and orients paralegals (permanent and temporary). When appropriate, assists in disciplinary actions and terminations.
  - Arranges continuing legal education (CLE) for paralegals by presenting in-house training programs and recommending specific CLE sessions run by bar associations, paralegal associations, etc.
  - Assigns projects to paralegals, coordinates workflow of paralegal assignments, and monitors billable and nonbillable hours of paralegals.
  - Prepares financial and statistical reports (including a yearly budget for the firm's paralegal program), periodic employee status reports, work assignment statistics, and profitability analyses to help the office assess the economic impact (e.g., profitability) of its paralegals.
  - Participates in periodic and yearly salary reviews and evaluations of paralegals.
  - Participates in long-range planning of the firm, with a focus on paralegal staffing needs.

- **Secondary Duties and Responsibilities**
  - Performs other administrative duties pertaining to paralegals, including solving personnel problems; administering existing policies and proposing new ones; complying with labor laws; and acting as a liaison among paralegals, attorneys, and the firm's Paralegal Committee in order to promote effective utilization of paralegals.

- **Relationships**
  - Reports directly to the paralegal committee, the personnel director, the executive director of administration, or the legal administrator.
  - Works with litigation support staff, personnel manager, outside consultants, placement offices, vendors, etc.

- **Minimum Qualifications**
  - Education: College degree, post-graduate degree or paralegal certificate preferred.
  - Experience: At least 3–5 years' experience as a paralegal. Previous management background preferred.
  - Special Skills: Computer skills, public speaking skills, financial reporting skills.

Reprinted with permission of the International Practice Management Association (www.paralegalmanagement.org).

OUTSOURCING

outsourcing Paying an outside company or service to perform tasks usually performed by one's own employees.

The vast majority of support staff in a law office are full-time employees who work at the office's main address or in one of the branches of the office. Part-time workers are hired on an as-needed basis. Increasingly, however, offices are considering the option of **outsourcing**, in which the office pays outside companies or service firms to perform tasks that would otherwise be performed by its own employees. Outsourcing by a law firm is called *legal process outsourcing* (LPO). Outsourcing is not new. Some tasks are regularly outsourced. *Third-party providers* such as printing companies, for example, are often hired to photocopy, print, and bind the office's appellate briefs. What is new is the increase of outsourcing due to technology that allows easy communication with English-speaking, technically proficient, low-wage workers in foreign countries. Outsourcing to foreign countries is called *offshoring*.

The most common tasks outsourced by law offices are accounting and word-processing (typing) tasks. Occasionally, discovery-related tasks are outsourced as well. It is relatively easy, for example, to use email and the Internet

- to send a transcript of a deposition to a service company in the Philippines and ask that the deposition be digested (summarized);
- to send a statement of facts from a client case to a service company in India and ask it to prepare a legal-research memorandum that uses U.S. laws, which are readily accessible online.

The U.S. Bureau of Labor Statistics estimated that 12,000 legal jobs were sent offshore in 2004; the number is expected to rise to 79,000 by 2015.[7] Some claim that any task that uses a computer can be outsourced. Although this claim is exaggerated, there is little doubt that outsourcing will continue to grow.

How will outsourcing affect paralegal employment in the United States? The National Federation of Paralegal Associations (NFPA) has issued a policy statement on the issue. It asserts that "since paralegals are highly trained and qualified professionals who provide efficient, cost-effective, and timely service to attorneys and clients, they should be utilized first and foremost for all non-attorney legal work."[8] The concern of NFPA is not limited to job protection. When client facts and documents are sent outside the office, client confidentiality could be at risk. Recently a woman in Pakistan threatened to post online the medical records she was transcribing for a law firm in the United States unless a payment dispute was resolved to her satisfaction.[9] As we saw in Chapter 5, there could also be conflict-of-interest problems if the same foreign company provides services to persons who have adverse interests.

Not all outsourcing is offshore. Some companies have set up centers within the United States, particularly in relatively small southern and Midwestern cities where labor costs for attorneys, paralegals, accountants, and clerical personnel can be substantially less than in large metropolitan areas. A few large law firms with many branches around the world have opened their own service offices in some of these low-cost American cities to take care of outsourcable functions that would otherwise have to be performed in the central and branch offices.

VIRTUAL LAW PRACTICE

As we saw in Chapter 13, technology allows attorneys to work outside a traditional office. Computers, the Internet, email, smartphones, etc. make it possible for attorneys to work at home or on the road and still be in regular communication with their main office. Some attorneys have abandoned the traditional office in favor of practicing as a **virtual law office**. They rarely or never meet with clients. All or substantially all communication is online. Most of these attorneys provide what is called **limited-scope representation**, meaning less than comprehensive or full representation of a client. The attorneys would not go to court to represent clients in litigation. Instead, they might draft agreements for a business transaction, prepare pleadings for plaintiffs who are representing themselves in divorce proceedings, or be available for as-needed advice by a construction company. Limited-scope representation is not limited to virtual law offices. Many brick-and-mortar offices offer it as well.

virtual law office An office in which an attorney provides limited-scope legal services mainly or exclusively through online communication.

limited-scope representation Less than comprehensive or full representation of a client. Example: an attorney drafts legal documents but does not provide court representation. Also called *unbundled legal services*.

COSTS OF RUNNING A LAW OFFICE

How does a law firm spend the fee income that it receives? In a recent survey, the average per-attorney gross receipts (meaning all income before expenses, salaries, and other distributions) at a large law firm was:

- $302,818 (for small firms)
- $499,518 (for larger firms)[10]

Another survey of 17,000 attorneys and 4,000 paralegals covered billable hours and expenses:[11]

Average Annual Billable Hours Worked

- 1,744 by equity partners/shareholders
- 1,842 by associates
- 1,400 by paralegals
- 1,486 by paralegal supervisors

Average Percentage of Gross Income Spent per Attorney on Expenses

- 2.3 percent of gross receipts spent for equipment
- 7.0 percent of gross receipts spent for occupancy
- 1.6 percent of gross receipts spent for promotion (marketing)
- 1.1 percent of gross receipts spent for library and research
- 4.0 percent of gross receipts spent for paralegals
- 14.8 percent of gross receipts spent for support staff
- 10.2 percent of gross receipts spent for other expenses, including malpractice insurance and the settlement of malpractice claims against the office

Average Percentage of Gross Income that Constituted Attorney Income after Expenses: *59 percent*

TIMEKEEPING

timekeeping Recording time spent on a client matter for purposes of billing and productivity assessment.

Abraham Lincoln's famous statement that a "lawyer's time is his stock in trade" is still true today. Effective **timekeeping** is critical to the success of a law firm. In some firms, it is an obsession, as typified by the following story. George, a senior partner in a prestigious Wall Street law firm, walked down the corridor to visit Howard, another senior partner at the firm. Upon entering the room, George was startled to find his colleague on the floor writhing in pain, apparently due to a heart attack. Standing there, he could think of only one thing to say to him: "Howard, are your time sheets in?"[12]

In some firms, the pressures of the clock on timekeepers (e.g., attorneys and paralegals) can be enormous:

[Y]oung lawyers often are shocked to discover their new employer's time expectations. Many firms in major cities require as many as 2,400 billable hours per year. When one considers that many full-time employees outside of the law only work 2,000 hours per year, the time commitment required by these firms is staggering.[13]

The cry for billable hours is thought by many to be at the heart of much of the problem. Many paralegals as well as attorneys have quotas of billable hours. Zlaket [the president of the State Bar of Arizona] stated that some firms require 2,200 hours a year and he deems this to be outrageous. He suggested that this only leads to padding of bills and time sheets, and it leads to unnecessary work that will be paid by somebody.[14]

Keep in mind that a requirement of 2,200 or 2,400 hours a year refers to *billable* hours. Most workers also spend a substantial number of nonbillable hours in the office. The ethical dimensions of these time pressures are considered in Chapter 5. Here, our concern is the administration of the timekeeping and billing system.

matter (1) A client issue. The reason a client hires or consults an attorney. (2) A case before the court.

new file worksheet A form used by some law offices that is the source document for the creation of all necessary accounting records that are needed when a law firm begins working on a new client case or matter. Also called a *new matter sheet*, *new business sheet*.

To gain an understanding of how a timekeeping-and-billing system might work in many law firms, you should know the accounting route taken by a client's *case* (sometimes called a **matter**) within a law firm. After the initial client interview, the starting point for accounting can be a **new file worksheet** (see Exhibit 14-4). It is also sometimes referred to as a *new matter sheet* or a *new business sheet*. The new file worksheet becomes the source document for the creation of all the necessary accounting records involved in working on a new client case or matter. As the example in Exhibit 14-4 demonstrates, the new file worksheet can also be used to record data that will help identify possible conflicts of interest. (See Chapter 5 for the ethical rules on conflicts of interest.)

As timekeepers, attorneys and paralegals must keep an account of the time they spend on behalf of a client. Time records are needed for accurate billing of every client who is

Exhibit 14-4	New File Worksheet

NEW CLIENT/MATTER/CONFLICT FORM

Client Number: *Matter Number:*   *Client Phone:*
                                                Client Fax:
                                                Client E-Mail Address:

Client Name and Address: Billing Name and Address:

Attn: **Attn:**

Biller			Originator			Responsible		
Name	Net ID	Pct	Name	Net ID	Pct	Name	Net ID	Pct
		%			%			%
		%			%			%
		%			%			%
		%			%			%
(Percent must = 100%)		100%			100%			100%

MATTER NAME:
CASE SYNOPSIS/COMMENTS:

PARENT/RELATED CLIENT:
CLIENT'S REF. NUMBER:
BUSINESS TYPE:
PRACTICE GROUP CODE:
INVOICE STYLE CODE:
COUNTRY CODE:
SIC CODE:
CASE CODE:

[NONSTANDARD FEE ARRANGEMENTS (OTHER THAN CONTINGENT) REQUIRE THE WRITTEN APPROVAL OF THE PRACTICE GROUP CHAIR. CONTINGENT FEE ARRANGEMENTS REQUIRE THE COMPLETION OF A CONTINGENT FEE INTAKE INFORMATION FORM AND WRITTEN APPROVAL OF THE CONTINGENT FEE COMMITTEE.]

FEE ARRANGEMENT	BILLING CYCLE

Billing Attorney:_____   Practice Group Chair:_____

September 17, 2015   Completed by :   /

CONFLICT CHECK

Billing Attorney:

Client Name:

Client Number, if not new:

Matter Name:

Matter Address (if matter name is a company different from client):

Standard Industrial Code (SIC), if known:

Case Synopsis/Comments: _____

These questions are designed to identify potential conflicts of interest. Examples given are for illustration only. Please be complete in responding to the questions. Additional Name/Relationship information may be added after the form is assembled by adding rows to the existing table.

CLIENT IDENTIFICATION (new clients only):

> If the client is a corporation, please provide, to the extent possible, the name(s) of all corporate parents and subsidiaries (including sister subsidiaries): If there is a different "real party in interest," *e.g.,* the beneficiary of our trustee or other fiduciary client, or the client of the law firm or accounting firm for whom we provide local or special representation, please provide, to the extent possible, the name of each such person or entity.

POTENTIALLY ADVERSE PARTIES:

> In *litigation,* please identify, to the extent possible, all other parties, including co-defendants, co-plaintiffs, intervenors and third parties. In *enforcement of remedies cases,* please identify, to the extent possible, all other lien claimants, etc. In *commercial or corporate transactions,* please identify, to the extent possible, all potentially adverse individuals or entities, such as the purchaser when we represent the seller; the lessee when we draft a lease for the lessor, etc. Please identify, to the extent possible, all other potentially adverse individuals or entities.

FOR ADMINISTRATIVE USE

New Business Department:

Conflict check performed and report attached — no potential conflicts found.

Signature _____

Date _____

OR

Potential conflicts found and report sent to Billing Attorney.

Signature _____

Date_____

Billing Attorney:

Sign only *after* resolving potential conflicts and forward to New Business Department.

Billing Attorney's Signature _____

Printed Name_____

Date _____

---

charged by the hour. Of course, all clients do not pay by the hour. A firm may be charging its client a flat fee under arrangements we will examine later in the chapter. Yet even in flat-fee cases, there are management reasons for keeping accurate time records. One of the ways to determine whether a particular case or client is profitable is to know how much time was needed to complete the work involved. Without time records, this is not always easy to determine, given that every individual in the office is probably working on more than one case simultaneously. Accurate time records are valuable management tools even in corporations where the corporate law office is financed out of the corporate treasury rather than out of fees. Decisions on whether to hire additional staff or to lay off present staff depend, in part, on knowing how much time is needed to complete certain tasks and who is and is not meeting those needs.

Many paralegals keep their own timesheets, even if they are not required to do so by their employer. In fact, some paralegals have two sets: the timesheets required by their employer and the even more detailed timesheets that they keep as part of their personal files. Comprehensive timesheets can allow the paralegal to track time spent on billable tasks (e.g., drafting a complaint) and nonbillable tasks (e.g., learning a new office filing procedure) and can be invaluable when making an argument for a raise or when someone raises questions about events that occurred weeks or months ago.

As we saw in the discussion of fee-shifting cases in Chapter 1, a losing party can be forced to pay the attorney and paralegal fees of the winning party in special **statutory-fee cases** such as those alleging violations of civil rights or environment laws. To claim such fees, the winning

statutory-fee case A case applying a special statute that gives a judge authority to order the losing party to pay the winning party's attorney fees (including paralegal fees) and costs.

substantive Nonclerical; requiring legal skills to perform.

side must be prepared to give the court detailed records of the time spent on the cases. Judges sometimes reject requests for paralegal fees because the requests fail to provide adequate documentation showing

- that the time spent by the paralegal was on **substantive** (as opposed to clerical) tasks, and
- that the work was not duplicative of the work of others in the office.

In the main, the documentation consists of detailed timesheets, which are offered into evidence when the attorney makes the fee request to the court.

There are two main ways that time is recorded: paper and computer. Some firms initially ask their timekeepers to record their time on paper forms, which are then coded into (i.e., transferred to) the computer for assessment and billing.

daily time sheet A form on which timekeepers record how much time they spend on particular client matters.

A commonly used form is the **daily time sheet** (see Exhibit 14-5). This form becomes the journal from which all time entries are posted to individual clients. Suppose, for example, that a paralegal spends some time summarizing or digesting a deposition. Using the abbreviations at the top of the daily time sheet, the "Description of Work" in the third column of Exhibit 14-5 might be "digesting DEPO." Note that the second entry in this column is drafting (DR) a complaint (COMP).

Exhibit 14-5	Daily Time Sheet

DAILY SERVICE REPORT OF: James O'Brien   DATE: 1/28/14

ANS	–Answer	DEPO	–Deposition	K	–Contract	O	–Order	RES	–Research
APP	–Appearance or Attending	DIC	–Dictation	L	–Legal	OP	–Opinion	REV	–Revision
ARG	–Argue or Argument	DOC	–Document	LT	–Letter to	P	–Preparation	S	–Settlement
BR	–Brief	DR	–Drafting	LF	–Letter from	PL	–Plaintiff	TF	–Telephone from
COMP	–Complaint	F	–Facts	MT	–Memorandum to	PR	–Praecipe	TT	–Telephone to
C–O	–Conference–Office	FL	–File	MF	–Memorandum from	PRT	–Pretrial	TR	–Trial
C–OO	–Conference–Outside Office	H	–Hearing	MOT	–Motion	R	–Reading and Review	TRV	–Travel
DEF	–Defendant	INV	–Investigation	NEG	–Negotiation	REL	–Release	W	–Witness
DEM	–Demurrer	INT	–Interview						

CLIENT (State billing division or department)	MATTER	DESCRIPTION OF WORK (Use abbreviations above)	TIME Minutes	TIME 10ths
AJAX, INC. (LITIGATION)	AJAX vs. SMITH	digesting DEPO	30	.5
AJAX, INC. (LITIGATION)	AJAX vs. SMITH	DR COMP	104	1.7

The last column of Exhibit 14-5 asks for the amount of time taken for each task. Law firms often use tenths of an hour (increments of six minutes) as the base unit for the measurement of time, although a few firms use one-fourth of an hour as their base. Time is recorded in fractions of an hour as follows:

Tenths of an Hour as Base

6 minutes = .1 of an hour
12 minutes = .2 of an hour
18 minutes = .3 of an hour
24 minutes = .4 of an hour
30 minutes = .5 of an hour
36 minutes = .6 of an hour
42 minutes = .7 of an hour
48 minutes = .8 of an hour
54 minutes = .9 of an hour
60 minutes = 1.0 hour

One-Fourth of an Hour as Base

15 minutes = .25 of an hour
30 minutes = .5 of an hour
45 minutes = .75 of an hour
60 minutes = 1.0 hour

If, for example, the paralegal spends an hour and thirty minutes digesting the transcript of a deposition in an office that records time in tenths of an hour, his or her time for this task would be entered as 1.5. Suppose the paralegal spent an hour and forty-four minutes on the project. Forty-four minutes does not evenly divide into tenths of an hour. In most offices, timekeepers are instructed to round up or down to the nearest increment. The nearest six-minute increment is forty-two minutes. Hence an hour and forty-four minutes would be recorded as 1.7. Other office policies may also exist on how to record travel time or short telephone conversations.

Suppose that a billable task takes a minute or two. Rounding down to the nearest six-minute would lead to a zero charge. Although some offices may follow this policy, the more likely billing practice is to have a minimum charge for every task, which would usually be .1 (or .25 of an hour if the quarter-hour system if timekeeping is used).

Time-and-billing software can automatically record time once the timekeeper clicks the start and stop buttons on the screen. Menus on the screen allow the timekeeper to tell the computer what client or matter is being worked on, whether the time is billable, and the nature of the work being performed. For an example of such a screen, see Exhibit 14-6. Time-and-billing software also helps the office generate the bills and administrative reports that we will examine later in the chapter.

Exhibit 14-6	Computer–Assisted Timekeeping

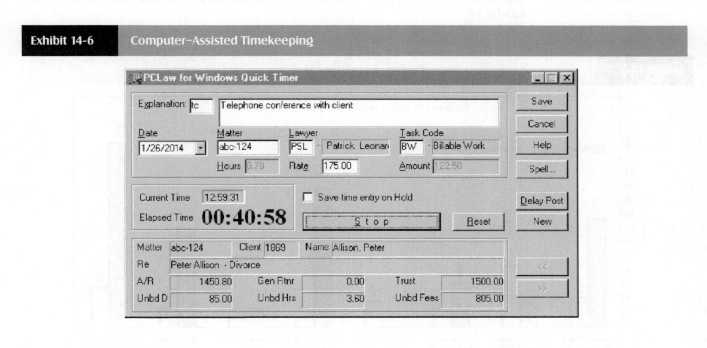

Source: Courtesy PCLaw by Alumni Computer Group, Inc. (www.pclaw.com)

If you have never kept close track of your time, you will find that the task requires a great deal of effort and discipline; it does not come naturally to most of us. The key to performing the task effectively is to do it consistently and comprehensively until it becomes second nature. A major recommendation of timekeepers is to record time **contemporaneously** rather than hours, days, or weeks after performing the task that must be timed. (Contemporaneous means happening or beginning at the same time or shortly thereafter.)

Here is how Tory Barcott, a paralegal in Anchorage, describes the process:

It "sometimes scares me a little to contemplate clients paying" for "for every six minutes of our time." To survive in this world, the paralegal must possess the accuracy and efficiency of a Swiss watch. "I keep one of those small, cheap, adhesive digital clocks where it can't be missed or covered with paperwork. Sticking it to my phone in the middle of my desk works best for me. The first step in performing any task is to record the time on my time

contemporaneous Existing or occurring in the same period of time; pertaining to records on events that are prepared as the events are occurring or very shortly thereafter.

sheet. I do this before retrieving the file, making a phone call," or going to meet a supervising attorney. The clock is also helpful in recording the time when a task is interrupted by anything unrelated to the current client matter. "I take notes on the start and stop times exactly as displayed on my digital clock." Some Saturdays, while absently attending to household chores, I'll glance at the clock and catch myself thinking, "that floor took only 0.4 to clean." This is a sure sign that the discipline of timekeeping has been internalized![15]

Time spent by paralegals and attorneys on tasks for which clients cannot be asked to pay is called **nonbillable time**. An example is the time spent by a paralegal helping to move furniture in the office. **Pro bono** work is also nonbillable. This consists of legal services provided without cost, usually for an **indigent** individual or for a public interest organization such as the Red Cross or a local group of community artists. (Someone is indigent if he or she does not have sufficient funds to hire a private attorney.) A firm's regular clients cannot be asked to pay for pro bono work the office does for others.

The firm needs to know how many billable and nonbillable hours paralegals and attorneys have accumulated over a particular time span. Computer programs are very helpful in allowing timekeepers to indicate which tasks fall into which category. They can also produce clear graphs that present this information in summary form. An example is the chart in Exhibit 14-7.

nonbillable time Time spent on tasks for which clients cannot be asked to pay.

pro bono Concerning or involving legal services that are provided for the public good (pro bono publico, shortened to *pro bono*) without fee or compensation. Sometimes also applied to services given at a reduced rate.

indigent Poor; without means to afford something such as a private attorney or filing fees.

Exhibit 14-7	Chart Showing Billable and Nonbillable Hours for Each Timekeeper

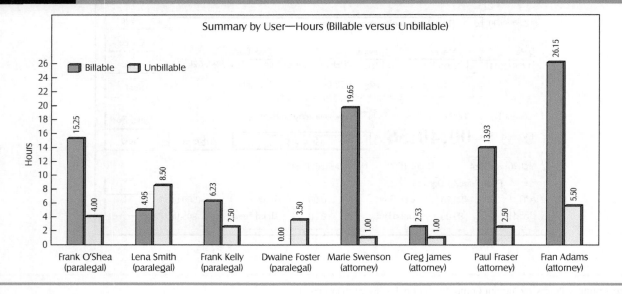

Law firms also set *targets* on how many billable hours they hope to obtain from partners, associates, and paralegals. Exhibit 14-8 shows different formats that computers can help generate to provide a graphic presentation of these expectations.

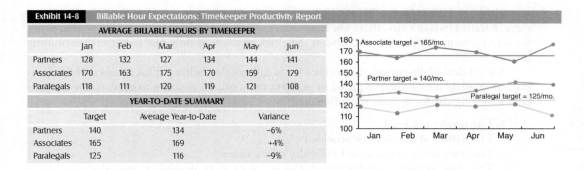

Exhibit 14-8	Billable Hour Expectations: Timekeeper Productivity Report

AVERAGE BILLABLE HOURS BY TIMEKEEPER

	Jan	Feb	Mar	Apr	May	Jun
Partners	128	132	127	134	144	141
Associates	170	163	175	170	159	179
Paralegals	118	111	120	119	121	108

YEAR-TO-DATE SUMMARY

	Target	Average Year-to-Date	Variance
Partners	140	134	−6%
Associates	165	169	+4%
Paralegals	125	116	−9%

Source: Jeff Coburn, *Creating Financial Reports That Partners Will Read*, 14 Legal Management 40 (November/December, 1995), reprinted with permission from the Association of Legal Administrators, Vernon Hills, Illinois (www.alanet.org).

CATEGORIES OF FEES

In Chapters 1 and 5 we covered different aspects of attorney and paralegal fees. Here is a closer look at the main categories of fees.

CLOCK-BASED FEES

■ Hourly Rate

An hourly rate fee is based on the number of hours worked. Paralegals have a separate (and usually substantially lower) hourly rate covering their time. An attorney's time, for example, might be billed at $375 an hour and a paralegal's time at $125 an hour.

■ Blended Hourly Rate

A partner and an associate who have different hourly rates may work on the same case. The bill to the client could break the fee down by rates. For example: $800 for two hours spent by Smith (a partner who bills at $400 an hour) and $600 for three hours spent by Jacob (an associate who bills at $200 an hour). An alternative is to charge a **blended hourly rate**. This is a single hourly rate that is based on a blend or mix of partner and associate rates. For example, to calculate the blended hourly rate, the firm might take the average of the normal rates charged by the partner and associate working on the case. If this is done with our $400 partner and $200 associate, the average hourly blended rate would be $300 an hour ($400 + $200 = $600 ÷ 2 = $300 an hour). In some states, the firm is allowed to add a paralegal's time into this blended hourly rate.

blended hourly rate A single hourly rate based on a blend or mix of the rates normally charged by different individuals, e.g., a partner, a senior associate, a junior associate, and sometimes a paralegal.

ALTERNATIVE FEES

Many individuals are not happy with billing that is controlled by the clock, as reflected in the following comments made by a business client who often retains law firms:

[We] have to look not only at the service and quality of law firms with which we do business but also at the linkage between price and performance. Hourly billing provides no such linkage. It is an accounting device. There is no credible economic theory underlying the hourly billing method, and for that reason, we no longer accept it as the sole, or even predominant, method of pricing legal services. In fact, hourly billing pushes the economic incentives in the wrong direction—weakening rather than strengthening the bonds between performance and pay. It also pushes law firms to a near obsession with billable hours. And this in turn supports the great unwritten rule of all law practices: those who want to get ahead must tally up the hours. This is, first and foremost, dubious economics. The number of hours spent on a matter is no measure of productivity. Productivity is better measured by results, including both outcome and time-frame. Linking the economic structure...to true measures of productivity, or value, will benefit both the firms and the client.[16]

Although billing by the hour is likely to remain the major method of financing legal services in most kinds of cases, there are alternatives, as suggested by this client. These alternative fee arrangements (AFAs) either abandon the clock or use it as only one factor in determining the fee.

A great deal of discussion centers on what is called **value billing**. This means that the fee is not based solely on the time required to perform the work. In addition to time, factors considered in setting the fee include the following.[17]

- The results achieved
- The nature of the services provided
- The complexity, novelty, and difficulty of the issues
- The time pressure under which the services were provided, including any time limitations imposed by the client
- The amount of responsibility assumed by the firm
- The extent to which the services precluded the firm from taking other clients
- The amount of money involved in the matter
- The nature and length of the firm's relationship with the client
- The efficiency with which the services were performed

Using factors such as these, a number of different fee arrangements have been devised. Here is an overview of these arrangements, some of which overlap.

- Fixed Fee

A **fixed fee** is a flat fee for the service—a set figure regardless of the amount of time needed to complete the service. The fixed fee can be a specific sum or a percentage of the recovery.

- Fee Cap

Under a **fee cap**, the parties set a maximum amount or maximum percentage that can be charged as a fee in the case. For example, the firm might bill an hourly rate, but the total bill will not exceed a preset budgeted amount.

- Task-Based Billing

Most attorney services consist of a mix or bundle of tasks such as legal advice, investigation, document review, document drafting, document filing, legal research, negotiation, and court representation. Collectively, these tasks are called **bundled legal services**. Suppose, however, that a client does not want (or cannot afford) the full range of attorney services. The client might be representing him or herself (**pro se**) but would like the attorney to perform specific tasks such as reviewing a document the client has prepared or making a phone call on the client's behalf. Attorneys who agree to provide discrete task representation of this kind are providing **unbundled legal services** (also called *limited-scope representation*, as we saw earlier). Charging for unbundled services is an example of **task-based billing**. A major ethical issue faced by attorneys who offer such representation is the requirement that clients understand that they are not receiving full (i.e., bundled) representation. See Chapter 5 for a discussion of this and related ethics issues.

There are different ways in which attorneys can charge clients for unbundled legal services:

- A set or fixed fee per task, regardless of how long it takes to perform the task,
- The same hourly rate the attorney charges for full (bundled) legal services, or
- A special hourly rate (called an *unbundled rate*).

Task-based billing for legal services is becoming increasingly popular as more consumers use the Internet to locate attorneys willing to provide such services. To find out more, run this search in Google, Bing, or Yahoo: aa "unbundled legal services" (substituting your state for aa).

- Hourly Plus Fixed Fee

With an **hourly plus fixed fee**, the firm charges an hourly rate until the nature and scope of the legal problem are identified. Thereafter, a fixed fee is charged for services provided.

---

value billing A method of charging for legal services based on factors such as the results achieved and the complexity of the case rather than solely on the number of hours spent on the client's case.

fixed fee A flat fee for services, regardless of the amount of time needed to complete the task.

fee cap A maximum amount or maximum percentage that can be charged as a fee in a case.

bundled legal services All tasks needed to represent a client; all-inclusive legal services.

pro se (on one's own behalf) Appearing for or representing oneself. Also called *in propria persona* (shortened to *in pro per*).

unbundled legal services Discrete task representation for which the client is charged per task as opposed to paying a single fee for all tasks to be performed. Also called *limited assistance representation*. Charging for such services is called *task-based billing, unit billing, project billing*.

task-based billing (1) Charging a specific amount for each legal task performed. Also called *unit billing, project billing*. (2) Paying for specifically performed tasks, often identified by using predefined categories of task codes.

hourly plus fixed fee An hourly rate charged until the nature and scope of the legal problem are known, at which time a fixed fee is charged for services provided thereafter.

■ Volume Discounts

The hourly or fixed fee might be reduced if the client gives the office a large amount of business, particularly when the office is able to reduce its own costs by standardization of work (e.g., for certain kinds of cases, the firm has developed standard forms that can be easily adapted to individual clients). A bill reduced for such reasons is called a **discounted hourly fee** or a volume discount.

■ Contingency Fees

The traditional **contingent fee** is a fee that is dependent—contingent—on the outcome of the case. It is paid only if the case is successfully resolved by litigation or settlement regardless of the number of hours spent on the case. The fee could be a fixed amount (e.g., $25,000) or a percentage of the amount the plaintiff wins in the litigation or settlement (e.g., 33 percent if the case is settled before trial, 40 percent if the case goes to trial, and 50 percent if the case is appealed). No fee is owed if the plaintiff loses, although he or she may still be responsible for the payment of expenses and court costs (discussed below) incurred by the office in the losing effort. Contingent fees are most often used in personal injury (PI) cases. Such fees, however, can also be used in other kinds of cases. Suppose, for example, an attorney is hired to handle a transaction such as a contract the client is negotiating with one of its suppliers. Under a contingent billing arrangement with the attorney, if "the transaction (in this case, the contract) fails to go through, the law firm bills the client either a pre-negotiated sum or a small portion of the actual billable hours. Conversely, if the deal is successful, the firm bills the client either a higher pre-negotiated sum or a premium."[18]

A premium is sometimes referred to as **incentive billing**. The attorney receives an increased fee for achieving an exceptional result such as settling a case for an amount that exceeds a target set by the client and attorney.

Most contingent fees are earned by the plaintiff's attorney. A **defense contingent fee** (also called a *negative contingency*) is a fee for the defendant's attorney that is dependent on the outcome of the case. Most often the fee is a fixed amount.

Contingent fees are not allowed in every case. See Chapter 5 for a discussion of when such fees are unethical in criminal and divorce cases.

■ Retroactive Negotiated Fee

Occasionally, a client and attorney might agree to finalize the fee *after* the services are provided. This is called a **retroactive negotiated fee**. When the case is over, the attorney and client agree on the value of the services provided and set the fee accordingly.

COURT COSTS

In addition to fees for services, a law firm usually recovers out-of-pocket expenses that the firm incurs while working on the case. Examples include witness fees, long-distance phone calls, and travel for the attorney or paralegal. The client also pays **court costs** imposed by the court. They include filing fees, jury fees, and special court taxes. When attorneys or paralegals incur expenses on behalf of a client, they often fill out an **expense slip** (see Exhibit 14-9), which goes into the office's accounting system.

In some cases, a court might order a party to pay court costs incurred by an *opposing* party. For example, if a defendant is forced to litigate what the court determines to be a

discounted hourly fee An hourly or fixed fee that is reduced because of the volume of business the client gives the office. Also called *volume discount.*

contingent fee A fee that is paid only if the case is successfully resolved by litigation or settlement, regardless of the number of hours spent on the case. The fee is also called a *contingency.*

incentive billing A fee that is increased if a designated target is met; an increased fee for achieving an exceptional result. Also called *performance bonus, success fee.*

defense contingent fee A fee received by the defendant's attorney that is dependent on the outcome of the case. Also called a *negative contingency.*

retroactive negotiated fee A client bill that is finalized after the services are rendered.

court costs Charges or fees imposed by and paid to the court that are related to litigation in that court. An example is a court filing fee.

expense slip A form used by an office to indicate that an expense has been incurred for which a client may or may not be billed.

Exhibit 14-9	Example of an Expense Slip

Client name _____ File number _____

Nature of expense incurred _____
_____

Billable or nonbillable _____
Expense code _____ Date incurred _____ Amount paid or due _____
Name/address of vendor _____
Person incurring the expense _____
Approved by _____

frivolous Lacking merit. Pertaining to a legal position that cannot be supported by a good-faith argument based on existing law or on the need for a change in existing law.

frivolous position of the plaintiff, the court might order the plaintiff to pay all court costs associated with the litigation of that position. (The ethical issues involved in asserting frivolous claims or defenses are discussed in Chapter 5.)

On when an a party must pay the attorney and paralegal *fees* of an opponent, see the discussion of fee shifting (e.g., statutory fee cases) in this chapter and in Chapter 1.

BILLING

The fees, expenses, and costs to be paid by the client should be spelled out in the attorney-client fee contract. (For an example of such a contract, see Exhibit 8-1 in Chapter 8.) If a **retainer** is involved, the contract should describe how it will work. The word *retainer* can mean the act of hiring or engaging the services of someone, usually a professional. ("Fred retained the firm of Hailey and Ava.") More specifically, a retainer is an amount of money (or other property) paid by a client as a deposit or *advance* against future fees, costs, and expenses of providing services. ("The firm asked for a retainer of $20,000.") Additional money is paid only when the deposit or advance runs out. The contract should specify whether such money or other property from the client is refundable if the client terminates the relationship because he or she fires the attorney or decides not to pursue the matter any further.

retainer (1) The act of hiring or engaging the services of someone, usually a professional. (The verb is *retain*.) (2) An amount of money (or other property) paid by a client as a deposit or advance against future fees, costs, and related expenses of providing services.

BILLING CODES

Some clients require law firms to use billing codes to describe the tasks they performed for the clients and the time it took to perform them. Standard codes have been developed to allow this to occur. Uniform Task-Based Billing (UTBB), for example, divides litigation into five phases:

- Case assessment and development
- Pre-trial pleadings and motions
- Discovery
- Trial preparation and trial
- Appeal

Within each phase, tasks are given a four-digit code (L450 hearing attendance, L520 appellate brief, A106 communication with client, etc.). Expenses are also assigned uniform codes (E109 local travel, E114 witness fees, etc.).

The goal of the codes is to give clients (particularly corporate clients) a better way to audit the bills they receive from law firms they hire and to compare how different firms charge.

BILLING STEPS

draft bill A billing memorandum that states expenses, costs, time spent, and billing rates of attorneys and paralegals working on a particular case or matter.

The actual billing process differs from firm to firm, and occasionally differs from case to case within the same firm. Client billing sometimes occurs only after the matter is completed. More commonly, a client is billed monthly or quarterly. An administrator in a large firm usually works with the billing attorney (the attorney doing the legal work for the client) to prepare the bill. When a matter is called for billing, the administrator may prepare a billing memorandum (the **draft bill**), which specifies the out-of-pocket expenses and costs incurred by the firm in connection with the matter, plus the amount of time each attorney and paralegal has spent on the matter (along with the billing rate of each). For the fee portion of the draft bill, here is an example covering three timekeepers who worked on the Davis matter:[19]

- *Attorney Thomas Jones: $1,750.* Billing rate: $350 an hour. Time spent on the Davis matter: 5 hours (5 × $350 = $1,750).
- *Attorney Kelly Sampson: $2,200.* Billing rate: $200 an hour. Time spent on the Davis matter: 11 hours (11 × $200 = $2,200).
- *Paralegal Harold Grondon: $1,320.* Billing rate: $110 an hour. Time spent on the Davis matter: 12 hours (12 × $110 = $1,320).

write down Deduct an amount from the bill. Also called a *discount adjustment*.

write up Add an amount to the bill. Also called a *premium adjustment*.

The billing attorney has three choices: (1) Bill the total of the actual amounts. In our Davis example, this would produce a bill of $5,270 ($1,750 + $2,200 + $1,320) plus expenses and costs, if any. (2) **Write down** the matter by subtracting a certain amount, e.g., $400. This would produce a bill of $4,870. (3) **Write up** the matter by adding an amount, e.g., $700.

This would produce a bill of $5,970. This adjustment downward or upward are among the possible conclusions when **valuing the bill**. An increase is sometimes called a *premium adjustment*; a decrease, a *discount adjustment*. The decision to adjust is based on factors such as the potential liability exposure of the firm (leading to a write-up if allowed under the attorney-client fee contract) and the relative inexperience of an attorney or paralegal working on the matter (leading to a write-down). If, for example, recently hired attorneys or paralegals take an unusually long time to complete a task they have not performed before, a write-down may be appropriate so that the client does not have to bear the full cost of their on-the-job training.

See Exhibit 14-10 for an example of a bill sent to a client covering work of attorneys and paralegals on a matter. The bill in Exhibit 14-10 is a traditional letter sent by regular mail. Increasingly, law firms are sending out bills electronically (e.g., as email attachments), particularly to corporate clients. The practice is referred to as **e-billing**.

valuing the bill Determining whether there should be a write-down, a write-up, or no adjustment of a bill to be sent to the client.

e-billing Sending out bills electronically (e.g., as email attachments).

Exhibit 14-10	Bill Sent to Client for Attorney and Paralegal Services

Rubin, Rinke, Pyeumac & Craigmoyle
1615 Broadway, Suite 1400
Oakland, California 94612–2115
(415) 444–5316
rrpc@bmt.com
www.rrpc.com

April 10, 2015

IBM Corporation
Norm Savage
3133 Northside Parkway
Atlanta GA 33033

Statement for Professional Services Rendered

Re: Chapter 11   (IBM-1)
      Liquidation

Description of services

Date	Description
04/17/15	Receipt and review of contracts regarding Armonk home office liquidation.
04/18/15	Meeting with opposing attorney regarding court appearance in Atlanta.
04/21/15	Receipt and preliminary review of depositions from seven hundred forty-three (743) claimants to Austin plant parking facilities.
04/22/15	Meeting with officers of the corporation to discuss liquidation of office furniture in all branch offices. Scheduling of 2,000 simultaneous garage sales in marketing managers' driveways to be advertised during next year's Varsity Bowl.

	Total for legal services rendered		$2,150.00
	Hours	Rate	
Partners	6.00	$300	1,800.00
Paralegals	3.50	$100	350.00

Reimbursable expenses and costs

Date	Description	Amount
04/17/15	Lunch meeting with three opposing attorneys.	185.17
04/27/15	Atlanta Bankruptcy Court filing fee due September 1 2015	55.00
04/29/15	Photocopies	5.69
04/29/15	Long-distance telephone charges	36.90
	Total expenses	$282.76
	Total current charges.	$2,432.76

Source: Computer Software for Professionals, Inc., Legalmaster (www.legalmaster.com)

Not all client bills are paid immediately upon receipt. Collection problems can sometimes be substantial. Furthermore, an increasing number of clients are carefully scrutinizing the bills that they receive. Business clients that frequently hire attorneys may use outside billing auditors to review attorney bills before paying them. The auditor will look for potential problems that should be brought to the attention of the client. Law Audit Services, for example, reviews bills from over 5,100 law firms hired by different insurance companies. Here are some of the more egregious irregularities flagged by this auditor:[20]

- An attorney bills for a thirty-eight-hour workday.
- An attorney charges 31¢ a mile for a rental car with unlimited mileage.
- An attorney bills 4.5 hours to look up addresses at a library.

When scrutinizing paralegal billing, clients might ask the law firm to explain:

- Why a particular task performed by an attorney (and billed at attorney rates) was not delegated to a paralegal
- Why paralegal fees are sought for clerical tasks performed by the paralegal

Even if a client does not use an outside auditor, it is wise to assume that someone in the client's office will be dissecting law firm bills for potential problems. Furthermore, the rules of ethics must always be kept in mind. For an overview of the major fee and billing ethical issues (e.g., padding), see Chapter 5.

In statutory-fee cases in which the court has authority to order the losing side to pay the attorney fees (including paralegal fees) of the winning side, conscientious judges are alert to improper fee requests. As we saw earlier, judges want to see accurate timesheet entries. A judge will not award an attorney's rate for paralegal tasks performed by that attorney. Nor will the judge want to award paralegal fees for clerical tasks performed by that paralegal.

CLIENT TRUST ACCOUNTS

client trust account A bank account controlled by an attorney that contains client funds that may not be used for general operating expenses or for any personal purpose of the attorney. Also called *lawyer's trust account, client account, escrow account*. In Washington State, the same obligation applies to accounts controlled by a Limited License Legal Technician (LLLT).

commingling Mixing what should be kept separate, e.g., depositing client funds into an account that also contains funds used for general operating expenses of the office.

Law firms must keep at least two separate bank accounts. One is the office account from which the office pays general operating expenses such as salaries, utility bills, and other overhead items. The second is the **client trust account**, which contains client funds that may not be used to cover office expenses or the attorney's personal expenses. Each client does not need its own client trust account. There can be one client trust account into which the funds of all clients are deposited. When deposits and withdrawals are made, careful records must indicate the client for which a particular deposit or withdrawal is made. Occasionally, an office may have individual client trust accounts for those clients whose cases involve large amounts of money.

There must be no **commingling** or mixing of office funds and client funds. It is unethical for the office to place everything in one account, no matter how meticulous the office may be about recording which funds in the single account belong to the office and which belong to clients. Furthermore, it is equally unethical for the attorney to use any client funds for a personal purpose (e.g., paying the attorney's home mortgage bill) or for an office purpose (e.g., paying the office rent) during a time when the attorney is experiencing a temporary cash-flow problem. This is unethical even if the attorney returns the client funds with interest. When attorneys are audited by the bar association, the auditor (or monitor) often gives careful attention to the accounting records in the office to determine whether these rules on separate accounts are being followed.

What funds must go into a client trust account? Here are some examples:

- A settlement check from an opposing party (or from its insurance company) when a case is settled
- A court award of damages paid by an opposing party (or its insurance company)
- Escrow funds from the sale of real property
- Prepayment of court costs
- Unearned attorney fees

The last category is particularly important. Where attorney fees must be deposited depends on what the fees are for and whether they have been earned. Suppose, for example, an attorney agrees to take a divorce case for a fee of $350 an hour upon the client's payment of an advance (retainer) of $25,000. If this advance is a deposit against future fees (which is often the case), it must be deposited in the client trust account because it has not yet been earned by the attorney. It is still the client's money; the attorney is holding it in trust for the client. Once the attorney earns the right to be paid by working on the case, funds can be transferred from the client trust account to the office account. For example, if the attorney spends twenty hours on the divorce case, he or she can bill the client for $7,000 (20 × $350) and instruct the bank to transfer this amount from the client trust account into the office account. This leaves $18,000 in the client trust account. If the client decides to discharge the attorney or wants to drop the case, the attorney must refund all unearned cash remaining in the client fund.

Some attorney fees, however, are not advances against future legal services. They may constitute a nonrefundable sign-up bonus that commits the attorney to be available to the client as needed over a designated period of time. Such fees can be deposited directly into the attorney's office account because they are considered earned when received.

To avoid disputes, the contract of employment (the fee agreement) between an attorney and client should clarify the purpose and nature of fees to be paid. Are they advances? Are they refundable or nonrefundable? When are they considered earned? Such questions should be answered and the answers understood by the client before the attorney-client relationship begins. The ethical rules of each state must also be carefully checked in this area of practice. Some states, for example, place restrictions on an attorney's right to nonrefundable fees, even if the client agrees to pay them.

Client trust accounts earn bank interest. In most states, law offices must send this interest to a public fund that makes grants to organizations that provide legal services to low-income clients. The use of these funds in this way is called the **IOLTA** (Interest on Lawyers' Trust Accounts) program.

IOLTA (Interest on Lawyers' Trust Accounts) A program that helps fund legal services for the poor with funds that attorneys are required to turn over from interest earned in client trust accounts containing client funds.

ADMINISTRATIVE REPORTS

The managers of a law office need to know what everyone in the office is doing. Many attorneys routinely complete a form similar to that illustrated in Exhibit 14-11, the work summary. It can be filled out by computer or on a paper form provided by the office. Paralegals also fill out work-summary reports, depending on the nature of the work they are doing. If they are working for several attorneys in one department, the department head and the paralegal supervisor, if any, often require copies of the work summary report in order to keep track of the work being done.

Exhibit 14-11	Work Summary

```
[ ]  Can Handle More Work                        C     (Work Completed
[ ]  Have All the Work                                  since Last Report)
     I Can Handle                              WP     (Work in Progress)
[ ]  Need Help                                 M/A    (Matter Is Inactive)
Report of:                                     Date:
```

Client	Matter	Description of Work	Date Assigned	Status

Various administrative reports are often based on the data in work summaries. For examples of administrative reports, see Exhibit 14-12.

| Exhibit 14-12 | Administrative Reports in a Law Office |

- *Accounts Receivable (A/R) Report.* A report showing all cases that have outstanding balances that are due and how long these balances are past due. For example, the report may state how many of the total accounts receivable (i.e., accounts due and payable) are less than 30 days old, how many are 30–59 days old, how many are 60–90 days old, and how many are more than 90 days old. (See Exhibit 14-13 for a partial A/R report.)
- *Timekeeper Productivity Report.* A report showing how much billable and nonbillable time is spent by timekeepers and the billable expectations the office has for each timekeeper. (See Exhibits 14-7 and 14-8.)
- *Case-Type Productivity Report.* A report showing which categories of cases in the office (e.g., bankruptcy, personal injury, or criminal) are most profitable. (Also called a *practice analysis report.*)
- *Fee Analysis Report.* A report on the fees generated, categorized by client, by area of law, by office (if the firm has branch offices), by individual attorney, and by individual paralegal. The report helps the office identify which cases, offices, attorneys, and paralegals are profitable and which are not.
- *Work-in-Progress (WIP) Report.* A report that provides details on cases each timekeeper has started but not yet completed. The report includes a list of all unbilled fees and expenses.
- *Cash Receipts Report.* A report that describes the income received in a specific day, week, month, quarter, or year. The cash receipts can be compared with the amount of projected income for a specific time period.
- *Client Investment Summary Report.* A report of the total amount billed and unbilled, with a calculation of the actual costs of providing legal services for a particular client.
- *Budget Performance Report.* A report that compares a firm's actual income and expenditures with budgeted or projected income and expenditures.[21]

| Exhibit 14-13 | Accounts Receivable (A/R): Bills Not Yet Paid |

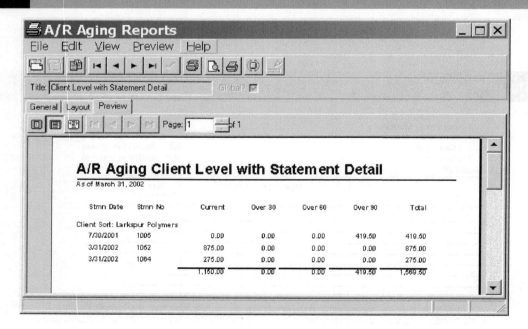

Source: Reprinted with permission of ProLaw Software (www.elite.com/prolaw).

Of particular interest to paralegals are reports generated from timekeeping records that analyze how much time paralegals are investing in client matters. This analysis is similar to the analysis the firm performs on the time invested by attorneys. Managers use these data to evaluate where the profit centers are, whether costs need to be contained, whether work is properly allocated among attorneys and among paralegals, which attorneys and paralegals are in line for salary increases and bonuses, etc.

CLIENT FILE MANAGEMENT

When you begin work in a law office, one of your early tasks will be to learn the office's system for organizing, locating, and storing client files. In some offices, particularly small ones, paralegals are given considerable responsibility for maintaining this system. Efficient file management is of critical importance. "Files are the nerve center of any office. Therefore, the proper storage, safekeeping, and expeditious retrieval of information from the files is the key to...efficient operation."[22] Attorneys and paralegals will tell you that few experiences are more frustrating than coping with a lost document or a missing file. "But the damage can run even deeper." Lost and misplaced files can cause deadlines to be missed, "leading to one of the most common causes of malpractice claims against attorneys."[23]

Many client files are in the computers of the office, often prepared and organized with the client-management software the office uses. In addition, a client's file will contain many *paper* documents, e.g., the attorney-client fee contract and answers to interrogatories. The following description covers file maintenance of these paper documents.

Documents are often placed in separate folders within the client's file. On the right side of one of the folders, you may find all incoming correspondence and copies of all outgoing correspondence. They will be in reverse chronological order, with the most recent correspondence always placed on top. To keep them all together, they will probably be two-hole punched and clipped to the right side of the folder. All other documents (e.g., copies of pleadings) might be similarly clipped to the left side of the folder. Large documents such as transcripts of depositions are often kept in separate folders.

Almost every law office has multiple clients. The location of the files of these clients will depend on factors such as the kind and size of cases the office handles, the number of attorneys in the office, the use of computers, and the availability of storage space. Large law firms often have a centralized filing area where all or most files are located. File clerks (perhaps under the direction of a **record information manager**) keep track of every file. Smaller offices tend to be more decentralized, allowing files to be located in or near the office of the attorney working on those files.

record information manager Someone in charge of client files in a large office.

FILING SYSTEMS

There are two major kinds of filing systems: alphabetical and numerical.

In an **alphabetical filing system**, files are arranged in alphabetical order by the surname or organization name of the client. For example, the file of George Bellman would go in front of the file of Kelly Motor Corp., which would go in front of the file of Mrs. John Thompson, etc. This system works relatively well if the office does not have a large number of clients. The more clients in the office, however, the more likely their names will be confusingly similar. Suppose, for example, that an office has the following clients, each with separate cases (or matters) handled by different attorneys and paralegals in the office:

alphabetical filing system A method of storing client files in alphabetical order by the surname or organization name of the client.

> A-1 North's Appliance Center (a tax case)
> North Central Bank (a securities case)
> Jason North (a divorce case)
> Sam North (Jason's father) (a landlord-tenant case)
> Northern Light, Inc. (a trademark case)

In an alphabetical filing system, there are rules that determine the order in which the files of these five clients would be kept in the file cabinet. Yet filing mistakes are fairly common in spite of the rules. Busy office workers do not always take the time to find out what the rules are. As documents in these files are used, returned, and reused throughout the day, the danger of misfiling is increased because of the similarity of some file names. A bank statement in Jason North's divorce case, for example, might end up in his father's landlord-tenant case or as one of the financial records in the unrelated North Central Bank securities case.

Color coding can help. To speed up the retrieval and return of files, the office can use colored file folders, colored file labels, or colored stickers. If, for example, colors are assigned to a particular area of the law, the folders and labels for all corporate law cases might be blue; those for all tax cases, orange; those for all family law cases, white; etc.[24] Alternatively, an office may use one color for every folder and file opened in a particular year regardless of the kind of case it is. When a new year arrives, new client cases go into folders and files of a different color.

A **numerical filing system** is substantially different from an alphabetical filing system. Numerical filing systems use numbers or letter-number combinations (rather than surnames or organization names) to identify files. Many varieties of numerical filing systems are in use. Here are five examples of how files might be identified in five different law offices:

- 12–778. The first two characters indicate the year the case was opened (12 is the year 2012) (778 is the number assigned to the client).
- LA11–55113. The first two letters indicate which branch office is handling the case (LA is the Los Angeles branch) (11 is the year 2011) (55113 is the number assigned to the client).
- PB–15-552. The first two letters indicate the type of case (PB is a probate case) (15 is the year 2015; 552 is the number assigned to the client). Other examples: TX (a tax case), WC (a workers' compensation case).
- JH.16.111. The first two letters indicate the particular attorney in charge of the case (JH is Jane Harrison, Esq.) (16 is the year 2016) (111 is the number assigned to the client).
- 37.007. The initial number indicates a particular client (for example, 37 is Avon Electronics), and the following numbers indicate how many matters are being handled for those clients (007 is the seventh matter the office has handled for Avon).[25]

Some offices will assign a range of numbers to a particular type of case or matter, e.g., all estate and trust cases will use the numbers 001–999; all tax cases will use the numbers 1,000–1,999; all criminal cases will use the numbers 2,000–2,999, etc. Other variations are also possible.

Index cards can be used to help locate particular files organized under a numerical filing system. For example, Avon Electronics would have its own card on which every file number assigned to it would be placed (37.001, 37.002, 37.003, etc.). These index cards would be kept in alphabetical order. If you want to read the file of a particular client, you would go to the index cards, find that client's name, jot down the numbers of the files that pertain to that client, and go to the file cabinets to locate those numbers. Additional cards allow for cross-indexing. For example, individual attorneys could have their own cards that contain all the case numbers they are handling or have handled. Also, cards for specific topics could be created (e.g., medical malpractice interrogatories and patent applications) on which the numbers for every case file containing documents on those topics would be written. If you wanted to look at medical malpractice interrogatories that the office has used in the past, you would go to the "m" cards, find the card on medical malpractice interrogatories, and jot down the number of every case containing such interrogatories.

Of course, a system of index cards can become cumbersome as the caseload of an office grows in volume and diversity. In many offices, therefore, special computer software is used to do the work of the index cards faster and more efficiently.

Some offices use bar coding to facilitate file management. Every file is assigned a **bar code**, which is a sequence of numbers and vertical lines that can be read by an optical scanner. Most supermarkets use this technology at checkout to record prices and provide inventory data to managers. Similarly, whenever you want to use a file that has been bar coded, you simply scan the bar code and take the file to your office. This is also done when you return the file to the file cabinet or storage room. The office thereby obtains an efficient computer record of who has which files, how long they have had them, and when they were returned.

In a bar-code system, you scan the bar code into a computer. Suppose you are also able to scan the contents of every document in every file into the computer. This amounts to a fully automated file-management system. Every attorney, paralegal, and secretary in the office can then be given instant (and simultaneous) computer access to any document in the files. Finding documents becomes substantially easier than combing through file drawers or boxes and carrying what you need to your desk. Search software allows you to define what you are looking for (e.g., the Ellerson deposition or all personal-injury complaints filed in Suffolk Superior Court after 2009). Not many law offices are sophisticated enough to have every document on computer. We have not yet reached the paperless office, although we are clearly moving in this direction.

numerical filing system A method of storing client files by numbers or letter-number combinations.

bar code A sequence of numbers and vertical lines of different shapes that can be read by an optical scanner.

CLOSED FILES

Once the office completes its work on a case, the file becomes a **closed file**, also called a *dead file* or a *retired file*. Some offices give the file a closed-file (CF) number to differentiate it from active files.[26] The file might be placed in storage boxes or, more likely, scanned into the computer. Important original documents (e.g., wills, estate plans, deeds, and tax returns) are usually returned to the client. The office keeps a copy.

Ethical rules in the state impose an obligation on the office to keep specified files for designated periods of time. "Firms should have policies on retention of files, turning files over to clients, destroying files, and security for files maintained in off-site storage. Since the client file is the property of the client, the attorney cannot destroy old files without informing the client and getting permission and/or giving the client the chance to keep the file."[27]

Finally, closed case files can often be of help to an office in future cases. To avoid reinventing the wheel, offices like to have closed-case files accessible. Whenever work on a current case involves drafting a document, for example, examining the same or a similar document prepared for a prior case can often be a good starting point. As we saw in Chapter 13, *knowledge-management* (KM) systems are being used by large law offices to enable them to locate, adapt, and reuse documents generated in prior cases.

> **closed file** The file of a client whose case is no longer active in the office. Also called *dead file, retired file.*

CHAPTER SUMMARY

Our examination of law-office administration began with an overview of statistics on attorneys and the different settings in which they practice. Most attorneys work in the private sector in sole proprietorships, office-sharing arrangements, partnerships, professional corporations, limited liability entities, or corporate law departments. Among the reasons attorneys choose one setting over another is taxation and whether the legal structure of the office imposes personal liability or limited liability. A sole proprietorship is a form of business that does not have a separate legal identity apart from the individual who owns all assets and assumes all debts and liabilities. The clients of many small or moderately sized offices are mostly or exclusively plaintiffs or are mostly or exclusively defendants. To save on expenses, several sole practitioners may enter into an office-sharing arrangement under which the attorneys practicing alone share the overhead costs of the office such as expenses for office space, secretarial help, etc.

A partnership is a business or other venture jointly owned by two or more persons who share its profits and losses. The equity or capital partners share in the profits and losses of the office and control its management, often through a committee or department structure. Associates are attorneys in the office who hope one day to become partners. There are, however, special categories of associates created for those who do not become partners, such as senior associate. Other categories of attorneys who might be hired by a law office include staff attorneys, of-counsel attorneys, and contract attorneys. For tax and estate-planning purposes, many states allow attorneys to practice law as a professional corporation. There is little practical difference, however, between the administration of a partnership and of a professional corporation. The newest format for law offices is the limited liability entity—the limited liability partnership (LLP). It combines the limited-liability feature of a corporation and the tax liability of a partnership. Some attorneys practice law in the

corporate law departments of corporations. They are employees of the corporation, which is their sole client.

Large law offices may have many nonattorney employees to help manage the office. Among the most prominent is the legal administrator. Also, if there are more than a few paralegals in the office, a paralegal manager is often hired to help administer the office's system for recruiting, hiring, training, and monitoring the progress of paralegals. Technology and a low-wage, skilled labor force abroad have encouraged some law offices to consider outsourcing law office tasks, although there are ethical problems that need to be considered. In a virtual law office, attorneys often provide limited-scope legal services, mainly or exclusively through online communication.

The main operational costs of running a law office are salaries, equipment, occupancy expenses, promotional (marketing) expenses, library and research expenses, support staff expenses, malpractice insurance, etc. The accounting foundation for new clients or matters is the new matter worksheet. There is considerable pressure on attorneys and paralegals to keep precise track of their time for billing purposes in hourly fee cases. For management purposes, accurate timekeeping records are important in all offices even if hourly fees are not involved.

A number of different fee arrangements exist: clock-based arrangements (e.g., hourly rate and blended hourly rate) and alternative fee arrangements (AFAs) that stress value billing (e.g., fixed fee, fee cap, task-based billing, hourly plus fixed fee, volume discount, contingent fee, and retroactive negotiated fee). Bundled services consist of the full range of tasks needed to represent a client on a matter. Unbundled legal services (limited-scope representation) consist of discrete tasks for which the client is charged per task, as opposed to being charged a single fee for all tasks to be performed.

The method of paying the bill (including expenses and court costs) should be spelled out in the attorney-client fee contract. Some clients require law firms to use billing codes. The amount actually paid by a client is not determined until there has been a valuing of the bill, which might result in a write-up, a write-down, or no change. Some business clients use an outside auditor to help them monitor law firm bills, particularly to identify irregularities.

Law firms must keep at least two separate bank accounts: the office account and the client trust account. There must be no commingling (mixing) of office and client funds. An efficient law office uses administrative reports to help it keep track of and manage the practice. Examples include work summary, accounts receivable (A/R) report, and timekeeper productivity report.

Correspondence in client folders is often filed in reverse chronological order, with the most recent item placed on top. Correspondence is clipped to the right of the folder and all other documents are clipped on the left. The location of client files in an office will be either centralized or decentralized. The two major kinds of filing systems are the alphabetical filing system and the numerical filing system. Some large offices use bar coding to facilitate file management. Once the office completes its work on a case, the file becomes a closed file. Practical considerations (e.g., space limitations) and the rules of ethics determine how long a firm must keep closed files. Important documents are returned to the client.

KEY TERMS

private law firm (p. 590)
fee-shifting (p. 590)
legal aid office (p. 590)
sole proprietorship (p. 590)
personal liability (p. 590)
limited liability (p. 590)
sole practitioner (p. 590)
general practitioner (GP)
 (p. 590)
PI cases (p. 590)
boutique law firm (p. 590)
law clerk (p. 591)
legal intern (p. 591)
office sharing (p. 591)
overhead (p. 591)
adverse interests (p. 591)
partnership (p. 591)
tort (p. 591)
pass-through entity (p. 591)
partner (p. 593)
rainmaker (p. 593)
nonequity partner (p. 593)

equity partner (p. 593)
draw (p. 593)
associate (p. 593)
lateral hire (p. 593)
senior associate (p. 593)
staff attorney (p. 593)
of counsel (p. 593)
contract attorney (p. 593)
professional corporation (P.C.)
 (p. 593)
limited liability entity (p. 594)
corporate law department
 (p. 594)
general counsel (p. 594)
managing partner (p. 594)
legal administrator (p. 594)
paralegal manager (p. 596)
outsourcing (p. 596)
virtual law office (p. 597)
limited-scope representation
 (p. 597)
timekeeping (p. 598)

matter (p. 598)
new file worksheet (p. 598)
statutory-fee case (p. 599)
substantive (p. 600)
daily time sheet (p. 600)
contemporaneous (p. 601)
nonbillable time (p. 602)
pro bono (p. 602)
indigent (p. 602)
blended hourly rate (p. 603)
value billing (p. 604)
fixed fee (p. 604)
fee cap (p. 604)
bundled legal services (p. 604)
pro se (p. 604)
unbundled legal services (p. 604)
task-based billing (p. 604)
hourly plus fixed fee (p. 604)
discounted hourly fee (p. 605)
contingent fee (p. 605)
incentive billing (p. 605)
defense contingent fee (p. 605)

retroactive negotiated fee
 (p. 605)
court costs (p. 605)
expense slip (p. 605)
frivolous (p. 606)
retainer (p. 606)
draft bill (p. 606)
write down (p. 606)
write up (p. 606)
valuing the bill (p. 607)
e-billing (p. 607)
client trust account (p. 608)
commingling (p. 608)
IOLTA (p. 609)
record information manager
 (p. 611)
alphabetical filing system
 (p. 611)
numerical filing system
 (p. 612)
bar code (p. 612)
closed file (p. 613)

ASSIGNMENTS

CRITICAL ANALYSIS

14.1 The chapter quotes a business client who says that "hourly billing pushes the economic incentives in the wrong direction."

(a) What did the client mean by this statement?

(b) Is the statement correct?

(c) When you work on cases as a paralegal, your attorney will charge clients for your work by the hour. Will you necessarily face incentives that go in the wrong direction?

PROJECT

14.2 In the practice of law, time is money. Hence you must develop the discipline of recording your time. Supervisors

will later decide what portions of your time are billable, and to what clients. Step one is to compile a record of your time.

To practice this discipline, fill out a daily time sheet for a day that you select. On a sheet of paper, record (in a chart form that you design) everything (approximately) that you do in six-minute intervals over a continuous eight-hour period. Use the six-minute decimals discussed in the chapter (e.g., 12 minutes =.2). When needed, round up or down to the nearest six-minute period. Once you design your chart, it should take you a total of no more than about fifteen minutes to fill it out during the eight-hour period. You do not, however, fill it out at one time; you fill it out contemporaneously as you go through the tasks you are keeping track of throughout the eight hours.

Select an eight-hour period in which you are engaged in a fairly wide variety of activities. Avoid an eight-hour period that contains any single activity lasting over two hours. Draw a chart covering the eight-hour period. At the top of the chart, place your name, the date of the eight-hour period that you used, and the starting/ending times of the eight-hour period. The period can be within a school day, a workday, a day of leisure, etc.

Using abbreviations, make specific entries on your activities within the eight hours in six-minute intervals. For example, "Reading a chapter in a real estate school text" might be abbreviated as RE-R. "Driving to school" might be abbreviated as D-Sch. All "purely personal matters" (such as taking a shower) might be abbreviated as PPM. You decide what the abbreviations are. On a separate sheet of paper, explain what the abbreviations mean. When an activity is repeated in more than one six-minute interval, simply repeat the abbreviation.

One format for the chart might be a series of vertical and horizontal lines on the sheet of paper. This will give you a small amount of space on which to insert your abbreviations for each six-minute interval. Design the chart any way that you want, keeping in mind the goal of the exercise: to enable someone else to know what you did within the eight-hour period.

In Exhibit 14-5, there is an example of a Daily Time Sheet used in a law office. You can adapt the format in Exhibit 14-5 so long as you follow the guidelines listed here. For example, place your abbreviations on a separate sheet of paper that you submit rather than at the top of the form.

14.3 Contact a private law firm in the area that is large enough to have an office manager or legal administrator. Ask this person if you can interview him or her on the phone, by email, or in person for several minutes. Explain that you are taking a paralegal course that requires you to interview a manager. Ask this person about the following topics:

(a) How the office is organized (partnership, sole proprietorship, or other)

(b) Major duties of the manager or administrator (use Exhibit 14-2 as a guide to some of the areas to cover)

(c) Categories of attorneys and other staff in the office, their duties, and the chain of command among them

(d) Kinds of fees the office charges

(e) Timekeeping methods

(f) How work is delegated and evaluated

(g) Filing system

(h) Law library size

Prepare a report on what you learned from this interview.

CORE SKILLS

Among the many skills a paralegal must have, five core skills stand out: writing (both basic English and legal drafting), research, ethics, computer use, and collaboration (working with others). The core-skill assignments introduce and reinforce these skills. Even if you are not asked to do all of the assignments as part of the course, you should do them on your own. Also, do not wait for the topics in the assignments to be covered in this course or in other courses. Successful paralegals are self-starters. A major characteristic of a self-starter is a thirst for independent study — learning on your own.

CORE SKILL: WRITING

14.4 Write a letter closing a case and asking the client what to do with the file. Your office has just closed the case of Leo Bradley. It was a negligence case in which Bradley sued John Noonan after an automobile collision. Bradley lost the case, but he has decided not to appeal. Draft a letter to be signed by your supervising attorney in which you inform the client of the balance owed by the client for expenses ($1,423). (No fees are owed because the office took the case on contingency.) State what documents you have in the files (e.g., medical records). Ask the client whether he would like to have these documents. Indicate that the office keeps records for three years after a case is closed and then destroys them. Make up any facts you need, such as the address of the client, the office file number for his case, the kinds of documents in the file, and the reasons for the expenses (e.g., witness fees, travel costs). For the format of the letter, see Exhibits 12-3 and 12-4 in Chapter 12.

CORE SKILL: RESEARCH

14.5 Run this search in Google, Bing, or Yahoo: how do attorneys use LinkedIn? Write a report in which you describe the different uses to which law firms have used LinkedIn for marketing. Your report must cite at least five different sources on the Web.

CORE SKILL: ETHICS

14.6 Dan Foley and Helen Davis are sole practitioners who have their own clients. They share an office, splitting the costs of rent, a secretary, and a paralegal. Both of their client files are in the same filing cabinet. When the secretary answers the phone, she says, "Foley & Davis, how many I help you?" In Google, Bing, or Yahoo, run this search: office sharing attorney ethics. Write a report of the ethical problems in the office of Dan Foley and Helen Davis.

CORE SKILL: COMPUTERS

14.7 In Google, Bing, or Yahoo, run this search: time billing software attorney. Compare two time-and-billing software programs. Cover price, features, etc.

CORE SKILL: COLLABORATION

14.8 In Google, Bing, or Yahoo, run this search: google hangout. Also run the same search in YouTube.

(1) What is Google Hangout?

(2) What are the steps to create a hangout?

(3) Create a hangout with as many of your classmates as possible. Invite fellow students to join the hangout. Items needed: a web camera (usually built into your laptop), a headset, a Google account, etc. Interview whoever joins the hangout about his or her hopes for a paralegal career. If you are invited to join another student's hangout, you will answer his or her questions in like manner.

THE JOB SEARCH

(The search for employment cannot wait until the end of a course or of a curriculum. It needs to begin now. The job-search assignments are designed to introduce you to different aspects of the job search and to build options for you to explore about employment.)

14.9 Use the job finding techniques in Exhibit 2-12 of Chapter 2 to find job listings for paralegal managers. Try to find at least three. Compare the duties of these positions with the list of duties in Exhibit 14-3.

REVIEW QUESTIONS

1. Approximately how many attorneys are there in the United States?
2. What percentage of attorneys work in private practice?
3. Name six settings in which attorneys practice law in the private sector.
4. What is a sole proprietorship?
5. What is the distinction between limited liability and personal liability?
6. What is the distinction between a plaintiff and a defendant law office?
7. What is a general practitioner (GP)?
8. What are law clerks and legal interns?
9. What is meant by an office-sharing arrangement?
10. What is overhead?
11. What is a partnership?
12. What are the liability and tax aspects of a partnership?
13. What are the different kinds of attorneys that might work in a partnership?
14. What is a rainmaker?
15. What are the two main categories of partners?
16. What is a partner's draw?
17. What is a senior associate?
18. What is a lateral hire?
19. Define the following categories of attorneys: staff attorney, of counsel, and contract attorney.
20. What is a professional corporation (PC)?
21. What is a limited liability entity?
22. What is a corporate law department?
23. What are some of the major responsibilities of the legal administrator?
24. List some of the main categories of administrative support staff in a large law office.
25. What are some of the major responsibilities of a paralegal manager?
26. What is outsourcing, and what ethical dangers does it pose?
27. What is a virtual law office?
28. What are the main expenses of running a law office?
29. What is a matter?
30. What is a new file worksheet?
31. Why are accurate time records important for offices that charge hourly fees as well as for offices that do not?
32. What is meant by recording time contemporaneously?
33. What is nonbillable time? Give some examples.
34. What is a statutory-fee case?
35. What is a daily time sheet?
36. Describe the following kinds of fees and billing arrangements: hourly rate, blended hourly rate, fixed fee, fee cap, hourly plus fixed fee, volume discount, contingent fee, incentive billing, and retroactive negotiated fee.
37. What is value billing?
38. What is the distinction between bundled and unbundled services?
39. What are the different meanings of *retainer*?
40. What are billing codes?
41. What are court costs?
42. What is a draft bill?
43. What is meant by valuing the bill?
44. What is the distinction between a write-down and a write-up?
45. What is the function of a billing auditor?
46. What is e-billing?
47. What is a client trust account, and why is it required?
48. What is the IOLTA program?
49. When can attorney fees be deposited in the attorney's personal account?
50. What is the function of the following administrative reports: accounts receivable (A/C) report, timekeeper productivity report, case-type productivity report, fee analysis report, work-in-progress report, cash receipts report, client investment summary report, and budget performance report?
51. Describe an alphabetical and a numerical filing system.
52. How can bar codes be used in file management?
53. How do offices handle closed case files?

HELPFUL WEBSITES

Statistics on the Legal Profession
- www.americanbar.com (in the search box, enter *legal profession statistics*)
- www.bls.gov/ooh/legal/lawyers.htm
- www.law.harvard.edu/programs/plp/pages/statistics.php

Occupational Outlook: Attorneys and Paralegals
- www.bls.gov/ooh/legal/lawyers.htm
- www.bls.gov/ooh/legal/paralegals-and-legal-assistants.htm

Law Office Management Resources
- www.americanbar.org/groups/law_practice.html

- www.americanbar.org/groups/gpsolo.html
- www.americanbar.org/portals/solo_home.html
- myshingle.com
- www.weilandco.com/manage.html
- lawlibguides.seattleu.edu/solo

Trust Account Handbook (example)
- www.ncbar.gov/PDFs/Trust%20Account%20Handbook.pdf

Lawyernomics
- lawyernomics.avvo.com

Office Sharing: Ethical Issues
- www.michbar.org/opinions/ethics/Articles/feb98.cfm

Marketing
- www.lawyermarketing.com
- www.ilawyermarketing.com

Outsourcing
- www.outsourcing.org/Directory/Legal
- en.wikipedia.org/wiki/Legal_outsourcing
- www.pangea3.com

Legal Consulting Firms
- www.altmanweil.com
- legalexecutiveinsights.com
- weilandco.com
- www.lawbiz.com
- www.robertdenney.com

Time and Billing Software
- na.sage.com/us/sage-timeslips
- www.lexisnexis.com/law-firm-practice-management/pclaw

- www.elite.com/prolaw
- www.legalmaster.com

"Greedy" Associates
- www.infirmation.com/bboard/clubs-top.tcl

Google, Bing, or Yahoo Searches
(On these search engines, run the following searches, using quotation marks and substituting your state for "aa" where indicated.)

- "law firm economics" aa
- "law office administration"
- "legal administrator" role aa
- billable hour attorney
- nonbillable attorney
- lawyer marketing
- legal process outsourcing
- outsourcing legal

- timekeeping in a law office
- billing software law
- client trust account
- "billable hour" lawyer
- American Bar Association Commission on Billable Hours Report

---

ENDNOTES

Portions of this chapter were originally written with Robert G. Baylor, business manager at Manatt, Phelps, Rothenberg, and Tunney. Others who have contributed valuable commentary include Michele A. Coyne, Shawn Jones, Dorothy Moore, Patsy Pressley, Kathleen Reed, and Deborah Thompson.

1. American Bar Association, *National Lawyer Population by State* (2012). See also endnote 4 and Bureau of the Census (www.census.gov) (type "statistics" in the search box).
2. American Bar Association Section on Legal Education and Admission to the Bar, *2012 Law Graduate Employment Data* (2013) (www.americanbar.org).
3. National Conference of Bar Examiners, *2012 Statistics* (www.ncbex.org).
4. Occupational Outlook Handbook, *Lawyers* (U.S. Department of Labor (2014) (www.bls.gov/ooh/legal/lawyers.htm).
5. *American Bar Association Releases Class of 2013 Law Graduate Employment Data* (www.americanbar.org) (April 9, 2014).
6. Robert Conroy and Robert Green, eds., *The Quality Pursuit* 69 (American Bar Association, 1989).
7. Ann Sherman, *Should Small Firms Get on Board with Outsourcing?* Small Firm Business (September 12, 2005).
8. *National Federation of Paralegal Associations, Position Statement on the Outsourcing of Paralegal Duties to Foreign Countries* (2005) (www.paralegals.org/associations/2270/files/outsourcing.pdf).
9. Eileen B. Libby, *Offshore Ripples Make Waves for US Paralegals*, 34 Facts and Findings 20 (May, 2007).
10. *2013 Report on the State of the Legal Market* (Georgetown Law Center for the Study of the Legal Profession, 2014).
11. Altman Weil, Inc., *2003 Survey of Law Firm Economics* (2004).
12. J. Margolis, *At the Bar*, N.Y. Times, September 7, 1990, at B13.
13. A. Walljasper, *I Quit!*, Wisconsin Lawyer 16 (March 1990).

14. Morris, *Join the Effort to Restore Respect to the Legal Profession*, The Digest 3 (Arizona Paralegal Ass'n, April 1989) [*legal assistant* changed to *paralegal* in quote].
15. Tory Barcott, *Time Is Money*, AALA News (Alaska Ass'n of LegalAssistants, April 1990).
16. Sherry Matteucci, *What the Heck Is "Value Billing" Anyway?*, 18 The Montana Lawyer 2 (November 1992). See also Darlene Ricker, *The Vanishing Hourly Fee*, 80 American Bar Ass'n Journal 66 (March 1994); Paul Marcotte, *Billing Choices*, 75 American Bar Ass'n Journal.
17. G. Emmett Raitt, *What if Your Client Used Value Billing?*, Orange County Lawyer 37 (April 1992).
18. Michele Coyne, *Alternatives to Customary Billing Practices*, The LAMA Manager 19 (International Paralegal Management Association, Summer 1991).
19. Darby, *Of Firms and Fees: The Administrator's Role*, 8 Legal Management 34, 39 (March/April 1989).
20. Milo Geyelin, *If You Think Insurers Are Tight, Try Being One of Their Lawyers*, Wall Street Journal, February 9, 1999, at Al.
21. Pamela Everett Nollkamper, *Fundamentals of Law Office Management* (5th ed. 2014); Brent Roper, *Practical Law Office Management* (3rd ed. 2002).
22. Paul Hoffman, *Law Office Economics and Management Manual* § 41:04, at 4 (1986).
23. Terry Light, *The Procedure Manual*, 26 The Practical Lawyer 71 (January 1980).
24. Pamela Everett Nollkamper, *Fundamentals of Law Office Management* 426 (5th ed. 2014).
25. Brent Roper, *Practical Law Office Management* (3rd ed. 2002).
26. Id. at 393.
27. Terry Cannon, *Ethics and Professional Responsibility for Legal Assistants* 258 (3rd ed. 1999).

CHAPTER 15

INFORMAL AND FORMAL ADMINISTRATIVE ADVOCACY

CHAPTER OUTLINE

- Nature of Advocacy
- Informal Advocacy
- Procedural Due Process
- Formal Advocacy

CHAPTER OBJECTIVES

After completing this chapter, you should be able to

- Define advocacy.
- Distinguish between informal and formal advocacy.
- List the major techniques of informal advocacy.
- Understand the importance of timing, evaluation, adaptation, and recordkeeping in advocacy.
- List the major components of procedural due process.
- Understand the role of a paralegal when allowed to represent clients at an administrative hearing.

NATURE OF ADVOCACY

Advocacy is the process by which an individual attempts to influence the goals or behavior of others. Advocacy is a basic component of everyday life. Note, for example, the advocacy involved, or potentially involved, in the following circumstances:

> **advocacy** The process by which you attempt to influence the goals or behavior of others.

- At a supermarket checkout counter, a clerk tells a customer that the price of tomatoes is 99¢ a pound. The customer replies, "But the sign back there said 89¢ a pound." The clerk says, "I'm sorry, but the price is 99¢."
- A student goes to the teacher to say that a term paper should have been graded "A" rather than "B."
- A tenant tells the landlord that a $900 a month rent increase is ridiculous because the building has been steadily deteriorating.
- A homeowner has been away on a vacation. Upon his return, he finds that his house has been burglarized. When he goes to the police station to report the crime, he asks the desk sergeant why his neighborhood has not been receiving better protection in view of all the burglaries that have been occurring in the area lately. The sergeant replies that there are not enough police available to patrol the neighborhood adequately. The homeowner is not satisfied with this response and asks to see the precinct captain.

The customer, student, tenant, and homeowner all have complaints. They are *complainants*. They are not satisfied with something. Their natural response is to make an argument for better service. In so doing, they become advocates for the objectives that they are seeking. Advocacy does not always require courtrooms, judges, and attorneys; all that is needed is a complaint, a person complaining (a complainant), and someone who may be able to act on the complaint.

Formal advocacy occurs in court trials and in court-like hearings held by administrative agencies. As we saw in Chapter 6, an administrative agency acts like a court when it holds hearings presided over by a hearing officer or **administrative law judge (ALJ)**. At such hearings, formal advocacy occurs through self-representation, attorney representation, and (where authorized) paralegal representation. Advocacy that takes place outside of court and court-like hearings is called *informal advocacy*.

> **administrative law judge (ALJ)** A government officer who presides over a hearing at an administrative agency. Also called *hearing examiner*. (Most, but not all, ALJs are attorneys.)

INFORMAL ADVOCACY

Paralegals often have contact with organizations that require the use of informal advocacy techniques. An example is responding to resistance when trying to convince a caseworker or a social worker that the action an agency has taken (or proposes to take) is illegal or ill advised. Exhibit 15-1 presents a summary of twenty-one techniques of informal advocacy that are sometimes used with varying levels of success when trying to obtain action from an administrative agency or from any large organization. Although some of the techniques overlap, they are listed in the approximate order of effectiveness. Of course, whether a particular technique will be effective depends on what you are trying to accomplish, whom the technique is directed against, and how well you execute the technique. In general, the techniques at the beginning of Exhibit 15-1 are more likely to be effective than those at the end. Do you agree?

Exhibit 15-1	Techniques of Informal Advocacy

1. *Put your cards on the table.* Be direct and completely aboveboard in telling the agency official what your position is and what you want.

2. *Insist on adequate service.* Point out to the agency official that the purpose of the agency is service and that this principle should guide the official's actions.

3. *Ask to see the authority they are relying on.* Insist that the agency official show you the regulation, law, or other authority that supports the action taken or proposed by the agency.

4. *Climb the chain of command.* "Can I speak to a supervisor?" Normally, everyone has a boss who can overrule decisions made by those beneath him or her. When you are dissatisfied with the decision or action of an employee, you can try to "appeal" or complain "up the chain of command" to the employee's supervisor and to the supervisor's supervisor, as needed.

5. *Insist on common sense.* Convey to the agency official the impression that common sense supports your position—in addition to or despite regulations or technicalities that might be cited against you.

6. *Take the role of the tired, battered, helpless citizen.* Do not insist on anything. Play dumb; act exhausted; act in such a way that the agency official will think, "This person needs help." Act as if everyone else has given you the runaround and you are praying that this official (whom you have not dealt with before) will finally give you a sympathetic ear—and some help.

7. *Cite a precedent.* Point out to the agency official (if it is true) that your case is not unusual because the agency has granted what you want to others under the same or similar circumstances in the past.

8. *Find the points of compromise.* Ferret out the negotiable points in the dispute, and determine whether you can bargain your way to a favorable result that gives you at least some of what you want.

9. *Uncover the realm of discretion.* Those in authority often want you to believe that their hands are tied, that there is only one way to apply the rule. In fact, some discretion is often involved in the application of rules. You need to find the realm of discretion and try to fit your case within it. The goal is to show that the discretion provides the agency official enough flexibility to give you what you are seeking.

10. *Look for an opening by asking a very broad question.* Pose a question to the official that is so broad that the answer may give you an opening. For example, "Has the agency ever granted xyz before?" "Are you telling me that in the thousands of cases your agency has handled, you have never granted a request like mine?"

11. *Demonstrate the exception.* Insist on the uniqueness of your client's situation. Show agency officials that the general rule they are using to deny your client a benefit is inapplicable.

12. *Cite the law.* Show the agency official that you know what administrative regulations apply to the case. Also cite statutes and other laws to demonstrate your point. Of course, if the law is clearly on your side, this technique (and number 13) would go at the top of the list.

13. *Interpret the law.* After citing a rule of law, explain to the official how the law applies to your situation.

14. *Be a buddy.* Show agency officials that you are not an enemy, that you respect and like them, and that you are aware of how difficult their job is.

15. *Make clear that you are going to fight this case "all the way up."* Make the official aware of how important the case is. Point out that you are thinking about taking the case to a formal agency hearing (if available) and that your office may go to court, if necessary.

16. *Redefine the problem.* If you can't solve a problem, redefine it, as long as you can still achieve the essentials of what you seek. For example, stop trying to qualify the client for program "A" if program "B" will serve the client equally well (or almost so), and if the problems of qualifying the client for "B" are not as great as those you face by continuing to insist on "A."

17. *Do a favor to get a favor.* Be willing to do something (within reason and the law) for the person from whom you are seeking something.

18. *Seek the support of third persons.* Gather the support of individuals or groups within and outside the agency so you can demonstrate that you are not alone.

19. *Preach.* Lecture the agency official about his or her responsibilities within the agency. Elaborate on the mission of the agency, making clear that the denial of what you are seeking violates or is inconsistent with that mission.

20. *Embarrass the official.* Show the agency official that you do not respect him or her. Do it in such a way that the official is made to look silly.

21. *Be angry.* Show your hostility. Be completely open about the anger you feel concerning what is being done or proposed.

Effective use of any informal technique of advocacy requires timing, evaluation, adaptation, and recordkeeping. (See Exhibit 15-2.)

A major threshold concern of an advocate is timing—deciding when to intervene with the advocacy techniques. The decision to intervene involves a strategic judgment about when it would be most appropriate to seek what you are after at the agency or organization. For example, suppose that you must contact the complaint bureau of an agency that is relatively new to you. One approach would be simply to walk up to the complaint bureau and delve right into the matter that brought you there. Another approach would be to try to find out something about the bureau before going to it. Online information about the structure of the agency will provide you with at least a general idea of what to expect. You may be able to talk to attorneys or other paralegals who have had prior contact with the bureau. Suppose you learn that two agency employees rotate their work at the bureau and that one employee has a reputation of being more cooperative than the other. You may decide not to go to the bureau until this employee is on duty. In short, you decide to postpone your contact with the bureau until circumstances are most favorable to the objective you are seeking.

Exhibit 15-2	Timing, Evaluation, Adaptation, and Recordkeeping

I. *Timing: Deciding When to Use Advocacy*
II. *Self-Evaluation of the Informal Advocacy Techniques Being Used*
   1. Are you making yourself clear?
   2. Are you creating more problems than you are solving?
   3. Are you accomplishing your goal?
III. *Adaptation.* Are You Flexible Enough to Shift Your Techniques as Needed?
IV. *Recording/Recordkeeping*
   1. Describe what you saw.
   2. Describe what you did.

As you use any of the techniques in Exhibit 15-1, you must simultaneously judge the effectiveness of the technique in light of what you are trying to accomplish. Are you making yourself clear? Are you complicating rather than resolving the problem? Are you getting through? Are you comfortable with the technique you are using? Does it clash with your personality? Are you pacing yourself properly? Is your insistence on immediate success encouraging a negative response that is counterproductive?

One of the major signs of ineffective advocacy is becoming so involved in the case that you begin to take roadblocks and defeat personally. Everyone agrees that objectivity is a good quality—and most of us claim to possess this quality in abundance. The unfortunate fact, however, is that we tend to lose objectivity as friction increases. We allow our careers and our lifestyles to be threatened when someone says to us, "You can't do that." We rarely admit that we can be thrown off balance in this way. We justify our response by blaming someone else for insensitivity, unfairness, or stupidity.

Once you have disciplined yourself to identify the techniques you are using and to evaluate their effectiveness, you must be flexible enough to adapt your techniques and shift to more effective ones as needed.

Finally, the paralegal usually will have a recording/recordkeeping responsibility. Almost every case you work on must be documented in the office files. Your efforts at informal advocacy, the steps you took, should be described in those files.

SAMPLE CASE

We now examine some of the informal advocacy techniques (Exhibit 15-1) in the context of the following fact situation:

> You are in your own home or apartment. You receive a letter from a local ISP (Internet service provider) stating that your Internet service will be shut off in ten days if you do not pay your bill. Your spouse tells you that all the bills have already been paid. You call the ISP, which has an office downtown. When you question the clerk, she says to you, "I'm sorry sir; our records reflect an unpaid bill of over sixty days. You must pay the bill immediately." To try to straighten matters out, you take a trip to the ISP office. In the dialogue that follows, the complainant is his own advocate. "C" is the complainant and "E" is one or more of the ISP company employees. As you read the dialog, ask yourself how effective C's informal advocacy is.

E: Can I help you?
C: Yes, I want to see someone about a problem with my bill.
E: I'm sorry, sir, but the customer complaint division closed at 2 p.m. You'll have to come back or call tomorrow.
C: Closed! Well, let me see someone about terminating the Internet service altogether.
E: All right, would you step over to that desk?

Technique: *If you can't solve a problem, redefine it, as long as you can still achieve the essentials of what you are seeking.* (See #16 in Exhibit 15-1.) The client is taking a risk. He cannot get to the complaint division, so he will try to achieve his objective through the termination division. He has substituted one problem (getting to the termination division) for another problem (getting to the complaint division) in the hope of expressing his grievance.

E: Can I help you?
C: Yes, I want to terminate my ISP service if I can't get this problem straightened out.
E: You'll have to go over to the bill complaint division, sir.
C: Look, stop sending me somewhere else! This has to be straightened out immediately!

Technique: *Demonstrate anger.* (See #21.) This is a dangerous tactic to employ. It is a fact of life, however, that some people respond to this kind of pressure.

C: Aren't you here to serve the public?

Technique: *Insist on adequate service.* (#2) Point out that the organization exists to serve and that you need better service.

E: There are rules and procedures that we all must abide by and...
C: Your responsibility is to take care of the public!

Technique: *Preach.* (#19) Perhaps the most common way people try to change other people is to lecture them, to tell them what they should or should not be doing.

Technique: *Embarrass the official.* (#20) Make the official look silly and unworthy of respect. At this point, has the complainant lost objectivity? What risks are being taken? Do you think the complainant is aware of what he is doing? If you asked him whether he was being effective, what do you think his response would be? Is he more involved with the "justice" of his case than with the effectiveness of his approach?

C: I'd like to speak to your supervisor. Who is in charge of this office?
E: Well, Mr. Adams is the unit director. His office is in Room 307.
C: Fine.

Technique: *Climb the chain of command.* (#4) Almost everyone has a boss who can overrule a subordinate's decisions. If you're unhappy about a decision, complain "up the chain of command," to the top if necessary.

E: Can I help you?

C: I want to speak to Mr. Adams about a complaint. Tell him that it is very important.

E: Just a moment. [She goes into Mr. Adams's office for a few moments and then returns.] You can go in, sir.

C: Mr. Adams?

E: Yes, what can I do for you? I understand you are having a little problem.

C: It's about this bill. I have been talking to person after person in this office without getting any response. I'm going in circles. I need to talk to someone who is not going to send me to someone else!

Technique: *Take the role of the tired, battered, helpless citizen.* (See #6)

E: Well, let me see what I can do. I've asked the secretary to get your file…Here it is. The records say that you haven't paid several months' bills. Our policy here is to terminate utility service if payment is delinquent sixty days or more.

C: What policy is that? Could I see a copy of this policy and what it's based on?

Technique: *Ask to see the authority they are relying on.* (#3) Make the agency show you the regulation, law, policy, or other authority that allegedly backs up the action it has taken or says it will take. What risk is the complainant taking by resorting to this technique? Is the complainant suggesting to Mr. Adams that he does not trust him? How would you have made the request in this situation? Does the request always have to be made in a hostile manner?

E: Well, I'll be glad to show you the brochure.

C: I would like to see it and also the law it is based on. You are a regulated service. And my position, Mr. Adams, is that my wife has paid the bills.

E: Well, our records don't reflect it.

C: All the canceled checks she used have not all come back from the bank yet. I would like a photocopy of your file on me. Under the law, I am entitled to it.

Technique: *Cite the law.* (#12) Demonstrate that you know what regulations and other laws apply to the case.

E: You do have this right, but only if you make the request in writing.

C: Let's be reasonable. I'm making the request in person. That should be sufficient.

Technique: *Insist on common sense.* (#5) Show the agency official that your position makes good common sense, even if regulations or technicalities go against you.

C: Surely, your rule calling for a written request can't apply when the person making the request is right in front of you.

Technique: *Interpret the law.* (#13) Regulations, statutes, and cases are often susceptible to more than one meaning. Identify and argue for the meaning most favorable to your cause.

Technique: *Demonstrate the exception.* (#11) Insist that your situation is unique, and not governed by the general rule.

C: Don't you have the power to waive this rule in such a case? Are you saying that the office never gives waivers?

Technique: *Uncover the realm of discretion.* (#9) Argue that rules do not exist until they are applied and that in the application of rules, officials often have some latitude in interpreting them in spite of their claim that their hands are tied by the rules.

Technique: *Look for an opening by asking a very broad question.* (#10) Pose a question to the official that is so broad that the answer may give you an opening.

E: Well, all right, I'll see if I can get a copy run off for you while you are here, but it will take a little time, and I must point out that it's highly irregular.

C: Now, Mr. Adams, I understand that you are a very busy man and that you have responsibilities more demanding than listening to people like me all day.

Technique: *Be a buddy*. (#14) Show the official that you are not his enemy, that you respect and like him, and that you are aware of how difficult his job is. Here the complainant has obviously shifted his tactic; he is no longer antagonistic. Consciously or unconsciously, he has made an evaluation of how successful his techniques have been thus far and has decided on a different course of action. What risk is he running in making this shift?

> C: All I want is a two-week extension of time so that I can collect the proof needed to show you that the bill has been paid.

Technique: *Put your cards on the table*. (See #1) Tell the agency official, directly and openly, what your position is and what you want.

> E: Well, we seldom give extensions. The situation must be extreme. I don't know…
> C: Mr. Adams, suppose we forget my request for a copy of the records for the time being. All I want is two weeks.

Technique: *Find the points of compromise*. (#8) Look for the negotiable points and figure out whether you can bargain your way to a good result.

> E: I don't think so.
> C: Well, Mr. Adams, it's either that or I'm going to go to court. All I'm asking for is some fair treatment. There's a principle involved and I intend to fight for it.

Technique: *Make clear that you are going to fight this case "all the way up."* (See #15) Make the official aware of how important this case is. When you have grounds to back you, point out that you are thinking about taking the case to court if necessary.

> E: I'm sorry you feel that way, but we have our rules here. It would be chaos if we broke them every time someone asked for it.
> C: Good day, Mr. Adams.

Has the complainant failed? Was he a "bad" advocate? Has he accomplished anything? Should he give up? Do you think he will? If he does not, do you think he has learned (or that he should have learned) enough about the agency to come back next time better equipped to handle his problem? If he comes back, what approach should he take and whom should he see? Should he see the supervisor of Mr. Adams, for example?

PROCEDURAL DUE PROCESS

Where paralegals are authorized by law to engage in *formal advocacy* by representing clients at administrative hearings (see Chapter 4), it is one of the great challenges that they enjoy. In the remainder of the chapter, we will explore some of the skills required to perform this task effectively after identifying the components of **procedural due process** when the advocacy involves a government agency.

When a government agency and a citizen have a serious dispute, basic fairness may require a number of procedural safeguards for the citizen. These safeguards are known as *procedural due process*. Let's look at an example:

> Tom is a civilian employee of the army. One day he receives a call from the manager of his division, who says, "I have just finished reading the report of the assistant manager. Based on my own observations and on this report, it is clear to me that you have been using the office computer for personal purposes in violation of agency policy. I have decided to terminate your employment."

As a matter of fairness and common sense, what is wrong with the manager's approach? Assume that Tom denies the charge and that this is the first time he has heard anything about an alleged improper use of an agency computer.

The resolution of a legal dispute requires the application of substantive and procedural law. **Substantive laws** are the nonprocedural laws that define or govern rights and duties, e.g., the duty to use reasonable care to avoid injuring someone. In our example, the substantive-law

procedural due process The constitutional requirement that the government provide fair procedures such as notice and an opportunity to be heard whenever the government seeks to deprive someone of life, liberty, or property.

substantive laws Nonprocedural laws that define or govern rights and duties, e.g., the duty to use reasonable care to avoid injuring someone.

procedural laws The rules that govern the mechanics of resolving a dispute in court or in an administrative agency, e.g., a rule on the time by which a party must respond to a complaint.

question is whether Tom violated any laws in his use of the computer. **Procedural laws** are the laws that govern the mechanics of resolving a dispute in court or in an administrative agency, e.g., a rule on the time by which a party must respond to a complaint. In our example, the procedural-law question is whether the agency's method of resolving the dispute with Tom is fair. The latter is a question of procedural due process.

In Exhibit 15-3, you will find some of the visceral responses that Tom or any citizen might make, plus their legal translation in terms of procedural safeguards.

Exhibit 15-3	Procedural Safeguards (Procedural Due Process)

Facts: Tom was fired on the day he was told he was suspected of improper computer use.

Note: The following overview of procedural rights covers challenges against something the *government* has done (here, firing a government employee). The overview does not cover procedural rights persons may have when the dispute is between private persons or entities.

VISCERAL RESPONSE TO TREATMENT OF TOM BY THE AGENCY	LEGAL PRINCIPLE INVOLVED	DEFINITIONS
"Before I was fired, I should have been told that the agency thinks I used the computer illegally."	■ *Notice.* To enable you to prepare a response, you should be given adequate advance notice of the charge against you.	**notice** Formal notification. (See glossary for another meaning.)
"Show me the report that the assistant manager wrote on me so that I can see what he's talking about. And tell me what made you [the manager] arrive at your conclusion about what I did."	■ *Examination of evidence.* In order to respond to the evidence against you, you should be able to see what that evidence is.	**evidence** Anything offered to establish the existence or nonexistence of a fact in dispute.
"Before you fire me, give me a chance to come before you to explain myself."	■ *Hearing.* You should be given a formal meeting or hearing where you can present your own evidence.	**hearing** (1) A proceeding designed to resolve issues of fact or law. (2) A meeting in which one is allowed to present or argue a position. (See glossary for additional meanings.)
"I want to present my case before someone other than the assistant manager or manager."	■ *Hearing officer free of bias.* The hearing officer should be uninvolved—free of bias. The person making the charge against you, or giving any evidence against you, should not be making the final decision as to whether the charge is true. (The accuser should not be the executioner.)	**bias** (1) An inclination, tendency, or predisposition to think or act in a certain way. (2) Prejudice for or against something or someone. (3) A danger of prejudgment.
"If people have something to say against me, I want to hear it from their own mouths, and I want to be able to ask them questions myself."	■ *Confrontation and cross-examination.* Whoever is accusing you or giving any evidence against you should be required to do so in your presence (confrontation). You should be able to ask this person questions about his or her allegations (cross-examination).	**confrontation** Being present when others give evidence against you and having the opportunity to question them. **cross-examination** Questioning of a witness at a hearing by an opponent after the other side has conducted a direct examination of that witness.
"I want to be able to bring my own counsel to help me."	■ *Legal representation.* You should have the right to representation by an attorney or (where allowed) by an attorney substitute of your own choosing.	
"I've had some unrelated troubles on the job in the past, plus some personal problems at home, but they have nothing to do with my use of the computer."	■ *Relevancy of evidence.* The hearing officer should consider only relevant evidence.	**relevant** Logically tending to establish or disprove a fact. Pertinent. (See glossary for another meaning.) The noun is *relevancy*.
"My coworker knows everything about my use of agency computers. I want to bring him to the hearing."	■ *Presentation of own witnesses.* You should be given the opportunity to present your own witnesses and any other evidence that supports your position.	
"I want to see the complete decision in writing."	■ *Written decision with reasons.* To enable you to prepare an appeal, you should be given the decision in writing as well as the reasons for the decision.	
"I want to be able to appeal."	■ *Appeal.* You should be given the right to appeal the decision to another individual or body.	**appeal** A proceeding in which a higher tribunal reviews or reconsiders the decision of an inferior tribunal.

Note, however, that a citizen is *not* entitled to all of the components of procedural due process outlined in Exhibit 15-3 in every dispute with a government agency. What procedural safeguards are required? The answer depends primarily on the seriousness of the dispute. In a hearing on terminating public assistance, for example, all ten safeguards listed in Exhibit 15-3 are required when the recipient is challenging the termination. This is so because of the extreme consequences that could result from termination. The more extreme the possible consequences, the more procedural safeguards the law imposes on the conduct of hearings to determine whether those consequences should be imposed.

FORMAL ADVOCACY

"What would it be like to stand before a judge, and it would be you—yes, *you*—standing (without a law degree) before a judge representing a client? A person in need would be depending on your ability as a representative to help win the case. What would it be like?"

Jeffrey S. Wolfe, U.S. Administrative Law Judge[1]

Judge Wolfe is referring to the right that nonattorneys have to represent their own clients before designated administrative agencies. In particular, he is referring to his own agency, the Social Security Administration (SSA), where you do not have to be an attorney to represent clients. As we saw in Chapter 4, there are a number of state and federal administrative agencies that allow paralegals to provide a full range of legal services, including representation of their own clients at administrative hearings. One of the largest agencies where this occurs is the SSA. Although formal administrative advocacy differs from agency to agency, an examination of a paralegal's role at the SSA can help us understand what is possible at many agencies.

One of the SSA's largest programs provides disability benefits to individuals who suffer from an "inability to engage in any substantial gainful activity by reason of any medically determinable physical or mental impairment."[2] Every year 2.5 million people apply for Social Security disability benefits under one of two programs:

- Disability Insurance Benefits (DIB) for individuals who have a qualifying work history
- Supplemental Security Income (SSI) for individuals who may have never worked

Approximately 1.7 million of these applications are denied. The denials lead to a staggering 600,000 annual appeals handled by federal administrative law judges (ALJs) like Judge Wolfe throughout the country. "The Social Security Administration…adjudicates more cases than all federal courts combined."[3] Social-security law, as many citizens know from first-hand experience, can be complicated. This is particularly true of disability law. Consequently, the need for legal assistance in the 600,000 annual disability hearings is enormous.

Unfortunately, not enough attorneys practice social-security law, although a growing number take social-security cases under the broader practice of **elder law**. Part of the reason many attorneys stay away from disability cases is that they do not generate enough revenue for the attorneys. In most cases, a representative can collect $6,000 or 25 percent of back-due disability benefits, whichever is less. The fee cannot be higher, even if the client agrees to pay more. Nationally, the average fee collected is $2,500.[4] This is not enough to interest many attorneys. Fortunately, claimants seeking legal representation have an alternative. Congress has specifically provided that persons: "other than attorneys" may represent "claimants before the Commissioner of Social Security."[5] Hence paralegals have a federal mandate to practice law before the SSA, including the right to charge fees for their services. To be a representative, the paralegal must know the "significant issue(s) in a claim" and have a "working knowledge" of social-security statutes, regulations, and rulings.[6]

One of the ALJs makes the following comment about the effectiveness of paralegal advocates in social-security cases: "It's not being a lawyer that makes a difference, but knowing what is a disability. [Nonattorney advocates] who know what they are doing, do a better job than an attorney who doesn't know disability."[7] Social-security representatives have formed the National Organization of Social Security Claimants' Representatives (NOSSCR), consisting of attorneys and "other advocates" (www.nosscr.org).

elder law An area of law covering the legal problems of the elderly. Examples include social security, estate planning, Medicare, and age discrimination.

Attorneys and paralegals have the same responsibilities as representatives in SSA hearings, but they are treated differently in the crucial area of fees. When attorneys win a disability case, their fee is deducted from the claimant's award by SSA and sent directly to the attorneys. When nonattorney representatives win a case, however, they must collect their fee on their own from the client *unless* they pass an exam on social-security law, obtain liability insurance, and take designated continuing legal education (CLE) sessions.[8] Nonattorney representatives who do not meet these qualifications must collect their fees directly from their clients.

The first step in being a representative is to be appointed by the client. See Exhibit 4-6 in Chapter 4 for the form that a social-security applicant must use to appoint a representative.

SAMPLE CASE

To gain a greater appreciation of paralegal representation at SSA disability hearings, we will examine a sample case involving a dispute on an overpayment to a recipient of disability payments under the Supplemental Security Income (SSI) program. Here are the major participants in the case:

- Mary O'Brien: SSI recipient and claimant
- George O'Brien: Mary's husband
- John Powell: paralegal representative of Mary
- Helen Davis: witness for Mary
- Alex Bolton: administrative law judge at SSA

BACKGROUND

Mary O'Brien is disabled. She suffers from depression, an affective disorder, and receives $531 a month in SSI. When Mary applied for SSI benefits, she told SSA that her husband, George O'Brien, earns $3,600 a year from a part-time job as a night watchman and that this amount was the total O'Brien income. The $531 a month awarded to Mary was based on this annual figure.

Mary and George have a strained relationship, although they continue to live together. She is not aware of what he does during the day. Indeed, when she questions him about his activities, he becomes hostile. He can be violent. On June 1, 2010, she called the police when he went into a rage. The police referred Mary to the County Domestic Violence Center. She went there and met with a counselor, Helen Davis. After describing what happened, Davis advised Mary to obtain a restraining order against her husband. Mary, however, did not want to involve the courts; she felt this would enrage her husband all the more. Hence she did not file for a restraining order, although she continued to come to the center to attend counseling sessions for abused women.

On September 1, 2011, SSA sends Mary a Notice of Overpayment. It states that according to information received from the Internal Revenue Service, George O'Brien reported taxable earnings of $12,000 during the year 2010. Her payment of $531 a month was based on a household income of $3,600. Since her husband was in fact earning considerably more, her 2010 entitlement has been recalculated. The SSA has concluded that Mary received an overpayment of $3,250 during 2010. To recoup this amount, SSA will deduct $53.10 a month from her disability check until the overpayment of $3,250 has been repaid.

This notice is quite distressing for Mary. She calls the local Neighborhood Legal Aid Office for help. On the phone, a receptionist determines that she is eligible for free legal services because of her low income. The receptionist tells Mary to come in the next day for an appointment with John Powell, a paralegal in the office who handles social-security cases.

John conducts an extensive interview of Mary. She tells John that her husband admits that he earned the extra money in 2010 but that it was "none of [her] business." He works as a night guard for a security firm that is managed by his cousin. She also describes his anger and violence over anything that questions or challenges his authority or that he considers an interference in his affairs.

PREHEARING ADVOCACY

John points out to Mary that if the extra money was earned, the only way she can avoid making the repayment is to file a Request for Waiver of Overpayment (www.ssa.gov/online/ssa-632.pdf) on the ground that she is without fault in causing the overpayment or in failing to report it and that requiring repayment will be a hardship and is against equity and good conscience. Furthermore, if they act quickly, they might prevent SSA from starting the deductions from her monthly disability check. Mary begins to feel relieved. She signs the SSA form appointing John as her representative and asks him to take whatever steps are necessary to try to avoid the repayment. He explains that if the request for waiver is denied, they can ask for a conference to explain their side and ultimately they can ask for a hearing before an administrative law judge (ALJ).

In the weeks following the meeting between John and his client, a number of events occur:

- John helps Mary fill out the Request for Waiver of Overpayment. The basis of the request is that Mary is without fault because she knew nothing about her husband's side job, he is secretive about his finances, and he is abusive, particularly when she questions him about anything he does outside the home.
- John sends this request to SSA along with a cover letter asking SSA not to begin deductions from Mary's monthly payment until the appeal process is complete. He makes this request as a precaution even though SSA's policy is not to begin "adjustment action" until the waiver issue is resolved.
- A month later, SSA sends Mary and John its response. The request for waiver is denied.
- John then asks the SSA field office for a personal conference during which he and Mary will explain their case before an SSA official who has not been involved in the initial decision to require the repayment of the overpayment. This request is granted.
- Five days before the personal conference, John exercises Mary's right to go to the SSA office in order to examine the file that contains the records used by the SSA to demand the return of the overpayment. He photocopies the records that he does not already have.
- By studying the SSA records in Mary's file, John identifies further evidence he needs to check in order to be better prepared to respond to the SSA's case against Mary.
- The personal conference takes place at the SSA office. It lasts about an hour. John goes over the details of what happened during 2010 and why Mary knew nothing about her husband's extra income. One of the reasons the conference is valuable (even if it does not result in a decision in Mary's favor) is that it gives John a clearer understanding of the SSA's case against her.
- A month later, Mary and John receive a notice from the SSA reaffirming the decision not to grant her the waiver.
- Further efforts to resolve the case (including use of reconsideration procedures) are unsuccessful. John then files a Request for Hearing before an ALJ (www.ssa.gov/online/ha-501.html).
- Several weeks later, John receives a call from the Office of Hearings and Appeals to arrange a date for the hearing. After John consults with Mary, a date for the hearing is set. John and Mary receive a formal Notice of Hearing indicating that the hearing will be held before U.S. administrative law judge Alex Bolton on the agreed-upon date.

CHARACTERISTICS OF DISABILITY HEARINGS

A disability hearing in SSA's Office of Hearings and Appeals is **nonadversarial** because it is a one-party proceeding. An official representing the SSA is not present. The only party at the hearing is the claimant. At a hearing, the following participants might be present:

- Claimant
- Representative of claimant (here, a paralegal)
- Witnesses (e.g., a vocational counselor, a relative)
- Reporter (often an SSA secretary) who makes a voice recording of the hearing
- Presiding ALJ

See Exhibit 15-4 for a typical arrangement of an SSA hearing room.

nonadversarial Pertaining to a conflict-resolution proceeding in which all opposing parties to the conflict or dispute are not present. See also *adversary hearing*.

| Exhibit 15-4 | Typical Social Security Hearing Room |

An administrative law judge (ALJ) presides over a social-security hearing. Present are the paralegal representative, the claimant, a witness, and a court reporter. Before the paralegal begins asking questions of the witness, the judge swears in the witness.

The absence of an SSA representative, however, does not mean that the claimant's representative will have an easy time establishing the position of the claimant. The ALJ is not an advocate, but he or she has an obligation to "develop the record." To fulfill this duty, the ALJ might take an affirmative role at the hearing such as by actively questioning the claimant and, if needed, arranging for a vocational expert to be present to give testimony.

The representative must convince the ALJ that the claimant's case fits within the guidelines of eligibility for a waiver of the overpayment. This is done primarily through the testimony of the claimant and other witnesses and the introduction of documentary evidence such as medical and vocational records. Medical records can be lengthy, complicated, incomplete, confusing, and, at times, contradictory. Nevertheless, most ALJs will not tolerate a sloppy presentation; they will hold a representative's feet to the fire by insisting on a coherent presentation of the claimant's case. The representative must be able to anticipate possible questions from the ALJ and provide answers by citing information on specific pages of exhibits in the record. Competent representation can be a challenge even though the other side (the SSA) is technically absent and unrepresented.

on the record Noted or recorded in an official record of the proceeding.

A disability hearing is similar to a court trial in that both are **on-the-record** proceedings in which testimony is given under oath. A reporter is present at the disability hearing to tape-record everything that is said. Yet unlike court trials, the rules of evidence do not fully apply to disability hearings. The ALJ will consider any evidence that is relevant (broadly defined) to the issues in the case. Judges in court trials are not as liberal on what is allowed in.

To a large extent, the conduct of a hearing depends on the style and personality of the presiding ALJ. Some ALJs will let the representative take the lead by making an opening statement, introducing documentary evidence, and questioning witnesses. The ALJ might ask his or her own questions after the representative has finished. Other ALJs take a more aggressive role. They might not allow the representative to take over until they ask their own questions of the claimant or other witnesses.

PREPARATION FOR THE HEARING

To prepare for Mary's hearing, John does the following:

- Asks Helen Davis to come to the hearing as a witness for Mary. Davis is the counselor at the County Domestic Violence Center where Mary went for assistance during 2010. (In the event Davis cannot come to the hearing, John will obtain her **affidavit**, which will state the circumstances of Mary's involvement with the center.)

- Obtains a letter from Mary's doctor, David Stepps, M.D., that describes the medication he prescribed for her due to the tension she was under at home.

- Researches this medication on the Internet and finds a report from the National Institute of Mental Health on the reasons the medication is prescribed and its side effects of lethargy and extreme sensitivity to conflict. John downloads this report and prints the pertinent section for use at the hearing.

- Researches **battered women syndrome** on the Internet and finds a medical study on the helplessness experienced by women faced with severe abuse from their husbands and significant others. He downloads and prints the study for use at the hearing.

- Researches SSA's policy manual (Program Operations Manual System [POMS]) on the Internet to make sure he has a full grasp of all of the procedures that SSA should be following in Mary's case.

- Prepares a complete summary of all Mary's assets and liabilities, showing monthly household income and expenses.

- Obtains copies of the O'Briens' federal and state tax returns for 2010.

- Compiles Mary's medical history, which will be relevant to the hardship issue (particularly the amounts she must pay for drugs and other medical care) and to her ability to handle stress and understand household finances.

- Prepares a set of notes in which he identifies Mary's theory of the case, together with citations to applicable regulations and supporting facts in the exhibits.

- Meets with Mary in his office to go over what is likely to happen at the hearing and to role-play her responses to the questions that he plans to ask her and that the ALJ might ask her. John comments on each of her responses, pointing out the importance of telling the truth and of giving detailed answers. He tells her that the hearing will be tape-recorded so she should speak clearly and answer questions verbally. The tape recorder will not know if she answers a question with a nod of her head.

affidavit A written or printed statement of facts made under oath by a person (called the *affiant*) before someone with authority to administer the oath.

battered women syndrome A woman's psychological helplessness or paralysis because of conditions such as financial dependence, loneliness, guilt, shame, and fear of reprisal from her husband or significant other who has repeatedly subjected her to physical, sexual, and/or emotional abuse in the past.

THE O'BRIEN HEARING

Judge Bolton begins the hearing by introducing himself and letting everyone know that a reporter will be recording the proceeding. He asks everyone to identify themselves for the record:

- Mary O'Brien: SSI recipient and claimant
- John Powell: paralegal representative of Mary
- Helen Davis: witness for Mary

Judge Bolton then turns his attention to the reports and other exhibits already in the file and those that anyone wants considered. They are all identified with an exhibit number. He asks John if he has any objections to any of the exhibits. John responds that he does not but that he hopes to have the chance during the hearing to comment on some of the SSA reports in the file.

Judge Bolton administers the oath (to tell the truth) to all witnesses who will be giving testimony (Mary O'Brien and Helen Davis) and tells John to present his case.

John begins by summarizing the position of his client: that she is without fault in receiving the overpayment because she had no knowledge of the extra earnings of her husband and that he has been physically abusive to her whenever she has tried to question him about any financial matters. He also says that forcing a repayment will be a severe hardship on Mary.

John then asks Mary a series of questions to elaborate on these and other relevant points. For example:

- Who takes care of the finances in the household?
- Is your name on any bank accounts with your husband?
- Describe the living expenses you and your husband have in the home.
- Explain whether it will be a hardship to have to repay the overpayment.

- Has your husband told you what he does during the day?
- When do you see him during the course of a typical day?
- Did your husband hit you during 2010?
- Did you call the police?
- Why were you referred to the County Domestic Violence Center?
- Did you meet with Helen Davis, a counselor there?
- What did she advise you to do?
- Did you ever consider obtaining a restraining order? If so, describe what happened.
- Why have you continued living with a husband who is abusive?
- Are any other living arrangements available to you if you leave your husband?
- Describe your health during 2010.
- Were you taking any medication?
- What effect did the medication have on you?

While asking such questions, John refers to specific exhibits such as the letter of Dr. David Stepps on why he prescribed the medication, the report on the side effects of the medication, and the study on the battered women syndrome.

When John finishes questioning Mary, Judge Bolton asks her several questions about her educational background and about the times at home when she is able to get along with her husband. After Mary answers, John asks her some follow-up questions designed to reinforce her inability to understand financial matters and her fear of her husband.

Finally, John questions Helen Davis, the counselor at the County Domestic Violence Center. John asks her to explain the services of the center and the level of agitation and fear Mary expressed when she came there for help. He asks her whether it is common for abused women to remain with their abusers. Finally, he asks her to explain why she recommended that Mary obtain a restraining order against her husband and whether it is unusual for an abused woman to be afraid to do so.

At the conclusion of all the testimony, Judge Bolton thanks everyone and says that he will render a decision as soon as possible.

Before leaving, John has one final request of Judge Bolton. He asks if he can submit a memorandum to the judge in which he presents the facts in the light of the applicable law. Judge Bolton says he will be glad to receive such a memorandum. John knows that ALJs hold many hearings and a memorandum of this kind might help influence the outcome of his case. Preparing it after the hearing gives John the opportunity to highlight those facts and legal matters that appeared to be of concern to the ALJ at the hearing.

Seven months after submitting the memorandum, John and Mary receive the decision of Judge Bolton. Mary is found to have been without fault in causing the overpayment and it would be an undue hardship to require repayment. Victory!

FURTHER APPEALS

If the decision had gone against Mary, the next step would have been a Request for Review by the Appeals Council (www.ssa.gov/online/ha-520.pdf). This is an appeal within the SSA. The claimant submits a brief to the Appeals Council indicating why the decision of the ALJ should be reversed. John would prepare the brief for Mary. A paralegal representative can write and sign these briefs. In the vast majority of cases, neither the party nor his or her representative makes a personal appearance before the Appeals Council.

If a claimant were dissatisfied by the decision of the Appeals Council, the next step would be an appeal to a U.S. district court. The case could be taken to court because the party had **exhausted administrative remedies.** At this point, an attorney would have to take over the case, although a paralegal could assist the attorney, as in any court case. The attorney could ask a paralegal to help prepare the pleadings and briefs that would be submitted to the court, but only an attorney could sign them. The federal authorization for paralegals to represent claimants within SSA does not include court representation.

exhaust administrative remedies To go through all dispute-solving avenues that are available in an administrative agency before asking a court to review what the agency did. Also called *exhaustion of remedies.*

CONCLUSION

As you can see from John Powell's role as a representative before the SSA, formal administrative advocacy by paralegals (where allowed) can be a major undertaking. Although most paralegals do not have the opportunity to engage in such advocacy in their everyday work, you might consider **pro bono** work where such advocacy is needed. There are neighborhood legal aid societies, senior citizen groups, and homeless projects in many cities that would welcome part-time volunteer work on social-security cases. Perhaps you could inquire about teaming with an experienced paralegal whom you could assist until you felt comfortable enough to venture out on your own cases. The need for legal help in this area is enormous. To find pro bono opportunities in your area, see the discussion of pro bono in Chapter 2 and run this search in Google, Bing, or Yahoo: pro bono paralegal aa (substituting your state or city for aa).

> **pro bono** Concerning or involving legal services that are provided for the public good (pro bono publico, shortened to pro bono) without fee or compensation. Sometimes also applied to services given at a reduced rate.

CHAPTER SUMMARY

Advocacy takes place all the time. It is an everyday process by which everyone—not just attorneys—attempt to influence or change the actions of others. Formal advocacy occurs in courts and other tribunals where hearings are held to resolve controversies that the participants were not able to resolve informally. Informal advocacy occurs outside of courts and formal hearings.

Advocates try many techniques of informal advocacy, with varying degrees of success. The techniques are as follows: put your cards on the table; insist on adequate service; ask to see the authority they are relying on; climb the chain of command; insist on common sense; take the role of the tired, battered, helpless citizen; cite a precedent; find the points of compromise; uncover the realm of discretion; look for an opening by asking a very broad question; demonstrate the exception; cite the law; interpret the law; be a buddy; make clear that you will fight the case "all the way up;" redefine the problem; do a favor to get a favor; seek the support of third parties; preach; embarrass the official; and be angry. While using any of these techniques, you need to evaluate your effectiveness and modify the techniques based on this evaluation.

Whenever the government takes an action that seriously affects a citizen, such as denying or removing a substantial benefit, basic fairness may require a number of procedural safeguards. These requirements are called *procedural due process*. Depending on the seriousness of what the government is accusing or depriving you of, the safeguards can include notice, examination of the evidence against you, a hearing where you can present your case, the absence of bias, confronting your accusers, questioning (cross-examining) witnesses, having representation, limiting the evidence to what is relevant, having the opportunity to present your own witnesses, receiving a decision in writing, and having an opportunity to appeal.

At some state and federal administrative agencies, paralegals are authorized to provide a full range of legal services, including representation of their own clients at administrative hearings. A major example of such an agency is the Social Security Administration (SSA), particularly in the representation of applicants at disability hearings. Competent representation at such hearings requires extensive preparation and skill in marshaling facts and coherently presenting them at the hearing in light of the applicable law.

KEY TERMS

advocacy (p. 618)
administrative law judge (ALJ)
    (p. 619)
procedural due process (p. 623)
substantive law (p. 623)
procedural law (p. 624)
notice (p. 624)

evidence (p. 624)
hearing (p. 624)
bias (p. 624)
confrontation (p. 624)
cross-examination (p. 624)
relevant (p. 624)
appeal (p. 624)

elder law (p. 625)
nonadversarial (p. 627)
on-the-record (p. 628)
affidavit (p. 629)
battered women syndrome (p. 629)
exhaust administrative remedies (p. 630)
pro bono (p. 631)

ASSIGNMENTS

CRITICAL ANALYSIS

15.1 In each role-playing exercise, there are two characters: C (the complainant) and E (the agency employee). Students from the class will be assigned one or the other role. In each setting, C is seeking something from E. E is

uncooperative. The objective of E is to antagonize C (within reason) to the point where C loses objectivity. The objective of C is to use effective advocacy techniques without losing objectivity. The members of the class who are not participating in the role-playing exercises should identify and evaluate the techniques of informal advocacy that C uses.

(a) At 4:30 p.m., C goes to the Department of Motor Vehicles to apply for a license. E tells C that the office closes at 5:00 p.m. and the application procedure takes forty-five minutes. E refuses to let C apply.

(b) C is filing a document at the clerk's office. The filing fee is $6. E tells C that the fee must be paid by check or the exact amount in cash. All C has is a $100 bill and must use some of it to take a long cab ride back to the office.

(c) C goes to the Bureau of Vital Statistics and requests a copy of his mother's birth certificate. E tells C that no citizen can obtain the birth certificate of another person without the written permission of the person. C's mother is ill in a hospital a thousand miles away. C wants the record without going through the bother of obtaining this permission.

PROJECT

15.2 Run this search in Google, Bing, or Yahoo: how do attorneys use Facebook? Write a report in which you describe the different uses to which law firms have used Facebook. Your report must cite at least five different sources on the Internet.

CORE SKILLS

Among the many skills a paralegal must have, five core skills stand out: writing (both basic English and legal drafting), research, ethics, computer use, and collaboration (working with others). The core-skill assignments introduce and reinforce these skills. Even if you are not asked to do all of the assignments as part of the course, you should do them on your own. Also, do not wait for the topics in the assignments to be covered in this course or in other courses. Successful paralegals are self-starters. A major characteristic of a self-starter is a thirst for independent study — learning on your own.

CORE SKILL: WRITING

15.3 Write a report in which you describe a dispute with a government agency or other large organization in which you used at least four of the techniques outlined in Exhibit 15-1. State the dispute, how you used the techniques, and the outcome.

CORE SKILL: RESEARCH

15.4 Find a list of state government agencies in your state. In Google, Bing, or Yahoo, run this search: government agency aa (substituting your state for aa). Pick any five of

these agencies that publish their administrative regulations online. State the names of the regulations and their Internet addresses. Also state whether you were able to tell how current the regulations are.

CORE SKILL: ETHICS

15.5 Read the ethical codes of the three national paralegal associations. See Appendix E. Prepare a chart in which in which you list major topics covered by the codes (e.g., confidentiality) and cite the sections of each code for each topic.

CORE SKILL: COMPUTERS

15.6 Run this search in Google, Bing, or Yahoo: how do attorneys use iPad tablets? Write a report in which you describe the different uses made by attorneys of iPads and tablet computers. Your report must cite at least five different sources on the Internet.

CORE SKILL: COLLABORATION

15.7 Assume that you are going to speak before a group of high school seniors on career day at the high school. You will give a presentation on paralegals. What paralegals are, where they work, why they exist, etc. Write out your presentation. Assume that your audience knows very little about the law and almost nothing about the practice of law. Be sure to avoid using any legal terms that you do not define. You want to give your audience enough information about the paralegal field to help them decide whether to consider such a career for themselves. Send your speech as an email attachment to every student in the class. For each speech you receive, send back a comment that includes two specific things you liked about the writer's speech.

THE JOB SEARCH

(The search for employment cannot wait until the end of a course or of a curriculum. It needs to begin now. The job-search assignments are designed to introduce you to different aspects of the job search and to build options for you to explore about employment.)

15.8 Run this search in Google, Bing, or Yahoo: independent paralegal nonattorney representation agency. Find three websites of nonattorneys in any state who represent clients at federal, state, or local administrative agencies. Describe the services offered by each, including the agencies involved.

REVIEW QUESTIONS

1. What is advocacy?
2. What is the distinction between formal advocacy and informal advocacy?
3. What is an administrative law judge (ALJ)?
4. What are the major techniques of informal advocacy?
5. What is meant by climbing the chain of command?
6. What are the roles of timing, evaluation, adaptation, and recordkeeping?
7. What is procedural due process?
8. What is the distinction between procedural and substantive law?
9. Depending on the seriousness of what the government is accusing or depriving someone of, what procedural safeguards may be required?
10. What is bias?
11. What is relevant evidence?
12. What roles can paralegals play in social-security hearings?
13. What is elder law?
14. When is a hearing nonadversarial?
15. What is meant by *on the record*?
16. What are some of the major steps a paralegal can take for effective representation of a client in a social-security hearing?
17. How does a client exhaust administrative remedies?
18. What is meant by pro bono?

HELPFUL WEBSITES

Advocacy Techniques
- www.cccnewyork.org (enter *advocacy* in the search box)
- en.wikipedia.org/wiki/Advocacy

Social Security Hearing Process
- www.ssa.gov/appeals/hearing_process.html

Social Security Representation
- www.ssa.gov/representation
- www.ssa.gov/appeals/hearing_process.html
- www.ssa.gov/pubs/EN-05-10075.pdf

National Organization of Social Security Claimants' Representatives
- www.nosscr.org

National Association of Disability Representatives
- www.nadr.org

Procedural Due Process
- en.wikipedia.org/wiki/Due_process
- law2.umkc.edu/faculty/projects/ftrials/conlaw/proceduraldue process.html

Google, Bing, or Yahoo Searches
(On these search engines, run the following searches, using quotation marks and substituting your state for "aa" where indicated.)

- administrative advocacy
- procedural due process
- "informal advocacy"
- Social Security hearings
- pro bono paralegal aa

ENDNOTES

[1] Jeffrey S. Wolfe, *Professional Service to the Beat of a Different Drum: Non-Lawyer Representation before Social Security's Office of Hearings and Appeals*, Facts & Findings 37 (May 2000). The assistance of Judge Wolfe and of Christopher J. Holly (an attorney and former Indiana independent paralegal) in the preparation of the Social Security materials in this chapter is gratefully acknowledged. See Judge Wolfe's book *Social Security and the Legal Professional* (Delmar, 2003) and Christopher Holly's Internet site (www.medicaidguide.com).

[2] 42 U.S.C. § 416 (i)(1)(A).

[3] Milton Carrow, *A Tortuous Road to Bureaucratic Fairness*, 46 Administrative Law Review 297 (Summer 1994).

[4] Wolfe, *supra*, note 1, at 39.

[5] 42 U.S.C. § 406 (a)(1).

[6] 20 C.F.R. § 404.1740 (b)(3)(I).

[7] Herbert M. Kritzer, *Legal Advocacy* 133 (1998).

[8] Direct Payment to Eligible Non-Attorney Representatives (www.ssa.gov/representation/nonattyrep.htm); (www.ssa.gov/OP_Home/ssact/title02/0206.htm).

BOOKS, ARTICLES, AND SOCIAL MEDIA ON PARALEGALISM

There are many excellent books, articles, and social media sites about paralegalism. Here are ways to find them:

MAJOR PATHWAYS

- Library of Congress Online Catalog
  catalog.loc.gov
  Searches to try on this site:
  - paralegal
  - "legal assistant"
  - paralegalism
  - "legal paraprofessional"

- Google Scholar
  scholar.google.com
  (select *Articles*)
  Searches to try on this site:
  - paralegal
  - "legal assistant"
  - paralegalism
  - "legal technician"
  - "legal paraprofessional"

- Amazon
  www.amazon.com
  Searches to try on this site:
  - paralegal
  - "legal assistant"

- Google, Bing, or Yahoo
  www.google.com
  www.bing.com
  www.yahoo.com
  Searches to try on these sites:
  - "paralegal book"
  - "legal assistant book"
  - "paralegal article"
  - "legal assistant article"

- ERIC
  eric.ed.gov
  Searches to try on this site:
  - paralegal
  - "legal assistant"

- Hathi Trust Digital Library
  www.hathitrust.org
  Searches to try on this site:
  - paralegal
  - "legal assistant"

- Criminal Justice Abstracts
  www.ncjrs.gov
  (covers more than criminal law)
  Searches to try on this site:
  - paralegal
  - "legal assistant"

- Highwire
  highwire.stanford.edu/cgi/search
  Searches to try on this site:
  - enter *paralegal* for "Title only" searches
  - enter *paralegal* for "Anywhere in text" searches

SPECIFIC SEARCHES

To any of the searches listed above, add a specific subject or state.
Examples:
- paralegal ethics
- "legal assistant" Florida bankruptcy

FINDING ARTICLES ONLINE

- www.wikihow.com/Find-Scholarly-Articles-Online
- www.ipl.org/div/farq/articleFARQ.html
- www.teachthought.com (enter "search engines" in the search box)

PARALEGALS ON FACEBOOK

- www.facebook.com/search/str/paralegal/pages-named
- www.facebook.com (enter *paralegal* in search box)

PARALEGALS ON LINKEDIN

- www.linkedin.com (enter *paralegal* in search box)

PARALEGALS ON TWITTER

- twitter.com/search?q=paralegal&src=typd
- twitter.com (enter *paralegal* in search box)

PARALEGALS ON GOOGLE+

- plus.google.com/people/find (enter *paralegal* in search box)

PARALEGAL, BAR, AND RELATED ASSOCIATIONS

A. Paralegal and Related Associations (State and Local)
B. Paralegal Associations (National)
C. Paralegal Associations (International)
D. More Related Associations
E. Bar Associations, Traditional
F. Bar (and Related) Associations (Specialty)

A. PARALEGAL AND RELATED ASSOCIATIONS (STATE AND LOCAL)

- Run these searches in Google, Bing, or Yahoo (substituting your state, county, or city for aa):
  - paralegal association aa
  - "legal assistant" association aa
  - legal professional association aa
  - Association of Legal Administrators aa
  - legal secretary association aa
  - American Association of Legal Nurse Consultants aa
- Lists of Paralegal Associations
  - www.paralegals.org/default.asp?page=2
  - www.nala.org/Aff_Roster.aspx
  - www.nals.org/?page_id=32
  - www.hg.org/assistants-assoc.html
  - www.criminaljusticedegreeschools.com/paralegal-association-directory
- Paralegal Associations on LinkedIn
  - www.linkedin.com (enter *paralegal association* in search box)
  - blog.linkedin.com/2007/07/15/5-tips-on-how-t
- Paralegal Associations on Facebook
  - www.facebook.com (enter *paralegal association* in search box)
  - www.facebook.com/search.php
- Paralegal Associations on Twitter (Once you have the name of an association, type it in the Twitter search boxes):
  - twitter.com (enter *paralegal association* in search box)
  - twitter.com/search-home
  - twitter.com/twittersearch
- Paralegal Associations on Google+
  - plus.google.com (enter *paralegal association* in search box)

B. PARALEGAL ASSOCIATIONS (NATIONAL)

- **National Association of Legal Assistants (NALA)**
  - www.nala.org

- **National Federation of Paralegal Associations (NFPA)**
  - www.paralegals.org

- **NALS the Association of Legal Professionals (NALS)**
  - www.nals.org

- **American Alliance of Paralegals (AAPI)**
  - www.aapipara.org

- **International Practice Management Association (IPMA)**
  - www.paralegalmanagement.org

C. PARALEGAL ASSOCIATIONS (INTERNATIONAL)

Alberta Association of Professional Paralegals (Canada)
- Alberta-paralegal.com

BC Paralegal Association (British Columbia)
- www.bcparalegalassociation.com

Canadian Association of Paralegals
- www.caplegal.ca

Institute of Law Clerks of Ontario (Canada)
- www.ilco.on.ca

Chartered Institute of Legal Executives (England)
- www.cilex.org.uk

Institute of Legal Executives (Australia)
- www.liv.asn.au/legalexecutives

International Association of Administrative Professionals
- www.iaap-hq.org

Irish Institute of Legal Executives (Ireland)
- iilex.ie

Legal Secretaries International
- www.legalsecretaries.org

New Zealand Institute of Legal Executives
- www.nzile.org.nz

Paralegal Society of Ontario (Canada)
- www.paralegalsociety.on.ca

Scottish Paralegal Association (Scotland)
- www.scottish-paralegal.org.uk

D. MORE RELATED ASSOCIATIONS

ABA Standing Committee on Paralegals
- www.americanbar.org/groups/paralegals.html

American Association for Justice (Affiliate Membership for Paralegals)
- www.justice.org (enter *paralegal* after clicking Search)

American Association for Paralegal Education
- www.aafpe.org

American Association of Law Librarians
- www.aallnet.org

American Health Lawyers Association
- www.healthlawyers.org

American Institute of Certified Public Accountants
- www.aicpa.org

American Pro Se Association
- www.legalhelp.org

Association of Bankruptcy Judicial Assistants
- www.abja.org

Association of Certified E-Discovery Specialists
- www.aceds.org

Association of Legal Administrators
- www.alanet.org

Association of Litigation Support Professionals
- alsponline.site-ym.com/general/register_member_type.asp
- www.linkedin.com/groups?trk=myg_ugrp_ovr&gid=50635

Court Appointed Special Advocates
- www.casaforchildren.org

Foundation for the Advancement of the Paralegal Profession
- www.paralegalfoundation.org

Healthcare Paralegals Federation
- healthcarepara.wordpress.com

International Paralegal Association
- www.paralegalinternet.com

International Process Servers Association
- www.iprocessservers.com

Legal Marketing Association
- www.legalmarketing.org

National Association of Freelance Legal Professionals
- freelancelegalprofessionals.blogspot.com

National Association for Law Placement
- www.nalp.org

National Association of Document Examiners
- www.documentexaminers.org

National Association of Enrolled Agents
- www.naea.org

National Association of Legal Investigators
- www.nalionline.org

National Association of Patent Practitioners
- www.napp.org

National Association of Professional Process Servers
- www.napps.org

National Association of Tax Professionals
- www.natptax.com

National Conference of Bar Examiners
- www.ncbex.org

National Court Reporters Association
- www.ncra.org

National Notary Association
- www.nationalnotary.org

National Organization of Legal Services Workers
- nolsw.org

National Organization of Social Security Claimants' Representatives
- www.nosscr.org

National Paralegal Association
- www.nationalparalegal.org

Navy Legalman Association
- navyln.wordpress.com

NOLO Press (self-help legal materials)
- www.nolo.com

Organization of Legal Professionals
- www.theolp.org

Women in E-Discovery
- www.womeninediscovery.org

E. BAR ASSOCIATIONS (TRADITIONAL)

- Run these searches in Google, Bing, or Yahoo (substituting your state, county, or city for aa):
  - bar association aa
  - lawyer association aa
  - attorney association aa
- Lists of State, County, and Local Bar Associations in Every State
  - www.washlaw.edu/bar
  - www.hg.org/bar-associations-usa.html
  - www.ilrg.com/non-profit.html
  - www.kautzlaw.com/links1.htm
  - www.citylegalguide.com/bar.cfm
  - www.americanbar.org/groups/bar_services/resources/state_local_bar_associations.html

F. BAR (AND RELATED) ASSOCIATIONS (SPECIALTY)

- **Lists of Specialty Bar Associations**
  - www.alllaw.com/legal_organizations
  - www.ilrg.com/non-profit.html
- **Individual Sites**

Academy of Legal Studies in Business
- www.alsb.org

American Academy of Estate Planning Attorneys
- www.aaepa.com

American Academy of Forensic Sciences
- www.aafs.org

American Academy of Matrimonial Lawyers
- www.aaml.org

American Agricultural Law Association
- www.aglaw-assn.org

American Arbitration Association
- www.adr.org

American Association for Justice (formerly Association of Trial Lawyers of America)
- www.justice.org

American Association of Attorney-Certified Public Accountants
- www.attorney-cpa.com

American Association of Law Libraries
- www.aallnet.org

American Association of Nurse Attorneys
- www.taana.org

American Bar Association
- www.americanbar.org/aba.html

American Civil Liberties Union
- www.aclu.org

American College of Family Trial Lawyers
- www.acftl.com

American College of Real Estate Lawyers
- www.acrel.org

American College of Trust and Estate Counsel
- www.actec.org

American Constitution Society
- www.acslaw.org

American Health Lawyers Association
- www.healthlawyers.org

American Immigration Lawyers Association
- www.aila.org

American Inns of Court
- www.innsofcourt.org

American Intellectual Property Law Association
- www.aipla.org

American Judges Association
- aja.ncsc.dni.us

American Judicature Society
- www.ajs.org

American Law and Economics Association
- www.amlecon.org

American Law Institute
- www.ali.org

American Masters of Laws Association
- www.amola.org

Group Legal Services Association
- glsaonline.org

American Pro Se Association
- www.legalhelp.org

American Society for Pharmacy Law
- www.aspl.org

American Society of Comparative Law
- www.comparativelaw.org

American Society of International Law
- www.asil.org

American Society of Law, Medicine & Ethics
- www.aslme.org

Animal Legal Defense Fund
- aldf.org

Association for Conflict Resolution
- www.acrnet.org

Association for Continuing Legal Education (CLE)
- www.aclea.org

Association of Attorney-Mediators
- www.attorney-mediators.org

Association of Corporate Counsel
- www.acc.com

Association of Family and Conciliation Courts
- www.afccnet.org

Association of Professional Responsibility Lawyers (ethics)
- www.aprl.net

Black Entertainment and Sports Lawyers Association
- www.besla.org

Canadian Bar Association
- www.cba.org

Center for American and International Law
- www.cailaw.org

Center for Law and Social Policy
- www.clasp.org

Christian Legal Society
- www.clsnet.org

Commercial Law League of America
- www.clla.org

Council on Law in Higher Education
- www.clhe.org

Criminal Justice Legal Foundation
- www.cjlf.org

Customs and International Trade Bar Association
- www.citba.org

Decalogue Society of Lawyers (bar association for Jewish attorneys)
- decaloguesociety.org

Defense Research Institute
- www.dri.org

Dominican Bar Association
- www.dominicanbarassociation.org

Education Law Association
- www.educationlaw.org

Environmental Law Institute
- www2.eli.org

Federal Communications Bar Association
- www.fcba.org

Federal Bar Association
- www.fedbar.org

Federal Circuit Bar Association
- www.fedcirbar.org

Federal Magistrate Judges Association
- www.fedjudge.org

Federation of Insurance & Corporate Counsel
- www.thefederation.org

Fully Informed Jury Association
- www.fija.org

Hellenic Bar Association
- www.hellenicbarassociation.com

Hispanic National Bar Association
- www.hnba.com

Home School Legal Defense Association
- www.hslda.org

Human Rights First
- www.humanrightsfirst.org

Inner Circle of Advocates
- www.innercircle.org

International Academy of Matrimonial Lawyers
- www.iaml-usa.com

International Air & Transportation Safety Bar Association
- iatsba.org

International Center for Not-for-Profit Law
- www.icnl.org

International Law Association
- www.ila-hq.org

International Masters of Gaming Law
- www.gaminglawmasters.com

International Technology Law Association
- www.itechlaw.org

Internet Attorneys Association
- internetattorneysassociation.org

Inter-Pacific Bar Association
- ipba.org

Italian–American Lawyers Association
- www.iala.info

Judge Advocates Association (military and veterans law)
- www.jaa.org

Justinian Society (Italian-American attorneys)
- www.justinian.org

Lambda Legal Defense and Education Fund (gay, lesbian, bisexual, and transgender issues)
- www.lambdalegal.org

Lawyer Pilots Bar Association
- www.lpba.org

Lawyers Without Borders
- www.lawyerswithoutborders.org

Legal Marketing Association
- www.legalmarketing.org

Licensing Executives Society
- les-europe.org

Lithuanian-American Bar Association
- javadvokatai.org

Million Dollar Advocates Forum (attorneys who have won $1,000,000+ in damages)
- www.milliondollaradvocates.com

Multilaw (Global Law Network)
- www.multilaw.com

National Asian Pacific American Bar Association
- www.napaba.org

NAACP Legal Defense and Education Fund
- www.naacpldf.org

National Academy of Elder Law Attorneys
- www.naela.org

National American Indian Court Judges Association
- www.naicja.org

National Association for Law Placement
- www.nalp.org

National Association for Rights Protection and Advocacy
- www.narpa.org

National Association of Assistant United States Attorneys
- www.naausa.org

National Association of Attorneys General
- www.naag.org

National Association of Bond Lawyers
- www.nabl.org

National Association of College and University Attorneys
- www.nacua.org

National Association of Consumer Bankruptcy Attorneys
- nacba.com

National Association of Criminal Defense Lawyers
- www.criminaljustice.org

National Association of Legal Search Consultants
- www.nalsc.org

National Association of Patent Practitioners
- www.napp.org

National Association of Retail Collection Attorneys
- www.narca.org

National Association of Secretaries of State
- www.nass.org

National Association of Women Judges
- www.nawj.org

National Association of Women Lawyers
- www.nawl.org

National Bar Association (African American attorneys)
- www.nationalbar.org

National Board of Trial Advocacy
- www.nbtanet.org

National Center for Lesbian Rights
- www.nclrights.org

National Center for Poverty Law, Sargent Shriver
- www.povertylaw.org

National Center for State Courts
- www.ncsc.org

National Crime Victim Bar Association
- www.victimbar.org

National District Attorneys Association
- www.ndaa.org

National Employment Lawyers Association
- www.nela.org

National Lawyers Association
- www.nla.org

National Lawyers Guild (civil rights group of lawyers, "jailhouse lawyers and legal workers")
- www.nlg.org

National Legal Aid and Defender Association
- www.nlada.org

National LGBT Bar Association
- lgbtbar.org

National Legal Center for the Public Interest
- www.nlcpi.org

National Native American Bar Association
- www.nativeamericanbar.org

National Organization of Bar Counsel
- www.nobc.org

National Right to Work Legal Defense Foundation
- www.nrtw.org

National Whistleblower Center
- www.whistleblowers.org

Network of Trial Law Firms
- www.trial.com

Phi Alpha Delta Law Fraternity
- www.pad.org

Philippine American Bar Association
- www.philconnect.com/paba

Rocky Mountain Mineral Law Foundation
- www.rmmlf.org

Rutherford Institute (civil and human rights)
- www.rutherford.org

Society of Corporate Secretaries and Governance Professionals
- www.governanceprofessionals.org

Sport and Recreation Law Association
- www.srlawebsite.com

Sports Lawyers Association
- www.sportslaw.org

Ukrainian American Bar Association
- www.uaba.org

FEDERAL GOVERNMENT ORGANIZATION CHART

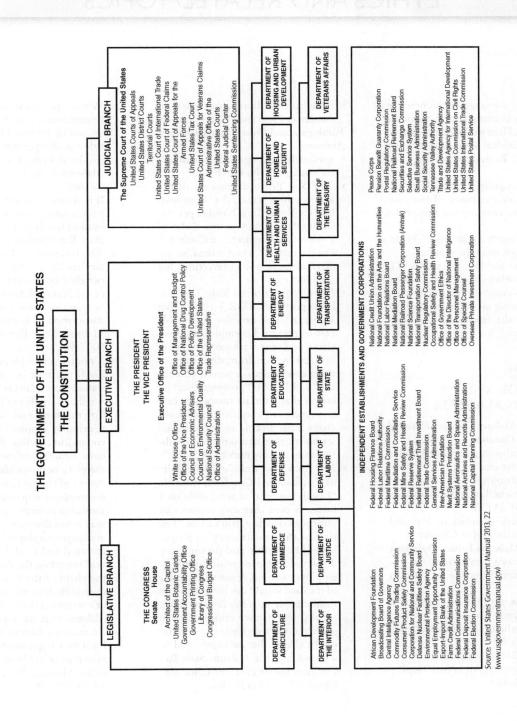

THE GOVERNMENT OF THE UNITED STATES

THE CONSTITUTION

LEGISLATIVE BRANCH

THE CONGRESS
Senate   House

Architect of the Capitol
United States Botanic Garden
Government Accountability Office
Government Printing Office
Library of Congress
Congressional Budget Office

EXECUTIVE BRANCH

THE PRESIDENT
THE VICE PRESIDENT

Executive Office of the President

White House Office
Office of the Vice President
Council of Economic Advisers
Council on Environmental Quality
National Security Council
Office of Administration

Office of Management and Budget
Office of National Drug Control Policy
Office of Policy Development
Office of the United States
Trade Representative

JUDICIAL BRANCH

The Supreme Court of the United States

United States Courts of Appeals
United States District Courts
Territorial Courts
United States Court of International Trade
United States Court of Federal Claims
United States Court of Appeals for the
Armed Forces
United States Tax Court
United States Court of Appeals for Veterans Claims
Administrative Office of the
United States Courts
Federal Judicial Center
United States Sentencing Commission

DEPARTMENT OF AGRICULTURE

DEPARTMENT OF COMMERCE

DEPARTMENT OF DEFENSE

DEPARTMENT OF EDUCATION

DEPARTMENT OF ENERGY

DEPARTMENT OF HEALTH AND HUMAN SERVICES

DEPARTMENT OF HOUSING AND URBAN DEVELOPMENT

DEPARTMENT OF THE INTERIOR

DEPARTMENT OF JUSTICE

DEPARTMENT OF LABOR

DEPARTMENT OF STATE

DEPARTMENT OF TRANSPORTATION

DEPARTMENT OF THE TREASURY

DEPARTMENT OF VETERANS AFFAIRS

DEPARTMENT OF HOMELAND SECURITY

INDEPENDENT ESTABLISHMENTS AND GOVERNMENT CORPORATIONS

African Development Foundation
Broadcasting Board of Governors
Central Intelligence Agency
Commodity Futures Trading Commission
Consumer Product Safety Commission
Corporation for National and Community Service
Defense Nuclear Facilities Safety Board
Environmental Protection Agency
Equal Employment Opportunity Commission
Export-Import Bank of the United States
Farm Credit Administration
Federal Communications Commission
Federal Deposit Insurance Corporation
Federal Election Commission

Federal Housing Finance Board
Federal Labor Relations Authority
Federal Maritime Commission
Federal Mediation and Conciliation Service
Federal Mine Safety and Health Review Commission
Federal Reserve System
Federal Retirement Thrift Investment Board
Federal Trade Commission
General Services Administration
Inter-American Foundation
Merit Systems Protection Board
National Aeronautics and Space Administration
National Archives and Records Administration
National Capital Planning Commission

National Credit Union Administration
National Foundation on the Arts and the Humanities
National Labor Relations Board
National Mediation Board
National Railroad Passenger Corporation (Amtrak)
National Science Foundation
National Transportation Safety Board
Nuclear Regulatory Commission
Occupational Safety and Health Review Commission
Office of Government Ethics
Office of the Director of National Intelligence
Office of Personnel Management
Office of Special Counsel
Overseas Private Investment Corporation

Peace Corps
Pension Benefit Guaranty Corporation
Postal Regulatory Commission
National Railroad Retirement Board
Securities and Exchange Commission
Selective Service System
Small Business Administration
Social Security Administration
Tennessee Valley Authority
Trade and Development Agency
United States Agency for International Development
United States Commission on Civil Rights
United States International Trade Commission
United States Postal Service

Source United States Government Manual 2013, 22
(www.usgovernmentmanual.gov)

STATE SURVEY: OPINIONS, RULES, STATUTES, AND REPORTS ON PARALEGAL ETHICS AND RELATED TOPICS

The primary coverage of the practice of law and ethics in every state is found in Chapters 4 and 5. Here we highlight specific provisions in individual states. Many court opinions are cited. To read the full text of an opinion,

- Go to scholar.google.com, select *Case law*, and enter the name of the case (if needed, try entering the rest of the citation).
- In a general search engine (e.g., Google, Bing, or Yahoo), enter the citation.
- Do the same for WL citations. WL refers to Westlaw. If you do not have access to this expensive research service, enter the citation in scholar.google.com and also try the citation in a general search engine.

ALABAMA

ETHICS CODE AND OPINIONS IN ALABAMA

- **Attorneys: Alabama Code:** *Rules of Professional Conduct*
  - judicial.alabama.gov/library/rules _bar_conduct.cfm
  - www.alabar.org/ogc
  - www.law.cornell.edu/ethics/al/code /AL_CODE.HTM
  - See also ethics links in Helpful Websites at the end of Chapter 5.
- **Attorneys: Alabama Ethics Opinions**
  - www.alabar.org/ogc/fopList.cfm
- **Unauthorized Practice of Law in Alabama**
  - www.alabar.org (enter *unauthorized practice of law* in search box)
  - judicial.alabama.gov/library/rules /cond5_5.pdf
  - *§ 34–3–1 (Michie's Alabama Code)*
  - www.alabar.org/ogc/fopDisplay .cfm?oneId=359

- ir.lawnet.fordham.edu/cgi/view content.cgi?article=3572&context=flr
- **Paralegals and Other Nonattorneys: Alabama**
  - www.alabar.org/ogc/fopList.cfm (enter *paralegal* in the search box)
  - *Rule 5.3.* For a discussion of the state's ethics Rule 5.3 ("Responsibilities Regarding Nonlawyer Assistants") in the Alabama Rules of Professional Conduct, see Chapter 5. For the text of 5.3 in Alabama, see judicial.alabama.gov/library/rules_bar _conduct.cfm.
  - *DR 4-101.* Prior to Rule 5.3, Alabama provided in DR 4-101(D) that a lawyer "shall exercise reasonable care to prevent his employees, associates, and others whose services are utilized by him from disclosing or using confidences or secrets of a client." DR 7-107(I) provided that "[a] lawyer shall exercise reasonable care to prevent his employees and associates from making an extrajudicial statement that he would be prohibited from making under DR 7-107."
  - *Rule 7.6.* Under Rule 7.6 of the Rules of Professional Conduct, the title "Legal Assistant" is acceptable on a business card that also contains an attorney's or a law firm's name. The title of the nonattorney employee should be legibly and prominently displayed in close proximity to the employee's name. A casual observer of the card should not be misled into thinking that it is the card of an attorney. (An earlier ethics opinion preferred the title *nonlawyer assistant* on the theory that *paralegal* could be a misleading title. Alabama State Bar, Opinion 86–04 (3/17/86). See also Opinion 86–120 (12/2/86).

- When a paralegal signs a letter to a nonattorney, the paralegal's name should be followed by one of these titles: nonlawyer assistant, nonlawyer paralegal, or nonlawyer investigator. Alabama State Bar, Opinion 87–77 (6/16/87).
- It is improper to include the name of a nonattorney assistant on the letterhead of law firm stationery. Alabama State Bar, Opinion 83–87 (5/23/83).
- The business card of a legal secretary can list the fact that she has been certified by passing an examination of the National Association of Legal Secretaries (now called NALS the Association of Legal Professionals). Alabama State Bar, Opinion 90–01 (1/17/90).
- A nonlawyer employee who changes law firms must be held to the same standards as a lawyer in determining whether a conflict of interest exists. A firm that hires a nonlawyer employee previously employed by opposing counsel in pending litigation would have a conflict of interest and must therefore be disqualified if, during the course of the previous employment, the employee acquired confidential information concerning the case. A firm may avoid disqualification if (1) the nonlawyer employee has not acquired material and confidential information regarding the litigation or (2) if the client of the former firm waives disqualification and approves the use of a screening device or Chinese wall. Alabama State Bar, Opinion 2002–01.
- An attorney cannot allow his paralegal to ask questions of debtors at meetings of creditors in bankruptcy cases. Alabama State Bar, Opinion 89–76 (9/20/90).

- Paralegals may draft documents if supervised by an attorney, but they cannot make court appearances or give legal advice. Alabama State Bar, Opinion 86–120 (12/2/86).
- An attorney engaged in collection work may not pay his lay employees on a commission basis. Opinion of the General Counsel (2/3/88, revised 2/14/90).
- Nonattorney independent contractors who sell legal research services to attorneys are not engaged in the unauthorized practice of law. Alabama State Bar, Opinion 90–04 (1/18/90).
- A law firm may not employ, retain, contract with, or hire a disbarred lawyer to provide legal services. This specifically includes paralegal services. A suspended lawyer may seek permission from the Disciplinary Commission to seek employment in the legal profession. In the event that permission is granted, the lawyer shall not have any contact with clients. Alabama Rules of Disciplinary Procedure, Rule 26. (See also Alabama State Bar, Opinion 1996–08.)
- Members of the bar, paralegals, or other personal assistants to members of the bar when accompanied by an attorney are permitted to bring laptops and personal digital assistants into the courthouse after such devices have been properly screened. Local Rules of the U.S. District Court, S.D. Alabama, Order 31.

Defining The Practice Of Law In Alabama

- *§ 34–3–6 (Michie's Alabama Code)*. . . (b) For the purposes of this chapter, the practice of law is defined as follows: Whoever, (1) in a representative capacity appears as an advocate or draws papers, pleadings or documents, or performs any act in connection with proceedings pending or prospective before a court or a body, board, committee, commission or officer constituted by law or having authority to take evidence in or settle or determine controversies in the exercise of the judicial power of the state or any subdivision thereof; or (2) For a consideration, reward or pecuniary benefit, present or anticipated, direct or indirect, advises or counsels another as to secular law, or draws or procures or assists in the drawing of a paper, document or instrument affecting or relating to secular rights; or (3) For a consideration, reward or pecuniary benefit, present or anticipated, direct or indirect, does any

act in a representative capacity in behalf of another tending to obtain or secure for such other the prevention or the redress of a wrong or the enforcement or establishment of a right; or (4) As a vocation, enforces, secures, settles, adjusts or compromises defaulted, controverted or disputed accounts, claims or demands between persons with neither of whom he is in privity or in the relation of employer and employee in the ordinary sense; is practicing law.

- *§ 6–5–572 (Michie's Alabama Code):* Paralegals and legal assistants as legal service providers. Under the Alabama Legal Services Liability Act, the term "legal service provider" is defined as follows: Anyone licensed to practice law by the State of Alabama or engaged in the practice of law in the State of Alabama. The term legal service provider includes professional corporations, associations, and partnerships and the members of such professional corporations, associations, and partnerships and the persons, firms, or corporations either employed by or performing work or services for the benefit of such professional corporations, associations, and partnerships including, without limitation, law clerks, legal assistants, legal secretaries, investigators, paralegals, and couriers.

Paralegals (And Others) In Alabama State And Federal Courts

(See the beginning of this appendix on how to find the full text of the opinions cited here.)

- *U.S. Gumbaytay*, 276 F.R.D. 671 (U.S. District Court, M.D. Alabama, 2011 (Information disclosed to housing advocate's paralegal by non-party victims was protected by attorney-client privilege.)
- *Pullum v. Pullum*, 58 So. 3d 752 (Supreme Court of Alabama, 2010) (A legal assistant made an error in the way in which 20 acres of land was stated in a deed; the court allowed the error to be corrected.)
- *Metropolitan Life Insurance Co. v. Akins*, 388 So. 2d 999 (Court of Civil Appeals of Alabama, 1980) (The failure of a "para-legal" to inform an attorney of a matter is not a sufficient excuse for the attorney's neglect of that matter.)
- *Browder v. General Motors Corp.*, 5 F. Supp. 2d 1267, 1275 (U.S. District Court, M.D. Alabama, 1998) (The attorney's carelessness included the failure to review a proposed pretrial order drafted by a paralegal.)
- *Ex Parte Moody*, 684 So. 2d 114 (Supreme Court of Alabama) (An indigent

defendant in a criminal case is not entitled to a court-appointed paralegal who is paid by the state or a court-appointed paralegal who works on a volunteer basis.)

- *Serra Chevrolet, Inc. v. General Motors*, 446 F.3d 1137 (U.S. Court of Appeals for the 11th Circuit) (General Motors hired fourteen paralegals to conduct a manual review of documents in 4,100 contract files.)
- *Allen v. Fountain*, 861 So. 2d 1104 (Court of Civil Appeals of Alabama, 2002) (Constitutional and statutory provisions allowing self-representation in civil court actions protect only natural persons, and do not allow for representation of separate legal entities, such as estates and corporations, by nonlawyers.)
- *Cormier v. ACAC*, 2013 WL 6499703 (U.S. District Court, S.D. Alabama, 2013) (Time spent by paralegals "receiving, reviewing, and indexing documents," "sending or receiving emails with documents attached," "preparing the civil cover sheet and summons," "receiving and indexing certified mail receipts," and "e-filing documents with the Court and receiving and indexing those documents" was not compensable time for the purposes of the fee petition. Courts in this district generally consider tasks such as mailing and telefaxing correspondence, making routing calls to clients, obtaining pleadings from the court's database and printing documents as secretarial functions.)
- *Hall v. Lowder Realty Co.*, 263 F. Supp. 2d 1352 (U.S. District Court, M.D. Alabama, 2003) (Paralegal work is compensable when it involves, for example, factual investigation, including locating and interviewing witnesses, assistance with depositions, interrogatories, and document production, compilation of statistical and financial data, checking legal citations, and drafting correspondence; but paralegal's hours spent reviewing documents and helping to prepare chart exhibits were clerical in nature and thus would be reduced.)

Doing Legal Research In Alabama Law

- **Statutes**: www.legislature.state.al.us
- **Cases**: www.findlaw.com/casecode /alabama.html
- **Court Rules**: judicial.alabama.gov (click *Rules of Court*)
- **General**: www.law.georgetown.edu /library/research/guides/alabama.cfm

Finding Employment In Alabama

- See Exhibit 2-12 in Chapter 2.
- legal.jobs.net/Alabama.htm

- www.indeed.com/q-Paralegal-1
  -Alabama-jobs.html
- www.careerbuilder.com/jobs/al
  /keyword/paralegal
- paralegal.jobs.net/jobs/alabama.aspx
- www.hg.org/legal_jobs_alabama.asp

ALASKA

ETHICS CODE AND OPINIONS IN ALASKA

- **Attorneys: Alaska Code:** *Rules of Professional Conduct*
  - www.courts.alaska.gov/prof.htm
  - www.touchngo.com/lglcntr/ctrules
    /profcon/htframe.htm
  - www.law.cornell.edu/ethics/alaska
    .html
  - See also ethics links in Helpful Websites at the end of Chapter 5.
- **Attorneys: Alaska Ethics Opinions**
  - www.alaskabar.org (click *Ethics /Discipline*)
- **Unauthorized Practice of Law in Alaska**
  - www.alaskabar.org (enter *unauthorized practice of law* in search box)
  - ir.lawnet.fordham.edu/cgi/view
    content.cgi?article=3572&context=flr
- **Paralegals and Other Nonattorneys: Alaska**
  - www.alaskabar.org (click *Ethics/ Discipline*, then *Topical Index* of Ethical Opinions, then *Legal Assistants*)
  - *Rule 5.3.* For a discussion of the state's ethics, see Rule 5.3 ("Responsibilities Regarding Nonlawyer Assistants") in the *Alaska Rules of Professional Conduct.* For the text of 5.3 in Alaska, see www.courts.alaska.gov/prof.htm.
  - *Rule 1.10 (Comment 4).* The rule of imputed disqualification in Rule 1.10 "does not prohibit representation by others in the law firm where the person prohibited from involvement in a matter is a nonlawyer, such as a paralegal or legal secretary." *Alaska Rules of Professional Conduct.*
  - *Rule 5.5* (Comment 2). Lawyers can employ the services of paralegals and delegate tasks to them "so long as the lawyer supervises the delegated work and retains responsibility for their work."
  - *Rule 5.5* (Comment 3). Lawyers can assist independent paralegals who are authorized to provide particular law-related services.
  - A suspended attorney may work as a paralegal but only under the supervision of an attorney in good standing. He or she may not have a direct relationship with a client. Alaska Bar Ass'n, *Ethics Opinion 84–6* (8/25/84).

Under Rule 15(c) of the Alaska Bar Association, attorneys who have been suspended solely for the non-payment of fees may represent another to the extent that a layperson would be allowed to do so.

- A law firm may ethically employ an accountant to advise and assist attorneys in the performance of legal services and to provide accounting services relating to or arising from legal services provided by the firm. An accountant so employed may not be a partner and shall be compensated by salary so as to avoid the prohibitions of Disciplinary Rules 3–102 and 3–103. Further, the letterhead, office sign, and professional cards of the law firm shall not indicate the availability of the accounting services to clients of the firm. Alaska Bar Ass'n, *Ethics Opinion 79–3* (10/26/79).
- Under the supervision or review of an attorney, a legal assistant can investigate claims and have contact with insurance agents regarding the settlement of claims in worker's compensation cases. Alaska Bar Ass'n, *Ethics Opinion 73–1* (10/6/73).
- Paralegal employees of attorneys may not conduct worker's compensation hearings. Alaska Bar Ass'n, *Ethics Opinion 84–7* (8/25/84). Note: this opinion was reversed on 11/9/84.

Defining The Practice Of Law In Alaska

- *Christiansen v. Melinda,* 857 P.2d 345, 347 (Supreme Court of Alaska, 1993): We have twice addressed the definition of "practice of law" in deciding whether a suspended attorney had impermissibly practiced law while on suspension. In each case we refused "to give a specific definition of the term 'practice of law'" because "[t]he practice of law may well be used in a different sense for various purposes. "Whatever the precise nuances of that definition may be for different "purposes," in-court representation of another — a paradigmatic function of the attorney-at-law — falls within that definition. See also 7 Am. Jur.2d Attorneys at Law § 1 (1980) ("practice of law . . . Embraces the preparation of pleadings and other papers incident to actions and special proceedings, the management of such actions and proceedings on behalf of clients before judges and courts"). (Internal cites omitted.)
- § 08.08.230 (*Alaska Statutes*): Unlawful practice a misdemeanor. (a) A person not an active member of the Alaska

Bar and not licensed to practice law in Alaska who engages in the practice of law or holds out as entitled to engage in the practice of law as that term is defined in the Alaska Bar Rules, or an active member of the Alaska Bar who willfully employs such a person knowing that the person is engaging in the practice of law or holding out as entitled to so engage is guilty of a class A misdemeanor. (b) This section does not prohibit the use of paralegal personnel as defined by rules of the Alaska Supreme Court.

- Rule 63. *Rules of the Alaska Bar Association:* For purposes of Alaska Statutes § 08.08.230 [making unauthorized practice of law a misdemeanor], "practice of law" is defined as (a) representing oneself by words or conduct to be an attorney, and, if the person is authorized to practice law in another jurisdiction but is not a member of the Alaska Bar Association, representing oneself to be a member of the Alaska Bar Association; and (b) either (i) representing another before a court or governmental body which is operating in its adjudicative capacity, including the submission of pleadings, or (ii), for compensation, providing advice or preparing documents for another which effect legal rights or duties.
- Rule 15(c). *Rules of the Alaska Bar Ass'n:* For purposes of the practice of law prohibition for disbarred and suspended attorneys, "practice of law" is defined as:. . . (B) rendering legal consultation or advice to a client; (C) appearing on behalf of a client in any hearing or proceeding or before any judicial officer, arbitrator, mediator, court, public agency, referee, magistrate, commissioner, hearing officer, or governmental body which is operating in its adjudicative capacity, including the submission of pleadings; (D) appearing as a representative of the client at a deposition or other discovery matter; (E) negotiating or transacting any matter for or on behalf of a client with third parties; or (F) receiving, disbursing, or otherwise handling a client's funds.

Paralegals (And Others) In Alaska State And Federal Courts

(See the beginning of this appendix on how to find the full text of the opinions cited here, including WL opinions.)

- *Welton v. State,* 2011 WL 2151850 (Court of Appeals of Alaska, 2011) It is true that paralegals are barred from independently giving legal advice to clients. *See* the American Bar Association's

Ethics Opinion No. 316 (1967). The ABA's *Model Guidelines for the Utilization of Paralegal Services* (2004) echoes this theme, declaring that clients "are entitled to their *lawyers'* professional judgment and opinion." *Id.* at 6 (emphasis added). Nevertheless, the *Model Guidelines* declares that paralegals may properly "communicate a lawyer's legal advice to a client" (as long as they do not "interpret or expand on that advice"), and that paralegals may also properly participate in "preparing the lawyer's legal opinion"—that is, participate in the process of *formulating* the lawyer's legal advice—so long as the lawyer makes the final assessment of what that advice should be. *Id.* at 6–7.)

- *Tracy v. State, Dept. of Health...*, 279 P3d 613 (Supreme Court of Alaska, 2012) (Under Rule 82 of the Rules of Civil Procedure, an award of attorney fees "shall include fees for legal work customarily performed by an attorney but which was delegated to and performed by an investigator, paralegal or law clerk.")
- *In re Zaruba*, 2010 WL 7374776 (U.S. Bankruptcy Court, Alaska, 2010) (Finally, HTC seeks disallowance of certain fees charged for paralegal Margaret Stroble, arguing that these services were primarily clerical in nature. Ms. Stroble's fees total $911.25, for miscellaneous entries in December, January, February, April and May of 2008. The services provided were the preparation of the debtors' required monthly operating reports. I disagree that these were clerical services. The preparation of monthly operating reports is an appropriate para-professional activity. No deduction for them is warranted.)
- *NCO Financial Systems Inc v. Ross*, 2012 WL 1232602 (Supreme Court of Alaska 2012) (NCO next asserts in a single sentence that some of Ross's requested itemizations for the Alaska Legal Services' paralegals "describe work that is clearly administrative work... not billable work by a paralegal." But NCO does not point to any examples of claimed paralegal charges that described work not "customarily performed by an attorney." The superior court was in the best position to determine whether the paralegals' work was properly considered attorney work. The superior court thus did not abuse its discretion by including paralegal work hours in the attorney's fee award.)
- *Marsingill v. O'Malley*, 58 P.3d 495 (Supreme Court of Alaska, 2002) (Paralegal was prohibited from asking jurors, during posttrial interview in a medical malpractice action, about jury's alleged confusion regarding an aspect of the jury instructions.)

Doing Legal Research In Alaska Law

- **Statutes**: www.legis.state.ak.us/basis/folio.asp
- **Cases**: courts.alaska.gov/search-cases.htm
- **Court Rules**: courts.alaska.gov/rules.htm
- **General**: www.courts.alaska.gov/aklegal.htm

Finding Employment In Alaska

- See Exhibit 2-12 in Chapter 2.
- www.alaskabar.org/servlet/content/46.html
- www.indeed.com/q-Legal-Assistant-l-Alaska-jobs.html
- www.simplyhired.com/k-paralegal-l-anchorage-ak-jobs.html
- anchorage.craigslist.org/lgl

ARIZONA

ETHICS CODE AND OPINIONS IN ARIZONA

- **Attorneys: Arizona Code: *Rules of Professional Conduct***
  - www.azbar.org/ethics/rulesofprofessionalconduct
  - www.law.cornell.edu/ethics/arizona.html
  - See also ethics links in Helpful Websites at the end of Chapter 5.
- **Attorneys: Arizona Ethics Opinions**
  - www.azbar.org/Ethics
- **Unauthorized Practice of Law in Arizona**
  - www.azbar.org (enter *unauthorized practice of law* in search box)
  - www.azbar.org/ethics/unauthorizedpracticeoflaw
  - ir.lawnet.fordham.edu/cgi/viewcontent.cgi?article=3572&context=flr
  - Arizona Certified Legal Document Preparers www.azcourts.gov/cld/LegalDocumentPreparers.aspx
- **Paralegals and Nonattorneys: Arizona**
  - *Rule 5.3.* or a discussion of the state's ethics Rule 5.3 ("Responsibilities Regarding Nonlawyer Assistants") in the Arizona Rules of Professional Conduct, see Chapter 5. For the text of 5.3 in Arizona and related ethics opinions, see www.azbar.org/ethics/rulesofprofessionalconduct.
  - *Rule 1.10 (Comment 4).* The rule of imputed disqualification in Rule 1.10 "does not prohibit representation by others in the law firm where the person prohibited from involvement in a matter is a nonlawyer, such as a paralegal or legal secretary." Arizona *Rules of Professional Conduct*.
  - *Rule 5.5 (Comment 1).* Lawyers can employ the services of paralegals and delegate tasks to them "so long as the lawyer supervises the delegated work and retains responsibility for their work."
  - The letterhead of an attorney or law firm can list nonattorney support personnel if their nonattorney status is made clear. State Bar of Arizona, *Ethics Opinion 90–03* (3/16/90). This overrules *Opinion 84–14* (10/5/84), which held to the contrary. The latter opinion also said that a separate letterhead for paralegals is not allowed.
  - A corporation consisting of independent contractor paralegals and a salaried attorney employee is impermissible. State Bar of Arizona, *Opinion 82–18* (12/1/82). It is unethical for an attorney to associate with a nonattorney-operated eviction service; there would be inadequate attorney supervision of the nonattorneys and improper sharing of fees with nonattorneys. State Bar of Arizona, *Ethics Opinion 93–01* (2/18/93).
  - An attorney ethically may contract with a paralegal to have the paralegal assist with conducting initial interviews of and signing of documents by estate planning clients, as long as: (1) the attorney supervises and controls the paralegal's activities to assure that the paralegal does not engage in the unauthorized practice of law; (2) there is no fee sharing; (3) the initial interviews are only with existing clients; and (4) there is no solicitation of new business by the paralegal. State Bar of Arizona, *Ethics Opinion 98–08* (10/98).
  - An Arizona attorney may permit his nonlawyer paralegal, who is a licensed tribal advocate, to represent clients in tribal court if that court's rules so permit. Such representations will not run afoul of the Arizona lawyer's duty to not assist in the unauthorized practice of law as long as the paralegal representation is limited to tribal court. State Bar of Arizona, *Ethics Opinion 99–13* (12/99).
  - Lawyers may not negotiate with an opposing party's nonlawyer public adjuster if the adjuster is not supervised by a lawyer. A lawyer may communicate directly with an opposing party who is "represented" by a public adjuster if the adjuster is not supervised by a lawyer or authorized

to practice law. State Bar of Arizona, *Ethics Opinion 99–07* (6/99).

- A law firm can compensate one of its nonattorney employees by a base monthly fee plus quarterly bonuses measured by a percentage of the firm's increased revenues derived from areas the nonattorney employee was hired to develop. State Bar of Arizona, *Ethics Opinion 90–14* (10/17/90).
- Lawyers may employ a disbarred lawyer in the same capacity as they would employ any nonlawyer assistant. State Bar of Arizona, *Ethics Opinion 87-27* (12/87).
- A judge did not have to recuse himself where his daughter was employed as a paralegal in a law firm appearing in a case before him unless his daughter's work on the case was extensive. Arizona Supreme Court Judicial Ethics Advisory Committee, *Opinion 77–1* (4/29/77).
- Other State Bar of Arizona Opinions involving nonattorneys: *Ethics Opinion 86–7* (2/26/86) (it is improper for an attorney to cooperate with a nonattorney "consulting service" that provided expert testimony to its customers for a contingent fee); *Ethics Opinion 82–18* (12/1/82) (it is improper for an attorney to be a salaried employee—not an owner—of a paralegal-run corporation that contracted with attorneys to provide legal services on an as-needed basis).

Defining Legal Assistants/Paralegals In Arizona

- Rule 31(a)(C) (*Arizona Supreme Court Rules*): "Legal assistant/paralegal" means a person qualified by education and training who performs substantive legal work requiring a sufficient knowledge of and expertise in legal concepts and procedures, who is supervised by an active member of the State Bar of Arizona, and for whom an active member of the state bar is responsible, unless otherwise authorized by Supreme Court rule.
- A legal assistant is a person, qualified through education, training, or work experience, who is employed or retained by a lawyer, law office, governmental agency, or other entity in a capacity or function which involves the performance, under the ultimate direction and supervision of an attorney, of specifically delegated substantive legal work, which work, for the most part, requires a sufficient knowledge of legal concepts that, absent such assistant, the attorney would perform the task. *Continental Townhouses E. Unit One Ass'n v. Brockbank*, 733 P.2d 1120, 1128 (Arizona Court of Appeals, 1986)

Defining The Practice Of Law In Arizona

- Rule 31(a)(A) (*Arizona Supreme Court Rules*) "Practice of law" means providing legal advice or services to or for another by: (1) preparing any document in any medium intended to affect or secure legal rights for a specific person or entity; (2) preparing or expressing legal opinions; (3) representing another in a judicial, quasi-judicial, or administrative proceeding, or other formal dispute resolution process such as arbitration and mediation; (4) preparing any document through any medium for filing in any court, administrative agency or tribunal for a specific person or entity; or (5) negotiating legal rights or responsibilities for a specific person or entity.

Legal Document Preparers In Arizona

- In 2003, the Supreme Court of Arizona adopted a new section of the Code of Judicial Administration, Section 7–208, and established the Legal Document Preparer Program. Supreme Court Administrative Order 2003–14 defines legal document preparers as nonlawyers who "prepare or provide legal documents, without the supervision of an attorney, for an entity or a member of the public who is engaging in self representation in any legal matter." Under Section 7–208 (F)(1) (b), certified legal document preparers may provide general legal information but may not give legal advice. Section 7–208 (D)(4) established the Board of Legal Document Preparers, which, in part, hears and adjudicates complaints against certified legal document preparers. *Sobol v. Alarcon*, 131 P.3d 487 (Court of Appeals of Arizona, 2006) (www.azcourts .gov/cld/LegalDocumentPreparers .aspx).*Regulation of Nonlawyers* (www .azbar.org/lawyerconcerns/non-lawyers).

Other Important Arizona Laws On Paralegals

- § 12–2234(A) (*Arizona Revised Statutes Annotated*): In a civil action an attorney shall not, without the consent of his client, be examined as to any communication made by the client to him, or his advice given thereon in the course of professional employment. An attorney's paralegal, assistant, secretary, stenographer or clerk shall not, without the consent of his employer, be examined concerning any fact the knowledge of which was acquired in such capacity. . . .
- R9–21–209 (B)(3) (*Arizona Administrative Code*): Mental Illness Records. An attorney, paralegal working under the supervision of an attorney, or other

designated representative of the client shall be permitted to inspect and copy the record, if such attorney or representative furnishes written authorization from the client or guardian.

Paralegals (And Others) In Arizona State And Federal Courts

(See the beginning of this appendix on how to find the full text of the opinions cited here, including WL opinions.)

- *Southern Calif. Edison v. Ariz. Corp. Comm'n*, 2011 WL 846568 (Court of Appeals of Arizona, 2011) (Fees for the services of legal assistants and law clerks are recoverable as attorneys' fees because legal assistants and law clerks have legal training and knowledge that can contribute to the attorney's preparation of a legal matter. A 1999 case (*Bach*) recognizes that some tasks are more properly performed by law clerks or legal assistants than an attorney and that such tasks are compensable.)
- *Agster v. Maricopa County*, 486 F. Supp. 2d 1005 (U.S. District Court, Arizona, 2007) (80 percent of the reasonable hours expended by plaintiffs' paralegals and legal assistants should be billed at a rate of $110, and the other 20 percent at $70. These rates more closely approximate the prevailing rates in this community; the court will deduct 933.82 hours from the time total for the fifteen paralegals/legal assistants because of duplication of effort, turnover of staff, and inefficiencies.)
- *Fouchia v. Carlota Copper Co.*, 2012 WL 2072673 (U.S. District Court, Arizona, 2012) (Plaintiff's counsel explained that he missed the April 12 expert disclosure deadline because his paralegal failed to enter that deadline into counsel's calendaring system. . . [The paralegal] is an experienced paralegal with over 20 years in litigation. Her standard operating procedure is to enter all dates into a calendaring system that notes the date something is due and also provides a reminder 30 days before the due date that follows the attorney's calendar every day until it was checked off by either the attorney or the paralegal. These deadlines were received by [the paralegal] but they were filed without putting them in the calendaring system.
- *Styles v. Ceranski*, 916 P.2d 1164 (Court of Appeals of Arizona, 1996) (Propriety of communication by a defense paralegal with an employee of the plaintiff without consent of the plaintiff's attorney.)
- *In the Matter of Miller*, 872 P.2d 661 (Supreme Court of Arizona, 1994) (Discipline of attorney for failure to supervise paralegals.)

- *Smart Industries Corp. v. Superior Court*, 876 P.2d 1176 (Court of Appeals of Arizona, 1994) (Disqualification of a plaintiff's attorney when he hired a legal assistant who once worked for the defendant's attorney.)
- *Samaritan Foundation v. Goodfarb*, 862 P.2d 870 (Supreme Court of Arizona, 1993) (Defendant's attorney hires a nurse paralegal who interviews hospital employees in a medical malpractice case. The statements of the employees are not within the hospital's attorney-client privilege.) See, however, § 12-2234(A) above.
- *Sobol v. Alarcon*, 131 P.3d 487 (Court of Appeals of Arizona, 2006) (A certified legal document preparer sued an attorney for defamation when the attorney sent a letter to the state bar accusing the document preparer of unauthorized practice of law and other improper conduct. The attorney's complaint was privileged.)
- *Oliver v. Long*, 2007 WL 623783 (U.S. District Court, Arizona 2007) (Judges have no obligation to act as counsel or paralegal to pro se litigants because requiring trial judges to explain the details of federal procedure or act as the pro se's counsel would undermine the judges' role as impartial decision makers.)
- *Miller v. Schriro*, 2007 WL 63613 (U.S. District Court, Arizona, 2007) (An Arizona inmate's legal access to the courts relies on designated staff, paralegals, legal access monitors, attorneys, and inmates.)

Doing Legal Research In Arizona Law

- **Statutes:** www.azleg.state.az.us /ArizonaRevisedStatutes.asp
- **Cases:** www.azcourts.gov/opinions /Home.aspx
- **Court Rules:** www.azcourts.gov /rules/Home.aspx
- **General:** www.superiorcourt .maricopa.gov/lawlibrary

Finding Employment In Arizona

- www.legalstaff.com/Common /HomePage.aspx
- www.azparalegal.org/jobbank.html
- www.indeed.com/q-Paralegal -l-Arizona-jobs.html
- phoenix.craigslist.org/lgl

ARKANSAS

ETHICS CODE AND OPINIONS IN ARKANSAS

- **Attorneys: Arkansas Code:** *Rules of Professional Conduct*
  - courts.arkansas.gov/administration
  - www.law.cornell.edu/ethics/ar/narr /AR_NARR_1_01.HTM

- See also ethics links in Helpful Websites at the end of Chapter 5.
- **Attorneys: Arkansas Ethics Opinions**
  - www.arkbar.com/pages/ethicsadv.aspx
- **Unauthorized Practice of Law in Arkansas**
  - www.arkbar.com (enter *unauthorized practice of law* in search box)
  - www.arkbar.com/Committee /CommitteeInfo.aspx?id=234
  - ir.lawnet.fordham.edu/cgi /viewcontent.cgi?article=3572&con text=flr
- **Paralegals and Other Nonattorneys: Arkansas**
  - *Rule 5.3.* For a discussion of the state's ethics Rule 5.3 ("Responsibilities Regarding Nonlawyer Assistants") in the Arkansas *Rules of Professional Conduct*, see Chapter 5.
  - *Rule 5.3.* (comment 3) A lawyer may use nonlawyers outside the firm to assist the lawyer in rendering legal services to the client. Examples include the retention of an investigative or paraprofessional service, hiring a document management company to create and maintain a database for complex litigation, sending client documents to a third party for printing or scanning, and using an Internet-based service to store client information. When using such services outside the firm, a lawyer must make reasonable efforts to ensure that the services are provided in a manner that is compatible with the lawyer's professional obligations. The extent of this obligation will depend upon the circumstances, including the education, experience and reputation of the nonlawyer; the nature of the services involved; the terms of any arrangements concerning the protection of client information; and the legal and ethical environments of the jurisdictions in which the services will be performed, particularly with regard to confidentiality. See also Rules 1.1 (competence), 1.2 (allocation of authority), 1.4 (communication with client), 1.6 (confidentiality), 5.4(a) (professional independence of the lawyer), and 5.5(a) (unauthorized practice of law). When retaining or directing a nonlawyer outside the firm, a lawyer should communicate directions appropriate under the circumstances to give reasonable assurance that the nonlawyer's conduct is compatible with the professional obligations of the lawyer.
  - *Rule 1.10 (Comment 4).* The rule of imputed disqualification in Rule 1.10 "does not prohibit representation

by others in the law firm where the person prohibited from involvement in a matter is a nonlawyer, such as a paralegal or legal secretary." Arkansas *Rules of Professional Conduct*.
- *Rule 5.5* (Comment 2). Lawyers can employ the services of paralegals and delegate tasks to them "so long as the lawyer supervises the delegated work and retains responsibility for their work."
- *Rule 5.5* (Comment 3). Lawyers can assist independent paraprofessionals who are authorized to provide particular law-related services.
- "The paralegal should never be placed in a position to decide what information takes priority over other information or to make decisions which affect the client." This function should never be delegated to a paralegal, even though "sometimes a fine line exists in the area of professional judgment." Paralegals need "specific guidelines," preferably in writing, in carrying out responsibilities. *The Paralegal in Practice* by A. Clinton, chairperson of the Paralegal Committee of the Arkansas Bar Ass'n, 23 Arkansas Lawyer 22 (January 1989).

Defining The Practice Of Law In Arkansas

- § 4-109-101(3) (Arkansas Code Annotated): (3) "Practice of law" means: (a) holding oneself out to the public as being entitled to practice law; (b) tendering or furnishing legal services or advice; (c) furnishing attorneys or counsel; (d) rendering legal services of any kind in actions or proceedings of any nature or in any other way or manner....
- § 2.02 (*Arkansas Code Annotated*): Defining the Practice of Law, Court Rules Regulations of the Arkansas Continuing Legal Education Board. Inactive Status. (2) Definition: Practice of Law. The practice of law shall be defined as any service rendered, regardless of whether compensation is received therefor, involving legal knowledge or legal advice. It shall include representation, provision of counsel, advocacy, whether in or out of court, rendered with respect to the rights, duties, regulations, liabilities, or business relations of one requiring the legal services.
- § 16–22–501 (*Arkansas Code of 1987 Annotated*): Unauthorized Practice of Law. (a) A person commits an offense if, with intent to obtain a direct economic benefit for himself or herself, the person:

(1) Contracts with any person to represent that person with regard to personal causes of action for property damages or personal injury;

(2) Advises any person as to the person's rights and the advisability of making claims for personal injuries or property damages;

(3) Advises any person as to whether or not to accept an offered sum of money in settlement of claims for personal injuries or property damages;

(4) Enters into any contract with another person to represent that person in personal injury or property damage matters on a contingent fee basis with an attempted assignment of a portion of the person's cause of action. . .

(6) Contacts any person by telephone or in person for the purpose of soliciting business which is legal in nature, as set forth above. . .

(e) This section shall not apply to a person who is licensed as an adjuster or employed as an adjuster by an insurer as authorized by § 23–64–101.

- § 4–109–101(3) (*Arkansas Code Annotated*): "Practice of law" means: (A) Holding oneself out to the public as being entitled to practice law; (B) Tendering or furnishing legal services or advice; (C) Furnishing attorneys or counsel; (D) Rendering legal services of any kind in actions or proceedings of any nature or in any other way or manner; (E) Acting as if or in any other manner assuming to be entitled to practice law; or (F) Advertising or assuming the title of lawyer or attorney, attorney at law, or equivalent terms in any language in such a manner as to convey the impression that one is entitled to practice law or to furnish legal advice, service, or counsel.

Paralegals (And Others) In Arkansas State And Federal Courts

(See the beginning of this appendix on how to find the full text of the opinions cited here, including WL opinions.)

- *Fink v. Neal*, 328 Ark. 646, 945 S.W.2d 916 (Supreme Court of Arkansas, 1997) (The mistakes made by an attorney's paralegal do not constitute an excuse for the attorney's own negligence.)
- *Brooks v. Central Arkansas Nursing Center*, 31 F. Supp. 2d 1151, 1154 (U.S. District Court, E.D. Arkansas, 1999) (The award

of attorney fees is reduced because "the Court is of the view these tasks could have been performed by a clerk or paralegal.")

- *Duvall v. City of Rogers, Arkansas*, 2006 WL 931908 (U.S. District Court, W.D. Arkansas, 2006) (One and one half hours charged for "Court Appearance to file Motions" will be disallowed because all filings in this court are handled electronically, and this task could have been accomplished in a few minutes by a secretary or paralegal.)

- *In re Seay*, 2007 WL 1623156 (U.S. Bankruptcy Court, E.D. Arkansas, 2007) (Work done by paralegals is compensable if it is work that would have been done by an attorney. If such hours were not compensable, then attorneys may be compelled to perform the duties that could otherwise be fulfilled by paralegals, thereby increasing the overall cost of legal services. Paralegal work that is purely clerical in nature is not reimbursable.)

- *Crump-Donahue v. U.S. Dept. of Agriculture*, 2007 WL 1702567 (U.S. District Court, E.D. Arkansas, 2007) (When a nonlawyer attempts to represent the interests of other persons, the practice constitutes the unauthorized practice of law and results in a nullity.)

- Herron *v. Jones*, 637 S.W.2d 569 (Supreme Court of Arkansas, 1982) (Conflict of interest allegation: an employee (a legal secretary) switches law firms in the same case. The court refuses to disqualify the current employer because confidentiality was not breached.)

- *In re Anderson*, 851 S.W.2d 408 (Supreme Court of Arkansas, 1993) (An attorney surrenders his license to practice law after a drug conviction and then goes to work as a paralegal in his father's law firm; readmission denied.)

Doing Legal Research In Arkansas Law

- **Statutes:** www.lexisnexis.com /hottopics/arcode/Default.asp
- **Cases:** opinions.aoc.arkansas.gov /WebLink8
- **Court Rules:** courts.arkansas.gov (click *Court Rules*)
- **General:** www.law.georgetown.edu /library/research/guides/arkansas.cfm

Finding Employment In Arkansas

- l.ar.bar.associationcareernetwork .com/Common/HomePage.aspx
- www.indeed.com/q-Paralegal-l -Arkansas-jobs.html
- www.simplyhired.com/k-paralegal-l -little-rock-ar-jobs.html

CALIFORNIA

ETHICS CODE AND OPINIONS IN CALIFORNIA

- **Attorneys: California Code:** *Rules of Professional Conduct*
  - rules.calbar.ca.gov/Rules /RulesofProfessionalConduct.aspx
  - www.law.cornell.edu/ethics/california .html
  - See also ethics links in Helpful Websites at the end of Chapter 5.
- **Attorneys: California Ethics Opinions**
  - ethics.calbar.ca.gov/Ethics/Opinions .aspx
  - www.lacba.org/showpage.cfm? pageid=427
  - www.sdcba.org/index.cfm?pg=Legal EthicsOpinionsIndex
- **Unauthorized Practice of Law in California**
  - www.calbar.ca.gov (enter *unauthorized practice of law* in search box)
  - § 6450(a) (California Business & Professions Code)
  - da.co.la.ca.us/pdf/UPLpublic.pdf
  - apps.calbar.ca.gov/mcleselfstudy /mcle_home.aspx?testID=29
  - ir.lawnet.fordham.edu/cgi/viewcontent .cgi?article=3572&context=flr
- **Paralegals and Other Nonattorneys: California**
  - *Rule 5.3.* California is considering the adoption of rules that would include Rule 5.3. For a discussion of the state's ethics Rule 5.3 ("Responsibilities Regarding Nonlawyer Assistants") in the California *Rules of Professional Conduct*, see Chapter 5.
  - Attorneys not in practice together who share office space and paralegal services must take reasonable steps to protect each client's confidences and secrets. State Bar of California, *Opinion 1997–150* (1997).
  - When a paralegal is authorized to represent a client before the Workers' Compensation Appeals Board, a law firm can use its paralegal to represent a client of the firm before this Board if the client consents and the firm supervises the paralegal. State Bar of California, *Opinion 1988–103*.
  - Attorneys must take steps to ensure that nonattorney employees understand their obligation not to disclose client confidences and secrets. State Bar of California, *Opinion 1979–50*.
  - A nonattorney can use a business card if it is used for identification rather than for solicitation of business. Los Angeles County Bar Ass'n, *Opinion 381*.
  - A law firm can pay a bonus to its paralegal as long as the bonus does not

involve a sharing of legal fees. Los Angeles Count Bar Ass'n, *Opinion 457* (11/20/89).

- A nonprofit legal services center for the elderly cannot advertise in a local newspaper the availability of "legal help" from "para-legal aides" trained by a local attorney. Legal help implies legal services. San Diego Bar Ass'n, *Opinion 1976–9* (7/1/76).
- A business that provides paralegal services to the public should have attorney supervision except for some purely ministerial tasks. San Diego Bar Ass'n, *Opinion 1983–7*.
- It is not the unauthorized practice of law for a paralegal to visit the homes of prospective clients for an attorney's estate and trust practice. She answers only those questions the attorney has trained her to answer. The attorney drafts any needed documents. Orange County Bar Ass'n, *Opinion 94–002*. (www.ocbar.org/AttorneyResources /EthicsOpinions.aspx).

Defining Legal Assistants/Paralegals In California

- § 6450(a) (California Business & Professions Code): "Paralegal" means a person who holds himself or herself out to be a paralegal, who is qualified by education, training, or work experience, who either contracts with or is employed by an attorney, law firm, corporation, governmental agency, or other entity, and who performs substantial legal work under the direction and supervision of an active member of the State Bar of California, as defined in Section 6060, or an attorney practicing law in the federal courts of this state, that has been specifically delegated by the attorney to him or her. Tasks performed by a paralegal include, but are not limited to, case planning, development, and management; legal research; interviewing clients; fact gathering and retrieving information; drafting and analyzing legal documents; collecting, compiling, and utilizing technical information to make an independent decision and recommendation to the supervising attorney; and representing clients before a state or federal administrative agency if that representation is permitted by statute, court rule, or administrative rule or regulation.
- *Business and Professions Code § 6450, Legal Malpractice Claims, And You: A Primer for Paralegals* (www.cel.sfsu.edu /paralegal/pdfs/6450.pdf).

Who Can Use the Title of *Paralegal* or *Legal Assistant* in California?

- § 6452(a) (California Business & Professions Code): It is unlawful for a person to identify himself or herself as a paralegal on any advertisement, letterhead, business card or sign, or elsewhere unless he or she has met the qualifications of. . . Section 6450 and performs all services under the direction and supervision of an attorney who is an active member of the State Bar of California or an attorney practicing law in the federal courts of this state who is responsible for all of the services performed by the paralegal. The business card of a paralegal shall include the name of the law firm where he or she is employed or a statement that he or she is employed by or contracting with a licensed attorney.

Legal Document Assistant And Unlawful Detainer Assistant In California

- § 6400 (California Business & Professions Code) Legal document assistant (LDA) and unlawful detainer assistant (UDA)
  - See Chapter 4
  - calda.org
  - www.lavote.net/clerk/unlawful _detainer_assistant.cfm

California Certification Of Paralegals

- www.cla-cas.org

Defining The Practice Of Law In California

- California *v. Landlords Professional Services*, 264 Cal. Rptr. 548, 550 (Court of Appeal, 4th District, 1990): Business and Professions Code section 6125 states: "No person shall practice law in this State unless he is an active member of the State Bar." Business and Professions Code section 6126, subdivision (a), provides: "Any person advertising or holding himself or herself out as practicing or entitled to practice law or otherwise practicing law who is not an active member of the State Bar, is guilty of a misdemeanor." The code provides no definition for the term "practicing law.". . . "[A]s the term is generally understood, the practice of law is the doing and performing services in a court of justice in any manner depending therein throughout its various stages and in conformity with the adopted rules of procedure. But in a larger sense it includes legal advice and counsel and the preparation of legal instruments and contracts by which legal rights are secured although such matter may or may not be [pending] in court.". . . [N]onetheless. . . "ascertaining whether a particular activity falls within this general definition may be a formidable endeavor.". . . In close cases, the courts have determined that the resolution of legal questions for another by advice and action is practicing law "if difficult or doubtful legal questions are involved which, to safeguard the public, reasonably demand the application of a trained legal mind."

- Becoming an attorney in California without going to law school § 6060 (e)(2)) (California Business & Professions Code): Studied law diligently and in good faith for at least four years in any of the following manners:

  (A) In a law school. . .
  (B) In a law office in this state and under the personal supervision of a member of the State Bar of California. . . It is the duty of the supervising attorney to render any periodic reports to the examining committee as the committee may require.

Paralegals (And Others) In California State And Federal Courts

(See the beginning of this appendix on how to find the full text of the opinions cited here, including WL opinions.)

- In *re Complex Asbestos Litigation*, 283 Cal. Rptr. 732 (California Court of Appeal, 1991) (A paralegal who switches jobs might cause the disqualification of his or her new employer to represent clients about whom the paralegal obtained confidential information while working at a prior (opposing) law firm. A rebuttable presumption exists that the paralegal shared this information with the new employer. The most likely way for the new employer to rebut this presumption, and hence for his employer to avoid disqualification, is to show that when the paralegal was hired, a Chinese wall was built around the paralegal with respect to any cases the paralegal worked on while at the prior employment.)
- *Devereux v. Latham & Watkins*, 38 Cal. Rptr. 2d 849 (California Court of Appeal, 1995) (A litigation paralegal sues her former law firm employer after the paralegal testified against the law firm in an overbilling case.)
- *Saret-Cook v. Gilbert, Kelly, Crowley & Jennett*, 88 Cal. Rptr. 2d 732 (California Court of Appeal, 1999) (A "fatal attraction" case. A paralegal loses her sexual-harassment case after having an affair with an office attorney.)
- People v. Gaines, 2004 WL 2386748 (California Court of Appeal, 2004) (It was not error for the prosecutor to

reject a paralegal as a juror. The paralegal had taken classes in criminal law and felt capable of informing people about criminal cases. The prosecutor may have reasonably believed there was a possibility that this juror would resist following the court's instructions in favor of his own conception of the law.)

- *In re White*, 18 Cal. Rptr 3d 444 (California Court of Appeal, 2004) (An attorney is disciplined. His health problems provide no excuse for authorizing a paralegal to sign his name on habeas corpus petitions that the attorney did not read.)
- *Rico v. Mitsubishi*, 10 Cal. Rptr. 3d 601 (California Court of Appeal 2004) (The attorney's work-product doctrine covers documents created not only by an attorney, but also by his agents or employees, including his paralegal.)
- *In re Hessinger & Associates*, 192 Bankruptcy Reporter 211 (U.S. Bankruptcy Court, N.D. California, 1996) (A law firm unethically allowed paralegals to complete bankruptcy petitions and to perform other work of a legal character without adequate attorney supervision. The firm was organized much like a production line, with little or no review by attorneys. The law firm argued that "everybody does it," that is, all large consumer bankruptcy firms rely on paralegals to perform a large amount of the work required for filing a bankruptcy petition, and in all such firms the paralegals do so with only minimal attorney supervision. While this may well be true, the court will not condone an unethical practice merely because most consumer bankruptcy firms are engaging in it.)
- *Oakland v. McCullough*; 53 Cal. Rptr. 2d 531 (California Court of Appeal, 1st District, 1996) (A claim for paralegal fees is rejected because of a failure to provide documentation in support of the claim.)
- *Sanford v. GMRI, Inc.*, 2005 WL 4782697 (U.S. District Court, E.D. California, 2005) (A request for paralegal fees is challenged in part because of doubts on whether the paralegal complied with the new California law on education and CLE requirements of paralegals.)
- *In re Stebbins*, 2007 WL 1877894 (U.S. Bankruptcy Court, E.D. California, 2007) (Paralegal fees are denied for basic services, such as entering data in the computer, preparing a transmittal letter, or faxing a letter. Such tasks are included in general office overhead and are not appropriately charged as paralegal or attorney time.)

- *Robinson v. Chand*, 2007 WL 1300450 (U.S. District Court, E.D. California, 2007) (Counsel seeks to bill at attorney rates work more appropriately handled by paralegals or secretaries. This work includes preparing cover sheets, converting files to PDFs, e-filing documents, mailing documents, arranging for service of documents, scheduling matters, researching nonlegal issues such as business ownership, preparing boilerplate documents, and organizing case files.)

Doing Legal Research In California Law

- **Statutes:** www.leginfo.ca.gov/statute .html
- **Cases:** www.courts.ca.gov/opinions .htm
- **Court Rules:** www.courts.ca .gov/rules.htm
- **General:** guides.library.harvard .edu/CaliforniaLegalResearch

Finding Employment In California

- p.ca.associationcareernetwork .com/Common/HomePage.aspx
- legal.jobs.net/California.htm
- losangeles.craigslist.org/lgl
- www.indeed.com/q-Paralegal-l -California-jobs.html

COLORADO

ETHICS CODE AND OPINIONS IN COLORADO

- **Attorneys: Colorado Code:** *Rules of Professional Conduct*
  - www.cobar.org (enter *Rules of Professional Conduct* in search box)
  - www.law.cornell.edu/ethics/colorado .html
  - See also ethics links in Helpful Websites at the end of Chapter 5.
- **Attorneys: Colorado Ethics Opinions**
  - www.cobar.org/index.cfm/ID/20202 /CETH/Ethics
- **Unauthorized Practice of Law in Colorado**
  - www.coloradosupremecourt.us (enter *Understanding Practice of Law* in the search box).
  - www.cobar.org (enter *unauthorized practice of law* in search box)
  - ir.lawnet.fordham.edu/cgi/viewcontent .cgi?article=3572&context=flr
- **Paralegals and Other Nonattorneys: Colorado**
  - Paralegals must disclose their nonattorney status to everyone at the outset of any professional relationship.

They should be given no task that requires the exercise of unsupervised legal judgment. They can write letters and sign correspondence on attorney letterhead as long as their nonattorney status is clear and the correspondence does not contain legal opinions or give legal advice. They can have their own business cards with the name of the law firm on them if their nonattorney status is made clear. The services performed by the paralegal must supplement, merge with, and become part of the attorney's work product. Colorado Bar Ass'n, *Guidelines for the* Utilization *of Paralegals* (1986) (www.cobar .org/index.cfm/ID/106/subID/23108 /CLAS).

- *Rule 5.3.* For a discussion of the state's ethics Rule 5.3 ("Responsibilities Regarding Nonlawyer Assistants") in the Colorado *Rules of Professional Conduct*, see Chapter 5. For the text of 5.3 in Colorado, see www.cobar.org /index.cfm/ID/22202.
- *Rule 1.10 (Comment 4)*. The rule of imputed disqualification in Rule 1.10 "does not prohibit representation by others in the law firm where the person prohibited from involvement in a matter is a nonlawyer, such as a paralegal or legal secretary." Colorado *Rules of Professional Conduct*.
- *Rule 5.5 (Comment 2)*. Lawyers can employ the services of paraprofessionals and delegate tasks to them "so long as the lawyer supervises the delegated work and retains responsibility for their work."
- *Rule 5.5 (Comment 3)*. A lawyer may employ or contract with a disbarred or suspended lawyer to perform services that a law clerk, paralegal or other administrative staff may perform so long as the lawyer directly supervises the work.
- *Rule 6.1. G. Paralegal Pro Bono Opportunities*. Approved pro bono legal work for paralegals includes: (1) work taken on in conjunction with and under the supervision of an attorney working on a specific pro bono legal matter, or (2) work handled independently for an organization that provides pro bono legal opportunities, provided, however, that such participation does not create an attorney-client relationship and/or involve the paralegal's provision of legal advice.
- The names of support personnel can be printed on law firm letterhead, and they can be given their own business card as long as they reveal clearly that they are not attorneys. Colorado

Bar Ass'n, *Formal Ethics Opinion 84* (4/1990).

- The Colorado Bar Association has also approved *Guidelines for Utilization of Paralegals* in over twenty-one specialty areas of the law:
  - Bankruptcy paralegal
  - Civil litigation paralegal
  - Collections law paralegal
  - Commercial law paralegal
  - Corporate law paralegal
  - Corporate securities paralegal
  - Criminal litigation paralegal
  - Elder law paralegal
  - Environmental paralegal
  - Estate planning paralegal
  - Family law paralegal
  - Immigration law paralegal
  - Intellectual property paralegal
  - Juvenile litigation paralegal
  - Labor and employment law paralegal
  - Natural resource paralegal
  - Real estate paralegal
  - Social security/disability law paralegal
  - Special district law paralegal
  - Water law paralegal
  - Workers' compensation paralegal

  (www.cobar.org/group/index.cfm?category=106&EntityID=CLAS)

- *What a Nonlawyer Cannot Do* (Nancy Cohen, Office of Attorney Regulation Counsel). You cannot give legal advice to another individual. You cannot choose legal documents which you believe are appropriate for another individual (without supervision of an attorney). You cannot draft legal documents on behalf of another (without supervision of an attorney). You cannot interpret law for another individual's situation (without supervision of an attorney). You cannot prepare cases for trial for another (without supervision of an attorney). You cannot teach law at an ABA accredited law school. You cannot represent another individual in any legal transaction or matter (unless specifically allowed by Supreme Court rule or statute).

- Attorneys not in the same law firm sometimes share offices. To ensure confidentiality in such situations, the attorneys should avoid the sharing of staff to the extent possible, particularly secretaries and paralegals. Colorado Bar Assn., *Formal Ethics Opinion 89* (1999).

- A law firm can use a paralegal to represent clients at administrative proceedings when authorized by statute and when the practice of law is not involved. To ensure competent representation, the attorney must train and supervise the paralegal. Colorado Bar Ass'n, *Opinion 79* (2/18/89).

- An attorney shall continually monitor and supervise the work of assistants to assure that the services they render are performed competently and efficiently. Colorado Bar Ass'n, *Ethics Opinion 61* (10/23/82).

- It is also generally improper for an attorney to direct or even authorize another, such as an investigator or legal assistant, to record conversations surreptitiously. Colorado Bar Ass'n, *Formal Ethics Opinion 112* (2003).

Defining Legal Assistants/Paralegals In Colorado

- Legal assistants (also known as paralegals) are a distinguishable group of persons who assist attorneys in the delivery of legal services. Through formal education, training and experience, legal assistants have knowledge and expertise regarding the legal system and substantive and procedural law which will qualify them to do work of a legal nature under the direct supervision of a licensed attorney. Colorado Bar Association, *Colorado Paralegals—Proposed Guidelines to the Next Century and Beyond: Part I*, 63 (1996) (www.nala.org/terms.aspx).

Defining The Practice Of Law In Colorado

- Colorado Supreme Court, Office of Attorney Regulation, Understanding Practice of Law Issues (2011): The Colorado Supreme Court has defined the "practice of law" as "act[ing] in a representative capacity in protecting, enforcing, or defending the legal rights and duties of another and in counseling, advising and assisting [another] in connection with these rights and duties." The Court's words make clear that providing legal advice to another person constitutes the practice of law, as does the selection and drafting of legal documents for use by another person. A non-lawyer's exercise of legal discretion on behalf of another's legal interest is prohibited because of potential harm to the public. Thus, a non-lawyer generally cannot:

  1) Provide legal advice to another person;
  2) Select legal documents on behalf of another person;
  3) Draft legal documents on behalf of another person;
  4) Interpret the law as it may apply to another person's situation;
  5) Represent another person in any legal transaction or matter;
  6) Prepare another person's case for trial.

     www.coloradosupremecourt.us (enter *Understanding Practice of Law* in the search box).

- *Unauthorized Practice of Law Committee of the Supreme Court of Colorado v. Prog*, 761 P.2d 1111, 1115 (Supreme Court of Colorado, 1988): The determination of what acts do or do not constitute the practice of law is a judicial function. . . . While recognizing the difficulty of formulating and applying an all-inclusive definition of the practice of law, we have stated that "generally one who acts in a representative capacity in protecting, enforcing, or defending the legal rights and duties of another and in counseling, advising and assisting him in connection with these rights and duties is engaged in the practice of law." See also Denver Bar Ass'n v. PUC, 391 P.2d 467, 471 (Supreme Court of Colorado, 2001.)

- Rule 201.3(2). *Court Rules Annotated* (*West's Colorado Revised Statutes Annotated*): For purposes of this rule, "practice of law" means:. . . (i) furnishing legal counsel, drafting documents and pleadings, and interpreting and giving advice with respect to the law, and/or (ii) preparing, trying or presenting cases before courts, executive departments, administrative bureaus or agencies. . . .

Paralegals (And Others) In Colorado State And Federal Courts

(See the beginning of this appendix on how to find the full text of the opinions cited here, including WL opinions.)

- *Robinson v. Colorado State Lottery Div.*, 155 P.3d 409 (Colorado Court of Appeals, 2006) (To the extent plaintiff objects to the award of fees for work performed by paralegals, we note that the supreme court has also allowed for the recovery of time charged for paralegal services. *Am. Water Dev., Inc. v. City of Alamosa*, 874 P. 352 (Colo. 1994).)

- *Ryals v. City of Englewood*, 2014 WL 2566288 (U.S. District Court, Colorado, 2014) (The time of paralegal Jill Coil was billed at $200 per hour. She is an experienced paralegal who joined Faegre in 2007. I have no doubt that her work was good, and that she contributed important value to the team effort. But that billing rate is significantly higher than the paralegal and legal assistant rates requested and approved in other cases in this district, and I have no good basis [other than that is what Faegre charges] to find that it was the prevailing rate for experienced paralegal work in the Denver metropolitan market in 2013.)

- *Carr v. Fort Morgan School District*, 4 F. Supp. 2d 998 (U.S. District Court, Colorado, 1998) (Fees involving paralegal time are reduced by 15 percent due to lack of detail as to the work done and apparent duplication of effort.)
- People v. Fleischacker, 2013 WL 174442 (Colorado Court of Appeals, 2013) (A prospective juror whose daughter was a paralegal in the prosecutor's office was not removable for cause for implied bias.)
- *In re Estate of Myers*, 130 P.3d 1023 (Supreme Court of Colorado, 2006) (A paralegal obtained a copy of a credit report through a ruse; the law firm denied allegations that the actions of the paralegal reflected the firm's normal practice.)
- *Carbajal v. American Family*, 2006 WL 2988955 (U.S. District Court, Colorado, 2006) (The court denied the defendant's motion to disqualify the law firm of the plaintiff on the basis of a brief social relationship between one of the plaintiff's attorneys and a paralegal for the defendant. Although the relationship was not wise, it was limited and no disclosure of information about the litigation occurred.)
- *People v. Smith*, 74 P.3d 566 (The Office of the Presiding Disciplinary Judge, 2003) (An attorney failed to supervise his paralegal, in violation of disciplinary rule requiring a lawyer with direct supervisory authority over a nonlawyer employee to make reasonable efforts to ensure that the employee's conduct is compatible with the lawyer's professional obligations. The attorney failed to review the client's marriage dissolution file to determine if the paralegal was attending to the case as she described to the attorney. The inadequate supervision allowed the paralegal to conceal problems developing in the case, including failure to comply with court orders, and allowed the paralegal to engage in the unauthorized practice of law. The measures that should have been taken, such as an informal program of instructing or monitoring the paralegal, must often assume the likelihood that a particular nonlawyer employee may not yet have received adequate preparation for carrying out that person's responsibilities.)
- *People v. Milner*, 35 P.3d 670 (The Office of the Presiding Disciplinary Judge,

Colorado, 2001) (Although lacking in tact, a paralegal's single impolite outburst toward a client, to "stop calling and bitching," would not be a separate basis for attorney discipline.)

- *In re Gomez*, 259 Bankruptcy Reporter 379 (U.S. Bankruptcy Court, Colorado, 2001) (A bankruptcy petition preparer, by its use of trade name that included the word *paralegals* on its letterhead and brochures, in answering telephone, and in its communications with prospective customers, violated the Bankruptcy Code provision barring any petition preparer from using the word *legal* or "any similar term" in its advertisements.)

Doing Legal Research In Colorado Law

- **Statutes:** www.lexisnexis.com /hottopics/Colorado
- **Cases:** www.courts.state.co.us (enter *opinions* in the search box)
- **Court Rules:** www.courts.state.co.us (enter *court rules* in the search box)
- **General:** libguides.law.du.edu/cat .php?cid=10931

Finding Employment In Colorado

- www.legalstaff.com/Common /HomePage.aspx
- www.indeed.com/q-Paralegal-l -Colorado-jobs.html
- legal.jobs.net/Colorado.htm
- denver.craigslist.org/lgl

CONNECTICUT

ETHICS CODE AND OPINIONS IN CONNECTICUT

- **Attorneys: Connecticut Code:** *Rules of Professional Conduct*
  - www.jud.ct.gov/publications /PracticeBook/PB.pdf
  - www.law.cornell.edu/ethics/ct/code
  - www.law.cornell.edu/ethics/connecticut .html
  - See also ethics links in Helpful Websites at the end of Chapter 5.
- **Attorneys: Connecticut Ethics Opinions**
  - www.jud.ct.gov/sgc/ethics/default .htm
  - www.jud.ct.gov/Committees/ethics /opinions.htm
  - www.jud.ct.gov/sgcdecisions
- **Unauthorized Practice of Law in Connecticut**
  - www.ctbar.org (enter *unauthorized practice of law* in search box)
  - § 51-88 (Practice of law by persons not attorneys) Connecticut

General Statutes Annotated (www .cga.ct.gov/current/pub/chap_876 .htm#sec_51-88)
- www.ethicsandlawyering.com/Issues /files/ConnUPL.pdf
- digitalcommons.law.yale.edu /cgi/viewcontent.cgi?article=2910 &context=fss_papers
- ir.lawnet.fordham.edu/cgi/viewcontent .cgi?article=3572&context=flr

- **Paralegals and Other Nonattorneys: Connecticut**
  - *Rule 5.3.* For a discussion of the state's ethics Rule 5.3 ("Responsibilities Regarding Nonlawyer Assistants") in the Connecticut *Rules of Professional Conduct*, see Chapter 5.
  - *Rule 1.10 (Commentary).* The rule of imputed disqualification in Rule 1.10 "does not prohibit representation by others in the law firm where the person prohibited from involvement in a matter is a nonlawyer, such as a paralegal or legal secretary." Connecticut *Rules of Professional Conduct*.
  - *Rule 5.5 (Commentary).* Lawyers can assist independent paraprofessionals, who are authorized to provide particular law-related services.
  - Connecticut Bar Association, *Guidelines for Lawyers Who Employ or Retain Legal Assistants* (www.ctbar.org) (enter *Legal Assistant Guidelines* in the search box) *Guideline 1*: A lawyer should take all reasonable supervisory measures to make sure the legal assistant acts in accordance with the lawyer's ethical obligations. *Guideline 2*: Legal assistants can perform many tasks with lawyer supervision and review. They cannot give legal advice, accept cases, reject cases, or set legal fees. They may appear before adjudicatory bodies if authorized to do so. They may act as a witness at will executions. They may attend real estate closings alone but can act only as a messenger to deliver and pick up documents and funds. They cannot express any independent opinion or judgment about execution of the documents, changes in adjustments or price, or other matters involving documents or funds. (See also *Informal Opinion 96–16* below.) *Guideline 3:* The lawyer should take reasonable measures to ensure that all client confidences are protected by the legal assistant. *Guideline 4:* The lawyer should take reasonable measures to ensure and that third persons are aware upon first contact with a legal assistant that the latter is not licensed to practice law. *Guideline 5:* The name

and title of a legal assistant may appear on the lawyer's letterhead and on business cards identifying the lawyer's firm. *Guideline 6:* A lawyer must take reasonable measures to ensure that the legal assistant does not create a conflict of interest due to current or prior employment, or to other business or personal interests. *Guideline 7:)* A lawyer shall not split legal fees with a legal assistant or pay a legal assistant for the referral of legal work. *Guideline 8:* If a client consents, the lawyer can charge a reasonable and separate charge for legal assistant work. *Guideline 9:* A lawyer shall not form a partnership with a legal assistant if any of the partnership's activities consist of the practice of law. *Guideline 10:* A lawyer should encourage the legal assistant's participation in continuing education and pro bono publico activities. See also *Lawyers' Professional Responsibility Obligations Concerning Paralegals*, 59 Connecticut Bar Journal 425 (1985).

- Section 51–86 of *Connecticut General Statutes Annotated* covers solicitation by nonattorneys: (a) A person who has not been admitted as an attorney in this state under the provisions of section 51–80 shall not solicit, advise, request or induce another person to cause an action for damages to be instituted, from which action or from which person the person soliciting, advising, requesting or inducing the action may, by agreement or otherwise, directly or indirectly, receive compensation from such other person or such person's attorney, or in which action the compensation of the attorney instituting or prosecuting the action, directly or indirectly, depends upon the amount of the recovery therein. (b) Any person who violates any provision of this section shall be fined not more than one hundred dollars or imprisoned not more than six months or both.

- An attorney may use a paralegal as a messenger to deliver and pick up already prepared documents and funds required for a real estate closing. The supervising attorney does not have to be present. The paralegal can communicate information or questions from an attorney in the firm to the buyer's attorney. The paralegal, however, must not provide information or give an independent opinion regarding the legal implications or sufficiency of any of the documents. Connecticut Bar Ass'n, *Informal*

Opinion 96–16 (7/3/96). See also Guideline 2 above.

- A government attorney is not relieved of the obligation to exercise independent professional judgment simply because the attorney is under the supervision and direction of a government paralegal (a "supervisory paralegal specialist"). Connecticut Bar Ass'n, *Informal Opinion 00–9* (4/27/00).

- A law firm can take a new case even though one of its nonlawyer assistants worked on the other side of the same case while employed at a different firm so long as the employee has not already disclosed confidential information about the case learned while at the other firm and is screened from the case at the current firm. It is important that the paralegal not disclose, intentionally or inadvertently, information relating to representation of the former client and not otherwise work against the interest of the former client on the same or a substantially related matter. Connecticut Bar Ass'n, *Informal Opinion 00–23* (12/27/00) (2000 WL 33157218).

- Other ethics opinions: Paralegals can have their own business cards if their nonattorney status is clear, *Opinion 85–17* (11/20/85). It is unethical for an attorney to instruct a nonattorney to make misrepresentations to the public, *Informal Opinion 95–4* (1/6/95).

Defining Legal Assistants/Paralegals In Connecticut

- A legal assistant is a person, qualified through education, training, or work experience, who is employed or retained by a lawyer, law office, governmental agency, or other entity in a capacity or function which involves the performance under the ultimate direction and supervision of an attorney, of specifically delegated substantive legal work, which work, for the most part, requires a sufficient knowledge of legal concepts that, absent such assistant, the attorney would perform the task. Connecticut Bar Ass'n, *Guidelines for Lawyers Who Employ or Retain Legal Assistants*, 1.

Defining The Practice Of Law In Connecticut

- Connecticut General Statutes, Rules for the Superior Court, § 2-44A (a) The practice of law is ministering to

the legal needs of another person and applying legal principles and judgment to the circumstances or objectives of that person. This includes, but is not limited to:. . . (2) Giving advice or counsel to persons concerning or with respect to their legal rights or responsibilities or with regard to any matter involving the application of legal principles to rights, duties, obligations or liabilities. (3) Drafting any legal document or agreement involving or affecting the legal rights of a person.

- *In re Darlene C*, 717 A. 2d 1242, 1246 (Supreme Court of Connecticut, 1998): While acknowledging that attempts to define the practice of law "have not been particularly successful," the court nonetheless observed that determining the legal theory of a case, drafting the papers necessary to commence a legal action, checking the various possible legal grounds, signing the pleadings and submitting them to the court are acts that are commonly understood to constitute the practice of law.

- *State Bar Ass'n of Connecticut v. the Connecticut Bank and Trust Co.*, 140 A.2d 863, 870, 69 A.L.R.2d 394 (Supreme Court of Errors of Connecticut, 1958): The practice of law consists in no small part of work performed outside of any court and having no immediate relation to proceedings in court. It embraces the giving of legal advice on a large variety of subjects and the preparation of legal instruments covering an extensive field. Although such transactions may have no direct connection with court proceedings, they are always subject to subsequent involvement in litigation. They require in many aspects a high degree of legal skill and great capacity for adaptation to difficult and complex situations. No valid distinction can be drawn between the part of the work of the lawyer which involves appearance in court and the part which involves advice and the drafting of instruments.

Paralegals (And Others) In Connecticut State And Federal Courts

(See the beginning of this appendix on how to find the full text of the opinions cited here, including WL opinions.)

- *Conn. State Dept. of Social Services v. Thompson*, 289 F. Supp. 2d 198 (U.S. District Court, Connecticut, 2003) (The better practice is for the paralegals to keep contemporaneous time records. Had they done so, the fees awarded in this case would be larger.)

- *Powell v. Harriott*, 2006 WL 2349450 (U.S. District Court, Connecticut, 2006) (The request for paralegal fees contains no information about the skills or experience of the firm's paralegals, rendering it difficult for the court to discern why they should be awarded above an average hourly rate.)
- *Haye v. Ashcroft*, 2004 WL 1936204 (U.S. District Court, Connecticut, 2004) (A suspended attorney may assist a licensed attorney as a paralegal so long as the attorney exercises close supervision and retains responsibility for the work of the suspended attorney.)
- *Statewide Grievance Committee v. Harris*, 239 Conn. 256, 683 A. 2d 1362 (Supreme Court of Connecticut, 1996) (Injunction against a paralegal charged with unauthorized practice of law in violation of General Statutes § 51–88. He ran an advertisement in the *Hartford Courant*, titled "Uncontested Pro Se Divorce," in which he represented that "Paralegals prepare all papers for your signing and step you through the self-help divorce.")
- *In re Darlene C*, 717 A.2d 1242 (Supreme Court of Connecticut, 1998) (Nonlawyer representatives who work for the state prepare, sign, and file petitions for termination of parental rights. Because a Connecticut statute authorizes these activities, they do not constitute the unauthorized practice of law.)
- *Rivera v. Chicago Pneumatic Tool Co.*, 1991 WL 151892 (Connecticut Superior Court, 8/5/91) (The trial court denies a motion to disqualify the plaintiff's attorney who hired a paralegal formerly employed by defendant's attorney even though the paralegal had been extensively involved in litigation concerning the defendant. There must be a sufficient Chinese wall built around such a paralegal to ensure that confidences are not divulged.)
- *Gazda v. Olin Corp.*, 5 CSCR 227 (1/18/90) (Legal secretary switches firms. Disqualification is denied where reasonable efforts were taken to ensure that the nonattorney employee would not divulge any confidences she might have acquired at the former firm.)

Doing Legal Research In Connecticut Law

- **Statutes:** http://www.cga.ct.gov/asp/menu/statutes.asp
- **Cases:** www.jud.ct.gov/jud2.htm
- **Court Rules:** www.jud.ct.gov/pb.htm
- **General:** www.jud.ct.gov/lawlib/legalresearch.htm

Finding Employment In Connecticut

- www.indeed.com/q-Paralegal-l-Connecticut-jobs.html
- www.careerbuilder.com/jobs/ct/keyword/paralegal
- www.careerjet.com/paralegal-jobs/connecticut-372.html
- newhaven.craigslist.org/lgl

DELAWARE

ETHICS CODE AND OPINIONS IN DELAWARE

- **Attorneys: Delaware Code:** *Rules of Professional Conduct*
  - courts.delaware.gov/Rules/DLRPCFebruary2010.pdf
  - www.law.cornell.edu/ethics/delaware.html
  - courts.delaware.gov/forms/download.aspx?id=39428
  - See also ethics links in Helpful Websites at the end of Chapter 5.
- **Attorneys: Delaware Ethics Opinions**
  - www.dsba.org/publications/ethics-opinions-index
  - www.dcbar.org/bar-resources/legal-ethics/opinions/index.cfm
- **Unauthorized Practice of Law in Delaware**
  - courts.delaware.gov/odc/uplr.stm
  - courts.delaware.gov/odc
  - ir.lawnet.fordham.edu/cgi/viewcontent.cgi?article=3572&context=flr
  - courts.delaware.gov/odc/rules.stm
- **Paralegals and Other Nonattorneys: Delaware**
  - *Rule 5.3.* a discussion of the state's ethics Rule 5.3 ("Responsibilities Regarding Nonlawyer Assistants") in the Delaware *Rules of Professional Conduct*, see Chapter 5.
  - *Rule 1.10 (Comment 4).* The rule of imputed disqualification in Rule 1.10 "does not prohibit representation by others in the law firm where the person prohibited from involvement in a matter is a nonlawyer, such as a paralegal or legal secretary." Delaware *Rules of Professional Conduct*.
  - *Rule 5.5 (Comment 2).* Lawyers can employ the services of paraprofessionals and delegate tasks to them "so long as the lawyer supervises the delegated work and retains responsibility for their work."
  - *Rule 5.5 (Comment 3).* Lawyers can assist independent paraprofessionals, who are authorized to provide particular law-related services.

- A law firm cannot allow its paralegal to represent a client before the Industrial Accident Board on a worker's compensation case. Delaware State Bar Ass'n, *Opinion 1985–3*.
- A nonattorney law clerk cannot work on a case where the other side is represented by the clerk's former employer. The clerk must be screened from involvement in the case. Delaware State Bar Ass'n, *Opinion 1986–1*.

Defining Legal Assistants/Paralegals In Delaware

- *McMackin v. McMackin*, 651 A.2d 778 (Delaware Family Court, 1993): Persons who, although not members of the legal profession, are qualified through education, training, or work experience, are employed or retained by a lawyer, law office, governmental agency, or other entity in a capacity or function which involves the performance, under the direction and supervision of an attorney, of specifically delegated substantive legal work, which work, for the most part, requires a sufficient knowledge of legal concepts such that, absent that legal assistant, the attorney would perform the task. (Citing the American Bar Association).

Delaware Certification Of Paralegals

- www.deparalegals.org/dcp-program.php

Defining The Practice Of Law In Delaware

- *Delaware State Bar Ass'n v. Alexander*, 386 A.2d 652, 661, 12 A.L.R.4th 637 (Supreme Court of Delaware, 1978): In general, one is deemed to be practicing law whenever he furnishes to another advice or service under circumstances which imply the possession and use of legal knowledge and skill. The practice of law includes "all advice to clients, and all actions taken for them in matters connected with the law.... Practice of law includes the giving of legal advice and counsel, and the preparation of legal instruments and contracts [by] which legal rights are secured.... Where the rendering of services for another involves the use of legal knowledge or skill on his behalf where legal advice is required and is availed of or rendered in connection with such services these services necessarily constitute or include the practice of law.".... "In determining what is the practice of law, it is well settled that it is the character of the acts performed and not the place where they are done that is decisive. The practice of law is not, therefore, necessarily limited to the conduct of cases in court but is engaged in whenever and wherever legal knowledge, training, skill and ability are required."

- Delaware Rules of Court, *Rules of the Board on the Unauthorized Practice of Law*, Rule 4: In evaluating possible unauthorized practice of law, the following types of conduct shall be examined: (i) giving legal advice on matters relating to Delaware law, (ii) drafting legal documents or pleadings for a person or entity (other than one's self) reflecting upon Delaware law, for use in a Delaware legal tribunal or governmental agency, unless the drafting of such documents or pleadings has been supervised by a person authorized to practice law in the State of Delaware, (iii) appearing as legal counsel for, or otherwise representing, a person or entity (other than one's self) in a Delaware legal tribunal or governmental agency, (iv) holding one's self out as being authorized to practice law in the State of Delaware, (v) engaging in an activity which has traditionally been performed exclusively by persons authorized to practice law. (courts.delaware.gov/odc/rules.stm)

Paralegals (And Others) In Delaware State And Federal Courts

(See the beginning of this appendix on how to find the full text of the opinions cited here, including WL opinions.)

- *In re Worldwide Direct*, 316 Bankruptcy Reporter 637 (U.S. Bankruptcy Court, Delaware, 2004) ("The past two decades have witnessed a remarkable transformation of the legal market. . . . A critical component of this transformed legal market is the incorporation of paralegals providing a wide range of legal services into the law firm tapestry, a component brought about by the cost-effectiveness of employing an intermediate level of professional to handle matters beyond the ken of the average legal secretary but not demanding the full education, experience, or skill of a licensed attorney." (quoting *Busy Beaver*, 19 F.3d 849 (3d Cir. 1994).)
- *In the Matter of the Estate of Ross*, 1996 WL 74731 (Court of Chancery of Delaware, 1996) ("In an age in which attorney fees are high, it is always welcome to see that good use is made of paralegals, with a resulting benefit to the client.")

- *Ciappa Const., Inc. v. Innovative Property Resources*, 2007 WL 1705632 (Delaware Superior Court, 2007) (Delaware courts have routinely included fees charged for a legal assistant's time when granting attorney's fees.)
- *Spark v. MBNA*, 289 F. Supp. 2d 510 (U.S. District Court, Delaware, 2003) (Counsel has submitted no evidence of the reasonable hourly rate for paralegal time to justify a charge of $175 per hour.)
- *Spark v. MBNA Corp.*, 157 F. Supp. 2d 330 (U.S. District Court, Connecticut, 2001) (The request for paralegal fees did not set out information on the education and experience of the paralegals or on comparable billing rates for this professional in the market.)
- *In re Hull*, 767 A.2d 197 (Supreme Court of Delaware, 2001) (Attorney is disciplined for failure to supervise her legal assistant and for paying the latter an improper commission.)
- *In re Arons*, 756 A.2d 867 (Supreme Court of Delaware, 2000) (It is the unauthorized practice of law for nonattorney lay advocates to represent families of children with disabilities in "due process" hearings held by Delaware Department of Public Instruction on federal disability issues; Congress did not authorize such lay representation.)
- *In re Feuerhake*, 89 A.3d 1058 (Supreme Court of Delaware, 2014) (A suspended attorney can act as a paralegal but cannot have any contact with clients, prospective clients, or witnesses.)
- *Dickens v. Taylor*, 464 F. Supp. 2d 341 (U.S. District Court, Delaware, 2006) (Prison authorities are required to assist inmates in the preparation and filing of meaningful legal papers by providing prisoners with adequate law libraries or adequate assistance from persons trained in the law—at least access to a prison paralegal or paging system by which to obtain legal materials.)

Doing Legal Research In Delaware Law

- **Statutes:** delcode.delaware.gov
- **Cases:** courts.delaware.gov/opinions
- **Court Rules:** courts.state.de.us
- **General:** www.law.georgetown.edu/library/research/guides/delaware.cfm

Finding Employment In Delaware

- delaware.craigslist.org/lgl
- www.indeed.com/q-Litigation-Paralegal-l-Delaware-jobs.html
- www.simplyhired.com/k-paralegal-l-wilmington-de-jobs.html

DISTRICT OF COLUMBIA

ETHICS CODE AND OPINIONS IN DISTRICT OF COLUMBIA

- **Attorneys: District of Columbia Code:** *Rules of Professional Conduct*
  - www.dcbar.org/bar-resources/legal-ethics/index.cfm
  - www.law.cornell.edu/ethics/dc.html
  - www.dcbar.org/attorney-discipline/disciplinary-decisions.cfm
  - See also ethics links in Helpful Websites at the end of Chapter 5.
- **Attorneys: District of Columbia Ethics Opinions**
  - www.dcbar.org/bar-resources/legal-ethics/index.cfm
- **Unauthorized Practice of Law in District of Columbia**
  - www.dcbar.org (enter *unauthorized practice of law* in search box)
  - ir.lawnet.fordham.edu/cgi/viewcontent.cgi?article=3572&context=flr
- **Paralegals and Other Nonattorneys: District of Columbia**
  - *Rule 5.3.* For a discussion of the state's ethics Rule 5.3 ("Responsibilities Regarding Nonlawyer Assistants") in the District of Columbia *Rules of Professional Conduct*, see Chapter 5.
  - *Rule 5.4.* A nonattorney *can* be a partner in a law firm. Hence a District of Columbia law firm *can* share fees with nonattorneys under the guidelines of Rule 5.4. For example, a lobbyist or an economist could form a partnership with an attorney. The nonattorney must agree to abide by the *Rules of Professional Conduct*. District of Columbia *Rules of Professional Conduct*.
  - *Rule 1.10 (Comment 19).* The rule of imputed disqualification in Rule 1.10 is treated differently with regard to a paralegal or legal assistant.
  - *Rule 5.5 (Comment 2).* Lawyers can employ the services of paralegals and delegate tasks to them "so long as the lawyer supervises the delegated work and retains responsibility for their work."
  - *Rule 5.5 (Comment 3).* Lawyers can assist independent paraprofessionals, who are authorized to provide particular law-related services.
  - A paralegal who switches firms must be screened from any cases involving clients represented by both firms. This will protect confidences and avoid imputed disqualification. D.C. Bar, *Opinion 227*, 21 Bar Report 2 (August/September 1992).

- A lawyer who employs a nonlawyer former government employee must screen that person from matters that are the same as, or substantially related to, matters on which the nonlawyer assisted government lawyers in representing a government client. D.C. Bar, *Opinion 285* (November 1998).
- Nonattorneys can have a business card that prints the name of the law firm where they work as long as their nonattorney status is clear. D.C. Bar, *Opinion 19*. See also *Speaking of Ethics*, Bar Report 2 (February/March 1988).
- A law firm can share a "success fee" with nonattorney experts on a case. "The fact that the portion of the "success fee" payable to the nonlawyer consultants flows from the client through the law firm does not result in a "sharing" by the law firm of legal fees with a nonlawyer proscribed by Rule 5.4" *Opinion 233*, Bar Report 2 (June/July 1993).
- A law firm may not compensate a nonlawyer employee, hired to work on designated class action claims against defendants who are members of a particular industry, based on a percentage of the profits earned from those cases. D.C. Bar, *Opinion 332* (February 2004).
- A nonattorney who is an officer, director, or employee of a corporation can appear for that corporation in the settlement of any landlord-and-tenant case. If, however, the corporation files an answer, cross-claim, or counterclaim, the corporation must be represented by an attorney. D.C. Court of Appeals, Rule 49(c)(8), *Rules of the District of Columbia Court of Appeals*.
- Law clerks, paralegals and summer associates are not practicing law where they do not engage in providing advice to clients or otherwise hold themselves out to the public as having authority or competence to practice law. D.C. Court of Appeals, Commentary to Rule 49, *Rules of the District of Columbia Court of Appeals*.

Defining The Practice Of Law In The District Of Columbia

- Rule 49(b)(2) (*Court Rules of the District of Columbia Court of Appeals*): "Practice of Law" means the provision of professional legal advice or services where there is a client relationship of trust or reliance. One is presumed to be practicing law when engaging in any of the following conduct on behalf of another: (A) Preparing any legal document, including any deeds, mortgages, assignments, discharges, leases, trust instruments or any other instruments intended to affect interests in real or personal property, wills, codicils, instruments intended to affect the disposition of property of decedents' estates, other instruments intended to affect or secure legal rights, and contracts except routine agreements incidental to a regular course of business; (B) Preparing or expressing legal opinions; (C) Appearing or acting as an attorney in any tribunal; (D) Preparing any claims, demands or pleadings of any kind, or any written documents containing legal argument or interpretation of law, for filing in any court, administrative agency or other tribunal; (E) Providing advice or counsel as to how any of the activities described in sub-paragraph (A) through (D) might be done or whether they were done, in accordance with applicable law. . . .

Paralegals (And Others) In District Of Columbia Courts

(See the beginning of this appendix on how to find the full text of the opinions cited here, including WL opinions.)

- *Minebea Co., Ltd. v. Papsti*, 374 F. Supp. 2d 231 (U.S. District Court, District of Columbia, 2005) (The party's counsel of record, their legal assistants, interpreters, and technical personnel were "essential" to the presentation of the party's case, and therefore could not be excluded from courtroom pursuant to a sequestration rule.)
- *Role Models America, Inc. v. Brownlee*, 353 F.3d 962 (U.S. Court of Appeals, D.C. Circuit, 2004) (Requested rates for the services of law clerks and legal assistants would be reduced by 25 percent, where the prevailing party did not submit information about the prevailing market rate in the Washington area, refer to either of two matrices upon which court had allowed reliance in past, or submit an affidavit dealing with the non-attorneys' experience and education.)
- *Palmer v. Rice*, 2005 WL 1662130 (U.S. District Court, District of Columbia, 2005) ("A paralegal, having performed classic paralegal duties such as drafting a letter to a client or cite checking a motion for summary judgment, may also make copies of those documents or send them in the mail once they have been approved by the supervising lawyer. In other words, it is impossible for a reviewing court to draw distinctions this fine and require that every task be delegated to the lowest competent level, no matter how small the task and no matter the time that may be wasted in accomplishing such delegation.")
- *In re Meese*, 907 F.2d 1192, 1202 (U.S. Court of Appeals, D.C. Circuit, 1990) (The rates billed for paralegals are reasonable; however, we deduct $4,253 for services billed at these rates that were of a purely clerical nature.)
- *Fonville v. District of Columbia*, 230 Federal Rules Decisions 38 (U.S. District Court, District of Columbia, 2005) (It is improper for a paralegal to sign answers to interrogatories, rather than the party to whom interrogatories are directed.)
- *In Re Ryan*, 670 A.2d 375 (District of Columbia Court of Appeals, 1996) (Attorney is disciplined in part because of her overreliance on paralegals who had no paralegal training.)
- *In Re Davis*, 650 A.2d 1319 (District of Columbia Court of Appeals, 1994) (Disbarred attorney ordered to perform 250 hours of community service as a paralegal.)

Doing Legal Research In District Of Columbia Law

- **Statutes:** dccouncil.us/legislation
- **Cases:** www.dccourts.gov/internet/welcome.jsf (enter *opinions* in search box)
- **Court Rules:** www.dccourts.gov/internet/appellate/dccarules.jsf
- **General:** www.law.georgetown.edu/library/research/guides/dc-in-depth.cfm

Finding Employment In The District Of Columbia

- www.indeed.com/q-Paralegal-l-Washington,-DC-jobs.html
- www.hg.org/legal_jobs_district-of-columbia.asp
- www.dcbar.org/about-the-bar/employment-opportunities/index.cfm

FLORIDA

ETHICS CODE AND OPINIONS IN FLORIDA

- **Attorneys: Florida Code:** *Rules of Professional Conduct*
  - www.floridabar.org (type *Rules of Professional Conduct* in the search box)
  - www.law.cornell.edu/ethics/florida.html
  - www.sunethics.com
  - See also ethics links in Helpful Websites at the end of Chapter 5.

- **Attorneys: Florida Ethics Opinions**
  - www.floridabar.org/tfb/TFBETOpin.nsf/EthicsIndex?OpenForm
  - www.floridabar.org (click *Ethics*)
- **Unauthorized Practice of Law: Florida**
  - www.floridabar.org (enter *unauthorized practice of law* in search box)
  - ir.lawnet.fordham.edu/cgi/viewcontent.cgi?article=3572&context=flr
- **Paralegals and Other Nonattorneys: Florida**
  - *Rule 4-5.3.* For a discussion of the state's ethics Rule 5.3 ("Responsibilities Regarding Nonlawyer Assistants") in the Florida *Rules of Professional Conduct*, see Chapter 5. Florida has added this section to 4-5.3: Ultimate Responsibility of Lawyer. Although paralegals or legal assistants may perform the duties delegated to them by the lawyer without the presence or active involvement of the lawyer, the lawyer shall review and be responsible for the work product of the paralegals or legal assistants (4-5.3(d)).
  - *Rule 4-1.10 (Comment).* The rule of imputed disqualification in Rule 4-1.10 "does not prohibit representation by others in the law firm where the person prohibited from involvement in a matter is a nonlawyer, such as a paralegal or legal secretary." Florida *Rules of Professional Conduct.*
  - *Rule 4-5.5 (Comment 2).* Lawyers can employ the services of paralegals and delegate tasks to them "so long as the lawyer supervises the delegated work and retains responsibility for their work."
  - Rule 10–2.1(a)(2) (Rules Governing... the Unlicensed Practice of Law): It shall constitute the unlicensed practice of law for a person who does not meet the definition of paralegal or legal assistant as set forth elsewhere in these rules to offer or provide legal services directly to the public or for a person who does not meet the definition of paralegal or legal assistant as set forth elsewhere in these rules to use the title paralegal, legal assistant, or other similar term in providing legal services or legal forms preparation services directly to the public. (www.floridabar.org/divexe/rrtfb.nsf/WContents?OpenView).
  - Paralegals can have their own business cards. They may also be listed on a law firm's letterhead, but a title indicating their nonattorney status should appear beneath their name. Attorneys should not hold their paralegals out as "certified" if they are not. Florida Bar, *Opinion 86-4* (8/1/86).

See also Florida Bar, *Opinion 71–39* (10/20/71) (nonattorney employee can use the law firm's name on his business card).
- Law firms can outsource paralegal functions to nonattorneys in India if adequate supervision is maintained, conflicts of interest are avoided, confidentiality is preserved, client consent is obtained, and billing arrangements are proper. *Proposed Advisory Opinion 07-2* (9/7/07).
- When a nonattorney changes jobs to an opposing law firm, the old and new employers must admonish him or her not to reveal any confidences or secrets obtained during prior employment, and the new employer must take steps to ensure there is no breach of confidentiality by this employee. Florida Bar, *Opinion 86–5* (8/1/86).
- A law firm can allow a nonattorney to conduct a real estate closing if certain conditions are met, e.g., an attorney is available (in person or by telephone) to answer legal questions, the nonattorney performs only ministerial acts (he or she must not give legal advice or make any legal decisions), and the client consents to having the closing handled by a nonattorney. Florida Bar, *Opinion 89–5* (11/1989) (overruling *Opinion 73–43*).
- Attorneys cannot delegate to lay persons the handling of negotiations with insurance company adjustors regarding claims of the attorney's clients. Florida Bar, *Opinion 74–35* (9/23/74).
- Preparing living trust documents constitutes the practice of law. It is the unauthorized practice of law for a nonattorney to decide whether a living trust is appropriate, and to prepare and execute the documents involved. *Florida Bar Re: Advisory Opinion on Nonlawyer Preparation of Living Trusts*, 613 So. 2d 426 (Supreme Court of Florida, 1992). See also *Florida Bar Re: Advisory Opinion on Nonlawyer Preparation of Residential Leases Up to One Year in Duration*, 602 So. 2d 914 (Supreme Court of Florida, 1992), and *Florida Bar Re: Nonlawyer Preparation of and Representation of Landlord in Uncontested Residential Evictions*, 605 So. 2d 868 (Supreme Court of Florida, 1992).
- It is ethically improper for a law firm to delegate to nonattorneys the handling of negotiations with adjusters on claims of the firm's clients. Florida Bar, *Ethics Opinion 74–35* (9/23/74).

But the nonlawyer employee can transmit information from the attorney. "For example, the nonlawyer employee may call the adjuster and inform the adjuster that the attorney will settle the matter for X. If the adjuster comes back with a counteroffer, the nonlawyer employee must inform the attorney. The employee cannot be given a range in which to settle." *Ethically Speaking.* The Florida Bar News, September, 15, 1991, at 15.
- An attorney can allow a supervised nonattorney to conduct an initial interview of a prospective client if his or her nonattorney status is disclosed to the client and only factual information is obtained. Florida Bar, *Opinion 88–6* (4/15/88).
- Other Florida Bar opinions involving nonattorneys: *Opinion 88–15* (10/1/88) (sharing office space with nonattorneys); *Opinion 87–11* (4/15/88) (nonattorney signing pleadings); *Opinion 70–62* (2/12/71) (a law firm cannot delegate anything that requires personal judgment to a nonattorney employee); *Opinion 68–58* (1/17/69) (nonattorney employees of a law firm can be part of a retirement plan funded from firm profits); *Opinion 73–41* (3/11/74) (nonattorneys cannot take depositions); *Opinion 76–33* (3/15/77) (an attorney must not overbill for paralegal time). *Opinion 02–1* (1/11/02) (attorney may not give a bonus to a nonlawyer employee solely based on the number of hours worked by the employee); *Opinion 02–8* (1/18/04) (attorney may not enter into a referral arrangement with a nonlawyer who is a securities dealer to refer the attorney's clients to the securities dealer, who would then pay the attorney a portion of the advisory fee for the clients referred).

Defining Paralegals/Legal Assistants In Florida

- Rule 10–2.1(b) (Rules Regulating the Florida Bar): A paralegal or legal assistant is a person qualified by education, training, or work experience, who works under the supervision of a member of The Florida Bar and who performs specifically delegated substantive legal work for which a member of The Florida Bar is responsible.
- § 57.104 (Florida Statutes Annotated): In any action in which attorneys' fees are to be determined or awarded by the court, the court shall consider, among other things, time and labor of any legal

assistants who contributed nonclerical, meaningful legal support to the matter involved and who are working under the supervision of an attorney. For purposes of this section "legal assistant" means a person, who under the supervision and direction of a licensed attorney engages in legal research, and case development or planning in relation to modifications or initial proceedings, services, processes, or applications; or who prepares or interprets legal documents or selects, compiles, and uses technical information from references such as digests, encyclopedias, or practice manuals and analyzes and follows procedural problems that involve independent decisions (www.leg.state.fl.us/statutes).

Who Can Use the Title of *Paralegal* or *Legal Assistant* in Florida?

■ Rule 10–2.1(a)(2) (Rules Governing . . . the Unlicensed Practice of Law): It shall constitute the unlicensed practice of law for a person who does not meet the definition of paralegal or legal assistant as set forth elsewhere in these rules to offer or provide legal services directly to the public or for a person who does not meet the definition of paralegal or legal assistant as set forth elsewhere in these rules to use the title paralegal, legal assistant, or other similar term in providing legal services or legal forms preparation services directly to the public (www.floridabar.org/divexe /rrtfb.nsf/WContents?OpenView).

Registration Of Paralegals In Florida

■ www.floridasupremecourt.org (click *Search* and enter *registered paralegal* in the search box)
■ www.flabar.org (enter *paralegal* in the search box)

Code of Ethics for Florida Registered Paralegals (FRP)

■ *Rule 20-7.1.* A Florida Registered Paralegal (FRP) shall adhere to the following Code of Ethics and Responsibility: *(a) Disclosure.* A FRP shall disclose his or her status as a Florida Registered Paralegal at the outset of any professional relationship with a client, lawyers, a court or administrative agency or personnel thereof, and members of the general public. Use of the initials FRP meets the disclosure requirement only if the title paralegal also appears. For example, J. Doe, FRP, Paralegal. Use of the word "paralegal" alone also complies. *(b) Confidentiality and Privilege.* A FRP shall preserve the confidences and secrets of all clients. A FRP must protect the confidences of a client, and it shall be unethical for a FRP to violate any statute or rule now in effect or hereafter to be enacted controlling privileged communications. *(c) Appearance of Impropriety or Unethical Conduct.* A FRP should understand the attorney's Rules of Professional Conduct and this code in order to avoid any action that would involve the attorney in a violation of the rules or give the appearance of professional impropriety. It is the obligation of the FRP to avoid conduct that would cause the lawyer to be unethical or even appear to be unethical, and loyalty to the lawyer is incumbent upon the FRP. *(d) Prohibited Conduct.* A FRP should not: (1) establish attorney-client relationships, accept cases, set legal fees, give legal opinions or advice, or represent a client before a court or other tribunal, unless authorized to do so by the court or tribunal; (2) engage in, encourage, or contribute to any act that could constitute the unlicensed practice of law; (3) engage in the practice of law; (4) perform any of the duties that attorneys only may perform nor do things that attorneys themselves may not do; or (5) act in matters involving professional legal judgment since the services of an attorney are essential in the public interest whenever the exercise of such judgment is required. *(e) Performance of Services.* A FRP must act prudently in determining the extent to which a client may be assisted without the presence of an attorney. A FRP may perform services for an attorney in the representation of a client, provided: (1) the services performed by the paralegal do not require the exercise of independent professional legal judgment; (2) the attorney is responsible for the client, maintains a direct relationship with the client, and maintains control of all client matters; (3) the attorney supervises the paralegal; (4) the attorney remains professionally responsible for all work on behalf of the client and assumes full professional responsibility for the work product, including any actions taken or not taken by the paralegal in connection therewith; and (5) the services performed supplement, merge with, and become the attorney's work product. *(f) Competence.* A FRP shall work continually to maintain integrity and a high degree of competency throughout the legal profession. *(g) Conflict of Interest.* A FRP who was employed by an opposing law firm has a duty not to disclose any information relating to the representation of the former firm's clients and must disclose the fact of the prior employment to the employing attorney. *(h) Reporting Known Misconduct.* A FRP having knowledge that another FRP has committed a violation of this chapter or code shall inform The Florida Bar of the violation.

Certification Of Paralegals In Florida

■ www.pafinc.org (click *Professions* and then *FCP*)
■ www.nala.org/cert-FL_certif.htm

Defining The Practice Of Law In Florida

■ State *ex rel. Florida Bar v. Sperry*, 140 So. 2d 587 (Supreme Court of Florida 1962) (vacated on other grounds 373 U.S. 379 (1963)). It is generally understood that the performance of services in representing another before the courts is the practice of law. But the practice of law also includes the giving of legal advice and counsel to others as to their rights and obligations under the law and the preparation of legal instruments, including contracts, by which legal rights are either obtained, secured or given away, although such matters may not then or ever be the subject of proceedings in a court. . . . In determining whether the giving of advice and counsel and the performance of services in legal matters for compensation constitute the practice of law it is safe to follow the rule that if the giving of such advice and performance of such services affect important rights of a person under the law, and if the reasonable protection of the rights and property of those advised and served requires that the persons giving such advice possess legal skill and a knowledge of the law greater than that possessed by the average citizen, then the giving of such advice and the performance of such services by one for another as a course of conduct constitute the practice of law.
■ Rule 10–2.2. *Rules Regulating The Florida Bar* (West's Florida Statutes Annotated): It shall not constitute the unlicensed practice of law for a nonlawyer to engage in limited oral communication to assist a self-represented person in the completion of blanks on a Supreme Court Approved Form. In assisting in the completion of the form, oral communication by nonlawyers is restricted to those communications reasonably necessary to elicit factual information to complete the blanks on the form and inform the self-represented person how to file the form. The nonlawyer may not give legal advice or give advice on remedies or courses of action.

Paralegals (And Others) In Florida State And Federal Courts

(See the beginning of this appendix on how to find the full text of the opinions cited here, including WL opinions.)

- *Stewart v. Bee-Dee Neon & Signs, Inc.*, 751 So. 2d 196 (Florida District Court of Appeal, 2000) (The disqualification of law firm that hired paralegal of an opposing firm was improper where no evidence was presented that the paralegal actually disclosed material confidential information to hiring firm, that the paralegal would necessarily work on case, or that screening measures would be ineffective) (compare *Koulisis v. Rivers*, 730 So. 2d 289 (Florida District Court of Appeal, 1999).

- *Eastrich No. 157 Corp. v. Gatto*, 868 So. 2d 1266 (Florida District Court of Appeal, 2004) (The fact that an individual, who had formerly worked as a legal secretary for plaintiff's counsel, was briefly used by defendant's counsel as an independent contractor in a nonlegal capacity did not require disqualification of defendant's counsel in this premise's liability action. The individual worked for defendant's firm for only ten hours, over two days, entering billing data into computer, and the billing records did not concern the underlying case.)

- *Miami-Dade County v. Walker*, 948 So. 2d 68 (Florida District Court of Appeal, 2007) (Plaintiff's counsel hired a paralegal who had previously worked for defendant's counsel. While employed by defendant's counsel, this paralegal worked on the plaintiff's lawsuit. The trial court granted defendant's motion to disqualify plaintiff's counsel.)

- *Acosta v. Deutsche Bank*, 88 So.3d 415 (Florida District Court of Appeal, 2012) (An attorney fails to attend a summary-judgment hearing due to a calendaring error made by his paralegal.)

- *Wells Fargo Credit Corp. v. Martin*, 605 So. 2d 531 (Florida District Court of Appeal, 1992) (Paralegal misreads her instructions and causes a $100,000 mistake.)

- *The Florida Bar v. Florida Service Bureau*, 581 So. 2d 900 (Supreme Court of Florida, 1991) (It is not the unauthorized practice of law for nonattorneys to give assistance to landlords by explaining what the eviction procedure entails as long they do not give legal advice. The "information given was no greater than that which anyone could glean from reading the eviction statute.")

- *The Florida Bar v. We The People Forms and Service Center of Sarasota*, 883 So. 2d 1280 (Supreme Court of Florida, 2004) (The providers of legal form preparation services engaged in the unlicensed practice of law when they provided customers with legal assistance in the selection, preparation, and completion of legal forms; corrected customers' errors or omissions; and assisted in the preparation of pleadings.)

- *In re Amendments to the Florida Rules of Judicial Admin.* 939 So. 2d 966 (Supreme Court of Florida, 2006) (The words "other person" in Rule 2.515(2) of the Florida Rules of Judicial Administration do not authorize nonattorneys to sign and file pleadings on behalf of another.)

- *The Florida Bar v. Shankman*, 908 So. 2d 379 (Supreme Court of Florida, 2005) (It is an improper sharing of fees with a nonattorney for an attorney to pay his paralegal a bonus of 7 percent of the fees generated in excess of overhead.)

- *In re Carter*, 326 Bankruptcy Reporter 892 (U.S. Bankruptcy Court, S.D. Florida, 2005) (A paralegal should be engaged in matters, under the supervision of an attorney, that require some independent judgment or are matters that an attorney would be expected to perform but can, under an attorney's supervision, be performed by an individual with specialized training or experience. Clerical functions such as typing, filing, photocopying, faxing, scanning, or filing documents either electronically or traditionally, are not such functions. Secretarial tasks are overhead expenses of the attorney and are not additionally compensable.)

- *Watson v. Wal-Mart Stores, Inc.*, 2005 WL 1266686 (U.S. District Court, N.D. Florida, 2005) (Plaintiff alleges that the paralegal time claimed by defendant for summarizing deposition transcripts was excessive. Plaintiff specifically complains of 9.1 hours for summarizing the 110-page deposition of the plaintiff. Defendant's attorneys say their paralegals usually summarize 14 to 18 pages per hour. At that rate, a paralegal should have completed plaintiff's 110-page deposition in 6.1 to 7.9 hours. Some attorneys still have paralegals summarize depositions (a practice that developed when transcripts came without indexes, and searchable text was unheard of), and the market still sometimes pays the charge. One might reasonably question why that is so. Searchable transcripts are now readily available, and laptop computers on counsel table are commonplace. Moreover, in a slip and fall case, one wonders how hard it could be to have a command of the depositions, perhaps with Post-It notes marking key passages, without the need for separate detailed summaries. It is perhaps no coincidence that some personal injury defense attorneys and commercial litigators [who typically charge by the hour, not only for their own time, but for paralegals] choose to have detailed summaries prepared, while most personal injury plaintiff's lawyers [who are paid based only on the result] do not. With the exception of a duplicative time entry, however, the time devoted to summarizing depositions in this case was a reasonable amount of time for completing the task.)

- *United States v. Pepper's Steel*, 742 F. Supp. 641 (U.S. District Court, S.D. Florida, 1990) (Although a paralegal accidentally delivered documents to the opposing party[!], the documents are still protected by the attorney-client privilege.)

- *The Florida Bar v. Neiman*, 816 So. 2d 587 (Florida Supreme Court, 2002) (Under Rule 3–6.1 of the Rules Regulating the Florida Bar, a suspended or disbarred attorney can be an employee of a law firm with the following restriction: "No employee shall have direct contact with any client.")

- *Florida Bar v. Furman*, 376 So. 2d 378 (Florida Supreme Court, 1979) (see discussion of this famous unauthorized-practice case in Chapter 4).

Doing Legal Research In Florida Law

- **Statutes:** www.leg.state.fl.us/Statutes
- **Cases:** www.floridasupremecourt.org/decisions/index.shtml
- **Court Rules:** www.llrx.com/courtrules-gen/state-Florida.html
- **General:** www.law.cornell.edu/states/florida

Finding Employment In Florida

- legal.jobs.net/Florida.htm
- miami.craigslist.org/lgl
- www.indeed.com/q-Paralegal-l-Florida-jobs.html
- l.fl.bar.associationcareernetwork.com/Common/HomePage.aspx

GEORGIA

ETHICS CODE AND OPINIONS IN GEORGIA

- **Attorneys: Georgia Code:** *Rules of Professional Conduct*
  - www.gabar.org/barrules/georgia-rules-of-professional-conduct.cfm
  - www.law.mercer.edu/academics/clep
  - See also ethics links in Helpful Websites at the end of Chapter 5.
- **Attorneys: Georgia Ethics Opinions**
  - www.gabar.org/barrules/ethicsandprofessionalism

■ **Unauthorized Practice of Law in Georgia**

- www.gabar.org (enter *unauthorized practice of law* in search box)
- www.gabar.org/committees programssections/programs/upl /opinions.cfm
- ir.lawnet.fordham.edu/cgi/view content.cgi?article=3572&context=flr

■ **Paralegals and Other Nonattorneys: Georgia**

- *Guidelines for Attorneys Utilizing Paralegals.* An attorney may delegate tasks to a paralegal that ordinarily comprise the practice of law, but only if the attorney has direct contact with the client and maintains "constant supervision" of the paralegal. The paralegal can render specialized advice on scientific or technical topics. The paralegal cannot negotiate with parties or opposing counsel on substantive issues. The paralegal's name may not appear on the letterhead or office door. The paralegal must not sign any pleadings, briefs, or other legal documents to be presented to a court. The paralegal can have a business card with the name of the firm on it if the word *paralegal* is clearly used to indicate nonattorney status. Unless previous contacts would justify the paralegal in believing that his or her nonattorney status is already known, the paralegal should begin oral communications, either face to face or on the telephone, with a clear statement that he or she is a paralegal employee of the law firm. State Disciplinary Board, *Advisory Opinion 21* (9/16/77, revised 1983) (www .gabar.org/barrules/handbookdetail .cfm?what=rule&id=469).
- *Rule 5.3.* For a discussion of the state's ethics Rule 5.3 ("Responsibilities Regarding Nonlawyer Assistants") in the Georgia *Rules of Professional Conduct*, see Chapter 5. For the text of 5.3 in Georgia, see www.gabar.org/barrules/hand bookdetail.cfm?what=rule&id=115.
- *Rule 5.3(d)* (suspended or disbarred attorneys). A lawyer shall not allow any person who has been suspended or disbarred and who maintains a presence in an office where the practice of law is conducted by the lawyer, to: 1. represent himself or herself as a lawyer or person with similar status; 2. have any contact with the clients of the lawyer either in person, by telephone or in writing; or 3. have any contact with persons who have legal dealings with the office either in person, by telephone or in writing.

- *Rule 5.5* (Comment 2). Lawyers can employ the services of paraprofessionals and delegate tasks to them "so long as the lawyer supervises the delegated work and retains responsibility for their work."
- *Rule 5.5* (Comment 3). Lawyers can assist "independent nonlawyers, such as paraprofessionals," who are authorized to provide particular law-related services.
- It is the unauthorized practice of law for a law firm to allow a nonattorney to conduct a real estate closing. Supreme Court of Georgia, *Formal Advisory Opinion 86–5* (5/12/89). It is not sufficient for the attorney to be available on the telephone during the course of the closing to respond to questions or to review documents. The lawyer's physical presence at a closing will assure that there is supervision of the work of the paralegal that is direct and constant. Supreme Court of Georgia, *Formal Advisory Opinion 00–3* (2/11/00).
- An attorney aids a nonlawyer in the unauthorized practice of law when the attorney allows his or her paralegal to prepare and sign correspondence that threatens legal action or provides legal advice or both. Supreme Court of Georgia, *Formal Advisory Opinion 00–2* (2/11/00).
- The payment of a monthly bonus by a lawyer to nonlawyer employees based on the gross receipts of his or her law office in addition to the nonlawyer employees' regular monthly salary is permissible. Also, nonattorney employees can be compensated pursuant to a plan that is based in whole or in part on a profit-sharing arrangement. *In re Formal Advisory Opinion 05–4,* 642 S.E.2d 686 (Supreme Court of Georgia, 2007).
- An attorney should not allow a paralegal to correspond with an adverse party (or the latter's agents) on the attorney's letterhead if the letter discusses legal matters that suggest or assert claims. Routine contacts with opposing counsel not involving the merits of the case are, however, permitted. State Disciplinary Board, *Advisory Opinion 19* (7/18/75).
- Nonlawyers who represent debtors in negotiations with creditors engage in unauthorized practice of law. *In re UPL Advisory Opinion 2003–1,* 623 S.E.2d 464 (Supreme Court of Georgia, 2006).

Defining Legal Assistants/Paralegals In Georgia

- [T]he terms "legal assistant", "paraprofessional" and "paralegal" are defined as any lay person, not admitted to the practice of law in this State, who is an employee of, or an assistant to, an active member of the State, who is an employee of, or an assistant to, an active member of the State Bar of Georgia or to a partnership or professional corporation comprised of active members of the State Bar of Georgia and who renders services relating to the law to such member, partnership or professional corporation under the direct control, supervision and compensation of a member of the State Bar of Georgia. State Bar of Georgia, State Disciplinary Board, *Advisory Opinion 21* (7/16/77) (www.gabar.org/barrules/handbook detail.cfm?what=rule&id=469).

Defining The Practice Of Law In Georgia

- § 15–19–50 (*Code of Georgia*): The practice of law in this state is defined as: (1) Representing litigants in court and preparing pleadings and other papers incident to any action or special proceedings in any court or other judicial body; (2) Conveyancing; (3) The preparation of legal instruments of all kinds whereby a legal right is secured; (4) The rendering of opinions as to the validity or invalidity of titles to real or personal property; (5) The giving of any legal advice; and (6) Any action taken for others in any matter connected with the law.
- § 15–19–51 (*Code of Georgia*): Unauthorized practice of law forbidden. (a) It shall be unlawful for any person other than a duly licensed attorney at law . . . (4) To render or furnish legal services or advice. . . (6) To render legal services of any kind in actions or proceedings of any nature. . . (8) To advertise that. . . he has, owns, conducts, or maintains an office for the practice of law or for furnishing legal advice, services, or counsel.

Paralegals (And Others) In Georgia State And Federal Courts

(See the beginning of this appendix on how to find the full text of the opinions cited here, including WL opinions.)

- *Hodge v. Ulfra-Sexton,* 758 S.E.2d 314 (Supreme Court of Georgia, 2014) (A paralegal switches sides and the former law firm seeks to disqualify the current law firm where the paralegal is now employed. Once a nonlawyers' new firm knows of the nonlawyer's conflict of interest from work at previous firm, the new firm must give prompt written notice to any affected adversarial party or their counsel, stating the conflict and the screening measures utilized. In order to warrant disqualification of a nonlawyer's new firm based on nonlawyer's conflict of interest due to work at previous firm, an adversarial party must show that the nonlawyer actually worked on a same or substantially related matter involving the adversarial party while the nonlawyer was employed at the former firm; if the moving party can show this, it will be presumed that the nonlawyer learned confidential information about the matter. Once a party moving for disqualification of a nonlawyer's law firm based on the nonlawyer's conflict of interest due to work at a previous firm establishes that nonlawyer worked on same of substantially related matter at previous firm, a rebuttable presumption arises that the nonlawyer has used or disclosed, or will use or disclose, the confidential information to the new firm. A nonlawyer's new firm may rebut the presumption that a nonlawyer with a conflict of interest due to work at previous firm has used or disclosed, or will use or disclose, the confidential information to the new firm by showing that it has properly taken effective screening measures to protect against the nonlawyer's disclosure of the former client's confidential information.)

- *In re Arp*, 546 S.E.2d 486 (Supreme Court of Georgia, 2001) (An attorney unethically pays a paralegal for the referral of cases and clients in violation of Standard 13 of Bar Rule 4–102, which prohibits an attorney from compensating a person or organization to recommend or secure employment by a client or as a reward for a recommendation.)
- *In re Eichholz*, 2007 WL 1223613 (U.S. Court of Appeals, 11th Circuit (Georgia), 2007) (An attorney fails to supervise his employees, allowing them to engage in activities that required legal knowledge such as explaining legal documents to clients.)
- *Peters v. Hyatt Legal Services*, 469 S.E.2d 481 (Court of Appeals of Georgia, 1996) (A paralegal is sued for legal malpractice along with the law firm.)
- *Cullins v. Georgia Dept. of Transportation*, 827 F. Supp. 756, 762 (U.S. District Court, M.D. Georgia, 1993) ("[P]aralegal costs are recoverable as a part of. . . attorney's fees and expenses but only to the extent such work is the type traditionally

performed by an attorney. Otherwise, paralegal expenses are separately unrecoverable overhead expenses".)
- *U.S. v. Patrol Services, Inc.*, 202 Federal Appendix 357, 2006 WL 2990211 (U.S. Court of Appeals, 11th Circuit (Georgia), 2006) (Paralegal fees were denied because no details were provided about the paralegal's experience.)
- *In re Golf Augusta Pro Shops, Inc.*, 2004 WL 768576 (U.S. Bankruptcy Court, S.D. Georgia, 2004) (The judge reviewed each entry of legal assistant time to determine which tasks required the use of independent paraprofessional judgment and therefore warranted inclusion in the Applicant's Fee Application. "I hold that tasks such as preparing certificates of service and preparing affidavits of service require the use of independent paraprofessional judgment. However, proofreading labels, proofreading service lists, processing notices of hearing, and processing the mail do not require that judgment. Labeling these tasks as paralegal time doesn't change the true nature of the task as secretarial and part of counsel's overhead expense included in the approved hourly rate.)
- *Morganactive Songs, Inc. v. Padgett*, 2007 WL 934609 (U.S. District Court, M.D. Georgia, 2007) (Employing *six* legal professionals (four attorneys and two paralegals) on what was, in this Court's view, a rather simple copyright infringement case, lead to an unreasonable accumulation of billed hours per task. Examples of overstaffing: the lead attorney and a paralegal spent 15.3 hours drafting a boilerplate complaint, preparing the scheduling order, and engaging in other preliminary matters; two attorneys and one paralegal spent 64.58 hours researching and writing a relatively simple motion for summary judgment.)

Doing Legal Research In Georgia Law

- **Statutes:** law.justia.com/codes /georgia
- **Cases:** www.loc.gov/law/help/guide /states/us-ga.php
- **Court Rules:** www.georgiacourts .org/index.php/court-rules
- **General:** www.romingerlegal.com /state/georgia.html

Finding Employment In Georgia

- www.careerbuilder.com/jobs/ga /keyword/paralegal
- www.indeed.com/q-Paralegal -l-Georgia-jobs.html
- legal.jobs.net/Georgia.htm
- atlanta.craigslist.org/lgl

HAWAII

ETHICS CODE AND OPINIONS IN HAWAII

- **Attorneys: Hawaii Code:** *Rules of Professional Conduct*
  - www.courts.state.hi.us/docs/court _rules/rules/hrpcond.htm
  - www.courts.state.hi.us/docs/court _rules/pdf/2013/2013_hrpc_ada.pdf
  - www.law.cornell.edu/ethics/hawaii .html
  - See also ethics links in Helpful Websites at the end of Chapter 5.
- **Attorneys: Hawaii Ethics Opinions**
  - www.odchawaii.com/Ethics_Advice .html
  - www.odchawaii.com/Consumer.html
- **Unauthorized Practice of Law in Hawaii**
  - codes.lp.findlaw.com/histatutes /4/32/605/605-14
  - ir.lawnet.fordham.edu/cgi/viewcontent .cgi?article=3572&context=flr
- **Paralegals and Other Nonattorneys: Hawaii**
  - *Rule 5.3.* For a discussion of the state's ethics Rule 5.3 ("Responsibilities Regarding Nonlawyer Assistants") in the Hawaii *Rules of Professional Conduct*, see Chapter 5.
  - *Rule 1.10 (Comment 4).* The rule of imputed disqualification in Rule 1.10 "does not prohibit representation by others in the law firm where the person prohibited from involvement in a matter is a nonlawyer, such as a paralegal or legal secretary." Hawaii *Rules of Professional Conduct*.
  - *Rule 5.5(c).* A lawyer shall not. . . allow any person who has been suspended or disbarred and who maintains a presence in an office where the practice of law is conducted by the lawyer to have any contact with the clients of the lawyer either in person, by telephone, or in writing or to have any contact with persons who have legal dealings with the office either in person, by telephone, or in writing. *Comment to the Rule*: In order to protect the public, strict prohibitions are essential to prevent permissible paralegal activities from crossing the line to giving legal advice, taking fees, or misleading clients and others who deal with the attorney's office.
  - *Rule 5.5 (Comment).* Lawyers can employ the services of paralegals and delegate tasks to them "so long as the lawyer supervises the delegated work and retains responsibility for their work."
  - An attorney may list a paralegal on professional cards, letterhead, and professional notices or announcement

cards as long as the employee is identified as a paralegal or legal assistant. A paralegal can use a business card identifying him or her as an employee of the law firm. A paralegal can sign correspondence as a paralegal. Hawaii Supreme Court Disciplinary Board, *Formal Opinion 78–8–19* (6/28/84). See also *Opinion 78–8–19–Supp.*

- The phrase "& Associates" cannot refer to nonlawyers, such as paralegals. Carole Richelieu, *Disciplinary Counsel's Report*, 1997 Hawaii Bar Journal 16 (March 1997).

Defining The Practice Of Law In Hawaii

- *Fought & Co., Inc. v. Steel Engineering and Erection, Inc.*, 951 P.2d 487, 496 (Supreme Court of Hawaii, 1998): The legislature has expressly declined to adopt a formal definition of the term practice of law, noting that "[a]ttempts to define the practice of law in terms of enumerating the specific types of services that come within the phrase are fruitless because new developments in society, whether legislative, social, or scientific in nature, continually create new concepts and new legal problems. . . . The legislature recognized that the practice of law is not limited to appearing before the courts. It consists, among other things of the giving of advice, the preparation of any document or the rendition of any service to a third party affecting the legal rights. . . of such party, where such advice, drafting or rendition of service requires the use of any degree of legal knowledge, skill or advocacy."

Paralegals (And Others) In Hawaii State And Federal Courts

(See the beginning of this appendix on how to find the full text of the opinions cited here.)

- *Schefke v. Reliable Collection Agency, Ltd.*, 32 P.3d 52 (Hawaii Supreme Court, 2001) (Courts should reduce an award of attorney's fees for excessive preparation time by a paralegal, duplicative efforts by the attorney and paralegal, and performance of clerical functions. Where there is no documentation for paralegal time, courts can decline to make award for fees.)
- *Blair v. Ing*, 31 P.3d 184 (Hawaii Supreme Court, 2001) (An award of paralegal fees is limited to charges for work performed that would otherwise have been required to be performed by a licensed attorney at a higher rate. This encourages cost-effective delivery

of legal services; the fees will be for legal work, not for secretarial work the paralegal may perform.)

- *Tirona v. State Farm Mutual Insurance Co.*, 821 F. Supp. 632 (U.S. District Court, Hawaii, 1993) (Paralegal fees denied when most of the services performed by paralegals were clerical in nature.)
- *Doe ex rel. Doe v. Keala*, 361 F. Supp. 2d 1171 (U.S. District Court, Hawaii, 2005) (Excessive fees: it is unreasonable to charge for a paralegal's time spent traveling to and attending a status conference when two attorneys are present.)
- *Office of Disciplinary Counsel v. Au*, 113 P.3d 203 (Hawaii Supreme Court, 2005) (Attorney disciplined for paying a nonattorney "runner" a fee in exchange for client referrals.)

Doing Legal Research In Hawaii Law

- **Statutes:** www.capitol.hawaii.gov /docs/HRS.htm
- **Cases:** www.courts.state.hi.us /opinions_and_orders/index.html
- **Court Rules:** www.llrx.com /courtrules-gen/state-Hawaii.html
- **General:** www.law.hawaii.edu /hawai'i-legal-research-guides

Finding Employment In Hawaii

- www.indeed.com/q-Attorney -l-Hawaii-jobs.html
- www.simplyhired.com/k-paralegal-l -honolulu-hi-jobs.html
- paralegal.jobs.net/jobs/honolulu, hawaii.aspx
- honolulu.craigslist.org/lgl

IDAHO

ETHICS CODE AND OPINIONS IN IDAHO

- **Attorneys: Idaho Code:** *Rules of Professional Conduct*
  - isb.idaho.gov/pdf/rules/irpc.pdf
  - www.law.cornell.edu/ethics/idaho .html
  - See also ethics links in Helpful Websites at the end of Chapter 5.
- **Attorneys: Idaho Ethics Opinions**
  - isb.idaho.gov/bar_counsel/formal _opinions.html
  - isb.idaho.gov/bar_counsel/formal _opinions_subject.html#subject
- **Unauthorized Practice of Law: Idaho**
  - isb.idaho.gov/pdf/rules/ibcr_sec08 _upol.pdf (unauthorized practice of law)
  - isb.idaho.gov (enter *unauthorized practice of law* in search box)

- isb.idaho.gov/bar_counsel/upol.html
- ir.lawnet.fordham.edu/cgi/viewcontent .cgi?article=3572&context=flr
- **Paralegals and Other Nonattorneys: Idaho**
- *Model Guidelines for the Utilization of Legal Assistant Services.* A lawyer is responsible for the professional actions of legal assistants and must take reasonable steps to ensure that they follow ethics rules governing attorneys. (Guideline 1) A lawyer can delegate tasks normally performed by lawyers unless the tasks are proscribed to one not licensed. (Guideline 2) Legal assistants cannot establish an attorney-client relationship, establish fees, or be responsible for giving a legal opinion to a client. (Guideline 3) The lawyer must take reasonable measures to disclose their nonattorney status. (Guideline 4) Their name and title can be on lawyer letterhead and on business cards that identify the lawyer's firm. (Guideline 5) The lawyer must take reasonable measures to ensure that legal assistants preserve confidentiality (Guideline 6) and do not create conflicts of interest based on other employment or interests. (Guideline 7) The lawyer can charge clients for the work legal assistants perform. (Guideline 8) A lawyer may not split fees with legal assistants nor pay them for referrals. Their pay cannot be contingent, by advance agreement, upon the profitability of the lawyer's practice. (Guideline 9) The lawyer should facilitate a legal assistant's participation in continuing legal education and pro bono work. (Guideline 10) *Model Guidelines for the Utilization of Legal Assistant Services.* (isb.idaho.gov/pdf/general/le-gasst.pdf)
- *Rule 5.3.* For a discussion of the state's ethics Rule 5.3 ("Responsibilities Regarding Nonlawyer Assistants") in the Idaho *Rules of Professional Conduct*, see Chapter 5. For the text of 5.3 in Idaho, see isb.idaho.gov/pdf/rules/irpc.pdf.
- *Rule 5.3 (Comment 3).* A lawyer may use nonlawyers outside the firm to assist the lawyer in rendering legal services to the client. Examples include the retention of an investigative or paraprofessional service, hiring a document management company to create and maintain a database for complex litigation, sending client documents to a third party for printing or scanning, and using an Internet-based service to store client information. When using such

services outside the firm, a lawyer must make reasonable efforts to ensure that the services are provided in a manner that is compatible with the lawyer's professional obligations.

- *Rule 1.10 (Comment 4)*. The rule of imputed disqualification in Rule 1.10 "does not prohibit representation by others in the law firm where the person prohibited from involvement in a matter is a nonlawyer, such as a paralegal or legal secretary." Idaho *Rules of Professional Conduct*.
- *Rule 5.5* (Comment 7). Lawyers can employ the services of paralegals and delegate tasks to them "so long as the lawyer supervises the delegated work and retains responsibility for their work."
- *Rule 5.5* (Comment 3). Lawyers can assist independent paraprofessionals, who are authorized to provide some kinds of legal services.
- An attorney must not share fees with nonattorneys. The attorney can request compensation for the work of a paralegal or other laypersons acting under his or her supervision as long as the request specifies that laypersons performed the work. Idaho State Bar, *Formal Ethics Opinion 125*.
- A law firm cannot list legal assistants on its letterhead. Idaho State Bar, *Formal Opinion 109* (11/30/81). (See, however, the Model Guidelines.)
- Attorneys must not split fees with nonattorneys. Idaho State Bar Committee on Ethics, *Opinion 117* (3/14/86).

Defining The Practice Of Law In Idaho

- *Idaho State Bar v. Meservy*, 335 P.2d 62, 64 (Idaho Supreme Court, 1959): The practice of law as generally understood, is the doing or performing services in a court of justice, in any matter depending [sic] therein, throughout its various stages, and in conformity with the adopted rules of procedure. But in a larger sense, it includes legal advice and counsel, and the preparation of instruments and contracts by which legal rights are secured, although such matter may or may not be [pending] in a court. . . . The drafting of. . . documents. . . or the giving of advice and counsel with respect thereto, by one not a licensed attorney at law, would constitute an unlawful practice of law, whether or not a charge was made therefor, and even though the documents or advice are not actually employed in an action or proceeding pending in a court.
- I.C. § 3–104. [A]ny person may appear and act in a magistrate's division of a district court as representative of

any party to a proceeding therein so long as the claim does not total more than $300, and so long as he or his employer has no pecuniary interest in the outcome of the litigation, and that he shall do so without making a charge or collecting a fee therefor.

Important Idaho Rules On Paralegals

- Rule 54(e)(1), *Rules of Civil Procedure*, (*West's Idaho Rules of Court*): Attorney Fees. In any civil action the court may award reasonable attorney fees, which at the discretion of the court may include paralegal fees, to the prevailing party or parties as defined in Rule 54(d)(1)(B), when provided for by any statute or contract.
- § 19–2705 (*Idaho Code*): A paralegal, as an agent of the attorney of record, is allowed to visit a defendant who has been sentenced to death. (Historical note: "The Legislature further recognizes that under American jurisprudence an adequate defense of a death penalty inmate is an interdisciplinary endeavor requiring the skills of counsel, experts, investigators and paralegals working together on the convict's behalf." (legislature.idaho.gov/legislation/1999/H0265.html)

Paralegals (And Others) In Idaho State And Federal Courts

(See the beginning of this appendix on how to find the full text of the opinions cited here.)

- *Defendant A v. Idaho State Bar*, 25 P.3d 846 (Idaho Supreme Court, *2001*) (Attorney disciplined for overcharging for a paralegal's work on a case.)
- *In re Castorena*, 270 Bankruptcy Reporter 504 (U.S. Bankruptcy Court, Idaho, 2001) (Bankruptcy attorneys may utilize paraprofessionals to assist them in rendering legal service to their clients but only if certain conditions are met: paralegals must be qualified, through training and experience, and capable of performing such services; must be adequately supervised; may not independently provide any legal advice; and may legitimately be delegated work only after attorney has first met with clients, determined what tasks need to be performed, and determined who may competently perform those tasks; also, neither attorneys nor paralegals may charge professional rates for clerical functions).
- *In re Doser*, 281 Bankruptcy Reporter 292 (U.S. Bankruptcy Court, 2002) (A bankruptcy petition preparer is charged with unauthorized practice of law). *In re*

Bush, 275 Bankruptcy Reporter 69 (U.S. Bankruptcy Court, 2002) (Bankruptcy petition preparer improperly calls himself a "certified" independent paralegal.)
- *P.O. Ventures, Inc. v. Loucks Family Irrevocable Trust*, 159 P.3d 870 (Idaho Supreme Court, 2007) (In this case, the trial judge applied the Rule 54(e)(1) restriction that fees may only be awarded for costs associated with attorney and paralegal work, distinguishing such costs from those incurred for clerical work. The trial judge struck those items that were not properly paralegal work.)
- *Medical Recovery Services, LLC, v. Jones*, 175 P.3d 795, 800 (Court of Appeals of Idaho, 2007) Case remanded for failure to consider a request for an award of paralegal fees under I.R.C.P. 54(e)(1).
- *Idaho State Bar v. Jenkins*, 816 P.2d 335 (Idaho Supreme Court, 1991) (An attorney was not sanctioned when his paralegal unethically solicited clients for the law firm, but without the knowledge or ratification of her attorney employer. Hence there was no violation of Rule 5.3 of the *Rules of Professional Conduct*.)
- *Kyle v. Beco Corp.*, 707 P.2d 378 (Idaho Supreme Court, 1985) (A party before the Industrial Commission must be represented by an attorney, if represented at all.)
- *Coleman v. Idaho*, 762 P.2d 814, 817 (Idaho Supreme Court, 1988) (Prison officials may not constitutionally prevent inmate paralegals from assisting illiterate inmates.)
- *Idaho State Bar v. Williams*, 893 P.2d 202 (Idaho Supreme Court, 1995) (Disbarred attorney as paralegal.)

Doing Legal Research In Idaho Law

- **Statutes:** legislature.idaho.gov /idstat/TOC/IDStatutesTOC.htm
- **Cases:** www.isc.idaho.gov /appeals-court/sccivil
- **Court Rules:** www.isc.idaho.gov /problem-solving/idaho-court-rules
- **General:** www.uidaho.edu/law /library/legalresearch/guides

Finding Employment In Idaho

- isb.idaho.gov/job_announce /announcements.cfm
- www.indeed.com/q-Legal-Assistant -l-Idaho-jobs.html
- www.simplyhired.com/job-search /l-Idaho/o-232000/t-Paralegal
- boise.craigslist.org/lgl

ILLINOIS

ETHICS CODE AND OPINIONS IN ILLINOIS

- **Attorneys: Illinois Code:** *Rules of Professional Conduct*
  - www.state.il.us/court/SupremeCourt/Rules/Art_VIII/default_NEW.asp
  - www.law.cornell.edu/ethics/illinois.html
  - See also ethics links in Helpful Websites at the end of Chapter 5.
- **Attorneys: Illinois Ethics Opinions**
  - www.isba.org/ethics
- **Unauthorized Practice of Law in Illinois**
  - www.isba.org (enter *unauthorized practice of law* in search box)
  - www.dcbabrief.org/vol140502art4.html
  - www.isba.org/resources/upl
  - ir.lawnet.fordham.edu/cgi/viewcontent.cgi?article=3572&context=flr
- **Paralegals and Other Nonattorneys: Illinois**
  - *Rule 5.3.* For a discussion of the state's ethics Rule 5.3 ("Responsibilities Regarding Nonlawyer Assistants") in the Illinois *Rules of Professional Conduct*, see Chapter 5.
  - *Rule 1.10 (Comment 4).* The rule of imputed disqualification in Rule 1.10 "does not prohibit representation by others in the law firm where the person prohibited from involvement in a matter is a nonlawyer, such as a paralegal or legal secretary." Illinois *Rules of Professional Conduct*.
  - *Rule 5.5* (Comment 2). Lawyers can employ the services of paraprofessionals and delegate tasks to them "so long as the lawyer supervises the delegated work and retains responsibility for their work."
  - *Rule 5.5* (Comment 3). Lawyers can assist independent paraprofessionals, who are authorized to provide particular law-related services.
  - Paralegal names can be printed on a firm's letterhead. The nonattorney status of the employee must be indicated. Illinois State Bar Ass'n, *Opinion 87–1* (9/8/87). This apparently overrules an earlier opinion that prohibited placing a nonattorney name on letterhead. *Opinion 350*.
  - Supervising attorneys must be sure their paralegals understand the rules of ethics governing attorneys. Paralegals can have contact with clients, but a direct attorney-client relationship remains primary. Paralegals must preserve confidentiality and make sure the paralegal's work does not

benefit the client's adversaries. Attorneys may charge clients for paralegal services, but they may not form partnerships with paralegals. Illinois State Bar Ass'n, *Recommendations to Lawyers for the Use of Legal Assistants* (1988).
- It is professionally improper to charge an hourly rate for a salaried paralegal as an expense in addition to a percentage of recovery on a contingent fee contract. Illinois State Bar Ass'n, *Opinion 86–1* (7/7/86).
- A paralegal cannot handle phone calls involving legal matters of her law firm while at a *collection* agency that is one of the clients of the law firm. The law firm would not be able to supervise the paralegal. Illinois State Bar Ass'n, *Opinion 88–8* (3/15/89).
- *Attorney* assistants can prepare standardized deeds and other real estate documents; correspond with any party, but only to obtain factual information. They can assist at real estate closings, but only in the company of a supervising attorney. Illinois State Bar Ass'n, *Position Paper on Use of Attorney Assistants in Real Estate Transactions* (approved by Board of Governors, 5/16/84).
- It is the unauthorized practice of law for a nonattorney to represent an employer before the Illinois Department of Employment Security in an unemployment compensation case in which the nonattorney prepares and presents evidence. The employer must be represented by an attorney. An attorney does not aid in the unauthorized practice of law by continuing to represent his client when the other side is represented by a nonattorney. Illinois State Bar Ass'n, *Advisory Opinion 93–15* (3/94).
- Sharing fees with a nonattorney via profit-sharing is proper provided the sharing is based on a percentage of overall firm profit and is not tied to fees in a particular case. Illinois State Bar Ass'n, *Opinion 89–5* (7/17/89).
- An attorney may not, pursuant to an arrangement with an organization that refers work to the attorney, employ the clerical or paralegal services of that organization. Illinois State Bar Ass'n, *Opinion 827* (4/1983). Also, it is professionally improper for a lawyer to participate in an arrangement with a nonlawyer whereby the lawyer obtains referrals in return for the payment of fees by the lawyer to the nonlawyer. Illinois State Bar Ass'n, *Advisory Opinion 99–02* (9/1999).

- In receiving a salary from the insurance company, the lawyer must take steps to avoid allowing the company to regulate or direct his professional judgment in representing the client (the insured). The lawyer must use his independent judgment in determining the level of clerical or paralegal support that is needed. In addition, all other aspects of representation must be determined by the attorney as is necessary to properly represent the insured. Illinois State Bar Ass'n, *Opinion 89–17* (1990).
- Upon entry of the final order of discipline, the disciplined attorney shall not maintain a presence or occupy an office where the practice of law is conducted. The disciplined attorney shall remove any indicia that he is a lawyer, counsellor at law, legal assistant, legal clerk, or similar title. Illinois Supreme Court Rules, Rule 764.
- A *paralegal* can conduct a real estate closing without his or her attorney-supervisor present if no legal advice is given, if all the documents have been prepared in advance, if the attorney-supervisor is available by telephone to provide help, and if the other attorney consents. Chicago Bar Ass'n (1983).
- Legal assistants can be listed on law firm letterhead or on the door as long as their nonattorney status is clear. Chicago Bar Ass'n, *Opinion 81–4*.
- *Code of Ethics of the Illinois Paralegal Association* www.ipaonline.org/?page=1

Defining Legal Assistants/Paralegals In Illinois

- "Paralegal" means a person who is qualified through education, training, or work experience and is employed by a lawyer, law office, governmental agency, or other entity to work under the direction of an attorney in a capacity that involves the performance of substantive legal work that usually requires a sufficient knowledge of legal concepts and would be performed by the attorney in the absence of the paralegal. A reference in an Act to attorney fees includes paralegal fees, recoverable at market rates. 5 *Illinois Compiled Statutes Annotated* 70/1.35.

Defining The Practice Of Law In Illinois

- *Continental Cas. Co. v. Cuda*, 715 N.E.2d 663 (Appellate Court of Illinois, 1999): Our supreme court has described the practice of law as: "[T]he giving of advice or rendition of any sort of service by any person, firm or corporation when the giving of such advice or rendition of such service requires the use of any degree of legal knowledge or skill." *People ex rel. Illinois State Bar Ass'n v. Schafer*, 87 N.E.2d 773 (Supreme Court of Illinois, 1949).

■ *In re Howard*, 721 N.E.2d 1126, 1134 (Illinois Supreme Court, 1999): Determining what conduct constitutes practicing law defies mechanistic formulation. It encompasses not only court appearances, but also services rendered out of court and includes the giving of any advice or rendering of any service requiring the use of legal knowledge.

■ § 205/1, chapter 705 (*Illinois Compiled Statutes Annotated*): Nothing in this Act [which restricts the practice of law to licensed attorneys] shall be construed to prohibit representation of a party by a person who is not an attorney in a proceeding before. . . the Illinois Labor Relations Board,. . . the Illinois Educational Labor Relations Board,. . . the State Civil Service Commission,. . . the University Civil Service Merit Board, to the extent allowed pursuant to rules and regulations promulgated by those Boards and Commissions.

Paralegals (And Others) In Illinois State And Federal Courts

(See the beginning of this appendix on how to find the full text of the opinions cited here, including WL opinions.)

■ *Hart v. Loan Kieu Le*, 995 N.E.2d 1002, 1005 (Appellate Court of Illinois, 2013) (The paralegal's affidavit fails, as a matter of law, to establish due diligence. The affidavit is vague with respect to the time of day when the paralegal made her second attempt to file plaintiff's complaint. The paralegal stated that she did so "prior to the close of business" on July 29, 2010. It is unclear, however, whether she was referring to the business hours of the clerk's office or those of her law firm. If the paralegal attempted to refile the complaint and summons after the clerk's office closed, those documents, even if accepted by the clerk, would have been deemed to have been filed on July 30, 2010, on which date the action was time-barred. The paralegal's affidavit is also vague with respect to the time of day when she learned that the first attempt to file the complaint had been unsuccessful. Thus, we cannot gauge whether the paralegal had a reasonable opportunity to refile before the clerk's office closed for the day.)

■ *Becker v. Zellner*, 684 N.E.2d 1378 (Appellate Court of Illinois, 1997) (Independent paralegals sue attorney for defamation for asserting that their work was worthless.)

■ *In re Estate of Divine*, 635 N.E.2d 581 (Appellate Court of Illinois, 1994) (Attorney supervisors are liable for the actions of their paralegals, but the latter should not be liable for the actions of their supervisors. A paralegal does not have an independent fiduciary duty to a law firm client.)

■ *Kapco Mfg. Co., Inc. v. C & O Enterprises, Inc.*, 637 F. Supp. 1231 (U.S. District Court, N.D. Illinois, 1985) (Disqualification of a law firm is not required simply because it hired a law office manager-secretary who had worked for opposing party at another law firm.)

■ *Johnson v. Thomas*, 794 N.E.2d 919 (Appellate Court of Illinois, 2003) (In general, overhead office expenses, namely expenses that an attorney regularly incurs regardless of specific litigation, including telephone charges, in-house delivery charges, in-house photocopying, check processing, newspaper subscriptions, and in-house paralegal and secretarial assistance, are not recoverable as costs of litigation.)

■ *Delgado v. Village of Rosemont*, 2006 WL 3147695 (U.S. District Court, N.D. Illinois, 2006) (Defendants argue that this court should not award fees for certain tasks that were not sufficiently complex to justify their completion by a paralegal. To award paralegal fees, a court must determine that "the work was sufficiently complex to justify the efforts of a paralegal, as opposed to an employee at the next rung lower on the pay-scale ladder." A court should disallow time spent on "clerical" or "secretarial" tasks. Courts have found organizing file folders, preparing documents, copying documents, assembling filings, electronically filing documents, sending materials, docketing or "logging" case events into an internal case tracking system, and telephoning court reporters to be clerical. In contrast, factual investigation, conducting legal research, summarizing depositions, checking citations, compiling statistical and financial data, preparing court documents, serving process, and discussing the case with attorneys are sufficiently complex.)

■ *Shortino v. Illinois Telephone Co.*, 665 N.E.2d 414, 419 (Appellate Court of Illinois, 1996) (Just because an experienced attorney is paid $350 an hour while appearing in court, he or she should not also be paid $350 per hour for tasks that could easily be done by. . . paralegals. . . at a lower hourly rate.)

■ *Boettcher v. Fournie Farms, Inc.*, 612 N.E.2d 969 (Appellate Court of Illinois, 1993) (Confidential communications made by a client to the paralegal of the client's attorney are protected by the attorney-client privilege.)

■ *Voris v. Creditor's Alliance*, 2007 WL 317033 (U.S. District Court, N.D. Illinois, 2007) (Waiver of attorney-client privilege is asserted when paralegal mistakenly faxes confidential client material.)

■ *Harrington v. City of Chicago*, 433 F.3d 542 (U.S. Court of Appeals, 7th Circuit, 2002) (Plaintiff attorney's paralegal could not participate in the on-the-record status conference. To the extent that the paralegal was carrying a message that the attorney was in trial and unable to attend, that message was too late and should have been provided to the court and opposing counsel before the hearing. The paralegal was not licensed to practice law and could not make an appearance in court.)

■ *People v. Alexander*, 202 N.E.2d 841 (Appellate Court of Illinois, 1964) (A *nonattorney* can appear in court for purposes of handling ministerial acts such as submitting agreed or stipulated matters.) (See discussion of this case in Chapter 4.)

Doing Legal Research In Illinois Law

■ **Statutes:** www.ilga.gov/legislation/ilcs/ilcs.asp
■ **Cases:** www.state.il.us/court
■ **Court Rules:** www.llrx.com/courtrules-gen/state-Illinois.html
■ **General:** www.rominger legal.com/state/illinois.html

Finding Employment In Illinois

■ legal.jobs.net/Illinois.htm
■ www.indeed.com/q-Paralegal-l-Illinois-jobs.html
■ www.linkedin.com/job/paralegal-jobs-chicago-il
■ chicago.craigslist.org/lgl

INDIANA

ETHICS CODE AND OPINIONS IN INDIANA

■ **Attorneys: Indiana Code:** *Rules of Professional Conduct*
  ■ www.state.in.us/judiciary/rules/prof_conduct/index.html
  ■ www.law.cornell.edu/ethics/indiana.html
  ■ See also ethics links in Helpful Websites at the end of Chapter 5.

- **Attorneys: Indiana Ethics Opinions**
  - www.inbar.org/PublicInformation /ISBALegalEthicsOpinions /tabid/81/Default.aspx
- **Unauthorized Practice of Law in Indiana**
  - www.inbar.org (enter *unauthorized practice of law* in search box)
  - ir.lawnet.fordham.edu/cgi/viewcontent .cgi?article=3572&context=flr
- **Paralegals and Other Nonattorneys: Indiana**
  - *Rule 5.3.* For a discussion of the state's ethics Rule 5.3 ("Responsibilities Regarding Nonlawyer Assistants") in the Indiana *Rules of Professional Conduct*, see Chapter 5.
  - *Rule 1.10 (Comment 4).* The rule of imputed disqualification in Rule 1.10 "does not prohibit representation by others in the law firm where the person prohibited from involvement in a matter is a nonlawyer, such as a paralegal or legal secretary." Indiana *Rules of Professional Conduct*.
  - *Rule 5.5* (Comment 2). Lawyers can employ the services of paralegals and delegate tasks to them "so long as the lawyer supervises the delegated work and retains responsibility for their work."
  - *Rule 5.5* (Comment 3). Lawyers can assist independent paraprofessionals, who are authorized to provide particular law-related services.
  - *Rules of Professional Conduct, Use of Legal Assistants* (1993). *Guideline 9.1*: An attorney must supervise the work of the legal assistant. Independent legal assistants, to wit, those not employed by a specific firm or by a specific attorney, are prohibited. *Guideline 9.2*: An attorney may delegate any task to a legal assistant so long as that task is not prohibited by law. The attorney must be responsible for the work product of the legal assistant. *Guideline 9.3*: An attorney cannot delegate to a legal assistant the tasks of establishing the attorney-client relationship, setting fees, or giving legal opinions to a client. *Guideline 9.4*: The attorney has the duty to make sure the client, the courts, and other attorneys know the legal assistant is not an attorney. *Guideline 9.5*: The legal assistant's name and title can appear on the attorney's letterhead and business card that also identifies the attorney's firm. *Guideline 9.6*: The attorney must take reasonable measures to ensure the legal assistant preserves client confidences. *Guideline 9.7*: The attorney can charge

for the work performed by the legal assistant. *Guideline 9.8*: An attorney may not split fees with a legal assistant or pay legal assistants for referring legal business. An attorney may compensate a legal assistant based on the quantity and quality of the legal assistant's work and the value of that work to a law practice, but the legal assistant's compensation may not be contingent, by advance agreement, upon the profitability of the attorney's practice. *Guideline 9.9*: An attorney who employs a legal assistant should facilitate the legal assistant's participation in appropriate continuing legal education and pro bono publico activities. *Guideline 9.10*: All attorneys who employ legal assistants in the State of Indiana shall assure that such legal assistants conform their conduct to be consistent with the following ethical standards: (a) A legal assistant may perform any task delegated and supervised by an attorney so long as the attorney is responsible to the client, maintains a direct relationship with the client, and assumes full professional responsibility for the work product. (b) A legal assistant shall not engage in the unauthorized practice of law. (c) A legal assistant shall serve the public interest by the improvement of the legal system. (d) A legal assistant shall achieve and maintain a high level of competence, as well as a high level of personal and professional integrity and conduct. (e) A legal assistant's title shall be fully disclosed in all business and professional communications. (f) A legal assistant shall preserve all confidential information provided by the client or acquired from other sources before, during, and after the course of the professional relationship. (g) A legal assistant shall avoid conflicts of interest and shall disclose any possible conflict to the employer or client, as well as to the prospective employers or clients. (h) A legal assistant shall act within the bounds of the law, uncompromisingly for the benefit of the client. (i) A legal assistant shall do all things incidental, necessary, or expedient for the attainment of the ethics and responsibilities imposed by statute or rule of court. (j) A legal assistant shall be governed by the American Bar Ass'n *Model Code of Professional Responsibility* and the American Bar Ass'n *Model Rules of Professional Conduct*. (www.state.in.us

/judiciary/rules/prof_conduct/index .html#_Toc341255509)
- *The* above rules (particularly Guideline 9.1) on the *Use of Legal Assistants* do not prohibit the use of paralegals through temporary services, contract services, and leasing firms so long as the work on a given project is under the direct supervision of the lawyer. Indiana Bar Ass'n, *Opinion 4* (1994).
- An attorney may properly hire a contract paralegal to assist with client matters if the attorney (a) maintains proper supervision and control over the paralegal's work and (b) takes such action as may be necessary to satisfy the requirements of Guidelines 9.1 through 9.10. Such steps should certainly address specifically the issues of client confidentiality and conflicts of interest. Indiana Bar Ass'n, *Opinion 3* (2000).
- An attorney can utilize a paralegal to conduct a negotiation session where no lawsuit has been filed so long as the paralegal is not responsible for rendering any legal opinions to the client. The attorney cannot however, delegate to a paralegal the representation of the client in mediation. Legal Ethics Committee of the Indiana State Bar Ass'n, *Opinion 1* (1997) (40 Res Gestae 22 (April 1997)).
- Paralegal names can be printed on a firm's letterhead if their nonattorney status is clear. The attorneys and nonattorneys must be distinguished clearly. Indiana Bar Ass'n, *Opinion 9* (1985) (overruling *Opinion 5*).
- Paralegals may have a business card as long as their capacity is stated and the identity of their employing attorney is disclosed. Indiana Bar Ass'n, *Opinion 8* (1984).
- An attorney aids an accountant in the unauthorized practice of law if the attorney prepares blank legal forms for the accountant who will help his clients fill them out without any attorney supervision. Indiana Bar Ass'n, *Opinion 2* (1995).
- Upon receiving notice of the order of suspension or disbarment, an attorney shall not maintain a presence or occupy an office where the practice of law is conducted. A respondent suspended for more than six months or disbarred shall take such action as is necessary to cause the removal of any indicia of lawyer, counselor at law, legal assistant, law clerk or similar title. Rule 23 (*Indiana Rules for. . . the Discipline of Attorneys*): § 26(b).

Defining Legal Assistants/Paralegals In Indiana

- § 6(a). As used in this section, "paralegal" means a person who is: (1) qualified through education, training, or work experience; and (2) employed by a lawyer, law office, governmental agency, or other entity; to work under the direction of an attorney in a capacity that involves the performance of substantive legal work that usually requires a sufficient knowledge of legal concepts and would be performed by the attorney in the absence of the paralegal. (b) A reference in the Indiana Code to attorney's fees includes paralegal's fees. *Indiana Code* 1–1–4–6 (www.state.in.us /legislative/ic/code/title1/ar1/ch4.html).

Defining The Practice Of Law In Indiana

- *Matter of Thonert*, 693 N.E.2d 559 (Supreme Court of Indiana, 1998): The *core* element of practicing law is the giving of legal advice to a client. Also, to practice law is to carry on the business of an attorney at law, and to make it one's business to act for, and by the warrant of, others in legal formalities, negotiations, or proceedings. A person who gives legal advice to clients and transacts business for them in matters connected with the law is engaged in the practice of law.
- *In the Matter of Fletcher*, 655 N.E.2d 58, 60 (Supreme Court of Indiana, 1995): It is the province *of* this Court to determine what acts constitute the practice of law. . . . The practice of law includes "the doing or performing services in a court of justice, in any matter depending therein, throughout its various stages. . . [b]ut in a larger sense it includes legal advice and counsel. . . ." The core element of practicing law is the giving of legal advice to a client and placing oneself in the very sensitive relationship wherein the confidence of the client, and the management of his affairs, is left totally in the hands of the attorney. . . . The practice of law includes the appearance in court representing another.

Paralegals (And Others) In Indiana State And Federal Courts

(See the beginning of this appendix on how to find the full text of the opinions cited here, including WL opinions.)

- *Smetzer v. Newton*, 2012 WL 1900118 (U.S. District Court, N.D. Indiana, 2012) (The attorney suggests that he missed the deadline because his legal assistant had not updated his calendar with e-mail correspondence from the Court, explaining that his assistant had never signed up to receive e-mails from the Court, a matter he has now rectified. But miscalendaring a date does not necessarily constitute good cause or excusable neglect.)
- Van Eaton v. Fink, 697 N.E.2d 490 (Court of Appeals of Indiana, 1998) (Paralegal sued for defamation by a witness who was accused by the paralegal or committing perjury in another lawsuit. Absolute privilege applied to the paralegal's statement made to the defendant's attorney before trial court entered final judgment for plaintiff. A qualified privilege applied to the paralegal's statement made by facsimile to plaintiff's attorney.)
- *Shell Oil Co. v. Meyer*, 684 N.E.2d 504, 525 (Court of Appeals of *Indiana*, 1997) (When one considers that attorneys utilize paralegals to perform tasks which might otherwise have to be accomplished by a lawyer with a higher billing rate, recovery for a paralegal's fees is hardly unreasonable.)
- *Daimler Chrysler Corp. v. Franklin*, 814 N.E.2d 281 (Court of Appeals of Indiana, 2004) (*In* this case, the paralegal's hourly rate was $100. We find that the trial court abused its discretion in including her fees for copying and mailing documents, which is work that requires no particular knowledge of legal concepts and is more in the nature of clerical or support staff work.)
- *Eli Lilly & Co. v. Zenith*, 264 F. Supp. 2d 753 (U.S. District Court, S.D. Indiana, 2003) (Defendant questions substantial amounts of time plaintiff's legal assistants spent shopping and coordinating travel arrangements and trial logistics, such as setting up the "war rooms." Defendant's criticisms are valid. Plaintiff's time records include a great deal of excessive time by legal assistants, including time devoted to clerical or other tasks for which a $100 rate is not remotely justifiable.)
- *Mayberry v. State*, 670 N.E.2d 1262 (Supreme Court of Indiana, 1996) (The statement to a paralegal is protected by attorney-client privilege.)
- *Whitehead v. Indiana*, 511 N.E.2d 284 (Supreme Court of Indiana, 1987) (Paralegal allowed to sit at counsel's table during trial.)
- *In re Blumenthal*, 825 N.E.2d 374 (Supreme Court of Indiana, 2005) (The attorney instructed her paralegal to alter one of the release forms the plaintiff had signed by adding the name of an unnamed physician, and to alter the execution date of the document, which had expired some months before.)
- *Exterior Systems v. Noble Composites*, 210 F. Supp. 2d 1062 (U.S. District Court, N.D. Indiana, 2002) (Mills is a paralegal. Strictly speaking, the conflict of interest rules do not apply to paralegals who are assisting the lawyers in a law firm. Instead, paralegals are governed indirectly by Rule 5.3, which imposes on the supervising lawyers the duty to ensure that their nonlawyer assistants' conduct is "compatible with the professional obligations of the lawyer.")

Doing Legal Research In Indiana Law

- **Statutes:** www.in.gov/legislative /ic/2010
- **Cases:** www.in.gov/judiciary/2730 .htm
- **Court Rules:** www.in.gov
- **General:** www.in.gov/judiciary /supreme/2329.htm

Finding Employment In Indiana

- www.indianaparalegals.org /jobbankpublic
- legal.jobs.net/Indiana.htm
- www.indeed.com/q-Paralegal-l -Indiana-jobs.html
- jobs.monster.com/v-legal-q -paralegal-jobs-l-indiana.aspx

IOWA

ETHICS CODE AND OPINIONS IN IOWA

- **Attorneys: Iowa Code:** *Rules of Professional Conduct*
  - www.legis.iowa.gov/docs/ACO /CourtRulesChapter/06-30-2014.32 .pdf
  - www.law.cornell.edu/ethics/iowa .html
  - See also ethics links in Helpful Websites at the end of Chapter 5.
- **Attorneys: Iowa Ethics Opinions**
  - www.iabar.net/ethics.nsf/Ethics%20 Opinions?OpenFrameset
  - www.iowabar.org/members/group .aspx?id=119858
- **Unauthorized Practice of Law: Iowa**
  - www.iowabar.org (enter *unauthorized practice of law* in search box)
  - ir.lawnet.fordham.edu/cgi/viewcontent .cgi?article=3572&context=flr
- **Paralegals and Other Nonattorneys: Iowa**
  - *Rule 32.5.3.* For a discussion of the state's ethics Rule 5.3 ("Responsibilities

Regarding Nonlawyer Assistants") in the *Iowa Rules of Professional Conduct*.

- *Rule 32.1.10 (Comment 4)*. The rule of imputed disqualification in Rule 1.10 "does not prohibit representation by others in the law firm where the person prohibited from involvement in a matter is a nonlawyer, such as a paralegal or legal secretary." *Iowa Rules of Professional Conduct*.
- *Rule 32.5.5* (Comment 2). Lawyers can employ the services of paralegals and delegate tasks to them "so long as the lawyer supervises the delegated work and retains responsibility for their work."
- *Rule 32.5.5* (Comment 3). Lawyers can assist independent paraprofessionals, who are authorized to provide particular law-related services.
- *Iowa Code of Professional Responsibility*. (www.paralegals.org/associations /2270/files/statedif.htm). The following six guidelines are based on the *Iowa Code of Professional Responsibility*, which has been replaced by the *Iowa Rules of Professional Conduct*. A lawyer often delegates tasks required in performance of the client's legal services to clerks, secretaries and other nonlawyer personnel employed by the lawyer. Such delegation which extends beyond duties merely ministerial in nature is proper under the following circumstances:

(1) If it is for the purposes of (a) investigation of a factual situation or consultation with a lawyer's client for the purpose, only, of obtaining factual information; or (b) legal research; or (c) preparation or selection of legal instruments and documents, provided, however, that in each such situation the delegated work will assist the employer-lawyer in carrying the matter to a completed service either through the lawyer's personal examination and approval thereof or by other additional participation by the lawyer. However, the delegated work must be such as loses its separate identity and becomes the service or is merged in the service of the lawyer.

(2) The lawyer must maintain an initial, continuing and direct relationship with the client, directly supervise the delegated work, and assume complete professional responsibility for the work product. This

requirement must not be ignored by a lawyer or given superficial recognition.

(3) The lawyer shall not permit employed laypersons to counsel the lawyer's clients about legal matters, appear in any court or administrative proceeding except to the extent authorized by court rule or administrative rule or regulation, or otherwise engage in the unauthorized practice of law. A lawyer should recognize the importance of being present, if practicable, when a client executes a will, contract, deed or other legal document, to insure that it is executed in compliance with the law and to answer the client's questions. A lawyer has a continuing affirmative duty to preserve and enhance the public's confidence in the legal profession. This is best accomplished when the client has direct access to a lawyer for the purpose of asking for and receiving legal advice prior to or at the time the client takes any contemplated legal action.

(4) A nonlawyer employed by a lawyer, law firm, agency or other employer may be referred to as a legal assistant if the majority of his or her job responsibilities include duties as defined in EC 3–6 (1). Such a legal assistant and the responsible supervising lawyer are at all times subject to all the provisions of EC 3–6. Such a legal assistant may be furnished with, and use, a professional card. The card must contain the following information on its face: Name; "Legal Assistant" centered immediately below the name; the name of the lawyer, law firm, agency or other employer whose lawyer is authorizing the issuance of the card; name of the employer or agency, if applicable; address and telephone number of the attorney, law firm, agency or other employer.

(5) When communicating with persons outside the law office, including other lawyers, a nonlawyer employed by a lawyer must disclose the nonlawyer's status. The disclosure must be made in a way that avoids confusion. With respect to oral communications, disclosure must

be made at the outset of the conversation. It is permissible for layperson office personnel to sign letters on the firm's stationery as long as the nonlawyer status is clearly indicated.

(6) The supervising lawyer must exercise care to insure nonlawyer personnel comply with all applicable provisions of the Code of Professional Responsibility. This includes the obligation referred to in DR 4–101 (D) and EC 4–2 to see that such employees preserve and refrain from using the confidence and secrets of the lawyer's clients.

- A legal assistant to an Iowa lawyer or law firm who has met the certification requirements of the National Association of Legal Assistants may add "Certified Legal Assistant" where his or her name properly appears, but not "CLA." Using CLA alone could mislead the public, even to the point of believing it to be a legal degree. Iowa Supreme Court Board of Professional Ethics and Conduct, *Opinion 04–01* (9/11/03). This opinion changes *Opinion 88–05*.

- It is proper to sign letters with the titles *legal assistant* or *paralegal*. Iowa Supreme Court Board of Professional Ethics and Conduct, *Opinion 88–22* (12/8/89).

- Paralegals and other nonattorney employees may not be listed on the law firm letterhead. Iowa Supreme Court Board of Professional Ethics and Conduct, *Opinion 87–18* (2/2/88). The office of the county public defender may not list the names of nonattorney personnel on its letterhead. *Opinion 89–35* (12/14/89).

- A sign outside the door of a law firm may not list the name of nonattorney employees even though they are called *legal assistants*. Iowa Supreme Court Board of Professional Ethics and Conduct, *Opinion 89–23* (12/26/88). A law firm may not list its paralegals or other nonattorney employees in law directories such as *Martindale-Hubbell*. Iowa Supreme Court Board of Professional Ethics and Conduct, *Opinion 92–33* (5/27/93).

- As an incentive, a law firm can pay a paralegal a percentage of the total income it earns as long as the compensation relates to the firm's profits and not the receipt of specific legal fees. Iowa Supreme Court Board of Professional Ethics and Conduct, *Opinion 90–9* (8/23/90).

- A law firm and a departing lawyer taking a contingency-fee file with him that originated with the law firm can enter into an agreement for a blanket formula to govern the value of services rendered by both attorney and legal assistants before and after the departure if the legal assistant services are computed in the formula at the usual rate charged to clients for legal assistant services and the legal assistants do not share in the allocations between the lawyers and the law firm under the formula agreement. Iowa Supreme Court Board of Professional Ethics and Conduct, *Opinion 96–11* (12/12/96).

■ It would be the unauthorized practice of law for a paralegal to represent a client in Small Claims Court. Iowa Supreme Court Board of Professional Ethics and Conduct, *Opinion 89–30* (12/8/89), and *Opinion 88–18* (2/20/89). Nor can a nonattorney represent someone before the city Civil Service Commission. *Opinion 92–18* (12/3/92).

■ It is unethical for an attorney to allow his or her paralegal to ask questions at a deposition even though the paralegal is supervised. Iowa Supreme Court Board of Professional Ethics and Conduct, *Opinion 96–03* (8/29/96).

■ In a Section 341 bankruptcy proceeding, a paralegal cannot sit with a debtor at the *counsel* table in the absence of the paralegal's supervising attorney. The paralegal can help the debtor find things in the schedule but cannot counsel the debtor. Iowa Supreme Court Board of Professional Ethics and Conduct, *Opinion 92–24* (2/28/93).

■ A retired attorney who is still licensed cannot function as a paralegal in a law office. Iowa Supreme Court Board of Professional Ethics and Conduct, *Opinion 94–1* (9/13/94).

Defining Legal Assistants/Paralegals In Iowa

■ *Iowa Code of Professional Responsibility*:
  ■ *EC 3–6(4).* A nonlawyer employed by a lawyer, law firm, agency or other employer may be referred to as a legal assistant if the majority of the nonlawyer's job responsibilities include duties as defined in EC 3–6(1).
  ■ EC 3–6(1). [Delegation is proper if for the purpose of] (a) investigation of a factual situation or consultation with a lawyer's client for the purpose, only, of obtaining factual information; or (b) legal research; or (c) preparation or selection of legal instruments and documents, provided, however, that in each such situation the delegated work will assist the employer–lawyer in carrying the matter to a completed service either through the lawyer's personal examination and approval thereof or by other additional participation by the lawyer. However, the delegated work must be such as loses

its separate identity and becomes the service or is merged in the service of the lawyer. Note: the *Iowa Code* has been replaced by the *Iowa Rules of Professional Conduct.*

Defining The Practice Of Law In Iowa

■ *Iowa Supreme Court Comm'n on Unauthorized Practice of Law v. Sturgeon,* 635 N.W.2d 679 (Supreme Court of Iowa, 2001). Ethical Consideration 3–5, *Code of Professional Responsibility* (*Iowa Code Annotated*): It is neither necessary nor desirable to *attempt* the formulation of a single, specific definition of what constitutes the practice of law. However, the practice of law includes, but is not limited to, representing another before the courts; giving of legal advice and counsel to others relating to their rights and obligations under the law; and preparation or approval of the use of legal instruments by which legal rights of others are either obtained, secured or transferred even if such matters never become the subject of a court proceeding. Functionally, the practice of law relates to the rendition of services for others that call for the professional judgment of a lawyer. The essence of professional judgment of the lawyer is the educated ability to relate the general body and philosophy of law to a specific legal problem of a client.

■ Iowa Court Rules, Rule 39.7: The practice of law as that term is employed in this chapter includes the examination of abstracts, consummation of real estate transactions, preparation of legal briefs, deeds, buy and sell agreements, contracts, wills and tax returns as well as the representation of others in any Iowa courts, the right to represent others in any Iowa courts, or to regularly prepare legal instruments, secure legal rights, advise others as to their legal rights or the effect of contemplated actions upon their legal rights, or to hold oneself out to so do; or to be one who instructs others in legal rights; or to be a judge or one who rules upon the legal rights of others unless neither the state nor federal law requires the person so judging or ruling to hold a license to practice law.

Paralegals (And Others) In Iowa State And Federal Courts

(See the beginning of this appendix on how to find the full text of the opinions cited here, including WL opinions.)

■ *Baker v. John Morrell & Co.,* 263 F. Supp. 2d 1161 (U.S. District Court, N.D. Iowa, 2003) ("[C]ounsel's efficient delegation of work to their experienced paralegal,

Ms. Collins, is in part responsible for keeping costs down in this case.")

■ *Northeast Iowa Citizens For Clean Water v. Agriprocessors,* 489 F. Supp. 2d 881 (U.S. District Court, N.D. Iowa, 2007) (The court approves $80 an hour for legal assistants. "Although the court is not familiar with any of the legal assistants, the requested rates do not exceed prevailing market rates for such professionals.")

■ *Foxley Cattle Co. v. Grain Dealers,* 142 Federal Rules Decisions 677, 681 (U.S. District Court, S.D. Iowa, 1992) (The attorney's claim for 8.8 hours to prepare a motion is excessive; this document "easily could have been prepared by a legal assistant in two to three hours.")

■ *Knudsen v. Barnhart,* 360 F. Supp. 2d 963 (U.S. District Court, N.D. Iowa, 2004) (The tasks of filing, serving summons, calendaring, and receiving and retrieving documents were administrative tasks, and therefore, could not be billed as paralegal time. Such tasks are clerical in nature and are considered part of overhead.)

■ *GreatAmerica Leasing Corp. v. Cool Comfort Air Conditioning and Refrigeration,* 691 N.W.2d 730 (Supreme Court of Iowa, 2005) (The district court abused its discretion insofar as it adopted a policy capping fees for all paralegals in civil cases. Iowa Code § 625.22 contains no such requirement.)

■ *The CBE Group v. Anderson,* 2007 WL 2120278 (Court of Appeals of Iowa, 2007) (We "note with concern the notion of a legal assistant representing a client at a pretrial conference.")

■ *Doyle v. First Federal Credit Union,* 2007 WL 1231809 (U.S. District Court, N.D. Iowa, 2007) (The notes taken by the legal assistant constitute attorney work product and are generally not discoverable.)

■ *Mlynarik v. Bergantzel,* 675 N.W.2d 584 (Supreme Court of Iowa, 2004) (A *contingency* fee agreement between a former client and a nonlawyer, under which the nonlawyer agreed to negotiate the settlement of a personal injury case, was unenforceable as against public policy. Accordingly, the former client was entitled to recover the fees paid pursuant to the illegal contract.)

■ *Committee on Professional Ethics v. Lawler,* 342 N.W.2d 486 (Supreme Court of Iowa, 1984) (Attorney disciplined for fee splitting with a nonattorney and failing to supervise his paralegal.)

Doing Legal Research In Iowa Law

■ **Statutes:** www.legis.iowa.gov/law /statutory/statutory

- **Cases:** www.iowacourts.gov (see links on page; also enter *opinions* in the search box)
- **Court Rules:** www.iowacourts.gov /Court_Rules__Forms/Overview
- **General:** libguides.law.drake.edu /IowaBasic

Finding Employment In Iowa

- legal.jobs.net/Iowa.htm
- www.ialanet.org/employment _listings.html
- www.indeed.com/q-Paralegal -l-Iowa-jobs.html
- desmoines.craigslist.org/search /lgl?query=+

KANSAS

ETHICS CODE AND OPINIONS IN KANSAS

- **Attorneys: Kansas Code;** *Rules of Professional Conduct*
  - www.kscourts.org (select *Court Rules and Forms* and then *Rules of Professional Conduct*)
  - www.law.cornell.edu/ethics/kansas .html
  - See also ethics links in Helpful Websites at the end of Chapter 5.
- **Attorneys: Kansas Ethics Opinions**
  - www.ksbar.org (enter *ethics* in the search box)
- **Unauthorized Practice of Law in Kansas**
  - www.ksbar.org (enter *"unauthorized practice of law"* in search box)
  - ir.lawnet.fordham.edu/cgi/viewcontent .cgi?article=3572&context=flr
- **Paralegals and Other Nonattorneys: Kansas**
  - www.nala.org/KSG_04.pdf
  - www.accesskansas.org/ksparalegals /ethics.html
  - *Rule 5.3.* For a discussion of the state's ethics Rule 5.3 ("Responsibilities Regarding Nonlawyer Assistants") in the Rules of Professional Conduct of Kansas, see Chapter 5. For the text of 5.3 in Kansas, go to www.kscourts .org, click *Court Rules and Forms*, and select *Rules of Professional Conduct*.
  - *Rule 5.3, Comment 3.* A lawyer may use nonlawyers outside the firm to assist the lawyer in rendering legal services to the client. Examples include the retention of an investigative or paraprofessional service, hiring a document management company to create and maintain a database for complex litigation, sending client documents to a third party for printing or scanning, and using an Internet-based service to store

client information. When using such services outside the firm, a lawyer must make reasonable efforts to ensure that the services are provided in a manner that is compatible with the lawyer's professional obligations. The extent of this obligation will depend upon the circumstances, including the education, experience, and reputation of the nonlawyer; the nature of the services involved; the terms of any arrangements concerning the protection of client information; and the legal and ethical environments of the jurisdictions in which the services will be performed, particularly with regard to confidentiality. See also Rules 1.1 (competence), 1.2 (allocation of authority), 1.4 (communication with client), 1.6 (confidentiality), 5.4(a) (professional independence of the lawyer), and 5.5(a) (unauthorized practice of law). When retaining or directing a nonlawyer outside the firm, a lawyer should communicate directions appropriate under the circumstances to give reasonable assurance that the nonlawyer's conduct is compatible with the professional obligations of the lawyer.

- *Rule 5.5* (Comment 2). Lawyers can employ the services of paraprofessionals and delegate tasks to them "so long as the lawyer supervises the delegated work and retains responsibility" for their work.
- *Rule 5.5* (Comment 3). Lawyers can assist "independent nonlawyers, such as paraprofessionals," who are authorized to provide particular law-related services.

Defining Legal Assistants/Paralegals In Kansas

- A legal assistant or paralegal is a person, qualified by education, training, or work experience who is employed or retained by a lawyer, law office, corporation, governmental agency or other entity and who performs specifically delegated substantive legal work for which a lawyer is responsible. Kansas Bar Ass'n, *Official Standards and Guidelines for the Utilization of Legal Assistants/Paralegals in Kansas* (2004) (www.nala.org/KSG_04.pdf).

Ethical Rules And Guidelines In Kansas

- Kansas Bar Ass'n, *Official Standards and Guidelines for the Utilization of Legal Assistants/Paralegals in Kansas* (2004) (www .nala.org/KSG_04.pdf). *Guideline I*: An attorney shall not permit a legal assistant/paralegal to give legal advice or to engage in the practice of law except

as provided for herein. *Guideline II*: An attorney shall not permit a legal assistant/paralegal to represent a client before any court or administrative agency, nor shall a legal assistant/paralegal sign any pleading, paper, or document filed on behalf of a client with any court or agency unless expressly permitted by statute or administrative regulation. *Guideline III*: An attorney should exercise care to prevent a legal assistant/ paralegal from engaging in conduct which would involve the attorney in a violation of the Kansas Rules of Professional Conduct (Rules) or which would result in the loss of designation for the legal assistant/paralegal. *Guideline IV*: Except as otherwise prohibited by statute, court rule or decision, administrative rule or regulation, or by the Rules or these guidelines, an attorney may permit a legal assistant/paralegal to perform services in representation of a client provided: A. the client is fully informed and understands that the legal assistant/paralegal is not an attorney; B. the attorney remains fully responsible for such representation, including all actions taken or not taken by the legal assistant/paralegal; C. the attorney maintains a direct relationship with the client; and D. the attorney supervises the performance of the legal assistant/ paralegal. *Guideline V*: An attorney shall instruct the legal assistant/paralegal to preserve the confidences and secrets of a client. *Guideline VI*: An attorney shall not share fees with a legal assistant/ paralegal. Comment: This guideline is not intended to deny legal assistants/ paralegals salaries, bonuses, or benefits, even though they may be tied to the profitability of the firm. It prohibits any form of compensation directly tied to the existence or amount of a particular legal fee. The legal assistant/paralegal should not be compensated for the recommendation of the attorney's services or be deprived of compensation because of the lack of such referrals. *Guideline VII*: An attorney shall not form a partnership with a legal assistant/paralegal if any of the activities of such partnership consist of the practice of law. *Guideline VIII*: A legal assistant/paralegal may have business cards and may be included on the letterhead of an attorney or law firm with their nonattorney status designated. *Guideline IX*: An attorney shall instruct the legal assistant/paralegal to disclose at the beginning of any professional contact that the legal assistant/ paralegal is not an attorney. *Guideline X*: An attorney is responsible to ensure that no personal, social, or business interest or relationship of the legal assistant/paralegal conflicts with the services rendered to the client.

- Legal assistants may be listed on law firm letterhead if their nonattorney status is clear and they have achieved some minimal training as a legal assistant over and above that customarily given legal secretaries. Supervised nonattorney employees may also have their own business cards. Kansas Bar Ass'n, *Opinion 92–15* (12/2/92). This overrules *Opinion 88–02* (7/15/88), which did *not* allow legal assistant names on attorney letterhead. See also *Opinion 82–38* (11/4/82).
- A legal *assistant* can use a business card that prints the name of his or her law firm if the legal assistant is identified as such. Kansas Bar Ass'n, *Opinion 85–4.* This overrules *Opinion 84–18.*
- A disbarred or suspended attorney can work as a paralegal if his or her functions are limited exclusively to work of a preparatory nature under the supervision of a licensed attorney-employer and does not involve client contact. *In re Juhnke*, 41 P.3d 855 (Supreme Court of Kansas, 2002).

Defining The Practice Of Law In Kansas

- *State ex rel. Stephan v. Williams*, 793 P.2d 234, 240 (Supreme Court of Kansas, 1990): In determining what constitutes the "practice of law" no precise, all-encompassing definition is advisable, even if it were possible. Every matter asserting the *unauthorized* practice of law must be considered on its own facts on a case-by-case basis. . . . "As the term is generally understood, the practice of law is the doing or performing of services in a court of justice, in any matter depending therein, throughout its various stages, and in conformity to the adopted rules of procedure. But in a larger sense it includes legal advice and counsel, and the preparation of legal instruments and contracts by which legal rights are secured, although such matters may or may not be depending in a court." . . . [T]he practice of law [is] "the rendition of services requiring the knowledge and application of legal principles and technique to serve the interests of another with his consent."

Paralegals (And Others) In Kansas State And Federal Courts

(See the beginning of this appendix on how to find the full text of the opinions cited here, including WL opinions.)

- *Zimmerman v. Mahaska Bottling Co.*, 19 P.3d 784 (Supreme Court of *Kansas*, 2001) (When a nonlawyer moves from one private firm to another where the two firms are involved in pending litigation and represent adverse parties, a firm may avoid disqualification if (1) the nonlawyer employee has not acquired material and confidential information regarding the litigation or (2) if the client of the former firm waives disqualification and approves of the use of a screening device or Chinese wall.)
- *In re Arabia*, 19 P.3d 113 (Supreme Court of Kansas, 2001) (Attorney gave his paralegals too little direction and supervision regarding the quantity of research they performed.)
- *Espy v. Mformation Tech.*, 2009 WL 2912506 (U.S. District Court, Kansas, 2009) (Finding excusable neglect where paralegal failed to recognize discovery requests were hand-delivered, and consequently the due date was not calendared correctly.)
- *Satterlee v. Allen Press*, 455 F. Supp. 2d 1236 (U.S. District Court, Kansas, 2006) (Although counsel contends that the documents were not filed because their large size exceeded the maximum amount allowed by the electronic filing system and this was the fault of his legal assistant, counsel bears responsibility for this oversight.)
- *MomsWin, LLC v. Lutes*, 2003 WL 21077437 (U.S. District Court, Kansas, 2003) (The legal assistant notarized a signature that she apparently knew was not genuine. "This is a serious violation of a notary's duties which the Court must report" to the state.)
- *In re Jones*, 291 Kan. 405, 420, 241 P.3d 90, 102 (Supreme Court of Kansas, 2010) ([T]his court has established guidelines for what suspended and disbarred attorneys may and may not do. With regard to limitations, we have emphasized: "[T]he better rule is that an attorney who has been disbarred or suspended from the practice of law is permitted to work as a law clerk, investigator, paralegal, or in any capacity as a lay person for a licensed attorney-employer if the suspended lawyer's functions are limited exclusively to work of a preparatory nature under the supervision of a licensed attorney-employer and does not involve client contact. Any contact with a client is prohibited. Although not an inclusive list, the following restrictions apply: a suspended or disbarred lawyer may not be present during conferences with clients, talk to clients either directly or on the telephone, sign correspondence to them, or contact them either directly or indirectly.") (See also In re Miller, 290 Kan. 1075, 238 P.3d 227 (Supreme Court of Kansas, 2010.)

- *In re Lady Baltimore Foods*, 2004 WL 2192368 (U.S. Bankruptcy Court, Kansas 2004) (The use of paralegals can be especially valuable when they render legal services, such as the research of legal issues or drafting legal pleadings, at less cost than if those same services were performed by an attorney. Yet counsel should explain why certain tasks in this case were delegated to a highly paid paralegal, instead of being *absorbed* in the firm's overhead by a competent legal secretary.)
- *Davis v. Miller*, 269 Kan. 732, 7 P.3d 1223, 1236 (Kansas Supreme Court, 2000) ("Davis also argues that some of the paralegal work was clerical in nature and should have been considered as part of the attorneys' overhead. Our view of the large record before us reveals that it would take a line-by-line review of records that are not descriptive enough for this court (or the district court) to separate paralegal work from clerical work to try and separate the two.")
- *Erickson v. City of Topeka*, 239 F. Supp. 2d 1202 (U.S. District Court, Kansas, 2002) (The prevailing party in this civil rights action was not entitled to recover fees for time spent by paralegal, where the paralegal did not itemize his billings, but instead lumped all his tasks together in a generalized description, and the tasks described were largely clerical in nature.)
- *Barker v. Grace, Unruh & Pratt*, 308 P.3d 31 (Court of Appeals of Kansas, 2013) (Barker was a senior legal assistant employed by Grace, Unruh & Pratt (GUP) when she filed her first application for hearing with the Division of Workers Compensation claiming that her left wrist and right elbow were injured by repetitive computer input and her dates of accident were from July 1, 1999, to July 27, 1999. Barker testified that the pain, primarily in her right arm, was brought on when she performed approximately 8 hours of constant typing. She reported the pain and was seen by several doctors. Her injuries are undisputed.)

Doing Legal Research In Kansas Law

- **Statutes:** www.kslegislature.org/li (click *Bills and Laws*, then select *Statute*)
- **Cases:** www.kscourts.org/Cases-and-Opinions/opinions

- **Court Rules:** www.kscourts.org (click *Court Rules and Forms*)
- **General:** www.washlaw.edu/uslaw /states/kansas.html

Finding Employment In Kansas

- See Exhibit 2-12 in Chapter 2.
- l.ks.bar.associationcareernetwork .com/Common/HomePage.aspx
- paralegal.jobs.net/jobs/overland -park,kansas.aspx
- www.careerbuilder.com/jobs/ks /keyword/paralegal
- www.simplyhired.com/k-paralegal-l -kansas-jobs.html

KENTUCKY

ETHICS CODE AND OPINIONS IN KENTUCKY

- **Attorneys: Kentucky Code:** *Rules of Professional Conduct*
  - www.kybar.org/237
  - www.law.cornell.edu/ethics/kentucky .html
  - See also ethics links in Helpful Websites at the end of Chapter 5.
- **Attorneys: Kentucky Ethics Opinions**
  - www.kybar.org/246
- **Unauthorized Practice of Law: Kentucky**
  - www.kybar.org (enter *unauthorized practice of law* in search box)
  - www.kybar.org/244
  - ir.lawnet.fordham.edu/cgi/viewcontent .cgi?article=3572&context=flr
- **Paralegals and Other Nonattorneys: Kentucky**
  - *Rule 5.3 (SCR 3.130).* For a discussion of the state's ethics Rule 5.3 ("Responsibilities Regarding Nonlawyer Assistants") in the Kentucky *Rules of Professional Conduct*, see Chapter 5. For the text of 5.3 in Kentucky, see www.kybar.org/237.
  - *Rule 1.10 (SCR 3.130) (Comment 4).* The rule of imputed disqualification in Rule 1.10 "does not prohibit representation by others in the law firm where the person prohibited from involvement in a matter is a nonlawyer, such as a paralegal or legal secretary." Kentucky *Rules of Professional Conduct.*
  - *Rule 5.5 (SCR 3.130)* (Comment 2). Lawyers can employ the services of paraprofessionals and delegate tasks to them "so long as the lawyer supervises the delegated work and retains responsibility for their work."
  - *Rule 5.5 (SCR 3.130)* (Comment 3). Lawyers can assist independent paraprofessionals, who are authorized

to provide particular law-related services.

- The letterhead of an attorney can include the name of a paralegal. An attorney's name can appear on the business card of a paralegal if the latter's nonattorney status is clear. An attorney shall not share, on a proportionate basis, legal fees with a paralegal. When dealing with a client, a paralegal must disclose at the outset that he or she is not an attorney. This disclosure must be made to anyone who may have reason to believe that the paralegal is an attorney or is associated with an attorney. Kentucky Paralegal Code, *Supreme Court Rule 3.700* (kybar.org/documents/scr /scr3/scr_3.700.pdf).
- A paralegal can communicate with clients outside the office if (1) it is made clear that the *paralegal* is not a lawyer; (2) the lawyer discusses the specific issues with the paralegal both before the paralegal-client discussions and afterwards; and (3) the attorney accepts full responsibility for the paralegal's actions and advice. Kentucky Bar Ass'n, *KBA U-47* (1994).
- Without client consent, it is unethical for an attorney to charge a client for paralegal services when the attorney's contract with the client calls for a statutory-set fee, a lump sum fee, or a contingent fee. The attorney who charges an hourly rate *can* charge for paralegal services, which may be separately stated. Kentucky Bar Ass'n, *Opinion E-303* (5/1985).
- To avoid disqualification, a law firm that hires a paralegal who brings a conflict of interest because of prior employment must screen the paralegal from the case in which the conflict arises and take other steps to avoid a breach of confidentiality. Kentucky Bar Ass'n, *Opinion E-308* (1985).
- A paralegal cannot appear in court on motion day or for the motion docket. Kentucky Bar Ass'n, *Opinion E-227* (1/80).
- A lay *assistant* cannot take (i.e., conduct) a deposition. Kentucky Bar Ass'n, *Opinion E-341* (1990).
- Independent paralegals cannot provide legal services to the public without attorney supervision. Kentucky Bar Ass'n, *Opinion U-45* (1992).
- A nonattorney cannot represent a corporation except in small claims court. Kentucky Bar Ass'n, *Opinion E-344* (1991).

- A nonattorney nurse ombudsman cannot represent a nursing home patient before an administrative agency unless federal law allows it. Kentucky Bar Ass'n, *Opinion U-46* (1994).
- An attorney can accept and follow insurance company guidelines on establishing an appropriate allocation of lawyer and nonlawyer/paralegal tasks, but cannot agree that all investigative work or all records review will be performed only by the insurer's employees or, if performed by the lawyer's firm, to be billed only at a paralegal rate. Kentucky Bar Ass'n, *Opinion E-416* (3/2001).
- A *suspended* attorney may work in a law firm as a paralegal after the period of his suspension has expired, even if he has not been reinstated. Kentucky Bar Ass'n, *Opinion E-336* (9/1989).

Defining Legal Assistants/Paralegals In Kentucky

- A paralegal is a person under the supervision and direction of a licensed lawyer, who may apply knowledge of law and legal procedures in rendering direct assistance to lawyers engaged in legal research; design, develop or plan modifications or new procedures, techniques, services, processes or applications; prepare or interpret legal documents and write detailed procedures for practicing in certain fields of law; select, compile and use technical information from such references as digests, encyclopedias or practice manuals; and analyze and follow procedural problems that involve independent decisions. Kentucky Paralegal Code, Supreme Court Rule 3.700 (www.kybar.org/documents/scr/scr3 /scr_3.700.pdf).

Defining The Practice Of Law In Kentucky

- § 3.020 (*Rules of the Kentucky Supreme Court*): The practice of law is any service rendered involving legal knowledge or legal advice, whether of representation, counsel or advocacy in or out of court, rendered in respect to the rights, duties, obligations, liabilities, or business relations of one requiring the services. But nothing herein shall prevent any natural person not holding himself out as a practicing attorney from drawing any instrument to which he is a party without consideration unto himself therefor. An appearance in the small claims division of the district court by a person who is an officer of or who is regularly employed in a managerial capacity by a corporation or partnership which is a party to the litigation in which the appearance is made shall not be considered an unauthorized practice of law.

Paralegals (And Others) In Kentucky State And Federal Courts

(See the beginning of this appendix on how to find the full text of the opinions cited here, including WL opinions.)

- *In re Paniagua de Aponte*, 364 S.W.2d 176, 183 (Supreme Court of Kentucky, 2012) ("No doubt, paralegals make much of the work of lawyers possible, and many of them could practice law as well as many lawyers, even without having attended law school. But we have a rule in place for a reason. The training of paralegals as a whole simply does not compare to that received by students at accredited American law schools.")
- Ziarko v. Crawford Law Offices, 2010 WL 5059569 (U.S. District Court, E.D. Kentucky, 2010) (A client (Joette Ziarko) loses a case because of the alleged negligence of her attorney in pursuing the client's claim. The client then sues the attorney, as well as his paralegal, Mary Vicini. A motion is made to dismiss the case against Vicini. The defendants argue that the client failed to state a claim against Vicini, who is a paralegal, not a lawyer. It may be true that Ziarko is precluded from suing Vicini for legal malpractice, but Ziarko has asserted claims against Vicini for garden-variety negligence. But wait, say the defendants. Before there can be negligence there must be a duty. And Vicini did not owe a duty to Ziarko because, according to the defendants, paralegals do not owe duties to the clients of the lawyers who employ them. The defendants do not cite to any Kentucky case establishing this "paralegal exception" to the general "duty of reasonable care which is owed by each of us to everyone else." Instead, the defendants ask the Court to fashion a paralegal exception out of whole cloth, relying on public policy. That is not this Court's role. And even if it were, the defendants have not identified what, exactly, is so sacrosanct about a paralegal's position that warrants a reprieve from the usual rule that everyone owes a duty of reasonable care to everyone else. Because the defendants have not established immunity of any sort for Vicini, Ziarko has stated a claim against her for negligence.)

- *Turner v. Kentucky Bar Ass'n*, 980 S.W.2d 560 (Supreme Court of Kentucky, 1998) (A statute authorizing nonlawyers to represent parties in worker's compensation proceedings violated the constitutional principle of separation of powers. Nonlawyer worker's compensation specialists did not engage in unauthorized practice of law when processing claims while supervised by an attorney. Nonlawyers, however, could not represent parties before any adjudicative tribunal.)
- *Wal-Mart Stores, Inc. v. Dickinson*, 29 S.W.3d 796 (Supreme Court of Kentucky, 2000) (Work product prepared by a paralegal is protected with equal force by the attorney work-product rule as is any trial preparation material prepared by an attorney in anticipation of litigation. Also, the attorney-client privilege applies with equal force to paralegals.)
- *Wyatt, Tarrant & Combs v. Williams*, 892 S.W.2d 584 (Supreme Court of Kentucky, 1995) (A paralegal works on tobacco litigation at a law firm. When the paralegal stopped working at the firm, he took copies of some of the tobacco litigation documents with him. The firm seeks an injunction against the paralegal to prevent disclosure of the contents of these "stolen" documents.) (See discussion of this case in Chapter 5.)
- *In re Belknap, Inc.*, 103 Bankruptcy Reporter 842, 844 (U.S. Bankruptcy Court, W.D. Kentucky, 1989) (In the award of fees, "[s]enior partners should not perform services which could be as competently performed by associates or paralegals; paralegals should not be used to perform tasks which are clerical in nature.")
- *Sawyer v. Mills*, 2007 WL 1113038 (Court of Appeals of Kentucky, 2007) (A paralegal's secret tape-recording of a conversation with an attorney in which the attorney promised to pay her a bonus of $1 million for her help on class action lawsuits did not satisfy the writing requirement of the statute of frauds.)
- *Countrywide Home Loans, Inc. v. Kentucky Bar Ass'n*, 113 S.W.3d 105 (Supreme Court of Kentucky, 2003) (A "real estate closing" is at best ministerial in nature. Some lawyers allow secretaries and paralegals to participate in closings. The closing, which consists mainly of financial matters, payments, schedules of payment, and insurance, is basically a nonlegal function. So long as the layperson avoids giving legal advice, there is no problem with a lay employee closing a real estate transaction. The rub

that frequently arises in a real estate closing situation is that often questions of a legal nature are posed to the layman who is closing the transaction. Any response would constitute legal advice and would be the unauthorized practice of law by the person answering the questions. In such an instance, the layperson should discontinue the closing and seek proper legal advice. It should be observed that many federal loans involve significant knowledge of the law, and questions as to what is meant in the documents would certainly involve the unauthorized practice of law.)

Doing Legal Research In Kentucky Law

- **Statutes:** www.lrc.ky.gov/statutes
- **Cases:** apps.courts.ky.gov/supreme/sc_opinions.shtm
- **Court Rules:** courts.ky.gov/courts/supreme/Pages/rulesprocedures.aspx
- **General:** www.law.georgetown.edu/library/research/guides/kentucky.cfm

Finding Employment In Kentucky

- loubar.org (click *Career Placement*)
- legal.jobs.net/Kentucky.htm
- www.indeed.com/q-Paralegal-l-Kentucky-jobs.html
- lexington.craigslist.org/lgl

LOUISIANA

ETHICS CODE AND OPINIONS IN LOUISIANA

- **Attorneys: Louisiana Code:** *Rules of Professional Conduct*
  - lalegalethics.org/louisiana-rules-of-professional-conduct
  - www.ladb.org/DR
  - www.law.cornell.edu/ethics/la/code/LA_CODE.HTM
  - See also ethics links in Helpful Websites at the end of Chapter 5.
- **Attorneys: Louisiana Ethics Opinions**
  - www.lsba.org/Members/EthicsAdvisary.aspx
- **Unauthorized Practice of Law: Louisiana**
  - www.lsba.org (enter *unauthorized practice of law* in search box)
  - www.lasc.org/rules/orders/2005/ROPC5.5_8.5.pdf
  - ir.lawnet.fordham.edu/cgi/viewcontent.cgi?article=3572&context=flr
- **Paralegals and Other Nonattorneys: Louisiana**
  - *Rule 5.3.* For a discussion of the state's ethics Rule 5.3 ("Responsibilities

Regarding Nonlawyer Assistants") in the Louisiana Rules of Professional Conduct, see Chapter 5.

- *Rule 1.10 (Comment 4).* The rule of imputed disqualification in Rule 1.10 "does not prohibit representation by others in the law firm where the person prohibited from involvement in a matter is a nonlawyer, such as a paralegal or legal secretary." Louisiana *Rules of Professional Conduct.*
- *Rule 5.5 (Comment 2).* Lawyers can employ the services of paralegals and delegate tasks to them "so long as the lawyer supervises the delegated work and retains responsibility for their work."
- *Rule 5.5 (Comment 3).* Lawyers can assist independent paraprofessionals, who are authorized to provide particular law-related services.
- *Rule 5.5(e)(1)(ii).* A lawyer shall not. . . employ, contract with as a consultant, engage as an independent contractor, or otherwise join in any other capacity, in connection with the practice of law, any person the attorney knows or reasonably should know is a suspended attorney, during the period of suspension, unless first preceded by the submission of a fully executed employment registration statement to the Office of Disciplinary Counsel, on a registration form provided by the Louisiana Attorney Disciplinary Board, and approved by the Louisiana Supreme Court. *Rules of Professional Conduct,* Rule 5.5(e)(1)(ii).
- *Rule 5.5* See also Defining the Practice of Law below.
- An attorney may pay a paralegal or legal assistant a salary and charge clients for their services at a rate greater than their actual salary. *Docket: 96–00068.*
- An attorney engaged in debt collection may not pay a nonlawyer a salary plus a bonus that is linked to increased revenues in the collections area. *Docket: 95–00098.*

Louisiana Certification Of Paralegals

- www.la-paralegals.org (click *LCP Certification*)

Defining The Practice Of Law In Louisiana

- *Rule 5.5.* For purposes of this Rule, the practice of law shall include the following activities: (i) Holding oneself out as an attorney or lawyer authorized to practice law; (ii) Rendering legal consultation or advice to a client; (iii) Appearing on behalf of a client in any hearing or proceeding, or before any judicial officer, arbitrator, mediator, court, public agency, referee, magistrate, commissioner, hearing officer, or governmental body operating in an adjudicative capacity, including submission of pleadings, except as may otherwise be permitted by law; (iv) Appearing as a representative of the client at a deposition or other discovery matter; (v) Negotiating or transacting any matter for or on behalf of a client with third parties; (vi) Otherwise engaging in activities defined by law or Supreme Court decision as constituting the practice of law.
- § 37:212 (*West's Louisiana Statutes Annotated*): A. The practice of law means and includes: (1) In a representative capacity, the appearance as an advocate, or the drawing of papers, pleadings or documents, or the performance of any act in connection with pending or prospective proceedings before any court of record in this state; or (2) For a consideration, reward, or pecuniary benefit, present or anticipated, direct or indirect; (a) The advising or counseling of another as to secular law; (b) In behalf of another, the drawing or procuring, or the assisting in the drawing or procuring of a paper, document, or instrument affecting or relating to secular rights; (c) The doing of any act, in behalf of another, tending to obtain or secure for the other the prevention or the redress of a wrong or the enforcement or establishment of a right; or (d) Certifying or giving opinions as to title to immovable property or any interest therein or as to the rank or priority or validity of a lien, privilege or mortgage as well as the preparation of acts of sale, mortgages, credit sales or any acts or other documents passing titles to or encumbering immovable property.
B. Nothing in this Section prohibits any person from attending to and caring for his own business, claims, or demands; or from preparing abstracts of title; or from insuring titles to property, movable or immovable, or an interest therein, or a privilege and encumbrance thereon, but every title insurance contract relating to immovable property must be based upon the certification or opinion of a licensed Louisiana attorney authorized to engage in the practice of law. Nothing in this Section prohibits any person from performing, as a notary public, any act necessary or incidental to the exercise of the powers and functions of the office of notary public, as those powers are delineated in Louisiana Revised Statutes of 1950, Title 35, Section 1, et seq.
C. Nothing in this Section shall prohibit any partnership, corporation, or other legal entity from asserting any claim, not exceeding five thousand dollars, or defense pertaining to an open account or promissory note, or suit for eviction of tenants on its own behalf in the courts of limited jurisdiction on its own behalf through a duly authorized partner, shareholder, office, employee, or duly authorized agent or representative. No partnership, corporation, or other entity may assert any claim on behalf of another entity or any claim assigned to it.

Paralegals (And Others) In Louisiana State And Federal Courts

(See the beginning of this appendix on how to find the full text of the opinions cited here, including WL opinions.)

- *Adcock v. Ewing,* 57 So.3d 434 (Court of Appeals of Louisiana, 2011) (The legal assistant's mistake in checking the "dismissal" option instead of the "default" option on the "drop-slip" in an original proceeding for breach of contract constituted a clerical mistake that was not tantamount to a judgment of dismissal.)
- *T.S.L. v. G.L.,* 976 So. 2d 793 (Court of Appeals of Louisiana, 2008) (A paralegal employed by the attorney for respondent had prior access to relator's privileged information while working for relator's former counsel. Therefore, because respondent's counsel is responsible for the conduct of her employees and because her paralegal has a direct conflict of interest in this case, the conflict disqualifies her from representing respondent.)
- *In re Watley,* 802 So. 2d 593 (Supreme Court of Louisiana, 2001) (An attorney's entry into a contract calling for fee splitting with an agency that provides secretarial and paralegal support violated the disciplinary rule prohibiting fee sharing with nonlawyers. See also *"We the People" Paralegal' Services v. Watley* 766 So. 2d 744 (Court of Appeals of Louisiana, 2000)).
- *State v. Diaz,* 708 So. 2d 1192 (Court of Appeal of Louisiana, 1998) (Paralegal tells authorities of possible fraud committed by her attorney supervisor.)
- *Louisiana State Bar v. Edwins,* 540 So. 2d 294 (Supreme Court of Louisiana,

1989) (An attorney can be disbarred for delegating too much to a paralegal and for failing to supervise the paralegal.)

- *Louisiana State Bar v. Lindsay*, 553 So. 2d 807 (Supreme Court of Louisiana, 1989) (An attorney charged with professional misconduct tries to shift the blame to his paralegal.)
- *United States v. Cabra*, 622 F. 2d 182 (U.S. Circuit Court, 5th Circuit, 1980) (It is improper to impound a paralegal's trial notes taken during a federal trial.)
- *In re Coney*, 891 So. 2d 658 (Supreme Court of Louisiana, 2005) (An attorney tries to convince his legal assistant to lie to a federal grand jury investigating the attorney.)
- *Kelly v. Housing Authority of New Orleans*, 826 So. 2d 571 (Court of Appeals of Louisiana, 2002) (A paralegal was allowed to testify for the sole purpose of introducing photographs he took of an alleged accident site. The only proof offered that these photographs were of the accident site was the paralegal's testimony that Ms. Kelly told him where she had fallen. What Ms. Kelly told the paralegal was clearly inadmissible hearsay.)
- *Stagner v. Western Kentucky Navigation*, 2004 WL 253453 (U.S. District Court, E.D. Louisiana, 2004) (The cost of paralegal services is to be included in the assessment and award of attorney's fees if the following criteria are met: (1) The services performed must be legal in nature. (2) The performance of such services by the paralegal must be supervised by an attorney. (3) The qualifications of the paralegal performing the services must be specified in the application or motion requesting an award of fees in order to demonstrate that the paralegal is qualified by virtue of education, training, or work experience to perform substantive work. (4) The nature of the services performed by the paralegal must be specified in the application/motion requesting an award of fees in order to permit a determination that the services performed were legal rather than clerical in nature. (5) The amount of time expended by the paralegal in performing the services must be reasonable and must be set out in the motion. (6) The amount charged for the time spent by the paralegal must reflect reasonable community standards of remuneration.)
- *Hanley v. Doctors Hosp. of Shreveport*, 821 So. 2d 508 (Court of Appeals of Louisiana, 2002) (In reviewing the time sheets for the paralegal services, we note numerous entries labeled as "summarize depositions," "preparation for trial," and

"work on exhibit books." Such general labels do not give the court sufficient information to determine the specific service performed or whether the work was reasonably necessary.)

Doing Legal Research In Louisiana Law

- **Statutes:** www.legis.state.la.us/lss/lss .asp?folder=75
- **Cases:** www.lasc.org/opinion_search .asp
- **Court Rules:** www.lasc.org/rules
- **General:** www.rominerlegal.com /state/louisiana.html

Finding Employment In Louisiana

- www.careerbuilder.com/jobs/la /keyword/paralegal
- legal.jobs.net/Louisiana.htm
- neworleans.craigslist.org/lgl
- www.indeed.com/q-Paralegal-l -Louisiana-jobs.html

MAINE

ETHICS CODE AND OPINIONS IN MAINE

- **Attorneys: Maine Code:** *Rules of Professional Conduct*
  - www.mebaroverseers.org/attorney _regulation/maine_conduct_rules .html
  - www.law.cornell.edu/ethics/maine .html
  - See also ethics links in Helpful Websites at the end of Chapter 5.
- **Attorneys: Maine Ethics Opinions**
  - www.mebaroverseers.org/index.html
- **Unauthorized Practice of Law: Maine**
  - www.mainelegislature.org/legis /statutes/4/title4sec807.html
  - ir.lawnet.fordham.edu/cgi/viewcontent .cgi?article=3572&context=flr
- **Paralegals and Other Nonattorneys: Maine**
  - *Rule 5.3.* For a discussion of the state's ethics Rule 5.3 ("Responsibilities Regarding Nonlawyer Assistants") in the Maine *Rules of Professional Conduct*, see Chapter 5. For the text of 5.3 in Maine, see mebaroverseers .org/attorney_regulation/bar_rules .html?id=88243.
  - *Rule 1.10 (Comment 4).* The rule of imputed disqualification in Rule 1.10 "does not prohibit representation by others in the law firm where the person prohibited from involvement in a matter is a nonlawyer, such as a paralegal or legal secretary." Maine *Rules of Professional Conduct.*

- *Rule 5.5* (Comment 2). Lawyers can employ the services of paraprofessionals and delegate tasks to them "so long as the lawyer supervises the delegated work and retains responsibility for their work."
- *Rule 5.5* (Comment 3). Lawyers can assist independent paraprofessionals, who are authorized to provide particular law-related services.
- The names of paralegals can be printed on a firm's letterhead as long as it is not misleading. Maine Board of Overseers of the Bar, *Opinion 34* (1/17/83).
- An attorney cannot form a partnership or professional corporation with a nonattorney to provide legal and nonlegal services to clients. Maine Board of Overseers of the Bar, *Opinion 79* (5/6/87).
- Attorneys have a responsibility to adequately train, monitor and discipline nonattorney staff on ethics. Here, a secretary revealed confidential information. Yet there is no indication that this was due to the attorney's failure to use reasonable care to prevent such disclosure. Maine Board of Overseers of the Bar, *Opinion 134* (9/21/93).
- Secretaries, paralegals and other non-legal staff members frequently leave one law firm and later work for another. A law firm must be sensitive to potential conflicts of interest when hiring non-legal staff members. Accordingly, the lawyer or law firm during the hiring process should make reasonable efforts to obtain information to determine whether there is a potential for conflicts and have systems and procedures in place to detect and manage conflicts after a new employee joins the firm. Assume that Law Firm A hires a new secretary. The secretary previously worked for Law Firm B. While at Law Firm B, the secretary worked on matters for Client X. After the secretary joins Law Firm A, the firm is retained to represent Client Y in litigation against Client X. The secretary was privy to confidential information pertaining to Client X that is relevant to the pending litigation and that was acquired through the prior employment with Law Firm B. We believe that screening of nonlawyer staff employed by a law firm is generally permissible to avoid conflicts of interest presented by that staff. The exceptions are when the confidential information has already been revealed by the non-legal staff member or when screening would be ineffective. Assume that a law firm

paralegal is a member of the Board of a non-profit entity against which the paralegal's law firm is now involved in litigation. The paralegal should be shielded from any involvement in or knowledge about the case, and should be instructed to abstain from any involvement in discussion or decision making in his or her capacity as a Board member of the non-profit entity with respect to issues related to the case. Other precautionary measures may also be necessary to avoid the risk that the personal interests of the paralegal or the paralegal's obligations to the non-profit entity might in some way adversely affect the representation provided by the lawyer or firm or might otherwise cause harm to the client. We also suggest that the Maine lawyer consider whether disclosure of conflict-like nonlawyer assistant relationships should be made to the lawyer's client. Maine Board of Overseers of the Bar, *Opinion 186* (7/22/04).

- A law firm can set up a profit-sharing compensation arrangement under which the firm will make quarterly distributions out of the profits of the partnership directly to nonattorneys employed by the firm in addition to their regular pay provided that the amounts paid to lay employees in addition to fixed salary (1) are not based upon business brought to the law firm by such employees; (2) are not based upon services performed by such employees in a particular case; and (3) do not constitute the greater part of the total remuneration of such employees. Maine Board of Overseers of the Bar, *Opinion 31* (9/22/82).

- The following arrangement is proper: An attorney proposes to accept a client by referral from a self-described "independent 'paralegal' advisor" who is not an employee of the attorney, and who does not receive any type of payment directly from the attorney. The attorney accepts the client's case on a standard contingent fee basis knowing that there is also a contract directly between the client and the "independent 'paralegal' advisor" whereby the advisor will receive 17% of any benefits received by the client as a result of the attorney's work. Thus, the attorney knows that the total fees to be paid by the client in the event of recovery would equal 50% of the amounts collected. Maine Board of Overseers of the Bar, Opinion 124 (5/6/92).

Defining Legal Assistants/Paralegals In Maine

- "Paralegal" and "legal assistant" mean a person, qualified by *education*, training or work experience, who is employed or retained by an attorney, law office, corporation, governmental agency or other entity and who performs specifically delegated substantive legal work for which an attorney is responsible. 4 *Maine Revised Statutes Annotated* § 921(1).

Who Can Use the Title of *Paralegal* or *Legal Assistant* in Maine?

- (1) A person may not use the title "paralegal" or "legal assistant" unless the person meets the *definition* in section 921, subsection 1. (2) A person who violates subsection 1 commits a civil violation for which a forfeiture of not more than $1000 may be adjudged. 4 *Maine Revised Statutes Annotated* §§ 922.

Defining The Practice Of Law In Maine

- *Board of Overseers of the Bar v. Mangan*, 763 A. 2d 1189 (Supreme *Judicial* Court of Maine, 2001): The term "practice of law" is a term of art connoting much more than merely working with legally-related matters. The focus of the inquiry is, in fact, whether the activity in question required legal knowledge and skill in order to apply legal principles and precedent. Even where trial work is not involved but the preparation of legal documents, their interpretation, the giving of legal advice, or the application of legal principles to problems of any complexity, is involved, these activities are still the practice of law. The practice of law includes utilizing legal education, training, and experience to apply the special analysis of the profession to a client's problem. The hallmark of the practicing lawyer is responsibility to clients regarding their affairs, whether as advisor, advocate, negotiator, as intermediary between clients, or as evaluator by examining a client's legal affairs. As attorneys' roles increase in complexity and overlap with other professions, the answer to [the question of what constitutes the practice of law] will continue to evolve. Ultimately, the question will turn on the specific facts of the work undertaken and the understanding of the parties.

- 4 *Maine Revised Statutes Annotated* § 807(1)&(3) No person may practice law unless that person has been admitted to the bar of this State. This section shall not apply to:
  - a nonattorney employee of a designated company who appears for the company in a small claims action;
  - a nonattorney who is represents a party in any hearing before the Workers' Compensation Board.

Paralegals (And Others) In Maine State And Federal Courts

(See the beginning of this appendix on how to find the full text of the opinions cited here, including WL opinions.)

- *Maine v. DeMotte*, 669 A.2d 1331 (Supreme Judicial Court of Maine, 1996) (Chinese wall built around paralegal to prevent disclosure of privileged communications and a conflict of interest.)

- *First NH Banks Granite State v. Scarborough*, 615 A.2d 248, 251 (Supreme Judicial Court of Maine, 1992) (Paralegal fees allowed. We "adopt no talismanic formula with regard to the inclusion of paralegal fees".)

- *Brennan v. Barnhart*, 2007 WL 586794 (U.S. District Court, Maine, 2007) (While counsel may have preferred to organize the files himself, the work could have been performed by a paralegal. Fee reduction ordered.)

- *IMS Health Corp. v. Schneider, 901 F. Supp. 2d 172, 197 (U.S. District Court, Maine, 2012)* (Hunton & Williams billed litigation support specialists and paralegals at the hourly rates of $200 and $180, respectively. In his Declaration, Mr. Montgomery states that at Bernstein Shur "[t]he hourly rate of litigation paralegals ranged from $75–$115 per hour at the time the work was performed." In [the *Desena* case, 847 F. Supp. 2d 207], the panel accepted the paralegal billing rate of $95 per hour. The Court accepts $95 per hour as the rate for paralegal and litigation support billing in Maine.)

- *St. Hilaire v. Industrial Roofing Corp.*, 416 F. Supp. 2d 137 (U.S. District Court, Maine, 2006) (Plaintiff requests $7,826 relating to work on discovery issues. Of this, $1,310 is attributed to paralegal work. As this court has previously held, such work is not recoverable as attorneys' fees).

- *Okot ex rel. Carlo v. Conicelli*, 180 F. Supp. 2d 238 (U.S. District Court, Maine, 2002) (This Court has previously expressed its view that charges for the work of paralegals "are properly included in firm overhead" and that, "[t]o the extent that paralegals are allowed to perform work that constitutes 'the practice of law' under Maine law, such practice is inconsistent with Maine law." *Weinberger*, 801 F. Supp. at 823. The Court continues to regard 4 M.R.S.A. § 807(1) as prohibiting the recovery of attorneys' fees for work done by paralegals that involves the legal judgment and analysis constituting the practice of law. Although the Court of Appeals for the First Circuit did affirm a district court's decision to grant fees for paralegal times in *Lipsett*, it did not hold that such fees were not required, and it did not address the unauthorized practice of law issue and the overhead inclusion rationale that have consistently motivated this Court's decisions to deny compensation for paralegal fees. The documentation submitted by Plaintiffs fails to distill tasks performed by Paralegal Tracy that do not involve the type of legal judgment properly performed by lawyers or that are not properly accounted for in firm overhead. The Court, therefore, will not award any attorneys' fees for the work that she performed.)

- *Currier v. United Technologies Corp.*, 2005 WL 1217278 (U.S. District Court, Maine, 2005) (My review of the entries on the challenged dates quickly reveals many entries which are the essence of paralegal work, *e.g.*, compile and redact exhibits, attention to exhibits for trial, preparation of trial and witness notebooks. I conclude that even the entries for preparation of a certificate of service and correspondence to the clerk of court fall into the gray area between purely clerical tasks and those properly entrusted to a paralegal, and recommend that they not be disallowed.)

Doing Legal Research In Maine Law

- **Statutes:** www.mainelegislature.org /legis/statutes/search.htm
- **Cases:** www.courts.maine.gov /opinions_orders/supreme
- **Court Rules:** www.courts.maine .gov/rules_adminorders/rules
- **General:** www.law.georgetown.edu /library/research/guides/maine.cfm

Finding Employment In Maine

- www.indeed.com/q-Paralegal-l -Maine-jobs.html
- www.careerjet.com/paralegal-jobs /maine-383.html
- maine.craigslist.org/search /lgl?query=+

MARYLAND

ETHICS CODE AND OPINIONS IN MARYLAND

- **Attorneys: Maryland Code:** *Rules of Professional Conduct*
  - www.msba.org/links/default.asp (scroll down to link to *Rules*)
  - www.courts.state.md.us/attygrievance /rules.html
  - www.law.cornell.edu/ethics /maryland.html
  - See also ethics links in Helpful Websites at the end of Chapter 5.
- **Attorneys: Maryland Ethics Opinions**
  - www.msba.org/members/ethics.asp
- **Unauthorized Practice of Law: Maryland**
  - www.msba.org (enter *unauthorized practice of law* in search box)
  - ir.lawnet.fordham.edu/cgi/viewcontent .cgi?article=3572&context=flr
- **Paralegals and Other Nonattorneys: Maryland**
  - *Rule 5.3.* For a discussion of the state's ethics Rule 5.3 ("Responsibilities Regarding Nonlawyer Assistants") in the Maryland *Rules of Professional Conduct*, see Chapter 5.
  - *Rule 5.3(d).* A disbarred or suspended attorney working in a law office cannot give legal advice to a client and must be directly supervised by an attorney.
  - *Rule 1.10 (Comment 4).* The rule of imputed disqualification in Rule 1.10 "does not prohibit representation by others in the law firm where the person prohibited from involvement in a matter is a nonlawyer, such as a paralegal or legal secretary." Maryland *Rules of Professional Conduct*.
  - *Rule 5.5 (Comment 2).* Lawyers can employ the services of paraprofessionals and delegate tasks to them "so long as the lawyer supervises the delegated work and retains responsibility for their work."
  - *Rule 5.5 (Comment 3).* Lawyers can assist independent paraprofessionals, who are authorized to provide particular law-related services.
  - Legal assistants can have business cards as long as their legal assistant status is designated. Maryland Bar Ass'n, *Ethics Opinion 77–28* (10/18/76).
  - An attorney can list the names of paralegals on office letterhead or on the office door as long as their nonattorney status is designated. Maryland Bar Ass'n, *Ethics Opinion 81–69* (5/29/81).
- A nonattorney once worked for attorney #A. She now works for attorney #B. These attorneys are opponents on a case in litigation. This case was underway when the nonattorney worked for attorney #A. If effective screening (i.e., a "Chinese Wall") is used to insulate the nonattorney from the case, attorney #B does not have to withdraw from the litigation. Maryland Bar Ass'n, *Ethics Docket 90–17* (1990).
- An attorney can hire a freelance paralegal as long as the latter is supervised at all times by the attorney who takes steps to ensure there is no disclosure of client confidences. Maryland Bar Ass'n, *Opinion 86–83* (7/23/86).
- It is unethical to pay a bonus to a paralegal for bringing business to the office. Maryland State Bar Ass'n, *Ethics Docket 86–57* (2/12/86).
- An attorney cannot divide a fee with a nonattorney. Maryland Bar Ass'n, *Opinion 86–59* (2/12/86).
- A legal assistant cannot be paid a percentage of the recovery in a case on which the assistant works. Maryland Bar Ass'n, *Ethics Opinion 84–103* (1984).
- An attorney can rent office space to a nonattorney as long as confidentiality of the attorney's clients is not compromised. Maryland Bar Ass'n, *Ethics Opinion 89–45* (6/12/89).

Defining Legal Assistants/Paralegals In Maryland

- A person qualified through education, training or work experience to perform work that requires knowledge or legal concepts and is customarily but not exclusively performed by a lawyer. This person shall be retained or employed by a law office, governmental agency or other entity or be authorized by administrative statutory or court authority to perform this work. A paralegal/legal assistant may apply for associate membership [of the Maryland State Bar Association] under rules prescribed by the Board of Governors if sponsored and employed by an active lawyer member of the Association. (www.msba.org /departments/membership/join.asp)
- A Legal Assistant is a person, qualified through education, training or work experience, who is employed or retained by a lawyer, law office, corporation, governmental agency, or other entity in a capacity or function which involves the performance, under the ultimate direction and supervision of an attorney, of specifically-delegated substantive legal

work, which work, for the most part, requires a sufficient knowledge of legal concepts that, absent such assistant, the attorney would perform the task. *Attorney Grievance Comm'n v. Hallmon*, 681 A.2d 510 (Court of Appeals of Maryland, 1996) (quoting the ABA definition).

Defining The Practice Of Law In Maryland

- § 10–101(h) (*Annotated Code of Maryland, Business Occupations & Professions Code*): Lawyers. (1) "Practice law" means to engage in any of the following activities: (i) giving legal advice; (ii) representing another person before a unit of the State government or of a political subdivision; or (iii) performing any other service that the Court of Appeals defines as practicing law. (2) "Practice law" includes: (i) advising in the administration of probate of estates of decedents in an orphans' court of the State; (ii) preparing an instrument that affects title to real estate; (iii) preparing or helping in the preparation of any form or document that is filed in a court or affects a case that is or may be filed in a court; or (iv) giving advice about a case that is or may be filed in a court.
- When defining the practice of law, the focus of the inquiry is whether the activity in question required legal knowledge and skill in order to apply legal principles and precedent. *Attorney Grievance Comm'n of Maryland v. Shaw*, 732 A.2d 876 (Court of Appeals of Maryland, 1999).
- On the distinction between legal information and legal advice, see the chapter 4 *discussion* of *Opinion 95–056*, Opinion of the Attorney General of Maryland.

Paralegals (And Others) In Maryland State And Federal Courts

(See the beginning of this appendix on how to find the full text of the opinions cited here, including WL opinions.)

- *Attorney Grievance Comm'n v. McDowell*, 93 A.3d 711, 439 Md. 26 (Court of Appeals of Maryland, 2014) (A partner is disciplined for failing to make efforts to ensure that the firm had in effect measures giving reasonable assurance that paralegals did not falsely notarize documents.)
- *Attorney Grievance Comm'n v. Brennan*, 714 A.2d 157 (Court of Appeals of Maryland, 1998) (It is permissible for a disbarred or suspended lawyer to work as a paralegal, provided that proper procedures and constraints are in place

to assure that no one is confused as to the person's status as a paralegal. Work performed by a paralegal constitutes the practice of law. Whether it is the unauthorized practice of law depends on the extent to which it is supervised by the lawyer.) (See also Maryland State Bar Ass'n, *Ethics 79–41*, *Attorney Grievance Commission of Maryland v. James*, 666 A.2d 1246 (Court of Appeals of Maryland, 1995), and Rule 5.3(d) above.

- *Sterling v. Atlantic Automotive Corp.*, 2005 WL 914348 (Circuit Court of Maryland, 2005) (Because there was no evidence that any of the "legal assistants" had paralegal degrees, the charge of $115 per hour was too high. Tasks not requiring legal training should not be billed to a client just because a "legal assistant" performs them. The court has conducted an independent review of the charges and disallowed those which in its view did not require legal training or experience, assuming that paralegal fees are recoverable under Article 49B, § 42 of the Maryland Annotated Code.)
- *In re Boyds Collection Ltd.*, 2006 WL 4671849 (U.S. Bankruptcy Court, Maryland, 2006) (Some of the time logged by paralegals is for clearly clerical work for which separate compensation will not be allowed. This includes time logged to print pleadings and prepare sets of orders.)
- *DiBuo v. Board of Educ. of Worcester County*, 2002 WL 32909389 (U.S. District Court, Maryland, 2002) (The plaintiffs may properly recover paralegal fees as an expense, given the relatively small amount of work done by the paralegal, which eliminated what would undoubtedly have been an even larger lawyer bill for the same work.)
- *In re Ward*, 190 Bankruptcy Reporter 242, 248 (U.S. Bankruptcy Court, Maryland, 1995) ("[w]hen seeking compensation for clerical services performed by an attorney or a paralegal, an applicant must provide sufficient information enabling the court to make a determination as to why such services were performed by an attorney or paralegal as opposed to a paralegal or secretary, respectively.")
- *Attorney Grievance Comm'n of Maryland v. Ward*, 904 A.2d 477 (Court of Appeals of Maryland, 2006) (A legal assistant illegally notarized a signature of a person who was not actually present at the moment of notarization.)
- *Attorney Grievance Comm'n of Maryland v. Zakroff*, 876 A.2d 664 (Court of Appeals of Maryland, 2005) (An attorney is disciplined for instructing his paralegal

to mislead clients' medical providers concerning the status of settled cases.)

Doing Legal Research In Maryland Law

- **Statutes:** www.lexisnexis.com/hottopics/mdcode
- **Cases:** mdcourts.gov/casesearch2/faq.html
- **Court Rules:** www.lexisnexis.com/hottopics/mdcode
- **General:** www.romingerlegal.com/state/maryland.html

Finding Employment In Maryland

- www.indeed.com/q-Paralegal-l-Maryland-jobs.html
- www.careerbuilder.com/jobs/md/keyword/paralegal
- p.md.associationcareernetwork.com/Common/HomePage.aspx
- baltimore.craigslist.org/search/lgl?query=+

MASSACHUSETTS

ETHICS CODE AND OPINIONS IN MASSACHUSETTS

- **Attorneys: Massachusetts Code:** *Rules of Professional Conduct*
  - www.mass.gov/obcbbo/rpcnet.htm
  - www.law.cornell.edu/ethics/massachusetts.html
  - See also ethics links in Helpful Websites at the end of Chapter 5.
- **Attorneys: Massachusetts Ethics Opinions**
  - www.massbar.org/for-attorneys/publications/ethics-opinions
- **Unauthorized Practice of Law in Massachusetts**
  - www.massbar.org (enter *unauthorized practice of law* in search box)
  - www.lawlib.state.ma.us/subject/about/lawyers.html
  - ir.lawnet.fordham.edu/cgi/viewcontent.cgi?article=3572&context=flr
- **Paralegals and Other Nonattorneys: Massachusetts**
  - *Rule 5.3*. For a discussion of the state's ethics Rule 5.3 ("Responsibilities Regarding Nonlawyer Assistants") in the Massachusetts *Rules of Professional Conduct*, see Chapter 5. For the text of 5.3 in Massachusetts, see www.mass.gov/obcbbo/rpc5.htm#Rule 5.3.
  - *Rule 5.5* (Comment 2). Lawyers can employ the services of paraprofessionals and delegate tasks to them "so long as the lawyer supervises the delegated work and retains responsibility for their work."

- An attorney fails to supervise his paralegal in making proper reconciliations for bank deposits. *In re: Stephen Follansbee*, 2014 WL 1689780 (2014).
- It is unethical for an attorney who represents insurance company to delegate tasks to paralegals without first determining that they are competent to perform those tasks even if the insurer requires such delegation. An insurer's guidelines on paralegal use cannot supplant the attorney's judgment on when such use is appropriate. Massachusetts Bar Ass'n, *Opinion 00–4* (9/29/00).
- Paralegal names can be printed on a firm's letterhead if their nonattorney status is clear. Massachusetts Bar Ass'n, *Ethics Opinion 83–10* (11/29/83).
- A paralegal can sign his or her name on law firm letterhead. Massachusetts Bar Ass'n, *Ethics Opinion 73–2.*
- A law firm cannot pay its office administrator (a nonattorney) a percentage of the firm's profits in addition to his fixed salary. Massachusetts Bar Ass'n, *Opinion 84–2* (1984).
- [N]o lawyer who is disbarred or suspended. . . shall engage in paralegal work, and no lawyer or law firm shall knowingly employ or otherwise engage, directly or indirectly, in any capacity, a person who is suspended or disbarred. Clerks' Committee on Ethical Opinions, Rule 4:01. See also *In re Bott*, 462 Mass. 430, 969 N.E.2d 155 (Supreme Judicial Court of Massachusetts, 2012).

Defining The Practice Of Law In Massachusetts

- *Massachusetts Conveyancers Ass'n, Inc. v. Colonial Title & Escrow*, Inc., 2001 WL 669280 (Massachusetts Superior Court, 2001) (Whether a particular activity constitutes the practice of law is fact specific. While a comprehensive definition would be impossible to frame, what constitutes "the practice of law", in general, consists of: "[D]irecting and managing the enforcement of legal claims and the establishment of the legal rights of others, where it is necessary to form and to act upon opinions as to what those rights are and as to the legal methods which must be adopted to enforce them, the practice of giving or furnishing legal advice as to such rights and methods and the practice, as an occupation, of drafting documents by which such rights are created, modified, surrendered or secured. . .")

- *In re Bonarrigo*, 282 Bankruptcy Reporter 101 (U.S. District Court, Massachusetts, 2002) (The "unauthorized practice of law" is prohibited, but not defined, by Massachusetts law. Massachusetts courts and courts in other jurisdictions have concluded that trying to express a comprehensive "definition of what constitutes the practice of law" is an impossibility and that "each case must be decided upon its own particular facts." *In re Shoe Mfrs. Protective Ass'n*, 295 Mass. 369 (1936). Generally speaking, the practice of law can include, "the examination of statutes, judicial decisions, and departmental rulings, for the purpose of advising upon a question of law. . . and the rendering to a client of an opinion thereon.")
- *In re Chimko*, 831 N.E.2d 316 (Supreme Judicial Court of Massachusetts, 2005) (We have rejected the proposition "that whenever, for compensation, one person. . . performs for another some service that requires some knowledge of law, or drafts for another some document that has legal effect, he is practicing law." Architects prepare building contracts, insurance agents prepare riders to policies, auctioneers prepare sale notes, and custom house brokers prepare important documents, all without practicing law.)

Paralegals (And Others) In Massachusetts State And Federal Courts

(See the beginning of this appendix on how to find the full text of the opinions cited here.)

- *U.S. Appolon*, 695 F.3d 44 (1st Cir. 2012) (A paralegal on the defense team has a romantic relationship with the postal inspector on the prosecution's team. Defendant's motion for a post-trial evidentiary hearing or discovery on this romantic relationship is denied. Seven affidavits submitted by the government asserted that the postal inspector did not share confidential information from paralegal with rest of prosecution team. The only people who were in a position to contradict that assertion were the postal inspector and, to a lesser extent, the paralegal, and the postal inspector and paralegal were likely to invoke their Fifth Amendment privilege against self-incrimination.)
- *Roggio v. Grasmuck*, ___ F. Supp. 2d ___, 2014 WL 991574 (U.S. District Court, Massachusetts, 2014) (Hourly rates of $290 for attorney and $190 for paralegal were reasonable in calculating award of attorney fees for a convicted felon

in an action against a detective and security guard under the Massachusetts Criminal Offender Record Information (CORI) Act. The attorney was an associate at law firm and and the paralegal had more than five years of experience.)
- *Matter of Eisenhauer*, 689 N.E.2d 783 (Supreme Judicial Court of *Massachusetts*, 1998) (Attorney is disciplined for charging attorney rates for paralegal time.)
- *Mogilevsky v. Bally Total Fitness Corp.*, 311 F. Supp. 2d 212 (U.S. District Court, Massachusetts, 2004) (A court must not permit an attorney to recover his standard hourly rate for work appropriate for a less experienced lawyer or a paralegal or secretary.)
- *Dixon v. International Broth. of Police Officers*, 434 F. Supp. 2d 73 (U.S. District Court, Massachusetts, 2006) (For purposes of calculating an award of attorney fees under Title VII and the Massachusetts discrimination statute, undetailed and general billing entries and duplicative work warranted a significant reduction of hours billed by the paralegal.)
- *Crance v. Commissioner of Public Welfare*, 507 N.E.2d 751 (Supreme Judicial Court of Massachusetts, 1987) (Paralegal fees are awarded where the paralegal's work was not merely ministerial but required the exercise of judgment.)
- *Deo-Agbasi v. The Parthenon Group*, 229 Federal Rules Decisions 348 (U.S. District Court, Massachusetts, 2005) (The neglect of a civil rights action by the plaintiff's paralegal, leading to the failure to timely respond to defendant's motion to dismiss, and attributed to paralegal's heavy caseload, did not constitute "excusable neglect" so as to warrant setting aside the dismissal.)
- *In re Rosario*, 493 Bankruptcy Reporter 292, 349 (U.S. Bankruptcy Court, Massachusetts, 2013) (Nonattorney bankruptcy petition preparer cannot be called a paralegal. The use of the word "paralegal" violates the law not only because it actually contains the prohibited word "legal," but also because it promotes the petition preparer's legal skills. Promotion of such skills leads a reasonable lay person to believe that the petition preparer offers the public legal advice or legal assistance regarding bankruptcy, which bankruptcy petition preparers are not authorized to provide.)
- *Rodriguez v. Montalvo*, 337 F. Supp. 2d 212 (U.S. District Court, Massachusetts, 2004) (If a nonlawyer paralegal established a confidential relationship with a client, that relationship may be imputed to the attorney supervisor and

consequently to the firm as a whole, for the purpose of a motion under Massachusetts law to disqualify an attorney based on a former representation.)

Doing Legal Research In Massachusetts Law

- **Statutes:** malegislature.gov /Legislation
- **Cases:** masscases.com
- **Court Rules:** www.lawlib.state .ma.us/source/mass/rules
- **General:** lawlibraryguides.bu.edu /masslawresearch

Finding Employment In Massachusetts

- legal.jobs.net/Massachusetts.htm
- www.indeed.com/q-Paralegal-l -Massachusetts-jobs.html
- boston.craigslist.org/lgl

MICHIGAN

ETHICS CODE AND OPINIONS IN MICHIGAN

- **Attorneys: Michigan Code:** *Rules of Professional Conduct*
  - www.michbar.org (enter *Rules of Professional Conduct* in search box)
  - www.law.cornell.edu/ethics/mi/code /MI_CODE.HTM
  - See also ethics links in Helpful Websites at the end of Chapter 5.
- **Attorneys: Michigan Ethics Opinions**
  - www.michbar.org/opinions /ethicsopinions.cfm
  - www.michbar.org/opinions/ethics /ethicsindex1.cfm
  - www.michbar.org/opinions /ethics/utilization.cfm (scroll down to *References*)
- **Unauthorized Practice of Law in Michigan**
  - www.michbar.org (enter *unauthorized practice of law* in search box)
  - www.michbar.org/professional/upl.cfm
  - ir.lawnet.fordham.edu/cgi /viewcontent.cgi?article=3572&con text=flr
- **Paralegals and Other Nonattorneys: Michigan**
  - *Rule 5.3.* For a discussion of the state's ethics Rule 5.3 ("Responsibilities Regarding Nonlawyer Assistants") in the Michigan *Rules of Professional Conduct*, see Chapter 5.
  - *Rule 5.5 (Comment).* Lawyers can employ the services of paralegals and delegate tasks to them "so long as the lawyer supervises the delegated work and retains responsibility for their work."

- *Rule 5.5 (Comment).* Lawyers can assist independent paraprofessionals, who are authorized to provide particular law-related services.
- State Bar Board of Commissioners, *Michigan Guidelines for the Utilization of Legal Assistant Services* (1993) (www .michbar.org/opinions/ethics/utiliza- tion.cfm). *Guideline 1:* An attorney must take reasonable steps to ensure that his or her legal assistant complies with the ethical rules governing Michigan attorneys. *Guideline 2:* The attorney must directly supervise and evaluate assigned tasks. A legal assistant may not convey to persons outside the law firm the legal assistant's opinion on the applicability of laws to particular cases. Legal documents on which a legal assistant works must be signed by an attorney. *Guideline 3:* An attorney cannot delegate to legal assistants the task of establishing an attorney-client relationship or the fee to be paid. *Guideline 4:* A legal assistant may be identified on attorney letterhead and on business cards that mention the law firm's name. *Guideline 5:* The attorney should take reasonable measures to ensure that no conflict of interest is presented arising out of the legal assistant's current or prior employment, or from the legal assistant's other business or personal interests. *Guideline 6:* An attorney can charge a client for legal assistant time if the client consents. *Guideline 7:* An attorney must not split fees with a legal assistant nor pay a legal assistant for referring legal business. A legal assistant can be included in a firm's retirement plan even if based on a profit-sharing arrangement. *Guideline 8:* The attorney should facilitate the legal assistant's participation in continuing legal education and public service activities.
- Where a paralegal has had access during prior employment to confidential or secret *information* concerning a legal matter substantially related and materially adverse to a matter in which the new law firm employer is representing a client, the law firm must promptly and adequately screen the nonlawyer from the matter in order to avoid disqualification. State Bar of Michigan, *Opinion RI- 285* (12/11/96). See also *Opinion CI- 1168* (12/10/86) and *Opinion RI-115* (1/31/92).
- When nonattorney employees with access to the files move to another law firm, a Chinese Wall may have to

be built around them to prevent the imputed disqualification of the new firm. State Bar of Michigan, *Opinion R-4* (9/22/89).

- Business cards and law firm letterhead can list the name of nonattorney employees with titles such as *legal assistant* or *paralegal*. The public must not be confused as to their nonattorney status. State Bar of Michigan, *Opinion RI-34* (10/25/89). See also *Opinion CI-1155*.
- A law firm may not list a nonlawyer on its letterhead, identifying the nonlawyer with the job title "Estate Administrator," indicating that the nonlawyer holds a MBA degree and interposing a horizontal line and a space between the last-listed lawyer's name and the nonlawyer's name, without doing more to indicate that the nonlawyer is not a lawyer. State Bar of Michigan, *Opinion RI-323* (6/5/01).
- A law firm may pay a legal assistant compensation based on a set salary and a percentage of the net profits of the practice area in which the legal assistant is involved as long as no payments are made based on fees generated from particular clients. State Bar of Michigan, *Opinion RI-143* (8/25/92).
- It is not possible for an attorney to give quality supervision to 24 paralegals located at six separate sites in the state. State Bar of Michigan, *Opinion R-1* (12/16/88).
- An attorney's paralegal can represent clients in administrative hearings where authorized by law. The attorney must make sure that this paralegal acts ethically in providing this representation. State Bar of Michigan, *Opinion RI-125* (4/17/92). See also *Opinion RI-103* (10/9/91).
- An attorney may not establish a business employing a paralegal who will sell will-and-trust forms where the paralegal will probably provide consultation and advice to clients. State Bar of Michigan, *Opinion RI-191* (2/14/94).
- As a matter of legal ethics, it is possible for a lawyer to represent a client relying on communications solely through a nonlawyer assistant. This Opinion supersedes *Informal Opinion RI-128* to the contrary. The assistant must be adequately trained and supervised by the lawyer; and the lawyer must carefully manage the communication and the handling of the matter to avoid

assisting in the unauthorized practice of law and failing to provide legal services competently, to communicate adequately with the client, and to provide candid advice. State Bar of Michigan, *Opinion RI-349* (7/26/2010).

■ An attorney is prohibited from representing a client if one of his nonattorney employees will become a witness who will give testimony that is not consistent with the interests of the attorney's client. State Bar of Michigan, *Opinion RI-26* (7/19/89).

■ Information collected by a legal assistant during an interview is protected against disclosure by the attorney-client privilege. State Bar of Michigan, *Opinion RI-123* (3/13/92).

■ A disbarred or suspended lawyer may not be employed as a "paralegal assistant" by a lawyer or law firm. State Bar of Michigan, *Opinion C-211* (7/72).

Defining Legal Assistants/Paralegals In Michigan

■ Any person currently employed or retained by a lawyer, law office, governmental agency or other entity engaged in the practice of law, in a capacity or function which involves the performance under the direction and supervision of an attorney of specifically delegated substantive legal work, which work, for the most part, requires a sufficient knowledge of legal concepts such that, absent that legal assistant, the attorney would perform the task and which is not primarily clerical or secretarial in nature. Article 1, Sec 6, of the *Bylaws of the State Bar of Michigan* Article 1, § 6 (jobs.michbar.org/home /index.cfm?site_id=11713)(www.michbar .org/opinions/ethics/utilization.cfm).

Defining The Practice Of Law In Michigan

■ *Dressel v. Ameribank*, 664 N.W.2d 151 (Supreme Court of Michigan, 2003) A person engages in the practice of law when he or she counsels or assists another in matters that require the use of legal discretion and profound legal knowledge. [Conducting cases in courts, preparing pleadings and other papers incident to actions, and managing such actions and proceedings on behalf of clients before judges and courts (these tasks demand the unique training and skills of an attorney). Giving legal advice in any action taken for others in any matter connected with the law even though unrelated to any action in court (this task requires a lawyer's training and skill). Drafting legal documents, such as wills, that require the determination of the legal effect of special facts and conditions (this task requires legal training and profound legal knowledge). Note, however, that the practice of law does *not* include drafting simple standardized legal documents, such as ordinary leases, mortgages, and deeds, that do not require legal training and knowledge — so long as the drafting does not entail giving advice or counsel as to their legal effect and validity.]

Important Michigan Rules On Paralegal Fees

■ *Rule 2.626 (West's Michigan Rules of Court)*: An award of attorney fees may include an award for the time and labor of any legal assistant who contributed nonclerical, legal support under the supervision of an attorney, provided the legal assistant meets the criteria set forth in Article 1, § 6 of the Bylaws of the State Bar of Michigan [governing eligibility to become an affiliate member of the State Bar of Michigan].

■ *Rates* charged must be commensurate with the level of skill required for a particular task. . . . Professional fees may not be charged for non-professional services such as copying or delivering documents, preparing or filing proofs of service, or for trustee duties generally performed without the assistance of an attorney or other professional. When paralegals are utilized to perform legal services for an estate, they may be compensated as paraprofessionals rather than treated as an overhead expense. *Local Bankruptcy Rules of the U.S. Bankruptcy Court for the Western District of Michigan*, LBR 9013–1.

Paralegals (And Others) In Michigan State And Federal Courts

(See the beginning of this appendix on how to find the full text of the opinions cited here, including WL opinions.)

■ *Michigan v. Hurst*, 517 N.W.2d 858, 862–63 (Court of Appeals of Michigan, 1994) (The "defendant's supplemental appellate brief. . . prepared by an apparently competent legal assistant, sufficiently apprised this court of the finer points of defendant's arguments.")

■ *In the Matter of Bright*, 171 Bankruptcy Reporter 799, 802 (U.S. Bankruptcy Court, E.D. Michigan, 1994) (A bankruptcy trustee charged a paralegal with the unauthorized practice of law in helping the debtor. A disclaimer that one is "only providing 'scrivener' or 'paralegal' services is irrelevant if the nonlawyer in fact engages in the unauthorized practice of law.")

■ *Cobb Publishing Co. v. Hearst Corp.*, 907 F. Supp. 1038 (U.S. District Court, E. D. Michigan, 1995) (Chinese wall set up to prevent disqualification of law firm due to a conflict of interest. A memo is sent to all attorneys, paralegals, and other staff to stay away from the contaminated employee.)

■ *Kearns v. Ford Motor Co.*, 114 Federal Rules Decisions 57 (U.S. District Court, E.D. Michigan, 1987) (A paralegal gives a copy of privileged litigation documents to someone with whom she was having a romantic relationship.)

■ *RVP Development Corp. v. Furness Golf Const.*, 2004 WL 1737589 (Court of Appeals of Michigan, 2004) (MCR 2.626 does not express that the award for time and labor of legal assistants be based upon [a] "reasonable hourly or daily rate." Legal assistants' wages are considered fixed overhead costs. Because wages of legal assistants are considered fixed and MCR 2.626 does not indicate otherwise, an award for the time and labor of legal assistants cannot exceed the actual charge.)

■ *Auto Alliance Intern., Inc. v. U.S. Customs Service*, 155 Federal Appendix 226 (U.S. Court of Appeals, 6th Cir. Michigan, 2005) (The billing records reflect that the vast majority of the paralegal work consisted of picking up and indexing documents. This is nonrecoverable clerical work, as contrasted with paralegal work that would be otherwise have to be done by an attorney.)

Doing Legal Research In Michigan Law

■ **Statutes:** www.legislature.mi.gov
■ **Cases:** courts.mi.gov/opinions _orders/Pages/default.aspx
■ **Court Rules:** courts.mi.gov (enter *court rules* in the search box)
■ **General:** www.michbar.org /generalinfo/libraries/michlaw.cfm

Finding Employment In Michigan

■ legal.jobs.net/Michigan.htm
■ www.indeed.com/q-Paralegal-l -Michigan-jobs.html
■ jobs.michbar.org/home/index .cfm?site_id=11713
■ jobs.michbar.org/jobseeker/search /results
■ detroit.craigslist.org/lgl

MINNESOTA

ETHICS CODE AND OPINIONS IN MINNESOTA

- **Attorneys: Minnesota Code: *Rules of Professional Conduct***
  - lprb.mncourts.gov/rules/Pages/MRPC.aspx
  - www.law.cornell.edu/ethics/minnesota.html
  - See also ethics links in Helpful Websites at the end of Chapter 5.
- **Attorneys: Minnesota Ethics Opinions**
  - lprb.mncourts.gov/rules/Pages/LPRBOpinions.aspx
- **Unauthorized Practice of Law: Minnesota**
  - msba.mnbar.org (enter *unauthorized practice of law* in search box)
  - ir.lawnet.fordham.edu/cgi/viewcontent.cgi?article=3572&context=flr
- **Paralegals and Other Nonattorneys: Minnesota**
  - *Rule 5.3.* For a discussion of the state's ethics Rule 5.3 ("Responsibilities Regarding Nonlawyer Assistants") in the Minnesota *Rules of Professional Conduct*, see Chapter 5.
  - *Rule 1.10 (Comment 4).* The rule of imputed disqualification in Rule 1.10 "does not prohibit representation by others in the law firm where the person prohibited from involvement in a matter is a nonlawyer, such as a paralegal or legal secretary." Minnesota *Rules of Professional Conduct*.
  - *Rule 5.5* (Comment 2). Lawyers can employ the services of paraprofessionals and delegate tasks to them "so long as the lawyer supervises the delegated work and retains responsibility for their work."
  - *Rule 5.5* (Comment 3). Lawyers can assist independent paraprofessionals, who are authorized to provide particular law-related services.
  - Paralegal names can be printed on a firm's letterhead, business cards, professional announcement cards, office signs, telephone directory listings, law lists, and legal directory listings if their nonattorney status is clear. Paralegals, so identified, may sign correspondence on behalf of the law firm if acting under an attorney's direction. But they cannot be named on pleadings under any identification. Minnesota Bar Ass'n, *Ethics Opinion 8* (6/26/74; amended 6/18/80 and 12/4/87). On letterheads, see also *Opinion 93* (6/7/84).

- It is improper for a lawyer to permit any nonattorney employee to accept a gratuity offered by a court reporting service or other service for which the client is expected to pay unless the client consents. Minnesota Lawyers Professional Responsibility Board, *Opinion 17* (6/18/93).

Defining The Practice Of Law In Minnesota

- *Cardinal v. Merrill Lynch Realty/Burnet, Inc.*, 433 N.W.2d 864 (Supreme Court of Minnesota, 1988): The line between what is and what is not the practice of law cannot be drawn with precision. Lawyers should be the first to recognize that between the two there is a region wherein much of what lawyers do every day in their practice may also be done by others without wrongful invasion of the lawyers' field. See also *Cowern v. Nelson*, 207 Minn. 642, 647, 290 N.W. 795, 797 (1940)
- § 481.02 (*Minnesota Statutes Annotated*):
  - Subdivision 1. Prohibitions. It shall be unlawful for any person or association of persons, except members of the bar of Minnesota admitted and licensed to practice as attorneys at law, to appear as attorney or counselor at law in any action or proceeding in any court in this state to maintain, conduct, or defend the same, except personally as a party thereto in other than a representative capacity, or, by word, sign, letter, or advertisement, to hold out as competent or qualified to give legal advice or counsel, or to prepare legal documents, or as being engaged in advising or counseling in law or acting as attorney or counselor at law, or in furnishing to others the services of a lawyer, or lawyers, or, for a fee or any consideration, to give legal advice or counsel, perform for or furnish to another legal services, or, for or without a fee or any consideration, to prepare, directly or through another, for another person, firm, or corporation, any will or testamentary disposition or instrument of trust serving purposes similar to those of a will, or, for a fee or any consideration, to prepare for another person, firm, or corporation, any other legal document, except as provided in subdivision 3. . . .
  - Subdivision 3. Permitted actions. The provisions of this section shall not prohibit. . . (2) a person from drawing a will for another in an emergency if

the imminence of death leaves insufficient time to have it drawn and its execution supervised by a licensed attorney-at-law. . . . (5) any bona fide labor organization from giving legal advice to its members in matters arising out of their employment. . . . (14) the delivery of legal services by a specialized legal assistant in accordance with a specialty license issued by the supreme court before July 1, 1995. . . .
  - Subdivision 3a. Real estate closing services. Nothing in this section shall be construed to prevent a real estate broker, a real estate salesperson, or a real estate closing agent, as defined in section 82.17, from drawing or assisting in drawing papers incident to the sale, trade, lease, or loan of property, or from charging for drawing or assisting in drawing them, except as hereafter provided by the supreme court. . . .
  - Subdivision 7. Lay assistance to attorneys. Nothing herein contained shall be construed to prevent a corporation from furnishing to any person lawfully engaged in the practice of law, such information or such clerical service in and about the attorney's professional work as, except for the provisions of this section, may be lawful, provided, that at all times the lawyer receiving such information or such services shall maintain full, professional and direct responsibility to the attorney's clients for the information and services so received. . . .

Paralegals (And Others) In Minnesota State And Federal Courts

(See the beginning of this appendix on how to find the full text of the opinions cited here, including WL opinions.)

- *State v. Wood*, 845 N.W.2d 239 (Court of Appeals of Minnesota, 2014) (At the trial of the defendant charged with petty misdemeanor traffic violations, defendant did not have a confrontation right to cross-examine prosecutor's paralegal who had signed criminal complaint.)
- *In Re Rubin*, 484 N.W.2d 786 (Supreme Court of Minnesota, 1992) (Attorney disciplined for permitting a legal assistant to back-date a signature on a deed.)
- *In re Petition for Disciplinary Action against Jeff D. Bagniefski*, 690 N.W.2d 558 (Supreme Court of Minnesota, 2005) (Attorney has his client sign a blank signature page and then has his paralegal notarize the signature.)

- *Minnesota v. Richards*, 456 N.W.2d 260 (Supreme Court of Minnesota, 1990) (A county attorney's office is not disqualified from prosecuting the defendant merely because the office hired a paralegal who had previously interviewed for a job with defense counsel.)
- *In re Disciplinary Action against Garcia*, 709 N.W.2d 237 (Supreme Court of Minnesota, 2006) (Attorney cannot be reinstated to the practice of law until he demonstrates to the director of the Office of Lawyers Professional Responsibility that he has established written office procedures designed to ensure that he is properly training and supervising nonlawyer employees.)
- *Silverman v. Silverman*, 2004 WL 2066778 (U.S. District Court, Minnesota, 2004) (Fee request is reduced by fifteen percent to reflect the underutilization of paralegals and less senior associates to research issues, prepare correspondence, draft simple motions, and other matters more properly billed at a lower rate.)
- *Macgregor v. Mallinckrodt*, 2003 WL 23335194 (U.S. District Court, Minnesota, 2003) (It is appropriate to bill for paralegal work at reasonable paralegal rates, but clerical duties do not justify attorney and paralegal rates. A few examples of clerical or nonlegal work performed by counsel or the paralegal and charged at those rates include: update witness addresses, file complaint in federal court for client, serve CT corporation for Mallinckrodt, schedule conference with defendant, serve subpoena, edit and type summary judgment brief.)
- *In re Reinstatement of Jellinger*, 728 N.W.2d 917 (Supreme Court of Minnesota, 2007) (Suspended attorney works as a paralegal during the suspension.)

Doing Legal Research In Minnesota Law

- **Statutes:** www.revisor.mn.gov/pubs
- **Cases:** caselaw.findlaw.com/courts /Minnesota
- **Court Rules:** www.mncourts.gov /default.aspx?page=511
- **General:** www.lawmoose.com

Finding Employment In Minnesota

- mnbenchbar.com/classifieds
- www.careerbuilder.com/jobs/mn /keyword/paralegal
- www.indeed.com/q-Paralegal-l -Minnesota-jobs.html
- legal.jobs.net/Minnesota -Minneapolis.htm
- minneapolis.craigslist.org/lgl

MISSISSIPPI

ETHICS CODE AND OPINIONS IN MISSIPPI

- **Attorneys: Mississippi Code:** *Rules of Professional Conduct*
  - courts.ms.gov/rules/msrulesofcourt /rules_of_professional_conduct.pdf
  - www.law.cornell.edu/ethics/ms/code /MS_CODE.HTM
  - www.law.cornell.edu/ethics /mississippi.html
  - See also ethics links in Helpful Websites at the end of Chapter 5.
- **Attorneys: Mississippi Ethics Opinions**
  - www.msbar.org/ethics-discipline /ethics-opinions.aspx
- **Unauthorized Practice of Law in Mississippi**
  - msbar.org/ethics-discipline /unauthorized-practice-of-law.aspx
- **Paralegals and Other Nonattorneys: Mississippi**
  - *Rule 5.3*. For a discussion of the state's ethics Rule 5.3 ("Responsibilities Regarding Nonlawyer Assistants") in the Mississippi *Rules of Professional Conduct*, see Chapter 5. For the text of 5.3 in Mississippi, see site above for the Rules.
  - *Rule 5.5* (Comment). Lawyers can employ the services of paraprofessionals and delegate tasks to them "so long as the lawyer supervises the delegated work and retains responsibility for their work."
  - We live in a world where attorneys and paralegals move from one firm to the other. Here, a paralegal switched firms. The prior and current firm had clients who opposed each other. It is the opinion of the Ethics Committee that disqualification of a paralegal is not imputed to the firm so long as the paralegal is screened to protect confidential information. The paralegal "must be screened by all supervising lawyers from information about or participating in matters involving the present clients" and must make the paralegal aware that no information relating to the representation of the clients of the former employer shall be revealed by the paralegal to any person in the current law firm. The paralegal should not be allowed to work on any matter in which he worked for the prior employer or respecting which the paralegal has information relating to the representation of the client of the former employer. The current law firm must take all necessary steps to ensure that

the paralegal takes no action and performs no work in relation to matters on which the paralegal worked in the prior employment unless a written consent is obtained by the client of the prior employer. Mississippi Bar Ass'n, *Opinion 258* (2011). See, however, the *Owens* case below where disqualification was ordered because screening was set up too late.
- It is permissible for an attorney to list the name of a paralegal or other nonlawyer on the attorney's letterhead. However, the listing of the names of the paralegals and other non-lawyer personnel should be accompanied by language stating that such persons are not lawyers. The paralegal should not be called a *paralegal associate*, because in common usage the term *associate* carries a connotation of being an attorney in a law firm. Mississippi Bar Ass'n, *Opinion 93* (1984, 2013).
- An attorney can pay a paralegal a bonus based on the number of her hours billed and collected in excess of a designated minimum. A nonattorney compensation or retirement plan can be based in whole or in part on a profit-sharing arrangement. Mississippi State Bar, *Opinion 154* (1988, 2013).
- Legal assistants can use the initials *CLA* (Certified Legal Assistant) or *CLAS* (Certified Legal Assistant Specialist) after their names on law firm letterhead as long as the designation is accompanied by language indicating that the legal assistant is not an attorney. These initials indicate the legal assistant has passed the test and met the other requirements of the National Association of Legal Assistants. Mississippi State Bar, *Opinion 223* (1995, 2013).
- A notary public who is not an attorney licensed to practice law is prohibited from representing or advertising that the notary public is an immigration consultant, immigration paralegal or expert on immigration matters unless the notary public is an accredited representative of an organization recognized by the board of immigration appeals pursuant to 8 CFR Section 292.2(a-e) or any subsequent federal law. *Mississippi Code Annotated* § 25–33–27.
- A *request* for a state or local hearing on eligibility for Medicaid must be made in writing by the claimant or claimant's legal representative. "Legal representative" includes the claimant's authorized representative, an attorney

retained by the claimant or claimant's family to represent the claimant, a paralegal representative with a legal aid services. . . . *Mississippi Code Annotated*, § 43–13–116(3)(b).

Defining The Practice Of Law In Mississippi

- *Mississippi Commission on Judicial Performance v. Jenkins*, 725 So. 2d 162 (Supreme Court of Mississippi, 1998): This Court defined the *practice* of law to include the drafting or selection of documents, the giving of advice in regard to them, and the using of an informed or trained discretion in the drafting of documents to meet the needs of the person being served. So any exercise of intelligent choice in advising another of his legal rights and duties brings the activity within the practice of the legal profession.

- *Mississippi Code Annotated*, § 73–3–55: It shall be unlawful for any person to engage in the practice of law in this state who has not been licensed according to law. Any person violating the provisions of this section shall be deemed guilty of a misdemeanor, and, upon conviction, shall be punished in accordance with the provisions of section 97–23–43. Any person who shall for fee or reward or promise, directly or indirectly, write or dictate any paper or instrument of writing, to be filed in any cause or proceeding pending, or to be instituted in any court in this state, or give any counsel or advice therein, or who shall write or dictate any bill of sale, deed of conveyance, deed of trust, mortgage, contract, or last will and testament, or shall make or certify to any abstract of title or real estate other than his own or in which he may own an interest, shall be held to be engaged in the practice of law. This section shall not, however, prevent title or abstract of title guaranty companies incorporated under the laws of this state from making abstract or certifying titles to real estate where it acts through some person as agent, authorized under the laws of the State of Mississippi to practice law; nor shall this section prevent any abstract company chartered under the laws of the State of Mississippi with a paid up capital of fifty thousand dollars ($50,000.00) or more from making or certifying to abstracts of title to real estate through the president, secretary or other principal officer of such company.

- *Darby v. Mississippi State Board of Bar Admissions*, 185 So. 2d 684, 687 (Supreme Court of Mississippi, 1966): The acts designated in Section 8682 [*Mississippi Code Annotated*, § 73–3–55] as constituting the practice of law are not all-exclusive nor all-inclusive. Manifestly there are many others which might be performed by an unlicensed person which may also constitute the practice of law. Section 8682 (Miss. Code Ann.) simply provides that the designated acts under the defined circumstances constitute the unlawful practice of law, but it does not encroach on the constitutional power of the judiciary to determine that other acts may also do so.

Paralegals (And Other Nonattorneys) In Mississippi State And Federal Courts

(See the beginning of this appendix on how to find the full text of the opinions cited here, including WL opinions.)

- *Owens v. First Family Financial Services*, 379 F. Supp. 2d 840 (U.S. District Court, S.D. Mississippi, 2005) (Defendants moved to disqualify attorneys for plaintiffs. Under Mississippi's Rules of Professional Conduct, a conflict of interest arising from a paralegal's prior work for the law firm that formerly represented defendants and subsequent work for the law firm during its representation of plaintiffs in their consumer fraud action against defendants had to be imputed to law firm representing plaintiffs for purposes of the defendants' motion to disqualify plaintiffs' counsel. Even if the device of a "Chinese wall" was available to shield the plaintiffs' law firm from imputed disqualification, that device did not apply, notwithstanding that the paralegal was no longer with the firm when disqualification was sought, given that the paralegal was involved in work on the plaintiffs' action against defendants for several months before the "Chinese wall" was erected.)

- *Shelton v. Lift, Inc.*, 967 So. 2d 1254 (Court of Appeals of Mississippi, 2007) (The court denied a motion to extend the time to serve process. There is no dispute that Shelton's attorney's paralegal incorrectly calculated the expiration date for the 120-day period. At the hearing, the paralegal testified that the miscalculation was simply "an honest mistake." Nevertheless, the law in this State is clear that "simple inadvertence or mistake of counsel" is neither good cause nor excusable neglect.)

- *Minnick v. Mississippi*, 551 So. 2d 77, 101 (Supreme Court of Mississippi, 1988) (Lawyer should not use a paralegal "to do his dirty work" in communicating with the other side.)

- *Mississippi State Chapter Operation Push v. Mabus*, 788 F. Supp. 1406, 1421 (U.S. District Court, N.D. Mississippi, 1992) (Award of paralegal fees criticized. It "is unnecessary to have three paralegals assisting at trial"; "using three paralegals when one would be sufficient.")

- *In re White*, 171 Bankruptcy Reporter 554 (U.S. Bankruptcy Court, S.D. Mississippi, 1994) (Attorney fees reduced. "[T]oo many lawyers are spending too much time on this case." They "used paralegals to perform secretarial tasks.")

- A disbarred attorney can be a paralegal under the supervision of an attorney in good standing, but must have no direct or indirect contact with clients and must be totally separated from his or her prior law practice. *In re Reinstatement of Parsons*, 890 So. 2d 40 (Supreme Court of Mississippi, 2003).

Doing Legal Research In Mississippi Law

- **Statutes:** www.sos.state.ms.us /ed_pubs/MSCode
- **Cases:** courts.ms.gov/appellate _courts/coa/coadecisions.html
- **Court Rules:** courts.ms.gov/rules /msrules.html
- **General:** www.law.georgetown.edu /library/research/guides/mississippi .cfm

Finding Employment In Mississippi

- paralegal.jobs.net/jobs/mississippi .aspx
- www.simplyhired.com/k-paralegal-l -jackson-ms-jobs.html
- www.indeed.com/q-Litigation -Paralegal-l-Mississippi-jobs.html
- jackson.craigslist.org/lgl

MISSOURI

ETHICS CODE AND OPINIONS IN MISSOURI

- **Attorneys: Missouri Code: *Rules of Professional Conduct***
  - www.courts.mo.gov/page.jsp?id=707
  - www.law.cornell.edu/ethics/missouri .html
  - See also ethics links in Helpful Websites at the end of Chapter 5.
- **Attorneys: Montana Ethics Opinions**
  - www.mobar.org/ethics /informalopinions.htm
  - www.mobar.org/ethics /formalopinions.htm
  - mo-legal-ethics.org
- **Unauthorized Practice of Law: Missouri**
  - www.mobar.org/ethics /formalopinions/supplement/ch9.htm

- www.moga.mo.gov/statutes/c400-499/4840000020.htm
- ir.lawnet.fordham.edu/cgi/viewcontent.cgi?article=3572&context=flr

■ **Paralegals and Other Nonattorneys: Missouri**

- *Rule 4-5.3.* For a discussion of the state's ethics Rule 5.3 ("Responsibilities Regarding Nonlawyer Assistants") in the Missouri *Rules of Professional Conduct*, see Chapter 5. For the text of 5.3 in Missouri, see www.courts.mo.gov/page.jsp?id=707.
- *Rule 4-1.10 (Comment 4).* The rule of imputed disqualification in Rule 4-1.10 "does not prohibit representation by others in the law firm where the person prohibited from involvement in a matter is a nonlawyer, such as a paralegal or legal secretary." Missouri *Rules of Professional Conduct.*
- *Rule 4-5.5* (Comment 2). Lawyers can employ the services of paralegals and delegate tasks to them "so long as the lawyer supervises the delegated work and retains responsibility for their work."
- *Missouri Bar Guidelines for Practicing with Paralegals* (enter the title in Google, Bing, or Yahoo). *Guideline I:* A lawyer is responsible for the professional and ethical conduct of a paralegal under his or her supervision. *Guideline II:* A lawyer shall not assist a paralegal in the performance of an activity that constitutes the unauthorized practice of law (UPL). A lawyer must supervise nonlawyer employees and ensure that their conduct is compatible with the professional obligations of the lawyer. Case law does not provide much guidance in defining where the actions of a paralegal cross the line from assisting a lawyer in the practice of law to actually performing acts that would violate the unauthorized practice of law statute. A paralegal is not practicing law if, under the ultimate direction and supervision of a licensed lawyer, the paralegal is applying knowledge of law and legal procedures in rendering direct assistance to a licensed lawyer. This assistance may include but is not limited to: (a) researching legal matters; (b) developing an action, procedure, technique, service or application; (c) preparing and interpreting legal documents; (d) selecting, compiling and using technical information; (e) assisting the lawyer in court; (f) handling administrative matters with the tribunal; (g) handling will attestations and real estate closings; and (h) analyzing and following procedural problems that involve independent decision. *Guideline III:* A lawyer shall not share legal fees with a paralegal, but may include paralegals in a compensation or retirement plan that is based on profit sharing. The prohibition against "fee splitting" is not intended to deny salary or bonuses to paralegals even though it is tied to the profitability of the firm. Rather, the prohibition is to any form of compensation directly tied to the existence or amount of a particular legal fee, where such fee splitting would influence the lawyer's professional independent judgment. To preserve a lawyer's independence, a lawyer and a paralegal cannot form a partnership that practices law. Nor can a lawyer practice law with a company or corporation in which a paralegal has an ownership interest or is a director or officer. *Guideline IV:* A lawyer must (a) develop policies that clearly define tasks paralegals can perform, (b) directly supervise the paralegal, (c) be responsible for the paralegal's work product, (d) give the paralegal copies of governing ethical rules and policies, (e) instruct the paralegal on ethical conduct, particularly the need to preserve client confidentiality, (f) check that the paralegal does not create a conflict of interest, and (g) check that the paralegal is qualified by education, training, or experience to act as a paralegal. *Guideline V:* A lawyer must (a) instruct the paralegal to disclose his or her paralegal status in all dealings with any other persons, (b) use the paralegal's title on all communications such as business cards and letterheads, and (c) instruct the paralegal to identify his/her title on written communications to others. A paralegal may sign correspondence on the law firm letterhead provided the signature is followed by an appropriate identifying designation as a paralegal. A paralegal's name can also appear on the letterhead of an office if clearly identified as a paralegal.
- *Missouri Bar Guidelines for Practicing with Paralegals* (more) enter the title in Google, Bing, or Yahoo).
- Generally paralegals may not appear as an advocate. However, specific exceptions to the unauthorized practice of law statute have been created through statutes and regulations that permit paralegals to represent clients in court.
- Paralegals can answer clients' questions by giving factual and procedural information. The paralegal cannot give legal opinions in response to client questions. When asked legal questions, paralegals must inform clients that they cannot give legal advice. Paralegals may relay advice specifically given to them by their supervising attorney.
- Paralegals can prepare and draft legal documents, but the lawyer is responsible for reviewing and approving the contents of the documents.
- Paralegals can engage in legal research.
- Paralegals cannot take a deposition, but they attend a deposition and assist the lawyer by taking notes and coordinating documents and exhibits.
- Paralegals can sit at the counsel table in court if permitted by local court rules. (Paralegals can be of great assistance to lawyers at trial and often sit at counsel tables if court rules do not restrict their presence.)
- Paralegals can have business cards on which they are clearly identified as paralegals.
- A paralegal's name can be included on law office letterhead if he or she is clearly identified as a paralegal.
- Paralegals can sign correspondence from a law firm as long as the paralegal's status is clearly identified. (Example: Very truly yours, TAYLOR & JONES By John J. Smith, Paralegal)
- Paralegals can be paid based upon the profitability of the firm. Law firms may give paralegals pensions, profit sharing plans and salary increases based upon the firm's profitability. These benefits can be given based upon individual performance and/or the firm's profitability. However, a firm may not base compensation upon the outcome of a case.
- The substantive legal work of a paralegal (work normally performed by an attorney in the absence of a paralegal) may be billed directly to the client in the same way an attorney's work is billed. To be billable, the work paralegals perform must not be clerical or ministerial. In circumstances where "attorneys fees" are reviewed or awarded by a court, the paralegal hours may be recovered as part of the attorney fee that is reviewed or awarded.
- A paralegal may not be a partner or shareholder in a law firm. Nonlawyers cannot have ownership or controlling interests in an entity where the lawyer practices law.
- The *Rules of Professional Conduct* and guidelines govern lawyers; they do not regulate paralegals.
- If a paralegal's activities violate the *Rules of Professional Conduct*, the

paralegal's employer is at fault. The employer (the lawyer) is responsible for the paralegal's direction and ethical guidance. The supervisory measures that the lawyer applies should take account of the fact that paralegals are not subject to professional discipline.

- At the beginning of all professional communications with others, the paralegal shall disclose that he or she is a paralegal. The lawyer shall instruct the paralegal to make this disclosure. If the lawyer is present, the lawyer should introduce the paralegal and identify him/her as a paralegal.
- An attorney who is licensed in another state but not in Missouri, can function in Missouri as a paralegal, but cannot engage in the practice of law. Missouri Bar Ass'n, *Informal Advisory Opinion 20030078*.
- A paralegal cannot answer a docket call of an attorney. Missouri Bar Ass'n, *Informal Opinion 1 (7/9/82)*.
- It would be an improper splitting of a fee with a paralegal if an attorney agrees not to pay a paralegal unless an entire particular fee is collected. Missouri Bar Ass'n, *Informal Opinion 20 (6/16/78)*.
- An attorney who hires a nurse to review medical records can list the nurse on the attorney's letterhead if it is clear she is not an attorney such as by calling her a legal assistant. Missouri Bar Ass'n, *Informal Advisory Opinion 970159*.
- An attorney can hire a disbarred attorney as a paralegal. Missouri Bar Ass'n, *Informal Advisory Opinion 960228*.
- An attorney can have a paralegal sign the attorney's name to correspondence and pleadings after the attorney has reviewed, approved the content, and supervised the production of the document. The paralegal should indicate that the paralegal signed attorney's name to the document. One method of indicating this fact is for the paralegal to initial the signature. Missouri Bar Ass'n, *Informal Advisory Opinion 950158*.
- Question: To what extent is an attorney disqualified from handling cases against attorneys in a firm which previously employed the attorney's paralegal? Answer: The attorney would not be required to withdraw from or decline cases adverse to clients of the paralegal's former firm as long as (1) the paralegal is screened from participation in those cases and (2) the paralegal does not reveal any confidential information from the former employment to any

person in the attorney's firm. These measures apply to all situations in the former firm, regardless of whether the paralegal had any involvement in those cases. Missouri Bar Ass'n, *Informal Advisory Opinion 930097*.

Defining Legal Assistants/Paralegals In Missouri

- A paralegal, qualified through education, training or work experience, is employed or retained by an attorney, law firm, government agency, corporation, or other entity to perform substantive and procedural legal work under the ultimate direction and supervision of an attorney or as authorized by administrative, statutory, or court authority. "Paralegal Experience" shall mean the performance of substantive legal work, non-clerical or non-administrative in nature, that absent a paralegal, an attorney would perform. (Missouri Bar Ass'n, *Practicing with Paralegals*.

Defining The Practice Of Law In Missouri

- § 484.010 (*Vernon's Annotated Statutes*): 1. The "practice of the law" is hereby defined to be and is the appearance as an advocate in a representative capacity or the drawing of papers, pleadings or documents or the performance of any act in such capacity in connection with proceeding spending or prospective before any court of record, commissioner, referee or any body, board, committee or commission constituted by law or having authority to settle controversies.
  2. The "law business" is hereby defined to be and is the advising or counseling for a valuable consideration of any person, firm, association, or corporation as to any secular law or the drawing or the procuring of or assisting in the drawing for a valuable consideration of any paper, document or instrument affecting or relating to secular rights or the doing of any act for a valuable consideration in a representative capacity, obtaining or tending to obtain or securing or tending to secure for any person, firm, association or corporation any property or property rights whatsoever.

Paralegals (And Others) In Missouri State And Federal Courts

(See the beginning of this appendix on how to find the full text of the opinions cited here, including WL opinions.)

- *Winsor v. Terex-Telelect-Inc.*, 43 S.W.3d 460 (Missouri Court of Appeals,

2001) (The court entered a default judgment after a recently hired paralegal failed to enter a case into the office database, but the default judgment was set aside when the court ruled that the error was negligent, not reckless.)

- *Logan v. Hyatt Legal Plans, Inc.*, 874 S.W.2d 548 (Missouri Court of Appeals, 1994) (A paralegal works for a law firm that represents the wife in a divorce action. The paralegal has an affair with the husband of this client(!). The paralegal is charged with disclosing confidential strategy information to her lover.)
- *Missouri v. Jenkins*, 491 U.S. 274, 109 S. Ct. 2463, 105 L.Ed. 2d 229 (U.S. Supreme Court, 1989) (Award of paralegal fees. See discussion of this case in Chapter 1.)
- *In re Kroh Brothers*, 105 Bankruptcy Reporter 515, 529 (U.S. Bankruptcy Court, W.D. Missouri, 1989) (In a request for attorney fees, the attorney fails to explain why some of the tasks performed by attorneys "were not performed by a paralegal.")
- *Carter v. Kansas City Southern Ry. Co.*, 2005 WL 1000078 (U.S. District Court, W.D. Missouri, 2005) (The Court will disallow the billing entries for the paralegal's performance of secretarial duties such as copying documents, making telephone calls, filing pleadings, and downloading pleadings. Organizing documents, however, is appropriate paralegal work.)
- *Johnson v. Barnhart*, 2004 WL 213183 (U.S. District Court, W.D. Missouri, 2004) (Purely clerical or secretarial tasks should not be billed at a lawyer or paralegal rate, regardless of who performs them. It is appropriate to distinguish between legal work, in the strict sense, and clerical work, and other work that can often be accomplished by nonlawyers but which a lawyer may do because he has no other help available. Such nonlegal work may command a lesser rate. Its dollar value is not enhanced just because a lawyer does it.)

Doing Legal Research In Missouri Law

- **Statutes:** www.moga.mo.gov/statutes/statutes.htm
- **Cases:** www.courts.mo.gov/page.jsp?id=12086
- **Court Rules:** www.courts.mo.gov/page.jsp?id=46
- **General:** www.law.georgetown.edu/library/research/guides/missouri.cfm

Finding Employment In Missouri

- legal.jobs.net/Missouri.htm
- www.careerbuilder.com/jobs/mo /keyword/paralegal
- www.indeed.com/q-Paralegal-l -Missouri-jobs.html
- stlouis.craigslist.org/lgl

MONTANA

ETHICS CODE AND OPINIONS IN MONTANA

- **Attorneys: Montana Code:** *Rules of Professional Conduct*
  - www.montanaodc.org/Portals/ODC /MRPC.2011.pdf
  - www.montanaodc.org/Portals/ODC /docs/rules_of_professional_conduct .pdf
  - www.montanaodc.org/Portals/ODC /RLDE.2005.DeskbookVersion.pdf
  - http://www.law.cornell.edu/ethics /montana.html
  - See also ethics links in Helpful Websites at the end of Chapter 5
- **Attorneys: Montana Ethics Opinions**
  - www.montanabar.org (enter *ethics opinions* in the search box)
- **Unauthorized Practice of Law in Montana**
  - www.montanabar.org (enter *unauthorized practice of law* in search box)
  - ir.lawnet.fordham.edu/cgi /viewcontent.cgi?article=3572&con text=flr
- **Paralegals and Other Nonattorneys: Montana**
  - *Rule 5.3.* For a discussion of the state's ethics Rule 5.3 ("Responsibilities Regarding Nonlawyer Assistants") in the Montana Rules of Professional Conduct, see Chapter 5.
  - Montana Code Annotated, § 25-10-305(2). An individual may use the title "paralegal" if the individual: (a) has received an associate's degree in paralegal studies from an accredited institution or a baccalaureate degree in paralegal studies from an accredited college or university; (b) has received a baccalaureate degree in any discipline from an accredited college or university and has completed not less than 18 semester credits of course work offered by a qualified paralegal studies program; (c) has received certification by the national association of legal assistants or the national federation of paralegal associations; (d) has received a high school diploma or its equivalent, has performed not less than 4,800 hours of substantive legal work under the supervision of a licensed attorney

documented by the certification of the attorney or attorneys under whom the work was done, and has completed at least 5 hours of approved continuing legal education in the area of legal ethics and professional responsibility; or (e) has graduated from an accredited law school and has not been disbarred or suspended from the practice of law by any jurisdiction.

- Montana Code Annotated, § 25-10-305(3). A person may not practice as a paralegal except under the supervision of a licensed attorney and is prohibited from engaging in the unauthorized practice of law. Montana Code Annotated, § 25-10-305.
- *Who Can Practice Law In Montana? (Can Paralegals Help?) State Bar of Montana.* (The only thing that a "non-lawyer" can legally do for you is sell you a pre-printed form and type in the information that you provide to them. They cannot tell you what information you should put on the form, what type of form to use, or fill out the form outside of the information that you provide to them.) (www.montanabar.org/?page=UPL& hhSearchTerms=%22paralegal%22)
- An attorney must not split a fee with a nonattorney. State Bar of Montana, *Opinion (1)* (9/13/85).
- It is unethical for a law firm to pay "runners" to recommend the law firm to injured railroad workers. State Bar of Montana, *Opinion 930927* (1994) (19 Montana Lawyer 15 (1/1994)).
- Paralegals employed by law firms cannot appear on behalf of creditors at section 341 hearings in bankruptcy proceedings to question and examine debtors. The appearance would constitute an unauthorized practice of law. State Bar of Montana, *Ethics Opinion 871008.*
- Attorneys are responsible for the work product of their paralegal employees. There is no need to establish a bureaucracy to provide additional regulation on who can be a paralegal and how they can be used. *In the Matter of the Proposed Adoption of Rules Relating to Paralegals and Legal Assistants*, No. 94–577 (Supreme Court of Montana, 7/17/95).

Defining Legal Assistants/Paralegals in Montana

- "Paralegal" or "legal assistant" means a person qualified through education, training, or work experience to perform substantive legal work that requires knowledge of legal concepts

and that is customarily but not exclusively performed by a lawyer and who may be retained or employed by one or more lawyers, law offices, governmental agencies, or other entities or who may be authorized by administrative, statutory, or court authority to perform this work. Montana Code Annotated, § 37–60–101(16).

- (1) As used in 25-10-304 [covering the award of paralegal fees] and this section, "paralegal" means a person qualified through education, training, or work experience who is employed or retained to perform, under supervision by a licensed attorney, substantive legal work that: (a) requires a substantial knowledge of legal concepts; and (b) in the absence of the paralegal, would be performed by an attorney.

Defining the Practice of Law in Montana

- *Pulse v. North American Land Title Co. of Montana*, 707 P.2d 1105 (Supreme Court of Montana, 1985): What constitutes the practice of law is not easily defined. "The line between what is and what is not the practice of law cannot be drawn with precision. Lawyers should be the first to recognize that between the two there is a region wherein much of what lawyers do every day in their practice may also be done by others without wrongful invasion of the lawyer's field." (citing *Cowern v. Nelson*, 290 N.W. 795 (Minnesota, 1940)) While there is a sizeable minority of cases which hold that the drafting or filling in of blanks in printed forms of instruments dealing with land may not constitute the unauthorized practice of law, the majority of cases take the contrary view. We agree with the majority.
- *Montana Supreme Court Comm'n on Unauthorized Practice of Law v. O'Neil*, 147 P.3d 200 (Supreme Court of Montana, 2006): A person who makes it his business to act and who does act for and by the warrant of others in legal formalities, negotiations or proceedings, practices law; and when his acts consist in advising clients touching legal matters pending or to be brought before a court of record, or in preparing pleadings or proceedings for use in a court of record, or in appearing before a court of record, either directly or by a partner or proxy, he is practicing law in a court of record.
- § 37–61–201 (*Montana Code Annotated*): Who is considered to be practicing law. Any person who shall hold himself out or advertise as an attorney or counselor at law or who shall appear in any court

of record or before a judicial body, referee, commissioner, or other officer appointed to determine any question of law or fact by a court or who shall engage in the business and duties and perform such acts, matters, and things as are usually done or performed by an attorney at law in the practice of his profession for the purposes of parts 1 through 3 of this chapter shall be deemed practicing law.

Montana Malpractice Law On Paralegals

- § 27–2–206 (*Montana Code Annotated*): Actions for legal malpractice. An action against an attorney licensed to practice law in Montana or a paralegal assistant or a legal intern employed by an attorney based upon the person's alleged professional negligent act or for error or omission in the person's practice must be commenced within 3 years after the plaintiff discovers or through the use of reasonable diligence should have discovered the act, error, or omission, whichever occurs last, but in no case may the action be commenced after 10 years from the date of the act, error, or omission.

Paralegals (and Others) in Montana State and Federal Courts

(See the beginning of this appendix on how to find the full text of the opinions cited here, including WL opinions.)

- *Jackson v. Board of Trustees. . .*, 2014 WL 1794551 (U.S. District Court, Montana, 2014) (Paralegal fees approved: 19.6 hours at $85 an hour. The rates for paralegals must be "consistent with markets rates and practices." $100 an hour was awarded in Education Logistics v. Laidlaw Transit, 2012 WL 1142674 (U.S. District Court, Montana, 2012).)
- *Sparks v. Johnson*, 826 P.2d 928 (Supreme Court of Montana, 1992) (Nonattorneys cannot practice in the justice's court on a recurring basis even though § 25–31–601 of the *Montana Code* says "any person" may act as an attorney in this court; the statute is a "one-time only" grant of a privilege of lay representation.)
- *State ex rel. Montana Dept. of Transportation v. Slack*, 29 P.3d 503 (Supreme Court of Montana, 2001 (award of paralegal fees; allegation of duplicative billing).
- *In re Sirefco, Inc.*, 144 Bankruptcy Reporter 495, 497 (U.S. Bankruptcy Court, Montana, 1992) (Paralegal fees disallowed; the paralegal's work in this case was duplicative and not beneficial; the attorney failed to establish that the

paralegal's work "was not merely secretarial in nature.")

- *Montana* Land *and Mineral Owners Ass'n, Inc. v. Devon Energy Corp.*, 2006 WL 1876859 (U.S. District Court, Montana, 2006) (Plaintiffs waived the work-product privilege regarding the preparation of the paralegals' summary; therefore, a deposition of the paralegals can be made concerning the preparation.)

Doing Legal Research in Montana Law

- **Statutes:** leg.mt.gov/bills/mca_toc/index.htm
- **Cases:** searchcourts.mt.gov
- **Court Rules:** courts.mt.gov/library/montana_laws.mcpx#judicial
- **General:** courts.mt.gov/library/montana_laws.mcpx

Finding Employment in Montana

- l.mt.bar.associationcareernetwork.com/Common/HomePage.aspx
- www.indeed.com/q-Paralegal-l-Montana-jobs.html
- montana.craigslist.org/lgl

NEBRASKA

ETHICS CODE AND OPINIONS IN NEBRASKA

- **Attorneys: Nebraska Code: *Rules of Professional Conduct***
  - supremecourt.ne.gov/10451/professional-ethics
  - supremecourt.ne.gov/supreme-court-rules/ch3/art5
  - www.law.cornell.edu/ethics/nebraska.html
  - See also ethics links in Helpful Websites at the end of Chapter 5.
- **Attorneys: Nebraska Ethics Opinions**
  - supremecourt.ne.gov/lawyers-ethics-opinions
- **Unauthorized Practice of Law: Nebraska**
  - www.nebar.com (enter *unauthorized practice of law* in search box)
  - ir.lawnet.fordham.edu/cgi/viewcontent.cgi?article=3572&context=flr
- **Unauthorized Practice of law in Nebraska**
  - *Rule 3-501.9 (d).* (paralegals as support persons) A lawyer shall not knowingly allow a support person to participate or assist in the representation of a current client in the same or a substantially related matter in which another lawyer or firm with which the support person formerly was associated had previously represented a client: (1) whose interests are materially adverse to the current client; and

(2) about whom the support person has acquired confidential information that is material to the matter, unless the former client gives informed consent, confirmed in writing. (e) If a support person, who has worked on a matter, is personally prohibited from working on a particular matter under Rule 1.9(d), the lawyer or firm with which that person is presently associated will not be prohibited from representing the current client in that matter if: (1) the former client gives informed consent, confirmed in writing, or (2) the support person is screened from any personal participation in the matter to avoid communication to others in the firm of confidential information that both the support person and the firm have a legal duty to protect. (f) For purposes of Rules 1.9(d) and (e), a support person shall mean any person, other than a lawyer, who is associated with a lawyer or a law firm and shall include but is not necessarily limited to the following: law clerks, paralegals, legal assistants, secretaries, messengers and other support personnel employed by the law firm.

- *Rule 3-501.10 (Comment 4).* The rule of imputed disqualification in Rule 1.10 "does not prohibit representation by others in the law firm where the person prohibited from involvement in a matter is a nonlawyer, such as a paralegal or legal secretary." Nebraska *Rules of Professional Conduct.*
- *Rule 3-505.5 (Comment 2).* Lawyers can employ the services of paraprofessionals and delegate tasks to them "so long as the lawyer supervises the delegated work and retains responsibility for their work."
- *Rule 3-505.5 (Comment 3).* Lawyers can assist independent paraprofessionals, who are authorized to provide particular law-related services.
- Paralegals can be listed on law firm letterhead if their nonattorney status is clear. Nebraska State Bar Ass'n, *Opinion 88–2.*
- Several attorneys who are not partners, associates, or otherwise affiliated with each other share office space and share nonattorney personnel. They represent clients who oppose each other in cases. This is not improper if the clients are aware of and consent to the arrangement and if steps are taken to ensure confidentiality – such as preventing common access to case files and preventing the nonattorneys from working both sides on a case. Nebraska State Bar Ass'n, *Opinion 89–2.*

- Hiring someone who has worked for an opposing law firm in matters related to a particular case automatically disqualifies the hiring firm from the case. A Chinese wall or cone of silence erected around an attorney, law clerk, paralegal, secretary or other ancillary staff member is insufficient to prevent disqualification due to a conflict of interest and appearance of impropriety. Nebraska State Bar Ass'n, *Opinion 94–4*. (See, however, Rule 3-501.9 above.)
- A suspended attorney may be employed as a paralegal. If there is client contact, the client must be told that the attorney cannot give legal advice or practice law. Nebraska State Bar Ass'n, *Opinion 11-01*.
- A suspended attorney may be employed as a paralegal if the employment is at a place and in such a manner as to not give the appearance of practicing law. A suspended attorney may not be employed as a paralegal at an office where he or she previously shared office space or practiced law. Nebraska State Bar Ass'n, *Opinion 96–1*. Affirmed in *Opinion 06–6*.

Defining the Practice of Law in Nebraska

- Nebraska Supreme Court Rules, § 3-1001: The "practice of law," or "to practice law," is the application of legal principles and judgment with regard to the circumstances or objectives of another entity or person which require the knowledge, judgment, and skill of a person trained as a lawyer. This includes, but is not limited to, the following:

  (A) Giving advice or counsel to another entity or person as to the legal rights of that entity or person or the legal rights of others for compensation, direct or indirect, where a relationship of trust or reliance exists between the party giving such advice or counsel and the party to whom it is given.

  (B) Selection, drafting, or completion, for another entity or person, of legal documents which affect the legal rights of the entity or person.

  (C) Representation of another entity or person in a court, in a formal administrative adjudicative proceeding or other formal dispute resolution process, or in an administrative adjudicative proceeding in which legal pleadings are filed or a record is established as the basis for judicial review.

  (D) Negotiation of legal rights or responsibilities on behalf of another entity or person.

- *State ex rel. Johnson v. Childe*, 23 N.W.2d 720 (Supreme Court of Nebraska, 1946) The power to define what constitutes the practice of law is lodged with this court. . . . It is the character of the act and not the place where the act is performed that constitutes the controlling factor. An all-inclusive definition of what constitutes the practice of law is too difficult for simple statement. We shall not attempt it here, but will follow the practice established by the previous decisions of this court and examine the facts and circumstances of each case and determine whether the defendant purported to exercise the legal training, experience and skill of an attorney at law without a license to do so. See Johnson v. Childe, 139 Neb. 91, 295 N.W. 381 (Supreme Court of Nebraska, 1941).
- *Nebraska. . . . v. Butterfield*, 111 N.W.2d 543 545 (Supreme Court of Nebraska, 1961): The Supreme Court of this state has the inherent power to define and regulate the practice of law in this state. . . . While an all-embracing definition of the term "practicing law" would involve great difficulty, it is generally defined as the giving of advice or rendition of any sort of service by a person, firm, or corporation when the giving of such advice or rendition of such service requires the use of any degree of legal knowledge or skill. . . . In an ever-changing economic and social order, the "practice of law" must necessarily change, making it practically impossible to formulate an enduring definition. . . . In determining what constitutes the practice of law it is the character of the act and not the place where the act is performed that is the controlling factor. . . . Whether or not a fee is charged is not a decisive factor in determining if one has engaged in the practice of law.
- Rule 5 (*West's Nebraska Court Rules and Procedure*): Admission of Attorneys: (3) For purposes of this rule, "practice of law" means:. . . (b) Employment as a lawyer for a corporation, partnership, trust, individual, or other entity with the primary duties of: (i) Furnishing legal counsel, drafting documents and pleadings, and interpreting and giving advice with respect to the law, or (ii) Preparing cases for presentation to or trying before courts, executive departments, or administrative bureaus or agencies. . . .

- *State ex rel. Johnson v. Childe*, 295 N.W. 381 (Nebraska Supreme Court, 1941): A layman may prepare simple, elementary documents of a routine character and may also advise persons as to matters of business, although minor legal questions are incidentally involved, without engaging in prohibited "practice of law" where the legal training, knowledge and skill required are not beyond range of average man.

Paralegals (and Others) in Nebraska State and Federal Courts

(See the beginning of this appendix on how to find the full text of the opinions cited here, including WL opinions.)

- State *ex rel. Counsel for Discipline of Nebraska Supreme Court v. Huston*, 631 N.W.2d 913 (Nebraska Supreme Court, 2001) (The charges that the attorney claimed for a legal assistant were excessive, given that much of the itemized work was secretarial in nature.)
- *Rockwell v. Talbott, Adams & Moore*, 2006 WL 436041 (U.S. District Court, Nebraska, 2006) (I also find that there was not a proper delegation of work from the attorney level to the legal assistant level, resulting in Mr. Cox doing work that arguably should have been performed in the first instance by a legal assistant. For example, drafts of the written discovery and summaries of the Defendant's discovery responses could have been prepared by legal assistants for the attorney's review. It is reasonable for a client to expect that work will be allocated within a law firm based on the level of expertise required of the task in order to provide efficiency and economy in the rendering of quality legal services.)
- *State ex rel. Creighton University v. Hickman*, 512 N.W.2d 374 (Nebraska Supreme Court, 1994) (Disqualification is ordered when a temporary clerical worker on a case for the defense had previously worked as an attorney for the law firm that represented plaintiff on the same case.)

Doing Legal Research in Nebraska Law

- **Statutes:** nebraskalegislature.gov /laws/browse-statutes.php
- **Cases:** supremecourt.ne.gov/sc /opinions
- **Court Rules:** supremecourt.ne.gov /rules
- **General:** www.findlaw.com/casecode /nebraska.html

Finding Employment in Nebraska

- www.indeed.com/q-Paralegal-l
  -Nebraska-jobs.html
- lincoln.craigslist.org/lgl
- nebraskaparalegal.org/careers
- l.ne.bar.associationcareernetwork
  .com/Common/HomePage.aspx

NEVADA

ETHICS CODE AND OPINIONS IN NEVADA

- **Attorneys: Nevada Code:** *Rules of Professional Conduct*
  - www.leg.state.nv.us/courtrules/RPC
    .html
  - www.nvbar.org/content/rules
    -lawyer-advertising
  - www.law.cornell.edu/ethics/nevada
    .html
  - leg.state.nv.us/courtrules/SCR.html
  - See also ethics links in Helpful Websites at the end of Chapter 5.
- **Attorneys: Nevada Ethics Opinions**
  - www.nvbar.org/node/98
- **Unauthorized Practice of Law in Nevada**
  - www.nvbar.org (enter *unauthorized practice of law* in search box)
  - ir.lawnet.fordham.edu/cgi
    /viewcontent.cgi?article=3572&con
    text=flr
- **Paralegals and Other Nonattorneys: Nevada**
  - *Rule 5.3.* For a discussion of the state's ethics Rule 5.3 ("Responsibilities Regarding Nonlawyer Assistants") in the Nevada *Rules of Professional Conduct*, see Chapter 5. For the text of 5.3 in Nevada, see http://www.leg .state.nv.us/courtrules/RPC.html.
  - A practicing lawyer can operate a collateral business through which he places temporary secretarial and clerical help in other law offices so long as (a) he does not place temporary help in offices with which he has matters pending; (b) the employees clearly understand they must preserve client confidences and avoid working on matters they have worked on for the lawyer or in other law offices; and (c) the lawyers who use the temporary secretarial service are told that the owner/operator of the service is himself an active lawyer. State Bar of Nevada, *Formal Opinion No. 6* (9/24/87).
  - The business card of an out-of-state attorney working in Nevada should state that he is a "legal assistant" or otherwise shows the nature of his employment. State Bar of Nevada, *Opinion No. 3* (3/19/75).

- Code of Ethics and Professional Responsibility of the Legal Assistants Division of the State Bar of Nevada (www.nvbar.org/sites/default/files /Code%20of%20Ethics.pdf).
- Legal Assistants Pledge of Professionalism (State Bar of Nevada) (www.nvbar.org/sites/default/files /Pledge%20of%20Professionalism .pdf)

Defining Legal Assistants/Paralegals in Nevada

- State Bar of Nevada, Legal Assistants Division: Definition. A legal assistant (also known as a paralegal) is a person, qualified through education, training or work experience, who is employed or retained by a lawyer, law office, governmental agency or other entity in a capacity or function which involves the performance, under the ultimate direction and supervision of an attorney, of specifically delegated substantive legal work, which work, for the most part, requires sufficient knowledge of legal concepts that, absent such an assistant, the attorney would perform the task. *ByLaws of the Legal Assistants Division of the State Bar of Nevada*, § 3 (www .nvbar.org/sites/default/files/Legal%20 Affidavit.pdf).

Defining the Practice of Law in Nevada

- Rule 51.5 (*Supreme Court Rules*): Admission to practice. 2. Practice of law. For purposes of this rule, the term "practice of law" shall mean:. . . (b) practice as an attorney for an individual, a corporation, partnership, trust, or other entity, with the primary duties of furnishing legal counsel, researching legal issues, drafting legal documents, pleadings, and memoranda, interpreting and giving advice regarding the law, or preparing, trying or presenting cases before courts, departments of government or administrative agencies. . . .

Paralegals (and Others) in Nevada State and Federal Courts

(See the beginning of this appendix on how to find the full text of the opinions cited here, including WL opinions.)
- *Leibowitz v. Eighth Judicial District. . .*, 78 P.3d 515 (Supreme Court of Nevada, 2003) (Screening of a nonlawyer employee may allow a hiring law firm to avoid imputed attorney disqualification based on the employee's acquisition, in the former employment, of confidences of the adversary of the hiring law firm's client. If the nonlawyer employee hired

by a law firm acquired, during the employee's former employment, confidences of an adversary of the hiring law firm's client, the hiring law firm must, at a minimum: (1) caution the employee not to disclose any information relating to the representation of the adversary; (2) instruct the employee not to work on any matter on which she worked during the prior employment or regarding which she has information relating to the former employer's representation; and (3) take reasonable steps to ensure that the employee does not work in connection with matters on which she worked during the prior employment, absent the adversary's consent, i.e., unconditional waiver after consultation.) (Overruling in part *Ciaffone v. Eighth Judicial District. . .*, 945 P.2d 950 (Supreme Court of Nevada, 1997).
- Brown *v. Eighth Judicial District Court ex rel. County of Clark*, 14 P.3d 1266 (Supreme Court of Nevada 2000) (Disqualification not warranted when legal secretary switches firms.)
- *McSmith v. Poker Productions*, 2011 WL 841350 (U.S. District Court, Nevada, 2011) (Plaintiff's attorney indicated that his paralegal had to leave the state for treatment for a serious medical condition and that the attorney did not discover that a response had not been filed until a later date. However, Plaintiff's attorney does not state when he discovered the error and how long he delayed before filing a response. Plaintiff's recitation of the events that led to his failure to respond (his paralegal failed to place this case on the list of active cases before he left) leaves a lot to be desired in the way of describing why the court should find excusable neglect. At worst, it appears that Plaintiff's counsel may have improperly allowed his paralegal to practice law without a license or failed to supervise and maintain sufficient control of cases bearing his mail.)
- *In re Ginji*, 117 Bankruptcy Reporter 983, 993 (U.S. Bankruptcy Court, Nevada, 1990) (Award of paralegal fees. Work that "was done by an attorney which should have been done by a paralegal. . . shall be billed at a lower rate.")
- *Trustees of Const. Industry and Laborers Health and Welfare Trust v. Redland Ins. Co.*, 460 F.3d 1253 (U.S. Court of Appeals, 9th Circuit (Nevada), 2006) (If the attorney's hourly rate already incorporates the cost of work performed by nonattorneys, then courts should not compensate for these costs as an additional "reasonable attorney's fee." The key is the billing custom in the relevant market. Thus, fees for work performed by nonattorneys such

as paralegals may be billed separately, at market rates, if this is the prevailing practice in a given community.)

- *Recio v. Clark County School Dist.*, 2006 WL 3149363 (U.S. District Court, Nevada, 2006) (Counsel seeks an award of paralegal fees for the work of Cheryl Jung but fails to offer evidence that Jung is qualified through education, training, or work experience to perform substantive legal work as a paralegal.)
- *Greenwell v. Paralegal Center*, 836 P.2d 70 (Supreme Court of Nevada, 1992) (Injunction granted against a typing service for the unauthorized practice of law, but the court orders the state bar to investigate the alleged unavailability of legal services for low- and middle-income Nevadans.)
- *Pioneer Title v. State Bar*, 326 P.2d 408 (Supreme Court of Nevada, 1958) (Some simple legal services may be so necessary that they could properly be provided by nonattorneys if they would otherwise be unavailable.)
- Gyger v. Sunrise Hosp. and Medical Center, 2013 WL 7156028 (U.S. District Court, Nevada, 2013) (The district court did not abuse its discretion by declining to dismiss a prospective juror for cause, even though the juror, who was a veterinarian, had previously exchanged business referrals with the husband of a paralegal of defendant's counsel.)

Doing Legal Research in Nevada Law

- **Statutes:** www.leg.state.nv.us/law1.cfm
- **Cases:** lawlibrary.nevadajudiciary.us
- **Court Rules:** www.leg.state.nv.us /courtrules
- **General:** www.clarkcountynv.gov (enter *legal research* in the search box)

Finding Employment in Nevada

- jobs.nvbar.org/jobseeker/search /results
- www.indeed.com/q-Litigation -Paralegal-l-Nevada-jobs.html
- careers.findlaw.com (select *Paralegal* and *Nevada*)
- lasvegas.craigslist.org/lgl

NEW HAMPSHIRE

ETHICS CODE AND OPINIONS IN NEW HAMPSHIRE

- **Attorneys: New Hampshire Code:** *Rules of Professional Conduct*
    - www.courts.state.nh.us/rules/pcon /index.htm
    - www.law.cornell.edu/ethics/nh.html
    - See also ethics links in Helpful Websites at the end of Chapter 5.

- **Attorneys: New Hampshire Ethics Opinions**
    - www.nhbar.org/legal-links/ethics1 .asp
- **Unauthorized Practice of Law: New Hampshire**
    - www.nhbar.org (enter *unauthorized practice of law* in search box)
    - www.nhbar.org/publications/ethics /rule-5-5.asp
    - ir.lawnet.fordham.edu/cgi /viewcontent.cgi?article=3572&con text=flr
- **Paralegals and Other Nonattorneys: New Hampshire**
    - *Rule 5.3.* For a discussion of the state's ethics Rule 5.3 ("Responsibilities Regarding Nonlawyer Assistants") in the New Hampshire *Rules of Professional Conduct*, see Chapter 5. For the wording of 5.3 in New Hampshire, see www.courts.state.nh.us/rules /pcon/pcon-5_3.htm.
    - *Rule 35*, New Hampshire Supreme Court Rules, *Guidelines for the Utilization by Lawyers of the Services of Legal Assistants under the New Hampshire Rules of Professional Conduct* (www .courts.state.nh.us/rules/scr/scr-35. htm). *Rule 1:* Paralegals must not give legal advice, but they can, with adequate attorney supervision, provide information concerning legal matters. *Rule 2:* An attorney may not permit a legal assistant to represent a client in judicial or administrative proceedings unless authorized by statute, court rule or decision, administrative rule or regulation, or customary practice. *Rule 3:* A paralegal shall not be delegated any task that requires the exercise of professional legal judgment. The attorney must supervise the paralegal. *Rule 4:* An attorney must take care that the legal assistant does not reveal information relating to representation of a client or use such information to the disadvantage of the client. *Rule 5:* An attorney shall not form a partnership with a paralegal if any part of the partnership consists of the practice of law. *Rule 6:* An attorney shall not share fees with a paralegal but can include the paralegal in a retirement plan based on a profit-sharing arrangement. *Rule 7:* A paralegal's name may not be included on the letterhead of an attorney. A paralegal can have a business card that prints the name of the law firm where he or she works, if the card indicates the paralegal's nonattorney capacity and the firm does not use the paralegal to solicit business for the firm improperly.

Rule 8: When dealing with clients, attorneys, or the public, the paralegal must disclose at the outset that he or she is not an attorney. *Rule 9:* An attorney must exercise care to prevent a legal assistant from engaging in conduct that would involve the attorney unethical conduct.

- A law firm cannot list legal assistants on its letterhead. New Hampshire Bar Ass'n, *Ethics Opinion 1982–3/20* (3/17/83).
- Without the prior written approval of the court, no person who is not a lawyer may represent a person other than himself or be listed on the notice of appeal or other appeal document, or on the brief, or sit at counsel table in the courtroom or present oral argument. *Rules Of The Supreme Court of the State of New Hampshire*, Rule 33(2).

Defining Legal Assistants/Paralegals in New Hampshire

- [T]he term "legal assistant" shall mean a person not admitted to the practice of law in New Hampshire who is an employee of or an assistant to an active member of the New Hampshire Bar. . . and who, under the control and supervision of an active member of the New Hampshire Bar, renders services related to but not constituting the practice of law. *Rules of The Supreme Court of the State of New Hampshire*, Rule 35(C) (www .courts.state.nh.us/rules/scr/scr-35.htm).

Defining the Practice of Law in New Hampshire

- *New Hampshire v. Settle*, 480 A.2d 6, 8 (Supreme Court of New Hampshire, 1984): The only statutory definition of the unauthorized practice of law is provided in RSA 311:7 which states: "No person shall be permitted commonly to practice as an attorney in court unless he has been admitted by the court. . . ." The defendant argues that unless an individual is actually practicing in court, his conduct is not proscribed by the statute. We cannot read RSA 311:7 to limit the unauthorized practice of law to those instances in which an individual has physically appeared in the courtroom to represent a litigant. At the very least, this provision also encompasses the filing of documents in the court system. . . . There is no "single factor to determine whether someone is engaged in the unauthorized practice of law. . . [Rather, such a] determination must be made on a case-by-case basis."

■ *Kamasinski v. McLaughlin*, 2003 WL 367745 (Superior Court of New Hampshire, 2003): For the purposes of this case, the Court defines the practice of law to include (but not be limited to) the following: 1. Giving advice or counsel to others as to their legal rights or the legal rights or responsibilities of others for fees or other consideration. 2. Selection, drafting, or completion of legal documents or agreements which affect the legal rights of an entity or person(s). 3. Representation of another entity or person(s) in a court, or in a formal administrative adjudicative proceeding or other formal dispute resolution process or in an administrative adjudicative proceeding in which legal pleadings are filed or a record is established as the basis for judicial review. 4. Negotiation of legal rights or responsibilities on behalf of another entity or person(s). HB 1420, Chapter 218:1, Laws of 2002, Task Force on the Definition of the Practice of Law.

■ Ethical Consideration 3–5 of the former *Code of Professional Responsibility*: It is neither necessary nor desirable to attempt the formulation of a single, specific definition of what constitutes the practice of law. Functionally, the practice of law relates to the rendition of services for others that call for the professional judgment of a lawyer. The essence of the professional judgment of a lawyer is his educated ability to relate the general body and philosophy of law to a specific legal problem of a client. . . .

Paralegals (and Others) in New Hampshire State and Federal Courts

(See the beginning of this appendix on how to find the full text of the opinions cited here, including WL opinions.)

■ *Tocci's Case*, 663 A.2d 88 (Supreme Court of New Hampshire, 1995) (§ 311.1 of the New Hampshire Revised Statutes says, "A party in any cause or proceeding may appear, plead, prosecute or defend in his or her proper person, that is, pro se, or may be represented by any citizen of good character." This section allows a nonlawyer to appear in an individual case; it does not allow persons "otherwise unable to practice law to act commonly, entering repeated appearances before the courts of this State.")

■ *Foley v. Huppe*, 2012 WL 5467527 (U.S. District Court, New Hampshire, 2012) (In awarding fees, "clerical or secretarial tasks ought not to be billed at lawyers' rates, even if a lawyer performs them." On this basis, 9 hours and 24 minutes of the attorney's entries have been challenged on the basis that the attorney should be reimbursed for the work at less

than her claimed customary hourly rates. These entries include: "revise and finish" the complaint, draft the motion to admit pro hac vice, draft the civil action cover sheet, "prepare" and "retype" the plaintiffs' interrogatory answers and send them to the plaintiffs for review; and "finish" those answers, as well as a response to a request for production of documents, and send them to opposing counsel. The attorney does not disagree with the characterization of these entries as "paralegal or secretarial-type work," arguing instead that they were "necessary" (which is probably true, but beside the point). The attorney has provided no reason to think that it was necessary for an attorney, as opposed to a paralegal or legal secretary, to perform these tasks. Accordingly, the court will allow the attorney to recover for the time she spent on these tasks, but at the reduced rate of $70 per hour.)

■ *Kalled's Case*, 607 A.2d 613 (Supreme Court of New Hampshire, 1992) (Excessive billing by an attorney: charging the client for 1,489 hours of paralegal time at $60 per hour.)

■ *Van Dorn* Retail *Management, Inc. v. Jim's Oxford Shop, Inc.*, 874 F. Supp. 476, 490 (U.S. District Court, New Hampshire, 1994) (Paralegal fees reduced. Attorneys and paralegals duplicated their efforts. Paralegals performed clerical functions.)

Doing Legal Research in New Hampshire Law

■ **Statutes:** www.gencourt.state.nh.us /rsa/html/indexes
■ **Cases:** www.courts.state.nh.us /supreme/opinions
■ **Court Rules:** www.courts.state .nh.us/rules
■ **General:** www.rominerlegal.com /state/newhampshire.html

Finding Employment in New Hampshire

■ careers.findlaw.com (select *Paralegal* and *New Hampshire*)
■ www.indeed.com/q-Paralegal-l -New-Hampshire-jobs.html
■ nh.craigslist.org/lgl
■ www.careerbuilder.com/jobs/nh /keyword/paralegal

NEW JERSEY

ETHICS CODE AND OPINIONS IN NEW JERSEY

■ **Attorneys: New Jersey Code:** *Rules of Professional Conduct*
■ www.judiciary.state.nj.us/rules /apprpc.htm

■ www.law.cornell.edu/ethics/nj.html
■ See also ethics links in Helpful Websites at the end of Chapter 5.

■ **Attorneys: New Jersey Ethics Opinions**
■ njlaw.rutgers.edu/collections/ethics /search.php

■ **Unauthorized Practice of Law: New Jersey**
■ www.njsba.com (enter *unauthorized practice of law* in search box)
■ ir.lawnet.fordham.edu/cgi/view content.cgi?article=3572&context=flr

■ **Paralegals and Other Nonattorneys: New Jersey**
■ *Rule 5.3*. For a discussion of the state's ethics Rule 5.3 ("Responsibilities Regarding Nonlawyer Assistants") in the New Jersey *Rules of Professional Conduct*, see Chapter 5. New Jersey has added an additional subsection to Rule 5.3 that is not is the ABA *Model Rules*. The N.J. addition is (c)(3), which provides that attorneys must make a "reasonable investigation of circumstances that would disclose past instances of conduct by the nonlawyer" that are "incompatible with the professional obligations of an attorney, which evidence a propensity for such conduct." For the text of 5.3 in New Jersey, see www.judiciary. state.nj.us/rules/apprpc.htm.

■ It is unethical for attorneys to hire a paralegal to screen calls of prospective clients to determine whether the case involves "good liability and damages." The paralegal would discuss the claims of the callers and make a determination of whether to refer the case to an attorney. This is the unauthorized practice of law. New Jersey Supreme Court Advisory Committee on Professional Ethics, *Opinion 645* (10/4/90) (njlaw.rutgers.edu/collections/ethics/acpe/acp645_1.html). In agreement: *Opinion 6* (10/4/90) of the New Jersey Supreme Court Advisory Committee on Attorney Advertising.

■ A paralegal can have a business card as long as the name of the employing law firm is also printed on it. New Jersey Supreme Court Advisory Committee on Professional Ethics, *Opinion 647* (1990) (njlaw .rutgers.edu/collections/ethics/acpe /acp647_1.html). See also the following opinions that allow nonattorney employees, e.g., office managers, to have business cards: *Opinion 471*, (2/12/81); *Opinion 553* (1/24/85).

■ The names of paralegals may be printed on attorney letterhead and in advertisements. "[T]he respect accorded paralegals and the work they perform has increased immeasurably over the last 10 to 15 years." New Jersey Supreme Court Committee on Attorney Advertising, *Opinion 16* (1/24/94) (njlaw.rutgers.edu /collections/ethics/caa/caa16_1 .html). This opinion superseded *Opinion 296* (1975). Compare *Opinion 330* (6/3/76).

- Nonattorney employees of the country welfare agency may represent litigants before the Office of Administrative Law. New Jersey Supreme Court Advisory Committee on Professional Ethics, *Opinion 580* (2/27/86) (njlaw.rutgers.edu /collections/ethics/acpe/acp580_1 .html).
- Paralegals can sign routine, nonsubstantive correspondence to clients, adverse attorneys, or courts, provided an attorney is supervising the paralegal and is aware of the exact nature of the correspondence, the paralegal's identity and nonattorney status is noted, and the name of the responsible attorney is set forth in the correspondence. New Jersey Supreme Court Advisory Committee on Professional Ethics and the Committee on the Unauthorized Practice of Law, *Opinion 46* and *Opinion 720* (3/23/11) (a joint opinion that revises *Opinion 611*) (www.judiciary.state.nj.us /notices/2011/n110328b.pdf)
- A paralegal switches jobs between law firms that opposed each other in litigation. The paralegal worked on the litigation while at the former firm. The new employer is not disqualified if a Chinese Wall is built around the paralegal and she would work for an attorney who has no involvement in the litigation. Also, her office would be located in another end of the building. New Jersey Supreme Court Advisory Committee on Professional Ethics, *Opinion 665* (8/3/92) (njlaw .rutgers.edu/collections/ethics/acpe /acp665_1.html), modifying the prohibition announced in *Opinion 546* (11/8/84).
- A law firm litigating tobacco cases can hire a nonattorney who had been involved in tobacco litigation at another firm if the nonattorney had no substantial responsibility in the tobacco litigation at the other firm, obtained no confidential information concerning the litigation, and is screened from such litigation at the present firm. New Jersey Supreme Court Advisory Committee on Professional Ethics, *Opinion 633* (11/2/89).

Special Rules an Paralegal Representation in New Jersey

- Nonlawyer representation. New Jersey Administrative Code, title 1, 1:1–5.4 Representation by nonlawyers: [T]he following nonlawyers may apply for permission to represent a party at a contested case hearing. . . 4. Legal service paralegals or assistants. (www.state. nj.us/oal/hearings/guide/#nbr5)
- Who May Appear. New Jersey Court Rules, Rule 1–21–1(f) Appearances Before Office of Administrative Law and Administrative Agencies. Subject to such limitations and procedural rules as may be established by the Office of Administrative Law, an appearance by a non-attorney in a contested case before the Office of Administrative Law or an administrative agency may be permitted, on application, in any of the following circumstances: (1) where required by federal statute or regulation; . . . (4) to assist in providing representation to an indigent as part of a Legal Services program if the non-attorney is a paralegal or legal assistant employed by that program; . . . (7) to assist an individual who is not represented by an attorney provided (i) the presentation appears likely to be enhanced by such assistance, (ii) the individual certifies that he or she lacks the means to retain an attorney and that representation is not available through a Legal Services program and (iii) the conduct of the proceeding by the Office of Administrative Law will not be impaired by such assistance. (www.judiciary.state. nj.us/rules/r1-21.htm)

Defining Legal Assistants/Paralegals in New Jersey

- [A paralegal is] a person qualified through education, training or work experience; is employed or retained by a lawyer, law office, government agency, or other entity; works under the ultimate direction and supervision of an attorney; performs specifically delegated legal work, which, for the most part, requires a sufficient knowledge of legal concepts; and performs such duties that, absent such an assistant, the attorney would perform such tasks. *In re Opinion No. 24*, 607 A.2d 962 (Supreme Court of New Jersey, 1992) (citing the definition of the American Bar Association).

New Jersey Certification of Paralegals

- www.sjpaparalegals.org /njcertifiedparalegal.php

Defining the Practice of Law in New Jersey

- *In re Opinion No. 24 of the Committee on the Unauthorized Practice of Law*, 607 A.2d 962, 966 (Supreme Court of New Jersey, 1992) (njlaw.rutgers.edu /collections/ethics/cuap/cua24_1.html): No satisfactory, all-inclusive definition of what constitutes the practice of law has ever been devised. None will be attempted here. That has been left, and wisely so, to the courts when parties present them with concrete factual situations. . . . What is now considered the practice of law is something which may be described more readily than defined. Essentially, the Court decides what constitutes the practice of law on a case-by-case basis. . . . The practice of law is not subject to precise definition. It is not confined to litigation but often encompasses legal activities in many non-litigious fields which entail specialized knowledge and ability. Therefore, the line between permissible business and professional activities and the unauthorized practice of law is often blurred. . . . There is no question that paralegals' work constitutes the practice of law. . . . However, N.J.S.A. 2A:170–81(f) excepts paralegals from being penalized for engaging in tasks that constitute legal practice if their supervising attorney assumes direct responsibility for the work that the paralegals perform. . . . Consequently, paralegals who are supervised by attorneys do not engage in the unauthorized practice of law.

Paralegals (and Others) in New Jersey State and Federal Courts

(See the beginning of this appendix on how to find the full text of the opinions cited here, including WL opinions.)

- *In re Opinion No. 24 of the Committee on the Unauthorized Practice of Law*, 607 A.2d 962 (Supreme Court of New Jersey, 1992) (Attorneys may delegate tasks to paralegals whether the paralegal is employed by the attorney or is an independent paralegal who is retained by the attorney as long as the attorney maintains a direct relationship with his or her clients, supervises the paralegal's work, and is responsible for the paralegal's work product). This opinion overruled *Advisory Opinion 24* (1990) of the New Jersey Unauthorized Practice of Law Committee, which said that attorneys cannot hire paralegals as independent contractors because of the difficulty of providing them with needed day-to-day supervision and the danger of conflict of interest because the paralegals work for different attorneys. (njlaw.rutgers.edu/collections/ethics/cuap/cua24_1.html)

- *Infante v. Gottesman*, 558 A.2d 1338 (Superior Court of New Jersey, 1989) (It is unethical for an attorney to form a partnership with and split fees with a paralegal/investigation service.)
- *Argila v. Argila*, 607 A.2d 675, 679 (Superior Court of New Jersey, 1992) (The application for paralegal fees failed to provide the qualifications of the paralegals and data on the prevailing market rate for paralegals.)
- *Deptford Tp. School Dist. v. H.B.*, 2006 WL 3779820 (U.S. District Court, New Jersey, 2006) (The attorney recorded 1.2 hours to review three certificates of service and to file a return of service with the court. These tasks (1) could have (and should have) been performed by a paralegal or capable legal assistant, or (2) billed at a much lower rate if the attorney performed them, or (3) absorbed as routine office overhead.)
- *Microsoft Corp. v. United Computer Resources of New Jersey*, 216 F. Supp. 2d 383 (U.S. District Court, New Jersey, 2002) ("54 hours in paralegal time spent preparing for an 8-hour hearing is excessive. Accordingly, the paralegal's time will be reduced.")
- *Buccilli v. Timby, Brown, Timby*, 660 A.2d 1261 (Superior Court of New Jersey, 1995) (A paralegal says she was fired after she complained of sexual harassment, a lack of attorney supervision of her work, and a request to forge her attorney's name on court documents, and after she told the firm she intended to file a workers' compensation claim.)
- *United States v. Barber*, 808 F. Supp. 361 (U.S. District Court, New Jersey, 1992) (disbarred attorney acts as paralegal).

Doing Legal Research in New Jersey Law

- **Statutes:** www.njleg.state.nj.us
- **Cases:** www.judiciary.state.nj.us/opinions
- **Court Rules:** www.judiciary.state.nj.us/rules
- **General:** www.law.georgetown.edu/library/research/guides/newjersey.cfm

Finding Employment in New Jersey

- www.indeed.com/q-Paralegal-l-New-Jersey-jobs.html
- newjersey.craigslist.org/lgl

- careers.findlaw.com (enter *Paralegal* and *New Jersey*)
- znjsba.legalstaff.com/Common/HomePage.aspx

NEW MEXICO

ETHICS CODE AND OPINIONS IN NEW MEXICO

- **Attorneys: New Mexico Code:** *Rules of Professional Conduct*
  - www.nmonesource.com/nmnxtadmin/NMPublic.aspx (click *OK*, then *Search New Mexico Rules*, scroll down to select *16*, and click *OK*)
  - www.law.cornell.edu/ethics/nm.html
  - See also ethics links in Helpful Websites at the end of Chapter 5.
- **Attorneys: New Mexico Ethics Opinions**
  - www.nmbar.org/legalresearch/ethicsadvisoryopinions.html
- **Unauthorized Practice of Law: New Mexico**
  - www.nmbar.org (enter *unauthorized practice of law* in search box)
  - ir.lawnet.fordham.edu/cgi/viewcontent.cgi?article=3572&context=flr
- **Paralegals and Other Nonattorneys: New Mexico**
  - *Rules Governing Paralegal Services*, New Mexico Rules Annotated
  - *Rule 20–101.* The employment of paralegals is a particularly significant means by which lawyers can render legal services more economically, in greater volume and with maximum efficiency while maintaining the quality of legal services.
  - *Rule 20–102.* Definition of a paralegal. See below.
  - *Rule 20–103.* A paralegal shall not provide legal advice; represent a client in court except to the extent authorized by law; select, explain, draft, or recommend the use of any legal document to or for any person other than the attorney who supervises the paralegal, unless the supervising attorney so directs; engage in conduct that constitutes the unauthorized practice of law; establish fees; perform any services for a consumer except as performed under the supervision of the attorney unless allowed statute or other law.
  - *Rule 20–104.* A lawyer will require the paralegal for whose work the lawyer is responsible to disclose to all persons with whom the paralegal communicates that the paralegal is not a lawyer. (Common sense would indicate that a routine disclosure

be made at the beginning of any conversation.)
- *Rule 20–105.* A lawyer has an affirmative obligation to ensure that the paralegal for whose work the lawyer is responsible preserves the confidences and secrets of a client.
- *Rule 20–106.* A lawyer will maintain active personal communication with the client. (This rule does not preclude a paralegal from meeting with or talking to the client, nor does it mandate regular and frequent meetings between the lawyer and client.)
- *Rule 20–107.* A paralegal may not act as an advocate on behalf of the client and cannot appear in court or any other tribunal, either in person or on record, as a representative of or advocate for the client, except to the extent authorized by law.
- *Rule 20–108.* A lawyer is responsible to ensure that no personal, social or business interest or relationship of the paralegal impinges upon, or appears to impinge upon, the services rendered to the client. (If a lawyer accepts a matter in which the paralegal may have a conflict of interest, the lawyer will exclude that paralegal from participation in any services performed in connection with that matter. Furthermore, the lawyer must specifically inform the client that a nonlawyer employee has a conflict of interest which, was it the lawyer's conflict, would prevent further representation of the client in connection with the matter.)
- *Rule 20–109.* The lawyer will not permit, encourage or influence the paralegal for whose work the lawyer is responsible to recommend that the lawyer or the lawyer's firm be retained by any person or entity, nor shall the lawyer condone such activity on the part of a paralegal.
- *Rule 20–110.* A lawyer is responsible to ensure that a paralegal is competent to perform the work which the lawyer delegates to the paralegal. (Commentary: The paralegal has a duty to inform the lawyer of any assignment which the assistant regards as being beyond his capability.)
- *Rule 20–111.* A lawyer will not form a partnership or other entity with a paralegal for the purpose of practicing law. (A lawyer will not share fees with a paralegal. The compensation of a paralegal may not include a percentage of profits, fees received generally or fees received specifically from a client who came to the lawyer or the firm by reason of acquaintance

or other association with the paralegal. But paralegals can be included in a retirement or profit-sharing arrangement plan, since such inclusion does not aid or encourage laymen to practice law.)

- *Rule 20–112*. The paralegal is directly accountable to the lawyer. The lawyer maintains ultimate responsibility for and has an ongoing duty to actively supervise the paralegal's work performance, conduct and product.
- *Rule 20–113*. The letterhead of a lawyer or law firm may not include the name of a paralegal. However, a lawyer or law firm may permit its name to appear on the business card of a paralegal, provided the paralegal's capacity is clearly indicated. (A lawyer may permit a paralegal to sign correspondence on his letterhead or on the letterhead of a law firm, as long as the nonlawyer status of the paralegal is clearly disclosed by a title accompanying the signature, such as "paralegal". The business card of a paralegal may contain the name, address and telephone number of the paralegal's employer. However, the card must on its face be clearly intended to identify the paralegal and not the lawyer or law firm.)
- *Rule 20–114*. A lawyer has an affirmative obligation to ensure that a legal assistant, paralegal or other nonlawyer support staff for whose work the lawyer is responsible does not engage in any activities which, if engaged in by the lawyer, would constitute a violation of the Rules of Professional Conduct.
- *Rule 20–115*. A paralegal shall meet specified educational, training or work experience qualifications. (www. nmbar.org/AboutSBNM/ParalegalDivision/PDrulesgovparalegalservices.html)
- *Rule 16.503*. For a discussion of the state's ethics Rule 5.3 (16.503) ("Responsibilities Regarding Nonlawyer Assistants") in the New Mexico *Rules of Professional Conduct*, see Chapter 5.
- *Rule 16.110 (Comment 4)*. The rule of imputed disqualification in Rule 16.110 "does not prohibit representation by others in the law firm where the person prohibited from involvement in a matter is a nonlawyer, such as a paralegal or legal secretary." New Mexico *Rules of Professional Conduct*.
- *Rule 16.505 (Comment 2)*. Lawyers can employ the services of paraprofessionals and delegate tasks to them

"so long as the lawyer supervises the delegated work and retains responsibility for their work."

- *Rule 16.505* (Comment 3). Lawyers can assist independent paraprofessionals who are authorized to provide particular law-related services.
- *Rule 16.505(C)*. A lawyer shall not employ or continue the employment of a disbarred or suspended lawyer "as a law clerk, a paralegal, or in any other position of a quasi-legal nature if the suspended or disbarred lawyer has been specifically prohibited from accepting or continuing such employment by order of the Supreme Court or the disciplinary board."
- Code of Ethics and Professional Responsibility, Paralegal Division, State Bar of New Mexico (www.nmbar. org/AboutSBNM/ParalegalDivision/ PDcodeethics.html)
- *CANON 1*. A paralegal must not perform any of the duties that only attorneys may perform nor take any actions that attorneys may not take.
- *CANON 2*. A paralegal may perform any task which is properly delegated and supervised by an attorney, as long as the attorney is ultimately responsible to the client, maintains a direct relationship with the client, and assumes professional responsibility for the work product.
- *CANON 3*. A paralegal must not: (a) engage in, encourage, or contribute to any act which could constitute the unauthorized practice of law; and (b) establish attorney-client relationships, set fees, give legal opinions or advice or represent a client before a court or agency unless so authorized by that court or agency; and (c) engage in conduct or take any action which would assist or involve the attorney in a violation of professional ethics or give the appearance of professional impropriety.
- *CANON 4*. A paralegal must use discretion and professional judgment commensurate with knowledge and experience but must not render independent legal judgment in place of an attorney. The services of an attorney are essential in the public interest whenever such legal judgment is required.
- *CANON 5*. A paralegal must disclose his or her status as a paralegal at the outset of any professional relationship with a client, attorney, a court or administrative agency or personnel thereof, or a member of the general public. A paralegal must act prudently

in determining the extent to which a client may be assisted without the presence of an attorney.

- *CANON 6*. A paralegal must strive to maintain integrity and a high degree of competency through education and training with respect to professional responsibility, local rules and practice, and through continuing education in substantive areas of law to better assist the legal profession in fulfilling its duty to provide legal service.
- *CANON 7*. A paralegal must protect the confidences of a client and must not violate any rule or statute now in effect or hereafter enacted controlling the doctrine of privileged communications between a client and an attorney.
- *CANON 8*. A paralegal must do all other things incidental, necessary, or expedient for the attainment of the ethics and responsibilities as defined by statute or rule of court.
- *CANON 9*. A paralegal's conduct is governed by the codes of professional responsibility and rules of professional conduct of the State Bar of New Mexico and the New Mexico Supreme Court. A member of the Paralegal Division of the State Bar of New Mexico shall be governed by the Rules Governing Paralegal Services (Rules 20-101 et seq. NMRA, as the same may be amended).
- Attorneys must tell clients how much services to be rendered by office nonattorneys will cost. Advisory Opinions Committee of the State Bar of New Mexico, *Opinion 1990–4* (6/9/90).
- The word "Associates" in a law firm's name cannot refer to or include paralegals, legal assistants, or other nonattorney employees. Advisory Opinions Committee of the State Bar of New Mexico, *Opinion 2006–1* (4/3/06).

Defining Legal Assistants/Paralegals in New Mexico

- *Rules Governing Paralegal Services*, New Mexico Rules Annotated
  - *Rule 20–102*. A. a "paralegal" is a person who: (1) contracts with or is employed by an attorney, law firm, corporation, governmental agency or other entity; (2) performs substantive legal work under the supervision of a licensed attorney who assumes professional responsibility for the final work product; and (3) meets one or more of the education, training or work experience qualifications set forth in Rule 20–115 NMRA of

these rules; and B. "substantive legal work" is work that requires knowledge of legal concepts and is customarily, but not exclusively, performed by a lawyer. Examples of substantive legal work performed by a paralegal include: case planning, development and management; legal research and analysis; interviewing clients; fact gathering and retrieving information; drafting legal documents; collecting, compiling, and utilizing technical information to make an independent decision and recommendation to the supervising attorney; and representing clients before a state or federal administrative agency if that representation is authorized by law. Substantive legal work performed by a paralegal for a licensed attorney shall not constitute the unauthorized practice of law. *Rules Governing Paralegal Services*, Rule 20–102, New Mexico Rules Annotated.

Using the Paralegal Title in New Mexico

- Persons not meeting the definition of a paralegal or attorneys who have been disbarred or suspended from the practice of law by the State of New Mexico or any other jurisdiction are discouraged from using the designation "paralegal." Attorneys are also discouraged from using the designation "paralegal" to identify nonlawyer support staff unless such staff qualifies as a paralegal pursuant to these rules. *Rules Governing Paralegal Services*, New Mexico Rules Annotated, *Rule 20–102* Committee Commentary.

Defining the Practice of Law in New Mexico

- *State ex rel. Norvell v. Credit Bureau of Albuquerque, Inc.*, 514 P.2d 40 (Supreme Court of New Mexico, 1973): [I]ndicia of the practice of law, insofar as court proceedings are concerned, include the following: (1) representation of parties before judicial or administrative bodies, (2) preparation of pleadings and other papers incident to actions and special proceedings, (3) management of such actions and proceedings, and non-court related activities such as (4) giving legal advice and counsel, (5) rendering a service that requires the use of legal knowledge or skill, (6) preparing instruments and contracts by which legal rights are secured. See also *Rules Governing Paralegal Services*, New Mexico Rules Annotated *Rule 20–102*.

Paralegals (and Others) in New Mexico State and Federal Courts

(See the beginning of this appendix on how to find the full text of the opinions cited here, including WL opinions.)

- *In re Montoya*, 150 N.M. 731, 266 P.3d 11 (New Mexico Supreme Court, 2011) (Attorney's conduct of allowing his paralegal to represent to life insurance company that deceased insured's girlfriend was decedent's wife under Utah law and to submit her affidavit to that effect, when attorney knew this was false violated rule prohibiting an attorney, while representing a client, from failing to disclose a material fact to a third party when disclosure is necessary to avoid assisting a criminal or fraudulent act by a client.)
- *In re Weaver*, 2011 WL 867136 (U.S. Bankruptcy Court, New Mexico, 2011) ("Clerical tasks are generally not compensable from the bankruptcy estate, even if such tasks are performed by paralegals or attorneys. Such tasks are considered part of office overhead. The Fee Application reflects time charged for filing documents electronically through the Court's CM/ECF system, and for time for electronically transmitting proposed orders to the Court for consideration. The Law Firm argued that filing electronically is not equivalent to hand-delivering documents to the clerk's office for filing, and that, because electronic filing requires selecting the proper document to file, navigating through the CM/ECF interface and preparing a docket entry, it is appropriate to bill for such work. This Court disagrees. Even though some training in using the Court's CM/ECF system is required, filing a document electronically is not a billable task, whether performed by the attorney or performed by a nonattorney under the direction and permission of the attorney with a CM/ECF account. It is the type of cost that should be absorbed in a legal firm's office overhead. Further, unless some explanation to the Court is required in connection with electronically transmitting proposed orders for entry, the task is clerical and not separately compensable. No evidence was presented relating to the submission of orders for entry. Accordingly, the time the Law Firm charged for filing documents through the Court's CM/ECF system and for the electronic submission of orders for entry in the amount of $160.00 will be disallowed.")
- *In re* Houston, 985 P.2d 752 (New Mexico Supreme Court, 1999) (Having a legal assistant conduct all meetings with the clients, during which the clients'

objectives and the means for pursuing them are discussed and decided, raises serious questions of unauthorized practice; the attorney needs instruction on the proper division of duties between lawyers and legal assistants and the ethical limits of the functions of a legal assistant.)
- *In the Matter of Martinez*, 754 P.2d 842 (New Mexico Supreme Court, 1988) (Attorney is suspended for failing to supervise a paralegal to ensure that the conduct of the paralegal comported with the ethical obligations of the attorney.)
- *Aragon v. Westside Jeep/Eagle*, 876 P.2d 235 (New Mexico Supreme Court, 1994) (Law firm failed to file a notice of appeal and the appeal was dismissed. The firm alleges that the failure to file was caused by a "clerical difficulty" of its paralegal who had a heavy workload and was busy training a new employee when the notice of appeal should have been filed.)

Doing Legal Research in New Mexico Law

- **Statutes:** law.justia.com/codes /new-mexico
- **Cases:** caselaw.findlaw.com/courts /New-Mexico
- **Court Rules:** www.llrx.com /courtrules-gen/state-New-Mexico. html
- **General:** www.supremecourtlawlibrary .org

Finding Employment in New Mexico

- www.indeed.com/q-Litigation -Paralegal-l-New-Mexico-jobs.html
- careers.findlaw.com (select *Paralegal* and *New Mexico*)
- albuquerque.craigslist.org/lgl
- www.nmbar.org/AboutSBNM /ParalegalDivision/PDjobbank.html

NEW YORK

ETHICS CODE AND OPINIONS IN NEW YORK

- **Attorneys: New York Code:** *Rules of Professional Conduct*
  - www.nysba.org/CustomTemplates /SecondaryStandard.aspx?id=26633
  - www.law.cornell.edu/ethics/ny.html
  - See also ethics links in Helpful Websites at the end of Chapter 5.
- **Attorneys: New York Ethics Opinions**
  - www.nysba.org/Ethics
  - www.nycbar.org/ethics/ethics -opinions-local
  - www.nycla.org (click *Ethics* then *Ethics Opinions*)

- www.nassaubar.org (enter *Ethics* in the search box)
- **Unauthorized Practice of Law in New York**
  - www.nysba.org (enter *unauthorized practice of law* in search box)
  - www.nysba.org/workarea/Download Asset.aspx?id=28147
  - ir.lawnet.fordham.edu/cgi /viewcontent.cgi?article=3572&con text=flr
- **Paralegals and Other Nonattorneys: New York**
  - *Rule 5.3.* For a discussion of the state's ethics Rule 5.3 ("Responsibilities Regarding Nonlawyer Assistants") in the New York *Rules of Professional Conduct*, see Chapter 5. The New York rule provides that a "law firm shall ensure that the work of nonlawyers who work for the firm is adequately supervised, as appropriate." The "degree of supervision required is that which is reasonable under the circumstances, taking into account factors such as the experience of the person whose work is being supervised, the amount of work involved in a particular matter and the likelihood that ethical problems might arise in the course of working on the matter."
  - *Rule 1.10 (Comment 4).* The rule of imputed disqualification in Rule 1.10 "does not prohibit representation by others in the law firm where the person prohibited from involvement in a matter is a nonlawyer, such as a paralegal or legal secretary." New York *Rules of Professional Conduct*.
  - *Rule 5.5 (Comment 2).* Lawyers can employ the services of paraprofessionals and delegate tasks to them "so long as the lawyer supervises the delegated work and retains responsibility for their work."

Ethical Rules and Guidelines in New York

- New York State Bar Ass'n, *Guidelines for the Utilization by Lawyers of the Services of Legal Assistants* (1997). (www .cdpa.info/files/NY_Paralegal_ guidelines.pdf). *Guideline I:* An attorney can permit a paralegal to perform services in the representation of a client if the attorney retains a direct relationship with the client, supervises the paralegal, and is fully responsible for the paralegal. *Guideline II:* An attorney must not assist a paralegal in engaging in the unauthorized practice of law. *Guideline III:* A paralegal may perform certain functions otherwise prohibited only to the extent authorized by law. An example would be a law that allows nonlawyer advocacy of clients at particular administrative agencies. *Guideline IV:* An attorney must take reasonable measures to ensure that all client confidences are preserved by paralegals and take appropriate measures to avoid conflicts of interest arising from their employment. *Guideline V:* An attorney shall not form a partnership with a paralegal if any part of the firm's activity consists of the practice of law, nor shall an attorney share legal fees with a paralegal. *Guideline VI:* An attorney shall require that a paralegal, when dealing with a client, disclose at the outset that the paralegal is not an attorney. The attorney shall also require such disclosure at the outset when the paralegal is dealing with a court, an administrative agency, attorneys, or the public if there is any reason for their believing that the paralegal is an attorney or associated with an attorney. *Guideline VII:* An attorney should promote the professional development of the paralegal. Examples include providing opportunities for continuing legal education, pro bono projects, and participation in professional associations.
- When a law firm hires a paralegal who has previously worked at another law firm, the law firm must adequately supervise the conduct of the paralegal. Supervisory measures may include (i) instructing the paralegal not to disclose protected information acquired at the former law firm and (ii) instructing lawyers not to exploit such information if proffered. In some circumstances, it is advisable that the law firm inquire whether the paralegal acquired confidential information from the former law firm about a current representation of the new firm or conduct a more comprehensive conflict check based on the paralegal's prior work. The results of such an inquiry will help determine whether the new firm should take further steps, such as seeking the opposing party's consent and/or screening the paralegal. New York State Bar Ass'n, *Opinion 774* (3/23/04).
- A judge should not preside in cases in which members of a law firm which employs the judge's spouse in a paralegal/clerical position, appear before the judge, but the disqualification is subject to remittal of disqualification. New York Advisory Committee on Judicial Ethics, *Opinion 99–87* (6/18/99).
- A part-time town judge who is employed as a paralegal by a law firm must recuse himself/herself in cases in which the law firm appears, but such cases may be heard by the other town judge. New York Advisory Committee on Judicial Ethics, *Opinion 94–108* (11/15/94).
- Paralegal names can be printed on a firm's letterhead if their nonattorney status is clear. New York State Bar Ass'n, *Ethics Opinion 500* (12/6/78). This opinion overturns *Opinion 261* (1972). A paralegal may sign letters on a lawyer's letterhead so long as the paralegal is clearly designated as a nonlawyer. New York State Bar Ass'n, *Opinion 255* (6/26/72).
- The titles *paralegal* and *senior paralegal* are acceptable, but the following titles are unacceptable because they are ambiguous: *paralegal coordinator, legal associate, public benefits advocate, legal advocate, family law advocate, housing law advocate, disability benefits advocate,* and *public benefits specialist.* The public might be misled about the non-attorney status of the people with these titles. New York State Bar Ass'n, *Ethics Opinion 640* (1992) (1992 WL 450730).
- An attorney may include on letterhead and other materials the identification of a nonlegal employee as a "Certified Legal Assistant," provided that term is accompanied by the statement that the certification is afforded by the National Association of Legal Assistants (NALA), and provided further that the attorney has satisfied himself or herself that NALA is a bona fide organization that provides such certification to all who meet objective and consistently applied standards relevant to the work of legal assistants. New York State Bar Ass'n, *Opinion 695* (8/25/97).
- A lawyer may allow a paralegal to use a signature stamp to execute escrow checks from a client trust account so long as the lawyer supervises the delegated work closely and exercises complete professional responsibility for the acts of the paralegal. New York State Bar Ass'n, *Opinion 693* (8/22/97).
- A nonlawyer should not independently advise a client of his or her rights or duties. New York State Bar Ass'n, *Opinion 44* (1/26/67).
- New York statutes allow nonlawyers to be licensed to represent claimants before the workers' compensation agency (McKinney's Workers' Compensation Law § 24-a). A lawyer can employ such a representative to appear on behalf of the lawyer's client in a workers' compensation proceeding in which the lawyer has entered an appearance. New York State Bar Ass'n, *Opinion 446* (12/3/76).

- An attorney may not accept referrals from an accounting firm in return for an agreement to share contingent fees with the accounting firm on a personal injury matter. New York State Bar Ass'n, *Opinion 727* (2/4/00).
- New York State Unemployment Insurance Appeals Board allows nonlawyers to serve as "registered representatives" of claimants seeking unemployment insurance benefits. (labor.ny.gov/forms docs/ui/LO424_4.pdf)
- There are circumstances in which an attorney can send his or her paralegal to attend a real estate closing alone. The attorney must determine that the closing calls for "merely ministerial" as opposed to discretionary duties, must be sure the background of the paralegal makes him or her suitable to attend, and must have a plan to cope with the unforeseen such as being available by telephone to the paralegal. "[F]rom an ethical standpoint, the lawyer who assigns a non-lawyer to work on a client's matter had better be right about the suitability of that task for delegation, and the suitability of that employee for the task at hand." New York State Bar Ass'n, *Opinion 677* (12/12/95).
- A paralegal cannot conduct a deposition or supervise the execution of a will. New York State Bar Ass'n, *Ethics Opinion 304* (1973) and *Ethics Opinion 343*.
- Nonlawyers may be compensated based on a profit-sharing arrangement but may not be paid a percentage of profits or fees attributable to particular client matters referred by the employee. New York State Bar Ass'n, *Opinion 733* (10/5/00), *Opinion 282* (1/25/73).
- Corporate legal department lawyers and paralegals have been asked to participate in the corporation's "compliance with law" program. The program requires all employees "to report all instances of unlawful or otherwise unethical behavior by any employee." Lawyers and legal assistants will staff and answer a "help line" telephone in the corporate legal department, taking reports from employees. Held to be ethical with qualifications. New York State Bar Ass'n, *Opinion 650* (6/30/93).
- A lawyer who continues to represent a client in a transaction in which the counter-party has chosen to be represented by a nonlawyer is not thereby aiding the unauthorized practice of law even if the representation by the nonlawyer is the unauthorized practice of law. New York State Bar Ass'n, *Opinion 809* (2/12/07).
- An attorney can give credit or recognition to a nonattorney for work performed in the preparation of a brief as long as his or her nonattorney status is clear. New York State Bar Ass'n, *Ethics Opinion 299*.
- An attorney cannot allow a nonattorney to engage in settlement negotiations or to appear at a pretrial conference. Bar Ass'n of Nassau County, *Opinion 86–40* (9/12/89).
- A nonattorney can attend a real estate closing to perform ministerial functions involving only formalities. His or her nonattorney status must be disclosed at the closing. Bar Ass'n of Nassau County, *Opinion 86–43* (10/21/86); reaffirmed in *Opinion 90–13* (3/18/90).
- As attorney cannot divide a fee with a paralegal who brings clients to the attorney. Bar Ass'n of Nassau County, *Opinion 87–37* (10/1/87).
- Nonattorneys cannot be referred to as *associates* of an attorney. Bar Ass'n of Nassau County, *Opinion 88–34* (9/29/88).
- Nonattorneys can be listed on attorney letterhead if such employees are clearly described and identified as nonattorneys. Bar Ass'n of Nassau County, *Opinion 91–32* (1991) (accountants); *Opinion 87–14* (1987) (paralegals).
- An attorney may not represent a defendant in a criminal case when the complainant in the case is an investigator whom the attorney used in an unrelated case. There would be an appearance of impropriety in such a representation. Bar Ass'n of Nassau County, *Opinion 89–1* (1/18/89).
- A New York lawyer may ethically outsource legal support services overseas to a nonlawyer, if the New York lawyer (a) rigorously supervises the nonlawyer, so as to avoid aiding the nonlawyer in the unauthorized practice of law and to ensure that the nonlawyer's work contributes to the lawyer's competent representation of the client; (b) preserves the client's confidences and secrets when outsourcing; (c) avoids conflicts of interest when outsourcing; (d) bills for outsourcing appropriately; and (e) when necessary, obtains advance client consent to outsourcing. Ass'n of the Bar of the City of New York, *Opinion 2006–3* (8/2006).
- An attorney cannot form a partnership with a nonattorney to practice law. An attorney who shares an office with a nonattorney must avoid misleading the public into believing the nonattorney is an attorney. Ass'n of the Bar of the City of New York, *Opinion 1987–1* (2/23/87).
- A law firm may issue an announcement that it has hired a law student or other nonattorney provided the announcement makes clear the fact that the person is not an attorney and is working in a nonattorney capacity. Ass'n of the Bar of the City of New York, *Opinion 1996–2* (2/26/96).
- It is improper for a law firm to send out an announcement listing a nonlawyer assistant as "associated" with the firm because this implies the person is a lawyer. Ass'n of the Bar of the City of New York, *Opinion 454* (1938).
- Attorneys must effectively supervise their nonattorney employees, refrain from aiding or encouraging them to engage in the unauthorized practice of law, and be sure that they maintain client confidences and that the public is not misled by their nonattorney status. Ass'n of the Bar of the City of New York, *Opinion 1995–11* (7/6/95). This opinion modifies *Opinion 884* (1974).
- It is improper for lawyer or law firm to employ a disbarred or suspended attorney in any capacity related to practice of law. Ass'n of the Bar of the City of New York, *Opinion 1998–1* (12/21/98).
- Paralegals can be listed on the letterhead of a law firm and on a business card that prints the name of the law firm (without printing the name of the supervising attorney) as long as their nonattorney status is indicated. New York County Lawyers' Ass'n, *Opinion 673* (12/23/89).
- A lawyer may not assign tasks to a legal assistant that involve the exercise of professional judgment. A lawyer may not hire in any capacity a disbarred or suspended lawyer. New York County Lawyers' Ass'n, *Opinion 666* (10/29/85).

Defining Legal Assistants/Paralegals in New York

- A legal assistant/paralegal is a person who is qualified through education, training or work experience to be employed or retained by a lawyer, law office, governmental agency, or other entity in a capacity or function that involves the performance, under the ultimate direction and supervision of, and/or accountability to, an attorney, of substantive legal work, that requires a sufficient knowledge of legal concepts such that, absent such legal assistant/paralegal, the attorney would perform the task. The terms "legal assistant" and "paralegal" are synonymous and are not to be confused with numerous other legal titles which have proliferated with the public and within the legal community. New York State Bar Ass'n, *Guidelines for the Utilization by Lawyers of the Services of Legal Assistants* (1997) (www.cdpa.info /files/NY_Paralegal_guidelines.pdf).

Defining the Practice of Law in New York

- *El Gemayel v. Seaman*, 533 N.E.2d 245, 248, 536 N.Y.S.2d 406, 409 (Court of Appeals of New York, 1988): The "practice" of law reserved to duly licensed New York attorneys includes the rendering of legal advice as well as appearing in court and holding oneself out to be a lawyer.
- § 118.1(g) (*McKinney's New York Rules of Court*): Registration of attorneys. For purposes of this section, the "practice of law" shall mean the giving of legal advice or counsel to, or providing legal representation for, [a] particular body or individual in a particular situation in either the public or private sector in the State of New York or elsewhere [;] it shall include the appearance as an attorney before any court or administrative agency.

Paralegals (and Others) in New York State and Federal Courts

(See the beginning of this appendix on how to find the full text of the opinions cited here.)

- *In the Matter of Feldman*, 785 N.Y.S.2d 600 (Supreme Court, Appellate Division, 3d Dept., 2004) (A laid-off paralegal is not required to accept a job as a legal secretary to qualify for unemployment compensation. "While both the paralegal position and the legal secretary position were characterized as legal support staff, the paralegal duties are more extensive and required different skills than that of a legal secretary.")
- *Fine v. Facet Aerospace Products Co.*, 133 Federal Rules Decisions 439 (U.S. District Court, S.D. New York, 1990) (Handwritten notes made by a paralegal on a document in the course of discovery in another case are protected from disclosure under the work-product doctrine.)
- *Glover Bottled Gas Corp. v. Circle M. Beverage Barn*, 514 N.Y.S.2d 440 (Supreme Court, Appellate Division, 2d Dept., 1987) (An attorney is disqualified after hiring a paralegal who worked on specific litigation while previously employed by the opposing counsel in the litigation.)
- *In the Matter of Lowell*, 784 N.Y.S.2d 69 (Supreme Court, Appellate Division, 1st Dept., 2004) (An attorney acted unethically by failing to create and maintain a Chinese wall separating a paralegal, who had formerly worked for law firm that represented the opposing party in a matrimonial action, from any association with the matrimonial matter while in attorney's office, by

requiring the paralegal to work on the case, and by questioning her about the adversary's litigation strategies.)

- *Mulhern v. Calder*, 763 N.Y.S.2d 741 (Supreme Court, Albany County, 2003) (Law firm's efforts to construct a Chinese wall around a secretary who had assisted the opponent's attorney on the case before being hired by the firm were sufficient to prevent the firm's disqualification. Automatic disqualification of law firms is not required simply because they hire nonlawyers who have had access to confidences of their opponents.)
- *NYC Medical & Neurodiagnostic, P.C.*, 784 N.Y.S.2d 840 (Civil Court, Kings County, 2004) (A clerk employed by the law firm in its mailroom will not cause the law firm to be disqualified from representing the plaintiff, simply because the clerk's testimony is necessary in establishing the elements of plaintiff's prima facie case. The disqualification rules governing lawyers do not apply to nonlawyer employees of law firm.)
- *First Deposit Nat'l Bank v. Moreno*, 606 N.Y.S.2d 938 (City Court of the City of New York, New York County, 1993) (A claim for paralegal fees must itemize what was done and how much time was spent by attorneys and by others. "[P]aralegals often competently perform certain services equivalent to those done by attorneys, while generally charging their time at a lesser rate than attorneys, thus benefitting those who pay the fees.")
- *United States v. Hooper*, 43 F.3d 26 (U.S. Court of Appeals, 2d Circuit, 1994) (A paralegal's mistake on the deadline for filing a criminal appeal is not "excusable neglect" justifying permission to file the appeal late. The paralegal thought she had thirty days to file rather than ten.)
- *In the Matter of Saltz*, 536 N.Y.S.2d 126 (Supreme Court, Appellate Division, 2d Dept., 1988) (An attorney is disciplined for lying when he claimed that his paralegal "doctored" divorce papers.)
- *Sussman v. Grado*, 746 N.Y.S.2d 548 (District Court, Nassau County, 2002) ("Regardless of her intentions to help the plaintiff, this independent paralegal operated without the supervision of an attorney. She tried to create a legal document without the required knowledge, skill or training. As a result the plaintiff may have lost the ability to execute against two bank accounts.")
- *Paralegal Institute, Inc. v. American Bar Ass'n*, 475 F. Supp. 1123 (U.S. District Court, S.D. New York, 1979) (Court dismissed paralegal school's antitrust charges against the American Bar Association.)

Doing Legal Research in New York Law

- **Statutes:** public.leginfo.state.ny.us /menugetf.cgi?COMMONQUERY =LAWS
- **Cases:** www.nycourts.gov/reporter /decisions.htm
- **Court Rules:** www.nycourts.gov/rules
- **General:** www.nycourts.gov /reporter/research.htm

Finding Employment in New York

- careers.findlaw.com (select *Paralegal* and *New York*)
- www.indeed.com/q-Paralegal-l -New-York,-NY-jobs.html
- www.linkedin.com/job/paralegal -jobs-new-york-ny
- www.simplyhired.com/k-paralegal-l -new-york-ny-jobs.html
- newyork.craigslist.org/lgl

NORTH CAROLINA

ETHICS CODE AND OPINIONS IN NORTH CAROLINA

- **Attorneys: North Carolina Code:** *Rules of Professional Conduct*
  - www.ncbar.com/rules/rpcsearch.asp
  - www.law.cornell.edu/ethics/nc.html
  - See also ethics links in Helpful Websites at the end of Chapter 5.
- **Attorneys: North Carolina Ethics Opinions**
  - www.ncbar.com/ethics
  - www.ncbar.com/ethics/propeth.asp
- **Unauthorized Practice of Law: North Carolina**
  - www.ncbar.com/programs/upl.asp
  - www.ncbar.com/PDFs/upl_statutes .pdf
  - ir.lawnet.fordham.edu/cgi /viewcontent.cgi?article=3572&con text=flr
- **Paralegals and Other Nonattorneys: North Carolina**
  - *Rule 5.3.* For a discussion of the state's ethics Rule 5.3 ("Responsibilities Regarding Nonlawyer Assistants") in the North Carolina *Rules of Professional Conduct*, see Chapter 5. North Carolina has added an additional comment to Rule 5.3 that is not is the ABA Model Rules. The comment says that a lawyer who discovers that a nonlawyer has wrongfully misappropriated money from the lawyer's trust account must inform the North Carolina State Bar. For the text of 5.3 in North Carolina, see http://www .ncbar.com/rules/rules.asp.

- *Rule 1.10 (Comment 4).* The rule of imputed disqualification in Rule 1.10 "does not prohibit representation by others in the law firm where the person prohibited from involvement in a matter is a nonlawyer, such as a paralegal or legal secretary." North Carolina *Rules of Professional Conduct.*
- Rule 5.5(e). A lawyer or law firm shall not employ a disbarred or suspended lawyer as a law clerk or legal assistant if that individual was associated with such lawyer or law firm at any time on or after the date of the acts which resulted in disbarment or suspension through and including the effective date of disbarment or suspension.
- *Rule 5.5* (Comment 9). Lawyers can employ the services of paraprofessionals and delegate tasks to them "so long as the lawyer supervises the delegated work and retains responsibility for their work."
- *Guidelines for Use of Nonlawyers in Rendering Legal Services,* North Carolina State Bar (2010) (www .nccertifiedparalegal.org/guidelines .asp) *Guideline 1:* A lawyer is responsible for the professional conduct of a paralegal performing services at the lawyer's direction. A lawyer must take reasonable measures to ensure that the paralegal's conduct is consistent with the lawyer's obligations under the Rules of Professional Conduct. *Guideline 2:* A lawyer shall not permit a paralegal to engage in the practice of law. To this end, a lawyer may not delegate the following responsibilities or activities to a paralegal: establishing a client-lawyer relationship and the terms of the relationship; giving oral or written legal advice or a legal opinion to a client; interpretation of legal documents for a client; or appearance in any court proceeding unless authorized by law. *Guideline 3:* A supervising lawyer is responsible for work product and for providing appropriate and active supervision to a paralegal. A lawyer may delegate to a paralegal any task normally performed by the lawyer except as set forth in guideline 2. *Guideline 4:* A lawyer is responsible for taking reasonable measures to ensure that client confidences are preserved and protected by a paralegal. *Guideline 5:* A lawyer may include the name of a paralegal on firm letterhead or other forms of communication, including advertising, provided the paralegal's title is clearly indicated. *Guideline 6:* A lawyer may charge for the work performed by a paralegal provided

the fee is not clearly excessive. *Guideline 7:* A lawyer may compensate a paralegal based on the quality and quantity of the paralegal's work but a legal fee may not be shared with a paralegal. The paralegal's compensation may not be contingent upon the outcome of a particular case or paid in exchange for referring clients. *Guideline 8:* A lawyer may delegate management of a trust account to a paralegal or other nonlawyer employee but the lawyer remains professionally responsible for the safe keeping of the funds deposited in the account and for compliance with the record keeping and accountings required by the *Rules of Professional Conduct. Guideline 9:* A lawyer shall take reasonable measures to prevent conflicts of interest resulting from a paralegal's prior employment, other employment, or personal interests. *Guideline 10:* A lawyer who employs a paralegal should facilitate the paralegal's continuing self-improvement by encouraging and supporting the paralegal's participation in professionalism, continuing education, and pro bono publico activities and encouraging certification by the North Carolina State Bar's Board of Paralegal Certification or other reputable program.
- A lawyer may not represent the beneficiary of the deed of trust in a contested foreclosure if the lawyer's spouse and paralegal own an interest in the closely held corporate trustee. North Carolina State Bar, *2011 Formal Ethics Opinion 5* (7/5/11).
- A person who is not an employee but who is formally affiliated with a firm, such as a contract paralegal, may use firm letterhead if the person is authorized to act on the firm's behalf and the affiliation is set forth on the letterhead or otherwise in the letter. North Carolina State Bar, *2011 Formal Ethics Opinion 9* (7/15/11).
- Opinion rules that a law firm may send a paralegal to meet with a prospective client and obtain a representation contract if a lawyer at the firm has reviewed sufficient information from the prospective client to determine that an offer of representation is appropriate. North Carolina State Bar, *2012 Formal Ethics Opinion 11* (7/19/13).
- A lawyer may have a nonlawyer employee deliver a message to a court holding calendar call, if the lawyer is unable to attend due to a scheduling conflict with another court or other

legitimate reason. The nonlawyer employee must be merely providing the court with information and not requesting or arguing for a particular action by the court. North Carolina State Bar, *2000 Formal Ethics Opinion 10* (7/27/01).
- A paralegal switches jobs. She now works for an attorney whose client opposes a party represented by the paralegal's former employer who says the paralegal worked on the case while there. The former employer seeks the disqualification of the current employer on the case. The request is denied. The imputed disqualification rules in Rule 5.11 [1.10] do not apply to nonlawyers. But the current employer "must take extreme care" to ensure the paralegal is "totally screened" from the case even if her involvement in the case at the prior employment was negligible. North Carolina State Bar, *RPC 176* (7/21/94). In agreement: *RPC 74* (10/20/89).
- An attorney may not pay a paralegal a percentage of fees as a bonus. A bonus for productivity can be given, but not as a percentage of fees. North Carolina State Bar, *RPC 147* (1/15/93).
- The compensation of a nonlawyer law firm employee who represents Social Security disability claimants before the Social Security Administration may be based upon the income generated by such representation. Nonlawyers are allowed to earn fees in Social Security agency cases. North Carolina State Bar, *Formal Ethics Opinion 6,* (10/21/05).
- Legal representation of a borrower requires the presence of the lawyer at the closing of a residential real estate refinancing. A nonlawyer may oversee the execution of documents outside the presence of the lawyer provided the lawyer adequately supervises the nonlawyer and is present at the closing conference to complete the transaction. North Carolina State Bar, *Formal Ethics Opinion 4,* (10/19/01). "The lawyer must be physically present at the closing conference and may not be present through a surrogate such as a paralegal." *Formal Ethics Opinion 8,* (10/19/01). See also *Formal Ethics Opinion 13* (7/21/00).
- With proper supervision, a real estate lawyer can engage a free-lance paralegal as an independent contractor to perform title searches for real estate closings. When working with him, the lawyer must check for conflicts of interest. North Carolina State

Bar, *RPC 216* (7/17/97) (1997 WL 331712).

- If warranted by exigent circumstances, a lawyer may allow a paralegal to sign his or her name to court documents so long as it does not violate any law and the lawyer provides the appropriate level of supervision. North Carolina State Bar, 2006 *Formal Ethics Opinion 13* (10/20/06).
- A legal assistant can communicate and negotiate with a claims adjuster if directly supervised by an attorney. However, "[u]nder no circumstances should the legal assistant be permitted to exercise independent legal judgment regarding the value of the case, the advisability of making or accepting any offer of settlement or any other related matter." North Carolina State Bar, *RPC 70* (10/20/89).
- An attorney can represent a client in an action to abate a nuisance even though his paralegal may be called as a witness against the opponent. North Carolina State Bar, *Revised RPC 213* (10/20/95).
- An attorney may not permit his paralegal to examine or represent a witness at a deposition. North Carolina State Bar, *RPC 183* (10/21/94).

Defining Legal Assistants/Paralegals in North Carolina

- A legal assistant (or paralegal) is a person, qualified through education, training or work experience, who is employed or retained by a lawyer, law office, corporation, governmental agency, or other entity, and who performs specifically delegated substantive legal work for which a lawyer is responsible. *Guidelines for Use of Nonlawyers in Rendering Legal Services*, North Carolina State Bar (2010).

North Carolina Certification of Paralegals

- www.nccertifiedparalegal.gov
- www.nccertifiedparalegal.org
- See Exhibit 4-11 in Chapter 4 for an overview of certification in North Carolina.

Defining the Practice of Law in North Carolina

- § 84–2.1 (General Statutes of North Carolina): The phrase "practice law" as used in this Chapter is defined to be performing any legal service for any other person, firm or corporation, with or without compensation, specifically

including the preparation or aiding in the preparation of deeds, mortgages, wills, trust instruments, inventories, accounts or reports of guardians, trustees, administrators or executors, or preparing or aiding in the preparation of any petitions or orders in any probate or court proceeding; abstracting or passing upon titles, the preparation and filing of petitions for use in any court, including administrative tribunals and other judicial or quasi-judicial bodies, or assisting by advice, counsel, or otherwise in any legal work; and to advise or give opinion upon the legal rights of any person, firm or corporation: Provided, that the above reference to particular acts which are specifically included within the definition of the phrase "practice law" shall not be construed to limit the foregoing general definition of the term, but shall be construed to include the foregoing particular acts, as well as all other acts within the general definition. The phrase "practice law" does not encompass the drafting or writing of memoranda of understanding or other mediation summaries by mediators at community mediation centers. . .or by mediators of employment-related matters for The University of North Carolina or a constituent institution, or for an agency, commission, or board of the State of North Carolina. (www .ncbar.com/PDFs/upl_statutes.pdf)

Paralegals (and Others) in North Carolina State and Federal Courts

(See the beginning of this appendix on how to find the full text of the opinions cited here, including WL opinions.)

- *Britt v. Cusick*, 753 S.E.2d 351 (Court of Appeals of North Carolina, 2014) (Limited discovery by the defendant of the plaintiff's paralegal is allowed (but not including a full deposition) concerning conversations the paralegal had with employees of the defendant's client.)
- *Nieto-Espinoza v. Lowder Const.*, 748 S.E.2d 8 (Court of Appeals of North Carolina, 2013) (A legal assistant's incorrect entry of the deadline for refiling a workers' compensation claim on the attorney's calendar was not excusable neglect, as would entitle claimant to relief from the deadline for refiling. The legal assistant incorrectly entered the deadline to refile the claim on the attorney's calendar as one year after the date the copy of the order was received, rather than one year after the date the order was entered. The attorney failed

to review the clearly marked entry date on the copy of the order of dismissal when it was received and failed to notice the paralegal's calendaring error until after deadline to refile the claim had passed. Hence the attorney did not demonstrate diligence in handling claimant's case.)

- *North Carolina v. Cummings*, 389 S.E.2d 66, 74 (Supreme Court of North Carolina, *1990*) (A paralegal is allowed to testify about a hearsay statement the victim made during an intake interview.)
- *Lea Co. v. North Carolina Board of Transportation*, 374 S.E.2d 868 (Supreme Court of North Carolina, 1989) (Paralegal fees denied. The paralegal work in this case was largely clerical in nature and therefore part of ordinary office overhead to be subsumed in the hourly attorney rate.)
- *Hyatt v. Barnhart*, 315 F.3d 239 (U.S. Court of Appeals, 4th Circuit, North Carolina, 2002) (Paralegal expenses are separately recoverable only as part of a prevailing party's award for attorney's fees and expenses, and even then only to the extent that the paralegal performs work traditionally performed by an attorney. Otherwise, paralegal expenses are separately unrecoverable overhead expenses.)
- *In re Thomas*, 2004 WL 2296550 (U.S. Bankruptcy Court, M.D., North Carolina, 2004) (Bankruptcy petition preparers are prohibited from providing paralegal services.)
- *In re Inquiry Concerning a Judge*, 614 S.E.2d 529 Supreme Court of North Carolina, 2005) (Censure is recommended for a judge who sexually harassed a paralegal.)

Doing Legal Research in North Carolina Law

- **Statutes:** www.ncleg.net/gascripts /statutes/statutes.asp
- **Cases:** appellate.nccourts.org /opinions
- **Court Rules:** www.nccourts.org /Courts/CRS/Policies/LocalRules
- **General:** cslguides.charlottelaw.edu /northcarolinalegalresearch

Finding Employment in North Carolina

- www.ncparalegal.org/careers
- careers.findlaw.com (select *Paralegal* and *North Carolina*)
- www.indeed.com/q-Legal-Assistant -l-North-Carolina-jobs.html
- raleigh.craigslist.org/search/lgl? query=+

NORTH DAKOTA

ETHICS CODE AND OPINIONS IN NORTH DAKOTA

- **Attorneys: North Dakota Code:** *Rules of Professional Conduct*
  - www.ndcourts.gov/Rules/Conduct/contents.htm
  - www.law.cornell.edu/ethics/nd.html
  - See also ethics links in Helpful Websites at the end of Chapter 5.
- **Attorneys: North Dakota Ethics Opinions**
  - www.sband.org/Ethics/default.aspx
- **Unauthorized Practice of Law: North Dakota**
  - www.ndcourts.gov/court/notices/20050353/adopted/rule5.5.htm
  - ir.lawnet.fordham.edu/cgi/viewcontent.cgi?article=3572&context=flr
- **Paralegals and Other Nonattorneys: North Dakota**
  - *Rule 5.3.* For a general discussion of ethics Rule 5.3 ("Responsibilities Regarding Nonlawyer Assistants"), see Chapter 5.
  - *Rule 5.3.* North Dakota's version of Rule 5.3 in its *Rules of Professional Conduct* adds the following provision: (d)(1) A lawyer may delegate to a legal assistant any task normally performed by the lawyer except those tasks proscribed to one not licensed as a lawyer by statute, court rule, administrative rule or regulation, controlling authority, or these Rules. (2) A lawyer may not delegate to a legal assistant: (i) responsibility for establishing a lawyer-client relationship; (ii) responsibility for establishing the amount of a fee to be charged for a legal service; (iii) responsibility for a legal opinion rendered to a client; or (iv) responsibility for the work product. (3) The lawyer shall make reasonable efforts to ensure that clients, courts, and other lawyers are aware that a legal assistant is not licensed to practice law. (www.ndcourts.gov/court/rules/Conduct/rule5.3.htm)
  - *Rule 5.3 (comment 3).* While appropriate delegation of tasks to legal assistants is allowed, a lawyer may not permit a legal assistant to engage in the "practice of law." The key to appropriate delegation is proper supervision, which includes adequate instruction when assigning projects, monitoring of the project, and review of the project. Lawyers should take care in hiring and choosing a legal assistant to work on a specific project to ensure that the legal assistant has the education, knowledge, and ability necessary to perform the delegated tasks competently.
  - *Rule 5.3 (comment 4).* Helpful guidelines in evaluating a legal assistant's qualifications include (1) graduation from a paralegal program that meets minimum standards, and (2) attaining paralegal certification that requires continuing legal education, work experience under attorney supervision.
  - *Rule 5.3 (comment 5).* A lawyer may not delegate responsibility to a legal assistant or other nonlawyer for deciding whether the representation will be undertaken or for any legal opinion rendered to a client.
  - *Rule 5.3 (Comment 6).* Nonlawyers may not hold themselves out as lawyers. It is the lawyer's responsibility to see that communications about services rendered by the law firm and its nonlawyers are not false, fraudulent, deceptive or misleading, and that nonlawyer employees of the firm understand those limitations. If the lawyer or a legal assistant becomes aware that the role of the legal assistant is unclear, the lawyer has an affirmative duty to clarify the legal assistant's role.
  - *Rule 5.5 (Comment 12).* Lawyers can employ the services of paraprofessionals and delegate tasks to them "so long as the lawyer supervises the delegated work and retains responsibility for their work."
  - *Rule 5.5 (Comment 12).* Lawyers can assist "independent nonlawyers" such as "paraprofessionals," who are authorized to provide some kinds of legal services.
  - *Rule 1.5 (f).* Lawyers may charge for the work performed by their legal assistants.
  - *Rule 1.5 (g).* A lawyer may not split legal fees with a legal assistant nor pay a legal assistant for the referral of legal business. A lawyer may compensate a legal assistant based on the quantity and quality of the legal assistant's work and value of that work to a law practice. The legal assistant's compensation may not be contingent, by advance agreement, upon the outcome of a case or upon the profitability of the lawyer's practice.
  - *Rule 1.5 (Comment 10).* In cases involving fixed fees or contingent fees, the total fees are agreed upon in advance and there should be no separate charge for legal assistant services. In matters charged on the basis of "fee for service" or "charge by the hour", a lawyer may include separate charges for work performed by legal assistants or otherwise include legal assistant hours in calculating the amount of fees to be charged. It may be appropriate to value such services at "market rates" rather than "actual costs" to the lawyer.
  - *Rule 1.5 (Comment 11).* The lawyer should disclose to the client, either at the outset of the representation or at the point during the representation when the lawyer determines a legal assistant should be used, that the lawyer proposes to use a legal assistant and obtain the client's agreement to any separate charges for legal assistant services.
  - *Rule 1.5 (Comment 12).* A lawyer may not split fees with a legal assistant, whether characterized as splitting of contingent fees, "forwarding" fees or other sharing of legal fees. The lawyer's obligation is to pay the legal assistant according to the employment agreement. There is no general prohibition against a lawyer recognizing the contribution of the legal assistant with a discretionary bonus. Likewise, a lawyer is not prohibited from compensating a legal assistant who aids materially in a practice with compensation greater than that generally paid to legal assistants in the geographic area working in less lucrative law practices.
  - *Rule 7.5 (e).* A lawyer may identify legal assistants on the lawyer's letterhead and on business cards identifying the lawyer's firm, provided the legal assistant's status is clearly identified.
  - An attorney who has been suspended from the practice of law may act as a paralegal, legal assistant, or other type of support staff to a licensed attorney, so long as the suspended attorney complies with the strictures of *In re Application of Christenson*, 215 N.W. 2d 970 (N.D. 1974) and Rule 5.3 of the North Dakota Rules of Professional Conduct. State Bar Ass'n of North Dakota, Opinion 01-02 (May 24, 2001). The *Christenson* case held that disbarred or suspended attorney engage in unauthorized practice of law when they perform services customarily performed by licensed attorneys which require legal expertise, though such acts might lawfully be performed by a layperson in some circumstances, unless their qualifications to perform such services derive from

sources other than their law training and law experience. "For example, a suspended lawyer who is also a public accountant may prepare tax returns as a public accountant. But a suspended lawyer may not prepare the papers necessary to incorporate a corporation merely because one of the stockholders of the corporation might also be able to fill in blanks on a printed form by himself." 215 N.W.2d at 926.

Defining Legal Assistants/Paralegals in North Dakota

- "Legal Assistant" (or paralegal) means a person who assists lawyers in the delivery of legal services, and who through formal education, training, or experience, has knowledge and expertise regarding the legal system and substantive and procedural law which qualifies the person to do work of a legal nature under the direct supervision of a licensed lawyer. *North Dakota Rules of Professional Conduct*, Rule 1.0(h) (www .ndcourts.gov/court/rules/conduct /rule1.0.htm)

Defining the Practice of Law in North Dakota

- *Ranta v. McCarney*, 391 N.W.2d 161, 162, 163 (Supreme Court of North Dakota, 1986): Practice of law under modern conditions consists in no small part of work performed outside of any court and having no immediate relation to proceedings in court. It embraces conveyancing, the giving of legal advice on a large variety of subjects, and the preparation and execution of legal instruments covering an extensive field of business and trust relations and other affairs. Although these transactions may have no direct connection with court proceedings, they are always subject to become involved in litigation. They require in many aspects a high degree of legal skill, a wide experience with men and affairs, and great capacity for adaptation to difficult and complex situations. These "customary functions of an attorney or counsellor at law". . . bear an intimate relation to the administration of justice by the courts. No valid distinction. . . can be drawn between that part which involves appearance in court and that part which involves advice and drafting of instruments in his office. . . . If compensation is exacted either directly or indirectly, "all advice to clients, and all action taken for them in matters connected with the law," constitute practicing law.

Paralegals (and Others) in North Dakota State and Federal Courts

(See the beginning of this appendix on how to find the full text of the opinions cited here.)

- *In re Disciplinary Action against Howe*, 843 N.W.2d 325, 330 (Supreme Court of North Dakota, 2014) (An attorney is disciplined for incompetent representation of a client. The attorney blamed a calendaring error by his paralegal. "Howe's arguments blaming his paralegal. . . are to no avail because he is responsible for ensuring his nonlawyer staff's conduct comports with his professional obligations as an attorney.")
- *In the Matter of Nassif*, 547 N.W.2d 541 (Supreme Court of North Dakota, 1996) (Attorney disciplined for allowing untrained "paralegals" to recruit *and* advise clients, negotiate fees, and perform unsupervised legal work for clients.)
- *In re Disciplinary Action against Hellerud*, 714 N.W.2d 38 (Supreme Court of North Dakota, 2006) (Attorney inappropriately charged his legal assistant's time at a rate of $275 per hour without disclosure to his client.)
- *State v. Niska*, 380 N.W.2d 646 (Supreme Court of North Dakota, 1986) (Nonattorney drafts pleadings and advises another on court actions in violation of § 27–11–01, practicing law without a license.)
- *In the Matter of Johnson*, 481 N.W.2d 225 (Supreme Court of North Dakota, 1992) (Disbarred attorney is not allowed to practice as a paralegal.)

Doing Legal Research in North Dakota Law

- **Statutes:** www.legis.nd.gov (click *Century Code*)
- **Cases:** www.ndcourts.gov/search /opinions.asp
- **Court Rules:** www.ndcourts.gov /rules
- **General:** www.ndcourts.gov/research

Finding Employment in North Dakota

- See Exhibit 2-12 in Chapter 2.
- l.nd.bar.associationcareernetwork .com/Common/HomePage.aspx
- www.indeed.com/q-Paralegal-l -North-Dakota-jobs.html
- careers.findlaw.com (select *Paralegal* and *North Dakota*)
- www.simplyhired.com/k-paralegal-l -fargo-nd-jobs.html

OHIO

ETHICS CODE AND OPINIONS IN OHIO

- **Attorneys: Ohio Code:** *Rules of Professional Conduct*
  - www.sconet.state.oh.us (Click *Disciplinary System*, then *Rules of Prof. Conduct*).
  - www.law.cornell.edu/ethics/ohio.html
  - See also ethics links in Helpful Websites at the end of Chapter 5.
- **Attorneys: Ohio Ethics Opinions**
  - www.sconet.state.oh.us/Boards /BOC/Advisory_Opinions/default.asp
  - www.clemetrobar.org/Committees /Ethics_Professionalism
  - guides.law.csuohio.edu/content.php? pid=406169&sid=3324025
- **Unauthorized Practice of Law: Ohio**
  - www.ohiobar.org (enter *unauthorized practice of law* in search box)
  - www.supremecourt.ohio.gov/Boards /UPL
  - ir.lawnet.fordham.edu/cgi /viewcontent.cgi?article=3572&con text=flr
- **Paralegals and Other Nonattorneys: Ohio**
  - *Rule 5.3*. For a discussion of the state's ethics Rule 5.3 ("Responsibilities Regarding Nonlawyer Assistants") in the Ohio *Rules of Professional Conduct*, see Chapter 5.
  - *Rule 1.10 (Comment 4)*. The rule of imputed disqualification in Rule 1.10 "does not prohibit representation by others in the law firm where the person prohibited from involvement in a matter is a nonlawyer, such as a paralegal or legal secretary." Ohio *Rules of Professional Conduct*.
  - *Rule 5.5 (Comment 2)*. Lawyers can employ the services of paraprofessionals and delegate tasks to them "so long as the lawyer supervises the delegated work and retains responsibility for their work."
  - *Rule 5.5 (Comment 3)*. Lawyers can assist independent paraprofessionals who are authorized to provide particular law-related services.
  - A law firm's letterhead and website may list the names of nonlawyer employees if the employees are clearly identified as nonlawyers through the use of job titles or other identifiers that differentiate the lawyers from the nonlawyers. Similarly, a law firm's business cards may bear the names of nonlawyer employees if the cards include job titles or other language indicating the employee is not licensed to practice law. *Advisory*

Opinion 89-16 is withdrawn. Board of Commissioners on Grievances and Discipline, *Opinion 2012-2* (6/8/12).

- A legal assistant can sign law firm correspondence on law firm stationery as long as his or her nonattorney status is clearly indicated. Board of Commissioners on Grievances and Discipline *Opinion 89–11* (4/14/89).

- Nonattorneys *cannot* be listed on law firm letterhead. They can, however, have business cards as long as their nonattorney status is clear. Board of Commissioners on Grievances and Discipline, *Opinion 89–16* (6/16/89).

- It is improper for an insurance defense attorney to abide by an insurance company's litigation management guidelines (e.g., on when to delegate tasks to a paralegal) in the representation of an insured when the guidelines directly interfere with the professional judgment of the attorney. Board of Commissioners on Grievances and Discipline, *Opinion 2000–3* (6/1/00).

- The words "Group" or "Law Group" should not be used in a law firm name to refer to paralegals or other non-attorney personnel. Board of Commissioners on Grievances and Discipline, *Opinion 2006–2* (2/10/06).

- A paralegal should not be referred to as an *associate*. Commissioners on Grievances and Discipline, *Opinion 1995–1* (2/3/95).

- It is unethical for an attorney to allow a paralegal to take a deposition or represent a deponent at a deposition. Board of Commissioners on Grievances and Discipline, *Opinion 2002–4* (6/14/02).

- Child support enforcement caseworkers do not engage in the unauthorized practice of law when they interview parents seeking child support enforcement and prepare paternity complaints. Board of Commissioners on Grievances and Discipline, *Opinion 1990–10* (6/15/90).

- It is unethical for an attorney to split a contingency fee with a nonattorney investigator. Board of Commissioners on Grievances and Discipline, *Opinion 1994–8* (6/17/94).

- Attorneys in separate practices can share nonattorney staff if they maintain office procedures that preserve client confidentiality. Board of Commissioners on Grievances and Discipline, *Opinion 1991–9* (4/12/91).

- A *retired* or inactive attorney may not perform the duties of a paralegal. Such attorneys "may not render any

legal service for an attorney" in active status. Board of Commissioners on Grievances and Discipline, *Opinion 92–4* (2/14/92). But a suspended or disbarred attorney can act as a paralegal. *Opinion 90–06* (4/20/90).

- Law firm letterhead can print the names and titles of nonattorney employees as long as their nonattorney status is clear and they are listed separately from the attorneys. Columbus Bar Ass'n, *Opinion (6)* (11/17/88).

- Law firm letterhead can list the names and titles of nonattorney employees, and the latter can also have their own business card as long as their nonattorney status is made clear. Cleveland Bar Ass'n, *Opinion 89–1* (2/25/89).

Defining Legal Assistants/Paralegals in Ohio

- A paralegal is a person, qualified by education, training or work experience, who is employed or retained by a lawyer, law office, corporation, governmental agency or other entity and who performs substantive legal work for which a lawyer is responsible. Ohio Bar Association (www.ohiobar.org) (*click For Legal Professionals* then *Certification* and the links to paralegal certification).

- A person qualified through education in legal studies that is employed by a lawyer or government entity to perform substantial legal work. Ohio Common Pleas Court of Greene County, Domestic Relations Division (www.co.greene .oh.us/documentcenter/view/74).

Ohio Certification of Paralegals

- www.ohiobar.org (enter *paralegal* in the search box)
- www.nala.org/StateCertif/Ohio.pdf

Defining the Practice of Law in Ohio

- *Cleveland Bar Assn. v. Pearlman*, 832 N.E.2d 1193 (Supreme Court of Ohio, 2005): The *unauthorized* practice of law is the rendering of legal services for another by any person not admitted to practice in Ohio. The term "rendering of legal services" has been defined further: "The practice of law is not limited to the conduct of cases in court. It embraces the preparation of pleadings and other papers incident to actions and special proceedings and the management of such actions and proceedings on behalf of clients before judges and courts, and in addition conveyancing, the preparation of legal instruments of

all kinds, and in general all advice to clients and all action taken for them in matters connected with the law." *Land Title Abstract & Trust Co. v. Dworken*, 193 N.E. 650 (Supreme Court of Ohio 1934).

Paralegals (and Others) in Ohio State and Federal Courts

(See the beginning of this appendix on how to find the full text of the opinions cited here, including WL opinions.)

- *Specht v. Finnegan*, 149 Ohio App.3d 201 (Court of Appeals of Ohio, 2002) (Paralegal fees are compensable as an element of attorney fees.)

- *Gibson v. Scott*, 2014 WL 661716 (U.S. District Court, S.D. Ohio, 2014) (Plaintiff's counsel seeks compensation for purely secretarial and nonlegal services. Plaintiff's counsel has attempted to bill for time associated with non-legal services, such as organizing file, get check for public records, copy and send documents to client, and get notebooks and dividers. The Court will not award attorney's fees for these services, as purely clerical or secretarial tasks should not be billed, even at a paralegal rate.)

- *Cleveland Area Bd. of Realtors v. City of Euclid*, 965 F. Supp. 1017, 1019 (U.S. District Court, N.D. Ohio, 1997) (It is beyond dispute that a reasonable attorney's fee includes compensation for the work of paralegals. Counsel contends that reimbursement for paralegal time must be limited to the amount actually paid to the paralegals. This is incorrect. Paralegal time, like attorney time, is measured in comparison to the market rate, if the prevailing practice in the area is to bill paralegal time separately at market rates.)

- *Alexander v. Local 496, Laborers' Intern. Union of North America*, 2000 WL 1751297 (U.S. District Court, N.D. Ohio, 2000) (The court deducted 10 percent of counsel's reported hours for his performance of tasks that could have been performed by a paralegal, including the making of numerous telephone calls and arranging schedules.)

- *Cincinnati Bar Assn. v. Statzer*, 101 Ohio St.3d 14 (Supreme Court of Ohio, 2003) (To avoid discipline, an attorney induced a former legal assistant to execute a false affidavit claiming that her law office had prepared a client's file for retrieval.)

- *Lorain Cty. Bar Assn. v. Noll*, 105 Ohio St.3d 6 (Supreme Court of Ohio, 2004) (The attorney's failure to adequately supervise his legal assistant, which resulted in client files being lost or destroyed, violated the disciplinary rule barring attorneys from engaging in actions that adversely reflect on the lawyer's fitness to practice law.)

- *Green v. Toledo Hosp.*, 94 Ohio St.3d 480 (Supreme Court of Ohio, 2002) (An attorney's secretary once worked for the attorney representing an opposing party on a current case. "In ruling on a motion to disqualify a lawyer based on that lawyer's employment of a nonattorney once employed by the lawyer representing an opposing party, a court must use the following analysis: (1) Is there a substantial relationship between the matter at issue and the matter of the nonattorney employee's former firm's representation? (2) Did the moving party present credible evidence that the nonattorney employee was exposed to confidential information in his or her former employment relating to the matter at issue? (3) If such evidence was presented, did the challenged attorney rebut the resulting presumption of disclosure with evidence either that (a) the employee had no contact with or knowledge of the related matter or (b) the new law firm erected and followed adequate and timely screens to rebut the evidence presented in prong (2) so as to avoid disqualification?")
- *Columbus Bar Assn. v. Thomas*, 846 N.E.2d 31 (Supreme Court of Ohio, 2006) (The legal assistant's conduct in preparing legal documents for the attorney's clients without the assistance or oversight of the attorney, and filing those documents before they had been reviewed and approved by the attorney constituted the unauthorized practice of law. R.C. § 4705.01; Government of the Bar Rule VII(2)(A). Although laypersons may assist lawyers in preparing legal papers to be filed in court and managing pending claims, those activities must be carefully supervised and approved by a licensed practitioner to avoid unauthorized practice of law.)
- *Cleveland Bar Assn. v. CompManagement, Inc.*, 818 N.E.2d 1181 (Supreme Court of Ohio, 2004) (In light of the informal setting of workers' compensation proceedings, nonattorneys can help someone file or respond to a claim at an agency hearing, but they cannot examine and cross-examine witnesses, give legal interpretations of laws or testimony, give legal advice to workers or employers, provide stand-alone representation at a hearing by charging a fee specifically associated with such hearing representation without providing other services. Nonattorneys who appear and practice in a representative capacity before the Industrial Commission and Bureau of Workers' Compensation within these restrictions are not engaged in the unauthorized practice of law.)

Doing Legal Research in Ohio Law

- **Statutes:** codes.ohio.gov
- **Cases:** www.supremecourt.ohio.gov/rod/docs
- **Court Rules:** www.supremecourt.ohio.gov/LegalResources/Rules/
- **General:** guides.law.csuohio.edu/ohio_primary_law

Finding Employment in Ohio

- www.legalstaff.com/Common/HomePage.aspx
- careers.findlaw.com (select *Paralegal* and *Ohio*)
- www.indeed.com/q-Paralegal-1-Columbus,-OH-jobs.html
- cleveland.craigslist.org/lgl

OKLAHOMA

ETHICS CODE AND OPINIONS IN OKLAHOMA

- **Attorneys: Oklahoma Code:** *Rules of Professional Conduct*
  - www.oscn.net/applications/oscn/Index.asp?ftdb=STOKRUPR&level=1
  - www.law.cornell.edu/ethics/oklahoma.html
  - See also ethics links in Helpful Websites at the end of Chapter 5.
- **Attorneys: Oklahoma Ethics Opinions**
  - www.okbar.org/members/EthicsCounsel/EthicsOpinions.aspx
- **Unauthorized Practice of Law: Oklahoma**
  - www.okbar.org (enter *unauthorized practice of law* in search box)
  - ir.lawnet.fordham.edu/cgi/viewcontent.cgi?article=3572&context=flr
- **Paralegals and Other Nonattorneys: Oklahoma**
  - *Rule 5.3.* For a discussion of the state's ethics Rule 5.3 ("Responsibilities Regarding Nonlawyer Assistants") in the Oklahoma *Rules of Professional Conduct*, see Chapter 5.
  - *Rule 1.10 (Comment 4).* The rule of imputed disqualification in Rule 1.10 "does not prohibit representation by others in the law firm where the person prohibited from involvement in a matter is a nonlawyer, such as a paralegal or legal secretary." Oklahoma *Rules of Professional Conduct*.

- *Rule 5.5 (Comment 2).* Lawyers can employ the services of paraprofessionals and delegate tasks to them "so long as the lawyer supervises the delegated work and retains responsibility for their work."
- Oklahoma Bar Association, *Minimum Qualification Standards for Legal Assistant/Paralegals*
- www.okparalegal.org/standards
- www.coala.cc/about-us/definitions-and-standards
- www.nala.org/Upload/file/PDF-Files/News-Articles/OK-qualifications.pdf
- A licensed supervising attorney may delegate to nonlawyers clerical assignments such as researching case law, finding and interviewing witnesses, examining court records, and delivering papers or messages. However, a licensed supervising attorney must not delegate to a nonlawyer, including a disbarred or suspended lawyer, tasks such as providing legal advice to clients, preparing legal documents for clients, or conducting court proceedings. Oklahoma Bar Ass'n, *Ethics Opinion 319* (12/13/02).
- Delegation of tasks that may require professional judgment to secretaries or any other nonlawyer employee is unethical. Oklahoma Bar Ass'n, *Ethics Opinion 260* (3/19/71).
- Lawyers must preserve client confidences. This duty outlasts the lawyer's employment, and extends as well to his or her employees. Oklahoma Bar Ass'n, *Ethics Opinion 238* (3/17/66).

Defining Legal Assistants/Paralegals in Oklahoma

- A legal assistant or paralegal is a person qualified by education, training, or work experience who is employed or retained by a lawyer, law office, corporation, governmental agency, or other entity who performs specifically delegated substantive legal work for which a lawyer is responsible, and absent such assistant, the lawyer would perform the task. Oklahoma Bar Ass'n, *Minimum Qualification Standards for Legal Assistants/Paralegals* (2000). (www.coala.cc/about-us/definitions-and-standards)

Defining the Practice of Law in Oklahoma

- *Edwards v. Hert*, 504 P.2d 407, 416, 417 (Supreme Court of Oklahoma, 1972): Practice of law: the rendition of services requiring the knowledge and the application of legal principles and technique to serve the interests of another with his consent.... [A] service which otherwise would be a form of the practice of law does not lose that character merely because it is rendered gratuitously.... [I]t is not a prerequisite that a fee should be paid before the relation of attorney and client may exist.... An unlicensed practitioner's performance of legal service is not sanctified by his failure to require pay.... It has been urged upon us that acts which properly are part of the lawyer's work also may form an integral part of the legitimate activity of another calling, and that, for performance of these acts by an unlicensed person, incidental to such an independent vocation, penalties should not be inflicted upon the theory that thereby he practices law. To a certain extent, this contention is sound. There is authority for the proposition that the drafting of documents, when merely incidental to the work of a distinct occupation, is not the practice of law, although the documents have legal consequences.... If the practitioner of the distinct occupation goes beyond the determination of legal questions for the purpose of performing his special service, and, instead, advises his patron as to the course to be taken to secure a desired legal status, he is engaged in the practice of law. The title searcher is exempt if he performs his task without giving opinion or advice as to the legal effect of what is found.... The work of the accountant is exempt only if it is dissociated from legal advice. One who, in the exercise of a commission to draw a conveyance, selects language designed to create a certain effect is practicing law.... So is one who draws estate plans, involving legal analysis.... A layman who draws a will for another necessarily is practicing law.... So is one who draws legal instruments or contracts.... A layman who evaluates a claim, and undertakes to settle it, based upon applicable legal principles, is practicing law.... A bank which furnishes legal information or legal advice with respect to investments, taxation, stocks, bonds, notes or other securities or property is involved in a considerable practice of law, despite the argument that this is an incident to the investment trade.

Paralegals (and Others) in Oklahoma State and Federal Courts

(See the beginning of this appendix on how to find the full text of the opinions cited here.)

- *Taylor v. Chubb Group of Insurance Companies*, 874 P.2d 806, 809 (Supreme Court of Oklahoma, 1994) (An award of paralegal fees is for substantive legal work, not for copying documents or for performing other secretarial tasks. A party must "prove that the charges made for nonattorney's time covered work that a lawyer would have had to perform but for the performance of such services by a legal assistant" at a lower total charge than a lawyer would have charged. A legal assistant may interview clients; draft pleadings and other documents; carry out conventional and computer legal research; research public documents; prepare discovery requests and responses; schedule depositions and prepare notices and subpoenas; summarize depositions and other discovery responses; coordinate and manage document production; locate and interview witnesses; organize pleadings, trial exhibits and other documents; prepare witness and exhibit lists; prepare trial notebooks; prepare for attendance of witnesses at trial; and assist lawyers at trials).
- *Cohlmia v. St. John Medical Center*, 906 F. Supp. 2d. 1188 (U.S. District Court, N.D. Oklahoma, 2012) (Reduction of attorney fees by $8,563 out of the claimed amount of $17,126 for paralegal time spent coding was warranted. Coding was not necessarily a legal skill.)
- *Hayes v. Central States Orthopedic Specialists*, 51 P.3d 562 (Supreme Court of Oklahoma, 2002) (The trial court erred when it found that Oklahoma law requires a firm to be disqualified when it hires a nonlawyer employee who had acquired confidential information while working on litigation for the firm's opponent's firm, although the firm has set up a "Chinese wall" screening device to insure that the nonlawyer employee did not reveal confidences and would be screened from exposure to the litigation.)
- *Jones v. Eagle-North Hills Shopping Centre*, 478 F. Supp. 2d 1321 (U.S. District Court, E.D. Oklahoma, 2007) (Counsel's legal assistant aptly "fell on the sword" for her employer, claiming that she made a typographical error when entering the deadline in their calendar program. It is this court's view, however, that the buck stops with counsel, not his loyal employees.)
- *State ex rel. Oklahoma Bar Ass'n v. Simank*, 19 P.3d 860 (Supreme Court of Oklahoma, 2001) (Failure to supervise a nonattorney employee.)

- *Brown v. Ford*, 905 P.2d 223 (Supreme Court of Oklahoma, 1995) (Paralegal alleges sexual harassment by attorney at work.)

Doing Legal Research in Oklahoma Law

- **Statutes:** www.oklegislature.gov /osstatuestitle.html
- **Cases:** oklegal.onenet.net/sample .basic.html
- **Court Rules:** www.llrx.com /courtrules-gen/state-Oklahoma.html
- **General:** oklegal.onenet.net

Finding Employment in Oklahoma

- www.indeed.com/q-Paralegal-l -Oklahoma-jobs.html
- www.simplyhired.com/k-paralegal-l -oklahoma-city-ok-jobs.html
- careers.findlaw.com (select *Paralegal* and *Oklahoma*)
- tulsa.craigslist.org/lgl

OREGON

ETHICS CODE AND OPINIONS IN OREGON

- **Attorneys: Oregon Code:** *Rules of Professional Conduct*
  - www.osbar.org/_docs/rulesregs/orpc .pdf
  - www.law.cornell.edu/ethics/oregon .html
  - See also ethics links in Helpful Websites at the end of Chapter 5.
- **Attorneys: Oregon Ethics Opinions**
  - www.osbar.org/ethics/ethicsops.html
  - www.osbar.org/UPL /advisoryopinions.html
- **Unauthorized (Unlawful) Practice of Law: Oregon**
  - www.osbar.org (enter *unauthorized practice of law* in search box)
  - www.osbar.org/upl
  - ir.lawnet.fordham.edu/cgi /viewcontent.cgi?article=3572&con text=flr
- **Paralegals and Other Nonattorneys: Oregon**
  - *Rule 5.3.* For a discussion of the state's ethics Rule 5.3 ("Responsibilities Regarding Nonlawyer Assistants") in the Oregon *Rules of Professional Conduct*, see Chapter 5. For the text of 5.3 in Oregon, see www.osbar.org/_docs /rulesregs/orpc.pdf.
  - Nonlawyer personnel can be listed, together with the positions they hold, on a lawyer's letterhead (e.g., John Doe, Legal Assistant) so long as the information is not misleading. Oregon State Bar, *Formal Opinion 2005–65* (8/05). See also *Formal Opinion 1991–65* (7/91).

- Two law firms can employ the same nonlawyer on a part-time basis if they take reasonable care to make sure that the nonlawyer does not work on or acquire information relating to the representation of a client with respect to any matter on which the two firms' clients are adverse. Oregon State Bar, *Formal Opinion 2005–44* (8/05). See also *Formal Opinion 1991–44* (7/91).
- A lawyer may comply with the insurance company guidelines that certain tasks be delegated to a paralegal if, in the lawyer's independent professional judgment, the particular task is appropriate for performance by a paralegal in the particular case. Oregon State Bar, *Formal Opinion 2002–166* (1/02).
- It is unethical for an attorney to let his legal assistant draft pleadings that the attorney would sign but not review prior to filing. Oregon State Bar Ass'n, *Formal Opinion 1991–20* (7/91).
- Nonattorneys in an estate-planning service are engaged in the unauthorized practice of law when they give legal advice to clients in connection with the service, even if an attorney reviews and executes the documents involved. Oregon State Bar, *Opinion 523* (3/89).
- Nonattorney employees can have their own business cards that contain the name of their attorney-employer. Oregon State Bar, *Opinion 295* (7/75).
- A *paralegal* can write and sign letters on attorney letterhead. Oregon State Bar, *Opinion 349* (6/77) and *Opinion 295* (7/75).
- A paralegal cannot take (i.e., conduct) depositions. Oregon State Bar, *Opinion 449* (7/80).
- A well-trained legal assistant can do almost anything an attorney can do. However, a legal assistant cannot accept a case, set a fee, give legal advice, or represent a client in judicial proceedings. The Legal Assistants (Joint) Committee of the Oregon State Bar, *The Lawyer and the Legal Assistant* (1988).
- A law firm can hire a suspended or disbarred lawyer as a legal assistant so long as they do not give legal advice or share in legal fees. Oregon State Bar, *Formal Opinion 2005–24* (8/05). See also *Formal Opinion 1991–24* (7/1991) (1991 WL 279165).

Defining the Practice of Law in Oregon

- *What is the Practice of Law?* Oregon State Bar, Unauthorized Practice of law (www.osbar.org/UPL/faq.html): The 'practice of law' is defined in decisions of the Oregon Supreme Court and generally includes, among other things: appearing on behalf of others in Oregon courts and administrative proceedings; drafting or selecting legal documents for another when informed or trained discretion must be exercised to meet the person's individual needs; advising someone of his or her legal rights in a particular situation; having a law office in Oregon regardless of where clients are located; acting as an immigration consultant unless authorized by federal law to do so; and holding oneself out as a lawyer. It is not necessary that money change hands in order for conduct to be the practice of law.
- *What Is the Practice of Law?* Oregon State Bar, Unauthorized Practice of Law (www.osbar.org/UPL/faq.html): Although it depends on the specific facts of each situation, some of these commonly occurring activities generally are not considered the unlawful practice of law in Oregon:
  - individual parties who represent only themselves in a case or legal dispute;
  - representation of others in justice courts;
  - out-of-state lawyers or collection agencies who send demand letters into Oregon, without more;
  - properly licensed out-of-state lawyers who limit their practice exclusively to certain areas of federal law, such as patent law or immigration law, when federal law specifically authorizes the lawyer's practice;
  - activities of licensed professionals whose actions are within the scope of their licenses; for instance, real estate professionals, title insurance companies, certified public accountants and other licensed tax professionals;
  - sale of generic do-it-yourself legal publications without any further personalized assistance in preparation of documents or court papers; and
  - Internet discussion groups or chat rooms that do not provide personalized assistance in preparation of documents or court papers.
- *Taub v. Weber*, 366 F.3d 966 (U.S. Court of Appeals, 9th Circuit, 2004) Thus, in Oregon, at a minimum "the 'practice of law' means the exercise of professional judgment in applying legal principles to address another person's individualized needs through analysis, advice, or other assistance." See also Oregon State Bar, *Formal Opinion Number 2005–101.*

- *Oregon State Bar v. Security Escrows, Inc.*, 377 P.2d 334, 337 (Supreme Court of Oregon, 1962): Documents creating legal rights abound in the business community. The preparation of some of these documents is the principal occupation of some lawyers. The preparation of business documents also occupies part of the time of accountants, automobile salesmen, insurance agents, and many others. The practice of law manifestly includes the drafting of many documents which create legal rights. It does not follow, however, that the drafting of all such documents is always the practice of law. The problem, as is frequently the case, is largely one of drawing a recognizable line. Here the line must be drawn between those services which laymen ought not to undertake and those services which laymen can perform without harm to the public.
- Rule 9.700 (Oregon State Bar, *Rules of the Unlawful Practice of Law Committee*): The practice of law includes, but is not limited to, any of the following:. . . appearing, personally or otherwise, on behalf of another in any judicial or administrative proceeding; 3) providing advice or service to another on any matter involving the application of legal principles to rights, duties, obligations or liabilities.

Paralegals (and Others) in Oregon State and Federal Courts

(See the beginning of this appendix on how to find the full text of the opinions cited here, including WL opinions.)

- *Precision Seed Cleaners v. County Mut. Ins.*, 976 F. Supp. 2d 1228 (U.S. District Court, Oregon, 2013) (Under Oregon law, a reasonable hourly rate for paralegal who assisted law firm in representing the insured seeking payment from insurer was $115 rather than $170 as requested by firm. The average hourly rate for attorneys in the same geographic area with zero to three years of experience was $182, recent decisions awarded much lower hourly rates for paralegal time, and the record contained no information regarding how long the paralegal had held her associate's degree in paralegal studies or how many years she worked in the field.)
- *Confederated Tribes of Siletz Indians of Oregon v. Weyerhaeuser Co.*, 2003 WL 23715982 (U.S. District Court, Oregon, 2003) (A significant portion of Kelly's time involved discovery matters: reviewing and organizing documents received from Weyerhaeuser and others, or preparing documents and

interrogatory responses for submission to Weyerhaeuser. That is classic paralegal work. Kelly also helped locate and interview witnesses, research and summarize the relevant facts, sift through a mountain of documents, and prepare demonstrative exhibits. Again, this is within the realm of paralegal tasks, particularly in a complex case.)

- *Mendoza v. SAIF*, 859 P.2d 582 (Court of Appeals of Oregon, 1993) (An attorney does not establish "good cause" for failure to file a request for a hearing by arguing that he told his legal assistant twice to file it but she failed to do so.)
- *Oregon State Bar v. Taub*, 78 P.3d 114 (Court of Appeals of Oregon, 2003) (For purposes of determining whether an unauthorized person has engaged in the practice of law, the application of legal principles to individual circumstances occurs, for example, when a paralegal gives advice to clients that is specific to the individual client or when a nonlawyer recommends particular legal forms tailored to the recipient's particular problems.)
- *In re Conduct of Morin*, 878 P.2d 393 (Supreme Court of Oregon, 1994) (It is not the unauthorized practice of law for paralegals to give seminars on living trusts and answer general questions about living trust packages. It is the unauthorized practice of law for the paralegal to advise clients or potential clients on legal matters specific to them or to help them select among the legal forms available.)
- *Robins v. Scholastic Book Fairs*, 928 F. Supp. 1027 (U.S. District Court, Oregon, 1996) Paralegal fees reduced; 210 hours spent by paralegals were excessive in a straightforward case.)
- *In the Matter of Griffith*, 913 P.2d 695 (Supreme Court of Oregon, 1995) (Disbarred attorney acts as paralegal at his old law firm.)

Doing Legal Research in Oregon Law

- **Statutes:** www.oregonlegislature .gov/bills_laws/Pages/ORS.aspx
- **Cases:** www.publications.ojd.state .or.us/Pages/index.aspx
- **Court Rules:** courts.oregon.gov /OJD/rules/index.page
- **General:** law.lclark.edu/library /research

Finding Employment in Oregon

- www.legalstaff.com/Common /HomePage.aspx
- careers.findlaw.com (select *Paralegal* and *Oregon*)

- www.indeed.com/q-Litigation -Paralegal-l-Oregon-jobs.html
- portland.craigslist.org/lgl
- eastoregon.craigslist.org/lgl

PENNSYLVANIA

ETHICS CODE AND OPINIONS IN PENNSYLVANIA

- **Attorneys: Pennsylvania Code:** *Rules of Professional Conduct*
  - www.pacode.com/secure/data/204 /chapter81/s81.4.html
  - www.padisciplinaryboard.org /attorneys/faqs
  - www.law.cornell.edu/ethics /pennsylvania.html
  - See also ethics links in Helpful Websites at the end of Chapter 5.
- **Attorneys: Pennsylvania Ethics Opinions**
  - www.pabar.org (click *Ethics Opinions*) (members only)
  - www.padisciplinaryboard.org /newsroom/cases
  - www.philadelphiabar.org (enter *Ethics* in the search box)
- **Unauthorized Practice of Law in Pennsylvania**
  - www.pbar.org (enter *unauthorized practice of law* in search box)
  - www.pacode.com/secure/data/204 /chapter81/s5.5.html
  - ir.lawnet.fordham.edu/cgi /viewcontent.cgi?article=3572&con text=flr
- **Paralegals and Other Nonattorneys: Pennsylvania**
  - *Rule 5.3.* For a discussion of the state's ethics Rule 5.3 ("Responsibilities Regarding Nonlawyer Assistants") in the Pennsylvania *Rules of Professional Conduct*, see Chapter 5.
  - *Rule 1.10 (Comment 4).* The rule of imputed disqualification in Rule 1.10 "does not prohibit representation by others in the law firm where the person prohibited from involvement in a matter is a nonlawyer, such as a paralegal or legal secretary." Pennsylvania *Rules of Professional Conduct*.
  - *Rule 5.5* (Comment 2). Lawyers can employ the services of paraprofessionals and delegate tasks to them "so long as the lawyer supervises the delegated work and retains responsibility for their work."
  - *Rule 5.5* (Comment 3). Lawyers can assist independent paraprofessionals, who are authorized to provide particular law-related services.
  - Pennsylvania Bar Ass'n, *Ethical Considerations in the Use of Nonlawyer Assistants, Formal Opinion Number 98–75*

(12/4/98). (1) A nonlawyer assistant who arrives with a disqualifying conflict of interest may be employed if she is screened and the client is notified. (2) A nonlawyer assistant cannot appear before a court or an administrative tribunal unless such appearance is authorized by statute, court rule or administrative regulation. This includes even routine matters such as seeking a postponement. (3) A nonlawyer assistant cannot conduct a deposition even with predetermined approval by the lawyer. (4) Attendance at a real estate settlement in the capacity of representing either the seller or the purchaser by anyone other than a lawyer constitutes the unauthorized practice of law. (5) Lawyers and their nonlawyer assistants should make certain that clients and other persons dealing with them are aware that the nonlawyer assistant is not a lawyer and cannot give legal advice. (6) Nonlawyers may not sign engagement letters, set fees, or solicit legal business for the lawyer or law firm. (7) The name of a nonlawyer assistant may appear on the lawyer's or law firm letterhead if her status is properly revealed. (8) Nonlawyer assistants may sign letters on firm stationery if they are properly identified, and the letters do not contain legal advice. (9) They may also have business cards with the name of the firm on it if they are properly identified and the information on the card conforms to the ethical rule on advertising. (10) A lawyer may not share particular fees with a nonlawyer. (11) It is proper to compensate a nonlawyer on the basis of a fixed salary plus a percentage of the firm's net profits. (12) The fees and expenses of legal assistants may be billed to a client who has consented to the arrangement. (13) A suspended or disbarred lawyer may be engaged as a nonlawyer assistant. See also Pennsylvania Bar Ass'n, *Ethical Considerations in the Employment of Legal Assistants* (Formal Opinion 1975–1) (4/9/75).

- Philadelphia Bar Ass'n, Professional Responsibility Committee, *Professional Responsibility for Nonlawyers* (1989). *Guideline 1:* Consider all work of the office confidential, even public knowledge about a client. Do not discuss the business of your office or your firm's clients with any outsider unless you have specific authorization from an attorney. It is illegal and unethical to disclose or to use any information about a company that might be of significance to the securities market in financial transactions such as the purchase or sale of stocks, bonds, or other securities. *Guideline 2:* A paralegal may not sign papers to be filed in court, ask questions at a deposition, or handle court appearances. A client with whom the paralegal has developed rapport will often ask the paralegal questions such as, "What do you think my chances of recovery are?" Such questions seek advice and the paralegal should refer them to an attorney. *Guideline 3:* If an attorney allows a nonattorney to sign letters on law firm stationery, a descriptive title such as *legal assistant* should be used to clearly indicate the nonattorney's position. *Guideline 4:* If you interview a witness who does not have his or her own attorney, explain who you are and who your office represents. You cannot give the witness any advice except to secure his or her own attorney. If the opposing party has an attorney, you cannot talk with that party without his or her attorney's permission. You might also need this permission to talk to any employees of the opposing party. *Guideline 5:* A paralegal must be truthful when dealing with others on behalf of a client. *Guideline 6:* If the law firm has possession of a client's money or other property, it must be kept completely separate from the attorney's or law firm's money or property, and a proper accounting must be maintained. (www.philadelphiabar.org/page /ProfessionalResponsibilityForNon Lawyers)

- It would be unethical for a law firm to give a nonattorney employee a day off for referring a new client to the office. Rule 7.2(c) of the *Rules of Professional Conduct* provides that an attorney shall not give "anything of value" to a person for recommending the lawyer's services. Pennsylvania Bar Ass'n, *Informal Opinion 2005–81* (6/28/05). See also *Informal Opinion 2006–41* (5/4/06), which prohibits giving a percentage of fees to a nonattorney for client referrals.

- A husband (H) has several conversations with Attorney B at a law firm about possible legal problems. Nothing formal comes of these conversations. Later, Attorney A at the firm represents the wife of H in a divorce action. Attorney B has since left the firm and now represents H in the divorce. Attorney A has inquired about

any ethical problems in continuing to represent the wife. The response included this comment: A conflict of interest "would exist if a paralegal or secretary at your firm worked with Attorney B on H's case and in so doing gained material information adverse to H. In that circumstance, the knowledge of the secretary or paralegal will be imputed to you and would create a conflict of interest for your firm." Pennsylvania Bar Ass'n, *Informal Opinion 2000–36* (5/16/00).

- A law firm, in an effort to educate itself in the event a particular case was retried, proposed to have a paralegal telephone jurors post-trial. The paralegals conducting the post-trial interviews would follow a script and, in the event any reluctance was encountered by any juror, the conversation would be terminated. This would be ethical. Pennsylvania Bar Ass'n, *Informal Opinion 2001–78* (10/18/01) (agreeing with *Informal Opinion 91–52* (4/3/91)).

- An attorney cannot hire an accountant on a contingent fee basis. This would be sharing a fee with a nonattorney. "If this arrangement was allowed, one could then have the paralegal or secretary be hired with similar type of arrangements and you could, obviously, see the problems that would create." Pennsylvania Bar Ass'n, *Informal Opinion 93–164* (10/17/93).

- It is permissible to place the name of a paralegal or legal assistant on the firm's letterhead so long as the nonlawyer is clearly identified to be a paralegal or legal assistant. Pennsylvania Bar Ass'n, *Informal Opinion 85–145*. The same is true of a properly identified employee who is a private investigator. *Informal Opinion 90–54* (4/23/90).

- A paralegal cannot conduct a deposition. Pennsylvania Bar Ass'n, *Informal Opinion 91–137* (10/18/91).

- Suspended attorneys can work in a law office so long as they perform no legal or paralegal work or law-related activities. They can perform administrative tasks. Licensed attorneys within the firm would be responsible to ensure that they did no legal, paralegal, or law-related work. Pennsylvania Bar Ass'n, *Opinion 2007–3* (3/07). See also *Opinion 2005–10* (7/05). Under Rule 217(j)(3) of the *Pennsylvania Disciplinary Rules of Enforcement*, "A formerly admitted attorney may have direct communication with a client. .

. only if the communication is limited to ministerial matters such as scheduling, billing, updates, confirmation of receipt or sending of correspondence and messages. The formerly admitted attorney shall clearly indicate in any such communication that he or she is a legal assistant and identify the supervising attorney." (42 Pa. Cons. Stat. Ann.)

- A law firm can pay nonlawyer employee collectors a bonus if the gross amount collected as a result of their efforts exceeds a predetermined figure provided the bonus is not tied to or contingent on the payment of a fee from a particular case or specific class of cases relating to a particular client or debtor. But the lawyer may not pay his non-law partnership for the services of the non-law partnership's collectors based upon the gross amount of money collected by the non-law partnership each month. Such an arrangement unethically shares fees with nonlawyers. Philadelphia Bar Ass'n, *Opinion 2001–7* (7/01).

- Nonattorneys are authorized to represent clients at Social Security agency hearings and to collect fees for such representation. A law firm can have its nonattorney employee represent Social Security clients at these hearings. The salary of the nonattorney, however, cannot be directly related to the fees derived from his cases. Philadelphia Bar Ass'n, *Guidance Opinion 98–1* (2/98).

- Paralegals can draft demand letters as long as an attorney has reviewed the work product for accuracy and completeness and the paralegal has identified his/herself as a paralegal. Philadelphia Bar Ass'n, *Guidance Opinion 90–5* (4/90).

- The paralegal title can be used on law firm letterhead to identify a nonattorney employee. Philadelphia Bar Ass'n, *Guidance Opinion 87–18* (6/25/87).

- This inquiry involves a solicitation issue. Physicians employ a consulting firm that monitors police reports and then contacts injured persons to see if they need medical treatment. The consulting firm through an investigator will also obtain relevant photographs and statements from the injured. The representative of the consulting firm inquires as to whether the injured person has an attorney. If not, the representative will obtain an executed fee agreement and forward the relevant documents to different attorneys on a revolving basis. The assigned attorney is then required to pay a flat fee to the consulting firm. The Pennsylvania Rules of Professional Conduct does not permit such an arrangement. . . . One of the rules violated is 5.3(c)(1). By accepting a referral obtained via unethical solicitation from the consulting firm, the attorney is ratifying the third party's conduct which conduct is in direct violation of the Rule. Philadelphia Bar Ass'n, *Ethics Opinion 2010-12* (2010).

Defining Legal Assistants/Paralegals in Pennsylvania

- "What is a paralegal?" The fifth edition of the manual of the Pennsylvania Bar Association's Unauthorized Practice of Law Committee answered this question by referring to two definitions that it "espoused": (1) A person not admitted to the practice of law, who acts as an employee or an assistant to an active member of the Bar. (2) A person qualified through education, training or work experience, who is employed or retained by a lawyer, law office, governmental agency or other entity in a capacity or function which involves the performance, under the ultimate direction and supervision of an attorney of specially-delegated substantive legal work, which for the most part, requires a sufficient knowledge of legal concepts that, absent such assistant, the attorney would perform. (www .pabar.org/public/committees/UNA01 /Opinions/uplmanual.pdf)

Defining the Practice of Law in Pennsylvania

- *Harkness v. Unemployment Compensation Board of Review*, 920 A.2d 162 (Supreme Court of Pennsylvania, 2007): [O]ur Court set forth three broad categories of activities that may constitute the practice of law: (1) the instruction and advising of clients in regard to the law so that they may pursue their affairs and be informed as to their rights and obligations; (2) the preparation of documents for clients requiring familiarity with legal principles beyond the ken of ordinary laypersons; and (3) the appearance on behalf of clients before public tribunals in order that the attorney may assist the deciding official in the proper interpretation and enforcement of the law. More recently, our Court expressed that the practice of law is implicated by the holding out of oneself to the public as competent to exercise legal judgment and the implication

that he or she has the technical competence to analyze legal problems and the requisite character qualifications to act in a representative capacity. Thus, the character of the actions taken by the individual in question is a significant factor in the determination of what constitutes the practice of law.

- § *2524*, title 42 (*Pennsylvania Consolidated Statutes Annotated*): [A]ny person, including, but not limited to, a paralegal or legal assistant, who within this Commonwealth shall practice law, or who shall hold himself out to the public as being entitled to practice law, or use or advertise the title of lawyer, attorney at law, attorney and counselor at law, counselor, or the equivalent in any language, in such a manner as to convey the impression that he is a practitioner of the law of any jurisdiction, without being an attorney at law or a corporation complying with 15 Pa.C.S. Ch. 29 (relating to professional corporations), commits a misdemeanor of the third degree upon a first violation. A second or subsequent violation of this subsection constitutes a misdemeanor of the first degree.

Pennsylvania Certification of Paralegals

- keystoneparalegals.org
- keystoneparalegals.org/index.php /pacp

Paralegals (and Others) in Pennsylvania State and Federal Courts

(See the beginning of this appendix on how to find the full text of the opinions cited here, including WL opinions.)

- *Brown v. Hammond*, 810 F. Supp. 644 (U.S. District Court, E.D. Pennsylvania, 1993) (A paralegal was dismissed for disclosing illegal billing practices.) (See text of case in Chapter 5.)
- *Anderson v. Boothe*, 1986 WL 6737, (U.S. District Court, E.D. Pennsylvania, 1986) (Judge awards $244,490 in fees for services performed by paralegals.)
- *In re Busy Beaver Building Centers*, 19 F.3d 833 (U.S. Court of Appeals, 3d Circuit, 1994) (Award of paralegal fees in bankruptcy case. The case has an extensive discussion of the role of the litigation paralegal as opposed to that of a legal secretary. An amicus brief in the case was filed by the National Federation of Paralegal Associations. The trial court disallowed compensation for services performed by paralegals that it considered "purely clerical functions" and therefore part of an attorney's overhead for which there can be no separate

payment. On appeal, this decision was reversed. If "the court were to disallow paralegal assistance on such matters, the paralegal profession would suffer a major setback, and attorneys would instead perform those services but at greater expense" to the client. The standard on what paralegal services are compensable will be whether such services are compensable in nonbankruptcy cases: whether nonbankruptcy attorneys typically charge and collect from their clients fees for the kind of services in question, and the rates charged and collected therefor. The case was sent back to the lower court to apply this standard.)

- *Harkness v. Unemployment Compensation Board of Review*, 920 A.2d 162 (Supreme Court of Pennsylvania, 2007) (A Pennsylvania statute allows claimants to be represented by nonattorneys at hearings of the Unemployment Compensation Board of Review (43 P.S. § 862). Nonattorneys can also represent the employer without engaging in the practice of law.)
- *German v. UCBR*, 489 A.2d 308 (Commonwealth Court of Pennsylvania, 1985) (Hearsay and the best-evidence rule objections were waived for the purposes of an appeal to the Commonwealth Court because the paralegal representing the claimant at the referee hearing failed to object.)
- *Baldauf v. UCBR*, 854 A.2d 689 Commonwealth Court of Pennsylvania, 2004) (A paralegal is fired for searching for a job during work hours (theft of company time) and is denied unemployment compensation.)
- *Tobia v. Bally Total Fitness Holding Corp*, 2013 WL 62=38290 (U.S. District Court, E.D., Pennsylvania, 2013) (Plaintiffs' counsel failed to check the docket for any case activity until the beginning of the Thanksgiving holiday. Counsel placed primary blame on his recently hired and inadequately trained paralegal, in whom he had vested sole responsibility for reviewing his emails during his two-week absence, during which the two motions to dismiss were filed. Counsel exhibited seriously questionable judgment in giving such important responsibility to an untested paralegal.)

Doing Legal Research in Pennsylvania Law

- **Statutes:** www.legis.state.pa.us
- **Cases:** www.pacourts.us/courts /commonwealth-court/court-opinions
- **Court Rules:** www.pacourts.us (enter *court rules* in the search box)
- **General:** www.pennsylvanialegalresearch .com

Finding Employment in Pennsylvania

- www.legalstaff.com/Common /HomePage.aspx
- careers.findlaw.com (select *Paralegal* and *Pennsylvania*)
- philadelphia.craigslist.org/lgl
- www.hg.org/legal_jobs_pennsylvania .asp
- www.indeed.com/q-Paralegal-l -Pennsylvania-jobs.html

RHODE ISLAND

ETHICS CODE AND OPINIONS IN RHODE ISLAND

- **Attorneys: Rhode Island Code; *Rules of Professional Conduct***
  - www.courts.ri.gov (select *Disciplinary Board* and then *Rules of Professional Conduct*)
  - www.law.cornell.edu/ethics/ri.html
  - See also ethics links in Helpful Websites at the end of Chapter 5.
- **Attorneys: Rhode Island Ethics Opinions**
  - www.courts.ri.gov (select *Attorney Resources* and *Ethics Advisory Panel*)
- **Unauthorized Practice of Law in Rhode Island**
  - www.courts.ri.gov (enter *unauthorized practice of law* in search box)
  - ir.lawnet.fordham.edu/cgi /viewcontent.cgi?article=3572&con text=flr
- **Paralegals and Other Nonattorneys: Rhode Island**
  - *Rule 5.3.* For a discussion of the state's ethics Rule 5.3 ("Responsibilities Regarding Nonlawyer Assistants") in the Rhode Island Rules of Professional Conduct, see Chapter 5. For the text of 5.3 in Rhode Island, see www.courts.ri.gov/PublicResources /disciplinaryboard/PDF/Article5.pdf.
  - *Provisional Order No. 18. Use of Legal Assistants.* This Order is printed after Rule 5.3 in the *Rules of Professional Conduct. Guideline 1:* A lawyer shall not permit a legal assistant to engage in the unauthorized practice of law. The lawyer shares in the ultimate accountability for a violation of this guideline. The legal assistant remains individually accountable for engaging in the unauthorized practice of law. *Guideline 2:* A legal assistant may perform the following functions, together with other related duties, to assist lawyers in their representation of clients: attend client conferences; correspond with and obtain information from clients; draft legal

documents; assist at closing and similar meetings between parties and lawyers; witness execution of documents; prepare transmittal letters; maintain estate/guardianship trust accounts; transfer securities and other assets; assist in the day-to-day administration of trusts and estates; index and organize documents; conduct research; check citations in briefs and memoranda; draft interrogatories and answers thereto, deposition notices and requests for production; prepare summaries of depositions and trial transcripts; interview witnesses; obtain records from doctors, hospitals, police departments, other agencies and institutions; and obtain information from courts. Legal documents, including, but not limited to, contracts, deeds, leases, mortgages, wills, trusts, probate forms, pleadings, pension plans and tax returns, shall be reviewed by a lawyer before being submitted to a client or another party. A legal assistant may represent clients before administrative agencies or courts where such representation is permitted by statute or agency or court rules. *Guideline 3:* A lawyer shall instruct the legal assistant regarding the confidential nature of the attorney/client relationship, and shall direct the legal assistant to refrain from disclosing any confidential information obtained from a client or in connection with representation of a client. *Guideline 4:* A lawyer shall direct a legal assistant to disclose that he or she is not a lawyer at the outset in contacts with clients, courts, administrative agencies, attorneys, or when acting in a professional capacity, the public. *Guideline 5:* A lawyer may permit a legal assistant to sign correspondence relating to the legal assistant's work, provided the legal assistant's nonlawyer status is clear and the contents of the letter do not constitute legal advice. Correspondence containing substantive instructions or legal advice to a client shall be signed by an attorney. *Guideline 6:* Except where permitted by statute, or court rule or decision, a lawyer shall not permit a legal assistant to appear in court as a legal advocate on behalf of a client. Nothing in this Guideline shall be construed to bar or limit a legal assistant's right or obligation to appear in any forum as a witness on behalf of a client. *Guideline 7:* A lawyer may permit a legal assistant to use a business card, with the employer's

name indicated, provided the card is approved by the employer and the legal assistant's nonlawyer status is clearly indicated. *Guideline 8:* A lawyer shall not form a partnership with a legal assistant if any part of the partnership's activity involves the practice of law. *Guideline 9:* Compensation of legal assistants shall not be in the manner of sharing legal fees, nor shall the legal assistant receive any remuneration for referring legal matters to a lawyer. *Guideline 10:* A lawyer shall not use or employ as a legal assistant any attorney who has been suspended or disbarred pursuant to an order of this Court, or an attorney who has resigned in this or any other jurisdiction for reasons related to a breach of ethical conduct.
- *Rule 1.10 (Comment 4).* The rule of imputed disqualification in Rule 1.10 "does not prohibit representation by others in the law firm where the person prohibited from involvement in a matter is a nonlawyer, such as a paralegal or legal secretary. . . . Such persons, however, ordinarily must be screened from any personal participation in the matter to avoid communication to others in the firm of confidential information that both the nonlawyers and the firm have a legal duty to protect."
- *Rule 5.5 (Comment 2).* Lawyers can employ the services of paraprofessionals and delegate tasks to them "so long as the lawyer supervises the delegated work and retains responsibility for their work."
- *Rule 5.5 (Comment 3).* Lawyers can assist independent paraprofessionals, who are authorized to provide particular law-related services.
- A law firm may not pay its adjuster/ paralegal a quarterly bonus based on the number of cases that the adjuster/ paralegal assists in settling and on the attorney fees generated from such cases. This would violate Rule 5.4(a) on fee-sharing with nonattorneys. Ethics Advisory Panel of the Rhode Island Supreme Court, *Opinion 2013-01* (February 14, 2013).
- A law firm's letterhead must place the title *legal assistant* after the name of an attorney who is licensed in another state but who is ineligible to sit for the Rhode Island bar examination because he graduated from an unaccredited law school. Ethics Advisory Panel of the Rhode Island Supreme Court, *Opinion 93–28* (5/12/93). See also *Opinion 92–6* (1992), where the

term *legal assistant* is preferred over *paralegal* for nonattorney employees.

- An attorney may not hire a suspended or disbarred attorney as a paralegal. Ethics Advisory Panel of the Rhode Island Supreme Court, *Opinion 90–12* (2/27/90); *Opinion 91–64* (9/19/91).

Defining Legal Assistants/Paralegals in Rhode Island

- A legal assistant is one who under the supervision of a lawyer, shall apply knowledge of law and legal procedures in rendering direct assistance to lawyers, clients and courts; design, develop and modify procedures, technique, services and processes; prepare and interpret legal documents; detail procedures for practicing in certain fields of law; research, select, assess, compile and use information from the law library and other references; and analyze and handle procedural problems that involve independent decisions. More specifically, a legal assistant is one who engages in the functions set forth in Guideline 2. Rhode Island Supreme Court, *Provisional Order No 18.*

Defining the Practice of Law in Rhode Island

- § 11–27–2 (*Rhode Island Statutes*): The term "practice law" as used in this chapter shall be deemed to mean the doing of any act for another person usually done by attorneys at law in the course of their profession, and, without limiting the generality of the foregoing, shall be deemed to include the following: (1) The appearance or acting as the attorney, solicitor, or representative of another person before any court, referee, master, auditor, division, department, commission, board, judicial person, or body authorized or constituted by law to determine any question of law or fact or to exercise any judicial power, or the preparation of pleadings or other legal papers incident to any action or other proceeding of any kind before or to be brought before the court or other body; (2) The giving or tendering to another person for a consideration, direct or indirect, of any advice or counsel pertaining to a law question or a court action or judicial proceeding brought or to be brought; (3) The undertaking or acting as a representative or on behalf of another person to commence, settle, compromise, adjust, or dispose of any civil or criminal case or cause of action; (4) The preparation or drafting for another person of a will, codicil, corporation

organization, amendment, or qualification papers, or any instrument which requires legal knowledge and capacity and is usually prepared by attorneys at law.

Paralegals (and Others) in Rhode Island State and Federal Courts

(See the beginning of this appendix on how to find the full text of the opinions cited here.)

- *Fedora v. Werber*, 84 A.2d 812 (Supreme Court of Rode Island, 2013) (A paralegal worked for a law office representing a doctor in a medical malpractice case. The paralegal then was hired by the law firm that was suing the doctor. The paralegal, however, was screened at the new firm.)
- *In re Low Cost Paralegal Services*, 19 A.3d 1229 (Supreme Court of Rhode Island, 2011) (Low Cost Paralegal Services engaged in the unauthorized practice of law in violation of § 11-27-12 by falsely holding itself out to Rhode Islanders, through Internet advertising targeting Rhode Island, as competent and qualified to prepare legal documents for uncontested divorce and to assist with a child support problem, which conduct constitutes "the practice of law" as defined in § 11–27–2(4).)
- *Schroff, Inc. v. Taylor-Peterson*, 732 A.2d 719 (Supreme Court of Rhode Island, 1999) (Award of paralegal fees; utilizing services *of* paralegals should result in reducing, rather than enhancing, attorney fees.)
- *Donovan v. Bowling*, 706 A.2d 937 (Supreme Court of Rhode Island, 1998) (Paralegal can be called as a witness to give testimony on possible prior inconsistent statements by a witness.)
- *In re Almacs*, 178 Bankruptcy Reporter 598 (U.S. Bankruptcy Court, Rhode Island, 1995) (Some of the paralegal charges are for tasks that are clerical in nature and should be treated as overhead rather than as separate paralegal fees.)
- *Unauthorized Practice of Law Committee v. State, Dept. of Workers' Compensation*, 543 A.2d 662 (Supreme Court of Rhode Island, 1988) (The statute authorizing employee assistants to assist injured employees in informal hearings before the Department of Workers' Compensation did not violate the Supreme Court's exclusive power under the Constitution to regulate practice of law.)

Doing Legal Research in Rhode Island Law

- **Statutes:** www.rilin.state.ri.us /Statutes/Statutes.html

- **Cases:** www.findlaw.com/casecode /rhode-island.htm
- **Court Rules:** www.courts.ri.gov (select *Courts* and then *Supreme Court* then *Supreme Court Rules*)
- **General:** www.loc.gov/law/help /guide/states/us-ri.php

Finding Employment in Rhode Island

- ribar.legalstaff.com
- careers.findlaw.com (Select *Paralegal* and *Rhode Island*)
- www.indeed.com/q-Paralegal-l -Rhode-Island-jobs.html
- providence.craigslist.org/lgl

SOUTH CAROLINA

ETHICS CODE AND OPINIONS IN SOUTH CAROLINA

- **Attorneys: South Carolina Code:** *Rules of Professional Conduct*
  - www.sccourts.org/courtReg (scroll down to *407*)
  - www.law.cornell.edu/ethics/sc.html
  - See also ethics links in Helpful Websites at the end of Chapter 5.
- **Attorneys: South Carolina Ethics Opinions**
  - www.scbar.org/MemberResources /EthicsAdvisoryOpinions
- **Unauthorized Practice of Law in South Carolina**
  - www.scbar.org (enter *unauthorized practice of law* in search box)
  - www.scbar.org/PublicServices /UnauthorizedPracticeofLaw.aspx
  - ir.lawnet.fordham.edu/cgi /viewcontent.cgi?article=3572&con text=flr
- **Paralegals and Other Nonattorneys: South Carolina**
  - *Rule 5.3.* For a discussion of the state's ethics Rule 5.3 ("Responsibilities Regarding Nonlawyer Assistants") in the South Carolina *Rules of Professional Conduct*, see Chapter 5.
  - *Rule 1.10 (Comment 4).* The rule of imputed disqualification in Rule 1.10 "does not prohibit representation by others in the law firm where the person prohibited from involvement in a matter is a nonlawyer, such as a paralegal or legal secretary." South Carolina *Rules of Professional Conduct.*
  - *Rule 5.5 (Comment 2).* Lawyers can employ the services of paraprofessionals and delegate tasks to them "so long as the lawyer supervises the delegated work and retains responsibility for their work."

- *Rule 5.5* (Comment 3). Lawyers can assist independent paraprofessionals, who are authorized to provide particular law-related services.
- South Carolina Bar, *Guidelines for the Utilization by Lawyers of the Services of Legal Assistants* (12/11/81). *Guideline I:* An attorney shall not permit his or her legal assistant to engage in the unauthorized practice of law. *Guideline II:* A legal assistant may perform certain functions otherwise prohibited when and to the extent permitted by court or administrative agency. *Guideline III:* A legal assistant can perform services for the lawyer if (a) the client understands that the legal assistant is not an attorney, (b) the attorney supervises the legal assistant, and (c) the attorney is fully responsible for what the legal assistant does or fails to do. *Guideline IV:* The attorney must instruct the legal assistant to preserve the confidences and secrets of a client and shall exercise care that the legal assistant does so. *Guideline V:* An attorney shall not form a partnership with a legal assistant if any part of the partnership consists of the practice of law. Nor shall an attorney share, on a proportionate basis, legal fees with a legal assistant. The legal assistant, however, can be included in a retirement plan even though based in whole or in part on a profit-sharing arrangement. A legal assistant shall not be paid, directly or indirectly for referring legal matters to an attorney. *Guideline VI:* The letterhead of an attorney may not include the name of a legal assistant, but a legal assistant can have a business card that prints the name of his or her attorney as long as the legal assistant's capacity or status is clearly indicated. A legal assistant can sign letters on an attorney's letterhead as long as the legal assistant's signature is followed by an appropriate designation (e.g., "legal assistant") so that it is clear the signer is not an attorney. *Guideline VII:* An attorney shall require a legal assistant, when dealing with a client, to disclose at the outset that he or she is not an attorney. This disclosure is also required when the paralegal is dealing with a court, administrative agency, attorney, or the public if there is any reason for their believing the legal assistant is an attorney or is associated with an attorney. This guideline applies even in administrative agencies where the legal assistant is allowed to represent clients. *Guideline VIII:* Except as otherwise provided by law, any grievances or complaints of the use of legal assistants by attorneys shall be referred for action to the Board of Commissioners on Grievances and Discipline.
- A compensation system in which a paralegal receives a bonus based on the charges billed to a client is a profit-sharing arrangement and expressly permitted under Rule 5.4(a)(3). A law firm, however, may run afoul of fee-splitting rules if the bonus is based on a percentage of a particular fee earned. South Carolina Bar, *Ethics Advisory Opinion 97–02* (3/1997).
- A paralegal, under the supervision and at the direction of the responsible attorney, can interview clients alone in order to gather information, but cannot alone assist clients in the execution of the documents. South Carolina Bar, *Opinion 02–12* (4/20/02) (2002 WL 2069864).
- A lawyer may employ the services of an independent paralegal assistance service provided the lawyer adequately supervises the work of the paralegals and remains responsible for their work product. In billing for the paralegal organization's services, the lawyer should comply with his fiduciary duty to disclose to his clients the basis of his fee and expenses. South Carolina Bar, *Ethics Advisory Opinion 96–13* (1996).
- A lawyer may not bill a client for paralegal services rendered by an individual who is not performing paralegal services. The issuance of paralegal certificates to a lawyer's staff does not transform all of the duties of those individuals into paralegal services. South Carolina Bar, *Ethics Advisory Opinion 94–37* (1/1995).
- A nonattorney switching jobs raises the possibility of disqualification of her new employer because of a conflict of interest. South Carolina Bar, *Ethics Advisory Opinion 93–29* (10/1993).
- A nonlawyer who works full time for a prosecutor can work part-time for a lawyer if she is strictly screened from any criminal matters and maintains confidentiality. South Carolina Bar, *Opinion 07–02* (4/20/07).
- A lawyer who represents a client in a matter adverse to a corporate party may hire as a paralegal a former employee of the corporate party, at least when the paralegal had no decision-making role while employed by the corporation, possesses no protected information, and is not likely to be called as a witness in the litigation. South Carolina Bar, *Opinion 91–12* (5/91)(1991 WL 787742).
- A full-time paralegal in a "Legal Services" office can also hold a position as a part-time magistrate within the same county. Any conflict with Legal Services cases could be avoided by the disqualification of the magistrate. South Carolina Bar, *Ethics Advisory Opinion 88–12* (1988) (1988 WL 582713).
- A lawyer who is disbarred, suspended, or transferred due to incapacity to inactive status shall not be employed by a member of the South Carolina Bar as a paralegal, as an investigator, or in any other capacity connected with the law. Appellate Court Rule 413, Lawyer Disciplinary Enforcement Rule 34.
- As long as the business card is not false or misleading, a legal assistant may have a business card with the name of the law firm placed on the card. South Carolina Bar, *Ethics Advisory Opinion 90–23* (10/90) (This opinion supersedes Opinion 88–06.)
- An attorney can hire nonattorneys to fill in preprinted real estate forms and do title searches as long as they are supervised by the attorney and the attorney maintains direct contact with clients. South Carolina Bar, *Opinion 88–2* (6/1988). On title searches, see also *Opinion 78–26* (10/1978).
- It is the unauthorized practice of law for a nonattorney to have an ownership interest, along with an attorney, in a corporation that drafts and provides real estate documents if the nonattorney controls any of the legal services provided. South Carolina Bar, *Opinion 84–3* (9/1985).

Defining the Practice of Law in South Carolina

- *The South Carolina Medical Malpractice Joint Underwriting Association v. Froelich,* 377 S.E.2d 306, 307 (Supreme Court of South Carolina, 1989): Conduct constituting the practice of law includes a wide range of activities. It is too obvious for discussion that the practice of law is not limited to the conduct of cases in courts. According to the generally understood definition of the practice of law in this country, it embraces the preparation of pleadings and other papers incident to actions and special proceedings and the management of such actions and proceedings on behalf of clients before judges and courts, and in addition conveyancing, the preparation of legal instruments of all kinds, and in general all advice to clients and all action taken for them in matters connected with the law.

Paralegals (and Others) in South Carolina State and Federal Courts

(See the beginning of this appendix on how to find the full text of the opinions cited here.)

- *In re Matthews,* 639 S.E.2d 45 (Supreme Court of South Carolina, 2006) (An attorney delegated the responsibility of reconciling his trust accounts to a nonlawyer assistant without providing proper training or supervision. As a result, significant errors were made.)
- *In re Ingalls,* 633 S.E.2d 512 (Supreme Court of South Carolina, 2006) (Attorney disciplined for allowing nonattorneys to conduct real estate closings without an attorney being present.)
- *Lucas v. Guyton,* 901 F. Supp. 1047, 1059 (U.S. District Court, South Carolina, 1995) (The "court observed Ms. Pope to be a diligent and very able paralegal who assisted in many respects during the trial, including reading the depositions of Plaintiff's death-row witnesses, taking notes throughout the proceeding and, on numerous occasions, conferring with counsel during his presentation of the case.")
- *In re Unauthorized Practice of Law Rules Proposed by the South Carolina Bar,* 422 S.E. 2d 123 (Supreme Court of South Carolina, 1992) (A business can be represented by a nonattorney employee in civil magistrate's court proceedings. A South Carolina state agency may authorize nonattorneys to appear and represent clients before the agency. An arresting police officer, a nonattorney, may prosecute traffic offenses in magistrate's court and in municipal court.)
- *In re Easler,* 272 S.E.2d 32, 32–33 (Supreme Court of South Carolina, 1980) (The activities of a paralegal do not constitute the practice of law as long as they are limited to work of a preparatory nature.)
- *South Carolina v. Robinson,* 468 S.E.2d 290 (Supreme Court of South Carolina, 1996) (Injunction against paralegal who advertises in the Yellow Pages ("If your civil rights have been violated, call me") as a paralegal and represents clients in court. Section 40–5–80 of the *South Carolina Code Annotated* allows a nonattorney to represent another in court if the permission of the court is first

obtained, but the paralegal in this case did not always obtain this permission.)
- *In the Matter of Jenkins,* 468 S.E.2d 869 (Supreme Court of South Carolina, 1996) (Attorney disciplined for asking her paralegal to notarize a forged signature.)
- *In re Chastain,* 587 S.E.2d 115 (Supreme Court of South Carolina, 2003). A law firm can hire a convicted felon as an in-house investigator if properly supervised. South Carolina Bar, *Ethics Advisory Opinion 92–26* (9/92).

Doing Legal Research in South Carolina Law

- **Statutes:** www.scstatehouse.gov/code /statmast.php
- **Cases:** www.judicial.state.sc.us /opinions/searchOpinion.cfm
- **Court Rules:** www.judicial.state.sc.us /courtReg
- **General:** www.law.georgetown.edu /library/research/guides/southcarolina .cfm

Finding Employment in South Carolina

- careers.findlaw.com (select *Paralegal* and *South Carolina*)
- www.indeed.com/q-Paralegal-l-South -Carolina-jobs.html
- charleston.craigslist.org/lgl
- www.careerjet.com/paralegal-jobs /south-carolina-20137.html

SOUTH DAKOTA

ETHICS CODE AND OPINIONS IN SOUTH DAKOTA

- **Attorneys: South Dakota Code: *Rules of Professional Responsibility***
  - http://www.sdbar.org/Rules/Rules /PC_Rules.htm
  - www.law.cornell.edu/ethics/sd.html
  - See also ethics links in Helpful Websites at the end of Chapter 5.
- **Attorneys: South Dakota Ethics Opinions**
  - www.sdbar.org/Ethics/ethics.shtm
- **Unauthorized Practice of Law: South Dakota**
  - www.sdbar.org/rules/Rules/rule_5_5 .htm
  - ir.lawnet.fordham.edu/cgi /viewcontent.cgi?article=3572&con text=flr
- **Paralegals and Other Nonattorneys: South Dakota**
  - *Rule 5.3.* For a discussion of the state's ethics Rule 5.3 ("Responsibilities Regarding Nonlawyer Assistants") in the South Dakota *Rules of Professional*

Responsibility, see Chapter 5. For the text of 5.3 in South Dakota, see www .sdbar.org/Rules/Rules/PC_Rules .htm.
- *Rule 1.10 (Comment 4).* The rule of imputed disqualification in Rule 1.10 "does not prohibit representation by others in the law firm where the person prohibited from involvement in a matter is a nonlawyer, such as a paralegal or legal secretary." South Dakota *Rules of Professional Responsibility.*
- *Rule 5.5* (Comment 2). Lawyers can employ the services of paralegals and delegate tasks to them "so long as the lawyer supervises the delegated work and retains responsibility for their work."
- *Rule 5.5* (Comment 3). Lawyers can assist independent paraprofessionals, who are authorized to provide particular law-related services.
- *South Dakota Codified Laws,* § 16–18–34.2(1). A legal assistant can assist in all aspects of the attorney's representation of a client, provided that:

  (a) The status of the legal assistant is disclosed at the outset of any professional relationship with a client, other attorneys, courts or administrative agencies, or members of the general public;

  (b) The attorney establishes the attorney–client relationship, is available to the client, and maintains control of all client matters;

  (c) The attorney reviews the legal assistant's work product and supervises performance of the duties assigned;

  (d) The attorney remains responsible for the services performed by the legal assistant to the same extent as though such services had been furnished entirely by the attorney and such actions were those of the attorney;

  (e) The services performed by the legal assistant supplement, merge with and become part of the attorney's work product;

  (f) The services performed by the legal assistant do not require the exercise of unsupervised legal judgment; this provision does not prohibit a legal assistant appearing and representing a client at an administrative hearing provided that the agency or board having jurisdiction does not have a rule forbidding persons other than licensed attorneys to do so and providing that the other rules pertaining to the utilization of legal assistants are met; and

(g) The attorney instructs the legal assistant concerning standards of client confidentiality.

- *South Dakota Codified Laws,* § 16–18–34.2(1). A legal assistant may not establish the attorney-client relationship, set legal fees, give legal advice or represent a client in court; nor encourage, engage in, or contribute to any act which would constitute the unauthorized practice of law.
- *South Dakota Codified Laws,* § 16–18–34.2(2). A legal assistant may author and sign correspondence on the attorney's letterhead, provided the legal assistant's status is indicated and the correspondence does not contain legal opinions or give legal advice.
- *South Dakota Codified Laws,* § 16–18–34.2(3). An attorney may identify a legal assistant by name and title on the attorney's letterhead and on business cards identifying the attorney's firm. *South Dakota Codified Laws,* § 16–18–34.2.
- *South Dakota Codified Laws,* § 16–18–34.3. The proper use of assistants who are not licensed attorneys significantly increases the ability of attorneys to provide quality professional services to the public at reasonable cost. An attorney cannot, however, delegate his or her ethical proscriptions by claiming that the violation was that of an employee. Thus, in order to secure compliance with the Rules of Professional Conduct:

(1) An attorney shall ascertain the assistant's abilities, limitations, and training, and must limit the assistant's duties and responsibilities to those that can be competently performed in view of those abilities, limitations, and training.

(2) An attorney shall educate and train assistants with respect to the ethical standards which apply to the attorney.

(3) An attorney is responsible for monitoring and supervising the work of assistants in order to assure that the services rendered by the assistant are performed competently and in a professional manner.

(4) An attorney is responsible for assuring that the assistant does not engage in the unauthorized practice of law.

(5) An attorney is responsible for the improper behavior or activities of assistants and must take appropriate action to prevent recurrence of improper behavior or activities.

(6) Assistants who deal directly with an attorney's clients must be identified to those clients as nonlawyers, and the attorney is responsible for obtaining the understanding of the clients with respect to the rule of and the limitations which apply to those assistants.

(7) A legal assistant should understand the Rules of Professional Conduct and these rules in order to avoid any action which would involve the attorney in a violation of chapter 16–18, or give the appearance of professional impropriety.

(8) An attorney takes reasonable measures to insure that all client confidences are preserved by a legal assistant.

(9) An attorney takes reasonable measures to prevent conflicts of interest resulting from a legal assistant's other employment or interest insofar as such other employment or interest would present a conflict of interest if it were that of the attorney.

(10) An attorney may include a charge for the work performed by a legal assistant in setting a charge for legal services.

(11) An attorney may not split legal fees with a legal assistant nor pay a legal assistant for the referral of legal business. An attorney may compensate a legal assistant based on the quantity and quality of the legal assistant's work and the value of that work to a law practice, but the legal assistant's compensation may not be, by advance agreement, contingent upon the profitability of the attorney's practice. *South Dakota Codified Laws,* § 16–18–34.3.

- *South Dakota Codified Laws,* § 16–18–34.4. The following persons shall not serve as a legal assistant in the State of South Dakota except upon application to and approval of the Supreme Court: (1) Any person convicted of a felony; (2) Any person disbarred or suspended from the practice of law; (3) Any person placed on disability inactive status; (4)

Any person placed on temporary suspension from the practice of law. *South Dakota Codified Laws,* § 16–18–34.4.
- It is unethical for an attorney to give 5 percent of the fees collected from clients referred by a nonattorney. State Bar of South Dakota, *Opinion 94–12.*
- A law firm can list paralegals on their letterhead (referring to graduates of law school who have not yet passed the bar exam). State Bar of South Dakota, *Opinion 90–10* (9/22/90).

Defining Legal Assistants/Paralegals in South Dakota

- Legal assistants (also known as paralegals) are a distinguishable group of persons who assist licensed attorneys in the delivery of legal services. Through formal education, training, and experience, legal assistants have knowledge and expertise regarding the legal system, substantive and procedural law, the ethical considerations of the legal profession, and the Rules of Professional Conduct as stated in chapter 16–18, which qualify them to do work of a legal nature under the employment and direct supervision of a licensed attorney. This rule shall apply to all unlicensed persons employed by a licensed attorney who are represented to the public or clients as possessing training or education which qualifies them to assist in the handling of legal matters or document preparation for the client. *South Dakota Codified Laws,* § 16–18–34.

Who Can Use the Title of Paralegal or legal Assistant in South Dakota?

- *South Dakota Codified Laws,* § 16–18–34.1. Any person employed by a licensed attorney as a legal assistant must meet minimum qualifications of formal training or in-house training as a legal assistant. (To see the qualifications, run this search in Google, Bing, or Yahoo: South Dakota 16-18-34.1)

Defining the Practice of Law in South Dakota

- *Persche v. Jones,* 387 N.W.2d 32, 36 (Supreme Court of South Dakota, 1986): Practicing law "is not limited to conducting litigation, but includes giving legal advice and counsel, and rendering services that require the use of legal knowledge or skill and the preparing of instruments and contracts by which legal rights are secured, whether or not the matter is pending in a court."

Paralegals (and Others) in South Dakota State and Federal Courts

(See the beginning of this appendix on how to find the full text of the opinions cited here, including WL opinions.)

- *Mock v. South Dakota Bd. of Regents*, 296 F. Supp. 2d 1061 (U.S. District Court, South Dakota, 2003) (Court comments on work of paralegal during the trial: "The Court observed Ms. Ford during the trial in this case and noted that she provided exceptional assistance to both Ms. Chanti and Mr. Jensen during their examinations of witnesses.")
- *Nienaber v. Citibank*, 2007 WL 2003761 (U.S. District Court, South Dakota, 2007) ($125 per hour for paralegals is approved as reasonable.)
- *In re Discipline of Mines*, 612 N.W.2d 619 (Supreme Court of South Dakota, 2000) (The disbarment of the attorney is warranted due in part to improper use of legal assistant and improper billing.)
- *In re Yankton College*, 101 Bankruptcy Reporter 151, 159 (U.S. Bankruptcy Court, South Dakota, 1989) (Paraprofessional Billing: if paralegal work is to be compensated, the qualifications of the paralegal should be established to justify the charge. "Simply classifying a secretary as a paralegal for billing purposes does not justify compensating secretary time" which should be part of overhead.)

Doing Legal Research in South Dakota Law

- **Statutes:** legis.sd.gov (click *Laws*)
- **Cases:** ujs.sd.gov/Supreme_Court/opinions.aspx
- **Court Rules:** ujs.sd.gov/Supreme_Court/rules.aspx
- **General:** www.law.georgetown.edu/library/research/guides/southdakota.cfm

Finding Employment in South Dakota

- careers.findlaw.com (select *Paralegal* and *South Dakota*)
- www.indeed.com/q-Paralegal-l-South-Dakota-jobs.html
- www.sdparalegals.com/sdpajobbank.html
- sd.craigslist.org/lgl

TENNESSEE

ETHICS CODE AND OPINIONS IN TENNESSEE

- **Attorneys: Tennessee Code:** *Rules of Professional Conduct*

- www.tsc.state.tn.us/rules/supreme-court/8
- www.law.cornell.edu/ethics/tennessee.html
- See also ethics links in Helpful Websites at the end of Chapter 5.
- **Attorneys: Tennessee Ethics Opinions**
  - www.tbpr.org/attorneys/ethicsopinions
  - www.tsc.state.tn.us (enter *ethics* in the search box)
- **Unauthorized Practice of Law: Tennessee**
  - www.tba.org (enter *unauthorized practice of law* in search box)
  - ir.lawnet.fordham.edu/cgi/viewcontent.cgi?article=3572&context=flr
- **Paralegals and Other Nonattorneys: Tennessee**
  - *Rule 5.3.* For a discussion of the state's ethics Rule 5.3 ("Responsibilities Regarding Nonlawyer Assistants") in the Tennessee *Rules of Professional Conduct*, see Chapter 5. For the text of 5.3 in Tennessee, see www.tsc.state.tn.us/rules/supreme-court/8.
  - *Rule 5.5(h).* A lawyer or law firm shall not employ or continue the employment of a disbarred or suspended lawyer as an attorney, legal consultant, law clerk, paralegal or in any other position of a quasi-legal nature. See also *Formal Ethics Opinion 83-F-50.*
  - *Rule 5.5* (Comment 2). Lawyers can employ the services of paralegals and delegate tasks to them "so long as the lawyer supervises the delegated work and retains responsibility for their work."
  - *Rule 5.5* (Comment 3). Lawyers can assist independent paraprofessionals, who are authorized to provide particular law-related services.
  - In the absence of the informed consent of all parties, a lawyer is ethically prohibited from representing litigants upon employment of a paralegal in instances wherein the paralegal had duties involving opposing parties while formerly employed by adverse counsel. The screening exception is disapproved as a method of preventing vicarious disqualification wherein there is a potential for harm. In this instance a potential harm exists. Supreme Court of Tennessee, *Formal Ethics Opinion 87-F-110* (6/10/87). See also *Clinard v. Blackwood* below.
  - If appropriate screening devices are in place and Client "A" consents, an entire law firm need not be disqualified from representing Client "A" simply because a "tainted" attorney

in the firm once worked at another firm that represented Client "B" in a case adverse to Client "A." Furthermore, "the disqualification rules and screening procedures are applicable to lawyer, law clerk, paralegal, and legal secretary." Board of Professional Responsibility of the Supreme Court of Tennessee, *Formal Ethics Opinion 89-F-118* (3/10/89). See also *Clinard v. Blackwood* below.

- It is the unauthorized practice of law for an attorney to allow his or her paralegal to appear at a section 341 meeting of creditors in bankruptcy cases to ask questions of debtors unless a court expressly authorizes it. Board of Professional Responsibility of the Supreme Court of Tennessee, *Advisory Ethics Opinion 92-A-473(a)* (5/12/92), confirming *Opinion 92-A-475* (1/1991). See *In re Kincaid* below, which *does* authorize it.

- It is the unauthorized practice of law for attorneys to allow their paralegals to appear in court at docket calls on behalf of the attorney to schedule cases. Board of Professional Responsibility of the Supreme Court of Tennessee, *Formal Ethics Opinion 85-F-94* (5/6/85).

- It is the unauthorized practice of law for an unsupervised independent paralegal to provide the public with the service of filling out legal documents such as bankruptcy petitions, uncontested divorce petitions, wills, and premarital agreements for a fee. Attorney General of Tennessee, *Opinion 92–01* (1/9/92).

Defining the Practice of Law in Tennessee

- § 23–3-101(3) (*Tennessee Code Annotated*): "Practice of law" means the appearance as an advocate in a representative capacity or the drawing of papers, pleadings or documents or the performance of any act in such capacity in connection with proceedings pending or prospective before any court, commissioner, referee or any body, board, committee or commission constituted by law or having authority to settle controversies, or the soliciting of clients directly or indirectly to provide such services.

- § 23-3-101(1) (*Tennessee Code Annotated*): (1) "Law business" means the advising or counseling for a valuable consideration of any person as to any secular law, or the drawing or the procuring of or assisting in the drawing for a valuable consideration of any paper, document or instrument affecting or relating to secular rights, or the doing of any act for a valuable consideration in a representative capacity, obtaining or tending to secure for any person any property or property rights whatsoever, or the soliciting of clients directly or indirectly to provide such services.

- Rule 9, § 20.2(e) (*Rules of the Supreme Court of Tennessee*): The term, "the practice of law" shall be defined as any service rendered involving legal knowledge or legal advice, whether of representation, counsel or advocacy, in or out of court, rendered in respect to the rights, duties, regulations, liabilities or business relations of one requiring the services. It shall encompass all public and private positions in which the attorney may be called upon to examine the law or pass upon the legal effect of any act, document or law.

Paralegals (and Others) in Tennessee State and Federal Courts

(See the beginning of this appendix on how to find the full text of the opinions cited here, including WL opinions.)

- *Clinard v. Blackwood*, 46 S.W. 3d 177 (Supreme Court of Tennessee, 2001) (A conflict of interest created by attorneys, law clerks, paralegals, and legal secretaries switching jobs does not lead to disqualification if appropriate screening procedures are followed.)
- *In re Kincaid*, 146 Bankruptcy Reporter 387 (U.S. Bankruptcy Court, W.D. Tennessee, 1992) (A nonattorney regularly employed by a corporate creditor could appear on behalf of the employer at a creditors' meeting in a bankruptcy case and question debtors without engaging in unauthorized practice of law.)
- *Alexander v. Inman*, 903 S.W.2d 686, 704 (Court of Appeals of Tennessee, 1995) (The request to the court for an award of fees for paralegal services explained the services they provided in such general terms "that no finder of fact would be able to determine whether they were required or reasonable.")
- *Hall v. City of Clarksville*, 2006 WL 2038004 (U.S. District Court, M.D. Tennessee, 2006) (Defendant objects to 18 paralegal time entries, for a total of 51.55 hours, for work such as making copies, preparing and disassembling witness and trial notebooks, gathering exhibits and burning CD-ROMs for trial, and copying exhibits. The court agrees that some reduction for clerical tasks is

warranted. Because some of the time entries involved work ordinarily performed by a paralegal, however, the court will reduce the challenged 51.55 hours by 15 hours. The court will award paralegal compensation for 165.65 hours at $75 per hour for a total of $12,423.75.)

- *Keisling v. Keisling*, 196 S.W.2d 703 (Court of Appeals of Tennessee, 2005) (A guardian *ad litem* may be an attorney or a specially trained nonlawyer such as the court-appointed special advocates (CASA). The role of the guardian *ad litem*, whether attorney or nonattorney, should be the same—to protect the child's interest and to gather and present facts for the court's consideration.)

Doing Legal Research in Tennessee Law

- **Statutes:** www.legislature.state.tn.us
- **Cases:** tncourts.gov/courts /supreme-court/opinions
- **Court Rules:** www.tsc.state.tn.us /courts/rules
- **General:** www.law.georgetown.edu /library/research/guides/tennesse.cfm

Finding Employment in Tennessee

- legal.jobs.net/Tennessee.htm
- careers.findlaw.com (select *Paralegal* and *Tennessee*)
- memphis.craigslist.org/lgl
- nashville.craigslist.org/search /lgl?query=+

TEXAS

ETHICS CODE AND OPINIONS IN TEXAS

- **Attorneys: Texas Code:** *Rules of Professional Conduct*
  - www.supreme.courts.state.tx.us /rules/atty_rules.asp
  - www.law.cornell.edu/ethics/texas .html
  - See also ethics links in Helpful Websites at the end of Chapter 5.
- **Attorneys: Texas Ethics Opinions**
  - www.law.uh.edu/libraries/ethics (click *Ethics Opinions*)
- **Unauthorized Practice of Law: Texas**
  - www.texasbar.com (enter *unauthorized practice of law* in search box)
  - www.supreme.courts.state.tx.us (enter *unauthorized practice of law* in search box)
  - ir.lawnet.fordham.edu/cgi /viewcontent.cgi?article=3572&con text=flr
- **Paralegals and Others Nonattorneys: Texas**

- *Rule 5.03.* For a discussion of the state's ethics Rule 5.3 ("Responsibilities Regarding Nonlawyer Assistants") in the Texas *Rules of Professional Conduct*, see Chapter 5.
- *Rule 5.05 (Comment 4).* Lawyers can employ the services of paralegals and delegate tasks to them "so long as the lawyer supervises the delegated work and retains responsibility for the work, and maintains a direct relationship with the client."
- *Code of Ethics and Professional Responsibility of the Paralegal Division of the State Bar of Texas* (1982) (txpd.org /page.asp?p=Professional%20Ethics). The paralegal profession is by nature closely related to the legal profession. Although the Code of Professional Responsibility of the State Bar of Texas does not directly govern paralegals except through a supervising attorney, it is incumbent upon the members of the Paralegal Division to know the provisions of the attorneys' code and avoid any action which might involve an attorney in a violation of that code or even the appearance of professional impropriety. *Canon 1.* A paralegal shall not engage in the practice of law as defined by statutes or court decisions, including but not limited to accepting cases or clients, setting fees, giving legal advice or appearing in a representative capacity in court or before an administrative or regulatory agency (unless otherwise authorized by statute, court or agency rules); the paralegal shall assist in preventing the unauthorized practice of law. *Canon 2.* A paralegal shall not perform any of the duties that attorneys only may perform or do things which attorneys themselves may not do. *Canon 3.* A paralegal shall exercise care in using independent professional judgment and in determining the extent to which a client may be assisted without the presence of any attorney, and shall not act in matters involving professional legal judgment. *Canon 4.* A paralegal shall preserve and protect the confidences and secrets of a client. *Canon 5.* A paralegal shall not solicit legal business on behalf of an attorney. *Canon 6.* A paralegal shall not engage in performing paralegal functions other than under the direct supervision of an attorney, and shall not advertise or contract with members of the general public for the performance of paralegal functions. *Canon 7.* A paralegal shall avoid, if

at all possible, any interest or association which constitutes a conflict of interest pertaining to a client matter and shall inform the supervising attorney of the existence of any possible conflict. *Canon 8.* A paralegal shall maintain a high standard of ethical conduct and shall contribute to the integrity of the paralegal profession. *Canon 9.* A paralegal shall maintain a high degree of competency to better assist the legal profession in fulfilling its duty to provide quality legal services to the public. *Canon 10.* A paralegal shall do all other things incidental, necessary or expedient to enhance professional responsibility and the participation of paralegals in the administration of justice and public service in cooperation with the legal profession.

- State Bar of Texas, *Texas Paralegal Standards* (2005). *A.* Attorneys should promote paralegal continuing legal education, certification, and bar division membership. If a person does not have formal paralegal education, it is suggested that they have at least four years of performing "substantive legal work" to be considered a paralegal. *B.* "Substantive legal work" includes, but is not limited to, the following: conducting client interviews and maintaining general contact with the client; locating and interviewing witnesses; conducting investigations and statistical and documentary research; drafting documents, correspondence, and pleadings; summarizing depositions, interrogatories, and testimony; and attending executions of wills, real estate closings, depositions, court or administrative hearings, and trials with an attorney. "Substantive legal work" does not include clerical or administrative work. Accordingly, a court may refuse to provide recovery of paralegal time for such non-substantive work. *C.* Consideration of Ethical Obligations. 1. *Attorney.* The employing attorney has the responsibility for ensuring that the conduct of the paralegal performing the services is compatible with the professional obligations of the attorney. It also remains the obligation of the employing or supervising attorney to fully inform a client as to whether a paralegal will work on the legal matter, what the paralegal's fee will be, and whether the client will be billed for any non-substantive work performed by the paralegal. 2.

Paralegal. A paralegal is prohibited from engaging in the practice of law, providing legal advice, signing pleadings, negotiating settlement agreements, soliciting legal business on behalf of an attorney, setting a legal fee, accepting a case, or advertising or contracting with members of the general public for the performance of legal functions (txpd.org/page. asp?p=Paralegal%20Definition%20 and%20Standards).

- State Bar of Texas, *General Guidelines for the Utilization of the Services of Legal Assistants by Attorneys* (January 22, 1993). *Guideline I:* An attorney should ensure that a legal assistant does not give legal advice or otherwise engage in the unauthorized practice of law. *Guideline II:* The attorney must take reasonable measures to ensure that the legal assistant's conduct is consistent with the Texas rules of ethics. *Guideline III:* An attorney may, with the client's consent, perform supervised functions authorized by law and ethics. *Guideline IV:* When dealing with others, the status of the legal assistant must be disclosed at the outset. *Guideline V:* The attorney must not assign functions to a legal assistant that require the exercise of independent professional legal judgment. The attorney must maintain a direct relationship with the client. The attorney is responsible for the actions taken and not taken by a legal assistant. *Guideline VI:* An attorney may not delegate to a legal assistant responsibility for establishing the attorney-client relationship, setting fees, or giving legal advice to a client. *Guideline VII:* An attorney must instruct the legal assistant to preserve the sanctity of all confidences and secrets and take reasonable measures to ensure that this is done. *Guideline VIII:* The attorney should take reasonable measures to prevent conflicts of interest resulting from a legal assistant's other employment or interests. *Guideline IX:* An attorney can charge and bill for a legal assistant's time but may not share legal fees with a legal assistant. *Guideline X:* An attorney may not split legal fees with a legal assistant nor pay a legal assistant for the referral of legal business. A legal assistant's compensation cannot be contingent, by advance agreement, upon the profitability of the attorney's practice. *Guideline XI:* The

legal assistant can have a business card that names the firm as long as the status of the legal assistant is included on the card. The attorney must take reasonable measures to ensure that the card is not used in a deceptive way for unethical solicitation. See also State Bar of Texas, Paralegal Division, *Code of Ethics for Legal Assistants* (Texas Center for Legal Ethics and Professionalism) at www.txethics.org/reference_ethics.asp. See also State Bar of Texas, Paralegal Division, *Canons of Ethics and Professional Responsibility* (txpd.org/page.asp?p=Ethics%20 Brochure).

- The Texas Disciplinary Rules of Professional Conduct also prohibit a Texas law firm from paying or agreeing to pay specified bonuses to nonlawyer employees contingent upon the firm's achieving a specified level of revenue or profit. Such a plan would provide an incentive for the firm's nonlawyer employees to increase revenues, which could be accomplished through soliciting clients, or to reduce expenses, which could be accomplished by interfering with a lawyer's independent judgment in practicing law. Furthermore, tying a bonus to achieving a specified level of profit is similar to tying a bonus to achieving a specified level of revenue because profit is a function of revenue and expenses. A Texas law firm may, however, consider its revenue, expenses, and profit in determining whether to pay bonuses to nonlawyer employees and the amount of such bonuses. Also, a law firm may not use the title officer for one of its nonattorney employees. Professional Ethics Committee for the State Bar of Texas, *Opinion No. 642* (May 2014).
- Law firm letterhead can include the name of legal assistants and can indicate that they have been certified (with a notation that they are legal assistants and are not licensed to practice law). State Bar of Texas, *Opinion 436* (6/20/86), which overrules *Opinion 390* (4/78).
- A legal assistant can write a letter on the law firm's letterhead as long as he or she signs as a legal assistant. The letter should not contain legal advice, judgment, strategy, or settlement negotiations. Such letters should be signed by an attorney. State Bar of Texas, *Opinion 381* (3/1975).

- A legal assistant may have a business card with the law firm's name appearing on it provided the status of the legal assistant is clearly disclosed. State Bar of Texas, *Opinion 403* (1982).
- The name of an employee can be printed on an outdoor sign of a law firm as long as the nonattorney status of the employee is clear on the sign. Professional Ethics Committee of the State Bar of Texas, *Opinion 437* (6/20/86). See, however, *Opinion 426* (9/85) that an outdoor sign of a law firm cannot include the name of an investigator who is an independent contractor.
- It is unethical for attorneys to take a case in which they know or believe that they may have to call their nonattorney employee as an expert witness. State Bar of Texas, *Opinion 516* (6/2/95).
- A legal assistant switches sides between law firms who are opposing each other on a case. The new employer is not disqualified if he takes steps to ensure there will be no breach of confidentiality by the legal assistant. State Bar of Texas, *Opinion 472* (6/20/91).
- A lawyer cannot agree with an insurance company to restrictions (e.g., when a paralegal should draft a document) that interfere with the lawyer's independent professional judgment in rendering legal services to the insured/client. State Bar of Texas, *Opinion 533* (9/2000).
- Ethical problems of supervision and professional judgment exist when a legal assistant (employed by a collection agency) sits in a lawyer's office making collection calls to debtors. Supreme Court of Texas, Ethics Committee, *Opinion 401* (1/82).
- When an attorney fails to supervise his paralegal, the attorney is responsible for the malpractice of the paralegal, such as the theft of client funds by the paralegal. "In the future, you should establish greater controls over your paralegals." Dallas Bar Ass'n, *Opinion 1989-5*.

Defining Legal Assistants/Paralegals in Texas

- A paralegal is a person, qualified through various combinations of education, training, or work experience, who is employed or engaged by a lawyer, law office, governmental agency, or other entity in a capacity or function which involves the performance, under the ultimate direction and supervision of a licensed attorney, of specifically delegated substantive legal work, which work, for the most part, requires a sufficient knowledge of legal principles and procedures that, absent such a person, an attorney would be required to perform the task. State Bar of Texas, *Texas Paralegal Standards* (txpd.org/page.asp?p=Paralegal%20Definition%20and%20Standards)

Texas Certification of Paralegals

- txpd.org/faqs.asp?p=Paralegal%20Certification

Defining the Practice of Law in Texas

- § 81.101(a) (*Vernon's Texas Statutes and Codes Annotated*): In this chapter the "practice of law" means the preparation of a pleading or other document incident to an action or special proceeding or the management of the action or proceeding on behalf of a client before a judge in court as well as a service rendered out of court, including the giving of advice or the rendering of any service requiring the use of legal skill or knowledge, such as preparing a will, contract, or other instrument, the legal effect of which under the facts and conclusions involved must be carefully determined.
- § 81.101(c) (*Vernon's Texas Statutes and Codes Annotated*): In this chapter, the "practice of law" does not include the design, creation, publication, distribution, display, or sale, including publication, distribution, display, or sale by means of an Internet web site, of written materials, books, forms, computer software, or similar products if the products clearly and conspicuously state that the products are not a substitute for the advice of an attorney.

Paralegals (and Others) in Texas State and Federal Courts

(See the beginning of this appendix on how to find the full text of the opinions cited here, including WL opinions.)

- *In re Columbia Valley Healthcare System*, 320 S.W.3d 819 (Supreme Court of Texas, 2010) (A law firm was disqualified from representing plaintiff in a medical malpractice action against a hospital, based on conflict of interest arising from firm's employment of a paralegal who had been employed by the hospital's attorney and who had previously worked on the same malpractice action. The plaintiff's firm did not effectively screen the paralegal from the malpractice matter and the paralegal actually worked on the malpractice case at the direction of an attorney at plaintiff's firm. The paralegal was told not to work on the malpractice file, but the firm did not take other institutional, formal measures to ensure that the paralegal did not work on the matter, such as removing file from the paralegal's access or providing the paralegal with a written policy about conflicts of interest.) (See also *In re Guar. Ins Services*, 310 S.W.3d 630 (Court of Appeals of Texas-Austin, 2010) in which disqualification was ordered when the new firm failed to rebut the presumption that the paralegal shared confidences.)
- *In re Mitcham*, 133 S.W.3d 274 (Supreme Court of Texas, 2004) (For purposes of determining whether attorney disqualification is warranted, there is an irrebuttable presumption that legal assistants gain confidential information only on cases on which they work, and a rebuttable presumption that they share that information with a new employer. The presumption is rebutted not by denials of disclosure, but by prophylactic (screening) measures assuring that the legal assistants do not work on matters related to their prior employment.)
- *In re TXU U.S. Holdings*, 110 S.W.3d 62 (Court of Appeals of Texas, 2002) (Unlike the irrebuttable presumption that exists for a disqualified attorney, a rebuttable presumption exists that a nonlawyer has shared the confidences of a former client with his new employer, for purposes of determining disqualification based on future representation that is adverse to former client. The presumption may be rebutted only by establishing that sufficient precautions have been taken to guard against disclosure of confidences.)
- *In re Bell Helicopter Textron*, 87 S.W.3d 139 (Court of Appeals of Texas, 2002) (Screening legal support staff that worked for counsel that represented an opposing party requires that the newly hired nonlawyer must be cautioned not to disclose any information relating to the representation of a client of the former employer, the nonlawyer must be instructed not to work on any matter on which she worked during the prior employment, or regarding which she has information relating to the former employer's representation, and the new firm should take other reasonable steps to ensure that the nonlawyer does not work in connection with matters on

which she worked during the prior employment, absent client consent after consultation.)

- *Phoenix Founders, Inc. v. Marshall*, 887 S.W.2d 831, 834 (Supreme Court of Texas, 1994) (There is a rebuttable presumption that a nonattorney who switches sides in ongoing litigation, after having gained confidential information at the first firm, will share the information with members of the new firm. The presumption may be rebutted to avoid disqualification upon a showing of sufficient precautions, e.g., building a Chinese wall, to guard against any disclosure of confidences). See also *In re American Home Products Corp.*, 985 S.W.2d 68 (Supreme Court of Texas, 1998).
- *All Seasons Window. . . v. Red Dot Corp.*, 181 S.W.3d 490 (Court of Appeals of Texas, 2005) (An award of attorney fees may include a legal assistant's time to the extent that the work performed has traditionally been done by any attorney. To recover such fees, the evidence must establish: (1) the qualifications of the legal assistant to perform substantive legal work; (2) that the legal assistant performed substantive legal work under the direction and supervision of an attorney; (3) the nature of the legal work performed; (4) the legal assistant's hourly rate; and (5) the number of hours expended by the legal assistant.)
- *Davis v. Mostyn Law Firm*, 2012 WL 163941 (U.S. District Court, S.D. Texas, 2012) (Class action sought by legal assistants who assert that they are entitled to overtime because none of the exemptions apply.) (See also *Black v. Settlepou*, 2011 WL 609884 (U.S. District Court, N.D. Texas, 2011), another case in which paralegal sought class-action status in an overtime case.)
- *Shaw v. Palmer*, 197 S.W.2d 854 (Court of Appeals of Texas, 2006) (A paralegal fails to prove the existence of a contract to accept a lower salary in exchange for bonuses based on increases in the firm's profits.)
- *State Bar of Texas v. Faubion*, 821 S.W.2d 203 (Court of Appeals of Texas, 1991) (It was unethical for an attorney to pay a paralegal/investigator up to one-third of the fees generated from particular cases on which the paralegal worked. A bonus is proper if it is not based on a percentage of the law firm's profits or on a percentage of particular legal fees.)
- *In re Witts*, 180 Bankruptcy Reporter 171, 173 (U.S. Bankruptcy Court, E.D. Texas, 1995) (The attorney cannot recover paralegal rates for such clerical

tasks as organizing files, proofreading and revising documents, faxing and copying.)

- *Jones v. Krown*, 218 S.W.3d 746 (Court of Appeals of Texas, 2007) (A will prepared by an attorney is void when it gives assets to a paralegal employed as an in-office independent contractor in the office of the attorney; to reach this result, the court applied Probate Code, § 58b.)
- *Cunningham v. Columbia/St. David's Healthcare Sys.* 185 S.W. 3d 7 (Court of Appeals of Texas, 2005) (Because lawyers are responsible for the actions of the legal assistants that they supervise, the procedural mistakes made by a legal assistant are imputed to the supervising attorney.)
- *Welch v. McLean*, 191 S.W.3d 147 (Court of Appeals of Texas, 2005) (A party tries to strike a paralegal as a juror in a malpractice case; he said he did not take paralegals on juries due to the "grave risk that they will get into the jury room and start telling folks about legal matters, of what the meaning of legal things is.")
- *Teague v. Dretke*, 384 F. Supp. 2d 999 (U.S. District Court, N.D. Texas, 2005) (In many prison disciplinary proceedings, a nonlawyer advocate known as "substitute counsel" is appointed to assist the inmate in presenting his defense.)
- *Petroleos Mexicanos v. Crawford Enterprises, Inc.*, 826 F.2d 392 (U.S. Court of Appeals, 5th Circuit, 1987) (Court appoints paralegal as a special master to monitor a company's discovery compliance.)
- *Rea v. Cofer*, 879 S.W.2d 224 (Court of Appeals of Texas, 1994) (Former client sues attorney and paralegal for legal malpractice.)

Doing Legal Research in Texas Law

- **Statutes:** www.statutes.legis.state .tx.us
- **Cases:** www.supreme.courts.state .tx.us/historical/recent.asp
- **Court Rules:** www.supreme.courts .state.tx.us/rules
- **General:** www.loc.gov/law/help /guide/states/us-tx.php

Finding Employment in Texas

- careers.findlaw.com (select *Paralegal* and *Texas*)
- l.tx.bar.associationcareernetwork .com/Common/HomePage.aspx
- www.careerjet.com/paralegal-jobs /texas-20747.html
- dallas.craigslist.org/lgl

UTAH

ETHICS CODE AND OPINIONS IN UTAH

- **Attorneys: Utah Code:** *Rules of Professional Conduct*
  - www.utcourts.gov/resources/rules /ucja/index.htm#Chapter 13
  - www.law.cornell.edu/ethics/utah .html
  - See also ethics links in Helpful Websites at the end of Chapter 5.
- **Attorneys: Utah Ethics Opinions**
  - www.utahbar.org/opc/eaoc
- **Unauthorized Practice of Law: Utah**
  - www.utahbar.org (enter *unauthorized practice of law* in search box)
  - www.utahbar.org/public-services /unauthorized-practice-of-law
  - ir.lawnet.fordham.edu/cgi /viewcontent.cgi?article=3572&con text=flr
- **Paralegals and Other Nonattorneys: Utah**
  - Paralegal Division of the Utah State Bar (paralegals.utahbar.org)
  - *Rule 5.3.* For a discussion of the state's ethics Rule 5.3 ("Responsibilities Regarding Nonlawyer Assistants") in the Utah *Rules of Professional Conduct*, see Chapter 5.
  - *Rule 1.10 (Comment 4).* The rule of imputed disqualification in Rule 1.10 "does not prohibit representation by others in the law firm where the person prohibited from involvement in a matter is a nonlawyer, such as a paralegal or legal secretary." Utah *Rules of Professional Conduct.*
  - *Rule 5.5 (Comment 2).* Lawyers can employ the services of paraprofessionals and delegate tasks to them "so long as the lawyer supervises the delegated work and retains responsibility for their work."
  - *Rule 5.5 (Comment 3).* Lawyers can assist independent paraprofessionals, who are authorized to provide particular law-related services.
  - Utah State Bar, Paralegal Division, *Guidelines for the Utilization of Paralegals*:
    A. Paralegals shall:
    (1) Disclose their status as paralegals at the outset of any professional relationship with a client, other attorneys, a court or administrative agency or personnel thereof, or members of the general public;
    (2) Preserve the confidences and secrets of all clients; and
    (3) Understand the Rules of Professional Conduct, as amended, and these guidelines in order to avoid any action

which would involve the attorney in violation of the Rules, or give the appearance of professional impropriety.

B. Paralegals may perform services for an attorney in the representation of a client, provided:

(1) The services performed by the paralegal do not require the exercise of independent professional legal judgment;

(2) The attorney maintains a direct relationship with the client and maintains control of all client matters;

(3) The attorney supervises the paralegal;

(4) The attorney remains professionally responsible for all work on behalf of the client, including any actions taken or not taken by the paralegal in connection therewith; and

(5) The services performed supplement, merge with and become the attorney's work product.

C. In the supervision of paralegals, attorneys shall:

(1) Design work assignments that correspond to the paralegal's abilities, knowledge, training and experience;

(2) Educate and train the paralegal with respect to professional responsibility, local rules and practices, and firm policies;

(3) Monitor the work and professional conduct of the paralegal to ensure that the work is substantively correct and timely performed;

(4) Provide continuing education for the paralegal in substantive matters through courses, institutes, workshops, seminars and in-house training; and

(5) Encourage and support membership and active participation in professional organizations.

D. Except as otherwise provided by statute, court rule or decision, administrative rule or regulation, or the attorney's Rules of Professional Conduct; and within the preceding parameters and proscriptions, a paralegal may perform any function delegated by an attorney, including but not limited to the following:

(1) Conduct client interviews and maintain general contact with the client after the establishment of the attorney-client relationship, so long as the client is aware of the status and function of the paralegal, and the client contact is under the supervision of the attorney;

(2) Locate and interview witnesses, so long as the witnesses are aware of the status and function of the paralegal;

(3) Conduct investigations and statistical and documentary research for review by the attorney;

(4) Draft legal documents for review by the attorney;

(5) Draft correspondence and pleadings for review by and signature of the attorney;

(6) Summarize depositions, interrogatories and testimony for review by the attorney;

(7) Attend executions of wills, real estate closings, depositions, court or administrative hearings and trials with the attorney;

(8) Author and sign letters provided the paralegal's status is clearly indicated and the correspondence does not contain independent legal opinions or legal advice; and

(9) Conduct legal research for review by the attorney.

- A lawyer may not split fees with a paralegal nor pay the paralegal for the referral of legal business. A lawyer may compensate a paralegal based on the quality of the paralegal's work and the value of that work to the law practice. A lawyer may not compensate a paralegal based solely upon a quota of revenues generated for the firm by a paralegal's work on a specific case or a group of cases within a certain prescribed time period, although a paralegal may participate in a firm's profit sharing plan.

- Utah State Bar, Legal Assistant Division and Board of Bar Commissioners, *Canons of Ethics for Legal Assistants* (www.utahbar.org/category/utah-bar-journal/legal-assistant-division)

- A lawyer may pay a nonlawyer employee for their clerical or case preparation work. But if the lawyer's payments to the nonlawyer employee are explicitly or even implicitly conditioned on that employee providing legal referrals, those payments must comply with Rule 7.2. Thus, a lawyer's paralegal could not be compensated for providing referrals, because such paralegal would not qualify as a "lawyer referral service" that is "hold[ing] itself out to the public" and funneling referrals to "multiple lawyers and law firms." But nothing prohibits a lawyer from accepting a referral from an employee, so long as the lawyer does not give the employee anything of value for the referral. Utah State Bar, *Opinion 03–03* (6/23/03).

- A lawyer can use nonlawyer paraprofessionals to provide representation of clients in hearings before a government agency (Social Security Administration) that authorizes nonlawyer representation. Utah State Bar, *Opinion 03–03* (6/23/03).

- Utah lawyers may hire outside paralegals on an independent-contractor basis, provided the paralegal does not control the lawyer's professional judgment. In addition, if the amounts paid for services are not tied to specific cases, Utah lawyers or law firms may share fees with nonlawyer employees in a compensation plan. Utah State Bar, *Opinion 02–07* (9/13/02). See also *Opinion 139* (1/27/94).

- An attorney can employ a paralegal who owns an interest in a collection agency the attorney represents as a client so long as there is no sham arrangement in which the paralegal would nominally own an interest in a collection agency that is in reality owned by the attorney. Utah State Bar, *Opinion 96–10* (12/6/96).

- A lawyer who negotiates or otherwise communicates with an opposing party's legal assistant representative on substantive matters affecting the rights of parties to a particular matter is not assisting in the unauthorized practice of law if that representative is supervised by a lawyer. Utah State Bar, *Opinion 99–02* (4/30/99).

- A lawyer may not use the word "associate" in its name if there are no associated attorneys in the firm even if it "employs one or more associated nonattorneys such as paralegals or investigators." Utah State Bar, *Opinion 138* (1/27/94).

- A nonattorney may be listed on the letterhead of an attorney as long as the nonattorney's status is clear. Utah State Bar, *Opinion 131* (5/20/93).

Defining Legal Assistants/Paralegals in Utah

- A paralegal is a person, qualified through education, training or work experience who is employed or retained by a lawyer, law office, governmental agency or other entity in a capacity or function which involves the performance, under the ultimate direction and supervision of an attorney, of specifically delegated substantive legal work, which work for the most part, requires a sufficient knowledge of legal concepts that, absent the [paralegal] the attorney would perform the task. Supreme Court of Utah, *In re Petition Creation of a Legal Assistant Division of the Utah State Bar* (3/26/96).

Defining the Practice of Law in Utah

- Rule 14–802 (*Supreme Court Rules of Professional Practice*):

  (a) The "practice of law" is the representation of the interests of another person by informing, counseling, advising, assisting, advocating for or drafting documents for that person through application of the law and associated legal principles to that person's facts and circumstances. . . .

  (c) Whether or not it constitutes the practice of law, the following activity by a nonlawyer, who is not otherwise claiming to be a lawyer or to be able to practice law, is permitted:

  (c) (1) Making legal forms available to the general public, whether by sale or otherwise, or publishing legal self-help information by print or electronic media.

  (c) (2) Providing general legal information, opinions or recommendations about possible legal rights, remedies, defenses, procedures, options or strategies, but not specific advice related to another person's facts or circumstances.

  (c) (3) Providing clerical assistance to another to complete a form provided by a [Utah court] when no fee is charged to do so.

  (c) (4) When expressly permitted by the court after having found it clearly to be in the best interests of the child or ward, assisting one's minor child or ward in a juvenile court proceeding.

  (c) (5) Representing a party in small claims court. . . .

  (c) (8) Acting as a representative before administrative tribunals or agencies as authorized by tribunal or agency rule or practice.

Paralegals (and Others) in Utah State and Federal Courts

(See the beginning of this appendix on how to find the full text of the opinions cited here, including WL opinions.)

- *Roth v. Joseph*, 244 P.3d 391 (Court of Appeals of Utah, 2010) (Due to an inadvertent error by a paralegal in the office of the law firm representing the hospital, the hospital's answer was calendared as due in forty-five days rather than the thirty days stated in the summons. Consequently, the hospital filed its answer on May 6, 2008, twelve days late.)

- *Spencer Law Office v. Dept. of Workforce Services*, 302 P.3d 1257 (court of Appeals of Utah, 2013) (The contention of the law firm that the legal assistant had been plotting with one of the firm's attorneys to leave, start a new practice, and take firm's clients was not supported by substantial evidence, as required to find that legal assistant was terminated for just cause and therefore was not entitled to unemployment benefits. There was no evidence that the legal assistant attempted to purposefully conceal his decision to leave so that he could steal firm's clients.)

- *State v. Garrido*, 314 P.3d 1014 (Court of Appeals of Utah, 2013) (The admission of out-of-court statements made by a kidnapping victim to the prosecutor that were overheard on a speakerphone by a paralegal, regarding victim's intention not to testify because of her fear of defendant, did not violate defendant's confrontation rights, where victim's statements were not accusatory, nor did they amount to bearing witness against defendant, but rather were simply declarations of victim's intention not to testify.)

- *Gold Standard, Inc. v. American Barrick Resources Corp.*, 805 P.2d 164, 169 (Supreme Court of Utah, 1990) (A nonattorney's work in preparation for litigation is protected by the attorney work-product rule.)

- *Barnard v. Utah State Bar*, 857 P.2d 917 (Supreme Court of Utah, 1993) (Attorney charged with unauthorized practice of law for using paralegals to help clients file their own divorces.)

- *Utah v. Long*, 844 P.2d 381 (Court of Appeals of Utah, 1992) (Attorney disciplined for failing to supervise his legal assistant who gave a client incorrect legal advice.)

- *Phillip M. Adams. . . v. Fujitsu*, 2010 WL 1064429 (U.S. District Court, Utah, 2010) (Attorneys should not do the work that can just as easily be done by a legal assistant, or clerical workers supervised by a legal assistant.)

- *Anderson v. Secretary of Health and Human Services*, 80 F.3d 1500 (U.S. Court of Appeals, 10th Circuit, 1996) (Paralegal costs denied where no documentation—other than the statement of the lead attorney—was submitted on what the paralegal did.)

- *Baldwin v. Burton*, 850 P.2d 1188, 1200 (Supreme Court of Utah, 1993) ("[A]llowing recovery for legal assistant fees promotes lawyer efficiency and decreases client litigation costs.")

Doing Legal Research in Utah Law

- **Statutes:** le.utah.gov/Documents /code_const.htm
- **Cases:** www.utcourts.gov/opinions
- **Court Rules:** www.utcourts.gov /resources/rules
- **General:** www.utcourts.gov /lawlibrary/research/utah.asp

Finding Employment in Utah

- www.indeed.com/q-Litigation -Paralegal-l-Utah-jobs.html
- careers.findlaw.com (select *Paralegal* and *Utah*)
- jobs.monster.com/v-legal-q -paralegal-jobs-l-utah.aspx
- saltlakecity.craigslist.org/lgl

VERMONT

ETHICS CODE AND OPINIONS IN VERMONT

- **Attorneys: Vermont Code:** *Rules of Professional Conduct*
  - www.vermontjudiciary.org (enter *Rules of Professional Conduct* in the search box)
  - www.law.cornell.edu/ethics/vermont .html
  - See also ethics links in Helpful Websites at the end of Chapter 5.
- **Attorneys: Vermont Ethics Opinions**
  - www.vtbar.org (select *For Attorneys* and click *Advisory Ethics Opinions*)
- **Unauthorized Practice of Law: Vermont**
  - www.vtbar.org (enter *unauthorized practice of law* in search box)
  - ir.lawnet.fordham.edu/cgi /viewcontent.cgi?article=3572&con text=flr
- **Paralegals and Other Nonattorneys: Vermont**
  - *Rule 5.3*. For a discussion of the state's ethics Rule 5.3 ("Responsibilities Regarding Nonlawyer Assistants") in the Vermont *Rules of Professional Conduct*, see Chapter 5.

- *Rule 1.10 (Comment 4)*. The rule of imputed disqualification in Rule 1.10 "does not prohibit representation by others in the law firm where the person prohibited from involvement in a matter is a nonlawyer, such as a paralegal or legal secretary." Vermont *Rules of Professional Conduct*.
- *Rule 5.5* (Comment 2). Lawyers can employ the services of paraprofessionals and delegate tasks to them "so long as the lawyer supervises the delegated work and retains responsibility for their work."
- *Rule 5.5* (Comment 3). Lawyers can assist independent paraprofessionals, who are authorized to provide particular law-related services.
- A paralegal may not sign court pleadings with an attorney's name and the paralegal's initials after the attorney's name. Vermont Bar Ass'n, *Opinion 01–5* (2001).
- A supervising attorney may permit a paralegal to conduct a loan closing on behalf of a lender client where the client consents, the paralegal's role is ministerial in nature, and the attorney is available for questions, at least by telephone. Vermont Bar Ass'n, *Opinion 99–3* (1999).
- Law Firm A may employ a paralegal who formerly was employed by Law Firm B, despite the fact that the two firms are engaged in litigation against each other in a matter in which the paralegal participated for Law Firm B. However, Law Firm A must now screen the paralegal from involvement in the pending litigation and any matter in which the interests of Law Firm B's client are adverse to those of any client of Law Firm A. Further, Law Firm A must ensure that no information relating to the representation of the client of Law Firm B is revealed by the paralegal to any person in Law Firm A. Vermont Bar Ass'n, *Opinion 97–9* (1997).
- A law firm cannot continue to represent a defendant in a civil case after hiring a nonattorney employee who had previously performed extensive work on the same case while employed by the law firm representing the plaintiff. Vermont Bar Ass'n, *Opinion 85–8* (1985). For other disqualification cases involving paralegals, see also *Opinion 79–28* (1979), *Opinion 89–4* (1989), *Opinion 87–15* (1987), and *Opinion 78–2* (1978).
- Law firms must supervise the independent paralegals they use. To prevent breaches of confidentiality, lawyers must check the systems used by the paralegal to prevent conflicts of interest. Once employed, the hiring firm must develop methods for effectively screening the independent paralegal from information concerning other clients. Vermont Bar Ass'n, *Opinion 2002–02*.
- The letterhead of a law firm may list certain nonlawyer employees such as paralegals and law clerks wherever the inclusion of such names would not be deceptive and might reasonably be expected to supply information relevant to the selection of counsel. Vermont Bar Ass'n, *Opinion 79–13*.
- In a conversation with a nonattorney employee, if a prospective client threatens to kill someone, the employee who believes the threat can warn the potential victim. Vermont Bar Ass'n, *Opinion 86–3*.

Defining Legal Assistants/Paralegals in Vermont

- A paralegal/legal assistant is a person qualified through education, training or work experience to perform substantive legal work that requires knowledge of legal concepts and is customarily, but not exclusively, performed by a lawyer. This person may be retained or employed by a lawyer, law office, governmental agency, or other entity or may be authorized by administrative, statutory or court authority to perform this work. Vermont Bar Association, Constitution. *Standards for Associate Membership*.

Defining the Practice of Law in Vermont

- *In re Welch*, 185 A.2d 458, 459 (Supreme Court of Vermont, 1962): In general, one is deemed to be practicing law whenever he furnishes to another advice or service under circumstances which imply the possession and use of legal knowledge and skill. The practice of law includes "all advice to clients, and all actions taken for them in matters connected with the law.". . . Practice of law includes the giving of legal advice and counsel, and the preparation of legal instruments and contracts [by] which legal rights are secured. . . . Where the rendering of services for another involves the use of legal knowledge or skill on his behalf—where legal advice is required and is availed of or rendered in connection with such services—these services necessarily constitute or include the practice of law. . . . We cannot over-emphasize the necessity of legal training in the proper drafting of legal documents and advice relating thereto. The absence of such training may result in legal instruments faulty in form and contents, and also lead to a failure of purpose, litigation, and expense.
- *In re Conner*, 917 A.2d 442 (Supreme Court of Vermont, 2006): [T]he essence of the practicing lawyer's function is the exercise of professional judgment, bringing to bear all of the lawyer's education, experience, and skill to resolve a specific legal problem for a particular client or case in controversy.

Paralegals (and Others) in Vermont State and Federal Courts

(See the beginning of this appendix on how to find the full text of the opinions cited here, including WL opinions.)

- *IMS Health Inc. v. Sorrell*, 2012 WL 2915845 (U.S. District Court, Vermont, 2012) (The average hourly rate of nearly $200 requested for Hunton & Williams's paralegals is exorbitant.)
- *In re Fibermark, Inc.*, 349 Bankruptcy Reporter 385 (U.S. Bankruptcy Court, Vermont, 2006) (A paralegal or other paraprofessional is eligible to be compensated from a bankruptcy estate, subject to the same scrutiny as that of a professional in the case. 11 U.S.C.A. § 330(a)(1)(A).)
- *In re S.T.N. Enterprises, Inc.*, 70 Bankruptcy Reporter 823 (U.S. Bankruptcy Court, Vermont, 1987) (Courts will reduce an attorney's rate of compensation for performing tasks that could have been performed by a paralegal at a lower rate.)
- *McSweeney v. McSweeney*, 618 A.2d 1332 (Supreme Court of Vermont, 1992) (It is not the unauthorized practice of law for nonattorney employees of the Office of Child Support to prepare and file complaints and motions in child support cases before a magistrate [4 V.S.A. § 464,] but they cannot handle URESA cases involving interstate support issues before a magistrate).
- *Hohman v. Hogan*, 458 F. Supp. 669 (U.S. District Court, Vermont, 1978) (paralegal assistance to inmates).
- *Berry v. Schweiker*, 675 F.2d 464 (U.S. Court of Appeals, 2d Circuit, 1982) (paralegal represents client at disability benefits hearing).

Doing Legal Research in Vermont Law

- **Statutes:** www.leg.state.vt.us /statutesmain.cfm
- **Cases:** libraries.vermont.gov/law /supct
- **Court Rules:** www.lexisnexis.com /hottopics/vtstatutesconstctrules
- **General:** www.loc.gov/law/help /guide/states/us-vt.php

Finding Employment in Vermont

- careers.findlaw.com (select *Paralegal* and *Vermont*)
- www.indeed.com/q-Paralegal-l -Vermont-jobs.html
- burlington.craigslist.org/lgl

VIRGINIA

ETHICS CODE AND OPINIONS IN VIRGINIA

- **Attorneys: Virginia Code:** *Rules of Professional Conduct*
  - www.vsb.org/pro-guidelines/index .php (hover the cursor over *Rules and Regulations)*
  - www.law.cornell.edu/ethics/virginia .html
  - See also ethics links in Helpful Websites at the end of Chapter 5.
- **Attorneys: Virginia Ethics Opinions**
  - www.vsb.org/site/regulation/ethics
- **Unauthorized Practice of Law: Virginia**
  - www.vsb.org (enter *unauthorized practice of law* in search box)
  - www.vsb.org/site/regulation /unauthorized-practice
  - ir.lawnet.fordham.edu/cgi/view-content.cgi?article=3572&context=flr
- **Paralegals and Other Nonattorneys: Virginia**
  - *Rule 5.3.* For a discussion of the state's ethics Rule 5.3 ("Responsibilities Regarding Nonlawyer Assistants") in the Virginia *Rules of Professional Conduct*, see Chapter 5. Virginia added the phrase ("or should have known") to the partner, manager, or direct supervisor's liability. Each is responsible if he or she "knows or should have known of the [paralegal's improper] conduct at a time when its consequences can be avoided or mitigated but fails to take reasonable remedial action."
  - *Rule 5.5* (Comment 2). Lawyers can employ the services of paraprofessionals and delegate tasks to them "so long as the lawyer supervises the delegated work and retains responsibility for their work."

- *Rule 5.5(b).* If a lawyer hires a suspended lawyer as a legal assistant, the lawyer shall not represent any client that the disciplined lawyer represented on or after the date when the disciplined lawyer's license was suspended (or revoked).
- A nonlawyer employee working under the direct supervision of a Virginia attorney may participate in gathering information from a client during an initial interview (a client intake), provided that this involves nothing more than the gathering of factual data and the nonlawyer renders no legal advice. In contrast, a nonlawyer employee may not determine the validity of the client's legal claim, as that determination appears to directly involve the application of legal principles to facts, purposes, or desires and is therefore considered the practice of law. The nonlawyer employee may transmit the attorney/client fee agreement to the client and obtain the client's signature on the document. While a nonlawyer employee is permitted to answer straightforward, factual questions regarding the fee agreement, such answers must not include any advice as to the legal ramifications of the contract provisions. Concerning settlement negotiations, a nonlawyer employee may transmit information and documents between the attorney and the client. For example, the employee could share with the client the latest settlement offer. However, it would not be permissible for the employee to evaluate the offer or to recommend to the client whether or not to accept an offer. In contrast, it would be permissible for the nonlawyer to communicate with the client the lawyer's evaluation or recommendation. Unauthorized Practice of Law Committee of the Virginia State Bar, *Opinion 191* (9/29/98).
- The paralegal, of course, cannot provide advice or service directly to the client or members of the general public, as that would clearly constitute the unauthorized practice of law. Unauthorized Practice of Law Committee, *Opinion 129* (2/22/89).
- A paralegal shall not communicate with clients, outside attorneys, or the public without disclosing his or her nonattorney status. *Code of Professional Responsibility,* DR 3–104(E).
- An attorney is not required to withdraw from a case as long as a

nonattorney employee does not disclose confidential information learned while she worked for an opposing attorney. Standing Committee on Legal Ethics of the Virginia State Bar, *Opinion 745* (1985).
- An attorney represents a client in a case in which the attorney's former nonattorney employee will testify against this client. The attorney is not disqualified from representing this client as long as the client is informed of this situation and still wants the attorney to represent him. Standing Committee on Legal Ethics of the Virginia State Bar, *Opinion 891* (4/1/87).
- A law firm can print the names of nonattorney employees on its letterhead as long as their nonattorney status is clear. These employees can participate in a profit-sharing plan of the firm as part of a compensation or retirement program. Standing Committee on Legal Ethics of the Virginia State Bar, *Opinion 762* (1/29/86). See also *Opinion 970* (9/30/87) (attorney may list name and title of firm's chief investigator as long as the listing includes an affirmative statement that the investigator is not licensed to practice law).
- An attorney must not split fees with nonattorneys, but they can be paid a bonus that is based on profit-sharing. Standing Committee on Legal Ethics of the Virginia State Bar, *Opinion 806* (6/25/86).
- A law firm engaged in collection work can pay its nonattorney employee a percentage of profits from the collections received plus a salary. Standing Committee on Legal Ethics of the Virginia State Bar, *Opinion 885* (3/11/87).
- It is unethical for a nonattorney employee of a law firm to contact prospective collections clients in order to suggest that they hire the law firm for their collections work. Standing Committee on Legal Ethics of the Virginia State Bar, *Opinion 1290* (10/25/89).
- A "real estate paralegal company" can provide assistance to an attorney in closing real estate loans that have been referred to this company by the closing attorney. This is not the unauthorized practice of law as long as designated procedures are followed. Unauthorized Practice of Law Committee, *Opinion 147* (4/19/91).

- It is not the unauthorized practice of law for a nonattorney to give a judicial officer information (present facts) that concerns the weight of the evidence in bail cases. Unauthorized Practice of Law Committee, *Opinion 186* (9/7/95).
- It is not the unauthorized practice of law for a paralegal to appear in court to collect monies resulting from a garnishment as long as this appearance involves only a ministerial or clerical act. Unauthorized Practice of Law Committee, *Opinion 72* (12/12/84).
- Under both the IDEA and Rehabilitation Act, the states and localities must comply with federal law and regulations requiring due process hearings for parents having disputes with local school boards. 34 C.F.R. §300.58 permits the aggrieved parents in IDEA hearings to be represented by counsel or a lay advocate, provided the lay advocate is a person having special knowledge or training concerning the problems of children with disabilities. No certification or training program is administered evaluate the competency or knowledge of a lay advocate. See Virginia's IDEA statute (§ 22.1–214C) Unauthorized Practice of Law Committee, *Opinion 187* (2/15/96).
- A paralegal cannot work for a suspended attorney because the paralegal would not have attorney supervision. Unauthorized Practice of Law Committee, *Opinion 137* (1/8/90).
- A paralegal's name can be printed on the door of the paralegal's private office as long as it does not create the impression that the paralegal is an attorney. Unauthorized Practice of Law Committee, *Opinion 225* (5/21/73) and *Opinion 326* (6/19/79).
- A private law firm employs a paralegal whose husband is an attorney who represents the government in cases against clients of the law firm. The law firm can continue to employ this paralegal, but it must tell its clients and the court of the relationship between the paralegal and the government attorney. Unauthorized Practice of Law Committee, *Opinion 358* (3/10/80).
- An attorney can instruct his paralegal to call a prospective defendant to ask if it manufactures a particular product. This does not violate the rule against contacting the other side,

since there is no litigation under way. The call is part of proper investigation. Unauthorized Practice of Law Committee, *Opinion 1190* (1/4/89). See also *Opinion 1504* (12/14/92) (paralegal can contact opponent to obtain information under the Virginia Freedom of Information Act) and *Opinion 1639* (4/24/95) (paralegal can contact the other side to provide information as a courtesy).
- A nonlawyer inmate of a correctional facility cannot represent a fellow inmate by way of in-court oral argument and out-of-court settlement negotiations in pending civil litigation. Unauthorized Practice of Law Committee, *Opinion 48* (12/1/83).

Defining Legal Assistants/Paralegals in Virginia

- Resolution of Standing Committee on the Unauthorized Practice of Law, March 8, 1996 (Virginia Bar Association) A legal assistant is a specially trained individual who performs substantive legal work that requires a knowledge of legal concepts and who either works under the supervision of an attorney, who assumes professional responsibility for the final work product, or works in areas where lay individuals are explicitly authorized by statute or regulation to assume certain law-related responsibilities.
- Virginia Alliance of Paralegal Associations. Recommended by the Virginia State Bar Standing Committee on Unauthorized Practice of Law by Resolution. The American Bar Association recognizes and has formulated guidelines for the utilization of paralegals. Although there are several formal definitions of a paralegal in general, a paralegal is a specially trained individual who performs substantive legal work that requires knowledge of legal concepts. Paralegals either work under the supervision of an attorney, who assumes professional responsibility for the final work product, or work in areas where lay individuals are explicitly authorized by statute or regulation to assume certain law related responsibilities. (www.vaparalegalalliance.org /about/educational-standards.)

Defining the Practice of Law in Virginia

- *Virginia Rules of Court, Rules of the Supreme Court of Virginia*: Part 6. Section

I. Unauthorized Practice Rules and Considerations. [O]ne is deemed to be practicing law whenever: (1) One undertakes for compensation, direct or indirect, to advise another, not his regular employer, in any matter involving the application of legal principles to facts or purposes or desires. (2) One, other than as a regular employee acting for his employer, undertakes, with or without compensation, to prepare for another legal instruments of any character, other than notices or contracts incident to the regular course of conducting a licensed business. (3) One undertakes, with or without compensation, to represent the interest of another before any tribunal —judicial, administrative, or executive—otherwise than in the presentation of facts, figures, or factual conclusions, as distinguished from legal conclusions, by an employee regularly and bona fide employed on a salary basis, or by one specially employed as an expert in respect to such facts and figures when such representation by such employee or expert does not involve the examination of witnesses or preparation of pleadings.

Paralegals (and Others) in Virginia State and Federal Courts

(See the beginning of this appendix on how to find the full text of the opinions cited here, including WL opinions.)

- *J.P. v.* County *School Bd. of Hanover County*, 2007 WL 840090 (U.S. District Court, E.D. Virginia, 2007) ($105 per hour for paralegal services comports with rates approved in other cases for paralegal fees in the Richmond area (for 2007) and reflects the skill and experience of these professionals.)
- *In re Hall*, 296 Bankruptcy Reporter 707 (U.S. Bankruptcy Court, E.D. Virginia, 2002) ($90 per hour is an excessive rate for paralegal time. Based on the court's general familiarity with prevailing 2002 rates in Alexandria, Virginia (derived from reviewing fee applications in other cases), the court determines that $75 per hour is currently the general market rate for paralegal time, and the court will allow compensation at that rate.)
- *County School Bd. of York County v. A.L.*, 2007 WL 756586 (U.S. District Court, E.D. Virginia, 2007) (It is appropriate to distinguish between legal work, in the strict sense, and investigation, clerical work, compilation of facts and statistics, and other work that can often be accomplished by nonlawyers but

that a lawyer may do because he or she has no other help available. Such non-legal work may command a lesser rate. Its dollar value is not enhanced just because a lawyer does it.)

- *In re Bryant*, 346 Bankruptcy Reporter 406 (U.S. Bankruptcy Court, E.D. Virginia, 2006) (The Court denies the time requested for a paralegal's services because of the lack of contemporaneous time records on the tasks performed.)
- *U.S. v. Smallwood*, 365 F. Supp. 2d 689 (U.S. District Court, E.D. Virginia, 2005) (Of course, most assistants. . . cannot themselves be held accountable for unethical behavior unless it also amounts to criminal conduct. Nonetheless, the fact that corrective measures cannot usually be implemented directly against these assistants does not mean that their conduct is beyond regulation. In certain circumstances, as here, it may be possible to sanction such assistants and investigators by reducing their compensation.)
- *Musselman v. Willoughby Corp.*, 337 S.E.2d 724 (Supreme Court of Virginia, 1985) (Paralegal negligence asserted in a legal malpractice case brought by client against attorney.)
- *Tanksley v. Garrett*, 175 Bankruptcy Reporter 434 (U.S. Bankruptcy Court, W.D. Virginia, 1994) (U. S. Trustee seeks to enjoin a law firm from allowing a paralegal to represent clients at Section 341 bankruptcy hearings.)

Doing Legal Research in Virginia Law

- **Statutes:** leg1.state.va.us/000/src .htm
- **Cases:** www.courts.state.va.us /search/textopinions.html
- **Court Rules:** www.courts.state .va.us/courts/scv/rules.html
- **General:** law.wm.edu/library /research/researchguides/virginia

Finding Employment in Virginia

- careers.findlaw.com (select *Paralegal* and *Virginia*)
- www.indeed.com/q-Paralegal-l -Virginia-jobs.html
- washingtondc.craigslist.org/nva/lgl
- www.simplyhired.com/k-paralegal-l -northern-virginia-va-jobs.html

WASHINGTON STATE

ETHICS CODE AND OPINIONS IN WASHINGTON STATE

- **Attorneys: Washington State Code:** *Rules of Professional Conduct*

- www.courts.wa.gov/court_rules/? fa=court_rules.list&group=ga& set=RPC
- www.law.cornell.edu/ethics /washington.html
- See also ethics links in Helpful Websites at the end of Chapter 5.

- **Unauthorized Practice of Law: Washington State**
  - www.wsba.org (enter *unauthorized practice of law* in search box)
  - ir.lawnet.fordham.edu/cgi /viewcontent.cgi?article=3572&con text=flr

- **Attorneys: Washington State Ethics Opinions**
  - www.wsba.org/Resources-and -Services/Ethics/Advisory -Opinions
  - www.wsba.org/Resources-and -Services/Ethics
  - www.courts.wa.gov/programs_orgs /pos_ethics

- **Paralegals and Other Nonattorneys: Washington State**
  - *Rule 5.3.* For a discussion of the state's ethics Rule 5.3 ("Responsibilities Regarding Nonlawyer Assistants") in the Washington *Rules of Professional Conduct*.
  - *Rule 5.5* (Comment 2). Lawyers can employ the services of paraprofessionals and delegate tasks to them "so long as the lawyer supervises the delegated work and retains responsibility for their work."
  - *Rule 5.5* (Comment 3). Lawyers can assist independent paraprofessionals, who are authorized to provide particular law-related services.

- **Limited License Legal Technician (LTTT)**
  - See Chapter 4 for the LTTT program. The Limited License Legal technician Board will be establishing "rules of professional and ethical conduct." (lib.law.washington.edu /content/guides/llltguide)
  - The titles "paralegal" or "legal assistant" can be used to designate employees on their business cards and on attorney stationery so long as it is clear they are not attorneys. Washington State Bar Ass'n, *Informal Opinion 1065* (1987).
  - There would not be a general conflict of interest between the attorneys who employed paralegals volunteering at a clinic and all clinic clients. A conflict of interest could exist between an attorney and a party with an adverse interest to the clinic client served by the paralegal regularly employed by that attorney. There would not be a conflict of interest for that attorney

that would prevent him or her from providing legal services to clinic clients served by other staff provided that there are adequate screening mechanisms in place at the clinic to insure that the paralegal does not have access to information from or about other clients served by the clinic. Washington State Bar Ass'n, *Informal Opinion 1861* (1999).

- An attorney cannot share fees with nonattorneys who are authorized to represent claimants before the Social Security Administration. Washington State Bar Ass'n, *Informal Opinion 1348* (1990).
- Serious ethical problems exist (e.g., sharing fees with a nonattorney) in a proposed arrangement with a paralegal company whereby the attorney would be referred clients by a financial planner to whom they had been referred by the paralegal company. Washington State Bar Ass'n, *Informal Opinion 1135* (1990).
- An attorney cannot let a collection agency use his name on court documents unless the attorney provides legal assistance on each particular case. Rubber-stamping legal papers of nonattorneys is unethical. Washington State Bar Ass'n, *Opinion 18* (1952) and *Opinion 76* (1960).
- An attorney can enter into a contract with an independent paralegal whereby the paralegal will receive a $250 flat fee for an initial file review and conference with the attorney. Compensation would be hourly after this initial review. (The client would be billed for these payments, even in contingency cases.) This flat-fee arrangement is not improper fee splitting with a nonlawyer. Washington State Bar Ass'n, *Informal Opinion 1774* (1997).
- A suspended lawyer is not allowed to serve as a paralegal, clerk or assistant in law-related matters. Washington State Bar Ass'n, *Informal Opinion 1772* (1997). See also *Informal Opinion 2003* (2002) and *Formal Opinion 184* (1990).

Defining Legal Assistants/Paralegals in Washington State

- A legal assistant is a person, qualified through education, training, or work experience, who is employed or retained by a lawyer, law office, governmental agency, or other entity in a capacity or function which involves a performance, under the ultimate direction and supervision of an attorney, of specifically delegated substantive legal work, which work, for the most part, requires a sufficient knowledge of legal concepts that, absent such assistant, the attorney would perform the task. *Absher Construction Co. v. Kent School District*, 917 P.2d 1086, 1088 (Court of Appeals of Washington State, 1995) (approving the definition of the American Bar Association).

Defining the Practice of Law in Washington State

- Rule 24 (*West's Washington Court Rules*): Part I, General Rules (GR).
  - (a) General Definition. The practice of law is the application of legal principles and judgment with regard to the circumstances or objectives of another entity or person(s) which require the knowledge and skill of a person trained in the law. This includes but is not limited to:
  - (1) Giving advice or counsel to others as to their legal rights or the legal rights or responsibilities of others for fees or other consideration.
  - (2) Selection, drafting, or completion of legal documents or agreements which affect the legal rights of an entity or person(s).
  - (3) Representation of another entity or person(s) in a court, or in a formal administrative adjudicative proceeding or other formal dispute resolution process or in an administrative adjudicative proceeding in which legal pleadings are filed or a record is established as the basis for judicial review.
  - (4) Negotiation of legal rights or responsibilities on behalf of another entity or person(s).
  - (b) Exceptions and Exclusions. Whether or not they constitute the practice of law, the following are permitted:
  - (1) Practicing law authorized by a limited license to practice pursuant to Admission to Practice Rules 8 (special admission for: a particular purpose or action; indigent representation; educational purposes; emeritus membership; house counsel), 9 (legal interns), 12 (limited practice for closing officers), or 14 (limited practice for foreign law consultants). . . .
  - (3) Acting as a lay representative authorized by administrative agencies or tribunals.
  - (6) Providing assistance to another to complete a form provided by a court for protection under RCW chapters 10.14 (harassment) or 26.50 (domestic violence prevention) when no fee is charged to do so. . . .
  - (c) Nonlawyer Assistants. Nothing in this rule shall affect the ability of nonlawyer assistants to act under the supervision of a lawyer in compliance with Rule 5.3 of the Rules of Professional Conduct.
  - (d) General Information. Nothing in this rule shall affect the ability of a person or entity to provide information of a general nature about the law and legal procedures to members of the public.

Paralegals (and Others) in Washington State and Federal Courts

(See the beginning of this appendix on how to find the full text of the opinions cited here, including WL opinions.)

- *Absher Construction Co. v. Kent School District*, 917 P.2d 1086 (Court of Appeals of Washington State, 1995) (Here are the relevant criteria for determining whether legal assistant services should be compensated: (1) the services performed by the nonlawyer personnel must be legal in nature; (2) the performance of these services must be supervised by an attorney; (3) the qualifications of the person performing the services must be specified in the request for fees in sufficient detail to demonstrate that the person is qualified by virtue of education, training, or work experience to perform substantive legal work; (4) the nature of the services performed must be specified in the request for fees in order to allow the reviewing court to determine that the services performed were legal rather than clerical; (5) as with attorney time, the amount of time expended must be set forth and must be reasonable; and (6) the amount charged must reflect reasonable community standards for charges by that category of personnel.)
- *Tumelson Family Ltd. Partnership v. World Financial News Network*, 2005 WL 2293588 (U.S. District Court, W.D. Washington, 2005) (Despite counsels' statement that they have endeavored to remove "clerical" work that their paralegals performed from their fee request, they have not gone far enough. Their invoices still include numerous entries for unquestionably clerical work (e.g., preparing copies, finalizing copies, scanning documents, creating compact discs). Even more entries describe time that might constitute legal services, and might be clerical (e.g., preparing exhibits, working on exhibits, making phone calls, reviewing transcripts). Some describe work that is probably legal (legal research, drafting pleadings). For the substantial majority of the paralegal time, the Tumelsons do not prove that the time is recoverable under the standards set forth in *Absher*. The court must therefore make a substantial deduction for paralegal time.)
- *Tegman v. Accident & Medical Investigations, Inc.*, 30 P.3d 8, 11 (Court of Appeals of Washington, 2001) (Paralegals charged with unauthorized practice of law and negligence. When a paralegal performs legal services with knowledge that there is no supervising attorney responsible for the case, the paralegal will be held to an attorney's standard of care. Non-attorneys who attempt to practice law will be held to the same standards of competence demanded of attorneys and will be liable for negligence if these standards are not met.)
- *Richards v. Jain*, 168 F. Supp. 2d 1195, 1200 (U.S. District Court, W.D. Washington, 2001) (Law firm is disqualified when its paralegal viewed privileged documents of the opponent. The supervising attorney failed to take reasonable steps to ensure that its nonlawyer employees complied with ethical rules. Paralegals are not held to a lower standard of ethical behavior than attorneys. "[N]onlawyers and lawyers are bound by the same ethical duties.")

Doing Legal Research in Washington State Law

- **Statutes:** apps.leg.wa.gov/rcw /default.aspx
- **Cases:** www.courts.wa.gov/opinions
- **Court Rules:** www.courts.wa.gov /court_rules
- **General:** lib.law.washington.edu /content/research/freelaw

Finding Employment in Washington State

- www.wsba.org/Job-Seekers

- careers.findlaw.com (select *Paralegal* and then Washington)
- www.acteva.com/booking .cfm?bevaID=44362
- seattle.craigslist.org/lgl

WEST VIRGINIA

ETHICS CODE AND OPINIONS IN WEST VIRGINIA

- **Attorneys: West Virginia Code:** *Rules of Professional Conduct*
  - www.wvodc.org/ropc.htm
  - www.law.cornell.edu/ethics/wv.html
  - See also ethics links in Helpful Websites at the end of Chapter 5.
- **Attorneys: West Virginia Ethics Opinions**
  - www.wvodc.org/leo.html
  - www.wvbar.org/public-information /advisory-opinions
- **Unauthorized Practice of Law: West Virginia**
  - www.wvbar.org/public-information /unlawful-practice
  - www.wvbar.org (enter *unauthorized practice of law* in search box)
  - ir.lawnet.fordham.edu/cgi /viewcontent.cgi?article=3572&con text=flr
- **Paralegals and Other Nonattorneys: West Virginia**
  - *Rule 5.3.* For a discussion of the state's ethics Rule 5.3 ("Responsibilities Regarding Nonlawyer Assistants") in the West Virginia *Rules of Professional Conduct*, see Chapter 5.
  - *Rule 5.5 (Comment).* Lawyers can employ the services of paraprofessionals and delegate tasks to them "so long as the lawyer supervises the delegated work and retains responsibility for their work."
  - Anything delegated to a nonattorney must lose its separate identity and be merged in the service of the attorney. When communicating with persons outside the office, a paralegal "must disclose his status as such." Nonattorneys can sign letters on law firm stationery as long as their nonattorney status is clearly indicated. *Legal Ethics Inquiry 76–7* (3 W.Va. State Bar Journal (Spring 1977)).
  - A corporation can be represented by a nonattorney in Magistrates Court. "Any party to a civil action in a magistrate court may appear and conduct such action in person, by agent or by attorney. . . . [T]he appearance by an agent shall not constitute the unauthorized practice of law. . . ." (*W. Va. Code* § 50–4–4a). West Virginia State Bar Committee on Unlawful Practice, *Advisory Opinion 93–001.*

Defining Legal Assistants/Paralegals in West Virginia

- A legal assistant is a person, qualified through education, training or work experience, who is employed or retained by a lawyer, law office, governmental agency, or other entity, in a capacity or function which involves the performance, under the ultimate direction and supervision of an attorney, of delegated substantive legal work, which work, for the most part, requires a sufficient knowledge of legal concepts that, absent such assistance, the attorney would perform the task. West Virginia State Bar (5/16/99)(www .wvbar.org).

Defining the Practice of Law in West Virginia

- *State Court Rules.* Definition of the Practice of law. [*Lawyer Disciplinary Bd. v. Allen*, 479 S.E. 2d 317, 333 (Supreme Court of Appeals of West Virginia, 1996).] In general, one is deemed to be practicing law whenever he or it furnishes another advice or service under circumstances which imply the possession or use of legal knowledge and skill. More specifically but without purporting to formulate a precise and completely comprehensive definition of the practice of law or to prescribe limits to the scope of that activity, one is deemed to be practicing law whenever (1) one undertakes, with or without compensation and whether or not in connection with another activity, to advise another in any matter involving the application of legal principles to facts, purposes or desires; (2) one undertakes, with or without compensation and whether or not in connection with another activity, to prepare for another legal instruments of any character; or (3) one undertakes, with or without compensation and whether or not in connection with another activity, to represent the interest of another before any judicial tribunal or officer, or to represent the interest of another before any executive or administrative tribunal, agency or officer otherwise than in the presentation of facts, figures or factual conclusions as distinguished from legal conclusions in respect to such facts and figures. Nothing in this paragraph shall be deemed to prohibit a lay person from appearing as agent before a justice of the peace or to prohibit a bona fide full-time lay employee from performing legal services for his regular employer (other than in connection with representation of his employer before any judicial, executive or administrative tribunal, agency or officer) in matters relating solely to the internal affairs of such employer, as distinguished from such services rendered to or for others. (See also Court Rules, *Michie's West Virginia Code Annotated* 535 (1996).)

Paralegals (and Others) in West Virginia State and Federal Courts

(See the beginning of this appendix on how to find the full text of the opinions cited here, including WL opinions.)

- *Stacy v. B.O. Stroud*, 845 F. Supp. 1135, 1145 (U.S. District Court, S.D. West Virginia, 1993) (Award of attorney fees. "Delegating appropriate tasks to paralegals reduces the overall costs of. . . litigation.")
- *Koontz v. Wells Fargo*, 2013 WL 1337260 (U.S. District Court, S.D. West Virginia, 2013) (Based on the Court's examples of paralegal work given by the United States Supreme Court in *Missouri v. Jenkins* (1989) the tasks the fee applicant claimed was "paralegal" work, it appears that the time entries here for "organizing", "calendaring", and "copying", are not within the realm of billable paralegal tasks. That is not to say that such tasks are never within the scope of a paralegals' work. Much has changed in law offices since *Missouri v. Jenkins* was decided. The advent of computer technology has brought a brave new world to the practice of law. With the advent of computerized legal research, electronic case filing, e-discovery, digital case processing, a myriad of case management and development software programs such as CaseMap, Masterfile, Summation, and Concordance, tasks such as "organizing" and "copying" (but likely not "calendaring") conceivably could involve 21st-century tasks that lie in that "gray area" of paralegal and lawyer work, such as conceiving of and constructing a CaseMap project. The Court need not answer that question today. Here, Plaintiff has offered no evidence to support a finding that Ms. Burdette's "organization" of a pleadings index or Ms. Johnson's "calendaring" and "copying" are anything other than secretarial tasks. The Court's analysis is frustrated by the fact that some of Ms. Johnson's entries contain references to multiple tasks, some plainly billable, some not. This practice is discouraged. Because Plaintiff

provides no evidence as to the percentage of time each task represents, the Court has no way of discerning how much time to disallow from the entry. Thus, the Court will discount the entry in its entirety.)

- *State ex rel. State v. Burnside*, 233 W.Va. 271, 757 S.E.2d 803 (Supreme Court of West Virginia, 2014) (Dissent: Consider the following: A large law firm in Huntington/Charleston employs an experienced and trusted paralegal. Unbeknownst to the law firm, paralegal is engaged in small-time bookmaking/selling small amounts of marijuana out of his office at the law firm. Law enforcement has probable cause and places a device to intercept oral conversations/telephone calls/email (pick one or more) in paralegal's office. As a result, the following scenarios occur: Scenario 1: Lawyer A is defending a highly contested criminal case. Lawyer A directs paralegal to interview potential witnesses who have not been listed in the prosecution's discovery or witness disclosure. Paralegal interviews witnesses who provide information which is potentially damaging to defendant's case. The interviews are not privileged under West Virginia law. Law enforcement shares the intercepted recordings of paralegal's interviews of said witnesses with the prosecutor, who then amends the State's witness list to include the witnesses not previously known to him. As a direct result of the new witnesses' testimony, defendant is convicted. [See text of opinion for the other scenarios.].)

- *Hughes v. Sears, Roebuck*, 2011 WL 2671230 (U.S. District Court, W.D. West Virginia, 2011) (The issue is whether paralegals can be questioned in a deposition. The answer in this case is yes, but the scope of the deposition must be limited. For example, the court will not permit plaintiffs to inquire into the litigation strategy known by Sears's paralegals.)

- *Lawyer Disciplinary Bd. v. Elswick*, 231 W.Va. 684, 749 S.E.2d 577 (Supreme Court of West Virginia, 2013) (Lawyer Disciplinary Board filed a statement of charges against an attorney, who was a public defender, alleging that she knowingly and intentionally directed or permitted her legal assistant to elicit a known false statement from a potential witness.)

- *State ex rel. Youngblood v. Sanders*, 575 S.E.2d 864 (Supreme Court of West Virginia, 2002) (A generalized discussion between the first codefendant's wife and the attorney's paralegal did not establish that the wife communicated confidential information so as to disqualify the attorney from representing the second codefendant, based on a conflict of interest, after the first codefendant decided not to hire attorney.)

- *Office of Disciplinary Counsel v. Battistelli*, 465 S.E.2d 644 (Supreme Court of Appeals of West Virginia, 1995) (Suspended attorney can work as a paralegal but must have no contact with clients.)

Doing Legal Research in West Virginia Law

- **Statutes:** www.legis.state.wv.us /wvcode/code.cfm
- **Cases:**www.courtswv.gov/supreme -court/opinions.html
- **Court Rules:**www.courtswv.gov /legal-community/court-rules.html
- **General:**www.romingerlegal.com /state/westvirginia.html

Finding Employment in West Virginia

- www.legalstaff.com/Common /HomePage.aspx
- careers.findlaw.com (enter *Paralegal* and *West Virginia*)
- www.indeed.com/q-Paralegal-l -West-Virginia-jobs.html
- wv.craigslist.org/lgl

WISCONSIN

ETHICS CODE AND OPINIONS IN WISCONSIN

- **Attorneys: Wisconsin Code:** *Rules of Professional Conduct*
  - www.legis.state.wi.us/rsb/scr/5200 .pdf
  - www.wicourts.gov/sc/rules/chap20a .pdf
  - www.wicourts.gov/supreme/sc_rules .jsp
  - www.law.cornell.edu/ethics /wisconsin.html
  - See also ethics links in Helpful Websites at the end of Chapter 5.
- **Attorneys: Wisconsin Ethics Opinions**
  - www.wisbar.org (enter *paralegal* in the search box)
- **Unauthorized Practice of Law in Wisconsin**
  - www.wisbar.org (enter *unauthorized practice of law* in search box)
  - ir.lawnet.fordham.edu/cgi /viewcontent.cgi?article=3572&con text=flr

- **Paralegals and Other Nonattorneys: Wisconsin**
  - *Rule 20:5.3.* For a discussion of the state's ethics Rule 5.3 ("Responsibilities Regarding Nonlawyer Assistants") in the Wisconsin *Rules of Professional Conduct*, see Chapter 5. For the text of 5.3 in Wisconsin, see www.legis.state.wi.us/rsb/scr/5200 .pdf.
  - *Rule 20:1.10 (Comment 4).* The rule of imputed disqualification in Rule 1.10 "does not prohibit representation by others in the law firm where the person prohibited from involvement in a matter is a nonlawyer, such as a paralegal or legal secretary." Wisconsin *Rules of Professional Conduct*.
  - *Rule 20:5.5 (Comment 2).* Lawyers can employ the services of paralegals and delegate tasks to them "so long as the lawyer supervises the delegated work and retains responsibility for their work."
  - *Rule 20:5.5 (Comment 3).* Lawyers can assist independent paraprofessionals, who are authorized to provide particular law-related services.
  - Wisconsin State Bar, Paralegal Task Force, *Proposed Ethics Rules for Paralegals.* (in the search box of www .wisbar.org, type "ethics rules for paralegals").
  - An attorney whose license to practice law is suspended or revoked or who is suspended from the practice of law may not engage in the practice of law or in any law work activity customarily done by paralegals. Rule 22.26 (f)(2).
  - Law firm letterhead can include the names of paralegals as long as their nonattorney status is made clear. State Bar of Wisconsin, *Opinion E-85–6* (10/1985). See also Opinion *E-83–3* allowing announcements of nonattorneys joining a firm (reversing *Opinion E-80–15*).
  - The office of the district attorney and the office of a circuit judge can share the services of a paralegal as long as the paralegal is supervised so as to maintain the confidentiality of each office. State Bar of Wisconsin, *Opinion E-86–13* (9/24/86).
  - A paralegal can have a business card containing the law firm's name but. State Bar of Wisconsin, *Opinion E-75–22*.
  - A paralegal can be listed on law firm letterhead. State Bar of Wisconsin, *Opinion E-85–6*.
  - A paralegal is allowed to attend a real estate closing on behalf of a

client without a supervising attorney being present if the paralegal is trained and the client consents, but the paralegal cannot give legal advice or legal opinions at the closing. Wisconsin State Bar, *Opinion E-95-3* (7/1998).

■ A paralegal who is a licensed real estate broker cannot appear at a real estate closing. "If a paralegal from the attorney's office appears at the closing, it will seem that he is there in a legal capacity." State Bar of Wisconsin, *Opinion E-80-2.*

■ A law firm can hire a litigation paralegal who will also provide court reporting services to other attorneys. State Bar of Wisconsin, *Opinion E-86-19* (12/12/86).

Defining Legal Assistants/Paralegals in Wisconsin

■ "Paralegal" means an individual qualified through education and training, employed or retained to perform substantive legal work and supervised by an attorney licensed to practice law in this state, requiring a sufficient knowledge of legal concepts that, absent the paralegal, the attorney would perform the work. State Bar of Wisconsin, Paralegal Practice Task Force, *Final Report* (2004) In Google, Bing, or Yahoo, enter this search Wisconsin Paralegal Practice Task Force.

Defining the Practice of Law in Wisconsin

■ § 757.30(2) *(Wisconsin Statutes Annotated)*: Every person who appears as agent, representative or attorney, for or on behalf of any other person, or any firm, partnership, association or corporation in any action or proceeding in or before any court of record, court commissioner, or judicial tribunal of the United States, or of any state, or who otherwise, in or out of court, for compensation or pecuniary reward gives professional legal advice not incidental to his or her usual or ordinary business, or renders any legal service for any other person, or any firm, partnership, association or corporation, shall be deemed to be practicing law within the meaning of this section.

Paralegals (and Others) in Wisconsin State and Federal Courts

(See the beginning of this appendix on how to find the full text of the opinions cited here, including WL opinions.)

■ *Ernst v. Narlock*, 314 Wis.2d 519, 822 N.W.2d 736 (Court of Appeals of Wisconsin, 2012) (State Farm then deposed the Estate attorney's legal assistant, who the Estate claimed had served State Farm. The legal assistant testified that she had never previously served legal process and was not instructed on what she was supposed to do. The legal assistant did not inform the receptionist that she was there to serve legal process. The assistant did not prepare an affidavit of service and could not confirm that the envelope she handed the receptionist contained an authenticated copy of the summons and complaint. The assistant testified that she did not know what "authenticated" meant.)

■ *In re Disciplinary Proceedings Against Weigel*, 342 Wis.2d 129, 810 N.W.2d 835 (Supreme Court of Wisconsin, 2012) (Attorney's conduct, paying firm's paralegal bonuses based in part on gross recoveries from personal injury cases paralegal had worked on, did not violate rule prohibiting attorney from sharing legal fees with a nonlawyer. Some of the nonlawyer personnel employed by the firm, including this paralegal, are compensated on an "incentive" or "bonus" system. The paralegal is compensated for her services as follows: She is paid a base hourly wage ($7.00 or $7.50 per hour) plus overtime pay for work in excess of 40 hours per week and on weekends, as mandated by the Fair Labor Standards Act. In addition to her base pay, the paralegal receives two forms of bonus: (1) thirty cents per thousand dollars (three-tenths of one percent) of the gross recoveries from personal injury cases she worked on; and (2) a quarterly bonus consisting of $1,500 plus $250 per thousand (25 percent) of the difference between a weekly average (computed quarterly, over 13 weeks) of gross recoveries from personal injury cases she worked on and her weekly goal of $127,500 per week.)

■ *In re Disciplinary Proceedings Against Compton*, 744 N.W.2d 78 (Supreme Court of Wisconsin, 2008) (Attorney's conduct in submitting bills to the office of the State Public Defender for work he alleged that he had performed, but was in fact performed by a paralegal, violated the professional rules that prohibited a lawyer from engaging in conduct involving dishonesty, fraud, deceit or misrepresentation and required a lawyer to make reasonable

efforts to ensure that his nonlawyer assistant's conduct was compatible with the professional obligations of the lawyer.)

■ *In re Disciplinary Proceedings Against Robinson*, 700 N.W.2d 757 (Supreme Court of Wisconsin, 2005) (Attorney's act in instructing a legal assistant to notarize a signature indicating that the signer of the deed was present when in fact he was not violated professional rule making an attorney responsible for conduct of nonlawyer assistants. SCR 20:5.3(c)(1).)

■ *Austin v. CUNA Mutual Insurance Society*, 240 Federal Rules Decisions 420 (U.S. District Court, W.D. Wisconsin, 2006) (Paralegals, called "law specialists," sue for failure to pay overtime compensation.)

■ *Abbott v. Marker*, 722 N.W.2d 162 (Court of Appeals of Wisconsin, 2006) (Nonlawyer's alleged agreement with attorney to refer potential clients in exchange for a percentage of the attorney fees violated public policy and statutes providing that it is illegal for a party to solicit retainers or agreements from another party for an attorney and illegal for an attorney to split legal fees with nonattorneys and, thus, was unenforceable.)

■ *In re Disciplinary Proceedings Against Bryan*, __ N.W.2d __, 2014 WL 2841959 (Supreme Court of Wisconsin, 2014) (An attorney whose license to practice law is suspended or revoked or who is suspended from the practice of law may not engage in this state in the practice of law or in any law work activity customarily done by law students, law clerks, or other paralegal personnel, except that the attorney may engage in law related work in this state for a commercial employer itself not engaged in the practice of law. SCR 22.26.)

■ *In re Webster*, 120 Bankruptcy Reporter 111 (U.S. Bankruptcy Court, E.D. Wisconsin, 1990) (Injunction issued against a nonattorney for engaging in the unauthorized practice of law in providing bankruptcy services.)

■ *Alexander v. City of Milwaukee*, 2006 WL 277114 (U.S. District Court, E.D. Wisconsin, 2006) ("I am well aware that counsel is more comfortable attending a deposition when the paralegal is at his or her side. However, when the deposition being taken is that of your own clients, generally speaking there is little need for the attendance of a paralegal. On the other hand, because of the voluminous material involved in this case, I will allow compensation for the paralegal's attendance at the deposition of the Defendants and others identified with the defense.")

- *Hutchison v. Amateur Electronic Supply*, 42 F.3d 1037, 1048 (U.S. Court of Appeals, 7th Circuit, 1994) (Fee award reduced for "failure to utilize paralegals.")
- *EEOC v. Accurate Mechanical Contractors, Inc.*, 863 F. Supp. 828 (U.S. District Court, E.D. Wisconsin, 1994) (Paralegal fees are limited to work performed by paralegals that would otherwise be performed by an attorney.)
- *Purdy v. Security Savings. . .*, 727 F. Supp. 1266, 1270 (U.S. District Court, E.D. Wisconsin, 1989) (It is "clearly excessive" to claim six and a half hours of paralegal time to cite check a document with only forty citations in it.)

Doing Legal Research in Wisconsin Law

- **Statutes:** legis.wisconsin.gov/rsb /stats.html
- **Cases:** legis.wisconsin.gov/rsb /wislawsources.html
- **Court Rules:** wicourts.gov/scrules /index.htm
- **General:** wilawlibrary.gov/learn /legalresearch.html

Finding Employment in Wisconsin

- l.wi.bar.associationcareernetwork .com/Common/HomePage.aspx
- careers.findlaw.com (select *Paralegal* and *Wisconsin*)
- www.indeed.com/q-Paralegal-l -Wisconsin-jobs.html
- www.careerbuilder.com/jobs/wi /keyword/paralegal
- milwaukee.craigslist.org/search /lgl?query=+

WYOMING

ETHICS CODE AND OPINIONS IN WYOMING

- **Attorneys: Wyoming Ethics Code:** *Rules of Professional Conduct*
  - www.courts.state.wy.us/WSC /CourtRule?RuleNumber=62
  - www.law.cornell.edu/ethics/wy/code /WY_CODE.HTM
  - www.wyomingbar.org/complaints /lawyers.html
  - See also ethics links in Helpful Websites at the end of Chapter 5.

- **Attorneys: Wyoming Rules on the Unauthorized Practice of Law**
  - www.courts.state.wy.us/WSC /CourtRule?RuleNumber=77
- **Unauthorized Practice of Law: Wyoming**
  - www.wyomingbar.org/bar_journal /article.html?id=43
  - ir.lawnet.fordham.edu/cgi /viewcontent.cgi?article=3572&con text=flr
- **Attorneys: Wyoming Ethics Opinions**
  - www.uwyo.edu/lawlib/research -guides/ethics.html
- **Paralegals and Other Nonattorneys: Wyoming**
  - *Rule 5.3.* For a discussion of the state's ethics Rule 5.3 ("Responsibilities Regarding Nonlawyer Assistants") in the *Wyoming Rules of Professional Conduct*, see Chapter 5. For the text of 5.3 in Wyoming, see www.courts.state.wy.us/WSC /CourtRule?RuleNumber=62.
  - *Rule 1.10 (Comment 4).* The rule of imputed disqualification in Rule 1.10 "does not prohibit representation by others in the law firm where the person prohibited from involvement in a matter is a nonlawyer, such as a paralegal or legal secretary." *Wyoming Rules of Professional Conduct.*
  - *Rule 5.5* (Comment 2). Lawyers can employ the services of paraprofessionals and delegate tasks to them "so long as the lawyer supervises the delegated work and retains responsibility for their work."
  - *Rule 8.4(g)* It is professional misconduct for a lawyer to "knowingly employ" or to contract with any person in the practice of law who has been disbarred or is under suspension from the practice of law in any position or capacity as a paralegal whether or not compensation is paid. *Wyoming Rules of Professional Conduct.*
  - *Mendicino v. Whitchurch*, 565 P.2d 460, 478 (Supreme Court of Wyoming, 1977) (A suspended attorney shall not participate in the practice of law as an attorney or paralegal.)

Defining the Practice of Law in Wyoming

- Rule 11 (*Wyoming Rules of Procedure Governing Unauthorized Practice* of Law):. . . (2) The core element of practicing law is the giving of legal advice to a client. Factors to be applied in determining between legal and non-legal

advice include: (A) the specificity of the advice; (B) the likelihood that the advice will be erroneous; and (C) the degree of harm to the recipient if the advice is erroneous. (3) Any activity which calls for the exercise of discretion, such as interviewing or advising another about the legal effect of certain choices, involves the practice of law. (4) Receiving money for drafting documents or performing other services involving legal matters constitutes the practice of law. (5) Holding one's self out as qualified to assist others in legal matters constitutes the practice of law. (www.courts.state.wy.us/WSC /CourtRule?RuleNumber=77)

Paralegals (and Others) in Wyoming State and Federal Courts

(See the beginning of this appendix on how to find the full text of the opinions cited here.)

- *Books v. Zebre*, 792 P.2d 196, 220 (Supreme Court of Wyoming, 1990) (A "lawyer who approaches a represented third party without going through counsel should be severely punished. And this is so though the lawyer uses a law representative or paralegal to do his dirty work").
- *Board of Professional Responsibility v. Kleinsmith*, 302 P.3d 1290, 1295 (Supreme Court of Wyoming, 2013) (The attorney violated Rule 5.3 when he failed to train and supervise his paralegal on appropriate filing procedures.)
- *In re NRF*, 294 P.3d 879 (Supreme Court of Wyoming, 2013) (The attorney failed to exercise billing judgment when he made many billing entries for clerical work (such as walking to and from the courthouse to file or retrieve documents) that was billed at attorney's regular hourly rate.)
- *Versteeg v. Bennett. . .*, 839 F. Supp. 2d 1238, 1242 (U.S. District Court, Wyoming, 2011) (Mr. Schroth has provided billing statements for time spent on this case. Those statements demonstrate [attorney] time that was spent on paralegal and secretarial tasks, including letters and conversations with process servers, serving and filing documents, including certificates of service. . . . Additionally, the billing records are cursory and it is often difficult to tell what work was done by the attorney. Rather than making a percentage cut across all the fees the Court has gone through the billing statement and disallowed

time that was spent on paralegal or legal secretary tasks, such as letters and calls to process servers, preparing certificates of service, filing documents and sending documents. While the Court has attempted to give counsel the benefit of the doubt regarding whether time was appropriately spent, there are some time entries that are so cursory that the Court has disallowed them because there is no basis for the Court to find these entries were for reasonable time spent on the case.)

Doing Legal Research in Wyoming Law

- **Statutes:** legisweb.state.wy.us /LSOWEB/wyStatutes.aspx
- **Cases:** www.courts.state.wy.us
- **Court Rules:** www.courts.state .wy.us/WSC/CourtRules
- **General:** www.romingerlegal.com /state/wyoming.html

Finding Employment in Wyoming

- See Exhibit 2-12 in Chapter 2.
- www.wyomingbar.org/job_bank /find_job.html
- www.simplyhired.com/k-paralegal-l -cheyenne-wy-jobs.html
- www.indeed.com/q-Legal-Assistant -l-Wyoming-jobs.html
- wyoming.craigslist.org/search /lgl?query=+

ETHICAL CODES OF NALA, NFPA, AND NALS

As indicated in Chapter 4, the major national paralegal associations have ethical codes. (See Exhibit 5-4 in Chapter 5.) Here are excerpts from these codes.

NALA CODE OF ETHICS AND PROFESSIONAL RESPONSIBILITY

NATIONAL ASSOCIATION OF LEGAL ASSISTANTS (WWW.NALA.ORG/CODE.ASPX)

Each NALA member agrees to follow the canons of the NALA Code of Ethics and Professional Responsibility. Violations of the Code may result in cancellation of membership. First adopted by the NALA membership in May of 1975, the Code of Ethics and Professional Responsibility is the foundation of ethical practices of paralegals in the legal community.

A paralegal must adhere strictly to the accepted standards of legal ethics and to the general principles of proper conduct. The performance of the duties of the paralegal shall be governed by specific canons as defined herein so that justice will be served and goals of the profession attained.

The canons of ethics set forth hereafter are adopted by the National Association of Legal Assistants, Inc., as a general guide intended to aid paralegals and attorneys. The enumeration of these rules does not mean there are not others of equal importance although not specifically mentioned. Court rules, agency rules and statutes must be taken into consideration when interpreting the canons.

Definition: Legal assistants, also known as paralegals, are a distinguishable group of persons who assist attorneys in the delivery of legal services. Through formal education, training and experience, legal assistants have knowledge and expertise regarding the legal system and substantive and procedural law which qualify them to do work of a legal nature under the supervision of an attorney. In 2001, NALA members adopted the ABA definition of a legal assistant/paralegal, as follows: A legal assistant or paralegal is a person qualified by education, training or work experience who is employed or retained by a lawyer, law office, corporation, governmental agency or other entity who performs specifically delegated substantive legal work for which a lawyer is responsible. (Adopted by the ABA in 1997)

Canon 1. A paralegal must not perform any of the duties that attorneys only may perform nor take any actions that attorneys may not take.

Canon 2. A paralegal may perform any task which is properly delegated and supervised by an attorney, as long as the attorney is ultimately responsible to the client, maintains a direct relationship with the client, and assumes professional responsibility for the work product.

Canon 3. A paralegal must not:

(a) engage in, encourage, or contribute to any act which could constitute the unauthorized practice of law; and

(b) establish attorney-client relationships, set fees, give legal opinions or advice or represent a client before a court or agency unless so authorized by that court or agency; and

(c) engage in conduct or take any action which would assist or involve the attorney in a violation of professional ethics or give the appearance of professional impropriety.

Canon 4. A paralegal must use discretion and professional judgment commensurate with knowledge and experience but must not render independent legal judgment in place of an attorney. The services of an attorney are essential in the public interest whenever such legal judgment is required.

Canon 5. A paralegal must disclose his or her status as a paralegal at the outset of any professional relationship with a client, attorney, a court or administrative agency or personnel thereof, or a member of the general public. A paralegal must act prudently in determining the extent to which a client may be assisted without the presence of an attorney.

Canon 6. A paralegal must strive to maintain integrity and a high degree of competency through education and training with respect to professional responsibility, local rules and practice, and through continuing education in substantive areas of law to better assist the legal profession in fulfilling its duty to provide legal service.

Canon 7. A paralegal must protect the confidences of a client and must not violate any rule or statute now in effect or hereafter enacted controlling the doctrine of privileged communications between a client and an attorney.

Canon 8. A paralegal must disclose to his or her employer or prospective employer any pre-existing client or personal relationship that may conflict with the interests of the employer or prospective employer and/or their clients.

Canon 9. A paralegal must do all other things incidental, necessary, or expedient for the attainment of the ethics and responsibilities as defined by statute or rule of court.

Canon 10. A paralegal's conduct is guided by bar associations' codes of professional responsibility and rules of professional conduct.

(Copyright 1975; revised 1979, 1988, 1995, 2007. Reprinted with permission of the National Association of Legal Assistants, www.nala.org, 1516 S. Boston, #200, Tulsa, OK 74119)

NFPA MODEL CODE OF ETHICS AND PROFESSIONAL RESPONSIBILITY

NATIONAL FEDERATION OF PARALEGAL ASSOCIATIONS (WWW.PARALEGALS.ORG) (CLICK *POSITIONS AND ISSUES* AND THEN *ETHICS.*)

1.1. A paralegal shall achieve and maintain a high level of competence.

EC 1.1(a) A paralegal shall achieve competency through education, training, and work experience.

EC 1.1(b) A paralegal shall aspire to participate in a minimum of twelve (12) hours of continuing legal education, to include at least one (1) hour of ethics education, every two (2) years in order to remain current on developments in the law.

EC 1.1(c) A paralegal shall perform all assignments promptly and efficiently.

1.2. A paralegal shall maintain a high level of personal and professional integrity.

EC 1.2(a) A paralegal shall not engage in any ex parte communications involving the courts or any other adjudicatory body in an attempt to exert undue influence or to obtain advantage or the benefit of only one party.

EC 1.2(b) A paralegal shall not communicate, or cause another to communicate, with a party the paralegal knows to be represented by a lawyer in a pending matter without the prior consent of the lawyer representing such other party.

EC 1.2(c) A paralegal shall ensure that all timekeeping and billing records prepared by the paralegal are thorough, accurate, honest, and complete.

EC 1.2(d) A paralegal shall not knowingly engage in fraudulent billing practices. Such practices may include, but are not limited to: inflation of hours billed to a client or employer; misrepresentation of the nature of tasks performed; and/or submission of fraudulent expense and disbursement documentation.

EC 1.2(e) A paralegal shall be scrupulous, thorough and honest in the identification and maintenance of all funds, securities, and other assets of a client and shall provide accurate accounting as appropriate.

EC 1.2(f) A paralegal shall advise the proper authority of non-confidential knowledge of any dishonest or fraudulent acts by any person pertaining to the handling of the funds, securities or other assets of a client. The authority to whom the report is made shall depend on the nature and circumstances of the possible misconduct, (e.g., ethics committees of law firms, corporations and/or paralegal associations, local or state bar associations, local prosecutors, administrative agencies, etc.). Failure to report such knowledge is in itself misconduct and shall be treated as such under these rules.

1.3. A paralegal shall maintain a high standard of professional conduct.

EC-1.3(a) A paralegal shall refrain from engaging in any conduct that offends the dignity and decorum of proceedings before a court or other adjudicatory body and shall be respectful of all rules and procedures.

EC-1.3(b) A paralegal shall avoid impropriety and the appearance of impropriety and shall not engage in any conduct that would adversely affect his/her fitness to practice. Such conduct may include, but is not limited to: violence, dishonesty, interference with the administration of justice, and/or abuse of a professional position or public office.

EC-1.3(c) Should a paralegal's fitness to practice be compromised by physical or mental illness, causing that paralegal to commit an act that is in direct violation of the Model Code/Model Rules and/or the rules and/or laws governing the jurisdiction in which the paralegal practices, that paralegal may be protected from sanction upon review of the nature and circumstances of that illness.

EC-1.3(d) A paralegal shall advise the proper authority of non-confidential knowledge of any action of another legal professional that clearly demonstrates fraud, deceit, dishonesty, or misrepresentation. The authority to whom the report is made shall depend on the nature and circumstances of the possible misconduct, (e.g., ethics committees of law firms, corporations and/or paralegal associations, local or state bar associations, local prosecutors, administrative agencies, etc.). Failure to report such knowledge is in itself misconduct and shall be treated as such under these rules.

EC-1.3(e) A paralegal shall not knowingly assist any individual with the commission of an act that is in direct violation of the Model Code/Model Rules and/or the rules and/or laws governing the jurisdiction in which the paralegal practices.

EC-1.3(f) If a paralegal possesses knowledge of future criminal activity, that knowledge must be reported to the appropriate authority immediately.

1.4. A paralegal shall serve the public interest by contributing to the improvement of the legal system and delivery of quality legal services, including pro bono publico services.

EC-1.4(a) A paralegal shall be sensitive to the legal needs of the public and shall promote the development and implementation of programs that address those needs.

EC-1.4(b) A paralegal shall support efforts to improve the legal system and access thereto and shall assist in making changes.

EC-1.4(c) A paralegal shall support and participate in the delivery of Pro Bono Publico services directed toward implementing and improving access to justice, the law, the legal system or the paralegal and legal professions.

EC-1.4(d) A paralegal should aspire annually to contribute twenty-four (24) hours of Pro Bono Publico services under the supervision of an attorney or as authorized by administrative, statutory or court authority to:

1. persons of limited means; or
2. charitable, religious, civic, community, governmental and educational organizations in matters that are designed primarily to address the legal needs of persons with limited means; or
3. individuals, groups or organizations seeking to secure or protect civil rights, civil liberties or public rights.

The twenty-four (24) hours of Pro Bono Publico services contributed annually by a paralegal may consist of such services as detailed in this EC-1.4(d), and/or administrative matters designed to develop and implement the attainment of this aspiration as detailed above in EC-1.41.4(a)(b)(c), or any combination of the two.

1.5. A paralegal shall preserve all confidential information provided by the client or acquired from other sources before, during, and after the course of the professional relationship.

EC-1.5(a) A paralegal shall be aware of and abide by all legal authority governing confidential information in the jurisdiction in which the paralegal practices.

EC-1.5(b) A paralegal shall not use confidential information to the disadvantage of the client.

EC-1.5(c) A paralegal shall not use confidential information to the advantage of the paralegal or of a third person.

EC-1.5(d) A paralegal may reveal confidential information only after full disclosure and with the client's written consent; or, when required by law or court order; or, when necessary to prevent the client from committing an act that could result in death or serious bodily harm.

EC-1.5(e) A paralegal shall keep those individuals responsible for the legal representation of a client fully informed of any confidential information the paralegal may have pertaining to that client.

EC-1.5(f) A paralegal shall not engage in any indiscreet communications concerning clients.

1.6. A paralegal shall avoid conflicts of interest and shall disclose any possible conflict to the employer or client, as well as to the prospective employers or clients.

EC-1.6(a) A paralegal shall act within the bounds of the law, solely for the benefit of the client, and shall be free of compromising influences and loyalties. Neither the paralegal's personal or business interest, nor those of other clients or third persons, should compromise the paralegal's professional judgment and loyalty to the client.

EC-1.6(b) A paralegal shall avoid conflicts of interest that may arise from previous assignments, whether for a present or past employer or client.

EC-1.6(c) A paralegal shall avoid conflicts of interest that may arise from family relationships and from personal and business interests.

EC-1.6(d) In order to be able to determine whether an actual or potential conflict of interest exists, a paralegal shall create and maintain an effective recordkeeping system that identifies clients, matters, and parties with which the paralegal has worked.

EC-1.6(e) A paralegal shall reveal sufficient non-confidential information about a client or former client to reasonably ascertain if an actual or potential conflict of interest exists.

EC-1.6(f) A paralegal shall not participate in or conduct work on any matter where a conflict of interest has been identified.

EC-1.6(g) In matters where a conflict of interest has been identified and the client consents to continued representation, a paralegal shall comply fully with the implementation and maintenance of an Ethical Wall.

1.7. A paralegal's title shall be fully disclosed.

EC-1.7(a) A paralegal's title shall clearly indicate the individual's status and shall be disclosed in all business and professional communications to avoid misunderstandings and misconceptions about the paralegal's role and responsibilities.

EC-1.7(b) A paralegal's title shall be included if the paralegal's name appears on business cards, letterhead, brochures, directories, and advertisements.

EC-1.7(c) A paralegal shall not use letterhead, business cards or other promotional materials to create a fraudulent impression of his/her status or ability to practice in the jurisdiction in which the paralegal practices.

EC-1.7(d) A paralegal shall not practice under color of any record, diploma, or certificate that has been illegally or fraudulently obtained or issued or which is misrepresentative in any way.

EC-1.7(e) A paralegal shall not participate in the creation, issuance, or dissemination of fraudulent records, diplomas, or certificates.

1.8. A paralegal shall not engage in the unauthorized practice of law.

EC-1.8(a) A paralegal shall comply with the applicable legal authority governing the unauthorized practice of law in the jurisdiction in which the paralegal practices.

(Reprinted with permission of National Federation of Paralegal Associations)

NALS CODE OF ETHICS

NALS THE ASSOCIATION FOR LEGAL PROFESSIONALS (WWW.NALS.ORG) (UNDER *JOIN*, CLICK *ABOUT NALS*)

Members of NALS are bound by the objectives of this association and the standards of conduct required of the legal profession. Every member shall:

- Encourage respect for the law and the administration of justice;
- Observe rules governing privileged communications and confidential information;
- Promote and exemplify high standards of loyalty, cooperation, and courtesy;
- Perform all duties of the profession with integrity and competence; and
- Pursue a high order of professional attainment.

Integrity and high standards of conduct are fundamental to the success of our professional association. This Code is promulgated by the NALS and accepted by its members to accomplish these ends.

Canon 1. Members of this association shall maintain a high degree of competency and integrity through continuing education to better assist the legal profession in fulfilling its duty to provide quality legal services to the public.

Canon 2. Members of this association shall maintain a high standard of ethical conduct and shall contribute to the integrity of the association and the legal profession.

Canon 3. Members of this association shall avoid a conflict of interest pertaining to a client matter.

Canon 4. Members of this association shall preserve and protect the confidences and privileged communications of a client.

Canon 5. Members of this association shall exercise care in using independent professional judgment and in determining the extent to which a client may be assisted without the presence of a lawyer and shall not act in matters involving professional legal judgment.

Canon 6. Members of this association shall not solicit legal business on behalf of a lawyer.

Canon 7. Members of this association, unless permitted by law, shall not perform paralegal functions except under the direct supervision of a lawyer and shall not advertise or contract with members of the general public for the performance of paralegal functions.

Canon 8. Members of this association, unless permitted by law, shall not perform any of the duties restricted to lawyers or do things which lawyers themselves may not do and shall assist in preventing the unauthorized practice of law.

Canon 9. Members of this association not licensed to practice law shall not engage in the practice of law as defined by statutes or court decisions.

Canon 10. Members of this association shall do all other things incidental, necessary, or expedient to enhance professional responsibility and participation in the administration of justice and public service in cooperation with the legal profession.

(Reprinted with permission of NALS the Association of Legal Professionals)

PARALEGAL BLOGS

- **LISTS OF ALL LEGAL BLOGS**
  (sometimes called blawgs)
  - blawgsearch.justia.com/blogs
  - www.abajournal.com/blawgs/by_topic
  - www.blogsearchengine.org (enter *paralegal* in search box)

- **PARALEGAL BLOGS**
  - **ABC's of E-Discovery**
    ediscoverybasics.blogspot.com
  - **Atlanta Paralegal Services**
    www.atlantaparalegalservices.com
  - **Bankruptcy**
    www.713bankruptcy.com
  - **California Family Law Paralegal**
    californiafamilylawparalegal.com
  - **The California Litigator**
    thecalifornialitigator.com
  - **California Paralegal**
    californiaparalegal.blogspot.com
  - **Digital Paralegal Services**
    www.digitalparalegalservices.com/blog
  - **The Empowered Paralegal**
    theempoweredparalegal.com
  - **The Estrin report**
    estrinlegaled.typepad.com
  - **Florida Paralegal**
    floridaparalegal.blogspot.com
  - **Haley's Law Blog (legal technology+)**
    haleyodom.com
  - **IPA Blog (Indiana)**
    indianaparalegals.blogspot.com
  - **Legaco Express for Paralegals**
    www.legaco.org
  - **Linda's Paralegal Services**
    miamifrp.com

  - **Mom-alegal's Blog**
    mom2tomtom.wordpress.com
  - **National Association of Freelance Legal Professionals**
    freelancelegalprofessionals.blogspot.com
  - **New York Paralegal**
    newyorkparalegalonline.blogspot.com
  - **New York Paralegal Blog**
    www.newyorkparalegalblog.com
  - **Ohio Paralegal**
    ohioparalegal.blogspot.com
  - **Pamela the Paralegal**
    pamelatheparalegal.com
  - **The Paralegal**
    theparalegal.wordpress.com
  - **Paralegal Blaw Blaw Blaw**
    lorijpaul.com
  - **Paralegalese**
    para-mel.blogspot.com
  - **Paralegal Essentials**
    paralegalessentials.wordpress.com
  - **Paralegal Ethics**
    paralegal-ethics.blogspot.com
  - **Paralegal Gateway**
    www.facebook.com/ParalegalGateway
    www.abajournal.com/blawg/paralegalgateways_weblog
  - **Paralegal Hell**
    paralegalhell.com
  - **Paralegal Illuminati (Property Laws)**
    paralegal-illuminati.com
  - **Paralegal-ish**
    paralegal-ish.blogspot.com
  - **Paralegalities**
    paralegalities.weebly.com
  - **A Paralegal's Life**
    aparalegalslife.blogspot.com

  - **The Paralegal Mentor**
    www.paralegalmentorblog.com
  - **Paralegal Pie**
    www.paralegalpie.com
  - **Paralegal Pundit**
    theparalegalpundit.wordpress.com
  - **Paralegal Scope (Canada)**
    paralegalscope.com
  - **The Paralegal Society**
    theparalegalsociety.wordpress.com
  - **Pennsylvania Paralegal**
    pennsylvaniaparalegal.blogspot.com
  - **The Poor Paralegal**
    thepoorparalegal.blogspot.com
  - **Practical Paralegalism**
    www.practicalparalegalism.com
  - **Purple Paralegal**
    purpleparalegal.wordpress.com
  - **The Researching Paralegal**
    researchingparalegal.com
  - **Scribe (Legal Document Assistants)**
    legaldocumentassistant.blogspot.com
  - **Sonoma Freelance**
    sonomafreelance.blogspot.com
  - **Parasec: The Source**
    parasec.wordpress.com
  - **Texas Paralegal**
    texasparalegalonline.blogspot.com
  - **Texas Paralegal Division Blog**
    blog.txpd.org
  - **Verbal Insanity**
    verbalinsanity.com

STARTING A FREELANCE PARALEGAL BUSINESS

INTRODUCTION

Sometime during their career, most paralegals wonder what it would be like to own their own business and be their own boss as a freelance paralegal.

There are two major kinds of businesses that paralegals have formed:

1. A business that offers legal and law-related services directly to the public without attorney supervision. These document service providers (DSPs) are independent contractors who are sometimes called *freelance paralegals, independent paralegals, or legal technicians*. (Some states, however, restrict the title of *paralegal* to persons who work under attorney supervision. See the discussion in Chapter 4 of the *legal document assistant* in California and the *legal document preparer* in Arizona.)
2. A business that offers services to attorneys who supervise the work done for them. These paralegals running this business are independent contractors who are sometimes called *freelance paralegals, independent paralegals, or contract paralegals*. They perform their services under attorney supervision even though they are not employees of attorneys.

Our focus in this appendix is the second category of business—the freelance paralegal who offers services to attorneys—although much of what is said will apply as well to the first category.

Running your own business is a major undertaking. Veteran freelance paralegals frequently comment on the time commitment that they must make. "You need to understand that you'll never work harder than when you own your own business."[1] If you become successful, nine-to-five work days will probably be rare. "There are no 'normal' work hours," reports a freelance paralegal in California who once had an attorney client show up on Sunday, December 24, 2000, "with paperwork that had to be prepared before the rules changed on January 1, 2001."[2] Another freelancer cautions that you need to subscribe to the "old adage that you work 80 hours a week just so you don't have to work 40 hours a week for someone else."[3] For most freelancers just starting out, patience is key. On a recent discussion on LinkedIn about freelance paralegals, one successful freelancer commented that "it usually takes between 1-2 years for any new business to really get going."

Yet the rewards of success in this endeavor can be substantial. In an article called *Following My Dream*, a freelance paralegal exclaimed, upon receiving her first check as a freelance paralegal, "I thought I had died and gone to entrepreneurial paralegal heaven."[4]

SHOULD I DO IT?

Is owning a freelance business a realistic option for you? Should you do it? Not many paralegals are in business as freelance paralegals. Surveys show that they constitute between 1 and 2 percent of paralegals in the country, although the percentage who have tried to start such a business without success is higher.

Check the competition. Be sure that you know who is already providing freelance services to attorneys in your area. Run this search in Google, Bing, or Yahoo: "freelance paralegal" aa (substituting the name of your state or city for aa). Find out:

- Who else is offering freelance services?
- What kinds of services are they providing?
- What are they charging their attorney clients?

Check their names in Yelp (www.yelp.com) and other social media rating sites to see what has been said about them. Check their names on Facebook and Twitter.

The two most important questions you need to ask yourself when deciding whether to start your own freelance business are as follows:

- Do you have the expertise that attorneys want?
- Can you survive without a steady cash flow during your first year in business?

Expertise

Attorneys expect you to be an expert in what they are asking you to do. They will take the time to tell you what they want done; *they will almost never take the time to explain to you how to do it*. You are expected to know. Consequently, the vast majority of successful freelance paralegals do not go into business until they have had years of experience, primarily as traditional paralegals employed by attorneys. Here are some examples of tasks commonly performed by freelance paralegals that you will need to know how to do *before* anyone is likely to hire you to perform them:

- Digest the transcript of depositions or other litigation documents.
- Collect and digest medical records.
- Prepare the 706 federal estate tax return.
- Prepare all the documents needed to probate an estate.
- Prepare trial exhibits.
- Incorporate a business.
- Search public records for assets of a debtor.

- Conduct a due-diligence search.
- Compile a chain of title to real property.
- Prepare and file trademark and patent applications.

Whether you are able to perform any of these tasks will, of course, depend on what specialties you developed while you were an employed paralegal.

There are, however, some freelance assignments that do not require great skill. For example:

- Bates stamp litigation documents.
- Encode litigation documents in a computer database.
- Complete service of process.
- File pleadings in court.

Yet these assignments usually pay the least, and there may not be enough of them to keep a full-time business running. You need to be able to offer *specialized* skills. If the tasks to be done did not require such skills, the attorney would not need a competent paralegal. A temporary secretary would be sufficient for many of them.

Cash Flow

If you depend on the security of a steady flow of income every week or month, it is too soon to start your freelance business. You need to have a cash reserve that will keep you in minimum survival mode until you find out whether your business will work. How long will it take to find this out? Although circumstances will differ from person to person, as a rule of thumb, you should have enough savings to sustain your personal life and your new business for six months to a year.

The cash-flow problem is not simply due to the fact that it will take time to develop attorney clients for your business. Payment delays also cause cash-flow headaches. A freelance paralegal may not be paid immediately upon completing an assignment. Law firms have their own cash-flow problems. An attorney might take the position that the freelance paralegal will be paid when the attorney is paid. In some cases, the attorney must wait months for payment. This, of course, can place great strains on the finances of a paralegal's business. On one of the paralegal electronic mailing lists, a freelance paralegal sent out the following call for help:

> "As a freelance paralegal, I find it very difficult to receive payment in a timely manner from attorneys. My terms are net/15 [meaning the net amount is to be paid within fifteen days]; however, some payments are not received for 30–60 days after the due date. Anyone have any collection tips?"

You need to know at the outset whether you may have to wait an extended period to be paid. If a satisfactory payment arrangement cannot be established with an attorney, you may have to decline the work from him or her. Many freelance paralegals require monthly payment in the agreement they sign with their attorney clients. (See the discussion of agreements below.) This, however, does not always eliminate the cash-flow problem.

BEGIN MODESTLY

Given these economic realities, you are strongly advised to begin modestly. Do not give up your day job too soon. Consider starting on a part-time basis. Find out if your current employer would have any objections to your taking some freelance cases from other law firms in the evening, on the weekend, or during your vacation. For several reasons, your employer needs to know if you are working on freelance cases. First there might be liability issues. If you are sued by one of your freelance clients for alleged negligence, your employer might be joined as a defendant in the suit even though the case of your outside client may have had nothing to do with your employer's cases. Second, there might be conflict-of-interest issues,

as we will see later. Hence, your employer must be fully informed of any outside work and reach the conclusion that the likelihood of liability or conflict is nonexistent or minimal.

Keep your overhead low. Work out of your home. The expenses of renting an office and paying a new set of utility bills can be substantial. Most freelance paralegals today are *virtual* paralegals, meaning that they communicate with their attorney clients primarily through email attachments and other online connections.

At a minimum, here is what you will need to start your business:

- A phone line dedicated to your business
- An answering machine
- Email communication
- A website that describes your services
- A LinkedIn page that describes your services and links to your website
- A Facebook page devoted to your business (separate from your personal page) that links to your other online business addresses
- A computer, word processing software such as Word, and a printer
- A basic accounting program such as Quicken
- A fax machine
- Business cards
- A flyer or brochure that lists your services

If you need a copier, start by purchasing one of the smaller ones without the expensive bells and whistles. Find out if your Internet service provider will allow you to set up a website at little or no additional charge. Although some freelance paralegals say their Internet site is not very useful for generating business, they like to have it in order to project a professional image.

Do not hire employees at the outset. You will have enough to do in getting your business off the ground and in sorting out the myriad of problems that you have probably never faced before. Even if you have enough work to justify bringing on help, it would be unwise to do so until you feel confident that the business is running smoothly. Obtaining good help is not always easy. You will have to supervise anyone who joins your staff. Too often the time required to train and monitor a new person outweighs the benefit that person provides as an assistant. Hence, you need to choose carefully. Consider these options when you are ready for help:

- Contact area paralegal schools to find out if they would be interested in having any of their students intern at your office. If you are unable to pay an intern, ask the school if an unpaid internship is possible.
- If you can pay someone, consider offering part-time work at the outset. This will give you an opportunity to assess the person's competence and the extent to which your personalities match. Terminating a full-time employee can be a wrenching experience.

YOUR MAIN WEBSITE

In addition to LinkedIn, Facebook, and perhaps Google+ accounts, you should have a website devoted to your business. Run this search in Google, Bing, or Yahoo: creating a website. Find out what the options are. Website developers can be expensive. Consider using a free website blog service that is easy to start and easy to develop. Examples include WordPress (wordpress.com) and Blogger (www.blogger.com). Free websites usually require your site to contain ads inserted by the company you used to create the site. You may have an option to avoid the ads by paying a monthly fee. For more options, run this search on Google, Bing, or Yahoo: creating an ad-free website.

LEGALITIES

You need to know the rules and regulations that govern businesses in your state. In Google, Bing, or Yahoo, run this search *starting a small business* aa (substituting your state for aa).

In addition, consult the information available from the Small Business Administration (www.sba.gov), SCORE (www.score.org), and your local chamber of commerce. Organizations such as these can often send you a packet or kit on starting a new business or can tell you where you can obtain one online, often at no cost. The organizations can also give you guidance on writing a business plan. Specialty groups in the area (e.g., professional women's groups, minority rights associations) may also be able to give you leads to available assistance for new businesses.

If you are starting out on your own, you will probably operate your business as a sole proprietorship, the simplest kind of business entity (see Chapter 14). In a sole proprietorship, one person owns all of the assets of the business and assumes all of its debts or liabilities. As a sole proprietor, you cannot separate your business debts from your personal debts. If you default on your business debts, your creditors can reach your personal assets (e.g., a car). Similarly, your business assets (e.g., a computer) can be reached to satisfy your personal debts. Other business formats exist, such as the corporation, partnership, and limited liability company. Although you should find out what the requirements, advantages, and disadvantages are for these other formats in your state, the simpler sole-proprietorship format will usually be sufficient to start a modest, one-person freelance business.

If you operate as a sole proprietorship and conduct a business under a name that does not include your surname, you may need to register your assumed or fictitious name with the state.[5]

One of your first steps should be to go to the phone book and look up the names and numbers of the agencies in your state, county, and city that have jurisdiction over businesses. They might be called the Department of Economic Development, Bureau of Licenses, Secretary of State, etc. Also look for these agencies on the websites for your state government, your county government, and your city or other local government. You want to obtain information on starting a business. For example:

- Do you need a business license from the local or state government? From both?
- As a business, what reporting requirements do you have?
- Can you operate your business out of your home? Are there any zoning restrictions on such businesses?

Almost all governments have agencies that provide information on the legal requirements for operating a business. They may also give you suggestions on the different kinds of business formats you can choose.

Also contact the tax departments of the federal, state, and local governments. You want to know what kind of tax returns you will have to file for your business. Don't wait until the end of the year (or until April) to find out. As a sole proprietorship, for example, you will probably report your income on Schedule C of your federal return. As a self-employed individual, you must make estimated tax payments every three months. Substantial social security taxes will have to be paid on your self-employment income. You may also have to pay personal property taxes on your business property. Obtain all the necessary forms and instructions well before filing time. Hiring a tax accountant to do your returns can be expensive. Even if you eventually use an accountant or other tax preparer, the best way to work intelligently with him or her is to know how to do the returns yourself.

The Internal Revenue Service (IRS) has information on tax obligations and record keeping for small businesses (www.irs.gov).

Find out if your state and local tax authorities have similar material on the Internet or that can be snail-mailed to you.

One of the tax issues faced *by attorneys* is whether they are trying to avoid paying employment taxes by using freelance paralegals who are not genuine independent contractors. The IRS may consider you to be an employee even if you have your own business license, have a home office, and are not on anyone's payroll. The test is not your title; the test is control. The more control the attorney has over the "manner and means" of the work assigned to you, the greater the likelihood that the IRS will treat you as an employee. The IRS uses 20 factors to decide whether someone is an employee as opposed to an independent contractor. For more on this issue, type *independent contractor* in the search box at www.irs.gov. Read Publication 15-A on the obligations of employers (www.irs.gov/pub/irs-pdf/p15a.pdf).

INSURANCE

Ask every attorney for whom you work whether you are covered by the firm's malpractice liability insurance policy. These policies usually cover independent contractors the attorney hires, such as freelance paralegals, but you should check. Because these policies often provide such coverage, not many freelance paralegals have purchased their own policy.

If you work out of your home, you may have a homeowners' policy that covers fire, theft, and liability arising out of the property. Although such insurance will not cover malpractice liability, you need to know to what extent it covers your business. For example, if any of your business equipment is stolen, is it covered? Do you need to tell your insurance carrier what equipment you have? How is portable equipment covered, e.g., a laptop computer that you take with you wherever you go? Does the policy cover a lawsuit brought against you because your dog bites the crosstown delivery person who comes to your home to deliver a deposition you will be digesting?

MARKETING

How do you market yourself? Where do you find attorney clients who will hire you? The most important initial source of clients will be the network of attorneys that you developed while you worked as a traditional paralegal. When you decide to leave your current employment, one of the first questions you should ask your employer is this:

After I leave, would you be interested in having me do some work for you on a freelance basis?

Many attorneys will see the advantages of such an arrangement. It lowers their overhead costs such as paying full-time salaries and benefits. They also avoid paying employment taxes (unless, as indicated, the IRS concludes that the freelancer is really still an employee). Furthermore, under a freelance arrangement, the attorneys are able to continue to work with someone who has proven his or her competence—you. Once this new arrangement proves to be successful, the attorney will often help you find additional attorney clients in the area's legal community. As mentioned earlier, you should explore the possibility of taking some freelance assignments from other law firms on your own time with the knowledge and cooperation of your employer. You want to try to line up as many attorney clients as possible before you quit your current job.

You'll need to be creative in reaching out to attorneys to let them know about your services. One freelancer went on Facebook to find people from her school who had become attorneys. She contacted each of them to let them know what her business could offer them.

Find out if your state or local bar association allows paralegals to become associate or affiliate members. If so, join. Even if such membership is not allowed, you may be able to attend continuing legal education (CLE) sessions of the bar in the areas of your specialty. You want to meet as many attorneys as possible who might be interested in the kind of services you offer. Don't be shy. Walk up to attorneys at these sessions, introduce yourself, and hand them your card or a flyer that lists your services. Extensive networking at such functions is a must. (See the techniques of assertive networking in Exhibit 2-8 in Chapter 2.)

A few paralegals place brief ads in the magazine or online newsletter that the bar association makes available to its members. The cost of such an ad, however, may be prohibitive. Furthermore, ads are rarely as effective as the networking you do on your own and the referrals obtained from the attorneys with whom you have worked.

When you meet with new attorneys who want to know more about your services, be prepared to show them

- samples of the kind of work you can do, e.g., the first page of a deposition digest, and
- a list of references.

Have a portfolio of samples readily available. If any of your writing samples come from a client document, be sure that actual names and other identifying information are blocked out (redacted) to preserve confidentiality. The list of references should consist primarily of your present and prior attorney clients who have told you that you can list them as references.

Develop a network among fellow freelance paralegals in the state. They can be a source of mutual referrals. A freelance paralegal may be willing to refer an attorney client to you because of a busy schedule, a conflict of interest, or a lack of expertise in the work sought by the client. You, of course, must be willing to make similar referrals. Whenever you are in the company of paralegals, ask them if they know of any freelance paralegals in the area. With persistence, you'll soon know the names of most of them. Some may be reluctant to talk with you because you might be viewed as a competitive threat. If, however, your willingness to share what you know becomes clear, many fellow freelance paralegals will be receptive to the idea of helping to create a mutual support network.

Join paralegal electronic mailing lists (listservs). Freelance paralegals are often members of such lists. You can direct questions to them. For example, on one list, someone could post the following question: "I'm trying to start a freelance business and want to write a promotional brochure to give out to attorneys. Have any of you had any luck with such brochures? I'd appreciate any suggestions." As a result of this email message, scores of responses might materialize from all over the country. You will also occasionally see messages posted such as the following: "Anyone know a good freelancer in Springfield who can track down some real property records for us at the county courthouse? If so, please contact me ASAP." A number of paralegal lists exist. For example, check the email list sponsored by Paralegal Today (www.paralegaltoday.com). Other options include searching for "freelance paralegal" at the following sites:

- www.groups.yahoo.com
- groups.google.com

Create profiles of your business on review sites such as the following:

- Yelp (www.yelp.com) (www.yelp.com/signup)
- Manta (www.manta.com)
- Yahoo Local (local.yahoo.com)
- For others, run this search in Google, Bing, or Yahoo: signing up for business review sites

FEES

How much should you charge attorneys for your services? Experienced paralegals determine their fees primarily on the basis of the complexity of the task and their own experience. Most bill by the hour, although a flat fee may be charged for some tasks, particularly those that can be completed within a predictable amount of time, e.g., filing papers in court. You need to find out what the market will bear. What is the competition charging? Do any of the freelance paralegals in your area have billing rate sheets that you can examine? Freelancers sometimes send fliers to attorneys advertising their services. Ask your attorney contacts if they have any in their files that you could examine. Some freelance paralegals charge two-thirds of the hourly rate that attorneys charge their clients for the time of their traditional paralegals.[6] Others try to charge one-half of the attorney's hourly rate.

Out-of-pocket expenses are usually paid in addition to hourly or flat fees. For example, if a freelance paralegal is asked to use an overnight shipping service or to take a cab to file a pleading in court, the costs of doing so should be separately charged to the attorney. Long-distance calls are also normal cost items. This needs to be made clear in the freelancer's agreement with the attorney.

The agreement that both the freelance paralegal and the attorney sign should state

- The tasks to be performed
- Due dates
- Fees and costs to be paid
- Time of payment

In your networking contacts with fellow freelance paralegals, find out if any standard service contracts are in use. If they are, you should consider adapting them to your own needs.

ETHICS

A freelance paralegal has the same ethical responsibilities as a traditional paralegal. Phrased another way, attorneys have the same ethical responsibilities working with freelance paralegals as they do working with their salaried paralegal employees.

Supervision

The ethical duty of supervision is particularly important. An attorney must supervise the paralegal, whether traditional or freelance. This is not always easy, particularly in a busy office. Some attorneys do an inadequate job of supervising the paralegal employees they work with in the office every day. Supervising freelance paralegals who work at their own offices or at home can be an even greater challenge. At one time, New Jersey considered making it unethical for attorneys to use freelance paralegals because of the great difficulty of supervising them from a distance. Although the New Jersey Supreme Court eventually rejected this extreme position, the court did caution attorneys that extra care was needed to fulfill their duty of supervising paralegals who do not work in the same office.[7]

Busy attorneys who have great confidence in the ability of freelance paralegals are likely to give them minimal supervision. Of course, you can't control the conduct of the attorneys who hire you. Yet, to protect yourself, you need to reinforce the importance of supervision whenever you can. Some freelance paralegals insert a clause in their agreement for hire stating that the attorney will provide adequate supervision on all assignments. Such a clause is not legally significant; the attorney has the supervision duty even in the absence of such a clause. Yet the clause helps communicate the message that you consider such supervision to be critical.

Ask for feedback as often as possible.

- "Have you looked at the deposition digest I prepared?"
- "What did you think of the complaint I drafted for you?"
- "I want to keep improving my skills, so I hope you'll let me know how it could have been better."

Focusing on your need for feedback will probably be more productive than pointing out the attorney's ethical duty to supervise you.

Unauthorized Practice of Law (UPL)

Be careful about the unauthorized practice of law (UPL). First of all, as pointed out in Chapter 5, if you do not receive adequate supervision, you are engaged in the unauthorized practice of law and the attorney for whom you are doing work is assisting in UPL. Another UPL area of concern is legal advice. Friends, relatives, clients, and strangers *regularly* ask freelance paralegals for legal advice or other help that only an attorney can provide. You may find it awkward to refuse their requests, particularly if you are an expert in the area of their need. Yet you must refuse. Your integrity and professionalism are on the line. If you have a list of attorneys that you feel comfortable recommending, have their phone numbers readily available to give out. If you do not have such a list, memorize the phone number of the local bar association's lawyer referral service so that you can give it to people who ask you questions that should be directed to attorneys.

Disclosure of Status

Disclose your status. Busy freelance paralegals often have contact with many people. You may think that someone you meet for the first or second time already knows you are not an attorney. Avoid making this assumption. Let everyone know that you are not an attorney. A clear communication might be as follows: "I am a paralegal. I am not an attorney, but I work under the supervision of one."

Confidentiality

Preserve client confidentiality. Treat everything you learn about an attorney's client the same way you would treat personal information about yourself that you do not want anyone to know. If you travel from office to office, be scrupulous about not letting strangers see your files, including the names of the parties on the front cover of any of the files. Carelessness in this area not only is an ethical violation but also can lead to a waiver of the attorney-client privilege. What a paralegal learns about a client may be covered by the attorney-client privilege. If, however, the information protected by the privilege is disclosed or inadvertently revealed, the privilege may be lost. (See Chapter 5.)

Be particularly careful about online communications that are not secure. Ask your attorney clients what can and cannot be transmitted by email attachments and whether encryption is needed. (See Chapters 5 and 13.)

Conflicts of Interest

Avoid conflicts of interest. Freelance paralegals who work for more than one attorney run the risk of creating a disqualifying conflict of interest. Attorney X, for example, may hire you for a project on a client's case without knowing that you now work or once worked on the case of Attorney Y's client, whose interests are adverse to Attorney X's client. To avoid a conflict of interest:

- Keep a *Career Client List* of parties and attorneys involved in all your present and prior paralegal work. For every case on which you have worked, the list should contain the names of the parties and attorneys for both sides, what you did on the case, and the dates of your involvement.
- Before you take a new assignment, ask for the names of the parties on both sides and all of their attorneys.

- Be ready to refuse to take the assignment if you once worked in opposition to the party you are now being asked to help, even if it was on a different case.
- Allow the attorney hiring you to see your list of parties and attorneys so that he or she can make an informed decision on whether hiring you might create a conflict of interest.

For an example of the format for a Career Client List, see Exhibit 5-9 in Chapter 5.

Also let the attorney know of any personal connection you might have to the case, e.g., that your brother works or once worked for the opponent of a current client or that you recently bought stock in the company of a client. Let the attorney decide whether these personal facts raise conflict issues.

KEEPING CURRENT

Finally, maintain your expertise. The main vehicle for doing so is continuing legal education (CLE). Often, CLE sessions will discuss the latest cases, statutes, and regulations that you need to know about in your specialty. In the middle of an assignment, a freelance paralegal never wants to have to say, "I didn't know the law changed on that." To maintain your expertise:

- Attend CLE sponsored by paralegal associations.
- Attend CLE sponsored by bar associations.
- Join the specialty section of your paralegal association; if one does not exist in your area of expertise, organize one.
- Read online blogs on your specialty. Use the RSS feeds described in Chapter 13.

HELPFUL WEBSITES

Independent Contractor Agreement
- www.cparalegalservices.com/icagreement.pdf

Are You Ready to Offer Freelance Paralegal Services?
- paralegaltoday.com/issue_archive/features/feature1_ma07 .htm

Independent Paralegals Improving the Quality and Delivery of Legal Services
- www.ldapro.com/Cregler-indep-para.pdf.

Freelance Paralegals: Trade Secrets of Success
- www.paralegals.org/associations/2270/files/freelance.htm

Could You Be One? Virtual Paralegals
- www.nala.org/Upload/file/PDF-Files/FactsFindings/virtual .pdf

Flying Solo (survey results)
- paralegaltoday.com/issue_archive/features/feature3_ma06 .htm

"Ten Signs You May Not Be Ready to Run a Freelance Paralegal Business"
- Type this title (in quotes) in Google, Bing, or Yahoo.

Colorado Freelance Paralegal Network
- www.paralegalsfreelance.com

Amazon
Run these book searches on www.amazon.com:
"freelance paralegal"
"independent paralegal"

Legal Document Assistants
- calda.org
- aldap.com
- www.independentparalegals.com
- en.wikipedia.org/wiki/legal_document_assistant
- www.saclaw.org/pages/legal-document-assistants.aspx

LinkedIn, Twitter, Facebook, Google+, and YouTube
On these sites (www.linkedin.com, www.twitter.com, www.facebook.com, plus.google.com, and www.youtube.com), enter these searches:

- virtual paralegal
- independent paralegal
- freelance paralegal

Virtual Assistants
- apps.americanbar.org/lpm/lpt/articles/mgt04062.shtml
- virtualassistants.com
- www.ivaa.org

Freelance Law
- www.freelancelaw.com

SCORE: Small Business Assistance
- www.score.org

Independent Contractor Resource
- www.guru.com

Entrepreneur
- entrepreneur.com

Internal Revenue Service
- www.irs.gov

National Association for the Self-Employed
- www.nase.org

Google, Bing, or Yahoo Searches
(On these search engines, run the following searches, adding the name of your city or state when you want local sites.)
freelance paralegal
independent paralegal
independent contractor
paralegal business
paralegal services
contract paralegal services
legal document assistant

ENDNOTES

[1] Cathy Heath, *Paralegal Services: How to Manage Your Own Firm*, vii (Rim Rock, 2000).

[2] *They Do It Their Way*, 15 National Paralegal Reporter 32 (April/May 2001).

[3] Chere Estrin, *When to Say "No (Thank You)" to Your Dream Job*, Recap 12 (California Alliance of Paralegal Associations, Spring 1999).

[4] Lee Davis, *Following My Dream*, 25 National Paralegal Reporter 5 (April/May 2001).

[5] Mary Willard, *Is It Time to Freelance?*, 28 Facts and Findings 18, 20 (National Association of Legal Assistants, May 2001).

[6] Mary Uriko, *Freelancing 101*, 18 Legal Assistant Today 83, 84 (September/October 2000).

[7] See *In re Opinion No. 26 of Committee on Unauthorized Practice of Law*, 654 A.2d 1344 (N.J. 1995), and *In re Opinion 24 on Unauthorized Practice of Law*, 607 A.2d 962 (N.J. 1992).

FINDING LAW OFFICES

INTRODUCTION

At some point when you are looking for employment, you may want to obtain an overview of the various law offices in the geographic area where you would like to work. Of course, if you already have the name of a law office, it is relatively easy to type the name of the office in any search engine in order to find information about it. What if, however, you have no names? You simply want to start canvassing an area. Earlier in the book, we covered various ways to find job openings with specific job-search sites. (See, for example, Exhibit 2-12 in Chapter 2.) Here we approach the employment search from a different angle. Suppose that you want to find information about clusters of law offices in your city or town. You want the websites of all (or most) of the attorneys where you live or hope to work.

GOALS

There are several reasons why you may want to spend time examining the websites of large numbers of law offices. Your goal might be

- to find law offices that practice in areas of law that are of particular interest to you
- to learn more about the variety of law offices that exist in order to begin identifying possible preferences
- to find law offices that list job openings on their websites (large law offices may have links on their websites called *Careers*, *Employment*, or *Openings*)
- to find law offices that list the names of paralegals they employ (sending an email to such persons inquiring about employment opportunities in their city might be productive)
- to obtain a list of offices that you will "cold call" to inquire about job openings (see Chapter 2 on cold calling)

ATTORNEY ADS OR JOB OPPORTUNITIES?

Most of the websites to which you will be led by the links in this appendix will be to attorneys and law offices that want to be hired—attorney ads. Yet these sites can be valuable to visit for the reasons indicated earlier: the sites will lead you to law practices in areas of law in which you have an interest, the sites may list job openings at the office, etc. Hence, don't be reluctant to scan through sites of law offices that are looking for clients. They can be good starting points in your own search for employment.

GENERAL SEARCHES

- On Google, Bing, or Yahoo, run this search: law office firm attorney aa (substituting your city or state for "aa"). (Example: law office firm attorney los angeles)
- On Google, Bing, or Yahoo, run this search: law office firm attorney aa bb (substituting your city or state for "aa" and an area of law for "bb"). (Example: law office firm attorney detroit corporate law)

LISTS OF LAW OFFICES

General

- www.llrx.com/features/locatinglawyers.htm
- www.ilrg.com/lawyers.html
- lawyers.findlaw.com
- www.martindale.com
- www.attorneylocate.com/default.asp
- www.lawyers.com
- pview.findlaw.com
- apps.americanbar.org/legalservices/lris/directory/home.html
- www.legaldirectories.com
- www.chambersandpartners.com
- www.bestlawyers.com
- www.avvo.com
- www.lawyerratingz.com
- In Google, Bing, or Yahoo, run this search: *lawyer rating services*

Large Law Offices

- www.ilrg.com/nlj250
- www.martindale.com/Press/Fortune-Mag.aspx
- en.wikipedia.org/wiki/List_of_100_largest_law_firms_by_revenue
- www.legal500.com/assets/pages/united-states/united-states.html

Categories of Attorneys

- research.lawyers.com/areas-of-law-definitions.html
- en.wikipedia.org/wiki/Category:Lawyers_by_type
- www.alllaw.com/topics/legal

Specialties (see also specialty associations in Appendix B)

Bankruptcy Attorneys
- www.nacba.org
- bankruptcy.lawyers.com
- www.attorneylocate.com/area.asp?catid=12
- www.martindale.com/Bankruptcy-lawyers-countries.htm
- pview.findlaw.com(type *bankruptcy law* in search box)

Commercial and Business Law Attorneys
- www.attorneylocate.com/area.asp?catid=17
- www.martindale.com/Commercial-Law-lawyers-countries.htm
- pview.findlaw.com (type *business law* in search box)
- business-law.lawyers.com

Consumer Law Attorneys
- www.naca.net

Corporate Law Attorneys
- www.martindale.com/Corporate-Law-lawyers-countries.htm
- pview.findlaw.com (type *corporate law* in search box)

Criminal Defense Attorneys
- www.nacdl.org
- afda.org
- www.nlada.org/About/About_Home

Elder Law Attorneys
- www.naela.org
- elder-law.lawyers.com
- pview.findlaw.com (type *elder law* in search box)

Employment and Labor Law Attorneys
- www.nela.org
- www.attorneylocate.com/area.asp?catid=28
- pview.findlaw.com (type *employment law* in search box)
- labor-employment-law.lawyers.com

Estate Attorneys
- www.aaepa.com
- www.actec.org
- trusts-estates.lawyers.com/estate-planning
- pview.findlaw.com (type *estate law* in search box)

Family Law Attorneys
- www.acftl.com
- www.attorneylocate.com/area.asp?catid=25
- pview.findlaw.com (type *family law* in search box)
- family-law.lawyers.com/divorce
- family-law.lawyers.com

Gay and Lesbian Attorneys
- lgbtbar.org/what-we-do/affiliates
- en.wikipedia.org/wiki/National_LGBT_Bar_Association
- civil-rights.lawyers.com/gay-and-lesbian-rights

Immigration Attorneys
- www.aila.org
- pview.findlaw.com (type *immigration law* in search box)
- immigration.lawyers.com

Insurance Law Attorneys
- pview.findlaw.com (type *insurance law* in search box)
- www.martindale.com/Insurance-lawyers-countries.htm

Intellectual Property Attorneys (patents, trademarks, etc.)
- www.martindale.com/Intellectual-Property-lawyers-countries.htm
- pview.findlaw.com (type *intellectual property law* in search box)

Medical Malpractice Attorneys
- www.justice.org
- www.pntla.org
- www.attorneylocate.com/area.asp?catid=44
- pview.findlaw.com (type *medical malpractice law* in search box)
- medical-malpractice.lawyers.com

Personal Injury Attorneys
- www.justice.org
- www.attorneylocate.com/area.asp?catid=47
- www.martindale.com/Personal-Injury-lawyers-countries.htm
- pview.findlaw.com (type *personal injury law* in search box)
- personal-injury.lawyers.com
- www.naopia.com

Real Estate Attorneys
- www.acrel.org
- www.martindale.com/Real-Estate-lawyers-countries.htm
- pview.findlaw.com (type *real estate law* in search box)
- real-estate.lawyers.com

Tax Attorneys
- www.attorneylocate.com/area.asp?catid=56
- www.martindale.com/Taxation-lawyers-countries.htm
- pview.findlaw.com (type *tax law* in search box)
- taxation.lawyers.com

Corporate Law Offices (in-house counsel)
- inhouse.law.com
- www.legal500.com/assets/pages/cc100/assets/images/inhouse/cc100.pdf

Legal Aid Offices
- www.lsc.gov
- www.lsc.gov/local-programs/program-profiles
- www.nlada.org/About/About_Home
- www.ptla.org/legal-services-links

STATE GOVERNMENT PARALEGAL JOBS

- **ALL STATES**
  - In Google, Bing, or Yahoo, run this search: state government paralegal aa (substituting your state for "aa")
  - In Google, Bing, or Yahoo, run this search: city government paralegal aa (substituting your city or town for "aa")
  - In Google, Bing, or Yahoo, run this search: county government paralegal aa (substituting your county for "aa")
  - In Google, Bing, or Yahoo, run this search: federal government paralegal aa (substituting your state for "aa")
  - www.governmentjobs.com

- **ALABAMA**
  www.personnel.state.al.us

  - **Legal Research Assistant** (Classification Code 11503)
  - **Docket Clerk** (Classification Code 11501)

  (www.personnel.state.al.us/Documents/Announcements/101690_A.pdf)
  (www.personnel.state.al.us/Documents/Announcements/100296_A.pdf)

- **ALASKA**
  doa.alaska.gov/dop

  - **Paralegal I** (Classification Code P10121)
  - **Paralegal II** (Classification Code P10122
  - **Legal Technician** (Classification Code CO128)

  (doa.alaska.gov/dop/classification)

- **ARIZONA**
  www.hr.state.az.us

  - **Legal Assistant I** (Classification Code 32201)
  - **Legal Assistant II** (Classification Code 32202)
  - **Legal Assistant III** (Classification Code 32203)
  - **Legal Assistant Project Specialist** (Classification Code 32204)
  - **Paralegal Specialist** (AUN02781)
  - **Legal Analyst** (AUN03357)
  - **Legal Administrator** (AUN04871)

  (www.hr.state.az.us/ClassComp/CC_Job_Titles_with_Ranges.asp)

- **ARKANSAS**
  www.dfa.arkansas.gov/Pages/default.aspx

  - **JDDC Paralegal** (Classification Code G230C)

- **Paralegal I** (Classification Code Q025U)
- **Supreme Court Paralegal OPC** (Classification Code Q208C)
- **Legal Assistant** (Classification Code Q002U)(R177)
- **Legal Support Specialist** (Classification Code C046C)
- **Legal Services Specialist** (Classification Code G179C)

(www.arkansas.gov/dfa/personnel_mgmt/jobs/view_classcode
.cgi?class=G230C)

- **CALIFORNIA**
  www.calhr.ca.gov

  - **Legal Assistant** (Classification Code JY66,1820) (www.calhr
    .ca.gov/state-hr-professionals/pages/1820.aspx)
  - **Legal Analyst** (Classification Code JY62, 5237) (www
    .calhr.ca.gov/state-hr-professionals/pages/5237.aspx)
  - **Legal Document Examiner** (Classification Code CW65,1829)
    (www.calhr.ca.gov/state-hr-professionals/pages/1829.aspx)

- **COLORADO**
  www.colorado.gov/dhr/jobs

  - **Legal Assistant I** (Classification Code H5E1XX)
  - **Legal Assistant II** (Classification Code H5E2XX)

  (Type the classification codes in the search box)

- **CONNECTICUT**
  www.das.state.ct.us
  das.ct.gov/HR/JobspecNew/JobSearch.asp

  - **Paralegal Specialist 1** (Classification Code (6140)
  - **Paralegal Specialist 2** (Classification Code (6141)

  (das.ct.gov/HR/JobspecNew/JobDetail.asp?FCC=6633)
  (das.ct.gov/HR/JobspecNew/JobDetail.asp?FCC=6038)

- **DELAWARE**
  delawarepersonnel.com

  - **Paralegal I** (Classification Code MAFD01)
  - **Paralegal II** (Classification Code MAFD02)
  - **Paralegal III** (Classification Code MAFD03)

  (www.jobaps.com/de/auditor/choosegroups.asp)
  (select *Legal Services*)

■ **DISTRICT OF COLUMBIA**

dcop.dc.gov

dchr.dc.gov/page/classification-and-compensation

- **Paralegal Specialist** (Classification Code DS-950) (type *paralegal* in the search box)
- **Judicial Assistant** (Classification Code 8310)

■ **FLORIDA**

jobs.myflorida.com/index.html

jobs.myflorida.com/joblist.html

- **Paralegal/Legal Assistant** (Classification Code 23-2011)
- **Law Clerk** (Classification Code 23-2092)
- **Judicial Assistant**

■ **GEORGIA**

doas.ga.gov/statelocal/hra/Pages/Home.aspx

www.gms.state.ga.us

- **Paralegal** (Classification Code 95412)
- **Legal Assistant** (Classification Code 95406)

■ **HAWAII**

www.hawaii.gov/hrd

- **Legal Assistant II** (Classification Code 2.141)
- **Legal Assistant III** (Classification Code 2.142)

■ **IDAHO**

dhr.idaho.gov

- **Legal Assistant** (Classification Code 05910)

(labor.idaho.gov/dhr/ats/statejobs/ClassificationData.aspx)

■ **ILLINOIS**

www2.illinois.gov/cms/Pages/default.aspx

- **Paralegal Assistant** (Classification Code 30860)

(www.state.il.us/cms/download/pdfs_specs/30860.pdf)

■ **INDIANA**

www.in.gov/spd

- **Legal Assistant 5** (Classification Code 001VA5)
- **Legal Analyst 3** (Classification Code 001VA3)

(www.in.gov/spd/files/job_titles.pdf)

■ **IOWA**

das.hre.iowa.gov/state_jobs.html

- **Paralegal** (Classification Codes 15004, 45004, 95004)

(das.hre.iowa.gov/class_and_pay.html)

■ **KANSAS**

da.ks.gov/ps/documents

- **Legal Assistant** (Classification Code 4093D3)

(admin.ks.gov/offices/personnel-services/compensation-and-classification)

■ **KENTUCKY**

personnel.ky.gov/Pages/default.aspx

- **Paralegal I** (Classification Code 9856)

- **Paralegal II** (Classification Code 9857)
- **Paralegal Advocate I** (Classification Code 9861)

■ **LOUISIANA**

www.civilservice.louisiana.gov

- **Paralegal 1** (Classification Code 165650)
- **Paralegal 2** (Classification Code 113470)

(www.civilservice.louisiana.gov/asp/OneStopJobInfo/default.aspx)

■ **MAINE**

www.state.me.us/bhr

- **Paralegal** (Classification Code 0884)
- **Paralegal Assistant** (Classification Code 0994)
- **Senior Paralegal** (Classification Code 0912)
- **Legal Administrator** (Classification Code 0912)
- **Workers' Compensation Advocate** (Classification Code 1007)

(www.state.me.us/cgi-bin/bhrsalary/jobs.pl)

■ **MARYLAND**

dbm.maryland.gov/Pages/home.aspx

- **Paralegal I** (Classification Code 0844)
- **Paralegal I OAG** (Classification Code 05176)
- **Paralegal II** (Classification Code 0885)

(www.jobaps.com/MD/auditor/classspecs.asp)

■ **MASSACHUSETTS**

www.mass.gov/portal/jobs-unemployment/finding-a-job

- **Paralegal Specialist** (Classification Code 10-R39)(J42134)
- **Paralegal Child Protection Unit** (J42390)
- **Legal Assistant** (Classification Code 1291)
- **Legal Assistant II** (Classification Code 1292)

■ **MICHIGAN**

www.michigan.gov/mdcs

- **Paralegal 8-11** (Paralegal-E) (Position Code PRLEGALE) (Paralegal-A) (Position Code PRLEGALA) (8020403)
- **Legal Assistant** (Position Code LEGLASTE)

(web1mdcs.state.mi.us/MCSCJobSpecifications/JobSpecMain.aspx)

(www.michigan.gov/documents/Paralegal_12243_7.pdf)

(www.michigan.gov/documents/LegalAssistant_12779_7.pdf)

■ **MINNESOTA**

www.careers.state.mn.us

statejobs.doer.state.mn.us/JobPost

- **Paralegal** (Classification Code 3611)
- **Legal Technician** (Classification Code 1541)
- **Legal Analyst** (Classification Code 2957)

■ **MISSISSIPPI**

agency.governmentjobs.com/mississippi/default.cfm

- **Paralegal Specialist** (Classification Code 1848)
- **Paralegal Specialist, Certified** (Classification Code 4916)
- **Workers' Compensation Legal Assistant** (Classification Code 4410)

MISSOURI

content.oa.mo.gov/personnel

- Paralegal or legal assistant positions are not found under the Missouri Merit System. Individual agencies not covered by the Merit System, however, may have such positions under the paralegal (9730) class. For example, the Missouri Office of the State Public Defender has a Paralegal Investigator I position.

MONTANA

doa.mt.gov
mt.gov/statejobs/default.mcpx

- **Paralegal** (13254-14AB)
- **Paralegal Assistant I** (Classification Code 119004; 249110)
- **Paralegal Assistant II** (Classification Code 119005)
- **Agency Legal Services Investigator** (Classification Code 16855).

NEBRASKA

das.nebraska.gov/personnel
das.nebraska.gov/personnel/classncomp

- **Paralegal I** (Classification Code A31121)
- **Paralegal II** (Classification Code V31122)
- **Legal Aide I** (Classification Code R31801)
- **Legal Aide II** (Classification Code R31802)

(das.nebraska.gov/personnel/classncomp/jobspecs/A/pdf/A31121.pdf)

NEVADA

hr.nv.gov
hr.nv.gov/Resources/Class_Specifications

- **Legal Assistant** (Classification Code 2.159)

NEW HAMPSHIRE

admin.state.nh.us/hr
admin.state.nh.us/HR/classindex_a_d.htm

- **Paralegal I** (Classification Code 6793-16)
- **Paralegal II** (Classification Code 6792-19)
- **Legal Aide** (Classification Code 6660-15)
- **Paralegal II** (Classification Code 5671-19)

(admin.state.nh.us/HR/classspec_p/6793.htm)

NEW JERSEY

www.nj.gov/csc
www.nj.gov/csc/seekers/jobs/announcements/title_search.html

- **Paralegal Technician 1** (Classification Code 30462)
- **Paralegal Technician 2** (Classification Code 30461)
- **Paralegal Technician Assistant** (Classification Code 30459)

(info.csc.state.nj.us/jobspec/30462.htm)
(The Legal Assistant position (36307) requires a law degree.)

NEW MEXICO

www.spo.state.nm.us

- **Paralegal & Legal Assistant-A** (Classification Code H2011A)
- **Paralegal & Legal Assistant-B** (Classification Code H20110)
- **Paralegal & Legal Assistant-O** (Classification Code H2011B)

(www.spo.state.nm.us/Past_Classifications_and_Pay_Listings.aspx)

NEW YORK

www.cs.ny.gov

- **Legal Assistant 1** (Classification Code 2522210)
- **Legal Assistant 2** (Classification Code 2522210)

(www.cs.ny.gov/tsplan/tsp_display2.cfm?speccode=2522210F)

NORTH CAROLINA

www.oshr.nc.gov
agency.governmentjobs.com/northcarolina/default.cfm

- **Paralegal I** (Classification Code 1422)
- **Paralegal II** (Classification Code 1423)
- **Paralegal III** (Classification Code 1424)

NORTH DAKOTA

www.nd.gov/hrms

- **Legal Assistant I** (Classification Code 0701)
- **Legal Assistant II** (Classification Code 0702)

OHIO

das.ohio.gov/Divisions/HumanResources.aspx

- **Paralegal/Legal Assistant 1** (Classification Code 63810)
- **Paralegal/Legal Assistant 2** (Classification Code 63811)
- **Certified Paralegal** (Classification Code 63811S)

(agency.governmentjobs.com/ohio/default.cfm?
action=agencyspecs)

OKLAHOMA

ok.gov/opm/State_Jobs/index.html

- **Paralegal** (Classification Code 140605-UNCE-73)
- **Legal Research Assistant** (Classification Code K101 FC:K10)(E30A)

OREGON

www.oregon.gov/DAS/CHRO/pages/index.aspx
www.oregon.gov/Pages/cgi-bin/ccrt.aspx?pg=ccrt

- **Paralegal** (Classification Code 1524)

(www.oregon.gov/DAS/CHRO/class/ccrt/spec/1524)

PENNSYLVANIA

www.employment.pa.gov/portal/server.pt/community
/pa_jobs/17638

- **Paralegal** (Classification Code 07010)
- **Legal Assistant 1** (Classification Code 07040)
- **Legal Assistant 2** (Classification Code 07020)

RHODE ISLAND

www.dlt.state.ri.us/webdev/JobsRI/statejobs.htm

- **Paralegal Aide** (Classification Code 02461300)
- **Legal Assistant**

SOUTH CAROLINA

www.ohr.sc.gov/OHR/OHR-jobs-portal-index.phtm
www.jobs.sc.gov./OHR/OHR-browse-class.phtm

- **Administrative Assistant** (Classification Code AA75)

SOUTH DAKOTA

bhr.sd.gov
bhr.sd.gov/classification

- **Legal Assistant** (Classification Code 11205)

(bhr.sd.gov/classification/ClassSpecs/011205.pdf)

■ TENNESSEE
www.tn.gov/dohr

- **Legal Assistant** (Classification Code 023350)
- **COT Legal Assistant** (Classification Code 02350)
- **Public Defender Legal Assistant** (Classification Code 029722)

■ TEXAS
www.hr.sao.state.tx.us

- **Legal Assistant I** (Classification Code 3572)
- **Legal Assistant II** (Classification Code 3574)
- **Legal Assistant III** (Classification Code 3576)
- **Legal Assistant IV** (Classification Code 3578)

(www.hr.sao.state.tx.us/Compensation/JobDescriptions/R3572.ht)

■ UTAH
www.dhrm.utah.gov

- **Legal Assistant (Paralegal) I** (Classification Code 85508)
- **Legal Assistant (Paralegal) II** (Classification Code 85510)
- **Legal Assistant I (Att Gen)** (Classification Code 09325)

■ VERMONT
humanresources.vermont.gov

- **Paralegal** (Classification Code 467400)
- **Paralegal Technician I** (Classification Code 081800)
- **Paralegal Technician II** (Classification Code 082300)

■ VIRGINIA
jobs.virginia.gov/emplJobListing.html
www.dhrm.virginia.gov/employmentandcareers.html

- **Administrative and Office Specialist III** (Classification Code 19013)
- **Legal Assistant** (Classification Code 21521)

■ WASHINGTON, D.C.
(See District of Columbia)

■ WASHINGTON STATE
dop.wa.gov/Pages/default.aspx

- **Paralegal 1** (Classification Code 426E)
- **Paralegal 2** (Classification Code 426F)
- **Paralegal 3** (Classification Code 426G)

(dop.wa.gov/CompClass/JobClassesSalaries/Pages/Specifications.aspx)

■ WEST VIRGINIA
www.personnel.wv.gov/Pages/default.aspx
agency.governmentjobs.com/wv/default.cfm

- **Paralegal** (Classification Code 1 (9500))
- **Child Support Paralegal** (Classification Code 9519)

(www.state.wv.us/admin/personnel/clascomp/spec/9500.pdf)

■ WISCONSIN
oser.state.wi.us
wisc.jobs/public/index.asp

- **Legal Assistant - Entry** (Classification Code 19201)
- **Legal Assistant - Objective** (Classification Code 19202)
- **Legal Assistant - Confidential** (Classification Code 19211)

■ WYOMING
www.wyoming.gov/loc/06012011_1/Pages/default.aspx

- **Legal Assistant** (Classification Code BALG08)

STATE RESOURCES

ABBREVIATIONS

AG: attorney general
CP: consumer protection
CS: court system of the state
GO: governor's office

LL: law library of the state (or alternative)
LR: legal research sources on state law
MV: motor vehicle laws of the state
PR: public records search in the state
SF: state forms, e.g., summons, will, or probate

SL: state legislature
SS: secretary of state (or equivalent office)
WC: workers' compensation in the state

ALABAMA

AG: www.ago.state.al.us
CP: www.ago.state.al.us/Page-Consumer-Protection
CS: judicial.alabama.gov
    caselaw.findlaw.com/courts/Alabama
GO: governor.alabama.gov
LL: www.washlaw.edu/statecourtcounty
LR: www.law.cornell.edu/states/alabama
    www.findlaw.com/casecode/alabama.html
MV: revenue.alabama.gov/motorvehicle/index.cfm
PR: publicrecords.onlinesearches.com/Alabama.htm
SF: www.alllaw.com/state_resources/alabama/forms
    forms.lp.findlaw.com/states/al.html
SL: www.legislature.state.al.us
SS: www.sos.state.al.us
WC: dir.alabama.gov/wc

ALASKA

AG: www.law.state.ak.us
CP: www.law.state.ak.us/department/civil/consumer/cpindex.html
CS: courts.alaska.gov
GO: www.gov.state.ak.us
LL: courts.alaska.gov/library.htm
LR: www.findlaw.com/casecode/alaska.html
MV: doa.alaska.gov/dmv
PR: www.publicrecordsfind.us/AlaskapublicrecordsAKrecords.html
SF: www.alllaw.com/state_resources/alaska/forms
    forms.lp.findlaw.com/states/ak.html
SL: w3.legis.state.ak.us/index.php
SS: commerce.alaska.gov/cbp/main/SearchInfo.aspx
WC: labor.state.ak.us/wc/home.htm

ARIZONA

AG: www.azag.gov
CP: www.azag.gov/consumer
CS: www.azcourts.gov
GO: www.governor.state.az.us
LL: www.azlibrary.gov/sla
    www.superiorcourt.maricopa.gov/lawlibrary
LR: www.findlaw.com/casecode/arizona.html
    www.loc.gov/law/help/guide/states/us-az.php
MV: www.azdot.gov/mvd
PR: publicrecords.onlinesearches.com/Arizona.htm
SF: www.alllaw.com/state_resources/arizona/forms
    forms.lp.findlaw.com/states/az.html
SL: www.azleg.gov
SS: www.azsos.gov
WC: www.ica.state.az.us

ARKANSAS

AG: www.ag.state.ar.us
CP: gotyourbackarkansas.org
CS: courts.arkansas.gov
GO: governor.arkansas.gov
LR: www.findlaw.com/casecode/arkansas.html
    www.loc.gov/law/help/guide/states/us-ar.php
MV: www.dfa.arkansas.gov/offices/driverServices/Pages/forms.aspx
PR: www.publicrecordsfind.us/ArkansaspublicrecordsARrecords.html
SF: www.alllaw.com/state_resources/arkansas/forms
    forms.lp.findlaw.com/states/ar.html
SL: www.arkleg.state.ar.us
SS: www.sos.arkansas.gov
WC: www.awcc.state.ar.us

CALIFORNIA

AG: oag.ca.gov
CP: oag.ca.gov/consumers
CS: www.courts.ca.gov
GO: gov.ca.gov/home.php
LL: www.washlaw.edu/statecourtcounty
LR: www.findlaw.com/casecode/california.html
    www.loc.gov/law/help/guide/states/us-ca.php

MV: www.dmv.ca.gov
PR: www.ca.gov/OnlineServices/OS_Government_records.html
SF: www.alllaw.com/state_resources/california/forms
forms.lp.findlaw.com/states/ca.html
SL: www.leginfo.ca.gov
SS: www.ss.ca.gov
WC: www.dir.ca.gov/DWC/dwc_home_page.htm

COLORADO

AG: www.coloradoattorneygeneral.gov
CP: www.coloradoattorneygeneral.gov/initiatives
/consumer_resource_guide
CS: www.courts.state.co.us
GO: www.colorado.gov
LL: www.washlaw.edu/statecourtcounty
LR: www.loc.gov/law/help/guide/states/us-co.php
www.findlaw.com/casecode/colorado.html
MV: www.colorado.gov/revenue/dmv
PR: www.publiclibraries.com/records/colorado.htm
SF: www.alllaw.com/state_resources/colorado/forms
forms.lp.findlaw.com/states/co.html
SL: www.leg.state.co.us
SS: www.sos.state.co.us
WC: www.colorado.gov/cs/Satellite/CDLE-Main
/CDLE/1240336821467

CONNECTICUT

AG: www.ct.gov/ag
CP: www.ct.gov/ag/cwp/view.asp?a=2093&q=482928
CS: www.jud.state.ct.us
GO: www.governor.ct.gov
LL: www.jud.state.ct.us/LawLib
LR: www.loc.gov/law/help/guide/states/us-ct.php
www.jud.state.ct.us/lawlib/state.htm
MV: www.ct.gov/dmv
PR: publicrecords.searchsystems.net/USA_State/Connecticut
SF: www.alllaw.com/state_resources/connecticut/forms
forms.lp.findlaw.com/states/ct.html
SL: www.cga.ct.gov
SS: www.ct.gov/sots
WC: wcc.state.ct.us

DELAWARE

AG: attorneygeneral.delaware.gov
CP: attorneygeneral.delaware.gov/fraud/cpu/complaint.shtml
CS: courts.state.de.us
GO: governor.delaware.gov
LR: www.findlaw.com/casecode/delaware.html
www.loc.gov/law/help/guide/states/us-de.php
MV: www.dmv.de.gov
PR: www.publicrecordsfind.us/DelawarepublicrecordsDErecords
.html
SF: www.alllaw.com/state_resources/delaware/forms
forms.lp.findlaw.com/states/de.html
SL: legis.delaware.gov
SS: sos.delaware.gov
WC: dia.delawareworks.com/workers-comp

DISTRICT OF COLUMBIA

AG: oag.dc.gov
CP: oag.dc.gov/consumerprotection
CS: www.dccourts.gov/internet
GO: mayor.dc.gov (mayor)

LL: www.law.georgetown.edu/library
LR: www.findlaw.com/casecode/district-of-columbia.html
www.loc.gov/law/help/guide/states/us-dc.php
MV: dmv.dc.gov
PR: www.publiclibraries.com/records/dc.htm
SF: forms.lp.findlaw.com/states/dc.html
SS: os.dc.gov
SL: www.dccouncil.washington.dc.us (City Council)
WC: does.dc.gov/page/workers-compensation-does

FLORIDA

AG: myfloridalegal.com
CP: myfloridalegal.com/consumer
CS: www.flcourts.org
GO: www.flgov.com
LL: library.flcourts.org
LR: www.findlaw.com/casecode/florida.html
www.loc.gov/law/help/guide/states/us-fl.php
MV: www.flhsmv.gov
PR: www.stateofflorida.com/Portal/DesktopDefault
.aspx?tabid=13
SF: www.alllaw.com/state_resources/florida/forms
forms.lp.findlaw.com/states/fl.html
SL: www.leg.state.fl.us
SS: dos.myflorida.com
WC: www.myfloridacfo.com/division/wc

GEORGIA

AG: law.ga.gov
CP: consumer.georgia.gov
CS: www.georgiacourts.org
GO: gov.georgia.gov
LL: www.washlaw.edu/statecourtcounty
LR: www.findlaw.com/casecode/georgia.html
www.loc.gov/law/help/guide/states/us-ga.php
MV: www.dds.ga.gov
PR: www.publiclibraries.com/records/georgia.htm
SF: www.alllaw.com/state_resources/georgia/forms
forms.lp.findlaw.com/states/ga.html
SL: www.legis.ga.gov
SS: sos.ga.gov
WC: sbwc.georgia.gov

HAWAII

AG: ag.hawaii.gov
CP: cca.hawaii.gov
CS: www.courts.state.hi.us
GO: gov.state.hi.us
LL: www.state.hi.us/jud/library/index.htm
LR: www.findlaw.com/casecode/hawaii.html
www.loc.gov/law/help/guide/states/us-hi.php
MV: www.dmv.org/hi-hawaii
PR: www.publiclibraries.com/records/hawaii.htm
SF: www.alllaw.com/state_resources/hawaii/forms
forms.lp.findlaw.com/states/hi.html
SL: www.capitol.hawaii.gov
SS: cca.hawaii.gov/breg (business registration)
WC: labor.hawaii.gov/dcd

IDAHO

AG: www.ag.idaho.gov
CP: www.ag.idaho.gov/consumerProtection/consumerIndex.html
CS: www.isc.idaho.gov

GO: gov.idaho.gov
LL: www.isll.idaho.gov
LR: www.findlaw.com/casecode/idaho.html
        www.loc.gov/law/help/guide/states/us-id.php
MV: itd.idaho.gov/DMV
PR: www.publicrecordsfind.us/IdahopublicrecordsIDrecords.html
SF: www.alllaw.com/state_resources/idaho/forms
SL: http://www.legislature.idaho.gov
SS: www.sos.idaho.gov
WC: www.iic.idaho.gov

ILLINOIS

AG: www.ag.state.il.us
CP: www.illinoisattorneygeneral.gov/consumers
CS: www.state.il.us/court
GO: www2.illinois.gov/Gov/Pages/default.aspx
LL: www.washlaw.edu/statecourtcounty
LR: www.findlaw.com/casecode/illinois.html
        www.loc.gov/law/help/guide/states/us-il.php
MV: www.cyberdriveillinois.com
PR: www.publiclibraries.com/records/illinois.htm
SF: www.alllaw.com/state_resources/illinois/forms
        forms.lp.findlaw.com/states/il.html
SL: www.ilga.gov
SS: www.cyberdriveillinois.com
WC: www.iwcc.illinois.gov

INDIANA

AG: www.in.gov/attorneygeneral
CP: www.in.gov/attorneygeneral/2336.htm#
CS: www.ai.org/judiciary
GO: www.state.in.us/gov
LL: www.in.gov/judiciary/supreme/2329.htm
LR: www.findlaw.com/casecode/indiana.html
        www.loc.gov/law/help/guide/states/us-in.php
MV: www.in.gov/bmv
PR: www.publiclibraries.com/records/indiana.htm
SF: www.alllaw.com/state_resources/indiana/forms
        forms.lp.findlaw.com/states/in.html
SL: iga.in.gov
SS: www.state.in.us/sos
WC: www.in.gov/wcb

IOWA

AG: www.state.ia.us/government/ag
CP: www.state.ia.us/government/ag/protecting_consumers
CS: www.iowacourts.gov
GO: governor.iowa.gov
LL: www.statelibraryofiowa.org/services/collections/law-library
LR: www.findlaw.com/casecode/iowa.html
        www.loc.gov/law/help/guide/states/us-ia.php
MV: www.iowadot.gov/mvd//index.htm
PR: publicrecords.onlinesearches.com/Iowa.htm
SF: www.alllaw.com/state_resources/iowa/forms
        forms.lp.findlaw.com/states/ia.html
SL: www.legis.iowa.gov
SS: www.iowa.gov
WC: www.iowaworkforce.org/wc

KANSAS

AG: ag.ks.gov
CP: ag.ks.gov/consumer-protection
CS: www.kscourts.org

GO: www.governor.ks.gov
LL: www.washlaw.edu/statecourtcounty
LR: www.findlaw.com/casecode/kansas.html
        www.loc.gov/law/help/guide/states/us-ks.php
MV: www.ksrevenue.org/vehicle.html
PR: publicrecords.onlinesearches.com/Kansas.htm
SF: www.alllaw.com/state_resources/kansas/forms
        www.megalaw.com/forms/ks/ksforms.php
SL: www.kslegislature.org
SS: www.kssos.org
WC: www.dol.ks.gov/WorkComp/Default.aspx

KENTUCKY

AG: ag.ky.gov
CP: ag.ky.gov (click *Consumer Complaints*)
CS: courts.ky.gov
GO: governor.ky.gov
LL: www.washlaw.edu/statecourtcounty
LR: www.findlaw.com/casecode/kentucky.html
        www.loc.gov/law/help/guide/states/us-ky.php
MV: transportation.ky.gov/motor-vehicle-licensing/Pages/default.aspx
PR: publicrecords.onlinesearches.com/Kentucky.htm
SF: www.alllaw.com/state_resources/kentucky/forms
        forms.lp.findlaw.com/states/ky.html
SL: www.lrc.state.ky.us/home.htm
SS: www.sos.ky.gov
WC: www.labor.ky.gov

LOUISIANA

AG: www.ag.state.la.us
CP: www.ag.state.la.us (click *Consumer Protection*)
CS: www.lasc.org
GO: www.gov.state.la.us
LF: www.lasc.org/rules/supreme.asp
LL: www.lasc.org/law_library/library_information.asp
LR: www.findlaw.com/casecode/louisiana.html
        www.loc.gov/law/help/guide/states/us-la.php
MV: omv.dps.state.la.us
PR: www.publiclibraries.com/records/louisiana.htm
SF: www.alllaw.com/state_resources/louisiana/forms
        forms.lp.findlaw.com/states/la.html
SL: www.legis.la.gov
SS: www.sos.la.gov
WC: www.laworks.net

MAINE

AG: www.maine.gov/ag
CP: www.maine.gov/ag (click *Consumer* links)
CS: www.courts.maine.gov
GO: www.maine.gov/governor/lepage
LL: www.state.me.us/legis/lawlib/index.htm
LR: www.findlaw.com/casecode/maine.html
        www.loc.gov/law/help/guide/states/us-me.php
MV: www.state.me.us/sos/bmv
PR: publicrecords.onlinesearches.com
SF: www.alllaw.com/state_resources/maine/forms
SL: www.maine.gov/legis
SS: www.state.me.us/sos
WC: www.state.me.us/wcb

MARYLAND

AG: www.oag.state.md.us
CP: www.oag.state.md.us/Consumer/index.htm

CS: www.courts.state.md.us
GO: www.gov.state.md.us
LL: www.lawlib.state.md.us
LR: www.findlaw.com/casecode/maryland.html
         www.loc.gov/law/help/guide/states/us-md.php
MV: www.mva.maryland.gov
PR: www.publiclibraries.com/records/maryland.htm
SF: www.oag.state.md.us/publications.htm
         www.alllaw.com/state_resources/maryland/forms
SL: mgaleg.maryland.gov
SS: www.sos.state.md.us
WC: www.wcc.state.md.us

MASSACHUSETTS

AG: www.mass.gov/ago
CP: www.mass.gov/ago/consumer-resources
CS: www.mass.gov/courts
GO: www.mass.gov/governor
LL: www.washlaw.edu/statecourtcounty
LR: www.findlaw.com/casecode/massachusetts.html
         www.loc.gov/law/help/guide/states/us-ma.php
MV: www.massrmv.com
PR: www.sec.state.ma.us/pre/preidx.htm
SF: www.alllaw.com/state_resources/massachusetts/forms
         forms.lp.findlaw.com/states/ma.html
SL: malegislature.gov
SS: www.sec.state.ma.us
WC: www.mass.gov/lwd/workers-compensation

MICHIGAN

AG: www.michigan.gov/ag
CP: www.michigan.gov/ag (click *Consumer Protection*)
CS: courts.mi.gov
GO: www.michigan.gov (click *Government* and
         Executive Branch)
LL: www.washlaw.edu/statecourtcounty
LR: www.findlaw.com/casecode/michigan.html
         www.loc.gov/law/help/guide/states/us-mi.php
MV: www.michigan.gov/sos
PR: www.publiclibraries.com/records/michigan.htm
SF: www.alllaw.com/state_resources/michigan/forms
         forms.lp.findlaw.com/states/mi.html
SL: www.legislature.mi.gov
SS: www.michigan.gov/sos
WC: www.michigan.gov/wca

MINNESOTA

AG: www.ag.state.mn.us
CP: www.ag.state.mn.us/Consumer/Complaint.asp
CS: www.mncourts.gov
GO: mn.gov/governor
LL: mn.gov/lawlib
LR: www.findlaw.com/casecode/minnesota.html
         www.loc.gov/law/help/guide/states/us-mn.php
MV: dps.mn.gov/divisions/dvs
PR: www.brbpublications.com/freesites/FreeSitesState
         .aspx?S1=MN
SF: www.lawlibrary.state.mn.us/forms.html
         www.alllaw.com/state_resources/minnesota/forms
SL: www.leg.state.mn.us
SS: www.sos.state.mn.us
WC: www.dli.mn.gov/workcomp.asp

MISSISSIPPI

AG: www.ago.state.ms.us
CP: www.ago.state.ms.us/divisions/consumer-protection
CS: courts.ms.gov
GO: www.mississippi.gov
LL: courts.ms.gov/state_library/statelibrary.html
LR: www.findlaw.com/casecode/mississippi.html
         www.loc.gov/law/help/guide/states/us-ms.php
MV: www.ms.gov/hp/drivers/license/Main.do
PR: www.publicrecordsfind.us
         /MississippipublicrecordsMSrecords.html
SF: www.alllaw.com/state_resources/mississippi/forms
SL: www.legislature.ms.gov
SS: www.sos.ms.gov
WC: www.mwcc.state.ms.us

MISSOURI

AG: ago.mo.gov
CP: ago.mo.gov/consumercomplaint.htm
CS: www.courts.mo.gov
GO: governor.mo.gov
LL: www.law.missouri.edu/library
LR: www.findlaw.com/11stategov/mo/index.html
         www.loc.gov/law/guide/us-mo.html
MV: dor.mo.gov/mvdl
PR: www.publicrecordfinder.com/states/missouri.html
SF: www.alllaw.com/state_resources/missouri/forms
SL: www.moga.mo.gov
SS: www.sos.mo.gov
WC: www.dolir.mo.gov/wc

MONTANA

AG: www.doj.mt.gov
CP: www.doj.mt.gov/consumer
CS: www.montanacourts.org
GO: governor.mt.gov
LL: courts.mt.gov/library
LR: www.findlaw.com/casecode/montana.html
         www.loc.gov/law/help/guide/states/us-wy.php
MV: www.doj.mt.gov/driving
PR: www.publicrecordsfind.us/Montanapublicrecords
         MTrecords.html
SF: www.alllaw.com/state_resources/montana/forms
         forms.lp.findlaw.com/states/mt.html
SL: leg.mt.gov
SS: sos.mt.gov
WC: wcc.dli.mt.gov

NEBRASKA

AG: www.ago.state.ne.us
CP: www.ago.ne.gov/consumer_protection
CS: supremecourt.ne.gov
GO: governor.nebraska.gov
LL: law.unl.edu/library
LR: www.findlaw.com/casecode/nebraska.html
         www.loc.gov/law/help/guide/states/us-ne.php
MV: www.dmv.state.ne.us
PR: www.publicrecordsfind.us/Nebraskapublicrecords
         NErecords.html
SF: www.alllaw.com/state_resources/nebraska/forms
         forms.lp.findlaw.com/states/ne.html
SL: nebraskalegislature.gov

SS: www.sos.ne.gov
WC: www.wcc.ne.gov

NEVADA

AG: ag.nv.gov
CP: ag.nv.gov/Complaints/File_Complaint
CS: www.nevadajudiciary.us
GO: gov.nv.gov
LL: www.washlaw.edu/statecourtcounty
LR: www.findlaw.com/casecode/nevada.html
www.loc.gov/law/help/guide/states/us-nv.php
MV: nevadadmv.state.nv.us/nvreg.htm
PR: publicrecords.onlinesearches.com/Nevada.htm
SF: www.clan.lib.nv.us/Polaris (Click *Nevada Legal Forms*)
nevadalegalforms.info/php/city.php
www.alllaw.com/state_resources/nevada/forms
SL: www.leg.state.nv.us
SS: nvsos.gov
WC: dirweb.state.nv.us/WCS/wcs.htm

NEW HAMPSHIRE

AG: doj.nh.gov
CP: doj.nh.gov/site-map/consumers.htm
CS: www.courts.state.nh.us
GO: www.governor.nh.gov
LL: www.courts.state.nh.us/lawlibrary
LR: www.findlaw.com/casecode/new-hampshire.html
www.loc.gov/law/help/guide/states/us-nh.php
MV: www.nh.gov/safety/divisions/dmv
PR: www.publicrecordsfind.us/
NewHampshirepublicrecordsNHrecords.html
SF: www.alllaw.com/state_resources/new_hampshire/forms
forms.lp.findlaw.com/states/nh.html
SL: www.gencourt.state.nh.us
SS: sos.nh.gov
WC: www.nh.gov/labor/workers-comp

NEW JERSEY

AG: www.state.nj.us/lps
CP: www.njconsumeraffairs.gov
CS: www.judiciary.state.nj.us
LL: www.washlaw.edu/statecourtcounty
LR: www.findlaw.com/casecode/new-jersey.html
www.loc.gov/law/help/guide/states/us-nj.php
MV: www.state.nj.us/mvc
PR: www.publiclibraries.com/records/newjersey.htm
SF: www.alllaw.com/state_resources/new_jersey/forms
forms.lp.findlaw.com/states/nj.html
SL: www.njleg.state.nj.us
SS: www.state.nj.us/state
WC: lwd.dol.state.nj.us/labor/wc/wc_index.html

NEW MEXICO

AG: www.nmag.gov
CP: www.nmag.gov/consumer
CS: www.nmcourts.com
GO: www.governor.state.nm.us
LL: www.fscll.org
www.washlaw.edu/statecourtcounty
LR: www.findlaw.com/casecode/new-mexico.html
www.loc.gov/law/help/guide/states/us-nm.php
MV: www.mvd.newmexico.gov

PR: www.publiclibraries.com/records/newmexico.htm
SF: www.alllaw.com/state_resources/new_mexico/forms
forms.lp.findlaw.com/states/nm.html
SL: www.nmlegis.gov/lcs
SS: www.sos.state.nm.us
WC: www.workerscomp.state.nm.us

NEW YORK

AG: www.ag.ny.gov
CP: www.ag.ny.gov/complaint-forms
CS: www.courts.state.ny.us
LL: www.washlaw.edu/statecourtcounty
LR: www.findlaw.com/casecode/new-york.html
www.loc.gov/law/help/guide/states/us-ny.php
MV: dmv.ny.gov
PR: www.publicrecordsources.com/new-york-public-records
SF: www.alllaw.com/state_resources/new_york/forms
forms.lp.findlaw.com/states/ny.html
SL: www.assembly.state.ny.us
www.nysenate.gov
SS: www.dos.ny.gov
WC: www.wcb.ny.gov

NORTH CAROLINA

AG: www.ncdoj.com
CP: www.ncdoj.com/Consumer.aspx
CS: www.nccourts.org
GO: www.governor.state.nc.us
LL: www.nccourts.org/Courts
LR: www.findlaw.com/casecode/north-carolina.html
www.loc.gov/law/help/guide/states/us-nc.php
MV: www.ncdot.gov/DMV
PR: www.peoplesmart.com/county-records/public-north-carolina
SF: www.alllaw.com/state_resources/north_carolina/forms
forms.lp.findlaw.com/states/nc.html
SL: www.ncga.state.nc.us
SS: www.secstate.state.nc.us
WC: www.ic.nc.gov

NORTH DAKOTA

AG: www.ag.nd.gov
CP: www.ag.state.nd.us/CPAT/CPAT.htm
CS: www.ndcourts.gov/court/courts.htm
GO: www.governor.nd.gov
LL: www.ndcourts.gov/lawlib/www6.htm
LR: www.findlaw.com/casecode/north-dakota.html
www.loc.gov/law/help/guide/states/us-nd.php
MV: www.dot.nd.gov
PR: www.publicrecordsfind.us/
NorthDakotapublicrecordsNDrecords.html
SF: www.alllaw.com/state_resources/north_dakota/forms
forms.lp.findlaw.com/states/nd.html
SL: www.legis.nd.gov
SS: www.nd.gov/sos
WC: www.workforcesafety.com

OHIO

AG: www.ohioattorneygeneral.gov
CP: www.ohioattorneygeneral.gov/Individuals-and-Families
/Consumers
CS: www.sconet.state.oh.us/JudSystem/trialCourts
GO: www.governor.ohio.gov

LL: www.sconet.state.oh.us/LegalResources/LawLibrary
LR: www.findlaw.com/casecode/ohio.html
      www.loc.gov/law/help/guide/states/us-oh.php
MV: www.bmv.ohio.gov/bmv.asp
PR: www.publiclibraries.com/records/ohio.htm
SF: www.alllaw.com/state_resources/ohio/forms
      www.uslegalforms.com/Ohio.htm
SL: www.legislature.state.oh.us
SS: www.sos.state.oh.us
WC: www.bwc.ohio.gov

OKLAHOMA

AG: www.ok.gov/oag
CP: www.ok.gov/oag/Legal_Resources/Forms_and_Publications
CS: www.oscn.net
GO: www.ok.gov/governor
LL: www.odl.state.ok.us/lawinfo
LR: www.findlaw.com/casecode/oklahoma.html
      www.loc.gov/law/help/guide/states/us-ok.php
MV: www.dps.state.ok.us/dls
PR: www.publiclibraries.com/records/oklahoma.htm
SF: www.alllaw.com/state_resources/oklahoma/forms
      forms.lp.findlaw.com/states/ok.html
SL: www.oklegislature.gov
SS: www.sos.ok.gov
WC: cec.ok.gov

OREGON

AG: www.doj.state.or.us
CP: www.doj.state.or.us/consumer/pages/index.aspx
CS: courts.oregon.gov
GO: www.oregon.gov/gov
LL: www.oregon.gov/soll
LR: www.findlaw.com/casecode/oregon.html
      www.loc.gov/law/help/guide/states/us-or.php
MV: www.oregon.gov/ODOT/DMV
PR: recordsproject.com/public/oregon.asp
SF: www.alllaw.com/state_resources/oregon/forms
      www.stevensness.com
SL: www.oregonlegislature.gov
SS: sos.oregon.gov
WC: www.cbs.state.or.us/wcd

PENNSYLVANIA

AG: www.attorneygeneral.gov
CP: www.attorneygeneral.gov/consumers.aspx
CS: ujsportal.pacourts.us
GO: www.governor.state.pa.us
LL: www.washlaw.edu/statecourtcounty
LR: www.findlaw.com/casecode/pennsylvania.html
      www.loc.gov/law/help/guide/states/us-pa.php
MV: www.dmv.state.pa.us
PR: publicrecords.onlinesearches.com/Pennsylvania.htm
SF: www.alllaw.com/state_resources/pennsylvania/forms
      forms.lp.findlaw.com/states/pa.html
SL: www.legis.state.pa.us
SS: www.dos.state.pa.us
WC: www.dli.state.pa.us

RHODE ISLAND

AG: www.riag.state.ri.us
CP: www.riag.state.ri.us/civil/consumer

CS: www.courts.ri.gov
GO: www.governor.state.ri.us
LL: www.olis.ri.gov/libraries/library.php?code=RLW
LR: www.findlaw.com/casecode/rhode-island.html
      www.loc.gov/law/help/guide/states/us-ri.php
MV: www.dmv.ri.gov
PR: www.publicrecordsfind.us/
      RhodeIslandpublicrecordsRIrecords.html
SF: www.alllaw.com/state_resources/rhode_island/forms
      forms.lp.findlaw.com/states/ri.html
SL: www.rilin.state.ri.us
SS: sos.ri.gov
WC: www.dlt.ri.gov/wc

SOUTH CAROLINA

AG: www.scag.gov
CP: www.consumer.sc.gov/Pages/default.aspx
CS: www.judicial.state.sc.us
GO: governor.sc.gov
LL: www.judicial.state.sc.us/supreme/library.cfm
LR: www.findlaw.com/casecode/south-carolina.html
      www.loc.gov/law/help/guide/states/us-sc.php
MV: www.scdmvonline.com/DMVNew
PR: www.peoplesmart.com/county-records/public-south-carolina
SF: www.alllaw.com/state_resources/south_carolina/forms
SL: www.scstatehouse.gov
SS: www.scsos.com
WC: www.wcc.state.sc.us

SOUTH DAKOTA

AG: atg.sd.gov
CP: atg.sd.gov/Consumers.aspx
CS: ujs.sd.gov
GO: sd.gov/governor
LL: www.usd.edu/law/lawlibrary.cfm
LR: www.findlaw.com/casecode/south-dakota.html
      www.loc.gov/law/help/guide/states/us-sd.php
MV: dor.sd.gov/Motor_Vehicles
PR: www.publicrecordsfind.us
      /SouthDakotapublicrecordsSDrecords.html
SF: www.alllaw.com/state_resources/south_dakota/forms
      www.findlegalforms.com/sitemap/state/SD
SL: legis.sd.gov
SS: www.sdsos.gov
WC: www.sdjobs.org/workerscomp/default.aspx

TENNESSEE

AG: www.tn.gov/attorneygeneral
CP: www.tn.gov/attorneygeneral/cpro/
      protectingconsumer.html
CS: www.tsc.state.tn.us
GO: www.state.tn.us/governor
LL: www.washlaw.edu/statecourtcounty
LR: www.findlaw.com/casecode/tennessee.html
      www.loc.gov/law/help/guide/states/us-tn.php
MV: www.state.tn.us/safety
PR: publicrecords.onlinesearches.com/Tennessee.htm
SF: www.alllaw.com/state_resources/tennessee/forms
      forms.lp.findlaw.com/states/tn.html
SL: www.legislature.state.tn.us
SS: www.state.tn.us/sos
WC: www.tn.gov/labor-wfd/wcomp.shtml

TEXAS

AG: www.texasattorneygeneral.gov
CP: www.texasattorneygeneral.gov/consumer/index.shtml
CS: www.courts.state.tx.us
GO: www.governor.state.tx.us
LL: www.sll.texas.gov
LR: www.findlaw.com/casecode/texas.html
www.loc.gov/law/help/guide/states/us-tx.php
MV: www.txdot.gov
PR: www.texas.gov/en/discover/Pages/records.aspx
SF: www.alllaw.com/state_resources/texas/forms
forms.lp.findlaw.com/states/tx.html
SL: www.capitol.state.tx.us
SS: www.sos.state.tx.us
WC: www.tdi.texas.gov/wc/indexwc.html

UTAH

AG: attorneygeneral.utah.gov
CP: www.consumerprotection.utah.gov
CS: www.utcourts.gov
GO: www.utah.gov/governor
LL: www.utcourts.gov/lawlibrary
LR: www.findlaw.com/casecode/utah.html
www.loc.gov/law/help/guide/states/us-ut.php
MV: dmv.utah.gov
PR: publicrecords.onlinesearches.com/Utah.htm
SF: www.alllaw.com/state_resources/utah/forms
forms.lp.findlaw.com/states/ut.html
SL: le.utah.gov
SS: www.utah.gov/government/secretary-of-state.html
WC: www.laborcommission.utah.gov

VERMONT

AG: www.atg.state.vt.us
CP: www.atg.state.vt.us/issues/consumer-protection.php
CS: www.vermontjudiciary.org
GO: governor.vermont.gov
LL: www.vermontlaw.edu/About_the_Library.htm
LR: www.findlaw.com/casecode/vermont.html
www.loc.gov/law/help/guide/states/us-vt.php
MV: dmv.vermont.gov
PR: publicrecords.onlinesearches.com
SF: www.vermontjudiciary.org/masterpages
/Court-Formsindex.aspx
SL: www.leg.state.vt.us
SS: www.sec.state.vt.us
WC: labor.vermont.gov

VIRGINIA

AG: www.oag.state.va.us
CP: www.oag.state.va.us/Consumer%20Protection/index.html
CS: www.courts.state.va.us
GO: www.governor.virginia.gov
LL: www.courts.state.va.us/courtadmin/library/home.html
LR: www.loc.gov/law/help/guide/states/us-va.php
MV: www.dmv.state.va.us
PR: www.publiclibraries.com/records/virginia.htm
SF: www.alllaw.com/state_resources/virginia/forms
forms.lp.findlaw.com/states/va.html
SL: virginiageneralassembly.gov
SS: commonwealth.virginia.gov
WC: www.vwc.state.va.us

WASHINGTON

AG: www.atg.wa.gov
CP: www.atg.wa.gov/FileAComplaint.aspx#.U7QsevldUXw
CS: www.courts.wa.gov
GO: www.governor.wa.gov
LL: www.courts.wa.gov/library
LR: www.loc.gov/law/help/guide/states/us-wa.php
www.findlaw.com/casecode/washington.html
MV: www.dol.wa.gov
PR: www.publiclibraries.com/records/washington.htm
SF: www.alllaw.com/state_resources/washington/forms
forms.lp.findlaw.com/states/wa.html
SL: www.leg.wa.gov
SS: www.sos.wa.gov
WC: www.lni.wa.gov/ClaimsIns/default.asp

WEST VIRGINIA

AG: www.wvago.gov
CP: www.wv.gov/residents/Pages/ConsumerProtection.aspx
CS: www.courtswv.gov
GO: www.governor.wv.gov
LL: www.courtswv.gov/public-resources/law-library
/law-library-home.html
LR: www.loc.gov/law/help/guide/states/us-wv.php
www.findlaw.com/casecode/west-virginia.html
MV: www.transportation.wv.gov/Pages/default.aspx
PR: www.50states.com/publicrecords/westvirginia.htm#
.U7LznPldUXw
SF: www.alllaw.com/state_resources/west_virginia/forms
forms.lp.findlaw.com/states/wv.html
SL: www.legis.state.wv.us
SS: www.sos.wv.gov
WC: www.wvinsurance.gov/WorkersCompensation.aspx

WISCONSIN

AG: www.doj.state.wi.us
CP: www.doj.state.wi.us/dls/consumer-protection
/consumer-protection
CS: www.wicourts.gov
GO: www.wisgov.state.wi.us
LL: wilawlibrary.gov
LR: www.loc.gov/law/help/guide/states/us-wi.php
www.findlaw.com/casecode/wisconsin.html
MV: www.dot.wisconsin.gov/drivers
PR: publicrecords.onlinesearches.com/Wisconsin.htm
SF: www.alllaw.com/state_resources/wisconsin/forms
forms.lp.findlaw.com/states/wi.html
SL: legis.wisconsin.gov
SS: www.sos.state.wi.us
WC: dwd.wisconsin.gov/wc/default.htm

WYOMING

AG: ag.wyo.gov
CP: ag.wyo.gov/cpu
CS: www.courts.state.wy.us
GO: governor.wy.gov/Pages/default.aspx
LL: courts.state.wy.us/LawLibrary
LR: www.loc.gov/law/help/guide/states/us-wy.php
www.findlaw.com/casecode/wyoming.html
MV: www.dot.state.wy.us
PR: www.50states.com/publicrecords
/wyoming.htm#.U7L4y_ldUXw

SF: www.alllaw.com/state_resources/wyoming/forms
SL: legisweb.state.wy.us
SS: soswy.state.wy.us
WC: wyomingworkforce.org (click Workers' Compensation)

MORE STATE RESOURCES

- **50 States: Age of Majority**
  www.acf.hhs.gov/programs/css/irg-state-map
  (Select *Program Category*)

- **50 States: Aging Services**
  www.statelocalgov.net/50states-aging.cfm

- **50 States: Agriculture Departments**
  www.statelocalgov.net/50states-agriculture.cfm

- **50 States: Budget Offices**
  www.statelocalgov.net/50states-budget-division.cfm

- **50 States: Child Support Enforcement**
  www.acf.hhs.gov/programs/css/irg-state-map

- **50 States: Doing Business in the State**
  www.irs.gov/Businesses/Small-Businesses-&-Self-Employed
  /State-Links-1

- **50 States: Education Departments**
  www.statelocalgov.net/50states-education.cfm

- **50 States: Government Sponsored Art**
  www.statelocalgov.net/50states-arts.cfm

- **50 States: Health Departments**
  www.statelocalgov.net/50states-health.cfm

- **50 States: Incorporation**
  indorgs.virginia.edu/portico/businesses.html

- **50 States: Insurance Departments/Commissions**
  www.statelocalgov.net/50states-insurance.cfm

- **50 States: Legislative Drafting Offices**
  www.oocities.org/iforstat/lrhp14.html

- **50 States: Paternity**
  www.acf.hhs.gov/programs/css/irg-state-map
  (Select *Program Category*)

- **50 States: Public Safety Departments**
  www.statelocalgov.net/50states-public-safety.cfm

- **50 States: Regulatory Boards**
  www.statelocalgov.net/50states-regulatory.cfm

- **50 States: State Employment Offices**
  www.statelocalgov.net/50states-jobs.cfm

- **50 States: Tax Authorities**
  www.statelocalgov.net/50states-tax-authorities.cfm
  www.irs.gov/Businesses/Small-Businesses-&-Self-Employed
  /State-Links-1

- **50 States: Unclaimed Property**
  www.unclaimed.org

- **50 States: Unemployment Insurance Offices**
  www.statelocalgov.net/50states-unemployment.cfm

NEWS STORIES, WAR STORIES, AND PARTING SHOTS

PARALEGAL ELECTED PROBATE JUDGE

In November 1987, Arleen G. Keegan, a paralegal, was elected probate judge in the town of Litchfield, Connecticut. (See Exhibit K-1.) A law degree is not required to be a probate judge in Connecticut. Judge Keegan's caseload is varied. In one case, for example, family members argued that their mother was incompetent when she prepared her will. "It was a tough decision because I had to get in the middle of a situation with family members pulling against a close friend of the decedent." "I get to deal with a lot of people, and I find people totally intriguing."[1]

PARALEGAL ARGUES BEFORE THE FLORIDA SUPREME COURT

Karen McLead is a prominent paralegal in Florida. When the Florida Supreme Court considered proposals to amend ethical rules governing attorneys and paralegals, Karen was invited to express her opinion of the proposals before the full bench of the Supreme Court. The proposed amendments placed limitations on who could be called a paralegal in Florida. Karen opposed the amendments because they were unduly restrictive. (See photos of Karen arguing before the court in Exhibit K-2). The court adopted the amendments. See Florida in Appendix D.

PARALEGAL CHAIRS A STANDING COMMITTEE OF A BAR ASSOCIATION COMMITTEE

The Colorado Bar Association appointed Joanna Hughbanks "to serve as chairman of the Legal Assistants Committee of the Colorado Bar Association." Ms. Hughbanks is an independent paralegal in Denver. She is believed to be the first nonattorney to chair a standing committee of a bar association.[2] The 2015 chair is litigation paralegal, Sydney Greenish. As more and more bar associations allow paralegals

Exhibit K-1	Judge Arleen Keegan, Former Paralegal

Probate Judge (and former paralegal) Arleen Keegan, at the courthouse in Litchfield, Connecticut.

Reprinted with permission of Arleen G. Keegan.

Exhibit K-2   Paralegal Argues Before the Supreme Court of Florida

Paralegal Karen McLead argues before the Supreme Court of Florida in opposition to proposed amendments that would restrict who can be called a paralegal in Florida.

Courtesy of the Florida Supreme Court.

to become associate members or affiliate members (see Chapter 4), roles for paralegals on select bar committees are becoming increasingly common. A recent dramatic example is paralegal Karen McLead, who served in the sensitive and high-profile position of chair of the Florida Bar's Unlicensed Practice of Law Committee between 1998 and 2000.[3] Karen is the paralegal mentioned earlier who made a presentation in Exhibit K-2 before the Supreme Court of Florida.

PARALEGAL APPOINTED BANKRUPTCY TRUSTEE

A Fort Worth paralegal, Twalla Dupriest, was appointed by the Bankruptcy Court as trustee for the estate of T. Cullen Davis, who was one of the wealthiest men in the United States. Twalla was responsible for gathering all of Davis's assets for the purpose of repaying creditors and presided at the meetings of creditors.[4]

NEW YORK PARALEGALS ON 9/11

Oliver Gierke, a Wall Street paralegal, remembers talking with a secretary when they both noticed paper flying around outside the window, some of it burned. Kristan Exner was in her law firm on the fiftieth floor of the North Tower when the planes struck. As she walked down the stairs to safety, she "passed countless firefighters climbing toward the fire." She remembers one fireman in particular about her age (twenty-two) pausing to rest. He looked terrified. "Of all the memories I have, that one stands out the most."[5]

PARALEGAL IN THE LEGISLATURE

Rosemary Mulligan, an Illinois paralegal, ran for a seat in the Illinois House of Representatives in 1990 against an incumbent. The election was held in a suburb of Chicago. The vote was so close that it was declared a tie. By law, such elections are decided by lottery — a toss of the coin. Although the paralegal won the toss, a court later declared her opponent the victor after reviewing some disputed ballots.[6] In 1992, Ms. Mulligan ran again, and this time she won outright. Prior to her election she was a paralegal with a specialty in municipal land development and family law. The first entry on her online biography says, "Paralegal."[7]

PARALEGAL CHARGED WITH INSIDER TRADING

A twenty-four-year-old paralegal was charged with insider trading by the Securities and Exchange Commission (SEC). The complaint

alleged that she had access to confidential information pertaining to the proposed merger of a client of the firm where she worked. She "tipped" her friends by giving them confidential information. The friends then used this information to earn over $800,000 through the purchase of 65,020 shares. A civil complaint sought damages of $3.29 million. The paralegal was fired by the law firm.[8]

A $90,000,000 MISTAKE!

A paralegal for Prudential Insurance Company inadvertently left off the last three zeros on a mortgage that was used to secure a $92,885,000 loan made by Prudential to a company that is now bankrupt. As a result of the mistake, Prudential was left with only a $92,885 lien. Prudential's attorneys have asked the U.S. Bankruptcy Court in New York City to ignore the mistake — and restore the zeros. To the paralegal's great relief, the zeros, after painful litigation, were restored.[9]

PARALEGAL CONVICTED

Mershan Shaddy was an independent paralegal in San Diego. He charged clients $180 to handle uncontested divorces, plus $50 if property had to be divided, and $30 for each child. He was arrested after an undercover investigator posed as a divorce client and secretly recorded him giving legal advice in violation of California law against the unauthorized practice of law. He was convicted and sentenced to forty-five days in jail.[10]

BILLIONAIRE PARALEGAL PREFERS PRISON TO FILLING OUT TIME SHEETS

Michael Milken, the billionaire "junk bond king," went to prison for illegal activities stemming from his Wall Street career. While still under the jurisdiction of federal prison and parole authorities, Milken worked as a "paralegal" in a law firm. He did not enjoy the experience. Comparing prison to the law firm, he told reporters that he would rather have other people keep track of his time than to have to "fill out those…time sheets every day."[11]

DID THE PARALEGAL WORK 43 HOURS ON JANUARY 10?

Hotel magnate Leona Helmsley (infamous for her wealth and her comment that "only little people pay taxes") sued a New York law firm for $35 million because she claimed they submitted fraudulent bills for fees and expenses. Among the allegedly fraudulent items cited in the suit was a bill for forty-three hours of work charged by a paralegal for one day—January 10.[12]

DON'T BE PHOTOGRAPHED IN THAT T-SHIRT

An insurance company challenged a bill for attorney and paralegal time submitted by the Los Angeles law firm, Latham & Watkins. During a court proceeding on the dispute, the company embarrassed the firm by introducing into evidence a photograph of the paralegal working on the case while wearing a T-shirt that read "Born to Bill."[13]

LAW FIRM SUES ITS FORMER PARALEGAL

Richard Trotter once worked as a paralegal for a Denver law firm. He wrote a book called *A Toothless Paper Tiger* about his experiences at the law firm. The book alleged that the firm improperly authorized him and other paralegals at the firm to perform the work of attorneys. The law firm sought an injunction to prevent the release of the book.[14]

PARALEGAL ORDERED TO PAY $925,000 IN ATTORNEY FEES

Los Angeles Superior Court Judge Arnold Gold dismissed the sexual harassment lawsuit brought by a paralegal, Elizabeth Saret-Cook, against her former law firm employer, Gilbert, Kelly, Crowley & Jannett. She alleged that she had been harassed after getting pregnant with the child of an attorney at the firm, Clifford Woosley. Calling her suit "frivolous" and "completely without merit," the judge ordered the paralegal to pay $925,000 in attorney fees to the law firm and to Woosley. This decision was affirmed on appeal.[15] According to court documents, the law firm had earlier offered to settle the suit for $400,000, but Saret-Cook refused the offer.[16]

HE'S NOT AN ATTORNEY?

"Brian T. Valery is our hero. He figured out a way to save $100K on a legal education — namely, by not getting one." While a paralegal at a New York City law firm, Valery told his superiors that he was going to night law school at Fordham. When he announced that he had graduated and passed the bar, no one had any reason to doubt him. The truth (that he never attended law school and never took the bar exam) was not discovered until two years later while Valery was litigating a case in Connecticut! "This story simply proves," said a reporter for the *Washington Post*, "you often don't really need a law degree to provide decent legal services to a client." His legal career in ruins, Valery now faces perjury charges.[17]

LAW FIRM SETTLES SUIT BROUGHT BY PARALEGALS

A class action was brought by paralegals and clerical workers who claimed that the Oakland firm where they worked failed to pay them overtime compensation. The case was eventually settled for $170,000, which was distributed among the paralegals and clerical workers.[18]

WILL THE LEGAL ASSISTANT PLEASE TELL THE COURT THE FACTS OF THE CASE?

At a paralegal association meeting in Houston, Judge Lynn Hughes, a federal district court judge, drew a "big laugh" concerning an incident in her courtroom. During a hearing, she watched a "Big Gun" senior partner constantly turn to his associate for information on the facts of the case. This associate, in turn, would ask his legal assistant for this information. Finally, Judge Hughes asked the legal assistant to stand up and tell the court the facts of the case![19]

"THEN YOU SHOULD HAVE USED A PARALEGAL!"

At oral argument before the U.S. Supreme Court in a case on paralegal fees, an attorney was interrupted by Justice Thurgood Marshall during the attorney's description of the custom of billing in New Orleans. In the following fascinating excerpt from the transcript of the oral argument, a clearly irritated Justice Marshall suggested that the attorney was unprepared because he did not have a paralegal working with him on the case:

JUSTICE MARSHALL:	Is all that in the record?
ATTORNEY:	I'm sorry …
JUSTICE MARSHALL:	Is that in the record?
ATTORNEY:	I'm not …
JUSTICE MARSHALL:	What you've just said, that the custom of billing and all in New Orleans, is that in the record?
ATTORNEY:	I think it is Justice Marshall.
JUSTICE MARSHALL:	You think? Didn't you try the case?
ATTORNEY:	I tried the case, but whether or not that particular item is in the record, it is certainly in the briefs, but …
JUSTICE MARSHALL:	Then you should have used a paralegal![20]

THE PERFECT RECIPE

"To one paralegal, add a pound of variety, eight ounces of flexibility, four ounces of creativity, and a healthy sense of humor. The result? One cost-effective, efficient litigation paralegal."[21]

PARALEGAL TRAPPED

A paralegal, on his way to an assignment on another floor, became trapped in an elevator just after getting on. Fellow employees gathered around the elevator door. The time-conscious paralegal called out from inside the elevator, "Is this billable or nonbillable time?"[22]

THE COST OF WHAT?

Recently, a paralegal was given an unusual assignment by her supervising attorney. She was asked to determine how much it would cost to purchase a penguin![23]

PARALEGAL WATCHES EXORCISM

Kevin McKinley is a paralegal at a West Palm Beach law firm that represented a defendant in a murder case. While working on the case, Kevin found an urn in the room of the defendant where the latter allegedly practiced voodoo and black magic. The family of the defendant was concerned that if the urn was opened in the courtroom, the spirit within it would harm those attending the trial. Hence an exorcism was performed to remove the defendant's control over this spirit. Kevin's assignment was to be a witness at this exorcism.[24]

THE PARALEGAL FLORAL STRATEGY

A litigation legal assistant was given the task of serving a subpoena on a defendant who was unlikely to open the door. She came up with a creative approach. On her way to the defendant's house, she stopped at a flower shop and picked up a plant. Upon her arrival, she rang the doorbell. The defendant looked out, saw a person with flowers, opened the door, and was presented with a plant…and a subpoena![25]

MORE UNUSUAL PARALEGAL ASSIGNMENTS

- Sandra Maness sat in the cab of a tractor trailer and videotaped its route along a narrow path in a land dispute over what constituted a road.
- Lisa McGibbon needed to obtain the VIN (vehicle identification number) of a boat that a client wanted to seize in order to satisfy a judgment. She went to the marina at night and obtained the VIN while "literally hanging off the side" of the boat.
- Anita Pollock crawled under cars to take pictures of frame damage that was not visible standing at the side of the car. She also videotaped medical exams.

WANTED: ADVENTUROUS PARALEGAL 107 POUNDS OR UNDER

The following want ad appeared in the classified section of a San Francisco legal newspaper. "ADVENTUROUS PARALEGAL. Travel in pvt. aircraft around the country up to 3 wks/mo. investigating franchise cases. Duties incl: client interviews, lgl research & witness invest. Your weight max: 107 lbs. (flight requirement)."[26]

URBAN LEGEND: A PARALEGAL'S SUSHI MEMO

In 2003, a paralegal made the front page of the *New York Times*. The story was about a memo that the paralegal had written about sushi restaurants in the Manhattan area of the law firm. The memo was three pages long, and replete with exhibits and footnotes. Is this what happens, the *Times* story suggested, when you ask a simple question ("Where's a good place for sushi?") to someone in the legal community? The memo soon became an urban legend as news of the memo spread around the world. Some believed that it was a parody or joke, but sources at the law firm (Paul, Weiss, Rifkind, Wharton & Garrison) insisted that it was genuine. They were quick to add, however, that the paralegal's time in drafting the memo was not billed to any clients.[27]

WANTED: PARALEGAL WITH MINIMUM OF 203 YEARS OF EXPERIENCE

A paralegal placement agency is seeking a person "w/at least 203 yrs exp in paralegal field." The ad was either a typo or the first step in getting recognition in the next edition of the Guinness record book.[28]

PARALEGAL BUMPER STICKERS

In Google Images, Bing Images, or Yahoo Images, type this entry: *paralegal bumper sticker*. Here are some entries for bumper stickers and tee shirts:

- Paralegals Rule
- My Paralegal Rocks
- The Few, the Proud, the Paralegals
- Because I'm The Paralegal, That's Why
- Do Not Disturb! Paralegal at Work!
- Have You Hugged Your Paralegal Today?
- Paralegal, The Real Power of Attorney

THE WORLD OF ATTORNEYS

- "I served with General Washington in the legislature of Virginia before the revolution, and during it, with Dr. Franklin in Congress. If the present Congress errs in too much talking, how could it do otherwise in a body to which the people send 150 lawyers, whose trade it is to question everything, yield nothing & talk by the hour?" *Autobiography 1743–1790*, Thomas Jefferson.

- If a man were to give another man an orange, he would say, simply, "Have an orange." But if the transaction were entrusted to an attorney, he would say: "I hereby give, grant, bargain and sell to you, all my right, title and interest in, of, and to said orange, together with all its rind, skin, juice, pulp, and pips, and all rights and advantages therein, with full power to bite, cut, and otherwise eat of the same, or give the same away, with or without the rind, skin, juice, pulp, and pips, anything hereinbefore or hereinafter, or in any other deed or deeds, instrument or instruments, of whatever kind or nature whatsoever to the contrary in any wise notwithstanding."[29]
- A document recently filed in the U.S. Bankruptcy Court in Tennessee contained the following language: "Debtors hereby amend the Amendment to Second Amended and Restated Disclosure Statement, Third Amended and Restated Plan of Reorganization, and Amendment to Third Amended and Restated Plan of Organization as follows. Wherever the name 'Mortgage Company' appears in the Amendment to Second Amended and Restated Disclosure Statement, Third Amended and Restated Plan of Reorganization and Amendment to Third Amended and Restated Plan of Organization, the name 'Bank' shall be inserted in lieu thereof."[30]
- Question: How many lawyers does it take to change a light bulb? Answer. Three senior partners to contemplate the history of light; two junior partners to check for conflicts of interest; ten associates to do the research on the antitrust implications of using a particular brand, on the cost-benefits of electric lighting versus candle light, on the health aspects of incandescent versus fluorescent bulb lighting, on the electric components that make light bulbs work, etc. And, of course, a paralegal to insert the bulb into the socket![31]

A SUIT TO COMPENSATE A TREE

In one of the oddest court opinions ever written, a three-judge panel in Michigan affirmed a lower court decision that denied relief for damage caused by the defendant's Chevrolet to the plaintiff's tree. The opinion is *Fisher v. Lowe*:[32]

> We thought that we would never see
> A suit to compensate a tree.
> A suit whose claim in tort is prest
> Upon a mangled tree's behest;
> A tree whose battered trunk was prest
> Against a Chevy's crumpled crest;
> A tree that faces each new day
> With bark and limb in disarray;
> A tree that may forever bear
> A lasting need for tender care.
> Flora lovers though we three,
> We must uphold the court's decree.
> Affirmed.

THE TWENTY-FIVE GREATEST LEGAL MOVIES

The American Bar Association Journal did a poll of its readers to identify the twenty-five greatest legal movies.[33] Here are the results:

- 12 Angry Men
- A Civil Action
- A Few Good Men
- A Man for All Seasons

- Amistad
- Anatomy of a Murder
- And Justice for All
- Breaker Morant
- Chicago
- Compulsion
- Erin Brockovich
- In the Name of the Father
- Inherit the Wind
- Judgment at Nuremberg
- Kramer vs. Kramer

- Miracle on 34th Street
- My Cousin Vinny
- Philadelphia
- Presumed Innocent
- Reversal of Fortune
- The Paper Chase
- To Kill a Mockingbird
- Verdict, The
- Witness for the Prosecution
- Young Mr. Lincoln

To see excepts any of these movies, type the title in YouTube. Also, run this search in Google, Bing, or Yahoo: *where can you see old movies for free?*

THE TWENTY-FIVE GREATEST LEGAL TV SHOWS

The American Bar Association Journal also did a poll to identify the twenty-five greatest TV shows.[34] Here are the results:

- *L.A. Law*
- *Perry Mason*
- *The Defenders*
- *Law & Order*
- *The Practice*
- *Ally McBeal*
- *Rumpole of the Bailey*
- *Boston Legal*
- *Damages*

- *Night Court*
- *Judging Amy*
- *Owen Marshall: Counselor at Law*
- *Jag*
- *Shark*
- *Civil Wars*
- *Harvey Birdman, Attorney at Law*

- *Law & Order: Criminal Intent*
- *Murder One*
- *Matlock*
- *Reasonable Doubts*
- *Law & Order: Special Victims Unit*

- *Judd for the Defense*
- *Paper Chase*
- *Petrocelli*
- *Eli Stone*

To see excepts, type the title in YouTube. Also, run this search in Google, Bing, or Yahoo: *where can you see old TV shows for free?*

THE TWELVE GREATEST COURTROOM DRAMAS PERFORMED ON STAGE

In another list, the American Bar Association Journal did a poll to identify the twelve greatest courtroom dramas performed on stage.[35] Here are the results:

- *The Merchant of Venice*
- *Twelve Angry Men*
- *Inherit the Wind*
- *Judgment at Nuremberg*
- *Witness for the Prosecution*
- *The Caine Mutiny*

- *A Man for All Seasons*
- *Anatomy of a Murder*
- *A Few Good Men*
- *Chicago*
- *Oedipus the King*
- *The Man in the Glass Booth*

To see excepts, type the title in YouTube.

AND FINALLY

Law offices often send out announcements. Exhibit K-3 are announcements collected by the Association of Legal Administrators.

Exhibit K-3	Announcements

The remnants of the once proud firms of
DAZZLE & DROWN
and
BETTEROFF, SOMEWHERE & ELSE
are pleased to announce the merger of what is left of their practices. They will continue under the name of
BETTEROFF & DROWN
The firm will continue to specialize in whatever it takes to survive.

DREAMS BEE & DASHED
A Professional Corporation
is pleased to announce
the relocation of its office to
Grant Avenue Safeway FoodMart
1001 Grant Avenue
Collegial, AZ
Telephone (393) 422-9987
The Firm will continue to seek subtenants for its penthouse suite in the Palace Tower

HAPPY & BLIND
is pleased to announce that
Truman R. Rightwig
formerly a partner for 27 years before being let go by
Shining, Star & Nomore
has joined the firm as a Contract Attorney
Mr. Rightwig will continue to specialize in litigating Nixon's 1971 Price Control Act

The Law Firm of
HURTING & SMARTING
is pleased to announce the terminations of

Harvey Notgood, Partner
Constance Reminder, Partner
Cynthia Snorz, Partner
Frederick Grating, Associate
Mildred Muddle, Associate
Eric Tomorrow, Paralegal
Janet Time, Secretary
Raymont Rabbit, Messenger

as part of its strategic plan to fit the size of the firm to its level of business.

GARGLE, MUMBLE & NUMB
Attorneys at Law

is pleased to announce
the cessation of its
recruiting program and
the decrease in its
first year associate starting
salary to $32,000

Applicants can
take it or leave it.

Source: Jim Cowan, Truth in Advertising, 10 ALA Newsletter 30 (Association of Legal Administrators, August/September 1991) (Reprinted with permission)

ENDNOTES

1. Howard, *A Legal Assistant Is Elected Probate Judge*, 5 Legal Assistant Today 32 (March/April 1988).

2. Letter from Christopher R. Brauchi, President of the Colorado Bar Association, to Joanna Hughbanks, June 27, 1989.

3. Mary Micheletti, *Karen McLead Serving with Distinction*, 17 Legal Assistant Today 52 (September/October 1999).

4. *Paralegal Appointed Trustee to Cullen Davis Estate*, Newsletter (Dallas Association of Legal Assistants, September 1987).

5. R. Hughes, *Five Years Later*, 24 Legal Assistant Today 66, 67, (September/October 2006).

6. *Toss of Coin to Decide Race in Illinois*, New York Times, July 18, 1990, at A12.

7. www.ilga.gov/house/rep.asp?MemberID=1402.

8. *Securities and Exchange Commission v. Hurton*, 43 S.E.C. Docket 1422, 1989 WL 991581 (May 16, 1989).

9. *17 At Issue* (San Francisco Paralegal Association, December 1990). *Prudential Ins. Co. of Am. v. SS American Lancer*, 686 F. Supp. 469 (S.D.N.Y 1988).

10. *Paralegal's Role in Legal System Stirs a Debate*, San Diego Union, March 29, 1990, at B-1.

11. *News across the Country*, KLAS Action (Kansas Legal Assistants Society, December/January 1994).

12. Andrew Blum, *The Empress Strikes Back*, The National Law Journal, July 11, 1994, at A6.

13. *Take Note of This*, California Paralegal 9 (January/March 1992).

14. Hicks, *Law Firm Fights Book by Former Employee*, National Law Journal, August 6, 1990, at 39.

15. *Saret-Cook v. Gilbert, Kelly, Crowley & Jennett*, 88 Cal. Rptr. 2d 732 (Cal. App. 2d Dist. 1999). To read the case online, go to scholar.google.com, select *Case law* and type *88 Cal. Rptr. 2d 732* in the search box.

16. Rebecca Liss, *Paralegal Ordered to Pay Fees in Harassment Case*, Los Angeles Daily Journal, September 27, 1996, at 2.

17. Enter this search in Google, Bing, or Yahoo: "Brian T. Valery".

18. Ziegler, *Firm Settles Suit on Overtime for Paralegals*, San Francisco Banner Daily Journal, January 25, 1989.

19. *National News ... Houston Legal Assistants Association*, 21 Outlook 5 (Illinois Paralegal Ass'n, Spring 1991).

20. *Official Transcript Proceedings before the Supreme Court of the United States, Arthur J. Blanchard, Petitioner v. James Bergerson, et al.*, Case 87–1485, at 25 (November 28, 1988).

21. Vore, *A Litigation Recipe*, On Point (National Capital Area Paralegal Association, November 1990).

22. *A Lighter Note*, MALA Advance 15 (Summer 1989).

23. *How Much Does a Penguin Cost?* SJPA Reporter 3 (South Jersey Paralegal Association September 1990).

24. *Exorcism of Urn Clears Way for Murder Trial*, The Tuscaloosa News, January 6, 1990 at 1F.

25. Anderson, *In the Line of Duty*, MALA Advance 17 (Minnesota Association of Paralegals, Spring 1991).

26. *Daily Journal Classifieds*, The Daily Journal, May 17, 1993, at 18.

27. *Sushi Memo* (en.wikipedia.org/wiki/Sushi_memo). Also, enter this search in Google, Bing, or Yahoo: paralegal sushi memo.

28. *Employment Registry*, Reporter, 11 (Los Angeles Paralegal Association, June 1993).

29. James Holland and Julian Webb, *Learning Legal Rules: A Students' Guide to Legal Method and Reasoning* 105 (Oxford University Press 2013).

30. *The Reporter* 15 (Delaware Paralegal Association, May/June 1991).

31. *On the Lighter Side*, ParSpectives 5 (Paralegal Association of Rochester, May 1990).

32. 333 N.W.2d 67 (Mich. Ct. App. 1983). To read the case online, go to scholar.google.com, select *Case law* and type *333 N.W.2d 67* in the search box.

33. A Richard Brust, The 25 Greatest Legal Movies, ABA Journal (August 1, 2008) (www.abajournal.com/magazine/article /the_25_greatest_legal_movies).

34. Stephanie Ward, *The 25 Greatest Legal TV Shows*, August 1, 2009 (www.abajournal.com/magazine/article /the_25_greatest_legal_tv_shows)

35. Jill Chanen, *The theater's 12 Greatest Courtroom Dramas*, ABA Journal *(August 1, 2012)* (www.abajournal.com/magazine/article /the_theaters_12_greatest_courtroom_dramas).

GLOSSARY

A

A. (1) Annotated. (2) *Atlantic Reporter*.

A.2d See *Atlantic 2d*.

AAfPE American Association for Paralegal Education (www.aafpe.org).

ABA American Bar Association (www.abanet.org).

abstract A summary or abridgment. See also *digest*.

abuse of process A tort consisting of the following elements: (1) the use of civil or criminal proceedings, (2) for a purpose for which the process is not designed, (3) resulting in actual damage.

a/c accounts receivable A list of who owes money to the office, how much, how long the debt has been due, etc.

accreditation A form of acknowledgment (other than certification, registration, or licensing) that a school or training program meets specified standards.

ACP (1) Advanced Certified Paralegal. See *specialty certification*. (2) See *attorney-client privilege*.

acquit To declare that the accused is innocent of the crime.

act See *statute*.

active voice The grammatical verb form in which the subject or thing performing or causing the action is the main focus. See also *passive voice*.

ad damnum clause A clause stating the damages claimed.

add-on question A question that is added to the end of another related question, both stated in one sentence. Also called *double-barreled question*.

adjourn To halt the proceedings temporarily.

adjudicate To resolve or decide by judicial process; to judge. The noun is *adjudication*; the adjective is *adjudicative*. See also *quasi-adjudication*.

ad litem For the purposes of this litigation. See also *guardian ad litem*.

administrative agency A governmental body, other than a court or legislature, that carries out (i.e., administers or executes) the statutes of the legislature, the executive orders of the chief executive, and its own regulations.

administrative code A collection of administrative regulations organized by subject matter rather than chronologically or by date.

administrative decision An administrative agency's resolution of a controversy (following a hearing) involving the application of the regulations, statutes, or executive orders that govern the agency. Sometimes called *ruling, administrative ruling*.

administrative hearing A proceeding at an administrative agency presided over by a hearing officer (e.g., an administrative-law judge) to resolve a controversy involving the application of the regulations, statutes, or executive orders that govern the agency.

administrative-law judge (ALJ) A government officer who presides over a hearing at an administrative agency. See also *hearing examiner*. (Most, but not all, ALJs are attorneys.)

Administrative Procedure Act (APA) The statute that governs procedures before federal administrative agencies. Many states have their own version of the APA for procedures before state administrative agencies.

administrative regulation A law written by an administrative agency designed to explain or carry out the statutes, executive orders, or other regulations that govern the agency. Also called *administrative rule*.

admiralty law An area of the law that covers accidents and injuries on navigable waters. Also called *maritime law*.

admissible Allowed into court to determine truth or believability.

admission (1) An assertion of the truth of a fact. (2) An official acknowledgment of someone's right to practice law.

admonition A milder form of private reprimand. Also called *private warning, private reproval*. See also reprimand.

ADR See alternative dispute resolution.

Advanced Certified Paralegal (ACP) The certification credential offered by NALA to paralegals who already have the CP/CLA credential.

advance sheet A pamphlet that comes out before (in advance of) a later volume.

adversarial Involving conflict and an adversary (opponent). See also *hearing*.

adversary system A method of resolving a legal dispute whereby the parties (alone or through their advocates) argue their conflicting claims before a neutral (impartial) decision maker.

adverse (1) Opposed. (2) Hostile. (3) Having an opposing position. (4) Harmful, unfavorable.

adverse interest A goal or claim of one person that is different from or opposed to the goal or claim of another person.

adverse judgment A judgment or decision against you.

advisement Careful consideration. If a decision is *taken under advisement*, it is delayed until the judge has time to consider it later.

advocacy The process by which you attempt to influence the goals or behavior of others.

AFA See *alternate fee arrangement*.

affidavit A written or printed statement of facts made under oath by a person (called the *affiant*) before someone with authority to administer the oath.

affirm To agree with or uphold the lower court judgment.

affirmative defense A defense raising facts or arguments that will defeat the opponent's claim even if the opponent's allegations in the claim are proven.

aged accounts receivable (A/R) report A report showing all cases that have outstanding balances due and how long these balances are past due.

agent (1) A person authorized to act for another; a representative. See also *principal*. (2) A power or force that produces an effect.

aggrieved Injured or wronged and thereby entitled to a remedy.

ALA Association of Legal Administrators (www.alanet.org).

allegation A claimed fact. A fact that a party will try to prove at trial.

alphabetical filing system A method of storing client files in alphabetical order by the surname or organization name of the client. See also *numerical filing system*.

A.L.R. See *American Law Reports*.

ALR Index The main index to annotations within the volumes of American Law Reports.

alternate An extra juror who will take the place of a regular juror if one is removed or becomes incapacitated during the trial.

alternate fee arrangement (AFA) Billing for services other than by standard hourly fees.

alternative dispute resolution (ADR) A method or procedure for resolving a legal dispute without litigating the dispute in a court or administrative agency.

ALWD Guide to Legal Citation A guidebook on citation form. It is the major competitor to *The Bluebook*.

ambulance chasing Approaching accident victims (or anyone else who might have a legal problem or claim) to encourage them to hire a particular attorney. If the attorney uses someone else to do the soliciting, the latter is called a *runner*. If this other person uses deception or fraud in the solicitation, he or she is sometimes called a *capper* or a *steerer*.

American Digest System Three digests of West (Thomson Reuters) that give summaries of every state and federal court that publishes its opinions: *Century Digest* covers opinions prior to 1897; *Decennial Digest* covers opinions during ten-year periods; and *General Digest* covers opinions since the last *Decennial Digest*.

American Jurisprudence 2d (Am. Jur. 2d) A legal encyclopedia of West (Thomson Reuters) that is national in scope.

American Law Reports (A.L.R., A.L.R.2d, A.L.R.3d, A.L.R.4th, A.L.R.5th, A.L.R.6th, A.L.R. Fed., A.L.R. Fed. 2d) A reporter of West (Thomson Reuters) that prints selected opinions and extensive annotations based on issues in the opinions. See also *annotated reporter*, *annotated statutory code*, *annotation*.

American rule Each party pays his or her own attorney fees (and paralegal fees) regardless of who wins the case. For exceptions, see *fee shifting*.

amicus curiae brief ("friend of the court" brief) An appellate brief submitted by a nonparty who obtains court permission to file a brief presenting its views on how the case should be resolved.

Am. Jur. 2d See *American Jurisprudence, 2d*.

analogize To determine whether something is sufficiently similar to justify a similar outcome or result.

analogous (1) Sufficiently similar to justify a similar outcome or result. (2) Sufficiently similar to lend support. (3) On point; germane. Involving the same or similar issues; involving facts and rules that are similar to those now under consideration.

analogy A comparison of similarities and differences.

ann. Annotated.

annotate To provide notes or commentary. A text is *annotated* if such notes and commentary are provided along with the text.

annotated reporter A set of books that contains the full text of court opinions plus notes or commentary on them called *annotations*.

annotated statutory code A collection of statutes organized by subject matter rather than by date, along with research references such as historical notes and summaries of court opinions (notes of decision) that have interpreted the statutes.

annotation (1) A note or commentary that summarizes or explains something. (2) A research paper in sets of volumes called *American Law Reports* (A.L.R.).

answer (1) The first pleading of the defendant in response to the plaintiff's claims. (2) To assume someone else's liability.

anticontact rule An advocate must not contact an opposing party without permission of the latter's attorney. Also called *no-contact rule*.

antitrust law The law governing unlawful interferences with competition such as through price fixing, monopolies, and other restraints of trade.

APA See Administrative Procedure Act.

appeal A proceeding in which a higher tribunal reviews or reconsiders the decision of an inferior tribunal.

appeal by right The appeal of a case that an appellate court must hear; it has no discretion on whether to take the appeal.

appearance Formally coming before a tribunal as a party or as a representative of a party.

appearance of impropriety Conduct that is unethical because it appears to violate ethical rules even though in fact no violation has occurred.

appellant The party bringing an appeal because of disagreement with a decision of a lower tribunal. Also called *petitioner*.

appellate brief A document that a party files with an appellate court (and serves on an opponent) in which the party presents arguments on why the appellate court should affirm (approve), reverse, vacate (cancel), or otherwise modify what a lower court has done.

appellate jurisdiction The power of a court to review and correct the decisions of a lower tribunal.

appellee The party against whom an appeal is brought. Also called *respondent*.

application (app) Software that performs tasks for an end user other than the major tasks of running the computer itself. The most commonly used apps today are downloaded on mobile devices.

application service provider (ASP) A provider of software through the Internet to users on an as-needed basis.

approval A form of acknowledgment that a school or training program meets specified standards. The acknowledgment may be based on different standards than those used for accreditation.

arbitration A method of alternative dispute resolution (ADR) in which the parties avoid litigation by submitting their dispute to a neutral third person (the arbitrator) who renders a decision resolving the dispute.

Arizona certified legal document preparer (AZCLDP) See *legal document preparer (LDP)*.

arraignment A pretrial criminal proceeding in which the defendant is formally charged with a crime and enters a plea. Arrangements are then made for the next proceeding.

arrest Taking someone into custody to bring him or her before the proper authorities, e.g., to answer a criminal charge.

Article III court See *constitutional court*.

ASP See application service provider.

assigned counsel An attorney (often in private practice) appointed by the court and paid by the government to represent an indigent person in a criminal or civil case. Attorneys who are government employees handling criminal cases might be called *public defenders*.

associate An attorney employee of a partnership who hopes eventually to be promoted to partnership. See also *law clerk* (1).

at common law (1) Referring to all the case law and statutory law in England and in the American colonies before the Revolution. (2) Pertaining to judge-made law. See also *common law*.

Atlantic Reporter 2d (A.2d) A regional reporter of West (Thomson Reuters) that prints state court opinions of nine states (Conn., Del., Me., Md., N.H., N.J., Pa., R.I., Vt., and Washington, D.C.).

A.2d The second series of Atlantic Reporter. The abbreviation of the first series is A.

attentive listening Affirmative, ongoing steps taken by an interviewer to let an interviewee know that you have heard what he or she just said and that you consider the meeting with him or her to be important.

attestation clause A clause stating that you saw (witnessed) someone sign a document or perform other tasks related to the validity of the document.

attorney attestation A signed statement by an attorney that a paralegal applying for membership in an association meets one or more of the criteria of the association, the most common of which is that the paralegal performs paralegal duties.

attorney-client privilege (ACP) A client or a client's attorney can refuse to disclose any confidential (private) communication between them if the purpose of the communication was to facilitate the provision of legal services to the client.

attorney general The chief attorney for the government. See also *opinion of the attorney general*.

attorney in fact One authorized to act in place of another, often in a business transaction.

attorney lien The right of an attorney to hold a client's funds or property (retaining lien) or to keep a part of funds coming to the client (a charging lien) until the attorney's fees and costs have been paid. See also *lien*.

attorney of record The attorney noted in court files as the attorney representing a particular party.

attorney work product See *work-product rule*.

at-will employee An employee who can be terminated for any reason that does not violate public policy. An employee with no union or other contractual protection.

authentication (1) The use of evidence that a writing or other physical item is genuine and that it is what it purports to be. (2) An official process by which the text of a law is certified as being complete and unaltered since the original version was approved. The verb is *authenticate*.

authority See *mandatory authority, persuasive authority, primary authority, secondary authority*.

award (1) The decision of an arbitrator. (2) A decision that grants damages.

AZCLDP See *legal document preparer (LDP)*.

B

backspace The key that allows you to delete the character to the left of the cursor.

backup A copy of your data stored in a different location for safekeeping.

bad faith Dishonesty or abuse in one's purpose or conduct.

bail (1) Money or other property deposited with the court as security to ensure that the defendant will reappear at designated times. Failure to appear forfeits the security. (2) Release of the defendant upon posting this security.

bailiff A court employee who keeps order in the courtroom and renders general administrative assistance to the judge.

bankruptcy petition preparer (BPP) A nonattorney who is authorized to charge fees for preparing (without attorney supervision) a bankruptcy petition or any other bankruptcy document that a self-represented debtor will file in a federal court.

bar Prevent or stop.

bar code A sequence of numbers and vertical lines of different shapes that can be read by an optical scanner.

barratry The crime of stirring up quarrels or litigation. Persistently instigating lawsuits, often groundless ones. The illegal solicitation of clients.

Bates stamp A tool with which to manually or digitally insert a number (usually sequential) on a page. After using the tool on a page, it automatically advances to the next number, ready to stamp the next page.

battered woman syndrome A woman's psychological helplessness or paralysis because of conditions such as financial dependence, loneliness, guilt, shame, and fear of reprisal from her husband or significant other who has repeatedly subjected her to physical, sexual, and/or emotional abuse in the past.

below (1) Pertaining to a lower level of court in the hierarchy of a court system. (2) Later in the document.

bench conference See *sidebar conference*.

bench trial A trial before a judge without a jury. Also called a *nonjury trial*.

beyond a reasonable doubt The standard of proof that is met when there are no doubts about the evidence that would cause prudent persons to hesitate before acting in matters of importance to themselves.

bias (1) An inclination, tendency, or predisposition to think or act in a certain way. (2) Prejudice for or against something or someone. (3) A danger of prejudgment.

bicameral Having two chambers in the legislature. If there is only one chamber, it is *unicameral*.

bill A proposed statute.

billable Pertaining to those tasks requiring time that can be charged to (and paid by) a client.

billable hours quota A minimum number of hours expected from a timekeeper on client matters that can be charged (billed) to clients per week, month, year, or other time period.

billing realization rate See *realization rate*.

bindover hearing See *preliminary hearing*.

black letter law A statement of a fundamental or basic principle of law.

blawg An Internet journal or diary on a mainly legal topic. See also *blog*.

blended hourly rate A single hourly rate based on a blend or mix of the rates normally charged by different individuals, e.g., a partner, a senior associate, a junior associate, and sometimes a paralegal. See also *fee*.

blind ad A want ad that does not give the name and address of the prospective employer. The contact is made through a third party, e.g., a newspaper or agency.

block A group of characters, e.g., a word, a sentence, a paragraph.

block billing Grouping multiple tasks under a single time charge rather than describing each task separately and assigning the actual time associated with each task. The timekeeper enters the total time spent working on blocks of tasks without itemizing the time spent on specific tasks for the case.

Block movement A feature of a word processor that allows the user to define a block of text and then do something with that block, e.g., move it or delete it.

blog An Internet journal or diary on any topic of interest to the blogger (writer) of the blog. Sometimes called *blawg* if the topic of the blog is mainly legal.

Bloomberg Law A major publisher of fee-based online legal research materials.

bluebook (also spelled *blue book*) (1) *The Bluebook: A Uniform System of Citation*, a guidebook on citation form. (2) The *National Reporter Blue Book*, a source for parallel cites in all states. (3) The *A.L.R. Bluebook of Supplemental Decisions*, a set of books that allows you to update the annotations in *A.L.R.1st*. (4) A directory of government offices and employees.

board of appeals The unit within an administrative agency to which a party can appeal a decision of the agency.

boilerplate Standard language that is commonly used in a certain kind of document. Standard verbiage.

bona fides Good faith.

bond An obligation to perform an act (e.g., pay a sum of money) upon the occurrence of a designated condition.

bonus A payment beyond one's regular salary, usually as a reward or recognition. See also *incentive billing*.

book (1) To enter charges against someone in a police register. The process is called *booking*. (2) To engage the services of someone.

booking Entering charges against someone in a police register.

Boolean search A search that allows words to be specifically included or excluded through operatives such as AND, OR, and NOT.

booting up Turning on or restarting the computer and loading the operating system.

bound over Held or transferred for further court proceedings.

boutique law firm A law firm that specializes in one main area of the law.

BPP See bankruptcy petition preparer.

breach of contract A cause of action seeking a court remedy (usually damages) for the alleged failure of a party to perform the term(s) of an enforceable contract.

brief (1) A summary of a court opinion that consists of ten parts: citation, parties, objectives of the parties, theories of the litigation, history of the litigation, facts, issues, holdings, reasoning, and disposition. Also called *case brief, brief of a case*. (2) Trial brief. See this term. (3) Appellate brief. See this term.

brief bank A collection of appellate briefs and related documents drafted in prior cases that might be adapted for current cases and used as models.

brief of a case See *brief*.

budget performance report A report that compares a firm's actual income and expenditures with budgeted or projected income and expenditures.

"bugs" Manufacturing or design errors that exist in products. Computer hardware or software glitches.

bundled legal services All tasks needed to represent a client; all-inclusive legal services. See also *unbundled legal services*.

burden of proof The responsibility of proving a fact at trial.

byte The storage equivalent of one space or one character of the alphabet typed into a computer.

C

calendar See *docket*.

calendar call The time in court when a case on the calendar (docket) is called for a determination by the judge of the next step in the proceeding. Also called *docket call*.

California Reporter 2d (Cal. Rptr. 2d) An unofficial reporter of West (Thomson Reuters) that publishes opinions of California state courts.

CALR See computer-assisted legal research.

Cal. Rptr. 2d See *California Reporter 2d*.

cap See *fee cap*.

capital partner See *equity partner*.

capper See *ambulance chasing*, *runner*.

caption The heading or introductory part of a pleading, court opinion, memo, or other document that provides identifying information such as the kind of document it is, the names of the parties, and the court involved, if any.

career client list A confidential list of every client or matter you worked on in any law office (as a paid employee or volunteer) from the beginning of your legal career to the present time. The list is used to help determine whether any of your future work might create a conflict of interest.

CARTWHEEL A technique designed to help you think of a large variety of words and phrases to check in online search engines and in book indexes.

CAS California Advanced Specialist, a person who has passed the California Advanced Specialty Examination.

case (1) A court's written explanation of how it applied the law to the facts to resolve a legal dispute. Also called *opinion*, *court opinion*, *judicial opinion*, *decision*. (2) A pending matter on a court calendar. (3) A client matter handled by a law office.

casebook A law-school textbook containing numerous edited court opinions and related materials assembled for a course.

case brief See brief.

case clerk (1) An assistant to a paralegal. (2) An entry-level paralegal.

case evaluation See *neutral evaluation*.

case-in-chief The main presentation of evidence by a party, not including any rebuttal evidence this party may want to present later.

case in point A court opinion whose facts are similar to the facts you are researching for a client's case. Also called *case on point*.

case management Software that combines multiple tasks in the control and management of a case. The tasks include calendaring, document control, document assembly, document tracking, and billing.

case method Learning law primarily by studying appellate court opinions in which the opinions are *briefed* (broken down into their issue, reasoning, and other essential parts), *synthesized* (read together with other opinions in order to identify rule patterns), and *applied* to new facts presented by the professor.

case reports See *reporter*.

case sensitive A search query that requires you to type uppercase or lowercase characters as instructed.

case synopsis See *syllabus*.

cause A legally sufficient reason to do something. Sometimes referred to as *just cause*, *good cause*.

cause of action (1) A legally acceptable reason for bringing a suit. A rule that constitutes a legal theory for bringing a suit. (2) The facts that give a person a right to judicial relief. When you *state a cause of action*, you list the facts that give you a right to judicial relief against the alleged wrongdoer.

central processing unit (CPU) The hardware of the computer that contains the processor chip that controls all computer parts.

Century Digest See American Digest System.

cert. See *certiorari*.

cert. denied The appellate court has refused to review the decision of a lower court. See also *certiorari*.

certificate of service See *proof of service*.

certificated Formally acknowledged as having met specified qualifications of a school or training program. Compare with *certified*.

certification A formal acknowledgment that a person or organization has met designated qualifications.

certified Formally acknowledged as having met specified qualifications of a certification program. (Say *certificated* rather than *certified* when the certification comes from a school or training program.)

certified legal assistant See CLA.

certified paralegal (CP) See CLA.

certiorari (cert.) An order (or writ) by a higher court that a lower court send up the record of a case because the higher court has decided to use its discretion to review that case. Also referred to as *writ of certiorari*.

C.F.R. See *Code of Federal Regulations*.

challenge for cause A request from a party to a judge that a prospective juror not be allowed to become a member of this jury because of specified causes or reasons. See also *peremptory challenge*.

chain of custody A list that covers the movement of evidence (and the persons who had it in their possession) from the time the evidence was obtained to the time it is offered in court.

champerty Promoting someone else's litigation, often by helping to finance the litigation in exchange for a share in the recovery.

character A letter, number, or symbol.

charge See *jury instructions*.

charging lien See *attorney lien*.

charter The fundamental law of a municipality or other local unit of government authorizing it to perform designated governmental functions.

checks and balances An allocation of governmental powers whereby one branch of government can block, check, or review what another branch wants to do (or has done) in order to maintain a balance of power among the legislative, executive, and judicial branches so that no one branch can dominate the other two.

Chinese wall Screening that prevents a tainted worker (attorney, paralegal, or other nonattorney) from having any contact with the case of a particular client in the office because the tainted worker has created a conflict of interest between that client and someone else. Also called *ethical wall*, *cone of silence*. A tainted worker is also called a *contaminated worker*. Once the Chinese wall is set up around the tainted worker, the latter is referred to as a *quarantined worker*.

chronological digest A summary of a deposition transcript that presents the events described in the deponent's answers in their chronological order.

chronological question A question designed to encourage the interviewee to describe what happened in the order in which events occurred—by date and time, step by step.

chronological résumé A résumé that presents biographical data on education, training, and experience in a chronological sequence starting with the present and working backward.

churning Providing services beyond what the circumstances warrant for the primary purpose of generating fees and commissions.

circumlocution The use of more words than are needed to express something.

circumstantial evidence Evidence of one fact from which another fact (not personally observed or known) can be inferred. Also called *indirect evidence*.

citation; cite (1) A reference to any authority printed on paper or stored in a computer database that will allow you to locate the authority. As a verb, to *cite* something means to give its location (e.g., volume number or Web address) where you can read it. The citation is the paper or online "address" where you can read something. (2) An order to appear in court to answer a charge. (3) An official notice of a violation.

citator A book or online service containing lists of citations that can (a) help you assess the current validity of an opinion, statute, or other item; and (b) give you leads to additional relevant materials.

cite See *citation*.

cite checking Examining citations in a document to determine their accuracy such as whether the format of the citation is correct, whether a parallel cite is needed, whether quoted material is accurately quoted, and whether the cited law is still valid.

cited Mentioned or discussed.

civil (1) Pertaining to the state or its citizens. (2) Noncriminal. (3) Nonmilitary. See also *civil-law system*.

civil cover sheet A form filed in court in a civil case that indicates the names and addresses of the parties and their attorneys, the kind of action being filed, etc. The form is filed with the complaint. Also called *civil action cover sheet*.

civil dispute A legal controversy in which (a) one private person or entity (e.g., a business) sues another, (b) a private person or entity sues the government, or (c) the government sues a private person or entity for a matter other than the commission of a crime.

civil law (1) The law governing civil disputes. Any law other than criminal law. See also *civil dispute*. (2) See *civil-law system*.

civil-law system The legal system of many countries in Continental Europe and Latin America (and Louisiana) that places a greater emphasis on statutory or code law than do countries (such as England and most of the United States) whose common-law system places a greater emphasis on case law.

civil service Nonmilitary government employment, often obtained through merit and competitive exams.

C.J.S. See *legal encyclopedia*.

CLA or CP The certification credential bestowed by the National Association of Legal Assistants. CLA: (Certified Legal Assistant); CP: (Certified Paralegal) (www.nala.org).

claimant A person asserting or making a claim.

claims-made policy Insurance that covers only claims actually filed (i.e., made) during the period in which the policy is in effect.

CLE See *continuing legal education*.

clear and convincing evidence A standard of proof that is met when the evidence demonstrates that the existence of a disputed fact is much more probable than its nonexistence. This standard is stronger than *preponderance of the evidence* but not as strong as *beyond a reasonable doubt*.

clerk The court employee who assists judges with recordkeeping and other administrative duties. See also *law clerk*.

CLI See *Current Law Index*.

client security fund A fund (often run by a bar association or foundation) used to compensate victims of designated kinds of attorney misconduct.

client trust account A bank account controlled by an attorney that contains client funds that may not be used for general operating expenses or for any personal purpose of the attorney. Also called *lawyer's trust account*, *client account*, *escrow account*. In Washington State, the same obligation applies to accounts controlled by a limited license legal technician (LLLT).

clinical education A training program in which students work on real cases under professional supervision.

closed-ended question A narrowly structured question that usually can be answered in one or two words, often yes or no. Also called a *directed question*.

closed file The file of a client whose case is no longer active in the office. Also called *dead file*, *retired file*.

closing The meeting in which a transaction is finalized. An example is the meeting to complete a real estate sale or other transaction. Also called *settlement*.

closing argument The final statement by an attorney to the jury (or to the judge alone in a bench trial where there is no jury). The statement summarizes the evidence that was presented during the trial and requests a favorable decision. Unrepresented parties make the argument themselves. Also called *closing statement, final argument, summation, summing up*.

cloud The part of the Internet where users can (a) obtain and update programs (apps) and (b) read, store, and manage data.

code (1) Any set of rules that regulates conduct. (2) A collection of laws or rules organized by subject matter regardless of when they were enacted. See also *statutory code*.

codefendants Two or more defendants who are sued in the same civil case or who are prosecuted in the same criminal case.

Code of Federal Regulations (C.F.R.) A publication containing many current federal administrative regulations organized by subject matter. See also *Federal Register*.

codify To arrange laws or rules in a systematic order, usually by subject matter, regardless of when the laws or rules were enacted. (The noun is *codification*.)

collaborative law A method of practicing law in which the attorneys refuse to continue representing the parties if they cannot settle their dispute through mediation or other method of alternative dispute resolution (ADR).

collection realization rate See realization rate.

combination question A question that has more than one part.

come-up system See *tickler*.

commingling Mixing what should be kept separate, e.g., depositing client funds in an account that also contains funds used for general operating funds of the office.

committee report A summary of a bill and a statement by the committee of the reasons for and against its enactment by the legislature.

common law (1) Judge-made law in the absence of controlling statutory law or other higher law. Law derived from court opinions. (2) The court opinions and statutes in England and in the American colonies before the American Revolution. (3) The legal system of England and of those countries such as the United States whose legal system is based on England's. See also *at common law, enacted law*.

common-law rule A rule created by the courts in the absence of controlling statutory law or other higher law.

common-law system The legal system of England and most of the United States that places a greater emphasis on case law than do countries that have a civil law system where a greater emphasis is placed on statutory or code law.

common representation See *multiple representation*.

compensatory damages See *special damages*.

competency See *competent* (2).

competent (1) Using knowledge, skill, thoroughness, and preparation that are reasonably necessary to represent a particular client. (2) Having the legal capacity to give

testimony because the person understands the obligation to tell the truth, has the ability to communicate, and has knowledge of the topic of his or her testimony. The noun is *competency*.

complaint (1) A plaintiff's first pleading, stating a cause of action against the defendant. Also called *petition*. (2) A formal criminal charge.

compliance paralegal A paralegal who works on cases in which clients must comply with statutory, administrative, and court rulings, regulations, guidelines, and other laws in regulated industries involving areas such as finance, health, worker safety, and the environment.

computer-assisted legal research (CALR) Performing legal research in computer databases.

conclusive presumption An assumption or inference of fact that a party will not be allowed to dispute or rebut. See also *rebuttable presumption*.

concurrent jurisdiction The power of more than one type of court to hear a particular kind of case.

concurrent representation The simultaneous representation of more than one current client who have adverse interests in the same litigated matter, in different litigated matters, in a negotiation, or in a transactional matter.

concurring opinion An opinion written by less than a majority of the judges hearing the case. The opinion agrees with the final conclusion or judgment of the majority opinion but wishes to add its own comments or reasoning. If the majority opinion has more than one holding, there can be a concurring opinion on only some of the holdings.

cone of silence See Chinese wall.

conference committee A temporary committee consisting of members of both chambers of the legislature that seeks to reach a compromise on two versions of the same bill each chamber passed.

confirmatory letter A letter that verifies or confirms that something important has been done or said.

conflict of interest Divided loyalties that actually or potentially harm (or disadvantage) someone who is owed undivided loyalty.

conflicts check Finding out whether a conflict of interest exists that might disqualify a law office from representing a prospective client or from continuing the representation of a current client. See also *conflicts specialist*.

conflicts specialist A law-firm employee, often a paralegal, who helps the firm determine whether a conflict of interest exists between prospective clients and current or former clients. Also called *conflicts analyst, conflicts technician*.

confidential (1) Pertaining to information that others do not have a right to receive. (2) Pertaining to all information related to the representation of a client whatever its source, including the fact that someone is a client.

confrontation Being present when others give evidence against you and having the opportunity to question them.

connectors Characters, words, or symbols used to show the relationship between the words and phrases in a database question or query.

consent (1) To agree to waive a right. (2) Voluntary agreement or permission, express or implied.

consideration Something of value that is exchanged between parties. It can be an act, a forbearance (not performing an act), a promise to perform an act, or a promise to refrain from performing an act.

constitution The fundamental law that creates the branches of government, allocates power among them, and defines some basic rights of individuals.

constitutional court A court that derives its jurisdiction from a provision of the constitution. (At the federal level, a constitutional court is called an *Article III court* because the court derives its jurisdiction from Article III of the U.S. Constitution.)

construction Interpretation (the verb is *construe*).

constructive service See *substituted service*.

construed Interpreted.

contaminate Cause a conflict of interest to exist in a law office because of prior employment, prior volunteer work, or other factors that could create the conflict.

contaminated Pertaining to an employee who brings a conflict of interest to the office. See also *Chinese wall*.

contemporaneous Existing or occurring in the same period of time; pertaining to records that are prepared on events as the events are occurring or very shortly thereafter.

contest (1) To challenge. (2) To raise a defense against a claim.

contingency case A case in which clients pay attorney fees only if they win through litigation or settlement.

contingent fee A fee that is paid only if the case is successfully resolved by litigation or settlement, regardless of the number of hours spent on the case. (The fee is also called a *contingency*.) A *defense contingent fee* (also called a *negative contingency*) is a fee for the defendant's attorney that is dependent on the outcome of the case. Hourly fees, on the other hand, are paid on the basis of the number of hours spent on the case regardless of who wins the case.

continuance The adjournment or postponement of a proceeding until a later date.

continuing legal education (CLE) Training in the law (usually short term) that a person receives after completing his or her formal legal training or after becoming employed.

contract attorney An attorney hired to work for a relatively short period, usually on specific cases or projects. Also called *project attorney*.

contract paralegal A self-employed paralegal who often works for several different attorneys on a freelance basis. See also *independent paralegal*.

contractual arbitration Arbitration that the parties have agreed (contracted) to use. Also called *private arbitration*. See also *arbitration, judicial arbitration*.

contributory negligence The failure of plaintiffs to use reasonable care for their own protection that an ordinary prudent person would have used in a similar situation and thereby helping to cause their own injury or other loss.

convention See *treaty*.

conversion A tort committed by an intentional interference with another's personal property, consisting of an exercise of dominion over the property.

cookie A small text file that a Website inserts on your computer when you visit the site with your browser, giving the site information about your browsing visit.

coplaintiffs Two or more plaintiffs who bring a suit in the same civil case.

copyright (©) The exclusive right for a fixed number of years to print, copy, sell, or perform original works.

corporate counsel An in-house attorney, often the chief attorney, of a corporation. Sometimes called *general counsel*.

corporate law department A law office within a corporation containing salaried attorneys (in-house attorneys) who advise and represent the corporation. Also called a *legal department*.

corroborative question A question designed to verify (corroborate) facts by seeking additional or supportive facts.

counteranalysis Arguments that support a different result or conclusion; counterarguments.

counterclaim A claim by one side in a case (usually the defendant) that is filed in response to a claim asserted by an opponent (usually the plaintiff).

court (1) The judge. (2) A government tribunal for the resolution of legal disputes.

court appointed special advocate (CASA) A volunteer appointed by the court to undertake special assignments pertaining to children in the court system. The CASA can be a nonattorney.

court costs Charges or fees (imposed by and paid to the court) that are related to litigation in that court. An example is a court filing fee.

court of appeals See *United States court of appeals*.

court of final resort The highest court within a judicial system.

court of first instance A trial court; a court with original jurisdiction.

court of record A court that is required to maintain a record of the proceedings before it, including a word-for-word account of what occurred.

court opinion See opinion (1).

court reporter See reporter (2) and (3).

court rules The procedural laws that govern the mechanics of litigation (practice and procedure) before a particular court. Also called *rules of court, rules of procedure, procedural rules*.

cover letter A letter indicating what is being sent in the same envelope or package and that often highlights its contents or purpose. Also called *transmittal letter*.

cover sheet See *civil cover sheet*.

CP Certified paralegal. See *CLA*.

credibility The extent to which something is believable or worthy of belief.

credible Believable.

crime Conduct the government classifies as a wrong that is serious enough to warrant a criminal proceeding and punishment if convicted.

criminal dispute A legal controversy in which the government alleges the commission of a crime.

cross-claim A claim brought by one defendant against another defendant or by one plaintiff against another plaintiff in the same action. Also called a *cross-action*.

cross-examination Questioning of a witness at a hearing by an opponent after the other side has conducted a direct examination of that witness.

cured Corrected. Removed a legal defect or error.

Current Law Index (CLI) A comprehensive index to legal periodical literature. An online version of CLI is called *LegalTrac*.

D

daily time sheet A form on which timekeepers record how much time they spend on particular client matters.

damages (1) Money claimed by a person to compensate for the harm caused by an alleged wrongdoer. (2) An award of money paid by the wrongdoer to compensate the person who has been harmed.

data Information that can be used by a computer.

database management Software that allows you to organize, search, retrieve, and sort data.

Decennial Digest See *American Digest System*.

decision See *administrative decision, opinion*.

declarant A person who makes a declaration or statement.

declaratory judgment A binding judgment that declares rights and obligations without ordering anything to be done.

declination A formal rejection.

deep pocket (1) An individual, a business, or another organization with resources to pay a potential judgment. (2) Sufficient assets for this purpose. The opposite of *shallow pocket*.

default (1) The failure to take action. (2) The failure to exercise a legal duty.

default judgment A judgment against a party for failure to file a required pleading or otherwise respond to an opponent's claim.

defendant The party against whom a civil or criminal action is brought in court.

defense (1) An allegation of fact or a legal theory offered to offset or defeat a claim or demand. (2) The defendant and his or her attorney.

defense contingent fee A fee received by the defendant's attorney that is dependent on the outcome of the case. Also called a *negative contingency*.

demand letter An advocacy letter that asks the recipient to take or refrain from specific action affecting the client, e.g., to compensate the client for harm allegedly caused by the recipient.

demurrer A motion to dismiss because a party has failed to state a claim on which relief can be granted.

de novo Anew; starting over.

deponent A person who is questioned in a deposition. See also *deposition*.

depose Ask questions of a witness in a deposition.

deposition (1) A method of discovery by which parties and their prospective witnesses are questioned by the opposing party before trial at a location other than the courtroom. (Judges are not present during depositions.). The purpose of discovery is to assist parties in trial preparation by allowing each side to uncover facts from the other side. The person questioned is called the *deponent*. (2) A posttrial method of discovery by which the winning party seeks to uncover facts that will help it enforce the judgment it obtained against the losing side.

depository library See *federal depository library*.

depo summarizer An employee whose main job is digesting (summarizing) discovery documents, particularly depositions.

derogation A partial repeal or abolishment of a law.

Descriptive Word Index (DWI) An index to the digests of West (Thomson Reuters).

detainer Keeping something in one's custody. See also *unlawful detainer assistant (UDA)*.

dictum (short for *obiter dictum*, "something said in passing") (1) A statement or observation made by a judge in an opinion that is not essential to resolve the issues before the court; comments that go beyond the facts before the court. (2) An authoritative, formal statement or announcement.

digest (1) A set of volumes that contain brief summaries of points of law in court opinions. The summaries come from headnotes at the beginning of court opinions. When the summaries are printed in digests, they are sometimes called *abstracts* or *squibs*. (2) An organized summary or abridgment.

digesting Summarizing transcripts and documents, often in preparation for litigation.

dilatory Causing delay, often without merit or justification.

directed question See *closed-ended question*.

directed verdict A judge's decision not to allow the jury to deliberate because only one verdict is reasonable. Called a *judgment as a matter of law* (see this phrase) in federal court and in some state courts.

direct evidence Evidence (based on personal knowledge or observation) that tends to establish a fact (or to disprove a fact) without the need for an inference. Also called *positive evidence*.

direct examination The first questioning of a witness at a hearing by the party who called the witness. Also called *examination in chief*.

directory A search tool in which you select from a list of broad subject categories and then keep clicking through subcategories of that subject until you find what you want.

disbarment The revocation or termination of the right to practice law as punishment for unethical conduct.

disbursements Out-of-pocket expenses.

discharge Extinguish; forgive a debt so that it is no longer owed.

Disciplinary Rule (DR) See *Model Code of Professional Responsibility*.

discount adjustment A write-down (decrease) in the bill.

discounted hourly fee An hourly or fixed fee that is reduced because of the volume of business the client gives the office. See also *fee*.

discoverable Pertaining to information or materials an opponent can obtain through deposition, interrogatories, or other discovery method.

discovery Methods used by parties to force information from each other before trial to aid in trial preparation. Examples of such devices include interrogatories and depositions. The methods can also be used to aid in the enforcement of a judgment.

discretion The power to choose among various courses of conduct based on one's reasoned judgment or preference.

disengagement See *letter of disengagement*.

disinterested (1) Not working for one side or the other in a controversy. (2) Not deriving benefit if one side of a dispute wins or loses; objective.

disposition (1) A court's final order that is reached as a result of its holding(s). (2) The transfer of something to another.

dispositive Pertaining to something that is essential to a decision; pertaining to a deciding factor or consideration.

disqualification See *imputed disqualification*.

dissent A judge's vote against the result reached by the judges in the majority (or plurality) on a case.

dissenting opinion An opinion that disagrees with part or all of the result or judgment reached by the majority (or plurality) opinion.

district court See *United States district court*.

diversity of citizenship The disputing parties are citizens of different states and the amount in controversy exceeds $75,000. This diversity gives subject-matter jurisdiction to a U.S. district court.

divided loyalty See *conflict of interest*.

docket (1) A court's list of its pending cases. Also called *calendar*. (2) A record containing brief notations on the proceedings that have occurred in a court case.

docket call See *calendar call*.

docketed Placed on a court's list of pending cases.

docket number A consecutive number assigned to a case by the court and used on all documents filed with the court during the litigation of that case.

document clerk An individual whose main responsibility is to organize, file, code, or digest litigation or other client documents.

document preparer A person who assists someone in the preparation of forms and documents using information provided by a self-represented person.

document service provider (DSP) (1) A nonattorney who works without attorney supervision to provide legal-document assistance to individuals who are representing themselves. Examples of DSPs include *bankruptcy petition preparer (BPP)* and *legal document assistant (LDA)*. (2) Someone who helps another prepare or process documents.

donee The person who receives a gift. The person who gives the gift is the *donor*.

donor The person who gives a gift.

double billing Fraudulently charging a client twice for the same service.

double jeopardy (1) A second prosecution for the same or substantially same offense after acquittal or conviction. (2) Multiple punishments for the same or substantially same offense.

download To move data from a remote computer (e.g., a central computer or Website) to your computer. Data is *uploaded* when you transfer it from your computer to the remote computer.

DR (Disciplinary Rule) See *Model Code of Professional Responsibility*.

draft (1) A document in one of its preliminary stages. (I was asked to proofread a *draft* of a contract before it was printed.) (2) To write. (She *drafted* a memorandum.) (3) See *draft bill*.

draft bill A billing memorandum that states expenses, costs, time spent, and billing rates of attorneys and paralegals working on a particular case or matter.

draw A partner's advance against profits or net income.

DSP See *document service provider*.

dual representation See *multiple representation*.

due diligence Reasonable efforts to find and verify factual information needed to carry out an obligation, to avoid harming someone, or to make an important decision, e.g., to determine the true market value of a potential investment, to decide whether a job prospect is worth pursuing.

duty of loyalty The obligation to protect the interests of a client without having a similar obligation to anyone else that would present an actual or potential conflict.

DWI See *Descriptive Word Index*.

E

e-billing Sending out bills electronically (e.g., as email attachments).

EC Ethical Consideration. See Model Code of Professional Responsibility.

EDD See e-discovery.

e-discovery The discovery by a party in litigation of an opponent's data generated by or stored in a computer or other digital device. The discovery of electronically stored information (ESI). Examples include email, instant messages (IMs), text messages, voice mail, social-media posts, spreadsheets, Web pages, digital video, and other digital data. Also called *electronic data discovery (EDD)*.

EEOC See *Equal Employment Opportunity Commission*.

e-evidence Evidence generated by or stored in a computer or other digital device. Examples include email, Web pages, digital spreadsheets, computer-generated memos, and other digital data.

e-filing Electronic filing in court of pleadings and other documents.

elder law An area of law covering the legal problems of the elderly. Examples include Social Security, estate planning, Medicare, and age discrimination.

electronically stored information (ESI) See *e-discovery*, *e-evidence*.

electronic citation A citation to online material.

electronic data discovery (EDD) See *e-discovery*.

electronic mail See email.

electronic mailing list A program that manages computer mailing lists so that members of the list can receive and send messages and read what other members send to each other. Also called elist, maillist, email list, listserv.

element A portion of a rule that is a precondition of the applicability of the entire rule. See also *element in contention*.

element in contention The portion of a rule about which the parties cannot agree. The disagreement may be over the definition of the element, whether the facts fit within the element, or both.

email Electronic mail. A message sent electronically.

empanel Select and swear in (referring to a jury). Also spelled *impanel*.

employment at will See *at-will employee*.

enabling statute The statute that allows (enables) an administrative agency to carry out specified delegated powers.

enacted law (1) Law written by a deliberative body such as a legislature or constitutional convention after it is proposed and often debated and amended. (2) Any law that is not created within litigation.

en banc ("on the bench") By the entire court.

encrypt Convert text into a code that renders the text incomprehensible until it is reconverted to a readable format by a recipient with the right software.

encyclopedia See *legal encyclopedia*.

endnote A numbered citation or explanatory text that is printed at the end of a document or chapter. If printed at the bottom of the page, the citation or text is a *footnote*.

engagement letter A letter that identifies the scope of services to be provided by a professional and the payments to be made for such services.

English rule The losing side in litigation must pay the winner's attorney fees. Also called *loser pays*.

engrossed bill The version of a bill passed by one of the chambers of the legislature after incorporating amendments or other changes.

enrolled agent A nonattorney who is licensed to represent taxpayers before the Internal Revenue Service. (Attorneys and certified public accountants can provide such representation without becoming enrolled agents.)

enrolled bill A bill that is ready to be sent to the chief executive after both chambers of the legislature have passed it.

enrollment See *registration*.

entry-level certification Certification acquired by meeting eligibility requirements that do not include work experience.

Equal Employment Opportunity Commission (EEOC) The federal agency that investigates employment discrimination that might violate federal law (www.eeoc.gov).

equitable (1) Fair; just. (2) Pertaining to any remedy available in an action in equity.

equity Justice administered according to fairness in a particular case, as contrasted with the strictly formalized rules once followed by common-law courts.

equity partner A full owner-partner of a law firm. Also called *capital partner*.

ESI (electronically stored information) See *e-discovery*, *e-evidence*.

estate (1) All of the assets and liabilities of a decedent at the time of his or her death. (2) An interest in real or personal property. (3) The extent and nature of one's interest in real or personal property. (4) All of the property of whatever kind owned by a person. (5) Land.

et al. And others.

Ethical Consideration (EC) See *Model Code of Professional Responsibility*.

ethical wall See *Chinese wall*.

ethics Rules or standards of behavior to which members of an occupation, profession, or other organization are expected to conform. Ethics governing attorneys are called *legal ethics*, *codes of professional responsibility*.

et seq. And following.

evidence Anything offered to establish the existence or nonexistence of a fact in dispute. Separate determinations must be made on whether a particular item of evidence is relevant or irrelevant, admissible or inadmissible.

evidence log An ongoing record that provides identification and related data about documents and other tangible objects that might eventually be introduced into evidence.

examination Questioning someone, who usually must answer under oath.

examination in chief See *direct examination*.

exclusive jurisdiction The power of a court to hear a particular kind of case, to the exclusion of other courts.

excuse the jury Ask the jury to leave the courtroom.

execution (1) Signing a document and meeting other requirements needed to finalize the document and make it legal. (2) Carrying out or performing some act to its completion. (3) Carrying into effect the orders in a judgment. (4) A command or writ to a court officer (e.g., sheriff) to seize and sell the property of the losing litigant in order to satisfy the judgment debt. Also called *general execution, writ of execution*. (5) Implementing a death sentence.

executive agreement An agreement between the United States and another country that does not require the approval of the Senate.

executive branch The branch of government with primary responsibility for carrying out, executing, or administering laws.

executive department agency An administrative agency that exists within the executive branch of government, often at the cabinet level.

executive order A law issued by the chief executive pursuant to specific statutory authority or to the executive's inherent authority to direct the operation of governmental agencies.

exempt Not subject to a requirement. The noun form is *exemption*.

exempt employee An employee who is not entitled to overtime compensation under the Fair Labor Standards Act because the employee is a professional, administrative, or executive employee.

exemption (1) Not subject to a requirement. (2) The right of a debtor to keep designated property rather than make it available to creditors to satisfy debts, particularly in bankruptcy.

exhaust administrative remedies To go through all dispute-solving avenues that are available in an administrative agency before asking a court to review what the agency did. Also called *exhaustion of remedies*.

exhibit A document, chart, or other object offered or introduced into evidence.

ex parte With only one side present (usually the plaintiff or petitioner) when court action is requested. An *ex parte order*, for example, is a court order requested by one party and issued before notice is given to the other party.

ex parte communication A communication with the court in the absence of the attorney for the other side.

ex parte hearing A hearing at which only one party is present. A court order issued at such a hearing is an *ex parte order*.

expense slip A form used by an office to indicate that an expense has been incurred for which a client may or may not be billed.

expert witness A person qualified by scientific, technical, or other specialized knowledge or experience to give an expert opinion on a fact in dispute.

ex rel. (ex relatione) Upon relation or information. A *suit ex rel.* is brought by the government in the name of the real party in interest (called the *realtor*).

external drive A drive that is outside your computer case or tower.

extranet The part of an intranet to which selected outsiders have been given access. See also *intranet*.

F

F.3d See *Federal Reporter*.

fact An actual event; a real occurrence. Anything that can be shown to exist, e.g., an incident, a relationship, an intention, an opinion, or an emotion.

fact issue (factual issue) See *legal issue*.

factor (1) One of the circumstances or considerations that will be weighted in making a decision. (2) One of the circumstances or considerations that will be weighted in deciding whether an element applies.

fact particularization (FP) A fact-gathering technique to generate a large list of factual questions (who, what, where, how, when, and why) that will help you obtain a specific and comprehensive picture of all available facts relevant to a legal issue.

failure to state a cause of action Failure of a party to allege enough facts that, if proved, would entitle the party to judicial relief. Sometimes called a *demurrer* or a *failure to state a claim upon which relief can be granted*.

Fair Labor Standards Act (FLSA) The federal statute that regulates conditions of employment such as when overtime compensation must be paid (29 U.S.C. § 201) (www.dol.gov/whd/flsa). See also *exempt employee*.

fair use The privilege of limited use of copyrighted material without permission of the copyright holder.

F. App'x. See *Federal Appendix*.

Federal Appendix (F. App'x.) A West (Thomson Reuters) reporter that prints unpublished opinions of some U.S. courts of appeals. See also *opinion* (1).

federal depository library A public or private library that receives free federal government publications (e.g., the statutes of Congress) to which it must allow access by the general public without cost. (In some states there is a comparable program for *state* government publications.)

federalism The division of powers between the federal government and the state governments.

federal questions Issues that arise from or are based on the federal constitution, federal statutes, federal administrative regulations, or other federal laws.

Federal Register (Fed. Reg.) A daily publication of the federal government that prints proposed federal regulations, notices of agency hearings, executive orders, and related information about federal agencies. See also *Code of Federal Regulations*.

Federal Reporter The West (Thomson Reuters) reporter currently containing opinions of the U.S. courts of appeals. Now in its third series (F.3d).

Federal Rules Decisions (F.R.D.) The West (Thomson Reuters) reporter that prints opinions of some U.S. district courts on procedural issues and related materials (e.g., speeches).

Federal Rules of Civil Procedure (FRCP) The rules that govern the mechanics of resolving a dispute by a U.S. district court, which is the main federal trial court (www.law.cornell.edu/rules/frcp).

Federal Supplement The West (Thomson Reuters) reporter currently containing opinions of the U.S. district courts. Now in its second series (F. Supp. 2d).

Fed. Reg. See *Federal Register*.

fee The amount charged for services rendered. An *hourly rate fee* is based on the number of hours worked. A *blended hourly rate* is a single hourly rate based on a blend or mix of rates normally charged by different individuals, e.g., a partner, an associate, and sometimes a paralegal. A *fixed fee* is a flat fee for the service regardless of the amount of time needed to complete it. A *capped fee* (fee cap) is an hourly rate leading to a total bill that will not exceed a predetermined amount. An *hourly plus fixed fee* is an hourly rate charged until the nature and scope of the legal problem are identified, at which time a fixed fee is charged for services provided thereafter. See also *contingent fee, fee splitting, incentive billing, task-based billing, value billing*.

fee cap A maximum amount or maximum percentage that can be charged as a fee in a case. See also *fee*.

fee shifting Requiring one party to pay another party's attorney fees and paralegal fees because of prior agreement, bad faith, or special statute.

fee splitting (1) The division or splitting of a single client's fee between two or more attorneys who are not in the same firm. (2) The division or splitting of a fee between an attorney and a nonattorney. Also called *fee sharing, division of fees.*

felony (1) Any crime punishable by death or imprisonment for a term exceeding a year. (2) A crime more serious than a misdemeanor.

fiduciary (1) Pertaining to the high standard of good faith and fair treatment that must be exercised on behalf of another (adjective). (2) A person who owes another good faith and fair treatment in protecting the other's interest (noun).

file (1) To deliver a document to a court officer so that it can become part of the official collection of documents in a case. (2) To deliver a document to a government agency.

final argument See *closing argument.*

final resort See *court of final resort.*

finder's fee See *forwarding fee.*

firewall A security program for computers on a network that analyzes incoming data to determine whether the data should be allowed into the network based on predetermined rules or criteria on what can be trusted.

first impression New; that which has come before the court for the first time.

first instance, court of A trial court; a court with original jurisdiction.

fixed fee A flat fee for services, regardless of the amount of time needed to complete the task. See also *fee.*

flextime A system that allows employees some control over aspects of their work schedule such as the times that they arrive at and leave from work during the day.

FLSA See *Fair Labor Standards Act.*

FOIA See *Freedom of Information Act.*

font The design or style of printed letters of the alphabet, punctuation marks, or other characters.

footer The same text printed at the bottom of every page beneath the main text on the page. (The same text printed at the top of each page before the main text is called the *header.*)

forensic (1) Pertaining to the use of scientific techniques to discover and examine evidence. (2) Belonging to or suitable in courts of law. (3) Concerning argumentation. (4) Forensics (ballistics or firearms evidence).

format (1) The way in which something is arranged, designed, or styled on a page. (2) In word processing, the layout of the page when printed, e.g., the font and margin settings.

formbook A collection of sample or model forms, often with practical guidance on how to use them. A legal treatises with an emphasis on the "how-to-do-it" practical dimensions of the law. Also called *practice guide, practice manual.*

forum (1) A court. (2) The place where the parties are presently litigating their dispute. (3) A court or other tribunal hearing a case.

forwarding fee A fee received by one attorney from another to whom the first attorney referred a client. Also called *finder's fee, referral fee.*

fraud An intentionally false statement of fact that is material, is made to induce reliance by the plaintiff, and results in harm because of the reliance. Also called *deceit, misrepresentation.*

FRCP See *Federal Rules of Civil Procedure.*

F.R.D. See *Federal Rules Decisions.*

Freedom of Information Act (FOIA) A statute that gives public access to certain information in the possession of the government. There is a FOIA for the federal government (www.foia.gov)(5 U.S.C. § 552) and equivalent FOIAs for state and local governments (www.nfoic.org).

freelance paralegal See *independent paralegal.*

frivolous Lacking merit. Pertaining to a legal position that cannot be supported by a good-faith argument based on existing law or on the need for a change in existing law.

F. Supp. 2d See *Federal Supplement.*

FTC *Federal Trade Commission* (www.ftc.gov).

full-text search A search of every word in every document in a database.

functional résumé A résumé that covers skills and experience regardless of when they were developed or occurred.

G

general counsel The chief attorney in a corporate law department. Also called *corporate counsel.*

General Digest See *American Digest System.*

general jurisdiction The power of a court to hear any kind of civil or criminal case, with certain exceptions.

general license Permission by a government body that allows a person who has met designated qualifications to engage in the full range of services that a specified occupation or profession is trained to provide. See also *limited license.*

general practitioner (GP) A professional who handles many different kinds of cases.

general schedule (GS) The pay scale system used in the federal government.

generic citation See *public domain citation.*

geographic jurisdiction See *territorial jurisdiction.*

gigabyte One billion bytes (approximately).

global In word processing, an instruction that will be carried out throughout the document.

GlobalCite An online citator of Loislaw (estore.loislaw.com). See also *citator.*

go bare To engage in an occupation or profession without malpractice (liability) insurance.

GOD Great Overtime Debate. See also *exempt employee.*

good cause A legally sufficient ground. A justifiable reason. Also called *cause, just cause, sufficient cause.*

good faith A state of mind indicating honesty and lawfulness of purpose; the absence of an intent to seek an undue advantage; a belief that known circumstances do not require further investigation. Bona fides.

government In a criminal case, the prosecutor.

government corporation A government-owned entity that is a mixture of a business corporation and a government agency created to serve a predominantly business function in the public interest. Also called a *quasi-government agency*.

GP see *general practitioner*.

grammar checker A computer software program that identifies possible grammatical errors in a document with suggested corrections.

grand jury A jury of inquiry (not a trial jury) that sits for a designated period of time (often a month), receives accusations in criminal cases, hears the evidence of the prosecutor (but not the evidence of the suspects), and issues indictments when satisfied that a trial should be held.

gratuitous (1) Pertaining to what is performed or given without a duty or obligation to do so. (2) Free.

grounds Reasons that are legally sufficient to obtain a particular remedy or result.

group legal services See *prepaid legal services*.

groupware Software that allows computers on a network to work together.

GS See *general schedule*.

guardian ad litem (GAL) A special guardian (often, but not always, an attorney) appointed by the court to appear in court proceedings on behalf of a person who is a minor, is insane, or is otherwise incapacitated.

Guideline (1) Suggested conduct that will help an applicant obtain accreditation, certification, licensure, registration, or approval. (2) A statement of policy, often with options on carrying it out.

H

hacker One who gains (or seeks to gain) unauthorized access to computer data.

harassment See *hostile-environment harassment*, *quid pro quo sexual harassment*.

hard copy A paper copy of what has been prepared on a computer. Also called *printout*. A *soft* copy of text is what exists on disk or on a computer screen.

hard drive A computer storage device for data that uses rapidly rotating platters inside a sealed casing. Also called *hard disk drive*.

hardware The physical equipment of a computer system.

header The same text that is printed at the top of every page.

headnote A short-paragraph summary of a portion of a court opinion (usually covering a single point of law) printed before the opinion begins. These headnotes will also be printed in digest volumes, which serve as an index to all court opinions. See also *digest*.

hearing (1) A proceeding designed to resolve issues of fact or law. An impartial officer presides at the hearing, the parties present evidence, etc. (2) A meeting of a legislative committee to consider proposed legislation or other legislative matters. (3) A meeting in which one is allowed to present or argue a position. (4) A proceeding convened to resolve a dispute during which parties in the dispute can present their case. The hearing is *ex parte* if only one party is present; it is *adversarial* if both parties are present.

hearing examiner One who presides over an administrative hearing and makes findings of fact and rulings of law, or who recommends such findings and rulings to someone else in the agency who will make the final decision. Also called *administrative-law judge (ALJ)*, *referee*, *hearing officer*.

hearing memorandum A memorandum of law submitted to a hearing officer.

hearing officer See *hearing examiner*.

hearsay An out-of-court statement quoted or reported by someone who did not make the statement when offered into evidence to prove the truth of the matter asserted in the statement.

historical note Information on the legislative history of a statute printed after the text of the statute.

holding A court's answer to one of the legal issues in the case. Also called *ruling*.

homophone Words that sound alike but have different meanings (e.g., aid/aide, prey/pray).

hornbook A legal treatise that summarizes an area of the law often covered within a single law-school course, designed primarily for the law school student.

hostile Unfriendly or antagonistic. See also *adverse*.

hostile-environment sexual harassment Pervasive unwelcome sexual conduct or sex-based ridicule that unreasonably interferes with an individual's job performance or that creates an intimidating, hostile, or offensive working environment, even if no tangible or economic consequences result.

hourly plus fixed fee An hourly rate charged until the nature and scope of the legal problem are known, at which time a fixed fee is charged for services provided thereafter. See also *fee*.

hypertext A method of displaying and linking information found in different locations on the same site or on different sites of the World Wide Web.

hypothetical (1) A set of facts assumed to exist for purposes of discussion or learning. (2) Not actual or real but presented for purposes of discussion or analysis; based on an assumed set of facts; based on a hypothesis.

I

icon A picture or graphic that is "clicked" on with a mouse in order to execute it.

id. The same as the immediately preceding cited authority.

identity theft Acquiring and using (or attempting to acquire and use) another person's private identifying information with the intent to commit any unlawful activity.

IFRAC An acronym that stands for the components of legal analysis: issue (I), facts (F), rule (R), application of the rule to the facts (A), and conclusion (C). IFRAC provides a structure for legal analysis. See also *IRAC*.

ILP See *Index to Legal Periodicals and Books*.

IM See *instant messaging*.

imaging The process by which a scanner digitizes text or images. Also called *document imaging*.

IME See *independent medical examination*.

impaired attorney An attorney with a drug or alcohol problem.

impanel See empanel.

impeach To challenge; to attack the credibility of.

imputed Attributed to.

imputed disqualification See *vicarious disqualification*.

incentive billing A fee that is increased if a designated target is met; an increased fee for achieving an exceptional result. Also called *performance bonus, success fee*.

income partner See *nonequity partner*.

independent contractor A self-employed person who operates his or her own business and contracts to perform tasks for others. In general, the latter do not control many of the administrative details of how the work is performed.

independent medical examination (IME) A method of discovery by which a party obtains a court order for a professional examination of a person whose physical or mental condition is in controversy.

independent paralegal (1) An independent contractor who sells his or her paralegal services to, and works under the supervision of, one or more attorneys. (2) An independent contractor who sells his or her paralegal services directly to the public without attorney supervision. Also called *freelance paralegal, legal technician*. In some states, however, the paralegal and legal assistant titles are limited to those who work under attorney supervision.

independent regulatory agency An administrative agency that regulates an aspect of society. The agency often exists outside the executive branch of government.

Index to Legal Periodicals and Books (ILP) A comprehensive general index to legal periodical literature. Available in paper volumes, in CD-ROM, and online.

indictment A formal document issued by a grand jury accusing the defendant of a crime. (If the state has no grand jury, the accusation is often contained in a document called an *information*.) See also *information, grand jury*.

indigent Poor; without means to afford something such as a private attorney or filing fees.

indirect evidence See *circumstantial evidence*.

inference A deduction or conclusion reached from facts.

inferior court (1) A trial court of limited or special jurisdiction. (2) Any court that is subordinate to the court of final resort.

infinitive A verb form that is usually preceded by *to*.

information A document accusing the defendant of a crime. The document is issued by a prosecutor when a grand jury is not used or does not exist. Also called *bill of information*.

informational interview An interview whose primary purpose is to gain a better understanding of an area of law or kind of employment.

informational letter A letter that provides or seeks information.

information and belief Good-faith belief as to the truth of an allegation, not based on firsthand knowledge.

informed consent Agreement to let something happen after receiving a reasonable explanation of the benefits and risks involved.

infra Below; mentioned or referred to later in the document.

in issue See *legal issue*.

initial appearance The first criminal court appearance by persons accused of a crime during which the court (a) informs them of the charges and of their rights, (b) makes a decision on bail, and (c) determines the date of the next court proceeding.

initiative The electorate's power to write a statute or constitutional provision or to force the legislature to vote on its proposals for such laws. See also *referendum*.

injunction A remedy that orders a person or organization to do or to refrain from doing something.

in personam jurisdiction See *personal jurisdiction*.

in propria persona (in pro per) In one's own proper person. See also *pro se, self-help*.

inquisitorial system A method of resolving a legal dispute in some countries in which the judge has a more active role in questioning the witnesses and in conducting the trial than in an adversary system.

In re In the matter of.

in rem jurisdiction The court's power over a particular *res*, which is a thing (e.g., a car) or a status (e.g., a marriage) that is located within the territory over which the court has authority.

insert mode When new text is typed in a line that already has text, the line opens to receive the new text. Nothing is erased or overtyped.

insider trading Improperly using or passing on to others any nonpublic information you learn about in the office in order to trade in the shares of a company.

instant messaging (IM) Electronic communication in real time. See also *real time*.

instructions See *jury instructions*.

instrument A formal written document that gives expression to or embodies a legal act or agreement, e.g., a contract, deed, will, lease, or mortgage.

insurance defense Representing insurance companies on claims brought against them or against their policy holders.

intake memo A memorandum that contains the facts given by a client during the initial client interview and comments by the interviewer about the client and the case.

intangible evidence See tangible evidence.

integrated bar association A state bar association to which an attorney must belong in order to practice law in the state. Also called *mandatory bar association, unified bar association*.

integrated package Software that contains more than one application (e.g., word processing, spreadsheet, and database management) in a single program.

intellectual property law The law governing patents, copyrights, trademarks, and trade names.

Interest on Lawyers Trust Accounts See *IOLTA*.

interlocutory appeal An appeal of a trial court ruling before the trial court reaches its final judgment.

intermediate appellate court A court with appellate jurisdiction to which parties can appeal before they appeal to the highest court in the judicial system.

intern See legal intern.

international law The legal principles and laws governing relations between nations. Also called *law of nations*, *public international law*.

International Practice Management Association (IPMA) An association of paralegal managers. Formerly called Legal Assistant Managers Association and Paralegal Managers Association (www.paralegalmanagement.org).

Internet A worldwide electronic network of networks on which millions of computer users can share information.

Internet service provider (ISP) A company that provides access to the Internet, usually for a monthly fee.

Interest on Lawyers Trust Accounts See *IOLTA*.

interoffice memorandum of law See *office memorandum of law*.

interrogatories ("rogs") A method of discovery by which one party sends written questions to another party. See also *discovery*.

interviewee The person being interviewed.

intra-agency appeal An appeal within an administrative agency, before the case is appealed to a court.

intranet A private network of computers for the sharing of data, software, and services within the organization using features similar to those of the World Wide Web.

introduce evidence To place evidence formally before a court or other tribunal so that it will become part of the record for consideration by the judge, jury, or other decision-maker.

investigation See *legal investigation*.

invisible web The part of the Internet that is not found by traditional search engines.

IOLTA (Interest on Lawyers Trust Accounts) A program that helps fund legal services for the poor with funds that attorneys are required to turn over from interest earned in client trust accounts containing client funds.

IRAC An acronym that stands for the components of legal analysis: issue (I), rule (R), application of the rule to the facts (A), and conclusion (C). IRAC provides a structure for legal analysis. See also *IFRAC*.

irrebuttable Conclusive; evidence to the contrary is inadmissible.

irrebuttable presumption An inference of fact that cannot be overcome (rebutted) because evidence to the contrary will not be considered. The presumption is conclusive.

ISP See *Internet service provider*.

issue (1) A question to be resolved. (2) A question of law. A question of what the law is, what the law means, or how the law applies to the facts. Also called *legal issue*, *issue of law*. (3) A question of fact. A dispute over the existence or nonexistence of the alleged facts. Also called *factual issue*, *issue of fact*, *question of fact*. (4) A single copy of a periodical pamphlet. (5) Offspring; lineal descendants.

issue of fact; issue of law See *issue, legal issue*.

issue on appeal A claimed error of law committed by a lower court.

issues presented See *questions presented*.

J

jailhouse lawyer An inmate, usually a self-taught nonattorney, who has a limited right to provide other inmates with legal services if the institution does not provide adequate alternatives to such services. Also called *writ writer*.

jargon Specialized or technical language used by a particular group or profession that may not be understood by the general public.

job bank A service that lists available jobs. The list is sometimes available only to members of an organization.

joint and several liability Legally responsible together and individually. Each wrongdoer is individually responsible for the entire debt or judgment. The injured party can choose to collect the full debt or judgment from one wrongdoer or from all of them until the debt or judgment is satisfied.

judgment The final conclusion of a court that resolves a legal dispute by declaring the rights and obligations of the parties or that specifies what further proceedings are needed to resolve it.

judgment as a matter of law A judgment on an issue in a jury trial that is ordered by the judge against a party because there is no legally sufficient evidentiary basis for a reasonable jury to find for that party on that issue. A judgment as a matter of law may be rendered before or after the verdict. In federal courts and in some state courts, this judgment is called a *directed verdict* if it is rendered before the jury reaches a verdict and is called a *judgment notwithstanding the verdict* (JNOV) if it is rendered after the jury reaches a verdict.

judgment creditor The person who wins and therefore has a right to collect a money judgment.

judgment debtor The person who loses and therefore must pay a money judgment.

judgment notwithstanding the verdict (JNOV) A judgment by the trial judge that is contrary to the verdict reached by the jury because the verdict was not reasonable, in effect overruling the jury. Called a *judgment as a matter of law* (see this phrase) in federal court and in some state courts.

judgment on the merits A judgment, rendered after evidentiary inquiry and argument that determines which party is in the right, as opposed to a judgment that is based solely on a technical point or procedural error.

judicial arbitration Court-referred or court-ordered arbitration. See also *arbitration, contractual arbitration*.

judicial branch The branch of government consisting of courts that have primary responsibility for interpreting laws by resolving disputes that arise under them.

judicial notice A court's acceptance of a well-known fact without requiring proof of that fact.

judicial review (1) The power of a court to determine the constitutionality of a statute or other law. (2) The power of a court to determine the correctness of what a lower tribunal has done.

jump cite See *pinpoint cite.*

jurisdiction (1) The power of a court to resolve a legal dispute. (2) A geographic area over which a particular court, legislature, or administrative agency has authority. The geographic area can be the entire country, a state, a group of states, a county, a city, etc. (3) The power or authority that a person, government, or other entity can exercise. See also *in rem jurisdiction, personal jurisdiction, quasi in rem jurisdiction, subject matter jurisdiction, territorial jurisdiction.*

Juris Doctor (J.D.) The law degree most American law schools grant its graduates. Also called *Doctor of Jurisprudence.*

jury instructions A statement of the law given to the jury by the judge for use in deciding the issues of fact in its verdict. Also called the *charge.*

jury panel A group of citizens who have been called to jury duty. From this group, juries for particular trials are selected. Also called *venire, jury pool.*

jury trial A trial in which a group of persons resolve the issues or questions of fact.

just cause See *good cause.*

justice gap The large numbers of people who do not have access to legal assistance, primarily because of the cost of such assistance.

justification In word processing, a feature for making lines of text even at the margins.

K

k A measure of capacity in a computer system.

KeyCite An online citator of West (Thomson Reuters) (www.westlaw.com). See also *citator.*

key fact A fact that was very important or essential in reaching a decision.

key number A general topic and a number. The number designates a subtopic of the general topic. For example, key number Divorce 204.5 refers to the subtopic covered in 204.5 of the general topic Divorce. Key numbers are used by West (Thomson Reuters) to organize millions of cases by topic in its multivolume digests.

kilobyte One thousand bytes (approximately).

KM See *knowledge management.*

knowledge management (KM) A productivity program for capturing and reusing the knowledge and work product of a law office. KM is a system of linking into the knowledge base of a law office embodied in the documents generated by all of the cases it has handled so that it can better meet the needs of current and prospective clients.

L

LAMA Legal Assistant Management Association. See *International Practice Management Association.*

landmen Paralegals who work in the area of oil and gas law. Also called *land technicians.*

laser printer A printer that uses a laser beam of light to reproduce images.

lateral hire A person hired from another law office.

law An authoritative rule written and enforced by one or more government bodies.

law clerk (1) A law firm employee who is in law school studying to become an attorney or who has graduated from law school and is waiting to pass the bar examination. Also called *clerk.* If law clerks work only in the summer, they are sometimes called *summer associates.* (2) One who provides research and writing assistance to a judge. (3) A nonattorney who is a "trained professional doing independent legal work" in Ontario, Canada.

law department The legal department of a corporation.

law directory A list of attorneys.

law journal See *law review.*

law review A legal periodical published by a law school. Sometimes called a *law journal.*

LCP Louisiana Certified Paralegal. A person who has passed the Louisiana Certified Paralegal Exam.

LDA See *legal document assistant.*

leading question A question that suggests an answer within the question.

L. Ed. 2d See *United States Supreme Court Reports, Lawyers' Edition 2d.*

left justified Every line of a paragraph on the left margin is aligned except for the first line if the first line is indented. See also *justification, right justified.*

legacy data Data that is no longer in regular use and that the organization may be getting ready to destroy.

legal administrator An individual, usually a nonattorney, who has responsibility for the day-to-day administration of a law office.

legal advice A statement or conclusion that applies the law or legal principles to the facts of a specific person's legal problem.

legal aid office An office of attorneys (and paralegals) that provides free or low-cost legal services to persons who cannot afford standard legal fees. Also called *legal services office.*

legal analysis The application of one or more rules to the facts of a client's case in order to answer a legal question that will help (1) avoid a legal dispute, (2) resolve a legal dispute that has arisen, or (3) prevent a legal dispute from becoming worse.

legal assistant A title that is usually synonymous with *paralegal* (see this word), although recently some individuals and organizations have argued that the legal assistant title has become more associated with secretarial tasks.

legal assistant clerk A person who assists a paralegal or legal assistant in clerical tasks such as document numbering, alphabetizing, filing, and any other task that does not require substantive knowledge of litigation or of a particular transaction.

legal dictionary An alphabetical list of legal words and phrases that are defined.

legal document assistant (LDA) A nonattorney in California who is authorized to charge fees for providing self-help assistance (without attorney supervision) to anyone representing himself or herself in a legal matter.

legal document preparer (LDP) A nonattorney in Arizona who is authorized to charge fees for providing self-help assistance (without attorney supervision) to anyone representing himself or herself in a legal matter. Also called *Arizona certified legal document preparer (AZCLDP)*.

legal encyclopedia A multivolume set of books that summarizes almost every important legal topic. The major national legal encyclopedias are published by West (Thomson Reuters): *Corpus Juris Secundum* (C.J.S.), available in volumes; and *American Jurisprudence 2d* (Am. Jur. 2d), available in volumes and online on Westlaw and LexisNexis. In addition, several single-state legal encyclopedias exist, e.g., *California Jurisprudence*.

legal ethics See *ethics*.

legal information Any statement about the law that is not directed at the facts of a specific person's legal problem.

legal insurance See *prepaid legal services*.

legal intern A student in a law office seeking practical experience.

legal investigation The process of gathering additional facts and verifying presently known facts in order to advise a client on how to solve or avoid a legal problem.

legal issue A question of law; a question of what the law is, what the law means, or how the law applies to specific facts. Also called *issue, issue of law*. If the dispute is over the existence or nonexistence of the alleged facts, it is a *question of fact* or a *factual question*.

legal malpractice (1) Malpractice committed by an attorney. (2) Attorney negligence, which is the failure to exercise the reasonable care expected of an attorney in good standing. See also *malpractice*.

legalman A nonattorney in the U.S. Navy who assists attorneys in the practice of law.

legal nurse A nurse, usually an employee of an attorney, who examines and evaluates facts involving the delivery of health care on behalf of an attorney.

legal nurse consultant (LSN) A nurse, usually an independent contractor, who examines and evaluates facts involving the delivery of health care on behalf of an attorney, health organization, or other entity.

legal periodical A pamphlet issued at regular intervals (e.g., quarterly) containing articles and notes on legal topics. The major examples are law reviews and bar journals.

legal services office See *legal aid office*.

legal technician A self-employed paralegal who works for several different attorneys, or a self-employed paralegal who works directly for the public. Sometimes called

an *independent paralegal* or a *freelance paralegal*. See also *limited license legal technician*.

LegalTrac See *Current Law Index*.

legal treatise A book written by a private individual (or by a public individual writing as a private citizen) that provides an overview, summary, or commentary on a legal topic.

legislation (1) The process of making statutory law. (2) A statute (see this term).

legislative branch The branch of government with primary responsibility for making or enacting laws.

legislative court A court created by the legislature. (At the federal level, they are called *Article I courts* because Article I of the U.S. Constitution gives Congress the authority to create special courts.)

legislative history Hearings, debates, amendments, committee reports, and all other events that occur in the legislature before a bill is enacted into a statute. Also part of the history are later changes, if any, made by the legislature to the statute.

legislative intent The design or purpose of the legislature in passing (enacting) a particular statute.

letterhead The top part of stationery, which identifies the name and address of the office (often with the names of owners and selected employees).

letter of disengagement A letter sent to a client formally notifying him or her that the law office will no longer be representing the client.

letter of nonengagement A letter sent to prospective clients that explicitly states that the law office will not be representing them.

leveraging Making profit from the income-generating work of others.

LexisNexis A fee-based system of computer-assisted legal research owned by Reed Elsevier. The most recent version is Lexis Advance (www.lexisnexis.com).

liable Legally responsible.

license Government permission to do something that would otherwise be unlawful. See also *occupational license*.

licensing The granting of a license. Also called *licensure*.

lien A security, encumbrance, or claim on property that remains until a debt is paid. See also *attorney lien*.

limine See *motion in limine*.

limited jurisdiction The power of a court to hear only certain kinds of cases. Also called *special jurisdiction*.

limited liability Restricted liability; liability that can be satisfied out of business assets, not out of personal assets of the debtor or wrongdoer. Protection from personal liability for business debts and claims.

limited liability entity A company or partnership whose owners are taxed like a partnership and have the limited liability of a corporation.

limited license Permission by a government body that allows a person who has met designated qualifications to engage in specified activities that are customarily (but not always exclusively) performed by another category of license holder. Also called *specialty license*. See also *general license*.

limited license legal technician (LLLT) A nonattorney in Washington State who is authorized to engage in the limited practice of law (without attorney supervision) in approved areas of practice.

limited practice officer (LPO) A nonattorney in Washington State who is authorized to select and prepare approved legal documents for designated property transactions.

limited-scope representation Less than comprehensive or full representation of a client. Example: an attorney drafts legal documents but does not provide court representation. Also called *unbundled legal services*.

Linux An open-source operating system. See also *open-source software, operating system*.

listserv See electronic mailing list.

litigant A party in a lawsuit.

litigation (1) The formal process of resolving a legal dispute through the courts. (2) A lawsuit.

litigation hold A notice that a legal dispute has occurred and that information pertinent to the dispute must be preserved by the person or organization in possession or custody of such information. The failure to do may result in sanctions for *spoliation* (see this entry).

litigation status The procedural category of a party during any stage of litigation, e.g., plaintiff, defendant, or appellant.

litigation support Software that stores, retrieves, and tracks facts, documents, testimony, and other litigation materials.

litigious (1) Inclined to resolve disputes through litigation. (2) Quarrelsome.

local area network (LAN) A multiuser system linking computers that are in close proximity to each other so that they can share data and resources.

lodestar A method of calculating an award of attorney fees authorized by statute. The number of reasonable hours spent on the case is multiplied by the prevailing hourly rate in the community for similar work by attorneys. Other factors might also be considered above the lodestar in setting the fee, such as the quality of representation, any delay in receiving payment, and the risk at the outset of the litigation that the prevailing attorney will receive no fee.

Loislaw A fee-based legal research service (estore.loislaw.com).

looseleaf service A law book with a binding (often three ringed) that allows easy insertion and removal of individual pages for updating.

loser pays See *English rule*.

LPO See *limited practice officer*.

LSN See *legal nurse consultant*.

lurking Reading online messages of others without sending any of your own.

M

macro The use one or a few keystrokes to insert frequently used text or to perform other repetitive functions. A keyboard shortcut to perform repetitive tasks.

magistrate (1) A judicial officer having some but not all the powers of a judge. (2) A government official of high rank.

majority opinion An opinion whose final conclusion or judgment is agreed to by more than half of the judges hearing the case. The agreement includes the holdings and reasoning for the holdings.

malicious prosecution A tort with the following elements: (1) The initiation (or procuring the initiation) of civil or criminal legal proceedings; (2) without probable cause; (3) with malice or an improper purpose; and (4) the proceedings terminate in favor of the person against whom the proceedings were brought.

malpractice (1) Any professional misconduct such as an ethics violation, breach of fiduciary duty, crime, tort, or other wrongdoing. (2) Negligence committed by a professional. See also *legal malpractice, negligence*.

malware Software that seeks to disable, disrupt, or otherwise damage computers. Examples include virus and Trojan horse.

managing partner A partner of a law firm who has day-to-day responsibility for the overall management of the firm.

mandate An order of a court.

mandatory authority Primary authority that is binding; it must be followed. Examples: the statutes of state "x" are mandatory authority in state "x"; opinions of the highest state court in state "x" are mandatory authority for every lower state court in state "x" so that all lower state courts must rely on the mandatory authority in reaching their decisions. See also *primary authority, persuasive authority*.

mandatory bar association See *integrated bar association*.

marital-communications privilege A person can refuse to testify and can prevent his or her spouse or ex-spouse from testifying about any confidential communications made between them during the marriage. Also called *marital privilege, husband-wife privilege*.

maritime law See *admiralty law*.

market rate The prevailing rate in the area.

markup (1) The process by which a legislative committee puts a bill in its final form. (2) An increase in price, usually to derive profit.

Martindale-Hubbell Law Directory A national directory of attorneys (www.martindale.com).

mass tort A general term for various causes of action asserted by a large number of persons who have been harmed by the same or similar conduct or product of a relatively small number of defendants. The causes of action include negligence, strict liability in tort, breach of warranty, misrepresentation, and violations of deceptive trade acts.

material (1) Serious and substantial. (2) Important enough to influence the decision that was made.

matter (1) A client issue. The reason a client hires or consults an attorney. (2) A case before the court.

matter of law See *judgment as a matter of law*.

matter of right See *appeal by right*.

MCLE Mandatory continuing legal education.

MCPR *Model Code of Professional Responsibility*, the earlier version of the *Model Rules of Professional Conduct (MRPC)* of the American Bar Association.

MDP See *multidisciplinary practice*.

med-arb A method of alternative dispute resolution (ADR) in which the parties first try mediation, and if it does not work, they try arbitration.

mediation A method of alternative dispute resolution (ADR) in which the parties avoid litigation by submitting their dispute to a neutral third person (the mediator) who helps the parties resolve their dispute, but does not render a decision that resolves it for them.

medium-neutral citation See *public domain citation*.

megabyte One million bytes (approximately).

memorandum (1) A short note. (2) A written record of a transaction. (3) A memorandum of law or legal memorandum, which is a written presentation of how one or more rules might apply to the facts of a client's case. The plural of memorandum is *memoranda*.

memorandum of law A written explanation of how one or more rules might apply to the facts of a client's case. Also called *memo, memorandum, legal memorandum*. The plural of memorandum is *memoranda*.

memorandum opinion (mem.) The decision of a court rendered with few or no supporting reasons, often because it follows well-known or established principles. Also called *memorandum decision*.

memory The internal storage capacity of a computer.

meritorious Having merit; having a reasonable basis to believe that a person's claim or defense will succeed.

merits See *judgment on the merits, on the merits*.

metadata Data about data. Data about an electronic document that are hidden within the document itself, e.g., earlier versions of the document.

metasearch A search for terms in more than one search engine simultaneously.

minimum-fee schedule A bar-association list of the lowest fees an attorney can ethically charge for specific kinds of legal services. Such lists (schedules) have been held to violate antitrust laws.

ministerial Involving a duty that is to be performed in a prescribed manner without the exercise of judgment or discretion.

minitrial See *summary jury trial*.

misdemeanor (1) Any crime punishable by fine or by detention (often for a year or less) in an institution other than a prison. (2) A crime less serious than a felony.

mitigate To reduce or minimize the severity of impact. To render less painful.

mock trial See *summary jury trial*.

model act See *uniform laws*.

Model Code of Professional Responsibility (MCPR) An earlier edition of the ethical rules governing attorneys recommended by the American Bar Association. The *Model Code* consisted of Ethical Considerations (ECs), which represented the objectives toward which each attorney should strive, and Disciplinary Rules (DRs), which were mandatory statements of the minimum conduct below which no attorney could fall without being subject to discipline.

Model Guidelines for the Utilization of Paralegal Services Ethical guidelines recommended by the American Bar Association for the ethical use of paralegals by attorneys.

Model Rule 5.3 The rule in the ABA *Model Rules of Professional Conduct* governing the responsibility of different categories of attorneys for the conduct of paralegals and other nonattorney assistants in a law office.

Model Rules of Professional Conduct (MRPC) The current set of ethical rules governing attorneys recommended by the American Bar Association. These rules revised the ABA's earlier rules found in the *Model Code of Professional Responsibility (MCPR)*.

modem A communications device that allows computers at different locations to exchange data using telephone lines, cables, or wireless connections.

motion An application or request made to a court or other decision-making body seeking to obtain a favorable action or ruling. The person making the motion is the *movant*. The verb is *move*.

motion for a judgment as a matter of law See *judgment as a matter of law*.

motion for a new trial A request that the judge set aside the judgment and order a new trial because the evidence is insufficient to support the judgment, newly discovered evidence, or errors committed during the trial.

motion for summary judgment See *summary judgment*.

motion in limine A request raised preliminarily such as asking the court for a ruling on the admissibility of evidence prior to or during trial but before the evidence has been offered.

motion to dismiss A request, often made before the trial begins, that the judge dismiss the case because the parties have reached a settlement or because of a serious procedural deficiency.

movant A party making a motion or request. See also *motion*.

move See *motion*.

move into evidence To request that an item be formally declared admissible.

MRPC See *Model Rules of Professional Conduct*.

multidisciplinary practice (MDP) A partnership consisting of attorneys and nonlegal professionals that offers legal and nonlegal services.

multiple-choice question A question that asks the interviewee to choose among two or more options stated in the question.

multiple representation Representation by the same attorney of more than one side in a legal matter or controversy. Also called *common representation, dual representation*.

multitasking Having the capacity to run several large programs simultaneously.

N

NALA National Association of Legal Assistants (www.nala.org).

NALS the Association for Legal Professionals (www.nals.org). The association was once called the *National Association of Legal Secretaries*.

National Reporter System The reporters of the West (Thomson Reuters) that cover the opinions of state courts (e.g., the seven regional reporters such as A.2d) and federal courts (e.g., S. Ct., F.3d). The reporters use key numbers to classify the issues in the opinions and later in the digests. See *key number*.

natural language Plain English as spoken or written every day as opposed to language that is specially designed for computer communication.

N.E.2d See *North Eastern Reporter 2d*.

negative contingency See *contingent fee*.

negligence The failure to use reasonable care that an ordinary prudent person would have used in a similar situation, resulting in injury or other loss.

negligent hiring Carelessly hiring an incompetent person who poses an unreasonable risk of harm to others.

negligent supervision Carelessly monitoring or supervising an incompetent person who poses an unreasonable risk of harm to others.

network (1) A group of computers that are linked or connected together by telephone lines, fiber-optic cables, satellites, or other systems. (2) Interconnected persons or things.

networking Establishing contacts and sharing information with people (a) who might become personal or professional resources for you and (b) for whom you might become a personal or professional resource.

neutral evaluation A method of alternative dispute resolution (ADR) in which both sides hire an experienced attorney or an expert in the area involved in the dispute who will listen to an abbreviated version of the evidence and the arguments of each side and offer an evaluation in the hope that this will stimulate more serious settlement discussions. Also called *case evaluation*.

new file worksheet A form used by some law offices that is the source document for the creation of all necessary accounting records that are needed when a law firm begins working on a new client case or matter. Also called a *new matter sheet, new business sheet*.

New York Supplement 2d (N.Y.S.2d) A reporter of West (Thomson Reuters) that publishes court opinions of state courts in New York.

NFPA National Federation of Paralegal Associations (www.paralegals.org).

no-contact See *anticontact rule*.

No contest A plea that does not admit guilt but that does not dispute the charge so that its effect is a conviction. Also called nolo contendere ("I will not contest.")

nolle prosequi (nol-pro) (nolle) ("not to wish to prosecute") A statement by the prosecutor that he or she is unwilling to prosecute the case. The charges, in effect, are dropped. (Abbreviated nol-pro or nolle.)

nominalization A noun formed from a verb or adjective.

nonadversarial Pertaining to a conflict-resolution proceeding in which all opposing parties to the conflict or dispute are not present. See also *adversary hearing*.

nonbillable time Time spent on tasks for which clients cannot be asked to pay.

nonengagement See *letter of nonengagement*.

nonequity partner A special category of partner who does not own the firm in the sense of an equity or capital partner. Also called *income partner*.

nonexempt employee An employee who must be paid overtime compensation.

North Eastern Reporter 2d (N.E.2d) A regional reporter of West (Thomson Reuters) that prints state court opinions of five states (Ill., Ind., Mass., N.Y., and Ohio). N.E.2d is the second series of this reporter. The first series is *North Eastern Reporter* (N.E.).

North Western Reporter 2d (N.W.2d) A regional reporter of West (Thomson Reuters) that prints state court opinions of seven states (Iowa, Mich., Minn., Neb., N.D., S.D., and Wis.). N.W.2d is the second series of this reporter. The first series is *North Western Reporter* (N.W.).

notary public A person who witnesses (i.e., attests to the authenticity of) signatures, administers oaths, and performs related tasks. In Europe, a notary often has more extensive authority.

notes of decisions Summaries of opinions that have interpreted a statute, usually printed beneath the text of the statute in annotated statutory codes.

notice (1) Formal notification. (2) Information about a fact; knowledge of something.

notice of appeal A party's notice given to a court (through filing) and to the opposing party (through service) of an intention to appeal.

notice of appearance A formal notification to a court by an attorney that he or she is representing a party in the litigation.

notice pleading A short and plain statement of the claim showing that the pleader is entitled to relief.

NOV See *judgment notwithstanding the verdict*.

numerical filing system A method of storing client files by numbers or letter-number combinations. See also *alphabetical filing system*.

N.W.2d See *North Western Reporter 2d*.

N.Y.S.2d See *New York Supplement 2d*.

O

oath A sworn statement that what you say is true.

obiter dictum See *dictum*.

objection A formal challenge usually directed at the evidence that the other side is trying to pursue or introduce.

objective Dispassionate; not having a bias. See also *bias*.

occupational license Government permission that is required to engage in a specified occupation.

occurrence policy Insurance that covers all occurrences (e.g., a negligent error or omission) during the period the policy is in effect, even if the claim is not actually filed until after the policy expires.

occurrence witness Someone who actually observed an event.

of counsel An attorney who is semiretired or has some other special status in the law firm.

office memorandum of law A memorandum that objectively analyzes the law; the memo is written for your supervisor or for other individual(s) in your office. Also called *interoffice memorandum of law*. See also *memorandum of law*.

office politics The interaction among coworkers who do not always have the same goals, powers, expectations, abilities, or timetables for performing the work of the office.

office sharing Attorneys who are sole practitioners but share the use and overhead costs of an office.

official reporter A volume (or set of volumes) of court opinions printed by or under the authority of the government. See also *reporter* (1).

official statutory code See *statutory code*.

OJT On-the-job training.

on all fours (1) Exactly the same, or almost so. (2) Being a very close precedent.

online (1) Connected to another computer or computer network, often through the Internet. (2) Residing on a computer and available for use; activated and ready for use on a computer.

on point (1) Raising or covering the same issue as the one before you. (2) Relevant to the issues of a research problem. See also *analogous*.

on the merits Pertaining to a court decision that is based on the facts and on the substance of the claim, rather than solely on a procedural ground or other technicality. See also *judgment on the merits*.

on the record Noted or recorded in an official record of the proceeding.

open-ended question A broad, relatively unstructured question that rarely can be answered in one or two words.

opening statement An attorney's statement to the jury (or to the judge alone in a bench trial where there is no jury) made before presenting evidence. The statement summarizes or previews the case the attorney intends to try to establish during the trial. Unrepresented parties make the statement themselves. Also called *opening argument*.

open-source software Software whose source code is freely available to the public for use and modification. An example is Linux.

operating software (OS) Software that tells the computer how to perform its major functions such as starting (executing) programs, managing its memory, and controlling printers and other attached devices (peripherals). The OS is the master or central software program that the hardware and all other software depend on to function. Also called *operating system*.

operating system (OS) See *operating software*.

opinion (1) A court's written explanation of how it applied the law to the facts to resolve a legal dispute. Also called *judicial opinion, case, decision*. Opinions are printed in volumes called *reporters*. See also *concurring opinion, dissenting opinion, majority opinion, plurality opinion*, and *unpublished opinion*. (2) A judgment, belief, or appraisal of something that may or may not be based on fact or proof. (3) A belief or conclusion expressing a value judgment that is not objectively verifiable.

opinion letter A letter to a client explaining the application of the law and providing legal advice based on that explanation.

opinion of the attorney general Formal legal advice given by the chief law officer of the government to another government official or agency.

optical storage device A device that uses laser light or beams to write data onto plastic disks. Examples include CDs, DVDs, and Blu-ray disks.

oral argument A spoken presentation to the court on a legal issue, e.g., telling an appellate court why the rulings of a lower tribunal were valid or were in error.

order An official command by a court requiring, allowing, or forbidding something.

ordinance A law passed by the local legislature (e.g., city council) that declares, commands, or prohibits something. (Same as a statute, but at the local level of government.) See also *statute*.

original jurisdiction The power of a court to be the first to hear a case before it is reviewed by another type of court. Also called a *court of first instance*.

OS See *operating software*.

outside counsel An attorney used by a company who is not an employee of the company.

outsourcing Paying an outside company or service to perform tasks usually performed by one's own employees.

outstanding Still unresolved; still unpaid.

overhead The operating expenses of a business (e.g., office rent, utilities, insurance, and clerical staff) for which customers or clients are not charged a separate fee. Some states, however, allow attorneys to charge clients for clerical or secretarial time if the client agrees and the amount charged is reasonable.

overreaching Taking unfair advantage of another's naïveté or other vulnerability, especially by deceptive means.

override (1) To supersede or change a result. (2) To approve a bill over the veto of the chief executive.

overrule (1) To decide against or deny. (2) To reject or cancel a holding in an earlier opinion by rendering an opposite decision on the same question of law in a different litigation. To *reverse* means to reject or cancel (overturn) a holding on appeal in the same litigation.

overview question An open-ended question that asks for a summary of an event or condition.

P

P.3d See *Pacific Reporter 3d*.

PACER (Public Access to Court Electronic Records) An electronic public access service that allows subscribers to obtain case and docket information from federal courts via the Internet (www.pacer.gov).

PACE Registered Paralegal See *RP*.

Pacific Reporter 3d (P.3d) A regional reporter of West (Thomson Reuters) that prints state court opinions of fifteen states (Alaska, Ariz., Cal., Colo., Haw., Idaho,

Kan., Mont., Nev., N.M., Okla., Or., Utah, Wash., and Wyo.). P.3d is the third series of this reporter. The second series is *Pacific Reporter 2d* (P.2d). The first series is *Pacific Reporter* (P.).

padding Adding something without justification; adding unnecessary material in order to make something larger. Example: claiming you worked three hours on a task that took only one hour.

page 52 debate A debate on whether there should be limited licensing for paralegals (based on a recommendation in favor of such licensing on page 52 of a report of an American Bar Association commission).

page/line digest A summary of a deposition transcript that presents the questions and the deponent's answers in the order in which the questions were asked along with the page and line numbers where the questions and answers appear.

panel (1) A group of judges, usually three, who decide a case on behalf of a court with a larger number of judges. (2) A list of individuals summoned for jury duty. From this list, juries for particular trials are selected. (3) A group of attorneys available in a group legal services plan. (4) Members of a commission.

paralegal (1) A person who performs substantive legal tasks on behalf of others when those tasks are supervised by an attorney who would be required to perform the tasks if the office did not have a paralegal. Some statutes provide special authorization for the performance of legal tasks even if they are not supervised by an attorney. (2) A person with legal skills who works under the supervision of an attorney or who is otherwise authorized to use those skills; this person performs tasks that do not require all the skills of an attorney and that most secretaries are not trained to perform.

Paralegal Advanced Competency Exam (PACE) The credential bestowed by the National Federation of Paralegal Associations for meeting its criteria such as passing a national certification exam for experienced paralegals.

paralegal code Rules and guidelines covering ethical issues involving paralegals.

paralegal division A bar association division that allows paralegals to join. An example is the Paralegal Division of the State Bar of Texas.

paralegal fee A fee that an attorney can collect for the nonclerical work of the attorney's paralegal. The fee covers the paralegal's substantive legal work on behalf of the client.

paralegal manager A paralegal who helps recruit, train, and supervise paralegals in a law office.

paralegal specialist The major civil service job classification for paralegals who work for the federal government and for some state and local governments.

parallel cite An additional citation where you can find the same written material in the library or online.

parallelism Using a consistent (i.e., parallel) grammatical structure when phrasing logically related ideas in a list.

parol evidence Evidence of an oral statement.

parol-evidence rule (PER) Prior or contemporaneous oral statements cannot be introduced to alter or contradict the terms of a written document if the parties intended the written document to be a complete statement of the agreement.

partner One who shares in the profits and losses of a jointly owned business or other venture. Partners make the ultimate decisions on how the business (e.g., law firm) should be managed.

partnership A business or other venture jointly owned by two or more persons who share its profits and losses.

passive voice The grammatical verb form in which the object of the action is the main focus. The emphasis is on what is being done rather than on who or what is performing or causing the action. See also *active voice*.

pass-through entity A partnership, limited-liability entity, or other business whose income tax is paid by the individual partners or owners of the entity rather than by the entity itself.

patch A software update that provides additional features and corrections to previous versions of the software.

patent agent A nonattorney licensed to prepare and submit patent applications before the U.S. Patent and Trademark Office. (If an attorney, he or she is more commonly called a *patent attorney*.)

P.C. See *professional corporation*.

PDF (portable document format) A file format consisting of an electronic image of a document that preserves the features and styles of the document (e.g., its line spacing, photograph placement, and font size) that existed before it was converted into a digital document.

pecuniary Relating to money. (A pecuniary interest is a financial interest.)

People The state or government as a party.

PER See parole-evidence rule.

percentage fee A fee that is a percentage of the amount involved in the transaction or award.

per curiam opinion An opinion issued "by the [whole] court," usually a short opinion that does not name the judge who wrote it.

peremptory challenge A request from a party to a judge asking that a prospective juror not be allowed to become a member of this jury without stating a reason for the request. Each side is allowed a limited number of such challenges. The request will be granted unless it is used to discriminate on the basis of race, sex, or ethnicity. See also *challenge for cause*.

performance bonus See *incentive billing*.

performance review An analysis of the extent to which a person or program has met designated objectives. Also called *performance appraisal*.

personal jurisdiction A court's power over a person to determine (adjudicate) his or her personal rights. Also called *in personam jurisdiction*. More limited kinds of jurisdiction include the court's power over a person's interest in specific property (*quasi in rem jurisdiction*), over the property itself (*in rem jurisdiction*), or over a status such as marriage (also *in rem jurisdiction*).

personal liability Liability that can be satisfied out of personal as well as business assets of a debtor or wrongdoer. See also *limited liability*.

personal recognizance Release of a defendant in a criminal case without posting a bond, based solely on a promise of the defendant to appear at all scheduled times. Also called *release on recognizance (ROR)*.

persuasive authority Any primary or secondary authority that is not binding, but that could be relied on by a court because it finds the authority helpful (persuasive) in reaching its decision. See also *mandatory authority, primary authority, secondary authority*.

petition (1) A formal request or motion. (2) A complaint.

petitioner One who presents a petition or complaint to a tribunal. See also *appellant*.

phishing The fraudulent attempt to obtain personal information by tricking the recipient of an email message into believing that the sender seeking the information is legitimate.

physical evidence That which can be seen or touched. Also called *tangible evidence*.

PI cases Personal injury (tort) cases.

pinpoint cite A reference to specific material within a document (e.g., a quote) in addition to the citation of the entire document. Also called a *jump cite*.

pirated software Software that has been placed ("loaded") in a computer that is not authorized by the terms of the purchase or lease of the software.

plagiarism Taking another's original ideas or expressions and using them as if they are one's own. One school defines plagiarism as "copying and representing as one's own the works of another in whole or in part regardless of whether such work is copyrighted; using the ideas of another without proper attribution; or any other effort to pass off the works of another, in whole or in part, as the work of the student." Cleveland-Marshall College of Law, *Student Handbook* 76 (2010–2011).

plaintiff The party who initiates a civil (and sometimes a criminal) action in court.

plea bargain An agreement whereby an accused pleads guilty to a lesser included offense or to one of multiple charges in exchange for the prosecution's agreement to support a dismissal of some charges or a lighter sentence. Also called a *negotiated plea*.

plead To file a pleading, make or enter a plea, or argue a case in court.

pleading A formal litigation document filed by a party that states or responds to the claims and defenses the parties have against each other. The main pleadings are the *complaint* and *answer*.

PL number Public law number.

PLS Professional legal secretary.

plurality opinion The opinion agreed to by the largest number of judges hearing the case when there is no majority opinion.

pocket part A pamphlet inserted into a small pocket built into the inside back (and occasionally front) cover of a hardcover volume. The pamphlet contains text that supplements or updates the material in the hardcover volume.

pocket veto The chief executive's "silent" rejection of a bill by not acting on it within 10 days of receiving it if the legislature adjourns during this period.

podcast An Internet audio file that the public can download and listen to through a browser or on audio devices such as iPods and MP3 players. Also called an *audioblog*.

point (1) A measure of the size of printed letters of the alphabet, punctuation marks, or other characters. One point is approximately $\frac{1}{72}$ of an inch tall. (2) A pertinent or relevant argument or issue. See also *on point*.

point heading A conclusion that a party wants a court to accept on one of the issues in the case.

points and authorities memorandum A memorandum of law submitted to a judge or hearing officer. Sometimes called a *trial memorandum*.

poll (1) To ask each member of a body (e.g., a jury) that has just voted to state how he or she individually voted. (2) To seek a sampling of opinions.

popular name A phrase or short title identifying a particular statute.

portable document format See *PDF*.

positional conflict A conflict of interest that exists (1) if an attorney asserts inconsistent legal positions while representing two current clients in separate, unrelated cases and (2) if success on behalf of a client in one case will harm or disadvantage the current client in the other case.

positive evidence See *direct evidence*.

post-occurrence witness Someone who did not observe an event but who can give an account of what happened after the event.

power of attorney (1) A document that authorizes another to act as one's agent or attorney in fact. (2) The authority itself.

PP (professional paralegal) The certification credential bestowed by NALS, the Association for Legal Professionals.

practice guide A legal treatise that provides practical advice on an aspect of the practice of law, often including standard forms and checklists. Also called *practice manual, formbook*.

practice of law Using or attempting to use legal skills to help resolve a specific person's legal problem.

praecipe A formal request to the court (usually made through the court clerk) that something be done.

prayer for relief The request in a pleading for damages or other form of judicial relief.

precedent A prior opinion or decision covering similar facts or issues in a later case that can be used as a standard or guide in a later case.

predictive coding A method of training software to find data that meets defined parameters.

preempt Displace or take precedence over. The noun form is *preemption*. Under the Supremacy Clause of the U.S. Constitution, federal laws take precedence over (preempt) any inconsistent state laws when Congress (1) expressly mandates the preemption, (2) regulates an area so pervasively that an intent to preempt the entire field may be inferred, or (3) enacts a law that directly conflicts with state law.

prejudice Harm or damage. See also *undue prejudice*.

preliminary hearing A pretrial criminal proceeding to determine if probable cause exists that the accused has committed a crime. Also called *probable-cause hearing*, *bindover hearing*.

pre-occurrence witness Someone who did not observe an event but who can give an account of what happened before the event.

prepaid legal services A legal-insurance plan by which a person pays premiums to cover future legal services that might be needed. Also called *legal plan*, *group legal services*.

preponderance of the evidence The standard of proof that is met when the evidence establishes that it is more likely than not that the facts are as alleged. Also called *fair preponderance of evidence*.

presentation graphics Software used to combine text with charts, graphs, pictures, video, clip art, and sound in order to communicate data more effectively.

presumption An assumption or inference that a certain fact is true once another fact is established. The presumption is *irrebuttable* (conclusive) if a party is not allowed to introduce evidence to show that the assumption is false. The presumption is *rebuttable* if a party is allowed to introduce evidence to show that the assumption is false.

pretexting Using online deception as a pretext to obtain information from another person.

pretrial conference A meeting of the attorneys and the judge (or magistrate) before the trial to attempt to narrow the issues, to secure stipulations, and to make efforts to settle the case without a trial. Also called a *trial management conference*.

prima facie (1) On the face of it, at first sight. (2) Sufficient.

prima facie case A party's presentation of evidence that will prevail unless the other side presents more convincing counterevidence.

primary authority A law written by one of the three branches of government.

principal (1) One who permits an agent to act on his or her behalf. (2) The amount of debt, not including interest. (3) The initial sum invested. (4) A perpetrator of a crime. (5) One with prime responsibility for an obligation.

private arbitration See *contractual arbitration*.

private judging A method of alternative dispute resolution (ADR) consisting of arbitration or mediation in which the arbitrator or mediator is a retired judge. Sometimes misleadingly called *rent-a-judge*.

private law A statute that applies to specifically named individuals or groups and has little or no permanence or general interest.

private law firm A law firm that generates its income mainly from the attorney (and paralegal) fees paid by individual clients.

private reprimand See reprimand.

private sector Offices in which operating funds come from client fees or the corporate treasury. See also *public sector*.

privilege (1) A special legal benefit, right, exemption, or protection. (2) The right to act contrary to the right of another without being subject to tort or other liability. A defense that authorizes conduct that would otherwise be wrongful.

privilege against self-incrimination A criminal defendant cannot be forced to testify. The right not to answer incriminating questions by the government that could directly or indirectly connect you to the commission of a crime.

privileged Protected by a privilege so that disclosure is prohibited or limited.

privilege log A list of data or documents claimed to be covered by privilege and, therefore, protected from disclosure in discovery or during trial.

probable cause (1) A reasonable belief that a specific crime has been committed and that the accused committed the crime. (2) A reasonable belief that a location contains items relevant to a crime. (3) A reasonable belief that good grounds exist to bring *civil* proceedings against someone.

probable-cause hearing See *preliminary hearing*.

probate (1) The procedure to establish the validity of a will and to oversee the administration of the estate. (2) To establish the validity of a will.

probation (1) Supervised punishment in the community in lieu of incarceration. (2) Allowing an attorney to continue to practice, but under specified conditions, e.g., submitting to periodic audits or making restitution to a client.

pro bono Concerning or involving legal services that are provided for the public good (pro bono publico, shortened to *pro bono*) without fee or compensation. Sometimes also applied to services given at a reduced rate. Shortened to *pro bono*.

procedural due process The constitutional requirement that the government provide fair procedures such as notice and an opportunity to be heard whenever the government seeks to deprive someone of life, liberty, or property.

procedural law The rules that govern the mechanics of resolving a dispute in court or in an administrative agency, e.g., a rule on the time by which a party must respond to a complaint.

procedural rules See *court rules*.

process The means (e.g., a summons, writ, or other court order) used by the court to acquire its power or jurisdiction over a person. See also *service of process*.

process server Someone who serves or delivers process.

professional corporation (P.C.) A corporation consisting of persons performing services that require a professional license, e.g., attorneys.

professional judgment Applying the law or legal principles to the facts of a specific person's legal problem. When communicated to this person, the result is called *legal advice*.

professional paralegal See *PP*.

project attorney See *contract attorney*.

project billing See *task-based billing*.

proof Enough evidence to establish the existence or nonexistence of an alleged fact.

proof of service A sworn statement (or other evidence) that a summons or other process has been served on a party in an action. Also called *certificate of service*, *return of service*.

pro per See *pro se*.

proposed findings and rulings Recommended conclusions presented to someone else in the administrative agency who will make the final decision.

pro se (on one's own behalf) Appearing for or representing oneself. Also called *in propria persona* (abbreviated *in pro per*).

prosecution (1) Bringing and processing criminal proceedings against someone. The words *prosecution* and *prosecute* can also refer to bringing and processing civil proceedings against someone, although the words are more commonly used in criminal proceedings. (2) The attorney representing the government in a criminal case. Also called the *prosecutor*.

prospective Governing future events; effective (having an effective date) in the future.

Public Access to Court Electronic Records See PACER.

public benefits Government benefits.

public defender An attorney appointed by a court and paid by the government to represent an indigent defendant in a criminal case.

public domain Work product or other property that is not protected by copyright or patent. A status that allows use by anyone without fee.

public-domain citation (1) A citation that is not dependent on the volume and page number of a reporter. (2) A citation that is both medium neutral (meaning that it can be read in a paper volume or online) and vendor neutral (meaning that it does not contain volume, page, or other identifying information created by particular vendors such as a commercial publisher). In a public-domain citation, each paragraph is consecutively numbered (e.g., ¶1, ¶2) so that you can refer to specific language in the opinion by paragraph number rather than by page number. Also called *vendor-neutral citation, generic citation, medium-neutral citation*.

public law A statute that applies to the general public or to a segment of the public and has permanence or general interest.

public policy The principles inherent in the customs, morals, and notions of justice that prevail in a state; the foundation of public laws; the principles that are naturally and inherently right and just.

public reprimand See *reprimand*.

public sector Offices in which operating funds come from charity or the government. See also *private sector*.

Q

qualify To present evidence of a person's education and experience sufficient to convince the court that the witness has expertise in a particular area.

quarantined Isolated or kept apart from a case because of a conflict of interest in connection with that case. See also *Chinese wall*.

quarantined employee See *Chinese wall*.

quasi-adjudication An administrative decision written by an administrative agency that has some characteristics of an opinion written by a court.

quasi-government agency See *government corporation*.

quasi-independent regulatory agency An administrative agency that has characteristics of both an executive department agency and an independent regulatory agency.

quasi in rem jurisdiction A court's power over a person, but restricted to his or her specific interest in property within the territory over which the court has authority.

quasi-judicial proceeding A proceeding within an administrative agency that seeks to resolve a dispute in a manner that is similar to a judicial (i.e., court) proceeding to resolve a dispute.

quasi-legislation An administrative regulation enacted by an administrative agency that has some characteristics of the legislation (statutes) enacted by the legislature. The adjective is *quasi-legislative*.

query A question that is used to try to find something in a computer database.

question of law/question of fact See *legal issue*.

questions presented A statement of the legal issues in an appellate brief that a party wants the appellate court to resolve.

quid pro quo sexual harassment Submission to or rejection of unwelcome sexual conduct used as a basis for employment decisions on promotion or other job-related benefits.

R

rainmaker An attorney who brings fee-generating cases into the office due to his or her contacts and/or reputation as a skilled attorney.

RAM See *random access memory*.

random access memory (RAM) Memory that stores temporary data that are erased (unless properly saved) whenever the computer's power is turned off.

ratify (1) To adopt or confirm a prior act or transaction, making one bound by it. (2) To give formal approval.

RE Regarding, concerning; in the matter of.

read-only Able to read data on a device but not to alter, remove, or add to the data.

read-only memory (ROM) Memory that stores data that cannot be altered, removed, or added to. The data can only be read by the computer.

read/write Able to read data on a device and write or insert additional data into it.

realization rate The percentage of total client billings of an attorney or paralegal that the office actually collects. Also called the *collection realization rate*. Because timekeepers often spend time on both billable tasks and nonbillable tasks, a further breakdown is a timekeeper's *billing realization rate*. This is the percentage of the timekeeper's total office time that is billable. For example, paralegals who spend half their time on nonbillable tasks and half on billable tasks have a 50 percent billable realization rate.

really simple syndication (RSS) A method of notifying subscribers of new content on an Internet site by syndicating (feeding) notice of the new content to subscribers.

real time Occurring now; happening as you are watching; able to respond or otherwise interact immediately or within seconds.

reasonable doubt Such doubt as would cause prudent persons to hesitate before acting in matters of importance to themselves.

reasonable fee A fee that is not excessive in light of the amount of time and labor involved, the complexity of the case, the experience and reputation of the attorney, the customary fee charged in the locality for the same kind of case, etc.

reasoning An explanation of why the court resolved an issue the way it did. The reasons the court reached its holding on an issue.

rebut To refute or oppose.

rebuttable Not conclusive; evidence to the contrary is admissible.

rebuttable presumption An assumption or inference of fact that can be overcome (rebutted) by sufficient contrary evidence but that will be treated as accurate if it is not rebutted. See also *conclusive presumption*.

receivables Accounts due and payable.

record (1) The official collection of all the trial pleadings, exhibits, orders, and word-for-word testimony that were part of the trial. (2) To make an official note of; to enter in a document. (3) The facts that have been inscribed or stored. (4) A collection of data fields that constitute a single unit, e.g., an employee record.

recordable DVD drive A drive that allows data to be recorded on DVD disks.

record information manager Someone in charge of client files in a large office.

recross-examination Another cross-examination of a witness after the witness has been through a redirect examination.

redact To edit or prepare a document for publication or release, often by deleting, altering, or blocking out text that you do not want disclosed.

redirect examination Another direct examination of a witness after he or she was cross-examined.

referee See *hearing examiner*.

referendum The electorate's power to give final approval to an existing provision of the constitution or statute of the legislature.

referral fee See *forwarding fee*.

regional reporter A West (Thomson Reuters) reporter that contains state court opinions of states within a region of the country. West has divided the country into seven regions.

register A regularly published collection of regulations and other documents of administrative agencies and the chief executive.

registered agent A nonattorney authorized to practice before the U.S. Patent and Trademark Office.

registered paralegal See *RP*.

registration The process by which the names of individuals or institutions are listed on a roster kept by a governmental or nongovernmental body. Also called *enrollment*.

regulation A rule or restriction designed to control the conduct of an organization or individual. The regulation can be issued by a governmental body (e.g., an administrative agency) or by a nongovernmental body (e.g., an association or club). See also *administrative regulation*.

rehearing A second (or later) hearing by a court to reconsider the decision it made after an earlier hearing.

release on recognizance (ROR) See *personal recognizance*.

relevant (1) Logically tending to establish or disprove a fact. Pertinent. Relevant evidence is evidence having any tendency to make the existence of a fact more probable or less probable than it would be without the evidence. (2) Contributing to the resolution of a problem or issue. The noun is *relevancy*.

rem See *in rem jurisdiction, quasi in rem jurisdiction*.

remand To send back. For example, to return a case to a lower tribunal with instructions from a higher tribunal on how to proceed.

remedial (1) Corrective; intending to correct. (2) Providing a remedy. See also *remedy*.

remedy (1) The means by which a right is enforced or the violation of a right is prevented, compensated for, or otherwise redressed. (2) To correct. The plural is *remedies*.

rent-a-judge See *private judging*.

reply A plaintiff's response to the defendant's counterclaim, plea, or answer.

reply brief (1) An appellate brief of the appellant that responds to the appellate brief of the appellee. (2) Any appellate brief that responds to an opponent's appellate brief.

reported Printed in a reporter.

reporter (1) A volume (or set of volumes) of court opinions. Also called *case reports*. An *official reporter* is printed by or under the authority of the government. An *unofficial reporter* is printed by a commercial publishing company without special authority from the government. (2) The person in charge of publishing the decisions of a court. Also called *reporter of decisions*. (3) The person who takes down and transcribes proceedings. The person is called a *court reporter*.

reprimand An official declaration that an attorney's conduct was unethical. The declaration does not affect the attorney's right to practice law. A *private reprimand* is not disclosed to the public; a *public reprimand* is.

reproval A disapproval or rebuke. See also *admonition*.

request for admission (RFA) A method of discovery by which one party sends a request to another party that the latter agree that a certain fact or legal conclusion is true or valid so that there will be no need to present proof or arguments about that matter during the trial.

request for production (RFP) A method of discovery by which one party requests that another party provide access to electronically stored data, paper documents, or other tangible things for copying or inspection. The method can also include a request to enter the party's land for inspection.

res A thing or a status. See *in rem jurisdiction*.

res judicata   ("a thing adjudicated") A defense raised (a) to prevent the same parties from retrying (relitigating) a claim that has already been resolved on the merits in a prior case or (b) to prevent the litigation of a claim arising out of the same transaction involved in the first case that could have been raised in the first case but was not.

respondeat superior   "Let the master [boss] answer." An employer is responsible (liable) for the wrongs committed by an employee within the scope of employment.

respondent   The party against whom an appeal is brought. Also called the *appellee*.

rest   To announce formally that you have concluded the presentation of evidence.

Restatement   A special legal treatise of the American Law Institute that states the law and indicates changes in the law that the Institute would like to see implemented. Example: *Restatement (Second) of Torts* (1965).

retain   To hire; to place or keep in one's service.

retainer   (1) The act of hiring or engaging the services of someone, usually a professional. (The verb is *retain*.) (2) An amount of money (or other property) paid by a client as a deposit or advance against future fees, costs, and related expenses of providing services.

retaining lien   See *attorney lien*.

retroactive   Applying to facts that arise before as well as after the effective date. See also *prospective*.

retroactive negotiated fee   A client bill that is finalized after the services are rendered.

return of service   See *proof of service*.

reverse   To reject or cancel a holding on appeal in the same litigation. See also *overrule*.

review   The power of a court to examine the correctness of what a lower tribunal has done. See also *judicial review*.

RFA   See *request for admission*.

RFP   See *request for production*.

right justified   Every line of a paragraph on the right margin is aligned except for the last line if it ends before the margin. See also *justification, left justified*.

roadmap paragraph   An overview or thesis paragraph at the beginning of a memorandum. It is an introduction to the entire memo. For example, it can tell the reader what issues will be covered and briefly state the conclusions that will be reached.

ROM   See *read-only memory*.

root expander   An exclamation mark (!) that stands for one or more characters added to the root of a term you are searching in Westlaw or LexisNexis.

ROR   See *personal recognizance*.

RP or PACE Registered Paralegal   The certification credentials bestowed by the National Federation of Paralegal Associations: RP (registered paralegal), PACE (Paralegal Advanced Competency Examination).

RSS   See *really simple syndication*.

rule   See *administrative regulation, court rules*.

Rule 5.3.   See *Model Rule 5.3*.

rule-making function   Writing administrative regulations.

rule of three   A general guideline used by some law firms to identify budget expectations from hiring paralegals: gross revenue generated through paralegal billing should equal three times a paralegal's salary.

rule on witnesses   A rule that requires certain witnesses to be removed from the courtroom until it is time for their individual testimony so that they will not be able to hear each other's testimony.

rules of court   See *court rules*.

rules of procedure.   See *court rules*.

ruling   The conclusion or outcome of a decision made by a court or administrative agency. See also *administrative decision*.

run   To cause a program to (1) be loaded into the computer from a disk drive and (2) begin to perform its task.

runner   (1) One who solicits business, especially accident cases. (2) An employee who delivers and files papers.

S

S.   See *Southern Reporter*.

sanction   (1) Penalty or punishment imposed for unacceptable conduct. (2) Permission or approval.

satisfy   To comply with a legal obligation. The noun is *satisfaction*.

scanner   An input device that converts text and images into an electronic or digital format that a computer can recognize.

scheduling order   A pretrial order of a magistrate or judge that sets time limits for discovery, filings, further pretrial conferences, and other related pretrial matters.

scope of employment   That which is foreseeably done by an employee for the employer's business under the employer's specific or general control.

screening   Steps taken by a law office to isolate a tainted worker from involvement in a case in order to avoid vicarious or imputed disqualification of the office from representation of a client in that case.

scrivener   A professional copyist; a document preparer.

scrolling   In word-processing and other programs, moving a line of text onto or off the screen.

S. Ct.   See *Supreme Court Reporter*.

search engine   A search tool that will find sites on the Internet that contain terms that you enter on any subject.

secondary authority   A nonlaw (e.g., a legal periodical article) that summarizes, describes, or explains the law but is not a law itself.

second chair   An assistant to the lead attorney at a trial. The assistant, usually another attorney, sits at the counsel's table in the courtroom.

self-help   (1) Self-representation. Representing oneself with or without some assistance from an attorney, document service provider (DSP), online legal site, manual, or other materials. (2) Acting on one's own to prevent or correct the effects of a tort or other wrong without using the courts or other public authority.

senior associate   An attorney who has been passed over for partner status but who remains at the firm.

separation of powers   The constitutional requirement that each of the legislative, executive, and judicial branches of government limit itself to the powers granted to it and not encroach upon the powers granted to the other two branches.

sequester (1) To separate or isolate a jury or witness. (2) To seize and hold funds or other property. Sometimes called *sequestrate*.

series A succession of numbered volumes in a set of books that will eventually use a new numbering order for volumes added to the set. The added volumes will not constitute a new edition.

server (1) A computer program that provides resources or services to other computers. (2) A system that manages resources on a network. (3) A computer that processes requests.

service company A business that sells particular services, usually to other businesses.

service of process A formal delivery of notice to a defendant that a suit has been initiated to which he or she must respond. *Process* is the means used by the court to acquire or exercise its power or jurisdiction over a person.

session (1) A continuous sitting of a legislature or court. (2) Any time in the day during which such a body sits.

session law A statute passed by the legislature and printed in volumes that are organized by date (chronologically) rather than by subject matter. Sometimes called *statute at large*.

set for trial To schedule a date when the trial is to begin.

settlement (1) An agreement resolving a dispute without full litigation. (2) Payment or satisfactory adjustment of an account. (3) Distributing the assets and paying the debts of an estate. (4) The meeting in which a transaction is finalized. Also called *closing*.

settlement work-up A summary of the major facts in the case presented in a manner designed to encourage the other side (or its liability insurance company) to settle the case. Also called a *settlement brochure*.

sexual harassment Unwanted and offensive sexual advances, contact, comments, or other interaction. See also *hostile-environment sexual harassment*, *quid pro quo sexual harassment*.

shadow jurors Persons hired by one side to observe a trial as members of the general audience (gallery) and, as the trial progresses, to give feedback to the trial attorney who will use the feedback to assess strategy for the remainder of the trial.

shallow pocket An actual or potential defendant without resources to pay a potential judgment. See also *deep pocket*.

shepardize To use *Shepard's Citations* (in book form and online) to obtain validation and other data on a case, statute, or other document you are shepardizing. See also *citator*.

Shepard's Citations A major citator that is available online and in paper formats. See also *citator*, *shepardize*.

short form citation An abbreviated citation format of an authority for which you have already provided a complete citation earlier in the document.

sidebar conference A discussion between the judge and the attorneys held at the judge's bench so that the jury cannot hear what is being said. Also called a *bench conference*.

skiptracing Efforts to locate persons (e.g., debtors) or assets.

slip law A single act passed by the legislature and printed in a single pamphlet.

slip opinion The first printing of a single court opinion.

So. 2d See *Southern Reporter 2d*.

social bookmarking An online service that allows users to share and comment on links to Websites.

Social media Websites that allow users to engage in different kinds of interaction or networking with each other such as by posting information about themselves and their interests and commenting on what others post.

software A computer program that tells or instructs the hardware what to do.

sole practitioner An attorney who practices alone. His or her office has no partners, associates, or employees who are attorneys.

sole proprietorship A form of business that does not have a separate legal identity apart from the one person who owns all assets and assumes all debts and liabilities.

solicitation (1) An appeal or request for clients or business. (2) An attempt to obtain something by persuasion or application.

source code The programming language of software.

South Eastern Reporter 2d (S.E.2d) A regional reporter of West (Thomson Reuters) that prints state court opinions of five states (Ga., N.C., S.C., Va., and W.Va.). S.E.2d is the second series of this reporter. The first series is *South Eastern Reporter (S.E.)*.

Southern Reporter 2d (So. 2d) A regional reporter of West (Thomson Reuters) that prints state court opinions of four states (Ala., Fla., La., and Miss.). So. 2d is the second series of this reporter. The first series is *Southern Reporter (So.)*.

South Western Reporter 3d (S.W.3d) A regional reporter of West (Thomson Reuters) that prints state court opinions of five states (Ark., Ky., Mo., Tenn., and Tex.). S.W.3d is the third series of this reporter. The second series is *South Western Reporter 2d (S.W.2d)*. The first series is *South Western Reporter (S.W.)*.

spam Unsolicited email messages, often consisting of commercial advertising. Unsolicited junk mail.

special damages Economic losses (e.g., medical expenses and lost wages) that must be alleged and proven. They are not presumed to exist. Also referred to as *specials*. Special damages is a category of *compensatory damages*, which is money paid to restore an injured party to his or her position prior to the injury or other loss.

special-interest group An organization that seeks to influence public policy in favor of a particular group or cause, often through lobbying.

special jurisdiction See *limited jurisdiction*.

specialty certification Recognition of competency in a particular area of law. The National Association of Legal Assistants, for example, has a specialty certification program to recognize a person as an ACP (Advanced Certified Paralegal).

specific performance A remedy for breach of contract that forces the wrongdoing party to complete the contract as promised.

speech recognition The ability of a computer to receive information (data) by talking into a microphone.

spell checker The identification of possible spelling errors in a computer-generated document with suggested corrections.

spoliation Intentionally destroying, altering, or concealing evidence.

spreadsheet Software that performs calculations on numbers and values that you enter.

squibs See *digest*.

staff attorney A full-time attorney employee who has no expectation of becoming a full partner. Also called *second-tier attorney*.

staffing agency An employment agency that places temporary workers, often directly paying the workers and handling all of the financial aspects of the placement.

stand-alone computer A computer that is not connected to a network.

standard of proof A statement of how convincing a version of a fact must be before the trier of facts (usually the jury) can accept it as true.

stare decisis ("stand by things decided") Courts should decide similar cases in the same way unless there is good reason for the court to do otherwise. When resolving an issue, courts should be reluctant to reject *precedent*—a prior opinion covering similar facts and issues.

Stat. See *United States Statutes at Large*.

statement of principles Guidelines negotiated by bar associations and specified law-related occupations that distinguish between those activities of the occupations that do not constitute the unauthorized practice of law and those that do.

statement of the case The portion of an appellate brief that summarizes the procedural history of the case to date and presents the essential facts of the dispute. It may also state the appellate court's subject-matter jurisdiction.

state questions Issues that arise from or are based on the state constitution, state statutes, state administrative regulations, state common law, or other state laws.

stating a cause of action Including facts in a pleading (e.g., a complaint) that, if proved at trial, would entitle the party to the judicial relief sought (assuming the other party does not plead and prove a defense that would defeat the effort).

status letter A letter that updates someone on a matter. Example: telling a client what has happened in the case thus far and what next steps are expected.

status line A message line that states the current position of the cursor and provides other formatting information.

statute A law passed by the state or federal legislature that declares, commands, or prohibits something. Also called *act, legislation*. (Statute, act, and legislation are sometimes used in a broader sense to include laws passed by any legislature, which would include ordinances passed by a city council.)

statute at large See *session laws*.

statute in derogation of the common law A statute that changes the common law.

statute of limitations A law stating that civil or criminal actions are barred if not brought within a specified time. The action is time-barred if not brought within that time.

statutory code A collection of statutes organized by subject matter rather than by date. An *official* statutory code is one published by the government or by a private company with special permission or authority from the government. An *unofficial* statutory code is one published by a private company without special permission or authority from the government.

statutory-fee case A case applying a special statute that gives a judge authority to order the losing party to pay the winning party's attorney fees (including paralegal fees) and costs.

stay The suspension or postponement of a judgment or proceeding.

steerer See *ambulance chasing, runner*.

stipulation ("stip") (1) An agreement between opposing parties about a particular matter. The verb is *stipulate*. (2) A condition or requirement.

STOP A writing technique alerting you to the need for a counteranalysis: after writing a Sentence that contains facts or analysis, Think carefully about whether the Other side would take a Position that is different from the one you took in the sentence.

stop words Common words (e.g., a, an, the) that some search engines do not recognize as part of the search query.

structured settlement An agreement in which a party fulfills a financial obligation (e.g., the payment of damages) by making periodic payments over a designated period. The payments are sometimes funded through an annuity.

subject-matter jurisdiction The court's power to resolve a particular type of legal dispute and to grant a particular type of relief.

subpoena (1) To command that someone appear at a certain time and place. (2) A command to appear at a certain time and place.

subpoena ad testificandum A command to appear at a certain time and place to give testimony.

subpoena duces tecum A command to appear at a certain time and place and bring specified things such as documents. (If ordered to give testimony, the subpoena would be a *subpoena ad testificandum*.)

subrogation The substitution of one person for another on a debt or insurance claim.

subscript A number (or other character) that is printed below the usual text baseline.

subscription (1) A signature. (2) The act of signing one's name.

substantive Nonclerical; requiring legal skills to perform.

substantive law Nonprocedural laws that define or govern rights and duties, e.g., the duty to use reasonable care to avoid injuring someone.

substantive legal work (1) Nonclerical tasks that require legal skills to perform. (2) Tasks for which a court would grant an attorney's application for paralegal fees.

substituted service An approved method of completing service of process other than by handing the process documents in person to the defendant or to the defendant's authorized representative in person (e.g., service by mail or by publication in a newspaper). Also called *constructive service*.

successive representation An attorney's representation of a current client who is opposing a former client of this attorney.

sufficient cause See *good cause*.

summary Quick, expedited, without going through a full adversary hearing.

summary judgment A judgment of the court that is rendered without a full trial because of the absence of conflict on any of the material facts.

summary jury trial A method of alternative dispute resolution (ADR) in which the parties present their evidence and arguments to an advisory jury, which renders a nonbinding verdict. Also called *mock trial*, *minitrial*.

summation See *closing argument*.

summer associate See *law clerk*.

summing up See *closing argument*.

summons A notice directing the defendant to appear in court and answer the plaintiff's complaint or face a default judgment.

sunshine law A statute that requires some government agencies to have open meetings and to provide public access to designated public records.

superior court Usually a trial court.

superscript A number (or other character) that is printed above the usual text baseline.

suppression Preventing evidence from being admissible.

supra Above; mentioned earlier in the document.

Supremacy Clause The clause in the U.S. Constitution (art. VI, cl. 2) that has been interpreted to mean that when valid federal law conflicts with state law, federal law controls.

supreme court The highest court in a judicial system. (In New York, however, the supreme court is a lower court.)

Supreme Court Reporter (S. Ct.) An unofficial reporter of West (Thomson Reuters) that prints opinions of the U.S. Supreme Court.

surety One who is liable for paying another's debt or performing another's duty.

surrogate court A special court with subject matter jurisdiction over wills, probate, guardianships, etc.

suspension The removal of an attorney from the practice of law for a specified minimum period, after which the attorney can apply for reinstatement.

sustain (1) To uphold or agree with. (2) To support or encourage. (3) To endure or withstand.

S.W.3d See *South Western Reporter 3d*.

syllabus A brief summary or outline. For court opinions, it is also called a *case synopsis* and is printed before the opinion begins. It is usually a summary of the entire opinion.

T

table of authorities (TOA) A list of primary authority (e.g., cases and statutes) and secondary authority (e.g., legal periodical articles and legal treatises) that a writer has cited in an appellate brief or other document. The list includes page numbers where each authority is cited in the document.

tainted Having or causing a conflict of interest; contaminated. See also *Chinese wall*.

tainted paralegal A paralegal who brings a conflict of interest to a law office because of the paralegal's prior work at another law office.

take under advisement See *advisement*.

TANF (Temporary Assistance for Needy Families) A federal-state welfare program.

tangible evidence Physical evidence; evidence that has a physical form. Evidence that can be seen and inspected. *Intangible evidence* (e.g., a right or belief) is evidence without physical form. Intangible evidence is sometimes embodied or evidenced by something physical, e.g., a written contract.

task-based billing (1) Charging a specific amount for each legal task performed. Also called *unit billing*, *project billing*. See also *fee*. (2) Paying for specifically performed tasks, often identified by using predefined categories of task codes.

task padding Inflating a client's bill by charging for tasks that were not performed.

telecommuting Working from home or other remote setting through the Internet, email, telephone, and other means of communication that do not require presence at a traditional office.

template A file containing text and a format that can be used as the starting point for creating frequently used documents.

term of art A word or phrase that has a special or technical meaning.

terms and connectors Relationships between terms in a search query that specify documents that should be included in or excluded from the search.

territorial jurisdiction The geographic boundaries within which a court has the power to act.

testator One who has died leaving a valid will.

test case Litigation that seeks to create a new legal principle or right.

testimony Evidence given by a witness under oath.

thesaurus A volume of word alternatives.

The Bluebook See *bluebook*.

third-party complaint A defendant's complaint against someone who is not now a party on the basis that the latter may be liable for all or part of what the plaintiff might recover from the defendant.

Thomson Reuters The publisher that acquired West Publishing Company. It publishes Westlaw and volumes such as the regional reporters.

tickler A paper or computer system designed to provide reminders of important dates. Also called a *come-up system*.

time-barred (1) Prevented or barred from bringing a civil or criminal action because of the passage of a designated period of time without commencing the action. (2) Being unable to sue because of the statute of limitations.

timekeeping Recording time spent on a client matter for purposes of billing and productivity assessment.

timeline A chronological presentation of significant events, often using text and diagrams.

timely Within the time set by contract or law.

time padding Inflating a client's bill by charging for time that was not spent.

tool bar A list of shortcuts (usually represented by icons) that can quickly execute commonly used functions.

topical digest A summary of a deposition transcript organized by specific topics covered in the answers of the deponent.

topic and key number See *key number*.

tort A civil wrong (other than a breach of contract) that causes injury or other loss for which our legal system deems it just to provide a remedy such as damages. Injury or loss can be to the person (a *personal* tort), to movable property (a *personal-property* tort), or to land and anything attached to the land (a *real-property* tort).

traditional paralegal A paralegal who is an employee of an attorney.

transactional matter Anything involving a transaction such as entering a contract, incorporating a business, closing a real estate sale, or planning an estate.

transactional paralegal One who provides paralegal services for an attorney who represents clients in transactions such as entering contracts, incorporating a business, closing a real estate sale, or planning an estate. A paralegal who does not work in litigation.

transcribed Taken down in a word-for-word account. The account is called a *transcript*.

transcript A word-for-word account of what was said. A written copy of what was said.

transmittal letter See *cover letter*.

treatise See *legal treatise*.

treaty A formal agreement between two or more nations. Also called *accord, convention, pact*. See also *executive agreement*.

trial binder See *trial notebook*.

trial book See *trial brief (2)*

trial brief (1) An attorney's written presentation to a trial court of the legal issues and positions of his or her client (also called *trial memorandum*). (2) An attorney's personal notes on how he or she will conduct a particular trial (also called *trial manual, trial book*).

trial de novo A new trial conducted as if a prior one had not occurred.

trial management conference See *pretrial conference*.

trial manual See *trial brief* (1).

trial memorandum See *points and authorities memorandum, trial brief*.

trial notebook A collection of documents, arguments, and strategies that an attorney plans to use during a trial. Also called *trial binder*.

truncated passive A form of passive voice in which the doer or subject of the action is not mentioned. See also *active voice, passive voice*.

trust account See *client trust account*.

typeover mode When new text is typed in a line that already has text, the old text is erased or overtyped with each keystroke. See also *insert mode*.

U

UDA See *unlawful detainer assistant*.

unanimous opinion An opinion in which all of the judges hearing the case agree with the final conclusion or judgment, including all of the holdings and reasoning.

unauthorized practice of law (UPL) (1) Using or attempting to use legal skills to help resolve a specific person's legal problem when the assistance is provided by someone who does not have a license to practice law and when the assistance requires such a license or other authorization. (2) A nonattorney's performance of tasks in a law office without adequate attorney supervision when those tasks are part of the practice of law. (3) Delegating tasks to nonattorney that only an attorney can perform.

unbundled legal services Discrete task representation for which the client is charged per task as opposed to paying a single fee for all tasks to be performed. Also called *limited-scope representation*. Charging for such services is called *task-based billing, unit billing, project billing*. See also *bundled legal services*.

uncodified Organized chronologically by date of enactment rather than by subject matter.

uncontested Unchallenged; without opposition or dispute.

undue influence Improper persuasion, coercion, force, or deception.

undue prejudice The persuasiveness of the evidence is outweighed by the harm it could cause a party because of the emotions the evidence could stir up in the minds of the jury.

unemployment compensation Temporary income from the government to persons who have lost their jobs (often after being laid off) and are looking for work. Also called *unemployment insurance*.

unicameral Having one chamber in the legislature. See also *bicameral*.

unified bar association See *integrated bar association*.

Uniform Electronic Legal Material Act (UELMA) A statute that provides a method of letting users of government sites know that the law contained on the sites is authentic.

uniform laws Laws proposed to state legislatures in areas where uniformity is deemed appropriate. Each state can adopt, modify, or reject the proposals. Sometimes called *model acts*.

uniform resource locator (URL) The address of a resource (or any page) on the Internet.

unit billing See *task-based billing*.

United States Code (U.S.C.) The official annotated statutory code containing the statutes of Congress published by the government.

United States Code Annotated (U.S.C.A.) An unofficial annotated statutory code containing the statutes of Congress published by West (Thomson Reuters).

United States Code Service (U.S.C.S.) An unofficial annotated statutory code containing the statutes of Congress published by LexisNexis.

United States court of appeals The main intermediate appellate court in the federal court system.

United States district court The main trial court in the federal judicial system.

United States Reports (U.S.) The official reporter for opinions of the U.S. Supreme Court.

United States Statutes at Large (Stat.) The session laws of Congress consisting of every public and private law, all printed chronologically.

United States Supreme Court The court of final resort in the federal judicial system.

United States Supreme Court Reports, Lawyers' Edition 2d (L. Ed. 2d) An unofficial reporter that prints opinions of the U.S. Supreme Court. The publisher is LexisNexis.

universal character A special character (e.g., *, !, ?) that can be used to represent one or more characters in a search query.

unlawful detainer assistant (UDA) A nonattorney in California who is authorized to charge fees for providing self-help assistance (without attorney supervision) to landlords or tenants in actions for the possession of land.

unofficial reporter A volume (or set of volumes) of court opinions printed by a commercial publishing company without special authority from the government. See also *reporter* (1).

unofficial statutory code See *statutory code*.

unpublished opinion An opinion designated by the court as not for official publication even though you may be able to read it online or in special reporters. Also called *unpublished case*.

UPL See *unauthorized practice of law*.

upload See *download*.

URL See *uniform resource locator*.

U.S. (1) The federal government. (2) United States. (3) *United States Reports*.

USB flash drive A portable memory drive that is inserted into and taken out of the computer's USB port. Also called *thumb drive*.

usurp To unlawfully exercise a position or power that belongs to another. The noun form is *usurpation*.

V

vacate (1) To cancel or set aside. (2) To surrender possession; to leave.

validation research Using citators and other legal materials to check the current validity of every primary authority (case, statute, etc.) you intend to rely on in the memorandum of law, appellate brief, or other document you are preparing.

value billing A method of charging for legal services based on factors such as the results achieved and the complexity of the case rather than solely on the number of hours spent on the client's case.

valuing the bill Determining whether there should be a write-up, a write-down, or no adjustment of a bill to be sent to the client.

vendor-neutral citation See *public-domain citation*.

venire See *jury panel*.

venue The proper county or geographical area in which a court with jurisdiction may hear a case. The place of the trial.

verdict The jury's finding or decision on the factual issues placed before it.

verification A formal declaration that a person has read a document (e.g., a complaint) and swears that it is true to the best of his or her knowledge.

veto A rejection by the chief executive of a bill passed by the legislature.

vicarious conflict A conflict attributed to every attorney in a law office solely because of an actual conflict caused by one of the attorneys in the office.

vicarious disqualification The disqualification of every attorney in a law office from representing a client solely because of an actual conflict caused by one of the attorneys in the office. Also called *imputed disqualification*.

vicarious liability Liability imposed on a person for the conduct of another, based solely upon the status of the relationship between the two (e.g., employer and employee). The person liable is not the person whose conduct led to the liability.

videoconferencing Meeting in more than one location between individuals who can hear and see each other on computer screens in real time.

virtual Carried out by computer. Existing in a computer-generated environment.

virtual law office An office in which an attorney provides limited-scope legal services mainly or exclusively through online communication.

virus A program that can reproduce itself and damage or destroy data on computers.

voir dire ("to speak the truth") A preliminary examination of (a) prospective jurors for the purpose of selecting persons qualified to sit on a jury or (b) prospective witnesses to determine their competence to testify.

volume discount See *discounted hourly fee*.

W

Wage and Hour Division The unit within the U.S. Department of Labor that administers the Fair Labor Standards Act, which governs overtime compensation and related matters.

waive To lose a right or privilege because of an explicit rejection of it or because of a failure to claim it at the appropriate time. The noun is *waiver*.

warrant An order from a judicial officer authorizing an act, e.g., the arrest of an individual or the search of property.

web browser A program that allows you to read pages on the World Wide Web.

West (Thomson Reuters) A major legal publisher of reporters and codes. Its online service is Westlaw.

Westlaw A fee-based system of computer-assisted legal research owned by West (Thomson Reuters). Its current version is WestlawNext.

whistleblower An employee who reports employer wrongdoing, usually to a government agency.

wholesale The purchase of goods in large quantities that will be retailed to consumers by others.

wide area network (WAN) A multiuser system linking computers over a large geographical area so that they can share data and resources.

wi-fi Technology that uses radio waves to allow wireless communication between computers (including the Internet) within a designated area.

wildcard A special character (e.g., *, !, ?) that can be used to represent one or more characters in a search query.

WIP See *Work in Progress*.

wireless See *wi-fi*.

word processor Software that allows you to enter and edit data in order to create and revise documents. It processes words, allowing you to write sentences, paragraphs, and pages on the computer.

work in progress (WIP) A list of tasks on which someone is currently working and the dates they are due.

work-product rule Notes, working papers, memoranda, or similar things prepared by or for an attorney in anticipation of litigation are not discoverable by an opponent, absent a showing of substantial need. They are protected by privilege.

World Wide Web (WWW) A system of sites on the Internet that can be accessed through hypertext links.

wrap-up question A question asked at the end of the interview (or at the end of a separate topic within the interview) in which the interviewee is asked if there is anything he or she thinks has been left out or inadequately covered.

writ A written court order to do or refrain from doing an act.

write down Deduct an amount from the bill. Also called a *discount adjustment*.

write up Add an amount to the bill. Also called a *premium adjustment*.

writ of certiorari (cert.) See *certiorari*.

writ writer See *jailhouse lawyer*.

wrongful discharge Terminating an employee for a reason that is illegal or a violation of public policy.

INDEX

A

A.2d, 508
AAfPE, 8
AAPI, 8, 14
ABA, 9, 11, 14, 26, 28, 158, 168, 184, 191
ABA associate membership,
ABA ethics rules, 214
ABA model code, 265
ABA model guidelines, 218
ABA model rules, 266
Abbreviations, xxvi, 83, 493
Abraham Lincoln, 26
Absence test, 14
Abstract, computer, 573
Abuse of process, 200, 233
Access to evidence, 233
Accident investigation, 419
Accomplishments, work, 144
Account, client trust, 608
Accountant, 26, 177
Accounting software, 568
Accounts receivable report, 610
Accreditation, 156
ACP, 188, 238, 425, 474
Acquit, 459
Act, 287
Action verbs, 97
Active listening, 143
Active studying, xxii
Active voice, 551
Actuarial associate, 122
Ad abbreviations, 83
Ad damnum clause, 444, 470
Adjourn, 452
Adjudicate, adjudication, 293, 299, 445
Administration, judicial, 64
Administration, law office, 66, 589
Administrative agency, 175, 180, 298, 459, 461
Administrative assistant/paralegal, 11

Administrative decision, 288, 460
Administrative dispute, 459
Administrative exemption, 196
Administrative hearing, 47, 459
Administrative law, 47
Administrative law judge (ALJ), 122, 300, 619
Administrative Procedure Act, 176, 177, 300
Administrative regulation, 288, 512
Administrative regulation, citation, 512
Administrative reports, 609
Administrator, legal, 44, 594
Admiralty law, 48
Admissible, 423
Admission, 424
Admission to practice, 25
Admonition, 216
ADR, 221, 465
Advanced certified paralegal, 192
Adversarial, 174, 293, 448
Adversary system, 175, 234, 293
Adverse, 139, 244
Adverse interest, 244, 591
Adverse judgment, 446
Advertising, 48, 190, 259
Advice, legal, 27, 158, 159, 272, 390
Advisement, 452
Advocacy, 77, 174, 618, 619
Advocacy, formal, 174
Advocate, lay, 160
Adware, 582
Affidavit, 471, 629
Affiliate membership, 8, 27
Affirm, 345, 455
Affirmative defense, 446, 471
Agency. See administrative agency
Agency advocacy, 626
Agency appeal, 460
Agency hearing, 626
Agency, kinds of, 299